The History of Mexico

The History of Mexico: From Pre-Conquest to Present traces the last 500 years of Mexican history, from the indigenous empires that were devastated by the Spanish conquest to the 2009 mid-term election. The book offers a straightforward chronological survey of Mexican history from the pre-colonial times to the present, and includes a glossary as well as numerous tables and images for comprehensive study.

In lively and engaging prose, Philip Russell guides readers through major themes that still resonate today including:

- The role of women in society
- Environmental change
- The evolving status of Mexico's indigenous people
- African slavery and the role of race
- Government economic policy
- Foreign relations with the United States and others.

The companion website provides many useful student tools including multiple choice questions, extra book chapters, and links to online resources, as well as digital copies of the maps from the book.

For additional information and classroom resources please visit *The History of Mexico* companion website at www.routledge.com/textbooks/russell.

Philip L. Russell is an independent historian and author of *Mexico Under Salinas*.

The History of Mexico

From Pre-Conquest to Present

Philip L. Russell

Routledge
Taylor & Francis Group
NEW YORK AND LONDON

First published 2010
by Routledge
270 Madison Avenue, New York, NY 10016

Simultaneously published in the UK
by Routledge
2 Park Square, Milton Park, Abingdon, Oxon OX14 4RN

Routledge is an imprint of the Taylor & Francis Group, an informa business

Typeset in Perpetua and Bell Gothic by
Florence Production Ltd, Stoodleigh, Devon, UK
Printed and bound in the United States of America on acid-free paper by
Edwards Brothers, Inc.

Library of Congress Cataloging in Publication Data
Russell, Philip L.
The history of Mexico: from pre-conquest to present/
Philip Russell.—1st ed.
p. cm.
Includes index.
1. Mexico—History. I. Title.
F1226.R94 2010
972–dc22 2009047308

ISBN13: 978–0–415–87236–2 (hbk)
ISBN13: 978–0–415–87237–9 (pbk)
ISBN13: 978–0–203–85127–2 (ebk)

Contents

Figures

Tables

Preface

This book will be published just as countless people north and south of the Rio Grande will be observing the hundredth anniversary of the Mexican Revolution and the two-hundredth anniversary of Mexican independence. To make the Revolution, independence, and other events more understandable, this book has been divided into nine parts and thirty chapters. Each of the sections discusses major events occurring during the period under consideration, as well as social change, the role of women, population growth, and economic and cultural development. The relationship between people and nature is stressed, from the dawn of Mexican civilization to twenty-first-century droughts and floods—considered by many to be harbingers of global warming.

The first part describes some of the myriad cultures that developed before the Spanish arrival in 1519. It then discusses how the Spanish were able to conquer the much more numerous Aztecs they encountered. A description of the administration the Spaniards established in their newly acquired domain follows. This part also considers how Europeans harnessed indigenous labor for their own ends and introduced Christianity and European-production techniques.

The first part emphasizes two significant differences between Spain's colony in Mexico and the settlement process occurring further north in the thirteen British colonies. The degree to which indigenous and European cultures fused to create a unique new Mexican culture stands in sharp contrast to what happened in the British colonies. Spaniards' diligent efforts to incorporate Mexico's indigenous population into the larger society also differ markedly from the approach of their British counterparts further north.

The second part discusses one of the events being commemorated in 2010—Mexican independence. It considers the many grievances against Mexico's colonizers and then describes how civil war engulfed Mexico after Father Hidalgo's 1810 call to arms. Finally, the role different groups played in the independence struggle and the war's impact on the economy are considered.

The third part describes how Mexicans endeavored to establish effective governance after independence. One of the major challenges was determining how far north and south the new nation extended. Building an economy outside the Spanish empire presented another formidable challenge. This part also discusses how the rise of a major power next door reshaped Mexico's boundaries.

The fourth part considers the place in Mexican history of two of its most famous figures, Benito Juárez and Porfirio Díaz—men who dominated late nineteenth-century Mexico. These presidents were successful in knitting Mexico into a coherent political and economic whole—something that had been sorely lacking during the first half-century of Mexican independence. This section also discusses how the economy at long last began to grow—surpassing even the growth rate of the U.S. economy.

Part Five considers another of the events being commemorated in 2010—the Mexican Revolution. It describes the grievances that led to violent upheaval, the various actors who eventually turned on each other, and the final outcome. A separate chapter considers how the United States attempted—sometimes successfully, sometimes unsuccessfully—to influence the course of the Revolution.

The sixth part considers how Mexicans once again faced the task of creating a new political apparatus, reviving their war-torn economy, and defining the role of foreign investment, especially in the politically sensitive oil industry. Each of these challenges was influenced by pressure from below for the government to deliver on many of the social reforms promised during the Revolution.

Part Seven considers how, between 1941 and 1970, Mexico created a smoothly functioning, though hardly democratic, political system that ensured political stability. This stability allowed decades of unprecedented economic growth. The final chapter of this part considers how the United States came to be accepted as a source of investment capital and as an ally, first in the context of the Second World War and later during the Cold War.

Part Eight considers Mexico's responses to falling economic growth and increased political instability. This part also discusses the new challenges presented by rapid population growth, massive emigration, and environmental contamination. In addition, it describes Mexico's shift to a new set of economic assumptions, often referred to as neoliberalism.

The final part considers how Mexico, after decades of one-party rule, embraced multiparty democracy. This section brings the reader to the present and raises the question of how to deal with the failure of the two great hopes of the 1990s—electoral democracy and the North American Free Trade Agreement (NAFTA)—to produce anticipated benefits.

This book will be successful to the extent that it better enables readers to understand Mexico's complex past. Another indicator of its success will be its contribution to understanding how two "Distant Neighbors" (to use Alan Riding's term) cope with such shared challenges as free trade, immigration, environmental pollution, and drug trafficking.

Following these nine parts is a list of Mexico's rulers, beginning at the middle of the nineteenth century, and a glossary containing terms that are largely unknown outside of Mexico. Finally an extensive bibliography, drawn from material published on five continents, allows readers to peruse more extensive discussions of issues considered in the text.

Any printed book has limitations as to the number of illustrations and tables and the length of text that can be included. To complement the material included in the book that is before you, there is a companion website. Material on the website includes translations of written documents, such as the January 1, 1994 declaration of the Zapatista Army of National Liberation (EZLN) in Chiapas. The website includes additional statistical tables, such as production figures that track Mexico's plummeting oil production. Other items on the website include photos and reviews of the book. The website also includes questions concerning the issues raised by events described in each chapter. Finally, a summary of events occurring after the publication of the book will allow readers to follow on-going events in Mexico.

I would like to thank a few of the many individuals who have contributed to making this book. Historians Alan Knight and Barbara Tenenbaum read parts of an earlier version of the manuscript and made valuable comments on the periods of their expertise. Carmen Ramos and Jodi Eineichner gave me valuable advice on interpreting women's history. Nancy Hamilton's reading of the entire manuscript resulted in numerous constructive suggestions on word choice and organization. Katherine Arens was invaluable in interpreting and translating all things Germanic.

This work would not have been possible without the efforts of the staff of the Benson Latin American Collection. They furthered the project in innumerable ways, including ferreting out information, keeping the collection stocked with recent publications, and shelving countless books, as I examined, checked, and rechecked sources.

Finally, credit is also due to the individuals who facilitated bringing the manuscript to book form. Linda Bathgate started the process by putting me in contact with Routledge. Kimberly Guinta then picked up the ball in her role as acquisitions editor. It was then a pleasure to work with Nicole Solano and Matthew Kopel as they helped put the book into its final form. Finally, I would like to thank two anonymous reviewers at Routledge for their suggestions for improving the manuscript.

Abbreviations

AFL	American Federation of Labor
AFL–CIO	American Federation of Labor–Congress of Industrial Organizations
AID	[U.S.] Agency for International Development
AMLO	Andrés Manuel López Obrador
APPO	Popular Assembly of the Peoples of Oaxaca
CDI	National Commission for the Development of Indigenous People
CGOCM	General Federation of Mexican Workers and Peasants
CGT	General Federation of Workers
CNC	National Peasant Confederation
CNDH	National Human Rights Commission
CNDP	National Committee of Proletarian Defense
CNH	National Strike Council
CNOP	National Federation of Popular Organizations
COFIPE	Federal Code of Electoral Institutions and Procedures
CONCAMIN	National Federation of Industrial Chambers
CONCANACO	National Federation of Chambers of Commerce
COPARMEX	Businessmen's Federation of the Mexican Republic
CROC	Revolutionary Federation of Workers and Peasants
CROM	Regional Federation of Mexican Workers
CSUM	Mexican Labor Federation
CTM	Mexican Workers Federation
DEA	Drug Enforcement Agency
ECLA	[U.N.] Economic Commission for Latin America
EZLN	Zapatista Army of National Liberation
FAT	Authentic Labor Front
FDI	Foreign direct investment
FDIC	Federal Deposit Insurance Corporation
FDN	Democratic National Front
FOBAPROA	Bank Savings Protection Fund
FUPDM	United Front for Women's Rights
G.I.	[U.S.] Government issue. (In the mid-twentieth century this term was widely used for U.S. soldiers and U.S. veterans, thus "G.I. Bill" and "G.I. Forum.")
GATT	General Agreement on Tariffs and Trade
GDP	Gross domestic product
IFE	Federal Electoral Institute
IMF	International Monetary Fund
INI	National Indigenous Institute
INS	[U.S.] Immigration and Naturalization Service
IRCA	[U.S.] Immigration Reform and Control Act
ISI	Import-substitution industrialization

IWW	Industrial Workers of the World
LULAC	League of United Latin American Citizens
MNC	multinational corporations
NAACP	[U.S.] National Association for the Advancement of Colored People
NAFTA	North American Free Trade Agreement
NAWU	National Agricultural Workers Union
NGO	Non-governmental organization
OAS	Organization of American States
OPEC	Organization of Petroleum Exporting Countries
PAN	National Action Party
PLM	Partido Liberal Mexicano—Mexican Liberal Party
PNR	Partido Nacional Revolucionario—National Revolutionary Party
PRD	Party of the Democratic Revolution
PRI	Revolutionary Institutional Party
PRM	Mexican Revolutionary Party
PROFEPA	Special Federal Prosecutor's Office for Environmental Protection
PRONAF	National Border Program
SAM	Mexican Food System
UNORCA	National Union of Autonomous Regional Peasant Organizations
UNT	National Workers Union
VAT	Value-added tax

Figure 0.1 *Map of Mexico*

Source: From Tenenbaum, *Encyclopedia of Latin American History and Culture*, vol. 4, 1E. Copyright Gale, a part of Cengage Learning, Inc.

Part One

The First Three Millennia

Chapter 1

Mesoamerica

THE FIRST MEXICANS

By 10000 BC, perhaps much earlier, humans had arrived in the area now forming Mexico. Our knowledge of Mexico's first inhabitants is limited since few of the utensils, clothes, or buildings they produced have survived.[1]

The best known of these early arrivals is an individual known as Tepexpan Man, found on the northeast edge of Lake Texcoco not far from modern Mexico City. The age of the skeleton was never established since it is unclear exactly what soil stratum it came from. In any case, the remains, actually those of a woman about 5 feet 3 inches tall, are often referred to as the first Mexican, since she is likely the earliest individual we know of.

Just to the southeast of Tepexpan Man, the remains of an imperial mammoth were discovered. It was butchered *in situ*, and flint projectile points were found associated with it. Knife marks scar the bone where meat was cut off. We know little of the culture of Tepexpan Man and of those who killed the mammoth, since no artifacts other than the projectile points were encountered at either site. Presumably these individuals had a widely varied diet in addition to mammoth, as is typical of hunter-gatherers who hunt big game.[2]

For millennia the descendents of the first arrivals in Mexico survived as hunter-gatherers. They formed loose, egalitarian groups, each one probably numbering fewer than one hundred members who were united by bonds of kinship. Such groups lived in caves and temporary campsites. These highly mobile groups possessed few material goods. They were constantly migrating, skirmishing, and intermarrying with other groups. The imposition of centralized control was impossible since disaffected people could too easily vote with their feet.

From what we know of hunter-gatherer peoples, they enjoyed a comfortable margin of existence and did not have to toil endlessly to survive. A key to their survival was low population density. They also developed superior weaponry. These early hunter-gatherers used the spear thrower, or atlatl, which could launch a projectile at fifteen times the speed of a hand-held spear, giving it more than 200 times the kinetic energy.[3]

Between 8000 and 2000 BC, the early Mexicans turned to planting, rather merely gathering, seeds. Various plants, including squash, corn, beans, and chile peppers were domesticated. The development of agriculture allowed the formation of permanent villages by the third millennium BC. These villages were quite small, having perhaps twelve households or sixty individuals. Residence in villages allowed the development of such arts as pottery making and loom weaving. Since they were no longer constantly on the move, village dwellers could accumulate a much wider range of goods. These included milling stones (*metates*) to grind corn, baskets, nets, cordage, mats, and wattle-and-daub huts. This early material culture is remarkably similar to the material culture still found in many homes of those living in isolated rural areas of Mexico.[4]

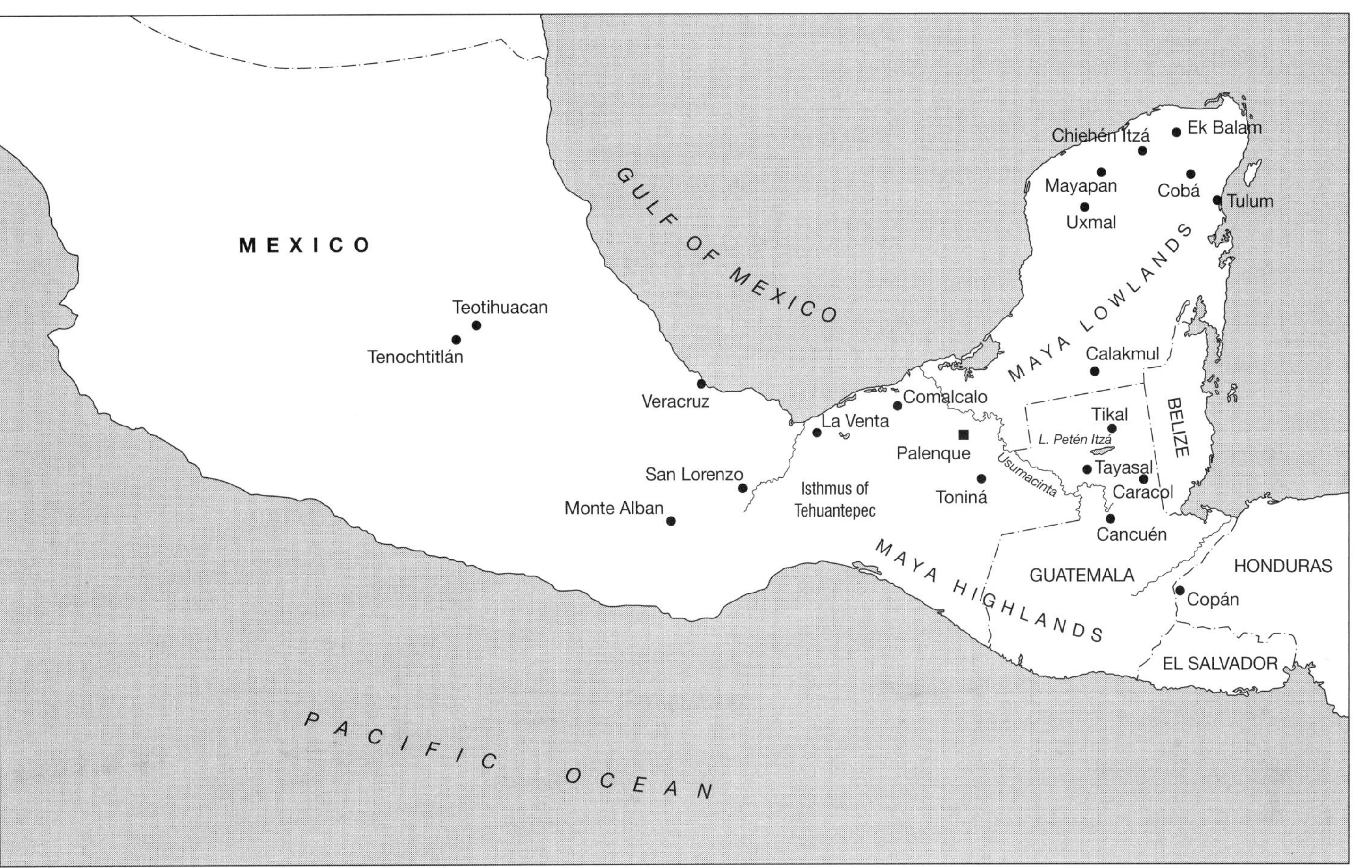

Figure 1.1 *Mesoamerica*

Source: Drawn by Philip Winton. From David Stuart and George Stuart (2008), *Palenque: Eternal City of the Maya*. London and New York: Thames & Hudson

The shift to agriculture occurred over a wide area and was a very slow evolutionary process occurring over millennia. Just as with their hunter-gatherer fore-bears, these early villages remained egalitarian for millennia. A major change produced by agriculture was increased population density.[5]

PRE-CLASSIC MESOAMERICA

These agricultural villages grew larger and developed a more sophisticated material culture. By roughly 1500 BC, there emerged a cultural area known as Mesoamerica, covering some 392,000 square miles. This area extended from the rugged snow-capped volcanoes of central Mexico south to present-day Nicaragua and included the mountains of Guatemala and the limestone plains of Yucatán. Mesoamerican cultures shared a religious tradition and had complex social, economic, and political organizations. Urban centers typically had public buildings arranged around a formal, open plaza adjacent to pyramidal temples. Another shared trait was human sacrifice. All of the Mesoamerican cultures relied on an agricultural surplus generated by cultivating corn. In Mesoamerican cultures, men would typically cultivate the corn, and women would grind the kernels and prepare tortillas—a division of labor that has persisted to the present. Corn was an ideal crop since it has a high yield per unit of land and is easily stored.[6]

The creation myth of the Quiché Maya indicates the intimate relationship between corn and the Mesoamerican societies that bred it. The Popol Vuh, the sacred book of the Quiché, describes how Xmucane, one of the divine grandparents, ground yellow corn and white corn nine times and then fashioned the flesh of the first human from the mixture.[7]

There are two theories concerning the origin of corn. One holds that early agriculturists bred a weed, teosinte, for a sufficiently long period to convert it into a greatly improved food source. Others think that the teosinte was crossbred with another plant to produce corn. In any case, in 7000 BC, an ear of corn only measured an inch long. After six millennia of cultivation, the ear attained a length of four inches. As a result of this transformation, the corn plant could no longer propagate itself without human intervention.[8]

Complex Mesoamerican cultures flourished between 2000 BC and AD 1519. Archeologists have divided this 3,500-year span into three time periods, each with its own characteristics. The earliest period, known as the Pre-Classic, lasted from roughly 2000 BC to AD 250. The Pre-Classic is distinguished from earlier village cultures by the emergence of large political entities that demanded that its inhabitants contribute material goods and labor. Entrance into and emergence from the Pre-Classic was a gradual evolutionary process that occurred at varying times in varying locations.[9]

The outstanding culture of the Pre-Classic period is known as the Olmec, a name given to its inhabitants by archeologists, since no one knows what they called themselves. The term means "dweller in the land of rubber," since rubber is a major export of the 125-by-50-mile area they inhabited in the steamy swamplands of coastal Tabasco. Between 1500 BC and 400 BC, the Olmec created one of the six pristine civilizations in human history. A pristine civilization is the earliest civilization in its respective region. The other pristine civilizations were the Chavin culture in Peru, China's Shang culture, the Indus civilization in modern Indian and Pakistan, and the Egyptian and Sumerian cultures in the Near East.[10]

Between 1500 BC and 1200 BC, the Olmec settled San Lorenzo, which was perhaps the first urban center in the Americas. San Lorenzo was a hilltop ceremonial center overlooking the Coatzacoalcos River. The site was several times larger than any other Mesoamerican urban center existing at the time. It covered roughly two square miles and had several thousand permanent residents. At San Lorenzo, highly skilled craftspeople produced planned public architecture and a variety of artistic works. Extensive interregional trade networks supplied these craftspeople with materials. Around 900 BC, San Lorenzo declined for reasons unknown.[11]

Radiocarbon dates indicate that a subsequent Olmec urban center, La Venta, flourished between 1200 BC and 400 BC. At its apogee, around 500 BC, its population was perhaps 2,000. It contained several plazas and the largest Mesoamerican structure yet built, whose original shape is still a matter of controversy. There the Olmec created awe-inspiring sculptures, finished without the benefit of metal tools. Much of the basalt they carved was quarried fifty miles away and presumably floated to La Venta on rafts. Today the most recognizable Olmec works are the magnificent stone heads representing their rulers. These sculptures measure as much as nine feet high and weigh up to forty tons.[12]

Even though they constructed San Lorenzo and later La Venta, most of the Olmec lived in small villages, fished, and raised corn, beans, squash, sweet potatoes, cotton, and various tree crops. Linking these villages was an elite that oversaw large-scale projects such as earthen and stone monument construction.[13]

Between 1300 BC and 500 BC, the Olmec culture influenced others throughout and beyond Mesoamerica. Trade routes, which connected areas of different resource endowments, were one of the main channels through which this influence spread. Recent archeological investigation has indicated that the Olmec influence in Mesoamerica was by no means unidirectional. Various other centers were developing and innovating at the same time and passing their knowledge to the Olmec. Major centers of this cultural network include the Valley of Mexico, the Valley of Oaxaca, and the area to the east of the Olmec where the classic Maya civilization would emerge.[14]

For reasons that are poorly understood, the Olmec centers collapsed. At La Venta, the altars and stone heads were systematically defaced and ceremoniously interred. Artisans ceased producing distinctive Olmec artistic works, and the extensive trade networks uniting the Olmec with surrounding regions no longer functioned. The causes for this decline have yet to be determined. Various explanations have been offered for this decline, including peasant revolt, disease, invasion, and agricultural exhaustion.[15]

THE CLASSIC PERIOD

The Classic Period of Mesoamerican culture extended from roughly AD 250 to AD 900 and saw two of the marvels of the pre-Conquest New World, the city Teotihuacan on the central Mexican plateau and the Mayan cities of southeastern Mexico. The AD 250 date corresponds to the earliest date in the Mayan calendar appearing on a carved monument, or stela, in the area. Classic cultures differed from their forebears in having more complex political organization, larger populations, full-time craft specialization, increased social stratification, and more centralized political authority.[16]

By the fourth century of the Christian era, a new civilization had emerged in central Mexico. When the Aztecs later encountered the remains of its capital, located thirty miles northeast of the present site of Mexico City, they named it Teotihuacan (the City of the Gods). The ethnic identity of the city's builders remains unclear. This city, with a population of 100,000 or more, covered eight square miles, an area larger than Rome, which flourished at the same time. Between AD 250 and AD 700, Teotihuacan's trading and tribute empire dominated central Mexico, and its influence was felt from present-day Guatemala to the dry non-agricultural areas far north of the city. The city relied on the highly fertile lands of the Valley of Mexico and a special resource—obsidian—for tool making. Obsidian was so far superior to other available stones for producing cutting tools that archeologist Robert Cobean noted that obsidian was to ancient Mesoamerica what steel is to modern civilization. More than 10 percent of the city's labor force appear to have been obsidian workers. In addition to the city's distinctive architectural style, its ceramic style influenced potters throughout Mesoamerica.[17]

The city's planners laid out more than 2,000 rectangular city blocks. Teotihuacan's Pyramid of the Sun, whose construction required an estimated 10,000 laborers working for twenty years, still inspires visitors. Its base covers an area equal to that of the pyramid of Cheops in Egypt. Archeological evidence also indicates that the notion of Quetzalcoatl, the plumed serpent, which had a temple built there in its honor, originated in the city. Along with the Virgin of Guadalupe, Quetzalcoatl is a quintessential symbol of Mexico.[18]

Figure 1.2 *Teotihuacan*
Source: Copyright Michael E. Calderwood

The city met its end in the seventh century through deliberate burning by the hand of unknown invaders. By AD 750, its population had fallen below 10,000. A likely culprit for the city's decline is deforestation. Trees were felled to supply fuel to burn the lime used in constructing the city. The loss of forests may have led to erosion and desiccation, thus undermining Teotihuacan's agricultural base.[19]

At the same time as the Olmec culture was flourishing, a distinctive Maya culture was emerging to its east. This culture developed over a 39,000-square-mile area extending from the Isthmus of Tehuantepec to modern Honduras. By 1000 BC the inhabitants of this region had settled in villages and were making pottery, and by 800 BC they were erecting small temples. Later, the population of this area soared, and a stratified social system emerged. Polities with centralized political power dominated the area.[20]

For a 650-year period, the area reached intellectual and artistic heights no other New World culture, and few in the Old World, could match. When Maya civilization was in full flower, it featured enormous ceremonial centers crowded with masonry temples and palaces facing spacious plazas covered with white stucco. These ceremonial centers, even though they shared a common culture, were never united into a single state. Rather they formed numerous small city-states, as was the case with classical Greece and Renaissance Italy. In the eighth century, these city-states numbered at least twenty-five.[21]

Maya urban centers, some of which may have exceeded 75,000 in population, had administrative, manufacturing, commercial, and religious roles. In each city-state there was a marked division of labor. Nearby peasants produced an agricultural surplus large enough to support an intelligentsia, craftsmen, traders, and corvée laborers who erected massive public structures such as temples. Maya potters achieved chromatic effects of great brilliance by firing their vessels at low temperatures. Traders distributed manufactured goods, including pottery, cotton cloth, and obsidian tools, over a wide area, using both overland trails and seafaring canoes. The urban intelligentsia used a numerical system employing the zero and was so sophisticated astronomically that its members could predict eclipses.[22]

These city-states were ruled over by individuals, including a few women, who formed a hereditary nobility. Rulers emphasized their connection to the supernatural world and controlled rituals that their subjects believed to be essential to life and prosperity. Such rituals were perceived to ensure water, food, and protection.[23]

Warfare was a staple feature of classic Maya society. Unlike the Inca to the south, the Maya did not use war to expand territorially. Extinguishing a vanquished kingdom and its dynasty was perceived as a threat to the world order. Rather, tribute obligations and vassalage were imposed. War allowed individual Maya rulers to display their prowess by sacrificing prisoners they had

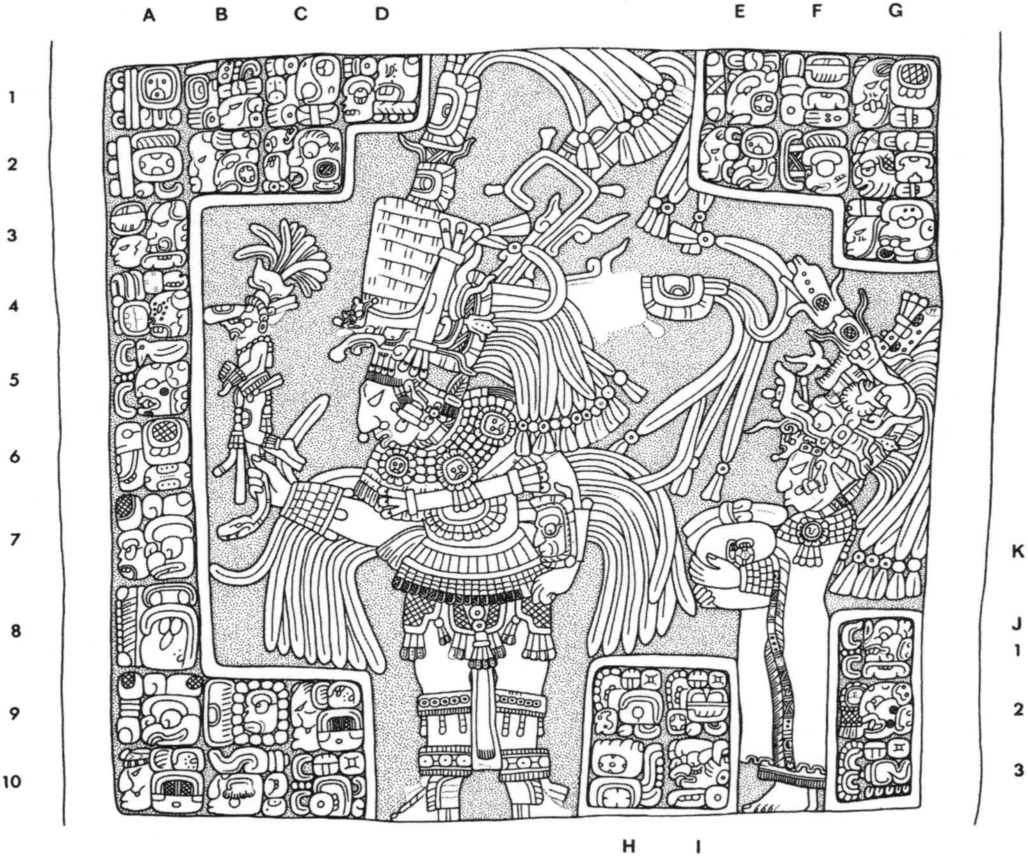

Figure 1.3 *Drawing from lintel 1, Yaxchilan temple 33, showing accession of Ruler Bird Jaguar IV, holding scepter, with his wife Lady Great Skull at right. Maya writing appears in corners and to left of the illustration*

Source: Drawings by Ian Graham, Corpus of Maya Hieroglyphic Inscriptions, vol. 3, Pt. 1, Yaxchilan, reproduced courtesy of the President and Fellows of Harvard College

THE MAYAN WRITING SYSTEM

Up until the middle of the twentieth century, a number of factors prevented the decipherment of Maya hieroglyphics:

- There was a prevailing racist assumption that the Maya were intellectually incapable of developing a complex writing system on a par with Egyptian hieroglyphics.
- Most of the scholars studying the Maya were unfamiliar with the early Old World writing systems, which would have given insight into how the Maya system functioned.
- It was assumed that if the Maya had phonetic writing, it would be alphabetic as is the case with European languages.
- Finally, Cold War rivalries delayed acceptance of a Russian's correct assertion that Maya writing combined symbols with phonetic value and those that conveyed ideas (logographs).

Progress on deciphering Mayan writing began in earnest with a 1952 publication by Yuri Knorosov, a Russian linguist who was familiar with early scripts such as the Egyptian, Mesopotamian, and Chinese, all of which combined phonetic symbols and logographs. He suggested that it was quite likely the Maya followed the same pattern. Once Knorosov's view became accepted, rapid progress at deciphering the hieroglyphs commenced. Anthropologist Michael Coe referred to the decipherment of Maya hieroglyphs as "one of the most exciting intellectual adventures of our age, on a par with the exploration of space and the discovery of the genetic code." Coe also commented on the vast collaborative effort that finally led to an almost complete understanding of the Maya hieroglyphs: "Hardly a day or week seemed to pass without some amazing new fact coming to light, or a new reading being made for a glyph, or someone coming forth with a revolutionary new interpretation of older data."[a]

Eventually it became clear that the Mayan hieroglyphs, which took the form of squares with rounded corners (see Figure 1.3), combined logographs with phonetic symbols that represented the classic Mayan language that was spoken at the time the writing system was codified. The logographs convey an idea, much as the "2" does in modern writing systems. The phonetic component is not alphabetic, with symbols corresponding to a given sound, as our letter "T" does. Rather each phonetic symbol corresponds to a consonant and to the vowel that follows, just as occurs in the modern Japanese writing system. The Maya had a distinct symbol for each consonant + vowel combination occurring in their language. As a result of deciphering the Maya hieroglyphs, the written history of the New World now extends back nearly 2,000 years.

a Coe (1999: 138, 7, 214) and Sharer (2006: 141).

captured on the battlefield. The blood and gore of this constant warfare was frequently depicted on stelae, which were erected to glorify rulers and their ancestors.[24]

At its peak in roughly AD 700, the Maya population numbered perhaps 10 million. Slash-and-burn agriculture produced much of the food they consumed. However, as population densities rose, more intensive practices were adopted to increase yields. These included terracing, household gardens, irrigation, raised-bed agriculture, and tree crops such as cacao, allspice, avocado, and papaya. The chief ground crops were corn, beans, squash, chile, and tomatoes.[25]

Perhaps the greatest cultural achievement of the Maya was the development of a hieroglyphic writing system (see the box on the Mayan writing system). Once modern scholars learned how to read the hieroglyphs in the late twentieth century, they gained insight into a dazzling panorama of Maya history, beliefs, and experiences. Hieroglyphs recorded information on Maya kings and queens, their claims to power, supernatural patrons, alliances, wars, triumphs, and defeats.[26]

One of the outstanding Maya city-states was Palenque, set in the lower foothills of the Sierra de Chiapas. The city occupied a commanding position overlooking the Gulf Coastal Plain. Maya architects working there in the seventh century AD had learned to construct lightly built vaults and mansard roofs, so the city has a spacious appearance lacking in earlier Maya sites. Carved stelae reveal the dynastic history of the city. Palenque expanded rapidly after AD 615 when K'inich Janab Pakal assumed the throne. During his reign, the city became the dominant political, religious, and cultural center of the area. The Maya erected at least thirty-five major building complexes at Palenque, and they walled stream banks and built aqueducts to manage the 120 inches of rain that fall on the city annually. The city's existence was long lost to Europeans. One of the early visitors to the rediscovered Palenque was American diplomat and lawyer John Lloyd Stevens, who visited the area between 1839 and 1842.[27] He observed:

> Here were the remains of a cultivated, polished, and peculiar people who had passed through all the stages incident to the rise and fall of nations; reached their golden age, and perished, entirely unknown . . . We lived in the ruined palace of their kings; we went up to their desolate temples and fallen altars; and wherever we moved we saw the evidence of their taste, their skill in arts, their wealth and power.[28]

A later Maya city-state, Chichen Itza, dominated the Yucatán peninsula between AD 850 and AD 1000. At its peak it was the most powerful and successful of the Maya city-states. It was more commercially oriented than earlier Maya city-states and traded with various regions within and beyond the Maya area. Much of its power was derived from its dominance of newly developed coastal trade networks using seafaring canoes.[29]

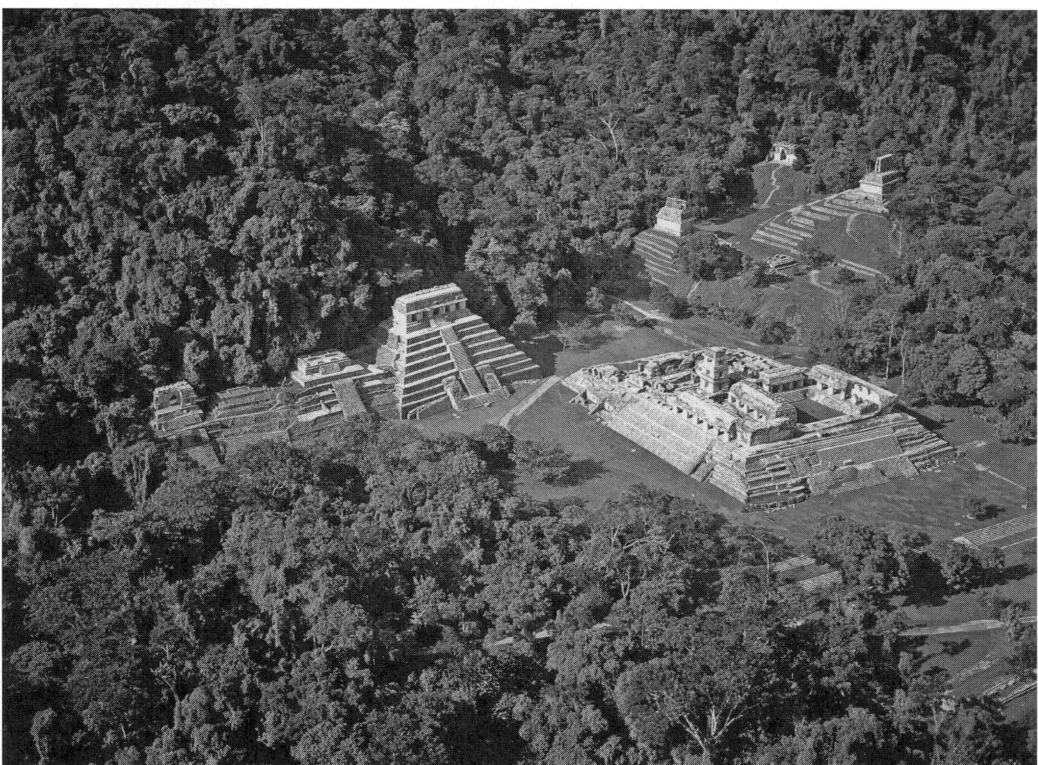

Figure 1.4 *Palenque, showing the palace, center right, with the Temple of the Inscriptions in the background*

Source: Copyright Michael E. Calderwood

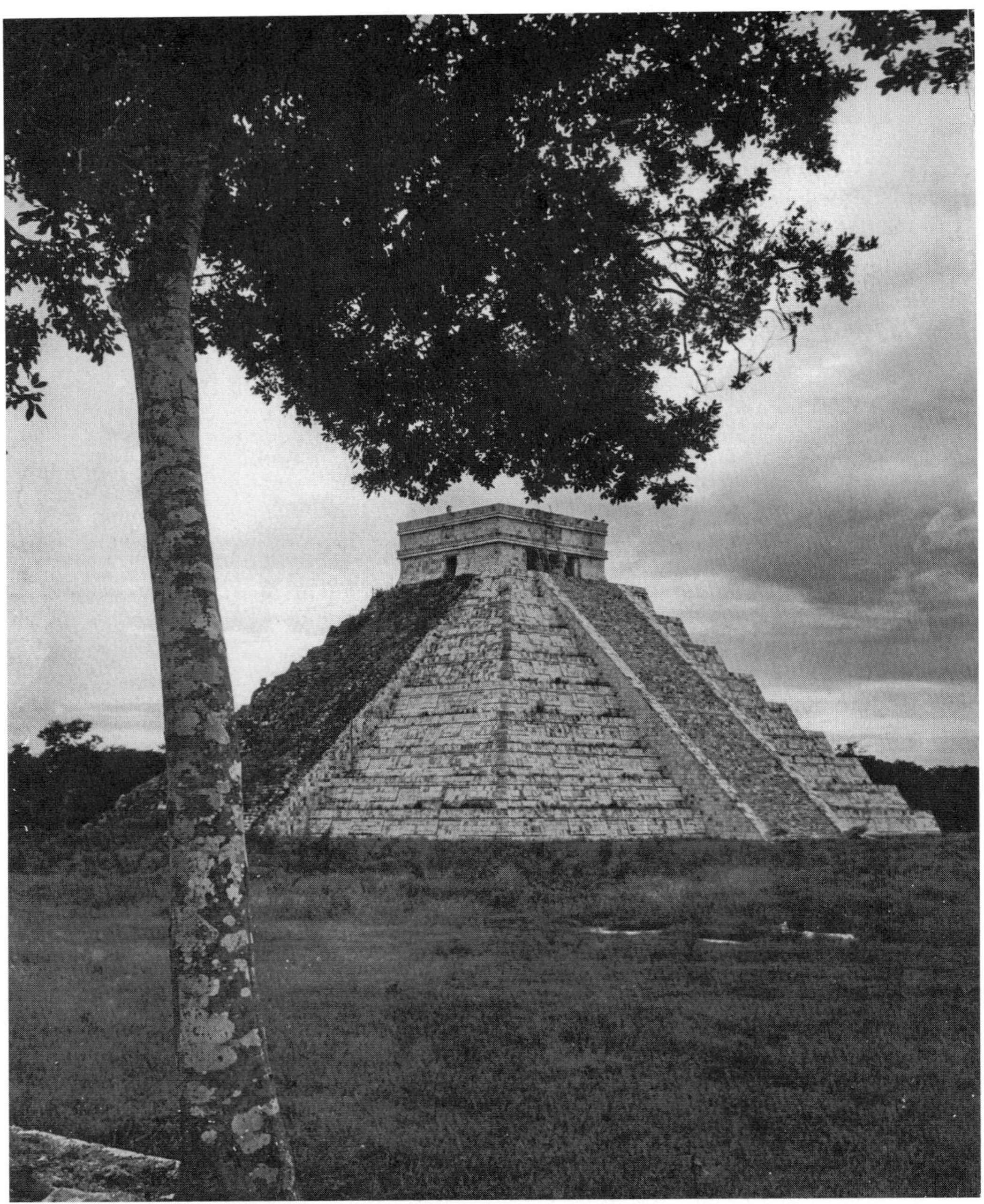

Figure 1.5 *El Castillo at Chichen Itza*

Source: Reproduced courtesy of the Benson Latin American Collection, the University of Texas at Austin

An enduring mystery is why the Maya city-states, which flourished for centuries, went into irreversible decline. This decline can be accurately dated since the production of monumental structures and stelae bearing dates ceased. The last date in the Maya calendar carved in stelae for Peten corresponds to January 15, 910. This decline did not follow a uniform trajectory and played out differently in different polities. However, the result was always the same—within 100 or 200 years of reaching their peak population levels, most of the central and southern Maya lowlands lost about 90 percent of their population.[30]

Apparently this decline in part resulted from overpopulation, which led to environmental degradation, whose impact was vastly amplified by climate change. As the Maya population expanded, formerly forested hillsides were cultivated. This resulted in erosion that exceeded the rate of soil formation. Rather than husbanding resources, Maya kings further depleted them by attempting to erect more grandiose monuments than their rivals did. Maya warfare, already endemic, peaked just before the collapse of the Classic Maya civilization. Greatly compounding the Maya's problems of overpopulation and resource scarcity was the worst drought in the last 7,000 years, which began in AD 760.[31]

At the same time as the Maya and Teotihuacan were flourishing, the Zapotecs developed Monte Alban in the Valley of Oaxaca. This city-state, whose population peaked at about 25,000, served as a political and religious center from which the Zapotecs dominated more than 1,000 smaller towns in the valley. Zapotec craftsmen constructed a very long, large plaza there as well as magnificent tombs with lovely murals on the walls. The Zapotecs also developed a writing system, but unlike that of the Maya, it has yet to be deciphered. While there is no sign that Monte Alban suffered a violent demise such as that suffered by Teotihuacan, by AD 900 most of the city was in ruins and the Valley of Oaxaca was divided into dozens of petty city-states.[32]

THE POST-CLASSIC

The period between AD 900 and the Spanish arrival in 1519 is known as the Post-Classic. It was characterized by renewed population growth, extensive commercial development, and the rise of the most powerful city-states yet seen in Mesoamerica. During this period, two city-states, Tula and later Tenochtitlan, the capital of the Aztec empire, dominated central Mexico. As was the case with the earlier periods, the onset of the Post-Classic occurred gradually and varied by location.[33]

For an extended period after the fall of Teotihuacan there was a power vacuum in central Mexico. As historian Enrique Florescano noted, "Wars pitting everyone against everyone else characterized that turbulent epoch." Several small city-states, such as Xochicalco in the modern state of Morelos and El Tajín in Veracruz arose to fill this power vacuum.[34]

After AD 900, the Toltec rose to dominance in central Mexico. The Toltec looked back to their first great ruler, Topiltzin, who was born in the first half of the tenth century. He was responsible for moving the Toltec capital to Tula, located fifty miles northwest of where Mexico City stands today. At its peak between AD 950 and 1150, the city had a population of 30,000–40,000 and covered 5.4 square miles. There the Toltec constructed an impressive formal plaza flanked by ball courts, altars, and pyramids topped by temples. From Tula, the Toltecs dominated central Mexico for two centuries. Toltec influence extended as far north as present-day Arizona and New Mexico and as far south as Yucatán.[35]

In Tula, military artistic motifs outnumbered religious ones. There were abundant images of both the ubiquitous Quetzalcoatl and of his enemy Tezcatlipoca (the Smoking Mirror). Toltec astronomers developed a superb calendar. Within the city there was a sizable community of artisans specializing in the production of pottery vessels, figurines, and obsidian blades. Their skill was reflected by the fact that the word "Toltec" was used in the Nahuatl language to mean artist. Farmers working irrigated, terraced fields supported these workers.[36]

Around AD 1175, a combination of drought, famine, and war led to the fall of Tula. All the evidence points to a sudden, overwhelming cataclysm. Ceremonial walls were burned to the ground. Soon the city was deserted.[37]

Aztec legends told of their coming from a place to the northwest of the Valley of Mexico known as Aztlan. Upon their arrival in the valley early in the twelfth century, this band of hunter-gatherers was scorned by more sophisticated agriculturists, such as the Colhuacan. For a short period, the Aztecs cultivated the lands of the Colhuacan as serfs. In 1323, the Aztecs' overlords provided one of their princesses to an Aztec chief as a bride. The Aztecs, rather than performing the anticipated marriage ceremony, sacrificed her in hopes she would become a war goddess. The enraged Colhuacan then expelled the Aztecs from their land. The Aztecs withdrew to an isolated, marshy area. There, according to their lore, in the year 1325, they founded the city of Tenochtitlan on the present site of Mexico City.[38]

An Aztec legend recounts that an eagle perched on a prickly-pear cactus, eating a snake, indicated the place where the Aztecs were to found Tenochtitlan. Today the Mexican flag and coat of arms depict this eagle.

The Aztecs constructed Tenochtitlan on roughly five square miles of land reclaimed from Lake Texcoco, which surrounded their capital. Its population reached as many as 250,000, making it larger than any city in Europe, except perhaps Naples and Constantinople, and four times the size of Seville. Only the cities of China, unknown to Spaniards and Aztecs alike, exceeded its population. Sophisticated systems provided food, trade goods, and potable water to the city's population.[39]

The difficulty of hauling grain in societies lacking wheeled vehicles and draught animals imposed size limits on Mesoamerican cities. Tenochtitlan could escape these limits since large cargo canoes, which came from distant waterfronts, provisioned the city with grain and other produce.[40]

In 1519, Tenochtitlan was the largest city that had ever existed in the New World. Its size and grandeur reflected its status as an imperial capital, and its large buildings made a statement about the might and control of its rulers, thus legitimizing and contributing to their power. In laying out the city, planners consciously adopted the model of Tula, since Tula and the Toltec practices served as the source of Aztec political and social legitimacy.[41]

With the exception of Tenochtitlan, most Aztec cities were not large. The second largest, Texcoco, had a population of 25,000. Secondary cities served as ceremonial centers of the Aztec territorial division known as the *altepetl*. Temples soared high above the plazas of these cities. The altepetl was the political unit responsible for collecting tribute from the villages and rural people within its boundaries. This tribute would then be distributed to the local elite and to Tenochtitlan. The altepetl also organized manpower in time of war and for construction projects. A hereditary leader known as a tlatoani, or speaker, headed each altepetl. Residents of each altepetl considered themselves a separate people from those elsewhere, even though all were Aztecs.[42]

By 1465, the Aztecs had the entire Valley of Mexico under their control. During the next half-century, the Aztecs extended their control across 140,000 square miles stretching from modern Querétaro and Guanajuato in the north to the Isthmus of Tehuantepec in the south. Divine sanction and generations of military triumphs bolstered Aztec confidence.[43]

Generally the Aztecs did not establish permanent garrisons in conquered territory. Merchants, known as *pochteca*, and tax collectors, known as *calpixtli,* were usually the only Aztec presence among the conquered. Recurrent bloody, punitive expeditions prevented disaffected subjects from challenging Aztec suzerainty or failing to supply demanded tribute. On the eve of the Spanish conquest, the Aztec empire constituted a massive agglomeration of 38 provinces, embracing a range of cultural and linguistic traditions.[44]

The Aztecs instituted a form of tributary despotism. They would rule conquered lands indirectly, leaving indigenous leaders and nobles in place, but subordinating them to the Aztec hierarchy. The tribute Aztec subjects sent to Tenochtitlan annually included 7,000 tons of corn, 4,000 tons each of beans, chia seed, and amaranth, and 2,000,000 cotton cloaks. The Aztecs also received as tribute shields, feather headdresses, and luxury products, such as amber, that were unobtainable in the central highlands. As a result of this tribute, as well as the Aztecs' well developed trading networks, the main Aztec market at Tlatelolco offered consumers pottery, chocolate, vanilla, copper, all sorts of clothing, cooked and unprepared food, gold, silver, jade, turquoise, feather products, and even slaves. Spaniard Bernal Díaz del Castillo visited the market, where 60,000 gathered daily, and expressed astonishment at "the number of people and the quantity of merchandise that it contained, and at the good order and control that was maintained, for we had never seen such a thing before."[45]

As was the case with other Mesoamerican civilizations, the Aztec empire was highly stratified socially. Most of the population were peasant farmers. They were responsible not only for their sustenance, but for providing tribute and labor for public works. The Aztec state then organized the redistribution of goods and labor on a massive scale, thus allowing the highly inegalitarian consumption by the nobility, which constituted roughly 5 percent of the population. Presiding over the Aztecs was an emperor who was selected from the nobility. Rather than having rigid rules of male primogeniture, as European monarchies of the time did, the top Aztec elite selected the royal family member they felt was most qualified. The last Aztec emperor to be selected before the Spanish arrival was Montezuma, who assumed the throne in 1502.[46]

Human sacrifice formed a salient characteristic of Aztec society. The Aztecs claimed that human sacrifices propitiated the god Huitzilopochtli (Humming Bird of the South) and thus prevented the destruction of the earth and the sun for a fifth time. Aztec belief held that humans had existed in four previous worlds and that all had perished when these worlds were destroyed. To reintroduce humans to the fifth world, Quetzalcoatl made a perilous journey to steal human bones from Mictlantecuhtli, the lord of the underworld. The gods then gave life to the bones by shedding blood on them.[47]

Modern scholars have yet to reach consensus on why Aztec sacrifice played such an important role. The threat of being sacrificed might have intimidated conquered subjects. Some modern scholars have attributed such frequent human sacrifice to the need for animal protein in a society lacking cattle. (Victims were eaten after the sacrifice.) Others maintain that sufficient protein existed and that sacrifice served to reduce the population. Aztec sacrificial practices were used by the Spanish to justify the Conquest. However, as archeologist Robert J. Sharer commented, "Before we decry practices such as human sacrifice, we should remember that Europeans of 500 years ago burned people alive in the name of religion and submitted 'heretics' to an array of tortures and protracted executions."[48]

The Aztecs perfected one of the most productive agricultural systems ever devised—the chinampa. Chinampas were artificial islands, located near lakeshores, which measured from fifteen to thirty feet in width and up to 300 feet in length. Aztecs grew crops in soil piled on these islands. Lake water penetrated the entire chinampa, moistening roots. Mud scooped up from the lake bottom and night soil brought from Tenochtitlan by canoe maintained fertility. Eventually chinampas covered 25,000 acres in the Valley of Mexico. Chinampa-produced food facilitated the rapid expansion of the Aztec empire.[49]

Chinampas formed part of the rich lacustrine culture that developed in the Valley of Mexico. Lakefront villages relied heavily on the abundant fish, crustaceans, mollusks, and 109 aquatic bird species that inhabited the 252 square miles of lakes in the Valley of Mexico. Canoes facilitated communication between villages and with Tenochtitlan. These canoes could transport a ton of grain, roughly ten times what the Spanish-introduced mule could carry.[50]

The charismatic megacivilizations, such as the Maya and the Aztec, only covered limited areas of present-day Mexico and only dominated their area of influence for relatively short periods. In addition, there were innumerable other ethnic groups. They adapted themselves to the widely varying environments in which they found themselves. Most lacked the attributes of civilization—social classes, states, and hieratic religion. They accumulated knowledge concerning a variety of terrestrial and aquatic species that furnished them with food, fibers, raw materials, and medicines.

Many such people lived in the deserts of northern Mexico. Even though they did not have a rich material culture, what they did have—projectile points, scrapers, milling stones, baskets, and mats—has been well preserved in desert caves.[51]

Even though the Aztec empire was truncated by the Conquest, Mesoamerica's ethnic diversity continued under Spanish rule, providing continuity to the area. This diversity is indicated by more than 100 distinct indigenous languages surviving until at least the end of the nineteenth century. Of these surviving languages, Nahuatl, the language of the Aztecs, presently has the largest number of speakers. Due to Aztec influence over Mesoamerica, Nahuatl loan words are found in many of Mexico's indigenous languages, and many Nahuatl place names are still used. Nahuatl loan words that have made their way into English include ocelot, coyote, tomato, chocolate, tamale, and avocado.[52]

Chapter 2

The Conquest of Mexico, 1519–1521

> The recent history of Mexico, that of the last five hundred years, is the story of a permanent confrontation between those attempting to direct the country toward the path of Western civilization and those, rooted in Mesoamerican ways of life, who resist.
>
> Guillermo Bonfil Batalla, 1996[1]

THE SPANIARDS ARRIVE

In 1517, the Aztecs received reports that strange men had landed in Yucatán. These "strange men" formed an expedition, led by Francisco Hernández de Córdoba, which had sailed from the Spanish colony of Cuba. This expedition, composed of three ships and 110 men, set in motion the conquest of Mexico. While on shore, twenty-five Spanish were killed in a clash with the Maya. Hernández de Córdoba himself was wounded and died of his wounds after returning to Cuba. Quite possibly the clash was touched off by Spanish attempts to capture Maya to take back to Cuba for sale as slaves. Ship-borne Spanish slave raids were common throughout the Caribbean at the time.[2]

When the Spanish arrived in Yucatán, the Mayan population was divided into sixteen city-states—each striving to expand its boundaries at the expense of its neighbors. Their society functioned at a lower cultural level than their ancestors had reached five centuries before.[3]

In 1518, news came of a second expedition that had sailed from Cuba to Yucatán. This 240-man expedition, commanded by Juan de Grijalva, followed the Mexican coast north to Cape Rojo, between the present cities of Tuxpan and Tampico. The expedition's four ships then returned to Cuba and whetted Spanish appetites with reports of gold and large Indian populations.[4]

In 1519, the Aztecs learned of the arrival of Hernán Cortés's fateful expedition in what an Indian observer described as "towers or small mountains floating on the waves of the sea."[5]

Cortés, who would forever change Mexican history, was born in the western Spanish region of Extremadura in about 1484.[6] Along with thousands of others, he came to the New World in search of gold and glory, joining a westward migration set in motion by Christopher Columbus. Such a search became especially attractive after 1492. After that year, due to the capture of the last Moorish position on the Iberian Peninsula, fighting the infidel no longer offered a path to status and wealth in Spain.[7]

At the age of fourteen, Cortés left home to study law at the University of Salamanca. He spent two years there without distinguishing himself and then left the University. Even though he abandoned law, the Latin and legal phraseology he learned in Salamanca lent an air of authority to his later writings.

In 1504, Cortés booked passage on a ship to the Caribbean island of Hispaniola. There he received land and benefited from the indigenous population living on it. During the seven years he lived on Hispaniola, Spanish authorities called upon him to suppress an Indian revolt. This gained him the reputation of being a formidable warrior, which in turn earned him an invitation to serve as secretary to Diego de Velázquez in the conquest of Cuba.

In 1511, the Spanish conquered, or, more accurately, occupied Cuba. The Indians there offered little resistance. Cortés was placed in charge of many indigenous people, whom he forced to mine gold. Overwork and cultural shock killed many of these indigenous people. However, the gold they produced made Cortés wealthy. His serving from 1516 to 1518 as one of the magistrates of Santiago de Cuba reflected his newly elevated status.

In late 1518, Velázquez, who had been appointed governor of Cuba, selected Cortés to lead a third expedition to Mexico. He felt that Cortés possessed the strong leadership that such an expedition would require. He also knew that Cortés had enough wealth to underwrite much of the cost of the expedition.

By the early sixteenth century, the Crown had privatized territorial expansion, since the cost of maintaining a standing army and conquering the enormous territory of the Americas exceeded its very limited financial means. In exchange for its granting a private individual a royal license, or contract, to conquer and settle a given area, the Crown was legally entitled to a fifth of the booty obtained. The remaining four-fifths were divided between financiers of the conquest and the conquistadores, who also received the right to control the indigenous population they encountered. Such an arrangement served the Crown since, in addition to the booty, it would receive taxes from subsequent economic activity in the conquered area.[8]

Velázquez issued Cortés with very detailed instructions, which were a model of jurisprudence. If they had been obeyed, Cortés would not have been the conqueror of Mexico. The instructions stated that the principal purpose of the expedition was to serve God, and thus blasphemy and sleeping with native women would not be allowed. If landing parties were needed to secure wood and water, on no account was anyone ever to sleep on shore. The instructions foresaw reconnaissance, gathering information on missing Spaniards, limited trade, and a return to Cuba. Velázquez felt information obtained from the voyage would facilitate his establishing a settlement on the mainland once formal authorization arrived from Spain.[9]

To raise capital for the expedition, Cortés mortgaged his estate, borrowed from wealthy merchants, bought what he could on credit, and begged from friends. He also showed his willingness to ignore the law when it served his interest. To obtain needed supplies, he simply appropriated a shipload of provisions.[10]

Shortly before his scheduled departure, Velázquez decided that Cortés would probably betray him and revoked his command. Cortés remained undaunted. He convinced officials to assist him in assembling the expedition, even though they had orders to stop him. Cortés even recruited for his expedition one of the messengers who had delivered the order revoking his command. No one in Cuba could mount a force to stop him.

On February 18, 1519, Cortés left Cuba with twelve ships, 530 Europeans, several hundred Cuban Indians, and a few black freemen and African slaves, as well as sixteen horses and fourteen cannons. The expedition included several women, who served as housekeepers and maids, as well as two sisters of conquistador Diego de Ordaz. The conquistadores had mixed goals. Expedition member Bernal Díaz del Castillo wrote that the Spanish came "to bring light to those in darkness, and also to get rich, which is what all of us men commonly seek."[11]

Upon arriving in Yucatán, Cortés found two Spaniards whose boat had been shipwrecked there in 1511 as it attempted to sail from Darien to Santo Domingo. Cortés picked up one of the survivors, Jerónimo de Aguilar, who had learned the Mayan language. The other Spaniard, Gonzalo Guerrero, who had married a Maya woman and fathered children, said he preferred the life of an Indian and remained behind.[12]

While Cortés was sailing up the Mexican coast, a Maya chief presented him with a woman as a gift. This woman, Malinche, formed a translation team with Aguilar. She translated from Nahuatl, the Aztec language, to Yucatecan Mayan. Aguilar then translated the Mayan into Spanish. Malinche

CURRENT VIEWS OF MALINCHE

Malinche was born to high status within the Aztec empire. However, while still a youth, she became a slave of the Maya. According to one version, after her father died, her mother remarried and bore her new husband a son. To avoid Malinche's claiming high status based on her deceased father, her mother and stepfather decided to remove her from the family, transferring her to the Maya on the Gulf Coast. There she learned the Mayan language, a second language in addition to her native Nahuatl. Upon Cortés's arrival, she was simply given to him as one might give an honored guest a parrot or a dog. Her knowledge of Nahuatl and Aztec life in general proved to be so valuable that Bernal Díaz del Castillo commented, "As Doña Marina [another form of her name] proved herself such an excellent woman and good interpreter throughout the wars in New Spain, Tlaxcala and Mexico . . . Cortés always took her with him . . ."[a]

Her role in facilitating the Conquest has earned her the opprobrium of the Mexican people since. Her name has even given rise to the Spanish adjective *malinchista*, which the dictionary of the Royal Academy of the Spanish Language defines as one who prefers the foreign to one's own. Nobel Prize-winning Mexican author Octavio Paz expressed the general Mexican opinion of her:

> Doña Marina becomes a figure representing the Indian women who were fascinated, violated or seduced by the Spaniards. And as a small boy will not forgive his mother if she abandons him in search for his father, the Mexican people have not forgiven La Malinche for her betrayal.[b]

The image of her as traitor to Mesoamericans and whore (she bore Cortés a son) was apparently etched in stone.

However, in the latter part of the twentieth century, feminists reconsidered of Malinche's place in history. The question was raised as to just what she owed the Aztecs who had cast her aside or the Maya who had given her away. Certainly she did not owe "Mexico" anything, since the concept did not yet exist. Similarly, it was only the Spanish who divided humanity into races. To the indigenous, one was Aztec or Mayan or Zapotec. In the indigenous word view of the time any obligation to race per se did not exist any more than Europeans or Africans owed loyalty to others from their respective continents.

As a result a revisionist view of her emerged as a resilient woman who overcame adversity early in life and employed her talents as translator and diplomat to rise to high position in the milieu into which she was thrust. This radical reinterpretation of Malinche, while not completely reversing old notions of her, at least provides an alternate view of her.[c]

a Díaz del Castillo (1996: 67).
b Paz (1985: 86).
c Townsend (2006), Karttunen (1994), Valenzuela (1988), and author's interview with Valenzuela, April 2009.

soon learned enough Spanish to dispense with Aguilar. Later she became Cortés's lover. See the box for current views on Malinche.[13]

Cortés's fleet arrived near the present site of Veracruz on April 21, 1519. Soon after arriving, some members of the expedition decided they should forego further exploration and sail back to Cuba. Cortés persuaded them to remain in Mexico, using his strong personality and payments of gold, which, as one conquistador noted, served as "such a pacifier!" No one knows when Cortés decided to act independently of Velázquez. His going into debt to finance an expedition four times as large as Grijalva's suggests that he had planned to reject Velázquez's authority even before leaving Cuba.[14]

Upon hearing of Cortés's arrival, Montezuma, the Aztec emperor, sent emissaries with a rich assortment of gifts, including food, silver- and gold-covered wooden disks the size of carriage wheels, gold nuggets, and ornate headdresses of green parrot feathers. The emissaries, in addition to providing gifts, attempted to glean as much information as possible about the newcomers.[15]

FROM VERACRUZ TO THE AZTEC CAPITAL

To legitimize his planned conquest of the Aztecs, which was in direct violation of Velázquez's orders, on June 28, 1519, Cortés established a town named Villa Rica de la Vera Cruz (Rich Town of the True Cross), complete with a municipal government. The Spanish then elected a town council composed of Cortés's friends. Cortés declared Velázquez's authority to be superseded by that of the new municipal government, which appointed him commander-in-chief. Cortés then sent Francisco de Montejo to notify Emperor Carlos V, the Spanish monarch, that he would serve the emperor directly "until such time as His Majesty provided anyone else." Given the slow communications of the time, Cortés knew that no royal response would come before he had had the opportunity to conquer the Aztecs and ingratiate himself to the Emperor.[16]

The Spaniards soon contacted the Totonac Indians, one of the many indigenous groups dominated by the Aztecs. Through them, they discovered that the Aztecs had created an empire that exacted tribute from non-Aztecs. The Spaniards saw how this imperial domination could be turned to their advantage and promised protection to the Totonacs in exchange for their allegiance.

Cortés treated the Totonacs as he would later treat other indigenous groups he encountered. He offered them the opportunity to accept Christianity and Spanish political control. If the offer was rejected, the Spanish attacked. If the offer was accepted, Cortés's men would destroy indigenous idols, which they declared to be the work of Satan. However, Cortés would prevent looting and physical abuse of Indians by the men under his command. Many villages, when faced with Spanish military might, decided Spanish control constituted a lesser evil than Spanish attack.

To prevent any faint-hearted Spaniards from returning to Cuba, Cortés scuttled his ships. Then on August 8, 1519, Cortés's 300-man force began to march inland, accompanied by roughly 250 Totonacs who served as porters, guides, and combatants. Even at this early date, the Indian-versus-European dichotomy was an oversimplification.[17]

As the expedition wended its way inland, the Spaniards marveled at the strange peoples and magnificent scenery. When they encountered Indians, the Spaniards would try to win their loyalty and Christianize them. They were quite successful at this since, as Cortés noted in a letter to the Emperor, the Indians "would rather be Your Highness' vassals than see their houses destroyed and their women and children killed."[18]

After a month of marching, the Spaniards reached Tlaxcala, a small resource-poor nation east of Tenochtitlan that the Aztecs had never conquered. The Tlaxcalans maintained their independence through tenacious defense of their homeland and the political convenience an "enemy" provided to the Aztecs.

Cortés realized he could benefit from the hostility between the Tlaxcalans and the Aztecs and commented:

> When I saw the discord and animosity between these two peoples I was not a little pleased, for it seemed to further my purpose considerably; consequently I might have the opportunity of subduing them more quickly, for, as the saying goes, "divided they fall."[19]

The Tlaxcalans debated the type of reception they should give the Spanish. Some felt they should be welcomed. Others argued that their coming from an Aztec tributary town indicated that they were secretly allied with the Aztecs. Upon deciding the Spanish had allied with the Aztecs, the Tlaxcalans mobilized to defend themselves.

As the Spanish approached, they read the *requerimiento*, a charge in Spanish directing Indians to lay down their arms and accept the Spanish king and Christianity or suffer the consequences. It notified the indigenous people of a chain of command from God to the pope to the emperor to the conquistadores. The latter, it noted, were merely implementing the divinely sanctioned donation of American lands and peoples by the pope to the Spanish monarch.[20]

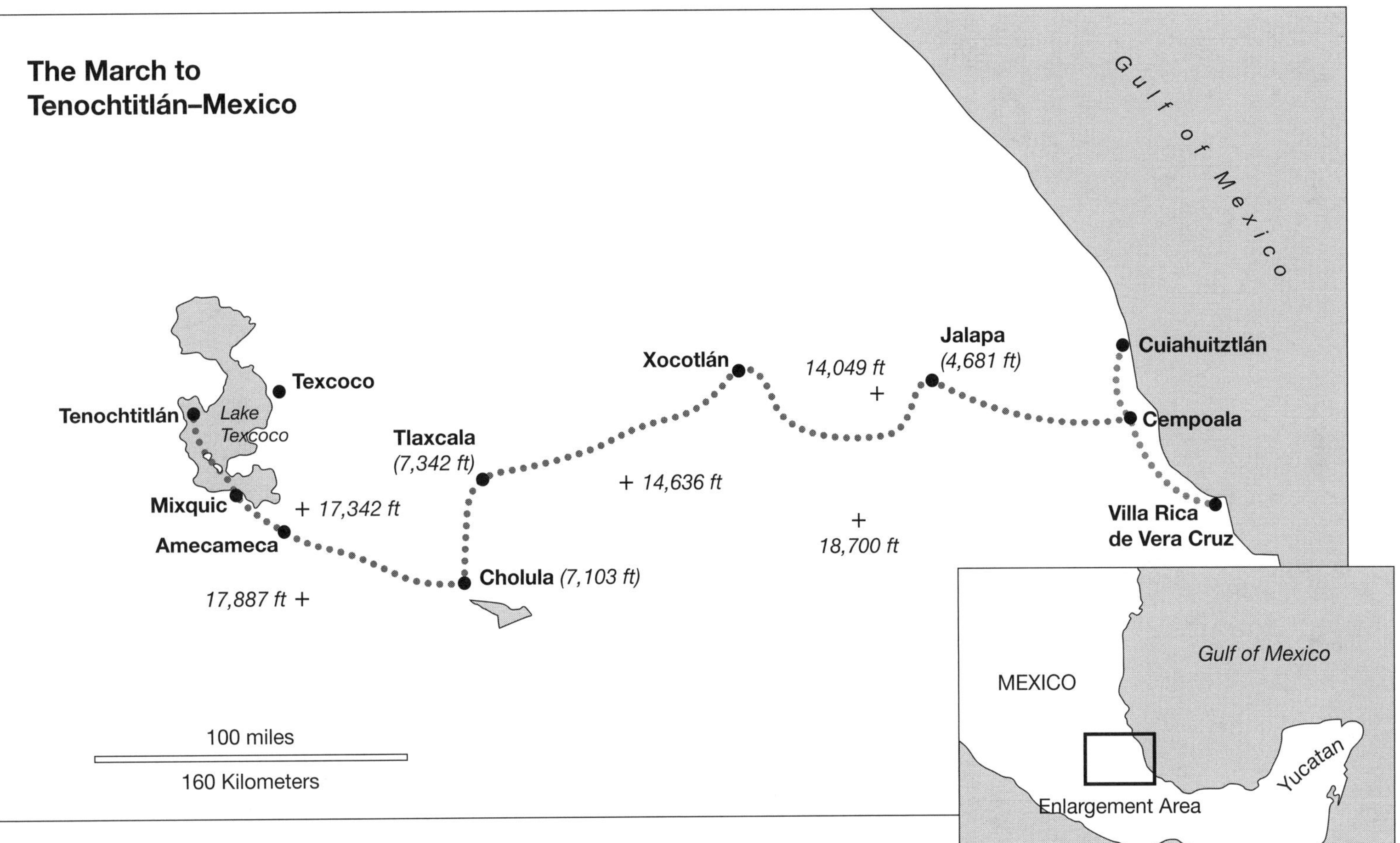

Figure 2.1 *Map of Cortés's march*

Source: From Tenenbaum, *Encyclopedia of Latin American History and Culture*, vol. 2, 1E. Copyright: Gale, a part of Cengage Learning, Inc. Reproduced by permission. www.cengage.com/permissions

It was immaterial that distance prevented the Indians from hearing the *requerimiento* and that they could not understand Spanish. Merely reading the charge fulfilled the Spanish requirement that infidels be given fair warning before being attacked. In conclusion, the *requerimiento* noted that if the Indians did not follow the order to accept Spanish rule and Christianity, the resulting havoc that would be wreaked on them would be their own fault, not the fault of the Spanish king, the reader of the *requerimiento*, or the Spanish soldiers.[21]

The right to conquest proclaimed by the *requerimiento* reflected legal doctrine in European international law that had been developing since the thirteenth century. Europeans claimed that Christians had the right to occupy the territory of the heathen if they assumed the responsibility for evangelizing those living there. This right was further elaborated with the notion of "just war," which could be waged against those who refused to accept Christianity or who later rebelled against Christian authority. Those captured in a "just war" could legally be executed for treason or sold into slavery.[22]

After the reading of the *requerimiento*, a series of battles ensued between the Tlaxcalans and the Spanish. Tlaxcalans provided stiff resistance to the conquistadores. In between battles with the Tlaxcalans, the Spanish would pillage the countryside, sowing fear by burning towns and mutilating civilians. Such tactics had proved to be especially effective on Hispaniola and Cuba.[23]

As a result of Spanish marauding and mounting battle casualties, the Tlaxcalans finally surrendered. The Spanish then entered Tlaxcala unmolested. Its citizens immediately accepted the Spanish offer to form an alliance against their perennial enemies—the Aztecs. Cortés showed his political skills by winning not only the Tlaxcalans' submission but their loyalty. This loyalty later saved the Spaniards' lives.

Cortés next marched to Cholula, an Aztec tributary town that had long served as a destination for religious pilgrimages. Further blurring the European versus Indian dichotomy, some 6,000 Tlaxcalans accompanied the Spanish. After Cortés's force arrived in Cholula, an informer told them that the Cholulans were preparing to attack them. Using this report as an excuse, the Spanish and the Tlaxcalans attacked the Cholulans.[24]

The Spanish priest, historian, and defender of Indian rights, Bartolomé de las Casas, later commented on the Spanish attack:

> Among other massacres was one which took place in Cholula, a great city of some thirty thousand inhabitants. When all the dignitaries of the city and the region came out to welcome the Spaniards with all due pomp and ceremony . . . the Spaniards decided that the moment had come to organize a massacre (or "punishment" as they themselves express such things) in order to inspire fear and terror in all the people of the territory.[25]

Even if a plot against the Spanish actually existed (evidence is mixed), the punishment inflicted by the Spanish was clearly excessive. Rather than targeting leaders believed to be involved in the plot, the Spanish slaughtered thousands of unarmed Cholulans.[26]

As the news spread that Spanish power rivaled that of the Aztecs, lords from several nearby cities approached Cortés and offered to reject Aztec sovereignty and fight with the Spanish. Cortés accepted such assistance, which later proved to be invaluable.

From Cholula, the Spanish departed for the nearby Aztec capital, which they entered by crossing a long causeway across Lake Texcoco. Causeways to the north, south, and west provided access to Tenochtitlan. A ten-mile-long dike divided the lake into fresh-water and salt-water sections. Streams flowed into the fresh-water section, enabling the Aztecs to fish and irrigate chinampas. Water then passed into the salty section, where it evaporated (as does water flowing into the Great Salt Lake in Utah), leaving salt to be collected.

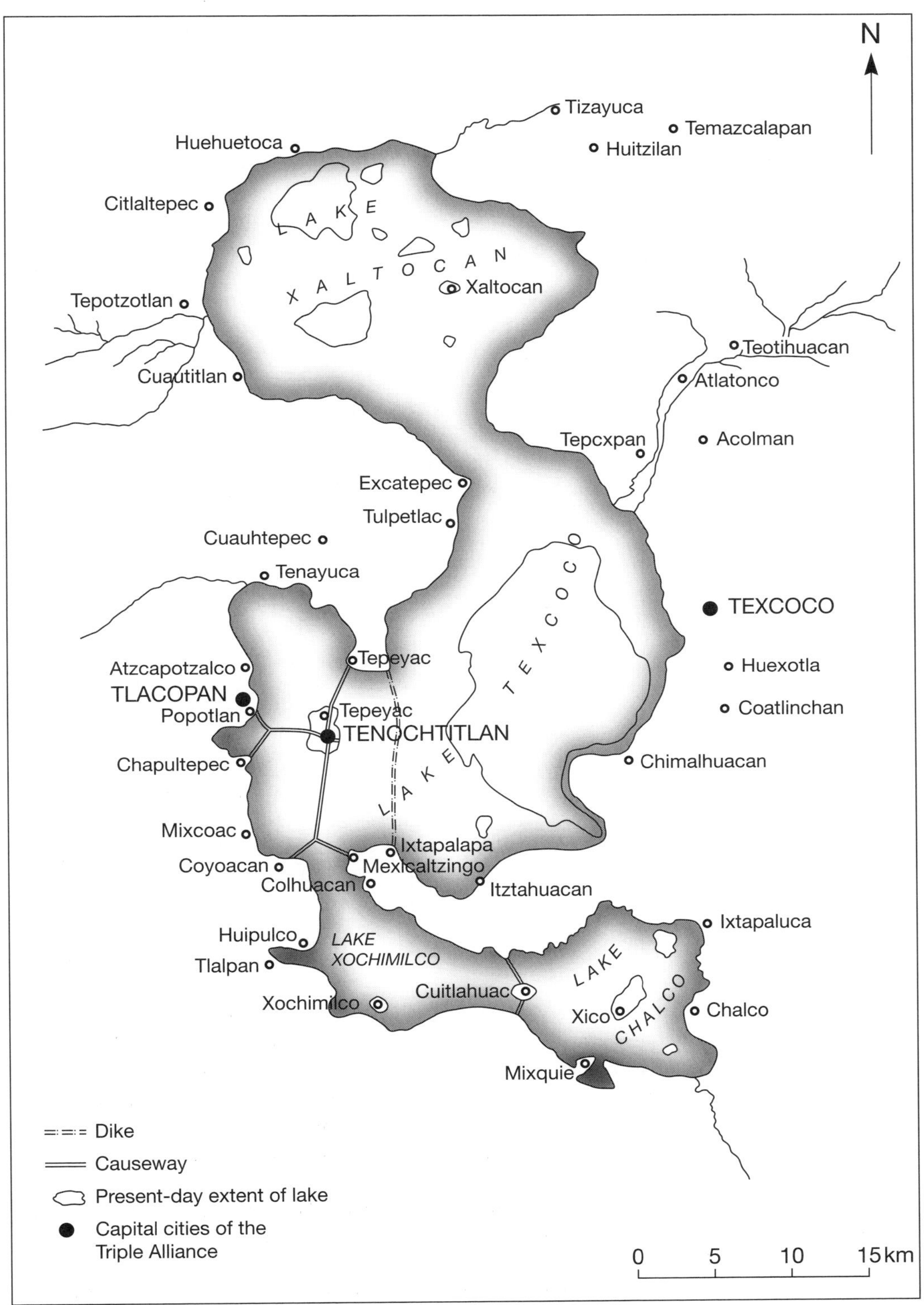

Figure 2.2 *The valley of Mexico in Aztec times*

Source: Reproduced courtesy of Michael D. Coe; map drawn by Patrick Gallagher

Díaz del Castillo commented on the Spaniards' reaction upon viewing Tenochtitlan:

> when we saw so many cities and villages built in the water and other great towns on dry land and that straight and level Causeway going towards Mexico, we were amazed and said that it was like the enchantments they tell of in the legend of Amadis, on account of the great towers . . . and buildings rising from the water, and all built of masonry. And some of our soldiers even asked whether the things we saw were not a dream.[27]

FROM ROYAL WELCOME TO SPANISH DEFEAT

Montezuma greeted the Spanish as they entered the city and invited them to be guests in a palace that had belonged to his father. To add to the impact of his arrival, Cortés had his cannons fired. One of the Aztecs, who had never heard cannon fire, said the sound had the same effect as psychedelic mushrooms.[28]

As the Spanish settled in as royal guests, they realized that they were not only failing to conquer the Aztecs but that they were in a precarious military position, surrounded by hundreds of thousands of warriors. Thus they decided to kidnap Montezuma and use him to gain control of the empire. A group of armed Spaniards went to Montezuma's palace and forced him to return to the palace where the Spaniards were lodged, threatening him with death if he resisted. Rather than risking his life at the hands of the Spaniards, Montezuma permitted them to take him prisoner, claiming he was their "guest."

Montezuma continued to rule the Aztec empire, even though Cortés controlled his actions. He announced that he was ruling in the name of the Spanish king and even turned the royal treasure over to the Spaniards.

Just as Cortés was seeing his ambitions fulfilled, he received word that a 900-man force sent by Cuban governor Velázquez had arrived on the Gulf Coast. Velázquez had instructed this force to arrest Cortés for not having returned to Cuba. Cortés placed the Aztec capital under the command of one of his officers, Pedro de Alvarado, and made a forced march to his rival's camp in Veracruz. Before he arrived in Veracruz, Cortés sent runners ahead to contact the men of the other force. Then through a combination of bribes, tales of riches forthcoming, and playing officers off against Pánfilo de Narváez, their unpopular commander, Cortés undermined the will of the opposing force. When Cortés finally attacked under the cover of a storm, resistance was minimal. Narváez later commented that he had been beaten by his own troops, not those of his rival.[29]

The newly arrived Spaniards, eager to share in the anticipated Aztec riches, joined Cortés, more than doubling his force. In addition he acquired many horses and weapons that Narváez had brought.

Soon after this victory, Cortés received word that Aztecs in Tenochtitlan had revolted. After receiving permission from the Spaniards remaining there, the Aztecs had staged a religious festival. During the festival, Alvarado had ordered his men to fire into the crowd in what modern strategists would term a preemptive strike. He claimed that the Aztecs had planned the festival as the prelude to an uprising. After this attack, the Aztec nation rose in arms and besieged the Spaniards' palace. Montezuma, still a captive, ordered the attacks to cease. The attacks then ended, leaving the Spaniards surrounded by the Aztecs.[30]

Cortés marched back to Tenochtitlan. The Aztecs allowed the returning force to cross their siege lines and join Alvarado in the palace, where they felt the Spaniards would be hopelessly trapped.[31]

From the roof of the palace, Montezuma again tried to quiet the Aztecs, but was met by jeers and rocks from the enraged attackers below. One of the rocks struck him, and he died shortly afterward, still a captive. The cause of Montezuma's death remains a mystery. Some claim the rock wound was fatal; others claim the Spaniards murdered him. In any case, Montezuma's death only heightened the fury of the besiegers.[32]

After enduring a month of siege, the Spaniards broke through the Aztec lines on the night of June 30, 1520. Cortés's troops had to swim the gaps their besiegers had dug in the causeway to prevent their flight. Aztec attacks forced the escaping Spaniards to fight their way to the mainland. Many Spaniards were so laden with stolen treasure that they could not defend themselves. Cortés's chaplain estimated that 450 Spanish died that night. In addition, several thousand Tlaxcalans probably died while fleeing the city. Mexicans refer to this Spanish defeat as la Noche Triste (the Night of Sorrows).[33]

Rather than engaging in hot pursuit, the Aztecs permitted the Spanish to regroup. The delay might be attributable to Alvarado having killed so many nobles that the Aztecs lacked a leader or to warriors being away tending their fields during the rainy season. The Aztecs might also have been observing a mourning period for those killed on la Noche Triste. Finally the Aztecs may have simply assumed the Spanish to be vanquished and unworthy of pursuit.[34]

Seven days later, as the battered Spanish forces headed for the protection of Tlaxcala, the Aztecs attacked them near the town of Otumba. They surrounded the beleaguered Spaniards. Then Cortés and five horsemen charged into the Aztec ranks, killed their commander, and triumphantly raised the captured Aztec imperial battle standard. For ancient Mesoamericans, battle standards served as both the representation of the state and the embodiment of a potent spiritual being whose presence and performance were critical to their success in battle. The Spanish were saved by Cortés's audacious action and by the open space at Otumba that permitted the effective use of horses. After the battle, Cortés's force marched on to Tlaxcala without further combat.[35]

THE FINAL SPANISH VICTORY

Once they arrived safely in Tlaxcala, the Spanish began preparations for the conquest of the Aztecs. Cortés ordered a fleet of sailboats built for use on the 238-square-mile Lake Texcoco. New arrivals from Spain and Cuba reinforced the Spaniards. Cuban governor Velázquez, unaware of Narváez's defeat by Cortés, sent additional men. At the same time, Cortés's Indian allies, especially the Tlaxcalans, assembled large armies. Once Cortés showed he was able and willing to protect his allies from Aztec retribution, additional Aztec tributaries joined his cause.

The Aztecs attempted to form an alliance with the Tlaxcalans against the Spanish. They noted that the two groups shared a common language, gods, and ancestry. The Aztecs also reminded the Tlaxcalans that the Spanish, even after having been warmly received by Montezuma, had repaid his kindness by imprisoning him. The Tlaxcalans, remembering past Aztec cruelty and arrogance, rejected such an alliance.[36]

While the Spaniards gathered strength, an insidious contribution inadvertently brought by the Spanish—smallpox—weakened the Aztecs. As the indigenous population had no natural immunity to the disease, epidemics swept the country, killing much of the population and demoralizing those who survived.

An Aztec account of the smallpox epidemic reported:

> It began to spread, striking everywhere in the city and killing many of the people. Sores erupted on their faces, breasts, bellies. They had so many painful sores over their bodies that they could not move, not even turn over in their litters, and if someone tried to move them, they screamed in agony. This pestilence killed untold numbers of people, many of them dying because there was nobody to feed them, so they starved. Those who survived had holes in their faces, or were left blinded.[37]

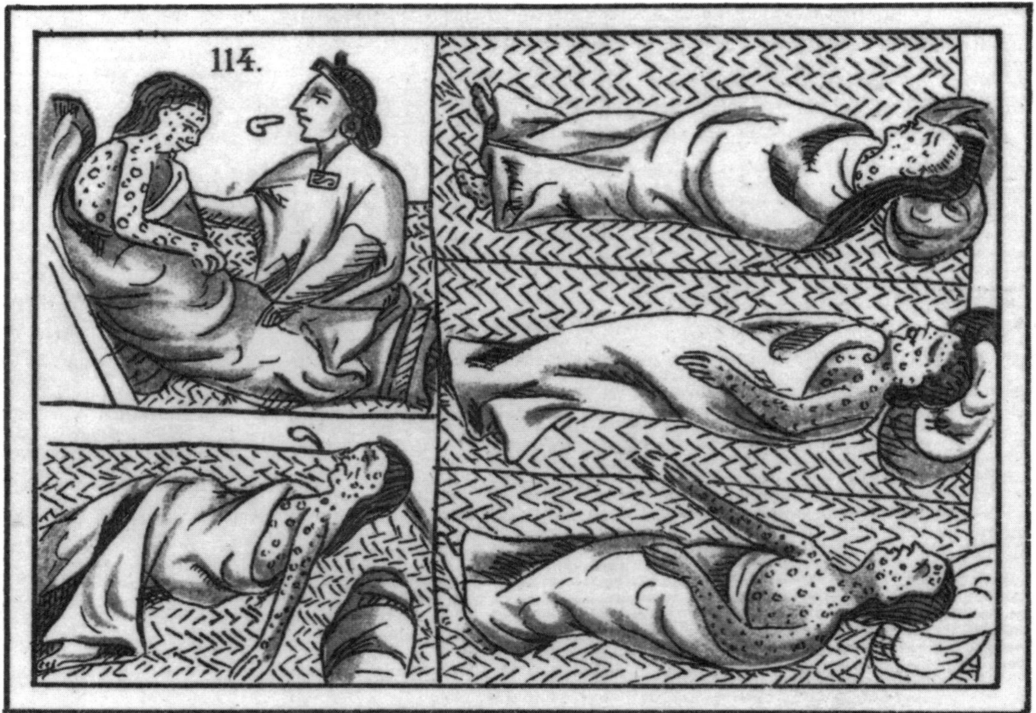

Figure 2.3 *Survivors' depiction of smallpox victims*

Source: Reproduced courtesy of the Benson Latin American Collection, the University of Texas at Austin

The fatalities from the epidemic included Montezuma's brother, Cuitláhuac, who had succeeded him as Aztec emperor. The Aztec elite then chose Montezuma's nephew, Cuauhtémoc, to be the last emperor of the Aztecs.[38]

After months of preparation, the Spaniards began their assault. Fifteen thousand porters carried portions of the newly constructed sailboats to Lake Texcoco, where they were assembled. Then the Spanish marched around the lake, subduing villages along the shore and cutting off aqueducts and food supplies to Tenochtitlan. Next they launched offensives down the causeways with the support of the boats, which had been armed with cannons. An estimated 200,000 Tlaxcalans and former Aztec subjects joined the offensive.[39]

The Aztecs stubbornly resisted the 85-day siege, forcing the attackers to fight for every inch of ground. To deny cover to the Aztecs, as well as to provide for the effective use of horses and cannons, the Spanish and their Indian allies filled all the canals and destroyed all the buildings they captured. The Aztecs chose to defend a fixed location, highly vulnerable to Spanish cannons and cavalry. Even if they had conceived of a guerrilla strategy, the Aztecs would likely have found little support among those they had previously tyrannized.[40]

During the siege, the Aztecs refused surrender offers, despite their high casualty rate, disease, and near starvation. To the horror of the Spanish, the Aztecs would sacrifice captured Spaniards, as well as their horses, in full view of the besieging force.

Finally, on August 13, 1521, Cuauhtémoc saw that the Spanish were closing in on the last Aztec-held section of the city. He tried to flee by canoe, but was captured and brought to Cortés as a prisoner.

After Cuauhtémoc's capture, Aztec resistance ceased. By one estimate, more than 240,000 Aztecs died during the siege. Of these, Cortés estimated that 100,000 died in combat. The rest succumbed to disease and starvation. Only 60,000 residents of Tenochtitlan survived. Between 500 and 1,000 of the Spaniards engaged in the Conquest died.[41]

The Spanish allowed the Aztec survivors to leave their once beautiful city, which had been reduced to rubble. Cuauhtémoc was not as fortunate as his former subjects. The conquerors imprisoned and tortured him in an unsuccessful attempt to make him reveal the location of additional Aztec treasure.

THE REASONS (VALID AND INVALID) FOR THE SPANISH VICTORY

The reasons why a handful of Spaniards were able to conquer millions of Aztecs include the following:

- The Spanish incited the Aztecs' subjects to rebel against their imperial masters. Rather than speaking of a Spanish victory, it would be more accurate to state that the Spanish led a successful rebellion. As noted above, 200,000 Indian allies supported the Spanish in the siege of Tenochtitlan. Other Indians fought with the Spanish elsewhere.
- The smallpox epidemic decimated the Aztecs and left them leaderless. Both Aztec defenders of Tenochtitlan and the Spaniards' Indian allies fell victim to the disease. However, the Spanish were largely immune, and their command structure remained intact. In contrast, Montezuma's successor, Cuitláhuac, died of the disease, thus plunging the Aztecs into a succession crisis during the siege.
- The Spanish used a variety of weapons unavailable to the Aztecs, including the crossbow, the notoriously inaccurate matchlock guns known as harquebuses, thundering cannons, and, especially, the long, sharp Castilian sword. After fighting in Tlaxcala, Díaz del Castillo commented, "It was only by a miracle of sword play that we could make them give way so that our ranks could be reformed."[42] Aztec swords, which were made of sharp stones slotted into wooden shafts, were intended to wound, but not to kill, so as to provide victims for sacrifice. Mesoamericans made little use of metal aside from bells and ornaments.[43]
- Spanish battle tactics, based on experience in European wars, allowed the Spaniards to successfully integrate infantry, artillery, and cavalry. In combat, the Aztecs, rather than attempting to destroy the enemy, would isolate and capture as many prisoners as possible for transport to the rear and eventual sacrifice in their capital.[44]
- Two animals contributed to the Spanish victory. The horse intimidated, provided a platform to impale and hack at natives, and allowed swift transportation. In addition, war dogs, probably mastiffs or Irish wolfhounds, felled many an Indian.[45]
- Cortés's talent for flattery, courtesy, eloquence, swift decision, improvisation, deviousness, and sudden changes of plan, as well as his will and courage in adversity, determined that he should lead the Conquest.[46]
- Cortés could draw on a variety of tactics that had been perfected during the Spanish Reconquest and the occupation of the Caribbean. These tactics included: 1) the wanton use of violence, as at Cholula; 2) kidnapping native rulers, a tactic that was also used in the Caribbean; and 3) allying with one non-Spanish group to conquer another, as was done both in the Caribbean and during the Reconquest of Andalucia. This third tactic was especially effective since Native American identity was highly localized. Native peoples saw themselves as members of a particular community or city-state and very seldom as members of a larger ethnic group. They certainly did not feel themselves to be anything even approaching the category of "Indians" or "natives."[47]
- Sixteenth-century European culture facilitated the Conquest. Writing allowed leaders of various Spanish forces to effectively communicate and for Cortés to request help from the rest of the Spanish realm. The wheel allowed the transport of the cannons used in the Conquest.

Improvements in the safety, price, and capacity of sea travel enabled the Spanish in Mexico to remain in communication with Europe and receive reinforcements.[48] As a result of their relative modernity, more than a year before the Conquest was complete, the Spanish were already exhibiting booty from Mexico and spreading information about Mexico thorough Europe.[49]

- Traditional accounts of the Conquest, such as William Prescott's classic *History of the Conquest of Mexico*, stressed that Montezuma was under the influence of strange portents that supposedly appeared during the last years of his reign. Rather than responding to portents, Montezuma appears to have accepted Cortés as what he said he was—an ambassador from a distant and unknown ruler. As such, Cortés had to be treated with respect and hospitality. After the Conquest, the Spanish had a vested interest in claiming that portents influenced the Aztecs, since that would establish their opponents as primitives in need of enlightenment by the Spanish. Indigenous informants who later spoke to the Spanish may have used portents to explain their humiliating defeat. Another possible explanation for Montezuma's call for the Aztecs to lay down their arms was that he recognized that resistance against Spanish technology was hopeless.[50]

THE CONQUEST IN RETROSPECT

The Spanish victory occurred with pontifical blessing. Pope Leo X sent bulls offering indulgences for those who engaged in war against the infidel. The conquistadores themselves fought with a clear conscience, certain that they were bringing civilization and Christianity. They believed their efforts would allow these newly discovered people to leave behind their backward conditions.[51]

However, the history that Bartolomé de las Casas published in 1552 did not share the view that the Conquest was religiously motivated. His history stated:

> The reason the Christians have murdered on such a vast scale and killed anyone and everyone in their way is purely and simply greed. They have set out to line their pockets with gold and to amass private fortunes as quickly as possible so that they can then assume a status quite at odds with that into which they were born.[52]

In Mexico, Cortés is now regarded as a ruthless invader. The conspicuous lack of his name on Mexican streets and monuments and Diego Rivera's portrayal of him as a cross-eyed, syphilitic hunchback in a mural in the National Palace indicate these feelings. On the other hand, Montezuma and Cuauhtémoc are national heroes, and innumerable streets and monuments bear their names.[53]

The five-hundredth anniversary of Columbus's arrival in the New World showed that the Conquest still arouses strong feelings. Heated debate occurred between those wanting a gala celebration of the anniversary and those wanting somber reflection. Mexicans did not even agree on whether Columbus's arrival should be referred to as a discovery, an encounter, or an invasion.[54]

Chapter 3

Three Centuries of Colonial Rule, 1521–1810

> Among the events that have done violence to Mexican history, none shook the foundations on which the indigenous peoples were based with as much force or was as decisive in the formation of a new society and a new historical project as the Spanish Conquest and colonization.
>
> Enrique Florescano, 1994[1]

FROM CONQUISTADOR TO ADMINISTRATOR

The fall of Tenochtitlan marked the end of the Aztec empire. However, outside the Valley of Mexico, the Spanish presence in the former empire was minimal. In even more distant parts of what is today's Mexico, this presence was virtually non-existent. Centuries would pass before effective Spanish control was established over many outlying areas.[2]

In 1524 Cortés made an ill-advised march to Honduras to arrest Cristóbal de Olid, one of his lieutenants, who had rejected Cortés's authority and begun communicating directly with Carlos V. Cortés brought Cuauhtémoc along as a hostage to prevent his leading a rebellion during the expedition's absence. En route, Cortés executed Cuauhtémoc, claiming he was planning an Indian revolt. Little evidence has ever been found to support this claim.[3]

Upon his arrival in Honduras, Cortés found members of Olid's colony had already overthrown and executed him, so he returned to Mexico City. During his twenty-month absence, Cortés's enemies had irreparably undermined his power, accusing him of keeping booty that legally belonged to the Crown and embezzling other funds. His enemies had also assumed political control and deprived those loyal to Cortés of their property and tribute rights.[4]

After Cortés's return from Honduras, the Crown dismissed the charges filed in his absence. His insubordination was also forgiven, which, after all, had involved only Governor Velázquez, not the monarch. Cortés, however, still presented the emperor with a dilemma. Carlos V wished to reward the conquistador for his services. Yet he wanted to keep Cortés's power in check so that he would not threaten the Crown. He resolved this dilemma by appointing a viceroy (administrator) for Mexico and then removing Cortés from formal administration. At the same time, he amply rewarded Cortés, granting him access to many thousands of acres of grazing land and more extensive *encomienda* (tribute and labor) rights than those of any other conquistador. Cortés's grant included 23,000 adult male tributaries in twenty-two towns and covered an area of more than 24,900 square miles. To prevent Cortés from using his tributaries as a power base, the emperor selected villages isolated from one another and distant from Mexico City, the seat of political power. The twenty-two towns granted to Cortés extended from the Valley of Mexico to the Valley of Oaxaca and from the Gulf to the Pacific Coast. Even this immense wealth failed to satisfy Cortés. The conquistador died in 1547 while on a return trip to Spain seeking additional reward.[5]

The Spanish organized various expeditions to extend their control. In 1523, 300 Spaniards and nearly 20,000 Indians, led by Pedro de Alvarado, marched south from Mexico City. Alvarado's force passed through Oaxaca and established Spanish rule in territory now forming Chiapas, Guatemala, and El Salvador.

In 1527, a 400-man force commanded by Francisco de Montejo attempted to impose Spanish rule on Yucatán. His force fought its way around the peninsula. In one single battle, the Spanish killed more than 1,200 Maya. However, unlike the Aztecs, the Maya lacked a centralized government, making it impossible for the Spanish to simply seize a ruler and, through him, control the Maya. The Maya responded to the Spanish with night attacks and by laying ambushes and traps. Their functioning as jungle guerrillas allowed some Maya to hold out until 1546. Revolts continued to plague the colonizers throughout the sixteenth century.[6]

In 1529, Nuño de Guzmán marched west through Michoacán. His foray, brutal even by the standards of the times, reached southern Sonora, burning villages, enslaving Indians, and executing Indian leaders, including Cazonci, the Tarascan king, who was accused of fomenting succession. Guzmán's expedition neatly illustrated the Crown's values. No one raised an objection to his having enslaved Indians to be sold in Spain's Caribbean possessions. The Crown simply levied taxes on their sale. However, royal authorities would not tolerate regicide and, in 1537, imprisoned Guzmán for his atrocities.[7]

These expeditions laid the basis for Spanish colonization, which was more pervasive than that of the Aztecs. Unlike the Aztecs, the Spanish imposed their culture and language on others. Spaniards also progressively deprived conquered Indians of direct control of their land. As Mexican historian Enrique Florescano noted:

> Pre-Hispanic man was totally integrated with the earth, his land, his community, nature, and the cosmos. This deep, inextricable integration began to disappear with increasing rapidity when the Spanish appeared and took the land. Upon losing their land, and as the nature of its use changed radically, the Indians also lost their place in the world and their relationship with other men, nature, and the cosmos.[8]

COLONIAL ADMINISTRATION

> The New World fell before a small group of enterprising conquistadores, yet force alone could not construct an empire. In the end, ideas relegated the conquerors to subordinate positions, and organized a vast and varied aboriginal population of different historical, cultural, and political traditions under royal control.
>
> Colin MacLachlan, 1988[9]

The Spanish monarch, who stood at the pinnacle of a highly centralized colonial administration, held title to all land, water, and mineral rights in his realm and was ultimately responsible for filling all public offices. The king assumed responsibility for both the spiritual and temporal well-being of his subjects. The Fuero Real, laws dating from 1255, declared the king to be the temporal interpreter of divine will. Thus questioning royal mandates implied not only a challenge to the political order but an attack on Christian faith.[10]

The monarch presented his kingdom as a political and territorial division within the universal church founded by Christ himself. Mundane considerations, however, prevailed. One individual, with or without divine sanction, could not administer an empire. The king readily acknowledged interest groups, such as merchant guilds, and often granted them self-policing powers and responsibilities now associated with a modern state. Various advisors, councils, and corporate groups surrounded the king. Petitioners, who inflated their own importance in an attempt to gain a hearing, constantly besieged him.[11]

The king's simple decree of divine sanction did not end political debate. In 1520, Castilian mayors, alderman, judges, professionals, craftsmen, and lesser clergymen revolted against Carlos V to prevent him from centralizing control, granting excessive privileges to foreigners, and spending money from Castile in his other realms. This movement, which he defeated, repeatedly raised demands concerning "the consent of all" and "the will of the people." The defeat of the uprising, known as the Comunero Revolt, greatly reduced the chances of imposing effective institutional restraints on the emperor.[12]

To cope with the increasingly complex demands of administering the New World lands claimed by Spain, Carlos V established the Council of the Indies in 1524. The Council consisted of a president and eight councilors who oversaw the political, ecclesiastical, and judicial affairs of Spain's New World colonies. These nine men answered only to the king.[13]

Along with the constraints imposed by the enormous area of the empire, poor communications, and the limited staff available, the Council's own self-image constrained it. Members saw themselves as a body of advisors to the monarch. Had they been charged with formulating and implementing policy, as the heads of modern semi-autonomous government agencies are, their actions would have had more direction.[14]

Since a round-trip voyage between Spain and Veracruz required six months, day-to-day administration obviously had to be vested in officials residing in the New World. Thus the Crown divided the Spanish empire into large administrative units called viceroyalties, each headed by a viceroy. The viceroyalty of New Spain, with its seat in Mexico City, included territory stretching from Costa Rica to California, and, in addition, Florida, the Philippine Islands, Spain's Caribbean colonies, and part of Venezuela. Throughout the colonial period, as a result of its being the seat of viceregal administration, Mexico City exercised a greater influence on Mexico than had Tenochtitlan before the Conquest.[15]

Given the influence of local economic interests, as well as isolation from Spain, the viceroy could carry out policy markedly at odds with royal decrees. The phrase "*Obedezco pero no cumplo*" ("I obey but I do not comply") summarized this attitude. To stall on implementing a matter at odds with local interests, the viceroy could simply request clarification and postpone action for a year or more. Viceroys also engaged in semantic evasion. For example, in 1585, a royal decree unequivocally prohibited the collection of tribute from Tlaxcala. Authorities in New Spain simply reclassified the tribute as a "*reconocimiento*" ("recognition") and continued to collect it. That way they could have access to Indian wealth without openly defying the king. Often the viceregal administration would yield part but not all of what the Crown demanded. As historian John Lynch commented, "Usually there emerged a workable compromise between what central authorities ideally wanted and what local conditions and pressures would realistically tolerate."[16]

The king appointed judges to a judicial body known as the *audiencia*, which served as Mexico's supreme court of appeals and as a consultative body. After a viceroy's death, *audiencia* judges, or *oidores*, administered the colony until the next viceroy arrived. Before the arrival of the first viceroy in 1535, the *audiencia* held both administrative and judicial power.

The *audiencia* limited the viceroy's actions and called him to account when necessary. In addition, the archbishop and the Mexico City municipal council were expected to prevent viceregal malfeasance. They both enjoyed the privilege of communicating independently with the king and the Council of the Indies and could report viceregal actions that countered the interests of the Crown.[17]

To facilitate administration, New Spain was divided into administrative entities known as *gobiernos*. Nueva Galicia, one of the best known and earliest of these subdivisions, encompassed the city of Guadalajara. Eventually twenty-two of these administrative units, also known as provinces or kingdoms (*reinos*), stretched from Costa Rica to California. A governor who served as political chief and military commander headed each province. In addition, he held judicial and civil authority and presided over the city council of the capital city. Distance and slow communications with Mexico City allowed governors to protest and delay orders from superiors with whom they disagreed.[18]

Districts embracing several municipalities, known either as *corregimientos* or *alcaldías mayores*, formed the next administrative layer. Such districts were under the jurisdiction, respectively, of a *corregidor* or an *alcalde mayor*—officials who formed the lowest rung of the colonial bureaucracy. These officials exercised discretionary executive and judicial powers and often engaged in the endemic corruption, bribery, and extortion that occurred at the local level. Normally such officials would serve three- to five-year terms after having been appointed or having purchased the position. Their duties included civil administration, justice, and tax and tribute collection. As with the viceroy, they also played a religious role, ensuring that Indians attended Mass and met religious obligations.[19]

The municipality *(municipio)*, which usually included a head town (*cabecera*) and outlying villages, formed the smallest significant administrative unit. Many of the early municipalities had the same boundaries as the Aztec altepetl, with the old ceremonial center becoming the *cabecera*. A municipal council (*cabildo*) of from four to fifteen members, depending on the local population, presided over municipal governments. Conquistadores and holders of *encomienda* grants initially selected *cabildo* members. Later, landowners and merchants made such selections. However, beginning with the reign of Felipe II, who ruled Spain from 1556 to 1598, the Crown began selling these positions, which could be inherited. By the late colonial period, a self-perpetuating oligarchy manned most municipal councils.[20]

While most municipalities remained small, some of them evolved into cities. These cities had varying origins. Veracruz served as a port, while others, such as León and Celaya, initially served as garrisons to protect against Indian raids. Zacatecas and Guanajuato began as mining centers. Puebla simply provided a place where Spaniards could live. Whenever possible, Spaniards preferred to live in cities, since they equated city dwelling with civilization, social status, and security. This preference notwithstanding, urban living remained the exception, not the rule. As late as 1800, only 9 percent of Mexicans lived urban areas.[21]

Royal decrees mandated that newly established cities must follow a general plan. Streets crossed at right angles in a checkerboard or grid pattern. A plaza surrounded by a church and government buildings formed the center of each city. Historian Robert Ricard commented on the importance of the plaza: "A Spanish American city is a main plaza surrounded by streets and houses, rather than a group of streets and houses around a main plaza."[22]

Most colonial cities, such as Mexico City, Guadalajara, and Puebla, shared a common commercial and residential pattern. Shops dominated the central plaza, and the homes of the wealthy occupied adjacent lots. A concentric ring around the wealthy housed the less affluent. On the edge of town, the homes of the poor—transient laborers, mulattos, and Indians—formed yet another ring.[23]

Rather than implementing a tax policy that would be judged sound by modern standards, the king and his top officials obtained revenue by auctioning positions in government to the highest bidder. Buyers expected that, through fees, bribes, tribute, and the ability to profit in business, they would recoup their investment and make a profit.[24]

The sale of office increased abuse, since in addition to the high costs of travel and setting up new households, office holders had to recoup the amount paid for office. Today this would be viewed as corruption. At the time, the populace regarded buying office as an investment in a revenue source that guaranteed the best men—those with a genuine stake in society—would occupy top positions. People judged officials not as honest or corrupt but by the degree to which they enriched themselves. Only flagrant excess brought condemnation.[25]

The Habsburg colonial administration, which lasted until 1700, was a creaking cumbersome engine that consumed great quantities of paper, energy, and cash payments. These payments—bribes and the sale of offices—were essential if the system was to function, given the lack of salaries.

The Habsburg regimes followed the dictum of letting sleeping dogs lie. They did not entertain grand visions of social transformation, being content with limited controls and limited fiscal benefit. Typically the Habsburgs relied on consensus, using repression only in a selective fashion. Loyalty to God and king undergirded governance. This loyalty was so pervasive that during the almost 200 years the Habsburgs ruled Mexico, no concerted challenge to the Crown emerged.[26]

THE SIXTEENTH CENTURY

> Assignment of encomiendas based on conquest contributions created a new gentry in New Spain including individuals who, had it not been for the chance of time and place, would never have risen above their plebeian origins.
>
> Robert Himmerich y Valencia, 1991[27]

The first viceroy, Antonio de Mendoza, came from a prominent Castilian noble house, ideal for offsetting Cortés's influence. Mendoza, who arrived in 1535, invested in commerce, textile manufacturing, and agricultural enterprises, thus setting a precedent for his successors. Sixteenth-century citizens readily accepted such investments. In fact Mendoza proved to be such an able administrator that he remained in office for sixteen years—a length of tenure that would never be equaled. At the end of his term, in recognition of his having stabilized the core and completed far-ranging reconnaissance, he was appointed viceroy of Peru.[28]

Fierce competition between the Crown, clergymen, and Spanish settlers for a shrinking amount of Indian labor and a dwindling supply of tribute dominated early colonial history. The Crown pursued the mutually exclusive goals of humanitarian treatment for Indians and maximizing income for the mother country. For example, in 1528, the emperor prohibited the use of Indian labor in gold mines to prevent the extinction of the indigenous population, something that was already occurring in the Caribbean. However, in 1536, he revoked the decree to "insure the expanding mining industry the labor it needs."[29]

Shortly after the Conquest, Cortés began awarding grants known as *encomiendas,* a practice copied from the Spanish colonies in the Caribbean. The Caribbean grants, in turn, resembled the grants made to Spaniards who had captured territory from the Moors during the Reconquest of Spain.[30]

Each *encomienda* grant gave Spaniards the right to collect tribute in the form of clothing, food, and other products from the Indians living in a certain area. While the grant allowed Spaniards to benefit from Indian labor, indigenous customs and local governments were largely unaffected. In exchange for receiving the fruits of Indian labor, Spaniards assumed responsibility for Christianizing the Indians included in the grant. The repeated sale and reassignment of *encomiendas*, however, indicated that the Spanish viewed the grant more as an economic asset than as a religious responsibility.

Spaniards did not acquire title to the land included in an *encomienda* grant nor could they legally control or sell Indians living there. These grants enabled the conquistadores to use the existing Indian production system to feed and clothe themselves. This dependence on the Indian reflected the conquistadores' aversion to manual labor as well as the lack of Spanish farmers and craftsmen.

The granting of *encomiendas* became a form of royal and viceregal patronage rewarding individuals who had not participated in the Conquest. These grants persuaded many adventurous Spaniards to remain in New Spain. They also provided a ready source of army recruits. Pedro de Alvarado employed many of the Indians from his Xochimilco *encomienda* in the conquest of Guatemala. The *encomienda* enabled the early Spaniards to accumulate enough wealth to establish their own enterprises. Recipients of these grants formed the first rudimentary rural administration before the establishment of conventional local government.[31]

The first of these grant holders, known as *encomenderos*, enjoyed quasi-seigneurial rights. They not only demanded material tribute but forced Indians to transport their goods and build their houses, roads, and farm buildings. Through the mid-1500s, the *encomienda* allowed the conquistadores to survive on a form of plunder economy.[32]

Early in the colonial period, the Crown feared *encomenderos* would form a hereditary aristocracy that would threaten its power. Christian humanists pressured the Crown to lessen the abuse of Indians, noting that *encomenderos* rarely fulfilled the reciprocal duty of evangelization. Finally, *encomenderos* collected tribute that Indians would otherwise have paid to the Crown. As a result, the king restricted the inheritability of the *encomienda*. Although Cortés's descendants retained their tribute rights, by about 1575 the descendants of most other *encomenderos* had lost their rights, and Indians paid tribute directly to the Crown. Between 1560 and 1642, the number of *encomenderos* declined from 480 to 140.[33]

Other factors led to the decline in the *encomienda*, which had dominated New Spanish society in the mid-1540s. After that date, the available tribute fell as the Indian population collapsed. Some *encomenderos* found a sedentary life uninteresting, abandoned their grants, and left for distant lands. The Crown capped the amount of tribute *encomenderos* could demand and, in 1549, made it illegal to demand labor, as opposed to goods, from those included in the grant. Finally, the relative position of *encomenderos* declined as new sources of income, such as silver mines, became available.[34]

The status of the *encomenderos* also fell as newcomers with close ties to the mother country obtained political positions and commercial concessions unavailable to long-time residents. These new arrivals opposed the *encomienda* since it denied them access to Indian labor. In 1599, Gonzalo Gómez de Cervantes, the son of a conquistador, complained:

> Those who only yesterday served in shops, taverns and other menial jobs are now holding the highest positions in the country, whereas the gentlemen and the descendants of those who conquered and settled it are poor, downcast, and out of favor.[35]

The New Laws of 1542 illustrate the conflict between the Crown's desire for humanitarian treatment of the Indian and colonial political reality. These laws prohibited enslaving Indians, even as punishment for resisting Spanish domination. They also prohibited new *encomienda* grants and stipulated that existing *encomienda* rights would terminate with the death of the current holder. Had this provision been enforced, the *encomienda* would have vanished within a generation.

In Peru, colonists rebelled and killed the viceroy sent to enforce the New Laws. Fearing such a response in Mexico, the viceroy refrained from enforcing the new regulations. *Encomenderos* alleged they could not survive without the *encomienda*. The Mexico City municipal government sent a delegation to Carlos V to protest the laws. The *encomienda* had powerful backers in Mexico, such as the Bishop of Mexico, Juan de Zumárraga, who held an *encomienda* grant. Given adamant opposition in the colonies, the Crown reversed itself and granted inheritance rights to the children and grandchildren of *encomenderos*. Even though authorities did not enforce the New Laws, legal restrictions on the *encomienda* continued to diminish its importance.[36]

The epidemics following the Conquest caused population loss exceeding that caused by the Black Death in fifteenth-century Europe. An eyewitness account estimated 60 to 90 percent mortality from the 1545–1548 epidemic alone. Compound epidemics and the rudimentary state of medical knowledge limited identification of specific diseases. Modern scholars consider the most lethal diseases to have been smallpox, typhus, measles, and influenza. Ironically, due to disease spreading in advance of the conquistadores, many Indians died of European diseases without ever having seen a Spaniard.[37]

Some modern estimates put the population *loss* at more than 95 percent of the pre-Conquest population of central Mexico. This loss was greatest in the low-lying tropical areas along the Pacific and Gulf Coasts, where hundreds of villages ceased to exist. In addition to European disease, mortality increased as excessive labor demands by Spaniards left villagers unable to provide for

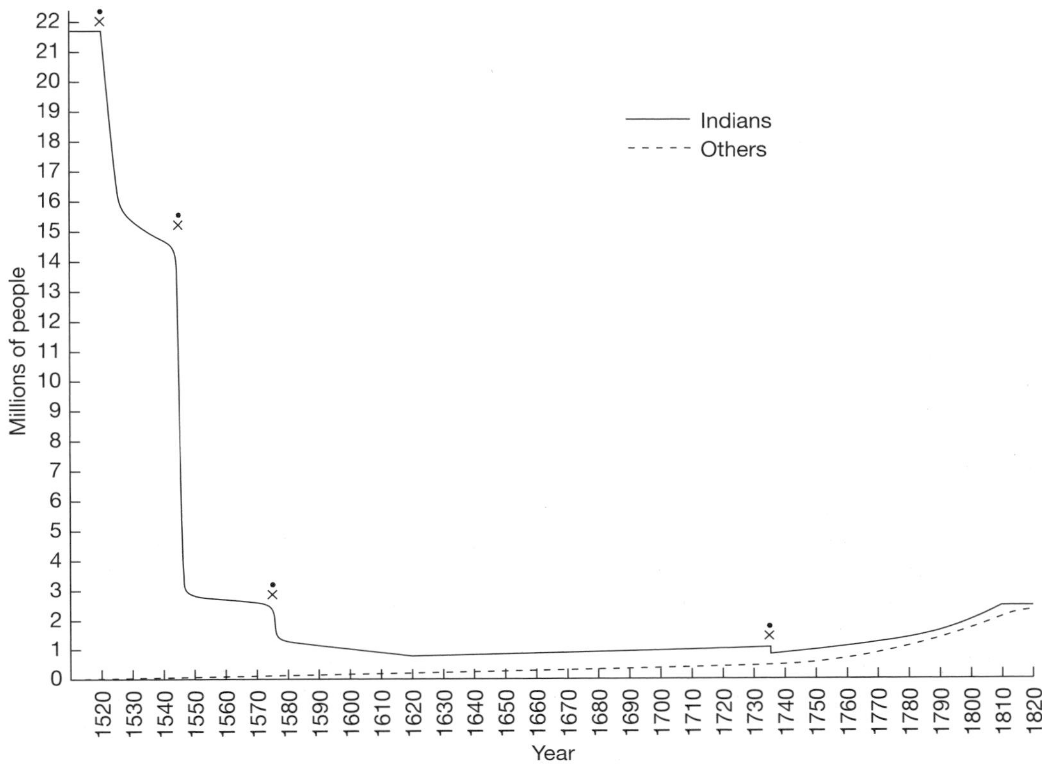

Figure 3.1 *The decline and recovery of the indigenous population*

Source: Adapted from Peter Gerhard (1993) *Guide to the Historical Geography of New Spain,* revised edition. Norman OK: University of Oklahoma Press. Copyright: the University of Oklahoma Press

themselves. Spanish atrocities, especially during the first wave of the conquest, also lowered population, as did the incorporation of Indian women (voluntarily and involuntarily) into the reproductive system of the whites.[38]

To meet their increasing labor needs at a time of Indian population decline, the Spanish adopted the *repartimiento* in 1549. This institution reflected the increasing scarcity of Indian labor and the establishment of enterprises by Spaniards who needed Indian workers. It forced Indians to work directly for Spaniards for a certain number of days a year. To meet its *repartimiento* obligation, a village supplied laborers who would march off for a week or two of work. Spanish authorities relied on Indian leaders to ensure that labor was delivered to Spanish employers. After the fulfillment of one group's labor obligation, the workers would return to their village and other workers would replace them. The Crown set the wage level for *repartimiento* workers and denied them the right to seek higher wages. These royally established wages were set at an extremely low level on the assumption that the cost of reproducing labor would be born by Indian communities. During the growing season, Indian villages normally supplied from 2 to 4 percent of their adult male laborers and, at harvest time, 10 percent. This institution placed Indian workers under Spanish supervision and exposed them to European agricultural techniques for the first time. However, it did not threaten the viability of the Indian community since each individual left the community for only a short period.[39]

The *repartimiento* had replaced the *encomienda* as the main source of Indian labor by the middle of the sixteenth century. It flourished between the 1550s and the 1630s and provided the Spanish with labor during the Indian population nadir. Spanish authorities subjected Indians who tried to escape *repartimiento* service and community leaders who failed to supply the demanded number of laborers to imprisonment, fines, and corporal punishment.[40]

Repartimiento laborers tilled Spaniards' fields, which allowed the provisioning of cities with products such as wheat, which the Spanish preferred to corn. These involuntary workers also engaged in mining and the construction of aqueducts, roads, and public buildings. Spaniards often abused their rights, forcing villages to supply more laborers than the amount legally stipulated and requiring workers to continue working longer than the law required.[41]

Well before the end of the sixteenth century, a triple alliance of the Crown, the Church, and the Indian elite was able to confront and roll back the power of the early Spanish conquistadores and settlers. However, the Crown's efforts to curb the colonial elite was often undermined by its own reliance on private individuals. This led to its repeatedly granting rich men lucrative concessions in exchange for their financing the expansion of the empire.[42]

THE SEVENTEENTH CENTURY

In contrast to the sixteenth century, which saw the grafting of a Spanish elite onto existing Indian societies, the seventeenth century saw a unique Mexican society emerge, an amalgam of previous cultures. Urban markets, mines, Spanish tribute demands, and a decline in the Indian population led to a relative decline in production for one's own consumption. There was a concomitant increase in the acquisition of goods through tribute, barter, and, increasingly, cash or credit.[43]

During the early seventeenth century, the indigenous population decline continued, especially in central Mexico. Indigenous communities were impacted by the Spaniards appropriating Indian land, the spread of grazing animals that fed on Indians' crops, and Indian males having to work to fulfill their *repartimiento* obligation rather than producing food for their own community.[44]

As a result of Indian population decline, in central Mexico large expanses of cultivated land were abandoned. Near towns, Spaniards moved onto vacated land and began producing wheat, corn, and fruit. Beyond these farms, Spaniards often raised sheep and cattle. Luis de Velasco, who served as viceroy from 1590 to 1595, commented on the interplay between a declining Indian population and increasing Spanish demand:

> The number of Spaniards grows apace each day; the resultant increase in importance of harvest lands and public works and building projects, secular and ecclesiastical, coupled with the alarming shrinkage of the native population, makes it extremely difficult to support so large a structure with so small a labor force.[45]

By the 1620s, the Indian population had begun to increase again since Indians had developed some immunity to European-introduced diseases. The surviving indigenous population could abandon marginal lands and plant only the best Indian-held land. Indian productivity also increased as they incorporated Spanish elements into their productive system. This population recovery came too late to prevent the Europeanization of Mexico. Rather than remaining a predominantly Indian nation, such as Guatemala or Bolivia, Mexico emerged as a predominately European and mestizo nation.[46]

In 1632, the *repartimiento* was abolished except in mining districts. By then, no major social group remained dependent on that institution. Humanists saw forced labor as wrong and abusive. The *repartimiento* led to a decrease in tribute paid to the Crown since many indigenous peasants left their community, temporarily or permanently, in favor of the hacienda, mine, and city to avoid *repartimiento* service. There, wages exceeded those paid for *repartimiento* labor. At the same time, an increasing number of mixed-race individuals began working on haciendas, lessening the demand for *repartimiento* labor.[47]

The end of the *repartimiento* reflected the Crown's declining power. Control of Indian labor passed from the hands of royal officials, who administered the *repartimiento*, to employers who became the workers' master, legislator, and judge. This shift to wage labor favored large growers since they had access to the cash needed to attract new workers by loaning them money. Laborers often remained on Spanish-owned estates because they needed wages to pay taxes or because they lacked any other attractive option. Often what passed as wage labor had little to do with cash. Landowners would provide the means of subsistence—food rations, housing, and the right to sow a plot of land—in exchange for an Indian's labor. With the possible exception of an initial loan, cash might never change hands.[48]

THE EIGHTEENTH CENTURY

In 1700, Spanish King Carlos II died without leaving an heir. After a power struggle known as the War of Spanish Succession (1702–1713), Felipe V, the grandson of French King Louis XIV, came to the Spanish throne, the first of the Bourbon dynasty. During the latter part of the eighteenth century, the Spanish government implemented a number of measures, generally known as the Bourbon reforms, since members of that dynasty carried them out. The Crown justified the resulting increase in state power by claiming that such an increase promoted the material prosperity and well-being of its subjects. The reforms led to substantial tax increases, which offended colonial taxpayers and undermined their stated aim of improving colonists' lives.[49]

Carlos III, the greatest of the Spanish Bourbon monarchs, ruled between 1759 and 1788. He and his ministers saw absolutism as the best means for introducing economic reform and government efficiency. They assumed that solving Spain's problems required an all powerful king rather than the social contract and balancing of special interests that the Habsburgs had relied on. Bourbons centralized power and effectively subordinated Church to state. The Habsburgs had perpetuated the notion New Spain enjoyed the same status as the various regions of Spain, such as Aragón and Castile. In contrast, the Bourbons viewed Mexico more as a modern colony, serving to provide revenue to the Crown.[50]

The notion of the monarch as the promoter of public well-being replaced the notion of the monarch as a simple upholder of natural law. The Bourbon reforms centralized imperial administration and finance, eliminated corporate privilege, political autonomy, and commercial monopolies. They also favored industries, such as mining, which would provide revenue to the Crown. Bourbon rulers expected Mexico to cover its administrative costs, subsidize defense costs throughout the viceroyalty, and still transfer a substantial surplus to Spain. Fulfilling these goals required limiting the power of the Creoles, a group that the Crown felt manipulated politics and retarded development. Administrative reforms already undertaken by the French and British provided a model for the Bourbon reforms.[51]

In 1767, following the example set by France and Portugal, Carlos III ordered the expulsion of Jesuits from the New World and the confiscation of the order's estates and other assets. This represented an attempt by the Spanish king, who resented Jesuit wealth, power and independence, to establish the supremacy of the state over the Church. He regarded the Jesuits as an autonomous, secretive international society, in much the same way as some small nations today regard multinational corporations (MNC). At the time of their expulsion, the 678 Jesuits in Mexico maintained haciendas, more than a hundred missions in northwestern Mexico, and the best schools, including twenty-three colleges and various seminaries.[52]

Given the Jesuits' importance in supplying credit and educating the Creole elite, they enjoyed widespread support in central Mexico. In response to their expulsion, rebellion broke out in Michoacán, San Luis Potosí, and Guanajuato. After the army quelled these protests, authorities hanged eighty-five persons and whipped and imprisoned hundreds more. This decision made it clear that the Crown expected submission, not discussion. Viceroy Marquis de Croix ordered Mexicans to accept the expulsion since "the subjects of the great monarch who occupies the throne of Spain should know once and for all that they were born to keep silent and obey, not to discuss or express opinion on high matters of government."[53]

In 1786, the Council of the Indies ordered that Mexico be divided into twelve new administrative districts known as intendancies. Most of these administrative units, such as Durango, San Luis Potosí, and Yucatán, remain as the modern states of Mexico. Within each intendancy, an intendant promoted economic growth and oversaw public administration, finance, justice, military preparedness, public works, and revenue collection. Intendants reported directly to the Minister of the Indies in Madrid, not the viceroy. The Crown modeled the office of intendant on the position of the same name and function in Louis XIV's France.[54]

The Crown felt that by appointing officials tied to Spain rather than to local economic interests, it could break the power of the regional oligarchies. However, newly appointed intendants found they could not govern without coming to some accommodation with existing elite interests, so little changed in this regard. The intendancy system did result in the disappearance of some 150 *alcaldías mayores*, which had allowed Creoles to control local government and in the process exploit the Indian population. The creation of the intendancy weakened the political links between the provinces and Mexico City. A tumultuous century would elapse before such links could be firmly reestablished.[55]

To the modern observer, many of the changes instituted by the Bourbons appear to be the epitome of sound administration. In 1755, the first free public school opened in Mexico City. During that decade, the Crown ceased to sell public office. In 1792, the Crown founded the Royal College of Mining, the first technical school in the New World. Professors there applied recent advances in physics, mineralogy, and chemistry to mining. This mining school provided a generation of Creoles with a sound technical and scientific education. In addition, the Bourbons sent foreign technology and mining missions to upgrade Mexican mines. In 1804, less than a decade after the discovery of the smallpox vaccination, the Spanish government dispatched teams of medical workers to carry out a massive immunization program in Mexico. Team members not only vaccinated tens of thousands, but trained Mexican doctors and *curanderos* in the technique.[56]

However, to the late eighteenth-century Creole observer, the reforms were an unwelcome intrusion. Creoles had grown accustomed to staffing the middle layers of the bureaucracy and resented their displacement by Spaniards. Only one of the twelve people appointed to head the newly created intendancies was a Creole. Peasants, as well as the elite, resented tax increases and the extension of tribute to new groups. The Crown assumed control of community funds previously beyond the reach of officials. In the name of equality and efficiency, Indians no longer received special protection.[57]

For most of the colonial period, the Spanish had not felt the need for a large standing army. Other institutions, especially the Church, maintained social control. As late as 1758, most of the 3,000 soldiers stationed in Mexico were in port cities or on the northern frontier. However, after the British occupied Havana during the Seven Years' War (1756–1763), the Crown decided Mexico needed protection from other European powers. As a result, by the turn of the nineteenth century, the regular infantry had increased to 10,000 and a 30,000-man militia had been formed. The infantry was concentrated in the Veracruz area to prevent British invasion, while militia forces were organized in practically all the cities of the viceroyalty. Colonial subjects were expected to bear the costs of the militia.[58]

The creation of a standing militia came at a time of rising rural tension. As silver production rose, mine owners bought more grain to support their operations. Agricultural exports, such as cacao, coffee, sugar, and hemp, increased. The increase in the area planted in cash crops forced many peasants from their ancestral lands. Increased demand from cities and mines caused the price of staples to rise, which led landowners to curtail the distribution of rations to their laborers. Protest, litigation, and occasional revolt followed. In many cases, those pushed from the countryside became the urban unemployed.[59]

Annual population growth during the eighteenth century averaged between 0.7 and 0.8 percent. In both 1742 and 1810, Indians comprised about 60 percent of Mexico's population, indicating that the Indian and non-Indian populations were increasing at about the same rate. Even though Mexico's total population had increased to 5.8 million by 1803, it remained considerably below the pre-Conquest level.[60]

The Bourbon dynasty tightened the colonial bond and extracted an ever-increasing surplus from Mexico. Between 1712 and 1798, revenue supplied by New Spain to the mother country increased from 3 million pesos to more than 20 million. The tribute Indians paid rose from 200,000 pesos in the 1660s to 1 million pesos in 1779. In 1790, New Spain contributed 44 percent more per capita to imperial coffers than did Spaniards. As historian John Lynch noted, by increasing the monetary demands on New Spain, the Bourbons "gained a revenue and lost an empire."[61]

COLONIAL STRATIFICATION

> Mexico is a country of inequality. No where does there exist such a fearful difference in the distribution of fortune, civilization, cultivation of the soil, and population.
>
> Alexander von Humboldt, 1811[62]

Social Stratification

During the colonial period, even disregarding the extremes of royalty and slavery, there was no assumption of individual equality. Rather, individuals' status derived from their membership in groups, each of which had distinct fiscal obligations, civil rights, and economic prerogatives. Heredity, occupation, and race (or the perception of race) formed the basis of these groups. Occupational groupings included the military and the Church, each of which enjoyed separate legal systems, or *fueros*. People of the same occupation formed guilds. The Crown expected each group to accept its assigned status and live in harmony with other groups.[63]

After the Conquest, Europeans and Indians formed the two major social groups. Europeans born in Spain held higher status than those born in the New World. The Spanish-born generally received appointments such as viceroy and archbishop, the highest positions in New Spain. All those considered European enjoyed privileged access into certain guilds and the university.

In what historian Nancy Farriss described as "a benevolent form of apartheid," the Crown prohibited non-Indians from living in Indian villages. This residential segregation policy attempted to protect Indians from what officials considered to be morally contaminating contact with non-Indians. Legally mandated spatial separation sought to minimize ill-treatment, which seemed inevitable in inter-racial relations. In the words of historian J. H. Elliott, "Indians were to be incorporated into, but not integrated with, the newly evolving colonial society."[64]

Black slaves occupied the lowest position in the social hierarchy. Although considered inferior to both Indian and European, many slaves worked in skilled occupations and served their masters in positions of trust that involved supervising Indian workers.[65]

In the period immediately after the conquest, children of mixed race simply moved into the community of one of their parents and did not seriously upset the system of racial classification. Later in the colonial period, mixed-race individuals formed a sizable group and generally intermarried.

Even though racial categories appeared to be rigid, in practice they could be manipulated. Individuals, or their children, would often declare themselves to be members of a racial category into which they or their parents were not born. Generally those changing racial category would declare themselves to be in the next whiter category than the one that had been ascribed to them or their parents.

Stratification by wealth existed alongside the racial hierarchy. Shortly after the Conquest, Indian nobles, Spanish conquistadores, and *encomenderos* formed the elite. Eventually with the decline of the Indian nobility, Indian stratification lessened. However, as Europeans made fortunes in commerce and mining, they became increasingly stratified. A strong, but not absolute, correlation existed between wealth and racial classification. A few Indians became wealthy, and many Spaniards remained or became poor. Nonetheless, wealth remained overwhelmingly in the hands of those of European descent. In 1792, there were only four non-whites in the 327-member elite of Antequera (today Oaxaca City).[66]

Colonial administrators desired neither legal nor economic equality. Rather, they rationalized social stratification as the key to stability. In an 1806 opinion, the Council of the Indies stated:

> It is undeniable that the existence of various hierarchies and classes is of the greatest importance to the existence and stability of a monarchical state, since a graduated system of dependence and subordination sustains and insures the obedience and respect of the last vassal to the authority of the sovereign. With much more reason such a system is necessary in America, not only because of its greater distance from the throne, but also because of the number of that class of people who, because of their vicious origin and nature, are not comparable to the commoners of Spain and constitute a very inferior species.[67]

The Social Elite

Colonial officials held the highest status, although not the greatest wealth. These officials not only profited from office but held significant power as well. They ceased to be household servants of the Crown and began to act as a semi-autonomous body that jealously guarded its prerogatives. These officials formed an interest group comparable to the landed aristocracy, the Church, and the urban elite. Although Spaniards almost always held the top posts, native-born Mexicans of Spanish descent, or Creoles, provided most of the staff for the colonial administration.[68]

Some plutocrats, bureaucrats, and officers received titles of nobility. The Crown benefited from granting titles by charging a hefty fee for ennobling the wealthy and by taxing the transfer of the title when it passed to the next generation. The Habsburgs ennobled conquerors, administrators, and colonizers. The Bourbons similarly honored administrators, the military, and entrepreneurs. At Independence, about fifty families resident in New Spain had been ennobled. The property of nobles could not be seized for overdue accounts nor could they be tortured or imprisoned for debt.[69]

Spaniards declared Creoles to be their inferiors to justify the disproportionate numbers of Spaniards serving as judges, provincial magistrates, chief aides to the viceroy, and leaders of missionary orders. They attributed this proclaimed inferiority to the malignant effect of New World land and climate, as well as to non-European genes among those claiming European status. Juan de Mañozca, the archbishop of Mexico from 1643 to 1650, attributed this perceived inferiority to Creoles' use of Indian wet nurses, so that "although creoles do not have Indian blood in them, they have been weaned on the milk of Indian women, and are therefore, like Indians, children of fear."[70]

By the end of the seventeenth century, Creoles began to identify with Mexico's pre-Hispanic past and take pride in the differences between Mexicans and Spaniards. However, they quite carefully separated the idealized Indians of the Aztec past from the abused Indians with whom they shared Mexico. This identification would later undergird the Creole struggle for independence. During the eighteenth century, Creole nationalism remained an elite construct, not a force that could mobilize the masses.[71]

The Creoles' ability to comply only partially with Spanish law or to defy it outright prolonged their tolerance for Spanish domination. This maintained the empire intact for centuries, despite its undeniably exploitative character.[72]

With a few exceptions, European ancestry united the elite. As historian James Lockhart commented, "Wherever wealth and Europeans congregated, things happened quickly; where they did not, slowly." Both the Spanish-born and the Creoles enjoyed elite status. While Spaniards controlled wholesaling, Creoles dominated retail sales. Elite Creoles also owned land, held positions in the colonial bureaucracy, and undertook military, professional, and ecclesiastic careers.[73]

Many wealthy families bridged the Creole–Spanish dividing line. Often newly arrived Spaniards married the daughters of wealthy Creoles. The Creoles' capital would finance Spanish-run ventures, which benefited from the Spaniards' family ties in Spain. Economic success relied on family ties, and old and new rich families constantly combined. As Lockhart commented, "One can emphasize either the continuity or the renewal; both are indispensable elements in the evolution of the society."[74]

The Economic Elite

The mine owners' income far surpassed that of high government officials. Mine-owning families in northern Mexico would buy titles of nobility and vie socially in Mexico City with Spaniards. In a society where 300 pesos a year provided a decent living, the Mexico City home of the great silver miner José de la Borda cost 300,000 pesos. Such mine owners often provided extravagant support for charities, while remaining blind to the material needs of the mineworkers who made possible this philanthropy.[75]

Only the fortunate struck it rich, since, according to lore, for every ten who invested in mines, eight failed. The limited number of Creoles and Spaniards who did become successful miners obtained the millions needed to open and expand their mines by borrowing from other elite groups, such as *hacendados*, merchants, and royal officials, who lent illegally.[76]

The *hacendados* formed another important sector of the elite, and as with the miners, they played a key role in the development of northern New Spain. They generally produced livestock and crops, processed what they produced, and marketed it. Wheat growers milled grain and distributed flour. Agave growers manufactured and sold intoxicants. Stock raisers slaughtered animals and sold meat. *Hacendados* created virtual feudal realms with their own jails. Owners routinely meted out corporal punishment to employees who displeased them. Typically *hacendados* established residences in Mexico City or a provincial capital and only visited the hacienda during the planting and harvest seasons. At other times, an overseer (*mayordomo*) administered the hacienda.[77]

Hacendados developed close ties with wealthy merchants and the most powerful colonial officials. They exploited their access to capital and their local predominance to provide credit and sell manufactured items and food to those living in the region. The Sánchez Navarro family, whose holdings in Coahuila at the end of the colonial period totaled more than 800,000 acres, provides a perfect example of the *hacendado* as merchant. The family supplied the Presidio de Río Grande and exercised a virtual monopoly on retailing in the capital, Monclova.[78]

Merchants solidified their control of urban markets by dealing only with major producers of grain, meat, and other commodities. This eliminated small producers who might undercut their prices. They lent to producers on the condition that the producer sold only to them. They also monopolized the sale of imported goods, so they could mark up the price 100 percent or more. Spanish-born wholesale merchants did not welcome the locally born, even if they were their own sons. They based their trade monopoly on their control of the merchant guild, kin ties, connections to Spain, and access to capital. Wholesale merchants only numbered 177 in 1689. That year, of the 1,182 adult male Spaniards in Mexico, only 124 served in government, compared to 628 in commerce.[79]

Merchants in Mexico City who acted as middlemen and the Spanish who shipped goods to Mexico and withdrew cash to Spain benefited from this system. The small and mid-sized farmers and the

Indian villagers who provided *repartimiento* labor and paid tribute lost out. As historian E. J. Hobsbawm noted, these merchants became the linchpin of the economic system linking Mexico and Europe:

> The key controller of these decentralized forms of production, the one who linked the labour of lost villages and back streets with the world market, was some kind of merchant . . . The typical industrialist (the word had not yet been invented) was as yet a petty-officer rather than a captain of industry.[80]

A merchant guild (*consulado*), which only accepted wholesalers, lobbied for its members and served as a commercial court, resolving disputes between traders as well as suits involving merchants and non-merchants. It also collected a sales tax known as the *alcabala* and received a 4 percent commission for its effort. The roughly 200 men in the *consulado* headed trading firms that regularly dealt with other firms scattered across both the Atlantic and the Pacific.[81]

Merchants invested much of their accumulated wealth in landed estates. Such estates provided a steady, if not spectacular source of revenue. Landowning merchants could accurately assess demand and adjust production. In the late colonial period, investment in land became especially attractive as demand for food increased and labor became cheaper. Merchant capital facilitated the construction of granaries, reservoirs, and irrigation canals.[82]

Merchants became a major source of credit in the late colonial period. They invested heavily in sugar production and textile weaving shops known as *obrajes* and provided miners with the necessary capital to purchase iron, steel, salt, mules, cattle, cloth, leather, and mercury. Others lent money to royal officials. They also bought refined silver and then coined it at the mint, which they controlled. Typically, they would keep as a fee one-ninth of the silver bullion that they had converted into coins. They made additional profits by minting silver and then smuggling it out of Mexico to avoid taxes. The merchants' control of the mint and their collection of the *alcabala* provide examples of private control of functions now accepted as valid government roles. The merchants' pervasive influence led Mexican historian Justo Sierra to comment, "The shopkeeper, and not the conqueror, is the true Spanish father of Mexican society."[83]

Frequently members of an extended family formed a trading partnership. Due to the difficulty in obtaining justice from a distant business associate, merchants relied on relatives or those whom they knew personally. The widespread use of credit buying necessitated a high degree of trust.[84]

Just as with miners, merchant families occupied a precarious social position. An often-cited proverb concerning merchants commented: "*Padre comerciante, hijo caballero, nieto pordiosero*" ("Merchant father, gentleman son, beggar grandson"). As with most proverbs, it contained an element of truth. Bequests to the Church drained capital from merchant families. Division among many children, conspicuous consumption, seasonal losses, and the inability to collect debts forming part of an inheritance all dispersed capital.[85]

Despite such loss of wealth, at least half of the merchant families studied by historian Louisa Hoberman managed to remain wealthy in the third generation. Families preserved wealth over the generations and maintained estates undivided by having a small number of children or by sending siblings into ecclesiastical careers. Marriage to descendants of other merchant families or to wealthy non-merchant families also maintained family fortunes. Finally, in the second and third generation, diversification into other careers, especially holding public office, maintained merchant wealth.[86]

Many elite families invested in mines, commerce, and haciendas. Frequently owners mortgaged their haciendas to obtain capital for commerce and mining ventures. Merchant families lacking capital frequently allied with land-owning families. This permitted land to be mortgaged to provide capital for commerce. Diversification permitted a family to retain its status in the event of a downturn in one economic sphere. It also permitted businesses to complement each other. Thus, a family's haciendas might provision its mine as well as supply its store.[87]

The economic elite's desire to have a voice in governance dovetailed with the Crown's view of the colonies as a revenue source. During the 1600s, municipal office could be bought in perpetuity. Thus wealthy Creoles would not only control local government but would will their positions to their children, who in turn would pass the position to the next generation. Beginning in 1687, posts in the *audiencias* were put up for sale. This allowed Creoles to buy their way into the central colonial administration and reinforce their social and economic dominance.[88]

The Indigenous Population

> Everything the Spaniards organized outside their own settlements in the sixteenth century—the encomienda, the rural parishes, Indian municipalities, the initial administrative jurisdictions—was built solidly upon individual existing altepetl.
>
> James Lockhart, 1992[89]

Between 1530 and 1550, the Spanish replaced the Indians' pre-Conquest altepetls with "Indian republics" modeled on the Spanish municipality. Residents of these republics enjoyed the right to use land held communally by the republic and had their own vigorous form of self-government. Such governments, which were recognized as legal entities, would collect taxes, organize collective labor for public works, and impart justice in cases involving minor offenses. The Indian republics effectively traded payment of tribute for ownership of communal land and local autonomy. This proved to be an effective survival mechanism, as the continued existence of some 4,000 Indian towns and villages through the eighteenth century indicates.[90]

The legal status of Indians differed markedly from that of Spaniards. The Crown considered indigenous people as minors needing protection and tutelage. The colonial government sharply limited Indians' ability to buy land, receive loans, or join a guild. Spanish law prohibited Indians from wearing European-style clothing or, for security reasons, riding horses. Those violating this latter provision received a hundred lashes and forfeited the animal if it belonged to them. Rather than admitting a fear of Indian revolt, José de Gálvez, Minister of the Indies, justified the prohibition by claiming that Indians should be kept "in that humble condition designed for them by the Creator."[91]

However, being an Indian carried with it certain advantages, such as being exempt from the compulsory tithe on agricultural produce non-Indians paid to the Church. Indians enjoyed exemptions from military service and remained outside the purview of the Inquisition. They also received more lenient criminal penalties than those meted out to non-Indians.

At a time when Creole town councils were essentially self-perpetuating oligarchies, Indian communities held often vigorous elections to select their local officials. These officials would safeguard land titles and population registers, protect the community's historical rights, and coordinate access to land, water, and forests in the area under their jurisdiction.[92]

Between 1592 and 1820, a special court, the *juzgado de indios,* adjudicated disputes between Indians or between an Indian and a non-Indian. The cases coming before this court mainly concerned: 1) land rights, 2) mistreatment or excessive demands made on Indians, and 3) criminal cases involving Indians.[93]

Early in the colonial period, the Crown protected indigenous communities, preferring to collect tribute rather than letting the *encomenderos* appropriate their wealth. The Crown also saw the Indian community as a useful counterweight to the elite of New Spain. At this time, the Spanish depended on indigenous producers for agricultural products since few Spaniards became farmers. Indigenous people seized upon the opportunities for self-defense provided by the Crown and soon became adept at playing individual and even institutional Spanish interests against each other.[94]

After the conquest, the Spanish officially recognized Indian ownership of lands they occupied and cultivated. The rate at which communities were dispossessed varied according to time and place. Indians first lost land in regions of heavy Spanish settlement. Colonists simply usurped land by force, especially in the decades after the Conquest. In other cases, Indians sold land. Most importantly, the plummeting Indian population emptied formerly settled and cultivated lands. During the first half of the seventeenth century, Indians still controlled 44 percent of New Spain. Another 30 percent was uncultivated desert or highlands technically owned by the Crown. Spanish colonists controlled the remaining 26 percent.[95]

Despite sincere efforts made by some viceroys to preserve a viable agricultural base for the Indian community, by the end of the colonial period, Indians remained in control of only 37 million acres, or about 8 percent of Mexico's land area. The amount of land left in Indian hands varied according to local resources and marketing opportunities. To take advantage of the well-developed food market in the Valley of Mexico, by the end of the colonial period, non-Indians had deprived Indians of virtually all their land. However, in Oaxaca, Indians retained substantial holdings due to the weak market for food and the survival of strong Indian communities to defend land titles. Of the 4,081 Indian pueblos remaining in 1803, 873 were in Oaxaca. Indians also retained more land in the south where they grew, but did not engage in the export of, crops such as indigo, cacao, and cochineal.[96]

Obligations imposed by both Church and state forced Indian peasants to earn cash. Contrary to modern orthodoxy that taxes stymie economic development, colonial officials imposed taxes to force Indians to engage in wage labor so they could meet their obligations. As long as they had access to subsistence plots, Indians doggedly (and rationally) refused to become wage laborers. Rather they sought to produce for their own consumption. In addition to producing their own food, Indians continued to weave cotton textiles on their backstrap looms, to the frustration of Spanish manufacturers, importers, and officials.[97]

Indians quickly adapted to their new situation as colonial subjects. As historian Susan Kellogg noted, "Far from simply being passive victims of the Spanish Conquest, the Mexica and other central Mexican groups proved to be significant social actors who helped shape the history of the early colonial state." Indian leaders exercised remarkable discretion in accepting or rejecting the diverse elements of Spanish colonial culture. They soon mastered such subterfuges as hiding infants and the bodies of the dead to avoid paying baptism and funeral fees. Indian farmers improved productivity by placing metal tips on their digging sticks (*coas*) and using the plow. Indigenous people soon began raising pigs and sheep and were the sole producers of cochineal dye. Between 1578 and 1598, 5 million pounds of this dye were exported from Veracruz to Seville.[98]

Indians engaged in the Spanish-introduced practice of litigation with considerable sophistication. If the occasion arose, Indians would even forge land titles to bolster their claims. Their success at litigation frequently vexed Spaniards, such as the curate of the Sagrario in Mérida, who complained to the government about Indians who contested land claims:

> The capriciousness, malice, and dishonesty of the Indians are well recognized in the sacred laws that govern us. If royal officials do not stand firm against their feigned humility and other tricks, we Spaniards will never be able to enjoy peaceful possession of our property, especially since they are led by the detestable proposition that they are on their own homeland, that all belongs to them, and other insolent notions.[99]

In the early post-conquest period, the Spanish relied on the Indian elite to maintain order and organize production. Members of this elite were allowed to maintain their positions as long as they provided *repartimiento* labor and collected and delivered tribute to Spaniards. With their status affirmed by the Spanish, many members of the indigenous elite acquired land and diversified economically. Some adopted Spanish economic practices, such as employing other Indians to raise pigs. Others, such as the Maxixcatzin family in mid-sixteenth century Tlaxcala, held extensive property farmed by lower-class Indian laborers. Shortly after the Conquest, a significant number of Indian noblewomen married Spaniards. This not only provided Spanish men with spouses but gave them access to Indian land and labor.[100]

Given their importance to the Spanish, during the early colonial period members of the Indian elite enjoyed a number of privileges. These privileges included special permission to wear Spanish clothes, ride horses, carry swords, and become priests. The colonial administration also exempted members of the Indian elite from paying tribute.[101]

As the colonial period progressed, Indian nobles became less useful to the Spanish since Indian labor became accessible through the *repartimiento* and wage labor. In many areas, such as Michoacán and the Valley of Mexico, by the middle of the eighteenth century, the Indian elite had lost Spanish backing, and its members had become virtually indistinguishable from commoners. In Oaxaca, caciques retained large land holdings and high social status throughout the colonial period since they faced little competition from Spaniards. Often noble "Indian" families intermarried with Europeans and mestizos, and their wealth determined their status more than their genealogy. As the status of Indian nobles declined and more Spanish women arrived, Spanish men ceased to marry Indian nobles.[102]

The Spanish colonial regime generally respected indigenous landholdings that were cultivated. The Indian village typically held lands communally and never placed them on the market. Its leaders assigned cropland to each household to work on an individual basis. Villagers enjoyed communal use of other lands for lumbering, hunting, and fishing. Residents sowed other plots communally to generate income to maintain the church and pay tribute.[103]

Although Indian communities enjoyed local autonomy, colonial officials held ultimate control. Spanish control passed from *encomenderos* to *corregidores* and *alcaldes mayores* after the middle of the sixteenth century. Spanish officials appropriated as much of the Indians' crops, community funds, and land as possible. The Indians, in turn, would use their communal structure to minimize transfer of wealth to these officials.[104]

Before the Conquest, most Indians lived in scattered homes near their fields, rather than in compact villages. However, late in the sixteenth century, the Spanish forced many Indians to move from their isolated farms to grid-pattern villages. This facilitated evangelization, social control, and tribute collection. From 1596 to 1606 alone, colonial authorities forced an estimated 250,000 Indians into 190 new towns. The crowding resulting from forced urbanization made Indians much more vulnerable to European disease than those remaining in isolated homes. Since Indians bitterly opposed such resettlement, in some instances authorities relented and permitted a return to old home sites. In other cases, Indians simply ran away and became even more dispersed, taking shelter in caves and inaccessible areas.[105]

This resettlement (*congregación*) played a major role in breaking down the old pre-Conquest indigenous culture and creating a new, distinct Indian culture. The newly emerging Indian culture, rather than mirroring Spanish culture, borrowed from both the Spanish and pre-Conquest traditions to form a unique blend. Often Indians retained their pre-Columbian festivals, but celebrated them on saints days. Most of the ancient Indian towns that currently exist were formed by *congregación*.[106]

A process known as *composición* facilitated non-Indians taking Indian lands. Those claiming land received legal title to it by paying a fee. When forced to choose between the hard cash charged for legalizing such titles and the long-range desire to maintain a viable Indian community, the Crown generally chose the former. Often these lands became vacant after the Indian population plummeted and *congregación* forced Indians out of rural areas.[107]

Most Indians in central and southern Mexico remained in Indian communities. However, some began to move to haciendas and Spanish towns to find employment and escape tribute, eroding the policy of racial separation. Abusive *encomenderos* and *corregidores*, as well as the destruction of crops by Spanish livestock, led to further out-migration. As the Indian population increased in the eighteenth century, still more Indian villagers moved to Spanish-run estates. The children of many of those who left their villages became Hispanized and joined the ranks of the mestizo, or mixed blood, population. In some cases, villagers would work seasonally on commercial estates without breaking their ties to their village.[108]

Some of these migrants settled in cities and towns and retained their Indian identity for generations. At the end of the seventeenth century, Indians in the city of Antequera worked in twenty-two occupations. Masons formed the most numerous occupational group, followed by bakers and tailors. Throughout New Spain, urban Indians also worked as laborers, carpenters, merchants, adobe layers, and in a variety of crafts. Even though Indians came to towns voluntarily, as historian John Chance noted, "With the exception of a handful of caciques, few Indians managed to escape their status as members of a lowly minority forced into the most menial of urban occupations."[109]

As the urban Indian population grew, the notion of "Indian" shifted from being a racial to a social concept. Individuals who so desired could shed their Indian identity and become mestizos. Individuals who accumulated wealth or married a non-Indian could more easily shed their Indian identity. Non-Indians expressed their contempt of such ethnic shifts, but could do little to stop them. In 1692, a priest in Mexico City commented on Indians shedding their identity: "Many of them wear stockings and shoes, and some trousers, and they cut their hair shorter. The women put on petticoats, become mestizos, and go to church at the Cathedral."[110]

Conflict with the Indigenous

Between 1700 and 1820, at least 150 village riots occurred. More than a hundred of these riots occurred after 1765, with the highest frequency between 1806 and 1810. They were generally characterized by violence, levity, and inebriation. Commonly such uprisings resulted from suppression of a local religious cult or abuses of power, often by a priest who had raised fees for baptism, marriage, burial, and the celebration of Mass. They were carried out with machetes, knives, clubs, axes, and hoes. Generally these riots burned themselves out with little intervention from the outside once they had achieved their immediate goal such as driving out a hated figure, freeing a prisoner, or getting a promise of action on a particular issue. Sometimes, after particularly severe outbursts, residents would abandon a town for a time to prevent retaliation.

Increased conflict in the late colonial period reflected demographic change. As the Indian population began to increase, conflicts erupted over land. If Indians wanted to put additional land under cultivation, they had to confront the hacienda, and when haciendas expanded to meet new market opportunities, they threatened Indian interests.[111]

Cultural and linguistic diversity and Indians' identity with village rather than with a wide-ranging cultural group, such as the Totonacs, led most rebellions to be highly localized. The Spanish prohibition on Indians owning firearms, swords, or daggers diminished their ability to resist government force. In addition, the lack of a vigorous, surviving indigenous elite to lead rebellions, as occurred in Peru, reduced the severity of uprisings.[112]

Authorities usually took a conciliatory stance toward such revolts, since they had limited ability to carry out counter-insurgency, sought taxes, and feared the spread of local revolts. These local revolts did not pose a major threat. Anthropologist William Taylor commented on such rebels, "They did not want to take power outside the local district, and, if they had, I suspect they would not have known what to do with it."[113]

More serious rebellions generally occurred after a miraculous occurrence, such as the claim that God had ordered the rejection of Spanish control and had promised mystical power and the establishment of a new, divinely mandated order. A charismatic leader, often a witness to the miracle, then transmitted the message. These movements often became regionalized, and their suppression involved heavy loss of life.[114]

In 1540, the Mixtón Rebellion erupted to the west of Mexico City, forcing the relocation of Guadalajara. This rebellion sought the elimination of any vestige of Christianity, the expulsion of Spaniards from Indian land, and the restoration of Indian religion and customs. Insurgents burned monasteries, churches, and crosses. They profaned religious objects, made sacrifices, and performed pagan dances. Many Spaniards, including conquistador Pedro de Alvarado, lost their lives suppressing this revolt. Thirty thousand Aztecs and Tlaxcalans assisted the Spanish in reasserting control.[115]

Conquest-era uprisings generally sought to eliminate everything Spanish, from Catholicism to orange trees. Their leaders promised a return to the old way of life. Spaniards repeatedly relied on other Indian groups to repress these uprisings. Since "Indian" was a European concept, Indian groups willingly participated in the suppression of other Indians. Such service could lead to booty, provide a chance to attack a traditional rival, or ingratiate a group to the Spanish.[116]

After the sixteenth century, millenarian movements indicated the degree to which Spanish culture had permeated Indian society. Rather than simply demanding a return to dimly remembered earlier beliefs, their leaders called for the replacement of Spaniards with Indian leaders who would oversee a new order that embraced many Spanish elements, such as worship of the Virgin.[117]

In 1712, a classical case of a millenarian rebellion occurred in Chiapas. There, a young Indian woman, María de la Candelaria, reported that the Virgin Mary had appeared to her and told her to build a chapel in her honor. When Spanish authorities attempted to suppress the cult that sprang up to honor the Virgin's appearance, Indians rebelled. The rebels organized their own political system and priesthood, which they reserved exclusively for Indians. They declared the Virgin to be supreme over God and heaven and that Spaniards were "Jews" who persecuted her. Members of their 5,000-man army referred themselves as "Soldiers of the Virgin." For three months, Indians sacked Catholic churches and Spanish estates, killing Spaniards and mestizos. Colonial authorities were only able to suppress the rebellion after heavily armed Spanish troops arrived from Guatemala.[118]

In 1761, another millenarian movement erupted in Yucatán, when Jacinto Canek led a rebellion brought on by forced labor, heavy taxes, tribute, and flogging. Canek established himself in a church, moved the silver crown from a statue of the Virgin Mary to his own head, and conducted religious ceremonies using the vestments and chalice of the Catholic clergy. A force of 500 well-armed Spanish finally defeated the 1,500-man Indian force led by Canek. After restoring control, the Spanish executed Canek. Spaniards publicly whipped other participants and cut off one of their ears. They leveled Canek's hometown of Quisteil so thoroughly that today no one knows its precise location.[119]

Spanish settlement slowly expanded northwards, largely as a result of mining operations. This led to a process that in some ways resembled the expansion of the U.S. frontier toward the west. In both cases, European settlement gradually eliminated independent Indian groups and channeled wealth into non-Indian hands. The Mexican experience differed from the U.S. experience in its emphasis on settling Indian groups and incorporating them into colonial life. The Spanish gave a major role in this process to other Indian groups that they had already dominated. Another contrast with the U.S. experience was that Spanish colonial exploration was carefully planned by the state. The 1573 Ordenanzas (statutes) even stipulated the death penalty for unauthorized exploration.[120]

As the Spaniards moved north to exploit mines in Zacatecas, warfare broke out with Indians known as Chichimeca, an Aztec term that translates roughly as "barbarian." Both the Spanish and the Aztecs used the term Chichimeca to refer to more than half a dozen distinct groups of nomadic people between San Juan del Río, Durango, Guadalajara, and Saltillo. Each group spoke, but did not write, a distinctive language. The Aztecs had never occupied the desert area the Chichimeca inhabited. The Chichimeca soon acquired horses and became expert riders. They mastered the ambush and established effective spy networks in Spanish-dominated villages, where they took advantage of the Spaniards' inability to distinguish them from other Indians.[121]

By the end of 1561, the Chichimeca had killed roughly 200 Spaniards and more than 2,000 of their Indian allies. In addition Chichimeca destroyed farms and robbed pack trains. In 1576, church officials in Guadalajara wrote the King:

> The damage and the murders done by the Chichimeca raiders daily—they are more daring and bloodthirsty than ever before—is causing the depopulation of many mines, cultivated lands, and *estancias* [ranches], and the highways are in the greatest danger.[122]

The wars with the Chichimeca dragged on for fifty years and provided the colonial administration with one of its greatest problems. As hunter-gatherers, the Chichimeca did not occupy a fixed location, making control extremely difficult. Before their domination, the Chichimeca cost the Spaniards more expense and lives than the conquest of the Aztecs. Peace with the Chichimeca came after Viceroy Álvaro Manrique de Zúñiga, who served from 1585 to 1590, realized that the soldiers responsible for pacifying Indians in fact exacerbated conflict. Soldiers would capture Indians and sell them into slavery. This served as the main source of income for many soldiers, who became more diligent at slaving than peacemaking.[123]

Viceroy Manrique de Zúñiga initiated a program called "peace by purchase." He provided the Chichimeca with food and clothes and encouraged them to form permanent settlements. To provide an example of settled Indians, the Spanish persuaded many Indians from Tlaxcala to settle in the Chichimeca area. Before the Tlaxcalans agreed to move, they demanded and received extensive land grants, freedom from personal tribute, and the right to carry arms and ride a horse with a saddle. As a result of the new Spanish policies, the Chichimeca and the Spanish coexisted peacefully after 1600.[124]

Peace with the Chichimeca did not end conflict with indigenous people. In 1687, an alliance led by the Toboso people embraced thirty indigenous groups resisting Spanish intrusion. This alliance threatened security (as defined by the Spanish) in broad areas of northeastern Mexico. In 1754, the bishop of Durango lamented to the king, "I have . . . heard much about uprisings of Indians and very little about new conversions."[125]

African Slaves

Before 1519, slavery existed on the Iberian Peninsula and in Mesoamerica, where Indians enslaved people as punishment or after their capture in war. Cortés and Narváez established hereditary slavery early on, as both brought African slaves to Mexico.[126]

In 1528, the Germans Heinrich Ehinger and Hieronymus Seiler bought monopoly rights, which lasted for four years, to import African slaves into Spanish America. Their serving as agents of the German banking house of Welsher indicates the close relation between the slave trade and international finance. The Crown received cash for granting slave-import monopolies and later taxed products produced by slave labor.[127]

During the second half of the sixteenth century, the demand for labor in commercial agriculture, urban industry, and, especially, silver mines soared, while the Indian labor supply plummeted. The lack of Indians to cultivate fields even raised the specter of famine. As a result, from about 1580 to 1620, New Spain imported more African slaves than any other locale in the Americas. That colony received approximately 36,500 African slaves between 1521 and 1594. During the seventeenth century, an annual average of 1,871 African slaves were brought to Mexico.[128]

Residents of New Spain had few moral qualms concerning the African slave trade. In the mid-fifteenth century, papal decrees, or bulls, had proclaimed African slavery acceptable since those enslaved would be converted to Christianity. Spaniards took at face value Portuguese slave traders' statements that, since they had been captured in just wars, those being sold into slavery had been legally enslaved. Once slavery began, slave owners rationalized the institution as a response to presumed black inferiority. A 1769 petition signed by virtually all the planters in the district of Córdoba, Veracruz, asserted: "If given freedom, blacks become increasingly more barbarous and bloodthirsty. The only proper condition for them is slavery." Free blacks and others of mixed African ancestry owned their own black slaves, indicating how widespread acceptance of slavery had become.[129]

Arguments based on economic necessity quashed lingering doubts on the issue of slavery. During the 1665–1700 reign of King Carlos II, a report by the Council of the Indies declared:

> First, the introduction of blacks is not only desirable, but absolutely necessary . . . The fatal consequences of not having them are easily deduced, for . . . they are the ones who cultivate the haciendas, and there is no one else who could do it, because of a lack of Indians.

The report concluded that without the slave trade Spanish America would face "absolute ruin."[130]

A few isolated individuals did speak out against slavery. In 1560, Alonso de Montúfar, archbishop of Mexico, wrote King Felipe II, "We do not know of any cause why the Negroes should be captives any more than Indians, since we are told that they receive the Gospel in good will and do not make war on Christians." Thirteen years later, Bartolomé Frías de Albornoz, a former law professor at the University of Mexico, wrote that Christianizing Africans did not constitute a sufficient reason for enslaving them. He declared that if indeed the Spanish wanted to convert heathens in Africa, it would be better to send missionaries. Not only did officials ignore his questioning of slavery, but the Inquisition placed his book dealing with the subject on its *Index of Forbidden Books*. Other isolated critiques would follow, but none had significant impact. Eventually, demographic change would halt the slave trade, not moral suasion.[131]

The Church, as an arm of the Crown, could not challenge slave policy. Dominicans and other orders worked African slaves on their haciendas. Other Church institutions, such as convents, owned slaves and financed others' purchase of them. In 1517, Bartolomé de las Casas, a priest who became famous for defending Indian rights, warned that unless indigenous people received some relief, they would soon disappear from Hispaniola. He proposed that each white resident of Hispaniola should receive permission to import as many as twelve African slaves.[132]

Initially African slaves were largely employed in urban areas. However, as the Indian population declined, African slaves increasingly worked in rural areas. Many worked in the port of Veracruz and on cattle ranches and sugar plantations along the east coast. Others worked to the north and west of Mexico City on ranches and in silver mines. Between Puebla and the Pacific Ocean, slaves worked in mines, on sugar plantations and ranches, and in the port of Acapulco. Slaves would work continuously, unlike Indian *repartimiento* laborers, who returned to their communities after an interval. The number of slaves in Mexico ranged between 20,000 and 45,000, a number far fewer than the 4 million slaves who would later labor in the U.S. south.[133]

In rural areas, slaves often served as intermediaries between whites and Indians, working in a supervisory capacity. They played a crucial role in the mining industry during the period of rapid Indian population decline. The 1570 Mexican mine census enumerated 3,690 slave workers, 1,850 Spaniards, and 4,450 Indians.[134]

Some slaves learned highly technical aspects of sugar production. Most commonly, though, rural slaves faced a lifetime of back-breaking labor in the fields. Slave labor came to dominate the sugar industry since the low-land Indian population had virtually vanished. The Spanish also felt that Africans withstood hot, heavy work better than Indians. King Felipe III's forbidding the use of Indian labor on plantations increased the reliance on slave labor.[135]

The Mexican slave population required constant resupply from Africa. So many slaves died due to poor nutrition, disease, high infant mortality, and the rigors of sugar production that they failed to reproduce themselves. Traffickers imported only one woman from Africa for every three men, thus limiting the number of slave women who could bear children.[136]

Black slaves and their descendants, who lacked a stable community to preserve their culture, assimilated Spanish culture more rapidly than the Indian. Male slaves often had children by, and married, Indian women. This reflected the fact that Indians were often the only available sexual partners and that male slaves were aware that free mothers gave birth to free children.[137]

The Spanish legal system specifically outlawed "bad treatment" of slaves, including mutilation or killing, except when the law authorized such treatment for an offense. Slaves also had the right to marry, regardless of their owners' wishes. Despite such legislation, as historian Colin Palmer noted, "Most masters were left to exercise their private power of discipline, whether excessively or not, with impunity." In some instances, the Inquisition prosecuted slaves for blaspheming while being beaten by their master, but did not punish the master for the beating.[138]

Creoles adamantly opposed the emergence of an Afro-Mexican elite that might compete with their own sons for the limited number of desirable jobs, such as civil and clerical appointments, so they prohibited anyone with African blood from enrolling in the university. Similarly Afro-Mexicans could not become masters in many craft guilds.[139]

More than 200,000 slaves were imported to Mexico during the colonial period. However, slavery never assumed the fundamental role that it did in the export-oriented plantation colonies of the West Indies. In contrast to these colonies, during the eighteenth century slavery virtually vanished from Mexico. In most instances, due to increases in the Indian and mixed-race populations, it became less costly to pay wages than to import and maintain slaves.[140]

After 1739, the slave trade declined to insignificance. Slavery only remained important in isolated areas, such as Córdoba, where the small Indian population could not supply sufficient labor. When the Prussian naturalist Alexander von Humboldt visited Mexico in 1803, he commented, "We may almost say that there are no slaves." While slavery ceased to be a major economic force well before the end of the colonial period, it provided crucial labor in the transition from Indian tribute to wages.[141]

Slave Rebellions

Frequent slave revolts resulted from the slaves' lack of freedom, unstable marital life, mistreatment, overwork, and their lack of effective legal means of obtaining freedom. The specter of slave rebellion kept the white population in fear. In 1553, former Viceroy Mendoza warned his successor, Luis de Velasco, "This land is full of Negroes and mestizos who exceed the Spaniard in great quantity, and all desire to purchase their liberty with the lives of their masters."[142]

As early as 1523, slaves revolted and erected crosses to celebrate their freedom and "to let it be known that they were Christians." In 1537, Viceroy Mendoza received warning of a plot by black slaves to kill all Spaniards and elect their own king. After eliciting confessions by torture, authorities identified leaders and had them drawn and quartered. Except for the "confessions," authorities found no evidence for the plot. In 1612, after the death of a slave woman in Mexico City, which blacks attributed to mistreatment by her owner, blacks plotted to kill all Spanish men and force Spanish women to serve them. When authorities learned of the conspiracy, they located an arms cache using information from tortured suspects. They hung twenty-eight black men and seven black women for their role in the plot.[143]

After the discovery of the 1612 plot, authorities placed restrictions on slaves, free blacks, and mulattos, none of whom they trusted. They ordered Afro-Mexicans off the streets after dark and prohibited them from carrying arms or gathering in groups of four or more.[144]

Officials viewed slave revolts in the countryside as even more of a threat to Spaniards due to the large concentrations of rural slaves, their lack of close scrutiny by owners, and their having none of the conflicting loyalties that domestic servants sometimes had for their masters. In 1735, a false rumor that the king had freed all slaves sparked a widespread slave rebellion in the Córdoba area. The revolt lasted five months and involved pitched battles between whites and slaves. Some thirty years later, planters in the area referred to the revolt as "a seditious movement and general uprising of all the slaves in that district, which cost much money, spilled much blood, and ruined the countryside to such a degree that even today it has not recovered." Between 1725 and 1768 alone, five major slave rebellions, each of which involved more than 2,000 slaves, broke out in the Córdoba area.[145]

Slaves often responded to their lack of liberty by running away from their owners. By the 1560s, fugitive slaves had allied with Indians to raid Spanish ranches. Other fugitives robbed pack-trains on the highway between Mexico City and Veracruz and retained their freedom by taking refuge in difficult terrain. Runaways would establish settlements, called *palenques*, which served as a base for their raids on plantations, roads, and towns. Owners attempted to discourage runaways by whipping captured fugitives, placing them in stocks, and other punishments. The Crown's efforts at preventing slaves from running away generally failed. In 1571, the viceroy decreed that slaves missing from work for four days would receive fifty lashes. Those absent for more than eight days received a hundred lashes and had iron fetters placed around their feet for two months.[146]

By 1600, the slopes of the Pico de Orizaba and the lowlands stretching to Veracruz teemed with small settlements of fugitive slaves. The colonial government organized counter-insurgency campaigns against the runaway bands, but had little success because the rugged terrain prevented the use of mounted troops. Rather than succumbing to Spanish soldiers, runaway settlements often died an evolutionary death. Unattached runaway males found, or sometimes captured, women, became husbands and fathers, and subsequently devoted less energy to raiding.[147]

Runaways founded the most successful fugitive settlement near the Pico de Orizaba in about 1580. It existed for thirty years and contained more than a hundred adults. Yanga, an escaped slave born in Africa, reportedly of a royal family, became its king. In 1606, the viceroy commented on the settlement, which bore the name of its king:

> I understood that many fugitive Negro slaves are gathered within the jurisdiction of Old and New Veracruz, Río Blanco, and Punta de Antón Lizardo. They act as if they were free and are quite daring. They have entered the town of Tlalixcoyan to rob and sack houses and have seized domestic Negroes from their masters' houses. They threaten Spaniards and set fire to their houses.[148]

Yanga taunted the Spanish, writing that his followers had fled the "cruelty and treachery of the Spaniards who, without any right, had become owners of their freedom." In 1609, Spanish authorities sent a 450-man military force to eliminate the settlement. After a bloody battle, the Spaniards captured the settlement, which had been abandoned. After further combat, the Spanish concluded that they would be unable to subdue the fugitives.[149]

As a result, the viceroy accepted Yanga's offer to stop raiding in exchange for his followers receiving not only their freedom but the right to found a legally recognized town. Yanga's followers realized their own limits and did not try to end slavery. Rather, they made a pledge—almost impossible to enforce—to return future runaways. Colonial authorities kept their word and permitted the fugitives to found San Lorenzo de los Negros, where they lived in freedom. However, the town did suffer constant harassment by local authorities who resented the slaves' successful struggle for freedom. Within a few generations, outsiders came into San Lorenzo and mingled with its original residents, making it racially indistinguishable from other settlements in the area.[150]

Racial Mixture

The social position of mixed-race individuals involved several factors, which changed over time. Initially, few of the parents of mixed-race children had married. These children were raised by either the Indian or Spanish parent. Later, as the number of mixed-race individuals increased, they intermarried and produced larger families than either Indians or Creoles. Racial status varied by region. In the north, with its meager Indian population, those of mixed race occupied a position near the bottom of the social scale and worked alongside the few remaining Indians. Thus, for example, in Nuevo León, by 1810, only 5.6 percent of the population was Indian, leaving those of mixed race as social inferiors to the 62.7 percent of the population considered Spanish. However, in areas such as Oaxaca, where 88.3 percent of the population was Indian, mixed race individuals enjoyed a higher social position.[151]

No single factor determined socio-racial status. Perceived ancestry comprised a key component. Those with light skin and more Caucasian features enjoyed higher status. They often insinuated themselves into the lower reaches of the priesthood and bureaucracy, worked as supervisors in mines and farms, or became small farmers, muleteers, petty merchants, and artisans. Similarly, greater wealth or marriage to someone of higher status would propel individuals upward. Close association with groups deemed African, European, or Indian would influence one's own ascription. Mestizos who appeared more Indian generally performed manual and menial labor.[152]

The various elements within the social hierarchy had differing views of it. Those forming the elite viewed racial divisions as rigid. Those at the bottom saw them as categories one could move into and out of to change status as the opportunity arose. Despite the ability of individuals, families, and even communities to change categories, especially from Indian to mestizo, these barriers were important, especially before the eighteenth century. In addition to maintaining the elite status of Europeans, the system of racial classification divided the non-European population and thus inhibited united opposition to European rule.[153]

In the early colonial period, as many as sixteen terms, including *pardo* (black and Indian) and *morisco* (Spanish and mulatto), described racial mixtures. One category, the *casta,* eventually embraced all mixed bloods, including mestizos (Spanish and Indian), mulattos (Spanish and black), and *zambos* (black and Indian). The *castas*, who lacked the constraints of the relatively static Spanish and Indian cultures, became more independent, more mobile, more innovative, and forged much of modern Mexico's distinctive culture.[154]

This 1811 statement that the merchant guild sent parliament (Cortes) reflects the elite's negative stereotype of non-Europeans:

> The castas whose lazy hands are employed in peonage, domestic service, trades, artifacts and the army, are of the same condition, the same character, the same temperament and the same negligence as the Indian . . . Drunken, incontinent, lazy, without honor, gratefulness, or fidelity . . .[155]

The elite not only held negative stereotypes of non-whites but formulated elaborate rules to prevent non-whites from competing with them for choice positions. Generally, those of mixed race were not allowed to hold public office, be members of municipal corporations, join religious orders and guilds, or enter the university. In 1757, persons of color were not even allowed to own or administer grocery stores in Mexico City.[156]

Table 3.1 *Colonial population, by race and ethnicity*

	1570	1646	1742	1793
Indians	3,336,860	1,269,607	1,540,256	2,319,741
Europeans	6,644	13,780	9,814	7,904
Mestizos	13,504	277,610	640,880	1,096,026
Blacks	20,569	35,089	20,131	6,100
Mulattos	2,435	116,529	266,196	369,790

Source: Aguirre Beltrán (1989a: 210, 219, 222, 230)

A few mestizo families, such as the Pimentel and Ixtlilxochítl families, descended on the Indian side from the royal household of Texcoco, enjoyed high social status. The majority, though, held much more modest status, working as shopkeepers and artisans. Others worked on haciendas where they frequently served as foremen, organizing the labor of Indians to meet the needs of Europeans. If caught using fraudulent scales for weighing meat, *castas* could receive a hundred lashes, while Spaniards merely received a fine. Policy makers rationalized these restrictions as a means of controlling those of bad character. Only a few individuals, such as Bishop-elect Manuel Abad y Queipo of Michoacán, declared that poverty and legal discrimination, not their inherent nature, caused *castas* to deviate from prescribed behavioral norms.[157]

The prejudice against mulattos exceeded the prejudice against either mestizos or Indians. They not only suffered from the legal restrictions imposed on mestizos and the stigma of slave ancestors but had to pay tribute, just as Indians did. In urban areas, they frequently worked as manual laborers.[158]

Despite the racial stereotypes and legally mandated isolation of racial groups, the actual lines became blurred. Many mestizos acquired wealth and status and gained acceptance as Creoles. A legal procedure allowed people to establish "purity of blood" ("*limpieza de sangre*") by paying a fee. Such a payment enabled them to consider themselves and to be considered Creole. Similarly many Indian leaders, despite their mixed ancestry, continued in their positions. Humboldt commented on the relation between race and social position: "In America, the greater or less degree of whiteness of skin decides the rank which man occupies in society. A white who rides barefooted on horseback thinks he belongs to the nobility of the country."[159]

Social mobility inevitably resulted in the absorption of many African and Indian genes into the segment of society culturally defined as white. Contemporary observers commented on this. In 1811, Father Beye Cisneros, trying to prevent the disenfranchisement of *castas* in America, told the Spanish parliament (Cortes):

> I have known mulattoes who have become counts, marquises, *oidores*, canons, colonels, and knights of the military orders through intrigue, bribery, perjury, and falsification of public books and registers; and I have observed that those who have reached these positions and distinctions by reprehensible means, have been granted the corresponding honors without repugnance, despite their mixed blood.[160]

Women

The restrictions imposed on women in colonial Mexico reflected the value system then prevalent in the Western world, of which Spain and its colonies formed a part. Gender inequality in countries bordering on the Mediterranean, such as Spain, exceeded that of northern Europe. Spanish society viewed the family as a miniature state, which had as its head the father, who exercised complete authority over his wife and children. He was legally entitled to administer corporal punishment to his wife and children as long as he did not endanger their lives.[161]

Many factors, such as wealth, divided colonial women, complicating generalizations about them. A contemporary observer commented:

> The luxury and munificence of the mine-owners is something wondrous to see. As a rule the wife of a mining man goes to church escorted by a hundred servants and twenty ladies and maids in waiting. She keeps an open house, and all who wish to do so may come to dine: a bell is rung for dinner and supper.[162]

Urban-rural, Indian–Creole (or mestizo), and slave-master divisions also separated women. Some men had Spanish wives and Indian mistresses. Some women lived on the northern frontier and others resided in Mexico City. Finally, the experience of women differed as the colony evolved over three centuries.[163]

Spanish law, a derivative of Roman Law, defined a woman's status. With a few exceptions, these laws remained in effect until the passage of the 1870 Mexican Civil Code. Women could not hold public office, vote, or be judges or priests. Regulations prohibited women from joining craft guilds, which prevented them from entering numerous occupations. Except for convents, women lacked groups that would further their interests in the way that the political system, the church structure, and guilds furthered male interests.[164]

Parents exercised authority over both male and female children until age twenty-five or until they married. However, after marriage, women only transferred their dependence, becoming subject to their husbands' authority. Married women required their husbands' permission to carry out legal proceedings, such as selling property, borrowing money, founding a charity, or freeing a slave. During the marriage, the husband administered communal property, including any income his wife might earn. He could dispose of this property without her consent. Wives could inherit property, but husbands had the right to administer it.[165]

Some laws did protect women's interests. Inheritance laws guaranteed female children an equal share of their parents' wealth, including land. Women could defend their interests, such as their right to an inheritance, in court. A widowed woman received half of the property accumulated during the marriage and any other personal property she might have brought to the marriage, such as her dowry.[166]

Unmarried women over age twenty-five, and, especially, widows, enjoyed the most freedom. They could carry out their own legal transactions, manage property, and choose their residence. The 1811 Mexico City census indicated that a fifth of women aged eighteen and over, primarily widows, headed their own households. The lucky minority of widows with assets could and did administer ranches, haciendas, shops, pulque taverns, and other urban businesses. They either exercised direct control of such properties or hired an administrator.[167]

The concept of honor exercised a strong influence on women of European ancestry, Creole and Spaniard. Honor demanded that women remain virgins until marriage. Male relatives, who suffered a loss of honor if a female relative lost her virginity, kept sisters and daughters under tight control to avoid this. After marriage, to preserve a wife's honor, a life of modest withdrawal was the ideal. As a result, upper-class women, who left business matters to their husbands, remained at home and supervised family members, administered money that the husband doled out for household expenses, and inculcated acceptance of these norms in their children. In addition, they administered servants, performed domestic tasks, embroidered, and read religious works.[168]

Income-generating activities for women, married and unmarried, varied according to class and ethnicity. The 1811 Mexico City census reported that only 13 percent of Spanish and Creole women declared an occupation, while 36 percent of mixed-race and 46 percent of Indian women did. Women frequently worked as domestics or as cigarette makers, wet nurses, washerwomen, and ambulatory vendors. Mine operations depended on women serving as cooks, servants, and prostitutes. Many slave women worked in sugar mills. Indian women produced and sold poultry, vegetables, and textiles in traditional weekly markets. Poor Creole and mestizo women worked as seamstresses, or sold cigars, sweets, candles, trinkets, and alcoholic beverages from small stalls. In the first half of the eighteenth century, women comprised a third of the textile labor force in Puebla. At the end of the colonial period, half of the 7,000 employees at the royal tobacco factory were women, a harbinger of the opening of salaried occupations for women in the nineteenth century.[169]

Elite women administered family property if no adult males were available. For example, the heiress to the Count of Santiago and Marquisate of Salvatierra, María Isabel de Velasco Altamirano y Ovando, was the unmarried holder of two titles and three entails, and ran the family business, along with a younger sister, between 1797 and 1809. In urban areas, women owned bakeries, print shops and textile workshops known as *obrajes*. Sixteen of the thirty convents founded in New Spain between 1600 and the end of the colonial period were the work of women. Upper-class women also administered nunneries.[170]

During the late colonial period, the Crown favored expanded female employment to increase family spending money, to provide a greater market for manufactured goods, and to free men for mining, farming, and military service. In 1799, to increase female employment, Viceroy Miguel José de Azanza decreed that women could hold a job regardless of guild rules excluding them. The percentage of the female workforce working as servants and seamstresses declined from 88 percent in 1753 to 54 percent in 1811, indicating an increase in female employment opportunities. With the exception of cigar making, women workers at the end of the colonial period predominated in the same sectors as today—domestic service, the apparel industry, and food processing and distribution.[171]

Indian women faced restrictions imposed by sex, class, and race. In the early colonial period, Spanish men sought Indian noblewomen as wives and took Indian women of lower status as concubines. Many early tribute obligations, such as grinding corn and making tortillas, fell upon Indian women.[172]

Throughout the colonial period, peasant families shared power more evenly than more affluent ones. Men cultivated the family cornfields, while women tended gardens, raised small animals, wove cloth, made clothing, and prepared meals. Peasant women often sold goods in local markets. The landed estates mainly hired men, leaving women with increased power in the home and the community. As a result, women constituted a majority of the participants in many of the local peasant rebellions that erupted during the eighteenth century. Women often led these movements, which protested encroachments on community autonomy.[173]

Marriage for the more affluent in colonial Mexico generally involved a dowry. The custom of providing dowries came from medieval Spain. The dowry could be in the form of cash, jewelry, slaves, clothing, household furnishings, or real estate. Upon marriage, the husband managed, but did not assume ownership of this wealth.

The dowry served as a means of parental control, since if the bride's parents disapproved of the marriage, they could deny a dowry. It also served to indicate social standing, since only the elite could afford a large dowry, which would attract a husband from a family of high standing. The dowry helped offset the cost of establishing the new household. When a couple legally separated or the husband died, the dowry reverted to the wife. As in other Latin American countries, in eighteenth-century Mexico, the use of dowries declined.[174]

The Church required married couples to live together. Religious authorities could force a wife to live with her husband, even if both spouses preferred to live apart. However, either spouse could petition for "ecclesiastical divorce," akin to a modern legal separation. Before the petition could be granted, a spouse had to present evidence of some specific offense. Grounds for an ecclesiastical divorce included: 1) one spouse being cruel or physically abusive; 2) a spouse having an incurable contagious disease, such as leprosy; 3) one spouse forcing the other to commit criminal acts, such as being a prostitute; 4) a spouse embracing paganism or heresy; 5) adultery; or 6) abandonment by the husband. The deterioration of the relationship alone could not serve as grounds for the divorce.[175]

This proceeding differed from divorce in the modern sense. The Church controlled both marriage and ecclesiastical divorce. Catholic doctrine regarded the couple as still married, so a spouse could only remarry upon the death of the other spouse. It did allow the spouses to establish separate households. In early nineteenth-century Mexico City, roughly 1 percent of marriages ended up in the divorce court.[176]

Reading and writing were deemed superfluous for poor women. Even the privileged elite girls of European ancestry received only a minimal education—in reading, writing, arithmetic, and domestic arts—which was considered all the knowledge they needed. Frequently nuns in convents imparted such instruction. In other cases, lay women taught girls until the age of eleven or twelve. The low educational level of these women, known as *amigas*, prevented them from dispelling the prevailing ignorance. Only the most fortunate received instruction from the *amigas*. In 1753, fewer than 25 percent of girls in Mexico City received any instruction at all.[177]

Even fewer educational opportunities existed in rural areas. Generally girls (and boys) received no formal schooling in rural Mexico, where the majority of the population lived. For Indian girls, family and community provided knowledge. Illiteracy among rural women remained the norm through the end of the nineteenth century.[178]

Educators did not design the curricula to uplift female status, but to foster acceptance of socially assigned roles. To prepare for the woman's assigned task of providing religious training to children, girls' schools emphasized memorizing catechism. Girls' education also stressed domestic skills such as weaving, embroidery, and sewing. As historian Asunción Lavrin emphasized, "Knowledge beyond these narrowly defined parameters was not for women."[179]

Colonial society considered marriage the norm. However, especially among the upper classes, many chose not to marry. Family wealth allowed affluent women to establish separate households. Other family members benefited by the reduction in the number of descendants who would claim the family wealth. Among the less affluent, especially those of mixed race, priests had less influence. This allowed many couples to simply begin living together. Throughout the colonial period, numerous adult women remained unmarried—living with a man, living alone, or widowed. An early eighteenth-century census in Guadalajara indicated that 64 percent of women were unmarried.[180]

By the end of the colonial period, the number of nuns in New Spain exceeded 2,400. Although only a small proportion of all women became nuns, a much higher percentage of the elite did. Convents generally accepted only daughters of the elite, since the convent required a substantial initial payment to cover the costs of a lifetime of care. To be admitted to the convent as a nun, aspirants had to prove pure Spanish ancestry— those whose ancestries included black, Indian, or Jewish bloodlines were excluded. *Castas* only entered convents as maids and servants. Convents often owned black slaves to perform communal tasks. In addition, nuns could bring in slaves who worked as personal servants.[181]

Convents played an economic as well as a religious role. They sold produce from their orchards and gardens to the public. The wealthy endowed or bequeathed assets to individual convents. Such wealth included haciendas, ranches, livestock, sugar mills and flourmills, and, especially, urban real estate. Convents often retained and managed this urban real estate. Other property was generally sold. As a result of selling such property, donations, income from real estate, and payments made by nuns upon entering the convent, convents amassed sizable amounts of cash. This money became an important source of credit for business activity.[182]

Sor Juana Inés de la Cruz

Despite the restrictions placed on women in New Spain, Sor Juana Inés de la Cruz remains the best remembered Mexican from the colonial period. Sor (sister) Juana was born as Juana Inés de Asbaje y Ramírez sometime between 1648 and 1651. Her Basque father, whom she may have never met, did not marry her Creole mother.[183]

Juana spent the first years of her life in the village of Nepantla, between Mexico City and the volcano Popocatépetl. She learned to read at age three by tagging along to the reading lessons of an older sister. Juana could read proficiently before her mother even learned of her class attendance. She had the good fortune to have access to books in her maternal grandfather's library. Though far from wealthy, her grandfather had amassed one of the few private collections of books in the colony. She indicated her early devotion to learning when she unsuccessfully attempted to persuade her mother to let her dress as a male so she could enter the university, which at the time banned women.

At age eight, Juana moved in with an aunt in Mexico City to increase her access to learning. At the age of thirteen, she received permission to live in the viceregal court as a maid-in-waiting, a common practice for favored children. During the five years she spent in court, she became an accomplished poet and the most learned woman in Mexico. Court life gave her a chance to mingle with the intellectual elite of Mexico.[184]

When she reached adulthood, Juana faced marriage, remaining single, or entering a convent. Given the values of her age, she almost certainly could not have found a husband willing to accept her intellectual activity. Had she been wealthy, remaining single might have been an option, but her family had little money. No unmarried women intellectuals in the colony served as role models. That left entering a convent as the only alternative to marriage.[185]

Juana entered the permissive Convent of Santa Paula of the Hieronymite order in 1669. She later wrote concerning that choice, "Given my total disinclination to marriage, it was the least unreasonable and most becoming choice I could make to assure my ardently desired salvation." She noted that another influence was her desire "to live alone, to have no fixed occupation which might curtail my freedom to study." Author Octavio Paz commented on her decision:

> It was a prudent decision consistent with the morality of the age and the habits and convictions of her class. The convent was not a ladder toward God but a refuge for a woman who found herself alone in the world.[186]

For the next twenty years, Sor Juana dedicated herself to intellectual pursuits. She commented on this activity:

> From my first glimmers of reason, my inclination to letters was of such power and vehemence, that neither reprimands of others—and I have received many—nor my own considerations—and there have been not a few of these—have succeeded in making me abandon this natural impulse which God has implanted in me.[187]

Within the convent, Sor Juana amassed one of the largest libraries in New Spain. She wrote in virtually every literary genre of the time, including ballads, drama, lyrics for lay and religious songs, love sonnets, the burlesque epigram, essay, drama, and religious works. The publication of her writings in Spain gave her renown throughout the Spanish-speaking world. She remained in close contact with the viceregal court and often received correspondence from abroad. As Paz commented, "Throughout the eighteenth and nineteenth centuries, there is no poet who used with such exquisite mastery so much variety in meter and form."[188]

Due to her biting comments on the subordinate role of women, many refer to Sor Juana as the first feminist in the Americas. In a frequently quoted poem, she commented on the double standard involving prostitutes:

> ¿O cuál es más de culpar,
> aunque cualquiera mal haga:
> la que peca por la paga
> o el que paga por pecar?
>
> Which is more to blame,
> Though each is a sinner:
> She who sins for pay,
> Or he who pays to win her?[189]

Science fascinated Sor Juana, and she wrote concerning various physical phenomena, ranging from the spinning of a top to the chemical changes produced by cooking food. Her observations in the kitchen led her to write, "If Aristotle had been a cook, he would have written much more."[190]

For twenty years, thanks to her ties to court and wealthy patrons financing her book purchases, Sor Juana continued her prodigious output. Her collected works total 876 pages.

In 1690, the Bishop of Puebla published Sor Juana's *Carta Atenagórica* (*Missive Worthy of Athens*), her criticism of a sermon by a Jesuit priest. In addition to publishing the critique, the bishop wrote a letter criticizing Sor Juana's scholarly activity. The letter bore the signature of Sor Filotea de la Cruz, a pseudonym for the bishop. In the letter, the bishop criticized Sor Juana for failing to confine her writings to religious topics, stating: "Letters that breed arrogance God does not want in women. But the Apostle does not reject them so long as they do not remove women from a position of obedience."[191]

The bishop's attack occurred at an inopportune moment for Sor Juana. Her benefactor, the former viceroy, had recently died in Spain. Archbishop Francisco Aguiar y Seijas, a misogynist who thought women should be scourging themselves, not writing plays and poetry, headed the church in Mexico.

Figure 3.2
Sor Juana de la Cruz

Source: Reproduced with permission of the General Secretariat of the Organization of American States

The bishop, who no doubt sought a humble retraction, found himself confronted with a refutation, known as the *Reply to Sor Filotea*. In it, Sor Juana commented that she and other women were just as entitled to write as males and inquired, "Is not my mind, such as it is, as free as his, considering their common origin?" In her response she cited numerous women from classical antiquity to the seventeenth century who had written and translated religious works.[192]

Shortly after she wrote *Reply to Sor Filotea*, Sor Juana renounced her literary activity, sold her library and musical instruments and donated the proceeds to the poor. She turned to the more conventional life of an ascetic nun. Sor Juana's renunciation of writing remains the great mystery of her life. Paz commented, "More likely it was due to the unwonted solitude in which she was living and to the anxiety caused by increasingly overt hostility on the part of her ill-wishers."[193]

When a plague broke out in her convent in 1695, Sor Juana cared for the afflicted and contracted the disease herself. As a result, she died in the convent, after twenty-six years of encloistration.

Sor Juana's life clearly reflects her times. She would not have been criticized if she had been a man engaged in the same pursuits. While she received severe criticism for being a scholarly woman, no one questioned the propriety of her owning the mulatto slave girl whom she brought to the convent as a servant.[194]

RELIGION

The Church as a Religious Institution

> By the middle of the eighteenth century the Catholic Church was by far the single most powerful institution in New Spain, rivaling even the royal Government.
>
> John Schwaller, 1985[195]

In 1493, Pope Alexander VI responded to Columbus's first voyage to the New World by issuing papal bulls that awarded Spain and Portugal sovereignty over the Americas. The bulls drew an imaginary line through the poles that ran one hundred leagues west of the Azores and the Cape Verde islands. Spain was granted the newly discovered lands west of this line. These bulls provided the religious justification for the Spanish Conquest and control of the New World. The Spanish jurist Juan de Solórzano y Pereyra succinctly stated this rationale in his *Política Indiana,* published in 1648. He claimed that the Indians:

> because they are so barbarous . . . needed somebody who, by assuming the duties of governing, defending and teaching them, would reduce them to a human, civil, social and political life, so that they should acquire the capacity to receive the Faith and the Christian religion.[196]

Since the Vatican did not have the resources to spread the Gospel in the New World, it transferred unprecedented control, known as the *patronato real* (royal patronage), over the Church to the Spanish monarchs as incentive for them to Christianize their colonies. In 1501, to compensate for the financial outlay required by missionary work in the New World, Pope Alexander VI allowed the Spanish monarchs to collect tithes in the New World. As a further incentive to evangelization, Spanish monarchs received the right to establish diocesan boundaries, administer church finances, nominate bishops, and review (or censor) all communications between the pope and the Church in Spanish America. Given the number of bishoprics, the Council of the Indies made the actual selection of bishops. While this transfer of power later had immense significance, at the dawn of the sixteenth century it did not seem as significant since little was known of the extent and wealth of the New World.[197]

In 1524, twelve Franciscan friars arrived in Veracruz and walked barefoot in patched robes to Mexico City. Upon their arrival, Cortés knelt in the dust and kissed their hands and the hems of their robes, to the amazement of nearby Indians. These friars began what has been called "the spiritual conquest of Mexico." By 1559, approximately 800 friars were working among a native population of 2.65 million. The mendicant orders—the Franciscans, the Dominicans, and the Augustinians—dedicated themselves to missionary work. Their devotion to preaching and teaching, and their flexibility, mobility, superior education, and intense zeal made them ideal for this task. Missionaries willingly endured harsh climate, new foods, disease, and even martyrdom. As historian Alan Knight remarked, "Like Castilian society as a whole, the Church was a crusading institution, newly invigorated by the heady triumph over Moorish Granada . . ."[198]

Clergymen vied with *encomenderos* for influence over Indians and protected them against extortion by merchants and abuse by *corregidores*. Priests supported the continued separation of the Indian and Spanish populations, believing they could create a new society under Church, not secular, control. The friars not only sought to uproot indigenous religious belief but to preserve the pristine, non-materialistic, and somewhat idealized Indian community. The desire to separate Indians from Spaniards reflected the clergy's concern that otherwise Spanish abuse would decimate Mexico's Indian population, as had already occurred in the Caribbean.[199]

Missionaries generally learned indigenous languages rather than preaching to their flock through an interpreter. They often formed the only communication channel between colonial authorities and the indigenous population. Indians were aware that conversion to Christianity allowed them to appeal to both the friars and the Crown for protection. Despite clerical efforts to isolate Indians physically and spiritually from the rest of colonial society, labor demands and the marketing of Indian products inexorably linked the two groups.[200]

The vast area of Spanish America, which stretched from Argentina to California, presented missionaries with a monumental challenge. The area's extreme linguistic diversity compounded the difficulty of their task. Missionary priests rejected imposing Spanish on Indians. They argued it would be better to convert infidels by learning indigenous languages and translating Christian precepts into these languages. Many languages they encountered lacked the vocabulary to express central concepts of Christianity such as "soul" and "devil." To facilitate their ministry, the Franciscans, who took the lead in learning native languages, published vocabularies and catechisms in such Indian languages as Tarascan, Nahuatl, Mazáhua, and Otomí. The 1571 Spanish–Nahuatl/Nahuatl–Spanish dictionary prepared by Franciscan Fray Alonso de Molina remains a prime reference for classical Nahuatl.[201]

In numerical terms, the early friars' efforts at converting Indians to Christianity proved fabulously successful. The Franciscan Fray Toribio de Benavente commented on early conversion efforts, "I believe that after this land was won, which was in 1521, up to the time I am writing this, which is in the year 1536, more than four million souls have been baptized." Another missionary, Pedro de Gante, boasted that in one day, with the aid of only one companion, he had baptized 14,000 Indians. The takeover of entire high cultures, such as the Tarascan, facilitated such mass conversion. In addition, the poverty and simplicity of the first friars impressed an indigenous population accustomed to deferring to an ascetic priesthood.[202]

Many of those baptized had only a rudimentary understanding of Christianity. Due to the lack of personnel and problems with translation, instruction dealt only with the fundamental tenants of Christianity. In one instance, Jesuits in northern Mexico used the example of a dammed soul surrounded by rings of fire and serpents to explain the concept of hell. Indians responded with smiles, noting that in such a place surely no one would suffer from cold nights or go hungry thanks to the snakes, which they considered a delicacy.[203]

Churchmen soon became aware that initial, euphoric conversions had been neither as pervasive nor as profound as the early missionaries had hoped. Persuading Indians to reject their old gods after they accepted the Christian one presented an enduring problem. Rather than simply switching religions, Indians frequently added or reworked Christian concepts and rituals according to their existing belief system. In 1530, Benavente commented that Indians concealed idols "at the foot of the crosses or beneath the stones of the altar steps, pretending that they were venerating the cross, whereas they were actually adoring the demon."[204] He also noted that the Indians' acceptance of the image of Christ merely resulted in the Indians having 101 idols, where a hundred had existed before. In 1581, the Dominican Diego Durán wrote, "They *believed* in God and at the same time *practised* the old ways and ritual of the devil."[205]

Despite the clergy's persistent efforts to eradicate them, pagan beliefs endured throughout the colonial period. Even though the Maya were baptized and thus officially converted, they continued old family rituals in the house and agricultural rituals in the fields. In Yucatán, even the wealthiest and most influential colonists acknowledged the superior supernatural powers of the Maya belief system and sought their help when in need to exorcise a bewitched cow, to remove a curse from a field, or to cure an ailment or infertility.[206]

In 1700, two Dominican fathers surprised the majority of the population of Francisco Cajonos, an Oaxacan village, as they sacrificed a deer and birds and said prayers in Zapotec. Two members of their own community, Juan Bautista and Jacinto de los Ángeles, had denounced them to the priests. The next day the two were savagely beaten and executed by their enraged fellow townspeople. In reprisal, the Spanish hanged fifteen people from the town.[207]

Even though the early friars plunged into mission work, from a theological point of view the Indians' nature remained unclear. Some conquistadores claimed the Indians were animals. This had more than theological implications. If indeed Indians were deemed to be animals, the clergy would be in no position to check the conquistadores' abuse of Indians and their property. As a result, the clergy waged a concerted effort to persuade the pope to declare unequivocally the Indians' humanity. As part of this effort, in about 1535, Julián Garcés, the bishop of Tlaxcala, lauded the Indians' intelligence and willingness to receive the faith and declared they were not "turbulent or ungovernable but reverent, shy and obedient to their teachers."[208]

Pope Paul III responded to these efforts by declaring the Indians' humanity in a 1537 bull entitled *Sublimis Deus*, which established that "Indians are truly men and that they are not only capable of understanding the Catholic faith but, according to our information, they desire exceedingly to receive it." The bull also stated, "The said Indians and all other people who may later be discovered by Christians, are by no means to be deprived of their liberty or the possession of their property, even though they be outside the faith of Jesus Christ."[209]

Within half a century, the early missionaries' zeal began to wane. In 1561, King Felipe II wrote:

> We have been informed that monasteries are built very close together, because the religious prefer to establish themselves in the rich green lands near the city of Mexico, leaving stretches of twenty to thirty leagues untended, because the religious avoid the rough, poor, and hot regions.[210]

During the early sixteenth century, there existed a genuine, though unequal, alliance between missionaries and Indians. Priests defended Indian rights and served as intermediaries between village authority and civil authority at higher levels. As time passed, this alliance weakened. In 1555, the First Provincial Council of Mexico prohibited the ordination of Indians. In 1571, the Church removed Indians from the authority of the Inquisition after deeming them mentally incapable of understanding the faith.[211]

Missionaries generally treated Indians in a paternalistic and sometimes abusive manner. The bishop of Michoacán, Vasco de Quiroga, commented that the missionaries:

> have inflicted and are now inflicting many mistreatments upon the Indians, with great haughtiness and cruelty, for when the Indians do not obey them, they insult and strike them, tear out their

> hair, have them stripped and cruelly flogged, and then throw them into prison in chains and cruel irons, a thing most pitiable to hear about and much more pitiable to see.[212]

Gradually the Church lost interest in native languages and became less optimistic about its ability to alter the indigenous world view. The missionaries' initial optimism gave way to viewing Indians as idle, barbarous, and backsliding in religious matters. Priests increasingly complained that rural assignments exiled them from the civil world they had known as students. Many priests would only settle in parishes where numerous non-Indians lived. Such priests made infrequent visits to remote villages to administer sacraments. This trend became more pronounced near the end of the colonial period. In 1791, seventy-five priests lived in the city of Querétaro and only thirteen lived in the rest of the *corregimiento*, despite its having twice the population of the city. Historian Colin MacLachlan commented, "The colonial church, increasingly institutionalized, became an enclave and sanctuary of European culture amid a no longer pliable mass of Indians who had drawn a line beyond which they would not go."[213]

The role of the Church evolved from initial conversion of Indians to ministering to long-established communities. Villagers depended on priests for spiritual consolation, for certain leadership and social welfare functions, and to mediate between community and state. These priests depended on their flock for sustenance and legitimacy.[214]

The Bourbons were not anti-clerical in the sense of questioning the validity of Catholicism. However, they did seek to curtail the power of the Church, which they considered politically offensive, economically retrograde, and culturally stultifying. As a result, priests' legal privileges—the ecclesiastical *fuero*—were reduced, and church courts were prohibited from inflicting corporal punishment. Popular religion came under increased official scrutiny, because it was associated with drink, degeneracy, sloth, profligacy, and backwardness. Many clerics shared this official view.[215]

The Church as an Educational Institution

Ironically Church action led to much of our knowledge of pre-Conquest cultures, as well as to much of our ignorance of them. Shortly after the Conquest, churchmen systematically gathered and burned pre-Columbian codices. As the Bishop of Yucatán Diego de Landa stated:

> We found a large number of books in these characters [Mayan hieroglyphs], and, as they contained nothing in which there were not to be seen superstition and lies of the devil, we burned them all, which they regretted to an amazing degree, and which caused them much affliction.

Subsequently, possession of such books was equated with idolatry, which was punished by hanging and burning at the stake.[216]

The attitude of the Church soon changed, and the clergy assumed the leading role in the study of pre-Conquest cultures. Fray Bernardino de Sahagún compared the study of indigenous beliefs to the study by a doctor of the cause of disease. He claimed that just as doctors needed to know the cause of disease, a priest, as a doctor of souls, needed to know the cause of idolatrous superstitions before he could cure the idolater.[217]

Sahagún's *Historia general de las cosas de la Nueva España* (*General History of the Things of New Spain*), also known as the Florentine Codex, is the outstanding example of such studies. In compiling his work between 1558 and 1569, Sahagún used methods that foreshadowed those of the modern ethnographer, including posing the same question in Nahuatl to different informants to corroborate the responses he received. His twelve-volume encyclopedia of pre-Columbian Aztec life included information on flora, fauna, history, and religious views and ceremonies. He included a long list of dishes with the ingredients, indicating the Aztecs' wide culinary variety. Included were dozens of ways to prepare tamales. Informants' replies in Nahuatl, transcribed for the book using the Latin alphabet, were included along with a translation. Accompanying the text were 1,852 illustrations drawn by indigenous informants. (One of these illustrations appears as Figure 2.3.)

While he felt the religious practices he documented indicated that Satan had possessed the Aztecs, Sahagún described with admiration Aztec architecture, medical knowledge, educational practices, and political organization. He did not, as far as is known, either suppress or censor any responses. Mexican historian Enrique Florescano described his work as "one of the most original books human ingenuity has ever produced."[218]

Many influential individuals in New Spain felt that Sahagún's work, served to perpetuate indigenous beliefs and rites, rather than eliminating them. In 1577, as a result of these individuals' denunciations, King Felipe II forbade research on Indian history and religion, thus halting Sahagún's work. This royal disfavor delayed the publication of his study in its full form until the twentieth century.[219]

The early church assumed the responsibility for educating the indigenous elite. Bishop Zumárraga and Viceroy Mendoza founded the Colegio de Santa Cruz in Tlatelolco to instruct the sons of Indian leaders in religion, reading, writing, rhetoric, philosophy, music, medicine, good manners, and Latin grammar. The Spanish hoped the school would become a seminary for training a native priesthood. The students, who numbered seventy in 1536, created a scholarly, written record of Aztec culture. They translated works directly from Nahuatl into Latin, a language they mastered so well that their compositions were compared to Cicero's. Some of the school's graduates remained to teach the next generation of students, and, in 1550, a native Mexican became rector. Other graduates became magistrates in Indian villages, skilled musicians and artisans, and teachers of indigenous languages.[220]

Later in the sixteenth century, the school fell into disfavor. Spaniards and Creoles, whose numbers continued to rise, became increasingly unwilling to share positions of influence with Indians. In 1585, the archbishop condemned teaching Indians Latin, rhetoric, and philosophy. By the end of the century, Creoles, but not Indians, received higher education in the University of Mexico.[221]

Missionaries assumed responsibility for the early primary education of Indian children. They not only imparted a basic education but also their class and gender values. Girls' schools sought to protect Indian girls and train them to be wives and mothers. They stressed sewing, catechism, and household tasks. Girls generally remained inside. When outside, someone accompanied them. The Franciscans separated the children of plebeian and aristocratic Indians. The latter attended boarding schools, stayed in school longer, and received more religious training. Many Indian leaders, unwilling to see their sons confined by the priests of the new religion, substituted the sons of their subjects or slaves for their own children, whom they kept at home.[222]

The Church was also responsible for much of the formal education imparted to non-Indians. Thanks to Jesuit education of the Creole elite, by the middle of the eighteenth century, modest pockets of Enlightenment could be found in all major cities in Spanish America. As a result of Church efforts, along with those of private teachers and the municipal government, roughly half of Mexico City's children of primary school age were receiving education by the end of the eighteenth century.[223]

The Church as a Financial Institution

During the colonial period, the Church emerged as a major financial institution. In addition to offerings in cash, the Church received income from agricultural tithes, which were an involuntary tax on crops and livestock produced by haciendas and *ranchos*. Income from Church-owned property and fees charged for sacraments and Masses further increased Church wealth. Often the dying would establish a trust fund for Masses to be said for the repose of their soul. Such trust funds would generate income paid to the priest who said the Masses. Some individuals, especially those who died childless, would bequeath land to the Church. The key to Church wealth was the Church's immortality as an institution. Over decades and centuries, bequests, donations from the faithful, and sound investments increased Church wealth.[224]

The fees priests charged for performing rites led to widespread conflict between clergy and parishioners. One priest wrote his lay assistant in an outlying village:

> Tell the sons of that *pueblo* that the clerical fees are by order of natural law, divine law, ecclesiastical law, and royal law. It is not a voluntary contribution, as you and the others seem to think. Just as I am obliged to give you spiritual care, you are obliged to care for my material needs, as St. Paul says.

This particular missive backfired. Indians obtained the letter and then used it as evidence of conduct unbecoming to a priest when challenging what they regarded as excessive fees.[225]

By the end of the colonial period, the Church had emerged as a major property owner. The Church rented some properties and managed others directly. At the time of their expulsion, Jesuits owned mines, large haciendas, and sugar cane plantations. These plantations, which employed black slave labor, were among the most efficient of the colonial period. The fact that the Mexican Church acquired more property than any other institution did not indicate that it was being especially acquisitive. It simply followed the example set in Europe where the Church owned more than any other landowner.[226]

As a result of donations and income from endowments, property ownership, mortgage payments, and land rental, the Church consistently amassed large surpluses of cash. Some of these funds financed hospitals, charitable works, colleges, and missions.[227]

Funds amassed by the Church also became the major credit source in the colony, which had no banks. Rather than Church wealth lying under a "dead hand," as critics charged, the Church kept money circulating through long-term, low-interest loans to *hacendados* and businessmen. By the eighteenth century, individual institutions— such as convents, monasteries, lay brotherhoods (*cofradías*), and Church hospitals—had become major credit facilities, handling several millions of pesos and employing trained staff who kept detailed accounts. The Marquesa de Selvanevada justified founding a convent in Querétaro specifically on the grounds that its construction would employ artisans and workers and that it would serve as a center for the circulation of money and as a stimulus to merchants, farmers, and industrialists. Such credit proved especially beneficial to small farmers in rural areas. Historian Michael Costeloe concluded, "It is difficult to imagine how any alternative credit system could have operated with greater success in the circumstances of the times . . ."[228]

In some instances, even by the standards of the time, Church control of property became excessive. In 1636, the members of the Mexico City municipal council commented on the Church's continued acquisition of property:

> Since the year fifteen hundred and seventy, this city has repeatedly entreated His Majesty to see fit to ban the mendicant orders of Dominicans and Augustinians and the fathers of the society of Jesus from acquiring houses and properties in this city, because the residents were now unable either to buy or even to leave inheritances to their children . . .

The council also noted that the Church owned much livestock and many grain and sugar mills.[229]

Given its enormous wealth, the Church often found itself involved in struggles over the most mundane of matters—power and money. In many cases, these struggles occurred within the Church. The mendicant orders vied with each other to control disputed areas. Archbishop Alonso de Montúfar commented on this rivalry: "They act as if they were disposing of their own vassals! And sometimes they even confront each other with battalions of Indians!"[230]

Figure 3.3
Mission Nuestro Señor Santiago, Jalpan de Serra, Querétaro, conceived and built (1751–1758) under the directions of Fray Padre Junípero Serra

Source: Photograph by Helga Teiwes, October 7, 1995

Church Architecture

Religious architecture forms a permanent legacy of the Church's wealth. As with colonial art, colonial architecture used imported styles, albeit in a freer manner modified to reflect Mexican reality. Large walled patios in front of churches accommodated multitudinous Indian converts. At the same time, the fortress-like design of many early monasteries reflected the danger of Indian attack.[231]

Church buildings often reflected a variety of stylistic influences. Indigenous craftsmen worked the materials, imparting their own decorative flourishes. As James Early remarked in his study of colonial architecture, "The energy of popular workmanship and the imaginative vitality of popular decorative taste have created much of the enduring appeal of Mexican viceregal architecture." These indigenous craftsmen took pride in their work and saw the church as the visual embodiment of their community.[232]

Early church architects in Mexico attempted, as did their Protestant counterparts, to emulate the simplicity of the primitive church of Christ. Protestant architects in Europe continued to stress simplicity, claiming that ornamentation should not distract worshippers from God. In contrast, Baroque church architects in Mexico felt that church adornment temporarily obliterated the misery of mundane life with a foretaste of paradise. The Augustinians, the most lavish mendicant builders, argued that if God had inspired Solomon to build a lavish temple, nothing should prevent them from doing likewise.[233]

Vasco de Quiroga's Hospitals

In the mid-sixteenth century, the secular priest Vasco de Quiroga, who had served as an *audiencia* judge, founded communal villages among the Tarascan Indians who lived around Lake Pátzcuaro in Michoacán. Each village, inspired by Sir Thomas More's *Utopia,* centered around a "hospital," in the medieval sense of the word. These hospitals not only cared for the sick but also welcomed the poor, the hungry, and travelers in need of shelter.

Although they were forced to renounce their old religion, village residents were housed, fed, and protected from the demands of *encomenderos*. The Tarascans could elect their own officials, and they shared communal lands. Quiroga stressed the need for all adults—men and women—to work a six-hour day and felt that well-rounded adults needed to combine urban and rural work. All residents had access to land and tools for artisanal activity. No one could hire domestic servants. Each village received instruction in a particular craft, such as weaving, ceramics, or woodcarving. Assigning one craft to each village avoided competition between villages and created a trade network throughout the Tarascan area. Villagers sold their crafts to obtain cash. Quiroga established almost a hundred of these new communities, where *corregidores* and *encomenderos* could not abuse Indians.[234]

Because of Quiroga's success with this, the Crown appointed him bishop of Michoacán. The Council of the Indies commented that his selection occurred because

> there is a good report of his life and example and he is much inclined to the conversion and good treatment of the Indians and to their instruction in the matters of our holy faith on which he has spent a large part of the salary that Your Majesty has commanded to be given him.[235]

Even though it rewarded Quiroga with a bishopric, the Crown was reluctant to extend his model since it removed Indian labor from Spanish control. The towns Quiroga founded continued to

Figure 3.4 *Surviving Quiroga-era hospital, Santa Fe de la Laguna*
Source: Philip Russell

function under the rules he laid down. Some of these towns, such as Santa Fe de la Laguna, still exist. The hospital and church Quiroga built there can still be seen. Today the people of Michoacán fondly remember Quiroga and still practice many of the crafts he introduced.[236]

Bartolomé de las Casas

> If Columbus, through a daring and momentous act, lessened the geographic and cultural distances between two worlds, it fell to Las Casas, a man driven by profound Christian beliefs and untamed humanism, to attempt to bridge the informational gap created by the forced incorporation of America into the Spanish empire.
>
> Daniel Castro, 2007[237]

Bartolomé de las Casas, one of the priests who influenced the pope to recognize the Indians' humanity, received an *encomienda* in Cuba. After becoming an *encomendero*, Las Casas began meditating on *Ecclesiasticus* 34: 24, "He that sheddeth blood and he that defraudeth the laborer of his hire are brothers." Las Casas soon absolved his *encomienda* Indians of tribute obligations and spent the rest of his ninety-two-year-long life defending the rights of Indians. The teachings of Las Casas, who became Bishop of Chiapas, had an impact throughout the New World and influenced the content of the New Laws of 1542.[238]

Las Casas argued that Indians were rational beings who had the right to freely choose their religion, their place of residence, and their job. For taking this relatively moderate stance, other Church officials, government administrators, and *encomenderos* bitterly attacked Las Casas. In some of his less moderate moments, Las Casas declared that instead of being hailed as heroes and receiving titles of nobility, Cortés and Francisco Pizarro (the conquistador of Peru) should have been hanged as common criminals. As bishop, Las Casas instructed priests not to give absolution to *encomenderos*.[239]

The following summarizes Las Casas's views on the Indian:

> Indians are free by law and by natural right and owe nothing to the Spanish nor to any other nation. Through unjust wars they were cruelly subjugated. After thus being subjugated, they were placed in the most extreme conditions of servitude, such as the encomienda and the repartimiento. Even the devils in hell could not invent such violations of natural and divine order. Encomiendas are inherently depraved, perverse, and beyond the bounds of law and reason. Why should free men be distributed against their will, ordered around like a herd of cattle, even if it were for a saint?[240]

In his most dramatic effort on behalf of the Indian, Las Casas debated the renowned Spanish scholar Juan Ginés de Sepúlveda. Prior to the debate, the king ordered that all further raids and expeditions be halted until the rights of Indians could be defined. The Crown intended that the debate, which occurred in the Spanish city of Valladolid in 1550 and 1551, would clarify the legal position of Indians. Even though the pope's 1537 decree established Indians' humanity, it did not state under what circumstances Spaniards could justifiably wage war against them.

Sepúlveda based his arguments on the fifth book of Aristotle's *Politics*. He declared that: 1) Indians were barbarous and that their natural condition was that of submission to more civilized peoples, 2) they were idolatrous and practiced human sacrifice, which justified intervention to prevent crimes against natural law, 3) intervention was justified to save innocent lives, and 4) intervention would facilitate Christian evangelization. In direct opposition to the principle later enunciated at Nuremberg, Sepúlveda claimed soldiers must not question the justice of a war, as that did not concern them.[241]

Las Casas, in a five-day oral presentation in Latin, argued that Indians should enjoy the same rights as Spaniards. He claimed that it insulted the Almighty and bordered on blasphemy to suggest that He would have peopled an entire hemisphere with people who were as brutish and incapable as Sepúlveda claimed they were. He also emphasized that Christianity could not properly be propagated by the sword. Rather than forcing Christianity on natives, Las Casas advocated conversion as it was carried out at the dawn of Christianity, when people were slowly shown the true way.[242]

Rather than facing each other, the debaters made oral arguments to a fourteen-man panel of judges. These judges never issued a collective decision. Sepúlveda so impressed the Mexico City municipal council that it voted to buy him 200 pesos worth of Mexican jewels and clothing to reward him for his efforts and "to encourage him in the future." Other observers felt Las Casas prevailed in the debate, noting that he could publish his views on the Conquest in 1552, while Sepúlveda did not receive permission to publish his.[243]

Las Casas was successful in that he created a moral climate in which the Crown was forcefully reminded of its obligation to defend Indians against their oppressors and to do what it could to improve their lot. His efforts led the Crown to pass legislation favoring the Indian and to take other steps to defend the indigenous population. This was a commitment for which, as historian J. H. Elliott noted, "It is not easy to find parallels in the history of other colonial empires."[244]

After the Valladolid debate, Las Casas remained in Spain to lobby in the royal court on behalf of Indians. After realizing that the immediate abolition of the *encomienda* was a political impossibility, Las Casas sought to prevent *encomiendas* from being inherited by the children of *encomenderos*. He continued his efforts on behalf of the Indian until his death in 1566.[245]

Las Casas must be recognized as one of the most vociferous critics of the Spanish colonization project and as one of the most prolific writers of treatises, histories, and countless other documents about colonial Indoamerica. He repeatedly raised questions few of his contemporaries considered. However, when judged by modern standards, Las Casas (and his contemporaries) can be faulted on several counts. He never questioned imposing an alien religious belief such as Christianity on peoples who already had well-defined theological beliefs. Although he acted on behalf of the oppressed, Las Casas never worked with the indigenous to transform them from passive objects to active subjects responsible for determining their fate. Finally, he accepted the proposition that subjecting native people to Spanish rule would leave them better off than they had been before the Conquest.[246]

The Inquisition

In 1571, the king removed the Inquisition from bishops' hands and decreed the establishment of the Tribunal of the Holy Office of the Inquisition in Mexico. The Holy Office enforced respect for religious principles and defended Spanish religion and culture against heretical views. Heretics were assumed to be traitors, and dissenters were assumed to be social revolutionaries attempting to subvert the political and religious stability of the community. Most cases investigated by the Inquisition in New Spain concerned bigamy, blasphemy, sodomy, witchcraft, solicitation in the confessional, healing (*curandismo*), misguided interpretations of the faith, and other offenses against the Catholic religion. Virtually none of these offenses—bigamy is the exception—would be cause for judicial action in modern Spain or Mexico.[247]

Bigamy and blasphemy formed the most frequent charges. The number of bigamy charges reflected the high degree of social and geographical mobility in New Spain. Often individuals abandoned wives back in Spain, remarried, and started a new life in Mexico. The Inquisition frequently charged people with heresy, a crime seen as a contagion requiring vigorous prosecution. Many such cases involved those whose Jewish ancestors had fled from Spain to Portugal after the expulsion of the Jews. During the 1580–1640 union of crowns of Spain and Portugal, many emigrated to Mexico. Their descendents were among the chief targets of the Inquisition in New Spain. Persons of African descent also received a disproportionate number of accusations.[248]

Since Protestantism had emerged from the Catholic clergy, enforcing clerical orthodoxy received special attention. This led to the Inquisition's delving into minute doctrinal matters, such as one's interpretation of the real presence in the Eucharist. In 1551, the Inquisition fined Dr. Pedro de la Torre a hundred golden pesos, exiled him from New Spain, and forced him to publicly abjure his heretical views for simply declaring that no difference existed between God and nature.[249]

The Inquisition's interest in keeping Catholicism pure led to an ever widening circle of concern. It frequently charged people with witchcraft and sorcery, which constituted two separate offenses. Non-Indians were frequently prosecuted for idolatry after they turned to pre-Columbian indigenous traditions to improve their status or procure wealth. Possessing the Koran or the Bible in a Romance language constituted an offense.[250]

The Inquisition created some offenses simply to facilitate its own operation. Those who failed to denounce an offense within the purview of the Inquisition could be excommunicated. Demeaning the Inquisition became an offense.[251]

Generally the Inquisition began proceedings only when it received a denunciation. It would then evaluate the charge to see if it had any foundation. If it found the charge plausible, it would order the accused arrested. Those arrested remained ignorant of the charges against them and did not know who had accused them. Those under investigation were asked which of their actions could have resulted in an accusation. The Inquisition maintained secret prisons where the accused could spend months during an investigation. The Inquisition did not use torture as a punishment, but frequently employed it in interrogation, as occurred in practically every country in the Western world at the time.[252]

The Inquisition could impose a wide range of punishments, including fines, forced labor, seizure of property, forced public confessions, whippings, and exile. In addition, the guilty could be sentenced to obligatory service working in a hospital or convent, on a state or city project, or in galleys. The Inquisition turned unrepentant heretics over to civil authorities to be burned at the stake. However, fewer than fifty people suffered that fate in New Spain.[253]

Although the Inquisition enjoyed extremely broad powers, the limitations imposed by its small staff and New Spain's geographical expanse restricted it. Between 1571 and 1700, it considered only 12,000 matters, of which fewer than 2,000 resulted in a trial. This amounted to only sixteen trials a year in the vast area stretching from Central America to California. Due to the Enlightenment's effect on the Spanish empire, the role of the Inquisition declined. In the 1700s, the Inquisition tried only 534 cases and put only one individual to death.[254]

During its existence, the nature of offenses considered by the Inquisition changed markedly. Bishop Zumárraga, the outstanding figure of the early Inquisition, headed it between 1536 and 1543. During this time, blasphemy, the most frequent charge, resulted in fifty-six trials.[255]

Under Zumárraga, the Inquisition also directed its attention to Indian religious practices. In one well-publicized case, the Inquisition tried Don Carlos, the cacique of Texcoco. He was definitely not a model citizen when judged by Spanish norms. He did not attend church and openly kept his niece as a concubine in addition to his wife. Don Carlos was convicted of declaring, "This is our land and our way of life and our possession and the rule of it belongs to us and will remain with us." The Inquisition declared him guilty of heretical dogmatism and he was burned at the stake.[256]

Attempts to enforce religious orthodoxy peaked between 1640 and 1650. During this time, the success enjoyed by those of Jewish ancestry in Mexico caused widespread jealousy. The Inquisition tried more than 200 individuals for Jewish practices during this decade. In 1649 alone, it had thirteen Jews burned at the stake in Mexico City.[257]

During the late colonial period, the Inquisition focused on political matters. In 1752, unfaithfulness to the Crown became an offense. Individuals committed this offense if they indulged "in the grievous error of disobedience, unfaithfulness, or defamation of the king our lord . . .." The Inquisition scrutinized works that popularized the libertarian principles of the French Revolution and lamented the "passion for the French books which have led so many to the abysm of corruption." It prohibited and confiscated books by Rousseau, Diderot, Voltaire, and Montesquieu.[258]

To evaluate the Inquisition, one must choose what criteria to use. The early Inquisition reflected Mexican society, which was a product of the Middle Ages. To the modern observer, the limits put on freedom of religion and expression offend human dignity. However, by European standards of the period, the Inquisition did not appear cruel. As historian William Manchester noted, at the time "men believed in magic and sorcery and slew those whose superstitions were different from, and therefore an affront to, their own."[259]

Even when judged by the standards of the times, the Inquisition was frequently abusive. Don Carlos of Texcoco was convicted solely on the uncorroborated testimony of one neophyte who lived with the Franciscans. Don Carlos claimed he was unjustly charged. Apparently the Council of the Indies agreed, since it severely reprimanded Zumárraga for his role in the trial and deprived him of inquisitional power. Early on, blasphemy charges against conquistadores formed part of a political campaign against Spaniards loyal to Cortés. Given the lack of safeguards to protect the accused, many individuals realized that false denunciations could be used to further their own interests. Indian nobles falsely accused rivals of idolatry. Convicted heretics denounced others in a desperate attempt to receive lighter sentences. Businessmen used charges of practicing Judaism to attack their competitors. Staffing the Inquisition with individuals who saw the tribunal as a path to personal wealth and selling confiscated goods to finance operations of the Inquisition also increased the possibility of abuse.[260]

MEXICO CITY

Once the Spanish completed the conquest of Tenochtitlan, they began rebuilding the city. Just as its Aztec defenders had prophesied, the reconstruction used forced Indian labor under Spanish supervision. Rebuilding a Spanish city on the ruins of Tenochtitlan created a monument to the Spanish triumph over the Aztecs. The new city, which had the same rectilinear plan as the old, borrowed from its predecessor in that it had a market plaza in Tlatelolco, a street of large houses leading to the west causeway, and an ensemble of structures surrounding the former central plaza of Tenochtitlan, today's Zócalo. The rebuilt city, known as Mexico City, became the capital of Mexico.[261]

Cortés established a municipal government to administer the newly founded colony. He asked that bishops and priests be sent from Spain to convert the Indian population to Christianity. Cortés specifically requested that Jewish and Moorish converts, physicians, and lawyers should not be allowed to come.[262]

By 1560, Mexico City had become New Spain's trade and financial center. It provided a substantial market for foodstuffs, fuel, textiles, and luxury goods. Not only was it New Spain's largest market but it was the nexus for a trading network extending from the Gulf of Mexico to the Pacific Ocean and from Guatemala in the south to northern mines. In addition, silks, porcelains, and other oriental goods passed through the city on their way to Europe, and slaves arrived there from Africa.[263]

During the sixteenth century, Mexico City became renowned for its architecture. A book published in 1554 by university professor Francisco Cervantes de Salazar wrote that the houses of the elite "match the nobility of those who reside in them" and that Tacuba Street "extends so far that the end cannot be seen, even by the eyes of a lynx." He noted that carpenters, blacksmiths, clocksmiths, weavers, barbers, bakers, painters, stone-cutters, tailors, shoe-makers, armorers, candle-makers, bow makers, sword cutlers, inn-keepers, and lath turners served the European population.[264]

While Spaniards in Mexico City replicated European civilization, some 20,000 Indians patronized the municipal market daily. The goods they traded included zapotes, beans, chiles, guavas, mameys, camotes, jícamas, prickly-pear cactus fruit, earthenware jars, atole, clothing, various seeds, medicinal plants, and aquatic worms for eating. Indians engaged in barter or used cacao beans as currency.[265]

A vast agricultural hinterland occupying most of the Valley of Mexico surrounded mid-sixteenth century Mexico City. Cervantes de Salazar described this area:

> Of the lands that approach nearest the city, some are common pastures that produce much herbage for cattle, mules, and herds. Others are bountiful in fruit-bearing trees, and so appropriate to every kind of cultivation that, save vines, whatever is planted brings forth returns with incredible interest. Among these are both rural and urban estates, individual ones being of such splendor and fertility that they refresh the mind and at the same time support families in sufficient abundance. Lest anything be wanting to make the spectacle the most pleasing of all, a lake abounding in fish . . . extends from the foot of the mountain and spreads out far and wide from the east toward the south and west, bearing many Indian barks with nets for catching fish.[266]

By the seventeenth century, the consequences of upsetting the ecological balance in the Valley of Mexico were becoming apparent. During the siege of Tenochtitlan, the Spanish dismantled dikes to allow their brigantines to sail freely. They also filled canals to allow for the passage of cavalry. Later, Spaniards' occupation of the fertile floor of the Valley of Mexico forced many Indians onto the surrounding hillsides where they engaged in slash-and-burn agriculture. This contributed to deforestation and erosion. The introduction of the Spanish plow led to additional erosion. Burning wood to make charcoal also contributed to deforestation, as did Spanish construction techniques. Builders required some 25,000 trees a year to provide pilings for construction on reclaimed lake beds. As these pilings rotted and had to be replaced, more trees were felled. Scaffolding, walls, roofs, and doors required additional wood. This deforestation inevitably resulted in erosion and increased run-off. As silt washed into the lakes, it reduced their storage capacity and exacerbated the problem of flooding.[267]

Conquistador Bernal Díaz del Castillo, who returned to Mexico City forty years after the Conquest, commented on his earlier visit:

> I was never tired of looking at the diversity of the trees, and noting the scent which each one had, and the paths full of roses and flowers, and the many fruit trees . . . Of all these wonders that I then beheld, today all is overgrown and lost, nothing is left standing.[268]

Shortly after Díaz del Castillo's return, Martín Enríquez, who served as viceroy between 1568 and 1580, described deforestation near Chalco southeast of Mexico City:

> In that the Indians of the village of Tlalmanalco have informed me that the Spanish and other people cut and destroy the forest in a manner in which if there is no remedy soon one will finish said forests, which would be of great harm and loss of all the republic being where principally one provides wood for the building of this city.[269]

In 1550, to prevent the cutting of wood for charcoal, authorities decreed that trees could only be felled with a permit. In 1570, they prohibited any cutting within five leagues of the city and banned slash-and-burn agriculture. Despite municipal and viceregal bans on felling trees, cutting continued.[270]

In 1607, to address the problem of flooding, excavation began on a channel to drain the closed basin formed by the Valley of Mexico. Some 40,000 Indians, working in shifts, toiled for ten months to excavate a 4.2-mile trench and a four-mile tunnel—the biggest single use of *repartimiento* labor.

The system diverted the Río Cuautitlán north from Lake Zumpango, the northernmost lake in the Valley of Mexico, into the Tula River valley. Humboldt, who visited Mexico early in the nineteenth century, commented that the drainage system constituted "a hydraulic operation which in our times, even in Europe, would claim the admiration of engineers."[271]

After 1623, authorities would not finance the maintenance of the drainage system. Soon debris and cave-ins rendered the trench and tunnel useless. In 1629, a flood that left the city under six feet of water demonstrated the folly of this neglect. After earlier floods, the waters receded. However, after the 1629 flood, the city remained submerged for five years. Priests held masses from the belfries of churches, shouting down to the faithful congregated in boats. At the time, officials seriously considered abandoning the capital. However, the owners of urban real estate, including the Church, successfully lobbied against the relocation.[272]

During the eighteenth century, Mexico City increased in influence and grandeur, a result of its being the seat of the viceregal government, the *audiencia*, the archbishopric, the Inquisition, and the mint and of its being surrounded by an extremely fertile valley. In the period before independence, as the Bourbons centralized power, Mexico City's population increased by 1.4 percent annually, well above the rate of population increase for Mexico as a whole. The city served as Mexico's major commercial crossroads. Some goods were transshipped to other locations. After entering the city, many of the raw materials, such as grain, meat, wool, and cotton, were transformed into products of utility to the urban population, such as bread and cloth. Merchants sold finished goods in a vast and diversified retail sector that supported thousands of business owners and even more managers, sales personnel, and commercial apprentices. Retail establishments, some general and some specialized, provided imported and domestic merchandise to all social classes. Most of Mexico's elite lived in the city and transacted business there.[273]

The population of the city increased during the second half of the eighteenth century as many migrated from neighboring areas due to crop failures, to population increase, and to haciendas encroaching on village lands. Its population of 137,000 surpassed that of any other city in the western hemisphere. Mexico City continued to be bicultural, although its racial proportions shifted. By the beginning of the nineteenth century, 2 percent of the population were native-born Spaniards, 48 percent were Creoles, 27 percent Indian, and 23 percent of mixed race.[274]

The magnificence of Mexico City's public buildings and the increase in its population and wealth caused Spaniards to worry that the capital of New Spain would eclipse Madrid. An upper class that not only possessed unprecedented wealth but had remarkably good architectural taste constructed many mansions. Some forty of these homes of the very rich still survive, the best known being the former home of the Conde del Valle de Orizaba, now known as the House of Tiles, in downtown Mexico City.[275]

THE INTELLECTUAL SCENE

With few exceptions, only those who could afford to arrange private tutors received an education. Mass education was frowned upon. In a 1785 *cédula* (decree), King Carlos IV declared that it was not desirable to "illustrate the Americans." He also proclaimed that "His Majesty did not need philosophers but good and obedient subjects."[276]

However, the need for an educated elite was recognized. In response, the Crown founded the Royal and Pontifical University of Mexico in 1553, eighty-three years before Harvard, "to serve God and the public welfare." A 1557 decree limited the number of students of mixed blood (mestizos) to six. In 1645, a constitution drawn up by Archbishop Palafox codified the racial make-up of the university. It excluded blacks, mulattos, slaves, Orientals, Jews, and Moors from enrollment. For the two-and-a-half centuries following its founding, the university provided New Spain with priests, lawyers, and doctors. By 1776, the university had granted 1,162 masters and doctorates and 29,882 bachelors degrees.[277]

Initially, the university, which was modeled on the renowned University of Salamanca, concentrated on four traditional faculties—law, the arts, theology, and medicine. Except for medical classes, professors taught in Latin and students wrote exams and theses in that language. Later, the university included such subjects as anatomy, surgery, mathematics, and astrology in the curriculum. Courses in Indian languages trained aspiring missionaries.[278]

University professors received little pay, even by the standards of the time. However, along with the student body, they did enjoy two privileges. The two groups formed a corporate body whose members were immune from judgment by civil authorities. Professors and students also elected the rector of the university, providing one of the few examples of democracy to be found in the colony.[279]

In 1539, an Italian who adopted the name Juan Pablos opened a print shop in Mexico City under the auspices of the first viceroy, Antonio de Mendoza, and the first bishop of Mexico City, Juan de Zumárraga. That year, Pablos printed *Doctrina cristiana* in Spanish and Nahuatl. Between 1524 and 1572, the mendicants published 109 books facilitating evangelization in various American Indian languages. By the end of the century, roughly 220 books had been published, and eight other printers had opened shops. Initially, publishing in the colony served to disseminate Christian doctrine and the King's laws. Later works included scholarly treatises and literature, including works of Sor Juana.

The Mexican publishing industry grew slowly through the colonial period. In 1810, the Mexican press published 275 titles (excluding newspapers) on religion, politics, literature, and other subjects. The number of copies of each book printed ran from a few hundred to several thousand. Several factors limited further increases in book publication. The high cost of paper and competition from imports limited demand for books printed in Mexico. The small number of copies printed increased the cost of each book. Low levels of literacy limited sales. Before a book could be published, the approval of a religious censor and civil authorities was required. Priests in religious orders also needed the approval of their order before they could publish their writings. Books dealing with the New World required authorization of the Council of the Indies.[280]

The first literature from Mexico, written by Spaniards, dealt with the Conquest itself. Cortés's *Cartas de México* (*Letters from Mexico*) and Díaz del Castillo's *Historia verdadera de la conquista de la Nueva España* (*True History of the Conquest of New Spain*), the two outstanding examples of this genre, continue to be read widely. These chronicles displayed a messianic sense of history, denigrated indigenous culture, and condemned native idolatry.[281]

During the seventeenth century, Mexico City remained the intellectual center of New Spain. Academies, literary groups, poetry readings, and musical performances complemented the university there. As in the previous century, rather than innovating, Mexico imported ideas and cultural norms from Europe. During this century, native-born Creole writers replaced the Spanish immigrants who had been the dominant writers of the sixteenth century.[282]

The expulsion of the Jesuits unintentionally resulted in the exiled Mexican priests making fundamental contributions to Mexican thought and culture. Much of their work responded to Europeans who proclaimed the "inferiority" of the geography and people of the Americas. The exiled Jesuits, who remained in Europe, compiled information on Mexico's ancient history, languages, geography, and ethnography.[283]

The Jesuit historian Francisco Javier Clavijero, born to Spanish parents in Veracruz in 1731, was the most eloquent and scholarly of these exiled authors. While in Mexico, he learned several indigenous languages. Clavijero did not begin writing history until after the Crown forced him and his fellow Jesuits from Mexico. His works defended pre-Hispanic civilization and Creole culture, which Europeans, most of whom had never even visited the New World, often misrepresented. Clavijero indicated his sympathies when he compared the Spanish destruction of Tenochtitlan to the Roman destruction of Jerusalem. His best known work, *Historia antigua de México* (*Ancient History of Mexico*), provided a scientific description of pre-Conquest cultures and nurtured Creole pride in Mexico's ancient heritage.[284]

Clavijero considered that pre-Conquest Mexico was shaped by social, geographic, and political forces, rather than its being the product of diabolic influence as previous historians had claimed. He readily acknowledged the role Indian labor played in the construction of colonial society. The tasks he mentioned as being performed by Indians, whom he referred to as *americanos*, included working the land, reaping wheat, lumbering, working stone, construction, road-building, mining, and herding.[285]

Mexico City remained the colony's outstanding intellectual center. Humboldt stated, "No city on the continent, without even excepting those of the United States, can display such great and solid scientific establishments as the capital of Mexico." In 1785, the Crown established the prestigious San Carlos Noble Arts Academy in the capital. There, European masters, highly influenced by prevailing neo-classic styles, taught drawing, sculpture, architecture, and mathematics. From 1805 to 1812, Carlos María de Bustamante published the first Mexican newspaper, *El Diario de México*. This Mexico City paper demonstrated Creole intellectual development, opening its pages to critical reflection on social and political matters as well as publishing substantial contributions concerning Indian history and antiquities.[286]

Chapter 4

From Corn to Capitalism, 1521–1810

> After the Conquest, New Spain became part of a much larger whole, the Spanish empire, and, through it, the capitalist mercantile system.
>
> Enrique Semo, 1993[1]

GEOGRAPHY

Mexico's central volcanic belt stretches from the Volcán de Colima in the west to the Pico de Orizaba in the east. The Pico's 18,855-foot elevation exceeds that of any peak in the lower forty-eight U.S. states. The permanently snow-capped volcanoes Iztaccíhuatl and Popocatépetl overlook 7,280-foot high Mexico City. These volcanoes produce earthquakes and an extremely fertile volcanic soil. One of the conquistadores who accompanied Cortés commented on conditions in the volcanic belt, "There are in this province of New Spain great rivers and springs of very good sweet water, extensive woods on the hills and plains of very high pines, cedars, oaks, and cypresses, besides live oaks and a great variety of mountain trees."[2]

North of Mexico City, two mountain ranges, the Sierra Madre Oriental and the Sierra Madre Occidental, extend in the direction of Texas and Arizona, respectively. The high, dry central plateau lies inside the inverted triangle formed by these two ranges. To the south of Mexico City, within the Sierra Madre del Sur, many isolated areas give rise to Oaxaca's wondrous diversity.

Due to soil fertility, abundant rainfall, and the availability of Indian labor, Spanish settlement was concentrated in central Mexico. Rampant diseases, to which newcomers had little resistance, discouraged settlement in low-lying coastal areas. The aridity of the north discouraged settlement there. Relatively few areas outside the central core could be used for agriculture, as roughly 31 percent of Mexico's land area is classified as desert and another 36 percent is semiarid.[3]

The availability of water, as well as topography, determined trade routes. In the early 1620s, Domingo Lázaro de Arregui commented on the 135-mile road from the silver-mining city of Zacatecas to the mining hamlet of Mazapil:

> If you took the direct route, you would arrive in two days at Mazapil. But traveling by the water holes and along the carting road, the journey takes five or six days. Going as the crow flies, there is no road or water, which is the reason for following such a roundabout path as people use.[4]

The lack of major rivers connecting New Spain's population centers had a profound impact on development. Transport by mule or cart was slow and expensive. As historians Arij Ouweneel and Catrien Bijleveld observed, "The severe climate, the difficult topography, the poorly paved roads, and the lack of good waterways between the population centers impeded the formation of an integrated market system."[5]

The transportation system in colonial Mexico stood in stark contrast to those of British North America and western Europe, whose economies were undergoing rapid economic growth and whose broad rivers made it possible to transport bulk goods to inland population centers inexpensively. In contrast to Mexico, much of the population of both these areas was located in port cities, so goods could be exchanged by sea, and relatively flat expanses and abundant water later made it possible to extend transport networks by building canals.

Population figures illustrate the impracticality of coastal shipping in New Spain. Tampico, the only coastal town of importance north of Veracruz, had only twenty-four Spanish citizens and 226 tributary Indians in 1570. At the end of the sixteenth century, Yucatán only had 300 Spanish citizens.[6]

Elevation change made transport difficult but yielded tremendous diversity. Thomas Gage, an English priest who traveled in New Spain between 1625 and 1636, passed through Jalapa and observed: "What makes it rich are the many farms of sugar, and some which they call *estancias,* rich farms for breeding mules and cattle; and likewise some farms of cochineal." After visiting Puebla, he commented: "Without it, there are many gardens, which store the markets with provision of salads. The soil abounds with wheat, and with sugar farms." In Oaxaca, he observed:

> The valley is full of sheep and other cattle, which yield much wool to the clothiers of the City of Angeles, store of hides to the merchants of Spain, and great provision of flesh to the city of Oaxaca, and to all the towns about . . . But what doth make the valley of Oaxaca to be mentioned far and near are the good horses which are bred in it, and esteemed to be the best of all the country. In this valley also are some farms of sugar, and great store of fruits, which two sorts meeting together have cried up the city of Oaxaca for the best conserves and preserves that are made in America.[7]

THE SIXTEENTH CENTURY

> Without labor, private landholding had limited value, and the accumulation of wealth, based on the utilization of economic resources, would be unlikely. The Europeans moved aggressively to establish both the concept of private property and its corollary, wage labor.
>
> Colin MacLachlan, 1988[8]

After the fall of Tenochtitlan, Spain began shaping the Mexican economy. The transition from feudalism to capitalism occurring in Europe and Spain's increasing insertion into the international market influenced this transformation. Spaniards set economic policy at all levels. The king set guidelines for the general course of the empire. Municipal governments allocated land, set prices, monitored markets, enforced guild regulations, and administered common land and public works.[9]

Sixteenth-century Mexico saw sweeping changes in technology. The long list of newly introduced items includes maps, the compass, pulleys, screws, the wheel for transport, and tools for blacksmithing and carpentry. Spaniards introduced some simple items, such as the nail. Others, such as ships used in transoceanic commerce, involved a complex combination of devices.[10]

The replacement of the digging stick with the plow led to increased productivity and to more erosion, as the plow loosened the entire surface of the earth. Plow-induced erosion led to the abandonment of entire estates. For example, the Jesuit-owned Jesús del Monte estate once produced 272,445 liters of wheat annually. Plow cultivation led to its fertile soil being washed away, leaving only bare rock. The Jesuits then converted the property from a wheat farm to a spiritual retreat.[11]

The introduction of European plants and animals produced a profound biological revolution. Plants intentionally introduced from the Old World include oranges, wheat, bananas, sugar cane, and mulberry trees for raising silk worms. Animals the Spaniards brought included chickens, pigs, donkeys, goats, sheep, cattle, and horses.[12]

European weeds proliferated and crowded out indigenous plants after Spaniards inadvertently introduced their seeds in cattle feed, horses' hooves, and cattle dung. These weeds thrived on plowed and overgrazed land. By 1600, many New World plants had become extinct, replaced by dandelions, nettles, and a host of grasses.[13]

A biological exchange in the opposite direction benefited the Old World. Corn and the potato were native to the New World and unknown in the Old World before Columbus. Other important plants introduced from the New World include sweet potatoes, peanuts, pineapples, vanilla, chiles, tomatoes, tobacco, long-stemmed cotton, and cacao (the source of chocolate).[14]

The Spaniards who came to Mexico during the sixteenth century had more experience with plunder, tribute, and slavery than they had with wages and market economies. The economy that emerged after the Conquest reflected this. It would be centuries before the labor force freely chose jobs based on working conditions and the wages received. In the period immediately after the Conquest, Spaniards demanded that Indians provided them with goods and that they performed certain tasks with little or no compensation.

In the decade after the Conquest, the Spanish enslaved many Indians. However, due to their high death rate, high initial purchase costs, and the availability of Indian labor through the *encomienda* and the *repartimiento*, Indian slavery soon diminished in importance.

The Crown had a financial interest in abolishing Indian slavery, since slaves did not pay tribute. This financial interest and humanistic concern resulted in the New Laws of 1542, which categorically prohibited Indian slavery. After this date, Indian slavery gradually disappeared in most areas. Exceptions, however, persisted. In 1643, Indians were still being bought and sold for work in the mines of Oaxaca.[15]

Indians not living within an *encomienda* paid tribute directly to the Spanish king. Such payments reflected the presumption that "discovered" lands belonged to the Crown. The king required the original inhabitants to pay him tribute to compensate him for generously allowing them to use his land. In 1570, roughly 800,000 Indians made such tribute payments.[16]

Tribute collection had a much greater impact than Indian slavery. In 1523, Carlos V wrote Cortés, "It is just and reasonable that the said Indians of the said land should serve us and pay tribute in recognition of the duty and service which, as our subjects and vassals, they owe us."[17] The Emperor's suggestion could easily be implemented since, as Rodrigo de Albornoz, the King's auditor in Mexico, wrote in 1525, "Indians here are very reasonable and orderly and accustomed to work for their living and contribute to Montezuma and his lords just like Spanish peasants."[18] The Crown's guaranteeing the survival of the Indian community by protecting its land from appropriation by Spaniards increased the Indians' willingness to pay tribute.[19]

Each head of a household in an Indian republic paid roughly two pesos a year tribute to the Spanish Crown. Non-Indians were exempt from this tax burden. As the Indian population declined more rapidly than the total amount of tribute demanded, per capita payments increased. This created a circular effect: more overwork, more population decline, and still more tribute per capita.[20]

Initially, Indians paid tribute in the form of food and clothing. Tribute payments in kind, such as corn, were generally sold at public auction to convert them into cash. However, most Indian-produced goods could not be readily converted to cash. As a result, treasury officials increasingly required Indians to pay tribute in cash. As this pressure increased, Indians became more integrated into the market economy, selling either their goods or their labor to raise the cash needed for tribute payments. To meet the Spaniards' cash demands, Indians produced and marketed silk, wheat, sheep, cattle, and pigs. The Spanish economy had little to offer the Indians that their own communities could not provide. The tribute requirement thus forced Indians to work for wages. In the absence of tribute, many would have produced to meet their own needs and avoided the cash economy.[21]

Rather than being consumed by local princes and lords, post-Conquest tribute embarked on a much more circuitous journey. In-kind tribute payments were sold for cash. The corn paid in tribute often nourished animals working in silver mines. Treasury officials sent the silver from the mines and cash tribute to Europe, where it circulated widely. The Spanish reexported some silver to the Orient in exchange for spices and other exotic imports.[22]

Given the lack of currency, the lack of Spanish-run enterprises, and the lack of European goods Indians desired, the Spaniards could not rely on wage labor. When Indians did receive wages, as in the case of *repartimiento* workers, they did not have the choice of rejecting employment. Luis de Velasco, who became viceroy in 1550, commented, "Indians must be forced to work for wages in the fields or in the towns to stop them from becoming vagrants."[23]

The Spaniards claimed Indians would not work voluntarily and that their lack of interest in consuming deprived them of interest in producing for the market. However, they did not test their assumption that Indians would not work for wages by offering them employment at wages that would attract voluntary workers. Rather, through the *repartimiento*, they forced Indians to work at wages well below those paid to voluntary workers.[24]

At the end of the sixteenth century, each of the major ethnic groups specialized in certain economic activities. The Indians produced corn, beans, chile, and the agave (*maguey*). They planted with the digging stick, and the same individuals produced crops and engaged in artisanal activity. The Spanish managed silver mines and estates producing wheat, cattle, and sugar cane. Fields were plowed, and mules and wagons carried goods. Most Spanish artisans did not engage in agriculture. These two groups were linked economically through tribute, the *encomienda*, and *repartimiento* labor.[25]

THE SEVENTEENTH CENTURY

During the seventeenth century, the pace of change slowed. In both the seventeen and eighteenth centuries, though, Spanish technology continued to permeate more deeply into the warp and woof of Mexican society.[26]

The *encomienda* ceased to be the dominant social institution. By the middle of the century, commerce, northern mines, and sugar refineries furnished considerably more revenue than the best encomiendas. This shift in the source of wealth led historian P. J. Bakewell to comment:

> In the sixteenth century, the white community lived on the surplus produced by a vast number of Indians working in a very primitive economic system. In the seventeenth, Spaniards lived on the product, broadly and ultimately, of their own enterprise and of an economy that was in its general outline of contemporary European design.[27]

Mexicans invested more capital locally, leading to an increase in production for Mexican use. This benefited the colony and led to greater economic diversity and autonomy. Given the high cost of land transportation, New Spain remained a patchwork of regional economies stitched together by trade and government. High taxes, piracy, privateering, and insecurity resulting from European wars limited trans-Atlantic trade.[28]

Between 1628 and 1724, silver production increased at an annual rate of 1.2 percent. At the same time, much to the chagrin of the Spanish, Mexicans appropriated more silver to finance their own production, administration, and defense, leaving less for the mother country. Due to increased smuggling, tax collection declined, further reducing remittances to Spain. In 1660, colonial authorities estimated that untaxed silver accounted for one-third more production than registered shipments. In the Philippines, merchants made purchases with Mexican silver. Finally, since Mexicans produced more goods for their own use, they sent less silver to Spain to purchase goods there.[29]

It is hardly surprising that Mexican economic growth proceeded at a snail's pace during the seventeenth century, since that was the prevalent condition in the world to which Mexico had been linked by the Conquest. Up to the beginning of the industrial revolution in the eighteenth century, growth was so slow that it might not be noticed within a lifetime. By one estimate, world per capita income only increased from $133 to $164 between AD 1000 and 1700. This imperceptible growth resulted from a very gradual increase in human population and from improvements in technology coming very slowly (by modern standards).[30]

THE EIGHTEENTH CENTURY

> The rise in royal revenues during the eighteenth century was truly spectacular, evidence perhaps of the effectiveness of the Bourbon reforms, a flourishing mining economy, diversification of productive activity, new taxes, and a rise in the population.
>
> John TePaske and Herbert Klein, 1981[31]

King Carlos III (1759–1788) emerged as the foremost proponent of economic reform during the eighteenth century. New economic ideas in vogue in France strongly influenced him. Carlos promoted commerce and production, and protected national industry from foreign competition. He sought to utilize Spanish American wealth and labor more efficiently. Rather than emphasizing mining, as his predecessors had, he promoted agriculture by relaxing the restrictions on slave imports and by facilitating the purchase of agricultural implements and seeds of selected crops. He also promoted better transportation, realizing that such a measure would increase agricultural exports.[32]

In 1777, Viceroy Antonio María de Bucareli commented on relaxed trade restrictions: "Never have the advantages been so visible as in the last few years." Due to the increased supply of labor and lower mercury prices, Mexican silver output increased substantially. Between 1699 and 1809,

Figure 4.1 *Xalpa aqueduct, about 15 km northwest of Tepotzotlán, built in the 1700s*

Source: William E. Doolittle

mine production rose by an average of 1.7 percent a year. In 1790, tax receipts totaled 11,493,748 pesos, 146 percent more than was collected in 1760. The mother country appropriated so much tax revenue that contemporaries spoke of a "river of silver" flowing from Veracruz to Havana and thence to Spain.[33]

During the eighteenth century, silver production increased at an annual rate of 1.8 percent, thus enriching mine owners and their financial backers in the merchant community, expanding employment directly and indirectly, widening the market for food and services, and providing the metallic basis for the local money supply. Long-distance trade increasingly monetized the economy as payment was made in silver. Ironically, even with record silver production, there were never enough silver coins since so many coins were exported.[34]

Economic growth resulted from eliminating restrictions on trade, the discovery of new silver deposits, an increase in agricultural production to supply mines, and increased demand generated by the creation of a standing army and an expanded government workforce. Increases in lumbering, shipbuilding, and mule transport also contributed to eighteenth-century economic expansion.[35]

This economic growth decreased the importance of the Indian community. The share of the colonial budget coming from tribute paid by Indians reflects this decline. In the sixteenth century, tribute provided the main source of Crown income, while by the middle of the eighteenth century it provided less than 5 percent. In the latter part of that century, half of Crown income was derived from taxes on mining and tobacco.[36]

After economic reforms were implemented, the mother country remained the main beneficiary of Spanish economic policy. In 1778, Spanish economist Gaspar de Jovellanos stated, "Colonies are useful in so far as they offer a secure market for the surplus production of the metropolis." To limit possible competition from colonial production, Spain went so far as to destroy cotton mills in its colonies. In 1801, a directive ordered Spanish colonial officials "to effect their destruction by the most convenient means they can devise, even if it means taking them over by the royal treasury on the pretext of making them productive."[37]

MINING

> A mining boom almost always caused a business upturn, but it seldom served as an instrument of structural change and intensive economic growth.
>
> Richard Garner, 1993[38]

From the Spanish point of view, mining provided New Spain's raison d'être. The 1550s take-off of Mexican mining, a result of the discovery of rich lodes such as those in Zacatecas (1546), Guanajuato (1550), Durango (1551), and Sombrerete (1558), more than met Spanish expectations.

Before 1553, silver miners used a charcoal fire fanned by a bellows to heat the ore and extract the silver. However, this process, known as smelting, required relatively rich ore to be profitable. After 1553, the introduction of a new process for refining silver paved the way for the subsequent increase in silver mining. Miners referred to the new process as the "patio process" since finely ground ore, water, mercury, and other reagents were mixed and allowed to react for weeks on the patio of the processing plant. Men or mules dragged poles through large piles of the mixture to stir it. This caused the mercury and silver to amalgamate. Refiners baked the amalgam in a kiln to drive off the mercury, leaving the silver. After the introduction of the amalgamation process, costs could be met if miners recovered only one and a half ounces of silver per hundred kilograms of ore concentrate.[39]

After the 1550s, silver production remained a key element of the colonial economy. In large part, a viceroy's reputation was based on the level of silver output during his administration. Silver never constituted less than 50 percent of Mexico's exports to Spain, and usually exceeded that figure. In the 1670s, New Spain permanently replaced Peru as the leading source of registered silver. By 1800, Mexico was producing almost two-thirds of the world's silver.[40]

For most of the colonial period, mine owners combined free and forced labor. Around 1590, there were 9,143 mine workers, of which 13.8 percent were African slaves, 68.5 percent free Indian workers, and 17.7 percent Indians working to fulfill a *repartimiento* obligation. Miners preferred to rely on forced labor, since that lowered their wage bill. However, later in the colonial period, due to the absence of docile Indian labor near the mines of northern Mexico, mine owners increasingly relied on wage labor. Given their high profit rates, they could afford to pay wages that would attract workers on a voluntary basis.[41]

During the sixteenth century, Spaniards introduced European techniques of deep shaft mining. Mine workers extracted the ore with brute force using hammers, mallets, picks, and crowbars, some of which weighed as much as 45 pounds. Human carriers then brought the rock to the surface in sacks weighing as much as 245 pounds. After the initial wave of European innovation, mining technology stagnated and fell behind European standards. Blasting powder and the animal-powered whim (*malacate*) for lifting ore and water did not become widely used until the eighteenth century.[42]

When Humboldt inspected the mines of Mexico in the early nineteenth century, their technological backwardness compared to German mines led him to write:

> A miner brought up in the mines of Freiberg, and accustomed to see so many ingenious means of conveyance practiced, can hardly conceive that, in the Spanish colonies, where the poverty of minerals is united to a great abundance of them, all the metal which is taken from the vein, should be carried on the backs of men. The Indian *tenateros* [ore carriers] who may be considered as the beasts of burden of the mines of Mexico, remain loaded with a weight of from 225 to 350 pounds for a space of six hours.[43]

His remarks on antiquated technology notwithstanding, the Valenciana mine in Guanajuato impressed Humboldt, who commented, "The piercing of this pit is one of the greatest and boldest undertakings to be found in the history of mines." In the early nineteenth century, the Valenciana mine had 3,332 workers and formed one of the greatest industrial enterprises in the Western world.[44]

Mexican silver undergirded the Crown's finances. Initially, miners paid a fifth of the metal produced, without deducting for expenses, as a tax. In 1548, the Crown reduced this tax to one-tenth. Silver financed the cost of colonial administration and defense, permitted Mexico to import goods, and enabled the Crown to engage in protracted wars. The Crown obtained additional revenue from its monopoly on the sale of the mercury used to refine silver. It not only marked up the price of mercury by 300 percent but used its control of the mercury supply to prevent cheating by silver miners. Those who did not pay taxes on production received no mercury to continue refining.[45]

The demand generated by the mines had an effect felt well beyond the shaft. As nineteenth-century historian Lucas Alamán commented, "The great sums poured into mining firms spread out for many leagues, promoting agriculture and industry by providing consumers for agricultural products and by the use of machinery for drainage and extracting and refining ore." Mines required mules for powering whims and for transport. The mines of Guanajuato alone used 14,000 mules in the amalgamation patios. The livestock and the workers in turn generated a demand for grain. Haciendas producing grain and livestock sprang up in mining districts. The sale of clothes to miners stimulated the textile industry. In 1802, Mexican mines consumed between 1.2 and 1.4 million pounds of domestically manufactured blasting powder. Around 1730, the Zacatecas mines annually consumed 80 tons of candle wax and more than 3,300 pounds of wick. Mine owners paid for all these inputs with silver coins, which then circulated throughout the colony.[46]

The rich silver mines of Zacatecas, located 325 miles northwest of Mexico City, stimulated colonization in the north. Within two years of its founding in 1548, Zacatecas had five churches and fifty operating mines. By the end of the sixteenth century, it vied with Puebla for the honor of being the second city of New Spain. In the early 1600s, it had a population of 1,500 Spaniards and 5,000 Indian and black laborers, and supported thriving shops and markets. Later discoveries of silver at Parral, Durango, and Chihuahua led to colonization still further north. Producers of livestock and cereals followed the miners north.[47]

In 1777, Bourbon reformers created the Mining Tribunal to handle educational, administrative, and judicial matters relating to mining and to distribute mercury and blasting powder. The Tribunal drafted the mining laws in effect until the late nineteenth century. Ironically, since California retained its mining laws after its cession to the United States, the Mexican colonial mining law remained in effect during the 1849 California gold rush.[48]

The mining industry boomed thanks to favorable legislation, such as the 1781 tax exemption on mine tools, and the Crown's lowering the prices of the mercury used in refining and of the gunpowder used for blasting. Mines owned by large corporations, which relied on elaborate credit networks, increasingly replaced owner-operated mines. Mine productivity increased due to new technology and the increased specialization of the labor force. Between 1769 and 1804, silver mintage increased from 11.99 million pesos to 26.13 million.[49]

The impact of mining must be kept in perspective. In 1800, mining contributed only 8.2 percent of the colony's gross domestic product (GDP) and never employed more than 50,000 people. Except for draft animals and livestock products, most of the domestically produced goods used by mines came from the immediate region of the mine. Finally, imports, such as mercury and ironware, which constituted 18 percent of mine purchases, did little to stimulate the economy.[50]

In the early sixteenth century, mines smelted ore, a process that required a constant supply of charcoal made from wood. Even after the patio process largely replaced smelting, miners used wood for beams to shore up tunnels and as a fuel to heat the amalgam. As a result, forests around mining areas were felled, leaving barren hillsides. While the patio process reduced the demand for wood, it created a new problem—mercury pollution. Each year hundreds of tons of mercury were released into the air, water, and soil surrounding the mining areas.[51]

Bishop Alonso de la Mota y Escobar commented on the deforestation that occurred in Zacatecas:

> There were lots of trees and bushes in the ravines when silver was discovered. They have all been felled, so that except for some small palm trees, nothing is left. And firewood is very expensive in town, since it has to be brought from eight or ten leagues away.[52]

Mine production by volume peaked in the 1790s, but profits peaked in the 1770s. Due to the exhaustion of rich ores, progressively more ore had to be mined to produce a pound of silver. Also, as deposits near the surface were exhausted, shafts had to be enlarged and sunk deeper. Often such deep shafts required expensive drainage operations. In the late colonial period, as costs increased, the market value of silver declined. Historian John Coatsworth noted, "Each mark of silver produced bought less and cost more to produce."[53]

AGRICULTURE

The hacienda evolved gradually from the first estates, which were based on grazing permits, not land ownership. These initial grants did not permit the owner of the herd to deny others access. Slowly, the old view of land as a common resource changed, and to guarantee a marketable surplus individuals began to prevent others from using pastures. By the mid-1600s, hacienda boundaries were becoming fixed. Owners invested heavily in buildings, machinery, storage facilities, and irrigation works. The capital for the initial development of the hacienda came from the *encomienda*, public office, mining, and commerce.[54]

In central Mexico, the birth of the hacienda responded to the decline of the Indian population. The food the hacienda supplied the city on a commercial basis replaced what the Indian had supplied on a tributary basis. To the north, haciendas initially supplied mines and then became institutions in their own right, especially when the mines they had supplied ceased operation.[55]

These estates initially relied on workers coming from nearby villages. Later, the hacienda began to appropriate Indian lands, forcing Indians to live and work on the hacienda. In the early colonial period, workers were in shorter supply than land, and *hacendados* were loath to offer attractive wages. Appropriating Indian land cost less than increasing wages. Haciendas further undermined Indian agriculture by monopolizing water supplies to irrigate wheat and sugar cane. As time passed, more and more hacienda workers lived on the hacienda, rather than in independent villages. Hacienda employment, on either a temporary or a permanent basis, served as the chief engine of Indian acculturation.[56]

In the 1630s, a member of the Mexico City municipal council observed that whereas fifty years earlier the city had been supplied by Indians, wealthy Spaniards had replaced them as food suppliers, and Indian cultivation had been reduced to local subsistence. As agriculture shifted from Indian to Spanish control, wheat cultivation replaced that of corn.[57]

Hacendados appropriated Indian grazing land, took land left ownerless when the Indian population declined, and occasionally resorted to brute force to expand their holdings. In other cases, they bought land from individual Indians or rented it from Indian nobles and later laid claim to it. Most hacienda land acquisition occurred before 1750. Although a few *encomienda* families acquired haciendas, generally no direct connection linked the *encomienda* and the hacienda.[58]

Although the great estate remained a fixture on the colonial landscape, individual estates constantly shifted in terms of their size, composition, ownership, and profitability. The pace of land turnover increased in the eighteenth century as swelling mercantile profits found their way into landholding.[59]

The hacienda's diversity allowed its survival. A typical hacienda produced corn, wheat, barley, beans, fruit, livestock, and the agave. This enabled it to be largely self-sufficient and minimized the effect blight, draught, or frost might have on any one crop. Large haciendas also minimized damage from a localized source, such as hail, by working non-contiguous holdings.[60]

Hacendados generally made rational responses to demographic, environmental, and economic change, effectively juggling variables to maximize profits. They would attempt to maximize income from crop sales and minimize cash outlay by operating sawmills and tanneries and producing food, building materials, and other supplies for their workers. Historian John Coatsworth described some of the reasons large estates were profitable:

> Estate agriculture enjoyed advantages not available to Indian villagers, small landowners, or tenant farmers: economies of scale, access to outside credit, information about new technology and distant markets, a measure of protection from predatory officials, and greater security of tenure.[61]

Records from one large hacienda, the Jaral, which employed 598 people, indicate the degree of internal stratification. Salaried resident administrators, a chaplain, a cashier, and storekeepers worked there. The Jaral also employed skilled workers such as bricklayers, weavers, millers, distillers, hatters, and tailors. The permanent labor force consisted of tenant farmers, wage laborers, and debt-peons.[62]

Haciendas, which sometimes had a resident population of as many as 1,000, played a commercial role, operating a commissary store (*tienda de raya*) which served both hacienda workers and other nearby residents. Hacienda residents also formed an alternative community, bound together by informal ties of loyalty and solidarity. The labor force resident on the hacienda sometimes received a guaranteed ration, even in years of bad harvests—a frequent occurrence in Mexico's semi-arid expanses. Residents would worship together in the hacienda chapel. The *hacendado* exercised a mediating role between his domain and the outside world. Within the confines of the hacienda, the colonial state allowed the *hacendado* to dispense justice, ordering corporal punishment or confinement in the hacienda jail.[63]

Taxes and the tithe and mortgage income paid to the Church often left *hacendados* strapped for cash. The increasingly strong position of merchants also drained cash from the hacienda. Merchants profited from selling locally produced goods in urban markets, by importing goods from Spain, and by exporting produce to Spain, leaving relatively little profit for the *hacendado*.[64]

In the early colonial period, the *encomienda* and the *repartimiento* served to exploit Indian labor. Then, after Indians lost most of their land, they came to work on haciendas. However, the Indians continued to work for, and enrich, non-Indians. By the eighteenth century, the *hacendado*-hacienda worker dichotomy had largely replaced the Spanish community-Indian community dichotomy as the major social divide.[65]

Haciendas played an especially important role in northern Mexico since they provided vital supplies to miners and few settled Indian communities existed to dispute the *hacendados*' land claims. Also, given the aridity of the area, estates needed to be larger to generate as much income as their central Mexican counterparts. Rather than being imposed on indigenous communities, as had occurred in central Mexico, northern haciendas started on land lacking a settled population. As a result of aridity and the absence of a sedentary population nearby to plant crops, northern haciendas concentrated on raising livestock.[66]

Compared to central Mexico, in northern Mexico a freer and more modern society evolved around haciendas. This unique character had limited impact during the colonial period. However, by the early twentieth century the north not only remained a center of modernization but became the locus of social revolution, overwhelming all of Mexico and having a profound impact.[67]

In 1810, 4,945 haciendas belonged to fewer than 4,000 families. As Humboldt noted, "The property of New Spain, like that of Old Spain, is in a great measure in the hands of a few powerful families, who have gradually absorbed the smaller estates." The hacienda supplied cities with grain and mines with animals for motive power, hides, leather, and tallow for illumination. By producing virtually everything it needed, the hacienda retarded monetization of the economy, kept markets small, and led to a low level of specialization. In contrast to capitalist societies in which production was overwhelmingly geared to market demand, only part of hacienda production entered the market, while the rest was consumed on the premises. The hacienda's control of the labor supply enabled it to pay less than the market price for labor and permitted the survival of an inefficient, technologically backward agricultural regime.[68]

Throughout the colonial period, Indian agriculture remained vigorous. Most Indians farmed on an individual basis. In addition, some village lands were communally farmed, thus giving the community cohesion and providing income for lay brotherhoods (*cofradías*).

Despite the dominance of the large estate, many smaller mestizo-owned holdings sprang up. These mid-sized holdings, known as *ranchos,* existed along aside the hacienda. By the middle of the sixteenth century, wheat was almost entirely produced on *ranchos* with Indian labor under European guidance. In northern Mexico, *ranchos* specialized in livestock.[69]

The sugar plantation stood in contrast to the hacienda in that it produced only one crop for sale. If the climate and availability of water permitted, landowners produced sugar rather than wheat since the value per acre of the sugar produced was more than four times that of wheat. Producers could sell sugar on the open market as a luxury, while wheat, considered a vital commodity, was subject to price ceilings and requisitions. During the sixteenth century, some sugar was exported to Seville and Peru, although most of it was consumed in Mexico. By the early seventeenth century, fifty or sixty large sugar mills produced between 7.7 and 11 million pounds of sugar a year, while additional sugar was produced by many small mills.[70]

Sugar plantations centered around sugar mills (*ingenios*), which were capital-intensive agro-industrial complexes requiring boilers, presses, and other refining machinery, as well as African slaves. Often seasonal wage laborers, Indians working to pay tribute, and African slaves, many of whom were highly skilled, formed the labor force. While the sugar plantations marketed only one product, they did maintain pastures for draft animals, large herds of cattle and sheep to provide meat and wool for their laborers, corn fields to feed animals and laborers, and woodlands and sawmills for fuel. Growers cleared extensive stands of highland tropical forests to permit cane planting and to provide fuel for heating the caldrons in which the cane sap was boiled. The mill at Tlaltenango, Morelos, consumed between 1,250 and 2,500 tons of wood a year for more than three centuries.[71]

Beginning in the 1540s, cattle spread like waves of a rising tide over the prairies of the north and the warm coastal lowlands. The number of grazing animals soared due to abundant vegetation and the lack of competition from indigenous species. As their numbers grew, cattle altered the vegetation mix, destroying plants they preferred and leaving plants such as cactus and palm. In 1563, a report informed the king that the herds had became so numerous that colonials ate more meat and spent more money on it in one city in the Indies than Spaniards did in ten on the peninsula.[72]

Prior to the Spaniards' arrival, no large herbivores existed, so crops could remain unfenced. Newly arrived cattle inflicted serious damage on the Indians' unprotected crops. In 1550, Viceroy Mendoza, who banned cattle ranches from the valleys around Oaxaca, wrote his successor: "The Spaniards are crying that I have ruined them, and they are right . . . but I could not do otherwise. May Your Lordship realize that if cattle are allowed, the Indians will be destroyed."[73]

Within a quarter of a century, the rapid expansion of the cattle population halted. This was largely due to the number of cattle exceeding the capacity of the grasslands. In addition, the slaughter of cattle increased as more humans, especially Indians, developed a taste for beef. Cattlemen, who had an interest in limiting damage to their forage base, became more effective land managers. Regulated grazing led to mosaics in the landscape that had greater plant diversity than woodlands—the other alternative for land left idle by the declining Indian population.[74]

Imported species had far-reaching effects. Pigs, fattened with corn that Indians paid in tribute, multiplied so quickly that, as historian François Chevalier noted, "The newcomers often had pork to eat while they were still going without bread." Animals replaced human cargo carriers, greatly increasing transport capacity. They also created entirely new industries, as sheep provided wool and cattle provided hides. Some newly introduced plants crowded out native species. However, newly introduced Mediterranean crops were adapted to winter growth and were harvested as the indigenous crops were just beginning to grow, thus providing a year-round food supply.[75]

Miners relied heavily on livestock production. Hides hauled water and ore out of the mine. Beef fed workers, while livestock pulled carts and powered machinery. An *audiencia* judge wrote in 1606, "If the mines have been worked at all, it is thanks to the plentiful and cheap supply of livestock."[76]

Hides became a major export, with 64,350 being shipped in 1587 alone. During the late colonial period, cattle supplied about 30 percent of the viceroyalty's GDP. Large-scale producers with herds of cattle and sheep in excess of 100,000 head dominated production.[77]

Sheep often proved more damaging to the environment than cattle, since they cropped grass closer to the ground and often grazed on erosion-prone slopes. After the late 1570s, the sheep population plummeted, since their number had exceeded the land's carrying capacity. Overgrazing permanently lowered the carrying capacity in some areas. Historian Elinor Melville described the impact overgrazing had on the Mezquital Valley north of Mexico City:

> The region was transformed from a complex and densely populated agricultural mosaic into a sparsely populated mesquite desert; and the indigenous populations were economically marginalized while the land and regional production passed into the hands of large landowners who were socially (if not always ethnically) Spanish.[78]

By the early seventeenth century, ecological equilibrium had been reestablished in Mexico. European plants had become a fixture on the landscape. Grazing animals had passed through boom-and-bust population cycles. The cattle population stabilized between 1570 and 1590, and the sheep population a little later. Indians responded to Spanish-introduced livestock by suing their owners for damages they caused, by killing the animals, and by taking advantage of their presence and using them for meat, wool, leather, and transport.[79]

In the late colonial period, as the prices for livestock and agricultural products rose, large estates appropriated more land to service growing urban markets. A substantial increase in the rural population provided more than enough labor for these estates. Historian Eric Van Young described the result:

> Gross indicators of agricultural prosperity—rising prices, rising tithe collections, increasing stability of ownership of large estates, rising levels of profits and investment in large-scale agriculture—pointed to economic growth, but signs of rural impoverishment and a fall in living standards for the rural masses in many parts of New Spain attested to how that growth was achieved.[80]

Just as had happened in the mining sector, at the end of the colonial period Mexican agricultural technology had fallen behind that of Europe. Low wages and the abundance of land, seven persons per square mile, as compared to 127 per square mile in France, reduced the pressure to introduce new technology. As a result of this technological backwardness, expanding agricultural production required cultivating larger areas.[81]

Despite its technological limits, agriculture remained the major economic sector. In 1800, agriculture accounted for 44.4 percent of the colony's production, compared to 22.3 percent for manufacturing and 8.2 percent for mining. In 1810, 75 percent of the population continued to work in agriculture.[82]

Several obstacles prevented agriculture from expanding further. Land held by the Church and entailed estates was inalienable. Courts were inefficient, and it was impossible to foreclose on land for debts. The widespread access to public and communally held lands made it difficult to attract labor to commercial agricultural enterprises.[83]

MANUFACTURING

Production in colonial Mexico combined indigenous and European practices. A few innovations in the artisan sector, such as the Indians' adoption of the Spanish loom, enabled them to weave wider cloth and to weave more rapidly. Generally, though, handicraft production retained traditional technology—and its low productivity. Early in the colonial period, Indian women produced cotton textiles to pay tribute. Throughout the colonial period, the Indian majority continued to produce most of the textiles it required. As late as 1817, the Veracruz merchant guild lamented, "The Indians spend nothing on cloth save what they make for themselves, and they produce their own raw materials." Artisan weavers consumed much of their production within their own household. However, some home production involved putting-out arrangements. In such cases, credit and raw materials would be supplied to a home weaver by a merchant or cloth producer.[84]

Butchers, bakers, weavers, hatters, pottery-makers, silversmiths, carpenters, tanners, and blacksmiths and producers of such items as saddles, candles, confections, shoes, and silk cloth each had their own guilds. Masters in each guild hired apprentices who would later become masters themselves. Guilds established detailed regulations concerning the type of product, production techniques, prices, and marketing. The bakers guild set the maximum number of bread shops in Mexico City at thirty-six and in Veracruz at fourteen. The needlemakers guild limited each master to only one store and rigorously fixed the price for each type of needle. To enhance their image and eliminate competition, some guilds prohibited the admission of mestizos, Indians, mulattos, or even the descendants of Jewish or Moorish converts. On occasion guild members such as painters engaged in public relations campaigns to puff up their image. Those who violated guild rules could be punished with fines, jail, whipping, destruction of tools and product, or even suspension from the profession.[85]

Mexico City, which had a population of 113,324 in 1790, illustrates the importance of the guild. In 1788, the city's workers belonged to fifty-five guilds with a total membership of 18,624. High-status guilds, such as those for silversmiths, architects, and coach makers, existed alongside more mundane ones, such as those for water drawers and pipe layers. Masons, who numbered 2,015, formed the largest guild.[86]

For most of the colonial period guilds enjoyed a legal monopoly on urban production and marketing. However, in the late colonial period, guild members had to compete with an increasing number of artisans, including women, who produced and marketed their products illegally. At the same time, policy makers, influenced by the Enlightenment, increasingly questioned the guilds' economic efficiency. Others felt the guilds' employment restrictions violated individuals' natural freedom to work in any job they desired. As a result of such doubts, an 1813 decree abolished the legal monopoly enjoyed by guilds, although it did not eliminate the guilds themselves. After that date, individuals could produce items regardless of their guild membership.[87]

Weavers' shops known as *obrajes* produced textiles for the domestic market. *Obraje* production resembled artisan production in that some *obrajes* had as few as three workers and employed technology similar to that of artisans. Their products were, however, more widely marketed than those of artisans. *Obrajes* resembled factories in their division of labor and larger scale of production. By putting several phases of production under one roof, the costs of supervision and transportation were reduced and control over the labor force could be increased.[88]

Obrajes differed from the factories that appeared with the industrial revolution in Europe in that they failed to introduce new technology. The lack of new technology limited profitability, making them unable to pay wages that would attract sufficient voluntary workers. Given their limited ability to hire voluntary workers, owners also employed slaves, convicts, vagrants, orphans, and indentured apprentices. The jail-like conditions of most *obrajes* also made it difficult to attract free laborers.[89]

Humboldt described an *obraje* he visited:

> Free men, Indians, and people of colour, are confounded with the criminals distributed by justice among the manufactories, in order to be compelled to work. All appear half naked, covered with rags, meagre, and deformed. Every workshop resembles a dark prison. The doors which are double remain constantly shut, and the workmen are not permitted to quit the house. Those who are married are only allowed to see their families on sundays. All are unmercifully flogged if they commit the smallest trespass, on the order established in the manufactory.[90]

Because of the poor working conditions, in 1601 King Felipe III forbade all Indian labor, forced or voluntary, in *obrajes*. Rather than improving working conditions, this restriction and others simply provided officials an opportunity to collect bribes for ignoring protective legislation. The same officials also profited from diverting convict and *repartimiento* labor to *obrajes*. As historian Richard Salvucci observed, "Some owners got labor, some officials got rich, and some workers got protection, but in distinctly different proportions."[91]

Even though the *obrajes* lacked the latest European technology, they did enjoy advantages over artisan production. In addition to being able to use political connections to obtain involuntary labor, they had sufficient capital to build up their wool inventory at shearing time, which allowed year-round production. Labor discipline and the division of work among such specialists as carders and washers increased productivity. The workforce at an individual *obraje* usually numbered between fifty and 150, although some *obrajes* employed as many as 700. The buildings housing *obrajes* ranged in size up to 39,000 square feet. Since artisans supplied most textile needs, the number of *obrajes* operating at one time in New Spain never exceeded thirty.[92]

In the sixteenth and seventeenth centuries, production of woolens centered on Puebla due to the availability of wool and water power and due to the market provided by nearby Mexico City and Puebla itself. Since mine labor required warm clothing produced from wool, the Crown sent Spanish artisans and sheep to Mexico and offered financial incentives for textile production. Later most production of woolens moved north to cities such as Querétaro, since *obrajes* there were closer to wool produced on the great sheep ranches of Coahuila and to the market provided by northern mines.[93]

Puebla remained as an important cotton weaving center, stimulating cultivation along the Gulf Coast. As late as 1808, the production of cottons supported some 20,000 people in the province of Puebla. Weaving in Mexico flourished, since prior to the end of the eighteenth century, imported textiles were beyond the reach of all but the most affluent.[94]

At the very end of the colonial period, Mexican cotton textile production declined as English textile imports, a product of the industrial revolution, appeared in Mexico. Mexican textile producers had been reluctant to invest in mechanization due to Mexico's low wage levels and their ability to coerce labor. In the late eighteenth century, a striking 84 percent of goods shipped from Spain to Mexico were textiles.[95]

In 1764, to increase revenue, the Crown established a monopoly on the manufacture and sale of tobacco products. To facilitate control, it limited tobacco cultivation to the region of Orizaba and Córdoba in the modern state of Veracruz. Monopolizing production increased royal income, as well as the income of a few privileged growers. The processed tobacco—cigars and cigarettes—could only be sold in government-licensed shops.

The monopoly reduced the income of those who had formerly grown the plant and those who had produced tobacco products. Before the Crown monopoly, many small growers and artisans had dominated tobacco growing and processing. This group lacked an effective lobby to defend their right to continue producing tobacco.[96]

The efficiency with which cigarettes and cigars were produced demonstrated Bourbon organizational ability. Factories were located in Guadalajara, Puebla, Oaxaca, Orizaba, Querétaro, and Mexico City. The largest, in Mexico City, employed almost 9,000 workers at its peak, an extraordinary size for a factory anywhere in the eighteenth century. By the 1790s, the tobacco monopoly employed almost 20,000, making it one of the largest organized industries in the colony, along with silver mining and textile production.[97]

Throughout the eighteenth century, the tobacco monopoly remained very lucrative. At its peak, it accounted for almost a fifth of government revenue, a figure surpassed only by silver mining.[98]

Management at the tobacco factories attempted to instill modern industrial labor values in workers, such as on-time arrival, not stealing materials, and abstaining from drunken or other "scandalous" behavior. It punished infractions of the rules by a stint in the factory stocks, suspension from the job, or permanent prohibition from employment.[99]

Women were encouraged to work in the tobacco factories, since one of the goals of the monopoly was providing desirable employment for poor urban women. Managers often preferred them as employees, since they felt men should be working in mines and fields. Women readily accepted such employment since many had worked in the tobacco industry before monopolization and because work there paid substantially more than the most common female occupation of the time—domestic service.[100]

In order to stimulate Spanish industry, Mexican producers were forced to rely on cigarette paper supplied by Spanish factories. As Spain's frequent wars interrupted the supply of paper, production declined or even halted, leaving workers jobless and the state without revenues. Despite the inescapable logic of building a paper mill in Mexico, this was never done, because it would compete with producers in Spain.[101]

Negotiation and compromise served as the basis of labor-management relations in the tobacco factories. This resulted from: 1) there being few alternatives for semi-skilled and unskilled male workers and fewer still for women; 2) the provision of an in-house dispute resolution mechanism; 3) management's desire for labor stability; and 4) the division of the labor force along the lines of gender, status, and ethnicity. Management also benefited from a general approval of the colonial regime. This became evident after management prohibited taking rolling papers home to meet their quota. Managers soon reversed the decision, leading workers to indicate their loyalty to the regime by sending the following message to the king: "... only with silence can we thank you. There is no other language more meaningful for a prince as perfect as your excellency."[102]

The elevated price of tobacco to the consumer reflected monopoly profit. This and the illegality of growing tobacco anywhere except in a small area inevitably led to widespread illegal dealing in contraband tobacco. Officials in some cases even justified illegal production by Indians on the grounds that it enabled them to earn money to fulfill tribute obligations.

Further north, away from the tobacco factories, authorities and citizens alike simply ignored the monopoly. Residents of New Mexico, Coahuila, and Texas cultivated tobacco extensively and bartered with it in the frontier economy.[103]

TRADE AND TRANSPORT

> Trade is the lifeblood of this kingdom, and from it flows the prosperity of the realm.
>
> Viceroy Cerralvo, 1634[104]

Colonial Mexico engaged in extensive trade with the mother country and emerged as the center of a large trading region including the Caribbean and extending south to Peru and west to the Philippines. The Crown structured Mexico's foreign trade to benefit Spain, disregarding and sometimes directly opposing the needs of the colony. The then-dominant mercantilist economic doctrine served to formulate trade policy. Mercantilism, in vogue from the fifteenth to the eighteenth centuries, held that national well-being required a continuous inflow of precious metals, or goods that could be exchanged for them. The mercantilist emphasis on trade surpluses led to severe restrictions on trade between the colonies and the rest of the world.[105]

Mercantilist thought influenced shipping regulations. For most of the colonial period, the Crown allowed only one port in Spain to trade with the colonies and required that trade to be carried in Spanish-built ships. Generally, Spanish colonies could not trade directly with each other or with other nations and their colonies. Shipping regulations limited the amount of goods sent to the New World and led to the shipment of luxury goods to maximize profits from the limited space available. Mercantilist regulations and the merchants' monopoly made commerce enormously profitable and solidified the merchants' dominant position in New Spain.[106]

During the sixteenth century, Spain supplied Mexico with food. As Creoles began to produce their own wheat and adapted to the indigenous cuisine, clothes, weapons, hardware, and tools replaced food imports. Clothing constituted roughly half of all imports. Other imported items included iron, steel, paper, honey, oils, cloth, liquors, medicines, olive oil, linen, brandy, beeswax (for candles), and spices such as cinnamon and pepper.[107]

Silver dominated Mexican exports to Spain. For 300 years, cochineal dye was the second most important Mexican export. This dye, extracted from an insect that feeds on the prickly-pear cactus, produced a brilliant red in fine fabrics used by popes, princes, nobles, and military officers. Ships returning to Spain also carried condiments, spices, sugar, leather, extracts, and purgatives.[108]

For most of the colonial period, the Crown required vessels carrying goods between Spain and Mexico to sail in convoys. Initially the convoys served as a defense against pirates and later they became a means of regulating trade and ensuring that New World silver arrived in Spain. A single convoy of from sixty to a hundred vessels would leave Spain each year. En route, it would divide, with ships sailing for various Spanish American ports. Between 1757 and 1776, ships arriving in Veracruz carried an annual average of 2,487 tons of merchandise.[109]

Roughly 1,000 muleteers would meet the convoy. They then hauled the merchandise to a giant trade fair, often in Jalapa, fifty miles northwest of Veracruz and 4,700 feet above it, safely removed from tropical disease. Merchants from Mexico City bought the goods in large lots and stored them in Mexico City warehouses. They then sold their purchases through their own outlets or to other retailers and street vendors.[110]

In order to increase the tax base and undercut smugglers, the Bourbons eliminated the requirement that ships sail in convoys. Between 1765 and 1776, the centuries-old prohibition on trade between Spanish colonies was also abolished, ushering in what was referred to as "free trade." Between 1784 and 1795, five times as many ships arrived in Veracruz as had arrived before the elimination of these restrictions. This resulted in an unprecedented influx of European goods, which soon saturated markets and caused a rash of merchant bankruptcies.[111]

Despite these reforms, heavy taxes remained on goods shipped from elsewhere in Europe to Spain and then from Spain to Mexico. This caused these items to be non-competitive with similar items shipped illegally. The price of a cask of brandy shipped from Barcelona to Veracruz rose in price 183 percent due to duties and taxes. Spaniards, who were the only merchants who could legally ship to the New World, would declare goods to be Spanish when they had in fact been produced elsewhere. This allowed such goods to avoid the 33 percent limit placed on the shipment of foreign goods to the colonies. Foreign traders often not only supplied the goods shipped but the financing, leaving the Spanish "merchants" as only front men. Ship captains failed to list foreign goods when presenting cargo manifests and then colluded with customs guards who boarded their ships on their arrival in Veracruz.

Heavy taxes and limited local production not surprisingly led to widespread smuggling. This smuggling provided colonials with inexpensive goods and colonial officials with bribes, but made local production less attractive and deprived the Crown of revenue. Estimates of contraband in the Atlantic trade ranged from 10 to 100 percent of registered cargo in the years between 1670 and 1700. Smugglers were well organized and savvy. They often appeared just before the arrival of the convoy from Spain, so they could take advantage of pre-convoy scarcity and increased prices.[112]

Humboldt commented on the smugglers' efficiency:

> A few days and frequently even a few hours are sufficient for the crews of fishing vessels to form connections with the inhabitants, for the sale of English goods, and to take in ladings of copper, Peruvian sheep, quinine, sugar and cacao. This contraband trade is carried on between persons who do not speak the same language, frequently by signs, with a fidelity very uncommon to the most polished people of Europe.[113]

Foreigners engaged in smuggling by illegally bringing goods to New Spain. Often goods arrived tax-free by being shipped directly from English ports to Jamaica and then being routed clandestinely to New Spain. Silver smuggled to Jamaica to pay for these goods avoided the legally mandated taxes and duties of 10.5 percent. In other cases, Spanish American merchants illegally shipped goods up and down the Pacific Coast of the Americas. Colonial subjects rationalized such illegality, noting it was better to provide local markets with needed goods at just prices than it was to pay taxes to a corrupt empire.[114]

Imperial reform, the general growth of Atlantic trade, and colonial prosperity created a shipping boom that lasted until 1795. New Spain's trade with the mother country increased in value from 13.3 million pesos in 1787 to 20.6 million in 1795. At the end of the century, the commercial sector comprised 16.7 percent of Mexico's GDP—more than that of mining. After 1795, Spain's European wars caused a decline in trade between Mexico and Spain.[115]

The Bourbon reforms undermined the old commercial elite. Mexico City merchants had grown comfortable with rules limiting their number, with restricted supply, and with high prices and high profits. When faced with real competition and provincial merchants being allowed to legally purchase goods in Veracruz for the first time, they petitioned the Crown to reestablish the convoy system and the requirement that goods be shipped through Mexico City. Viceroy Revillagigedo responded that eliminating convoys had produced a notable increase in trade and prosperity. He also noted that some individuals had suffered due to ignorance, poor financial administration, and poor mining investments, but that free trade should not be abandoned because of such individual misfortune. Many established merchants moved their capital into agriculture and mining rather than facing real competition, and were replaced by an increased number of more competitive merchants.[116]

Finally, it was a misnomer to describe the replacement for the convoy system as "free trade." Strict volume limits kept the fabulous potential of trade with Asia in check. Spanish merchants feared they would lose control of trade with Spanish America entirely and successfully lobbied against unlimited trade with Asia. Even more importantly, the prohibition remained on trading outside the Spanish empire, despite the North Atlantic's emergence as the hub of world commerce. These prohibitions were an obstacle to trade with the rest of the world and therefore seriously constrained Mexico's growth.[117]

Free trade reversed the seventeenth-century trend of entrepreneurs producing for the internal market. Instead a trans-Atlantic focus reemerged, retarding continued internal development. Increased taxation resulting from the Bourbon reforms also slowed internal development. Tax collection decreased coinage in circulation, thus complicating business transactions.[118]

During the early colonial period, given the extreme scarcity of mules and horses, Indian bearers (*tlamemes*), as in pre-Conquest times, hauled freight. Carlos V felt such a practice to be inhuman and banned it, even if the Indians worked on a voluntary basis. However, Indians continued to haul freight since no replacement for them existed. The Crown later accepted this and tried to prevent abuses. Finally, in the seventeenth century, an increased supply of mules and burros allowed the replacement of human carriers.[119]

After 1550, carts were introduced, although since they required good roads and bridges, they did not replace mules. In the north, flat land and the small number of rivers permitted the extensive use of carts. Bad roads elsewhere limited their use. A contemporary observer commented on the highway between Mexico City and Veracruz, the most important road in the colony: "It is a disgrace to the Spanish nation, that at the end of two centuries and half, this road continues to be as neglected as at the time of the Conquest, full of dangers, embarrassments, and a thousand inconveniences." The deplorable condition of the roads resulted from the great differences in altitude and torrential rains falling on areas that the roads crossed and from the Crown's failure to understand the vital role roads played in economic development.[120]

Since carts could not traverse the roads, mules carried freight from the ports of Acapulco and Veracruz to Mexico City. At the close of the eighteenth century, 75,000 mules plied the Acapulco–Mexico City route and 70,000 hauled cargo between Veracruz and Mexico City. These beasts of burden competed with humans for available corn. Some haciendas specialized in breeding mules and growing fodder for them.[121]

Mule teams became a feature of the Mexican landscape. Indians and *castas* found that becoming a muleteer was one of the few routes open for an Indian commoner to accumulate wealth. Each mule carried roughly 350 pounds. Having to follow routes that provided water and pasture slowed mule trains. The trip by mule train from Veracruz to Mexico City required sixteen to twenty days.[122]

This reliance on expensive mule transport prevented the formation of an integrated market system, added to the cost of Mexican exports, and greatly increased the prices of goods sold in

Mexico. Transporting imported wine from Veracruz to Mexico City added 70 percent to its price. A third to a half of the cost of grain used in the mines of Zacatecas resulted from transport charges. Transport costs precluded the shipment of low-cost agricultural products much beyond a hundred miles. Only luxury products and high-value goods could be sold colony-wide. In addition to silver, goods transported for sale over long distances included leather and suede produced in Jalisco and woolens from Guanajuato. Further to the north, the main trade items were leather, livestock, and silver.[123]

Only in the eighteenth century, with technical improvements in shipbuilding, did shipping around the southern tip of South America became commonplace. As a result, for 250 years before that, from 1565 to 1815, it was Mexico that linked Spain with the Philippines, then a Spanish colony. Goods and personnel would cross the Atlantic to Veracruz, travel by land to Acapulco, and continue to the Philippines. In addition to its transshipment of cargo to and from Spain, Mexico supplied goods to the Philippines and consumed goods shipped from there. To prevent an excessive loss of silver to the Orient and unwelcome competition with Spanish products, the Crown taxed these shipments heavily, limited the amount that could be carried, and only permitted one or two galleons to sail from Mexico to the Philippines each year. Colonists unsuccessfully lobbied for the removal of restrictions on trade with the Philippines (and Peru). As with Atlantic shipping, the Crown could not prevent colonists from engaging in widespread smuggling.[124]

Each year the ship or ships known as the Manila Galleons would leave Acapulco carrying church and government personnel, along with mail, silver, Spanish wine, Saltillo wool, cochineal, and cocoa. Upon arriving in Manila, these products would be exchanged for goods, most of which were brought to Manila from around Asia on Chinese junks. The Galleons, built in the Philippines from local teak, returned to Mexico laden with silk, brocades, linen, porcelain, furniture, cottons, velvets, satins, damasks and taffetas, jewelry, ivory, furniture, pearls, gold- and silverwork, and spices from the East Indies. When the Galleons returned, the population of Acapulco would swell from 4,000 to 9,000 as merchants flocked in to snap up the imports.[125]

The Spanish colonization of the New World accelerated globalization. Asian-African maritime trade had persisted for centuries before Europeans rounded the Cape of Good Hope. Then, in 1498, Portuguese sailor Vasco de Gama reached India, and his countrymen began trading with Africa, India, and China. Beginning in the sixteenth century, silver, largely obtained in Peru and New Spain, linked Portuguese and Spanish commerce. The Portuguese paid for textiles in India with silver and then traded the textiles for African slaves who were brought to the New World. Later in the sixteenth century, ships sailing between Acapulco and Manila added a trans-Pacific component to globalization. New World silver also facilitated the expansion of intercontinental trade in which the main participants were England, France, and the Netherlands.

The Spanish silver peso, which circulated in the Americas, Europe, and Asia, became the first truly international currency. In its role as both commodity and currency, the peso facilitated the rapid expansion of world trade. Given its ubiquitous nature, the Congress of the newly independent United States adopted the Spanish peso, under the name "dollar" (which comes from the German *Thaler*), as its unit of currency.[126]

THE COLONIAL MODEL

> Spain never developed a coherent economic policy; the imperial bureaucracy acted simply as a conduit of wealth into Italian, South German, and Dutch coffers.
>
> Eric Wolf, 1982[127]

Mexican silver underwrote Spain's cost of governance and war, formed the base of the currency, and paid for such Asian imports as spices, jewels, silks, and pepper. While mining stimulated the region adjacent to the mine, it did not stimulate the economy as a whole. Mexican mining technology changed little after the sixteenth century, so mines created less demand for iron goods, such as boilers, than mines in Europe did. Referring to eighteenth-century silver miner José de la Borda, Salvucci commented, "Perhaps God gave to the miner Borda, and Borda gave back to God, but neither divine providence nor beautiful churches provide a basis for economic development."[128]

During the last decades before independence, Mexico generated wealth on a scale unmatched elsewhere else in Spanish America. Its diversified economy in large part served the needs of the Mexican elite, despite the Crown's attempts to shape it to meet the needs of the mother country. Between 1796 and 1820, exports only averaged 4.3 percent of the GDP.[129]

Much eighteenth-century economic growth resulted from a doubling in population from 3.3 million in 1742 to 6.1 million in 1810. However, unlike growth in Europe at the time, Mexico did not acquire new technology. Rather, Mexico added more land and labor to increase production. With much of the domestic wealth falling into the hands of a small number of wealthy miners, merchants, and *hacendados*, little remained to trickle down. As historian Richard Garner noted, "Growth in output from mining, agriculture, and manufacturing had not visibly enhanced the material lot of the ordinary citizen."[130]

The Bourbons administered more efficiently than the Habsburgs. They also appropriated more of Mexico's wealth to subsidize Spain, the Philippines, and Spanish colonies in the Caribbean. They remained convinced that state intervention was needed to spur economic growth and to keep the state financially solvent. In some cases, such as supplying mercury, salt, and tobacco, the state controlled economic activity directly. In most cases, though, the state influenced the economy through taxes and detailed regulations. Policymakers felt market regulation would eliminate sharp price fluctuations, shortages, and the consequent social tension. Rather than taxing wealth or income, taxes fell heavily on the movement of goods. These taxes, such as a tax on sales and barter, on the movement of goods from one tax district to another, and on exports and imports, retarded the creation of large markets.[131]

In an exchange remarkably similar to those occurring two centuries later, miner José de la Borda argued in 1765 that a decrease in mining taxes would stimulate investment and increase the treasury's income. Viceroy Bucareli rejected this advice, declaring that the increase in mining that had followed a pervious decline in the price of mercury resulted, not from the price decrease, but from new ore discoveries.[132]

The society created under Spanish tutelage retarded industry. Concentrated income and high commercial profits led to an emphasis on the import of luxury goods. With the exception of tobacco and mine workers, few wage earners could afford mass-produced goods.[133]

The Crown's policy of protecting Spanish industry retarded Mexican industrialization. Authorities tolerated some Mexican industrialization, such as the production of ordinary fabrics and textiles. Generally, however, they prohibited investment that competed with Spanish manufactured imports. Some of these restrictions led to economic absurdities. Until the 1794 economic reform, sugar brandy could not be produced in Spanish America. Molasses would be shipped to Spain for distillation into spirits, and the product would then be shipped back to Mexico for sale. This reflected the Crown's desire to have the colonies supply Spain with raw materials so that Spanish labor could convert them into finished goods and return them to the colonies.[134]

The Crown made independence appear less attractive by impeding the industrialization of its colonies, thus prolonging their dependence on the mother country for industrial goods. In 1790, perhaps in response to the successful revolt of Britain's North American colonies, the Viceroy of Nueva Granada (today Venezuela and Colombia), Francisco Gil de Taboada, stated:

> It's clear that the security of America can be measured by the degree of dependence on the mother country, a dependency which is based on the distribution of merchandise. When the day comes that the colonies have all they need, their dependency will be voluntary, and neither the armed forces we have there, nor government generosity, nor a better system of justice will be sufficient to assure our possession.[135]

Each guild regulated in detail the type of raw materials used, the shape and form of articles produced, and the tools used. While these measures served their stated purpose of protecting consumers from inferior products, they impeded improved design and the introduction of new production technology. Guild regulations, which excluded certain racial groups, such as Indians, prevented efficient utilization of labor.[136]

The shortage of coins provided a further impediment to developing the colonial economy. (Paper money did not exist during the colonial period.) Not only was silver hoarded but there was a massive outflow—partly to pay for imports but also because taxes and profits from government monopolies were remitted to Spain and other Spanish colonies and because wealthy Spaniards retired back to the mother country with their personal fortunes. Given the scarcity of coins, in the late colonial period an estimated two-thirds of commercial transactions involved letters of credit.[137]

The coin shortage also affected the retail trade. Colonials often purchased items as insignificant as bread and clothing on credit. As late as 1800, cacao beans still served as currency. Merchants and *hacendados* would also issue their own local currency made of wood, copper, or even soap. As the distance from its issuer increased, the value of this currency declined. This served as yet another barrier to increasing the size of the market.[138]

The wealthy frittered away much of the economic surplus they accumulated, rather than reinvesting it. Historian José Durand commented that among the descendants of the conquistadores, "From a very early date, riches financed such manifestations of Renaissance exquisiteness as Plateresque architecture, clothing, jewels, paintings, and the lifestyle of a courtesan." Some *hacendados* invested in ostentatious homes, titles of nobility, dowries for daughters to enter convents, and lavish social gatherings. The Church, while it did facilitate credit, also diverted much of its wealth into temples and convents adorned with paintings, altars, and images, many of which were made with precious metals and jewels that had once belonged to women of aristocratic lineage.[139]

Between 1792 and 1820, the Bourbons transferred roughly 7.2 percent of colonial income to the mother country—a tax burden that by today's standards is remarkably light. Institutional problems resulting from Spanish colonization provided a greater obstacle to development than did taxation. These obstacles included inefficient judicial institutions and pre-modern land tenure. The existence of privileged corporate bodies, such as the military and the Church, whose members operated with their own rules and sat in judgment of one another, raised the costs and risks of enterprise for the rest of the population. The Crown failed to develop a financial infrastructure capable of supporting productive long-term investment. The system of racial classification forced mestizos and Indians into a straightjacket of approved activities.[140]

Ironically, despite having the largest empire in the world, Spain failed to benefit significantly from its colonies. The 1492 expulsion of the Jews deprived Spain of much of its financial expertise, just when the inflow of New World wealth increased the need for such knowledge. Given the anti-entrepreneurial values among Spain's Castilian elite, the expulsion of Jews created a catastrophic financial vacuum. Before 1492, foreign bankers had played virtually no role in Spain. The expulsion of Spain's Jews destroyed the primary source of credit, leaving Spain completely dependent on Dutch, German, French, and especially Genoese bankers.[141]

France, England, and the Netherlands, lacking mines, focused on obtaining gold and silver by manufacturing for export. Many of the taxes and guild regulations that plagued Mexican industry of the time also stifled Spanish industry. The massive inflow of precious metals to Spain led to 400 percent inflation between 1500 and 1600, pricing Spanish goods out of the market. In 1521, Spanish clergy, monarchy, and aristocrats cut off the growth of the class that developed industry elsewhere in Europe when they defeated the *comunero* rebels at the Battle of Villalar. This shaped Spanish values and, as a result, until 1772 engaging in manufacturing could cause one to lose noble status. Because of these factors, by 1600 the core of the world economy had shifted to Holland, England, and France.[142]

Spain fell further behind northern Europe in the seventeenth century, in large part due to enormous military expenditure. In the early 1600s, King Felipe IV had 300,000 men under arms. The seemingly endless wars left Spain with little to invest productively. These conflicts resulted from: 1) the Habsburg monarchy inheriting possessions in territory now forming parts of Italy, Holland, Belgium, France, and Germany, and waging costly, futile battles to retain them; 2) the Crown perceiving its duty as combating Protestantism in Northern Europe and Moslems in the Mediterranean area; and 3) the Crown protecting its New World claims and its shipping from the French, Dutch, and English. In retrospect, imperial Spain never recovered from its wasting seventeenth-century conflicts.[143]

Spain acted as a conduit for commerce between its colonies and the rest of Europe. Increasingly Spain bought inexpensive manufactured goods from North Atlantic nations and then shipped them to the colonies. By the end of the seventeenth century, only 5 percent of the merchandise shipped from Spain to its American colonies came from Spain. France supplied 25 percent, Genoa 22 percent, Holland 20 percent, Flanders 10 percent, Great Britain (a latecomer to trans-Atlantic trade) 10 percent, and Germany 8 percent. During the last third of the eighteenth century, the percentage of exports to the New World produced by Spain increased. However, such an increase could not reverse the ascendancy of northern Europe.[144]

By the end of the colonial period, profit-oriented Mexican entrepreneurs, who were increasingly relying on wage labor, owned and directed the major means of production. This was especially true along a spinal column of commercial capitalism that extended west from Veracruz through Jalapa and Mexico City and then north to the mining districts of Zacatecas and Durango.[145]

Elsewhere in the colony, various factors prevented the formation of vigorous markets. At the end of the colonial period, most work was not performed by free wage labor. High transport costs, the Church tithe, and internal customs (*alcabala*) also hampered the development of large markets. Mexico's increasingly being milked by a greedy and belligerent metropolis further stymied the development of markets.[146]

The colonial period saw the depletion of many of Mexico's natural endowments. Precious metals, mined and lost forever to Mexico, facilitated European development. Similarly, Mexico's forest stock declined during the colonial period. Forests covered roughly three-quarters of New Spain at the time of the Conquest. By the end of the colonial period, as a result of using wood for fuel, construction, shipbuilding, and mining, forest cover had declined by one-third. This loss occurred despite efforts to protect Mexican forests. For example, in 1765, King Carlos III decreed that licenses would be required to cut wood on private as well as on common land and that for each tree cut three more had to be planted.[147]

Chapter 5

The Far North, 1598–1810

THE NORTHERN BORDERLANDS

> The northern frontier of New Spain—this new desert into which they ventured—was much more varied than its counterpart in Andalucia and Castile. It had a wider range of altitudes, soils, animal life, drought-resistant vegetation, and even more capricious cycles of annual rainfall. The mountains were more rugged and towering, and the barrancas or canyons more impenetrable.
>
> Michael Meyer, 1984[1]

The term "borderlands" refers to the area that formed the northern border of the Spain's American empire. Some use the term to describe Spanish claims stretching along the Gulf of Mexico from Florida to Texas and to the states on both sides of the present U.S.–Mexican border. Others restrict the term to the states presently on each side of the U.S.–Mexican border. The area included in this latter definition was administered from Mexico City, explored and settled from Mexico, and traded almost exclusively with Mexico. Even if one restricts the definition of borderlands to the present border states—six in Mexico and four in the United States—the borderlands cover more than 960,000 square miles, an area considerably larger than western Europe.[2]

Water scarcity limited the possible sites for missions, *presidios*, towns, and farms. It also placed constraints on travel. For example, the 1775 colonizing expedition that marched overland from Sonora to California had to be divided into three groups so waterholes could refill after the passage of each group. The available water could not support large concentrations of humans and animals. Closely related to water scarcity was low population density. In 1810, Coahuila had six inhabitants per square league, less than 1 percent of the population density of Guanajuato.[3]

Sheep, cattle, and horses introduced into this arid region trampled grass, or ate it, and made trails. This led to erosion, quicker run-off, and gullying. The gullies carried rainwater away rapidly, rather than letting it soak into the soil. This, in turn, lowered water tables and led to desertification.[4]

Conflict in the borderlands often revolved around water, not land. As the number of cattle increased, conflict intensified. An eighteenth-century census of the lower Rio Grande valley found that the human population numbered 2,273, compared to a cattle population of 209,000. Conflict occurred not only between species and between ethnic groups, but within them. Spanish clergymen and soldiers each proclaimed their water rights to be supreme. As historian Michael Meyer commented, "Each group rationalized that its own presence was needed to assure the happiness and tranquillity of the surrounding Indian population, but the documentation suggests forcefully that in most cases Indian water interests were served by neither."[5]

Borderland settlement occurred after Spain had lost the vigor that had characterized it during the early Conquest period. This led to a chronic shortage of military support and financial subsidy in the distant borderlands. Due to its isolation, neither Mexico City nor Madrid could exercise control over everyday affairs in the north. If an official in Santa Fe wrote his superior in Mexico

City asking for direction, and if the superior answered promptly, the reply would arrive six months later. The same official would usually have to wait a year or longer for a response from Madrid.[6]

The Spanish borderland population consisted of missionaries, soldiers, and settlers. When their tour of duty ended, many of the soldiers remained and joined the ranks of the settlers, who soon outnumbered both soldiers and missionaries. Unlike his countrymen in central Mexico, a Spaniard in the north could not live from wealth accumulated by Indians. Nor did the scant indigenous population provide a plentiful source of labor as in central Mexico. As a result, as historian Oakah Jones, Jr. commented, "The large majority of the people of the Spanish frontier in the colonial period consisted of real settlers, established in formal communities, and absolutely dependent on tilling the soil and raising livestock for their livelihood."[7]

On the frontier, as a result of lax record keeping, mestizos, mulattos, and Hispanized Indians found it rather easy to transcend official racial categories. Indians and mulattos declared themselves to be mestizos, and mestizos to be Spaniards. A priest in Santa Barbara, California, commented on its residents, "Although it is well known that not all are genuine Spaniards, if they were told to the contrary they would consider it an affront." In Texas, perhaps to avoid giving offense, census takers simply listed all military personnel as "Spaniards," regardless of their racial origins. "Spanish" became such an elastic term that Texas census reports mention "a Spaniard from Canada," "a Spaniard from France," and "a Spaniard from Corsica." In contrast to central Mexico, continual warfare against Indians gave those with "impurities of blood" the opportunity to distinguish themselves and acquire prestige and status.[8]

Mixed-bloods from other parts of Mexico, not Spaniards, comprised the majority of the arrivals to the borderlands. Only a third of the men and a fourth of the women who founded San Jose and San Francisco identified themselves as "Spanish." Only two of the initial forty-six residents of Los Angeles did so.[9]

STRATEGIC IMPERATIVES

Individuals' desire for wealth and the opportunity to convert Indians to Christianity led to the settlement of Central Mexico. The settlement of the northern borderlands, in contrast, responded

Figure 5.1 *Native pictograph of Spaniards on horseback on the walls of Cañon del Muerto, Arizona*

Source: Arizona State Museum, University of Arizona, neg. #28883

to perceived French, English, and Russian threats to Spanish control. Only after the Crown ordered settlement to begin did individuals sign on in hopes of acquiring wealth. Given their strategic origins, the borderland settlements had a strong military component.

Rather than supplying the Crown with revenue, as central Mexico did, borderland settlements relentlessly drained royal coffers. Since most indigenous residents of the borderlands lived near the subsistence level, efforts to exact surplus from them cost more than they yielded.[10]

New Mexico

The appearance of Sir Francis Drake, who landed on the California coast in 1579, galvanized the Crown into settling New Mexico to prevent England from encroaching on it. The Spanish thought Drake had found a passage through North America, connecting the Atlantic and the Pacific and that New Mexico would be close enough to this passage to control it.[11]

The Crown appointed Juan de Oñate to carry out its preemptive colonization of New Mexico. Oñate had inherited wealth from his father, Cristóbal de Oñate, who had discovered the fabled silver lodes of Zacatecas, and this made him ideal for the task. He hoped to find mineral wealth on a par with Zacatecas. The Franciscans promoted the expedition, since they sought to convert the sedentary Indians living in New Mexico.[12]

In exchange for his financing the expedition, the Crown promised Oñate the governorship of New Mexico, tax exemptions, and *encomiendas* that would last for three generations. Notions of geography were so vague that Oñate's instructions directed him to survey New Mexico's coastline and harbors. Many Spaniards still clung to the notion that somewhere not far to the north there lay a water route connecting the Atlantic and the Pacific.[13]

Oñate's colonizing expedition left Chihuahua in 1598, with some 500 people, including eight Franciscan priests, two Franciscan lay brothers, and 129 soldiers, as well as wives, children, personal servants, herders, and drivers of various ethnic backgrounds. The expedition consisted of eighty-three supply wagons and a thousand head of stock—sheep, cattle, oxen, horses, and mules—some for work and some for nourishment.[14]

Once Oñate had established a colony, it became apparent there was disappointingly little wealth the Spanish could appropriate. However, the Spanish did not abandon New Mexico, since that would have removed the strategic barrier that prevented other European powers from making incursions directed at the rich mines of northern Mexico. Nor did the Spanish want to abandon Indians that they had Christianized to reprisals by heathens.[15]

Texas

> Geographically isolated and economically marginal, the province's sole reason for existence was as a buffer against encroachments, whether from European rivals or hostile Indians, into the more valuable interior of the viceroyalty.
>
> Jesús F. de la Teja, 1995[16]

For nearly a century and a half after shipwrecked Spaniard Alvar Núñez Cabeza de Vaca traversed it in the 1530s, Texas remained without permanent European settlement. That only changed with the arrival of one of the foremost explorers of French North America, René Robert Cavelier, Sieur de La Salle. In 1682, La Salle followed the Mississippi from Canada to the Gulf of Mexico. At the mouth of the Mississippi, he claimed for France the same land Spanish conquistador Hernando de Soto had claimed for Spain 140 years earlier and named the area Louisiana, in honor of King Louis XIV of France. La Salle's expedition resulted from the French observation that the British, moving from the east, and the Spanish, moving from the south, would soon eliminate the possibility of further French expansion into the Mississippi Valley.[17]

Louis XIV later appointed La Salle as commander of Louisiana and instructed him to establish a settlement on the Gulf of Mexico. In 1684, La Salle sailed from France with 300 men, women, and children in four ships, *Le Joly, L'Aimable, La Belle*, and *St. François*.

La Salle's colonists established a primitive settlement named Fort St. Louis, five miles up Garcitas Creek, which flows into an extension of Matagorda Bay northeast of Corpus Christi. Hard labor, privation, and sickness soon reduced the population of Fort St. Louis by one sixth. In January 1687, La Salle and seventeen of his men began walking to the Mississippi to seek assistance from other Frenchmen. Shortly after their departure, La Salle's nephew berated some of the men in the group walking east. This criticism exacerbated old animosities among the frustrated Frenchmen accompanying La Salle. In response, they killed both the nephew and La Salle somewhere between the Brazos and Trinity Rivers. A few members of the group trudged on to French Canada to report the fate of the colony.[18]

Once the Spanish learned that La Salle had established a settlement in territory claimed by Spain, officials ordered that the settlement be located and destroyed. Five land and six sea expeditions set out in fulfillment of this order. On March 23, 1689, one these expeditions, led by Alonso de León, governor of Coahuila, left Monclova. De León's expedition included eighty-five soldiers, twelve mule drivers, thirteen servants, an unspecified number of Indians, and more than 700 horses, 200 head of cattle, and pack mules.[19]

The Spanish found that after the remaining members of La Salle's colony had been ravaged by disease, Karankawa Indians had killed the few adult survivors and appropriated their clothes, which they were wearing when the Spanish arrived.[20]

To check further French expansion, in 1690 De León and Fray Damián Massanet, a Franciscan from the Apostolic College of Querétaro, established the Missions of San Francisco de los Tejas and Santísimo Nombre de María. They located these missions, the first in Texas, among the Caddoan-speaking Indians in present-day Houston County in east Texas. In 1693, since no further French intrusions into the area had occurred, the Spanish abandoned these missions.[21]

At the beginning of the eighteenth century, Texas was again devoid of European settlement. Even though Texas had been only temporarily occupied, the land and sea expeditions launched in response to La Salle vastly increased Spanish knowledge of the area. The Tejas people they encountered near the Neches River made a strong impression on expedition members. These Indians raised corn, beans, squash, and watermelon, and weeded their fields with wooden hoes. They sat on wooden benches and slept on raised canopy beds. The word that would become the name of the Lone Star State came from these Indians. The Spanish heard their word of greeting as "tejas," which meant roughly "friend" or "our own people." They soon used that term to refer to the region, and, Anglicized, it now refers to Texas.[22]

Despite the failure of La Salle's colony, the French continued to strengthen their presence in central North America. In 1700, they established Ft. Mississippi, thirty miles below present-day New Orleans. This fort split in two the Spanish land claim that stretched from Florida along the Gulf Coast to Texas and on down to Mexico. It gave France a rival claim that ran orthogonally from the mouth of the Mississippi north to French Canada.[23]

The east Texas missions were rebuilt in the early 1700s to prevent French expansion. After the 1762 transfer of Louisiana to Spain, the French threat vanished, as did the raison d'être for the Spanish presence in east Texas. The Spanish again abandoned their east Texas missions and ordered that the 167 Hispanic families in east Texas be relocated to San Antonio, where a *presidio* and missions had been established earlier.[24]

California

The long process of exploring and settling California began in 1533, when Spanish pilot Fortún Jiménez sailed into a placid Baja California bay and named it La Paz. By the 1540s, the land he visited, which was thought to be an island inhabited entirely by women, was known as California. That name derived from a popular sixteenth-century tale of chivalry that told of an island called California that was home to a race of valiant women. Once Baja California was determined to be a peninsula, both the peninsula and the coast to the north of it became known as California.[25]

Others' interest in California served to awaken Spanish interest in settling the remote province. Russian fur traders, moving down the Pacific Coast from Alaska, seemed poised to seize California. In 1759, a Spanish Franciscan published a book with the title *Muscovites in California* to alert Spanish authorities to the danger. The Spanish also became concerned that the Manila Galleon, which sailed close to the Californian coast on the eastbound leg of its journey, was vulnerable to attack. To ensure the safety of the Galleon, as well as to prevent other European powers from encroaching, in 1768 Carlos III ordered the occupation of Alta California, as the modern U.S. state of California was then known.[26]

Two ships sailed north to found settlements. Capt. Gaspar de Portolá, a minor Catalonian nobleman with thirty years' military experience, commanded the expedition. The first ship arrived at San Diego on April 11, 1769. The second ship arrived eighteen days later, after many of its crew had died of scurvy.[27]

An overland expedition from Baja California soon reinforced the Spaniards. Since so few able-bodied sailors remained, in July sixty men and a pack train of mules set out on foot for Monterey Bay. They failed to recognize it and instead stumbled on San Francisco Bay, whose narrow mouth, the Golden Gate, had been previously overlooked by mariners. Fray Juan Crespi, who accompanied them, described the bay as being so large that "doubtless not only all the navies of our Catholic Monarch, but those of all Europe might lie within the harbor."[28]

In 1770, Portolá ventured back north, located Monterey Bay, and established a *presidio* there "to occupy the port and defend us from attacks by the Russians, who were about to invade us." Despite the bravado, the token force in Monterey, 450 miles north of San Diego, could have done little to stop the Russians.[29]

Visitor-General José de Gálvez organized the occupation of Alta California with an eye to minimizing the costs to the royal treasury. He ordered California's missions, which were under the supervision of Father Junípero Serra, a Spanish-born Franciscan, to supply the *presidios*. To further lower costs, Gálvez directed the Franciscans to strip their missions in Baja California to provide supplies. As a result, hundreds of head of livestock, built up carefully over the years, were slaughtered to feed the new settlements.[30]

Spain's northward thrust on land ended in 1776 with the establishment of the *presidio* and mission of San Francisco, the northernmost permanent Spanish settlement in California. Ultimately, the Franciscans would found twenty-one missions in California, most of which were located near the coast, since they were founded in conjunction with the *presidios*, which sought to prevent foreign incursions. Due to their strategic importance in reinforcing Spain's claim to California, the Crown subsidized the missions until they could produce their own food.[31]

Spanish control over California remained tenuous. The long supply lines were stretched so thin that a 1774 report noted some *presidial* soldiers had only guns, some had only swords, and some had neither. Fortunately for Spain, the only military action the *presidios* engaged in was firing a lone cannon shot at an unidentified ship that appeared in San Francisco harbor in 1792. The ship sailed away, never identified.[32]

Arizona

Arizona indicates the importance of strategic motivation in settling the borderlands. The area now known as Arizona never faced a foreign threat, and, therefore, little settlement occurred. In fact, the use of the term Arizona imposes a contemporary view. Arizona never formed an administrative division of either colonial New Spain or independent Mexico. The U.S. government carved Arizona Territory out of New Mexico territory in 1863.[33]

During the colonial period, territory now included in Arizona formed part of Sonora. In the seventeenth century, Spaniards who moved up the east coast of the Gulf of California from river valley to river valley laid the groundwork for settling Sonora. The advance into Sonora proceeded slowly, as there were few resources to aid settlement. During the colonial period, Sonora remained an arid, sparsely populated area dotted with missions, farms, and mines.[34]

Spaniards only settled the extreme southern part of Arizona, which formed the northern part of an area known as the Pimería Alta, home to the Pima, Pápago, and Yuma people. The Pápago were typical of the indigenous peoples of the area. They planted corn, beans, and squash along flood plains and channeled water to their fields with crude brush dams. They became semi-nomadic during the dry season, subsisting on hunting and gathering. The lack of permanent water sources prevented them from becoming sedentary.[35]

Only in 1775 did the Spanish empire put down permanent roots in what is today Arizona. In that year, a military garrison was transferred to a newly constructed *presidio* on the Santa Cruz River, across from the long-established Pima village known as San Agustín. The *presidio* attracted other Pima, Pápago, pacified Apache, and Spanish, who together numbered 1,104 in 1804. Initially, Indian raids and aridity inhibited expansion of the community, which became known as Tucson. Aridity remained as a constraint, while after a 1786 peace with the Apache, Indian raids ceased, permitting an expansion of ranching, mining, and trade with Sonora.[36]

TRADE

Settlements in each of the present U.S. border states were isolated from one other, and all relied on supply lines extending back to Mexico City. As Humboldt observed early in the nineteenth century, "There has been hitherto no permanent communication between Sonora, New Mexico, and New California." Humboldt also noted that no one had yet traveled from New Mexico to the California coast.[37]

Spanish trade policy stifled development along the northern border. In the late colonial period, foreign products were burdened with a 36 percent tax upon arrival at Veracruz. Other taxes led to a tax burden of 75 percent by the time goods reached consumers. Due to long supply lines, as well as duties, some goods would quadruple in price between their arrival in Veracruz and their sale on the frontier.[38]

Due to Spanish shipping restrictions, settlers in Texas could not use their ports on the Gulf of Mexico to export mules, hides, lard, tallow, wool, grain, flour, meats, and salt. To obtain manufactured goods legally, Texas depended on a supply line running from northern Europe, through Spain, to Veracruz, and then to Texas. North of the Rio Grande, the need for a military escort to protect from Indian attack further increased costs. As a result of its being tied to long, cumbersome supply lines, Texas led a marginal economic existence throughout the eighteenth century and was only loosely tied to the broader colonial economy.[39]

This circuitous route for supplying the colony created enormous pressure to smuggle manufactured goods in through French Louisiana. Since no other practical source of manufactured goods existed, many Texas governors ignored such smuggling. Others participated in the smuggling.[40]

Since Texans could not ship goods out, they relied on products that could move themselves—horses and cattle. Exporting livestock eventually overshadowed other aspects of the Texas economy. Herds were driven southward to Nuevo León and Coahuila and often, illegally, eastward to Louisiana. In exchange for their livestock, Texans would receive from Louisiana luxury items such as silk shawls, ribbon, and braid, as well as such basics as nails.[41]

Even after Louisiana was transferred to Spain, trade was not permitted with Texas. Louisiana was administered from Cuba and had lower taxes. If trade had been permitted between Louisiana and Texas, fewer taxes would have flowed to Mexico City. In addition, entrenched commercial interests in Veracruz and Mexico City lobbied against permitting Texas–Louisiana trade. As one would expect, smuggling across the Texas–Louisiana border continued.[42]

Father Mariano Sosa commented that trade restrictions in Texas created "the lack of an incentive to raise larger or better crops." Sosa suggested that if farmers could sell their crops in Louisiana they would be more productive. He also suggested that it would stimulate production if troops garrisoned in Texas were paid in cash and allowed to purchase locally produced goods, rather than being forced to purchase all their supplies at the commissary.[43]

Isolation also delayed New Mexico's development. The nearest real market was more than 700 miles to the south. Unfavorable terrain separated it from that market. Unpredictable weather and attacks by indigenous nomads plagued the road south. Heavily armed convoys of roughly thirty-two wagons, each carrying up to 4,000 pounds, provided the main trade link with the south. Sometimes years elapsed between convoys. These wagons took nine months to reach Mexico City. Exports to the silver mining regions to the south included blankets, raw wool, Indian slaves, *piñón* nuts, and, during the last decade of Spanish control, roughly 200,000 head of sheep, which were driven south annually.[44]

Chihuahua merchants, who reaped enormous profits from their trade monopoly, controlled New Mexico's commerce with the rest of Mexico. Much of the money the Crown spent maintaining its New Mexico colony ended up in their pockets. In 1804, New Mexico exported $60,000 worth of goods and imported $112,000.[45]

Governor Diego de Vargas remarked that New Mexico was "remote beyond compare." This remoteness led to the formation of a largely self-sufficient economy. Hispanic farmers adopted the methods of Pueblo farmers, raising corn, beans, and chiles. As the eighteenth century progressed, livestock raising became more important. Due to a shortage of coins, New Mexicans relied heavily on barter.[46]

The lack of supplies made life in California so harsh that in 1769 Portolá declared that if the Russians wanted California, he would let them have it. After a Yuma revolt closed the overland route from Sonora, California again became dependent on ships coming from San Blas, a port west of Guadalajara. This tenuous supply line discouraged colonization and retarded development.[47]

By the end of the eighteenth century, Alta California was wealthy in grain, meat, and hides, but could not convert these products into cash or use them to barter for needed items. The domestic market for agricultural produce was minuscule, since most of the population produced food. The Spanish forbade trade with other Spanish colonies and ships of other nations.

Despite this official prohibition, toward the end of the colonial period Californians began trading with U.S., Russian, and British ships. Their crews illegally provided manufactured goods in exchange for otter pelts. California governors realized the official supply system had broken down and that some substitute, albeit an illegal one, had to be accepted. Governor José Darío Argüello reasoned, "Necessity makes licit that which is not licit by law."[48]

THE HISPANIC POPULATION

Few Hispanics settled the economically stagnant frontier areas on their own initiative. To induce colonization, the Crown provided new arrivals with seeds, tools, land, free transport, and tax exemptions. Late in the colonial period, these incentives virtually halted since the Crown could no longer afford them. Due to the lack of identifiable mineral wealth and readily exploitable Indians, the Crown had always viewed the northern border in terms of defense, not in terms of its economic potential. Trade policy, weak links to major markets, and attacks by Indians also limited settlement in the borderlands.[49]

Between 1731 and 1760, Texas's Hispanic population increased from 500 to 1,190, of whom 580 lived in San Antonio. In 1777, the first Texas census enumerated 3,103 Spanish, mixed bloods, and peacefully settled Indians.[50]

The lack of easily exploitable wealth slowed population growth in New Mexico. Writing to King Felipe III in 1602, Viceroy Gaspar de Zúñiga y Acevedo, Conde de Monterrey, observed that New Mexico's settlers

> have nothing to sell from which they can obtain cash, and poverty is everywhere. It therefore seems to me that these conditions, especially the lack of money, will discourage anyone from going there, or, if already settled, would discourage anyone from remaining there. . . . Neither will the food be lavish nor the clothing dignified.[51]

Thanks in large part to the availability of irrigated land, two centuries after the settlement of New Mexico, its Hispanic population numbered 30,000, more than twice the combined Hispanic population of California, Arizona, and Texas.[52]

California, after losing its overland access, became in effect an island. It failed to attract settlers since the missions had appropriated the best land and indigenous labor. Even though immigration to colonial California never amounted to more than a trickle, the Hispanics multiplied and incorporated some Indians into their numbers. Between 1791 and 1800–1805, official census figures indicate that California's population increased from 8,431 to 19,945. (This count excludes the far more numerous population of non-mission Indians.) No Hispanic settlement was further inland than Soledad, thirty miles from the sea.[53]

Mission work and the 1736 discovery of a silver mine known as the Real de Arizonac, located a few miles southwest of present-day Nogales, attracted a few settlers into the Pimería Alta. The name of the mine was corrupted into Arizona, yielding the name of the modern state. Given the scant Indian population and desert conditions, in the 1760s the Hispanic population of Sonora barely exceeded 8,000. Fewer than 1,000 Hispanics lived in territory now included in Arizona.[54]

MISSIONS

> Although staffed by members of the Catholic Church, the mission was fundamentally a government institution funded by the Crown. The government had to authorize the establishment of each new mission.
>
> Robert H. Jackson, 1998[55]

The mission became the dominant Spanish presence in many areas of northern Mexico. The lack of a sedentary indigenous workforce made it unfeasible to institute the *encomienda* and the *repartimiento*. Priests gathered widely scattered, often nomadic, Indians into the mission complex. Mission Indians led a semi-communal existence and learned catechism, crafts, and European agricultural techniques. The friars attempted to impose such non-religious cultural traits as the Spanish language, adobe or stone houses, men's trousers, a political organization focused on loyalty to the Spanish king, and the acceptance of colonial labor drafts and tribute payments.[56]

Friars would replace recalcitrant indigenous leaders with more pliant figures. They concentrated on the youth and then used them to undermine the older generation. They organized Indian men, women, and children to build mission complexes and engage in daily routines such as ringing bells, preparing food, tending livestock, and tilling mission fields. The missionaries attempted to introduce what they considered desirable occupations—mining, plow agriculture, and raising livestock.[57]

In contrast to central Mexico, mission priests provided Indians with a fixed residence and a source of livelihood. Since the mission as an institution replaced either widely scattered settlement or the lack of a fixed settlement at all, it represented a much greater change for the Indians involved than did earlier efforts at evangelization. Mission Indians were more tightly controlled than Indians in central Mexico in that they lived at the mission complex and their movement was restricted. Economic activities at the mission, such as farming, ranching, and the production of textiles and leather goods, relied on indigenous workers under the supervision of priests.[58]

San José mission, in San Antonio, provides an example of a typical mission. Priests assembled hunter-gatherers from the surrounding area and provided them with religious instruction, housing, and employment. The mission formed a village in miniature within a walled compound measuring 611 feet on each side. The compound contained living quarters, a chapel, and shops for weaving, tailoring, carpentry, and blacksmithing. It also contained a granary and lime and brick kilns. To provide security, the compound was fortified and soldiers were stationed there. Between 1777 and 1794, roughly 300 Indians lived at San José. Later this number declined. San José produced corn, beans, lentils, melons, peaches, potatoes, sweet potatoes, and sugar cane for residents' consumption and for nearby Spanish settlements and *presidios*. The mission's nearby ranch raised cattle, sheep, and goats.[59]

In marked contrast to missionaries' early successes in central Mexico, their experiences in the borderlands were hardly cause for celebration. Only a handful of the missionaries in the north learned indigenous languages. Their scant numbers also limited conversions. Between 1769 and 1848, only 138 Franciscans served in Alta Californian missions.[60]

The California mission culture, once viewed rather romantically, came under heavy criticism in response to the beatification of Junípero Serra. Critics noted that while missions provided places of refuge for Indians threatened by war and drought, they also uprooted cultures and exposed Indians to harsh regimentation and European disease. The missionaries forced Indians into residence at the mission so they could more effectively convert them and exact labor from them. Missionaries assumed indigenous labor was an endowment to which the mission was entitled. Acting on this assumption, they forced Indians to produce crops to sustain the *presidios*. This transferred the burden of supporting colonization from the Crown to the indigenous population. They also rented Indians to work for Hispanic settlers who needed labor and retained the fee paid for this labor. Indians were whipped when their behavior and labor output did not meet the friars' standards.[61]

From a demographic point of view, the impact of the mission was catastrophic. Between 1771 and 1820, the average birth rate in missions was 41 per 1,000, while the death rate was 78 per 1,000. The Spaniards were aware that missions contributed to high Indian mortality, but did not abandon the system. In 1820, the fifth father president of the California missions, Mariano Payeras, wrote that in the missions Indians "become extremely feeble, lose weight, get sick and die."[62]

Many California Indians responded to poor sanitary conditions and the friars' labor demands by fleeing the mission. Usually flight involved only individuals or families. However, in a single incident in 1795, 280 escaped the San Francisco mission together, followed by 200 the next year. The reasons Indians gave for fleeing included overwork, harsh punishments, hunger, not being allowed to eat their traditional food, and being denied permission to visit relatives living outside the missions. In response, the military mounted expeditions into interior areas to capture fugitives.[63]

Another response to mission life was rebellion. Anthropologist Daniel Reff noted, "Almost without exception, native peoples throughout northwestern Mexico rebelled at one time or another against Jesuit tutelage." Such criticism of the missions notwithstanding, Indians' living conditions further deteriorated after the abolition of the missions left them to the mercy of a hostile society.[64]

The mission experience on the borderlands reflected the geopolitical and environmental situation of each individual mission. In east Texas, the Caddo achieved a decent (by their standards) livelihood and obtained arms and trade goods from the French in Louisiana. In exchange, they provided the French with chamois, tallow, horses, and bear- and deerskins. The Spanish friars sent there were unable to persuade any Indians to live in the missions. The undermanned Spanish *presidios* could not force compliance. As historian David Weber noted, "Indians who had viable alternatives tended to avoid life in missions."[65]

A few hundred miles to the southwest of the Caddo, the missions obtained their greatest success (as defined by the Spanish). There, the Coahuiltecans living to the south of San Antonio benefited from being protected from attack by the Lipan Apache and from abandoning their hunter-gathering existence and integrating themselves into the missions' irrigation-agricultural regime. Even though they enjoyed an increased standard of living, the indigenous at the mission suffered from high mortality and frequently fled. The Coahuiltecans who remained learned the Spanish language and Spanish crafts so well that they and their descendants ultimately merged into Hispanic society.[66]

Given California's geopolitical importance, missions there flourished even though the Bourbons deemphasized them elsewhere on the borderlands. Between 1769 and 1783, the missions stretching from San Diego to San Francisco housed more than 4,000 Indians. These missions were well supplied with indigenous labor despite the high Indian mortality rate, since Spanish troops repeatedly brought in Indians from the heathen population. This forcible recruitment of Indians, who could quite easily provide for themselves, was rationalized in 1801 by the head of a Franciscan contingent who declared that only through forcible means could friars rescue a people "of vicious and ferocious habits who know no law but force."[67]

Due to California's isolation, colonization was impractical. As a result, the major productive unit remained the mission, which provided sustenance for the *presidios*. The productive success of the mission resulted from land grants by the king, who, according to Spanish law, owned all of California. These grants allowed missionaries to select the best land. This land, combined with forced Indian labor, produced sufficient food for both mission and *presidio*. Given the small number of colonists, the *presidios* became dependent on mission produce. Once this dependency was established, missionaries justified their control of California land and Indian labor as the only feasible way to supply the *presidios*. Lay Californians resented this, but were too few in number to pressure the Crown into changing policy.[68]

THE 1680 PUEBLO REVOLT

The Spanish assumed that Christianizing the urbanized Pueblo they encountered in New Mexico would be an easy task. The Pueblo produced sophisticated pottery and lived in solidly constructed, multi-storied, terraced apartment buildings with as many as 2,000 residents. They hunted game, gathered plants, and grew corn, squash, beans, and cotton in irrigated fields. Between 110 and 150 functioning Pueblo villages existed at the time of Spanish contact. These villages maintained extensive trade networks with other pueblos and with neighboring nomadic people.[69]

The pueblos looked deceptively similar, but were in fact inhabited by people belonging to five major language groups—Piro, Hopi, Zuñi, Tano, and Keresan. In 1609, this linguistic diversity led the viceroy to comment that New Mexico "is populated by a variety of nations, with very few people in each one of them, who speak various difficult and barbarous languages." Only a few of the Franciscans mastered the Pueblo languages well enough to minister without an interpreter. The pueblos' isolation from Spanish settlement presented missionaries with the challenge of living and teaching in communities that were alien and indifferent, if not hostile.[70]

Forcing Pueblos to relinquish their indigenous religion proved to be a never-ending task for the friars. After 1630, Franciscans began to seize and destroy native religious objects and imprison, torture, and publicly whip those who maintained indigenous religious practices. Civil authorities occasionally hanged alleged Indian sorcerers. In 1660, Fray Nicolás de Freitas declared, "It has been impossible to correct their concubinage, the abominable crime of idolatry, their accursed superstitions, idolatrous dances, and other faults."[71]

Tribute collection increased tension between Spaniards and Pueblos. *Encomenderos* legally exacted salt, nuts, hides, and clothing from Indians and illegally appropriated their land and labor.

Figure 5.2 *Taos Pueblo, north house block, by John K. Hillers, 1879*
Source: Courtesy of Museum of New Mexico, #16096

The Spanish appropriated so many goods that the Pueblos could no longer maintain trade ties with nomadic people in the region. Nomads, who had grown dependent on Pueblo supplies, began raiding to seize what they could no longer obtain by trade. [72]

Conditions for the Pueblo deteriorated in the late 1660s. A severe drought between 1667 and 1672 led to famine and increased raids by starving nomads. When Spaniards' prayers failed to deliver rain, the Pueblo turned to traditional religious leaders. The Spanish responded by hanging three Pueblo religious practitioners and lashing forty-three others deemed guilty of sorcery and sedition. The combination of draught, epidemics, attacks by neighboring nomads, and Spanish labor and tribute demands pushed the Pueblo to the breaking point.[73]

Popé, a Tewa religious leader from San Juan Pueblo who had been flogged by the Spanish in 1675 for his attempts to reinvigorate native religious practices, organized the Pueblo response. Over a period of several years, he coordinated plans for a rebellion. He united speakers of six languages from two dozen independent towns spread over several hundred square miles. Popé's success was based on his organizational skill and his promising that the old gods would restore happiness and prosperity after Christians and their god were ousted. He promised his followers that after the revolt the Pueblo could reclaim the choice lands held by Spaniards and that there would be no more forced labor.[74]

The conspirators set the revolt for August 11, 1680, the first night of the new moon. They timed it to occur just before the arrival of the supply caravan, which would bring additional ammunition and horses for the Spanish. A series of knots tied in cords carried to conspiring villages communicated that date. One knot was to be untied each day. The revolt was set for the day no knots remained. Spanish officials only learned of the rebellion on its eve, too late to prevent it.[75]

The Indians simultaneously attacked isolated missions and ranches in northern and central New Mexico. Given the element of surprise and their overwhelming numerical advantage, the Indians soon had all of northern New Mexico, except for Santa Fe, under their control. Using guns and horses captured in outlying areas, they besieged that Spanish stronghold. Just as the Spanish had cut the water supply when they had besieged Tenochtitlan, the rebels cut the water supply to the Spaniards in Santa Fe. Rather than attempting to withstand a siege by a vastly superior force, after nine days, the 1,000 people massed in Santa Fe retreated south to El Paso. The rebels did not attempt to prevent their flight. Even in the face of rebellion, Spanish oppression did not cease. The Spanish forced 500 of their Pueblo and Apache slaves to accompany them as they fled.[76]

During the rebellion, the rebels killed at least 400 Spaniards, including thirty-two friars, whom they encountered in isolated areas. They specifically targeted anything associated with Christianity. The Pueblo slew priests at their altars, desecrated holy furnishings with human excrement, and burned missions. Leaders instructed their followers to wade in streams and scrub themselves with yucca root to wash away Christian baptism. The rebels resumed worship of their old gods, after declaring the Christian god and St. Mary dead. Rebels prohibited speaking Spanish in areas they controlled. The Pueblo emptied and resacralized kivas that had been desecrated and filled with sand.[77]

Once the Spanish retreated, the rebels faced no immediate military threat, since 300 miles of rugged terrain, much of which was under Apache control, separated them from El Paso. However, after having ridded themselves of the Spanish, problems did not simply vanish. Old rivalries between Pueblo resurfaced, and epidemics continued. Since Spanish soldiers no longer offered protection, raids by nomadic Indians increased.[78]

Popé began to affect the role of a Spanish governor and demanded tribute. His actions, in the eyes of some Pueblo, smacked of extremism. He forbade the sowing of Spanish-introduced plants and demanded that long hours be devoted to religious ceremonies. After resentment built up against Popé, a coup finally ousted him.[79]

To reassert Spanish control, in August 1692 Spanish nobleman Diego de Vargas marched north from El Paso with fifty presidial soldiers, their officers, ten armed citizens, a hundred Pueblos, three Franciscan friars, pack animals, livestock, several wagons carrying provisions, a small cannon, and a mortar. De Vargas's force stopped at each pueblo and offered its residents the opportunity to return to Christ and the Crown. After a pueblo accepted his offer, priests would absolve Indians of their sins and baptize the children who had been born since 1680. Indians who had occupied Santa Fe agreed to submit after the cross and the banner of the Blessed Virgin were displayed. From the Spanish point of view, De Vargas's mission was a resounding success. Without a shot being fired, twenty-three pueblos pledged to return to the Christian fold and the Spanish empire. Priests baptized some 2,214 Indians, mostly children.[80]

De Vargas's success in the 1692 campaign resulted from his willingness to accept submission without exacting revenge and his moving so quickly that pueblos did not have the chance to reunite. No leader emerged to replace Popé, who had died. De Vargas also enjoyed the support of the Crown, which financed the reoccupation of New Mexico, since it was reluctant to abandon those who had converted to Christianity. It also feared that if New Mexico was not reoccupied, the French would usurp Spanish territorial claims and invade the silver-producing regions of northern Mexico. Multiple crises, such as the appearance of La Salle, left the Crown overextended and delayed support for recolonizing New Mexico.[81]

Once he had received pledges of submission to the Crown, De Vargas returned to El Paso. In September 1693, he accompanied 800 settlers and their livestock back to New Mexico. Almost immediately, Spanish demands for scarce food supplies led to violence. De Vargas, in mid-winter, demanded that the Pueblo turn over accumulated food supplies and vacate buildings in Santa Fe so the Spanish could occupy them. Their refusal led to combat. In the ensuing battle to reoccupy Santa Fe, eighty-one Indians died, including seventy who were executed after having surrendered. An additional 400 men, women, and children were seized as slaves. This produced resistance in other pueblos. In early 1694, De Vargas traveled from pueblo to pueblo and forced them to submit once again. Even with the Spanish force in their midst, the pueblos never reunited. Not only did the Pueblo lack leaders to replace Popé, but some pueblos, such as Pecos, actively supported the Spanish.[82]

After reoccupying New Mexico, Christian religious practices were reimposed. However, the Spanish (those who survived the rebellion) did learn some lessons. They became more tolerant of Pueblo religious practices. Spanish priests, who numbered only twenty in 1776, were spread so thin that Indians enjoyed more religious freedom. The Spanish also realized that to prevent another revolt, they would have to become more self-sufficient and cease relying on the Pueblo to produce for them. Spanish governors in Santa Fe became more attentive to Pueblo complaints of abuse by friars and settlers. As the eighteenth century wore on, trade and intermarriage between Hispanics and Pueblo increased. In the late 1700s, the Hispanic population surpassed that of the Pueblo, who realized they would have to learn to live with non-Indians.[83]

GUERRA A SANGRE Y FUEGO

> Northern New Spain never enjoyed the long, if flawed, social peace of the centre; Spanish hegemony was, at best, patchy and frequently contested.
>
> Alan Knight, 2002[84]

During the late colonial period, the borderlands were distinguished from central Mexico by the presence of independent Indian groups that refused to accept what the Spanish defined as appropriate behavior—conversion to Christianity and permanent settlements. Indians could successfully reject Spanish tutelage since: 1) they had acquired the horse and become expert horsemen; 2) they could acquire firearms from traders of other nationalities, especially the French; and 3) they had ready sources of food, such as buffalo, which permitted survival without submitting to the Spanish.

The European presence in North America led to massive destabilization, even among Indians who had never seen a white man. Epidemics spread far ahead of European settlement, wreaking havoc. Later, horses spread from the southwest, as they strayed or were stolen. Firearms obtained from traders flowed from the northeast. When Indian groups acquired both horses and firearms, the existing balance of power changed radically. After European settlement forced one group of Indians into the territory of another, food supplies were often inadequate for both groups, leading to raids on third parties, often the Spanish, for food.[85]

The Comanche, perhaps the most transformed of all Indian groups affected by, but not dominated by Europeans, originated in the mountainous country of contemporary Colorado and Wyoming and emerged onto the plains in the late seventeenth century. The combination of the horse, the gun, and the buffalo allowed them to remain independent of Europeans. They lived a fully nomadic life, trading, raiding, and hunting buffalo, which made them exceedingly difficult to control. The Comanche moved into the lush grasslands of eastern New Mexico and from there launched devastating raids against settlements along the Rio Grande. In the late 1700s, the area under Comanche control, known as the *comanchería,* covered some 240,000 square miles and formed a formidable barrier against Spanish efforts to expand north and west of San Antonio. At the height of their power, the Comanche boasted that they only allowed Spaniards and Mexicans to remain in northern Mexico to raise horses for them to steal.[86]

At the time of European contact, the Apache occupied southern New Mexico and adjacent areas of Texas. They engaged in horticulture, which provided a reliable food supply. The Apache never formed a tribe, in the sense of having one chief or a definable structure. Rather, they formed an ethnic group, which had at least twenty subdivisions, known by such names as Gileño Apache and Jicarilla Apache.[87]

The newly empowered Comanche forced the Apache to abandon their land and their way of life by denying them access to Spanish markets in New Mexico and by preventing them from establishing spring farming camps. Some Apache were displaced west into what is now southeastern Arizona and to the south and west into what is now northern Chihuahua and Sonora. The Lipan Apache moved into the area between the Big Bend and the lower Rio Grande Valley in Texas. Some of the northern Apache groups, such as the Faraones, disappeared entirely. The area under Apache domination, known as the *gran apachería*, extended from today's northern Sonora and southern Arizona to west Texas and Coahuila—750 miles from east to west and as much as 550 miles from north to south. During the middle of the eighteenth century, Apache control created a barrier to northward Spanish expansion.[88]

Sandwiched between the Comanche to the north and the Spanish to the south, the Apache perfected the raid as a means of survival. As historian Donald Worcester noted:

> The Apaches successfully resisted all attempts to conquer them from the early seventeenth century until the last quarter of the nineteenth. They avoided pitched battles if possible, but when cornered fought to the death. As guerrilla fighters they were without peers; unlike the Plains tribes, they could not be starved into submission by extermination of the bison or any other animal.[89]

As the strength of independent Indian groups increased, the Spanish began to see themselves not as conquistadores but as underdogs. In 1758, the presidial commander at La Bahía del Espíritu Santo on the Texas coast commented that the surrounding Indians were so "superior . . . in firearms as well as in numbers, that our destruction seems probable."[90]

The cycle of raid and counter-raid developed into a state of low-intensity warfare. Emphasis shifted from saving Indians' souls to killing them. Spanish punitive expeditions often struck innocent groups. The ready market for booty and slaves did not lead punitive expeditions to be very discriminating concerning their choice of targets. Nor did they need to worry about Spanish officials enforcing laws against slavery. In 1752, New Mexico Governor Vélez Cachupín reminded colonists that Indian slavery was illegal but tolerated in New Mexico so that captives "can be instructed in Our Holy Catholic Faith and made cognizant of the Divine Precepts, so that they may win their own salvation in honor and glory of God, our Lord."[91]

By the 1770s, Apaches were subjecting the entire province of Nueva Vizcaya to attack, and many of its villages had been abandoned. The region was described as being in a state of "permanent warfare." Governor Felipe Barri reported that between 1771 and 1776, Indian raids had resulted in 1,674 persons being killed, 154 captured, 116 haciendas and ranches abandoned, and 68,256 head of livestock stolen.[92]

To supplement the *presidio*, in Chihuahua the Crown established a series of fortified settlements inhabited by armed peasant freeholders. Migrants from Spain and central Mexico, as well as local Indians who settled in these colonies and participated in military action against nomadic Indians, received extraordinary benefits. These included extensive land holdings and exemptions from paying taxes for ten years. Indians who settled in the colonies, in contrast to Indian peasants in central Mexico, who were considered wards of the Crown, were given full rights of Spanish citizenship. Namiquipa, Cruces, Casas Grandes, Janos, and Galeana, the first five of these military colonies, were established in 1776, and each received 277,527 acres of land.[93]

Under the leadership of Teodoro de Croix, who commanded Spanish forces in northern New Spain, a three-pronged strategy for countering Indians was developed: 1) missionaries would encourage Indians to lay down their arms and settle peacefully; 2) failing that, the Spanish would adopt a scorched-earth military policy known as "*guerra a sangre y fuego*" ("war by fire and blood"); and 3) if war proved too expensive or futile, the Crown would bribe or buy off Indians who posed a threat. This third option proved especially favorable to the Comanche, who received gifts, weapons, and ammunition as bribes not to attack the Spanish.[94]

Croix organized troops who had previously cowered in *presidios* into mobile strike forces, or "flying companies" that would ride out in pursuit of Indians. He reformed the internal administration of *presidios* and increased the number of border troops to more than 3,000. These troops suffered high mortality, but unlike the Apache, Croix could bring in replacements from afar.[95]

Rather than considering the indigenous population as a monolithic entity, Spaniards began to exploit age-old ethnic antagonisms between groups, such as those between Comanche and Apache, and divisions within ethnic groups. They successfully formed an alliance with the Lipan Apache against the Mescalero Apache. Pedro de Nava, who served as general commander of the Interior Provinces from 1793 to 1802, commented on the divide-and-conquer policy in a letter to Texas Governor Manuel Muñoz:

> One of the maxims that should always be observed on our part, with respect to the nations of Indians, is to allow them to make reciprocal war on each other in order in this way to bring about a diminution of their forces, to energize their mutual hatreds, and to avoid their union and alliance.[96]

Beginning in the 1780s, the Spanish began to pursue the Apache, destroy their settlements, and kill as many of them as possible. The Apache faced the alternatives of continued combat with the Spanish, a return north to face their hereditary enemies, the Comanche, or agreeing to settle near a mission.[97]

Just as had occurred with the Chichimeca, the Spanish eventually concluded that the key to peace in the northern borderlands lay not in waging war but in supplying independent Indians with sufficient merchandise so that they would refrain from attacking Spanish settlements. Even though this merchandise transfer was referred to as "gift giving," it was de facto tribute paid by the Spanish to independent Indian groups.

In 1786, the Comanche and Spaniards signed a formal peace accord at Pecos, amidst festivity and flattering oratory. The 1786 peace held and became one of the most enduring treaties signed between Indians and Spaniards. That year, the first installment of the promised gifts destined for the Comanche arrived in San Antonio from Louisiana. The shipment included thirty-seven boxes of imported European goods as well as 474 bundles of tobacco. In addition to receiving gifts, the Comanche benefited from the peace, trading to the Spaniards captives, buffalo hides, and jerked meat.[98]

The Comanche willingly ceased raiding at this time since: 1) they had greater difficulty obtaining guns after the Spanish assumed control of Louisiana; 2) they had suffered a major smallpox epidemic in 1780–1781; and 3) Spanish forces had just destroyed a Comanche camp in southeastern Colorado and killed prominent war chief Cuerno Verde. The Comanche not only refrained from attacking Spaniards but joined the Spanish in attacking the Lipan.[99]

The peace with the Comanche became so cordial that in 1806 when U.S. troops stood poised on the Texas–Louisiana border to support inflated American claims that the Louisiana Purchase extended as far as the Rio Grande, thirty-three Comanche chiefs offered their support to Spanish Governor Antonio Cordero in San Antonio.[100]

As a result of combined Spanish and Comanche attacks, in 1791 the Spanish were able to sign a peace treaty with the Lipan. Raiding was to cease in exchange for gifts, including weekly supplies of corn, meat, tobacco, and sweets. The Spanish created *establecimientos de paz* (peace establishments), where many Apache settled and received food. Pedro de Nava, who was serving a commander in chief of the Interior Provinces, expressly forbade missionary proselytizing in peace establishments, fearing it would annoy the Apache and cause them to flee. Since peace establishments cost less than war, the Spanish maintained them for rest of the colonial period.[101]

Apaches who promised to settle peacefully received not only food but seeds, farm tools, and protection from the Comanche. They also received copious amounts of liquor. As anthropologist Edward Spicier noted:

> It was a frankly cynical policy based on the view that the Apaches could never be civilized, and thus represented a very sharp alteration of what had been the Spanish approach, namely, the belief that all Indians were capable through moral suasion of changing from barbarians to civilized Christians.[102]

Peace remained tenuous. Sometimes peace treaties would only bind Indians not to attack a specific Spanish settlement. Villages that regularly purchased booty or captives would be spared attack. This encouraged villages to make such purchases, but also encouraged attacks on other villages. In addition, lack of warfare did not necessarily mean Spanish control, as historian John Coatsworth noted: "Colonial frontiers were ill-defined, and virtually undefended. Although progress was achieved in settling and pacifying parts of the northern areas, vast regions remained entirely outside the control of Spain at the time of independence."[103]

THE INDIGENOUS POPULATION

> The Christian mission as a frontier institution that emerges in this chapter is not a romantic pastoral scene peopled by happy converts led by congenial pastors. Rather, it is the grim story of rapid population decline.
>
> Henry Dobyns, 1976[104]

The borderland Indian population suffered the same catastrophic numerical decline that Indians had in central Mexico. Mission Indians, the population for which the best records exist, had a high level of mortality due to a combination of malnutrition, disease, crowding, and poor sanitation. Bones recovered from mission Indians are significantly smaller than those of their predecessors from pre-Spanish times, indicating malnutrition and disease.[105]

A few examples indicate the magnitude of Indian population decline. By 1690, European-introduced diseases had reduced the population of east Texas to only about 10 or 20 percent of what it had been in 1542. In 1581, the Pueblo population totaled 130,000. By 1706, it had declined to 6,440. Burial books indicate that the eastern pueblos, such as Pecos, suffered major epidemics during every decade from 1695 to 1828. Between 1540 and 1590, there were roughly seventy-five to ninety pueblos in the Rio Grande drainage. By 1643, only forty-three were still occupied.[106]

California has often been cited as the shining example of the Spanish mission system. The mission population there grew three-fold between 1790 and 1820, with the establishment of ten new missions and the addition of neophytes at all missions. The missions' numerical "success" resulted from forced recruitment from the large pool of non-mission Indians. Alta California's Indian population numbered 300,000 in 1769. By the end of the colonial period, it had fallen to 200,000.[107]

As a result of disease and unsanitary conditions, life expectancy at birth in California missions was only 4.5 years. High mortality rates resulted from congregating Indians in one location, which facilitated the spread of diseases such as influenza, diphtheria, measles, pneumonia, whooping cough, small pox, malaria, typhoid, cholera, tuberculosis, dysentery, syphilis, and gonorrhea. Forced relocation to the cool, damp, foggy seashore exacerbated health problems. Neither the missionaries nor the Indians understood the causes of the high mortality rate among mission Indians. This led mission historian Robert Archibald to comment, "This destruction was inexcusable but it was not intentional." Archibald also observed, "The missionaries would have preferred to have dead Christians rather than live pagans."[108]

Part Two

Independence, 1810–1821

Chapter 6

The End of Spanish Rule, 1810–1821

Latin American independence came in the midst of an era of sweeping change in the Western world. It was indeed part of that change. The Enlightenment, in advertising the potency of human reason, had accustomed those whom it touched to the notion that change was a normal state of being; for what was dangerous, damaging, or demeaning in the human condition could be remedied by the proper application of the mind's power.

P. J. Bakewell, 1997[1]

EARLY NINETEENTH-CENTURY GRIEVANCES

Throughout most of the colonial period, the vast majority of New Spain's residents remained loyal to the king, just as, being good Catholics, they were loyal to the pope. Gradually, however, colonists became disenchanted with royal administration. Eventually, after grievances accumulated, most politically aware Mexicans welcomed a clean break with both royal administration and the monarchy.

The Crown's 1767 expulsion of the Jesuits irreparably damaged elite loyalty to the mother country. Of the 680 Jesuits expelled from Mexico, about 450 were Mexican. Their life-long exile caused resentment not only among themselves but among the families and sympathizers they left behind. For the first time, the viceroy required a formally organized army to suppress the violent protests that the expulsion provoked.[2]

In most instances, inefficiency, incapacity, and corruption permitted early eighteenth-century Creoles considerable flexibility, autonomy, and even a modicum of self-government. The 1786 creation of intendancies directly targeted local officials and their illegal, but widely tolerated, commercial monopolies. The Bourbon state regarded the ending of Creole participation and its corollary, government by compromise, as necessary steps toward control and revival. Residents of New Spain perceived these same measures as the issuance of non-negotiable demands from an imperial state. As historian John Lynch commented, "To creoles this was not reform."[3]

In the short term, royal agents successfully fulfilled their goal of increasing colonial revenue. The Bourbons increased the *alcabala* from 4 percent to 6 percent and tapped new revenue sources, such as the tobacco monopoly. New taxes were placed on various commodities such as grains, cattle, and distilled beverages (*aguardiente*). Tax collection increased from an average of 6.5 million pesos annually during the 1760s to 17.7 million pesos in the 1790s, as growth in mining, commerce, and the internal market enlarged the tax base. Between 1779 and 1820, the cost of trade restrictions and taxes equaled 7.2 percent of Mexico's income. In 1775, British colonialism only cost its North American colonies 0.3 percent of their income.[4]

Even contemporary observers felt that taxes had exceeded the prudent level. Humboldt reported that New Spain contributed ten times as much revenue to Spain, on a per capita basis, as India did to Britain. These taxes fell upon all social groups.[5]

For Spain, trade policy provided revenue, protected Spanish industry and influential merchants, and ensured that the colonies remained a part of the empire. In 1794, Viceroy Revillagigedo commented on this last function:

> It should not be forgotten that this is a colony which must depend on its mother country, Spain, and must yield her some benefit because of the protection it receives from her; and thus great skill is needed to cement this dependence and to make the interest mutual and reciprocal; for dependence would cease once European manufactures and products were not needed here.[6]

Creoles resented economic restrictions, such as the prohibition on producing paper, which protected Spanish producers. Except in colonies such as Cuba and Venezuela, which could produce export crops, landowners received little benefit from Bourbon trade reforms. Lowered trade barriers hurt Mexico's relatively unsophisticated manufacturers. By 1810, European imports were competing with textiles produced in Querétaro and Puebla. Finally, Spanish trade policy failed to recognize that Mexican mining, agriculture, and commerce had few economically rational links to Spain. The mother country could not supply the American market nor could it absorb goods produced in the New World. As historian Colin MacLachlan noted, "American economies could not be sustained by an obsolete trading system regardless of how it was reformed."[7]

Military forces in Mexico were largely recruited locally and sustained by local taxes. Not surprisingly, this drain on resources created resentment. The defense strategy deemed most cost-effective—a cadre of Spanish officers who trained Mexican soldiers—inevitably produced resentment, as Spaniards filled top posts. Between 1798 and 1800, of the thirteen colonels and lieutenant colonels in New Spain's regular army, only one had been born in Mexico. Spaniards stationed in Mexico acted as an arrogant occupation force. Thanks to the *fuero*, all military personal had the right to be tried in courts martial, even in civil matters.[8]

Compulsory military service created still more resentment. Few felt any interest in Spain's conflicts with European powers. Poorly paid soldiers often could not afford to bring their families with them when they were transferred. Militiamen lived in mortal fear of being sent to garrison duty in Veracruz and having to face the threat of yellow fever. Soldiers feared death from this disease, known as *vómito negro*, more than death in combat. Volunteers for military service were never sufficient.[9]

Economic growth under the Bourbons did not translate into improved living standards for the majority of Mexicans. Higher taxes and the concentration of income left little for the majority. Cash crops increasingly relegated corn farming to marginal lands, while the population increased from 4.48 million in 1790 to 6.12 million in 1810. Not surprisingly, agricultural prices rose 50 per cent between 1780 and 1811. Food, housing, and clothing all increased in price more rapidly than wages after the 1780s.[10]

As large estates devoured increasing amounts of land and the population increased, the rural poor were caught in a Malthusian vice. Population increase led to an oversupply of rural labor, which resulted in a 25 percent decrease in the buying power of wages between 1775 and independence. This produced a steady migration of unskilled workers to cities, especially to Mexico City. In 1786, Viceroy Bernardo de Gálvez declared that the many beggars, vagabonds, and unemployed in Mexico City threatened religion, the state, and public tranquillity.[11]

FROM BAD TO WORSE

Repeated changes in Spanish shipping policy, a result of Spain's nearly constant wars, added to resentment in the New World. From 1793 to 1795, Spain fought France in a futile attempt to reverse the French Revolution. In addition, Spain and England were at war for most of the years from 1796 to 1807.[12]

When Spain and Britain were at war, the British fleet blockaded Spain's ports, cutting off trade with Spanish America. Its ships would attack Spanish ships after they left Veracruz. In 1797, to allow its colonies to export and receive supplies, the Spanish Crown allowed trade with neutral countries. Two years later, it prohibited trade with neutrals, claiming such trade only benefited Britain. In 1804, war again interrupted shipping, and Spain again permitted trade with neutrals.[13]

The high cost of war between 1793 and 1808 and the loss of trade and bullion shipped from the colonies contributed to Spanish decline. By 1808, the Spanish fleet had been largely destroyed in battle, and colonial trade increasingly benefited neutral shippers, rather than Spanish merchants and manufacturers. The interruptions in shipping devastated the Mexican mining industry. As the stocks of mercury imported from Spain were exhausted, many silver mines suspended operations. Allowing neutral nations to trade with its colonies put Spain in a no-win situation. Consumers benefited from obtaining inexpensive imports. Producers could get exports to market. However, both groups were then reluctant to accept the reimposition of trade restrictions after the restoration of peace.[14]

In 1804, to ease its war-induced financial woes, the Crown ordered that all debts owed to the Mexican Church should be repaid immediately and that the funds collected should be sent to Spain. Abad y Queipo estimated that credit extended by the Church totaled 44 million pesos, two-thirds of Mexican capital in active circulation—money used to pay salaries and grow crops. He predicted the withdrawal of this capital would severely damage agriculture, mining, and commerce. Less than a week after the publication of the decree, the Mexico City government declared the measure "totally impractical," since "it would inevitably bring ruin to these dominions and cause enormous damage to the state." The Crown's desperate need for funds caused it to ignore such warnings.[15]

Spanish officials had assumed that the decree, known as the Consolidation Decree, would have an effect comparable to that of a similar 1798 decree issued in Spain, where the Church owned large tracts of property. However, unlike in Spain, where 90 percent of church wealth was invested in real estate and only 10 percent was liquid, in New Spain only 12 percent was invested in real estate, and the rest was liquid. Church loans financed the operations of New Spain's 200,000 entrepreneurs, only 5 percent of whom operated entirely with their own capital.[16]

The Consolidation Decree damaged the interests of miners, *hacendados*, merchants, and artisans who operated on borrowed capital. Many businesses were closed as buildings were seized and sold at auction. Medium-sized and small landowners who could not obtain cash to liquidate debts suffered the most. They were forced to sell their houses, *ranchos*, and haciendas to repay loans just when others' sales had caused the value of real estate to decline by half. The decree devastated schools, hospitals, and social welfare institutions, such as orphanages, which income from Church investment had sustained. It also embittered the lower clergy, since many of its members lived on interest from chaplaincies and loaned capital. Commenting on the European conflict that motivated the Consolidation Decree, Mexican priest Fray Servando Teresa de Mier lamented: "The war is more cruel for us than for Spain, and is ultimately waged with our money. We simply need to stay neutral to be happy."[17]

In 1808, Napoleon sent French troops into Spain to further his imperial ambitions. He forced King Fernando VII off the throne and imprisoned him in France. He then installed his own brother Joseph to replace the Spanish monarch. In Spain, various groups, or "juntas," sprang up to fight Napoleon's forces. They claimed that in the absence of the king, they were the true representatives of the Spanish nation. For a brief period the invasion of Spain united New Spain, as its residents, regardless of which side of the Atlantic they had been born on, rallied around the deposed Fernando and declared their opposition to the French occupation of the Mother Country.[18]

Soon representatives of different juntas began arriving in Mexico seeking funds to finance the struggle of their respective juntas, each of which was fighting for the restoration of Fernando.

Figure 6.1
Father Miguel Hidalgo

Source: Reproduced courtesy of the Benson Latin American Collection, the University of Texas at Austin

Two commissioners from the Seville junta appeared in Mexico City and declared that the Seville junta represented all of Spain and demanded that authorities in Mexico should recognize it as the legitimate government.[19]

To fill the power vacuum in Mexico, a junta central, composed of Viceroy José de Iturrigaray, the archbishop, members of the Mexico City government, various other administrators and distinguished persons including representatives from Puebla and Jalapa, began meeting in Mexico City. The junta confirmed its support for Iturrigaray and announced that it would only subordinate itself to a junta in Spain that was appointed by Fernando. Since he was a prisoner in France, that was tantamount to saying the junta in Mexico City would manage New Spain's affairs until such time as the Spanish monarch returned to the throne.[20]

Creoles who convened the Mexico City junta operated on the premise that Mexico was not a colony of Spain, but a kingdom co-equal to Spain under the monarchy. They reasoned that with the monarch absent, the link uniting Spain and New Spain ceased to exist.[21]

Spaniards in Mexico did their best to quash notions that Mexicans might assume sovereignty. On August 27, 1808, the Inquisition declared any theory that sovereignty resided in the corporations or the people at large to be heretical. The *audiencia* claimed that the declarations by members of the Mexico City municipal government that sovereignty was based on a pact between the governed and the monarch only served as a smokescreen for their desired independence.[22]

Many Spanish-born people believed that Iturrigaray's cooperation with the junta indicated that he sought to separate Mexico from Spain. No evidence has been found to support that assumption, but that did not prevent Spaniards from acting on it. The two commissioners who had come to demand loyalty to the Seville junta encouraged their fellow countrymen in Mexico City to take action.[23]

Shortly after midnight on September 16, 1808, wealthy Spanish *hacendado* Gabriel de Yermo assembled a force numbering roughly 300. It was largely composed of immigrant Spanish merchants who swept into the viceregal palace and arrested Iturrigaray. The coup enjoyed the support of the archbishop of Mexico, *consulado* members, representatives of the Inquisition, and justices of the *audiencia*, almost all of whom were Spaniards. The plotters also imprisoned the leading figures in the municipal government. The audiencia then appointed seventy-seven-year old Field Marshal Pedro Garibay as viceroy and sent Iturrigaray back to Spain to face trial for treason.[24]

Garibay immediately recognized the junta in Seville as the legitimate ruler of Mexico. In doing this, he made a giant intellectual leap. Creoles had asserted that if the monarch was absent, Mexicans were Mexico's sovereign. Garibay's recognition of the Seville junta, however, asserted that the absence of the monarch justified a self-proclaimed ruling junta of Spaniards becoming Mexico's sovereign.[25]

The coup against Iturrigaray reminded Creoles of their secondary status. They chaffed under successive viceroys, whom, after 1808, they viewed as illegal, even according to Spanish norms. The coup closed the possibility of obtaining independence as the elite wanted it—a change only in relations between elite groups, without popular participation or violence. In the short run, the coup was a success, since it halted the slide toward Creole autonomy. However, in the long run, the coup destroyed what survived of the mystique surrounding Spanish power. It became even clearer that naked force, not the divine right of kings, formed the basis of Spanish rule.[26]

THE HIDALGO REVOLT, 1810–1811

In May 1810, Abad y Queipo predicted a colonial revolt due to colonial grievances and the "electric" example of the French Revolution. He urged the Crown to appoint an enlightened military man as viceroy and that competent military officers, field cannons, cannon balls, and grapeshot also be sent to Mexico.[27]

This warning indicated Abad y Queipo's prescience, since, unbeknownst to him, residents of the Bajío, northwest of Mexico City were plotting to free Mexico. The Bajío, a vast high plain in the state of Guanajuato, had become one of the most prosperous and densely populated areas in Mexico. The population of the Bajío, which contained few Spaniards or traditional Indian villages, was more socially mobile than the Mexican population as a whole. Its mixed economy, based on mining, herding, manufacturing, farming, and artisanal production, was the most developed in New Spain. Mining created a demand for both manufactured goods and agricultural products.[28]

Upon visiting the Bajío, Humboldt observed:

> In Mexico the best cultivated fields, those which recall to the mind of the traveler the beautiful plains of France, are those which extend from Salamanca towards Silao, Guanaxuato, and the Villa of Leon, and which surround the richest mines of the known world.[29]

The 1810 conspirators met regularly in Querétaro, 125 miles northwest of Mexico City, under the guise of attending a literary society. The most distinguished conspirator was Miguel Domínguez, from an elite local family, who served as the *corregidor* of Querétaro. Other conspirators included his wife, Josefa Ortiz de Domínguez ("La Corregidora"), and various lawyers, military officers, and commercial and religious figures. Neither members of the central elite nor the poor joined the Querétaro conspiracy. The conspirators hoped to strike a quick blow against the Spanish, that is, do to the Spanish what they had done to Iturrigaray. The planned uprising was initially set for December.[30]

Miguel Hidalgo, one of the conspirators, served as the priest of Dolores, a Bajío town of 15,000. Hidalgo, the son of a hacienda manager, read prohibited books and loved wine, dance, and other worldly pleasures. He served as a one-man community development project promoting tanning, carpentry, beekeeping, the weaving of wool, and the production of silk, pottery, tiles, and wine. In addition, he produced theater, sometimes his own translations of French works. In 1804, after the recall of Church loans, the Crown temporarily seized and rented out Hidalgo's small hacienda to generate income to repay the 7,000 pesos he owed.[31]

Spanish authorities, who received a report concerning the 1810 plot, sent officials to arrest the conspirators. After arriving in Querétaro, they jailed La Corregidora to prevent information leaks. However, she managed to get word to her jailer, a fellow conspirator, who sent riders off, Paul Revere style, to warn other plotters.[32]

Upon learning that the Spanish were coming, Hidalgo decided to launch the rebellion immediately. Evidently he had not been a driving force behind the plot up to this point. Early on the morning of September 16, 1810, he issued his famous Grito de Dolores (Cry of Dolores), which set Mexico into rebellion. There are almost as many versions of what he said as there are historians. Some claim Hidalgo only attacked Spanish misrule; others saw his revolt as favoring Fernando VII against France; while still others saw it as a call for complete independence.[33]

The people of Dolores immediately rallied behind Hidalgo, who freed and armed the seventy prisoners in the town jail. He next ordered the newly freed prisoners to arrest and jail all Spaniards in the town. Hidalgo's hastily gathered throng of urban and rural workers armed with lances, machetes, rakes, slings, and sticks then set out to liberate Mexico. This force first marched to San Miguel el Grande (today San Miguel de Allende), twenty-four miles away. On the way they passed Atotonilco, a frequent destination for religious pilgrimages. There they appropriated an image of the Virgin of Guadalupe and mounted it on a pole, creating a standard. The Virgin became the symbol of the insurgency and a potent force for mobilizing support for the independence cause.[34]

Many working in the fields joined the insurgency as Hidalgo's force passed. Their standard of living had fallen, and they were suffering from unaccustomed insecurity and famine. The participation of local leaders, such as Hidalgo, indicated splits in the elite that would open a role for the masses. The obvious enrichment of local landowners who produced cash crops added to the anger of the majority.[35]

Hidalgo's force took San Miguel el Grande, the home of fellow conspirator Ignacio Allende, without firing a shot. There the contradictions within the movement became apparent. Indians and mestizos began looting the town despite the efforts of Hidalgo and Allende—a wealthy Creole who had served as the captain of a Spanish cavalry regiment—to stop them. The insurgents spent two days in San Miguel gaining additional recruits.

The rebels then marched south, took Celaya, and turned back north toward Guanajuato. As Alamán commented, "In each village, Father Hidalgo needed only to appear in order to recruit the masses."[36]

On September 28, the insurgents, 20,000 strong, arrived at Guanajuato, a mining center of 60,000. For six days, Juan Antonio Riaño, the city's Spanish intendant, had trained militia forces and organized the digging of defensive trenches. However, at the last minute he lost his nerve and ordered wealthy Spaniards and Creoles to take refuge in La Alhóndiga, a fortress-like granary. An observer noted that those taking refuge in the granary brought with them "money, silver bars, precious jewels, the most valuable goods from their chests, trunks of clothes, gold and diamond jewelry, and other valuables from their homes."[37]

Miners and prisoners freed from the local jail joined the rebels. Riaño's decision to take refuge in La Alhóndiga intensified the class nature of the struggle, since he allowed only the wealthy inside the granary. Five hours after the insurgents attacked, they broke through the doors, killing men, women, and children and making off with clothing, bullion, and jewelry. Hidalgo's men killed at least 300 Spaniards in the granary and during the subsequent looting of the city. For Hidalgo, this was a Pyrrhic victory, since the looting and brutality ended any chance of his gaining widespread Creole support.[38]

Hidalgo's 70,000-man force then marched to Valladolid (today Morelia), took it on October 17 without firing a shot, and looted it. The disorderly crowd that formed Hidalgo's army filed through the streets shouting, "Long live the Virgin of Guadalupe," and "Death to the Spaniards." The officers, many of whom had defected from the royalist army, commanded poorly armed and poorly dressed peasants. At this stage of the rebellion, the insurgency had the festive air of a pilgrimage.[39]

Until this point, the independence movement had been in the hands of Creoles, who wanted only to replace the Spaniard with the Creole, leaving the social and economic structure unchanged. However, the Indians and mestizos had other ideas. Alamán described what happened as Hidalgo's force passed haciendas:

> The Indians would fan out into the cornfields and take the corn. They broke open granaries. The grain inside soon vanished. The shops, found on most haciendas, were stripped down to the beams. Killing all the oxen was de rigueur. If there happened to be an Indian village nearby, even the hacienda buildings were destroyed, so the beams and doors could be taken to the village.[40]

On October 29, the insurgents occupied Toluca. Hidalgo's force of some 80,000, the largest army assembled in Mexico since Aztec times, continued east. As the insurgents approached Mexico City, they met their first major resistance from royalist forces in the Battle of Monte de Las Cruces. A force of 2,500 well disciplined royalists with artillery almost held Hidalgo's force off. Finally after heavy losses on both sides, the insurgents surrounded the royalists. The royalists then fought their way out of the encirclement, and their badly mauled force retreated to Mexico City.[41]

Instead of proceeding on to take Mexico City, Hidalgo paused at the battle site for three days and then ordered his army back to the west. This decision remains one of the most controversial in Mexican history and probably resulted from the insurgents' lack of ammunition, the strength of Mexico City's royalist garrison, the approach of royalist reinforcements from the north, and the weakness of Hidalgo's own poorly trained army. Hidalgo may also have feared his army would loot Mexico City.[42]

The failure of Indians living in the area to support the insurgency may also have deterred Hidalgo. In central Mexico, outside the Valley of Mexico, strong paternalistic ties remained between Indian laborers and *hacendados* who employed them. They considered *hacendados* as benefactors, not exploiters. Villages there, which retained substantial amounts of land, continued to accept the status quo.[43]

Hidalgo also failed to attract Mexico City's artisans, since after the looting of Guanajuato, they correctly judged him to be the leader of a peasant-based movement favoring rural interests. Since half of his 80,000-man force had either been killed at the Battle of Monte de Las Cruces or had deserted, Hidalgo desperately needed new recruits.[44]

Despite massive military spending after 1762, the viceroy had virtually no forces he could mobilize against the rebels. On October 2, Brigadier Félix Calleja, the royalist commander in San Luis Potosí, wrote the intendant of Puebla: "My troops are short in numbers and of the same quality as yours. I lack artillery, infantry officers, and I am in a country so undermined by sedition that I cannot abandon it without exposing it."[45]

Rather than wringing his hands, Calleja energetically began forming units, collecting arms, and requisitioning provisions. Only on October 24 did he march south with 3,000 cavalry, 600 infantry, and four cannons founded during the weeks after the rebellion began. Calleja mainly drew his men from the cattle estates of San Luis Potosí. Since these estates offered secure employment, employees there remained loyal to landowners and the Crown.[46]

On November 7, soon after the insurgents turned west, their 40,000-man army met Calleja's force at Aculco. When confronted by the royalist force, the rebels panicked and fled the battlefield, abandoning most of their artillery and supplies. The royalists at Aculco were not seasoned troops, just better disciplined and better armed than Hidalgo's.

The defeat at Aculco forced Hidalgo to the west. His force paused briefly in Valladolid. While there, the rebels marched small groups of Spaniards out of the city daily to be executed. The rebels then continued west to Guadalajara, which had already been taken by the rebel leader José Torres.[47]

Hidalgo remained in Guadalajara from November 26, 1810, to January 14, 1811. While there, the insurgents established a rudimentary government, murdered many of the Spanish who fell into their hands, and rebuilt their army. The insurgents again found an ample supply of recruits. The hinterland surrounding Guadalajara had been subject to the same sudden commercial pressure that the Bajío had. After 1750, many villages had lost their access to land, which the elite used to grow cash crops for the Guadalajara market. This market demanded ever more produce to feed the city's mushrooming population.[48]

After Aculco, Calleja also turned west, taking San Miguel, Dolores, and Guanajuato. In retaliation for the rebels killing so many Spaniards in Guanajuato, Calleja ordered the execution of sixty-nine Mexicans for having collaborated with the rebels. Calleja soon found that counter-insurgency presented far more of a challenge than simply reoccupying cities. He commented, "The insurrection is far from calm, it returns like the hydra, in proportion to the number of times its head is cut off."[49]

In zones supporting the rebels, royalist commanders stripped villages, haciendas, and ranches of horses, arms, and weapons, including small kitchen knives. They rounded up all blacksmiths and destroyed forges, which could be used to make lance points and other weapons. Royalists shot individuals apprehended with arms who could not produce proper documents or who acted suspiciously. Their bodies were displayed at the point of execution. Such tactics terrorized some people into compliance, while others became even more implacable foes of the regime.[50]

When he learned of Calleja's approach, Hidalgo ordered his army out to meet the royalists. The insurgents had 80 cannons, 3,500 soldiers, 2,000 mounted ranch hands armed with lances, and 50,000 Indians on foot with lances, slings, and bows and arrows. Calleja commanded 6,000 men, mostly cavalry, and had ten cannons. The battle near the Puente de Calderón (Calderón Bridge) lasted all day, January 11, 1811, and involved hard fighting on both sides. The royalists finally managed to fight their way up onto the high ground occupied by the insurgents, at which point Hidalgo's force fled. Historian Christon Archer remarked, concerning both Aculco and Calderón: "The insurgent commanders committed the tragic error of believing that they could engage in conventional battle with the royalist army. They lacked the arms, leaders, and discipline." This defeat ended the threat to the Crown posed by Hidalgo.[51]

With their force in disarray, Hidalgo and Allende retreated north through Aguascalientes and Saltillo. Feeling Hidalgo had bungled the military campaign, the rebels stripped him of his military command, but kept him as a figurehead. This reflected the conflict between Hidalgo and Allende, who, as a military officer, had consistently advocated the use of a smaller, more disciplined force. Subsequent observers have seconded Allende's judgment, noting that Hidalgo lacked an overall military strategy and did not carry out tactical maneuvers in battle. His inexperienced generals had neither seen combat nor studied military tactics.[52]

While the initial leaders of the movement fled north, many others, inspired by Hidalgo's example, continued to fight. They did not attempt to confront the royalist forces directly, but carried out fragmented, regionalized campaigns. Rebels so intimidated the Spanish in Zacatecas that many of them, including the intendant, simply fled.[53]

On March 21, 1811, north of Saltillo, royalists captured the remnants of the insurgent army as its leaders attempted to reach the United States and obtain sanctuary and support. A former rebel officer, who had been angered by his failure to receive a promotion, facilitated the capture.[54]

Royalists shot several hundred of the captured rebels and condemned others to *presidios* or assigned them to labor in haciendas and mines. Royalists took Hidalgo to Chihuahua, where a court composed of four Spaniards and five Creoles tried him. Members of the court unanimously voted to execute him. Authorities placed his head, Allende's head, and those of two other executed rebels in metal cages on the granary in Guanajuato as a warning to potential rebels.[55]

While a prisoner, Hidalgo signed a highly controversial repentance, which included the following:

> I see the desolation of these lands which I have caused, the destruction of property, the many orphans which I have left, and the blood which has flowed with such profusion and temerity. The souls of many of those who followed me dwell in the abyss.[56]

While he did sign the statement of repentance, possibly under duress, Hidalgo never stated he regretted having furthered the cause of independence, only the means used to reach that goal. As has since been argued, these means might have done more harm than good for the independence cause.[57]

The lack of written manifestos makes it difficult to know exactly what sort of society Hidalgo and his associates envisioned. To further confuse matters, leaders of the movement attempted to conceal their intentions. Allende provides an example of such deceit. He wrote Hidalgo on August 31, 1810:

> We decided to work with our intentions carefully concealed, since if the movement was openly revolutionary, it would not be supported by the general mass of the people. . . . Since Indians are indifferent to the word "liberty," it is necessary to make them believe the uprising is being carried out only on behalf of Fernando VII.[58]

It is also difficult for modern readers to interpret the insurgents' declarations since "Mexico" is a post-independence construct. At the dawn of the nineteenth century, the area now forming Mexico was a conglomeration of cities, towns, and Indian villages with no clearly defined northern or southern boundary. Similarly the term "independence" is ambiguous, since some used it to refer to Mexican independence from Spain, while others used it to refer to the Spanish empire's independence from France and Great Britain. At the time, "independence" was also used to refer to "autonomy."[59]

Hidalgo and his close allies had hoped for a Creole coup, but failed to attract sufficient military support for that. Hidalgo praised Fernando VII and condemned Spaniards and the French, declaring them to be enemies of God and humanity. Religion would serve as the major justification of the revolution, not Enlightenment ideals.[60]

Hidalgo issued several reformist decrees, which increased his lower-class following. On October 19, 1810, he decreed the abolition of slavery and threatened those not emancipating slaves with the death penalty. The next month, he decreed an end to the tribute paid by Indians and mulattos and abolished the monopoly on tobacco and gunpowder production. In December, he abrogated existing agreements for the rental of Indian land, since renters often used such agreements to usurp Indian holdings. Hidalgo never controlled sufficient territory to implement these policies. Nor did he ever issue decrees dealing with such basic issues as wages and land ownership.[61]

Hidalgo relied on a mass-based movement that he could not or would not discipline. He and his subordinates had no way of anticipating that his rebellion against Spanish rule would become a

D. JOSÉ MARIA MORELOS Y PABON, nació en la ciudad de Valladolid el 30 de Set.e de 1765
y murió fusilado en S. Cristobal Ecatepec el 21 de Diciembre de 1815
V. de Murguia é hijos

Figure 6.2
José María Morelos

Source: Reproduced courtesy of the Benson Latin American Collection, the University of Texas at Austin

race war that threatened both the Creoles and others who aspired to replace the Spanish. Arousing Indians to revolt and placing all property and established social relations in jeopardy drove Spaniards and Creoles alike into the royalist camp. Hidalgo condoned pillaging by his forces and the murder of numerous Spanish prisoners as a legitimate means to attract new peasant recruits and retain his followers.[62]

Had Hidalgo concentrated solely on independence and guaranteed the lives and property of Creoles and Spaniards, he would doubtlessly have won. Calleja, who later served as viceroy, commented:

> This vast kingdom weighs too heavily upon an insubstantial metropolis; its natives and even the Europeans themselves are convinced of the advantages that would result from an independent government; and if the absurd insurrection of Hidalgo had been built upon this base, it seems to me as I now look at it, that it would have met with little opposition.[63]

Hidalgo presents historians with sharply conflicting images, just as the slave-owning Thomas Jefferson as an advocate of democracy does. Historians on both sides of the Rio Grande have criticized Hidalgo. For example, Mexican historian and politician Lorenzo de Zavala (1788–1836) wrote: "He operated without a plan, a system, or a fixed objective. Viva la Señora de Guadalupe was the only basis of his campaign; the national flag on which her image was printed, his code of law and institutions."[64]

THE MORELOS REBELLION, 1811–1815

The executions of Hidalgo and Allende shifted the focus of the insurgency to southern Mexico. There, José María Morelos y Pavón, a priest from Carácuaro, a backwater, hot-country village in Michoacán, led the struggle. Morelos, the mixed-race son of a carpenter, came from more humble origins than the original leaders of the rebellion. He had worked for years as a mule driver before entering the priesthood at age thirty-two. This experience gave him an intimate knowledge of southern Mexican terrain.[65]

Morelos, a former student of Hidalgo's, met with him as the rebel army marched east toward Toluca and then joined the insurgents. Hidalgo ordered him south, where he proved to be an astute guerrilla leader. The social programs he proposed went beyond Hidalgo's. Morelos called for racial equality, declaring, "Slavery will be forbidden forever, as well as caste distinctions, leaving everyone equal, and the only thing that will distinguish one American from another is vice and virtue." Morelos's emancipation proclamation facilitated his recruiting the large Afro-Mexican population in his area of operations.[66]

Morelos absolved Creoles of paying debts to Spaniards, but left unaffected debts owed by Spaniards to Creoles. He said agriculture should be

> based on many cultivating small plots separately, with their own industry and labor, with no one individual having large expanses of unused land and enslaving thousands to work that land which was cultivated.[67]

The rebellion reached its high point between 1812 and 1814, with insurgents operating over much of southern and western Mexico. During these years, rebels felt they could destroy the colonial government by conquering increasing amounts of territory and establishing civil administration in the areas they controlled.[68]

Both sides followed a scorched-earth policy that destroyed substantial wealth. The insurgents burned haciendas, looted towns, and drove off cattle in areas supporting the Crown. The royalists, in turn, burned villages and crops in areas supporting the insurgents. Alamán reported that every day in the early months of 1814 an average of twenty-five insurgents, or suspected insurgents, faced firing squads. Many Spanish officers excelled at counterinsurgency, since they had been guerrillas during the Spanish struggle against the French. Royalist officers recognized that effective counterinsurgency demanded mobility, speed, and flexibility. They combined the use of exemplary terror and "flying detachments," which chased down and punished guerrilla bands and the civilian population that supported the insurgency. The royalist captain general of Nueva Galicia, Brigadier José de la Cruz, wrote in April 1811: "We must spread terror and death everywhere so that not a single perverted soul remains in the land . . . These bandits will learn what war to the death really means." Despite the terror, the royalists found that the traditional social ties and habits of obedience, once broken, could not be reestablished.[69]

Morelos's small army, which never exceeded 6,000 men, attacked swiftly and then vanished in classic guerrilla style. In coastal areas, Morelos's ability to recruit blacks and mulattos who were already skilled with firearms contributed to his success. Morelos energetically suppressed any outbreak of looting or racial warfare. The insurgents had learned that they could not challenge disciplined royalist units in conventional battles, and so there were no battles such as occurred at Aculco.[70]

By the end of 1812, the insurgents controlled territory stretching north from the Isthmus of Tehuantepec to Acapulco (under siege) and toward Veracruz, Puebla, and Mexico City. In November of that year, the rebels had taken Oaxaca. Morelos's mountainous domain provided an ideal location for waging guerrilla war. It contained a large Indian and mixed-race population and few Creoles.[71]

During 1813, the rebels consolidated their gains. However, the following year, a royalist offensive penetrated deep into rebel territory and recaptured Oaxaca, Chilpancingo, and Acapulco. In addition, the rebels lost key leaders. Other rebel leaders began to act independently of Morelos.[72]

In an attempt to unite the scattered insurgent groups and to project a favorable image to Creoles outside rebel territory, insurgent leaders convened a Congress on September 14, 1813, at Chilpancingo, the capital of the modern state of Guerrero. At its inauguration, Morelos declared that indigenous leaders such as Montezuma, who had resisted Cortés, were national heroes. He linked Montezuma and the independence movement, referring to the latter as "the auspicious movement in which your illustrious children have gathered to revenge the outrages and abuses committed against you and free ourselves from the grasp of the tyranny . . . ." The unelected Congress never actually legislated. Given the military situation, elections could be held for only two of its members, while the rest were appointed to represent areas where the rebels could not hold elections.[73]

On November 6, 1813, the Congress issued a declaration of independence, definitively laying to rest the notion that the rebels were fighting for Fernando VII. In social matters, the Congress generally ratified the decrees Morelos had already issued concerning the abolition of class distinctions, slavery, and tribute.[74]

The Congress did write a constitution, which it promulgated on October 22, 1814, at Apatzingán, where it had been forced to move by royalist forces. The constitution declared all Mexicans to be legally equal and divided powers into executive, legislative, and judicial. The drafters' fear of absolutism led them to grant the legislative branch the power to choose a three-man executive and appoint justices of the supreme court. The document resembled the Spanish constitution in that it declared the Catholic Church as the official and only religion of Mexico. Given that the rebellion was in decline by the time of its promulgation, the constitution never served as the law of the land.

Despite Morelos's efforts to prop up a civilian administration, the Congress never managed to unite the scores of guerrilla bands and military satrapies resisting the colonial regime. Rather than enhancing the rebels' stature, it weakened them by introducing politics, debate, and divisions within rebel ranks and by weakening Morelos's position.[75]

During 1815, the rebel Congress spent much of its time fleeing from one small town to another to avoid royalist troops. In the fall of that year, Congress members decided to seek refuge among rebel forces in the Puebla–Veracruz area east of Mexico City, feeling that would facilitate the rebels' communications with groups abroad. In November, royalists captured Morelos while he was fighting a rearguard action to protect the Congress during its move.[76]

The Inquisition tried Morelos on twenty-six charges, which included: 1) carrying out priestly functions after being excommunicated; 2) attacking the king and his ministers; 3) executing prisoners; 4) possibly being tainted with atheism for espousing principles of anti-Catholic authors and of the U.S. Constitution; 5) imitating Luther and other heretics in criticizing the Church; and 6) sending his thirteen-year-old son to the United States, where, it noted, there was religious toleration. The indictment declared that Morelos's low birth *(baja extracción)* aggravated the charges. The court convicted Morelos on all counts, defrocked him, and sentenced him to death.[77]

While Morelos showed tactical brilliance, he did commit one strategic mistake—the prolonged siege of Acapulco in the summer of 1813. Hit-and-run attacks on mule trains would have effectively interrupted shipping from that port. Instead, by tying up his men there for months until he finally took the city, he gave the royalists time to regroup in the north, receive reinforcements from Spain, and then turn south from a position of strength that he could never overcome.[78]

Morelos and Hidalgo failed to impose twentieth-century values on a colonial, politically underdeveloped, conservative society. As with Hidalgo, Morelos failed to attract substantial Creole support, even though he sought such support by preventing peasant land-takeovers, which would have alienated wealthy Creoles, and by promising to respect property and give Creoles high military and civil posts. Morelos's elimination of racial categories and his proclaiming the right of Indians and peasants to land prevented Creoles from embracing his cause. Even though Morelos retained control of his army, Creoles did not trust it. A royalist soldier held prisoner by Morelos commented on the social background of his force: "None of them came from a decent family . . . there are Indians, Negroes, mulattos, and delinquents, fugitives from their homelands." The issues Hidalgo and Morelos raised would not be seriously addressed until a century later in the Mexican Revolution.[79]

HEARTS AND MINDS

Even before the Spanish could seize the military initiative, they acted to quell the rebellion. In October 1810, without waiting for permission from Spain, Viceroy Francisco Javier de Venegas, who had taken office only forty-eight hours before Hidalgo launched his rebellion, abolished tribute for Indians and those of mixed race. He ordered that the decree abolishing tribute be published in Nahuatl, as well as Spanish, so that the literate Indian elite could read it in their own language. Publishing the decree in Nahuatl to reach out to the indigenous community reversed a 1770 ban on the official use of Nahuatl and other Indian languages, implemented in the name of Bourbon efficiency.[80]

The Church also entered the fray. On September 24, 1810, Bishop-elect of Michoacán Abad y Queipo declared Hidalgo and three other rebel leaders excommunicated. The Church automatically excommunicated all who joined the rebellion after that date. Abad y Queipo justified the excommunications by declaring that the rebels were "violators of public order, seducers of the people, sacrilegious perjurers who merited the highest level of excommunication: *Siquis Suadente Diábolo*." He also declared it sacrilege to use the Virgin of Guadalupe to promote insurrection.[81]

The church hierarchy consistently backed the royalist cause. The Archbishop of Mexico declared Hidalgo the "precursor of the Antichrist." In 1816, when it became apparent that Spanish American rebellions would continue, Pope Pius VII issued the encyclical *Etsi longissimo,* which urged bishops and clergy in Spanish America to inform the faithful of the dreadful consequences of rebellion against legitimate authority.[82]

Hidalgo responded to Abad y Queipo's charges, noting that had he not attempted

> to liberate our country from the great evils which afflict it, and from even worse misfortunes which are about to befall it, I would never have been accused of heresy. . . The oppressors reacted by excommunicating us. However, they are well aware that the excommunications serve to frighten the unwary and terrorize the ignorant, and sow fear of excommunication, even though there is no reason to be afraid . . . Do they really feel that one cannot be a true Catholic if one is not subject to Spanish despotism?[83]

Initially, royalists controlled all the printing presses in the country. Royalists used them to print appeals to Catholicism, to urge support for the restored monarchy (after 1814), to call for harmony in a society produced by the intermarriage of Creoles and Spanish, and to emphasize the shared social and economic interests of the colonial elite. By modern standards, the propaganda lacked subtlety. The title page of an 1813 collection of Abad y Queipo's works stated that the book had been published

> to further the general welfare of New Spain and the happiness of its inhabitants, especially the Indians and castas, and to expose the atrocious calumnies that have been published by insurgent ringleaders, in order to make them odious to the public, and to refute, by this means, writings that have been published since the start of the insurrection. [84]

When royalists addressed those of European descent, they claimed non-whites threatened to destroy society. In other cases, they made broad appeals to racial unity. In one appeal, Agustín Pomposo Fernández, one of the most skillful of royalist pamphleteers, wrote:

> All of us, Spaniards, Indians, castas, are a single nation, of a single religion, of a single society, of a single family governed by a single prince. We are now one with the Spaniards born in the Old World. . . . There is no position or honor, however elevated it may be, that cannot be achieved by a loyal Indian or even the son of an Indian man and a Spanish woman or the son of a Spaniard and an Indian woman.[85]

Pro-Spanish priests manned most of the pulpits and often formed the principal source of information for their parishioners. The Spanish exercised control of the presses, the paper supply, and the pulpits in the Valley of Mexico. This also limited support for Hidalgo, even after his victory at Monte de las Cruces.[86]

The royalists required people to obtain official permission to change residence. New dependants, servants, or guests could only be admitted to households after notifying officials and providing an explanation. Residents could not spend more than two days away from home without permission, and innkeepers had to compile lists of their guests. Government-issued (G.I.) passports attempted to limit movement to those authorized to travel. However, the number of merchants requiring passports overwhelmed local bureaucracies, and shipments of blank printed passports on their way to regional officials repeatedly fell into insurgent hands. Government officials further undermined the passport system by supplying rebels with passports due to their sympathizing with them or receiving bribes from them.[87]

After capturing a printing press in Guadalajara, the rebels launched their own propaganda effort. There they published six issues of the newspaper *El Despertador Americano*, which denounced Spaniards for controlling the colony's wealth, occupying top Church and government positions, and marrying rich heiresses. Later, in other locations, the rebels published the *Ilustrador Nacional,* the *Ilustrador Americano,* the *Semanario Patriótico,* and the *Correo Americano del Sur*. None of these papers appeared after 1813. While they portrayed the insurgents in a favorable light, for logistical reasons, they never had the impact of royalist propaganda.[88]

Fray Servando Teresa de Mier undertook another propaganda effort single-handedly. He wrote a book, the *History of the Revolution of New Spain*, to justify rebellion against Spanish rule and refute Spanish critiques of the insurgency. Rather than portraying the Spanish presence in Mexico as three centuries of Christian enlightenment, he chronicled the destruction Spaniards had wrought and portrayed their rule as a dark age. By rejecting both Spanish political control and the Spanish monarch, he sought to break the mental bonds that still linked many Creoles to Spain. Teresa de Mier published his work in England since even before the outbreak of rebellion he had been exiled for publicly questioning whether the Virgin of Guadalupe had actually appeared.[89]

Given the prevailing illiteracy, information (true and false) propagated at markets, drinking establishments, and areas where women drew water and washed clothes. The difficulty either side

Figure 6.3
Leona Vicario

Source: Reproduced courtesy of the Benson Latin American Collection, the University of Texas at Austin

had in communicating with the rural population was compounded by the inability of many indigenous people to speak Spanish.[90]

The Guadalupes, a secret society of rebel sympathizers in Mexico City, supported the insurgency. Its members acted as an informal political party during the 1813–1814 elections for the Spanish parliament (Cortes). They helped elect sympathetic Creoles, whom they felt could further the cause of Mexican independence while serving in the Cortes. They also helped obtain a press and materials for insurgent publishing operations, sheltered refugees, furnished recruits, provided information, and smuggled arms to insurgents. They infiltrated the viceregal palace and pilfered correspondence from the office of the viceroy's secretary. The Guadalupes' activities so peeved Viceroy Calleja that he referred to them as a "diabolic assembly."[91]

The most famous member of the Guadalupes was Leona Vicario, a member of an elite Creole family who received a good education by the standards of the time. She began to aid the independence movement by using her Mexico City home as a meeting place for insurgent sympathizers. She later sent arms to rebels, used her family inheritance to finance the insurrection, and recruited and armed rebels. Late in 1813, authorities intercepted letters she had written the rebels, investigated her activity, and confined her under the authority of nuns at the Colegio de Belen.[92]

A group of rebels soon freed Vicario, enabling her to join the insurgents. After joining Morelos's army, she administered its finances and supervised care of the ill and injured. She soon married another rebel, her uncle's former law clerk, Andrés Quintana Roo, and gave birth to their first child in a cave in Achipixtla. Royalist authorities responded by confiscating her goods and declaring her a traitor.[93]

THE WAR DRAGS ON

Following Morelos's death, the nature of the independence struggle changed dramatically. No formal structure united the rebel groups. After the rebel Congress arrived in Puebla, the local rebel commander refused to accept its authority and simply dissolved it. The movement became more atomized, more rural, and lost its appeal to the urban elite. Guadalupe Victoria, in the Puebla-Veracruz area, and Vicente Guerrero, in Oaxaca, commanded the most substantial rebel forces. In 1818, royalist commanders still reported that bands of 200 or 300 insurgents attacked Querétaro haciendas daily. Other small units operated in Veracruz, Michoacán, Guanajuato, Puebla, the Mexico City area, and in the Pacific lowlands in the modern states of Michoacán and Guerrero.[94]

Rebels employed guerrilla tactics and took advantage of terrain to avoid royalist soldiers. They attacked, withdrew, and then hit another place. In each locale, if the royalist army showed signs of weakness, guerrilla bands would reemerge and operate again. Due to both geography and the aspirations of local leaders, the rebels never managed to coalesce over large areas. This weakened them militarily, but made it impossible to snuff out the insurgency.[95]

After 1815, royalist officers assumed de facto control of many areas, displacing civilian officials. As historian Virginia Guedea commented, "Civil order ceased to exist and the armed struggle, the guerrilla war, became the new way of life for everyone." Legality became a victim of the war effort. The viceroy tolerated royalist officers who confiscated and sold property of supposed rebels, keeping the proceeds for themselves. Others traded with insurgents and pocketed special taxes they levied. Authorities tolerated all but the most egregious cases of royalist enrichment. By the end of the decade, this process resulted in regional commanders having created a series of semi-autonomous military satrapies.[96]

The number of unemployed increased as commercial traffic and industrial output declined during the war. Many who lost their jobs joined the rebel cause. Others joined the insurgents after fleeing royalist tax collectors who were desperately attempting to finance the war effort. De facto redistribution of land abandoned by *hacendados* repeatedly occurred as individuals moved into rebel zones to be able to farm and raise stock. The expulsion of wealthy *hacendados* and their overseers did not always result in declining production. Royalist officers on long-range patrols expressed shock at reentering insurgent-controlled districts and finding the countryside well ordered and sometimes apparently more prosperous than before 1810.[97]

Many observers dismissed the remaining insurgents as "bandits." As historian Eric Van Young noted, "In the revolutionary period, the rather fluid boundary between crime and rebellion was continually crossed back and forth by thousands of Mexicans." The elite considered any act of collective appropriation, destruction of property, or violence against royalists as "banditry." In contrast, when viewed from below, in social terms, vague but discernible notions of social justice, retributive or redistributive in nature, generally sustained these attacks.[98]

DEMOCRACY, SPANISH STYLE

After the 1808 French invasion of Spain, the Spanish people responded to the absence of their king by falling back on their long tradition of provincial and municipal power. They established juntas in many Spanish cities not under French control. By September 1808, the various juntas formed the Supreme Central Junta to coordinate resistance to the French and administer areas the French did not occupy.[99]

As French troops advanced, junta members fled to Seville in southwestern Spain. In January 1810, a five-man Regency replaced the Junta Central. Its members fled further southwest to Cádiz, where they could act under British protection. The Regency then convened a Cortes, or parliament, to administer during Fernando's absence.[100]

While Spanish aristocracy and royalty had controlled previous governments, the Junta Central attracted the most liberal elements of Spanish society. The Junta Central desperately needed support from Spanish America, so it elevated the Spanish colonies to the same legal status as that enjoyed by Spain. The junta instructed the municipal government of each provincial capital (*cabecera*) to select three individuals "endowed with probity, talent, and learning and without any blemish." Of these three, one, chosen by lot, would serve in the Cortes. In keeping with these instructions, eighteen representatives, of whom thirteen were priests, were selected to represent New Spain in the Cortes.[101]

Since the opening date of the Cortes, September 24, 1810, did not allow time for newly elected delegates from the New World to cross the Atlantic, twenty-six persons from the Americas residing in Spain served as temporary substitutes for those selected as delegates but who had not yet arrived.[102]

The Cortes took several steps to keep the colonies loyal. In October 1810, it ended tribute for Indians and *castas* and declared the judicial equality of all inhabitants of Spanish America and the Spanish mainland. In February of the following year, it abolished monopolies. In November 1812, the Cortes prohibited the *repartimiento* and all other forms of personal servitude and ordered the distribution of Crown lands to married Indians residing on them.[103]

The Cortes sought reform, but not an end to colonialism. Representatives from Spain always far outnumbered those from the colonies. Although their number varied, roughly 158 deputies represented Spain while only fifty-three came from the Americas. This did not reflect the relative population of the two areas. The population of Spanish America totaled roughly 16 million, compared to only 10.5 million in Spain.[104]

In 1812, the Cortes promulgated a new constitution that granted the right to vote to most adult males living within the Spanish empire. Drafters of the constitution considered that Indians were fully capable of integration into the mainstream of society and that the material progress of Spanish America required such integration. However, the constitution denied those of African descent the right to vote. Such individuals could be granted that right on an individual basis, based on meritorious service. The failure to enfranchise those of African descent reflected politics as well as prejudice. Since most people of African descent lived in the colonies, enfranchising them en masse would tip the scales toward New World control.[105]

The constitution eliminated literacy and property restrictions for voting and so restrained the king that it virtually created a republic. It also established freedom of the press and provided for the election of all municipal officers and the removal of those who had inherited or bought seats on municipal councils. Indian tribute, forced labor, and the Inquisition were eliminated. In a major concession to tradition, Article 12 declared Catholicism the one official religion and prohibited the exercise of any other religion.[106]

Several rounds of elections in Mexico chose representatives to the Cortes and to institutions created by the constitution. In November 1812, the first popular elections in Mexican history selected twenty-five electors to choose members of the Mexico City municipal council. There was widespread grassroots participation, including the successful candidacy of those who had headed the recently disbanded Indian community governments. All those chosen as electors in Mexico City were born in Mexico and favored political change.[107]

Once again, the residents of New Spain received a lesson in realpolitik. Claiming electoral fraud, the Viceroy and the Archbishop simply nullified the elections. It became apparent, though, that the birthplace of those elected and their political sympathies, not voting irregularities, caused the annulment.[108]

In December 1812, elections selected representatives to the Cortes. Each parish chose one elector for each 200 citizens in the parish. These electors met at the district level to choose district electors, who met in the provincial capital and also selected a representative to the Cortes. As occurred at the municipal level, the electors did not choose a single Spaniard. The Spaniards' failure to be elected, despite their efforts to gain office, reflected: 1) resentment due to the 1808 coup, 2) the increasingly repressive nature of the colonial government fighting the insurgency, 3) voters' sympathy with the insurgents, and 4) support for candidates known to favor autonomy.[109]

These elections were allowed to stand, and the duly elected deputies took their seats in the Cortes. They had to tread lightly, though, because if they were too candid, they might be arrested. The three main issues raised by the New World deputies were: 1) the reserving of half of all offices for Creoles, 2) opening colonial ports to foreign shipping, and 3) extending voting rights to all those born in the New World, including those of African descent. Spaniards not only opposed a further expansion of voting rights but bitterly resented the expansion that had already occurred. The Spanish-dominated Mexico City *consulado* declared New Spain to be "a province the home of five million automatons, of a million disloyal vassals, and of a hundred thousand citizens addicted to order."[110]

To decentralize the formerly monolithic Spanish governing structure, the 1812 constitution created provincial deputations to administer local affairs in each province. These deputations pitted residents of the New World against Spanish colonial officials. The Spanish considered the deputations merely as advisory bodies without legislative power. However, Mexicans felt they represented the will of each province's citizens. The Mexicans staffing these bodies performed many local administrative, judicial, and fiscal functions and in the process enhanced citizens' sense of territoriality.[111]

In addition to creating provincial deputations, the 1812 constitution granted municipalities with a population of more than 1,000 the right to elect their own town councils. As a result, by 1814, the number of town councils in Mexico had increased from a mere 55 to nearly 900. Most of the newly created councils were in indigenous and mestizo communities. These elections not only created new city councils but transformed previously established ones, since from the early seventeenth century on, they had become closed, self-perpetuating oligarchies.[112]

After prolonged resistance, the French withdrew from Spain due to: 1) the success of Spanish guerrillas, 2) victories by Portuguese troops under British command who fought Napoleon's troops, and 3) Napoleon's 1812 defeat in Russia. Without a French force to sustain him, Joseph abdicated on January 7, 1814, paving the way for Fernando to reclaim the throne. Both sides of the Atlantic rejoiced when the recently released Spanish monarch assumed full powers in May.[113]

This rejoicing came to an abrupt end when Fernando abolished the Cortes, which he claimed had usurped his power and forced a constitution on the Spanish people. He assumed absolute power and abolished all the institutions, such as the provincial deputations and elected municipal governments, created by the 1812 constitution. Policymaking became dominated by hardliners who rejected compromise with Spanish America. Indians were once again required to pay tribute. Many liberal leaders, including some of the Mexican deputies, were jailed.[114]

In the final months of 1819, Fernando ordered Spanish troops to Cádiz so they could be sent to the New World to fight rebels. Rather than engaging in a colonial war, the troops rebelled and joined forces with liberals opposed to Fernando's absolutism. By March of 1820, they had gained sufficient strength to force the reestablishment of the Cortes and the reimposition of the 1812 constitution.[115]

The 1820–1821 session of the reconvened Cortes saw Spain fail to seize upon its last chance to keep the empire intact. In June 1821, the Spanish American deputies presented a plan that would have created a new *corte* (parliament) in Mexico and two new ones in South America. This would have in effect created three new governments, which would have been presided over by Bourbon princes and which would have been free to trade with any nation. They would have maintained commercial and foreign policy ties to the Spanish Crown, which they would help finance. The deputies making this proposal cited Canada as an example of an area that had administrative autonomy without rejecting its sovereign.[116]

Spanish liberals and absolutists agreed upon one thing—the ports of Spanish America must remain closed to all except Spanish ships. They rejected the proposal of the New World deputies and in the process made a mockery of the vaunted equality—proclaimed by the Cortes—of Spaniards and overseas citizens.[117]

The 1812 constitution served to convert Mexicans from subjects to citizens. Between 1810 and 1822, Mexico held five elections for deputies to the Spanish Cortes, each of which was held at three levels. In addition, Mexicans elected municipal councils and provincial deputations. Those elected learned parliamentary procedure, the value of compromise, and debating skills, and voters learned to value the ballot. The twenty-two Mexicans who served in the Cortes occupied important positions and gained invaluable experience. Freedom of the press exposed Mexicans to new ideas. Documents published in the Mexican press included the U.S. Constitution and the manifesto of the government of independent Buenos Aires. In fact, Mexicans so fully took advantage of freedom of the press that Viceroy Venegas canceled the freedom after two months.[118]

BREAKING THE STALEMATE

The 1820 reimposition of the 1812 Constitution dramatically affected the war effort in New Spain. The newly reconstituted municipal governments ceased supporting the royalist counterinsurgency effort with tax revenue. Royalist Colonel José Barradas, serving in Veracruz, reported that the "constitutional municipalities have openly refused me any aid . . . I only receive frivolous excuses." The lack of local financial support caused the disbanding of many militia units that had been engaged in counterinsurgency operations.[119]

Early in 1821, virtually no constituency favored the status quo. Royalist forces were suffering from battle fatigue and a lack of finances, which literally reduced some units to rags. Military levies and continued destruction prevented economic recovery. The Creole elite and the ecclesiastical hierarchy, both staunch opponents of the insurgents, felt the reimposition of constitutional rule in Spain threatened their ancestral privileges. Surviving rebel units were still far from victory. The moribund economy and the mass mobilization prevented countless Mexicans from obtaining jobs and getting on with their everyday lives.[120]

Agustín de Iturbide, the son of a noble Basque merchant in Valladolid, facilitated the break-up of the political-military logjam. His father-in-law was the wealthiest and most powerful man in that city. When the independence war began, Iturbide was serving as a lieutenant in the Provincial Regiment of Valladolid. He later claimed that Hidalgo offered him the rank of lieutenant general if he would join the insurgents but that he declined, claiming Hidalgo's movement "would produce only disorder, massacre, and devastation, without accomplishing the object which he had in view."[121]

Iturbide cast his lot with the royalists and was promoted to captain for outstanding service at Monte de las Cruces. By 1813, he had reached the rank of colonel and became commander of Guanajuato, one of the main theaters of the rebellion. Iturbide not only rose rapidly through the ranks but developed a reputation for brutality, excessive even by the standards of the conflict.[122]

In 1816, Iturbide's meteoric rise through the ranks ended when he was relieved of command for financial impropriety and cruelty to non-combatants. Authorities in Spain considered the complaints against him and eventually exonerated him of all charges. However, he did not receive another command until 1820.[123]

Denied the opportunity to advance his military career, Iturbide turned increasingly to politics. In November 1820, four years after being relieved of his command in Guanajuato, Viceroy Apodaca appointed him as Commander of Southern Mexico, hoping this would enable the royalists to defeat Guerrero's forces.[124]

Rather than pursuing military victory, Iturbide sent Apodaca false reports about his "progress" and requested additional troops and supplies. At the same time, he corresponded extensively with various factions of the urban elite in Mexico City and Veracruz, sounding out the possibility of a political solution to the military stalemate.[125]

On February 24, 1821, after it became apparent that a political solution was viable, Iturbide signed a document stating his intentions in Iguala, a village in the modern state of Guerrero. On March 1, Iturbide formally presented his new proposal, known as the Plan of Iguala, to his officers. Iturbide and his men then took an oath to support the independence of Mexico. The ceremonies ended with a Te Deum chanted at the local church.[126]

The Plan of Iguala called for an extremely broad coalition, including both royalists and insurgents, to unite against Spain to achieve Mexican independence. Article 1 of the Plan of Iguala established the Roman Catholic Church as the official religion "to the exclusion of all others." Article 2 proclaimed the "absolute independence" of Mexico. Article 3 called for Mexico to be ruled by a constitutional monarchy. Article 4 invited Fernando, a member of his family, or a member of another ruling dynasty to govern. Article 5 established an interim government until a *corte* could meet. Article 12 granted citizenship to "all the inhabitants" of New Spain. Article 14 guaranteed the *fuero* and property of the clergy.[127]

The Plan of Iguala was as conciliatory as possible in keeping with its goal of independence. To attract conservatives, it declared Spain to be the "most Catholic pious, heroic, and magnanimous nation on earth." The Plan offered each interest group some of what it desired. It offered all citizens, including Spaniards, security of property. Government, military, and religious officials accepting the Plan could continue in their posts. The most radical proposal, in addition to that of independence itself, was civil equality for all ethnic groups. This served to win over insurgents, many of whose bloodlines had previously been declared to be inferior.

With the advantage of hindsight, one can marvel at the political acumen of the Plan of Iguala. However, early in 1821, the response to Iturbide's Plan remained in doubt. In many places, people evaluated Iturbide's program and his capacity to win a definitive victory. Slow communications, especially with a place as isolated as Iguala, gave the newly announced plan the appearance of having settled in limbo. The Puebla newspaper *La Abeja* partly resolved Iturbide's problem with disseminating the Plan when it printed it "by mistake."[128]

On March 10, insurgent leader Vicente Guerrero, whose forces had repeatedly defeated Iturbide's, announced his alliance with the former royalist. After having exacted an assurance that citizenship would be extended to men of all races, Guerrero declared Iturbide to be "*primer jefe de los ejércitos nacionales*" ("commander-in-chief of the national armies") and placed his forces at Iturbide's disposal. Then on March 19, Colonel Anastasio Bustamante, one of the leading royalist commanders, joined the cause. Still, at the end of March, Iturbide's troops numbered only 1,800, many of whom were irregulars who had been in Guerrero's force.[129]

Once it became apparent that the Plan of Iguala would attract officers of Bustamante's stature, an avalanche of royalist defections followed. Sometimes officers joined Iturbide, bringing their units with them. In other cases, royalist units simply melted away. At the beginning of March 1821, the royalist force in Valladolid numbered more than 3,500, but by April 4, only 1,500 remained.[130]

As both royalist and insurgent forces joined Iturbide's movement, they formed the Army of Three Guarantees (Ejército Trigarante). This force took its name from the three main provisions of the Plan of Iguala, the guarantees of independence, of the Roman Catholic religion, and of civil equality. This army won repeated victories, not so much due to its effectiveness but to the collapse of the royalist forces. As historian Christon Archer observed, "Exhausted by eleven years of conflict, the old order simply crumbled without much fighting and faded away." During April, May, and June of 1821, large parts of the Bajío and Nueva Galicia accepted the Plan of Iguala. On August 2, 1821, the city of Puebla surrendered to Iturbide's forces.[131]

Viceroy Apodaca was an able administrator, but proved to be a poor military commander. Initially, he responded to Iturbide by concentrating his veteran troops in Mexico City in anticipation of an attack. This enabled Iturbide to build his forces with little opposition. Apodaca could not even trust the loyalty of the troops he commanded.[132]

Military officers were attracted by Iturbide's offer to let them keep their rank and by his pledge to reestablish the military *fuero*, which had been abolished by the Cortes. Many Creole officers, such as Antonio López de Santa Anna, switched allegiance, feeling they had been neglected in the provinces and often left without pay. Many Spanish soldiers accepted the Plan, too, since it promised them safe conduct back to Spain. Other Spanish officers, who had been in Mexico so long that they had developed extensive financial interests, joined Iturbide with the intention of remaining in Mexico. Others disliked the anti-military aspects of the reimposed 1812 constitution.[133]

Juan O'Donojú, the last viceroy sent over from Spain, arrived on July 30, 1821, just as royalist forces were on the verge of collapse. By August, the Army of Three Guarantees controlled almost all of Mexico except Mexico City, the port of Veracruz, Acapulco, and the fortress of Perote. O'Donojú, a liberal who had been jailed after Fernando reimposed absolutism in 1814, realized he could not save Mexico as a colony.[134]

O'Donojú accepted Iturbide's invitation to meet in the town of Córdoba on August 23, 1821. The following day, the two signed the Treaty of Córdoba. As Iturbide later commented, O'Donojú accepted his proposal "as if he had helped me write the plan." With the treaty, O'Donojú felt he could save Mexico for the Bourbon dynasty, if not for Spain, and lay the foundation for cordial relations between the two nations. Accepting the treaty also preserved the wealth and lives of Spaniards then living in Mexico. O'Donojú had other motivations for quickly accepting Iturbide's terms. Within weeks of his arrival, two of his nephews, seven officials traveling with him, and a hundred crewmen of the battleship *Asia*, which had brought him to Mexico, had died of yellow fever at Veracruz. He was also promised a life-time pension, allowing him to remain in Mexico rather than returning to Spain where he would be stigmatized for having lost Mexico.[135]

The seventeen articles of the Treaty of Córdoba, signed on August 24, largely reiterated the provisions of the Plan of Iguala. Article 2 declared that Mexico would be governed by a moderate constitutional monarchy. Article 8 provided for the immediate establishment of a Governing Provisional Junta, to include O'Donojú, which would function until a Mexican *corte* could be convened. Article 11 provided for a three-man regency to serve as the executive power. O'Donojú agreed to use his authority to persuade Spanish troops in Mexico City to lay down their arms.[136]

The Spanish force in Mexico City presented the only remaining obstacle for the Army of Three Guarantees. On September 14, O'Donojú informed its commander that under Spanish law, he remained subject to the viceroy and that resistance was absurd. The commander then ordered his men to lay down their arms. As his final official act, O'Donojú assumed responsibility for marching Spanish troops out of the city.[137]

On September 27, 1821, Iturbide's thirty-eighth birthday, he and his 16,000-man Army of Three Guarantees triumphantly entered Mexico City, passing under a magnificent triumphal arch constructed for the occasion. Also present, commanding a division, was Vicente Guerrero. A huge popular festival celebrated the consummation of independence. Indians danced in streets strewn with flowers. Official Mexico celebrated with a Te Deum and a banquet. After Iturbide's arrival, Mexico enjoyed a period of euphoria, rejoicing, and hope.[138]

On the following day, September 28, 1821, the Governing Provisional Junta issued a formal Declaration of Independence. Thirty-eight people signed it, none of whom were former insurgents. However, some of the signatories included members of the Guadalupes, former deputies to the Cortes, and a member of the feisty 1808 Mexico City municipal council.[139] The declaration read:

> The oppression, which the Mexican nation has suffered for 300 years without being able to act freely or being able to express itself, ends today. . . . The rights granted by the author of nature

> and which are recognized as inalienable and sacred by the civilized nations of the world have been restored. Mexico is now free to form the government which will best ensure its well-being. Mexico solemnly declares that it is a sovereign nation and independent of Old Spain.[140]

Iturbide provided a political program around which various groups could rally to end the war. As historian Timothy Anna noted:

> In the short run, the Plan of Iguala swept the whole nation before it precisely because it was a workable compromise. Of course, different adherents to the plan had different motives for supporting it and different ideas about what form of government should be created.[141]

SOCIAL ROLES

> To interpret any process of large-scale, protracted political violence or nation-building as monolithic . . . whether or not a revolution in the classic sense of the term, is folly.
>
> Eric Van Young, 2001[142]

Internal divisions and opinion shifts complicate any discussion of the role groups played in the independence struggle. The Enlightenment influenced some of the members of the elite. Other Mexicans reflected the thinking of another era. For example, insurgent troops commanded by General Mariano Matamoros fought under a banner inscribed, "Die for ecclesiastical immunity," an expression of their demand that special legal privileges be restored to the clergy. In so far as the rebels fought for the concept of a nation, it was a Creole notion, since *castas* had at best a vague notion of nationhood, and Indians and blacks none at all. Indian communities, which supplied the majority of insurgent troops, were deeply conservative and sought to defend community lands and other assets that were under pressure from commercial agriculture and increased taxes. Sometimes one community would support the insurgency largely because an adjacent, rival community opposed it.[143]

The failure of the Creoles, by and large, to rally behind Hidalgo prolonged the independence struggle. The examples of Creole rebellion provided by Hidalgo and Allende were the exceptions, not the rule. Even Hidalgo's own brother José María Hidalgo fought in the area of Pénjamo, Guanajuato, as a royalist officer. In contrast to the elite in the thirteen British North American colonies, the Creole elite lived in a predominantly non-white society. While they sought autonomy, its members did not necessarily wish to sever their ties with the mother country. They not only respected the monarchy but feared that radical change might upset the existing social hierarchy that placed them close to the top of the social order.[144]

Creoles in Angangueo, Michoacán, provided a more typical response than that of Father Hidalgo. They wrote Viceroy Venegas two weeks after the revolt began:

> As soon as we learned . . . that some of our brothers had raised their voices to start an insurrection contrary to the national character, and diametrically opposed to the maxims of our holy religion, we were filled with the greatest bitterness, and became fired with the flame of loyalty and patriotism.[145]

Generalizations about the rural lower class are hampered by the extreme variation of its members and their not having left as abundant a written record as members of the elite. Much of what we know of their thinking was recorded in their testimony when royalists put them on trial for having joined the insurgents.

Most of the population of late colonial Mexico did not have a world view that extended far enough beyond their own locality to even conceive of a state, let alone contemplate the nature of the state they desired. Evidence from trials of rebels fails to indicate that the notion of "autonomy" made its way down to rural combatants. Rather than a cohesive rebellion, Mexico saw regional insurrections motivated by myriad grievances explode in thousands of directions at once. None of these insurrections responded to any such thing as "Mexico." Rather than fighting for land per se, as revolutionaries would a century later, rural insurgents concentrated more often on defending themselves from voracious administrators and their representatives and protecting existing land holdings and water and grazing rights. Although a majority of the population was poor, only a minority joined Hidalgo's rebellion or later uprisings.[146]

Indian attitudes ranged from support for the insurrection, loyalty to the Crown, and indifference. The Indian community had become highly dependent on Church and Crown for its existence, so colonial ties were not cast off lightly. Generally the more "Indian" individuals were in culture and self-identification the less likely they were to move much beyond their villages for collective political action.[147]

Some Indians joined the insurgents to preserve the autonomy of their communities from new market and fiscal pressures and based their actions on entirely different assumptions than the elite. Indian insurgents of both sexes captured in November 1810 clearly believed they were following the orders of the King of Spain, who was physically present in Mexico, riding about the countryside in a mysterious black coach. They testified that he had commanded Father Hidalgo to take up arms against the Spanish colonial authorities. Furthermore, they believed that the headman of their village had ordered them to kill the viceroy and all other Spaniards and divide their property among the poor. Some of the testimony supported the notion that the Virgin of Guadalupe was working hand in hand with Fernando. In December 1810, Hidalgo ordered the Indians of Juchipila, Zacatecas (directly north of Guadalajara), not to sack the estates of the local Spanish tax administrator. The Indians refused to obey, even after direct orders from their parish priests. After plundering the estate, they claimed to have acted with the permission of the Virgin of Guadalupe. What was unthinkable before could be accomplished under the higher authority of the Virgin.[148]

The Virgin also inspired Indians who fought on the royalist side. Indigenous combatants supporting the Crown in Zacapoaxtla, Puebla, attributed each victory to her. At the village of San Miguel Tomatlán, near Orizaba, patriotic Indians and mestizos volunteered to serve in royalist militias shouting, *"¡Viva la religión, Viva el rey, Viva la patria, Muera todo traidor!"* ("Long live religion, Long live the King, Long live the homeland, Death to Traitors!").[149]

The decade of insurrection had a profound effect on many Indian communities, which for the first time became involved in massive social movements that lasted for years and broke the boundaries of individual villages. In his study of the Indians of northern Veracruz, Michael Ducey found that early in the insurrection Indian demands centered on what he described as a "naive monarchism" and reflected dissatisfaction with particular officials. A decade later, the same Indians had borrowed elements from the discourse of the elite and began asserting their right to appoint and control local officials. In contrast, Indian leaders in Amecameca early on showed a sophisticated grasp of the situation. They threatened to join Hidalgo if a case involving land ownership was not resolved in their favor. The *audiencia* promptly delivered the verdict they desired.[150]

The clergy formed a pivotal group in the insurrection. One study found that priests comprised 27.5 percent of the rebel leadership, the largest single occupational group. By 1815, more than a hundred priests had been executed for supporting the insurgency and many more had been excommunicated. The clergy played such an important role in the insurrection that Abad y Queipo complained that the rebellion "is almost entirely the work of ecclesiastics, since they are its chief authors and those who started and sustain it."[151]

In contrast to the lower clergy, the ecclesiastical hierarchy, almost all of whom were Spaniards, feared they would lose their status and supported the Crown until the issuance of the Plan of Iguala. While many priests actively supported the insurrection, not more than a tenth of them played an active role on either side.[152]

After the proclamation of the Plan of Iguala, the clergy rallied around Iturbide's cause since he promised them the ecclesiastical immunity that had been abolished by the Spanish Cortes in 1820. The Cortes had also restricted the right of the Church to own property. Soon churchmen were preaching sermons denouncing the Spaniards and announcing that the war for independence would be a religious war to defend the old order.[153]

As with other groups, Mexican women lent support to both sides of the conflict. Their involvement led to a permanent shift in socially accepted roles for women. Some took up arms, such as Manuela Medina, an Indian from Taxco, who reached the rank of captain fighting with the insurgents. More commonly, though, women smuggled messages and weapons under their full skirts. In one celebrated instance, a group of women, accompanied by children and picnic baskets in a carriage, smuggled a printing press out of Mexico City so rebels could publish a newspaper. Other women served as spies, accompanied troops to prepare food and care for the wounded, and made cartridges for insurgent combatants. Royalists executed many women for supporting the independence cause. While the total number of women involved in the independence struggle remains unknown, almost 250 have been identified.[154]

La Corregidora, by far the best known of the women serving the insurgency, sent the warning to Hidalgo that their conspiracy had been discovered and later continued to supply information to the insurgents. Authorities arrested her in 1814 and placed her in a convent. They later released her, rearrested her, and, in 1816, sentenced her to four years' seclusion. However, she was released again after she reported that she was pregnant with her fifteenth child. After independence, Iturbide honored La Corregidora. She was offered the title of lady of honor to the empress, but declined the honor, stating she was too busy at home.[155]

In 1815, Leona Vicario accepted a royalist pardon, which permitted her and her husband to survive until independence. In recognition of her contribution to the independence cause and to compensate her for the financial losses she had suffered, the first Congress of independent Mexico granted her a hacienda and several houses in Mexico City. When Vicario died in 1842, President Antonio López de Santa Anna led her funeral procession.[156]

Women also actively supported the royalist cause. In late 1810, when Hidalgo was poised to take Mexico City, they formed the first known secular female organization in Mexico, the Patriotas Marianas. Its more than 2,000 members watched over the image of the Virgin of Remedios, the patroness of the royalist army, and sewed banners with her image. These banners countered the insurgents' banners with the image of the Virgin of Guadalupe. This group later raised funds for the royalist cause and published pamphlets proclaiming their loyalty to the Crown.[157]

There is little evidence that agrarian conflicts were the driving force of the independence war. Although rebels would frequently farm abandoned land, they never clearly called for the systematic transfer of land from *hacendados* to the landless, as Emiliano Zapata would a century later.[158]

During the war years, rural residents acquired arms, fighting experience, and above all, consciousness of their strength. Municipalities proliferated and appropriated judicial and fiscal powers. This allowed their residents to play an essential role in Mexican political life in subsequent years.[159]

The independence war in Mexico was much more bitter than the U.S. war for independence due to the lack of consensus among the elite, which led to mass rural insurrection and class and race conflict. The conflict in Mexico also lasted longer than the U.S. conflict due to Mexico's lack of foreign support— the forces fighting for U.S. independence had the assistance of 10,000 French troops, for example. In addition, Spanish and French ships neutralized the British fleet, while Spanish troops attacked the British along their long common border in North America. Throughout Spanish America, pro-independence forces were unable to play other European powers against Spain.[160]

Estimates of the number who died during the Mexican independence conflict range from a low of 200,000, or 3 percent of the population, to 600,000, or 10 percent of the population. In any case, Mexico paid an inordinately high price. The movement led by Iturbide was essentially a counter-revolution designed to defend the established order, which was no longer guaranteed by its traditional protector, the Spanish Crown. For almost half a century, generals whose careers began with the independence struggle would rule Mexico. With changed names and slightly altered institutions, Mexico began its independent life without having solved any of the basic questions behind the struggle. These remained for the future.[161]

THE ECONOMIC IMPACT

> As the state became more costly and intrusive, the New World equilibrium so carefully constructed over a quarter of a millennium began to break down.
>
> John Coatsworth, 2006[162]

By the beginning of the nineteenth century, Britain's economic growth and its burgeoning trade with the New World were making the Spanish empire a hollow shell. British Admiral Horatio Nelson's 1805 naval victory over Spain in the Battle of Trafalgar, which virtually destroyed Spanish sea power, further weakened the empire. As Spanish sea power declined, smuggling increased. Trinidad and Jamaica increasingly served as transshipment points for British goods destined for Spanish America. Smuggling not only deprived the Crown of revenue but demonstrated the advantages of trade outside the empire.[163]

After the 1808 French invasion of Spain, trade between Britain and Spanish America increased. While the British fleet blockaded Spanish ports, British exporters met the resulting shortages in the colonies either directly or through smuggling and neutral intermediaries. Between 1809 and 1811, 35 percent of all British exports went to Latin America. The opening of Latin American markets compensated the British for markets lost in Europe due Napoleon's ascendancy.[164]

Even before the Grito de Dolores, the Mexican economy was in trouble. To maintain mining output at a high level, the Crown provided massive financial subsidies for the purchase of the mercury used to refine silver. As trade barriers were lowered, legally imported textiles, as well as smuggled ones, ruined local producers. Buyers found imported British cottons especially attractive since the mechanization of carding and spinning reduced the cost of producing them—and therefore their market price—by nearly 70 percent between 1790 and 1812. The 1804 Consolidation Decree eliminated the major source of credit. After that date, miners lacked the capital needed to sink deep shafts, could not purchase drilling equipment, and had difficulty buying supplies from merchants.[165]

After the Grito de Dolores, the insurgency damaged the economy in innumerable ways. Well before rebels appeared, mine owners would flee to cities controlled by royalists. Mine workers joined the rebels, died, or moved away. Many wealthy Spaniards not only departed but took their capital back to Spain with them, exacerbating the credit crunch. Higher taxes to finance the royalist war effort increased costs. Royalist officers speculated with merchandise under their control, further increasing prices and damaging the economy.[166]

The independence struggle most affected mining, with its complex system of supply and financing. Since the insurgents were especially active in mining areas, these areas suffered a precipitous withdrawal of capital. To finance the war, the Crown shifted from subsidizing mining to heavily taxing it, further exacerbating the capital shortage. In 1811, the Crown ended its monopoly on the supply of mercury. However to the mine owners' chagrin, private suppliers charged as much as five times more to supply mercury than the Spanish government had charged. Also private vendors ceased to provide mercury on credit, as the Crown had. The isolation of mining towns not occupied by rebels often prevented them from obtaining supplies. The population of the mining-dependent Guanajuato area decreased from 70,600 in 1802 to 35,733 in 1822 as that industry declined.[167]

Mexican silver production peaked at 24.7 million pesos in 1809. By 1812, it had plummeted to 4.0 million due to the independence struggle. After 1812, as the intensity and locale of rebel activity shifted, mintage rebounded. However, between 1813 and 1820, it remained at less than half the 1809 level. The decline in Mexican silver exports caused the price of silver in London to increase by 10 percent.[168]

As with mining, the textile industry depended on extended raw material and marketing networks. *Obraje* owners complained of an "almost absolute lack of necessary materials" because of the "present barbarous and destructive insurrection" that had "annihilated the ranchers that supplied the wool" and obstructed the roads for the transport of what little remained. Given their isolation from *obrajes*, many ranchers began to rely on homespun wool. In the fifteen months after the Grito de Dolores, the number of *obrajes* in Querétaro fell from nineteen to eight. Machine-made fabrics from Europe and cheap cloth from the Orient displaced local production after they entered Mexico in substantial quantities without the heavy duties established under Spanish trade regulations. As a result of tariff-free textile imports through Pacific ports, Guadalajara's cotton textile industry was virtually eliminated.[169]

Some of the richest agricultural areas, such as Jalisco and the Bajío, also saw of some of the heaviest combat and destruction. Hacienda owners often fled to the safety of the city, and many of their workers joined the insurgent cause. Rebel bands in Querétaro killed hacienda administrators, ran off livestock, and pillaged, leaving many haciendas ruined. As mines closed, small farmers lost their markets and left the land. Morelos's troops specifically targeted Veracruz tobacco fields for burning, since they supplied the royal tobacco factory, a major revenue source for the Crown. Agricultural production during the insurgency fell by roughly 50 percent.[170]

The insurgency disrupted trade routes for prolonged periods. Many small villages were abandoned to the insurgents. After royalist troops garrisoned cities, their residents complained about the loss of contact with rural areas. As early as 1811, the Chihuahua municipal government noted the interruption of trade had led to shortages of clothing, paper, sugar, chocolate, medicine, and even tobacco, which led to the smoking of local herbs. Due to rebel activity, bullion often could not be shipped to Mexico City to be minted, so the viceroy authorized regional mints to convert bullion into coins.[171]

Traders who remained in business had to pay the high cost of military escorts to accompany mule trains. As many as 1,000 soldiers guarded the caravans that carried goods from Veracruz to Mexico City. Muleteers operating without royalist military escort often had to pay rebels protection money. The scarcity of beasts of burden and of coins to pay for goods further reduced trade. As a result of the reduction in trade, between 1810 and 1818 the population of Veracruz declined from 15,000 to 8,934.[172]

In Mexico, the independence conflict resulted in economic and fiscal changes that lasted longer than mere physical destruction, which could be repaired in a relatively short period (witness post-Second World War Europe). Local officials spent more on defense than before the Grito de Dolores. The Guanajuato district transferred roughly 80 percent of all taxes to Mexico City between 1791 and 1807. However, between 1812 and 1816, tax receipts declined to half of the pre-war level and, due to military spending, only 28 percent were transferred to Mexico City. Eliminating Indian tribute deprived the government of 2 million pesos a year. Military spending by the provinces deprived the central government of both resources and political power. Reestablishing the fiscal ties with the provinces that had existed for almost three centuries presented a monumental challenge for nineteenth-century Mexico.[173]

The interruption of trade routes also deprived Mexico's core of its traditional power. Tariff revenue fell since between 1811 and 1820 the level of foreign trade was 41 percent below that of the previous decade. Since transport through central Mexico was often impossible during the war, new trade routes opened. Spanish, Panamanian, and South American merchants flocked to the Pacific port of San Blas. These merchants, with commercial ties to Kingston, Jamaica, and access to British capital, provided a preview of the economic forces that would shape post-independence Mexico. Opening new trade routes decentralized power and the tax base.[174]

THE U.S. REACTION

The war of 1812 minimized the U.S. ability to play a role in the Latin American independence struggles. Combat at home and British control of the seas left the United States with little influence over Spanish America. During the war, the British had an almost entirely free hand in consolidating their political and economic influence throughout Latin America. British diplomacy effectively headed off Spanish attempts to secure the intervention of other European powers to prevent the loss of Spanish sovereignty and the increase of British influence in the Americas.[175]

While the independence struggle was being waged in Mexico, the United States and Spain negotiated a border treaty known as the Adams–Onís Treaty. The treaty, signed in 1819, recognized the Spanish claim to Texas in exchange for Spain's ceding to the United States its claim to Florida, which it obviously could not defend. The newly delineated boundary separating New Spain and the United States ran along the present east boundary of Texas, up the Red River, and then north along the one-hundredth meridian (the present east boundary of the Texas panhandle) to the Arkansas River. It followed the Arkansas to its headwaters and then ran to the forty-second parallel and then west along that parallel (the present northern boundary of California) to the Pacific. Since no one knew if the Arkansas originated north or south of that line, the treaty stipulated the boundary would run either north or south from the headwaters of the Arkansas to the forty-second parallel.

The treaty pleased both the Spanish and U.S. governments. Spain secured its claim to Texas and lost only Florida, which it had in fact already ceased to control. The United States obtained not only title to Florida but its first solid claim extending to the Pacific. Previously Spain had claimed territory north of the forty-second parallel. Since the treaty gave the United States access to the Pacific, it is also referred to as the Transcontinental Treaty.

Other European powers lost out as their prospects for acquiring territory on the Pacific Coast dimmed. Of course, the area's indigenous population suffered the biggest loss. Without even their knowledge, much less their consent, those of European descent divided their land among themselves.

The unwillingness to jeopardize the delicate negotiations that led to the Adams–Onís Treaty shaped the U.S. response to the Spanish American independence struggle. The two-year delay between the 1819 signing of the treaty and its ratification by Spain ensured that the United States would not openly support pro-independence forces. Also, after 1776 Cuba's trade with the United States surpassed Cuba's trade with Spain. The United States was unwilling to risk being excluded from the Cuban market by supporting independence struggles in other Spanish colonies. By 1821, U.S. exports to Spanish America had reached $8 million a year, or 13 percent of all U.S. exports.[176]

Officially, the United States remained neutral during the struggle for Spanish American independence. However, by allowing roughly thirty-seven insurgent-flagged privateers to operate from U.S. ports and prey on Spanish commerce, President James Monroe virtually recognized the rebels' belligerency. Spain urged that these rebel ships be considered as pirate ships, just as many Americans during the U.S. Civil War felt Confederate cruisers should be treated as pirates.[177]

In 1817, the United States ignored the organization of an invasion force assembled on U.S. territory. In New Orleans, Francisco Javier Mina, a Spanish liberal, openly recruited for an invasion force to wrest Mexico from Spanish rule. He had fought against the French in his home country and then turned against the Crown after Fernando reimposed absolutism and the Inquisition. In violation of U.S. neutrality laws, Mina obtained recruits, boats, military supplies, and financing from merchants seeking access to Mexican markets. Mina's force sailed for Mexico with seven ships and 300 men. He landed on the Gulf Coast and reached the Bajío. In response to his force, the royalists launched a 6,000-man offensive. Rebels provided little support for Mina since they resented his having assumed command and did not trust a Spanish military man to free them from Spain. Royalists eventually dispersed Mina's force, captured him, and ordered him shot in the back as a traitor.[178]

Despite the U.S. government's declared neutrality, American citizens generally sympathized with the cause of Spanish American independence. They sold weapons to insurgents and sent propaganda and copies of the U.S. Constitution south. Roughly 90 percent of the captains who carried letters of marque for the government of Buenos Aires were U.S. citizens. Henry Clay described the Spanish American independence movement as a "glorious spectacle of eighteen millions of people, struggling to burst their chains and be free."[179]

Since the United States and Britain both sought to control Spanish American markets and keep the French out, they maintained very similar policies toward independence movements. The British and the Americans largely formulated policy for the Spanish empire as a whole and only rarely designed measures directed specifically at Mexico. Since both the United States and Great Britain were formally allied with Spain, they sought to maintain at least the appearance of neutrality. The British enacted laws making it almost impossible for British subjects to render any assistance to Spanish American rebels, then demurely ignored the systematic violation of these laws. In 1818 alone, six expeditionary forces illegally departed from Britain to South America's north coast. The Mina expedition also obtained a shipload of arms in Britain before stopping in New Orleans to recruit.[180]

Part Three

Early Nineteenth-Century Mexico, 1821–1855

Chapter 7

Nationhood, 1821–1855

A NATION IS BORN, 1821–1823

> The eighteen months of Iturbide's rule is one of the most fascinating periods in Mexico's history, for it was then that leaders of the new society had to face the challenge of creating a government and forging a nation out of a vast territory that was until then a colony of Spain.
>
> Timothy E. Anna, 1990[1]

The Plan of Iguala and the Treaty of Córdoba laid the groundwork for Mexico's first government, which was largely copied from the Spanish model. These documents provided for a Sovereign Provisional Junta, which functioned until the election of a Congress, and for a Council of Regency, which served as an executive body. At its first session, the Junta chose five men to serve on the Council of Regency and named Iturbide as its president. For the next eight months, Iturbide ruled the country as president of the Regency.[2]

In accordance with the Treaty of Córdoba and the Plan of Iguala, elections were held for a unicameral Congress, which first met in February 1822. As had been the case with the Cortes, three-tier elections selected Congressional representatives. Common citizens only voted for electors, who then chose another elector at the district level. Electors chosen at the district level then met to choose a representative to Congress. Those establishing these rules assumed that members of local elites would be chosen in the first round of voting and that these electors would keep power in the hands of the elite. This permitted the enfranchisement of the masses without their empowerment.[3]

On the night of May 18, 1822, a Mexico City army garrison declared Iturbide to be emperor of Mexico. Mass demonstrations in the streets supported Iturbide's ascension to the throne. That night, Iturbide declined to accept the Crown. The next day, the sixty-two highest ranking military officers in the capital called on Congress to proclaim Iturbide as emperor.[4]

On May 19, Congress met in special session to consider proclaiming Iturbide emperor. As Iturbide made his way to the session through crowds in the streets, celebrants unhitched his horses and pulled his carriage to the Congressional hearings.[5]

That same day, under pressure from the mobs and the military, Congress declared Iturbide as emperor of Mexico. For a short period, Congress and the new emperor enjoyed a political honeymoon. On May 23, Congress bestowed Iturbide with the title "Agustín, by Divine Providence and by the Congress of the Nation, the First Constitutional Emperor of Mexico." Congress even added the date of Iturbide's election, May 19, to the list of national holidays, along with the emperor's birthday and those of his children.[6]

Congress's embracing of Iturbide reflected the prevailing national mood. Liberal historian Lorenzo de Zavala reported that support for Iturbide becoming emperor came from "the clergy, the miserable nobility of the country, the army in its greater part, and the common people who saw in that chief nothing more than the liberator of their country." As has been repeatedly noted since, that constituted the majority of Mexico's population.[7]

The honeymoon between Congress and Iturbide was short-lived. In its haste to proclaim Iturbide emperor, Congress did not specify what powers he would be delegated. Apparently its members had assumed that the restrictions placed on the Spanish monarch by the 1812 Spanish constitution would also apply to Iturbide. Congress declared Iturbide had no veto power over its legislation, while Iturbide claimed he did. Similarly, a dispute arose when both Congress and Iturbide claimed the power to appoint supreme court justices. There soon emerged what has been termed a crisis of "dual sovereignty," with both Congress and Iturbide claiming ultimate power.[8]

Congress had assumed Iturbide would serve as a constitutional monarch. However, after his coronation, Mexico's new emperor proved incapable of restraint and plunged into partisan politics. He became one of the first Latin American military dictators and soon began closing critical newspapers and jailing their writers and dissenting legislators.[9]

Eight months after its convening, Congress had made no progress at writing a constitution nor had it devised a way to finance the newly independent government. Since Iturbide considered Congress obstinate, unrepresentative of the national will, and incapable of directing the nation, on October 31, 1822, he simply dissolved it, threatening the use of military force if its members did not accept his decree. Iturbide described his motivation for dissolving Congress: "Being responsible for perfecting the work that I began and which the nation by its general vote confided in me, I cannot permit [Congress] to ruin [this work.]"[10]

After the abolition of Congress, a semblance of normalcy settled over Mexico. Iturbide observed, "At this period, the empire was tranquil, the government was actively engaged in consolidating the public prosperity, and our interior grievances were removed."[11]

During 1822, Iturbide received many letters accusing Brigadier Antonio López de Santa Anna, the commander of the port of Veracruz, of insubordination, unjust acts, and embezzlement of regimental funds. In response, Iturbide summoned Santa Anna to Jalapa, located between Mexico City and the port of Veracruz, and personally informed him that he had been relieved of his command. Iturbide felt he had resolved the matter, not realizing that he had come up against the all-time political survivor of Mexican history.[12]

Before news of his having been relieved of command arrived in Veracruz, the twenty-eight-year-old Santa Anna raced back to the port and launched a rebellion. On December 6, 1822, he issued a verbose, poorly organized political declaration known as the Plan of Veracruz, which called for restoring the dissolved Congress. Santa Anna's plan was so muddled that the Iturbide government published it in Mexico City in an attempt to discredit him.[13]

Iturbide ordered General José Antonio Echávarri, the commander of troops in the states of Veracruz, Puebla, and Oaxaca, to capture the port of Veracruz, which Santa Anna continued to control. Rather than attacking Santa Anna, who had better artillery and whose troops had higher morale than his own, Echávarri issued the Plan of Casa Mata, which called for the election of a new Congress, with one deputy for each 100,000 population. By basing representation on population he sought to eliminate the overrepresentation Mexico's sparsely populated north had enjoyed in the initial Congress. Echávarri apparently assumed that a new Congress, with each member representing the same number of people, would restore confidence in government. Significantly, both plans, rather than calling for Iturbide's removal, only sought to limit his power.[14]

The Plan of Casa Mata struck a chord with a wide range of provincial and regional interest groups that had been asking why, if power was transferred from Spain to Mexico City, it should not be transferred from Mexico City to regional centers such as Veracruz and Durango. Article 10 of the Plan of Casa Mata played to these interests by declaring that until the election of a new Congress, the provincial deputations would administer the country.[15]

The Plan of Casa Mata rapidly attracted followers, just as the Plan of Iguala had two years earlier. After issuing his Plan, Echávarri joined forces with Santa Anna. Many regional commanders supported the Plan because it decentralized the army command, facilitating the advancement of junior officers. The Plan not only challenged Iturbide's absolutism, but represented a major power shift from the old colonial center of power, Mexico City, to the provinces.[16]

The conflicting demands on Iturbide complicated his response. Some sought the restoration of the dissolved Congress; others demanded that a new Congress be elected. The emperor decided not to fight the rebels. His war record clearly indicates his decision did not result from cowardice. Perhaps his decision reflected his fear of anarchy, of plunging the nation into civil war.[17]

On March 19, 1823, Iturbide submitted his abdication. Even though none of the forces opposing him had demanded his removal, when faced with the choice of compromise or abdication, Iturbide chose the latter. Iturbide fell from grace so rapidly and so completely because he had forgotten where independence had come from and what had caused it. He turned his back on the provinces and threatened provincial autonomy, especially by dissolving Congress, which represented the interests of the provincial elites. His scornful treatment of former insurgents ensured they would not rally to his defense.[18]

With Iturbide's abdication, the question of how to organize the nation still remained unanswered. Historian Nettie Lee Benson wrote, "By the middle of March, 1823, Mexico, instead of being a united country, was broken into virtually autonomous provinces." The Plan of Casa Mata not only effectively destroyed the central government but it created a power vacuum that would not soon be filled. None of the leaders who followed Iturbide had the degree of public support that he himself had enjoyed.[19]

After his abdication, Iturbide sailed to exile in Italy. He soon tired of inaction there and moved to England, where he received letters from Mexico urging him to return. When news arrived that several of Mexico's states had proclaimed themselves sovereign, Iturbide saw this as the prelude to the balkanization of Mexico. As a result, he decided to return to assist in uniting his country. He left a letter with British Foreign Secretary George Canning declaring that, on the invitation of several groups, he was returning to help consolidate an effective government. He specifically disavowed any intention of reestablishing his empire.[20]

On July 14, 1824, Iturbide landed at Soto la Marina on Mexico's northeast coast. Unknown to him, two weeks before he left England, the Mexican government had decreed that if Iturbide as much as set foot on Mexican soil, he should be subject to the death penalty. Such a measure attempted to prevent Iturbide from enacting a Napoleonic return from Elba to reclaim the Mexican throne.

Authorities took Iturbide into custody and transferred him to Padilla, where the Tamaulipas legislature met. Adhering to strict legality, the legislature declared the law clearly indicated that Iturbide should be executed merely for having returned to Mexico. He was not even accused of any other offense.[21]

Iturbide was executed by firing squad and buried in Padilla's roofless parish church. He underwent partial posthumous rehabilitation in 1838 when his remains were taken to Mexico City and buried in a chapel. His epitaph read:

> Agustín de Iturbide,
> Author of Mexican Independence.
> Compatriot, weep for him.
> Passerby, admire him.
> This monument guards the ashes of a hero.
> His soul rests in the bosom of God.[22]

Mexicans remember Iturbide more for his faults than for his contribution to their independence. His household expenses were nearly five times those of the viceroys. His dissolving Congress not only indicated disdain for democracy but provided a concrete issue for his enemies to rally around.

He compounded the new government's financial problems by lowering taxes to increase his popularity. Finally, Iturbide failed to accommodate the newly empowered provincial elites.[23]

Iturbide faced many grave problems, such as financing his government, that would stymie Mexico's leaders until the latter part of the century. During the period that Iturbide led Mexico, members of the elite, the only Mexicans with liquid capital, were loath to support the government financially. None of the governments in succeeding years managed their finances more effectively, but at the time this could not be foreseen. After Santa Anna challenged him, the provincial elite, which correctly perceived the Plan of Casa Mata as their key to empowerment, overwhelmed Iturbide's support among senior army officers, high clergy, the colonial nobility, and Mexico City plutocrats.[24]

GUADALUPE VICTORIA AND VICENTE GUERRERO

> The only legitimate authority, the crown, and its colonial representative, the viceroy, disappeared. Intense political conflict ensued as various groups sought to legitimize their political philosophies.
>
> Roderic Ai Camp, 2003[25]

In late March 1823, the Congress that Iturbide had dissolved was reconvened. Initially its members assumed that they would write Mexico's first constitution. However, some states, including Jalisco and Zacatecas, withdrew support from Congress and declared they would not be bound by its actions. These states demanded that elections be held to select a new Congress that would better represent regional interests. The reconvened Congress ordered a military force to Jalisco to reassert control. In response, Jalisco and Zacatecas mobilized their militias to defend local sovereignty.

When the force sent from Mexico City reached the Jalisco border, its commander agreed to parlay with Jalisco's leaders. After a face-saving concession by Jalisco, on May 20 Congress agreed to new Congressional elections. Congress hoped this concession would avoid the disintegration of the country—a highly probable event. By mid-1823, ten of Mexico's nineteen provinces as well as the five provinces of Central America had declared themselves either sovereign or self-governing. The forming of alliances among the states themselves without consulting Mexico City also alarmed Congress.[26]

Elections then chose representatives to Mexico's second Congress, which convened in November 1823 specifically to write a constitution. The new Congress found favor in the hinterlands because it represented the provincial elite rather than the Mexico City elite. Lawyers (39.1 percent) formed the largest occupational group among the deputies, followed by clerics (29.8 percent). Military officers (16.9 percent) and *hacendados* (12.5 percent) comprised the next largest occupational groups. Thirty-five percent of the deputies had also been elected to the first Congress. Most deputies favored federalism and rejected a monarchy.[27]

This attempt to keep Mexico intact was only partially successful. In 1822, the Central American elite had opted to join Mexico, attracted by Iturbide's empire. However, after Iturbide abdicated, they opted for independence. For a short period, Central America remained as a single nation and then divided into the present republics of Central America.[28]

The second Mexican Congress drafted a new constitution, which it promulgated in 1824. Mexico's first constitution, modeled on the 1812 Spanish constitution, abolished the monarchy and shifted power to the states. The military and the Church retained special privileges such as their *fueros*. The constitution prohibited all religions except Roman Catholicism. The framers were so sure they were on firm religious ground that they specifically prohibited amending the article concerning religion. In most cases, the provincial deputations created by the 1812 Spanish constitution became states in the new republic. These states received the exclusive right to administer affairs within their borders. This reflected the consensus that, due to Mexico's enormous size and geographic diversity, local problems could be best addressed locally.[29]

The constitution divided government into executive, legislative, and judicial branches. Between 1824 and 1835, as a result of the constitution's enfranchising males without regard to wealth, literacy, or ethnicity, Mexico enjoyed broader suffrage than the United States, France, or Great Britain—the nations usually cited as the maximum achievement of liberal democracy in the early nineteenth century. Indirect elections, as under the 1812 Spanish constitution, chose one member of the lower house of Congress for each 80,000 residents. Each state legislature chose two members of the national senate and elected supreme court justices. The state legislatures also elected the president, with each state casting one vote, regardless of its population. Given the framers' fear of absolutism, they created a weak presidency and a weak federal government that was dependent on states for troop recruitment and tax collection. For the same reason, a president had to sit out a term before he could be reelected. The person who received the second highest vote in the presidential election became vice-president.[30]

Awarding the vice-presidency to the candidate receiving the second highest vote total contributed to instability, since it left a president with his chief political opponent serving as vice-president. With only one exception, all the vice-presidents elected under the 1824 constitution revolted against the presidents they served under.

Guadalupe Victoria, a respected insurgent combatant, was elected Mexico's first president in 1824. As was the case after Iturbide's triumphant entry into Mexico City two years earlier, optimism ran high. Historian Lucas Alamán commented: "President Victoria found himself in the best of circumstances. The republic was calm; the political parties were under control; and all expected a bright future."[31]

Due to Victoria's non-assertive political style, to this day he remains something of a cipher. Liberal Lorenzo de Zavala commented that he became "an entirely null personage and the instrument of the men who surrounded him." During Victoria's term, the real initiative in public affairs did not lie in Mexico City. The 1824 constitution, which created a weak presidency, left initiative to the states. Victoria's outstanding grace was his willingness to respect state autonomy, just as the constitution mandated.[32]

In 1829 President Victoria completed his term, an event that would not occur again for decades. The stability that enabled Victoria to finish his term resulted from the acceptance of his cabinet choices and his actions by most members of the elite. The receipt of British loans, which temporarily filled government coffers, also increased stability.[33]

The 1828 presidential election pitted General Manuel Gómez Pedraza, a former royalist officer who had joined Iturbide, against the former insurgent commander, Vicente Guerrero. During the campaign, Guerrero's opponents referred to him as "El Negro," a comment on his dark skin. Centralists supported the more moderate Gómez Pedraza, a rich, cultivated Creole.

Gómez Pedraza won the election, which was decided by each state legislature casting one vote for its preferred candidate. This procedure, while strictly legal, did not reflect popular will, in that Guerrero, a hero of independence, was far more popular than his opponent.[34]

Rather than accepting defeat, Guerrero decided to take the presidency by force. From his power base in Veracruz, Santa Anna supported Guerrero's assuming the presidency, charging that "pro-Spanish" interests had backed Gómez Pedraza. Then the two main military commanders in Mexico City seized the Acordada Armory and called for Guerrero to assume the presidency. Soon crowds took to the streets in support of Guerrero, charging Gómez Pedraza with fraud. A pro-Guerrero mob of 5,000 looted the Parián market in Mexico City. The market, with its many Spanish-owned shops, catered to the wealthy, thus making it a symbol of class privilege.[35]

In January 1829, Congress, responding to both military and mass support for Guerrero, annulled votes for Gómez Pedraza, confirmed Guerrero as president, and installed Anastasio Bustamante as vice-president. Guerrero served as president from April 1, 1829, to December 28 of that year. His presidency represented the high-water mark for the locally based, non-white, populist forces that Hidalgo had mobilized.[36]

During the Guerrero administration, decentralization of power reached its high point. Municipalities demanded and received the same rights to participation and autonomy over their affairs and resources that states had demanded in 1823. This municipal autonomy reaffirmed the traditional role played by the village, dating from the colonial period and before.[37]

The abolition of African slavery remains as Guerrero's major accomplishment. By 1800, for economic reasons, slavery had fallen into disuse in all but a handful of areas. High slave mortality, their high initial purchase costs, and the uncertainty of future slave purchases led to a reliance on Indian and mestizo wage labor.[38]

Shortly after independence, a national commission on slavery estimated that only 3,000 slaves remained. In contrast to the United States, the 1829 abolition of slavery produced little controversy, given the small slave population. Again, in contrast to the experience of the United States, the role of blacks in the post-slavery era has not been a significant issue. Miscegenation has so thoroughly blurred the differences between blacks and other mixed-race Mexicans that the number of Mexicans with identifiable African ancestry has become socially insignificant.[39]

The other major social enactment of the 1820s—the expulsion of Spaniards—was far more controversial. Resentment against Spaniards had its roots in their haughty treatment of Mexicans during the colonial period. Counterinsurgency campaigns during the war for independence exacerbated anti-Spanish sentiment. Spain's rejection of the Treaty of Córdoba and its continued occupation of San Juan de Ulúa, the island fortress offshore from Veracruz, increased resentment. Mexicans regarded the Spanish merchants remaining after independence as usurious and monopolistic and felt their massive imports threatened the livelihood of artisans. They considered the Spanish to be a virtual fifth column, maintaining loyalty to the Spanish empire and exploiting Mexico's wealth. The discovery of an 1827 plot by the Spanish friar Joaquín Arenas to restore Spanish rule exacerbated such fears. Nationalist Creoles found Spaniards a satisfying scapegoat for Mexico's post-independence economic decline. The number of choice jobs Spaniards held increased support for their expulsion. As Zavala, a contemporary observer of these events, noted, "It is difficult to determine as to what point one can call an emotion patriotic which can be easily confused with a desire for jobs held by others."[40]

Congress passed the first of several Spanish expulsion laws in 1827. Such laws, which required Spaniards to leave Mexico, continued to be in force until 1836, when Spain finally recognized Mexican independence. The expulsion did not proceed smoothly, since some Spaniards had clearly supported Mexican independence, some had Mexican families, and some could not afford passage out of Mexico. Still others were ill or feigned illness and paid physicians to certify their inability to travel.

As a result of expulsion legislation, roughly three-fourths of the 6,600 Spanish men in Mexico departed between 1827 and 1834. While the granting of many exemptions permitted some Spaniards to remain in Mexico, the expulsion virtually eliminated Spaniards from the military, government service, the mining industry, and the Church. Spaniards managed to survive, to a degree, in commerce and as property owners. Forcing Spaniards out of Mexico impoverished the economy since those expelled took substantial specie with them, as well as their productive energy. Expelled Spaniards, though a small percentage of the workforce, were among the most experienced and highly trained of the professional, commercial, and artisan classes. Ironically, the Americans, the French, and the British, but not the Mexicans, filled the gap left by departing Spanish merchants.[41]

Spain's launching of a 3,000-man Bay of Pigs-style invasion in July 1829 further increased anti-Spanish feelings. Just as with the Bay of Pigs, invasion planners felt the mere presence of the invading force would produce a popular uprising to restore the status quo ante. The Spanish press referred to the force's commander, Isidro Barradas, as the "second Cortés." After sailing from Spanish-held Cuba, the invaders landed on the Gulf Coast and marched north to occupy Tampico. Barradas was so confident that he ordered his troop transport ships back to Cuba, thus cutting off his retreat. He then waited in vain for spontaneous pro-Spanish uprisings to occur.[42]

The invasion allowed Santa Anna to demonstrate his ability to rapidly muster improvised armies. In less than a week, he assembled 1,644 men and commandeered some merchant ships to take his men north. Santa Anna then landed and encircled the Spanish force. Additional Mexican forces later arrived to reinforce Santa Anna. In September, the Spanish force surrendered, battered not only by Mexican attacks but by a lack of supplies and by yellow fever, which spread rapidly in the unhealthy coastal climate. Due to poor conditions, fifteen to twenty invaders died each day even after they had surrendered. Surviving members, roughly half of the original force, were allowed to return to Cuba.[43]

Militarily, the Spanish invasion was not of great consequence. However, Santa Anna's organization of the force that countered the invasion elevated him to national prominence above the other figures of the independence war. Santa Anna realized that the Spanish invasion furthered his own interests. In his autobiography, he commented, "When fortune smiles on Santa Anna, she smiles fully!"[44]

In response to the invasion, Congress granted emergency war powers to President Guerrero. Once he assumed these extraordinary powers, which he used to abolish slavery, he refused to relinquish them even after the invaders had surrendered. This provided the military, leading clerics, and business interests with a rationale for ousting him.[45]

However, conservatives did not oust Guerrero due to his retention of emergency powers. His Finance Minister, Lorenzo de Zavala, had announced a progressive income tax, which left the poor untaxed and imposed a 10 percent tax on rent for property worth more than $500. Proponents of this tax justified it as a means of paying the cost of defeating the Spanish invasion. However, the elite considered the measure dangerous populism. The elite was also concerned that Indian peasants in the present-day state of Guerrero interpreted anti-Spanish legislation as authorization to expel non-Indians from their lands, continuing their long struggle over land rights. Guerrero's ties to the masses, his dark skin, country mannerisms, and lack of polish added to resentment against him. Guerrero's support for village autonomy also threatened elite interests. The military turned against Guerrero, not on ideological grounds, but because its pay was in arrears due to the lack of government funds.[46]

In late 1829, Vice-President Anastasio Bustamante rebelled with the backing of the military, the high clergy, and major landowners. Guerrero, unable to quell the uprising, abandoned the presidency. Those who ousted Guerrero portrayed themselves as fighting the war of "civilization against barbarism, of property against thieves, of order against anarchy."[47]

After Guerrero left the presidency, his followers waged guerrilla war against the central government from southern Mexico. From that vantage point, the central government in Mexico City served as an aristocratic cabal undermining Mexican independence and handing the nation back to Spain. Guerrero's supporters fought for a vaguely defined people's democracy and the overthrow of the usurper Bustamante. The Bustamante administration, in turn, claimed it was fighting for its self-proclaimed objectives—civilization and order. This would become the classic dichotomy of nineteenth-century Mexico.[48]

Since Guerrero symbolized the rebellion, the government paid a Genoese ship captain who brought supplies to the rebels 50,000 pesos to capture Guerrero. The captain invited Guerrero aboard his ship for dinner in Acapulco, imprisoned him, and delivered him to the Bustamante government, which promptly executed him.[49]

Without Guerrero, the rebellion quickly faltered. Had other areas of Mexico supported the rebels, they might have succeeded. However, the government's ability to concentrate all its forces on rebels in the area that later became the state of Guerrero doomed the rebellion.[50]

Many consider the execution of Guerrero and other captured leaders to have been an effort by the Creole elite to ensure that those of mixed race who enjoyed mass backing did not aspire to the presidency. Previously, failed rebels of European ancestry were not executed. Mexicans still honor their second president for his prominent role in the independence struggle. Historian Justo Sierra wrote this epitaph for Guerrero, who came from a humble background and had virtually no formal

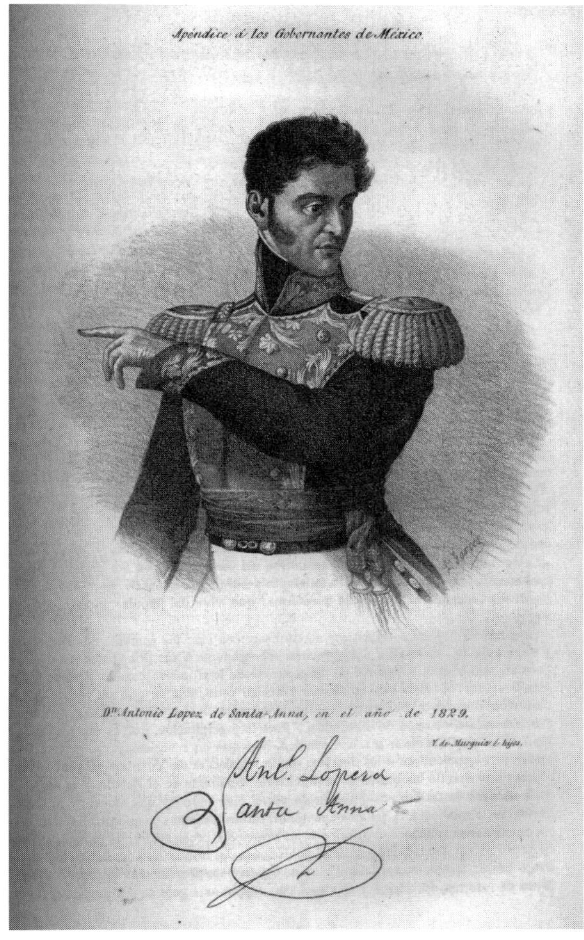

Figure 7.1
Antonio López de Santa Anna

Source: Reproduced courtesy of the Benson Latin American Collection, the University of Texas at Austin

education: “Ambitious partisans had tried to make a politician out of a man who was only a great Mexican.”[51]

While he made a major contribution to the cause of independence, Guerrero did initiate the seizure of power by force in the fledgling republic. Upon hearing how Guerrero had seized the presidency, South American liberator Simón Bolívar lamented, “The casual right of usurpation and pillage has been enthroned in the Mexican capital and countryside as if it were king.”[52]

Bustamante’s assumption of the presidency gave conservatives their first opportunity to curtail the political role of the common man and peasant communities. Lucas Alamán, who served as Bustamante’s minister of interior and foreign affairs, emerged as the driving force behind the administration. Since the constitution vested so much power in state legislatures, Alamán concentrated on deposing legislatures hostile to the conservative agenda. He would induce elements of the state militia to revolt against state governments. Since the states were not organized to defend their interests, they could be picked off one by one.[53]

Bustamante established an authoritarian, elitist, pro-clerical, highly centralized government that alienated many by arresting and imprisoning critics. To allay the rising fear of the upper classes, Bustamante curtailed peasant movements and used the colonial administration as a model for his own. He promised to cut government deficits through efficient management rather than new taxes. However, he spent more on the army than his predecessors—spending that he financed by secretly borrowing from domestic moneylenders (*agiotistas*). The Bustamante administration closed the lively newspapers of the republic's early days if they opposed the president. To render ineffective criticism by writers too distant from Mexico City to intimidate, it banned the sale in Mexico City of periodicals from outside the city.[54]

In November 1831, the federal military commandant general of Jalisco ordered the arrest and execution of the printer responsible for anti-government pamphlets. In response, the Jalisco state government issued a call for other states to rebel in defense of states' rights. Santa Anna was asked to lead the rebellion, which was financed by Veracruz and Tampico customs receipts and backed by state militias. The rebellion, under Santa Anna's leadership, quickly gathered support since Bustamante was held responsible for executing Guerrero and was viewed as arbitrary and despotic. Bustamante soon saw that his position was untenable and abandoned the presidency.[55]

Santa Anna, rather than assuming power, ensured that Gómez Pedraza served the last months —December 1832 to April 1833—of the 1829–1833 term to which he had been elected. This created the façade of legality and left Santa Anna's reputation unsullied. Santa Anna received almost all the credit for overthrowing the Bustamante regime, and as a result, enjoyed overwhelming popularity.[56]

The 1832 war to oust Bustamante left Mexicans exhausted in spirit and pessimistic about the future. It also made it abundantly clear that continued state autonomy required state-controlled militias and that those controlling the instruments of force would determine Mexico's future.[57]

ANTONIO LÓPEZ DE SANTA ANNA

> The long and painful transition from colony to independent republic, from absolutist monarchical rule to constitutional government, from corporatist-feudal society to one that privileged individualism, from tradition to modernity, unfolded during Santa Anna's lifetime. His career, his successes and his failures, his rises and falls and the choices he made were all reflections of the times in which he lived.
>
> Will Fowler, 2007[58]

In 1794, Santa Anna was born in Jalapa, Veracruz, the son of a minor official in the colonial administration. At age sixteen, he joined a Veracruz-based infantry militia unit. Between 1811 and 1815, he fought pro-independence forces in northeastern Mexico and later commanded 500 troops in the Veracruz area. In contrast to many of his timid colleagues in the royalist officer corps, Santa Anna was a vigorous commander. On his own initiative, he made land available to amnestied insurgents to provide them with an alternative to warfare.[59]

Even at the age of twenty-eight, Santa Anna impressed future U.S. Ambassador Joel Poinsett, who commented that he possessed "a very intelligent and expressive countenance." Santa Anna showed a charismatic quality of leadership and the ability to gain control of the Veracruz customs receipts. He first rose to prominence when he issued his Plan of Veracruz calling for limits on Iturbide's power. His defeat of the 1829 Spanish invasion and his leading the forces that ousted President Bustamante further increased his stature. Before he passed from the political scene, Santa Anna had served as president of Mexico six times.[60]

In 1833, Mexico's state legislatures provided Santa Anna with sixteen of the eighteen votes cast, thus electing him president for the 1833–1837 term. He immediately put his personal stamp on the presidency by retiring to his 220,000-acre Veracruz hacienda, Manga del Clavo (Clove Spike), and leaving governance in the hands of Vice-President Valentín Gómez Farías. This enabled Santa Anna to avoid instituting the reforms his liberal constituency expected. Such reforms would inevitably divide society and undermine his popularity.[61]

Gómez Farías was the model of a liberal, middle-class provincial. A native of Guadalajara, he had practiced medicine in Aguascalientes and then served as a congressman from Zacatecas. Upon assuming power, he attempted to impose the values of the Enlightenment upon his reluctant countrymen. He believed members of society should be free to rise or fall according to their ability and that the primary responsibility of government was to ensure that freedom.[62]

Gómez Farías and his allies in Congress introduced sweeping changes affecting the whole society. Following liberal tenets, he shifted the responsibility for education from Church to the states and secularized Franciscan missions in the north. He made payment of agricultural tithes to the Church voluntary. To replenish the national treasury, the government ordered the Church to sell all non-essential property and levied a 6 percent tax on such sales. Priests were forbidden to bring politics into their sermons. Gómez Farías canceled the *fueros* of both the Church and the army. He also reduced the size of the military, placed governors in command of military forces serving in their state, and strengthened state militias. Finally, he launched an intense propaganda campaign against wealthy aristocrats, claiming that wealth should circulate and not remain in the hands of the few.[63]

By 1834, Gómez Farías had not only instituted sweeping change but had accumulated a formidable list of political opponents without having consolidated a power base. To devout common people, his measures affecting the Church constituted rampant anti-clericalism. The Church and the military resented both the end of their *fueros* and their reduced role in society. Many wealthy individuals, who in the abstract supported free enterprise, resented their loss of monopoly and privilege.

Santa Anna possessed a keen sense of the politically possible that bore no relation to ideology. In 1834, he seized upon opposition to Gómez Farías and staged a coup. The elite, the military, and the clergy supported the coup. Santa Anna also drew support from some individuals who had previously favored federalism, but who had decided Mexico required a strong central government to maintain control of Texas, impose order, adequately finance the government, and keep the nation whole. In April 1834, Gómez Farías resigned and the left the country, ending the first great attempt to reform the Church and the army.[64]

Santa Anna then began to restructure government in a manner more sweeping than Gómez Farías had attempted. He dissolved Congress after it granted him the power "to make as many changes in the Constitution of 1824 as he should think needful for the good of the nation without the hindrances and delays which that instrument prescribed."[65]

A new constitution, promulgated in 1836, required voters to have an income of at least a hundred pesos a year or "honest, useful" employment. Such a requirement reduced male suffrage by 60 percent. The constitution also introduced a minimum income requirement for members of the chamber of deputies, senators, and the president. States, which lost their political and financial autonomy, were downgraded to "departments," whose governors were appointed by the president. Santa Anna appointed many aristocratic militia officers as department governors. State legislatures were eliminated. Officials appointed by department governors assumed most municipal functions, greatly limiting peasants' ability to compete for local power and protect their interests. Federal army officers took command of state militias, rendering these forces incapable of defending state interests.[66]

Santa Anna's scrapping of the federalist political structure won him the support of a broad range of interests. The army and the Church supported him for having returned to them the power and privilege that they had previously enjoyed. *Hacendados* supported him for his having denied peasants access to local political power. The Mexico City elite supported him because he restored power to the capital, enabling them to protect their interests in the provinces. Many others supported Santa Anna simply because he promised an end to insecurity and political strife.[67]

As has so often been the case, those promising to rule with a firm hand to end strife have only increased conflict. Provincial interests in Yucatán, Zacatecas, and Texas refused to accept Santa Anna's centralization of power. Many Yucatecans considered Mexico a greater liability than Spain since it lacked the mother country's wealth, stability, and trade connections. Zacatecas sought to keep the federal government at arm's length so more wealth from its rich silver mines would remain in the state, rather than disappearing into federal coffers. In Texas, Anglo settlers who had been allowed to colonize the area after Mexican independence formed the nucleus of the opposition. Some in Texas preferred to remain a part of Mexico, but under the decentralized government provided by the 1824 constitution. Others saw their opposition to Santa Anna as a wedge issue they could use to wrest sovereignty from Mexico and join the United States, from where the overwhelming majority of the colonists had come.[68]

Santa Anna's decisive responses to these movements left permanent changes in the map of Mexico. Since Zacatecas was the closest of the upstarts, he advanced on the state with a 4,000-man force and delivered an ultimatum, declaring that the state militia should lay down its arms or be attacked. Zacatecans rejected the ultimatum since they knew Santa Anna would abolish their state militia, and by so doing, render the state unable to resist the new order. Santa Anna's forces took the state capital in a pre-dawn surprise attack. He not only allowed his troops to plunder the city but removed Aguascalientes from the jurisdiction of Zacatecas, making it a federal territory. Zacatecas never again played a major role on the national political scene.[69]

Texas presented a greater challenge due to its distance from Mexico City. Nonetheless, Santa Anna marched his troops through the central Mexican desert to arrive in San Antonio in February 1836. There, a defiant, largely Anglo force held an old mission now known as the Alamo. Santa Anna's forces stormed the Alamo, killing all its defenders. Feeling this victory ended the Anglo military threat, he very unwisely divided his forces so they could drive what remained of the Anglo opposition east back into Louisiana. On April 21, his 1,200-man force was camped at San Jacinto, near the present city of Houston. There, 910 Texas rebels under the command of Sam Houston routed his force in a surprise attack. Santa Anna was captured and, in order to secure his release, he agreed to recognize Texas's independence from Mexico. After the fall of the Alamo, Anglo colonists had unequivocally embraced separation from Mexico. Even though the Mexican government refused to recognize Texas's independence, the rebels had won de facto independence.

Following his release from Texas, Santa Anna returned to Manga del Clavo—as often occurred when his fortunes declined. In 1838, luck favored Santa Anna in the form of a French invasion. As was the norm in international diplomacy of the time, the French government demanded the payment of damage claims made by its citizens against the Mexican government—a sum of $600,000. These claims included compensation for a French-owned pastry shop destroyed when the mob sacked the Parián market. When the bankrupt Mexican government failed to honor the claims, France landed troops in Veracruz. This incident is known as the Pastry War because of the pastry shop claim.

Santa Anna assembled a force that pushed the French back to their ships. Mexico later met the French monetary claims, but did not yield to other French demands, such as the dismissal of officials the French claimed had mistreated French citizens. This action came at a high personal cost for Santa Anna, since French artillery riddled his leg with shrapnel. Doctors amputated his left leg below the knee after it turned gangrenous. However, Santa Anna's rallying of troops to save Mexico's honor did restore his reputation.[70]

Having redeemed himself politically, Santa Anna returned to the presidency in 1839. To consolidate his position, he attempted to muzzle the press, referring to reporters as "a race of delinquents" and urging state governors to "take the most energetic measures available . . . to purse and apprehend" those responsible for all "seditious" printing.[71]

Neither Santa Anna nor any other Mexican could effectively govern. Between 1839 and 1847, there were twenty-one presidencies, with Santa Anna repeatedly returning to the National Palace. Since presidents came and went with such frequency, none could reshape Mexico. A new constitution, promulgated in 1843 in an attempt to correct the flaws in the two previous constitutions, failed to provide stability.[72]

During these revolving presidencies, ceremony replaced substance. In 1842, Santa Anna staged an elaborate funeral parade to Santa Paula Cemetery, where his severed leg was solemnly interred. He also established a holiday of national sacrifice on the anniversary of the day he lost his leg. The next year, Santa Anna was serving as president when the new constitution was proclaimed. A day-long round of parades, processions, and speeches, a Te Deum, and a bull fight were capped by filling the fountains of the Alameda park with sangría so the poor could celebrate publicly while the wealthy held private parties.[73]

An 1844 coup ousted Santa Anna, who had fallen out of favor due to the bankrupt state of the treasury, his despotic measures, excessive military spending, and the lack of progress on retaking Texas, which was the rationale for increased taxes. Mobs then invaded the Santa Paula Cemetery, destroyed the cenotaph marking the resting place for Santa Anna's leg, and gleefully dragged the leg through the streets.[74]

Santa Anna continued to swirl into and out of the presidency, and, when his fortunes plummeted, into exile. He assumed personal command of the army facing the U.S. forces during the Mexican–American War. With Mexico's defeat and its loss of New Mexico and California, Santa Anna again went into exile.

Following the Mexican–American War, Mexico hit a low point. Losing half its territory demoralized the nation, Yucatán was in rebellion, there were revolts in the heartland, and the Apache and Comanche raided far into northern Mexico and took refuge north of the newly established U.S.–Mexican border. Communications remained poor, and little industry had developed.

This formed the backdrop for a victorious conservative rebellion in 1852. Conservatives claimed that embracing foreign ideas such as federalism and rejecting Mexico's Spanish heritage had resulted in the moral and political disintegration of the nation. The victors wanted to create a government modeled on the old colonial order and saw Mexico's defeat in the Mexican–American War as validation of their views. They also felt that economic growth required a strong central government.[75]

In March 1853, given the power vacuum, eighteen of the twenty-three state legislatures voted to select Santa Anna as president. He returned to the presidency, established a military dictatorship, and promised stability. On this basis, most of the elite backed him. All state legislatures and most town councils were abolished. Santa Anna governed without a constitution and became a monarch in all but name, assuming the title of "His Extremely Serene Highness." During one eight-month period, military spending accounted for 93.9 percent of the government budget. In trying to resurrect the old colonial model, Santa Anna reestablished compulsory payment of agricultural tithes to the Church.[76]

His Extremely Serene Highness tolerated no political dissent and exiled those who refused to kowtow to him, including the liberal governor of Oaxaca, Benito Juárez. In 1854, John Black, the American consul in Mexico City, commented on the Santa Anna administration: "There is no doubt generally speaking that it is the most unpopular government that has ever existed in this country since their independence, although nothing dare be said against it."[77]

Santa Anna's final administration did improve highways, reform the judicial system, and promote education. Medals were given to outstanding educators. Visiting Spanish poet José Zorrilla wrote that all bandits had been caught and executed, leaving only Santa Anna to rob.[78]

Once again, dictatorial control imposed by Santa Anna led to revolt. Juan Álvarez, who had fought royalists in the area now forming the state of Guerrero, led the rebellion. From 1820 to 1862, Álvarez controlled this area, maintaining a political fiefdom. During this period, he protected Indian land rights and provided tax relief. Those he protected formed his power base.

The rebels' March 1854 manifesto became known as the Plan of Ayutla. It promised the removal of Santa Anna, the writing of yet another constitution, and constituting the nation "in a stable lasting manner" to guarantee individual liberty.[79]

Some of the rebels' proclamations were more radical. They accused Santa Anna of having resurrected the "oligarchic" ruling class that had murdered Guerrero and that was sucking Mexico's blood dry. The rebels emphasized the need for a political system that included all of Mexico's citizens, not the just wealthy Creoles.

Santa Anna's intemperate spending for government and the military made inevitable the imposition of new taxes, which further undermined him. These taxes fell on, and alienated, landholders and the Church. By the early 1850s, many moneylenders had invested in factories and sought stability and access to national markets. When they realized that Santa Anna could not guarantee these, they supplied funds to Álvarez. At the same time, thousands in small towns and villages rallied against Santa Anna in the hope that the Plan of Ayutla would allow the restoration of federalism.[80]

In August 1855, as his elite support crumbled and the heterogeneous coalition of creoles, Indians, and mestizos opposing him continued to grow, Santa Anna resigned and went into exile, sailing on a warship named *Iturbide.* In 1874, he was allowed to return to Mexico, where he died two years later impoverished and nearly forgotten.[81]

The rebels' 1855 victory represented the triumph of the periphery over the center, of militia units over the regular army, and of the countryside over the city. A broad coalition facilitated victory, and like all such alliances, once it had accomplished its original purpose, it required some sorting out to determine its direction. What distinguishes the Ayutla movement from other uprisings of the period was that its triumph ushered a new political generation into power. This group would radically change existing political structures.[82]

In the early nineteenth century, Santa Anna used his impressive political talents to repeatedly assume the presidency. One of the keys to his success was his ability to appear to be above partisan interests in a bitterly divided environment, to be beholden to no faction, and to assume power reluctantly. Santa Anna understood the importance of propaganda in a way none of his antagonists did. He and his followers converted his campaigns into epic legends and his questionable triumphs into dazzling victories. His political longevity did not result from military prowess, since his defeats outweighed his victories. However, his showering the military with promotions, pay raises, pensions, and prestige during each of his administrations facilitated his repeated return to power. Finally, his strong regional base in Veracruz gave him control over the Veracruz customs receipts, upon which the national government depended.[83]

At the end of his final presidency in 1855, many held Santa Anna responsible for Mexico's impoverishment, its being decreased in size by half, and its being overwhelmed by economic woes and profiteering. As a result, Santa Anna has joined the man he helped depose, Iturbide, in Mexico's pantheon of anti-heroes.[84]

However, Mexico's early nineteenth century ills were more of a reflection of the times than of Santa Anna, who occupied the presidency for a total of less than six years. Almost all other Spanish American republics experienced similar shake-out periods. The collapse of colonial control led to a power vacuum that Santa Anna repeatedly filled. In a similar manner, caudillos filled power vacuums from Guatemala (Rafael Carrera) to Argentina (Juan Manuel de Rosas).[85]

CAUSES OF INSTABILITY

> As the nation struggled to overcome the effects of a ruinous decade of civil war that had given it life, it continued to stagger under repeated economic crises, quarrels between Church and State, the machinations of predatory and often illiterate army officers, the defiance of local leaders whose regional interests ran deeper than their allegiance to the nation, and the threats of foreign invasion.
>
> David J. Weber, 1982[86]

Between 1829 and 1855, there were forty-eight changes in the presidency and 319 in the four-member cabinet. However, since the executive branch had not become the all-pervasive hydra it was to become in the twentieth century, such changes were not as devastating as they might appear. While the executive resembled a merry-go-round, members of the national Congress demonstrated considerable courage and determination to sustain the independence of the legislative branch, often in the face of open hostility from the military men who dominated the executive.[87]

State governments, which affected individuals more directly, were neither chaotic nor anarchic. After independence, the national government did not have sufficient strength to challenge village councils and mayors, leaving them with a high degree of local autonomy. While those applying European notions of sound governance saw only chaos, the regions functioned with far more efficiency. Regular elections were held at the state and local level. As historian Timothy Anna observed:

> One has the strongest sense that it mattered very little who occupied the National Palace and that brief sojourns in office should not be counted as "regimes" . . . It is not clear if any president could get his orders obeyed beyond the outer patio of the palace.[88]

Despite its remoteness from the lives of most Mexicans, it is worth considering why the executive branch remained so unstable.

Regional Interests

> The history of Mexico is a history of its states and regions; its identity is an identity based on states and regions.
>
> Timothy Anna, 1998[89]

At the time of independence, Mexico, in the sense we normally use the term today, did not exist. At the time, the term "Mexico" referred to the immediate area surrounding Mexico City, not the area stretching from Chiapas to California. Nor did "Mexico" refer to what had been the Viceroyalty of New Spain, since that area included Central America, Florida, several Caribbean islands, and part of Venezuela.[90]

In 1821, the people of central Mexico, where Aztec culture had held sway, were the only people considered "Mexicans." Further from the capital, people generally felt themselves to be Oaxaqueños, Jaliscenses, or Sonorenses. It would take centralizing forces decades to extend the notion of being "Mexican" to outlying regions. The lack of a term to address citizens of the new nation is illustrated by the Plan of Iguala, which opened by addressing "*americanos*," not "*mexicanos*".[91]

At independence, little bound the hinterland to the capital or induced its residents to follow policy set in Mexico City. Iturbide's choice of the term "empire" for his creation indicated the general belief that the new entity would be an aggregation of distinct jurisdictions.[92]

For decades, the provincial elites felt that there were no advantages to be gained by submitting to a strong central government. Rather than submitting, as historian David W. Walker noted, "*empresarios* and other groups that made up the emerging dominant class in Mexico ruthlessly manipulated the state for private gain, to the detriment of class interests, economic growth, and political stability." Eventually these elites did accept that a strong national government would be advantageous. As a result, after the middle of the century, they sought to forge a nation, just as, over the centuries, the kingdoms and provinces on the Iberian Peninsula were forged into the Spanish nation.[93]

New Spain miraculously resisted the fragmentation that the other Spanish viceroyalties underwent after independence. Since the area that became Mexico was divided into two *audiencias*, two autonomous governments, twelve intendancies, and one captaincy general, it was by no means a foregone conclusion that Mexico would remain whole.[94]

Centralists vs. Federalists

> The provinces generally believed that sovereignty had reverted to them when the Iturbide regime ceased to exist.
>
> Jaime E. Rodríguez O., 1992[95]

Much of the instability of the early republic resulted from the Mexico City elite's attempting to concentrate power in the capital. Opposing them were the provincial elites who felt that shifting power from Madrid to Mexico City was only a marginal improvement over colonialism. This later group wanted regional centers, not the old viceregal capital, to exercise power. The conflict between Mexico City and Guadalajara, which had long chafed under control from the viceregal capital, was especially pronounced.[96]

Those desiring devolution of power to regions were known as federalists. They assumed they were victorious when the 1824 Constitution placed extensive power, including electing the president, in the hands of state governments. However, powerful interests representing Mexico City—the centralists—were far from vanquished. Beginning in late 1823, the federal government began sending military forces against state governments, especially those in Puebla and Jalisco, which appeared to pose the greatest challenge to centralized power. The centralists also imposed themselves by interpreting the meaning of federalism in a manner that favored centralized control.[97]

Even after the scrapping of the 1824 Constitution, federalists remained more numerous then the centralists. However, since they were never unified, their strength did not match their numbers. This permitted the centralists to increase their strength by abolishing state militias, increasing the strength of the federal army, and allying with the Church.[98]

The center's efforts to reassert hegemony over all aspects of government in the early republic became the major cause of political turmoil. The regional elites, which opposed this reassertion, derived much of their influence from ties to town-based groups in their region. Nothing indicates that the federal government was more socially enlightened than state or local governments in this period. The federalists attempted to thwart centralizing efforts by: 1) maintaining control of revenue sources, 2) fracturing the political power of the center by separating the Federal District from the State of Mexico, 3) expelling the Spanish who were seen as a major source of the central elite's power, and 4) maintaining state-controlled militias.[99]

The 1824 constitution created a de jure federalist system. However, federalism lasted only five years since centralism was so deeply rooted, as was the tendency to depend on the will of a single man. During the Victoria and Guerrero administrations, the states never acted in concert against the center, state militias were unable to confront the central government's army, and the clerical and military *fueros* lent strength to centralism. Because Guerrero had taken the presidency by force, he was left with little political support among moderates who might otherwise have sustained him. The radicals, who had organized the coup that put him into power, were unable to keep him in office. He did not build an organized base of support during his short administration. As a result, Guerrero's federalist administration was easy prey to a centralist coup. Once in power, centralists used the state to solidify their control.[100]

FINANCIAL CRISES

> The new republic was caught in a vicious cycle: financial problems caused political turmoil, which in turn unsettled an already shaky economy.
>
> Ruth Olivera and Liliane Crété, 1991[101]

A lack of revenue severely constrained government effectiveness and the incumbents' ability to resist challenges to their power. When revenues fell, the government could not meet defense costs and became vulnerable to challenge by regionally based military strongmen. If taxes on outlying areas were increased, those being taxed might rebel. If the government could not meet its international financial obligations, it risked foreign intervention to collect debts owed to foreigners.

In 1825, President Victoria's budget totaled 21 million pesos, of which the military received 90 percent. This proposed expenditure amounted to four times government income, since between 1806 and 1824, government revenue declined from 39 million pesos to 5.4 million. To further add to its financial woes, the national government accepted the debts of the colonial administration. Even after dubious claims were disallowed, the colonial debt assumed by the republic totaled 45 million pesos. Accepting the colonial debt favored those who had lent the most to sustain the colonial regime—the Church and the elite.[102]

The traditional sources of revenue the colonial government had relied on were either greatly reduced or unavailable. Both the mining tax and Indian tribute, which together had supplied 30 percent of colonial revenue, were abolished. In addition, the *alcabala* and the pulque tax were transferred from the federal to state governments. Customs receipts formed the only reliable source of federal government revenue. However, the government pledged much of these receipts to liquidate debts, leaving little for day-to-day operations. When protectionists were ascendant, imports declined, reducing tariff collection. Smuggling and the seizure of customs receipts by military officers to pay troops further decreased tariff revenue. Also, since Mexican exports did not generate enough revenue to finance large-scale importation, there were few imports to levy tariffs on. Imports fell at an average rate of 3 percent a year from the mid-1820s to the mid-1840s, thus undermining customs duties as a revenue source. Despite these limitations, between 1826 and 1831 levies on foreign trade generated 54 percent of tax revenue.[103]

Financial solvency was undermined by the fallacious assumption that the tax structure that had functioned so well during the colonial period could finance the republic. Officials simply assumed that the new government would inherit the legitimacy of the Crown. However, the elite, which had willingly financed the Crown, refused to pay taxes since it regarded the newly created federal government as a greedy consumer of its wealth, not as a partner in the development of the nation. Between 1824 and 1867, financial policy was in constant flux, as is indicated by fact that the average term of finance ministers was less than five months.[104]

Since the old colonial tax collection system had collapsed, states assumed the responsibility for collecting taxes and then transferring revenue to the federal government. However, this often resulted in delayed payment. In other cases, states simply failed to report what they had collected. In desperation, the federal government responded to its fiscal problems with ad hoc measures such as forced loans, confiscation and sale of assets, including those of the Church, and a wide variety of tax increases.

Some decisions that individually appeared to be sound further undermined government finances. The tobacco monopoly was eliminated to please the citizenry. In the name of equality, the tribute paid by Indians was abolished. Taxes on silver production were sharply reduced to reinvigorate mining.

For a brief period in the 1820s, the government remained solvent by borrowing aboard. However, after it defaulted on its foreign loans and could no longer borrow abroad, it turned to domestic moneylenders (*agiotistas*). The *agiotistas* produced a vicious cycle of mortgaging future income to secure funds at ever higher interest rates. This reduced even further the revenue available for daily needs and necessitated increased borrowing from the moneylenders.[105]

In the context of a shrinking economy, government borrowing at annual interest rates as high as 536 percent created a veritable Ponzi game. Since the government had no solid revenue base, it used new loans to liquidate old debts. Since the loans were so risky, interest rates were exorbitant. When the amount borrowed reached untenable levels, as it frequently did, the whole system would collapse. Sometimes new governments would repudiate loans to previous governments. In other cases, they lowered interest rates by decree. Often, when all obligations could not be met, certain sets of lenders were paid, and others were not. Lenders would use all their political leverage, domestic and foreign, to ensure they were among those repaid.

The *agiotistas* became one of the most influential groups, utterly unaccountable to any constituency. They would lend money to those contemplating a coup if they felt that their chances of having previous loans repaid would be enhanced by the coup. These financiers often obtained their initial capital in foreign commerce, profited from lending to the government, and then diversified into other activities, notably the textile industry and agriculture. In 1844, historian Carlos Bustamante observed they constituted a "class of people cursed by God and abhorred by the whole nation."[106]

The Military

> The praetorian bands of Mexico like those of Rome must have money and indulgences and those who promise fairest secure their aid, until one promise fails or a better one is made.
>
> Anthony Butler, U.S. Chargé d'affaires, 1830[107]

The military impaired government effectiveness by consuming the majority of government revenue. Officers repeatedly installed governments that they felt would better serve their financial and other interests. The military's size alone made it inevitable that it would be a major consumer of government income. Both the insurgent and royalist forces were kept under arms after independence, yielding a force of some 75,000. The 22,750 men still under arms in 1825 continued to place a tremendous drain on government finances.[108]

Valid reasons existed for maintaining military strength. Until 1825, the Spanish continued to occupy San Juan de Ulúa and interfere with operations of the port of Veracruz. Even after that date, the military faced the real threat of Spanish reconquest. Soon after Spain recognized Mexican independence and the danger of reconquest faded, Mexicans expected the military to reoccupy Texas.

Military spending and influence, however, went far beyond Mexico's needs. Between 1821 and 1851 only six civilians served as president—for a total of 947 days—and fifteen generals occupied the presidency. Generals who commanded a division received three times the salary of governors. A high level of military spending was required to prevent officers from revolting and installing a patron who would provide increased funding. This was reflected in a saying of the time, "When salaries are paid, revolutions fade."[109]

The many coups of the period mobilized no more than a few thousand men, and none attracted mass popular support. A successful coup provided virtually the only access to the presidency. Junior officers would support coups in response to explicit promises of promotions and wealth if the coup succeeded. Coups were not formed exclusively within the army. Regional factions of army officers formed alliances with tobacco and cotton farmers, textile manufacturers, and merchants, promising them the requisite government permits to ensure their business success in exchange for their support. Once they seized power, military men relied on civilian politicians to administer the country since the officers had little administrative experience.[110]

In addition to seeking financial favor, the military establishment openly opposed the maintenance of state militias, which it saw as a threat to its privileged status. This led to conflict, since outside Mexico City, people considered militias to be protectors of states' rights and checks on the power of the army.[111]

Since there were few avenues to acquiring wealth in early nineteenth-century Mexico, the seizure of state power became an accepted avenue of upward mobility. Senior military officers, despite their lack of inherited wealth, repeatedly acquired substantial rural holdings.[112]

Despite its massive consumption of government revenue and its strong political role, the army never formed an effective fighting force, as became apparent during the Mexican–American War.

While officers used the military as a path to wealth and political power, its ranks were formed by the forced enlistment of vagabonds and criminals in cities and Indians from rural areas. Before the middle of the century, the military never emerged as a cohesive body. Many army commanders became autonomous political operatives, forming political alliances with individuals and factions to suit their own and their region's aims. State militia units, which liberals felt would offset the political power of the regular army, were similarly divided along partisan and social lines.[113]

Caudillos

> There was a ruralization as well as a militarization of power, which represented a shift in the center of political gravity from the city to the countryside, from the intellectuals to the interest groups, from the bureaucrats to the rural militias, and from the politicians to the caudillos.
>
> John Lynch, 1994[114]

The weakness of the central government created a political vacuum filled by regional strongmen known as *caudillos*. They were generally of humble origins and had achieved prominence by leading their men in combat, especially in isolated rural areas. These strongmen emerged during the independence war when the colonial government could not impose its will throughout Mexico. Some of these caudillos were insurgent leaders while others were royalist officers who had operated without direct control from Mexico City. Both royalists and insurgents built personal followings and emerged as caudillos. The most famous of all the caudillos, Santa Anna, expanded his influence from his Veracruz power base to the national scene.[115]

Caudillos exercised so much power at the local and regional level that they undermined the authority of the central government. Often they defended local interests that the national government either ignored or opposed. Juan Álvarez, the insurgent leader from Guerrero, maintained regional power to the almost total exclusion of the national government. Eventually he used his home region as a power base to oust Santa Anna. Caudillos retained local power and aspired to national power by promising offices and other rewards to followers once they triumphed. They were the legitimate and perhaps even natural leaders of their home provinces, whether the central government (and later historians) liked it or not. Although a few caudillos, such as Santa Anna, achieved national power, most operated at the regional level and buttressed regional Creole elites.[116]

Divided Elites

> It is precisely because no school of thought, no ideological force, decisively carried the field in nineteenth-century Mexico that unanimity and consensus were not possible.
>
> Timothy Anna, 1993[117]

The elite lacked consensus on the direction the country should move in. During the early post-independence period, it formed factions that became known as federalists and centralists. Mexicans who had favored continued colonial rule generally advocated a monarchy after independence. When they failed to establish a monarchy, they became centralists. Those who had favored independence from Spain sought a republic after the end of Spanish rule. After the establishment of the republic, they advocated federalism.[118]

The centralists advocated a strong central government with Mexico City in control, as in colonial times. They felt the army and the Church should play major political roles. The centralists were generally supported by the military, which could count on receiving a large part of the revenues raised by centralist governments. Centralists also advocated developing industry, rather than purchasing manufactured goods aboard. As Lucas Alamán noted, "Manufacturing stimulates agriculture just as mining does, but in a more stable manner."[119]

The federalists wanted to loosen the old system so they might advance more rapidly. State governments tended to be federalist, since they wanted power to be exercised at the state level, rather than at the national level. They wanted colonial institutions reformed and special privileges for the Church and the army abolished. Federalists turned their back on their Spanish heritage, claiming it should be put behind them. When in power, federalists often acted like centralists in an attempt to spread their notions nationwide. As with most of the interest groups of the time, federalism was based on broad, heterogeneous, shifting alliances. Often federalists were united only by a common enemy.[120]

By the middle of the century, the federalists and centralists had evolved into groups known, respectively, as liberals and conservatives. The term "liberal," as used in nineteenth-century Mexico, meant limited government, a capitalist economy, and a low level of government regulation, especially of foreign trade.[121]

The free individual, unrestrained by government or corporate bodies and equal to his fellows under the law, was the liberal ideal. They felt a constitution should limit government authority and advocated the strengthening of state-controlled militias to break the regular army's control over politics. With such limits, liberals felt, the individual would thrive after being freed from the constraints imposed by traditional corporate entities—the Church, the army, guilds, and Indian communities. Since the Church was the strongest of these entities, liberals targeted its wealth, judicial privileges, and control over education and the events of life itself—birth, marriage, and death. Similarly, they felt that restrictions affecting the sale of property should be removed, including those imposed by the traditional Indian community.

In this atmosphere, they assumed free individuals could apply their initiative, using land placed on the market, to increase wealth. Liberals based their hopes on international trade, feeling that the country would best be served by an international division of labor. Under such a scheme, Mexico would export raw materials and agricultural products and import manufactured goods. Rather than redistributing wealth to the poor, as twentieth-century liberals often advocated, their nineteenth-century predecessors strove to create as many independent economic actors as possible, each competing on equal terms, in an attempt to maximize market efficiency. They felt this would lead to the liberal ideal—a nation of yeoman farmers and master craftsmen unhindered by restrictive laws.[122]

Liberalism was not a defined political party, but rather a broad shifting coalition of rural strongmen, state governments, old insurgents, new radicals, ideologues, and their mass bases. They shared a common desire to tame the three icons of the Plan of Iguala—the Church, the Spanish community, and the military.[123]

The conservatives continued the centralist tradition and were backed by *hacendados*, militarists, monarchists, and the Catholic hierarchy. They felt their social position reflected their better bloodlines and their natural superiority over those with non-European ancestors—the majority of the nation. They looked to Europe as a model for development, rather than to the United States.[124]

Conservatives advocated a strong military and the maintenance of Church privileges. They also felt that the government should play a major role in determining the course of economic development. Power, conservatives felt, should be in the hands of the prosperous class, the group they perceived as most able to manage the affairs of state. To keep power there, they advocated restricting access to the ballot box through such means as property requirements for voting.[125]

Remnants of the dominant class in colonial times formed the most important conservative group. Its members had major investments in central Mexican commerce and agriculture. They felt centralism would increase their political power, enabling them to protect their interests and manipulate markets. Former royalist officers allied with them to take advantage of their newly acquired political power.[126]

Liberalism was the more diverse of the two ideological currents, mixing a variety of beliefs, each with its own regional, class, and ethnic dimension. The category liberal became so broad that it came to embrace groups that were often in conflict.[127]

Although liberals and conservatives considered themselves as being at opposite ends of the political spectrum, they agreed on more than they disagreed. Leaders of both groups came from the urban middle and upper classes, roughly the top 20 percent of the income strata. Neither group sought to build a base among the rural majority. Although they were less elite-oriented than the conservatives, liberals still held the common citizen in low regard. For example, liberal Lorenzo de Zavala commented, "The proletarian class of citizen lacks even the capacity necessary to distinguish between the candidates it ought to nominate." The elite saw the excesses of the French Revolution, as well as the looting of the Parián market, as examples of the political chaos that resulted from too much empowerment of the masses.[128]

The elite also agreed that the hacienda should remain intact. Most *hacendados* were conservatives, so conservatives not surprisingly supported the institution. Liberals were reluctant to force the subdivision of the hacienda, feeling market forces would best harmonize the interests of the individual and society. They failed to realize the contradiction in their own beliefs. They accepted the Jeffersonian dream of agrarian democracy. However, since they failed to force the partition of haciendas, little land was available for small farmers.[129]

Liberals and conservatives failed to agree on what nation to emulate. Conservatives looked to Spain and its Catholic heritage. In contrast, nineteenth-century liberals viewed the United States much as twentieth century Marxists viewed the Soviet Union, considering it as the land of progress and of the future.[130]

These ideological groupings, federalist, centralist, liberal, and conservative, were only the most prominent of the period. Other groups abounded, known as anarchists, aristocrats, and innovators, as well as groups named for their leaders, such as Santa Anna. None of these groups formed formal political parties and all were quite fluid. Individuals often moved from one political camp to another. Since they shared so many beliefs, individuals could change sides without losing credibility. Many formed alliances based, not upon ideology, but on personal networks of power (*caciquismo*), village or locality, corporate or peer group, or profession. This explains in part why some leaders, such as Santa Anna, could draw such a politically disparate following.[131]

Nation vs. Village

Much of the early nineteenth-century instability resulted from unsuccessful attempts to reconcile two powerful ideals—the sovereignty of the nation and the sovereignty of villages. Neither centralists nor federalists were able to create a functional national government and simultaneously respond to villagers' desire to control their own resources. Elites of any persuasion seeking power often mobilized locally based militia forces to claim power. After the elites took power, the communities that had been mobilized would retain their arms and demand concessions, such as the confirmation of community lands and municipal sovereignty, which those in power were loath to grant.[132]

Early Mexican history differs sharply from that of the United States, which had become independent less than half a century earlier. In New Spain, the entire government had been built on a top-down basis, with power coming from the Crown. When this single legitimating institution disappeared in 1821, nothing bound Mexicans together. Not only did Mexicans have to create new institutions, but people had to learn to respect them.[133]

Simón Bolívar commented on Spanish Americans' poor preparations for democracy:

> As long as our countrymen do not acquire the political talents and virtues which distinguish our brothers to the north, wholly popular systems, far from working to our advantage, will, I greatly fear, come to our ruin. Unfortunately, these characteristics are beyond our reach in the degree

> to which they are required. On the contrary, we are dominated by the vices contracted by rule of a nation like Spain, which has only distinguished itself by ferocity, ambition, vindictiveness and greed.[134]

In British North America, there had been a significant degree of self-government. The institutions the British created, such as J.P. courts, country courts, houses of burgesses, and town meetings in New England, remained intact after U.S. independence and provided a stable framework for the new government. Similarly, the colonies had enjoyed a relatively free press, which continued after independence. Economic diversity—shipbuilding, farming, and some manufacturing—led to internal trade ties that held the former colonies together. Britain's 1783 recognition of U.S. independence minimized the danger of recolonization and decreased the need for military spending. Finally, the elite in the United States enjoyed a high degree of cohesion through the first five U.S. presidencies.[135]

THE CHURCH

As with other institutions in Mexico, independence had a profound impact on the Church. Its financial strength had been undermined by the 1767 seizure of Jesuit property, the 1804 Consolidation decree, and war damage to remaining Church property. The Church also suffered because of the close association between the Church hierarchy and the Crown during the independence struggle.[136]

Even though its wealth had declined, the Church did retain title to vast properties, urban and rural. It continued to charge fees for marriages, baptisms, and other religious services and receive the agricultural tithe. To the extent it was possible with its diminished resources, the Church continued to provide credit. In addition, as in colonial times, the Church maintained birth, marriage, and death records.[137]

Independence produced a sharp decline in the number of priests, as some priests sympathizing with the rebels had been executed during the independence war, some Spanish priests were expelled, priests ceased to arrive from Spain, and the number of native-born clergy declined. Many parishes were left unattended, and, as a result, Mass and sacraments were often unavailable. The number of clergy fell from 7,341 in 1810 to 4,008 by the 1830s.[138]

With the authority of the Crown gone, the Church acted with little restraint from civil authority. Nevertheless, it worked in relative harmony with civil officials to pursue the common goal of social control. The Church emerged as one of the few cohesive forces in Mexico, transcending regional and class differences. Lucas Alamán commented that the Church formed "the only common bond which united all Mexicans, when all the rest have been broken."[139]

Toward the middle of the century, as the Church regained its strength, anti-clericalism became a potent force. Many politicians envied the Church, which was obviously more stable, wealthier, and more popular than the government. Thus they sought to tax and control it to restore the balance between Church and state. They also felt Church power and privileges retarded economic growth. This feeling was especially strong among young, upwardly mobile professionals who viewed the Church as an obstacle to nation-building and to their own economic and social aspirations. The more radical liberals (*puros*) viewed an all-out attack on remaining Church wealth and power as a necessary condition for change. The notion that the Church hindered growth and undermined national sovereignty was largely restricted to the elite and to those aspiring to that status.[140]

To fend off liberal attacks, the Church allied with political conservatives and became more conservative itself. Since conservatives felt the Church provided spiritual certainty and bore a long social and cultural tradition that bound society together, they responded vigorously to attacks on the religious establishment.[141]

MEXICAN SOCIETY AFTER INDEPENDENCE

The New Order

After independence, Article 12 of the Plan of Iguala, which declared all Mexicans to be legally equal, guided government policy. Not only were Mexicans legally equal, the official usage of racial categories was discontinued. No longer did census, marriage, or baptismal documents indicate one's ethnicity. An 1822 marriage register in a Mexico City church contained the following notation:

> By order of the superior government a proclamation was made public on the 14th of this month of January ordering that the qualities of Spaniards, Indians, Mulattoes, etc. no longer be specified in parish registers, but that everybody receive the qualification of American, and this order will be carried out from today onwards.[142]

Though race disappeared from official documents, not surprisingly it did not vanish as a social concern. Race simply became an unwritten component of Mexican culture, with roughly the same significance as before. In the 1840s, U.S. Ambassador Waddy Thompson remarked, "At one of these large assemblies at the President's palace, it is very rare to see a lady whose color indicates any impurity of blood."[143]

A society based on class replaced legally mandated racial categories, leaving individuals, in most cases, with the same social standing as they had enjoyed before independence. The white man remained on top of society, with the Creole replacing the Spaniard. Especially favored were Creoles who had served in the royalist army and then followed Iturbide.[144]

The abolition of racial categories did provide for increased social mobility. Mestizos began to take advantage of new opportunities to rise on the social scale. Non-whites, in general, could obtain better jobs and interact more freely with other groups at all but the upper levels of society. Former slaves and their descendants began to vote, run for, and be elected to public office. A few Indians, most notably Benito Juárez, also took advantage of increased opportunity for social mobility.[145]

In rural areas, large estates remained in the hands of a relatively small group of Creoles, who were often bound together by kinship ties, which they used to dominate rural labor and resources. In many areas where severe combat had occurred, diverse rural peoples challenged Creole dominance. In some areas of the Bajío, where commercial agriculture had been abandoned after heavy fighting, tenants enjoyed much greater autonomy than before as they became responsible for producing their own crops.[146]

In other parts of rural Mexico, as throughout Spanish America, the new order brought little in the way of improved material circumstances, let alone electoral democracy. The independence movement had been essentially conservative. Debt peonage increased after independence due to a labor scarcity resulting from the number of war dead. Historians' interpretations of debt peonage vary. Some see it as an oppressive force trapping rural workers in a never-ending cycle of poverty and exploitation. Others see it as reflecting rural workers having sufficient bargaining power to demand a cash advance during times of labor scarcity. At the time, a few liberals, such as Melchor Ocampo, denounced the immorality of debt peonage. However, he and other liberals were afraid of social conflict, so they took no action on the issue.[147]

No longer did taxes fall on specific social groups, such as the tribute born by the Indians in colonial times. Nor were special taxes levied to finance corporate groups, such as the merchant guild. Policy makers embraced laissez faire economic policies, assuming that a free market would enable all citizens to prosper. However, as historian Richard Graham noted, "Those reformers could not have been expected to know that when superimposed on still remaining hierarchical and elitist traditions, these policies would mean merciless exploitation."[148]

The government, having eliminated ethnic classification, tried to inculcate allegiance to the state and nation rather than to the Indian village. Communities countered the state's effort by striving to retain their indigenous cultures. Their success in large part resulted from the limited coercive power of the modernizers. At the same time, rural violence increased, as peasants responded to the weakness of the state by attempting to forcibly resolve conflicts with landowners. Similarly, landowners felt that without a strong state they could dispossess peasants by force. In addition, both liberals and conservatives would mobilize peasants to bolster their political projects, using them as cannon fodder.[149]

The government did make a valiant attempt to provide universal public education, although such an undertaking clearly exceeded the resources available. An 1842 law made education obligatory for boys and girls aged seven to fifteen. As has often been the case in Mexican history, this law reflected more a statement of good intentions than a change in educational practice. Schools were simply not available for all the children the law compelled to attend. In 1844, only 4.8 percent of children were in school.[150]

Between independence and the middle of the nineteenth century, Mexico's population grew slowly due to war, famine, poor sanitation, lack of medical care, and the failure to attract immigrants. During this period, births equaled roughly 4 percent of the population each year, while deaths equaled 3 percent. Between 1820 and 1854, Mexico's population increased from 6.2 million to 7.9 million.[151]

Most of Mexico's mestizo population lived in rural areas or in small villages. Such villages had dirt streets, few amenities, and were dominated by the village church, both architecturally and spiritually. Retail sales were largely transacted in weekly open-air markets held in the principal square, where a wide variety of wares were offered for sale. As was the case in Indian villages, residents of mestizo villages had little contact with the outside world, which increased the difficulty of inculcating a sense of national identity. Village life had changed little since the late colonial period.[152]

The collapse of colonial rule ended royal efforts to protect Indian lands. However, a weakened central government gave villagers more room to maneuver. Their goals included minimizing taxes, protecting individual and collective land holdings, and limiting interference in village life by state and national governments. To further these goals, they promoted local leaders whom they felt would further their interests, went to court, and resorted to violence. They influenced events at the regional and national level by supporting aspirants to power whom they felt would serve their interests.[153]

About 1850, Carl Sartorius, a German who had lived in Mexico for decades, described a typical rural home:

> Inside the hut, upon a floor of earth just as nature formed it, burns day and night the scared fire of the domestic hearth. Near it, stand the *metate* and *metlapil*, a flat and a cylindrical stone for crushing the maize, and the earthen pan (*comal*) for baking the maize bread. A few unglazed earthen pots and dishes, a large water pitcher, a drinking cup and dipper of gourd-shell constitute the whole wealth of the Indians' cottage, a few rude carvings, representing saints, the decoration. Neither tables nor benches cumber the room within, mats of rushes or palm leaves answer for both seat and table. They serve as beds for their rest at night, and for their final rest in the grave.

In dry areas, homes were often built of adobe. Few homes were made of wood, since, due to its scarcity, it was too expensive. The price of wood, the only available fuel, also made the use of kiln-baked bricks prohibitively expensive. In wetter areas, logs often supported a thatched roof while wickerwork, which allowed air and light to enter, formed the walls.[154]

Cities differed from villages not only in population size but in the number of amenities, the presence of retail shops, and in their having a substantial Creole population. Creoles typically served

Figure 7.2 *Hut near Córdoba, Veracruz*

Source: Reproduced courtesy of the Benson Latin American Collection, the University of Texas at Austin

as craftsmen, government officials, physicians, lawyers, merchants, manufacturers, and mine operators, and in the higher orders of the clergy. The affluent lived near the central square in multistory houses. The sides of the main square not occupied by the church or official buildings had ground floor arcades where warehouses, wine and coffee shops, and retail stores supplied a wide variety of goods, many of which were imported. Larger cities had numerous convents and monasteries and some, such as Puebla, Guanajuato, and Guadalajara, had permanent theaters. For the less sophisticated, there were bullrings.[155]

The one-story dwellings of the less affluent stood further from the city square. As in colonial times, the poorest residents occupied city fringes. Sartorius commented on these outlying areas:

> In Mexico, the suburbs are mean and dirty, and inhabited by the lowest classes. Refuse and filth, carcasses of animals and rubbish of buildings are found piled up at the entrances of the streets, by the side of wretched hovels, the abode of ragged vagabonds or half naked Indians.[156]

Policy Towards the Indigenous

In keeping with Enlightenment ideals, Indians (but not the military or priests) were declared legally equal to other citizens. Official documents referred to residents of the abolished communities as "those previously called Indians."[157]

Not only were indigenous people denied separate status, but their communal land-holding system came under legislative attack. An 1826 Veracruz law decreed that "all the land of indigenous communities, forested or not, will be reduced to private property, divided with equality to each person . . . who belongs to the community." Veracruz *hacendados* attempted to accelerate land privatization by releasing cattle to forage on Indian cornfields and by laying claim to land occupied by Indians for countless generations but for which they had no legal title. By the late 1820s, twelve Mexican states, including the central highland states of Mexico, Puebla, and Michoacán, had passed laws mandating the division of communal holdings into private plots.

This legislation sought to replace Indian owners, who had adapted to their environment and co-evolved with it, with owners who attempted to control nature and reshape it for their own purposes. In northern Veracruz, the elite sought to remove a biologically diverse tropical forest where Indians engaged in slash-and-burn agriculture and replace it with grasslands that fed one species—cattle.[158]

Despite the enactment of privatization legislation, states were politically divided, so they could not implement the radical changes in land tenure they had mandated. The fact that states were legislating for changes in land tenure rather than the federal government indicates the active role played by state governments of the period. These states saw no reason why they should wait for officials in Mexico City to formulate agrarian policy.[159]

Economics provided one of the rationales for the compulsory division of Indian communal lands. Legislators felt that the nation would benefit from having communal land with Indian labor becoming subject to market forces. Those smugly accepting this notion declared that such land would remain in the hands of individual Indians.

Others viewed ending the special status enjoyed by Indians as the elimination of a pernicious colonial legacy. Benito Juárez, as governor of Oaxaca, claimed that the Indian community must be broken at all costs, so that individual initiative and modern forms of representative government could prevail. Liberal Gómez Farías viewed the existence of different races in the same society as an eternal cause of conflict. Not only did he refuse to recognize distinctions between races but he sought to hasten the fusion of Indians with the rest of Mexican society.[160]

Fear of the Indian and outright racism also motivated legislative changes. Conservative Lucas Alamán claimed that teaching Indians to read was dangerous, since if they knew how to read, subversive material might fall into their hands and increase their discontent and rebelliousness. In 1824, a clerical member of the Veracruz Congress described Indians as "downright savages, who had successfully resisted every attempt to educate them."[161]

Changes in the status of the Indian were significant not only because of the radical change demanded in the lives of these affected but because, as late as 1850, Indians constituted roughly half of Mexico's population. As municipal governments replaced Indian community governments, Indians had less direct control over their everyday affairs and had to share administration with others who were more powerful and more knowledgeable in the mechanisms of formal electoral government. In many cases, Indians had to pay taxes not formerly levied on them—taxes whose amount could exceed that of the abolished tribute. Finally, after independence, as a result of their being declared legally equal to their fellow citizens, Indians were subject to compulsory military service for the first time.[162]

Dividing Indian lands into individually owned plots inevitably resulted in much of the divided land falling into the hands of non-Indians. Those acquiring such lands enjoyed far greater economic power and had closer ties to the judiciary, which would rule on disputed land claims. In some cases, Indians were required to submit land titles to authorities who failed to return the documents. After independence, the government failed to accept as a responsibility the Crown's practice of providing legal assistance to Indians.[163]

Although legislators rationalized legal equality as a step to benefit the Indians, the reality was far from that. In general terms, the nation preserved the social structure built up over the three previous centuries, and Indians remained a dominated group. In 1841, Fanny Calderón de la Barca, the wife of the first Spanish ambassador to Mexico, wrote: "Certainly no visible improvement has taken place in their condition since independence. They are quite as poor and quite as ignorant and quite as degraded as they were in 1808 . . ."[164]

The Indians' Response

Creoles felt they were not only in keeping with the times but were doing the Indians a favor by declaring them to be legally equal to other citizens, by refusing to even use the term "*indio*" in government records, and by placing their land on the market. However, the record does not indicate that indigenous people were consulted concerning these changes or that they desired to be incorporated into the new social order, where, in any event, they would occupy an inferior economic status. In fact, Indians almost unanimously opposed such changes. In Tlacotalpan, Veracruz, they protested their having being declared "equal" and demanded a return to Indian village government. Authorities rejected their petition, characterizing it as "illegal and unjust."[165]

As non-Indians extended their landholdings at the expense of indigenous communities, Indians turned from formal protests to rebellion. In northern Veracruz, Indian rebels successfully fought government forces to a stalemate, thus ensuring continued control of their land and the survival of the tropical forest in which they lived. Usually, though, Indians did not prevail. In 1832, dozens of villages revolted, beginning with Nochistlan in Oaxaca. The revolt spread to southern Guerrero and Michoacán before it was finally suppressed. As historian John Lynch succinctly stated, "The Indians were losers from independence."[166]

Ten years later an even more serious revolt spread over 60,000 square miles, extending from Michoacán to the Isthmus of Tehuantepec. Indians there violently rejected the changes in language, ecosystem, diet, work regimen, religion, politics, and local autonomy associated with commercial agriculture. In 1845, General Nicolás Bravo described the rebels as "miserable Indians, incapable of understanding the benefits of civilization, returned to a barbarous state worse than that of savage tribes."[167]

Rebellions launched during the Mexican–American War often forced both the federal and the state governments to direct military forces away from advancing Americans and towards other Mexicans. After U.S. troops occupied Mexico City, villagers of Xochitepec, south of Cuernavaca, attacked the nearby hacienda of Chiconcuac to repossess lands, taking advantage of the breakdown of the Mexican army. *Hacendados* turned to the commander of the U.S. occupation force stationed in Cuernavaca, who sent troops. The U.S. troops drove away local insurgents and remained encamped at the hacienda to prevent further attacks. U.S. officers sought a stable Mexico, not social justice.[168]

In 1847, the most serious nineteenth-century Indian conflict broke out in Yucatán as the Maya also took advantage of the opportunity presented by the Mexican–American War. There, the lines were still sharply drawn between dominant Creoles and indigenous Maya. Debt servitude and civil and religious taxes were forced on the indigenous population. Creoles were rapidly increasing the area planted in sugar cane and henequen. They were also producing increased amounts of food for Yucatán's population, which rose from 358,000 in 1800 to 580,000 in 1845. Creoles asserted control over land and water holes (*cenotes*) to which the Maya had previously enjoyed unrestricted access. This expansion of commercial agriculture deprived the Maya of land for growing corn.[169]

To bolster Yucatán's secessionist movement against the central government, Indians had been offered land and tax exemptions to induce them to fight alongside Yucatán's white elite. This provided Indians with arms and combat experience. Creoles then very unwisely broke the promises they had made to Indians. The Indians soon rebelled, hoping to expel or kill all whites, in a conflict named the War of the Castes.[170]

In one of first few recorded statements by Indian leaders at any time in Mexican history, an Indian wrote to a non-Indian priest, asking rhetorically:

> Why didn't you remember us or sound the alarm when the governor began to kill us? Why didn't you protect us or protest when the whites killed so many of us? Why didn't you react when Father Herrera abused poor Indians. He put a saddle on a poor Indian, and rode him, and began to whip him; and spurred him in the stomach. Why didn't you complain when this happened? Now you appeal to the true god. Why didn't you appeal to the true god when they were doing that to the Indians?[171]

By 1848, Indians controlled four-fifths of the Yucatán Peninsula, and had Mérida, the capital, under siege. The Maya in Yucatán could effectively resist the Creole elite since they had access to rifles smuggled in from British Honduras (today's Belize).[172]

The Creole-run government offered Great Britain, the United States, or Spain "domination and sovereignty" in exchange for protection against the Indians. When none of these powers accepted the offer, Yucatán's Creole elite once again embraced the Mexican government.[173]

Just when the Maya forces appeared to be on the verge of taking Mérida and some Creoles were fleeing by boat, the rebels turned back, for reasons that are still poorly understand. Suggested explanations include: 1) Maya peasants wanting to return to their fields at the beginning of planting season; 2) disagreement on goals; 3) the whites having received shipments of rifles, artillery, food, and money from Cuba, Veracruz, and New Orleans; and 4) the distance from Maya supply sources in British Honduras.[174]

Creole-led forces eventually drove the Maya into the jungle with the aid of guns from Spain and a shipment of U.S. arms and munitions brought from Veracruz by Commodore Matthew C. Perry—later to gain fame by opening up Japan to U.S. commerce. In the absence of an official response to the request for a U.S. military force, Yucatecans simply hired U.S. troops demobilized after the Mexican–American War. Several hundred of these troops served for $8 a month and the promise of 320 acres of land. Between 300 and 400 Americans fighting in Yucatán were killed or wounded. This casualty rate of almost 40 percent was roughly double the American casualty rate during the Mexican–American War.[175]

The 16,000-man army defending the Creoles triumphed in part due to the Creoles' ability to recruit Maya living on haciendas. Rather than being strictly a race war, the War of the Castes pitted those tied to the modern cash economy against those tied to the indigenous subsistence economy.

Creoles took some 2,000 Maya prisoners and sold them into servitude in Cuba. They rationalized this as bringing an improvement to lives of the Maya, although they never scrutinized the deportees' condition in Cuba. The Creoles in Yucatán were not only ridded of an enemy but received 25 pesos for each prisoner delivered.[176]

As advancing troops of the Yucatán government pushed the Maya back, Indian rebels embraced a Maya–Christian religious cult that had as a central icon a cross representing the ancient Maya world tree or flowering cross. They believed their crosses spoke, issuing instructions to followers of the movement. The crosses, called *santos*, were dressed in Maya garments, replacing the images of saints with Caucasian features and European clothing, which had previously been venerated.[177]

Inspired by the voices from the crosses, the Maya retired into the jungle of the eastern Yucatán peninsula and maintained their independent existence. Fighting continued at different levels of intensity for decades, with raids, massacres, and reprisals occurring repeatedly. The indigenous there were not subjugated until 1901, when Porfirio Díaz's machine-gun equipped army occupied the last independent rebel town, Santa Cruz. The severity of the struggle is indicated by the fall in Yucatán's population from 582,173 in 1837 to 320,212 in 1862.[178]

Women

The Mexican government redefined the status of both Afro-Mexican slaves and Indians. In contrast, the legal status of women during the early nineteenth century underwent only slow evolution. Sometimes this benign neglect, such as the continued enforcement of the Spanish law guaranteeing women and men equal inheritance rights, favored women. In most cases, though, it hurt women. A woman's only remedy to a failed marriage remained, as in colonial times, an ecclesiastical divorce—a form of Church-sanctioned separation.[179]

The labor of poor, rural women played a crucial role in the economy, even though their efforts never appeared in the detailed hacienda account books of the period. Wives rose before dawn to prepare tortillas for the family. Once that was done, they tended gardens, raised small livestock, and "helped" work the estate fields, with their labor being credited to the accounts of their fathers, sons, or husbands. They earned cash by spinning; in the household they converted crops to food, wool to yarn, and yarn to family clothing, and they raised the next generation.[180]

In Mexico City, women over age eighteen who worked outside the home increased from 32 percent of the labor force in 1811 to 37 percent in 1848. Throughout the early nineteenth century, domestic service remained the main source of female employment. Domestics were often on call twenty-four hours a day, and many received only room and board. An endless stream of young women coming from rural areas ensured that pay for domestics remained low. As other opportunities for women became available, the percentage of Mexico City's female labor force working as domestic servants declined from 54 percent in 1811 to 30 percent in 1848. Increasingly, women were being hired in commerce, food preparation, and service industries. Seamstresses increased from 3 to 14 percent of Mexico City's working women during this period. Women prepared food for sale, sewed, opened small retail establishments, peddled in the streets, and sold in local markets, where they dominated.[181]

As a more modern vision of womanhood gained acceptance, legal and social barriers to women joining the labor force declined. At the same time, economic trends worked against increased female employment. Massive imports undermined industries, such as textiles, in which women worked. Similarly, mechanization deprived women of employment. Machines operated by men deprived many seamstresses of employment.

In 1836, Mexican writer and politician José María Luis Mora noted that "the progress of Mexican civilization is especially evident in the Fair Sex." He also noted that women's education had improved since colonial times when instruction was "reduced to the barest essential required to fulfill domestic obligations."[182]

In 1838, only 3,280 girls were registered in the eighty-two convent, parish, municipal, and private schools in Mexico City. This represented only one-sixth of school-aged girls. During the next two decades, enrollment doubled, and girls attended school in roughly the same percentage as boys. By 1850, 150 women were teaching in Mexico City.[183]

In 1841, after visiting some of the institutions where women she knew volunteered, Fanny Calderón de la Barca commented:

> With the time which they devote to these charitable offices, together with their numerous devotional exercises, and the care which their houses and families require, it cannot be said the life of a Mexican señora is an idle one—nor, in such cases, can it be considered a useless one.[184]

Even though they were banned from public office, women did attempt to influence public policy. More than fifty Mexican women signed an 1829 petition that protested the expulsion of Spaniards—their husbands were threatened with deportation. A delegation of women personally presented the petition to President Guerrero. Women were so active in the all-volunteer Junta Patriótica, which organized the annual commemoration of Mexican independence, that, in 1849, its bylaws were revised to explicitly state that women could be members.[185]

Entrenched male attitudes toward women changed slowly. In 1843, the liberal writer Guillermo Prieto expressed a widely held view when he described an ideal wife: "She should know how to sew, cook, sweep, . . . find pleasure and utility in virtue, [and] be religious, but never neglect my dinner for mass . . . The day she discusses politics, I'll divorce her." Many believed that ending wives' subordination to husbands would upset the social order.[186]

MEXICO CITY

As people fled the tumult of the independence wars, Mexico City's population mushroomed from about 100,000 in the 1790s to 167,000 in 1821, preserving its position as the largest city in the western hemisphere. Between 1824 and 1857, the city's population increased at less than half the rate of the nation as a whole. Even though Mexico City covered a 2-mile-by-1.5-mile area and had a population of 200,000 in 1857, its relative importance diminished. The growth of Mexico City, and of Mexican cities in general, slowed as highly urbanized Spaniards departed, the commercial influence of foreigners increased, and political power shifted to *hacendados*.[187]

Migration from the countryside, not urban births, led to increases in Mexico City's population. Partially offsetting this migration was the toll taken by disease—a reflection of the malnutrition and poor sanitation of most of the city's inhabitants. Diarrhea and dysentery were among the major killers. A smallpox epidemic killed more than 2,000 children in 1840, and cholera epidemics killed almost 6,000 in 1833 and 9,000 in 1850.[188]

The capital inherited by newly independent Mexico formed one of the positive legacies of Spanish colonialism. Just as Mexico's colonial masters had feared, Mexico City emerged as a city larger, richer, and more beautiful than Madrid. Mexico City's grandeur underlay the optimism of the early independence period. As in colonial times, Mexico City housed the National University, the College of Mining, and the San Carlos Fine Arts Academy. The Academy, and other cultural centers, continued to imitate Europe, rather than encouraging innovation. As author Carlos Fuentes noted:

> By the time independence was won from Spain three centuries after the conquest, we did have a new mestizo culture, but did not give ourselves credit for it; we wanted to become just like France or the United States as quickly as possible.[189]

Naturalist Jean Louis Berlandier described Mexico City in 1827:

> It is not until penetrating the interior of the city that one encounters those beautiful streets and lovely civil and religious edifices which constitute one of its principal beauties. Because of its wealth and climate, Mexico City has justly been ranked among the most beautiful cities in the New World, and the Spaniards may always glorify themselves with its having been the work of their bravery and their constancy.[190]

Poinsett, who lived in Mexico City during the same decade, noted a less glamorous aspect of the city—the contrast between rich and poor: "In front of the churches and in the neighborhood of them we saw an unusual number of beggars, and they openly exposed their disgusting sores and deformities to excite our compassion."[191]

The benefits of independence were most readily apparent in the press, as Mexicans took advantage of their newly acquired freedom of expression. Newspapers published in Mexico City became increasingly influential. They made their cases to the public, printing notices, decrees, laws, minutes of special meetings, election results, and statements by prominent politicians. This information circulated widely, reaching the hands of the public within days of an event's occurrence. The openly partisan papers of the era, such as *El sol de México*, favored centralism, while others, such as *El Águila mexicana*, advocated provincial autonomy. The best known paper of the period, *El siglo XIX,* promoted expanded suffrage and a federal republic.[192]

As remains the case today, Mexico City papers were the most influential. Nonetheless, provincial papers proliferated. In 1847, German botanist Karl Heller visited Mérida, Yucatán, population 25,000, and noted that the city supported four newspapers as well as two book printers.[193]

Incumbents paid lip service to freedom of expression and repeatedly infringed upon it, jailing editors and banning certain publications. Often political cartoons expressed notions that, if openly stated, would result in censorship. The chorus of anti-government publications became so strident under Bustamante that he began to subsidize pro-government papers—a tactic widely used by his twentieth-century successors.[194]

THE MEXICAN ETHOS

> Bankruptcy and political inexperience were shaky foundations on which to construct a new state over an immense territory without effective communications and a heterogeneous, badly distributed population.
>
> Josefina Vázquez, 2000[195]

The English settlers in North America brought with them the ideals of the Reformation and the Enlightenment. By the time of their arrival, the power of the British monarchy had been limited, a robust private sector flourished, and the religious monopoly of the Roman Catholic Church had been broken. Mexico lacked these influences since the Spanish settled New Spain earlier and then closed it to new ideas.[196]

The United States was relatively homogenous in the early nineteenth century as a result of the English having eliminated or pushed aside the indigenous population and then created small farms. After independence, townships organized and funded basic public education. In contrast, the Spanish superimposed themselves on the existing Indian population. After independence, the small Creole population maintained its privileges, denying power to the vast majority and refusing to finance a broad-based educational system.[197]

The differences between Mexico and the United States at independence reflect more their economic foundations than any grand colonial design. Given New Spain's endowment of precious metals, fertile tropical land, and a sedentary indigenous population, the Spanish constructed the highly inegalitarian society that Humboldt commented on. In contrast, in British North America, the colonizers found neither precious metals, nor a subordinate labor source comparable to the Mesoamericans, nor land suitable for crops such as sugar, best produced on plantations. This resulted in a society where land ownership was more equitable. The examples of Jamaica and the British Caribbean islands, where harsh slave regimes prevailed, indicates that what shaped New World colonies was not an abstract colonial model but the nature of the colony's economy.[198]

Mexican writer Carlos Fuentes commented on the differences between Mexico and the United States:

> We did not acquire freedom of speech, freedom of belief, freedom of enterprise as our birthright, as you did. We had to fight desperately for them. The complexity of the cultural struggles underlying our political and economic struggles has to do with unresolved tensions, sometimes as old as the conflict between pantheism and monotheism, or as the rift between tradition and modernity. This is our cultural baggage, both heavy and rich.[199]

Chapter 8

The Dawn of Industrialization, 1821–1855

Mexico could not get needed capital without stability, it could not establish stability without capital.

Daniel Levy and Kathleen Bruhn, 2001[1]

EARLY OPTIMISM

The euphoria surrounding political independence also extended to economic matters. Since Mexico had been the jewel of Bourbon Spain's American empire, most observers assumed it would soon recover from the ravages of the independence war. In addition to its endowment of natural riches, independence allowed Mexico to use foreign capital to accelerate economic recovery, to sell in the best-paying markets, and to buy where prices were lowest. Tribute formerly paid to Spain could be invested in Mexico. The stability of the four-year-long Guadalupe Victoria administration increased this optimism and attracted foreign investors.[2]

MINING

Mines were the source of much of the 1820s optimism concerning Mexico's economy. Mexican mines, such as La Valenciana, had become worldwide symbols of wealth. Humboldt's description of late colonial Mexico had been disseminated widely in Europe, further enhancing Mexico's image as a mother lode of silver.

Clearly considerable effort would be required to restore the mining industry to its former glory. The mines themselves had suffered from more than a decade of cave-ins and flooding. On the surface, financiers and suppliers had disappeared, and skilled labor had dispersed. The mines still in operation were only a shadow of their former selves. In 1822, Joel Poinsett, an unofficial U.S. envoy sent by President Monroe, found that employment at La Valenciana mine had declined from more than 3,000 to 1,000.[3]

In 1823, since Mexico lacked capital to quickly rehabilitate mines, the government enacted legislation opening mining to foreign investment for the first time. Other 1820s legislation encouraged mining. A modest 3 percent tax on silver production replaced the more burdensome colonial taxes on mining. A newly enacted law permitted the tax-free importation of mercury to refine silver.[4]

This welcoming of foreign mining investment occurred at a propitious time. In 1824 and 1825, a wave of speculative interest carried capital from a prosperous Britain throughout the world. By 1827, seven British, one German, and two American mining companies had begun operations in Mexico. British investment alone totaled some £3 million. In addition to capital, England sent negotiators, mine experts, skilled mine workers, and a variety of tools, implements, vehicles, and machines to Mexico.[5]

The Real del Monte Company, established in London in 1824, overshadowed other British mining ventures. Its investors were convinced that the application of modern capital and technology to the largely ruined Mexican silver mines would both revive the Mexican mining industry and reap handsome profits. The company purchased the Real del Monte mines from Mexican silver magnate Pedro Romero de Terreros. Enthusiasm ran so high in the speculative euphoria of the day that by the end of 1824 Real del Monte mine shares were worth ten times their initial selling price.[6]

Mexicans shared this enthusiasm. A British Real del Monte employee reported that when his countrymen first arrived at the mine, "The people at our arrival envinced every demonstration of joy by ringing the bells; and a deputation of the priest and principal inhabitants of the place immediately waited on us." A special Mass was said for the success of the new enterprise.[7]

In May and June of 1825, 1,500 tons of supplies were unloaded at Veracruz, including nine steam engines for stamping ore, operating sawmills, and pumping out the mine. The company also sent sawmills, pumps, iron-working tools, 150 wagons, 760 sets of mule harnesses, and 123 mine employees, about a score of whom died of fever on the tropical coast before even reaching the mine. The company hired fifty men to improve the road from Veracruz to the mine, which was located near Pachuca, fifty miles northeast of Mexico City. It purchased 200 horses and 500 mules to haul the equipment to the mine, a task that took eleven months.[8]

Once the British arrived, they plunged into a flurry of activity. Two years of day-and-night work enabled to them to retimber the drainage tunnel and bring it to the vein. The British also built roads to connect mine entrances and mills and established a hacienda to supply food to the 7,000 Mexicans they employed in the mines and mills.[9]

Figure 8.1 *"La Dificultad" mine, Real del Monte, Hidalgo*

Source: Reproduced courtesy of the Benson Latin American Collection, the University of Texas at Austin

The Real del Monte Company introduced steam power to drain its mines and improved the patio technique of refining silver ore. Such innovations paved the way for massive technological change in the Mexican mining industry.[10]

Unfortunately for the shareholders, despite this Herculean effort, the mine lost millions as mineshafts flooded and workers demanded more pay. By 1849, the company had produced $11 million worth of silver at a cost of $16 million. Shareholders felt they were throwing good money after bad, so they sold their interest for $30,000 to a group of Mexican investors. Real del Monte investors were not alone in suffering financial loss. By 1850, all but one of the British silver-mining companies in Mexico had failed.[11]

In an ironic twist of fate, Real del Monte's Mexican investors, using the expensive improvements left by the British, soon discovered a rich ore deposit. These investors became some of the richest Mexicans of the era.[12]

Even though it did not reward shareholders, the massive investment by British mining companies did inject badly needed cash into the Mexican economy. This investment also created many jobs in the production of mining equipment in Great Britain and in Mexican mining and agriculture.[13]

Beginning in the 1830s, the rehabilitation of old mines and the opening of new ones resulted in a slow recovery of silver production. By the middle of the century, Mexican silver production approached pre-independence levels. At this time, Mexico produced 50 to 60 percent of the world's silver. In large part, this recovery resulted from the discovery of new mines in Zacatecas and other states.[14]

With the benefit of hindsight, one can understand why the high expectations of early mine investors were dashed. Repeated changes of government and of policy replaced the stability that the colonial mine operations had enjoyed. Mine operators faced falling silver prices and operated in an economy with poorly functioning commercial and credit networks. Wealthy Mexicans continued to withdraw capital from Mexico. Only rarely could the British successfully combine necessary credit arrangements, political contacts, labor, transport, and imported equipment, and, at the same time, find profitable lodes.[15]

Labor problems plagued the mining companies. Initially they relied heavily on Cornish miners. Soon, in part due to these miners' unbridled consumption of alcohol, mine operators switched from a reliance on much more costly foreign labor to European management and local labor. Such a shift, though, only substituted one set of problems for another.[16]

Epidemics, a product of inadequate sanitation, often decimated the Mexican mine-labor force. British managers were reluctant to allow Mexicans to hold positions involving machinery or the supervision of other employees. These foreign managers had little experience working with Mexican miners and failed to understand their élan. Mexican miners formed part of the labor elite and showed remarkable unity when it came to preserving traditional privileges. They adamantly demanded that they should continue to receive, as in colonial times, a share of the ore produced (the *partido*) as well as wages in cash. At Real del Monte, mine workers hired their own lawyer to prevent the company from cutting their wages as it sought to reduce costs.[17]

Various unanticipated problems arose. Mercury prices increased spectacularly between 1825 and 1850 as a result of the Rothschilds monopolizing the world mercury market. Mine operators believed the application of steam power to drain mines, raise ore to the surface, and crush it would revolutionize mining. However, they underestimated the problems involved in transferring the latest British technology to Mexico. Transportation from the port to the mine, as the Real del Monte experience indicated, was extremely expensive and time consuming. The lack of wood to fuel boilers limited the application of steam. British technology required the importation not only of machinery but also of spare parts and technicians. The lack of workers familiar with steam-powered equipment created problems. French botanist Jean Louis Berlandier reported that at the Real de Catorce mine: "About six years ago the English brought in a steam engine to draw up water, but the man who was charged with its care did not understand it and allowed it to blow up."[18]

The decline and slow recovery of silver mining reduced both mine employment and the silver-based money supply. During the first half of the nineteenth century, mining contributed between 8 and 9 percent to Mexico's gross domestic product (GDP).[19]

MANUFACTURING

Postindependence political instability, civil violence, and foreign invasion did not provide an environment for good industrial policy.

Rafael Dobado González, Aurora Gómez Galvarriato, and Jeffrey G. Williamson, 2008[20]

Manufacturing in the early post-independence period suffered from many of the same problems faced by the mining industry. In 1824, after visiting Querétaro, which formerly had been a major textile producer, the American consul in Veracruz reported: "I was much disappointed in visiting the manufacturing establishments at Querétaro. They have now fallen into ruin." Entrepreneurs wishing to reestablish and expand their facilities faced capital shortages, political instability, and poor transport. In addition, manufacturers faced competition from imports, which caused a decline in Mexican textile production during the 1820s.[21]

After independence, the position of shop artisans and self-employed craftsmen became increasingly precarious. They faced competition from imports, *obrajes*, and the few mechanized factories established after independence. The guilds, which no longer enjoyed legal protection, declined. Even the strongest guilds, such as those of the gold- and silversmiths, passed out of existence before the middle of the century.[22]

The passing of the guilds decreased upward mobility for artisans. In 1842, the 11,229 artisans working in Mexico City represented 28 percent of the city's workforce. The percentage of the workforce comprised by artisans had changed little since 1794, when they made up 29.3 percent of the workforce. By the middle of the nineteenth century, most artisans worked in the shops of others since they lacked the resources to open their own workshops.[23]

During the middle of the nineteenth century, due to the lack of modern factories and the high cost of shipping goods from Veracruz to central Mexico, production by artisans continued to dominate Mexico City manufacturing. Artisan shops failed to evolve into true factories since they lacked capital and the necessary political clout to obtain favorable tariff policies. Moreover, they relied heavily on family labor, which limited their size. As a result of this reliance on artisanal techniques, much of the labor force had a very low level of productivity.[24]

Mexican liberals felt that the country could rely on export revenue to purchase manufactured goods from abroad, and that, in any case, the market would resolve production problems. Conservatives, in contrast, favored deliberate government action to stimulate industry. In 1830, to further industrial development, the conservative Anastasio Bustamante administration founded a government-owned industrial development bank known as the Banco de Avío. Tariffs levied on imported cotton goods financed the bank. The government directed the bank to lend money to Mexican entrepreneurs so that they could establish factories, especially textile mills, improve technology, and make Mexico less dependent on imports.[25]

A $146,000 loan from the Banco de Avío partially financed the La Constancia Mexicana (Mexican Perseverance), a water-powered textile mill. The plant, located in Puebla, bore little resemblance to the colonial *obraje*. Fanny Calderón de la Barca described it:

> It is beautifully situated, and at a distance has more the air of a summer palace than of a cotton factory. Its order and airiness are delightful, and in the middle of the court, in front of the building, is a large fountain of the purest water. A Scotchman, who has been there for some time, says he has never seen anything to compare with it, and he worked six years in the United States.[26]

La Constancia Mexicana's progressive owner, Esteban de Antuñano, built schools for workers' children and established a medical fund to provide a doctor and an apothecary. He challenged conventional wisdom and allowed women to work alongside men in his factory. He published a pamphlet to justify his then-controversial decision to hire women to work in his factory. The pamphlet noted that modern machinery did not require great strength to operate. The main advantage claimed for female employment was increasing family income. Antuñano argued that female morality would be better preserved in his well supervised factory than it would be by having young women idle and alone at home. Finally he noted that women worked in factories in industrially advanced countries such as England.[27]

The problems Antuñano faced were typical of those facing manufacturers of the period. He had to employ "foreign workmen at exorbitant prices" to build his mill. A year after it was shipped from Philadelphia, textile machinery arrived for the mill, but it proved to be unworkable. Only after losing two subsequent shipments to shipwrecks and having had another shipment delayed by a French blockade could he begin operating his mill.[28]

Before its liquidation in 1842, the Banco de Avío had lent $509,000 for textile mills in Puebla, Veracruz, Querétaro, and the State of Mexico. It lent to thirty-one enterprises, of which twenty-one became operational, ginning cotton and producing lumber, honey, silk, paper, glass, earthenware, and textiles. Of the enterprises the bank financed, 65.8 percent produced cotton textiles and 14.3 percent produced iron and machinery.[29]

The problems of the Banco de Avío were representative of early nineteenth-century Mexico. Liberals opposed it, claiming it distorted the market. The government had so little cash that it ceased providing funds to the bank years before formally liquidating it. Its record keeping led one inspector to conclude that the bank "had never been staffed by employees even modestly trained in the principles of bookkeeping." The bank also suffered from its being led by amateurs in a rapidly changing world, from its inability to rely on courts to recover from defaulting borrowers, and in some cases from political pressure determining who would receive loans. During coups, the seizure of funds and the halting of transport between Veracruz and Mexico City often delayed bank-financed projects.[30]

During the 1830s, thanks to tariffs and the introduction of mechanized mills, textile production rebounded. As a result of British investment, as well as that of the Banco de Avío, Mexico possessed the most highly developed textile industry in Latin America and became almost self-sufficient in cotton textiles. Between 1837 and 1845, the number of spindles in Mexican mills increased from 8,000 to 113,813. Due to high transport costs, foreign textiles could not compete with domestic production.[31]

In 1854, the 10,316 textile workers wove 5,482 tons of cotton into cloth. The cotton-textile industry produced $12 million worth of fabric, roughly equal in value to the mintage of precious metals—quite an accomplishment in a nation where mines were universally regarded as the principal source of wealth.[32]

Domestic cotton-textile producers suffered due to a political decision. They assumed that if they allied with domestic cotton growers, they would create a solid lobby for tariffs and import prohibitions on raw cotton, yarn, and cloth. However, in striking this deal, they saddled themselves with the very high costs of Mexican cotton. Speculators profited handsomely by buying the domestic crop and then selling it to textile producers.[33]

Labor relations in the newly established textile mills were smoother than in the mining industry, where miners had a much longer tradition of defending their interests. In the textile industry management could generally impose its will, which included ten- to sixteen-hour shifts. Numerous religious holidays relieved this tedium. Since as many as one day in five was designated as a religious holiday, the Mexican government obtained papal consent in 1836 to reduce the number of holidays. Pope Gregory XVI issued a brief allowing Mexicans to work on all days except Sundays and sixteen other specified days.[34]

A few foreigners invested in manufacturing outside the textile sector. Juan Corbière established a brandy (*aguardiente*) factory, two Englishmen opened a felt-hat factory, and Arísteo Mainet established Mexico's first beer factory. Most industrial activity involved construction, producing textiles and beverages, and processing food, tobacco, and leather. The median size of the workforce at the five foundries reported in the 1853 census was only fourteen.[35]

As in the rest of Latin America, extremely low manufacturing productivity increased the cost of goods at a time when the population had little buying power. At the same time, the high cost of transporting goods over poor roads created many small markets. State and local governments continued to impose regional trade taxes (the *alcabala*), which further reduced market size. This served to protect local producers and fill local government coffers, but made economies of scale impossible.[36]

Little capital remained to finance industry, since it had been dispersed, exported, or invested in government securities. Merchants did not consider manufacturing as a profitable activity to invest in, Church lending was under liberal attack, and past failures and political instability deterred foreign investors. Foreigners were also loath to finance Mexican production that would compete with their own operations. Neither the liberal model, based on international trade, nor the conservative model—tariff protection and government financing for industry—were maintained for a sufficiently long period to permit success.[37]

AGRICULTURE

The independence struggle resulted in extensive damage to the dams, wells, and aqueducts that had provided water for Mexico's 1,729,000 irrigated acres. Even haciendas that remained physically intact suffered from a loss of markets as the buying power of miners and city dwellers declined. In order to repay loans, some *hacendados* were forced to sell their land to former tenants or administrators. A village in the Huasteca region of San Luis Potosí purchased a 40,000-acre hacienda in 1826. Each of the 187 members of the community contributed twenty pesos to acquire the land they had once rented.[38]

As an institution, though, the hacienda emerged unscathed after independence. Since mining and commerce were largely in the hands of foreigners, generals and politicians often invested their newly acquired wealth in haciendas. In the 1850s, liberal Ponciano Arriaga commented on the *hacendado*:

> With some honorable exceptions, the rich landowners of Mexico . . . resemble the feudal lords of the Middle Ages. On his seigniorial lands, with more or less formalities, the landowner makes and executes laws, administers justice and exercises civil power, imposes taxes and fines, and has his own jails and irons, metes out punishments and tortures, monopolizes commerce, and forbids the conduct without his permission of any business but that of the estate.

These estates were largely self-sufficient, with resident artisans producing saddlery, furniture, tiles, and pottery. Such production further reduced the incentive to invest in industry.[39]

The hacienda continued to be the dominant rural institution. The well-documented hacienda El Maguey in Zacatecas, which covered 416 square miles, was only the seventh or eighth largest in the state. It centered around a cluster of stone buildings, where most of the 500 to 900 employees lived. In 1835, 89,000 sheep, 4,000 horses and mules, 12,000 goats, and a hundred head of cattle grazed on El Maguey. Workers lived on hacienda land and worshipped in its chapel. Their children attended the hacienda school. El Maguey sold wool as well as goat and sheep tallow used to make candles to illuminate mines. The hacienda attracted and kept labor by offering security in an insecure rural environment.[40]

Further north, where there was abundant land and few if any sedentary Indian communities, even larger estates predominated. After the Sánchez Navarro family bought out the Marquisate de Aguayo in 1840, their holdings totaled at least 25,780 square miles—an area larger than Connecticut, Massachusetts, New Jersey, Rhode Island, and Delaware combined. As part of the purchase, the buyers acquired not only land, buildings, and livestock but also indebted workers. By way of comparison, the fabled King Ranch of Texas covered only 1,719 square miles. In 1846, an American army captain commented on the Sánchez Navarro ranch, whose size was extensive even for Mexico, "More than half the whole State of Coahuila belongs to the two brothers Sanchez, who also own some thirty thousand peons."[41]

Many hacienda workers owed the *hacendado* debts. Sometimes these debts resulted from cash advanced to attract the worker. *Hacendados* were most reliant on debt to hold workers in the labor-scarce north and in areas where people had access to land to farm on their own. Often workers never emerged from debt due to their low wages and to dishonest bookkeeping by the *hacendados*. Indebted workers would respond by working for short, irregular periods, knowing their wages would be reduced accordingly. However, since they were hopelessly in debt, it did not matter. In one reported instance, an indebted shepherd fled the Sánchez Navarro estate. He was forcibly brought back, soundly beaten, and, to add insult to injury, the cost of retrieving him was added to his debt.[42]

A number of factors limited production on the hacienda. High transport costs restricted market size. Costs prohibited shipping grain to Guanajuato if it was grown more than thirty-four miles away. Transport problems created a national mosaic of agricultural surplus and shortage with wild price fluctuations between even nearby localities. Up until 1833, the government required agricultural estates to pay a tithe to the Church. Bandits in central Mexico and Indian attacks in the north also limited agriculture.[43]

Mid-sized holdings, or *ranchos*, mostly owned or rented by mestizos, existed alongside the large estates. The *rancho* differed from the hacienda in that the owner lived on his land and relied on his own labor and that of his family and of seasonal employees. Unlike the *hacendados*, who were often seen as vain and idle, *rancho* owners were widely admired. Fanny Calderón de la Barca observed, "It is impossible to see anywhere a finer race of men than these rancheros—tall, strong, and well made, with their embroidered shirts, coarse sarapes, and dark blue pantaloons embroidered in gold."[44]

Between independence and the mid-nineteenth century, the number of *ranchos* increased substantially. Some Mexicans, taking advantage of the instability of the period, moved into isolated uplands and established *ranchos*. In other cases, people bought plots from financially weak haciendas, converting them into *ranchero* communities. By 1854, there were 15,085 *ranchos*.[45]

Small farms recovered from the independence war relatively rapidly. As early as 1824, Poinsett noted, "The buildings are in ruins, yet the country appears to be cultivated as extensively and as carefully as ever." Reduced demand in cities and mines did not have a significant effect on small farmers, since they mainly produced for local markets or their own use. The vitality of this sector is indicated by the degree to which multi-village peasant movements, in alliance with other actors, became a major force shaping the Mexican state in the nineteenth and early twentieth centuries.[46]

TRADE

Independence transformed foreign trade more than any other sector of the economy. Under the colonial system, merchant-exporters in Spain shipped merchandise to Veracruz and from there to mining centers or to retailers. Credit was supplied at the top of the system. Merchants obtained hefty profits at each level. In such a system, commercial profit could not easily be separated from usury.[47]

The British merchants who arrived in the 1820s succeeded due to their access to capital. They could pay for goods they bought in Mexico with cash. More importantly, they could extend long-term credit. They replaced the Spanish at the top rung of the distribution system, but would often sell to a Spanish middleman, who in turn would sell to retailers and peddlers. By virtue of being British citizens, these merchants could live a relatively normal life, even in the midst of political turmoil. They were generally protected by the widespread fear of British retaliation against those who harmed them or their property. In addition, the British fleet moved their wealth in safety. As early as 1819, a British naval vessel reportedly docked at San Blas to collect "a large amount of treasure" belonging to a British subject and then safely remove it from Mexico.[48]

Given these advantages, between 1819 and 1825 the value of Mexico's trade with Great Britain soared from £21,000 to more than £1 million. By 1831, more than twenty British import-export houses were operating in Mexico. These commercial houses remained dominant from the 1820s to the 1850s. During this period, British merchants were among the wealthiest individuals in Mexico. In describing Jalapa, Fanny Calderón de la Barca remarked on the expensive homes with "the best as usual belonging to English merchants." British merchants even replaced their Spanish counterparts in matrimony. They would marry into leading Mexican families, creating win-win marriages that matched British capital with the local contacts of the bride's family.[49]

In the early nineteenth century, neither France nor the United States ever threatened British commercial dominance. The British supplied the elite with a wider variety of manufactured goods of better quality, at lower prices, and usually on better terms, than any other merchants.[50]

Gaining access to Spanish American markets became a key element of British foreign policy. George Canning, who served as British foreign secretary from 1822 to 1827, proclaimed, "The deed is done, the nail is driven, Spanish America is free; and if we do not mismanage our affairs sadly, she is *English*." To bolster their exports, the British promoted free trade, an advantage to their already established industries. They opposed tariff protection for industries being established in Latin America. They would respond to trade restrictions by threatening to press for debt payments, impose economic sanctions, suspend relations, or invade.[51]

Trade shifted north to the port of Tampico, because for years the Spanish occupied San Juan de Ulúa, the island fortress off Veracruz, and shelled the city from that island. The port of Tampico became established and, even after the Spanish departed Veracruz, Tampico continued to ship silver, cattle, cotton, produce, and ixtle for rail-road seat cushions.[52]

Once freed from Spanish regulation, trade flourished on the Pacific Coast. Acapulco, the port of the Manila Galleon, was forgotten in its tropical splendor, since few affluent buyers lived in the hinterland adjacent to it. Further north, San Blas served Jalisco, Mazatlán served Sinaloa, and Guaymas served Sonora. The principal Asian goods shipped to these ports were textiles from Calcutta and Canton.[53]

Despite this trade diversification, Veracruz remained Mexico's principal port and maintained close shipping links with Havana and New Orleans. Its continued prosperity resulted from it being the closest port to the locus of Mexican population, economic activity, and politicking.[54]

The same items were traded as in colonial times. Silver accounted for 70 percent of exports, followed by cochineal dye, which accounted for 7 percent. During the first sixty years of independence, 90 percent of imports were consumer goods for the wealthy, including textiles, wine, food, perfume, hats, and some durables, such as furniture and mirrors.[55]

Foreign trade had a mixed impact. Consumers benefited from cheaper goods. Due to technological progress, in 1850 inexpensive imported cotton cloth cost only a quarter of what it had cost between 1810 and 1820. Import tariffs also provided the government with an easily collected source of revenue that created little popular protest. Trade also created jobs. Dressmakers and tailors fashioned imported textiles into clothing for the elite. Foreign trade meant travel, so more innkeepers and others catering to the traveler found employment.[56]

Foreign trade also carried liabilities. To pay for imports, scarce coinage left the country, thus depriving Mexico of a medium of exchange. The British industrial revolution reached out to ruin textile artisans in Puebla, Querétaro, and Oaxaca. Between 1800 and 1827, the number of working looms in Oaxaca declined from 800 to thirty. Unlike Europe, where factories offered jobs to displaced artisans, there were few factory jobs available.[57]

Once foreigners quit lending to Mexico, the nation's ability to import was largely determined by its production of the silver used to pay for imports. During the 1820s, international trade totaled only 67.1 percent of the 1801–1810 level. At mid-century, Mexico's annual exports totaled only $3.20 per capita, well below the Latin American average of $5.20.[58]

With most of its production and population in the central volcanic belt or in the mountainous south, Mexico could not rely on water transport for domestic trade, as was occurring in the United States and Western Europe. That left traders dependent on roads, which were generally in poor condition, if in fact any roads existed at all. Road conditions were so bad that it was cheaper to import wheat flour from Kentucky and Ohio to Veracruz than to transport it from central Mexico. In the early nineteenth century, as a result of poor roads, mules continued to haul the bulk of Mexican goods. The perpetually bankrupt governments of the period spent little to improve or even maintain roads.[59]

As in colonial times, smuggling sharply limited the government's ability to tax imports. In 1834, liberal leader José Luis Mora estimated that two-thirds of Mexico's imports entered the country illegally. Mexico's 10,000 miles of coastline made it impossible to prevent smuggling. In 1826, only five vessels guarded Mexico's coastal waters. One Mexican observer noted, "The savings from evading increased taxes allow merchants to offer bribes of such magnitude that few men have the honor to refuse them."[60]

A variety of other problems plagued commerce. Many veterans of the independence struggle became bandits and preyed on travelers. One merchant wrote that "a fly cannot pass from Guanajuato to Silao without losing its little wings." A lack of coinage led to a proliferation of cumbersome bills of exchange and promissory notes. Given the difficulty of transport and the *alcabala*, Mexico continued to be divided into numerous small markets. As economist Clark Reynolds observed, "It is highly probable that interregional trade and internal commerce in Mexico were more highly developed at the time of the Aztecs than they were in mid-nineteenth century." Mexico would have to await the arrival of the railroad in the late 1870s for its national market to achieve the integration it had enjoyed in 1800.[61]

THE FOREIGN DEBT

After the Napoleonic wars, London emerged as the world's leading financial center. In the early 1820s, English financiers, riding an economic boom, eagerly invested surplus capital in the newly independent nations of Latin America. At the same time, Latin American leaders were luxuriating in their newly acquired right to obtain capital from wherever they chose. The disruption of local credit networks by the independence wars made foreign capital especially attractive. The interest rates charged by foreign lenders were far lower than interest rates charged by domestic lenders. As long as they could obtain loans, Mexican leaders borrowed abroad.[62]

British bankers received substantial commissions, in the 4 to 8 percent range, for bond issues they arranged. They usually assumed little risk, since they sold bearer bonds to individual investors who bore the risk. Bankers often used their profits to finance merchandise exports to Latin America. The British press both favored and fueled the investment frenzy.[63]

Investors plunged into the Mexican bond market for a variety of reasons. Humboldt's works, which continued to circulate, created the impression of great wealth available for the asking. In the mid-1820s, the general euphoria characteristic of financial market peaks led investors to feel there would no limit to profiteering. Bankers and agents for foreign nations had every reason to present rosy prospectuses. Investors assumed that debts backed by governments, as opposed to individuals, would always be safe. Investors assumed Mexico, with its abundant sub-surface wealth, to be an especially good credit risk.[64]

Mexico arranged its first bond issue through the banking firm of B. A. Goldschmidt & Co., which sold bonds with a face value of 16 million pesos. Goldschmidt charged an 8 percent commission on the transactions. Francisco Borja Migoni, a Mexican merchant long resident in London, also benefited from the bond sale. The Mexican government had authorized him to arrange the bond sale. As a monarchist and partisan of Iturbide, he had no scruples about defrauding the new republic and lining his own pockets.[65]

Initially, Borja Migoni's cronies bought the bonds secretly for an artificially low price. The Mexican government received only the proceeds from this initial sale. An eager public then bought the bonds for 3.5 million pesos more than Borja Migoni's collaborators had paid. Borja Migoni split the difference between the secret sale price and the public sale price with the initial purchasers. Of the 16-million-peso face value of the bonds, the Mexican government only received 5,866,157 pesos. The Mexican government pledged a third of its customs receipts to repay the 16 million pesos, plus interest.[66]

The first bond package failed to meet Mexico's financial needs, so the Mexican government arranged for additional bonds to be issued by Barclay's, another English banking house. Due to Mexico's good image and its no longer relying on Borja Migoni, the Mexican government received 11.3 million pesos, or 85 percent of the face value of the bonds sold.[67]

The government allocated about 20 percent of these bond proceeds to liquidate claims by British merchants, 15 percent to finance the state tobacco monopoly, and 15 percent to the military. The other 50 percent paid salaries and pensions, which went overwhelmingly to military men.[68]

Mexican bond issues formed part of a boom in Latin American lending. Between 1822 and 1825, more than £20 million of Latin American government bonds were sold in the London capital market. In addition, shares were sold in companies capitalized at more than £36 million. These companies engaged in mining, commerce, and other ventures. Buyers were so eager to buy Latin American stocks and bonds that they purchased bonds of the non-existent nation of Poyais, supposedly located on the Mosquito Coast of Central America. An imaginative con artist offered the Poyais bonds.[69]

Mexico's expenditure of bond money doomed it to default, since none of the funds enabled it to increase its export capacity. After spending the proceeds from the bonds, the government was saddled with debt liquidation as well as the everyday operating costs that it could not meet before the bond sales.[70]

Not surprisingly, Mexico defaulted on scheduled bond payments in 1827. Except for Brazil, by 1827 all Latin American nations issuing bonds had defaulted. Brazil could continue payments because its economy had been spared the ravages of an independence war and because of the ready market for its exported sugar.[71]

Default caused the trust and goodwill that had initially characterized Mexico's relations with Great Britain to be replaced by disillusionment and resentment. Subsequent Mexican administrations had to rely on much more costly credit from local lenders, since, until Maximilian assumed power in the 1860s, foreigners refused to lend to Mexico.[72]

Mexico repeatedly renegotiated its foreign debt, adding unpaid interest to unpaid principal to arrive at new, higher, and even more unpayable totals. By 1850, the renegotiated total reached more than \$55 million. To partially satisfy this debt, Mexico transferred \$2.5 million of the indemnity funds received after the Mexican–American War to British bondholders. Payments to bondholders continued for three years, until the Revolution of Ayutla, when the government once again went into default.[73]

DASHED HOPES

> Mexico lagged behind Chile, Brazil, or Argentina because of its cycle of civil wars and foreign invasions was more severe and protracted, while its economy and topography were more resistant to commercial penetration.
>
> Alan Knight, 2008[74]

The early optimism concerning Mexico's economy soon turned to despair as Mexico found itself in a downward spiral. The lack of capital, foreign or domestic, presented a seemingly insurmountable obstacle to growth. Without growth, the government would remain weak, so it could not defend itself from internal or external attack. This inability to defend the nation exacerbated the very conditions that retarded growth. Between 1800 and 1850, the per capita GDP declined at an average rate of 0.7 percent.[75]

The reestablishment of a sound legal climate was long delayed. The ponderous and exacerbating colonial judicial system was a model of efficiency compared with the process following independence. The break with Spain destroyed many of the institutions that provided credible commitments to rights and property within the Spanish empire. The wealthy preferred to keep their wealth in cash, or export it, rather than investing it where property rights were insecure. Some of the laws that would have stimulated investment were simply not on the books. For example, only in the 1890s did the government pass legislation permitting the formation of a limited liability corporation.[76]

The Mexican economy suffered from losing its sophisticated colonial financial markets, especially those based on Church lending. With interest rates on government loans generally fluctuating between 30 and 200 percent, capital was siphoned away from long-term productive investment. As was the case in most of Latin America, through the middle of the century Mexico was plagued by a lack of banking institutions and the non-existence of formal stock markets.[77]

Railroads would have lowered transport costs and created a national market. However, the attempts at railroad building only indicated the ineffectiveness of both government and private enterprise. In 1837, the government granted Veracruz merchant Francisco Arrillaga the first concession to build a railroad from Veracruz to Mexico City. It canceled this concession in 1840, since he had failed to lay a single mile of track. A new concession was granted in 1842 and was then canceled in 1849 since only three miles of track had been laid. By the time another decade had passed, only fifteen miles of track had been completed.[78]

In the early nineteenth century, the British were the world's supreme industrial power and the only naval power. Backed by this strength, the British Foreign Office often used its power to support British businessmen in Mexico, usually at the expense of Mexican development. While Mexicans considered building factories, British consuls situated at ports encouraged smuggling. When the Mexican government urged the creation of a national bank, British merchants actively opposed the measure so they could continue lending to the Mexican government. Such loans and the diplomatic power to enforce their repayment weakened Mexico's fragile fiscal structure. The British willingness to utilize all means at their disposal compromised the weak political system even further. As historian Barbara Tenenbaum concluded, "The British in Mexico, therefore, in pursuit of riches for themselves, only made Mexico poorer and more powerless."[79]

Early nineteenth century Mexico underwent little environmental change. The ecological equilibrium of the late colonial period continued through the first half of the nineteenth century. This ecological balance resulted from the lack of large enterprises and the reliance on traditional technology rather than from environmental awareness. Most labor continued to be performed with simple hand tools.

Some enterprises, however, proved to be highly destructive. Operators of the Real del Monte Mine, for example, cut so much wood that it became necessary to fell trees as far as twenty miles away to obtain fuel and timbers. In 1848, the company's three steam engines were burning 2,600

350-pound loads of wood a month. This reliance on wood to fire boilers highlights yet another problem facing Mexico at the time—its lack of industrial fuels.[80]

Mexico's economic experience during the early nineteenth century differed sharply from that of the United States. As historian Leandro Prados de la Escosura noted, the economic performance of the United States should not be used to judge Mexico, since the United States was exceptionally well endowed with natural resources and enjoyed economic growth that exceeded that of most other nations of the period.[81]

In addition to its natural resources, the United States enjoyed economic diversity—shipbuilding, farming, and some manufacturing—which stimulated internal trade. Such trade moved along the Atlantic Coast, along a rapidly expanding network of canals, and along the Mississippi and its tributaries. This trade, unhindered by the *alcabala*, allowed the integration of regional markets into a national market.[82]

The United States also enjoyed a vastly greater agricultural endowment than Mexico. Mexico's entire agricultural area covered about 15 percent of its territory, or an area about the size of Kansas. Millions of English, Scots, Irish, and Germans emigrated to the United States before its Civil War, accelerating development, while Mexico lacked immigrants. Capital from abroad, not available to Mexico after its default, also spurred U.S. development. In the 1830s, Europeans held nearly two-thirds of U.S. state and municipal bonds, and as late as 1853, Europeans still owned more than a third of America's public debt. In that year, the U.S. Treasury estimated total foreign investment in the United States at $222 million.[83]

Although U.S. independence preceded Mexican independence by less than half a century, the United States found much more favorable circumstances. The British recognized U.S. independence in 1783, which allowed the new nation to concentrate on economic growth, not defending itself from its former colonizer. Conflict in Europe during the two decades following the French Revolution in 1789 created an insatiable demand for U.S. goods. As a neutral, the United States could supply all nations. This allowed the U.S. merchant fleet to expand and enabled the United States to become the sixth industrial power of the developed world, with a nearly fifty-fold increase in manufacturing by 1830. The invention of the cotton gin gave the United States an added stimulus. During the 1820s, cotton mill production in the northeast United States increased by 600 percent.[84]

When Mexico became independent, not only had wartime demand ended but Europe was importing far less than it had in previous decades, especially after 1826 market crash in London. Rather than finding a ready market for exports as the United States had during its first years of independence, Mexico's first years of independence saw both Europe and the United States attempting to flood Mexico with their own manufactured goods.[85]

The years before 1850 had a marked influence on Mexico's subsequent economic relationship with the United States and other North Atlantic nations. In 1700, Mexico's per capita income was 43 percent greater than that of the thirteen British colonies that would form the United States. By 1800, it was only 55 percent of the U.S. per capita income, and by 1850 it was only 33 percent. Since then, Mexico has grown at roughly the same rate as the United States, but it has never been able to close the income gap that opened up before 1850.[86]

Chapter 9

The Diplomats Arrive, 1822–1855

JOCKEYING FOR POSITION

By the beginning of 1822, the U.S. position on recognizing the Spanish American republics was ripe for change. Diplomatic recognition, which earlier might have been interpreted as a partisan act, would simply reflect a fait accompli. The House of Representatives responded to this new situation on January 30, 1822, when it asked President James Monroe to provide information so Congress could make a decision on diplomatic recognition. The House requested correspondence from U.S. agents in Spanish America, correspondence from Spanish American agents in the United States, and information on independence wars in Spanish America.[1]

On March 8, 1822, Monroe forwarded to Congress the correspondence requested and observed that five Spanish American countries—Mexico, Chile, Argentina, Peru, and Colombia—were "in full enjoyment of their independence" and deserved recognition.[2]

On March 19, 1822, the House resolved "that the American provinces of Spain, which have declared their independence, and are in the enjoyment of it, ought to be recognized by the United States, as independent nations." Soon after this resolution, Congress appropriated funds to establish diplomatic missions in the five nations referred to in Monroe's message.[3]

On April 23, 1822, U.S. Secretary of State John Quincy Adams wrote José M. Herrera, Mexico's secretary of foreign affairs, stating Monroe's willingness to receive an envoy from Mexico. In response, Emperor Iturbide dispatched José Manuel Zozaya to Washington. On December 12, 1822, Adams presented Zozaya to Monroe as envoy extraordinary and minister plenipotentiary from the Mexican empire. With that ceremony, the United States formally acknowledged the independence of Mexico. The United States was the first nation to recognize Mexico, a reflection of the U.S. fear that if it did not move quickly, a strong Great Britain would replace a weak Spain, leaving little benefit for Americans.[4]

Despite having recognized Mexico in 1822, the United States did not send an ambassador until 1825. The initial nominees were either caught up in political turmoil or declined the post. As a result, the distinction of being the first U.S. ambassador to Mexico fell upon Joel Poinsett. His name was later given to the poinsettia, which he introduced to the United States from Mexico, where it is known as the *nochebuena*.[5]

In 1825, Poinsett arrived as ambassador carrying a triple mandate: 1) to negotiate a treaty of commerce; 2) to obtain territorial concessions from Mexico; and 3) to foster democratic institutions. He faced a difficult situation. Mexican officials were already suspicious of U.S. territorial aspirations. The fact that Poinsett arrived after Henry Ward, Britain's highly effective chargé d'affaires in Mexico, also left him at a disadvantage. Ward had already negotiated a commercial treaty with Mexico and did his best to prevent the Mexican government from granting the United States any privileges not accorded Britain. Ward was in an advantageous position since: 1) Britain was not attempting to acquire Mexican territory, 2) the British had a strong navy to which Mexico might look for protection, and 3) the Mexican elite had already established strong cultural and commercial ties with the British.[6]

The British were generally more successful at advancing their trade interests since the finished goods and low-cost capital they exported were in greater demand than the raw materials and foodstuffs exported by the United States. In addition, the British were simply better diplomats. As Mexican historian Josefina Vázquez noted, "They were good observers, and they learned to utilize friendships and pressure to achieve their demands, without violent confrontations, and thus functioned efficiently in Mexican political circles."[7]

British diplomatic success also reflected the priority they gave to foreign affairs. In the 1824 and 1828 U.S. elections, foreign affairs was a marginal issue. In contrast, as the major world trading power, Britain was vitally concerned with Spanish America in general and Mexico in particular. British Foreign Secretary George Canning commented on Mexico's unique position in an 1824 memorandum:

> I believe we now have the opportunity (but it may not last long) of opposing a powerful barrier to the influence of the U.S. by an amicable connection with Mexico, which from its position must be either subservient to or jealous of the U.S.[8]

While the British were advancing their trade interests, Poinsett was repeatedly offending Mexicans by offering to buy their territory rather than accepting the existing boundary between the United States and Mexico. This insistence was hardly Poinsett's fault since Washington repeatedly instructed him to buy land. Poinsett's attempts to acquire Mexican territory were undermined by British chargé d'affaires Ward. In 1827, Ward wrote Canning:

> I have no hesitation . . . in expressing my conviction, both publicly and privately, that the great end of Mr. Poinsett's mission . . . is to embroil Mexico in a Civil War, and to facilitate . . . the Acquisition of the Provinces to the North of the Rio Bravo [Río Grande].[9]

Poinsett eventually concluded that badgering Mexico to sell land to the United States was damaging relations between the two nations and refrained from pressing the issue further. Upon his return from Mexico, he reported to President Andrew Jackson that there was not the remotest possibility of buying Texas, since the Mexicans were a proud people who would never sell a single foot of their territory.[10]

Poinsett did successfully negotiate a commercial treaty. During negotiations, the question arose as to whether Mexico should return runaway slaves to their U.S. owners. Poinsett argued that if Mexico did not return them, respectable people, that is, slave owners, would not settle near the border. The Mexicans responded that a free republic should never assume the role of sending slaves to their merciless and barbarous masters in North America. The treaty was finally ratified under Poinsett's successor, with the United States dropping its demand that runaway slaves be returned. Mexico agreed not to give any other nation more favorable trade privileges than it gave the United States.[11]

Poinsett also negotiated a border treaty. American officials sought to move the border south and west. However, the Mexicans stood firm. Finally the U.S. government recognized the boundary established in the 1819 treaty between the United States and Spain as the boundary between the United States and Mexico. The Mexicans argued that if the 1819 treaty did not determine the boundary, then the previously agreed upon 1795 borderline between the United States and New Spain must determine the dividing line between the United States and Mexico, leaving Florida in Mexican hands. As with the commercial treaty, this treaty was negotiated by Poinsett, but not ratified until after his successor had arrived.[12]

Poinsett's involvement in Mexican politics often overshadowed his diplomatic activity. He openly sided with those advocating democracy at a time when many members of the elite did not want power in the hands of the masses.[13] Just before the 1827 Mexican presidential election, he wrote Guerrero, "You know how much I want you to be placed in a position which you deserve, due to your service in favor of liberty."[14]

Eventually, Poinsett's meddling in domestic politics inflamed passions in Mexico. The Veracruz legislature passed a resolution declaring Poinsett to be "more dangerous than 20 battalions of the Spanish tyrant." President Guerrero responded to popular sentiment and requested Poinsett's recall on July 1, 1829, declaring:

> The public clamor against Mr. Poinsett has become general, not only among the authorities, and men of education, but also among the vulgar classes; not only among individuals who suspected him, but also among many of those who have been his friends.[15]

Poinsett was replaced by Anthony Butler, who served from 1830 to 1835. As a result of his investments in Texas land, Butler had a personal financial interest in the transfer of this territory to the United States. He was chosen not because of his diplomatic tact but because he was an old friend and comrade-in-arms of President Jackson. Butler received explicit instructions from Jackson:

> Let a listening ear, a silent tongue, and a stedfast [*sic*] heart, the three jewels of wisdom, guard every advance which you make on the subject of *Texas.* The acquisition of that territory is becoming every day an object of more importance to us . . .[16]

While Butler served in Mexico, U.S.–Mexican relations deteriorated. The Mexican ambassador in Washington, José María Tornel, reported that the United States was openly advocating the acquisition of Texas without considering Mexican rights. Since it was public knowledge that Butler was attempting to buy Texas, he was not popular in Mexico. In turn, he made no secret of his negative view of Mexicans. In 1832, he wrote, "These people will not be prepared for self government in 50 years to come . . ."[17]

Finally Butler exceeded the limits of Mexican tolerance. While returning to Mexico City after a visit to the United States, he visited a group of Texans whose loyalty to Mexico was highly questionable. As a result, in 1835, the Mexican government requested Butler's recall, noting he was involved in "intrigues unbecoming a diplomatic agent."[18]

Americans made no secret of their desire for Texas. Former U.S. vice president and then-Senator John C. Calhoun declared in the Senate in May 1836 that there were "powerful reasons why Texas should be part of this Union." Calhoun noted that the acquisition of Texas would prevent events there from undermining the slave system in the U.S. south. He also noted that "the navigating and manufacturing interests of the North and East were equally interested" in acquiring Texas.[19]

None of the other U.S. ambassadors to Mexico before the Mexican–American War left much of a mark. Butler's successor, Powhatan Ellis, devoted himself to collecting damage claims filed against the Mexican government by U.S. citizens. The claims issue was closely tied to the territorial issue. Many Mexicans felt that claims against Mexico had been deliberately inflated to force Mexico into ceding territory to settle them.[20]

Finally, Mexico and the United States agreed to arbitrate the claims. In 1842, the arbitrators awarded the United States just over $2 million, which Mexico agreed to pay in twenty equal quarterly installments. Payments continued until mid-1844. Mexico then suspended payments since relations with the United States continued to deteriorate, and, as usual, the government had no money.[21]

EVOLVING TRADE RELATIONS

Trade between the United States and Mexico increased after Mexican independence. The United States replaced Spain as a transshipment point for British goods, which arrived in Mexico via New York or New Orleans. Flour and cotton were the major U.S. exports to Mexico.

Once Spanish-imposed commercial restrictions were removed, U.S. merchants began landing goods at northern Mexican ports and taking them inland. Much of this trade funneled through Matamoros, near the mouth of the Rio Grande. New Orleans soon became the main port supplying Matamoros, since lighter, shallow-draft ships, suitable for landing along the gulf shore, could sail from there. Ships coming from ports on the U.S. east coast had to be larger to survive the rigors of the Atlantic. In Matamoros, U.S. merchants unloaded American and European goods and returned with cowhides, mules, wool, and coins. Between 1820 and 1837, as a result of commercial restrictions being removed, the population of Matamoros surged from 2,320 to 16,372.[22]

Charles Stillman, of a Connecticut mercantile family, was one of the foremost Matamoros traders. He promoted his trading there, which he began in 1828, by declaring: "There's nothing down there but the Rio Grande. There's nothing across the Rio Grande but Matamoros. There's nothing in Matamoros but the gateway to all Mexico for cotton, hides and gold!"[23]

In 1835, U.S. exports to Mexico reached $9 million, or 7 percent of all U.S. exports. U.S. imports from Mexico were not as significant. Before the Mexican–American War, Mexico only supplied about 1 percent of U.S. imports. As conflict over Texas intensified, trade between the two nations declined and remained low for decades.[24]

Chapter 10

The North Adrift, 1821–1845

> Powerful centrifugal forces—regionalism, isolation, and foreign influence—began to swirl the frontier out of the Mexican orbit in the years following independence while the central government seemed unable to exert a countervailing force to pull the region back again.
>
> David J. Weber, 1982[1]

GOVERNANCE

Unfortunately for residents of the northern frontier, the neat lines the 1824 Constitutional Convention traced on the map were not conducive to sound governance. The national government was weak and enmeshed in constant conflict. As a result, it could not shoulder the burden of defending Hispanics from Indian raids, and it neglected other matters, such as trade promotion. Since local governments were at least as impoverished as the national one, they could not defend the citizenry. By default, the main burden of defense fell on members of low-status groups, such as free peasants and hacienda cowboys, who assumed the burden of combat, while the more affluent subsidized its costs. After independence, troops received less pay, worse provisions, and poorer mounts, and were less effective than they had been before independence. At one time or another, troops in each frontier province were furloughed so they could support themselves by hunting, farming, or ranching.[2]

Distance and slow communications inevitably created a sense of isolation from the central government. That government's failure to address defense needs heightened the sense of alienation and frustration. Resentment toward the central government mounted as politicians in a far away capital made key decisions. The income qualifications included in the 1836 constitution only added insult to injury, since it reportedly excluded every Californian from serving as a senator or deputy. In 1833, California Governor José Figueroa, born in what is today Morelos, noted that California's Hispanics looked upon Mexicans with the same hostility that Mexicans had viewed Spaniards. Mexican officials treated frontier people with condescension and described them as undereducated rustics, which intensified this feeling.[3]

At the time of Mexican independence, many leaders on the frontier took greater pride in their region than in their nation and saw themselves as socially distinct from central Mexico. The military and the Church, the bastions of institutional strength in the north during the Spanish era, had lost much of their effectiveness. As a result, before 1845, in California and New Mexico, dissatisfaction with the central government in Mexico City grew to serious proportions.[4]

In 1845, Antonio Comadurán, the first justice of the peace and military commander at Tucson, reflected widespread frontier sentiment when he declared:

> Our leaders pay no attention to even the most basic of their own laws. Weary of taxes and other burdens placed on them for no good reason, our people feel that the nation has lost its sovereignty and independence. To say that we are Mexicans means nothing anymore.[5]

SECULARIZATION

One of the few coherent national policies implemented along the frontier was the disbanding of the mission system, a process known as secularization. Control of mission chapels was transferred from state-supported religious orders to parish priests. Mission Indians were legally entitled to mission livestock and farm and ranch land. Any surplus land was transferred to others.

Secularization occurred for several reasons. Enlightenment notions of racial equality conflicted with the reality of having distinct religious and social communities established specifically for the indigenous population. The government had a vested interest in disbanding missions since neophytes would not only become tax-paying citizens but support their parish priests, relieving the government of that responsibility. In California, officials saw the missions as an obstacle to economic development since they had a near monopoly over indigenous labor and land on the coastal strip. Without access to land and labor, settlers would not come. Policy makers felt that removing Indians from mission tutelage would promote individual responsibility and initiative. Finally, many policy makers supported secularization since they wanted to transfer the lands held by missions to non-Indian hands.[6]

Secularization of the Texas missions began before Mexico's independence. San Antonio de Valero (the Alamo) was inventoried and disbanded in 1793. The San Antonio missions were fully secularized by 1823–1824. The city government distributed mission lands to a host of eager petitioners. The chapels themselves remained church property, but priests no longer used them for religious services. The last Texas mission, Nuestra Señora del Refugio, north of present-day Corpus Christi, struggled along until 1829, when its goods were finally auctioned off.[7]

In California, secularization proceeded at a much slower pace since the mission played a vital role in the California economy. Governor José María Echeandía even refused to enforce the Spanish expulsion laws, since twenty-five of the twenty-eight padres in California were Spanish-born Franciscans. He argued that their departure would not only ruin the missions but if the missions ceased producing food as a result, "the rest of the inhabitants and the troops would perish."[8]

When secularization began in earnest in the 1830s, few California Indians received legal title to the land they had worked. Protests by former neophytes went unheeded. Mission San Gabriel provides a typical example. In 1834, Bernardo Yorba, the son of the colonial grantee of Rancho Santiago de Santa Anna, petitioned for a grant of property adjoining his ranch. A priest protested that the land belonged to Indians of San Gabriel. The Los Angeles town council ignored the priest and lauded Yorba as an exemplary citizen who was one of the most industrious people in California. Its members then declared that he had every right to the property.[9]

Secular administrators whose sympathies lay with Hispanic ranchers desirous of increasing their holdings frequently thwarted Indian access to California mission land to which they were legally entitled. This left Indians with the options of rejoining Indians living in interior valleys, moving to Hispanic cattle ranches, or establishing themselves in emerging towns, where they would be landless and impoverished. The majority, who had not assimilated the cultural patterns of coastal Hispanic society, chose a return to a semi-nomadic Indian way of life. A few Indians, especially those born in the missions, remained as a part of Hispanic society.[10]

In California, the availability of land and cheap Indian labor from recently secularized missions gave rise to a class of nouveau riche cattle barons. Despite federal legislation to the contrary, Hispanic Californians gained control of the land and cattle of disbanded missions. The appropriation of additional land occupied by heathen Indians added to Hispanic ranch holdings. Ninety-three of these California ranches measured in excess of 24,700 acres. In 1839, Governor Juan Bautista Alvarado tried to check what nearly every writer has termed the "plunder" of the mission, but it was too late. "All is destruction, all is misery, humiliation, and despair," wrote one padre in 1840.[11]

COMMERCE

After Mexico became independent, trade in northern Mexico shifted from a north–south axis to an east–west axis. A trade route developed between New Mexico and California. Each year, roughly 200 men on horseback, plus mules laden with sarapes and blankets, would depart from New Mexico. In California, they exchanged these goods for California mules, pelts, Asian silks, and various Chinese goods. New Mexican Hispanics carried on most of this trade, although a few U.S. citizens took part.[12]

Another trade route became known as the Santa Fe Trail. Before Mexican independence, Spanish authorities had prohibited trade between New Mexico and the United States. Under Spanish rule, authorities jailed traders from the United States and confiscated their goods. With independence, this trade was welcomed.[13]

In the fall of 1821, William Becknell and five associates set out from Missouri to trade with Indians. They unexpectedly met a detachment of soldiers from New Mexico, who guided them to Santa Fe. There Governor Facundo Melgares welcomed them and encouraged further commercial ventures. Becknell and his companions sold their merchandise and returned to Missouri with handsome profits, giving birth to the Santa Fe Trail.[14]

The next year, three more expeditions, including one led by Becknell, arrived in Santa Fe. Soon traders introduced wagons on the Santa Fe Trail, which stretched from Missouri to New Mexico. In 1824, twenty-five wagons left Missouri, carrying $35,000 worth of merchandise that was exchanged for $190,000 of gold, silver, and furs. By 1825, New Mexico was buying more from Missouri than from the rest of Mexico. Independence, Missouri, had a customs house, and as a result of this trade, Mexican silver coins dominated the currency circulating in that state.[15]

By 1825, due to the saturation of the New Mexico market, many U.S. traders were venturing south to Chihuahua. This wagon-borne trade converted Chihuahua's capital into a major trade center. Mexicans bought imported goods with the some of the 500,000 pesos of coins minted there each year from locally produced silver. Poinsett even reported having seen in Mexico City four wagons that Americans had driven south from Santa Fe through Chihuahua.[16]

The early trading expeditions that arrived in Santa Fe reported profits of as high as 2,000 percent. Later, as the market became saturated, profits declined to 40 to 50 percent. To keep profit margins high, traders would evade customs duties by engaging in the time-honored practice of bribery or by placing high-value goods on mules and bringing them in through back-country trails. Much of the merchandise, of course, was declared at customs offices, and surviving declarations provide a wealth of information on what was shipped, who shipped it, and its destination.[17]

Since the United States had little industry, U.S. traders imported much of the merchandise and then shipped it to New Mexico. Such reexported goods included French cotton shawls, German linens, silk stockings, and handkerchiefs from India. The main items the caravans transported were cotton goods. In addition, they brought a wide range of manufactured goods—everything from jewelry to mirrors, from writing paper to champagne. New Mexicans eagerly sought these goods due to their variety, their higher quality, and their prices, which were up to two-thirds less than those charged by Mexican merchants.[18]

In Santa Fe, traders would retail goods themselves, sell to Hispanic and Anglo wholesale merchants, or proceed on to Chihuahua. Traders returned home with specie, livestock, and beaver and otter pelts. This trade, worth nearly $1 million a year, converted New Mexico into a virtual economic satellite of the United States even before the Mexican–American War.[19]

The Santa Fe Trial stimulated job creation in New Mexico. Since the importation of ready-made clothes was prohibited, the cloth brought into New Mexico produced a dramatic increase in the number of tailors and seamstresses. New Mexicans enjoyed a reputation for being excellent muleteers and horsemen and were frequently recruited to work in the caravans that traveled from Missouri to interior Mexico. Even Anglos, who so often found fault with Hispanics, acknowledged their superlative skills in packing and handling beasts of burden.[20]

By the end of the 1830s, New Mexican Hispanics were venturing east along the trail to buy goods in places as far removed as Baltimore, Philadelphia, and Pittsburgh, where wholesale houses sought their business. The 1843 caravan of New Mexicans that left Santa Fe for the east indicates the magnitude of Hispanic participation on the Santa Fe Trail. The caravan included 180 men, forty-two wagons, 1,200 mules and carried between $250,000 and $300,000 in bullion and a substantial amount of furs. Eleven of the traders continued on to New York to make purchases. New Mexican traders not only traveled east but continued on west to California and south to Chihuahua with the goods they had acquired in the United States. They often formed partnerships with Anglo traders, resulting in firms bearing names such as Browne and Manzanares. Hispanic traders also employed Anglos as *mayordomos* (wagon bosses).[21]

Trade on the Santa Fe Trail soon became institutionalized. Steamboats brought goods up the Missouri River. From Missouri, caravans of as many as 175 wagons traveled to Santa Fe, making the 770-mile trip in about eight or nine weeks. Wagon trains remained as cohesive units so they could defend themselves against Indian attack. Within a decade, control of trade shifted from individual traders to wealthy merchants with hired workers. As the size of the shipments grew, it became necessary to search for additional capital and make credit arrangements, tap new sources of merchandise, seek competitive prices for goods, and insure shipments.[22]

The U.S. government supported the Santa Fe Trail by appointing consuls in Santa Fe and Chihuahua and providing cavalry escorts to protect traders from Indian attack. As one of his last public acts, U.S. President James Monroe signed a bill providing $10,000 to survey and mark the trail and $20,000 to pay Indians to allow peaceful passage of traders. Finally, the U.S. government refunded customs duties paid on goods that had been imported into the United States and then subsequently reexported on the Santa Fe Trail.[23]

New Mexico's residents welcomed commerce on the Santa Fe Trail since it ended the commercial monopoly of Chihuahua, something that had vexed them for generations. One trader noted, "In all their principal towns, the arrival of Americans is a source of pleasure, and the evening is dedicated to dancing and festivity."[24]

Given its relative proximity to the United States, Americans influenced New Mexico more than areas further west. In 1832 an American commented, "Santa Fe may be considered, in some sense, an American town, the stores being filled with American goods and the streets with American people." Some of the Americans who arrived via the Santa Fe Trail settled and took Hispanic wives. These settlers formed a strong pro-American block in New Mexico. As historian Warren Beck noted, "The Americans entered New Mexico to trade, but ultimately remained to take over."[25]

As soon as Spanish trade restrictions were lifted, a flotilla of U.S. traders arrived in California, furnishing desired goods that never arrived from Mexico, including cloth, axes, shoes, fishing lines, and even Boston rum. In exchange, traders accepted products from the burgeoning ranching industry. Between 1826 and 1848, Boston traders alone purchased more than 6 million hides and 7,000 tons of tallow. In 1843, California exported 2,000 barrels of wine and brandy. In 1846, a British resident of Monterey commented on the U.S. domination of California's commerce, "There is not a yard of tape, a pin, or a piece of domestic cotton or even thread that does not come from the United States."[26]

For a short period, New Englanders purchased California sea otter pelts, which were ten to twenty times more valuable than cow hides. The number of sea otter hunters soared, as the easy money attracted Aleuts, Kodiaks, Mexicans, and Americans. The hunters' effectiveness also increased as they began to employ guns rather than spears. By the early 1840s, the animals had been hunted nearly to extinction.[27]

Between 1835 and 1845, four-fifths of the boats arriving in California were foreign. Data on trade during this period are spotty since much of the exchange was carried on clandestinely to avoid import taxes, which totaled roughly 80 percent of the value of the merchandise.[28]

ETHNIC CONFLICT

> From California to Texas, Mexico's northern border with independent Indians became a far more violent place than it had been in the late Spanish era.
>
> David J. Weber, 2005[29]

In what is now the U.S. southwest, Indians came under increasing pressure as American settlers moved west. These settlers either occupied an indigenous group's land or the lands of an adjacent group. In the latter case, the adjacent group would then move west. The presence of both groups would exceed the land's carrying capacity. The obvious survival option was to supplement what the land supplied with plunder from Mexicans. The weak Mexican governments of the period had neither the means nor the will to fight the Indians. Nor did they have the economic strength to shower the indigenous population with gifts in exchange for remaining peacefully settled.[30]

The Comanche war trail extended south from west Texas into Durango, Zacatecas, San Luis Potosí, Nuevo León, and Tamaulipas. On one occasion, a group of Comanche was reported at Querétaro, 135 miles north of Mexico City. The Comanche and their allies killed an estimated 2,000 Mexicans in the twelve years before the Mexican–American War.[31]

Beginning about 1830, the Apache raided into Sonora and Chihuahua. In a single 1840 raid, Lipans raided Agualeguas, Nuevo León, killing sixty, wounding sixty, capturing twenty-eight, and rustling 300 head of cattle. Between 1820 and 1835, Apache raiders killed an estimated 5,000 Mexicans along the frontier.[32]

Northern Mexico lacked money, mounts, arms, and ammunition to effectively check attacks by independent indigenous groups. In any case, raiding parties as large as 800–1,000 made effective defense of isolated rural locations virtually impossible.[33]

As a result of the Indian onslaught, such previously dominant institutions as the state, the army, the Catholic Church, and wealthy landowners had largely disappeared along the northern border of Chihuahua by the 1830s The effectiveness of the few remaining trinkets Mexicans continued to supply Indians declined as American traders offered, in exchange for booty, a broad range of goods, including liquor.[34]

Indians who obtained modern weapons from American traders became far more formidable than they were with old Spanish-supplied muskets. These traders also gave Indians a motive to raid Mexican settlements since they would readily buy booty acquired in Mexico—no questions asked. In some cases, Indians would pass weapons to other indigenous groups that had no direct contact with American traders.[35]

By 1826, arms supplied by American traders had become such a concern that Mexico's secretary of state asked Poinsett to stop the "traders of blood who put instruments of death in the hands of the barbarians." The plea was of no avail, leading one high-ranking Mexican official to wonder if it was U.S. policy "to use savage Indians to menace defenseless Mexicans in order to force them to abandon their lands or. . . request the protection of the United States government." Rather than suppressing the arms trade, in the mid-1830s, the U. S. government signed trade and amity treaties with the Comanche and the Kiowa, which facilitated Americans' purchase of plunder and livestock from Mexico.[36]

Although increased conflict with Indians largely resulted from forces beyond the control of Hispanics on the frontier, their behavior further exacerbated Hispanic-Indian relations. From California to Texas, Hispanics continued the Spanish colonial practice of taking captives in Indian campaigns and purchasing or ransoming Indians from other Indians. They justified the bondage imposed by claiming that their actions allowed Indians to receive the blessings of Christianity and that, in some cases, they had spared captives from death or a life of servitude at the hands of "pagans." In 1838, New Mexico Governor Manuel Armijo entered Navajo territory, ostensibly to free a New Mexico settler captured on a raid. Armijo freed the settler and noted that, in addition, he had enslaved seventy-six Indians and seized 226 horses, 2,060 sheep, six sarapes, and 160 buckskins.[37]

In California, no single Indian group posed a threat comparable to the Apache or the Comanche. Small groups, however, did raid settlements with increasing intensity. As raids were increasing, the number of troops in *presidios*, including retirees, declined from 710 in 1821 to only 125 in 1841. As a result of these raids, between 1830 and 1840 San Diego's population declined from 520 to about 150.[38]

Mexicans sought out Indians and signed peace treaties. Political divisions on both sides of the ethnic divide complicated such treaty making. In 1842, Chihuahua signed peace treaties with several Apache bands. The treaties only bound the bands that signed them and were in effect only in Chihuahua. Apache signatories not only raided in Sonora, which was not involved in the negotiations, but sold the loot openly in Chihuahua. Treaties signed with Indians provided for the return of captives and the transfer to Mexican authority of any individual Indian who violated the peace. In exchange, Indians received a defined territory for hunting and the right to engage in commerce. Treaty making became a significant policy instrument. The 1824 constitution gave the government the power to make treaties with Indians—its sole mention of Mexico's indigenous population.[39]

Each individual state developed its own Indian policy. The governor of Sonora offered a hundred pesos for each Apache scalp and allowed scalp hunters to keep the plunder and livestock they recovered. In 1849, Chihuahua offered 200 pesos for an Indian warrior's scalp, 250 pesos for an adult male prisoner, 200 pesos for a dead woman or child under fourteen, and 150 pesos for a captured woman or child. Instead of ending conflict, scalp bounties only made the Apache fight more desperately. The bounty policy gave scalp hunters virtually free rein. Military historian William DePalo, Jr. commented on these bounty hunters: "Needless to say, these outlaws exercised few scruples in discriminating between hostile and friendly Indians."[40]

None of these strategies, which enjoyed minimal support from the central government, proved effective. As a result, northern Mexico lived in fear of Indian attack. An 1846 statement of the Chihuahua legislature reflected these feelings:

> We travel the roads . . . at their whim; we cultivate the land where they wish and in the amount they wish; we use sparingly things they have left to us until the moment that it strikes their appetite to take them for themselves.[41]

Chapter 11

Shifting Boundaries, 1845–1855

THE OUTBREAK OF WAR, 1845–1846

> What Polk's intentions were regarding Mexico—and whether he even had any clear notion of what he wanted and how to get it—are a bit of a mystery even today. Texas was already a state, and while its southern boundary was a matter of dispute, no one but the Texans themselves thought it worth a war. That is why most historians believe that Polk really aimed from the start at the richest prize left in North America: the derelict province of Alta California.
>
> Walter A. McDougall, 1997[1]

In October 1845, the Mexican government stated it would receive a U.S. representative to negotiate outstanding differences. In response President Polk sent John Slidell, a Spanish-speaking politician from Louisiana, to Mexico. Polk instructed Slidell to negotiate the purchase of Alta California and New Mexico.

In a sense, Slidell's mission was doomed before it started, since he was not authorized to negotiate on the two points that Mexicans felt it was necessary to discuss: 1) whether Mexico still had any residual claims to Texas; and 2) if it did not, what the boundary between Texas and Mexico was. An additional factor dooming his mission was his arriving with the title of "minister," the equivalent of a diplomat arriving today with the title of "ambassador." That title implied that Mexico and the United States had reestablished diplomatic relations—broken after the 1845 U.S. annexation of Texas—and that the Texas question was behind them. This view that contrasted sharply with the Mexican perception of relations with the United States.[2]

In his 1844 State of the Union Address, President Tyler had addressed the first point, noting that Mexico's claim to Texas was extinguished because Texans had organized themselves into an independent republic recognized by several of "the leading powers of the earth" and because Mexico had failed to reconquer Texas after nine years.[3]

The U.S. claim to Texas was much stronger than its assertion that the Rio Grande formed Texas's southern border. Slidell's instructions on that question stated, "In regard to the right of Texas to the boundary of the del Norte [Rio Grande], from its mouth to the Paso, there cannot, it is apprehended, be any very serious doubt."[4]

The U.S. claim to the Rio Grande boundary was based on: 1) the claim the United States had obtained via the Louisiana Purchase, and 2) the December 1836 claim by the Texas Congress that the Rio Grande formed the border. The Adams–Onís Treaty extinguished whatever rights might have been acquired via the Louisiana Purchase. The claim by the Texas Congress neither reflected the historic boundary of Texas nor the de facto situation during the existence of the Republic of Texas. Even after the U.S. annexation of Texas, Mexicans continued to collect customs duties at Point Isabel (today's Port Isabel), north of the Rio Grande.[5]

At the time Texas was annexed to the United States, many viewed the Rio Grande as a promising trade route to New Mexico. Some Texans hoped the Rio Grande would replace the Santa Fe Trail.

Anglo settlers compared the Rio Grande to the Hudson and the Mississippi. Traders were aware that Matamoros served as a port for San Luis Potosí and other parts of northern Mexico. While the commercial and residential center of Matamoros was on the south side of the river, the actual port was just north of the mouth of the Rio Grande at Point Isabel. Control of land north of the Rio Grande would give control of the port. In fact, soon after the Mexican–American War, the port was handling $10 to $14 million worth of cargo a year. In addition to desiring the area between the Nueces and the Rio Grande for its port, ownership of this land became a matter of national pride for both countries.[6]

On November 30, 1845, Slidell arrived in Mexico. His instructions to acquire additional Mexican territory conflicted with Mexican nationalism. There is no indication Slidell foresaw this difficulty. He shared Polk's view that the matter would be simple. Mexico was bankrupt, impotent, and isolated. Seemingly the easiest solution for both parties would be for Mexico to sell California, recognize the annexation of Texas, and use the money received to resolve its problems.

The Mexicans had a very different view of the situation. They felt threatened by a nation that they had seen steal land from Indians and enslave blacks and whose citizens were marching inexorably toward Mexico. The Mexicans did not share the U.S. notion that frontiersmen were the noble precursors of civilization. Rather, they saw them as barbaric, shiftless wretches who paved the way for more sophisticated operators. Many felt that if they did not take measures to stop U.S. expansion, the Mexican nation would cease to exist.[7]

Since Polk instructed Slidell to purchase additional territory at a time when Mexicans felt the most pressing issue was Texas, a final chance for peace was lost. To further complicate matters, Mexican firebrands were more than ready to oust any government that could be considered as kowtowing to the Americans. Any Mexican government that simply accepted the Texas question as settled and then negotiated further territorial loss, in keeping with Slidell's instructions, would have set itself up for a coup. As historian Karl Schmitt commented: "Could any regime, administration, or leader have surrendered Texas, and then survived to make it stick? It seems highly unlikely."[8]

Since Mexico had threatened to go to war if Texas was annexed, the United States was preparing its military option while Slidell was in Mexico. In 1844, a force commanded by General Zachary Taylor, who had already made a reputation as an Indian fighter, was assembled at Fort Jesup, just east of the Sabine River in Louisiana. On June 15, 1845, Taylor received orders to move southwest so that he could "protect what, in the event of annexation, will be our [south] western border."[9]

In response to this order, Taylor moved his troops to Corpus Christi, a small Mexican village of fewer than a hundred people located on the Gulf Coast. An American trading post there sold goods to Mexican smugglers. Taylor's dragoons came overland via San Antonio. Most of the rest of his men came by steamship from New Orleans. There followed six months of boredom interspersed with drills, parades, and breaking horses.[10]

Whether Polk wanted war, or simply wanted to negotiate from a position of strength, has been disputed since by historians. It is not an either-or question, though, since, as Polk's biographer Charles Sellers noted, Polk thought peaceful coercion would get him what he wanted. However, if it did not, he would "not shrink from war to accomplish his purposes."[11]

Events in Mexico made it appear that war could still be avoided. Despite his bellicose statements, President Paredes took no action, since he lacked an effective army and the money to finance one. Eventually, after harsh criticism in the press, he sent troops north under the command of General Pedro Ampudia. They reinforced the Mexican position on the lower Rio Grande, but did not cross to the north side of the river.[12]

If the Polk administration intended only to bluff the Mexicans, it pushed the situation too far. On January 13, 1846, after receiving word that Mexicans were unwilling to negotiate other matters before settling the Texas question, Secretary of War William Marcy ordered Taylor to move his force to "positions on or near" the Rio Grande.[13]

Taylor received his orders on February 3, 1846. After scouting the area, he began to move his forces on March 8. Taylor's 4,000 men represented half of all U.S. army forces since at the time the United States did not feel it necessary to maintain a large standing army. Taylor assembled the largest U.S. force since the War of 1812.[14]

Regardless of whether Mexicans considered Texas to still be a part of Mexico, the virtually unanimous opinion in Mexico was that the State of Tamaulipas extended north to the Nueces River. In this light, Mexicans viewed Polk's actions as an invasion, or a provocation, or both. Mexicans were not the only ones to consider Taylor's move a deliberate provocation. Ulysses S. Grant, who served as a lieutenant in the war, wrote in his memoirs, "We were sent to provide a fight, but it was essential that Mexico should commence it." Polk, however, said troops were ordered into the disputed territory due to the "urgent necessity to provide for the defense of that portion of our country."[15]

As U.S. troops reached the north bank of the Rio Grande across from Matamoros, Mexican cotton farmers living there fled to the south side. In the U.S. Senate, anti-slavery Ohio Senator Thomas Corwin commented that Mexicans successfully grew cotton there without slaves. By Mexican reckoning, the land they farmed on the north side of the river did not lie in Texas, but in the Mexican state of Tamaulipas.[16]

In mid-April, General Ampudia demanded that Taylor withdraw his troops from south of the Nueces, threatening war if he failed to. Taylor replied that his orders would not permit a withdrawal.[17]

Taylor not only refused to withdraw, claiming that boundary problems should be left to diplomats, but he took at face value General Ampudia's statement that his failure to do so would bring about a state of war. He ordered the mouth of the Rio Grande to be blockaded. This forced Ampudia to either withdraw or attack, since he depended on supplies brought in by ship from New Orleans. The blockade, which began April 12, was the first act of war in what is now known as the Mexican–American War.[18]

On April 4, in response to what Mexicans considered an invasion and to Taylor's refusal to withdraw, Minister of War and Marine General José María Tornel ordered an attack on U.S. forces along the Rio Grande.[19]

On April 26, Taylor ordered an eighty-man detachment of the Second Dragoons to investigate a report that Mexican troops had crossed to the north side of the Rio Grande upstream from his position. The 1,600 Mexican soldiers who had indeed crossed the river then ambushed the detachment fifteen miles upstream from present-day Brownsville, Texas, killing or wounding seventeen Americans and taking the rest prisoner.[20]

Taylor wrote to Washington the next day, "Hostilities may now be considered as commenced." His message arrived in Washington on May 9, leading Polk's cabinet to unanimously vote to support a declaration of war. In fact, before he received news of the attack, as he recorded in his dairy, Polk had already decided to request a declaration of war based on Mexico's failure to negotiate with Slidell, its unwillingness to sell land, its failure to resolve matters concerning Texas, and its failure to meet claims made against the Mexican government by U.S. citizens. The claims resulted from repudiated bonds, revoked concessions, and damage to American-owned property during civil strife. These claims were, Mexicans felt, a hodgepodge of reasonable demands, exaggerated claims, and the absurd. Just as was the case in the Pastry War, the failure to resolve claims was regarded as a major provocation.[21]

Polk reworked his already partly written war message and, on May 11, submitted it to Congress, noting that Mexicans had "shed American blood on American territory." In addition to simply assuming that "American territory" extended to the Rio Grande, Polk rewrote history when he stated, "It is absurd for Mexico to allege as a pretext for commencing hostilities against the United States that Texas is still part of her territory." It was the U.S. occupation of the area between the Nueces and the Rio Grande, not Mexico's claim to Texas, that led to war.[22]

Paredes stated his motives for not accepting U.S. occupation of this area:

> The defense of Mexican territory which the troops of the United States are invading is an urgent necessity, and my responsibility before the nation would be immense if I did not order the repulse of forces which are acting as enemies; and I have so ordered.[23]

Since not all members of the U.S. Congress favored war with Mexico, the declaration of war was included with the same bill that appropriated funds to support Taylor's force. Those voting against a declaration of war also voted to deny support for American forces under attack. This was likely unnecessary, since the declaration of war passed overwhelmingly. Only fourteen of the 188 votes cast in the House, all of them by abolitionist Whigs, were against the declaration. In the Senate, the declaration passed by a vote of forty to two, with three abstentions.[24]

If, in fact, Polk was trying to provoke a war, he was successful. If his goal was brinkmanship, he failed due to: 1) his acceptance at face value of Mexicans' bellicose statements, which were demanded by the Mexican public, 2) considering Slidell's rejection frivolous, without realizing how delicate Paredes' position was, and 3) defining as settled the border between Texas and Mexico.

THE MONTERREY CAMPAIGN, 1846–1847

When Taylor learned that additional Mexican troops were crossing to the north side of the Rio Grande, he withdrew most of his force to Point Isabel on the Gulf of Mexico and waited for supplies and reinforcements.

On May 7, 1846, after receiving the anticipated supplies and reinforcements, Taylor started back toward Matamoros with 2,228 officers and men, followed by 270 ox- and mule-drawn wagons loaded with supplies. On May 8, he encountered 3,709 Mexicans, commanded by General Mariano Arista, blocking the road at Palo Alto, ten miles northeast of Matamoros. The Mexican force formed a mile-long line perpendicular to the road.

Cannon fire began immediately. Solid Mexican cannonballs often fell short of the U.S. line and rolled by like bowling balls, permitting the Americans to dodge them. Horse-drawn U.S. cannons were advanced at full gallop, fired on the Mexican line, and then moved to another position. U.S. artillery was not only more mobile than that of the Mexicans, but it fired explosive shells and had greater range. Mexican attempts to advance on Taylor's force failed due to marshy ground, dense vegetation, and withering cannon fire. After suffering some 257 casualties, mostly resulting from cannon fire, the Mexicans withdrew.[25]

The next day the Mexicans regrouped at Resaca de la Palma, three miles north of the Rio Grande. The Resaca was an old channel of the Rio Grande, roughly ten feet deep and 200 feet wide. Since brush covered the area, the battle differed from Palo Alto. The dense chaparral prevented effective use of artillery. Combat involved small parties and hand-to-hand fighting. The outcome of the battle was still in question until U.S. troops found a trail around the west end of the Mexican line. When they appeared at the Mexican rear, the Mexicans broke and ran for the Rio Grande. The retreating force abandoned eight cannons and General Arista's baggage, writing desk, silver service, and papers.[26]

Matamoros, on the south side of the Rio Grande, was fortified. However, Mexican troops withdrew, permitting U.S. forces to enter it on May 18, 1846, without firing a shot. Upon occupying the city, the Americans found 400 sick and wounded Mexican troops that Arista had abandoned.[27]

On July 7, 1846, nearly two months after the occupation of Matamoros, Mexico declared war. The first article of the declaration stated, "The government, in legitimate defense of the nation, will repel aggression initiated by the United States of America and sustained against the Mexican republic, which has had several of its states invaded and attacked."[28]

A few locally procured ox-carts, 175 wagons, 1,500 Mexican pack mules, and shallow-draft steamships that had been plying the Ohio and Mississippi rivers moved Taylor's force eighty miles up the Rio Grande to Camargo, the head of navigation. His force, which had swelled to 15,000, spent four miserable months there in mud from a recent flood and heat as high as 112 degrees Fahrenheit. Estimates place the number of deaths resulting from poor sanitation there at more than 1,000. A lack of supplies, not Mexican resistance, delayed Taylor. Since the United States was not on a war footing, supplying Taylor's army required a massive logistical effort. The supplies necessary for an offensive did not arrive until September. Even then, Taylor only had supplies to outfit 6,230 men when he began his advance.[29]

Taylor's first major objective was Monterrey, a city of 10,000, which guarded a key mountain pass through the Sierra Madre Oriental. Beyond that pass lay Saltillo and the interior of Mexico. The Americans faced a difficult task, as the city was protected by a river to its south, mountains to the west, and by fortresses to the north, east, and west. The 7,303-man Mexican force in Monterrey outnumbered Taylor's force.

After meeting stiff resistance in the city, Taylor settled for less than total victory. He agreed to permit the Mexicans to retreat to Saltillo with their arms, rather than fighting to the last man. Taylor's forces were running low on ammunition and had suffered 120 killed and 368 wounded, or 8.5 percent of the men fighting. This exceeded the Mexican casualty rate of 5 percent.[30]

While Taylor was waging his campaign, Polk attempted to end the war through non-military means. Santa Anna, then in exile in Cuba, sent his confidential representative Alexander Atocha to Polk with a deal. Atocha claimed that if Polk would permit Santa Anna to pass through the U.S. blockade at Veracruz, Santa Anna would save lives and money by arranging for the cession of territory and a peaceful settlement of the conflict.[31]

Polk accepted Atocha's proposal and ordered that Santa Anna be allowed to sail from Cuba to Veracruz. In August of 1846, Santa Anna landed at Veracruz and then made a triumphal entry into Mexico City, only two years after he had been exiled "for life." In the previous two years, Mexico had had four different governments and even more finance ministers, none of whom had enjoyed any credibility. The nation needed a savior and looked to Santa Anna, who once again received an invitation to serve as president.[32]

Two weeks after his arrival in Mexico City, on September 28, 1846, Santa Anna ordered the Mexican army north toward Taylor's force. This act added Polk to the long list of those betrayed by Santa Anna.

Santa Anna paused in San Luis Potosí to gather supplies and additional troops. The Mexican force that had defended Monterrey joined him. Rather than defending Saltillo, Santa Anna had ordered the troops who left Monterrey to regroup in San Luis Potosí. A lack of money hampered Santa Anna's efforts. The refusal of the states of Jalisco, Durango, and Zacatecas, which in the past had opposed Santa Anna, to supply men and matériel presented yet another obstacle.[33]

After four months in San Luis Potosí, Santa Anna decided to attack Taylor's force. This decision was based on a captured U.S. dispatch that revealed that much of Taylor's army had been withdrawn to take part in a planned amphibious landing at Veracruz. On January 27, 1847, Santa Anna's force started north, some 21,553 strong—another tribute to his organizational capacity. In twenty-seven days, his force marched 240 miles and decreased to 15,142, not due to hostile fire, but cold weather, poor food, and desertion. A large contingent of *soldaderas*, who prepared food, maintained clothing, provided medical care, and on occasion, engaged in combat, accompanied the force north. Their presence was a major factor in stemming desertion.[34]

Santa Anna's still formidable force approached Taylor's position ten miles south of Saltillo. Each nation engaged gave the battleground where they met different descriptive names. To the Americans, the place was Buena Vista, referring to the fine view south from the high plateau that the Americans were defending. The Mexicans called the battlefield Angostura (the narrows), referring to the narrow pass through which the Saltillo-San Luis Potosí road passed. Mountains lined the road to both the west and east. Steep gullies crisscrossed the area alongside the road, forming a natural barrier.

The ensuing battle lasted two days, February 22 and 23, 1847. On one occasion, the Mexicans broke through the east side of the U.S. line. Reinforcements thrown into the breach saved the Americans. Later Mexican attacks were turned back by light artillery, which proved decisive due to its ability to shift rapidly to check Mexican infantry advances. Finally, after two days of hard fighting and heroism on both sides, Santa Anna's forces turned back. Taylor lost 272 killed, the highest U.S. death toll of any battle in the war, and 387 wounded, or about 14 percent of the men engaged. The Mexicans lost more than twice that number. Although Taylor's 4,594-man force was mainly composed of green volunteers, they were well rested, well fed, and enjoyed effective artillery support.

Had Santa Anna persisted a third day, he might have broken through U.S. lines. However, he decided his men were incapable of fighting for another day. Rather than risking a decisive defeat, Santa Anna pulled his men back. He justified quitting a battlefield where he claimed to have won, noting that his troops had not eaten or slept in forty-eight hours and were dying of thirst, hunger, and fatigue.

Strategically the battle accomplished little, since both armies returned to their initial positions, Santa Anna in San Luis Potosí and Taylor in Saltillo. However, the battle did stir the fires of patriotism in the United States as reports arrived of Taylor's turning back of Santa Anna's superior force.[35]

FROM VERACRUZ TO MEXICO CITY, 1847

The battle at Buena Vista left the Americans in a quandary. Taylor's campaign had permitted U.S. forces to occupy territory from the Gulf of Mexico to Saltillo. However, it did not immediately lead to peace, since distance prevented U.S. forces from pressuring the central government in Mexico City.

U.S. Senator Thomas H. Benton wrote in his memoirs of Polk's dilemma:

> They wanted a small war, just large enough to require a treaty of peace, and not large enough to make military reputations, dangerous for the presidency. Never were men at the head of a government less imbued with military spirit, or more addicted to intrigue.[36]

Polk's hopes for a short, neatly executed war were never met. Even though they had defeated the Mexicans on the battlefield, after almost a year peace was still elusive.

After Buena Vista, Taylor suggested maintaining his position in northern Mexico and then waiting for the Mexicans to tire of the U.S. presence. This, he felt, would lead to a negotiated withdrawal.

Polk rejected this strategy, claiming that it would necessitate a long defensive line and provoke guerrilla attacks. He also rejected the idea of moving Taylor's force south since he deemed the desert between Saltillo and Mexico City too formidable an obstacle to march across.[37]

Even before Buena Vista, Polk had decided on an amphibious invasion of Veracruz followed by an attack on Mexico City, with the invaders retracing Cortés's footsteps. Taking Veracruz would prevent the Mexican government from importing arms and deny it revenue from the Veracruz customs house.[38]

Polk also feared that if the war dragged on, criticism from the home front would escalate. As Senator Benton noted, a defensive strategy would "prolong the war and ruin the Democratic party." U.S. opponents of the war included those opposed to the military, abolitionists, those feeling their businesses would be harmed, opponents of a powerful presidency, Whigs opposed to the incumbent Democrats, and those feeling the war was unjust.[39]

Robert E. Lee and Ulysses S. Grant, who would lead the armies of the U.S. Civil War, both criticized the Mexican–American War. Grant stated the war was "the most unjust war ever waged by a stronger against a weaker nation." Similarly, Abraham Lincoln commented on Polk's 1847 State of the Union message, "How like the half-insane mumblings of a fever dream is the whole war part of his late message!"[40]

The best remembered criticism of the war by a private citizen came from Henry David Thoreau, who was briefly jailed for his refusal to pay taxes to support the war. In his book *Civil Disobedience*, Thoreau linked both slavery and the Mexican–American War to "a hundred thousand merchants and farmers here, who are more interested in commerce and agriculture than they are in humanity . . ."[41]

Though opposition did not seriously undermine the war effort, the war did become a major political issue in the 1846 Congressional elections. Polk responded to war critics in his December 1846 State of the Union Address: "A more effectual means could not have been devised to encourage the enemy and protract the war than to advocate and adhere to their cause, and thus give them 'aid and comfort.'" The words "aid and comfort" were a pointed allusion to the constitution's treason clause.[42]

Polk selected General Winfield Scott to lead the force invading Veracruz. Scott was general-in-chief of the army and had served in the military for almost thirty-seven years. As a result of his distinguishing himself as a commander in the War of 1812, he was promoted to brigadier general at the age of twenty-nine. Later he remained in the limelight as an Indian fighter. In choosing Scott to command the invasion force, Polk, a Democrat, attempted to neutralize Taylor's popularity. Nonetheless Taylor parlayed his military victories into the 1848 Whig nomination and was elected president.[43]

On March 9, 1847, the campaign to take Veracruz began with an amphibious landing three miles south the city. At the time, it was the largest amphibious landing in the annals of war. More than 10,000 troops went ashore in sixty-five heavy surf boats towed close to the shore by steamers. In addition, artillery and supplies were landed. Horses were thrown overboard and forced to swim.[44]

The Americans landed unopposed. As Frederick Zeh, a Bavarian emigrant who served with U.S. forces, noted in his first-person account of the landing, "The Mexicans had plenty of time to prepare a forceful response for us, but they neglected everything; and from beginning to end, their entire military leadership was devoid of energy and strictly defensive." It was a serious military error for the Mexicans not to oppose the landing since the U.S. troops were most vulnerable as they were disembarking.[45]

Rather than attacking Veracruz from the sea, as the Mexicans had anticipated, the Americans encircled the city after they landed, cutting off supplies. Then, rather than storming the city and suffering heavy casualties, Scott ordered a prolonged shelling. The shelling lasted four days. During this period, Scott would not permit the evacuation of women, children, and non-combatants, since he correctly felt their continued presence in the city would increase pressure for surrender. Finally, after 6,700 rounds—463,000 pounds—had been lobbed into the city, Veracruz surrendered. During the siege some 600 Mexican soldiers and 400 to 500 civilians died. U.S. dead numbered only about thirteen.[46]

The approach of the yellow fever season provided an incentive for a rapid move inland. Initially logistics presented more of a problem than hostile fire. The supplies included roughly 300,000 horse- and mule-shoes, and 300,000 bushels of oats, and 200,000 of corn. On April 8, after Scott's force had acquired sufficient mules and wagons, his troops began to move toward Mexico City.[47]

At Cerro Gordo, fifty miles northwest of Veracruz, Scott found his way blocked by a Mexican force commanded by Santa Anna. The situation was the reverse of Buena Vista. Santa Anna was entrenched on high ground, while U.S. forces were coming from below. The Mexicans trained their artillery on the road, assuming that the U.S. force, with its heavily laden supply wagons, would follow it inland.

On April 17, rather than pushing through the concentrated fire directed toward the road, the Americans turned north. Troops under the command of a young captain named Robert E. Lee pushed their way through ravines and thickets north of the road. The Mexicans had considered this area impassable. This permitted them to occupy the top of a hill, Cerro Atalaya. Santa Anna had failed to post troops on the hill, even though his military engineer had advised him to do so. Then with artillery support from Cerro Atalaya, U.S. troops stormed up another hill, Cerro Gordo, which overlooked Mexican forces. Other U.S. troops continued through woods and across ravines behind Cerro Gordo. As they emerged behind the Mexican line, Mexicans, feeling American forces would envelop them, broke and ran.

The Battle of Cerro Gordo lasted only three hours. There were 431 U.S. casualties, while Santa Anna lost more than 1,000. Scott's force took more than 3,000 prisoners, so many that they could not be cared for, so they were released. Santa Anna barely escaped capture.

Santa Anna retreated to Puebla, a city of 80,000 lying seventy-five miles east–southeast of Mexico City. There he requested funds from Bishop Francisco Pablo Vázquez so he could strengthen his army. Vázquez said no Church money should be used for the war and retired to his country home. After he failed to obtain the financial support he was seeking, Santa Anna continued on to Mexico City.[48]

Rather than immediately following Santa Anna into Mexico City, Scott stopped in Puebla, where the clergy welcomed him. No one attempted to organize a defense of the city. Scott remained in Puebla for nearly three months. His forces were low on ammunition, and many of his men were wounded or sick. Others had enlisted for only a short period and returned home. While he awaited supplies and additional troops in Puebla, Scott spent at least $10,000 trying to bribe Santa Anna to hold peace talks. He rationalized this payoff, noting that since the United States bribed American Indians and Barbary pirates, it was appropriate to bribe Mexican officials.[49]

On August 7, after deciding he could not obtain peace through negotiation, Scott ordered his 10,738-man force to advance on Mexico City. To many, Scott's mission seemed impossible. A force of 30,000 troops on their own ground was defending his objective—a fortified city of 200,000. As in Aztec times, lakes and swamps protected Mexico City.[50]

After evaluating intelligence reports, Scott decided to turn south of Lakes Chalco and Xochimilco, enabling him to bypass Santa Anna's strong outlying position at El Peñón. This placed his force at the extreme southern end of the Valley of Mexico. In response, Santa Anna shifted his men to his southern defensive positions.

Once again, Captain Lee outflanked the Mexicans. He managed to lead a force across an almost impassable lava bed, today's fashionable suburb of El Pedregal. This placed the Americans southwest of Mexico City. At Contreras, a force commanded by General Gabriel Valencia awaited them. Valencia remained isolated from other Mexican forces due to his refusal to obey Santa Anna's order to combine his forces with Santa Anna's. He feared that Santa Anna would get credit for saving Mexico City if the two forces were combined.

As it turned out, the credit Valencia received differed from what he had anticipated. Americans moved up a ravine running behind his force and then staged a surprise attack with fixed bayonets. Valencia's force broke and ran. U.S. forces suffered sixty casualties, while 700 Mexicans died and 800 were captured. The Mexicans also lost twenty-two artillery pieces, 700 pack mules, and other supplies.[51]

Later the same day, August 20, U.S. troops approached Churubusco, where a former monastery formed one of the strong points of Santa Anna's defensive line. An eight-foot-thick adobe wall had been constructed there as part of the defenses. After meeting some of the most determined resistance of the war, the 6,000 American attackers finally forced the 1,980 Mexican defenders to surrender. The victory resulted from a breach of the defensive wall by the U.S. artillery, the élan of the U.S. troops, and the Mexicans' ammunition shortage. After the Mexicans surrendered Churubusco, U.S. General David Twiggs met the Mexican commander General Pedro María Anaya, who uttered the most celebrated sentence of the war, "If we'd had enough ammunition, you wouldn't be here."[52]

Rather than advancing on Mexico City, five miles north of Churubusco, Scott ordered a halt. His troops were tired and hungry and an attack might have scattered the Mexican government, leaving no one to negotiate a peace treaty with. In a single day, Santa Anna lost 4,000 killed or wounded, and 3,000 captured, including eight generals, two of whom were former presidents of Mexico. Scott lost 1,053, of whom 139 were killed. Santa Anna's forces suffered not only heavy casualties south of Mexico City but also hopeless demoralization among those remaining.[53]

After Churubusco, peace talks began. The Mexicans offered to renounce their claims to Texas and declare the area between the Nueces and the Rio Grande neutral territory. This was not, however, what the Americans were looking for. Polk commented on the unwillingness of the Mexicans to cede further territory in his December 1847 State of the Union address:

> The doctrine of no territory is the doctrine of no indemnity, and if sanctioned would be a public acknowledgment that our country was wrong and that the war declared by Congress with extraordinary unanimity was unjust and should be abandoned—an admission unfounded in fact and degrading to the national character.[54]

After rejecting the Mexicans' initial proposal, U.S. negotiators proposed the transfer to the United States of New Mexico and most of the present state of California. This time the Mexicans rejected the proposal. The hawks in Santa Anna's cabinet refused to part with that much territory.[55]

On September 8, Scott concluded that there was little possibility of a peace accord, so he ordered his troops to attack Mexico City from the west, just the opposite of what Santa Anna had initially anticipated. His first targets were two buildings, Molino del Rey (King's Mill), a hundred yards west of Chapultepec Castle, and the Casa Mata, a stone fortress 500 yards west of that. Chapultepec, in turn, was three miles southwest of the center of Mexico City. Repeated infantry charges took Molino del Rey, and artillery reduced the Casa Mata.

The Americans then assaulted Chapultepec. Despite its impressive appearance, perched high on a hill, Chapultepec Castle had been built as a summer home for the viceroys, not as a heavily constructed fort. On September 13, the attack began with more than twelve hours of artillery bombardment followed by an infantry assault. As Major General John Quitman later wrote: "The assault forces advanced like a flood. The Mexicans stood in the parapets with rare firmness. For a brief time, they struggled arm to arm, wielding swords and bayonets, as well as rifles." Finally, the Americans prevailed.[56]

The battle at Chapultepec has been immortalized in both countries. Mexicans annually commemorate the valor of the *niños héroes*—the cadets at the military academy located in the castle. They died defending Chapultepec rather than surrendering to the Americans. The U.S. Marine Corps hymn keeps the battle alive in American memory with its reference to "the halls of Montezuma."

Chapultepec formed the last defensive position between the Americans and Mexico City. Santa Anna still had roughly 5,000 troops in the Ciudadela, a tobacco factory that had been converted into a fort, and perhaps another 7,000 elsewhere in the city. Rather than defending the capital, he marched his troops out of the city. As a parting gesture, he opened the prisons, loosing hundreds of felons on the populace and the invaders.[57]

The entire world recognized Scott's defeat of Santa Anna as an impressive military feat. The Duke of Wellington, Europe's most distinguished solder, commented, "His campaign was unsurpassed in military annals."[58]

The conservative Mexico City government decided on its own to surrender the city to avoid combat damage. However, many residents did their best to turn back U.S. troops. Lacking firearms, they bombarded American troops with boiling oil, stones, flowerpots, and other objects flung from rooftops. This harassment lasted for three days. In some cases, houses sheltering such attackers were reduced by firing eight-inch howitzers at them.[59]

Figure 11.1 *General Winfield Scott riding into Mexico City's main square, the Zócalo, in 1847*
Source: Reproduced courtesy of the Benson Latin American Collection, the University of Texas at Austin

A grim aspect of the U.S. victory was the hanging of fifty U.S. deserters, many of whom were impoverished Irish immigrants who had been forced out of their homeland by crop failure and heavy-handed British rule. Before they had joined the U.S. army, they had faced anti-Irish sentiment and, in come cases, had been the target of rioters in the United States.[60]

Once the Irish arrived in Mexico, the Mexicans began to play on both ethnic and religious antagonisms. Mexicans addressed them as "Sons of Ireland, a noble race," and sent messages in English, such as:

> Can you fight by the side of those who put fire to your temples in Boston and Philadelphia? Come over to us! May Mexicans and Irishmen, united by the sacred ties of religion and benevolence, form only one people.[61]

In addition to appealing to ethnic loyalty and their Catholicism, deserters were promised money and 320 acres of land.

As a result of these appeals and harsh treatment from their officers, several hundred U.S. soldiers deserted and were incorporated into the Mexican army as the San Patricio Brigade. Roughly 40 percent of its members were Irish born, while 20 percent were U.S. born, and 14 percent were German born. Brigade members fought capably and bravely at Monterrey and Buena Vista. At Churubusco, they were among the staunchest defenders, knowing what fate would befall them if they were captured.[62]

After marching his troops out of Mexico City, Santa Anna sought funds and munitions to continue opposing the Americans. However the government, which reorganized itself after fleeing Mexico City, relieved Santa Anna of command. Given Santa Anna's dismissal, combat was essentially over after the U.S. occupation of Mexico City.[63]

The war resulted in the deaths of 10,000 Mexicans, of whom 4,000 to 5,000 died in battle. U.S. combat deaths numbered 1,721, while another 11,155 died from accidents, disease, and other causes. This gave the Mexican–American War the dubious distinction of being the deadliest war the United States ever fought in terms of the percentage of troops who died. In this war, 15.3 percent of U.S. troops died. In the next most deadly U.S. conflict, the Civil War, 9.8 percent died. The war also had the highest desertion rate of any U.S war.[64]

PEACE

After American forces occupied Mexico City, the remnants of the Mexican government fled northwest to Querétaro. A period of political instability followed. No Mexican wanted to take responsibility for admitting defeat and signing away territory.

Polk had sent Nicholas Trist, the chief clerk of the State Department, to Mexico along with Scott's force. Trist, whose position today would be called under-secretary of state, was authorized to negotiate a peace treaty. Polk's negotiator, who spoke Spanish and had served as U.S. consul in Havana, carried with him a draft treaty that made demands similar to those made by Slidell. He could offer $15 million for California and New Mexico, the minimum territorial concession acceptable to Polk. If Baja California and transit rights across the Isthmus of Tehuantepec were also ceded, he could offer $30 million. Before the transcontinental railroad and the Panama Canal, the Isthmus of Tehuantepec provided a relatively easy way to cross from the Caribbean to the Pacific.[65]

On October 5, 1847, given the unwillingness of any Mexicans to begin the negotiation process, Polk ordered Trist to return home. Polk's order did not arrive in Mexico until six weeks later. Just as he received his recall order, a new Mexican political party was formed for the express purpose of negotiating a peace treaty. Trist decided to remain and negotiate since he feared that if he did not negotiate then, the central government might collapse. When Polk learned of Trist's disobedience, he called him "an impudent and unqualified scoundrel."[66]

The Mexican delegates negotiating the peace treaty did their best to minimize territorial loss. They held Trist to his minimal demand and preserved for Mexico a land bridge between Baja California and Sonora. Given that the United States could have taken whatever it wanted, limiting U.S. acquisitions constituted a triumph for Mexican diplomacy.[67]

Mexican negotiators not only had to defend Mexican interests against Trist, but had to contend with the *puro* (pro-war) faction in Mexico, which advocated continued war against the United States, not only to avoid loss of territory but to bring about economic and political reforms. The pro-peace faction finally prevailed, arguing that failure to ratify a peace treaty would result in continued American military occupation, the probable loss of additional territory, and prolonged financial disaster for the Mexican government, which received no customs receipts from American-occupied ports.[68]

On February 2, 1848, a peace treaty was signed in the village of Guadalupe Hidalgo, four miles north of Mexico City. The Treaty of Guadalupe Hidalgo established a new U.S.–Mexican boundary that started at the mouth of the Rio Grande. It ran up that river until it met the southern border of New Mexico. It then ran west along that line and turned, following the western border of New Mexico north until it intersected the Gila River or reached the closest point to that river. No one knew if the Gila crossed into New Mexico. Then the border ran down the Gila to its junction with the Colorado River. From there the boundary ran to a point on the Pacific Coast one marine league south of San Diego, forming the present southern boundary of California.

Mexico received $15 million, and, in addition, the Mexican government was relieved of responsibility for meeting past damage claims filed by U.S. citizens. Throughout the war, Polk had insisted that Mexico should cede territory to the United States to pay for the war it forced the United States to fight. At the same time, the United States wanted to avoid the appearance of stealing land, so it paid for the territory it acquired. U.S. historian Glenn Price noted, "It was all

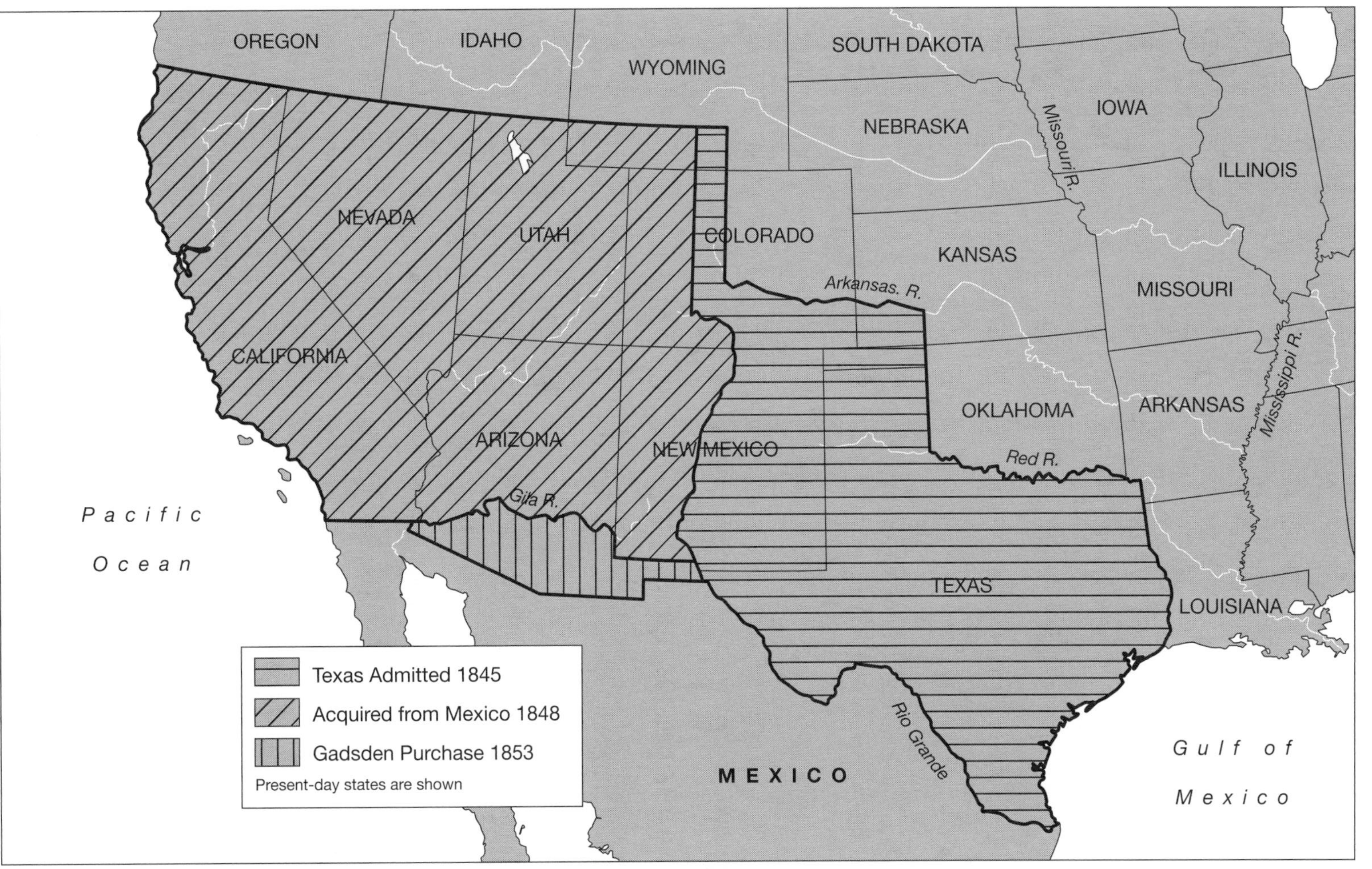

Figure 11.2 *Mexican border with the United States c.1855*

Source: Reprinted by permission of HarperCollins Publishers

very odd logic." At the time, Mexican President Manuel de la Peña y Peña commented that Mexico did not cede California and New Mexico for $15 million but rather to get U.S. troops out of Mexican cities and ports.[69]

British bondholders, who ultimately received $2.5 million of the $15 million indemnity payment, supported the settlement. *Agiotistas*, wanting to be paid in hard cash, also supported a settlement. One of the *agiotistas* who had the biggest stake in the settlement was British consul Ewen MacKintosh, who received $600,000 of the first $3 million indemnity payment.[70]

The Treaty of Guadalupe Hidalgo gave the roughly 85,000 Hispanics in the area transferred to the United States the option of moving to Mexico to keep their Mexican citizenship. If they remained for more than a year in the territory acquired by the United States, they automatically became U.S. citizens and were guaranteed possession of any property they owned.

Mexicans were lucky to retain as much territory as they did. A strong "all of Mexico" movement in the United States advocated taking the entire country. Advocates of the "all of Mexico" position were not confined to the United States. Some Mexican liberals who admired the United States proposed to General Scott that he should become dictator of Mexico. They wanted that to be the first step towards annexation by the United States.[71]

Proponents of seizing "all of Mexico" did not prevail for a variety of reasons. Former ambassador Poinsett warned that taking all of Mexico would require a large occupation force and would inflame Mexican nationalism, increasing resistance to the United States. Since the legality of slavery in any Mexican territory acquired had not been settled, abolitionists opposed absorbing Mexico since they feared that all the land annexed would become slave territory. Others opposed annexation because they did not want 7 million Mexicans of mixed race to be cast into the U.S. racial melting pot. William Prescott, author of the classic account of the Spanish conquest of Mexico, commented, "The Spanish blood will not mix well with the Yankee."[72]

BEHIND THE U.S. VICTORY?

As had been the case a decade earlier in Texas, "Manifest Destiny" formed the leitmotif of the Mexican–American War. In his biography of Polk, Eugene McCormac observed:

> Determined from the beginning to add California and New Mexico to our national domain, he pursued his object with a dogged persistence which neither opposition nor denunciation could weaken. Whatever may be thought of his motives or his methods, to him is due the credit (or censure, if you please) of extending to the Pacific the boundaries of the United States.[73]

The Mexican press limited the possible actions of Mexico's leaders by urging war on them and whipping up public sentiment to favor war. Mexicans' failure to accurately assess the relative military strength of the United States and Mexico impaired their decision-making ability. Finally, many in Mexico felt that if Mexico did not take a strong stance against its northern neighbor, the United States would continue to press claims forever, nibbling away at Mexican territory until the nation ceased to exist.[74]

Given that the United States had long supply lines, a pre-industrial economy, and a small standing army, and that it was forced to attack the strong defensive position offered by the Sierra Madre Oriental, it is worth considering why the United States triumphed over Mexico. The U.S. victory amazed European observers. A British journalist commented, "There must be some mystery—some leading cause, imperfectly understood on our side of the Atlantic."[75]

Factors contributing to the U.S. victory include:

- The U.S. population at the time of the war consisted of 17 million whites and 3 million slaves, more than double the number of Mexicans. This enabled the United States to draw on a much larger population for soldiers and war production.

- African Americans formed a significant element of the U.S. presence in Mexico, performing labor in camp and serving white soldiers. The Mexican–American War is the only U.S. war in which African Americans were not mobilized as combatants—an indicator of the racial sensitivities of the time. Far outweighing African Americans' contribution in Mexico, black slaves in the United States produced food and cotton for military uniforms and for export.[76]
- The United States made extensive use of light "flying" artillery that could be moved rapidly, keeping up with the troops and advancing to fire on enemy positions. Artillery officers were permitted to move and fire without having to wait for orders from a central command. The U.S. artillery played a crucial role in several battles, such as those as Palo Alto, Monterrey, and Veracruz. At Buena Vista, General John Wool stated, "Without our artillery we would not have maintained our position a single hour."[77]
- The smooth-bore muskets that were the standard U.S. infantry weapon were among the world's most advanced shoulder weapons. The milling machines used in their manufacture produced interchangeable parts and uniform barrel diameter. U.S. muskets had a range of 220 yards, considerably greater than the hundred-yard range of the Mexicans' muskets.[78]
- By the time of the Mexican–American War, the majority of the lieutenants and captains were West Point graduates. Years of campaigning against elusive Indian guerrillas on the western frontier accustomed these officers to rapid, decentralized decision-making. Such officers were especially valuable when U.S. forces were operating in small units, as at Resaca de la Palma. After the war, Scott commented:

  > I give it as my fixed opinion that but for our graduated cadets the war between the United States and Mexico might, and probably would, have lasted some four or five years, with, in its first half, more defeats than victories falling to our share, whereas in two campaigns we conquered a great country and a peace without the loss of a single battle or skirmish.[79]

- The élan of the all-volunteer U.S. force was crucial. Many existing militia units volunteered en masse, reinforcing camaraderie. Initial American victories lifted spirits and additional triumphs kept them high. This élan and patriotism was evident in one officer who saw the U.S. flag at Monterrey and commented, "A glow of honest pride lit up my face, and I thanked God I was an American, and that he had endowed my own country with so much to love and venerate."[80]
- Even though some Americans opposed the war, the United States was much more united than Mexico. The desire to acquire California was a generally shared goal, just as expansion into the Mississippi Valley had been a generation earlier. Herman Melville described the pro-war feeling in a small New York town: "People here are all in a state of delirium about the Mexican War. A military ardor pervades all ranks. . . and 'prentice boys are running off to the wars by scores.—Nothing is talked of but the 'Halls of the Montezumas.'"[81]
- The U.S. economy, unlike the Mexican economy, which had yet to recover ground lost during the struggle for independence, was beginning its industrialization. The United States could achieve what, for the times, were prodigious logistical feats. For example, within a four-month period, forty-nine ten-inch mortars and 50,000 shells were ordered, manufactured, and transported to Veracruz.[82]

A number of factors contributed to the Mexican loss:

- The Mexican population of seven million was substantially smaller than the U.S. population. Only a small proportion of Mexico's population was mobilized, some 70,000 out of 7 million, or 1 percent. This contrasts with the U.S. Civil War in which roughly 3 million, or 10 percent of the population, were mobilized for the Union and Confederate armies.[83]
- Mexican statesmen failed to see in time that the United States constituted a threat to Mexico. As late as 1825, the Mexican government convened a special commission to advise on developing

California. It warned not of danger from the United States but from Russia. Even the normally perceptive Humboldt wrote in the first decade of the nineteenth century that

> the principles of wisdom and moderation by which the government of the United States is animated, lead us to hope that a friendly arrangement will soon fix the limits between the two nations, who both possess more ground than they can possibly cultivate.[84]

Some Mexicans did see the danger posed by the United States before war broke out. For example, former President Valentín Gómez Farías wrote in 1843 that Texas was the key, which if it should fall into American hands, would unlock the last barrier to the rest of northern Mexico. By taking this "giant step" toward California, he wrote, the United States would be extended "from sea to sea" and Mexico's hopes for a prosperous future would be gone. By then it was too late to save California.[85]

- The frequent changes in government in the mid-1840s undermined the government's already weak financial structure. The U.S. occupation of the Veracruz, Tampico, and Matamoros customs houses further impoverished the government.[86]
- The ever present possibility of a coup made presidents keep one eye on the United States and the other on possible rivals. The most serious internal conflict, known as the Revolt of the Polkos, occurred just before the invasion of Veracruz when conservatives rebelled against liberals in the capital. Rather than rushing to defend the port, Mexicans engaged in an artillery duel in downtown Mexico City. The revolt was triggered by liberal Acting President Gómez Farías authorizing the government to confiscate Church property to finance the war.[87]
- The actions of individual Mexican states also weakened the war effort. Yucatán declared itself independent on January 1, 1846. This renegade state not only failed to contribute to the war effort but sold supplies to U.S. naval forces blockading Veracruz before the invasion. California, Tabasco, Sinaloa, and Chihuahua were unable to contribute to the national war effort because they were fighting what amounted to internal civil wars. By default, much of the defense burden fell on the individual state being invaded. Puebla failed to accept this defense burden, and the State of Mexico, which U.S. forces had to pass through to enter Mexico City, declared itself to be neutral. Many state governors were reluctant to raise militia units due to the long-standing perception that military commanders were abusive and authoritarian. Conservative governors were reluctant to see militia units recruit politically unreliable members of the lower classes. The Mexico City municipal government opposed attempts to fortify the city.[88]
- Political, class, and racial divisions hampered the war effort. In 1848, the newspaper *El Siglo XIX* commented:

  > The forces of disintegration—formerly civil strife and more recently foreign war—have been building up in our country. They have gathered so much force, are so numerous, and are so palpable that at first glance one can doubt if our republic is really a society rather than simply a gathering of men without bonds, rights, and duties.[89]

- Many wealthy Mexicans not only failed to contribute to the war effort but actually welcomed the invaders. Often merchants preferred Scott to Santa Anna and his forced loans. Santa Anna complained that the wealthy went into hiding as U.S. troops approached Mexico City, so they could avoid contributing to its defense. Certainly the sight of the rich attending the opera and bullfights did nothing to encourage the defenders of Mexico City, who ate poorly and were practically dressed in rags.[90]

The wealthy and the Church wanted to maintain their properties and prerogatives. The United States made it clear that none of these interests would be jeopardized. After taking Veracruz, Scott published a manifesto declaring that Americans were friends of the Mexicans and that the Catholic Church and property rights would be respected. He and his staff attended Mass at the Cathedral in full dress uniform. He ordered his men to salute priests. President Polk requested that Catholic bishops in the United States inform their Mexican counterparts that the United States would respect the Church.[91]

- Unlike slaves in America, Mexican Indians, roughly half the population, produced little surplus that could support the war effort. They had little in common with the rest of Mexico and little sense of belonging to a "nation." Taking advantage of the national crisis to advance their own causes, indigenous people staged widespread uprisings in the central and southern regions following the U.S. invasion. In northern Veracruz, Indians under pressure from encroaching cattlemen rose up, burning towns and haciendas. *Hacendado* Manuel Soto wrote, "Blood ran in torrents, and for ten months the Huasteca [region of Veracruz] was the stage for the most horrible scenes." Suppressing such uprisings diverted men and arms away from fighting Americans.[92]
- Prolonged conflict with independent Indian groups such as the Apache had left large areas of northern Mexico unable and unwilling to resist the U.S. army. American troops frequently encountered abandoned homes, overgrown fields, and hastily finished graves—a result of Indian raids—in the parts of northern Mexico they occupied. Prior to the Battle of Buena Vista, the states of Chihuahua, Durango, and Zacatecas ordered soldiers to remain at home to protect against Indian raids.[93]
- The civilian population frequently reacted as if the war was being waged by two foreign powers. U.S. officers and Mexican landowners frequently fraternized. Other landowners, such as the Sánchez Navarro family in Coahuila, sold massive amounts of livestock, corn, and wheat to the U.S. army. To insure that the U.S. forces did not antagonize landowners, Generals Scott and Taylor insisted that all food and supplies needed by U.S. troops were paid for in voluntary, negotiated sales. Other Mexicans served U.S. troops as guides, teamsters, and spies and supplied them with mules, cattle, and corn.[94]
- The army reflected the chronic financial problems of early nineteenth-century Mexican governments. The lack of finances resulted in an army that was poorly equipped at the outbreak of hostilities and made it difficult to amass war matériel later on.[95]
- The professional army that defended Mexico reflected Mexican society as a whole. The army was poorly led, since individuals with little military training used bribes or political influence to obtain leadership positions. The officer corps was conservative and elitist. Of the 137 most senior officers, all but about twenty had fought on the Spanish side in the independence struggle. Changes in government generally resulted in changes in the army's command structure. These repeated personnel shifts impaired fighting ability. Mexico's bloated army had 24,000 officers commanding 20,000 enlisted men. The British ambassador wrote home in 1846 that the army was "the worst perhaps to be found in any part of the world." Zeh, while marching on Mexico City, commented, "The enemy cavalry now had a marvelous opportunity to capture our generalissimo; but to do this required courage and a spirit of daring-do which, fortunately, they lacked."[96]
- Morale among Mexican troops was low, since they were often impressed or taken from prisons. They received little training and, as a result, could not perform tactical maneuvers in large groups.[97] Historian Josefina Vázquez described the army defending Mexico as

  > a ghost comprised of untrained conscripts who deserted as soon as the opportunity presented itself, and led by officers who dedicated themselves to politics. The cavalry and artillery, which had acquired a certain fame, had declined due to the lack of funds and failure to maintain proper levels of enlistment.[98]

  Waddy Thompson, the U.S. ambassador to Mexico from 1842 to 1844, noted that Mexican recruitment consisted mainly of capturing Indians, of whom no more than one in ten had ever seen a gun and not one in a hundred had fired one.[99]
- The effectiveness of Mexican cannons was limited by their being of a variety of calibers and by poor logistics. The solid shot used by Mexicans was less effective than the grape and canister

shot used by Americans. Mexican muskets had been purchased from British stocks after they had been declared obsolete and often unserviceable. Zeh commented that after Cerro Gordo, "The captured muskets usually were collected into huge piles and set afire, because they were of no value."[100]

- Mexican officers tended to view battles like chess games. They expected events to unfold within a clearly defined area. The Americans would repeatedly extend the limits of the battlefield, and win. This occurred at Resaca de la Palma, Cerro Gordo, and Contreras.[101]
- Mexican forces repeatedly withdrew before they were attacked. The list of such abandoned positions includes Matamoros, Tampico, Jalapa, Mazatlán, Tucson, El Paso, Santa Fe, and Chihuahua City. No military force existed in other cities such as Puebla. Others, such as Veracruz, Monterrey, and Mexico City, were defended for a time, and then surrendered. The fortress at Perote was abandoned along with a sizable amount of war matériel. A more determined defense would have increased the number of U.S. casualties, thus possibly undermining American support for the war.[102]
- Guerrilla warfare might also have defeated the United States. However, Santa Anna opposed a guerrilla strategy, feeling he could win on the battlefield. The wealthy opposed guerrilla warfare since the resulting disruption and social mobilization would be prejudicial to their interests. This, and the lack of a credible leader, prevented the creation a strong guerrilla force comparable to the force opposing Maximilian in the 1860s. The most serious action by irregulars was an attack on a supply train between the Rio Grande and Monterrey. In that attack, forty to fifty teamsters were killed, and 110 wagons and 300 pack mules were captured. Taylor referred to that attack as "an atrocious barbarism unprecedented in the existing war."[103]

  Scott did his best to stamp out any outbreak of guerrilla warfare. During his six-year struggle against the Seminole, he had learned how hard it was to suppress a full-scale guerrilla insurrection. He ordered the summary execution of partisans and the destruction of villages supporting them. In addition, he held local mayors responsible for capturing and turning over to Americans anyone killing or robbing U.S. soldiers. Mayors who failed to capture such attackers faced heavy fines. To avoid antagonizing Mexicans, Scott also took special care to see that his forces avoided the repeated atrocities committed by some of Taylor's forces.[104]

  Scott commented on these atrocities:

  > Our militia & volunteers, if a tenth of what is said to be true, have committed atrocities—horrors—in Mexico, sufficient to make Heaven weep, & every American, of Christian morals blush for his country. Murder, robbery & rape on mothers and daughters, in the presence of the tied up males of the families, have been common all along the Rio Grande.[105]

- Many of Mexico's problems resulted from its failure to have formed a national consciousness in the quarter century after independence. In 1848, statesman Mariano Otero commented, "There has not been, nor could there have been a national spirit, for there is no nation."[106]

To this date, Mexicans resent the loss of roughly 40 percent of "their" territory. However, just as was the case with the Adams–Onís Treaty, those most affected by the Treaty of Guadalupe Hidalgo were not the roughly 85,000 Hispanics on land ceded to the United States but the 160,000 Indians whose ancestral lands passed to U.S. control without their having been consulted.[107]

In Mexico, the war was a painful but perhaps necessary shock to the nation, provoking self-examination. The questions raised by the war shaped a new generation and led to a consolidated state and increased nationalism, evident in the 1860s during the struggle against Maximilian. In the aftermath of the war, the dominance of the army, the Church, and the *hacendados* began to be questioned more strongly than ever before.[108]

For most of the twentieth century, the Mexican Revolution of 1910–1917 overshadowed the Mexican–American War. However, by the end of the century the effects of the Revolution had largely run their course. The results of the Mexican–American War, in contrast, remain glaringly apparent. The four states—California, Arizona, New Mexico, and Texas—that form the bulk of the territory lost to the United States had a GDP almost four times that of Mexico in 2000.[109]

THE LAST STEP OF MANIFEST DESTINY

Before the Mexican–American War, Mexico for the United States was a distant and little known area, just as Africa was for Europe. The war changed that forever. After the war, Americans began appearing in Mexico with increasing frequency. Some were wanderers; others were entrepreneurs, speculators, and financiers. Many brought their skills and capital to Mexico.[110]

Charles Stillman, who pioneered shipping through Matamoros in the 1820s, was one of the most conspicuous of these Americans. By the 1850s, he had interests in copper, iron, lead, and silver mining in Nuevo León and Tamaulipas. He even sold shares on the New York Stock Exchange for his Vallecillo Mine, located between Nuevo Laredo and Monterrey. Soon men like him would dominate much of the Mexican economy.[111]

American merchants, whose appetite for trade with Mexico had been whetted during the Mexican–American War, responded to increased Mexican tariffs after the war by smuggling. Historian J. Fred Rippy commented, "Practically every Anglo-American along the [border] line chose the pursuit of a merchant rather than that of stock-raising or agriculture, and smuggling, ceasing to be blameworthy, soon became meritorious."[112]

Soon after the Mexican–American War, a new element—filibustering—began to complicate U.S.–Mexican relations. Filibusterers wanted to either provoke war with Mexico to pave the way for U.S. annexation of territory or to create ostensibly independent "republics" that could later be annexed by the United States. They mainly targeted Baja California and Sonora in isolated northwestern Mexico.

Filibusterers were the romantics of the age, mainly U.S. southerners and Frenchmen who had come to California in search of gold. When they failed to find fame and fortune there, they turned their sights south. They claimed the United States had a right to occupy northwestern Mexico to raise the standard of living and end corruption and dictatorship.[113]

Filibusterers complicated the normal course of diplomatic relations, making it difficult for the United States to acquire more Mexican territory or secure transit rights and trade treaties. Consequently Washington did not favor their actions. Local officials, however, often showed quite a different attitude, which reflected strong public support for filibustering in border areas. Even if zealous prosecutors indicted filibusterers, it was virtually impossible to find a jury that would convict them. The 1818 Neutrality Act set penalties for filibustering after it had occurred. However, it failed to provide authorities a legal mechanism for stopping expeditions before they left U.S. soil, making the prevention of filibustering even more difficult.[114]

William Walker, a lawyer from Tennessee who arrived in California in 1850, overshadowed the other filibusterers. Walker worked briefly as an editor for the *San Francisco Herald* and then began filibustering. In November 1853, he occupied La Paz, Baja California, with forty-five men. Walker arrested the Mexican governor and proclaimed the establishment of the Republic of Lower California. He even announced his "republic" would restore slavery to Baja California.[115]

After losing twelve men to Mexican attacks at La Paz, Walker withdrew to Ensenada, sixty miles south of Tijuana. While in Ensenada, Walker received additional arms, supplies, and enough recruits from the United States to bring his force up to 200 men. He founded a government while there, complete with a cabinet and himself as president.

In January 1854, Walker declared Sonora to be part of his republic, which he renamed the Republic of Sonora. In February, he started overland to occupy that state. By then, desertions had reduced his force to twenty-five. As soon as Mexicans threatened an attack, he retreated back to the United States.

After returning to California, Walker was arrested and charged with filibustering. However, his activities were quite popular and, as a result, a San Francisco jury took eight minutes to declare him not guilty.[116]

Walker might well have returned to Mexico on another filibustering expedition if he had not learned that Guaymas, Sonora, had already been occupied by the 400-man force of French filibusterer Gaston de Raousset Boulbon, the self-styled "Sultan of Sonora." After sixty-seven died in combat between the filibusterers and Mexican forces, the Mexicans captured Raousset de Boulbon and executed him. This did not have any long-lasting effect on Walker, though. He later declared himself to be president of Nicaragua and was finally executed for filibustering in Honduras.[117]

In addition to trying Walker for filibustering, the United States government did confiscate a boat loaded with arms that Walker was to have taken to Mexico. Despite such actions, the Mexican response proved to be the most effective deterrent to filibustering. In 1857, Henry A. Crabb, another Tennessee lawyer, led a force from California to Sonora. Mexicans captured his force and executed sixty-eight of its members, all except a fourteen-year old boy. Although filibustering expeditions never posed a military danger to Mexico, given the experience of Texas and the Mexican–American War, Mexicans viewed them as a major threat.[118]

In 1848, the Apache found themselves in a changed world, with an international boundary dividing the area where they had traditionally ranged. They could not understand why the U.S. government claimed to own the part of the Apache range north of the border just because it had conquered the Mexicans. The Apache noted that the Mexicans had never defeated them, and therefore could not cede to the United States what they had never controlled.[119]

The Apache and other groups continued raiding into Mexico, creating a diplomatic problem. The Treaty of Guadalupe Hidalgo shouldered the United States with the responsibility for preventing such raids. However the United States soon found preventing cross-border raids was easier said than done. The problem became especially severe as U.S. settlers continued to push westward, displacing Indians from their traditional lands.

After the Mexican–American War, military colonies were established just south of Chihuahua's newly delineated border with the United States to protect the state from Indian raids. Those who volunteered to live in these colonies and fight Indians for six years received land, tax exemptions, and other benefits.[120]

Despite its treaty obligations, the United States rejected Mexican monetary claims resulting from Indian raids. The U.S. government simply responded that it had tried to prevent such raids with diligence and energy. U.S. officials also noted that since American citizens received no compensation for damages resulting from Indian raids, there was no reason to compensate Mexicans.[121]

As north–south sectional tensions in the U.S. increased, it became clear that the federal government was unlikely to devote much attention to Indians in the southwest. From 1848 to 1852, not more than 180 U.S. mounted troops were within immediate reach of the border at any one time. Congress simply would not appropriate enough funds to provide for cavalry and Indian agents in the territory transferred to the United States in 1848.[122]

Sometimes U.S. efforts to prevent raids into Mexico would backfire. In 1850, an Apache told a U.S. army captain investigating a raid on Doña Ana, New Mexico, that, "We must steal from somebody; and if you will not permit us to rob the Mexicans, we must steal from you, or fight you."[123]

Many Anglos in the southwest came to an understanding with Indians. They would not interfere with Indian raids into Mexico, and in exchange, Indians would not bother them. Often Americans' willingness to purchase plundered goods provided the incentive for the Apache to raid into Mexico. In 1859, the editor of the Tucson *Arizonian* commented:

> We make treaties with the Indians to protect ourselves, and at the same time allow them to plunder our neighbors across the line, which they do to an extent almost beyond belief. The whole State of Sonora is ravaged by marauding bands of Apaches, who find safe retreat, and often a market for their booty, in Arizona Territory. It is, in fact, nothing more nor less than legalized piracy upon a weak and defenseless State, encouraged and abetted by the United States government.[124]

Though most Indian raids moved from U.S. territory into Mexico, some crossed the border in the opposite direction. Residents on both sides of the border claimed that the opposite nation was failing to prevent cross-border raiding and the disposal of booty from such raids. After 1848, Apaches used the border to their advantage, eluding Mexican pursuit by crossing into the United States, and visa versa.[125]

The raids heavily impacted Sonora, where 167 were killed in 1851 alone, more than in any other state. Residents of one of the military colonies, Namiquipa, noted that in Chihuahua "all neighbor haciendas had been abandoned because of the constant danger of aggression by the barbarians between 1832 and 1860 and only Namiquipa remained to fight the barbarians and to constitute a lonely bastion of civilization in this remote region." In Coahuila, between 1849 and 1853, the Apache and Comanche killed 191, captured sixty-three, and wounded 121.[126]

After the Mexican–American War, U.S. planners began to consider possible transcontinental rail routes. One of the most promising routes lay in the area, still in Mexican hands, just south of the Gila River in what is today southern Arizona. Mexico came under intense pressure to cede this territory to the United States. In 1853, President Franklin Pierce appointed James Gadsden, a prominent railroader and proponent of a southern transcontinental rail route, as U.S. ambassador to Mexico. He was instructed to negotiate a treaty with Mexico that would move the border south to include the future rail route. As with his predecessors, he was authorized to pay according to the amount of Mexican territory ceded. He could pay up to $50 million for Coahuila, Chihuahua, Sonora, and Baja California. Gadsden expressed his confidence in accomplishing his mission, informing Secretary of State William Marcy:

> The Mexican government needs money—their necessities are great, and their pretensions very extravagant. The most serious difficulty in the way of extension of Territory will be: *The consideration* to be paid.[127]

Mexicans greeted renewed U.S. territorial demands with resignation. They could do little to stop the United States since the government teetered on the edge of bankruptcy and lacked popular support. President Santa Anna commented on the situation he faced, "Our neighbors to the north were threatening another invasion if the boundary question was not settled to their satisfaction." Santa Anna desperately needed money to fight the pintos, as Álvarez's rebels were known. He rationalized the loss of further territory by claiming that it was of little use to Mexico.[128]

Foreign Relations Minister Lucas Alamán's inability to organize a French-British-Mexican alliance to stop U.S. encroachment thwarted Mexico's only hope to avoid ceding territory. The threat of war in Europe prevented France and Great Britain from taking any action. Since such European actions would violate the Monroe Doctrine, the United States condemned the plan. That led Mexico to claim that excluding Europe from the western hemisphere was only a cover for aggression by Americans, who were referred to as "the new Vandals and Goths."[129]

Given Santa Anna's desperate financial situation and his inability to confront the U.S. militarily, he signed what is known as the Gadsden Treaty, which the United States ratified in 1854. For $10 million, Mexico ceded 29,640 square miles that now form southern New Mexico and Arizona, including Tucson. Since this was the last land acquisition by the United States at Mexican expense, it has been referred to as the final step of Manifest Destiny.[130]

In addition to securing the desired rail right of way, the Gadsden Treaty relieved the United States of the responsibility for preventing Indians raids across the border.[131]

Mexicans strongly condemned the sale of the Gadsden Purchase. The Plan of Ayutla commented on Santa Anna's role in the sale:

> Despite having a duty to preserve the territorial integrity of the Republic, he sold a considerable part of it, sacrificing our brethren on the northern border, who from now on will be foreigners in their own land, just as occurred in California.[132]

Mexico and U.S.–Mexican relations both underwent major changes in the 1850s. After the 1850s, the Mexican government became more stable thanks to revenues obtained from the export of raw materials. At the same time, the U.S. interest in territorial acquisition waned. Instead, the United States sought to acquire raw materials and invest in the mines that produced them and in the railroads that transported them to the United States.[133]

Part Four

Late Nineteenth-Century Mexico, 1856–1909

Chapter 12

Juárez and Díaz, 1856–1909

THE LIBERALS TRIUMPHANT, 1855–1857

> If our Independence movement cut the ties that bound us to Spain, the Reform movement denied that the Mexican nation as a historical project should perpetuate the colonial tradition.
>
> Octavio Paz, 1985[1]

Santa Anna's overthrow in 1855 ended the alternation between liberal and conservative governments that dominated the first years of Mexico's independence. A liberal juggernaut that soon linked its fortunes to the rapidly increasing export of minerals and agricultural products overwhelmed the conservatives, who still looked back to the Spanish colonial model. Even though they had vanquished the conservatives, uniting their country provided liberals with a formidable challenge. During the middle of the century, the trip from Mexico City to the capital of Sonora required two weeks, and the trip to Yucatán, which included a voyage by sea, required a similar time. Moving an army required much more time.[2]

As their power grew, the liberals sought to dismantle the system based on the Church, the army, and regional strongmen (caudillos). In its place, they hoped to modernize U.S. style, establish civil liberties, build railroads, break down barriers to internal commerce, and put the immense land holdings of the Church and Indian villages on the market. Liberals saw themselves as nation-builders, feeling Mexicans' principal allegiance should not be to villages, communities, or corporate bodies, including the ecclesiastical estate, but to the nation. For the liberals, allowing males to vote without income restrictions was the sine qua non of democracy. The liberal ideal was a Jeffersonian agrarian democracy where large numbers of smallholders formed a stable citizenry. The liberal program, as well as that of the conservatives, lacked any measure to address extreme inequalities of wealth.[3]

While liberals did share core beliefs, they differed on application and emphasis. Sub-factions of the liberal movement included the *puros* (pure ones) and the *moderados* (moderates). The *puros* sought the participation of the rural poor in the political process, especially at the local level. In contrast, the *moderados* shared the conservatives' reluctance to grant significant power to the lower classes. Rather than being a true political party, liberals were associates brought together more by friendships, acquaintances, and affiliations than by an agreed program.[4]

When the 1824 constitution was promulgated, the burning issue was the degree of federalism Mexico was to enjoy. By 1857, the role of the Church had become the most controversial issue.[5] For example, liberal Melchor Ocampo, the former governor of Michoacán, wrote:

> What is the purpose of so many churches in a village which can barely support one? Why are there so many festivals? . . . Why force villagers to bear the cost of these festivals, sucking up what little money they may have amassed. Their wealth goes up in the smoke of candles, censers, and fireworks![6]

Ocampo felt that oppressive clerical fees served to entrench debt servitude. This belief stemmed from priests charging agricultural workers fees for sacraments. The employer would pay the priest for administering the sacraments to his employees and then add the amount paid to their debts.[7]

An anonymous priest from Michoacán responded to Ocampo:

> Michoacán, beware of where Mr. Ocampo is unwittingly leading us—to *freedom of religion and freedom of conscience.* These two notions, as ungodly as they are lamentable, currently serve as rallying points for European socialism. If God decides to punish us by spreading them among us, our total destruction will certainly follow.[8]

Most liberals were not as anti-clerical as Ocampo and would have preferred a harmonious co-existence with the Church. However, they did feel that the sacred should return to the intimacy of one's conscience and the interior of church buildings.[9]

After the liberal army overthrew Santa Anna, a group of radical liberals met in Cuernavaca and, on October 4, 1855, chose Juan Álvarez, the leader of the revolt against Santa Anna, to be Mexico's next president. This selection pre-empted the efforts of more moderate liberals to gain the presidency and set the stage for political and religious conflict with conservatives.[10]

In November 1855, Álvarez finally entered Mexico City. His ragged troops, with their swarthy complexions, alarmed the elite. Many were shoeless and poor, including the officers. From the elite point of view, this was the most dangerous force to enter Mexico City since Guerrero's arrival twenty-five years earlier.[11]

As a life-long resident of rural, southern Mexico, Álvarez, who had only three years of formal schooling, never felt at home in the capital. Even after he assumed the presidency, the Mexico City elite denigrated him and his indigenous backers. A moderate politician of the time, Manuel Siliceo, described Álvarez's followers as "wretched and indecent rabble . . . a horde of savages," words similar to those that would be used to describe Emiliano Zapata's forces when they entered Mexico City some sixty years later. To complicate Álvarez's position, moderate and *puro* liberals in his own cabinet constantly differed on whether they should compromise with conservatives or impose change.[12]

In December 1855, Álvarez, who had no ideological axe to grind, realized that fighting suited him better than governance and resigned. He turned the presidency over to Ignacio Comonfort, a moderate liberal who, as a Puebla *hacendado* and retired militia colonel, functioned more effectively in Mexico City than Álvarez.[13]

The month before he resigned, Álvarez implemented by decree the Juárez Law (Ley Juárez), named for his appointee as secretary of justice, ecclesiastical affairs, and public instruction, Benito Juárez. This law abolished the special courts established for clergy and the military. After the law went into effect, priests and the military charged with common crimes or facing civil suits were tried in ordinary courts.[14]

Strong opposition developed to ending the clergy's special legal status, known as the ecclesiastical *fuero*. The notion that priests could be jailed along with common criminals offended many rural people. When the bishop of Michoacán requested that the application of the law be suspended until the pope's opinion was known, Juárez responded that it was not becoming to the dignity of government to discuss with its subjects the compliance or disobedience of the law.[15]

The next major enactment, the Lerdo Law (Ley Lerdo), also affected the Church, which owned roughly a fifth of national property, including half the houses in Mexico City. This law, named for Miguel Lerdo de Tejada, the secretary of development who drafted it, prohibited both the Church and Indian villages from owning land. The law did not affect Church property used for strictly religious purposes, such as monasteries, convents, and church buildings. Liberals felt both indigenous communities and the Church stymied development and curbed individual initiative by removing land from commerce. The Lerdo Law provided that tenants could buy Church land they were renting. The government auctioned Church property the tenant could not or would not buy and turned the proceeds over to the Church, after collecting a 5 percent tax. Many of the Church's tenants refused to buy the land they were legally entitled to purchase because they felt such a purchase would be a betrayal of their religious faith.[16]

The Lerdo Law did undercut the power base of the Church. However, most sales failed to benefit the small farmer and rancher, whom the liberals proclaimed to be the basis of the ideal society. Wealthy landowners, including some of the liberal legislators who voted for the law, acquired most of the large tracts that were auctioned.[17] As journalist Anselmo de la Portilla noted in 1858:

> The number of landowners did not increase. Some speculators took advantage of the law to engage in unethical practices, some of the rich increased their fortunes, and none of the poor ceased being poor.[18]

Even though the law failed to convert community-based peasants into yeoman farmers, it did meet two other liberal policy goals— generating tax revenue and placing more land on the market.[19]

Within a generation, many Indian villages that had lost their land also lost their indigenous identity.[20] Liberals felt the abolition of communal land tenure would enable these Indians to improve their standard of living. It never occurred to the liberals that they should consult the indigenous population on whose behalf they claimed to act. However, they soon received a response on the matter. In September 1856, Interior Minister José María Lafragua sent a letter to governors that reported:

> In the states of Michoacán, Querétaro, Veracruz, and Puebla there have been uprisings in Indian towns. Their residents mistakenly feel the principles of liberty and progress, which the current administration proclaims, destroy the social order. They not only question property titles, but destroy them and divide the lands of others . . .
>
> The government, which feels its greatest duty is the defense of property, can in no way tolerate these disorders, which besides being serious crimes, cause the government severe problems . . .[21]

The government avoided still more serious conflict with villages owning communal land by delaying implementation of the law.[22]

Young liberal ideologues who assumed leadership of the revolution against Santa Anna implemented these reforms. The revolution had began as a non-ideological insurrection. However, the new generation that gained control after its triumph used the revolution to impose its political beliefs. These young liberals, many of whom were unemployed or underemployed lawyers, had strong ties to the middle class and provincial leaders. However, few had links to the majority of the population—the rural poor.[23]

In February 1856, 157 deputies, mostly young liberal lawyers, met to draft a new constitution. Despite their being considered anti-Catholic by many, all but one (a deist) were professing Catholics. Since conservatives had opposed the coalition toppling Santa Anna, they were largely unrepresented in the constitutional Congress. The new charter, drafted by some of the best liberal minds of the period, was promulgated on February 5, 1857. It created a state that claimed power based on popular will, not on divine right or the pope's blessing. Since only half of the political spectrum drafted it, not surprisingly, the document did not produce political consensus.[24]

Mexico's new constitution removed the prohibition against religions other than Roman Catholicism, which had been included in the 1824 constitution. Liberals felt that it would be politically unwise to openly declare freedom of religion in a nation comprised largely of traditional rural Catholics. As a result, they simply omitted a declaration that Catholicism was to be the religion of the land. The constitution also guaranteed freedom of press, of association, and of travel, and protected the right to bear arms.[25]

To prevent another Santa Anna-like dictator from assuming power, Convention members deliberately weakened the presidency by denying the executive veto power over legislation. They viewed a bicameral legislative branch as an opportunity for the executive to divide and weaken Congress, so they created a unicameral body, which they felt would maintain legislative supremacy over the executive.[26]

By 1857, as a result of Mexico's loss in the Mexican–American War and rebellions in Texas and Yucatán, many liberals had accepted the need for a strong central government. They also wanted to recoup for the federal government powers assumed by state governors after the collapse of the Santa Anna dictatorship. Finally, they felt a strong federal government would be necessary to strip the Church of its temporal power. To accomplish these goals, the 1857 constitution increased the power of the central government at the expense of states and municipalities. The liberals' use of state power to force the sale of Church- and Indian-owned land clearly violated their declared belief in local autonomy.[27]

The constitution's lofty ideals and its provision for the separation of powers never had much to do with reality. Despite its positive provisions, such as civil liberties and voting rights for males without regard to land ownership or wealth, it failed to deal with Mexico's single greatest problem—the grossly inequitable distribution of land. Liberals felt that a constitution alone would reform a society composed of people who for the most part could not read and whose life was governed by tradition, not by legislators seated comfortably in Mexico City.[28]

The delegates debated the land question. Liberal Ponciano Arriaga stated that society had granted the right of land ownership and could withdraw this right. He advocated government action to subdivide haciendas, declaring:

> A few individuals have immense uncultivated tracts of land, which could support many millions of men. This leaves the overwhelming majority of the citizens to languish in the worst squalor, without property, home, or job.[29]

The liberals, given their respect for private property, took no action, hoping market forces would eventually lead to the subdivision of the hacienda.

Conservatives felt liberal measures, such as abolishing the clerical *fuero* and the forced sale of Church property, were attacks on religion. They wanted a strong role in society not only for the Church but for the army. They felt the constitution should have imposed wealth restrictions on suffrage. Governance was best accomplished, they felt, by a strong executive, just as it had been in colonial times.[30]

At the time of its promulgation, many viewed the 1857 constitution as just one more document in a series of failed attempts to effectively govern Mexico. However, during the liberals' subsequent struggles against both conservatives and foreign intervention, it became a symbol of Mexican nationalism. Mexican historian Daniel Cosío Villegas looked back to the drafting of the 1857 Constitution:

> Mexican history has its dark, shameful pages which we wish could be erased. It has heroic pages that we would like to see highlighted. However, our history has a single page in which Mexico appears as a mature nation rising to the democratic standards and liberalism of modern western Europe. That page is the 1856 Constitutional Convention.[31]

THE CONSERVATIVES STRIKE BACK, 1857–1860

In December 1857, a group of moderate liberals proclaimed the Plan of Tacubaya, which called for another constitutional convention in three months. The Plan declared Roman Catholicism to be Mexico's sole religion and restored Church control over its property and reestablished the *fuero* for priests. Drafters of the Plan cemented an alliance with industrialists by reinstituting high tariffs. They then dissolved Congress and rescinded the constitution, leaving Comonfort as president. The moderates felt if they replaced the 1857 constitution with a more moderate charter designed to reconcile tradition and reform they could avoid a civil war.[32]

President Comonfort, hoping to prevent liberal reforms from escalating into civil war, accepted the provisions of the Plan of Tacubaya. This cost him the support of radical liberals. In January 1858, a second coup, led by General Félix Zuloaga, deposed Comonfort. The ousted president, by having accepted the Plan of Tacubaya, had already lost the support of radical liberals. Given the opposition of conservatives and weak support from his own liberal base, Comonfort resigned and went into exile. This marked the demise of the broad alliance of anti-Santa Anna forces that had supported Álvarez.[33]

Conservatives and the regular army supported the coup and recognized Zuloaga as president. The 1857 constitution, however, provided that Benito Juárez, who was serving as the chief justice of the Supreme Court, should assume the presidency. Juárez had been elected to this position during the Comonfort administration. Soon, both Zuloaga and Juárez were claiming the presidency.[34]

Juárez's birthplace, the isolated Oaxacan village of Guelatao, had neither a school nor a church. As was the case with the other twenty families in the village, the family of Mexico's future president spoke the Zapotec Indian language, not Spanish. As an impoverished orphan, Juárez worked as a sheepherder until age thirteen. Fortunately for Juárez, and for Mexico, he then decided to broaden his horizons and walked fifty miles barefoot to the Oaxaca City household where his sister worked. Her employer, Antonio Maza, a merchant who had immigrated from Italy, found him work with a bookbinder who became his benefactor. The bookbinder advised a seminary education, feeling that no other doors were open for an impoverished Indian, regardless of his education and talent.[35]

Juárez briefly studied for the priesthood, but soon disregarded his benefactor's counsel and enrolled to study law at Oaxaca's Institute of Arts and Sciences, a hotbed of liberal ideas. For the rest of his life, Juárez would proudly wear the liberal mantle. In 1843, he married Maza's seventeen-year-old daughter Margarita, despite his being twenty years her senior. Even though indigenous men rarely married women of European ancestry, the marriage received the blessing of the Maza family. This marriage not only created a long-lasting relationship but provided Juárez with access to Oaxaca's elite, which he would not otherwise have enjoyed.[36]

Beginning in 1832, with his membership in the Oaxaca City municipal council, Juárez rose steadily through public-sector positions. As Mexican historian Enrique Krauze observed, "In each of these public positions (and as a deputy to the federal Congress as of 1847) he demonstrated a sense of responsibility that was rare, especially in those frivolous times." During this time, Juárez defended Indian villagers from abuse by priests. By the middle of the century, Juárez had broken with the indigenous world into which he was born and had adopted the world view of the Hispanic city of Oaxaca. From then on, Juárez was viewed, and viewed himself, not as an Indian, but as a liberal Mexican.[37]

In 1847, Juárez received an appointment as interim governor of Oaxaca, an office to which he was later elected—the first time an Indian was elected as a state governor in independent Mexico. As governor, Juárez introduced a style of governance that stressed budgetary discipline, regular payment of public employees, and arbitration of disputes in a spirit of conciliation. During his administration, Juárez opened more schools than any of his predecessors. Many events, such as securing the clergy's collaboration in building schools and roads, showed his willingness to work with the Church. As would be the case with his presidency, he adopted a stoic, austere style and only reluctantly shared power, even though he did exercise power within a legal framework.[38]

During his last presidency, Santa Anna sent Juárez into exile in New Orleans. While there, Juárez, who survived by rolling cigarettes, fell under the tutelage of two fellow exiles—liberal ideologues Melchor Ocampo and Ponciano Arriaga. This cemented his belief in the separation of Church and state. As with most liberals, Juárez remained a Catholic who attended Mass, married in the Church, and baptized his daughters.[39]

Figure 12.1
Benito Juárez

Source: Reproduced courtesy of the Benson Latin American Collection, the University of Texas at Austin

D. BENITO JUAREZ.
Disuelta por D. Ignacio Comonfort la Representacion Nacional el 17 de Dbre. de 1857, D.
to Juarez, Presidente de la Suprema Corte de Justicia, estableció en Guanajuato la
del Poder Ejecutivo Constitucional en 19 de Enero de 1858. Despues estuvo en
y Veracruz y en este puerto dió las leyes de nacionalizacion de bienes
monio civil y tolerancia de cultos. En 1861 fué nombrado Presidente constitucional
la Intervencion francesa y gobernó hasta su muerte acaecida en 18 de Julio
1872.
Benito Juarez

Liberal exiles in New Orleans arranged for Juárez to return to Mexico via Havana, Panama, and Acapulco as a representative to Álvarez, thus positioning themselves for a return to power upon Álvarez's triumph. Juárez's journey to Acapulco lasted six weeks.

By the time Juárez arrived in Acapulco, liberal forces had driven Santa Anna from office. After Álvarez met Juárez, he appointed the Oaxacan as his minister of justice, ecclesiastical affairs, and public instruction (one of only six cabinet positions). Juárez was serving in this position when the Juárez Law was promulgated. His subsequent election as chief justice of the Supreme Court placed him first in the line of presidential succession. The 1857 constitution had scrapped the position of vice-president—vice-presidents were considered too prone to lead revolts against the presidents they served under.[40]

In January 1858, after the issuance of the Plan of Tacubaya, Juárez realized that he had little support in Mexico City and abandoned the capital. He retreated north to Guanajuato, where a resident commented: "An Indian by the name of Juárez, who calls himself the President of the Republic, has arrived in this city." From there, Juárez continued on to the Pacific Coast and sailed to Panama. He crossed the isthmus and finally arrived in Veracruz, where he established a liberal government.[41]

The strongest support for the conservatives came from Mexico City, Querétaro, and traditionally conservative Puebla. In addition, many rural people supported the conservatives because they resented urban, liberal lawyers imposing their views on others through legislation. Often urban renters of Church property backed conservatives, since they assumed that if the Church lost its holdings, their rents would increase. Conservatives drew support from the Church, military officers, and Indian villages wishing to retain communal land holdings. Residents of central Mexico, especially *hacendados*, hoped conservatives would perpetuate that region's dominance of the periphery. The traditional nature of Mexican society also favored the conservatives. In 1861, there were only 443 engineers and architects in Mexico, while there were 9,344 priests and 42,578 in the military.[42]

The Veracruz customs house, the major source of government revenue, financed the liberal cause. Liberals used customs duties to purchase foreign arms, which were shipped to Veracruz.

At the leadership level, urban professionals such as lawyers, doctors, teachers, and journalists, dominated liberalism. State governors tended to favor the liberals, whom they felt would permit more power to be retained at the state level. Businessmen who stood to benefit from free trade also backed the liberals. Miners, merchants, teachers, cattlemen, and professionals embraced the liberal cause as a way to gain a political voice, especially in north-central Mexico. Entrepreneurs, merchants, low-level government employees, radical intellectuals, and clerks felt liberals would promote their advancement.[43]

In July 1859, Juárez nationalized all remaining Church lands without compensating the Church. He blamed the civil war on the Church and accused it of financing the conservative war effort with income from its land holdings. The liberal government in Veracruz sought to separate church and state by secularizing cemeteries, declaring marriage a civil contract, and assuming responsibility for birth registrations. Liberals also decreed the nationalization of the Church's investment capital, which exceeded the value of its real estate. These measures, the Juárez Law, the Lerdo Law, and the changes embodied in the 1857 constitution are known as the Reforma, for which Mexico City's Paseo de la Reforma is named.[44]

The liberal government hurriedly sold the nationalized Church property to finance the war. Since the sales were so hasty and the titles so shaky, in many cases the government received only a quarter or a third of the value of the land. Such sales had the advantage of winning allies for the liberals since, if the conservatives were to win the war, these sales would be declared invalid, and the Church would recover the properties.[45]

The military overwhelmingly supported the conservatives. As a result, during 1858 conservative generals Miguel Miramón, Tomás Mejía, and Leonardo Márquez led their forces to a string of victories over the militarily inexperienced liberals. Since they lacked access to the Veracruz customs receipts, the conservatives borrowed abroad. One such loan from the Swiss banking house of Jecker netted 1 million pesos. For this sum, the conservatives committed Mexico to redeem bonds totaling 15 million pesos.[46]

Liberals recruited those favoring the abolition of compulsory military service, freedom of commerce, army reorganization, and, in areas where the Catholic clergy had lost its legitimacy, religious liberty. Eventually, liberal tenacity, the support of state militias, and the arms bought with Veracruz customs revenues overwhelmed the conservatives. Liberal commander Santos Degollado suffered repeated defeats. However, after each defeat, he would rally his forces, suffer another defeat, and then rally his forces once again. Even though both sides resorted to conscription, there were never more than 25,000 men under arms. This, in a nation of 8 million, did not represent total war. As historian Enrique Krauze noted, "The War of Reform was not a popular war in either sense of the word."[47]

Liberal historian Justo Sierra commented on Degollado, who felt that limitations should be placed on the power of the Church: "He tried to limit the power of the Church because it had gone astray and was no longer faithful to the teachings of Christ. He was the Catholic, the canon lawyer, the theologian. The bishops were the impious."[48]

Liberal forces reoccupied Mexico City on Christmas Day of 1860, thus ending the War of the Reform, as the 1857–1860 civil war is known. Once again, war had devastated the country. The U.S. consul at Veracruz reported, "Haciendas are abandoned, *ranchos* deserted, and even whole villages pillaged and sacked, leaving nothing but desolation wherever the armies of the contending parties have made their tracks."[49]

THE SECOND EMPIRE, 1861–1866

The victory over the conservatives allowed Mexico to hold elections. Three candidates presented themselves—Acting President Juárez, Miguel Lerdo de Tejada, author of the Lerdo Law, and General Jesús González Ortega, a war hero. Due to his reputation achieved during the War of Reform, as well as rising anti-military sentiment, Juárez defeated González Ortega. Lerdo de Tejada died of natural causes just before the election.[50]

Even after the defeat of the conservative army, turmoil continued. There were several peasant uprisings in central Mexico. In June 1861, U.S. Ambassador Thomas Corwin sent a dispatch from Mexico City describing the conservative irregulars who continued to attack Juárez's forces:

> Since my last dispatches the country has been in a state of great disorder. Bands of armed men, in numbers varying from fifty to four thousand, have been ravaging the country in this and two or three adjoining States, pushing their operations to the very suburbs of this city.[51]

Given the unrest and destruction, Mexico could not make payments on its public debt. In July 1861, the Mexican Congress recognized this and, as an emergency measure to permit internal reconstruction, it unilaterally suspended payments on its foreign and domestic debts for two years, but it did not repudiate the debts. This act, coming as it did during the U.S. Civil War (which prevented the United States from enforcing its Monroe Doctrine and keeping Europeans out of Latin America), gave Europe the pretext for massive intervention in Mexico.[52]

Spain, England, and France formed an alliance to collect the debt, including the amount due on the Jecker bonds approved by conservatives battling Juárez's forces in the War of Reform. Representatives of the three creditor nations met in England and signed the Tripartite Convention of London. Its signatories declared that they would occupy Mexico's customs houses so they could collect funds to retire the debt owed them. However, they pledged not to "interfere in Mexico's internal affairs in such a manner as would impair that nation's right to freely elect and constitute its own government."[53]

The French, who were already expanding their empire into Algeria and Indo-China, had the most far-reaching plans. French Emperor Napoleon III planned to impose a monarchy that would provide France with markets and raw materials and prevent the spread of U.S. influence into Latin America.[54]

Mexican conservatives welcomed France's monarchical pretensions. Having lost in the War of Reform, they were more than willing to allow foreigners to restore them to power. They felt the early 1860s were an ideal time to install a monarchy since the United States, preoccupied with its own civil war, could not oppose an empire to its south. Also, as long as the United States remained at war, it would not compete with Mexico for European investment capital. Conservatives felt the circumstances were finally at hand to fulfill Lucas Alamán's dream of a monarchy that would produce stability—the key to attracting foreign capital for development.[55]

In December 1861 and January 1862, Spain landed 6,000 troops and Britain sent 800 marines. As occurred with the U.S. invasion fifteen years earlier, Mexicans failed to oppose the landing. Unlike their American predecessors, though, the European invaders remained on the coast too long and fell victim to yellow fever.[56]

The British and Spanish soon realized that the French, the Tripartite Convention of London notwithstanding, were planning a much greater undertaking than debt collection. After the Mexican government pledged to resume debt payments as soon as possible, the British and Spanish departed.[57]

The French commander, General Charles Latrille, Count of Lorencez, began an advance on Mexico City. On April 25, 1862, he wrote his minister of war, "We are so superior to the Mexicans in race, organization, morality, and devoted sentiments that I beg your excellency to inform the Emperor that as head of 6,000 soldiers I am already master of Mexico."[58]

Ten days after this was written, the French force fought its first major battle at Puebla, where its advance was blocked by two forts, Loreto and Guadalupe, perched on hilltops connected by a 3,500 foot-long ridge. The 4,500-man French force had to traverse a two-mile wide plain. Then they faced withering Mexican cannon fire as they scrambled up the hills. Eventually combat extended along the ridge connecting the two forts. The French approaching the ridge were exposed to crossfire from both forts. After 475 of the attackers were killed, wounded, or taken prisoner, the French force withdrew. Mexican casualties totaled 227.[59]

The battle fought on May 5, 1862, brought together diverse elements of Mexico's population. Not only did units come from numerous states but indigenous units from north Puebla towns fought alongside mestizos, distinguishing themselves in bitter hand-to-hand combat. The victory at Puebla remains the outstanding military victory in Mexican history. Each year Mexicans, and many Americans, celebrate the Cinco de Mayo (Fifth of May), and Ignacio Zaragoza, who commanded the defending forces, is widely honored.[60]

This defeat affected the outcome of the intervention since the French had to await reinforcements before they could advance. This delayed the establishment of a puppet government by a year, which left relatively little time for that government to consolidate itself before the end of the U.S. Civil War. After its own civil war ended, the United States could credibly threaten France for violating the Monroe Doctrine.[61]

After their defeat at Puebla, the French retreated and awaited the arrival of additional troops. By January 1863, the interventionist force totaled 30,976. Then the French advanced and besieged Puebla for seventy-four days. Its residents were reduced to eating house pets and small animals that they trapped. After a lack of food and ammunition forced Puebla to surrender to the French, starving children stole corn from the fodder bags of French cavalry mounts.[62]

As the French approached Mexico City, Juárez abandoned the practically defenseless capital and moved his government north to San Luis Potosí. For the next three years, he would govern by decree, using the extraordinary powers Congress had granted him to prosecute the war.[63]

After arriving in Mexico City, the French created an interim government. Its officials invited all Mexicans to unite around it and urged them to cease considering themselves liberals or conservatives. Conservatives forming the interim government felt a foreign Catholic monarch would bring Mexico's polarized society together. As a result, they invited the Austrian archduke, Ferdinand Maximilian, to become emperor of Mexico.[64]

The person invited to assume the throne was the brother of Austrian Emperor Franz Joseph and the son-in-law of King Leopold of Belgium. His invitation resulted from pressure exerted on Napoleon's wife Eugénie by conservative Mexican exiles in Europe who had engaged in a prolonged lobbying effort to have a European power install a monarchy in Mexico. Eugénie influenced her husband, who insured that Maximilian received the invitation.[65]

Maximilian did insist that a plebiscite be held in Mexico to determine whether he should assume the throne. The French obliged, allowing individuals favoring the monarchy to act as local representatives who could "vote" for the rest of the population. Sometimes the French claimed that voting, which only occurred in a state capital, represented the entire state's population. Ultimately the French claimed that all important Mexican cities and towns had accepted the empire, even though the French had yet to extend its control to many areas.[66]

The future emperor of Mexico accepted the plebiscite at face value. However, a somewhat more skeptical Sir Charles Wyke, the former British chargé d'affaires in Mexico City, remarked that Maximilian had been "elected" to the throne by a "majority vote from places inhabited by two Indians and a monkey."[67]

In April 1864, Maximilian signed a secret treaty with the French, making Mexico a virtual French colony. He agreed to pay not only the inflated debt claims of the French but also the cost of French troops occupying Mexico. Napoleon agreed to keep French troops in Mexico until 1870.[68]

Before leaving Europe, Maximilian received the personal blessings of Pope Pius IX. The pope felt Maximilian would restore the Church to its former position in Mexico. Pius commented, "Although the rights of nations are great and must be respected, those of religion are much greater and holier."[69]

Even before arriving in Mexico, Maximilian began courting liberals by granting pardons to republican prisoners and reducing their prison sentences. To broaden his support, he shifted tax burdens to the rich and ended debt servitude. He also showed his moderate European liberalism by refusing to return to the Church the property it had formerly owned and by allowing freedom of worship. He abolished corporal punishment, limited hours of work, and guaranteed a minimum wage to agricultural workers. He mandated that those employing more than twenty families should provide free primary education and that Indian schools should be bilingual. He anticipated twentieth-century land reform efforts by ordering that unused government land should be provided to the landless. Maximilian's failure to embrace the conservative agenda reduced his conservative backing and won him few liberal supporters. His enactments might have been sound policy. However, quite often imperial hegemony did not extend beyond the edge of Mexico City, leaving his decrees unenforced.[70]

Maximilian attempted to hold himself above the liberal-conservative fray and invited all Mexicans to join his government. Moderate liberals did accept appointments to serve as ministers of foreign relations, interior, and justice. Again, this cost him conservative support and did little to attract other liberals.[71]

In 1863, French General François Bazaine, who had learned counter-guerrilla tactics while imposing French colonial rule in Algeria, assumed command of imperial forces in Mexico. The next year, he wrote Napoleon to say that Maximilian was "putting on airs; that he fails to remember that he is still dependent—dependent on France, dependent on General Bazaine, and dependent on General Bazaine's army."[72]

After occupying Mexico City, the French moved north, taking Saltillo and Matamoros. Juárez retreated, eventually taking refuge in Paso del Norte (today, in his honor, Ciudad Juárez). By mid-1864, French-installed governments controlled eighteen of the twenty-four Mexican states. By the following year, all state capitals flew the imperial flag. Imperial forces totaled 60,000 troops, of whom 30,000 were French, 24,000 Mexican, and the rest Austrian and Belgian. These forces confined Juárez's regular forces to a small area bordering on west Texas and New Mexico. In December 1865, the U.S. consul in Paso del Norte reported that Juárez's forces numbered only 300. In addition, 200 to 300 men in Guerrero and Oaxaca, led by the wily guerrilla fighter Porfirio Díaz, supported Juárez. Unlike Santa Anna in the Mexican–American War, Juárez realized that guerrilla warfare was the only way to confront a powerful foreign army.[73]

The French occupation made elections impossible when Juárez's presidential term expired in 1865. Juárez used the extraordinary powers granted him by Congress in 1861 to simply extend his term. Some liberals, especially those seeking power themselves, criticized this as a violation of liberal principles. Undaunted, Juárez continued to rule by decree.[74]

Even though Juárez's regular forces verged on annihilation, the French could not extend their control into the countryside. As soon as their troops withdrew, popular uprisings occurred. The French-organized counter-guerrilla forces were effective, but lacked sufficient numbers to dominate an area as large as Mexico.[75]

The imperial government's fragmentation prevented it from implementing policies that might have won it adherents. The French dominated the military and occupied the customs houses. Maximilian's cabinet contained both conservatives and liberals and had to share power not only with Maximilian's European-dominated private cabinet but with the French ambassador and the head of the French financial mission.[76]

Maximilian established a royal court complete with what he considered fitting pomp and ceremony. The manual describing court etiquette, the *Relgamento para el servicio y ceremonial de la corte (Regulations for Court Service and Ceremony)*, filled almost four hundred pages. His elaborate lifestyle made previous Mexican presidents seem positively frugal. Guadalupe Victoria had a pair of carriages, while Maximilian had thirty-three. During his last presidency, Mexicans had widely criticized Santa Anna for his spending some 8,000 to 10,000 pesos a month to maintain himself in regal style. Maximilian and his wife Carlota received an annual allowance of 1.7 million pesos for living expenses and maintaining the court, palace, and grounds.[77]

Feeling the republican forces were almost defeated, on October 3, 1865, Maximilian signed the infamous black flag decree, published in Spanish and Nahuatl and posted throughout the empire. It decreed that any person apprehended bearing arms against the empire would be executed within twenty-four hours. Despite its widespread application to prisoners of war, this measure drove more Mexicans into the arms of the republic.[78]

In 1866, Napoleon decided to withdraw French troops from Mexico. His decision resulted from: 1) the high cost of the war in Mexico; 2) its unpopularity in France; 3) Maximilian's failure to develop an independent base; 4) the fear that the United States would support Juárez after its own civil war ended; and 5) Napoleon's need for troops in Europe to respond to the threat posed by an increasingly militarized Prussia.[79]

Upon learning that the French had decided to withdraw their troops, Carlota returned to Europe to persuade Napoleon and the pope to continue supporting her husband's empire. Before leaving, she appealed to Maximilian to stay in Mexico and uphold Habsburg honor. The empress not only failed to rally support in Europe but suffered a mental breakdown there from which she never recovered.

At the time, Maximilian felt he could end the raging civil war by convening a national Congress that would invite both liberals and conservatives to sit down and amicably resolve their disputes. However, any chance of Juárez's compromising with his foe had vanished, since the French departure opened the way for a liberal victory without compromise.[80]

Bazaine sailed from Veracruz with the last French forces in March 1867—three years earlier than the departure date agreed to by Napoleon. After the French departure, Maximilian's empire began to disintegrate with increasing rapidity. Juárez's forces, taking heart at the French withdrawal, moved south, aided by U.S. arms and veterans who appeared in Mexico after the end of the U.S. Civil War. In January 1867, liberal forces took Guadalajara, San Luis Potosí, and Guanajuato. They occupied Cuernavaca, Morelia, and Zacatecas the following month.[81]

The imperial forces made their final stand at Querétaro. In February, General Mariano Escobedo besieged the city with 30,000 liberal troops. Maximilian had already come north from Mexico City to personally lead his 9,000-man force. The siege lasted until May, when liberals captured the city and took Maximilian prisoner. Shortly afterward, Porfirio Díaz came from the east and captured Mexico City for the liberals.

Juárez ordered that Maximilian be tried by court martial. The former emperor faced the same criminal charges of rebellion that he had decreed Juárez's supporters captured in battle should face. The court found him guilty and sentenced him to be executed by firing squad, along with two of his generals, Tomás Mejía and Miguel Miramón. Juárez resisted intense pressure from around the world to issue a pardon, feeling that a live Maximilian would only serve to promote further uprisings and prolong internal strife. Juárez knew that conservatives pardoned after the War of Reform had supported the empire. Liberal journalist Juan José Baz wrote, "This example will ensure in Europe we are respected and will remove any desire on the part of any other adventurer to come here."[82]

In July 1867, after an absence of four years, Juárez returned to Mexico City. His wife Margarita Maza de Juárez, who had spent the war years in the United States, soon rejoined him. During these years she had not only rallied support for the liberal cause in Washington but had done her best to keep her family together. Despite her efforts, two of her children died while in exile, one of dysentery and one of cholera.[83]

Compared to Mexican resistance in the Mexican–American War, resistance to the empire was, as historian Alan Knight noted, "more prolonged, dogged, and above all, successful." Liberal strongmen provided Juárez with crucial support at the regional level, just as they had in defeating the conservatives during the War of the Reform. Rural people generally supported the liberal cause, feeling liberalism offered greater local autonomy. Much of Juárez's appeal was based not on his program but on his once having been a poor Indian who rose thorough the ranks to govern the country.[84]

Another reason for the fall of the empire was the less than total support from France. In 1808, Napoleon I had sent more than 200,000 French troops to support his brother Joseph in Spain. Since these troops failed to keep Joseph on the throne, it is not surprising that 27,000 French troops failed to keep Maximilian on the throne in Mexico—a nation twice as large as Spain. The effectiveness of these troops was greatly reduced because guerrilla forces opposing them refused to fight the set-piece battles the European-trained military expected. Rather, they simply outlasted the French in a prolonged war of attrition.[85]

The forging of a Mexican national identity, a spirit sorely lacking in 1847, forms a lasting legacy of the struggle against the French. After the collapse of the empire, Creoles no longer defined Mexican nationality. This role shifted to Juárez's generation of mestizo politicians, journalists, writers, poets, legislators, and historians. They created republican institutions and a wide range of newspapers, magazines, and scientific and literary academies. They felt that history and education should form national character and wrote novels with mestizo characters and scenes.[86]

The enhanced national identity resulting from the war came at a high cost. Approximately 300,000 died as a result of the French intervention. In addition, Mexico's already abused and neglected infrastructure suffered extensive damage, and marketing arrangements were once again disrupted.[87]

THE RESTORED REPUBLIC

> Juárez defined Mexico, in opposition to Catholic and Conservative thought, as a secular and federal republic with a liberal political system in which civil power was to be supreme.
>
> Brian Hamnett, 1997[88]

With Maximilian's defeat, many felt that internal stability was finally at hand. Liberalism had become a unifying myth almost synonymous with patriotism, since it had been the liberals' tenacity that had defeated the French. However, once liberals no longer faced a common enemy, forging a consensus became a major challenge. The following constituencies vied for influence in the restored republic: 1) landowners who wanted to acquire Church and Indian lands; 2) the middle class; 3) workers, including textile workers, blacksmiths, and artisans; and 4) peasants who had supported the 1855 revolt against Santa Anna. Conflicts erupted between personalities and generations, as those who took up arms to defeat the empire vied with the older generation that had passed the Reform laws while in Veracruz.[89]

The 1867 presidential elections involved indirect voting, as was provided in the 1857 constitution. Juárez, who was at the peak of his popularity, obtained 72 percent of the 10,371 electoral votes cast. His young rival, General Porfirio Díaz, who only obtained 26 percent of the votes, found he could not convert military prowess into electoral victory.[90]

The hoped for post-war calm never became a reality. Rather, the years after the liberal victory were ones of rebellion, with men being pressed into military service, civil discord, and the opposition of almost all the press to Juárez. National guard officers, who resented demobilization, led many uprisings. Disgruntled peasants and demobilized soldiers, lacking land, often turned to banditry. An estimated 1,000 bandits plagued the Guadalajara area alone. Highwaymen, kidnappers, and bandits posed a constant threat to peace. Congress granted Juárez extraordinary powers, allowing him once again to govern by decree, so that he could suppress bandits and guerrilla movements.[91]

Differences within the liberal camp—whose significance rivaled the differences between liberals and conservatives—increased unrest. Liberals disagreed on what powers should be retained at the state level, on whether elections should be direct or indirect, on whether Congress should be unicameral or bicameral, and on the proper role of the Church. After 1867, the general exclusion from government of those ordinary Mexicans, including Indians, who had taken up arms to defeat European intervention, further destabilized the Juárez government.[92]

No one attempted to curb the power of the *hacendado*, who continued to administer corporal punishment, to jail at his whim, and to collect debts from descendants of debtors. Such abuses were frequently noted, but rarely challenged. In 1868, even though liberals exercised total political dominance, Congress rejected a proposal to prevent landowners from: 1) establishing private jails; 2) inflicting corporal punishment; and 3) collecting from children debts inherited from their parents.

The failure, once gain, to address the land issue, increased unrest. At the time, Juárez could have distributed unused national lands or lands that had been owned by the Church, villages, and conservatives such as the Sánchez Navarros. However authorities either returned estates to conservatives or sold them to politically powerful liberal landowners. In addition, the government retained ownership of extensive tracts in the hope that they could be used to attract European immigrants. The inability of the landless peasant and the demobilized war veteran to obtain land contrasted sharply with the U.S. experience after the Civil War. The Homestead Act there provided free public lands to settlers.[93]

Juárez's failure to change the tax structure added to unrest. The *alcabala* and a tax known as the personal contribution placed the tax burden on the poor. The personal contribution required all tax payers, *hacendados* and hacienda laborers alike to pay a sum equivalent to six to twelve days' wages for an agricultural laborer.[94]

Juárez's collection of these taxes reflected his desperate financial plight. The war-ravaged economy yielded little tax revenue, and the army devoured much of the government budget. Although \$45 million worth of Church property had been nationalized, less than \$2 million had reached the treasury, and that was soon spent. At the time, the government owed more than \$80 million. Increased state control over tax revenues generated outside Mexico City exacerbated the central government's financial problems. Impoverished state governments frequently failed to make the legally mandated transfer of tax receipts to the federal government.[95]

Between 1867 and 1877, the federal government repeatedly intervened to suppress insurrections mounted by villages and districts to assert local sovereignty. Such conflicts only subsided after Porfirio Díaz assumed the presidency and successfully centralized power.[96]

In 1871, against the advice of many friends, Juárez sought reelection. The propriety of his reelection became a major issue. Even though the 1857 constitution did not prohibit reelection, many felt it ran counter to the liberal ethos. There was little precedent on the issue since during the first half century of Mexico's independence, so few had even finished one term, let alone aspired to a second one. Only in 1878 did a constitutional amendment prohibit immediate presidential reelection.[97]

Juárez faced challenges by two of his former supporters, Porfirio Díaz and Sebastián Lerdo de Tejada, whose brother wrote the Lerdo Law. Both of his opponents attacked Juárez's reelection, after thirteen years in office, as a violation of liberal principles. Díaz claimed that Juárez's mission had been fulfilled after Maximilian's defeat and that he was attempting to personalize the presidency. Juárez responded that Díaz was a military adventurer in the tradition of Santa Anna.[98]

The country was at peace, and it was difficult to justify Juárez's staying in office once Mexico's independence and integrity were assured. Also, the country had little to show for the liberal triumph, as most of the population still lived in grinding poverty. Historians Michael C. Meyer and William L. Sherman commented on Juárez's 1871 candidacy: "he had allowed his very human desire for power and accomplishment to impugn his earlier ideals."[99]

In the 1871 election, whose fairness was questioned, Juárez received 5,837 electoral votes, Díaz 3,555, and Lerdo de Tejada 2,874. The law stipulated that if no candidate received a majority of the votes, Congress would select the next president. Juárez retained office when Congress selected him for the 1871–1875 term.[100]

In 1872, Juárez died of a heart attack in the National Palace. During his fourteen and a half years as president, Mexico underwent greater change than under any previous president.

Juárez strengthened Mexicans' feelings of nationhood and unity. Rather than seeking vengeance on Maximilian's vanquished supporters, he implemented a broad amnesty that embraced all but those who had held the highest positions in the empire.[101] He commented on his policy after the defeat of the empire:

> Neither in the past nor at the moment of victory has the government desired vengeance against those with whom it fought. Its duty is now, and has been, to temper justice with mercy . . . Let the people and the government respect everyone's rights. Among individuals, as among nations, peace is respecting the rights of others.[102]

During his presidency, Juárez greatly expanded the power of the federal government as he confronted not only foreign invasion and civil war, but the task of unifying his fragmented nation. The reality of many interest groups and small markets demanded a strong government to integrate the country. To obtain badly needed revenues, Juárez instituted higher tariffs.[103]

The Juárez presidency began a trend towards a strong executive with little regard for the written constitutional model. Liberals concluded that no government could bring order without strong central authority and a powerful executive. By the end of the Juárez administration, power had shifted from the Church, local caudillos, and the military establishment to a modern nation state. Power also shifted from states to the federal government. Under Juárez, the presidency became the lynch-pin of the political system, perhaps his most lasting legacy.[104]

Since his death, Juárez has been regarded in much the same way as Lincoln in the United States. His austere life-style stood in sharp contrast to Santa Anna's and Maximilian's profligacy. Juárez never presented a concrete program for dealing with social inequality. Rather he merely declared all men to be equal before the law. This reflected the emphasis classical liberalism placed on the role of the individual in society, while failing to present a positive theory of government.[105]

During Juárez's presidency, Mexicans enjoyed greater freedom of expression than at any previous time in their history, as hundreds of newspapers flourished. As historian Enrique Krauze noted: "The constitution of 1857—for a brief shining moment—was put into practice. Never before had Mexico been closer to democracy than it was during this period of the Restored Republic."[106]

In an 1866 interview in the *New York Herald*, Juárez explained that the objective of liberal policies was to take government out of the hands of the class dominated by the ecclesiastical hierarchy and army officers. His success in replacing these groups and opening the door wide for mestizos to occupy high positions was one of his great accomplishments. Between 1860 and 1870, democracy was also broadened, as direct voting to elect governors was instituted in thirteen of Mexico's twenty-seven states.[107]

Juárez viewed the elementary school as a means of transferring Mexicans' primary loyalty to the republic from corporate and ethnic groups and kin and patron-client networks. In 1867, the First Law of Public Instruction established free, compulsory primary education for "the poor" and specifically excluded religious instruction from the curriculum. Despite Juárez's vision of education as a force of change, the reality of recurrent insurrection and financial limitations prevented widespread provision of secular schooling. During his presidency, school attendance increased from 10 percent to 15 percent of school-age children.[108]

Higher education was even more a preserve of the elite. In 1878, when Mexico's population totaled 9.3 million, slightly more than 3,000 students attended secondary schools and fewer than 5,000 were enrolled in professional schools.[109]

Democracy had yet to take root everywhere, especially in areas far removed from Mexico City. The leader of an 1869 rebellion in Chiapas told the officer commanding troops sent to suppress the rebellion:

> The constitution and the laws which you cite with such emphasis state that all of us citizens have the right to elect the authorities which govern us. However, neither I nor my comrades-in-arms have had the slightest role in selecting the authorities which form the farcical government which you serve. As a result, we have no obligation to obey them nor to continue supporting them with the fruits of our labor which they so arbitrarily deprive us of.[110]

The next in line of presidential succession upon Juárez's death was the chief justice of the Supreme Court, Sebastián Lerdo de Tejada. Lerdo de Tejada took office in July 1872 and called elections for October. He won these elections with 92 percent of the vote.

Lerdo's 1872–1876 term was more peaceful than Juárez's last term. Economic development and the completion in 1873 of the Veracruz–Mexico City railroad added to Lerdo's prestige. He continued the trend towards a strong presidency. The 1874 division of legislative power between a Chamber of Deputies and a Senate added to presidential power, as did granting the president, with Senate approval, the power to remove state governors and appoint provisional governors in their place.[111]

PORFIRIO DÍAZ ASCENDANT, 1876–1884

Porfirio Díaz became president of Mexico in 1876. Mexico's new president was born in 1830, the son of a modest mestizo innkeeper and an Indian mother. The turmoil in the decades after his birth permitted social mobility. He followed the career path of his fellow Oaxacan Benito Juárez and began studying for the priesthood. Also like Juárez, he later studied law at the Institute of Arts and Sciences in Oaxaca City.[112]

Díaz practiced law briefly, but was forced into hiding in 1854 for opposing Santa Anna. He joined a group of Indians combating the dictator and proved to be a brilliant guerrilla fighter. During the War of Reform, Díaz fought on the liberal side. In 1862, his reputation reached almost mythical proportions when as a young general he led a cavalry charge during the Battle of Puebla. This maneuver forced an already retreating French army to break in disarray. Díaz added to his reputation by twice escaping from the French after being captured. By the time the thirty-six-year old Díaz took Mexico City for Juárez in 1867, he had fought thirty-seven battles.[113]

When President Lerdo de Tejada announced his intention to stand for reelection in 1876, Díaz responded with his Plan of Tuxtepec, which emphasized "No reelection." Díaz's manifesto claimed that Lerdo de Tejada had trampled on the constitutional rights of Mexican citizens. He claimed that by preventing Lerdo de Tejada from serving another term, he would spare Mexico another experience with prolonged one-man rule.[114]

Díaz obtained the support of the army, which disliked Lerdo de Tejada's anti-military policies. Caciques who joined his effort early on saw their control over their respective states confirmed. A wide range of Díaz's personal acquaintances rallied to his cause since they felt he would further their own careers. Others backed Díaz due to Lerdo de Tejada's persecution of the Church. At the time, Díaz was considered to be a radical opposed to the elite.[115]

For symbolic reasons Díaz named his *plan* for the small Oaxaca town of Tuxtepec, even though his revolt began early in 1876 in Brownsville, Texas. Some Texas landowners and U.S. railroad tycoons, bankers, and holders of Mexican bonds, who felt Díaz would pave the way for their future operations in Mexico, openly supported him with arms and cash. In the United States, Díaz obtained cash contributions of at least $500,000, 300 rifles, 350 carbines, 250,000 rounds of ammunition, horses, mules, uniforms, cattle, and forage to start his revolt. Additional support came later. Americans made up as many as half of the armed force that Díaz led into Mexico. With this support, for six months Díaz sustained his revolt along the Rio Grande between Nuevo Laredo and Matamoros.[116]

Díaz's ability to wage prolonged guerrilla warfare undermined the already bankrupt Lerdo de Tejada government, which was unable to obtain loans to purchase arms. Given the multiple centers of rebellion, Lerdo de Tejada's government could not suppress the revolt. As members of the provincial elite saw that he could not suppress the revolt, they began to jump on Díaz's bandwagon.[117]

Ignacio Mariscal, Mexico's ambassador in Washington, strongly protested the use of U.S. soil to stage a revolt against a government with which the United States enjoyed cordial relations. The U.S. government not only allowed Díaz to continue receiving supplies from north of the Rio Grande but permitted him to retreat back to Texas after he met unexpected resistance in Mexico. Díaz then traveled to New Orleans and sailed to Oaxaca to continue his revolt.[118]

In November 1876, Lerdo de Tejada resigned, and Díaz assumed power as a hero of the popular resistance to the French intervention. The general, who enjoyed the support of various regionally based movements that had grown up in the power vacuum left by Maximilian, then called for elections to legitimize his rule. Díaz, who ran unopposed, was elected to serve the 1877–1880 term. As president, he faced the challenge of establishing peace and stability in a nation plagued by poverty, illiteracy, social inequality, political turmoil, financial penury, and a woefully inadequate infrastructure—the same problems Juárez and Lerdo de Tejada had faced. In theory, the federal government was supreme, though in practice many state governors and local political bosses with their own militias governed independently and in defiance of the federal government.[119]

At the end of his term, Díaz abided by his "no reelection" pledge. He did, however, promote a stand-in to succeed him in 1880. He showed his political savvy by choosing not a distinguished liberal general who might build his own independent power base but General Manuel González, one of his least able protégés. Since González had fought as a conservative during the War of Reform, his position depended entirely on Díaz's favor.[120]

Díaz's selection of González inaugurated the *dedazo*, the practice of the incumbent president handpicking his successor and ensuring his election. This practice would dominate presidential politics in the last half of the twentieth century.

During González's term, the first rail line to the United States was completed, linking El Paso and Mexico City. Various trends emerged during his administration that would characterize Mexico for the rest of the century. The executive became increasingly important, eclipsing Congress. The press and political opponents came under increasing attack, and the economic elite's influence over the government increased. Finally, foreign investment began to enter Mexico at an ever-increasing rate.[121]

In 1881, after his first wife died in childbirth, Díaz married seventeen-year old Carmen Romero, who was thirty-four years his junior. She was the daughter of Manuel Romero Rubio, Lerdo de Tejada's minister of foreign relations. She devoted herself to imparting social graces to Díaz and managed to covert him from a rough country soldier into a polished gentleman who could mix freely with the cream of Mexican society. This proved to be an invaluable skill, especially after Díaz returned to the presidency and increasingly relied on Mexico's elite for support.

THE PORFIRIATO, 1884–1900

> Himself a Mixtecan from Oaxaca who had risen through local and provincial office, both civil and military, Díaz had a profound understanding of how Mexico functioned at its most basic levels. Mexico City-based intellectual and political figures rarely understood this.
>
> Brian Hamnett, 1999[122]

Díaz's reelection in 1884 allowed him to assume the presidency again. During his extended administration, known as the Porfiriato, Porfirio Díaz created a political apparatus over which he kept tight personal control. For decades, the smooth functioning of this machine indicated his political genius. Díaz atomized power so no individual could challenge him. Power at the regional level was divided among governors, military commanders, and 300 district chiefs, known as *jefes políticos*. All owed their position to Díaz. The responsibility for maintaining order was divided between two separate bodies, the army, under the secretary of war, and the *rurales*, under the secretary of the interior. The *rurales* dated back to 1861 and were modeled on the Spanish Civil Guard.[123]

The army received the latest European military technology, which made it prohibitively expensive for local warlords to challenge Díaz. The creation of a national rail network permitted Díaz to deploy troops to distant trouble spots and nip opposition in the bud. During the Porfiriato, the army provided the order necessary for economic development, and economic development provided the revenues necessary to keep the army loyal and well equipped.[124]

At their peak, the *rurales*, who received better pay than the army, were made up of eleven corps, each numbering 300 men. Once banditry ceased to be a threat, the *rurales* provided security for trains and payrolls, served as spies, suppressed working-class opposition, punished those who defied the dictator, and guaranteed that candidates favored by Díaz won elections.[125]

Since Díaz felt that members of the middle class were likely to cause trouble if not attended to, Díaz simply put them on the government payroll. The government hired several generations of intellectuals to draft statements and speeches, while many others found openings in the diplomatic corps. Promising talent received government scholarships. One such recipient was Diego Rivera, who achieved international recognition in Paris as a Cubist painter while on a government scholarship. By one estimate, more than 70 percent of the literate population was working for the government at the end of the Porfiriato.[126]

Díaz let bygones be bygones. He accepted liberals, conservatives, and the clergy alike into his ruling coalition. These groups, along with military leaders, landowners, foreign investors, and positivist intellectuals, formed a coherent dominant class. Even Díaz's later rival Francisco Madero conceded that Díaz was "quite successful at eliminating old hatreds."[127]

Before 1900, Díaz faced little opposition. Of the handful who were arrested for opposing his repeated reelection, many would become members of the Chamber of Deputies—a testimony to Díaz's ability at political co-optation. The few who opposed Díaz received little publicity, since journalists and newspapers that did not give Díaz favorable coverage were denounced and persecuted, ushering in a dark age for journalism.[128]

In 1878, to shore up his democratic credentials, Díaz had pushed through a constitutional amendment banning the reelection of an incumbent president. In 1887, near the end of his second term, he ensured the passage of an amendment allowing a single consecutive reelection, thus paving his way for his election to the 1888–1892 term. In 1890, with his position secure, he ensured that yet another amendment eliminated all restrictions on presidential reelection. During the Porfiriato, it was Díaz's will, not the constitution, that determined the course of political events.

Figure 12.2
Porfirio Díaz

Source: Reproduced courtesy of the Benson Latin American Collection, the University of Texas at Austin

In appearance, the old federal structure was maintained. However, Díaz held all the reins of power. The courts simply responded to the dictates of the president, the governor, or the local *jefe político*. As the Porfiriato wore on, congressmen, whose positions were virtually assured for life, aged. One legislator commented that the Senate "housed a collection of senile members in a state of lingering stupor." After 1886, Congress became for all practical purposes a rubber stamp. Díaz approved congressional candidates before their election or reelection. As historian Alan Knight observed, "A large proportion of Porfirian governors—maybe 70%—were presidential favourites, imported into alien states, where their prime allegiance was to their president and maker, rather than to their provincial subjects." Incumbency in state legislatures was usually permanent, interrupted only by death or promotion. In Sonora, during the thirty-two years of the Porfiriato, 208 legislative seats came up for election. Only seventy-four individuals served in the legislature during this period. Considering that some legislators died and others received promotions, this left little room for electoral defeat.[129]

Despite power being concentrated in the federal executive, as historian Michael Johns noted, "No other Latin American country combined the oppression of dictatorship with such an obsession for the appearance of legality and legitimacy." Election fraud became a way of life, a ritual to sanctify an incumbent, not a method of selecting a leader. Once this became accepted practice, it was hard for Mexico to shake it during the twentieth century.[130]

The surviving papers of Puebla Governor Rosendo Márquez illustrate how Díaz micromanaged elections. The president wrote Márquez informing him who should be elected as federal deputies from Puebla. Márquez then wrote Puebla's *jefes políticos*, telling them who should be elected in their respective jurisdictions. They, in turn, informed the mayors what the outcome of the elections should be. Márquez's papers indicate how smoothly the whole arrangement functioned. The mayors wrote the *jefes políticos*, who in turn informed the governor, who in turn informed Díaz, that his instructions had been carried out.[131]

Unlike earlier liberal presidents, Díaz had the financial wherewithal to reward large numbers of potential rivals. By the late nineteenth century, transport facilities and soaring world demand permitted massive raw material exports. From 1876–1877 to 1892–1893, federal tax revenue rose from 17.2 million pesos to 38.6 million, vastly increasing the power in Díaz's hands. The government was finally able to break out of the vicious cycle of weak government leading to chaos, leading to reduced revenue, leading to weak government.[132]

Díaz publicly proclaimed his regime to be guided by the liberal principles that had guided Benito Juárez and kept the 1857 constitution and the laws of reform on the books. However, in practice Díaz abandoned much of the liberal agenda. He welcomed the military into the ruling elite and dispensed with the anti-clerical policies of previous decades. The government, rather than limiting itself to creating a favorable business climate, actively promoted railroad development and drafted a mining code that encouraged foreign investment. The traditional liberal ideal of the small property owner as the key to rural progress was replaced by the reality of large landowners who, with government approval, vastly increased their holdings.[133]

A small group of advisors called *científicos* surrounded Díaz and formulated policy. They were so named because of their supposedly "scientific" management practices. Díaz and the *científicos* set policy for decades. They emphasized that wealth had to be created before it could be divided, thus rationalizing its concentration. The *científicos* argued that the country's problems could be solved by the application of statistics and rational thought. The very small number of *científicos* exercised enormous power due to their holding top government positions and thus controlling government economic policy. They had close dealings with major industrial and commercial firms and often were important businessmen in their own right.[134]

By the end of the nineteenth century, positivism had replaced liberalism as the guiding philosophy of the Mexican political and economic elite. Auguste Comte (1798–1857), the French social philosopher who formulated positivist doctrine, believed that societies passed through three stages—the early primitive stage, then the metaphysical stage, and finally the scientific or positivist stage. The positivist stage was based on reason and empirically verifiable scientific knowledge. Comte considered the advanced nations of the nineteenth century were entering the positivist stage.[135]

Gabino Barrera, who was influenced by Comte while studying in Paris, returned to Mexico, where Juárez appointed him as an advisor on educational reform. Barrera promoted positivism in his journal *La Libertad*, which had as its motto, "order and progress," a phrase that appears on the flag of Brazil, which also fell under positivist influence. In Mexico, positivism's greatest impact was in shaping the higher education curriculum. Positivist educators stressed science and mathematics, while downplaying the arts and social and religious studies. [136]

By the turn of the century, Díaz had already ruled Mexico longer than anyone before, including Santa Anna. His lengthy tenure in office resulted from, above all, the overwhelming desire for peace. Writing in the 1890s, historian Justo Sierra commented: "The country's real desire, manifested everywhere, was peace . . . Seldom in history has there been a people with a more unanimous, more anguished, more determined aspiration."[137]

Initially, it appeared that Mexico could have both democracy and peace. Díaz pledged no reelection in 1876. Then, in 1884, he was elected for a single additional term. By 1888, when it had become obvious that he intended to remain in the presidency, reelection seemed a small price to pay for peace and economic growth. Many Mexicans assumed that Díaz was personally responsible for economic progress—an assumption that suited him perfectly.[138]

A final element prolonging Díaz's tenure was hope. Although the material rewards of Porfirian development were highly concentrated, the belief that development would soon lead to a general increase in the standard of living was far more widespread.[139]

Rather than trying to oust Díaz or modify his policies, humble Mexicans shared a deep belief in Díaz's enormous power and often assumed that his personal will was all that was needed for their needs to be met. Supplicants wrote him letters, often accompanied by a photo, to ask for a favor or a job, just as they wrote viceroys in colonial times. Government employees sought back pay or promotions. Aging soldiers or their widows requested pensions. Impoverished students sought scholarships. Litigants sought his intervention to obtain favorable judicial rulings. Some wrote simply to reiterate their loyalty to him.[140]

PORFIRIO DÍAZ DESCENDENT, 1901–1911

The first decade of the twentieth century saw the decline of the Porfiriato. Until then, a combination of economic growth and repression had prevented nationwide opposition to the dictator. However, after 1900 splits among the elite, economic recession, and jockeying for presidential succession undermined the Díaz regime.[141]

As Díaz aged, those he had placed in high positions not only aged but acquired an air of permanence. By 1910, of Mexico's twenty-four governors, only one was under fifty, and sixteen were over sixty. The chief justice of the Supreme Court was eighty-three, and six of the ten justices were over seventy. Ignacio Mariscal had served as secretary of foreign relations since 1885, and José Yves Limantour had served as treasury secretary since 1893. Fresh blood was seldom infused into Díaz's inner circle. This extended tenure in office reflected the changed nature of the Díaz regime. It had shifted from reliance on regional strongmen and peasants who had fought alongside Díaz early in his career to reliance on a Mexico City-based entrepreneurial class and the foreign investors associated with it.[142]

Newly affluent industrialists, merchants, professionals, and intellectuals, the product of economic growth, were excluded from political power, as were miners, industrial workers, and schoolteachers. The generation coming of political age at the turn of the century no longer viewed Díaz as the national hero who had saved Mexico from France, but as an aging tyrant clinging to power. Aspirations rose along with educational levels. As historian Roger Hansen noted, "The co-opted grew richer and older; the outsiders grew older and increasingly resentful."[143]

Díaz's permitting the Church to reassert its influence became one of the most obvious departures from the liberal cannon. This galvanized Camilo Arriaga, nephew and intellectual heir to liberal ideologue Ponciano Arriaga, into action. Arriaga, an engineer who had served as a deputy until 1900, came from a wealthy mining family. As part of the elite, he was an unlikely rebel, even though his family's mines were performing poorly and his family felt pressure from foreign investors. The Arriagas were typical of many elite families in northern Mexico in that they felt that those close to Díaz received favors that were denied to them.[144]

In response to what he felt was ill-advised tolerance of Church activity, Arriaga called for like-minded Mexicans to form liberal clubs. By the end of 1900 fifty such clubs had been founded in thirteen states. Members of liberal clubs formed part of the elite, as 68 percent of their members had professional training in law, engineering, or medicine, and another 16 percent were teachers.[145]

The liberal clubs never assumed a prominent political role, in large part due to their focus on enforcing anti-clerical laws, long after popular concern had shifted to political democracy and economic issues. The rapid proliferation of the clubs reflected the degree to which modernization had broadened the set of political actors.[146]

In February 1901, club members held a convention that drew fifty-six delegates—fifty-two men and four women—representing forty-nine clubs and four newspapers. The delegates founded the Mexican Liberal Party (PLM—Partido Liberal Mexicano). Díaz and the *científicos* tolerated such activity, which appeared to represent a narrow faction of the political elite that was miffed because it did not enjoy official favor.[147]

The PLM provided a forum for a variety of individuals, many of whom did not represent the elite. One of Díaz's strongest critics at the convention was Ricardo Flores Magón, who was born to Indian parents in the Oaxaca town of San Antonio Eloxochitlán. He soon became cut off from his Indian roots as his family sent him to Mexico City to receive the best possible education. At the convention, he attacked the status quo and demanded justice, democracy, and freedom of speech and press. He described the Díaz administration as a "den of thieves." By the middle of the decade, he had became Díaz's foremost opponent.[148]

Under the influence of younger, less affluent leaders, such as Flores Magón, the PLM soon became far more radical than the Juárez liberals ever had been. The party advocated forcing those who invested in Mexico to become Mexican citizens, ending presidential reelection, and land reform. It targeted industrial workers, demanding the eight-hour day, a minimum wage, equal pay for equal work, accident compensation, and other reforms workers themselves had been seeking. *Regeneración*, which Flores Magón founded along with his brother Enrique, became the unofficial journal of the party. This paper dealt with such politically volatile issues as the administration of justice, freedom of the press, and labor conditions. Flores Magón was soon jailed for his criticism of the regime. The paper continued to appear for four months after his arrest, after which time financial problems and the discovery of its clandestine press forced its closure.[149]

In 1904, Flores Magón, who was released after spending twenty-two months in jail, faced a difficult choice. He could continue organizing in Mexico, where he was prohibited from publishing and where he felt he was likely to be murdered, or he could challenge Díaz outside Mexico. He chose the latter course and went into voluntary exile in the United States, where he and a small group of followers resumed publication of *Regeneración*. Although the paper was banned in Mexico, 25,000 copies of each issue were smuggled in and circulated widely. Chihuahua Governor Enrique Creel, who remained puzzled over the eagerness with which workers received *Regeneración*, remarked, "Had they had to pay a 25 centavos tax to the government . . . they would have cried to high heaven, but many of them have deprived their children of bread in order to send five pesos to the Flores Magón."[150]

In 1906, exiled PLM members published a manifesto that called for revolution and laid out plans for a post-Díaz Mexico. The PLM manifesto demanded guaranteed job security, an end to child labor, and universal free education. It declared:

> No longer will there be present the Dictatorship, always at hand to advise the capitalists who rob the worker or to use the Armed Forces as protection for foreigners who reply to peaceful petitions of Mexican workers with showers of bullets.[151]

The PLM leaders envisioned acquiring arms in the United States, attacking across the border, and being joined by PLM-affiliated clubs throughout Mexico. Before the plan could be implemented, joint action by U.S. and Mexican authorities prevented the revolt. With its leaders in exile, the PLM soon lost influence. In 1906 the PLM's calling for government intervention in education, labor relations, and land distribution was considered wildly radical. However, within a generation, this had become an accepted role for government in Mexico.[152]

A number of factors limited the effectiveness of the PLM. As it became increasingly radical, affluent members, such as Arriaga and Francisco Madero, who had financed the publication of *Regeneración*, left the party. Mexicans associated with Díaz forced the closing of *Regeneración* by suing for libel in U.S. courts. U.S. authorities intercepted mail addressed to exiled PLM leaders and turned copies of their correspondence over to the Mexican government. Chihuahua Governor Creel's successful infiltration of the PLM provided him with information on its plans for uprisings. He passed this information to U.S. authorities, permitting the arrest of plotters for violating U.S. neutrality laws. PLM organizing, following more of a European intellectual tradition, relied heavily on the written word, which was effective with workers but almost totally bypassed the illiterate rural population. Finally, the PLM call for revolt came during an economic boom. For many industrial workers and dissatisfied members of the middle class, economic opportunities diminished the oppressive burden of government policy.[153]

As the 1904 presidential elections approached, Díaz ensured the passage of a constitutional amendment extending the presidential term from four to six years, which only added to the speculation that he might not live out his term. The amendment also created the position of vice-president. Díaz selected Ramón Corral, an unpopular former governor of Sonora, and at the time, secretary of the interior, to fill that position. The selection of Corral, a confident of Díaz, made it apparent that even if Díaz were to die in office, the same clique would remain in power.[154]

In 1906, workers struck at the copper mines in Cananea, Sonora, twenty-three miles south of the Arizona border. The mines there had contributed to the rapid change characteristic of Mexico's northern border. Cananea barely had a hundred inhabitants in 1891. By 1906, it had 25,000, making it the largest city in Sonora. As with so many Mexican mines, the Cananea mine was owned by an American, Colonel William Greene. Like many foreign investors, Greene enjoyed a cozy relationship with local officials. The state government not only guaranteed him a supply of inexpensive, non-union labor but contributed 15,000 pesos to construct a road that allowed Greene to transport machinery to his mines. Greene enjoyed tax exemptions on copper production, on the construction and operation of his physical plant, and on the importation of building materials, which by his own estimate saved him more than $1 million a year.[155]

Greene's Cananea Copper Company employed 3,521 Mexicans and 1,178 foreigners, most of whom were Americans. The Americans received wages two to four times higher than did Mexicans performing the same tasks. Cananea became highly Americanized, as houses were built U.S. style with wood, rather than adobe, and stores sold Milwaukee beer and Levi Strauss jeans. Workers rested on Thanksgiving Day, since the mining company observed it as a holiday.[156]

On June 1, 1906, rather than allowing the company to lay off miners and accept a shift from hourly wages to piece work, workers called a strike, demanding equal pay with Americans, access to American-held jobs, the eight-hour day, and the dismissal of two abusive foremen.[157]

After fire hoses were turned on the strikers, generalized violence erupted, resulting in the death half a dozen Americans and thirty Mexicans. Rafael Izábal, the governor of Sonora, called in 275 armed American volunteers from Arizona. The volunteers remained in Cananea for only a few hours, since the 2,000 Mexican troops and *rurales* who were sent to the area had no trouble restoring order.[158]

The strike collapsed after General Luis Torres, who commanded the Mexican troops sent to the scene, gave striking workers an ultimatum—return to work or be drafted into the army to fight Yaqui Indians. Except for the dismissal of one foreman, none of the workers' demands were met. A number of leaders were sentenced to the notorious San Juan de Ulúa prison from which they only emerged after Díaz's fall.

The presence of armed American volunteers inflamed Mexican nationalism. Díaz's failure to take action against the governor who allowed American volunteers to enter Mexico indicated to the public that the aging dictator supported foreign investors, not Mexicans. Rather than attempting to ingratiate himself to his outraged constituents, after the strike Governor Izábal stated that Americans at the mine deserved higher wages than Mexicans since they performed better than Mexican workers.[159]

In January 1907, Díaz issued an arbitration decree that sought to end a textile workers' strike that protested new management-imposed work rules. Workers were scheduled to return to the mills on January 7. However, when the steam whistle summoned workers back to the Santa Rosa mill in Río Blanco, Veracruz, some workers refused to accept the arbitration decree. The exact sequence of events that followed remains unclear, but likely those refusing to work blocked mill entrances. Soon several thousand workers gathered outside the mill. Stone throwing began, and a group of workers headed for the company store a block away. Employees inside the store panicked and fired on the unarmed workers, killing several and converting a hostile crowd into a raging mob that looted and burned the store. Troops were called in, and before calm returned, between fifty and seventy workers were killed, including some taken prisoner and summarily executed. Sending other strike leaders to the fever-ridden work camps of Quintana Roo added to the death toll.[160]

Díaz's failure to resolve labor conflicts peacefully tarnished his image and weakened him politically as his regime later went into crisis. Negotiation and compromise, which had characterized the early decades of Díaz's administration, were conspicuously absent. The regime had apparently lost its ability to adapt.[161]

The 1907 recession in the United States spread to Mexico, threatening banks and causing the finance minister to tighten loan requirements. This eroded the cheap credit *hacendados* had relied upon. Restricting credit also lowered mine output, as did reduced demand in the United States. Between 1900 and 1909, the price of silver fell 17 percent and that of copper by 23 percent. The effects of the crisis were most keenly felt in the north, which had the closest ties to the U.S. economy. The mills, mines, railroads, and cattle ranches of northern Mexico all began laying off workers. Since an unprecedented number of Mexicans, especially in the north, worked for wages, subsistence farming provided less of a cushion. In 1907, a draught-induced crop failure resulted in soaring food prices. Since food purchases often constituted a majority of a household's expenditures, many suffered a dramatic decline in their standard of living. Resentment against Díaz increased as the *científicos* were held to blame for these economic problems.[162]

As Díaz prepared for the 1910 elections, he found his traditional supporters divided. Since Díaz obviously would not live forever, the question inevitably arose concerning the transition from one-man rule to the rule of law in a nation where only 22 percent of the population over age ten could read and write.[163]

Díaz set the stage for the 1910 presidential elections by telling journalist James Creelman that he would not be a candidate. The interview containing this statement appeared in the March 1908 issue of *Pearson's Magazine* and was widely reproduced in Mexico.

In the interview, Díaz stated:

> I have waited patiently for the day when the people of the Mexican Republic would be prepared to choose and change their government at every election without danger of armed revolutions and without injury to the national credit or interference with national progress. I believe that day has come . . . I retire when my present term of office ends, and I shall not serve again.[164]

Díaz also commented on his form of governance:

> We were harsh. Sometimes we were harsh to the point of cruelty. But it was all necessary then to the life and progress of the nation . . . It was better that a little blood should be shed that much blood should be saved. The blood that was shed was bad blood; the blood that was saved was good blood.[165]

Later Díaz reversed himself, claiming that many people had implored him to stand for reelection. He stated that the interview expressed only his personal desire. Díaz may have changed his mind or he may have used the interview to bring opposition into the open. The aging dictator might also have hoped that Mexicans would shower him with demands that he run for another term. In any case, Díaz was never to effectively dominate the political scene again.[166]

When he let it be known, the Creelman interview notwithstanding, that he would be a candidate for the 1910–1916 term, Díaz said nothing about whether he would retain Corral as vice-president. This omission, whether deliberate or inadvertent, focused the attention of aspiring politicians on the vice-presidency.[167]

Francisco Madero, a member of one of the oldest aristocratic families in the north, soon moved into the political vacuum created by Díaz's age. As with so many elite families in the north, the Maderos were being challenged by foreign investors. Madero family interests included the largest Mexican-owned smelter, which competed directly with those of the Guggenheims—a U.S. family that owned mining and smelting interests around the world. Other family investments included banking and agriculture.[168]

Madero first achieved national prominence with the January 1909 publication of his 321-page book *Presidential Succession in 1910*. The book criticized the lack of democracy in Mexico. Madero's repeated reference to the "government of the center" indicated his regional viewpoint. Finally, his quoting from Montesquieu and making repeated references to classical antiquity indicated his elite background.[169]

Madero first challenged Díaz by campaigning for the vice-presidential nomination. When Díaz began to openly support the vice-presidential candidacy of incumbent Ramón Corral, Madero changed tactics and challenged Díaz for the presidency. He soon engaged in something unheard of in Mexico—campaign tours across the country. These tours, financed with personal funds, drew large crowds of disenchanted industrial workers, intellectuals, radical liberals, schoolteachers, members of the middle class, and even *hacendados*.[170]

As Madero toured the country, it became clear that he enjoyed widespread support. Many members of the urban middle class, who had seen their income decline due to the 1907 recession, joined his campaign. Support came from groups that had long felt shut out of power and opportunity. Students, seeing little future under the old regime, flocked to his cause. Industrial workers around the nation generally favored him. He sought labor support by visiting Orizaba, Veracruz, a textile-mill town where he pledged support for workers' freedom and their right to unionize. Madero was the first Mexican to awaken popular consciousness in thirty years.[171]

Tolerance turned to repression as Madero's campaign gained momentum. Municipal officials denied him permission to hold rallies, and police broke up the crowds that did appear. The government closed Madero's paper *El Antireelecionista*. Authorities warned other newspapers not to give him coverage and closed them if they failed to heed the warning. By May, numerous leaders of the anti-reelection movement had been jailed or sent to military service in Quintana Roo. By June, repression, which specifically targeted Madero's working class followers, had increased. That month, authorities arrested Madero himself, charging him with fomenting rebellion and insulting authorities.[172]

Madero remained in a San Luis Potosí jail on election day, June 26, 1910. By the official count, Madero received the votes of only 221 electors nationwide. Díaz, credited with the votes of 18,829 electors, began his eighth term as president of Mexico. Once the elections were over, authorities released Madero from jail, assuming that he no longer posed a threat. Unwilling to give up the struggle against Díaz, Madero eluded Mexican authorities by disguising himself as a rail worker. He crossed the border into Texas and began to rebuild his movement to oust Díaz in San Antonio.[173]

MEXICAN SOCIETY

Social Change

In the late 1890s, roughly 1 percent of the population formed the upper class, while the middle class encompassed 8 percent. The remainder included soldiers, miners, industrial workers, vendors, hacienda workers, sharecroppers, and beggars. By the dawn of the twentieth century, Mexico, rather than simply replicating mid-nineteenth century society, albeit with more population and wealth, had produced a qualitatively different society.[174]

As artisan production declined, and, as Church, Indian, and untitled lands (*baldío*) were transferred to private ownership, a massive migration from rural areas to Mexico City and other urban areas occurred. Between 1895 and 1910, the number of cities whose population exceeded 20,000 increased from twenty-two to twenty-nine, and their total population increased by 44 percent. Mexico's four largest cities, Mexico City, Guadalajara, Puebla, and Monterrey, underwent even more rapid population growth.[175]

A number of factors caused newly created wealth to be highly concentrated. As Mexico entered the world market, fewer artisans produced for home or local use, while the wealth of factory owners and merchants increased. Population increase put downward pressure on wages, as did the expropriation of village land, which forced peasants into the labor market. New technology, while increasing production, displaced labor with machines. An increasing number of Mexicans lost the networks that had served to protect them on the hacienda and in the village as they moved into new surroundings.[176]

Rather than improving during the first decade of the twentieth century, economic conditions worsened. Between 1903 and 1910, the average cost of corn, beans, rice, wheat, sugar, and coffee rose by 20 percent. Wages failed to keep abreast of the inflation that ravaged incomes. The 1907 recession in the United States spilled over into Mexico. As the export market for commodities collapsed, miners were laid off.[177]

In the north, after attacks by nomadic Indians ceased, the railroad facilitated the export of cattle and minerals. Population increase there far surpassed that of Mexico as a whole. Between 1877 and 1910 the population of the border states of Sonora, Chihuahua, Coahuila, Nuevo León, and Tamaulipas increased by 227 percent. In 1910, 31.7 percent of the population of Coahuila had been born outside the state. The north was less urban than the rest of Mexico and more arid and isolated. Few sedentary Indians lived there, and the Catholic Church exercised less influence than in the rest of the Mexico. Between 1877 and 1910, some 300,000 displaced peasants, ruined artisans, and adventurers moved to this area from central Mexico. The same individuals often moved from mine labor to agriculture to the railroad in search of employment.[178]

The north's proximity to the United States influenced the area in a number of ways. Americans invested massively in railroads, lumbering, mining, and ranching. Employers in the north were forced to increase wages to attract workers from central Mexico and to prevent them from continuing on the United States in search of still higher wages. As early as 1891, visiting Englishwoman Mary Jaques remarked that Monterrey was rapidly becoming Americanized. In 1910, a Guaymas, Sonora newspaper, *El Noticioso,* observed that "the learning of English had become a real avocation, because young people who speak it are assured good paying jobs in any business."[179]

In central Mexico, cities underwent the most conspicuous change. There, electricity, street cars, paved streets, street lamps, the telephone, sewage treatment plants, the sewing machine, and drinking water systems resulted in urban life being qualitatively different from what it had been in colonial times and in the early nineteenth century. The telegraph vastly increased the speed and volume of long-distance communication between both businesses and private citizens. Mexico's newly created wealth was most prominently displayed in these urban areas. Mary Jaques noted that "average" city homes employed from ten to twenty servants, while the larger ones employed from thirty to thirty-five.[180]

While change swept into urban areas and the north, tradition continued to exercise a strong grip on rural central and southern Mexico. In 1910, 71 percent of Mexico's population lived in communities with a population below 2,500. Many who lived in larger communities still engaged in agriculture. The 85 percent of the population living in towns with fewer than 10,000 residents gives a better measure of rural Mexico. Most of those living in rural areas rarely saw a mine, a railroad, a foreigner, a Mexico City resident, or a politician. One of the first harbingers of change in rural areas was the increased use of basic consumer goods, which indicated that a substantial number of individuals were joining the money economy.[181]

During the later part of the nineteenth century, in most rural areas, the means of communication remained excruciatingly slow. Most people traveled only to nearby towns and markets and only rarely to state capitals. Generally, any affairs that could not be settled in one's own town could be settled in the municipal head town (*cabecera*) As historian Alan Knight observed, even as late as 1910 Mexico was "less a nation than a geographic expression, a mosaic of regions and communities, introverted and jealous, ethnically and physically fragmented, and lacking common national sentiments."[182]

In his eponymous study of his home village in western Michoacán, historian Luis González y González chronicled how the slow pace of village life only reluctantly yielded to modernity. Well into the 1860s in villages such as San José de Gracia, only the season marked time, no one read, and the town functioned without a school, jail, or judge. González y González remarked:

> None of the modern methods of communication and transport fostered by the regime reached that far. Technical innovations and foreign capital were lacking. Not one of the national products for export was produced there. The area had been forgotten by the government . . .

In 1900, only 3,251 people resided in the vicariate of San José, of whom only 894 lived in the town itself. The 9,000 cattle grazing there far outnumbered the humans. The town boasted a plaza shaded with large trees, a church seating 500, a parish house, several shops, and 150 houses.[183]

In 1910, while Mexico's elite was celebrating the centennial of Hidalgo's Cry of Dolores with great fanfare, much of village Mexico was still infused with traditional values and practices. Colorful pre-Hispanic markets, or *tianguis,* with their profusion of herbs, crafts, and foods, supplied villagers.

Eventually, even small towns such as San José de Gracia began to feel the winds of change. The number of non-agricultural jobs increased. By 1901, eighteen people in San José de Gracia engaged solely in buying and selling. Traveling salesmen began appearing with increasing frequency, selling not only traditional goods but such technical innovations as Singer sewing machines. A postal service was established, and newspapers, phonographs, cameras, and factory-made goods made their appearance.[184]

As the experience with San José de Gracia indicates, to a greater or lesser degree, all areas underwent transformation. The Reform era in the middle of the century brought into prominence a generation of mestizo and Indian leaders trained and hardened by the exigencies of war. Beginning in the last third of the nineteenth century, income generated by the export of coffee, sugar, and copper enabled those who benefited from this trade to import the goods needed to enter the European world of fashion. The cachet of foreignness enhanced the appeal of imports. As an increasing percentage of the population was integrated into the national and international economy, caste identity was supplanted by class identity. Many ethnically distinct Indians were transformed into an ethnically indeterminate peasantry. At the dawn of the twentieth century, the railroad had eroded if not broken rural isolation, the printed word had become far more influential than before, thanks to an expanded educational system, and Mexicans had become more conscious of being Mexicans.[185]

The Elite

> The growing wealth of Porfirian elites came from diversified investments in real estate, in financial markets, and in export-related enterprises, not from manufacturing industry.
>
> Edward Beatty, 2001[186]

Díaz wooed the upper classes with riches beyond the imagination of previous generations. Newly created wealth surpassed old wealth to such a degree that the traditional elite families, such as the Fagoagas, were referred to as the "poor rich." Many Mexican members of the new elite bore foreign names, such as Creel, Limantour, and Braniff. Wealthy members of the French, American, British, and Spanish communities resident in Mexico also formed part of the elite.[187]

Those enjoying Díaz's favor received public positions, which enabled them to increase their wealth. Control of state governments, or the favor of those who did exercise control, allowed the purchase of public lands and former Church and Indian lands at bargain prices. A privileged few received lucrative government contracts, tax exclusions, tariff exemptions, favorable judicial rulings, and concessions to exploit natural resources. Well-placed members of the upper class, including state governors, federal cabinet members, and Díaz's family members, received high salaries for serving on boards of directors of foreign corporations. This was not mere window dressing—they would arrange the necessary permits, tax exemptions, rights of way, and contracts upon which the investors' success depended. Corruption was encouraged, since that made government positions so valuable that officeholders would not risk losing their positions by revolting. Such arrangements continued the close linkage between public office and private enterprise that had long characterized Mexico.[188]

The Díaz administration sought to keep wages depressed, feeling that would attract foreign investors. Low wages permitted high profits. The company owning the Santa Rosa textile factory in Río Blanco paid 12 to 14 percent dividends between 1902 and 1907. Profits could be further increased by the use of forced labor. Olegario Medina, who had grown fabulously wealthy in the henequen business in Yucatán, used his position as minister of development to arrange for the deportation of Yaqui Indians from northern Mexico to work in the henequen fields of his home state.[189]

Control of vast amounts of land formed one of the keys to elite wealth. The size of land holdings increased substantially during the late nineteenth century. Landowners used their already immense power to acquire land put on the market as a result of the Reforma. To further increase their holdings, they would violate the agrarian rights of peasant villages. After the defeat of the Yaqui Indians who had previously lived on the land, a single company, the Compañía Constructora Richardson, acquired 993,650 acres, extending from just north of Guaymas to the Mayo River and eighty miles inland. Toward the end of the Porfirato, 835 families owned 95 percent of the arable land.[190]

The Terrazas family of Chihuahua provides a classical example of how politics and business were inseparable. Family patriarch Luis Terrazas, the son of a butcher, rose through the ranks combating Apache raiders. Terrazas, a member of the last generation for which fighting Indians offered a path to upward mobility, then protected Benito Juárez during his stay in Chihuahua and, in the process, insinuated himself onto the national political scene. As governor he expropriated property of another *hacendado*, Pablo Martínez del Río, who had supported the French intervention, and then allocated the property to himself.

Terrazas, who served as governor of Chihuahua at various times between 1860 and 1904, assembled 10 million acres of land on which 500,000 head of cattle grazed. His ownership of more than twenty haciendas made him the largest Mexican landowner. Since Terrazas controlled the state government, he not only granted himself and his son-in law Enrique Creel a charter for the Banco Minero in 1882 but exempted the bank from state taxes. His control of government assured that family members would be invited to become partners with foreign corporations investing in the state.[191]

The Middle Class

> Porfirian schools were more important in their production of middle-class talent for the post-revolutionary educational and cultural efforts than they were in transforming popular behavior and eradicating illiteracy.
>
> Mary Kay Vaughan, 2006[192]

During the Porfiriato, the middle class included physicians, lawyers, engineers, midwives, pharmacists, petty merchants, *rancho* owners, journalists, politicians, the lower clergy, and junior military officers. Government employees also joined the middle class in increasing numbers. Between 1876 and 1910, the government payroll increased by 900 percent. In 1876, only 16 percent of the middle class worked for the government, while by 1910, 70 percent did. As in the colonial period, the private sector was not hiring the new generation of the educated.[193]

The 1907 depression closed the gates for social mobility and undercut the middle class, whose members disproportionally lived in the hard-hit northern states. Lawyers, physicians, engineers, and small merchants saw their dreams vanish in its wake. Foreign-owned corporations cut wages and jobs, and small merchants went out of business. Widespread bank failures occurred after growers failed to make mortgage payments. Unemployment, lower wages, and a sharp rise in the cost of living threatened to pull many down from middle class status.[194]

The middle class resented its inability to gain access to public offices held by Díaz's cronies and to mid-level private-sector jobs held by foreigners. White-collar workers resented receiving wages only slightly above those of industrial workers. Modest middle-class incomes were heavily taxed, since the government kowtowed to the domestic oligarchy and foreign investors, leaving them virtually tax free. After 1907, the specter of downward mobility increased discontent. For these reasons, members of the middle class ultimately rebelled against the regime that had fathered them.[195]

Workers

> No longer ignored, the men and women who made up Mexico's first generation of industrial workers demanded not only higher wages and better working conditions, but respect from their fellow citizens as well.
>
> Rodney D. Anderson, 1976[196]

With some notable exceptions, during the Porfiriato, the government assumed a hands-off stance in labor disputes. In 1877, Interior (and later Treasury) Minister Trinidad García expressed this view, "The government should grant private enterprise complete freedom of action with respect to labor." Nonetheless, labor leaders, realizing that they could never match the economic power of industrialists, frequently demanded government regulation of labor relations in hopes of improving their bargaining position.[197]

With a virtually inexhaustible labor supply, management felt little pressure to increase wages or even to keep them abreast of inflation. Wages for the unskilled plateaued just above subsistence. In 1893, a newspaper in the textile town of Orizaba, Veracruz, noted: "There is poverty, great poverty, and the struggle for a living is . . . painful (but not so for those who have capital). In addition to this, the cost of living increases daily, and labor is compensated disgracefully." The worst conditions existed in urban areas where workers were crowded together with no plumbing or safe water supply, amid filth and diseases. At the turn of the century, the newspaper *El País* referred to Mexico City's working-class neighborhoods as "centers of sickness and death."[198]

In addition to low wages, labor had a number of grievances. In the 1890s, with the advent of electric lighting in mills, the fourteen-hour day became common and the sixteen-hour day was not unusual. Miners and textile workers were often paid in script only redeemable at the company store. Despotic treatment by supervisors, many of whom were foreign, produced widespread resentment. Workers' safety, especially in mines, emerged as an issue, since the lack of compulsory workers compensation laws provided management with little incentive to invest in safety.[199]

At least 250 strikes occurred during the Porfiriato. Those striking most frequently were workers in textile mills and cigarette factories—two groups with a long labor tradition. Miners and rail workers also used the strike to further their demands. As was the case with strikes in earlier decades, strikers most often demanded higher wages. Most of these strikes failed due to the workers' lack of strike funds.[200]

By the turn of the century, labor militancy was increasing. As manufacturing shifted from artisan shop to factory, increasingly large numbers of workers were thrown together, thus facilitating a higher degree of working-class consciousness, much of which was tinged with nationalism—a response to the abuses of foreign owners. More workers were the children of other workers, not transplants from rural areas. These second-generation workers measured their lot in life not by comparing themselves with agricultural workers but by comparing their situation with that of the Porfirian elite. The contrast between workers and the elite became all the more galling as the purchasing power of industrial wages in central Mexico declined 38 percent between 1898 and 1908. Mexican workers also protested that they were being discriminated against in their own country. As U.S. investment increased, especially in railroads and mining, Mexicans often found themselves working alongside U.S. workers. Almost invariably, the best jobs were reserved for Americans. U.S. workers also received substantially higher pay for doing the same work as Mexicans. Increased exposure to U.S. workers, who were better organized than their Mexican counterparts, and the message of radical labor organizers added to labor militancy.[201]

Strikers during the first decade of the twentieth century faced a number of obstacles. As had been the case during the nineteenth century, the lack of sizable strike funds remained an almost insurmountable hurdle. The economic downturn after 1907 reduced strikes as anxiety over job loss increased. Management exploited national divisions. When U.S. locomotive engineers struck the Monterrey–Nuevo Laredo rail line, their strike was broken by replacing them with Mexican engineers, inevitably raising the issue of why Mexicans were not regularly employed by the railroad as engineers. Unions were frequently infiltrated. In Monterrey, Governor Bernardo Reyes's supporters packed the rail workers' local, rejected their union newspaper *El Ferrocarrilero,* revised the local statutes, and named the governor honorary president of the local.

Labor effectiveness was also undermined by the government's subsidizing pro-government labor organizations and rewarding pliant labor leaders—two practices that would figure prominently in post-revolutionary government-labor relations. One of the pliant labor leaders cultivated by the Díaz administration was Pedro Ordóñez, an activist since the 1870s. He was elected to the Mexico City municipal council, a position to which he was reelected for more than two decades. He also served as alternative deputy in the National Congress. He justified his serving in this position by claiming that his holding public office allowed him to voice labor's concerns.[202]

Until the end of the Porfiriato, the government officially maintained its hands-off attitude toward labor disputes. This attitude was justified by writer and presidential advisor Francisco Bulnes, who declared:

> The words "just remuneration" have no meaning in political economy. In political economy nothing is just or unjust as far as remuneration is concerned. Labor is a product, like any other, such as corn, wheat, flour, and is subject to the law of supply and demand.[203]

Official declarations not withstanding, organized labor repeatedly suffered repression. Such oppression frequently occurred in the mining industry where workers were often concentrated in isolated areas, removed from the public view, and where mining companies were wont to share their wealth with local officials. One mine manager wrote:

> There is no objection to a man or any number of men striking, but the moment these began to interfere with other men taking their places, or the moment they began to destroy property, the Federal Government takes a hand, and the leaders will, in all probability, be shot without trail.[204]

During the Porfiriato, many first generation workers maintained the rural tradition of short-term wage labor. Later, as an increasing number of workers were the children of other workers,

Mexican labor became more stable, and workers increasingly viewed themselves as full-time industrial workers, not as farmers sporadically working in industry to supplement their income. By 1910, the nearly 750,000 workers in modern industry, frustrated in their efforts at reform, came to favor Díaz's removal.[205]

Rural Mexico

> During the sixty years following 1870, the rural people of Spanish America probably underwent a greater change than at any previous time in their history except for the conquest of America itself.
>
> Arnold Bauer, 1986[206]

During the late nineteenth century, agricultural workers were linked to the land through a variety of arrangements. Some, known as *peones acasillados*, lived full time on haciendas. Others lived in villages that owned land that they could cultivate. A few villages retained enough land to support all their residents. More commonly, though, villagers would work part time for wages on a nearby hacienda to earn cash, which allowed them to purchase what their village plot could not provide them. The landless formed the lowest rung of the rural social ladder. The number of landless rural laborers regularly exceeded the demand for their labor, leaving them with little bargaining power. These workers, known as *jornaleros*, frequently moved from region to region to find work. Increasingly, the landless began to migrate to the United States in search of work, and, after 1910, joined revolutionary armies.[207]

Porfirian economic development did not produce a uniform transformation from communal landholding to wage labor. Peasants were most likely to lose their land in states such as Veracruz, Morelos, Oaxaca, and Chiapas, where there was a rapid expansion of capitalist agriculture. While many villages lost land, 92 percent of the villages of Oaxaca retained communal lands in 1910. This was especially true in isolated regions that offered few marketing opportunities. There were few dispossessed peasants in some parts of Oaxaca who could be attracted by the low wages offered. Plantation owners there resorted to forced labor. Muckraking investigative reporter John Kenneth Turner, who visited one such area posing as a potential investor, exposed the forced labor system on Valle Nacional's tobacco plantations. He described the abuses he witnessed there in his book *Barbarous Mexico*. Workers would be attracted by false promises of high salaries, shanghaied off the streets of urban centers, or sent from jails.[208]

Villagers across Mexico did not accept liberal rhetoric and strenuously opposed the legally mandated sale of communal lands. Uplands, which provided pasturage and firewood, would be closed to the community if privatized. Other holdings were dedicated to generating income to support local government and religious life. Auctioning them would necessitate new fees and taxes to replace income from village-owned land. If land were privatized, local officials would no longer have an interest in defending municipal lands and resources. Finally, villagers felt that privatization of land would greatly increase social stratification, as some individuals would inevitably control more land than others.[209]

Through their access to political leaders and their ability to summon armed force, *hacendados* exercised power that extended well beyond the market. They maintained close ties to the local priest, supported the hacienda school, meted out their own justice, and brought in the only merchandise available, which was supplied at the hacienda store. The hacienda set the pattern for rural wages and working conditions generally. The hacienda also formed the principal link between rural Mexico and the city.[210]

Most of those working on haciendas did so because they had no better alternative. In some instances, though, if high profits were anticipated and labor was scarce, the state willingly supported planters who forced laborers to work their land. Officials also supplied the planters with convicts, "vagrants," and political dissidents. The henequen fields of Yucatán and the tobacco fields of Valle

Nacional, Oaxaca, provide classic examples of the use of such forced labor. In other cases, planters secured labor to work under dangerous or harsh situations by providing a worker, often when drunk, with an advance of goods or future wages. This obligated him to work until he liquidated the debt.[211]

During the Porfiriato, several factors shifted the balance of power between the village and the hacienda in favor of the latter. Policy makers regarded the villages of southern and central Mexico as relics of the colonial past, which formed an obstacle to national development. They felt progress required that the peasant be transformed into a wage laborer or a capitalist agricultural entrepreneur. In the north, villages were no longer needed to protect against raids by nomadic Indians. As Díaz built a stable, solvent regime, his need for rural backing diminished, and the paternalism he had shown rural people faded. Throughout Mexico, the railroad provided distant markets for agricultural produce, thus providing an incentive for the appropriation of village land. After 1870, the growth of the market became a bigger threat to the village than liberal legislation. The seizure of village land by sugar-producing *hacendados* in Morelos so they could meet increased market demand provides a classic example of this. Such a fragment of economic history would be long forgotten if it had not been for Emiliano Zapata, who rebelled in defense of these lands.[212]

The loss of community lands deprived villages of communal income used to finance education and provide social services. This reduced the number of hospitals and schools well before the state could fill the void in education and medical service. The loss of communal land also reduced villagers' access to wood, pasture, and charcoal. As villages lost land, their residents further swelled the ranks of the rural unemployed. Village life, even though it might have been lacking in monetary terms, was far superior to the impersonal market forces residents faced after losing their land.[213]

Between 1877 and 1879, 300 villages in central Mexico formed a coalition and hired a lawyer to appeal to the Supreme Court in an attempt to regain their lands. Other peasants rejected the legal process and rebelled, seriously undermining Juárez's efforts to reestablish the supremacy of civil law. Most of these rebellions occurred in densely populated central Mexico, where villages attempted to cling to their ancestral holdings. Rebellions between 1878 and 1883 were spurred by the coming of the railroad, land privatization, and road building. Federal troops suppressed these uprisings without addressing their root cause.[214]

In Chihuahua, many lived in communities that had been established in the eighteenth century as a means of defending against Indian attack. By the late nineteenth century, the Chihuahuan elite no longer needed military colonies to defend against Indians. As a result, a 1905 law permitted wealthy ranchers, *hacendados*, and public officials to purchase the land of these villages, including house lots where people lived. This created bitter enemies who would bring down both Terrazas and Díaz in 1911.[215]

Rural Mexico, whose inhabitants were overwhelmingly illiterate, hungry, ill-housed, and marked for an early death due to disease, bore the brunt of the Porfirian economic development model. Rural people not only lost land but control of their community and social life. In 1910, only 2.4 percent of rural household heads owned land. The corresponding figure for the United States was almost 70 percent.[216]

As a result of increased corn prices, increased population, and number of those seeking wage labor after losing access to land, the purchasing power of agrarian wages declined 17 percent between 1895 and 1910. In that last year, peasants, more than 70 percent of Mexico's population, received only 3.3 percent of Mexico's national income.[217]

The Indigenous Population

The 1857 constitution denied Indian communities the juridical recognition they needed to defend village lands and provided no social legislation to favor them. Maximilian reversed this trend, restoring to Indian communities the right to own land. In 1866, the empire published two decrees, in Spanish and Nahuatl, establishing a mechanism for towns to recoup lost village land. In the end, imperial decrees concerning redress of grievances backfired. Hopes raised by such decrees were dashed when those asserting their rights were repressed.[218]

Neither the 1857 constitution nor Maximilian's decrees had any discernible impact on nomadic Indians in the north. In 1861, Captain Charles P. Stone, the U.S. consul in Guaymas, described Sonora as "the great Apache *rancho*, where they went when they needed cattle or horses."[219]

Between 1861 and 1870, Sonora's population declined by 25,000 as the state's residents fled from Indians and moved on to greener pastures in the United States. The war with the Apache dragged on into the 1880s, especially in Chihuahua.[220]

Finally, the combined military action of Mexican and U.S. armies defeated the Apache. Geronimo surrendered in 1886, virtually ending the Apache threat. A few Apache, who attempted to avoid contact with outsiders, survived in Sierra Madres, perhaps as late as the 1950s.[221]

After 1850, Comanche incursions into Coahuila declined due to U.S. forts near the border and the extinction of game such as buffalo. In addition, settlements of Kickapoo, Seminole, and Mascogo Indians were established to serve as a barrier to the Comanche, who also suffered from such contributions of the white man as liquor, small pox, and cholera.[222]

Unlike the Apache and the Comanche, the Yaqui living along the coast of Sonora were sedentary. During colonial times, the Yaquis were the only Indian group in the area willing to perform wage labor, and after independence, the Yaqui remained an integral part of Sonora's labor force. After 1850, outsiders sought to exploit not only Yaqui labor but their lands. In 1860, Sonoran governor Ignacio Pesqueira, who established a company to exploit Yaqui land, declared:

> It is not part of the elevated policies of the state to exterminate at one time the Yaqui Indians. Its only objective is to subdue them and subordinate them to the progress of civilization. They would always have sufficient land to cultivate for their own subsistence. But it is very essential for the prosperity and well being of the state that the unused land of the Yaqui River be cultivated.[223]

To facilitate the appropriation of Yaqui land, the government began their forced removal. In 1861, the prefect of Hermosillo received a party of more than 150 captured Yaqui women and children whom he sent to the prefect of Altar so they could be dispersed in his district as servants. As a result of this policy, in urban areas of Sonora, abducted Yaqui children formed a great percentage of household servants.[224]

The Yaqui's fertile, irrigated land came under increased pressure from commercial farmers after the railroad made it possible to transport crops grown on Yaqui land to markets in the United States. When the Yaqui defended their lands against encroachment, the Mexican army supported the interlopers in a genocidal war that lasted for decades.

A 1903 report on the Yaqui published by the Mexican War Department noted:

> The primordial tendency of these Indians is to maintain their independence from the white race, to live apart and govern themselves with their customs, habits, and ceremonies. Due to tradition, instinct, and the education they receive from birth, they hate civilized people.[225]

The report commented on Yaqui tactics:

> The Yaqui have staged large and small uprisings, and hide in haciendas, towns, and mines when they are pursued or defeated. In towns, they mingle with Yaqui workers who are hired since they are the only workers found there. There, the warriors rest, obtain supplies, and rebel again, always protected and aided by their fellow Yaqui who send them what they can and replace them. Thus, the war has no end.[226]

Figure 12.3 *Yaqui prisoners in penitentiary*
Source: Reproduced courtesy of the Benson Latin American Collection, the University of Texas at Austin

The author of the report concluded the Yaqui wars could be ended in three ways: 1) exterminate the population; 2) deport the Yaqui from Sonora; or 3) colonize their lands. The author rejected the first as too brutal. He rejected the second not only because of its brutality but because it would deprive Sonora of a labor force. Thus he recommended the third choice.[227]

In 1897, the eight Yaqui pueblos expressed their views in a letter to the Mexicans after signing a peace treaty with Mexicans at Ortiz. The letter was addressed to Mexican General Luis Torres:

> What we want is that whites and soldiers leave. If they leave willingly, then we will have peace; if not, then we will declare war. The peace we signed in Ortiz provided that whites and soldiers leave, and this condition has not been met.[228]

This plea fell on deaf ears, and later General Torres boasted:

> Thousands of prisoners taken of the Indians have been remitted to diverse parts of the Republic, so that under the vigilance of the federal government and the supervision of the state authorities, they could be adapted to the uses and customs of civilized life.[229]

For each Yaqui received, *hacendados* in Yucatán paid a bounty, which was divided between the Ministry of War and the military officer in charge. Colonel Francisco B. Cruz received ten pesos for each of the 15,700 Yaqui he was credited with deporting. By 1908, a quarter to a half of the Yaqui population had been sent out of the state by rail. Other Yaquis fled across the border to

Arizona. By the end of the Porfiriato, these massive deportations had broken the back of Yaqui resistance.[230]

With the exception of using the military against Indians in northern border states, Mexico did not have a coherent Indian policy in the late nineteenth and early twentieth centuries. Liberals associated the white man with technology, a spirit of enterprise, good manners, and progress. They associated the Indian with lethargy and treachery. Policy makers felt that the Indians' extensive land holdings formed the patrimony of all Mexicans and resented Indian attempts to cling to their ancestral domains.[231]

The political elite disapproved of the Indians' high degree of self-sufficiency and sought to make Indians consumers as well as producers for the market. In 1870, Veracruz Governor Francisco Hernández y Hernández stated:

> Indians have a fanatical adoration for the land, and yet their only benefit from it is their constant communion with it. They are rich due to their surroundings. Strictly speaking, they have no needs. Their ambition is satisfied by a contemplative gaze at their land sowed with various flowers and fruits. They know nothing else and want nothing else. Theirs is an easy life because within their reach is all the food they need. A handful of corn thrown on the ground they tread provides enough for their table. They do not want to participate in public affairs nor do they want anything from the government . . . The government continues to insist on subdividing land, convinced as it is, that once these Indians become landowners, they will soon become worthy citizens. Today they are neither producers nor consumers and they only serve as cannon fodder.[232]

Díaz realized that rural peace depended on defending Indian rights to land in central and southern Mexico. He favored Indian communities by failing to enforce the Lerdo Law, which required villages to subdivide their land. By 1882, only four or five communities in Veracruz had divided their lands, and they had transferred ownership to large groups of co-owners. As late as 1910, an estimated 41 percent of indigenous communities in Mexico retained some of their ancient lands. In some communities, residents purchased land that had been communally owned and became small-scale agricultural entrepreneurs.[233]

In 1901, Article 27 of the constitution was amended to allow non-religious groups, such as villages, to legally own land. Neither the constitution as written in 1857 nor the constitution as amended in 1901 actually determined land ownership. As historian Charles Gibson observed: "In Mexican history significant changes have rarely occurred as a consequence of law. Law provides an approximation of historical happening, or a commentary upon it."[234]

Some explanations for the income disparity between indigenous people and non-Indians were based on race. In 1910, papers presented at the Seventeenth Congress of Americanists meeting in Mexico City expressed the academic consensus that Indians were racially inferior, as indicated by bone measurement of their skulls. Bulnes claimed that Indian poverty resulted from a lack of energy-releasing nitrogen in their corn-based diet. Positivist writer Luis Mesa claimed the Indian suffered from the negative impact of the Church, and suggested the Indians' redemption lay not in more nitrogen but in less religion. Others, such as Justo Sierra, felt Indian poverty resulted from inadequate education. He stated that "given the equality of circumstance, of two groups of people, the one that is less educated is inferior."[235]

Elite discourse centered on bringing the Indian into contemporary society. Historian and philologist Francisco Pimentel stated that Indians must "forget their customs and even their language." Mestizos and Creoles felt assimilation would benefit not only the Indian but also the nation as a whole, since cultural homogenization would lead to true nationhood. As was the case with most liberals, Juárez himself believed that full citizenship for indigenous peasants could only be achieved by cultural assimilation, as he had shown with his own example.[236]

Figure 12.4
Tehua woman

Source: Reproduced courtesy of the Benson Latin American Collection, the University of Texas at Austin

Efforts at Indian education were generally limited to teaching Spanish. Expressed interest in Indian education remained largely intellectual rhetoric. While most Mexicans at least paid lip service to the desirability of educating Indians, others, such as Francisco Cosmes, editor of the positivist daily *La Libertad,* stated that Indians should not be subjected to compulsory education laws, since they were "impervious to all civilization." Cosmes also stated the state should not deprive Indian families of child labor in a futile effort to educate them. Opposition to the introduction of alien ways from within the Indian community further complicated the meager effort at Indian education. In 1909, the Kickapoo burned a school that had been built for them on the day it was to be inaugurated. Such rejections occurred in other parts of Mexico.[237]

Depriving villages of communal lands and the Indians' increased incorporation into the national market caused many Indians to lose their Indian identity and to be considered henceforth mestizos. As a result, after the middle of the nineteenth century, the Indian population began to decline. In 1877, 38 percent of Mexico's population spoke an Indian language, while, in 1910, only 13 percent did.[238]

During the latter part of the nineteenth century, systematic academic study of Mexico's Indians began. Such studies emphasized that, rather than there being a monolithic Indian culture, the indigenous population was highly differentiated by village, language, and ethnic group. Their loyalty to community above loyalty to nation and their poverty provided their thread of commonality. Francisco Pimentel provides an example of such scholarship with his *Cuadro comparativo de las lenguas indígenas de México (Chart of the Indigenous Languages of Mexico)*. In it, he identified 108 indigenous languages, which he grouped into twelve families based on their structure.[239]

Mexico's indigenous people did not reject the varied forces of modernity outright, but negotiated, innovated and adopted those that they felt would meet their needs. Growing coffee is an example of an innovation that Indians wholeheartedly embraced. Under Indian control, raising coffee became an important income source. As a result of this selective embrace of elements of alien cultures, the designation "Indian" did not automatically denote a poor peasant. In some areas, especially in Oaxaca, there were comfortable indigenous artisans and wealthy indigenous landowners.[240]

Women

In contrast to the 1824 Constitutional Convention, delegates to the 1857 Convention at least considered the status of women. Liberal politician Ignacio Ramírez stated that granting women the vote would serve no purpose since their fathers and husbands adequately represented them. Convention members apparently agreed, since they took no action on the matter.[241]

As a result of the 1857 constitution remaining silent on gender-related issues, women remained disenfranchised. Given the tumult of the 1860s, only in 1870 did a national civil code define the status of women.

The 1870 Civil Code left most of the colonial practices concerning women intact. They remained excluded from politics and were punished for transgressions, such as adultery, according to a double standard. As historian Silvia Arrom observed, "The new codes often repeated ancient patriarchal provisions almost verbatim."[242]

The 1870 Civil Code declared that the husband had a duty to feed and protect his wife and the wife should "obey her husband as much in domestic affairs as in education of the children and in the administration of property." A wife's capacity for legal self-representation was contingent on her husband's permission, except in criminal cases or when her husband was involved.

The 1870 legislation not only wrote into law the long-standing inferior social position of women but attempted to enforce a nuclear family prototype with a single line of inheritance. As historian Carmen Ramos-Escandón noted, "The liberal model for the family, one in which the family is formed solely by a monogamic couple and its children, was not prevalent in Porfirian Mexico, and legalized marriages were not the rule."[243]

Canon law governed marriage until 1859, when the Law of Civil Matrimony became effective. The new legislation provided little change, even though the power to define marriage shifted from Rome to Mexico City. The law declared marriage to be a civil contract. However, it continued Catholic practice by declaring that neither party could remarry until the death of the other party in the marriage. This gave the contract the unique status of not being rescindable even though both of the parties to the contract might desire its rescission. The law included a passage, known as the Epistle of Melchor Ocampo, whose reading was required at all civil marriage ceremonies. It included the following passage:

> The woman, whose principle sexual endowments are self-denial, beauty, comprehension, perspicacity, and tenderness, should and will obey the husband and provide pleasure, assistance, consolation, and counsel.[244]

Laws, such as the 1857 constitution, the 1859 law on matrimony, and the 1870 Civil Code, lagged behind changing Mexican social reality. Though denied the vote, women repeatedly took part in political movements. More than 1,000 women signed a petition opposing the freedom of religion that the 1857 constitution provided for. The petitioners qualified their position, stating, "We have not come to meddle in the difficult question of politics, completely foreign to our sex." When two women arrived to serve as delegates to the 1876 General Congress of Workers, heated debate arose over where they should be seated. Those opposed declared that women had never been seated before and that seating them would violate a precedent. Finally, after heated debate, they were seated to a standing ovation. This opened the way for more extensive female participation in the labor movement. In 1879, Carmen Huerta was elected president of the Congress, a position to which she was reelected in 1880. In 1900, a number of women answered Arriaga's call to become active in liberal clubs. In Veracruz, an all-women liberal club was formed with Concepción Valdés as president.[245]

More women joined the labor force, since few urban male workers could support a family on one income and many single or widowed women sought employment. Increased migration from rural to urban areas undermined the traditional nuclear family. In Mexico City, 70 percent of births were to unmarried women. The low rate of marriage also reflected the high cost of a formal marriage and the slow acceptance of civil, as opposed to religious, marriage.[246]

The urban upper classes frowned on women working outside the home. They did, however, approve of upper-class women who founded social-benefit institutions since Porfirians viewed philanthropy as one of the few proper activities for upper-class women. In 1904, President Díaz reflected this view when he stated, "The mission most worthy of society matrons is to provide the sustenance, education, and training of orphaned girls through efforts to replace moral despair with examples of virtue." In their organizing of philanthropic efforts, elite women exercised significant power and influence. These efforts to provide assistance to workers and indigents were especially important as Church-sponsored charities declined.[247]

Women's educational opportunities expanded as their role in society evolved. As late as 1874, education remained not only a preserve of the elite, but of males, as only 22 percent of students were women. Only in 1892 did the Escuela Normal de Profesores in Nuevo León accept women. The large number of women enrolling in that school led to the establishment of a separate Escuela Profesional para Señoritas, which offered courses in pedagogy, telegraphy, accounting, and natural and social sciences, in both day and night shifts. Between 1878 and 1907, the number of teachers' colleges increased from twelve to twenty-six. At the same time, other professions were slowly opening to women. In 1886, the first woman dentist graduated, and in 1887, the first surgeon did.

Once they graduated, women professionals still faced obstacles in a male-dominated world. At the turn of the century, María Asunción Sandoval de Zarco, the first woman law school graduate, could not practice criminal law, her initial area of interest, and was forced to practice civil law. Public litigation was viewed as an unseemly role for a woman. Women school teachers were dismissed if they married.[248]

Economic expansion greatly increased the need for education, and, as in the rest of the Western world, teaching became one of the first professions to open its doors to women. By 1895, 51.3 percent of teachers were women, and, by 1910, this figure had risen to 64.4 percent. Many middle-class women found jobs in the growing commercial sector and in government, working as clerks, secretaries, typists, and bookkeepers.[249]

The number of women enumerated as a part of the formal labor force increased steadily until 1900. Then, with the economic downturn, the decreased cost of male labor removed the economic incentive to hire women who previously had been willing to work for even lower wages than men. As a result, the number of working women declined by 1910 (see Table 12.1).

Women were almost entirely excluded from some areas of the economy, such as mining. However, in the industry of transformation, which included textile and cigar factories, women comprised a third of the workforce. As women increasingly joined the industrial labor force, the

Table 12.1 *Female labor force participation, 1895–1910*

	1895	1900	1910
Working women	850,087	872,978	778,559
Women in industry of transformation (includes textiles and tobacco)	182,000	210,000	199,000

Source: Ramos-Escandón (1990b: 29) and Towner (1977: 99)

idealized notion of a woman evolved from that of a frail, helpless person to one who should be allowed to work as long as her job did not interfere with her domestic duties.[250]

In some cases, women workers struck making demands specifically as women. They would often address a letter to a powerful public figure and then have the letter published so their grievances could be aired. In 1881, female cigar rollers struck four factories in the Federal District—La Niña, La Mexicana, El Modelo, and El Borrego—after management raised the daily quota from 2,304 to 2,600 cigars. Strikers posted placards, which they signed "Las Cigarreras," declaring, "We have to work from six in the morning until nine at night . . . We don't have one hour left to take care of our domestic chores, and not a minute for education." In this case, the governor of the Federal District intervened and set the daily quota at 2,400 cigars.[251]

While some women moved into new areas of employment in the professions and industry, many others continued to work in traditional occupations. The 1895 census found 190,413 women (and 82,887 men) working in domestic service. Indigenous women in urban areas, who were frequently separated from their families and cultures, often worked as domestics. They worked in an environment where they received little pay, toiled long hours, and were vulnerable to sexual abuse. Home sewing was another common form of female employment. Many other women worked as street vendors and tortilla makers.[252]

The 1910 census indicated that women made up only 14 percent of the work force. This figure in part reflects employment practices in still largely rural Mexico. The low percentage of women reported to be in the labor force also indicates census takers' blindness to many economic activities undertaken by women but not generally included in employment statistics.[253]

In the late nineteenth century, women's periodicals provided space for women to share ideas with other women. Unlike early nineteenth-century periodicals for women, Porfirian women generally wrote and edited the magazines targeting them. *El álbum de la mujer* reported on social and artistic events, life in Europe, fashion, the theater, poetry, hygiene, and the role of women in Mexican society. A weekly magazine *Las violetas de Anáhuac* spoke out on behalf of women's suffrage and equal opportunity. In 1904, three women, a doctor, a lawyer, and a teacher began publishing a feminist monthly, *La mujer mexicana.* All of these journals faced financial problems, and as a result none lasted more than a decade.

Laureana Wright de Kleinhans, born to a Mexican mother and an American mine owner in Taxco in 1846, was an early critic of the status quo. She founded *Las violetas de Anáhuac* and vigorously attacked the notion of female intellectual inferiority. Wright argued that women failed to match men's intellectual achievement because they were denied an adequate education. To buttress this argument, she cited the National Preparatory School, the incubator of the late nineteenth-century Mexican elite, which only accepted its first female student fifteen years after its founding. Wright minced no words, declaring, "Men aren't content with subjugating all other species, they also subjugate half of their own species—women."[254]

During the Porfiriato, Mexican feminists concentrated on eliminating the inferior status for women codified in the civil code and in expanding women's access to education. Even these rather tepid, by modern standards, demands put women on the defensive. In response to the charge that such changes would destroy the family, women noted that increased education would allow them to obtain better jobs and thus improve their families' living standard.[255]

The changing role of women inevitably produced a backlash. Even though female employment in the federal bureaucracy was burgeoning, Treasury Secretary Limantour opposed hiring women, claiming they not only lacked the mental capacity for treasury jobs, but that they would distract men from doing their jobs. The treasury department remained closed to women until the end of the Porfiriato.[256]

In 1909, Horacio Barreda, whose father founded the National Preparatory School, declared that feminism, by preaching the equality of rights for men and women "threatened to uproot the very foundation of the family and society."[257] Leading *científico* Francisco Bulnes warned:

> Feminism has entered into Mexico as an extremely disruptive force. It is well known that in Latin countries it is only the unattractive women, despairing widows, and indigent spinsters, when they are susceptible to hysterical emotions, who consecrated themselves to the social cause. A woman . . . is in great social peril if her energies are not channeled into religious and charitable channels. Those reforming women are the generators of a hatred against society more dangerous than that fulminated by a Barcelona anarchist.[258]

Population

Between 1855 and 1875, Mexico's population only increased from 7.5 to 8.4 million. Beginning in the 1870s, and especially in the 1890s, population growth accelerated due to political peace, medical advances, improvements in sanitation, railroads moving cereal during times of famine, and improved living conditions for some sectors of the population. Between 1875 and 1910, the population increased from 8.3 million to 15.1 million—an increase of 1.7 percent a year. This moderate population increase, given the lack of immigrants, almost entirely resulted from the birthrate exceeding the death rate. During the first decade of the twentieth century, the birth rate was 46.3 per 1,000, while the death rate was 33.2 per thousand.[259]

During the middle of the nineteenth century, more than 300 out of every 1,000 children born died before their first birthday.[260] A Protestant missionary recalled his experience during the Porfiriato:

> I used to ask, "How many of you, fathers and mothers, have children in heaven?" Usually all hands would promptly go up, while the replies came, "*Tengo cinco.*" "*Tengo ocho,*" I have five, I have eight, etc. Deplorable ignorance as to proper sanitary conditions in the home and the care of children is responsible for a large proportion of this death harvest among the little ones.[261]

At the end of the Porfiriato, only 0.8 percent of Mexico's population was foreign-born, compared to 30 percent that was foreign-born in Argentina at the time of the First World War. Liberal policy makers attempted to attract immigrants since they felt the only salvation for Mexico lay in attracting European Catholics whose industry and intelligence could develop the country. Despite this welcoming attitude, Mexico, with its low wages and densely populated central plateau, could not compete with the United States and Argentina, which offered higher wages, attractive climate, and abundant, free, fertile land.[262]

In 1910, 116,527 foreigners lived in Mexico. Many were members of the U.S. upper and middle classes who worked in northern Mexico as merchants and technicians. Those who did come to do manual work had less choice than European Catholics. Some indebted Korean laborers harvested henequen in Yucatán. In Sonora, Chinese came to work as miners, cooks, gardeners, washers, and domestics. A 1903 report noted that 2,464 Chinese lived in the state.[263]

THE CHURCH

> Opinion became so polarized by the middle of the nineteenth century that Catholicism ceased to be the principal factor of national unity.
>
> Anne Staples, 1989[264]

Most of the drafters of the 1857 constitution were Catholics who wanted to end close Church-state ties. They felt that only by eliminating the Catholic Church as a political and economic force, though not as a religious one, could Mexico become a modern nation. Others thought the Church too prone to support abusive centralized power.[265]

The Church responded as if the authors of the constitution belonged to a satanic cult, when, in fact, they had taken their oath to the constitution before a crucifix and the first line of the document mentioned God. In response to the Lerdo and Juárez Laws, Pope Pius IX declared:

> We raise our Pontifical voice in apostolic liberty . . . to condemn, to reprove, and declare null and void the said decrees and everything else that the civil authority has done in scorn of ecclesiastical authority and of this Holy See.[266]

The Church also condemned the 1857 religious toleration implied (but not explicitly stated) by the 1857 constitution. The Archbishop of Mexico presented a petition to Congress demanding the prohibition of any religion other than Roman Catholicism.[267]

The Church subsequently made what were, from a political point of view, two disastrous mistakes. Its rejection of the reform laws led to the War of Reform. Then the Church responded to the liberal victory in the War of Reform by promoting French intervention, hoping to regain from a Catholic prince what it had lost to Mexican liberals. The Archbishop of Mexico even served as a member of the French-imposed triumvirate that offered the throne to Maximilian.[268]

After Maximilian's defeat, the Church's standing plummeted, since it not only lost its material wealth but was stigmatized for having cast its lot with those whom the victorious liberals branded as reactionary enemies of the state. The nation as whole lost out because it suffered two wars. In addition, before the Church's wealth was nationalized, much of it had been used to support social services. Many of these assets were transferred to the landed classes, leaving the poor without hospitals, foundling homes, schools, and orphanages. The nation also lost out because priests were denied a role in politics. In early independent Mexico, they had been an integral part of public life. After the French intervention, priests, who were among the best educated in Mexico, were denied a political role.[269]

After the defeat of the empire, the Church benefited from Juárez's conciliatory policy. The right to vote was returned to the clergy and an amnesty removed the threat of prosecution from those who had supported Maximilian. In 1868, Pope Pius IX designated six new bishops to fill vacant sees in Mexico. Rather than pursuing old vendettas, Juárez concentrated on reconstructing the nation and fighting off military rivals.[270]

During the Porfiriato, toleration and reconciliation between Church and state reflected Díaz's general policy of not letting old antagonisms needlessly interfere with current governance. Nuns in convents were warned of inspections, so when government inspectors arrived to see if illegal convents were being maintained, they found nothing and could file a report stating the law had been upheld. By 1907, the Church was operating 586 primary schools. That same year, the old Palafox Seminary became a degree-granting Catholic university. The Church maintained loose links with more than twenty-three newspapers. By the end of the Porfiriato, the Church had again become a landowner, with lands and buildings registered in the names of intermediaries. Whenever Díaz dedicated a government project, a robed priest stood at his side to add his blessing. The number of clergy increased from 3,576 in 1895 to 4,533 in 1910. Díaz's approach to improved relations with the Church was typically Mexican: he did not repeal anti-clerical legislation— he simply did not enforce it.[271]

Rural priests resumed their positions—or in some cases retained them—as the true authorities in many villages. Only rarely were laws restricting fiestas and religious processions enforced in rural Mexico. Historian Luis González y González noted that in San José de Gracia, during the first decade of the twentieth century:

> Padre Othón was the highest authority. The political leaders who were called "peace officers," and the judges, known as *jefes de acordada,* recognized and bowed to the priest's supremacy; they consulted with him about what was to be done, and they worked closely with him in providing the few public services required by the village.[272]

In 1900, Monsignor Montes de Oca, bishop of San Luis Potosí, declared, "The religious pacification . . . has been achieved in Mexico despite the laws remaining unchanged, thanks to the wisdom and valor of the illustrious man who governs us." Even though a few doctrinaire liberals, such as Camilo Arriaga, took umbrage at the Church's resurgence, the majority of Mexico's population welcomed it. Díaz's rapprochement with the Church made a political ally of a traditional foe and avoided renewed conflict between liberals and conservatives that would have sidetracked political consolidation and economic development.[273]

While doctrinaire liberals continued to demand suppressing the Church as a reactionary body, within the Church a current developed in response to the social problems of an emerging industrial society. This current became known as the Catholic Social Action Movement. It originated during the last years of the nineteenth century and drew inspiration from Pope Leo XIII's 1891 encyclical *Rerum Novarum*, which called for Catholics to combat the evils of both "savage" capitalism and socialism. Rather than accepting either ideology, it proposed a third path based on small and medium-sized family properties.[274]

As American influence increased and religious freedom was allowed by the 1857 constitution, Protestantism became a significant religious force in Mexico. Hundreds of American lay preachers took up residence in Mexico. By 1910, an estimated 700 Protestant congregations with roughly 70,000 members had been established. They were concentrated in major urban areas and in areas where economic transformation had been most profound, especially those areas associated with the railroad and mining. Protestants adopted not only different religious beliefs but embraced modernity, education, and the view that the world was an orderly place marching to progress. Díaz actively encouraged Protestantism since he felt it would break the Catholics' religious monopoly and that the presence of Protestant churches would make U.S. investors feel more welcome.[275]

MEXICO CITY

Maximilian left his lasting mark on Mexico City by ordering the construction of a broad avenue, the Calzada de la Emperatriz (Causeway of the Empress), modeled on Paris' Champs-Elysées, which linked Chapultepec Castle with downtown Mexico City. He took other steps to create a city worthy of being an imperial capital, including realigning streets, planting a thousand ash trees, extending water pipes, and providing gas illumination, public squares, new fountains, and parks.[276]

After the fall of the empire, Mexico City's elite and their exclusive shops clustered around the city's massive plaza, known as the Zócalo, just as they had in colonial times. However, during the 1870s, the elite began to abandon the north and east sides of the Zócalo for its west side. By 1880, the Zócalo had become the eastern terminal of an axis of power, wealth, and culture that ran west to Alameda Park. San Francisco Street, also known as Plateros (today's Francisco Madero), was the principal street of this eight-block by five-block area. Most of the city's landlords, businessmen, and politicians lived in or near this area. In the early 1880s, almost a quarter of the country's retail purchases occurred in this zone, which included roughly a dozen modern Parisian-style department stores located just off the southwest corner of the Zócalo. At these stores, the best known of which was the French-owned Palacio de Hierro, the Francophile elite bought the luxurious wares ostentatiously displayed in gleaming windows.[277]

This first westward shift was only the prelude for further westward movement into new suburbs lining the Paseo de la Reforma—the renamed Calzada de la Emperatriz. This shift was facilitated by the easy access to downtown offices and businesses provided by the Paseo itself and by the economic dynamism of the Porfiriato providing the elite with sudden riches.[278]

Early in the Porfiriato, the colonial model of elite housing still prevailed. House walls abutted the street and only an exterior wall, a solid wooden door, and grilled windows were visible to the public. Such homes, which were three or four times as long as they were wide, contained patios with wells, gardens, and fruit trees and housed both servants and an extended family. As the elite moved west to subdivisions along Reforma, they built multi-story mansions set back from the street to openly display their inhabitants' wealth and prestige.[279]

As with much of the economy, suburban development involved foreigners. Large American companies working with local businessmen and government officials built many of these subdivisions. Treasury Secretary Limantour owned land along Bucareli Street, on the western edge of the city, and awarded contracts for providing urban services to the land he owned. Other top officials collected fees for linking foreign real estate, paving, and utility companies with the functionaries dispensing government licenses and contracts. As a result, American, Canadian, German, and English firms paved streets, laid sewers, and installed electric lines. Some 400 tramway cars facilitated rapid travel from new subdivisions to the urban core. (Factory workers could not afford the fare.) They were property of the Canadian-owned Mexican Tramways Company.[280]

As the affluent were moving west of the city, the city's near west side saw the construction of monumental public buildings. The Italian architect Adamo Boari designed Mexico City's Italian Renaissance-style post office, which still remains in service. Work began on the neoclassical

Figure 12.5 *Mexico City's main plaza, with cathedral in background*

Source: Reproduced courtesy of the Benson Latin American Collection, the University of Texas at Austin

legislative palace. (Its unfinished dome was later converted into the Monument to the Revolution.) Construction of the National Theater, now the Palace of Fine Arts, began with marble imported from Italy. Since the Revolution interrupted its construction, it was only competed in 1934. Such monuments to Mexico's progress were designed not only to highlight the progress of Profirian Mexico but to induce foreign capitalists to invest there. As historian Stanley Ross noted, "The capital became a showplace, a solid and silent testimony to the greatness of the Mexican leader who had accomplished so much."[281]

During the first half of the nineteenth century, the Church had foreclosed on numerous homes of those who had lost fortunes, leaving the Church as the owner of half of the city's buildings. In the late 1850s, the Reform laws placed Church-owned buildings on the market. Just as liberal planners had hoped, some 9,000 new property owners emerged. These new owners, however, sought profit, not architectural preservation. Many colonial buildings, such as such as the monastery of San Francisco, were destroyed, as were magnificent colonial homes. These colonial masterpieces were leveled so that streets could be extended or the land on which they stood sold to speculators. Destroying colonial buildings in the name of progress became practically synonymous with public service, as one writer noted in *El Imparcial*:

> In the name of progress, it is necessary to destroy these ancient mansions of counts and marquises, those manorial homes which display shields and coats of arms on their outside walls, those "palaces" with wide corridors and magnificent patios which were praised by the famous Baron Humboldt in his *Political Essay on the Kingdom of New Spain.* These homes and palaces, which date back to the first two centuries of the Spanish colony, must inevitably cede their place to modern four- and five-story buildings with steel frames and showy facades, true labyrinths of residential rooms, stairways, passages, elevators, and commercial offices, which replace sun-filled patios in deference to the square meter, whose value we are only now beginning to realize.[282]

While Mexico City was modernizing and its elite was moving west, the city's poor and urban workers formed a crescent to the north, east, and south of the old colonial center. The urbanized area east of the Zócalo doubled between 1880 and 1900, as its population grew many times over. At least a dozen distinct barrios (neighborhoods), each with its own market, church, and residential identity, formed the eastern part of the city. Within each of these barrios, sprawling warrens of adobe huts, wooden shacks, and one-story brick tenements housed the city's labor force. Observers frequently commented that rather than appearing as part of a world-class city, the eastern barrios were simply a Mexican village writ large.[283]

Residents in the eastern barrios faced a different reality from those in the west. A survey of one working class district at the turn of the century found 2,550 rooms with 18,523 residents, an average of seven per room. Some tenements packed as many as twenty into a room. The east was home to servants, laborers, peddlers, and innumerable one-room shops manufacturing items such as hats, coffins, matches, chairs, glue, and soap. The eastern barrios lacked sewers and potable water. Open drainage ditches ran alongside cramped, poorly ventilated, shoddy tenements—most of which violated the unenforced building code. As a result, in the easternmost districts, mortality rates exceeded those of Cairo or Madras.[284]

In the late nineteenth century, Mexico City emerged as a major industrial center. Previously factories had been located near sources of water power. The introduction of electricity allowed factories to be located near available labor and their largest market. The number of factory workers in the city rose from 2,000 in 1895 to 10,000 in 1910. At the end of the Porfiriato, Mexico City was also home to 18,000 skilled construction workers and 6,700 tramway employees.[285]

In 1899, the English firm of S. Pearson & Son received a £2 million contract to alleviate flooding. The project included a system of channels to collect sewage and storm run-off. These channels drained into a great canal that carried the run-off thirty miles to the north. The canal, whose depth varied from sixteen to seventy-two feet, required the excavation of 16 million cubic yards of earth. At the north end of the canal, a six-mile long tunnel allowed the collected water to drain into the Tula River basin.[286]

The canal and tunnel drained six square miles of lake, which had been created after lava had sealed the valley some two million years earlier. The successful completion of the project greatly alleviated flooding and was heralded as a symbol of Mexican modernity. However, lake drainage produced several unforeseen results. The indigenous waterfront culture along the lake shores disappeared. There was a great reduction in the number of water fowl. As sediment under the city dried out, it contracted. The dried lakebeds became an enormous salt flat, above which clouds of dust swirled. During the twentieth century, Mexico City expanded east into the area that had been drained by the canal.[287]

Due to improved transportation and communication, during the Porfiriato, Mexico City dominated Mexico as never before. In 1856, Mexico City's population was 185,000, or 2.4 percent of the national population. By 1910, it had risen to 471,066, or 3.1 percent of national population. The city's footprint expanded from three square miles in 1858 to more than fifteen square miles in 1910.[288]

Despite its rapid growth, Mexico City had ceased to be the largest city in the Americas well before the end of the nineteenth century. By 1900, Buenos Aires had 756,000 inhabitants, a sixth of Argentina's population. New York and Rio de Janeiro had also surpassed Mexico City in population. In the late nineteenth century, these cities grew even more rapidly than Mexico's capital since they handled voluminous ocean shipping and provided an entryway for millions of European immigrants.[289]

As the centennial of Hidalgo's Cry of Dolores approached, Mexico City began to preen itself for a huge celebration to commemorate the event and enhance Mexico's image as a strong, stable nation deserving international recognition. For a decade, the federal and municipal governments spent huge sums rebuilding downtown Mexico City, including paving streets, renovating the municipal palace, and constructing new buildings. As the centennial approached, uniforms were put on the city street sweepers and trash haulers, and police cleared those deemed undesirable out of the town center.[290]

Nearly every country that maintained diplomatic relations with Mexico sent special envoys to witness the banquets, patriotic ceremonies, garden parties, outdoor festivals, and parades staged in honor of the centennial. Spain even returned the sword and uniform of Morelos, who had died before a Spanish firing squad. The event was almost as much a tribute to Díaz as it was to Mexico.[291]

During the September 1910 centennial celebration, optimism infused the city, and the Porfiriato appeared destined to continue well into the future. The following December, German envoy Karl Bünz expressed that feeling, "I consider general revolution to be out of the question as does public opinion and the press."[292]

THE INTELLECTUAL SCENE

In their efforts to reduce the influence of the Church, liberals often destroyed functioning institutions without offering any replacement. Liberals closed what had been known as the Royal and Pontifical University in 1833, 1857, and 1861, since they considered it a bastion of clericalism. Conservatives would reopen it when they took power.[293]

The University remained closed from the 1860s until 1910. In that year, it reopened as the National University with 1,969 students, combining museums, libraries, a graduate school, the National Preparatory School, and the existing schools of law, medicine, engineering, and architecture. The reopening of the University was heralded as a sign of Mexico's entrance into the modern world.[294]

During the nineteenth century, rather than being a vehicle for providing news, the Mexican press served as a means for Mexico's intellectual elite to express itself on political and philosophical matters. Politicians and intellectuals did not view newspapers supporting rivals as institutions exercising freedom of the press but as political rivals that, in one way or another, had to be neutralized.[295]

Following a brief press renaissance during the restored republic, Díaz began to either punish or reward newspapers, depending on the coverage he received. A writer could be jailed and a newspaper closed for even the mildest criticism of his regime. Newspaperman Filomeno Mata was jailed thirty-four times. Of course, the fact that Mata survived so many terms in jail indicates that the Díaz regime was not as brutal as others that would follow in Latin America.[296]

Díaz's approach to the press was sometimes more subtle than merely jailing writers and raiding print shops. Papers providing favorable coverage, such as *El Universal*, received subsidies of as much as 70,000 pesos a year. Writers who praised the regime often received well-paying jobs. Eventually, massive subsidies to pro-Díaz papers made financial survival for those not receiving subsidies difficult, if not impossible.[297]

Journalists responded to the dictatorship in a variety of ways. Some, such as Filomena Mata, doggedly continued to criticize and be jailed. Some writers published under pseudonyms. The political cartoon flourished, since much could be alluded to in pictures that could not be explicitly stated.[298]

Justo Sierra (1848–1912) was perhaps the Porfiriato's most influential man of letters. His prolific work included poetry, literature, essays, plays, and history. In typical Latin American fashion, he played a major role in government, serving as secretary of public instruction and fine arts. He believed virtually all people, including Indians, could be educated and that without effective, free, compulsory education, corruption and tyranny would prevail.[299]

Sierra become something of an in-house historian for the Porfiriato and promoted the notion that liberalism was the equivalent of the Mexican nation and that conservatism and Catholicism had become somewhat irrelevant, discredited, dead-end branches of the Mexican family tree. The last sentence of Sierra's best known work, *The Political Evolution of the Mexican People,* indicates that he did not entirely buy into official dictum, "Mexican social evolution will have been wholly abortive and futile unless it attains the final goal: liberty."[300]

Another important commentator was Andrés Molina Enríquez, who is best known for his *Los grandes problemas nacionales (The Great National Problems),* which was probably the second most important book of the Porfiriato (after Madero's *Presidential Succession* in 1910). In this book, he anticipated various post-revolutionary points of view. He viewed the Mexican mestizo as a new race, endowed with its own character and inner force. He noted that the low wages Mexican workers received would not create a vibrant domestic market and that the reliance on exports exposed Mexico to boom-and-bust cycles. He anticipated the land reform by calling for widespread government-mandated changes in the Mexico's land ownership. Molina Enríquez even warned that the concentration of wealth, especially concentrated land ownership, could lead to violence if not remedied.[301]

Through the end of the Porfiriato, Mexican literature continued to be torn between dealing with local themes and aping the European. While elite tastes remained staunchly pro-European, the authentically Mexican occasionally emerged. Manuel Altamirano (1834–1895) addressed the search for Mexico's literary roots. Altamirano was born to Indian parents in Guerrero and up until the age fifteen he did not speak Spanish. He was one of the fortunate few Indians who could continue his education, thanks to his having won a scholarship to the Scientific and Literary Academy in Toluca, where he studied Spanish, Latin, and French.

In 1869, after serving in the War of Reform and fighting Maximilian, Altamirano founded *El Renacimiento*, a literary journal that attempted to foster cordiality between writers of various ideological backgrounds in a conscious search for a national culture. He remarked that Mexico had

Figure 12.6
Posada's drawing of Porfirio Díaz

Source: Reproduced courtesy of the Benson Latin American Collection, the University of Texas at Austin

"still not heard the Cry of Dolores" in her literature and commented: "The cult of the virgin is the only thing which unites us. If we lose it, we will lose our Mexican nationality." Altamirano served in Congress and wrote two celebrated novels dealing with Mexican themes, *Clemencia* (1869) and *El Zarco* (1888). In *Clemencia*, a dark skinned protagonist emerged as a hero, while the Creole character was flawed—a daring literary statement for the day.[302]

A few Mexican painters, such as José María Velasco (1840–1919), broke with convention and painted typically Mexican themes. Velasco, who specialized in magnificent landscapes of the Valley of Mexico, is considered to be Mexico's most important nineteenth-century artist. He left a strong artistic legacy and, as an instructor at the San Carlos Fine Arts Academy, taught Diego Rivera.[303]

Artist José Guadalupe Posada (1852–1913) also concentrated on typically Mexican themes. As the son of a baker in Aguascalientes, Posada never formally studied graphic design. He simply apprenticed himself in a lithography shop at age sixteen. In 1888, he moved to Mexico City, where he soon began to work for a broadsheet publisher, at a time when the publication of broadsheets flourished.

Posada became one of the most prolific artists in history. His plates number in the thousands and encompass chapbook covers, cartoons, announcements, newspaper and magazine mastheads, and even cigar box lids. His illustrations often accompanied the printed text of a narrative ballad (*corrido*), which might deal with a cockfight, a stabbing, or a merciful intervention of the Virgin of Guadalupe. He was so typically working class and his themes so Mexican that he was ignored by the city dandies and established artists. When he died in 1913, he was buried in a pauper's grave by his neighbors, only one of whom could sign his own name.[304]

Mexican leaders had long paid lip service to education. However, only during the Porfiriato did mass education become a reality. Between 1878 and 1907, primary school enrollment increased from 141,178 to 657,843. In 1910, Mexico's 21,017 teachers outnumbered doctors, lawyers, and priests combined. Between 1878 and 1910, states increased their education spending from 10.52 percent of their budgets to 23.08 percent, making education the largest budget item. Outstanding students in rural areas received scholarships to be trained as teachers. As a result of the increased emphasis on education, between 1895 and 1910 literacy increased by 37 percent.[305]

Despite such increases, the educational effort fell far short of what was needed to sustain economic growth. In part, this resulted from the government having broken what it considered a "clerical monopoly" on education. However, after largely forcing the Church out of education, the government failed to fill the vacuum. The rural and urban poor had little opportunity to attend school at all. The educational opportunities that did exist were highly truncated. In 1910, the state of Puebla had 1,091 schools offering grades one to four, but only one offering grades five and six. The lack of funding remained as a permanent obstacle to expanding the school system. In 1884, when the Puebla legislature attempted to force *hacendados* to finance schools on their haciendas, they protested that such utopian plans could be afforded only by those landlords who owned estates "the size of certain independent nations of Europe."[306]

Educational spending strongly favored the already educated. In 1900, the government spent twenty centavos per primary school student, 105 pesos per secondary student, and 126 pesos for each person enrolled in higher education. Such spending provided a sizable government subsidy for the few who could afford to remain in school for an extended period. In additional to attending publicly funded institutions of higher education, the elite used private schools to maintain its social position from one generation to another.[307]

While teachers outnumbered other professionals, their status and wages lagged behind considerably. Teachers' wages barely exceeded those of factory workers and hacienda day-laborers. Not surprisingly, scores of teachers became leaders in the Revolution, including future presidents Álvaro Obregón and Plutarco Elías Calles, as well as Otilio Montaño, who helped Emiliano Zapata draft the Plan de Ayala in 1911.[308]

Chapter 13

Plunging into the International Market, 1856–1909

> Where the Bourbon boom depended upon Spanish demand for bullion, coupled with Mexican demographic growth, the Porfirian boom derived from the far more potent stimuli of a global—though primarily North American—industrial economy, richly endowed with capital and technology and greedy for industrial raw materials and consumer goods.
>
> Alan Knight, 1998[1]

BREAKING WITH THE PAST

The victory over Maximilian did not automatically lead to economic development as the liberals had hoped. Mexican society remained very traditional, with 61 percent of its workers employed in agriculture and mining. Some 64,000 artisans dominated manufacturing. Church wealth, which liberals had hoped would provide a stimulus to the economy once it was transferred to private hands, had been largely dissipated by war.[2]

The restored republic faced many of the same economic obstacles Mexico had faced earlier in the century. Mexican entrepreneurs were lacking, especially those devoted to technological change and long-term growth. Forced loans, banditry, and property destruction continued to deter investment. Finally the appalling transportation system prevented the creation of integrated markets. Austrian Lt. Ernst Pitner, who fought on the French side in the 1860s, commented on the all-important transport route between Mexico City and Veracruz:

> The mud between Orizaba and Córdoba reaches in places to a pedestrian's armpits. Laden mules in large numbers get stuck in it and suffocate. On the route one sees at least twenty such dead animals. At times soldiers with packs had to be pulled out with ropes slung under their arms.[3]

Juárez felt economic development would create a strong state that could defend Mexican interests. Given the lack of local capital to spur development, his administration sought foreign investment. That led to a conundrum—how to attract foreign capital without inviting the foreign intervention that development was designed to prevent.[4]

After the 1820s, British lenders maintained a loan embargo on Mexico due to its bond defaults. Obtaining foreign capital was further complicated when France, Spain, and Great Britain broke diplomatic relations with Mexico after the execution of Maximilian. Almost by default, Mexico turned to the United States for the investment capital Europeans would not provide. In 1873, Ignacio Mariscal, Mexico's ambassador the United States, made this opening explicit:

> It should be clear to any impartial observer that Mexico fervently desires the investment of foreign capital, and especially that of the United States, to develop its wealth and uncover the immense treasures which lie hidden in its valleys and mountains and which await the effort of intelligent industry to be converted into inexhaustible sources of life and wealth.[5]

Throughout Latin America, the elite shared the view that economic development would occur by Latin American nations': 1) exporting commodities, 2) receiving foreign investment, and 3) attracting European immigrants. Before 1880, the Mexican government did not assume an active role in the development process due to the general feeling that development would be almost spontaneous. Even if it had desired to do so, the government's meager budget would not have allowed it to play an active economic role.[6]

When Díaz became president in 1876, the government lacked the resources to buy off regional warlords or to cow them into submission. In the short run, he could not solve his financial problems by raising taxes since the government did not have the administrative structure necessary for effective taxation. In addition, the economy was simply too small to provide much revenue.[7]

Díaz pulled Mexico out of a self-replicating cycle of violence, predation, and zero growth by granting special privileges to certain businessmen. These special privileges, such as protecting bankers from competition and establishing high tariffs on imports competing with Mexican producers, allowed the operations of certain individuals to be so profitable that they assumed the risk of investing in Mexico. Díaz ensured that the property rights of those enjoying his favor were respected. As these privileged individuals prospered, they provided financial and political support for Díaz, enabling him to defeat or buy off his rivals.[8]

After 1880, the Mexican economy began sustained economic growth. U.S. investment began flowing into Mexico, in part due to an effective public relations campaign undertaken by the Mexican government. In 1879, Development Secretary Vicente Riva Palacio arranged for a delegation of U.S. journalists and merchants to visit Mexico at the Mexican government's expense. Díaz and his cabinet received them in a calculated effort to create a favorable impression and thus attract investment. At the world's fairs in 1889 and 1892, the government invested substantial sums to project a modern, positive image of the country.[9]

Increased mining activity became economically feasible due to the construction of railroads to haul ore and metal to foreign markets. These foreign markets were especially buoyant, because the demand for raw materials was soaring as the North Atlantic nations were undergoing rapid industrialization.[10]

Technological change played a major role in the post-1880 economic expansion. Steamships facilitated the export of raw materials and the import of machinery. By 1888, the American-organized Mexican Telegraph Company had installed more than 19,200 miles of telegraph line. Later in the Porfiriato, the introduction of electricity revolutionized the mining and textile industries. Between 1900 and 1911, installed electrical generating capacity increased from 22,430 kilowatts to 165,100 kilowatts. In turn, electricity allowed for streetcars, which made large cities workable. By 1905, Mexico City's 190-mile long streetcar system had an annual ridership of 48,000,000.[11]

After 1880, the government began to play a more active role in promoting development. Under the González administration (1880–1884), for the first time a government agency—the Department of Development (Fomento)—had a larger budget than the War Department had. Legislative changes encouraged investment. The 1884 commercial code paved the way for joint-stock companies (*sociedades anónimas*). This legislation limited investors' liability to the amount invested in the corporation. Until that time, an investor's entire assets were liable in case of corporate loss or damage claims. By 1900, some twenty-five large joint-stock companies operated in the tobacco, textile, brewing, and metallurgy sectors.[12]

The formation of the Banco Nacional de México (Banamex) in 1884 provided the government with access to funds, including money to subsidize the construction of railroads. Díaz allowed those lending to the government to extract benefits from the rest of society. This allowed his administration to avoid paying high interest rates to compensate for the risks of lending to a government with a deeply flawed credit history. To induce it to lend to the government, Banamex was allowed to manage the mint and collect customs and excise taxes. The government protected Banamex by not granting charters to rival banks and allowing it to avoid taxes and reserve requirements imposed on other banks. Only two banks—one of which was Banamex—were allowed to branch freely across state lines. These privileges made it well worth Banamex lending to the government. The bank averaged 30.5 percent profits on equity between 1885 and 1898.[13]

After returning to power in 1884, Díaz established a solid reputation as a friend and protector of investors, and by the dawn of the twentieth century, that image provided a strong inducement for investment. To maintain his investment-friendly image, Díaz offered investors low taxes, liberal concessions, cheap labor, police protection, predictably pro-business judicial rulings, and laws adjusted to the international legal order of the developed countries. This occurred as the home markets of the industrialized nations were becoming saturated, leading to increased export of capital, much of which was invested in Mexico. In 1895, American mine operator Alexander Shepherd proclaimed Díaz to be the greatest man in North America because he had made property "twenty times safer in Mexico than it is in the United States."[14]

Mexico finally put the Maximilian era behind it. By 1884, Spain, France, and Great Britain had restored diplomatic relations with Mexico. After the resumption of diplomatic relations and after having consolidated past debts, Mexico again began to receive foreign loans. A crucial step to obtaining this credit was the government's placing of all its foreign debt operations in the hands of Banamex. The bank, with its influential European and North American financiers, was crucial for gaining the confidence of foreign lenders.[15]

Later in the Porfiriato, banks proliferated. Between 1897 and 1903, twenty-four banking concessions were granted. Unlike Mexican mines and industries of the time, the banks sold stock on the Mexican and European capital markets. Although banks operated under Mexican management, between 60 and 70 percent of the capital invested in them was foreign, with the French being the principal investors.[16]

Banks played a major role in economic development by providing long-term, low-interest financing for cotton-textile factories, metallurgical firms, and railroad companies. Their issuance of banknotes freed commerce from its old bugaboo of lacking a medium of exchange. Between 1882 and 1897, the amount of paper money in circulation increased by 21.5 percent a year.[17]

The banking structure inhibited more robust economic growth. Just two banks, Banamex and the Bank of London and Mexico, held more than 60 percent of banking system assets. Those without connections to the banking elite rarely received loans. Only ten of the forty-seven banks existing in 1911 were legally allowed to lend for terms of more than one year.[18]

By the beginning of the twentieth century, Mexico was inexorably linked to U.S. and world markets. When the 1907 recession hit the United States, the *Commercial and Financial Chronicle*, a Wall Street paper, declared, "Of course Mexico could not escape being affected by business depression in the United States." The price of silver and copper fell, mine production declined, and mine workers were laid off. Since mines and railroads were the main consumers of manufactured goods, recession rippled through the Mexican economy. Between 1900 and 1910, the proportion of the population working in agriculture rose, as those forced out of mines and factories returned to the farm. The 1907 recession even brought down the financially overextended Colonel Greene, who lost control of his Cananea mines, which were valued at $25 million.[19]

The 1907 recession notwithstanding, the elite expressed satisfaction with the course of Mexican development. Mexico was enjoying low-cost credit as Treasury Secretary José Limantour had balanced the budget and renegotiated Mexico's foreign debt. Also under Limantour, the *alcabala,* a form of internal tariff, was abolished, facilitating the creation of a national market. The heavy reliance on foreign investment, which increased from $200 million at the beginning of the Porfiriato to between $1.5 billion and $2 billion at its end, was seen as a transitory stage. In 1905, Limantour told Congress:

> The day will come, as has been exemplified by the history of other modern nations, when the population, increased by the multiplication of the means of livelihood and trained in more

> laborious habits, will by degrees redeem itself from indebtedness, and when that happens, the bonds, shares, and other securities of our most flourishing enterprises will be held at home and will not be allowed again to leave the country.[20]

In sharp contrast to the period before 1870, during the Porfiriato Mexican economic growth exceeded that of the United States. In 1870, Mexican gross domestic product (GDP) per capita was 27.6 percent of that of the United States. By 1910, it had risen to 34.1 percent.[21]

RAILROADS

> Railroad construction did not take off until the Porfirian state seized the initiative by providing hefty subventions to encourage British and U.S. investment and by promoting the development of the North.
>
> Allen Wells, 2000[22]

During the nineteenth century, the railroad occupied the same position that steel plants would occupy in the twentieth—it symbolized a better tomorrow. Rail fever swept over Mexico. In 1881, the *Diario Oficial* noted that it "was indeed with the greatest of enthusiasm that, in all sections of the country, the building of the railroads is being prosecuted."[23]

For some, building railroads was practically a matter of faith. For others, it became the way to accumulate wealth. Bankers realized they could profit from the sale of securities and from lending for the purchase of railway equipment. Merchants and landowners favored the railroad because it would facilitate the production of commodities. For politicians, the railroad represented a way to increase the power of the state and win the support of constituencies via recourse to the pork barrel. The railroad also contributed to politicians' personal wealth. For example, Manuel Romero Ancona, the governor of Yucatán between 1878 and 1881, found no conflict of interest when he granted concessions to two of the state's rail lines and then served on their boards of directors.[24]

Throughout the Porfiriato, festivities accompanied the opening of a rail line. In 1892, Oaxacan businessmen raised 40,000 pesos for a fiesta to celebrate the driving of the last spike on the line to their city. President Díaz, Interior Secretary Manuel Romero Rubio, the British contractors, and a carload of newsmen traveled to Oaxaca City for the inauguration ceremonies. In 1907, an even more elaborate inaugural bash celebrated the opening of the rebuilt Tehuantepec Railroad. Four special trains carried guests, including Díaz, three state governors, ambassadors, and other diplomatic representatives. The event received national and international coverage from newsmen, who were provided with their own special train.[25]

While virtually all policy makers favored railroads, heated debate erupted concerning questions raised by rail construction. Many Mexicans warned that if rail lines connected the United States and Mexico, Mexico would be overwhelmed by the Colossus of the North. In 1878, Deputy Alfredo Chavero argued eloquently in Congress against building rail lines to Mexico's northern border:

> You, the deputies of the States, would you exchange your beautiful and poor liberty of the present for the rich subjection which the railroad could give you? Go and propose to the lion of the desert to exchange his cave of rocks for a golden cage, and the lion of the desert will reply to you with a roar of liberty.[26]

President Lerdo de Tejada initially shared this fear of being overwhelmed by the United States. Eventually, though, he concluded that rail links to the United States would lead to economic expansion in Mexico, which, in turn, would provide the strength to resist the United States.[27]

Table 13.1 *Miles of railroad in Mexico, 1870–1910*

Year	Number of miles
1870	259
1880	666
1890	5,917
1900	8,441
1910	11,954

Source: Summerhill (2006: 302)

Paying for railroad construction provided the political elite with a conundrum. After the fall of Maximilian, Juárez promised the Imperial Railroad Company, Ltd. a 560,000-peso annual subsidy, agreed to purchase 3.7 million pesos of the company stock, granted the company the right to import material duty free, and exempted it from numerous taxes so it would continue construction of the Veracruz–Mexico City line. To avoid any delay in the construction of the railroad, Juárez made an exception to his policy of canceling all concessions granted by Maximilian. The British-managed Imperial Railroad Company, which had received its initial concession from the emperor, was allowed to continue construction.[28]

Subsequent administrations turned to domestic sources of financing after concluding that allowing foreigners to build railroads would inordinately increase their influence in Mexico. During Díaz's first administration, the federal government built thirty-one miles of line, but then ran out of resources. President González also attempted federally financed rail construction, but could only muster funds to build twenty-four miles of line.[29]

The federal government encouraged states to build rail lines. Between 1877 and 1880, states received twenty-eight concessions to build rail lines. However, the only significant construction occurred in Morelos and Guanajuato, where a total of ninety-two miles of track was laid.[30]

The Mexican private sector proved equally incapable of carrying out railroad construction. Between 1860 and 1880 eleven concessions were awarded to private Mexican interests to build railroads. Only one, in Hidalgo, was completed. Despite attempts to raise money through such novel means as a lottery, the capital and managerial requirements of rail construction overwhelmed Mexican builders, private and public.[31]

By the end of Díaz's first term, it had become apparent that if Mexico was to have railroads within the near future, foreign interests would build them. To entice foreigners to build railroads the government had to ensure construction in Mexico was more attractive than in Cuba, Argentina, or the United States, which were rapidly expanding their rail networks. The government attracted foreign rail companies by offering subsidies that ultimately paid a quarter to a third of construction costs. As one of his last acts during his first term, Díaz granted the U.S.-owned Central Railroad Company a concession to build a rail line connecting Mexico City with El Paso, Texas. The concession included a subsidy of 7,000 pesos per kilometer of track completed. In addition to cash subsidies, rail builders were promised bonds, generous land grants, and certificates that could be used to pay customs duties.[32]

Since Mexicans could not finance rail building and Europeans were reluctant to invest in Mexico, the United States supplied 80 percent of the capital used to build Mexico's major railroads. By 1883, the Central Railroad Company was employing 22,000 workers in rail construction. Employing such large numbers of workers on projects before they began to yield revenue required access to vast financial resources. The amount required exceeded the resources of individual U.S. companies. The Central Railroad and the National, which received the concession to link Mexico City and Laredo, Texas, sold shares on the Boston and New York exchanges to raise capital. When funds raised there proved insufficient, they turned to the London exchange. The government paid roughly 40 percent of the construction costs of the Central Line.[33]

The use of foreign capital permitted the more rapid development of railroads and allowed Mexicans to invest their scarce capital in other areas. Sometimes the generous subsidies promised by the government remained unpaid, because in times of financial crisis the amount pledged exceeded available funds.[34]

Once the decision had been made to allow foreigners a dominant role in rail construction, rail mileage soared. When Díaz first took office, Mexico had only 416 miles of track. In 1884, Mexico City was connected with El Paso, Texas, amid predictions that the new line would stimulate the Mexican economy and open new markets for U.S. products. By 1910, rail mileage had soared to 11,954 as political stability and generous government subsidies attracted foreign capital and innovations in metal production (such as the Bessemer process) reduced the cost of steel.[35]

Between 1878 and 1910, the railroad produced an 80 percent decrease in freight costs. Thanks to the railroad, the cost of shipping a ton of cotton goods from Mexico City to Querétaro declined from $61 to $3 between 1877 and 1910.[36]

While the cost of transport plunged because of the railroad, setting rail rates would have challenged Solomon. Since the first Veracruz–Mexico City rail line had a monopoly, it charged almost much as muleteers did. The British consul candidly observed that a railway "that could be beaten in point of cheapness by pack animals is naturally not the railway to develop a country."[37]

Even though rival U.S. interests owned the rail lines connecting Mexico City with the U.S. border, Limantour feared that cut-throat competition would lead to bankruptcy. That would hurt Mexico's image and allow Mexico's railroads to fall into the hands of unscrupulous foreign financiers. As a result, in a nationalistic move more commonly associated with post-revolutionary governments, the government began to purchase shares of foreign-owned rail companies. In 1908, the journal *El Economista Mexicano* observed, "If the state does not exercise control over the railroads, the railroads will exercise control over the state." Due to the railroads' financial weakness, it would have been easy for a single owner to take them over. Limantour's fears were well founded, since rail monopolization had already resulted in ruinous rate increases in the United States.[38]

Limantour borrowed in France to obtain the funds he used to purchase rail shares. In 1908, he formed a government-owned rail company that controlled two-thirds of the nation's rail system, including the all-important Central and National lines leading to the United States. The partnership of Scherer-Limantour Banking House purchased the shares and then sold them to the government at a profit. Limantour's brother served as a partner in the firm and both the secretary and his brother were among the firm's chief stockholders.[39]

The railroad had a profound social impact. In 1910, in a nation of 12 million, 15.8 million rail passengers were transported more than 1 billion kilometers. Many of these travelers used the railroad to relocate from central to northern Mexico. Travel time between Veracruz and Mexico City decreased from days to thirteen hours. A special train allowed Puebla residents to leave for Mexico City in the morning, shop or transact business in the capital, and return home for a late dinner.[40]

Only with the coming of the railroad did Mexico regain the degree of economic integration that it had enjoyed in 1800. Although railroads were largely foreign-built, they did link most inhabited regions, crossed the best agricultural districts, and reached the richest mineral deposits. The railroad's linking of different areas not only allowed shipment of agricultural surplus from one area to another but also created a synergistic effect. New firms created new demand and new products. To supply railroad builders, Monterrey's steel mills produced rails. In northern Mexico, coal mines supplied locomotive fuel, and ranches expanded so they could supply the U.S. market. As a result, between 1883 and 1911, rail freight increased at an average annual rate of more than 10 percent.[41]

The railroad facilitated the expansion of the mining industry. Without rail service it would not have been economically feasible to mine metals such as copper, zinc, and lead. Since the rail system linked most major urban areas and agricultural, mining, and industrial centers, it provided a powerful stimulus to the domestic economy. As a result, the railroad's greatest impact was local. Between 1898 and 1905, less than 2.5 percent of total rail cargo went to the United States.[42]

Figure 13.1 *Native people leaving a train at Amecameca, Mexico, 1907, by Sumner Matteson*

Source: Reproduced courtesy of the Science Museum of Minnesota, photo #A 84: 16: 29

The railroad allowed cattle and crops, such as cotton, tobacco, and henequen, to be shipped to distant markets. It also allowed the development of previously underutilized regions. In 1884, Navojoa, in the agricultural heart of Sonora, had a population of 1,344. After the arrival of the Southern Pacific Railroad, its population jumped to 10,822, as growers began shipping their produce out by rail. In 1884, the Laguna region, on the Coahuila–Durango border, shipped less than 5,000 tons of cotton. In 1901, the railroad hauled more than 120,000 tons of cotton from there, mainly to mills in central Mexico.[43]

The impact of railroads rippled throughout the areas they served. Historian Allen Wells described the impact of the railroad on Yucatán:

> Property values skyrocketed; large landholdings were concentrated near railway lines; imported goods—grains, manufactured wares, and luxury items—flooded local markets; and migration within the peninsula exploded as *campesinos* took advantage of the railroad to seek employment in the burgeoning state capital, Mérida, and in the principal port, Progreso.[44]

The railroad would have had even greater economic impact if Mexican industry had been able to supply the construction material and rolling stock used. Mexico not only imported rail cars, locomotives, air brakes, and telegraph equipment but even rails and wood and coal for fuel. In 1910, 57 percent of gross railroad revenue left Mexico to pay for railroad equipment, consumer goods for railroad personnel, skilled foreign supervisors and engineers, profits, and interest on loans. Finally, rather than strengthening financial institutions as they did in the United States and Europe, railroad builders in Mexico largely ignored local banks and turned to foreign capital.[45]

Cities benefited from the railroad, as their residents could enjoy inexpensive agricultural goods produced in distant areas. Owners of large estates and factory producers also benefited as they could dominate large markets. Before the coming of the railroad, if agricultural capacity exceeded local needs, it could not be used. The United States also benefited, since the railroad shifted Mexico from a dependence on European goods to a dependence on U.S. goods. Innumerable other Mexicans benefited by being employed in endeavors that would not have existed without the railroad.[46]

Small farmers and artisans often suffered as the railroad led to ruinous competition with large-scale producers. Preferential shipping rates for exporters and high-volume shippers put the small producer at an even greater disadvantage. In the 1880s and 1890s, as marketing opportunities provided by the railroad led to an increase in cash crops, many subsistence farmers were forced off the land they had occupied. Some cities and regions lost out as trade patterns changed. Guaymas was displaced as the main supplier of imports to Sonora after rail lines connected the state to the United States via Nogales. In the 1870s, Tampico suffered economic collapse due to competition provided by the opening of the Veracruz–Mexico City line. In 1890, the city enjoyed an economic revival after rail service was established. This allowed the transshipment of European coal to foundries in Aguascalientes, San Luis Potosí, and Monterrey.[47]

Railroads consumed enormous amounts of wood for station construction, ties, bridges, posts, and fuel. An 1880 circular published by the Secretariat of Development reported that forest destruction had caused erosion, climate change, air pollution, increased flooding, the drying up of springs, and the loss of agricultural land.[48]

FOREIGN TRADE

> Too often the expansion of the export sector was achieved on the back of the rural poor, at the expense of traditional landholding arrangements, and was dominated by foreign capital. The social dislocations and resentment were severe and widespread.
>
> Edward Beatty, 2000[49]

Several factors contributed to the dramatic increase in Mexico's foreign trade during the Porfiriato. The booming North Atlantic economies drew in raw materials to manufacture a wide range of new goods, including electrical machinery, chemical dyes, and vehicles with internal combustion engines. The demand for raw materials continued to increase as the rising population of the industrialized nations led to ever increasing consumption.[50]

Mexican exports increased as transport improved. Between 1815 and 1900, freight rates for shipping commodities across the Atlantic declined almost 95 percent due to innovations such as the screw propeller, the compound engine, steel hulls, larger ship size, and shorter turn-around time in port. The port of Veracruz was modernized to facilitate trade with Europe, thus offsetting U.S. influence, which was increasing as a result of the railroad.[51]

The mines of northern Mexico exported to the United States by rail. Products such as coffee and vanilla from southeastern Mexico were distributed to U.S. and European buyers. Although exports were more varied than in colonial times, precious metals continued to dominate. In 1913, 75.2 percent of Mexican exports went to the United States, followed by the United Kingdom, which absorbed 13.5 percent.[52]

Increased exports generated revenue that was shared by merchants, bankers, landowners, the urban middle class, and especially, the government. Export revenue partially financed rail construction and increased the capacity of the government, allowing it to promote industrialization.[53]

Export revenue also enabled Mexicans to import on a massive scale. The import trade was dominated by immigrants whose success was based on: 1) their foreign contacts, especially in their country of origin, 2) the necessary social contacts and strategic marriages in Mexico, and 3) political contacts, which permitted them to obtain permits and favorable legislation. German merchants took advantage of the rupture in diplomatic relations between Mexico and Spain,

Table 13.2 *Composition of Mexican exports, 1880–1910, by value*

Type of goods	Percentage of total exports
Gold and silver	65
Coffee, henequen, precious woods, tobacco, and vanilla	20
Animal products	10
Manufactured goods	5

Source: INEGI (1994: 785–86)

France, and Great Britain and began importing goods into Mexico. By 1878, Hanseatics controlled two-thirds of Mexico's foreign trade. With the completion of rail links to the United States, Americans quickly became the major force in foreign commerce, especially in northern Mexico.[54]

International, national, and regional elites concurred in orienting Mexico's economy towards the export of minerals and agricultural raw materials. The assumption prevailed that in some ill-defined fashion export growth would enhance productivity and lead to structural change throughout the economy. Little consideration was given to just how the rest of the economy would be transformed, even though the domestic sector produced far more and employed far more people than the export sector.[55]

Government officials favored exports since export taxes on silver, gold, and copper formed an important element of public finance. Revenue earned by exports allowed the purchase of imports, which then could be subjected to a tariff, providing another politically acceptable source of government revenue. At the turn of the century, customs revenue provided 44 percent of government income.[56]

Mexico experienced positive trade balances every year from 1892 to 1910. In the heyday of Mexico's export growth—1890 to 1912—Mexico's exports increased at an annual rate of 5.2 percent. If this rate had been sustained, Mexico's economy would have been transformed. The pre-First World War experience of other Latin American nations indicates that exports led to economic growth. Those nations that exported had the highest rate of per capita economic growth. Those that failed to export failed to grow.[57]

During the Porfiriato, foreign trade played an ever increasing role in Mexican development. In 1860, the sum of exports and imports equaled only 9.8 percent of GDP. This figure increased to 18.6 percent in 1888 and 30.5 percent by 1910.[58]

MINING

After the War of Reform and the French intervention, mines were again flooded, labor had dispersed, and investors were lacking. As late as 1884, mining remained at a virtual standstill. American companies were working only forty mining concessions. The British had become so disillusioned that they had largely withdrawn from mining.[59]

By 1904, miners were working 13,696 active concessions that covered 552,534 acres. Silver exports, a third of all exports, increased from 607,000 kilograms in 1877–1878 to 2.3 million in 1910–1911. Gold, a sixth of exports, rose from 1,000 to 37,100 kilograms during the same period. In 1911, Mexican mines produced 32 percent of the world's silver, 11 percent of its lead, and 7 percent of its copper.[60]

This boom in mining combined all the elements that led to rapid economic growth in other sectors. Before 1884, all mineral wealth belonged to the nation. Those wishing to begin mining were required to obtain government permission. Government control over minerals represented a continuation of the colonial tradition. The national government simply claimed ownership of the mineral wealth that had belonged to the Crown in colonial times.[61]

The Mining Law of 1884 law allowed private ownership of subsoil wealth—ownership rights that were separate from those of the surface owner. An 1892 law allowed miners to claim as much land as they could pay taxes on and to open or close mines as they saw fit. As a result of these laws, which followed the U.S. model, not only was the right to exploit mineral wealth granted to private individuals but it could also be sold on the open market independently of the ownership of the surface property.[62]

British investors returned to Mexico, drawn by this legislation, as well as political stability and favorable publicity in England. Americans invested even more, especially in the north. By 1902, Sonora had become Mexico's most prosperous state and received more U.S. mining investment—$27.8 million—than any other state. By 1910, U.S. mine investment totaled $200 million, while the British had $50 million invested.[63]

The introduction of electricity into the mines produced huge savings in hoisting, drilling, and illumination. Electricity permitted the use of winches, hoists, electric locomotives, and pneumatic drills. As historian Marvin Bernstein noted, "Peons no longer had to carry 200-pound loads up ladders in suffocating temperatures; hoists did the lifting and ventilating fans could make the mines more livable."[64]

The use of cyanide revolutionized the refining of silver ore. To extract the silver, ore was crushed to a powder and then mixed with water and cyanide. The silver bonded with the cyanide. Then zinc was added to the mixture, causing the silver to precipitate out. The use of cyanide permitted the recovery of as much as 92 percent of the silver contained in the ore, compared to 60 percent with the patio process. It also made it economically feasible to mine ores with a lower silver content and to rework previously accumulated mine tailings that still contained substantial amounts of silver. This new refining technique, which almost entirely replaced the patio process, reduced costs and processing time.[65]

Although cyanide did not last long in the environment, its short-term impact could be disastrous. Mining journals frequently discussed cyanide poisoning of miners. The American-owned El Rey del Oro Mining Company discharged waste near the town of Mulatos, Sonora, causing the death of cattle that drank the water. The village mayor filed a complaint with the superintendent of the mine. When the superintendent failed to respond to the complaint, the mayor ordered the company to either shut down or build a pipeline so the poison would at least be discharged downstream from the town. In response, the mine owners visited Sonora's governor, who overruled the mayor and allowed the mine to continue operating and discharging waste in the same way as before.[66]

As the world industrialized, a shift occurred in the metals mined in Mexico. Electrification worldwide produced a tremendous increase in the demand for copper. Between 1891 and 1905, Mexican copper production increased more than eleven-fold, not only providing increased exports but also copper for Mexican electrification. Industrialization also increased the demand for lead, whose production more than tripled during this same period.[67]

In 1910, mining produced 8.4 percent of the GDP, roughly what it had produced at the end of the colonial period. At its peak, the industry employed 126,900 miners.[68]

Mines increased demand for domestically produced lumber, leather, food, explosives, tools, and structural iron and steel. However, several factors limited the impact of mining on the rest of the economy. Much of the machinery and other mine inputs was imported, especially in the states adjoining the U.S. border, where 75 percent of mining occurred. At the Cananea mine, technology, capital, and daily supplies came from the United States, and the entire product was exported there. Foreign mine owners often sent profits out of Mexico rather than reinvesting them locally. Since most of the minerals were exported, no further jobs were created in processing and converting minerals into manufactured items. Finally, due to decreased world demand and increased production, the price of silver steadily declined during the Porfiriato. As a result, miners had to produce ever-increasing amounts of silver just to maintain the same income.[69]

Increased mining led to increased deforestation. In 1865, a member of the scientific commission of Pachuca, Hidalgo, commented that "the axe of the woodcutter has become a terrible enemy of these forests." He noted that the Real del Monte Mining Company caused the most deforestation and that, as a result, springs were drying up. Later, the mining boom in Sonora produced wholesale deforestation, which led to desertification. Sonoran mining also left the countryside dotted with mountains of mine waste and allowed the toxic chemicals used to process ores to seep into aquifers.[70]

INDUSTRIALIZATION

> Before 1870 markets were still too small, the energy supply too unreliable, and transport costs too high to permit more than a handful of large-scale factories to be built to serve the home market.
>
> Victor Bulmer-Thomas, 1994[71]

In 1862, there were more than 20,000 artisan shops in Mexico, while only 207 factories operated. Toward the end of the nineteenth century, artisan production began to decline as railroads brought inexpensive imports into the Mexican interior and Mexican factories began production. Few artisan shops evolved into modern factories since their owners lacked access to capital, had little political clout to influence public policy, and often relied on a very limited supply of family labor.[72]

Given the lack of an institutional framework to transfer capital from lenders to borrowers, industrial firms were generally financed by families channeling funds into a new industry from some other existing business, such as commerce. Since immigrant families dominated large-scale commerce, they financed much of Mexico's early industry by reinvesting commercial profits.[73]

To stimulate industrial investment, entrepreneurs received tax exemptions, federal subsidies, production monopolies, and protective tariffs. Between 1893 and 1911, Limantour rewarded industrialists who supported Díaz by setting high import tariffs on products they produced, while everyone else was left out in the cold. Since those who benefited from these inducements faced no competition, their profit rate was unusually high. Thanks to protective tariffs, domestic manufacturing expanded just as foreign manufacturers were most aggressively pursuing Mexican markets.[74]

In the 1880s, tariffs were repeatedly reduced on certain raw materials, while duties were increased on such products as textiles, beer, cement, and iron and steel to encourage their production in Mexico. Several other factors favored industrialization. Displaced artisans and agricultural laborers provided an abundant supply of inexpensive labor. Railroads allowed factory-produced goods to be distributed nationwide. As the value of the silver-based Mexican peso declined relative to the gold-based North Atlantic currencies, imports cost more, thus encouraging domestic production. Finally, between 1877 and 1900, industry benefited from the introduction of new manufacturing technology and steam and hydroelectric power.[75]

Between 1895 and 1910, manufacturing increased by 106 percent. During that period, the number of industrial workers only increased from 45,806 to 58,838, indicating an increase in productivity associated with new technology. Consumer-oriented industries produced textiles, beverages, clothing, paper, soap, footwear, and food and tobacco products. Factories produced cement, bricks, paints, chemicals, and iron and steel for use in extractive and manufacturing processes.[76]

Mexican textile factories, which employed 32,147 workers in 1910, were the largest modern enterprises in Mexico. Rail transport made larger mills profitable, and electrically powered looms

Figure 13.2
Cigarette factory

Source: Reproduced courtesy of the Benson Latin American Collection, the University of Texas at Austin

and spindles replaced water powered ones. French investors, who supplied almost 80 percent of the capital in the industry, facilitated this expansion. The expansion of the textile industry did not lead to increased employment since the number of handloom weavers declined from 41,000 to 12,000 between 1895 and 1910.[77]

The textile industry produced inexpensive cotton cloth for Mexico's expanding work force, successfully combining foreign capital, transport, and imported technology. In 1901, it transformed 43,040 tons of cotton into cloth, up from 5,842 tons in 1854. In 1899, 32 percent of the textile products consumed in Mexico were imported, while in 1911, only 3 percent were imported.[78]

During the Porfiriato, as had been the case since colonial times, most industry was located along the axis from Veracruz to Mexico City, where it had access to transportation, markets, political influence, and hydropower. However, by the dawn of the twentieth century, a new industrial center had emerged—Monterrey. The city enjoyed an ideal location for industry, since rail lines linked it with both the United States and central Mexico. Water from the Santa Catarina River and nearby deposits of iron ore and coal enticed industry to locate there. The Nuevo León state government spurred industrialization by granting tax exemptions of up to twenty years for new investments. An impressive financial sector, which developed in the 1890s, financed new industry. In 1901, the city proudly inaugurated La Fundidora de Fierro y Acero, Mexico's first iron and steel mill. Thanks to the Fundadora and other industries, Monterrey received the nickname "the Pittsburgh of Mexico."[79]

Unlike the rest of Mexico, Monterrey's industry largely remained in Mexican hands. In 1900, Mexican capital, much of which came from wealthy commercial families, comprised 80 percent of the city's industrial investments. Isaac Garza (1853–1933), the patriarch of the most prominent of these families, married into the Sada family. In 1891, Garza-Sada interests began producing beer in Monterrey. Within a decade, the brewery workforce increased from fifty to more than 500. In 1899, to supply bottles for their brewery, the Vidriera Monterrey was established. By 1909, this factory was producing 24,000 bottles a day. These firms continued to expand, eventually creating Mexico's most famous industrial empire, which was based on beer, glass, and steel.[80]

Garza-Sada success resulted, in part, from bucking some prevailing trends. Rather than associating with foreign capital, they retained Mexican control, and to demonstrate their patriotism, they named their brewery for Cuauhtémoc. To encourage the training of Mexican technicians, they paid them the same wages foreign technicians received. By 1900, when most other industries remained dependent on foreigners, their entire staff, including brewers, mechanics, and electricians, were Mexicans.[81]

Often, in response to individual influence, the government granted special tax and tariff exemptions, monopoly privileges, and concessions to exploit natural resources. These privileges, granted to individuals, were so valuable that they gave the recipient a virtual monopoly in a given industry, thus discouraging efficiency and preventing competition. In 1902, the *New York Times* reported, "Nearly all of the principal branches of industry in Mexico are now controlled by trusts and combines, the greatest of them being the Guggenheim Exploration Company . . ."[82]

Mexico's lack of energy sources hampered industrialization. Domestic coal and hydropower only partly met industrial energy needs. Some coal was imported. At the very time energy needs were increasing, the supply of wood, the traditional fuel source, was becoming exhausted. It became increasingly costly to bring in wood from ever-greater distances as nearby supplies were exhausted. As historian Fernando Rosenzweig noted: "Deforestation occurred around the large cities where demand was greatest and along the principal transport routes."[83]

By 1910, Mexico's manufacturing base contributed 10 to 12 percent of the national economy and employed roughly 10 percent of the labor force. Between 1876 and 1911, as more items were produced locally, consumer goods fell from 75 percent of Mexico's import bill to 43 percent. In 1910, Mexican manufacturing produced $713 (in 1970 U.S. dollars) per worker, far above the production of agricultural workers. When the Revolution broke out, Mexico was well ahead of other Latin American nations in developing its paper, cigarette, glass bottle, and basic chemical industries.[84]

Despite its impressive gains, Porfirian industry failed to achieve the synergy found in the industrialized nations. Typically, almost everything in a factory was imported. Thus, for example, a new textile factory would incorporate imported construction materials, spindles, and looms. Only in the latter part of the twentieth century would Mexico produce the capital goods needed to construct factories.[85]

Low demand presented the single biggest obstacle to industrialization. Peasants' low income largely excluded them from the cash economy. The oversupply of industrial labor and its repression eliminated upward pressure on wages. For individual industrialists, this meant higher profits. However, for the nation as a whole, it limited further industrialization. Despite Adam Smith's notion of the invisible guiding hand, as historian Alan Knight noted, "Individual profit will not redound to collective development."[86]

AGRICULTURE

The agricultural sector was divided between those who produced primarily for their own consumption, that is, the subsistence sector, and those who produced for sale. Commercial agriculture increased in importance during the Porfiriato as the railroad opened the way to distant markets and exports. The subsistence sector was closely associated with the small farmer, while commercial agriculture was closely associated with the roughly 7,000 *hacendados* in Mexico. Some 45,000 to 50,000 *rancheros*, who worked, but did not necessarily own, properties in the 100 to 1,000 hectare range (247 to 2,470 acres), formed a middle stratum.[87]

A variety of factors led to the increased concentration of land ownership during the Porfiriato. The railroad increased marketing opportunities and provided incentive to displace peasants. Lands that in the past had been set aside to attract colonists to fight Indians were no longer needed for that purpose. Díaz's advisors believed that large landowners, particularly those who engaged in commercial agriculture, were more efficient and productive custodians of land than Indian villagers and peasants. They reasoned that for nature to be transformed and for the economy to be developed, both the land and the labor of the peasant had to be placed on the market.[88]

The actual mechanism for transfer of property to large landowners varied. Sometimes property was simply purchased. In other cases, individual landowners illegally appropriated land. The government intervened to remove the Yaqui and open the way for commercial agriculture in Sonora. Sociologist Andrés Molina Enríquez noted that some *hacendados* simply litigated spurious claims until the legitimate, but financially strapped, owner was overwhelmed.[89]

Through the 1870s, informal land titles, or the lack of land titles, kept much land off the market. A Mexican geologist hired by oil companies commented on the informal arrangements by which land was held in many places:

> The boundaries were not well defined [and] no one bothered to measure or to fence his property; the transfer of ownership was done from fathers to sons, almost by tradition and [transfers] done by sales or exchanges followed a vague and at times uncertain specification of the boundaries. In other cases, the actual extension of land was hid in order to escape the tax collector and finally, as the majority of the land remained uncultivated and covered by virgin jungle, the proprietors did not actually know the size of their [properties].[90]

Laws passed in 1883 and 1894 allowed privately owned surveying companies *(compañías deslindadoras)* to identify unclaimed lands, survey them at their own expense, and then turn two-thirds of the land surveyed over to the national government. To compensate the surveying companies for their efforts, the remaining third would become company property, which was usually sold. The government felt that the surveying process would: 1) promote growth by attracting capital once titles were regularized, 2) raise money for the government, which could auction the two-thirds of surveyed land it received title to and later collect taxes on all the land surveyed, 3) attract European immigrants who could be lured by secure land titles, and 4) attract Mexicans to border areas by offering land with clear titles.[91]

During the Porfiriato, the surveying companies received 52 million acres of land in compensation, that is, 10.7 percent of Mexico's territory. This implies that 157 million acres, 32 percent of Mexico's territory, were surveyed under the program.[92]

The transfer of this surveyed land to private individuals represented a tremendous concentration of wealth, and, as was desired, served to create a modern capitalist economy. Without secure titles, no one would invest in natural resources or agriculture. This land surveying had the unintended effect of increasing deforestation. Previously, forests had been considered as a common village resource complementing informally held agricultural properties. After these informally held properties were surveyed and transferred to others, those who had cultivated them would increase their timber cutting to support themselves. In 1905, a journalist commented, "The forests are being destroyed by peons who would rather gather roots in the mountains than work on the haciendas."[93]

Communities that claimed to have had their property rights infringed by the surveying companies could appear before a judge and claim ownership to land the survey companies deemed vacant or untitled *(baldío)*. In some cases, large-scale commercial farmers in alliance with local elites used the surveying process to seize the land of small farmers. However, court records indicate that most community protests were upheld. The government, in upholding these claims, was responding to conflicting interests. It wanted land surveyed and placed on the market, yet it wanted to maintain rural peace, something that it felt would be impossible if large numbers of rural people felt dispossessed. The government knew that rural peace was essential to attracting foreign investors. Both the government and the surveying companies were willing to yield to peasant claims due to the abundance of land surveyed. If a few thousand acres were declared the property of villagers in one locality, tens of thousands in another locale were in fact unclaimed and uncultivated.[94]

As an institution, the hacienda rebounded from its post-independence slump due to: 1) political stability, 2) the markets offered by mines and cities, 3) railroads to move crops and cattle, 4) access to bank credit, and 5) access to land provided by reform laws and surveying companies. Some estates contained large expanses of unproductive land, maintained close ties to nearby villages, and retained a deeply feudal quality. These entities consumed their own products and were more aristocratic luxuries than business ventures. Other haciendas were managed as modern commercially oriented enterprises. Haciendas often lost their feudal qualities when new interests purchased them and introduced more commercially minded management.[95]

Critics of the hacienda often claimed unused land indicated a lack of entrepreneurial spirit. However, in many cases, such land reflected a lack of capital or the inability to market crops. In such cases, *hacendados* would allow renting and sharecropping, since that did not require capital and shifted the risk of crop failure away from the *hacendado* in case of drought or other natural calamity. *Hacendados* sometimes held excess land to deny local peasants the opportunity to grow their own crops, thus forcing them to work on the hacienda. Idle land was also held as a reserve, should market opportunities improve. Recent scholarship has done much to dispel the notion of *hacendados* as not being commercially oriented. Generally *hacendados*, or their administrators, quickly adjusted to new markets offered by the railroad and brought in machinery on the same railroad tracks that carried away their crops.[96]

Hacienda agriculture differed from U.S. agriculture, which faced a labor shortage. In the United States, farmers made massive investment in laborsaving technology. This resulted in the United States becoming a world leader in the design and production of farm machinery and provided a stimulus to the U.S. capital goods industry. In Mexico, the solution to agricultural labor shortages in areas such as Valle Nacional was not to introduce better technology but to coerce labor.[97]

During the first decade of the twentieth century, agricultural exports totaled more than a third of export value, which was amazing considering the resurgence of mining. This agricultural boom was closely associated with the railroad. Before the building of the railroad, *hacendados* lobbied to have a rail line built near their land and subsequently they lobbied the government to mandate lower freight rates for their produce.[98]

At the beginning of the Porfiriato, Mexico was still relying on such agricultural exports as vanilla and tobacco. This changed as the railroad opened new marketing opportunities. Between 1891–1892 and 1901–1902, cattle exports increased by 493 percent, rubber by 95 percent, and beans by 127 percent. Growers in Mexico's Pacific Northwest appropriated Indian lands and constructed irrigation works, allowing them to use the railroad to supply U.S. markets with sugar and fresh vegetables. Investment in farming former Yaqui land led Sonora to have the second highest rate of U.S. capital investment in Mexico (after Veracruz with its oil).[99]

Unlike mining and manufacturing, technological change did not revolutionize agricultural production. It did, however, influence the demand for Mexico's agricultural exports. The discovery of aniline dyes in 1856 eliminated the demand for cochineal dye. As a result of the development of the mechanical reaper/binder in the United States, Yucatán began exporting henequen, a fiber obtained from a cactus-like plant. Binders used twine made from twisted henequen fibers. Between 1900 and 1910, as a result of cheap labor and a booming international market, profits on henequen investments ranged between 50 and 600 percent. U.S. and Canadian binders consumed an average of 235,000 tons of twine a year between 1900 and 1930.[100]

International Harvester, which dominated 99.8 percent of the henequen market in 1910, sought to maintain low henequen prices so farmers would buy their harvesters. Despite this, and their suffering through boom and bust production cycles, a small number of henequen producers became fabulously rich. Historian Allen Wells commented on their life style:

> Looking to the far-off capitals of the Western world for inspiration and design, the prosperous *henequeneros* built ornate palaces with marble pillars, intricately carved façades, and ostentatious stained-glass enclosed porticos . . . In addition to engaging in pleasant after-dinner conservation while sipping imported French wines on his shaded veranda, the henequen oligarch also spent considerable time keeping abreast of current stock quotations from the Paris *bourse* and dabbling in urban and rural real estate.[101]

As with most agricultural commodities, henequen came at a steep price. Growers used state power to break down communal village land ownership and coerce the Maya to produce the fiber, which permitted the use of labor-saving machines in Canada and the U.S. midwest. To limit their mobility, henequen workers were encouraged to take on debt. England's Anti-Slavery and Aborigines Protection Society reported that henequen workers toiled "in a bondage at once as cruel and hopeless as almost any form of slavery within knowledge of the society."[102]

Henequen cultivation shifted 9,000 square miles from more biologically diverse cattle and corn-raising to mono-crop plantations. The steam-powered machines used to extract the fiber from the henequen leaf were fueled by wood, which in turn led to deforestation and erosion on additional land. In 1903, to address this deforestation, the State of Yucatán created a forestry commission. However, henequen producers neither understood its mission nor cooperated with it.[103]

U.S. investment in land came late in the Porfiriato. Between 1902 and 1912, such investment increased from $30 million to $80 million. In 1910, Americans held about 130 million acres, or 27 percent of Mexico's surface area. Fewer than a hundred American interests held nearly 90 million of these acres in tracts larger than 100,000 acres.[104]

Through 1910, American ownership of Mexican property rarely resulted in conflict. In some cases, though, authorities refused to remove squatters and defaulted renters from American-owned properties. In other cases, those occupying lands to which Americans had acquired legal title were forced off. For example, in 1908, the federal cavalry received orders to clear settlers from land that the Hearst family had purchased at auction. In addition to the large holders, some 15,000 American "pioneers," brandishing rifles and titles to small farms, displaced thousands of Mexican peasants and rancheros.[105]

In 1910, Mexico had 3,581,000 people in its agricultural labor force, or 63.7 percent of workers. However, due to their low productivity, they only produced 24.0 percent of GDP, an average of only $230 per capita (in 1970 U.S. dollars). The almost universal illiteracy of agricultural workers made increasing their productivity difficult.[106]

While agricultural exports boomed, production for domestic use was neglected. Between 1877 and 1907, per capita corn production declined from 282 kilograms to 144. Imports from the United States made up part of this shortfall. However, few mechanisms existed to match grain supplies with the increased number of people thrust into the grain market. A 1901 corn famine in Michoacán illustrated this. Speculators raised the price of corn beyond the means of many, leading residents of Puruandías to storm a grain warehouse. The hungry were driven off by armed guards, leaving twenty wounded, including seven women and four children.[107]

Porfirio Díaz's understanding of rural Mexico served to maintain peace through the first decade of the twentieth century. To limit rural unrest, he instructed government officials to ensure that village land rights be respected. In 1901, a constitutional amendment allowed villages, but not the Church, to hold communal property. Ending the prohibition on village land ownership eliminated a major source of rural discontent.[108]

OIL

> The Porfirio Díaz dictatorship (1876–1911) had strong incentives to develop this industry because Mexico faced high energy costs.
>
> Stephen Haber, Noel Maurer and Armando Razo, 2003[109]

In 1859, the modern petroleum era began in Titusville, Pennsylvania, with the discovery that oil could be drilled for, much like water. Petroleum derivatives replaced candles and whale oil for illumination and wood and coal for fuel. Lubricants derived from petroleum facilitated the rapid expansion of shipping, railroads, and manufacturing. By the end of the nineteenth century, the United States had become the world's leading producer of oil as well as the major exporter to world markets, including Mexico. U.S. oil exports to Mexico increased from an annual average of 400 barrels between 1880 and 1884 to 670,000 barrels between 1905 and 1909.[110]

Mexicans rapidly increased their use of oil for the same reasons Americans had. At the beginning of the twentieth century, British rail companies operating in Mexico imported Welsh coal, while the American ones relied on coal from West Virginia and Alabama. These imports totaled 4.5 million tons annually. Mexico's lack of a domestic fuel source also affected manufacturing, as the U.S. consul in Chihuahua reported in 1908: "It will thus be seen that the matter of fuel makes the cost of manufacturing so high as to offer very little encouragement to such industries."[111]

An independent American oilman, Edward Doheny, was largely responsible for breaking Mexico's dependence on oil imports. He had prospected for minerals in the U.S. southwest for fifteen years before moving to Los Angeles. There he entered the fledgling U.S. oil business by digging a well, using picks and shovels. The well yielded seven barrels a day, bailed out by hand. Other more productive wells soon followed, and Doheny grew rich producing oil in California, much of which he sold to the Southern Pacific and Atchison, Topeka, and Santa Fe Railroad Companies to fuel their locomotives.[112]

After A. A. Robinson, the president of the Mexican Central Railroad, informed Doheny that oil was seeping from the ground near Tampico, Doheny made a trip to Mexico, prospecting for oil from the back of Robinson's private rail car. Doheny considered the area so promising that he began to buy land near the seeps to obtain oil rights. He soon purchased 450,000 acres of land and leased an additional million acres. As he later admitted, he often bought land for $1 an acre from owners who knew nothing of its oil prospects.[113]

In the northern Veracruz region, known as the Huasteca, where Doheny prospected, as late as 1885 a majority of the population spoke an indigenous language. Many lived within a tropical forest, replete with vines and epiphytes. In 1909, travel writer Philip Terry described the Huasteca as a "primitive biblical region flowing with milk and honey."[114]

The indigenous population readily agreed to lease their land to oil companies since, before drilling began, petroleum extraction did not seem as invasive as the milpa-eating cattle from nearby haciendas. Oil company agents offered undreamed-of cash payments for leases and promised residents they could continue their slash-and-burn agriculture. If Indian residents refused to sign, companies were not averse to resorting to violence to obtain the leases they sought. Local *hacendados*, who understood the notion of land titles, oil leases, and royalties far better than the indigenous population, sold or leased their property simply because the sums oil companies offered far exceeded the potential income from cattle raising.[115]

Before it marketed any crude, Doheny's company, the Huasteca Petroleum Company, laid 125 miles of eight-inch pipe and constructed ten pumping stations and twelve 55,000-barrel steel tanks. For a time, Doheny's drilling at El Ébano, forty miles west of Tampico, produced only dry holes. As Doheny teetered on the verge of bankruptcy, well number six came in at 15,000 barrels a day and soon filled all available storage facilities. Then number seven came in at 60,000 barrels a day. When workers tied to cap it, oil sprung forth from a fissure in the earth 300 feet from the well. Workers feverishly constructed a 750,000-barrel earthen reservoir to contain the oil.[116]

Doheny signed a contract to supply the Mexican Central Railroad with 6,000 barrels of fuel a day and soon began supplying Mexican smelters. After investing more than $4 million, and nearly going bankrupt, Doheny began to earn about $10 million a year from his Mexican oil holdings.[117]

The Mexican government welcomed Doheny's oil venture, since domestic oil production replaced expensive imported fuels. To stimulate oil investments, the government waived import duties on machinery and granted him a ten-year exemption on all taxes except the stamp tax.[118]

Doheny cultivated a personal relationship with Díaz, who became a close friend. To seal this friendship, he made 508 preferred shares of his company available to him. Governors of the states in which he operated received similar attention. He also hired as his attorney, Joaquín de Casasús, a former Mexican ambassador to the United States and a close associate of Díaz.[119]

Although the Díaz administration welcomed Doheny's efforts to produce Mexican petroleum, it felt that Mexico was becoming dangerously dependent on the United States and sought to offset U.S. influence by turning to Weetman Pearson, a successful British businessman and engineer. Pearson first visited Mexico in 1889, at age thirty-three, and for more than twenty years continued to spend considerable time there. In England, where he held a seat in the House of Commons, Pearson was known as the "Member for Mexico," which is also the title of his biography by Desmond Young.[120]

To encourage Pearson, who had no prior oil experience, Díaz granted him a fifty-year oil concession on national lands, lakes, and lagoons in six states including oil-rich Veracruz. Enrique Creel, the governor of Chihuahua, Guillermo de Landa y Escandón, the governor of the Federal District, and Porfirio Díaz, Jr. sat on the board of Pearson's Compañía Mexicana de Petróleo "El Águila." By 1906, Pearson reported owning "about 600,000 acres of land in the oil country and hav[ing] royalty leases for 200,000 or 300,000 acres." Pearson's early wells were dry holes, just as Doheny's had been. He began to make a profit from oil production only after investing £5 million of his own money.[121]

Pearson's first discoveries were quite dramatic. In 1908, one of his wells blew in at Dos Bocas, midway between Tampico and Tuxpan. The American consul at Tampico described the ensuing gusher, which was set on fire by flames from a nearby steam boiler:

> The heat was so intense that it is impossible to go nearer than several hundred feet. Considering the great quantity of oil coming out, there is little gas. The internal pressure is tremendous. The height at which the oil first ignites is forty feet. The steady height of the column of oil is 850 feet while gusts of wind are constantly deflecting the main flame and portions of the burning air to an immense height, oftentimes exceeding fourteen hundred feet. The flame itself is visible at thirty miles while the light, under favorable atmospheric conditions, can be seen [at a distance of] two hundred miles.[122]

The gusher flowed at the rate of 100,000 barrels a day, in ten days equaling Mexican production for 1907. Burning crude floated as far as thirty-one miles from the well. Since there were no Red Adairs at that stage of the oil industry, the well burned from July 4 to August 30, 1908, when the fire finally exhausted itself.[123]

A gaping, bubbling crater of salt water and sulfur gas remained. A 1913 visitor to Dos Bocas reported:

> The potent hydrogen sulfide gas had killed everything. What had been a lush *monte* was now a gaunt specter of dead trees. The air stunk with the smell of rotten eggs. There was no sign or sound of animal, bird or insect life. Nothing stirred in the breeze. The silence was appalling. It was eerie and frightening.[124]

Pearson's next big strike came on a hacienda named Potrero del Llano, fifty miles northwest of Tuxpan. In 1910, a 250-foot gusher erupted there. Unlike the gusher at Dos Bocas, it did not catch fire. The 100,000 barrels a day that shot out of the well flowed into the Tuxpan River and fouled the Gulf Coast as far as Tampico, 200 miles to the north. More than 3 million barrels of oil were lost. When it was finally controlled, the well produced 30,000 barrels a day, more than many entire fields. That single well became the most productive well in the world, yielding 117 million barrels of oil in twenty-eight years.[125]

Pearson, who is said to have made more money in Mexico than any foreigner since Cortés, enjoyed access to Mexico's political insiders. He learned such social graces as leaving a case of whisky with the appropriate Mexican officials. His firm paid retainers to prominent politicians not only to ensure cooperation but also to avoid making political enemies. His leasing land from elite families, including Díaz's in-laws, ensured that he would not fall from official favor.[126]

Pearson's insider contacts gained him tax benefits, generous concessions, and contracts to sell fuel to the national railway. He also received insider information on bids, often by U.S. contractors, so he could successfully underbid them. This, combined with good business sense, the latest technology, and the financial resources of London bankers, allowed him maintain his business momentum for an entire decade while he competed against more experienced American oilmen.[127]

By the end of the Porfiriato, the oil industry had become Mexico's star economic performer. In 1901, only 10,345 barrels were produced. By 1910, Mexico had become the seventh largest producer in the world, and production had reached 3.6 million barrels. The next year production jumped to 12.6 million barrels. Doheny and Pearson together controlled 90 percent of this production.[128]

Early Mexican production was concentrated in an area along the Gulf Coast south of Tampico called the Faja del Oro, or Golden Lane. Further south, Pearson drilled in, but missed what became the fabulously rich, but deep, Reforma Field of the 1970s. The cable tool drilling apparatus used in 1905 could not drill below 3,000 feet. In the 1970s, wells drilled in the same area perforated as deep as 30,000 feet.[129]

During the first decade of Mexican oil production, Doheny produced roughly 10.5 million barrels out of the total Mexican production of 12.3 million barrels. Much of the remainder came from Weetman Pearson's oil company and Oil Fields of Mexico, a company started by another Englishman, Percy Furber. In 1911, Great Britain had 57.2 million pesos invested in Mexican oil production, while the United States had 40.0 million, and France had 6.8 million. This production saved Mexico the considerable cost of imported fuels.[130]

Thanks to favorable legislation and the example provided by early strikes, nearly 500 oil companies, almost all foreign, opened offices in Mexico. Oil development would remain in the hands of foreigners for decades since Mexicans lacked the technical expertise for oil production. In addition, the costs of refineries, pipelines, and drilling exceeded Mexicans' investment capital. New oil fields almost invariably required extensive investment in transportation and oil storage facilities for their successful exploitation. The isolation of most fields forced oil companies to absorb the costs of warehouses, saw mills, electric generators, roads, ice plants, and hospitals.[131]

Working in the oil fields provided many Mexicans with an escape from rural poverty and *hacendados*' tyranny. Oilfield workers received as much as two pesos a day, to the consternation of highland *hacendados*, who complained that oil companies were stealing their labor. Skilled workers came either from the highlands or from abroad since very few skilled laborers lived near the Golden Lane. Ninety percent of the adult population of Tuxpan, the nearest population center, was illiterate, and no manufacturing whatsoever existed there. As a result of the unprecedented influx of labor, the area's indigenous population was soon displaced in number and social importance.[132]

By the end of the Porfiriato, Mexico had become the fourth largest oil producer in the world. The petroleum industry bolstered Mexican development in a number of ways. Railroads and other industries could operate at lower costs thanks to the use of petroleum fuels and lubricants. Paying workers in cash stimulated the development of local industry.[133]

Much of the potential stimulus to the economy, however, was never realized. As with railroads, most of the equipment used in the production of oil was produced outside Mexico. Even many of the oil workers' daily necessities were imported, since most of the work occurred near a port. As with the mines, profits were sent out of Mexico, rather than being reinvested locally. Finally, the bulk of oil produced in Mexican fields during the first decade of the twentieth century was refined in the United States.[134]

CONCLUSION

Between 1877 and 1910, Mexico's per capita income (expressed in 1950 U.S. dollars) increased from $62 to $132. From 1860 to 1910, Mexico's rate of per capita economic growth exceeded that of such economic powers as France, Germany, and Great Britain. This economic growth resulted from: 1) railroads lowering transport costs, 2) political stability, and 3) banks supplying credit to both private interests and the government. Between 1877 and 1910, federal government revenue increased by 437 percent, while the population only increased by 60 percent.[135]

Mexico's exports were too low to lift the whole economy, as occurred in Argentina, Latin America's star economic performer. In 1890, Mexico exported $4.40 per capita, while Argentina exported $32.40 per capita. In addition, Mexico's exports generated relatively few jobs and had limited links to other sectors of the economy. Exports were often generated in rather small enclaves, such as mines. In contrast, Argentina's agriculture- and cattle-based exports were more closely integrated to the rest of the economy. Cattle raising, for example, generated jobs in processing meat for export and in the leather, shoe, and chemical industries.[136]

The government's failure to invest in educating the labor force prevented sustained economic growth. In the short term, this kept taxes low and made enterprises profitable. However, in the long term it choked off development by denying Mexico a skilled labor force that could absorb technical innovation from advanced countries and produce manufactured exports.[137]

While Mexico had no clear alternatives to the acceptance of foreign investment, such investment could have been more effectively regulated. The elite rationalized the virtual carte blanche given to foreign investors as a necessary measure to attract foreign capital. The experience of Brazil and Argentina, however, contradicted this. These two countries not only had more nationalistic investment policies but also received more British investment than Mexico during the Porfiriato.[138]

While some statistics paint a positive picture of the Porfiriato, others indicate the opposite. Mexico failed to break out of the colonial development model. As late as 1910, three metals—gold, silver, and copper—comprised almost three-fifths of Mexico's exports. That year, 67 percent of the labor force remained in the primary sector (agriculture, cattle, forestry, hunting, and fishing).[139]

At the end of the Porfiriato, the roughly $2 billion of foreign investment denied Mexicans control of mining, oil, banking, commerce, public utilities, cattle ranching, and railroads (until their nationalization). This led historian James Cockcroft to conclude, "The single most influential economic group was neither a rural aristocracy nor an urban bourgeoisie, but rather a *foreign* bourgeoisie." Foreign capital also generated wealth that fell into the hands of the local elite, thus solidifying its position in power.[140]

Some problems that became apparent during the Porfiriato have yet to be adequately addressed. Factories, mines, and other extractive industries could not absorb the surplus of workers produced by land consolidation, population increase, and the declining need for artisans.[141]

Regional disparity increased during the Porfiriato. Electricity permitted the location of industry in Mexico City, rather than near sources of hydropower. Chihuahua, Sonora, Coahuila, and the Federal District alone received 86 per cent of foreign investment. Government investment was concentrated in Mexico City. This left many entire states with little benefit from Porfirian economic development. As historian Leticia Reina commented, "The majority of people were left out of the national project."[142]

Tariff protection led to industrial investment since investors knew they would not have to compete with foreign goods at prevailing world prices. Since so many machines and components were imported and economies of scale were often lacking, Mexican production costs were higher than in the developed world. Consumers were the most obvious group hurt by tariffs as they paid nearly 70 percent more for manufactured goods than they would have if imports had been allowed to enter freely. The reliance on tariffs set the pattern for Mexican industrial development for most of the twentieth century and resulted in an industrial plant with high costs and low productivity.[143]

Díaz successfully broke the cycle of impoverished governments and coups by favoring a few banks, such as Banamex, with special privileges and restricted competition. While this allowed the government to obtain credit, the forty-two banks that existed in Mexico in 1910 were insufficient to meet credit needs. Operating under much less stringent rules, the United States had 18,723 banks and trust companies that year.[144]

A fatal flaw in the way Mexico based development on industrialization, commercialization of agriculture, and internationalization of capital was that the lower classes were denied returns to labor commensurate with the new wealth being created. As historian Mark Wasserman stated, "Mexico's last and greatest civil war, the Mexican Revolution (1910–1920) was essentially a protest against this system."[145]

Chapter 14

A Superpower Emerges Next Door, 1856–1909

> Prior to the Civil War, the United States had constructed an empire on the North American continent; following the conflict, the focus shifted to a "New Empire" of foreign trade. By the 1890s, the makers of U.S. foreign policy sought markets rather than extensive new territories.
>
> Joseph Fry, 1996[1]

AFTER THE GADSDEN PURCHASE

Expansionism continued to shape U.S. political thinking after the United States acquired the Gadsden Purchase from Mexico in 1854. In 1858, Sam Houston, who by then was serving in the U.S. Senate, proposed making all of Mexico a U.S. protectorate to secure for its people "the benefits of orderly and well-regulated republican government."[2] John Forsyth succeeded Gadsden as U.S. ambassador to Mexico. He staunchly believed in Manifest Destiny and felt that "our race, I hope our institutions—are to spread over this continent and that the hybrid races of the West must succumb to, and fade away before the superior energies of the white man . . ."[3]

Despite the beliefs of men such as Houston and Forsyth, the United States would acquire no more territory at Mexican expense. This resulted in part from an increase in sectional rivalry. The north began to view any territorial acquisition on the southern boundary of the United States as conferring an advantage on the south and thus would oppose such acquisitions. Also, many Americans felt that desirable lands with few Mexicans, such as California, had already been acquired. They felt further territorial acquisition would involve the incorporation of less desirable land as well as larger numbers of non-Europeans.[4]

THE WAR OF REFORM, 1857–1860

> At times during the cruel, onerous War of Reform, U.S. economic and military support for the liberals was a decisive factor in their victory . . .
>
> Enrique Krauze, 2006[5]

The decade 1857 to 1867 proved to be the most complicated period for U.S.–Mexican relations since the independence of the two nations. For most of that period, Mexico had two governments, one liberal and one conservative. Then, during the early 1860s, the U.S. Civil War raged.

In 1857, Ambassador Forsyth received instructions to offer President Comonfort $12 million for Baja California and part of Sonora and Chihuahua. Mexico rejected the offer.[6]

Forsyth recognized Zuloaga immediately after he had seized power, feeling that Mexico's new leader would facilitate the territorial acquisition that Comonfort had resisted. The rest of the diplomatic corps in Mexico also recognized Zuloaga on the grounds that he controlled the capital city.[7]

In 1858, Forsyth proposed to Zuloaga's Foreign Relations Minister Luis G. Cuevas that Mexico transfer territory to the United States for a cash payment and that it cede perpetual transit rights across the Isthmus of Tehuantepec.

Invoking Manifest Destiny, Forsyth stated that Mexico should sell the land, since the "inscrutable" designs of the Creator included U.S. acquisition of that territory. Cuevas rejected the offer, noting that indeed the designs of the Lord might be inscrutable, but that in order for countries to live harmoniously together, they should respect each other's territorial rights.[8]

After Cuevas rejected his offer to purchase territory, Forsyth broke diplomatic relations with the conservative government, which had levied a 1 percent property tax on all residents of Mexico, including foreigners. An American citizen refused to pay the tax, leading the conservatives to expel him from the country. Forsyth used this expulsion to justify breaking relations.[9]

Forsyth's departure left the United States without diplomatic representation in Mexico. Since this interrupted the flow of information to Washington, President James Buchanan sent William Churchwell to Mexico as a special agent to report on conditions there. Churchwell reported that the Juárez government claimed to be recognized by sixteen of the twenty-one Mexican states and that it enjoyed the support of 70 percent of the population. The liberals indicated to Churchwell that they would "negotiate affirmatively" the cession of Baja California, the granting of transit rights, claims adjustment, and reciprocal trade.[10]

Buchanan, upon receiving Churchwell's report, sent Robert McLane to Mexico as U.S. ambassador and instructed him to recognize whichever of the two governments in Mexico that he felt offered the best prospects for acquiring Baja California and transit rights across Mexican territory. McLane landed in Veracruz, and, since the liberal government there appeared willing to negotiate, McLane recognized it in April 1859.[11]

The positive liberal responses to Churchwell and McLane reflected Juárez's realization that support from Washington could be advantageous. Juárez felt that obtaining U.S. recognition would not only allow his beleaguered government to receive economic aid but would also guarantee maritime security in the Veracruz area.[12]

McLane and liberal Foreign Relations Minister Melchor Ocampo then began negotiating a treaty on transit rights and territorial cession. Since the sale of Baja California was most strongly opposed in northern Mexico, where Juárez enjoyed his firmest support, that sale was not included in the resulting treaty, known as the McLane–Ocampo Treaty. The transit rights enumerated in the treaty reflected not the liberals' desire to open Mexico's doors to unregulated crossings of its territory but the financial and military pressures they felt at the time of McLane's arrival and their hope that signing the treaty would be the key to obtaining U.S. aid.[13]

The McLane–Ocampo Treaty granted the United States perpetual transit rights: 1) across the Isthmus of Tehuantepec, 2) from the lower Rio Grande to Mexico's west coast, and 3) from Guaymas to Nogales, Arizona. Americans not only viewed these transit rights as desirable but also felt they would pave the way for the formal incorporation of these areas into the United States. The treaty granted the United States the right to intervene militarily to protect people and goods in transit along the routes included in the treaty. In exchange for these rights, the United States was to pay the liberal government \$4 million, of which \$2 million was to be retained to settle damage claims against Mexico filed by U.S. citizens.[14]

Fortunately for Mexico, and Juárez's historical reputation, the U.S. Senate rejected the McLane–Ocampo Treaty. Senators from northern states felt slave interests would benefit if U.S. influence extended into Mexico. Twenty-seven senators opposed the treaty, while eighteen favored it. Northern senators cast twenty-three of the negative votes. Southern senators cast fourteen of the votes in favor.[15]

Since the U.S. Senate rejected the treaty, the liberal government did not receive the desperately needed cash that the treaty would have provided. The liberals' willingness to negotiate with the

United States did provide some crucial military support. In early 1860, conservative General Miguel Miramón surrounded Veracruz with an army of 7,000. To prevent the liberals from being supplied by sea and thus force their surrender, the conservatives bought two ships and ammunition in Cuba, then still a Spanish colony. The two ships, the *General Miramón* and the *Marqués de la Habana,* sailed to Mexico and anchored at the small port of Antón Lizardo, fourteen miles south of Veracruz.

Juárez, lacking either naval or land forces to attack Antón Lizardo, declared the boats to be "pirate ships" and then sought U.S. aid in subduing the "pirates." The claim that the conservative boats were pirate ships was obviously a sham. Nevertheless, U.S. navy ships proceeded to the port and captured the two vessels with the loss of one American and fifteen Mexican lives. The ships were then taken to New Orleans where an admiralty court ruled that they were not pirate ships. By that time, the conservative ground forces threatening Veracruz had been withdrawn, so the ships could not force the surrender of the city.[16]

Late in 1860, Juárez's army took Mexico City. In January 1861, John Weller, the new U.S. ambassador presented his credentials and a long list of damage claims filed by U.S. citizens.[17]

THE SECOND EMPIRE

After Maximilian's arrival in Mexico City, the European powers soon recognized his government. However the United States maintained diplomatic relations with Juárez throughout the intervention. Even though the Juárez government enjoyed U.S. recognition, the outbreak of the Civil War thwarted Juárez's hopes for U.S. aid. In November 1862, the United States imposed a ban on the export of military supplies since they were needed for Union forces and U.S. authorities feared that exported arms might end up in Confederate hands.[18]

Both the United States and the Confederacy were willing to make deals at the other's expense. The United States offered to buy Baja California, claiming such a purchase would keep the Confederacy from seizing it. The Confederates, in turn, promised to return New Mexico and California to Mexico if the liberal government would sign a peace treaty with the Confederacy. The liberals rejected the offer, noting that the Confederacy offered to give Mexico territory it did not control, while failing to offer Texas, the former Mexican territory that it did control.[19]

Lincoln's Secretary of State William Seward proved to be quite effective at preventing France from supporting the Confederacy—the major U.S. foreign policy goal during the Civil War. To avoid antagonizing Napoleon, complaints about violations of the Monroe Doctrine were muted. The United States gave the French an incentive to remain neutral by permitting them to buy mules, food, and other supplies at U.S. ports to support their military effort in Mexico.[20]

In April 1861, President Lincoln decreed a blockade of Confederate ports, thus interrupting the sale of southern cotton to Europe. To circumvent the blockade, Confederate cotton was carted to the Rio Grande. It was then brought into Mexico and exported through Bagdad, a makeshift port at the mouth of the Rio Grande. Since Bagdad—whose population reached as many as 12,000—lacked a harbor, small craft would brave the surf to carry the cotton to freighters waiting offshore in Mexican territorial waters. Rather than creating an international incident, Union warships did not interfere with such shipments.[21]

The Confederates exported an estimated 300,000 to 350,000 bales of cotton through Bagdad. In early 1865, Union General Ulysses S. Grant commented, "There is never a day that there are not 75 to 150 vessels off Bagdad, discharging and receiving cargos." The same carts that brought cotton south would return north laden with rifles, medicine, uniforms, and other military supplies brought to Bagdad by sea.[22]

Ships sailing from Bagdad carried Confederate cotton to Liverpool, Barcelona, Le Havre, and even New York City. After leaving Bagdad, ships sometimes stopped in ports such as Nassau or Havana to hide the origin of the cotton. As historians Milo Kearney and Anthony Knopp noted:

> Profit knows no political loyalty, and New York traded heavily with Matamoros [adjacent to Bagdad], including in carbines, pistols, and ammunition on the transparent fiction that these goods were destined only for Mexico and would not find their way into Texas.[23]

The blockade of Confederate ports during the U.S. Civil War also led to a commercial boom in northeastern Mexico. In exchange for cotton, Mexico sent the Confederacy flour, hides, wool, lead, silver, salt, footwear, cloth, blankets, gunpowder, and potassium nitrate (to produce gun-powder). Monterrey served as the distribution center for Mexican goods bound for the Confederacy. Thousands of carts carried goods between Monterrey and Texas.[24]

As the Confederacy collapsed, some 8,000 to 10,000 Confederates moved to Latin America to avoid Union rule. Most of them went to Mexico, where they felt Maximilian's empire would be preferable to Reconstruction. Maximilian's official publication, the *Diario del Imperio*, invited large-scale southern immigration, hoping that the immigrants would introduce new agricultural methods.

Maximilian designated 500,000 acres in Veracruz for Confederate resettlement. Confederates arriving there founded a community, which they named for Empress Carlota. Few Confederates fared well there. Many were felled by disease after having being weakened by poor diet. Liberal forces attacked their community, which also suffered earthquake damage. After the fall of the empire, most of the surviving Confederates returned to the United States.[25]

After the U.S. civil war ended, Secretary of State Seward stepped up the pressure on France to withdraw its troops from Mexico. The specter of a French alliance with the Confederacy no longer restrained U.S. action. Seward sought to obtain French withdrawal without involving the United States in another war. To accomplish this, U.S. General Philip Sheridan was sent to the Rio Grande with 50,000 veteran troops. Sheridan encouraged rumors that his force was preparing to invade Mexico, sent scouts into northern Mexico, and provided extensive support, including 30,000 muskets, to liberal forces.[26]

On their own initiative, several thousand Americans crossed the border to serve with Juárez. They converted Juárez's force—some of whom were armed with bows and arrows—into one armed with the most modern arms. Americans who had experience with repeating rifles and artillery proved to be especially valuable. While some former Confederates served with Maximilian's forces, they were too few to offset former members of the Union army serving with Juárez. After President Andrew Johnson revoked the ban on arms exports in May 1865, additional arms were sold to Mexico.[27]

In November 1865, the United States sent the French a note declaring, "The presence of a French army in Mexico which maintains a government imposed by force and against the free will of the Mexican people, is a source of serious preoccupation for the United States." Napoleon replied that he was pulling his troops out as fast as transport allowed.[28]

Although Mexicans had hoped for direct U.S. assistance after the Civil War ended, the Mexican ambassador to the United States, Matías Romero noted later that Mexico probably benefited from the U.S. failure to intervene. He commented that U.S. pressure "accomplished its object without entailing on Mexico the curse which usually falls on nations who call in a more powerful neighbor to relive them from a present danger . . ." The United States did receive official thanks from Juárez, who stated that U.S. efforts against Maximilian "justly deserve the sympathy and the regard of the people and government of Mexico."[29]

THE RESTORED REPUBLIC

After peace was reestablished in Mexico, relations between Mexico and the United States were as warm as they had ever been. U.S. Ambassador Marcus Otterbourg, who arrived in 1867, was instructed not to press the damage claims of U.S. citizens so that the liberals would have time to put their affairs in order. The liberals, firm believers in international trade, sought U.S. investments and technology to develop the Mexican economy.[30]

Juárez commented on U.S.–Mexican relations during his 1867 state of the nation address:

> The same cordial relations are now maintained with the United States as existed during the Mexican people's struggle against the French republic. Americans' sympathy and the moral support the U.S. government lent the Mexican nation merited and still merits the sympathy and respect of the people and government of Mexico.[31]

An incident in May of 1870 indicated the degree of cordiality in U.S.–Mexican relations. The U.S. Navy steamship *Mohican,* under the command of Captain W. W. Low, was sailing along the Pacific Coast of Mexico. Upon learning that a pirate boat was pillaging the coast, the *Mohican* gave chase. The smaller pirate boat took refuge in the Teacapan River, seventy-five miles north of San Blas. Since the larger *Mohican* could not enter the river, some of its crew took to whale boats, rowed forty miles up the river, and captured and burned the pirate boat. The Mexican government simply accepted this as welcome assistance, even though it was unauthorized by either government. To show their gratitude, fourteen villages in the area the pirates had victimized melted down silver coins, had them converted into a silver service, and presented it to Low as a token of appreciation.[32]

During the early 1870s, border conflict began to undermine the existing goodwill between Mexico and the United States. From an American perspective, border conflict resulted from Mexican cattle rustlers who would cross to the north side of the Rio Grande, steal cattle, and retreat back across the river. In 1872, Texas rancher Mifflin Kenedy testified to a congressional committee that along the 135-mile strip of the river between Roma and the Gulf of Mexico, 400,000 head of cattle and 20,000 horses had been stolen since the end of the Civil War. In one spectacular 1875 raid, some fifty mounted Mexicans made their way to the Corpus Christi area and looted stores. Women and children were sent out to sea for their protection. U.S. forces repeatedly crossed the border into Mexico in "hot pursuit" of rustlers and raiders during the Lerdo de Tejada administration.[33]

Claims for damages that U.S. and Mexican citizens filed against the opposite nation also soured relations. In 1868, a Joint Claims Commission was established to handle the claims that had accumulated since 1848. Many of these claims had their origins in Indian raids. The commission worked for almost a decade, evaluated more than 2,000 claims, and dismissed the vast majority of them. The value of claims by U.S. citizens that were upheld exceeded the value of upheld Mexican claims by $3.975 million. Mexico agreed to pay this sum in annual installments of $300,000, beginning in 1877.[34]

Relations between the United States and Mexico remained almost quaintly simple. In 1873, when U.S. Ambassador John Foster (the grandfather of John Foster Dulles) arrived in Mexico, only 130 American adults lived in the Federal District. Ships sailing at what Foster described as "rare intervals" provided communication between the two nations. That year, trade with Mexico only accounted for about 1 percent of U.S. foreign trade. In the 1870s, U.S. exports to Mexico totaled between $6 million to $8 million a year, below the peak reached before the Mexican–American War. The United States imported from Mexico even less—never more than $5 million a year in the 1870s.[35]

Even though trade between the United States and Mexico remained low during the Lerdo de Tejada administration, U.S. commercial interests were producing a shift in U.S. policy toward Mexico. The U.S. Civil War dramatically shifted the balance of power between the United States and Mexico. Virtually all the fighting in the United States was confined to the south, allowing the north to make unprecedented industrial advances. In contrast, the War of Reform and the French intervention devastated the Mexican economy. U.S. factories and mechanized farms were soon producing more than the United States could consume. In response, U.S. producers turned to overseas markets. As a result, economic goals replaced territorial aspirations. As Seward stated, the United States should "value dollars more, and domination less."[36]

The Homestead Act, post-Civil War reconstruction, rapid industrialization, and the shifting of the United States' attention to its own west absorbed vast amounts of U.S. capital and human resources, reducing expansionist pressure. Neither the Republican nor the Democratic platforms of 1868, 1872, 1876, and 1880 contained a word about Latin America. Both parties broke their twenty-four-year silence in 1884, but then only to voice support for trade with the region.[37]

RECOGNIZING DÍAZ

Porfirio Díaz seized power in November 1876, the waning months of the Ulysses Grant administration. Rather than following the policy established by Thomas Jefferson of recognizing new governments once they had assumed de facto power and had indicated an ability to fulfill their international obligations, the United States withheld recognition from Díaz in an attempt to gain concessions. Ambassador Foster explained the delay, noting that the United States "waits before recognizing General Díaz as president of Mexico, until it shall be assured that his election is approved by the Mexican people." Never before had the United States required a Latin American nation to hold a legitimizing election in order to receive recognition.[38]

When Rutherford Hayes was inaugurated as U.S. president in March 1877, Díaz remained unrecognized. On June 1, 1877, U.S.–Mexican relations were further complicated by an order authorizing U.S. General Edward Ord to cross the Texas–Mexico border at his own discretion in pursuit of bandits or Indians. Rather than allowing the United States to trample upon Mexican sovereignty in an attempt to ingratiate himself to the Hayes administration, Díaz responded by sending General Gerónimo Treviño north with orders to cooperate with U.S. officers but to use force to block any U.S. crossing of the border. Fortunately, both Ord and Treviño favored cooperation rather than confrontation. Ord directed his force to cross the border only when no Mexican troops were in the area, and Treviño worked to coordinate movements of his troops with those of Ord. General Ord's order enraged Mexicans, but did cause them to invigorate their campaign to suppress Indian raiding across the border. Foster noted that "no effort was made by Mexico to suppress the outlaws until after the instructions to General Ord were issued." Eventually, not only did the two generals establish a working relationship to suppress lawlessness but Treviño also married Ord's daughter.[39]

Díaz mounted a publicity offensive in the United States to promote trade with and investment in Mexico. He invited American investors to Mexico and granted them huge concessions and subsidies. Not surprisingly, these investors then lobbied in the United States for improved relations between the two countries. In 1878, Díaz sent Manuel Zamacona, an experienced diplomat, to the United States to publicize Mexico's resources. He also hired two American journalists to produce books and articles supporting the recognition of Mexico.[40]

Recognition finally came on April 9, 1878. The pressure of American bankers, miners, and potential railroad investors played a major role in the decision to recognize the Díaz administration. U.S. efforts to force Díaz into making concessions backfired, since Mexico's president refused to concede on any of the U.S. demands, such as the right to "hot pursuit," an end to forced loans from American citizens living in Mexico, and the elimination of the duty-free zone along the border. U.S. pressure, which Mexicans viewed as heavy handed, soured U.S.–Mexican relations. Díaz enhanced his already solid record as a patriotic war hero by standing up to the United States.[41]

By the 1870s, recognition by the United States had become a key to stability throughout Latin America. Such recognition signaled that it was safe to make investments and that nations enjoying recognition might obtain loans. It was presumed that the United States would not actively undermine administrations it recognized. Lack of recognition indicated instability and inadvisability for investment, and the possibility of dissidents obtaining U.S. aid to topple the incumbents. The United States, realizing that its recognition had become a valuable commodity, began to charge accordingly.[42]

U.S.–MEXICAN RELATIONS DURING THE PORFIRIATO, 1884–1908

> The most powerful foreign influence in Mexican affairs was of course the United States, whose proximity and overwhelming superiority in wealth, technology, and population were both welcomed and feared.
>
> Robert Holden, 1994[43]

During the Porfiriato, U.S.–Mexican relations became more complicated. Old concerns, such as exacting forced loans from American citizens, vanished as the Mexican government became more stable and solvent. New concerns arose as trade and investment increased. Trade between the two nations, which only totaled $4 million in 1855, soared to $117 million by 1907. The number of Americans living in Mexico steadily increased, reaching 75,000 by 1910. In 1911, more than 45 percent of total U.S. foreign investment was in Mexico.[44]

Smuggling into the United States from the tariff-free zones along the border slowly declined as U.S. industry began manufacturing high-quality, competitively priced goods. The railroad also allowed low-cost transport of U.S.-produced goods to the border area. This eliminated the incentive to smuggle anything into the United States.

Indians, bandits, and rustlers continued to raid across the border through the 1880s and 1890s, with both sides accusing the other of making inadequate efforts to secure the border. Díaz, realizing that a peaceful border was key to gaining U.S. support and investment, ruthlessly suppressed banditry along the border. In response to this effort to control border lawlessness, the U.S. order allowing Ord to engage in "hot pursuit" was withdrawn in 1880. In 1882, the United States and Mexico signed a treaty stipulating that "regular Federal troops of the two Republics may reciprocally cross the boundary line of the two countries, when they are in close pursuit of a band of savage Indians." The signing of the 1882 treaty indicated that Mexico no longer viewed U.S. border crossings as the prelude to control or conquest of its territory. Tensions resulting from border lawlessness slowly decreased as the border area became more settled, and, especially on the U.S. side, land was fenced.[45]

Since France, Spain, and Great Britain lacked diplomatic relations with Mexico after the fall of Maximilian, the United States had little difficulty increasing its trade with Mexico. In 1883, when Great Britain was negotiating the reestablishment of diplomatic relations, an Englishman commented, "The commercial influence of the U.S.A. is being so rapidly extended that it bids fair before long, unless some stimulus and encouragement is given to British commerce there, to drive it out altogether." By 1885, the United States had replaced Great Britain as the main supplier of goods to Mexico.[46]

U.S. imports from Mexico were chiefly gold, silver, ores, rubber, non-ferrous metals, hides, coffee, and fibers such as henequen. The United States shipped Mexico lard, provisions, beer and wine, canned goods, tobacco, lumber, petroleum, cotton, flour, coal, iron and steel, and cereals, especially corn. It was only after the First World War that capital goods and sophisticated manufactured products dominated U.S. exports to Mexico.[47]

In 1900, the United States supplied 51.1 percent of Mexico's imports, while Great Britain supplied 17 percent, and Germany supplied 11.5 percent. During the next decade, as U.S. manufacturing increased and rail transport improved, the United States supplied between 55 and 60 percent of Mexico's imports and absorbed between 65 and 75 percent of its exports.[48]

From the 1870s to roughly 1912, Mexico absorbed more U.S. direct foreign investment than any other country. Thanks to legal reforms south of the border that replicated institutional structures in the north, the border nearly ceased to exist as an obstacle to trade and investment. By 1910, the United States, which accounted for 38 percent of total foreign investment in Mexico, had surpassed the British, who supplied 29 percent. Mining, railroads, and the petroleum industry accounted for roughly 80 percent of U.S. direct investment. As U.S. investment increased,

***Table 14.1** U.S.–Mexico trade, 1855–1910*

Year	U.S. exports to Mexico ($ million)	U.S. imports from Mexico ($ million)
1855	3	1
1876	6	5
1886	8	11
1896	19	17
1907	66	57
1910	58	59

Source: U.S. (1976: 903–07)

U.S. investors developed a vested interest in stability and in Díaz remaining in office. In 1907, Secretary of State Elihu Root declared Díaz to be "one of the great men to be held up for the hero worship of mankind."[49]

By the end of the Porfiriato, as historian W. Dirk Raat noted, "U.S. capital and markets had created the commercialization of agriculture, the proletarianization of the peasantry, and the expansion of an export-oriented economy." In general, Mexicans' desire for better-paying jobs outweighed any doubts they had about the foreign influences accompanying U.S. trade and investment. The higher wages Americans generally offered laborers led Mexican landlords to believe that "contact with the United States, and even with individual Americans, spoils the peons." In northern Mexico, the upper class often sent its children to the United States so they could learn English and receive a good education.[50]

Others were not so pleased with the U.S. presence. Mexican historian Justo Sierra was not alone in voicing concern about the triple economic, legal, and cultural threat of "Americanism." He feared that by blindly imitating American values and institutions, Mexico would sacrifice its cultural integrity. Mexican professionals resented their often being deemed incapable of filling jobs above that of clerk simply because they were Mexicans. Anti-Americanism came to transcend any single class or occupational group. The U.S. consul in Jalapa, John B. Richardson, commented on these anti-American feelings: "The Mexican loves his country and does not love the foreigner. He does not like to have his work done by foreigners at double the wage he gets. He is uneasy over innovation which he does not value or understand . . ." To this day, heated debate continues about the degree to which the Mexican Revolution was motivated by anti-American feelings.[51]

Along with American investment and trade came new ideas, the harbinger of even greater U.S. cultural and intellectual influence. Protestantism began to make inroads in cities. Young converts were sent to the United States to further their studies. Anarchism as a political philosophy influenced Mexican labor organizers and political dissidents such as Ricardo Flores Magón. Finally, the progressive movement influenced other Mexicans such as Madero.[52]

DON PORFIRIO TEETERS

> It is not clear that the Taft administration [1909–1913]—or the U.S. interests it sought to represent—stood to gain from the ouster of Díaz, or that they rejoiced at his fall.
>
> Alan Knight, 1998[53]

In the early twentieth century, Díaz attempted to balance U.S. and European investment to prevent Mexico from becoming too dependent on its northern neighbor. Also, for historical reasons, Mexican politicians did not want to appear to be dominated by American interests. In 1902, the Austrian ambassador to Mexico observed, "The Mexican government has now formally taken a position against the trusts formed with American capital." Loans were placed with European banks, and the British-owned El Águila Oil Company was favored over its American competitors. This search for European investment indicates that Díaz's action was not motivated by opposition to foreign capital per se.[54]

At the turn of the century, the United States did not have separate polices for each Latin American nation. President Taft, like Roosevelt, sought to maintain existing markets and find new outlets for U.S. capital and goods. The U.S. government saw its role as protecting private American entrepreneurs threatened by local political crisis. In the United States, this appeared to be a very even-handed approach. To Latin American countries, the United States appeared to be overwhelming them, often earning itself the "imperialist" label.[55]

By 1909, events were forcing the United States to formulate a separate Mexico policy. In October 1909, aware of rumblings of discontent, President William Howard Taft sought to bolster Díaz's stature by meeting with him in El Paso and Ciudad Juárez, the first visit to Mexico by an incumbent U.S. president. Taft wrote his wife that Díaz:

> is very anxious to strengthen himself with his own people by a picturesque performance in which we show our friendship for him and his government, and I am glad to aid him in that matter for the reason that we have two billions of American capital in Mexico that will be greatly endangered if Díaz were to die and his government go to pieces.

Taft also commented on Díaz, "I can only hope and pray that his demise does not come until I am out of office."[56]

In 1910, after Madero fled to the United States, the U.S. government was noticeably lukewarm in the application of U.S. neutrality laws to Madero's supporters. However, little evidence indicates that the U.S. desired Díaz's removal. The tension resulting from Díaz's pro-European tilt and foreign-policy independence notwithstanding, the U.S. delegation to Mexico's 1910 centennial celebration declared: "Just as Rome had its Augustus, England its Elizabeth and Victoria, Mexico had Porfirio Díaz. All is well in Mexico. Under Porfirio Díaz, a nation has been created."[57]

EMIGRATION

Although it was only a trickle compared to a century later, the latter half of the nineteenth century saw sustained Mexican emigration to the United States. Before the completion of rail links across the border, Texas was the principal destination of Mexican emigrants. By 1880, there were 43,161 Mexican-born residents of Texas. In 1855, while visiting Texas, traveler Frederick Olmsted commented: "The Mexicans appear to have almost no other business than that of carting goods. Almost the entire transportation of the country is carried on by them, with oxen and two-wheeled carts." As late as 1900, almost three-quarters of all Mexican-born residents of the United States—some 71,062 individuals—lived in Texas.[58]

By the 1880s, rail links to the U.S. southwest increased the number of Mexicans emigrating to the United States. The railroad not only facilitated passage across the northern Mexican desert but it also permitted easy access to New Mexico, Arizona, and California. Labor recruiters in Mexico, known as *enganchadores*, aggressively recruited workers for the rail companies and other U.S. enterprises that they represented. The railroad also permitted the shipment of minerals and produce from the southwest to the eastern United States, causing the demand for labor to soar.[59]

Opposition to this migration largely came from south of the border, where the loss of low-cost labor was viewed with concern by landowners. In 1906, *El Correo de Chihuahua* reported with alarm that 22,000 Mexicans had entered Texas through Ciudad Juárez. As would be the case well into the twentieth century, the overwhelming majority of these emigrants came from rural areas.

Between 1900 and 1910, the number of Mexican-born residents living in the United States increased from 103,393 to 221,915. By 1912, Mexicans had become the main source of labor on railroads west of Kansas City. In addition to those Mexicans who established permanent residency in the United States, by the early twentieth century roughly 60,000 to 100,000 would cross the border each year to work on a seasonal basis. Employers came to depend on seasonal Mexican labor for certain tasks, such as clipping sheep. Some of the suggested reasons for Mexican emigration include: 1) political repression; 2) the high birth rate in Mexico; 3) easy access to the United States by rail; 4) higher wage levels in the United States; and 5) escaping the rigors of hacienda life.[60]

During the first decade of the twentieth century, the U.S. government adopted a neutral policy to immigration from Mexico, trying neither to stimulate it nor to limit it. American employers welcomed Mexican workers since they assumed them to be temporary sojourners who would not aggressively demand better wages and working conditions.[61]

The wave of Mexican immigrants, most of whom remained in the U.S. southwest, upset the modus vivendi reached there after 1848. The abuse of Mexican citizens increased, and English literacy requirements were established to disenfranchise Mexicans. Mexicans were often forced to trade their dignity for higher pay, since, as a U.S. government study reported, they claimed "the treatment they got in Texas sometimes was very humiliating to them, and they were called 'niggers' and 'greasers,' but nevertheless they got good pay." In Arizona, the racism of U.S. miners and their unions and Arizona's own version of the dual wage scale confronted Mexicans.[62]

Part Five

The Mexican Revolution, 1910–1916

Chapter 15

The Revolution, 1910–1916

> The Revolution . . . unlike its Russian counterpart, arose in the provinces, established itself in the countryside, and finally conquered an alien and sullen capital. And, unlike its Chinese counterpart, it failed to produce either a vanguard party or a coherent ideology.
>
> Alan Knight, 1986[1]

THE FALL OF THE DÍAZ ADMINISTRATION

> Although Mexicans had fought over land since colonial times, during the Porfiriato the unprecedented convergence of land consolidation, population growth, and inflation in food prices resulted in a groundswell of protest that resulted in revolution.
>
> Michael Gonzales, 2002[2]

In October 1910, after fleeing Mexico and taking refuge in San Antonio, Texas, Madero issued his Plan of San Luis Potosí, which declared:

> A tyranny, the likes of which we Mexicans have not suffered since we won our independence, oppresses us in a manner which has become intolerable. In exchange for that tyranny we have been offered peace, but it is a shameful peace for the Mexican people. It is based on force, not law. Its goal is not the greatness and prosperity of our homeland, but the enrichment of a small group which, by abusing public positions, has converted them into sources of personal wealth, unscrupulously exploiting concessions and lucrative contracts.[3]

Madero's Plan called for a revolt against Díaz on November 20, 1910, free elections, and a legal review of previous land thefts.

Before November 20, the government seized lists of Madero's urban supporters, which permitted mass arrests in various states, undermining the rebellion. Nevertheless, several uprisings, most of which were suppressed, did occur on November 20.

The most successful uprisings occurred in Chihuahua, where the initial revolt spread. Soon more than 1,000 men were fighting under the command of Pancho Villa and a prosperous muleteer named Pascual Orozco. For nearly two months they held out against the army of what was considered to be one of the strongest states in Latin America.

Rebellion in Chihuahua responded to the Terrazas family having converted the entire state into a virtual company town. In 1907, draught and recession had hit the state especially hard. Many Mexicans returning from the United States, where they had lost jobs, found no employment south of the border. Unlike other parts of Mexico, Chihuahuans opposing Díaz formed a heterogeneous urban-rural, middle- and lower-class coalition because so many had suffered under Terrazas.

Rural lower-class leadership of the revolt in Chihuahua came as a surprise to Madero. He had assumed the November 20 revolt would be an urban affair that would soon topple Díaz and permit a smooth change at the top—very tidy. However, to the consternation of the better classes, other social groups with other objectives suddenly appeared.[4]

By December 1910, rebels controlled the Sierra Madre Occidental stretching from Chihuahua towards Zacatecas and Tepic. Then the fighting spread to Durango and the Laguna area on the Durango–Coahuila border, where the rapid increase of cotton production had resulted in peasants being displaced from their fertile, well watered land. The insurgency was overwhelmingly rural, popular, and agrarian. While Díaz had many urban opponents, they were vulnerable to repression and, unlike the Chihuahuans, they lacked ready access to horses and guns.

For months, Díaz failed to take the revolt seriously and referred to the rebels as "bandits." As the British chargé noted, Díaz "quite ignored the very possibility of an imperfection in his administration."[5]

On February 14, 1911, Madero returned to Mexico from the United States to assume command of the Revolution. As would be the pattern throughout the Revolution, rebellions continued to spring up without their being tied to any major leaders. By April 1911, insurrection had spread to eighteen states and most of the countryside was in the hands of revolutionaries. Examples of such rebellions include the uprising in the Laguna region and the occupation of Baja California by the Partido Liberal Mexicano (PLM).[6]

The army, staffed by aged generals commanding unwilling conscripts, could not stop Madero. Díaz had purposely let the army decline, feeling it might oust him. In 1910, of the 20,000 soldiers serving in the army, only 14,000 were available for counter-guerrilla operations. Money had been budgeted for thousands of additional troops, but rather than recruiting, commanders had simply pocketed their salaries. Between 1877–1878 and 1910–1911, military spending declined from 42 percent of the federal budget to 22 percent. Until 1910, a small number of troops dispatched by rail had been able to quell local uprisings.[7]

However, when revolts sprang up in many areas early in the Revolution, the army soon became overextended. Ironically, in 1910 and 1911, rebels adopted Díaz's 1876 strategy—undermine the central government by using guerrillas to start brushfires in as many places as possible. Army commanders failed to form mobile brigades such as those that had successfully reduced the Indian threat in the nineteenth century.[8]

On May 10, rebel troops under Villa and Orozco captured Ciudad Juárez, across the Rio Grande from El Paso, Texas, even though Madero had ordered that the city should not be attacked. He had feared that stray bullets might cross the river into El Paso and that the resulting damage and deaths might alienate the United States. This unauthorized capture greatly improved Madero's negotiating position since Ciudad Juárez's rail links facilitated his obtaining military supplies from the United States.

While Madero was challenging Díaz in the north, opposition was developing in the state of Morelos, just south of Mexico City. There, sugar planters had deprived villages of their water and their land, and peasant demands for restitution were the most threatening. In many cases, the lack of water, not access to land, limited increased sugar production. This appropriation of peasant resources responded to the pressure of the world sugar market and was facilitated by a tight alliance between Morelos' governors and local planters.[9]

The railroad arrived in Morelos in the 1880s, facilitating the shipment of sugar out of the state. In the late 1890s, much Cuban and Puerto Rican sugar production capacity was destroyed during the independence struggles there, increasing the demand for sugar from Morelos. Sugar production in Morelos quadrupled between 1880 and 1910.[10]

The international demand for sugar severely undermined the traditional peasant economy. Then recession led to a decline in world sugar purchases. After the Spanish-American War, Cuban production rebounded. As a result, between 1908 and 1910, sugar production in Morelos declined from 115 million pounds to under 107 million pounds. Layoffs and reduced pay and working hours followed. These layoffs exacerbated an already critical employment situation that had resulted from the installation of labor-saving machinery in sugar mills and Morelos' 12 percent population increase between 1895 and 1910. A massive enclosure movement by large estates reduced the land area available for traditional uses. Sugar producers fenced irrigation ditches with barbed wire and hired armed guards to prevent villagers from diverting water to the fields they still did retain. Towns filled with displaced agricultural workers—future recruits for the Revolution.[11]

Resistance erupted in Anenecuilco, Morelos, a village that had appeared on Aztec tribute lists before the Spanish Conquest. The town was the home of Emiliano Zapata, whose family owned horses, mules, and a small plot of land. Although far from being wealthy, Zapata had escaped the grinding poverty of most Morelos residents and had learned to read and write, which was considered enough formal education in his milieu. By 1910, all the lands of his village, in an area where land had traditionally been communally owned, had been appropriated by *hacendados*. A neighboring hacienda was taking over part of the village, and sugar cane was being planted where homes once stood.[12]

In 1909, at age thirty, Zapata was chosen as chief of village defense. Zapata, who spoke Nahuatl, the language of the Aztecs, shared the deeply rooted Indian heritage of Anenecuilco. Along with eighty armed men, he began reclaiming and distributing to villagers land usurped by the hacienda. Previously, those who challenged the theft of land in or out of the courts had been sent to forced labor in Yucatán. However, by 1910, the political climate had changed. Díaz was preoccupied with Madero in the north, so Zapata's land distribution not only went unchallenged but his example also spread to other parts of the state.[13]

Early in 1911, Díaz responded to the inexorable spread of the revolution with a series of reforms. In March, he replaced his most unpopular governors and six of his cabinet members. In April, he removed more government officials, promised an independent judiciary, and once again declared there would be no more gubernatorial or presidential reelection. He even called for the subdivision of the great estates on terms that were fair both for the landless and the landowners. With these sweeping reforms, Díaz felt he would undercut Madero and bring the revolt to a close. Had he attempted these measures a year earlier, they might have worked. However, by April 1911, they were viewed as a sign of Díaz's weakness, not as a harbinger of democracy.[14]

After the defeat of Díaz's forces at Ciudad Juárez, his traditional power base began deserting him. The financial elite felt that Díaz's remaining in office would cause foreigners to lose confidence, thus cutting off investment and low-interest loans. As large parts of the countryside fell under the control of revolutionaries, *hacendados* decided that they would undercut the more radical rural *insurrectos* by yielding to the political demands of Madero, who, after all, shared their upper-class background. The guerrillas would win the war, not by overpowering the federal army but by denying Díaz the military supremacy he needed to assure his political base.[15]

Díaz's abandonment by his traditional power base led him to agree to the Treaty of Ciudad Juárez, which called for him to resign and go into exile. Francisco León de la Barra, his foreign affairs minister, would serve as interim president until elections could be held. The treaty stipulated that Díaz's federal army would remain intact, while the rebel forces that had supported Madero would be disbanded. This agreement, which sought to end the Revolution, disarm the peasants, and maintain the social system upheld by the federal army, did not mention land reform.[16]

Díaz agreed to the treaty due to the hemorrhaging of his support and his desire to resign and leave in dignity, rather than facing rebel hordes at the gates of Mexico City. Madero was pressured to bring the revolt to a halt by conservative family members and his desire to avoid a devastating civil war and possible U.S. intervention.[17]

With the benefit of hindsight, Madero has frequently been criticized for allowing Díaz's legislature, judiciary, and, most significantly, his army to remain intact. However, a major restructuring was not Madero's agenda. He sought to reform, not destroy, Mexico's socioeconomic system. This, he felt, could be brought about by reopening the political process. For this reason, the treaty has been characterized as the triumph of Madero's idealism over reality. Madero had forced Díaz's

Figure 15.1 *Francisco Madero*

Source: El Paso Public Library, Aultman Collection, photo #A 1458

resignation, but the regime lived on in institutions and behavior patterns with roots too deep to fall with the old caudillo.[18]

Díaz kept his word, resigned on May 25, 1911, and went into exile. Supposedly, as he was leaving Mexico Díaz commented, "Madero has unleashed a tiger, let's see if he can control it." Unlike the typical Latin American dictator, Díaz did not loot the treasury, and he lived to the end on the charity of friends. In 1915, he died in exile in France.

Díaz's departure was hardly lamented at the time. Subsequent governments had a vested interest in portraying his government as a bad regime that deserved to be overthrown. While this is true, Díaz did lay the foundation of modern Mexico. As revolutionary General Felipe Ángeles observed:

> Díaz was a glorious soldier who struggled for independence and national sovereignty. He was an able administrator, but took advantage of his prestige as a caudillo and used the army to impose his will on the nation. He did not respect our democratic institutions nor did he obey the law. He usurped authority and became a dictator.[19]

THE MADERO YEARS, 1911–1913

Upon Díaz's resignation, Madero left Ciudad Juárez for Mexico City. He made a triumphal march to the capital, cheered by enthusiastic crowds along the way. An estimated 200,000 witnessed his Mexico City arrival in a coach complete with bewigged, liveried, and powdered footmen.[20]

As agreed in the Treaty of Ciudad Juárez, Francisco León de la Barra assumed the presidency. During his short time in office, he implemented reforms in education and labor relations.

To adjudicate land disputes and return land unjustly taken, he created the National Agrarian Commission. Elections carried out under De la Barra, while not perfect, were far more honest than those under Díaz and sometimes selected candidates not favored by either De la Barra or Madero. De la Barra ended subsidies to pro-government newspapers and allowed the press to publish freely. Finally, he rapidly demobilized the revolutionary forces that had toppled Díaz.[21]

In August 1911, Madero, who was campaigning for the October presidential elections called for in the Treaty of Ciudad Juárez, went to Morelos to negotiate with Emiliano Zapata. There, Zapata agreed to demobilize his forces in exchange for Madero's promise of land reform. However, as the Zapatistas were turning in their arms, De la Barra declared that he would not negotiate with "bandits" and ordered troops under General Victoriano Huerta to move into Morelos and disarm remaining Zapatistas.

Fighting broke out between the Zapatistas and Huerta's force. Despite further negotiation with Madero, Zapata said no more guns would be turned in until land reform became a reality. Huerta attempted to wrest Morelos from Zapatista control, but was unable to suppress Zapata's forces. De la Barra's heavy-handed response to the Zapatistas left Madero with a problem that he would be unable to resolve during his fifteen-month-long presidency.[22]

In October 1911, voters selected electors to choose a president. These electors then chose Madero and José María Pino Suárez to be president and vice-president, respectively. Pro-Madero sentiment was overwhelming. While the elections were free, they served only to ratify what had been achieved earlier by force of arms. De la Barra resisted pressure to become a candidate, since he felt the tradition of reelection should be broken. It would be another eighty-nine years before an election actually selected a president, rather than ratifying a military victory or the choice of an incumbent.

By the time Madero assumed the presidency in November 1911, popular enthusiasm had already waned. As president, rather than dismantling the old Porfirian bureaucracy, Madero merely changed the personnel at the top. He neglected sound politics, leaving former foes in office, while failing to reward those who had fought for him. At the same time, millions of peasants continued stoop labor on the haciendas of the Terrazas, the Creels, and other *hacendados*, just as they had under Díaz.[23]

Madero never realized his slogans "effective suffrage" and "no re-election" meant little to the impoverished, illiterate majority of the population. Even when offered the opportunity, few voted. Less than 10 percent of the eligible voters outside Mexico City cast a ballot in the 1912 congressional elections.[24]

The National Agrarian Commission continued to study the land issue. The Commission concluded that only through buying hacienda land and then distributing it could land be provided for the landless. However, money was never appropriated for such purchases. Madero felt that large holdings provided the best route to agricultural modernization and thus did not feel it was in Mexico's best interest to subdivide large estates to provide peasants with subsistence plots. In June 1912, he stated that it was "one thing to create small property by dint of hard work and another to redistribute large landholdings, something I have never thought of doing or offered in any of my speeches or programs."[25]

Madero's mere mention of the land issue turned members of the elite against him. They correctly felt that any consideration of land distribution would legitimize the concept and lead to future problems for them. Madero soon found himself in the same position as Maximilian, clinging to the middle of the road and lacking a strong base of support.[26]

Madero's experience with the press illustrated his problematic position. In keeping with his liberal beliefs, he allowed the press, which remained almost exclusively in the hands of wealthy conservatives, to flourish without restraint. With few exceptions, publishers used their freedom to undermine his administration. A typical remark, from *El Heraldo,* referred to Madero as "a reptile which should be stepped upon." Political cartoonists joined in the Madero-bashing, discrediting the president even with illiterates. They frequently played upon Madero's small stature by portraying him as a child. President Madero's brother Gustavo commented that the press "bit the hand which had removed its muzzle."[27]

Given Madero's failure to initiate land reform, in late November 1911, Zapata issued his Plan of Ayala, which withdrew recognition from the President and called for his overthrow. The Plan charged Madero with abandoning the Revolution and siding with the *hacendados*. It called for action since:

> the immense majority of Mexican pueblos and citizens are owners of no more than the land they walk on, suffering the horrors of poverty without being able to improve their social condition in any way or to dedicate themselves to Industry or Agriculture, because land, timber, and water are monopolized in a few hands . . . .[28]

The Plan reflected the enormous gulf between the elite, literate, legalistic Madero and the parochial, egalitarian, and largely illiterate Zapatista movement.[29]

The Plan of Ayala declared that peasants should take the initiative to reclaim stolen lands and defend them with armed force. Dispossessed *hacendados* could take matters to court *after the Revolution* if they wished. In addition, one-third of each legally owned hacienda was to be purchased for the landless. Lands of those opposing the Plan were to be confiscated, thus depriving them of an economic base. Income from such confiscated lands was to support widows and orphans of revolutionaries. The Plan did not demand political power for Zapata's followers. Rather, it called for elections to select a new government after Madero's overthrow.

With the Plan of Ayala as its standard, by early 1912, the Zapatista rebellion had spread into nearby states, despite a constant shortage of money, guns, and ammunition. General Juvencio Robles, Madero's commander in Morelos, responded by forcing rural residents to move to government-controlled resettlement camps.[30]

In addition to the Zapatistas, Madero faced other challengers. In December 1911, former governor of Nuevo León Bernardo Reyes launched a rebellion. In March 1912, his former supporter Pascual Orozco, rebelled in Chihuahua, charging him with having betrayed the principles of the Plan of San Luis Potosí. In October 1912, Porfirio Díaz's nephew Félix Díaz rebelled in Veracruz. Together these rebellions sapped government resources and undermined Madero's credibility.[31]

To add to Madero's woes, peasant-initiated violence, which had never stopped after the Treaty of Ciudad Juárez, continued to sweep the country. Armed peasants seized land and fought with local authorities in several states. Díaz's many-layered repressive apparatus was too damaged and overextended to respond to these peasant initiatives. In the countryside, the revolution had mutated and taken root among people with no patience for parliamentary procedure, little interest in candidates and ballots, and scant faith in politicians. In Durango, peons of the Santa Catarina Hacienda, which had been ruled by an iron hand, began an unprecedented strike. They demanded a pay increase from thirty-seven centavos to one peso, the abolition of the company store, a shorter working day, and payment in cash instead of kind. A Veracruz landowner complained that about 150 Indians had invaded his finca "with the depraved idea of making changes in my property."[32]

Deep crisis gripped the Madero government at the end of 1912. Madero could not satisfy the aspirations of peasants and industrial workers without betraying his closest associates. Throughout rural Mexico, strikes and spontaneous land seizures challenged his administration. The failure of the old repressive mechanisms that had allowed Madero to seize power also meant that his administration was incapable of maintaining law and order in the countryside. Industrialists, landowners, and foreign investors felt their property was unprotected. Army officers considered Madero a non-military upstart.[33]

Madero also failed to live up to the traditional macho stereotype of a leader. He was a small man with a squeaky voice, a vegetarian, and a spiritualist, and he did not womanize. He abstained from alcohol and tobacco and had a childless marriage. This added to the impression that a power vacuum existed around him.

On February 9, 1913, military officers responded to what they felt to be Madero's inability to govern. They initiated a coup and released from jail Félix Díaz and Bernardo Reyes, whom they planned to install as president. Reyes was killed as he approached the National Palace on horseback, thinking it was in rebel hands. It was actually held by Madero loyalists, and he was cut down by a burst of machine-gun fire.

With their anticipated leader slain and in the face of unexpected resistance, Félix Díaz and his fellow rebels took refuge in the Ciudadela, a stoutly built Mexico City fortress that contained most of the local supply of artillery shells. Madero appointed General Huerta to crush the rebels. However Huerta had little sympathy for Madero and deliberately protracted a military stalemate. The rebels remained in the Ciudadela for ten days, a period known in Mexican history as "La Decena Trágica" ("The Ten Tragic Days"). During this period, the two forces engaged in artillery duels in downtown Mexico City, carefully avoiding the cannons of the "enemy" and creating a climate in which the population would welcome any settlement. Huerta neutralized troops loyal to Madero by ordering hopeless frontal assaults into Díaz's machine-gun fire. Despite receiving repeated warnings of Huerta's disloyalty from family and advisors, Madero failed to revoke Huerta's command.[34]

Finally, Huerta and Félix Díaz formally agreed to join forces. Huerta was to be the interim president until elections could be held to elect the younger Díaz as president. Madero and Pino Suárez were arrested and were promised that their lives would be spared if they resigned their offices.

On February 22, while being taken from the National Palace to prison, Madero and Pino Suárez were killed, although it remains unclear just who gave the orders to kill them. The government claimed they died when Madero supporters attempted to free him. The car in which Madero was riding was riddled with bullets to support the story. Few accepted the official version.[35]

During his brief administration, Madero permitted the formation of political and labor organizations, shortened the work day, and outlawed punishment by factory owners. He instituted Mexico's first taxes on producing and exporting oil and made Spanish the official language of the Mexican railway system, replacing English. Finally, as he had promised, he democratized Mexico by introducing universal male suffrage. Bringing the middle class into the political process via honest elections was Madero's major break with *científico* practices.[36]

Madero expected Mexicans to put down their guns, join political parties, and elect local, state, and national leaders who would legislate reform programs. He never moved beyond the view that his movement had been purely political and that all that was needed was to set aside the fraudulent 1910 presidential elections and hold new democratic elections.[37]

Madero failed to solve Mexico's social problems due to his sharing with the *científicos* the belief that the existing socioeconomic system was the only rational one and that it should be preserved. This system relied on a continual inflow of foreign capital to modernize Mexico. In addition, it relied on large estates for agricultural production. Preservation of the system required suppressing radical peasant movements that demanded immediate land reform. To accomplish this he left the federal army intact.[38]

Madero failed to use the masses as a power base. He was not interested in them, and soon after he took office, they lost interest in him. He failed to allow his rural supporters to freely participate in local politics and to manage their own community affairs. Furthermore, his short regime was marred by nepotism and the placing of his associates in office. Madero was never able to go beyond the ideas acquired during his privileged nineteenth-century upbringing.[39]

Madero's accomplishments include ending the Porfiriato, initiating direct elections for public office, opening the door for the massive reforms of the twentieth century, and launching a generation of Mexican leaders into the political arena. Unlike so many movers and shakers of Mexican history, Madero is still remembered favorably. Historian Stanley Ross wrote of Madero, "His martyrdom accomplished, at least for a time, what he had been unable to do while alive: unite all the revolutionists under one banner."[40]

THE HUERTA DICTATORSHIP, 1913–1914

> It was far too late for . . . a facile attempt to turn back the clock and restore an old-style regime.
>
> Timothy Henderson, 1998[41]

Huerta established a government with the backing of *hacendados*, bankers, rich merchants, high clergy, the federal army, British oil interests, and the U.S. business community. Many, including Mexico City residents, supported the coup since it ended violence in the city and was seen as a way to restore order in the countryside and maintain the flow of foreign investment. Huerta's backers felt that Mexico needed a firm hand like Díaz's and that Madero had failed due to too little repression, not too little reform.

Initially, Huerta's administration did not swing sharply to the right. His educational budget spending exceeded that of Díaz. However, the exigencies of war soon led to increased repression, forced military recruitment, and attempts to squeeze more resources out of the citizenry to wage war. Huerta put his men in governorships around the country. He soon dispelled the old adage of honesty among thieves by failing to permit Félix Díaz to become president as he had agreed.[42]

Response to the coup was not long in coming. In the northern state of Coahuila, Venustiano Carranza, a *hacendado*, declared Huerta's government to be illegal. Carranza had served as a senator under Díaz. He had fallen out of favor with Díaz, leading him to support Madero. After Díaz's resignation, Madero had appointed Carranza as governor of Coahuila, a position to which he was later elected. Carranza's distance from Mexico City afforded protection that permitted his survival. Carranza, then fifty-three years old, had flowing white whiskers worthy of an Old Testament prophet. He stood over six feet tall and very much fit the image of a revolutionary leader.

In March 1913, Carranza issued a written call for resistance to Huerta known as the Plan of Guadalupe. The Plan, named for the hacienda where it was drafted, deliberately avoided all social issues in order to build the broadest possible coalition against Huerta. Its sole demand was that constitutional rule, usurped by Huerta, be reestablished. The Plan provided for the formation of an army, whose members were known as Constitutionalists, with Carranza at its head. It withdrew recognition from the federal army that had served under Díaz and declared the Constitutionalist army to be the only legitimate military force.[43]

Historian Friedrich Katz commented on Carranza's defiance of Huerta:

> It required courage to be the only governor to openly defy the military regime. In part, Carranza was certainly impelled by ambition. History had suddenly thrust the chance of assuming the presidency into his lap. He probably also felt that he had no choice. The murders of Madero, Pino Suárez, and [Chihuahua governor Abraham] González could well be seen as foreshadowing his own fate.[44]

In July, Huerta's forces took the military initiative, forcing Carranza to retreat. He made a symbolically important seventy-nine-day ride on horseback to Sonora, rather than traveling by rail through the United States—his other option. Distance and its lack of a direct rail link with central Mexico protected Sonora from Huerta's forces. Its border with the United States provided a ready source of arms.

As opposition to Huerta swelled, members of the middle class raised armies and acquired national prestige. They differed from Madero in that they were backed by armed men—a force that Madero either had not known how to use or had not wanted to use when he held office. Also, they began a style of mass politics that Madero had never imagined. This populism began with the offering of concessions and reforms to the masses in exchange for their support in achieving political and military aims. Despite the mass support so freely given, the promises and concessions would rarely see the light of day.[45]

Huerta's coup also brought peasant leaders into the forefront, removing them from the obscurity to which years of Díaz oppression and Madero inaction had condemned them. In the south, Zapata continued to defend his version of the Revolution. Huerta felt it would be relatively easy to suppress the Zapatista movement. He assured sugar planters in Morelos, "The government is going, so to speak, to depopulate the state, and will send to your haciendas other workers." Huerta created free-fire zones and removed "recruits" for his army by the boxcar load, a practice that closely resembled the government procedure in the wars against the Yaqui in Sonora and the Maya in Yucatán.[46]

In Chihuahua, Abraham González, the governor at the time of the coup, refused to recognize Huerta. The local military commander put him on a train bound for Mexico City. González was murdered before the train arrived.

González's death left a power vacuum in Chihuahua that Pancho Villa soon filled. He built a force of artisans, workers, shopkeepers, small farmers, miners, peasants, muleteers, peddlers, bandits, and the unemployed. Residents of Chihuahua's military colonies joined Villa in hopes of reasserting their old position. Villa's ability to make payrolls at a time when jobs were scarce made military service even more attractive. These men from the highly mobile, recently developed north reflected a society quite different from the villages of Morelos, where the population had had its roots in the same area since before the Spanish Conquest.[47]

Villa was of the same background as his followers. In 1878, he was born into a sharecropper family on a hacienda in the state of Durango. Before answering the call to join Madero's November 20 uprising, Villa seems to have lived in the twilight zone between legal occupations and cattle rustling. He was widely viewed, perhaps correctly, to have lived the life of a Robin Hood bandit. No record exists of his having engaging in political activity before 1910.[48]

As Villa's army gained strength, another general, Álvaro Obregón, organized anti-Huerta forces in Sonora. Obregón was a self-made man, typical of northern Mexico. After working as a carpenter and mechanic, he became a small-scale chickpea farmer. During Madero's presidency, he was elected mayor of Huatabampo after sympathetic *hacendados* brought in farm laborers from outside the municipality to vote at least once, sometimes twice. After Madero's overthrow, Sonora's governor, who did not recognize Huerta, appointed Obregón to command the state's military forces. It soon became apparent that he was a self-taught military genius.[49]

The northern armies, except for Villa's, were led by middle-class officers who commanded plebeian masses. By the summer of 1913, rebels controlled the entire state of Sonora except for the port of Guaymas, protected by federal gunboats. In Sonora, rebels began to collect taxes and show more interest in order than radical change.[50]

By early summer, rebels controlled most of rural Chihuahua. Only the cities remained in Huerta's hands, protected by artillery. By that time, rebellion had broken out in thirteen states in addition to Sonora, Chihuahua, and Coahuila. As these rebellions spread, the anarchy that the Huerta coup was supposed to end inexorably increased.[51]

In October 1913, Huerta abolished Congress and arrested 110 of its members. The reason—Congress had decided to investigate the death of Senator Belisario Domínguez, murdered for speaking out against Huerta. After Congress was dissolved, the U.S. chargé d'affaires stated that Huerta could "be considered as an absolute military dictator."[52] The German ambassador commented on another aspect of the regime—corruption:

> The government displays a corruptibility and depravity that exceeds anything known in the past. Everyone seems to want to steal as fast as he can, because he now knows that he does not have much time for it.[53]

As opposition mounted, Huerta increased the federal army from its 50,000-man level under Madero to more than 200,000. This was accomplished by drafting into the army poor people found on the street or in movie theaters, bullrings, and bars at closing time. He kept his regime in power through systematic assassination of dissenters and press censorship. Huerta's main goal was the pacification of the country, and everything, including the rule of law, fell before it. This created a vicious circle. As militarization increased, opposition grew stronger and so still more militarization was required. Huerta tried to solve all conflict with force, in contrast to Díaz, who employed compromise and diplomacy.[54]

On November 14, Villa intercepted one of Huerta's coal trains traveling south from Ciudad Juárez. He forced a telegraph operator to report that the track had been cut. An unsuspecting dispatcher then ordered the train back to Ciudad Juárez. That night the train arrived with 2,000 of Villa's troops aboard. Given the element of surprise, they easily took the city. This provided a major psychological boost to the Constitutionalists and enabled Villa to trade cattle across the border for U.S. arms.[55]

By March 1914, Villistas controlled the entire state of Chihuahua, giving Villa an opportunity to carry out reforms. He ordered the confiscation of haciendas and other properties of the wealthiest families, including those of the Terrazas and the Creels. These estates were kept intact, but under Villista management, so they could produce marketable products, such as cotton and cattle, to sell in the United States. Revenue from such sales allowed Villa to purchase arms, meet army payrolls, and make payments to war widows and orphans. Income from the undivided estates also benefited the entire population of Chihuahua, the majority of whom were not peasants. Subdividing the haciendas would have had little effect on the non-peasant majority. After the cessation of hostilities, Villa envisioned establishing military agricultural colonies modeled on the colonies that had been established in colonial Chihuahua to ward off Indian attack.[56]

In large part due to income from confiscated estates, Villa's army became the strongest and best equipped of the armies opposing Huerta. Arms purchased in the United States enabled Villa to begin a rapid southward advance that gave him and his army, the Northern Division, fame as the strike force of the Revolution. At the height of his power in October 1914, Villa commanded 40,000 men. Villa's popularity, and thus his ability to raise large armies, resulted from his appearance of invincibility, his extensive distribution of goods and money to the lower classes, his promise that veterans would receive land after Huerta's defeat, and the perception that he could not lose due to U.S. backing.[57]

While Villa controlled Chihuahua, peasants' lives did not undergo significant change, and only one spontaneous land seizure was recorded. The major piece of legislation limited payments by sharecroppers to 50 percent of their crop.[58]

After the Revolution, Villa planned to distribute land to revolutionary veterans, war widows, and those whose lands had been stolen by *hacendados*. He wanted to create a society of small agrarian communities in which individuals owned private plots. If he had distributed land to his soldiers immediately, it would have been difficult to motivate them to leave the state and fight. Subdividing estates would also have ended the income source that financed arms purchases in the United States.[59]

The social content of the Villa administration can be gleaned from reports of Villa's activities that appeared in the *El Paso Times*. He gave to the poor clothing, shoes, and other apparel from El Nuevo Mundo, the large department store that he confiscated from Spaniards. He also reduced the price of beef from one peso to fifteen centavos a kilo. Those who had lost their jobs due to the Revolution could collect free food at army commissaries. Villa personally ordered free supplies

Figure 15.2 *Villista troop train*

Source: El Paso Public Library, Aultman Collection, photo #A 2457

for day-care centers. When food prices rose, Villistas sold wheat and corn from confiscated estates at reduced prices.[60]

After taking control of Chihuahua, Villa and the Northern Division moved south in a veritable folk migration, accompanied by the famed *soldaderas*, musicians, beggars, photographers, and whores. It formed a microcosm of mobile, heterogeneous northern Mexico.[61]

In April 1914, 16,000 Villistas besieged well-entrenched federal troops at Torreón. After three days, the federal troops withdrew, providing Villa with his greatest victory to date. The 2,000 casualties suffered by Villa's forces indicate the intensity of the fighting. Villa demonstrated an ability to maneuver and supply a large army in the field as well as to use artillery effectively. The sudden professionalization of Villa's forces amazed most observers. One such observer noted that the Villistas "for the first time resembled real soldiers instead of [the] unkempt ragged peons that one is accustomed to associate with revolutions in northern Mexico."[62]

Uprisings inspired by Villa's example were typically led by local, uneducated men not formally linked to any of the major revolutionary leaders. In the north, they generally acknowledged Carranza as their leader, even though he had no means of exercising command. Often demands concerned local autonomy as much as land ownership. In Zongolica, Veracruz, for example, an official commented on the leader of a revolt there:

> He is not a Carrancista, nor does he have any links with any contending party, but what he desires is that the Indians of the region whom he leads be given possession of their lands, and likewise those who are said to have been despoiled by hacienda proprietors, and they be left in complete liberty . . . to name local authorities from among individuals of their own patch of land, and of their own estimation and trust.[63]

Revolts such as the one at Zongólica sapped the vitality of the Huerta regime. First, federal troops abandoned mountain areas, hamlets, and villages, leaving cities increasingly isolated.

Alan Knight, author of a magisterial work on the Mexican Revolution, noted that it is possible to plot the southward movement of armies on a map but that general rural rebellion can only be conveyed metaphorically—a rising water level lapping around islands of the Huerta regime and finally covering all like Noah's flood. As this tide rose, the economy atrophied, and income needed to finance Huerta's army declined.[64]

As Villa's forces moved south, antagonism between him and Carranza increased. Historian G. M. Joseph contrasted the two leaders' forces, noting that Villa's were "underdogs and outcasts of the great Chihuahuan expanses, they espoused a freewheeling brand of populism that clashed with Carranza's more gradualist, aristocratic notions of reform."[65]

In June 1914, Villa's 22,000 men then attacked Zacatecas' 12,500-man garrison, producing the largest and bloodiest battle that occurred during the revolt against Huerta. The fall of Zacatecas left 6,000 federal troops and 1,000 Villistas dead and sealed the fate of the Huerta regime.[66]

After the victory at Zacatecas, Carranza and Villa remained openly at odds, even though they were both fighting to topple Huerta. Subsequently Carranza denied Villa ammunition and the coal his locomotives required to move further south, thus preventing him from taking Mexico City. Carranza refused to even contact Zapata, whom he called a "bandit."[67]

Despite their differences, the armies closing in on Mexico City did force Huerta into resigning on July 15, 1914. The federal army backing Huerta was never defeated in set battle. Rather it was simply undermined by surprise attacks and the frequent defection of garrisons.

Huerta left Mexico for exile in Barcelona, where he soon tired of inaction. He then traveled to Texas, where he hoped to launch another revolt. In January 1916 he died there—a death resulting from cirrhosis of the liver induced by a lifetime of hard drinking.[68]

With Villa immobilized by a lack of coal for his locomotives, Obregón continued to advance. He had marched south along Mexico's west coast. He then captured Guadalajara, turned east, and triumphantly marched into Mexico City in August. As had been previously arranged with Huerta's forces, positions facing south towards Morelos were turned over to Obregón's men, thus preventing the Zapatistas from entering Mexico City.

The Constitutionalists demanded and obtained the unconditional surrender and disbanding of the federal army that had served under Díaz, Madero, and finally Huerta. As Obregón's troops entered Mexico City, the national government ceased to exist. The Constitutionalists had learned from Madero that half a victory was no victory at all—the enemy had to be destroyed. Even though the federal army was finally dismantled, neither Díaz's fall nor that of Huerta produced a revolution. These events merely opened the door for more change.[69]

At this point, Mexico was again rid of a dictatorship, but the major leaders—Zapata, Villa, Obregón, and Carranza—strongly disagreed on the kind of society to construct. This reflected their different class origins and the varied social and economic make-up of the regions from which they came. In addition, sharp personal rivalry existed between these leaders.[70]

Middle-class leaders who had taken over state governments in the north soon began carrying out reforms, indicating the future course of the Revolution. Minimum wages were set and hacienda-owned stores, which had mercilessly exploited employees, were outlawed. Conspicuously absent from this list of reforms was any ratification of peasant-initiated land seizures that had already occurred.[71]

CIVIL WAR, 1914–1916

Once Díaz and Huerta were removed in 1914, the Revolution lacked any national goal.
John S. D. Eisenhower, 1993[72]

In an attempt to resolve the question of who should head the government that was to replace the Huerta dictatorship, a convention was called at Aguascalientes, midway between Mexico City and

Villa's Chihuahua bastion. It opened on October 10, 1914, with representatives of the armies of Obregón, Villa, and Carranza declaring the Convention sovereign and beholden to none of the leaders who had sent representatives. Delegates then invited the Zapatistas to Aguascalientes. Each group's uniforms clearly indicated their social background. The Constitutionalists' uniforms were neatly pressed and had shiny buttons. The Villistas wore dirty, sloppy rural clothes. The Zapatistas' attire was similar, but in worse condition.[73]

While they lacked snappy uniforms, the Zapatistas brought what the Convention was seeking—a political program. Their Plan of Ayala, as limited in scope as it was, at least provided a blueprint, and the Convention accepted the provision for taking one-third of each hacienda for peasants. During the Convention, the most revolutionary, popular, and democratic debates of Mexican history occurred. Issues such as women's rights and an activist, interventionist state were seriously considered for the first time in Mexican political history.[74]

The Convention chose as its President Eulalio Gutiérrez, a former mine foreman who had joined Madero in 1910. Although he had later fought with Carranza and become a skilled dynamiter of railroad trains, he was a neutral figure who did not threaten any of the revolutionary leaders. Earlier in 1914, he had served as provisional governor of San Luis Potosí.

While the Convention was meeting, Villa and Carranza continued to build up their forces. Carranza moved reinforcements from the Isthmus of Tehuantepec to Mexico City. Late in October, Villa began to mass his troops around Aguascalientes. Instead of letting the Convention run its course, both leaders ordered troops to approach Aguascalientes in an attempt to influence the Convention's deliberations.[75]

The Convention resolved that Villa and Carranza should resign their commands simultaneously. Villa agreed to resign, but was challenged by Carranza, who questioned whether he had actually relinquished command of his forces. Carranza refused to recognize the Convention's authority and recalled his representatives. Gutiérrez, in the only major decision of his presidency, declared Carranza to be in rebellion and reinstated Villa as head of the Northern Division. With his mantle of legality restored, Villa advanced on Mexico City.[76]

The Convention failed to impose its will on the two recalcitrant rivals and could not overcome personal ambition and regional and class interests. Both Villa and Carranza share blame for the Convention's failure. Most directly, Villa used his troops to threaten the Convention while Carranza never relinquished his command and only agreed to send representatives to the Convention when it appeared that the United States was backing Villa and that Obregón was uncommitted. Whether either leader would have yielded power if they had felt their rival was doing likewise is open to question.[77]

To avoid Villa's forces, Carranza transferred his army from Mexico City, where he had been ruling by decree, to Veracruz. This left a political vacuum in the capital. Despite having driven the oligarchy from power, Villa and Zapata failed to take power for themselves. They just bided their time and finally turned power over to the middle-class leaders of the Convention. Each of these peasant leaders wanted to leave national politics to the Convention while retaining control of their home areas. Carranza, in contrast, viewed himself as the leader of the entire Mexican nation.[78]

Following Carranza's withdrawal, Mexico City was occupied by the armies of Villa and Zapata in the legal role of representatives of the Convention government. On December 4, 1914, Zapata and Villa met at Xochimilco on the outskirts of Mexico City. They could only agree to leave the Convention in power. The possibility of an effective military alliance between the two was diminished since Zapata's guerrilla force, virtually unbeatable on its home turf, lacked the ability or the desire to project force long distances to help Villa. While they discussed land reform, they failed to consider the working class or relations with the United States and other nations. After the meeting, Villa and Zapata decided to abandon the center of the country and return to their own regions whose limited horizons they had never been able to overcome.[79]

Figure 15.3 *Francisco Villa and Emiliano Zapata*
Source: El Paso Public Library, Aultman Collection, photo #A 5648

This decision not to advance on Carranza is one of the most important of the Revolution. Villa's army numbered roughly 40,000, Zapata's 25,000, and another 20,000 or 30,000 were loyal to the Convention. These troops far outnumbered those serving under Carranza.[80]

At this stage, the urban population, especially in Mexico City, was largely uninvolved in the Revolution. Its experience with the Revolution had been to witness the indecision of the Convention government. It saw the Convention's representatives govern using the tactics of guerrilla warfare. For example, when Villista General Tomás Urbina needed operating funds, he kidnapped wealthy individuals and held them for large ransoms, rather than taxing them. Similarly, Villa responded to his critics, especially Huerta supporters, by having some 150 of them assassinated. When Convention President Gutiérrez tried to act independently, Villa ordered his execution. Gutiérrez then fled Mexico City and, powerless, made peace with Carranza.[81]

Within a week of Carranza being declared in rebellion by the Convention, almost all the important military leaders of the northwest and northeast, including Obregón, had joined him. Most of these men were up-and-coming entrepreneurs and public officials. Obregón probably joined Carranza because: 1) he was socially and ideologically closer to him than to Villa and Zapata; 2) he harbored resentment against Villa resulting from their previous encounters in Chihuahua; 3) most of his commanders would not have followed him if he had joined Villa; and 4) Carranza, but not Villa, was willing to allow him to maintain a regional power base in Sonora.[82]

Carranza was hemmed in on the Gulf Coast without a political base. However, he had a world view that was both national and international in scope. During the respite provided by the failure of the Convention army to pursue him, Carranza reorganized. He had access to income from Veracruz customs duties, the sales of Yucatán henequen, and Gulf Coast oil—revenue sources that would not run short as did the revenue Villa obtained from selling cattle to the United States.

Carranza's first major move was political. On January 6, 1915, in a complete reversal of the non-ideological stance he took during the anti-Huerta campaign, Carranza announced his own land reform. Carranza's land reform differed from Zapata's Plan of Ayala in that it called for the reform to be implemented by local, regional, and national agrarian commissions, not peasants themselves—a difference that proved to be fundamental.[83]

After arriving in Veracruz, Carranza created a civilian cabinet, bringing in distinguished men, mainly from the middle class, who represented various regions and activities. Key states, such as Jalisco, Puebla, and Chihuahua, were all represented. The Constitutionalists showed an attention to administrative detail sorely lacking with the representatives of the Convention—who were known as Conventionists. Examples include vaccinating for smallpox and sending teachers for training in the United States. Constitutionalists, though lacking a written manifesto such as the Plan of Ayala, envisioned a modern, capitalist, secular, outward-looking state that would bring Mexico into the modern world.

The Constitutionalists' former allies, the Conventionists, sought autonomous, locally controlled communities carrying out reforms to reinforce traditional patterns of life. They were less involved with organized labor and industry and did not share the Constitutionalists' anti-clericalism. Any analysis of the Conventionists, as well as that of the Consitutionalists, is complicated by each faction's being composed of various, constantly changing groups.[84]

Once they had reorganized in Veracruz, the Constitutionalists launched a military offensive. In late January 1915, Obregón moved west and occupied Mexico City, left practically defenseless by Villa's withdrawal to the northwest.

Obregón upstaged Villa and Zapata by passing out food to the urban poor, something the Convention government had failed to do. In addition, merchants were ordered to sell their goods to the poor at reduced prices. In contrast to the ineffective Convention government, Obregón ruled Mexico City by decree, which both offended and impressed Mexico City dwellers and provided far more decisive governance.[85]

Obregón then advanced northwest to fight Villa, once again abandoning Mexico City to the Zapatistas. By this time, Carranza had established an appreciable following. In addition to a formal alliance with the organized working class, he was supported by many members of the middle class who saw him as a promoter of economic development. Similarly, many *hacendados* and wealthy city dwellers, feeling that Carranza was their best bet, lent support to the Constitutionalists.

Carranza drew peasant support in many areas where Villa and Zapata were seen as far removed from local affairs and lacking a land reform program such as Carranza's, the "legality" of which was constantly emphasized. ("Legality" meant it was in written form to guide authorities.) Carranza astutely played on Villa's failure to distribute land. He claimed that he himself was the real revolutionary and that he would distribute land "during the struggle."[86]

The impending conflict between Obregón and Villa would result in a qualitatively different type of warfare—that of professional armies in conventional battles. Charisma counted for less, and there was no guarantee the most popular leader would win. The Villa–Obregón struggle has been compared to a cockfight, where the only question is who will win, not the issues involved.[87]

In three months of fighting, Obregón advanced 150 miles from Celaya to Aguascalientes. Villa suffered his greatest losses at Celaya where he repeatedly ordered his cavalry to charge Obregón's force, which was protected by elaborate barbed-wire networks and the then-novel machine gun. In these battles, more than 50,000 men were involved on both sides, and 20,000 were killed or wounded. Cool generalship triumphed over élan and charisma. After a final defeat at Aguascalientes, the remaining elements of Villa's force straggled back to Chihuahua, where they reverted to guerrilla warfare.[88]

Villa's defeat resulted from several mistakes. He ignored the advice of his professional military advisor, Felipe Ángeles, to pursue Carranza to Veracruz before he could regroup. Villa also failed to concentrate his forces to defeat Obregón. At the time of the battle of Celaya, his forces were divided and off fighting for control of territory in other areas. Finally, Villa failed to draw Obregón further north, which would have enabled him to sever Obregón's supply lines, which stretched back to Veracruz.[89]

With Villa's army out of the picture, Obregón began occupying territory, and by October 1915 he controlled most of northern Mexico. The Constitutionalists permanently occupied Mexico City. Then they turned their attention toward Morelos, where events had gone almost unaffected by the Carranza-Obregón-Villa struggle.

The Zapatistas had been driven back to the south as Obregón passed through Mexico City in pursuit of Villa, whom he judged to be the greater of his enemies. The Zapatistas correctly felt they had little in common with Carranza. Historian John Womack Jr. commented on how Carranza differed from Zapata, "Rebel and revolutionary he might now be, but in another world—an established and civilized world of clean linen, breakfast trays, high politics, and ice buckets for wine."[90]

While the Constitutionalists were fighting the Villistas, the Zapatistas turned inward and began to create the society they had long envisioned. After Gutiérrez fled Mexico City, the Zapatistas administered Morelos as they saw fit. Reforms went far beyond the Plan of Ayala. Entire haciendas were expropriated without compensation. As soon as the remnants of the old government upheld by Díaz, Madero, and Huerta were swept away, each village in Morelos carried out land reform on its own.[91]

In March 1915, Zapata reported: "The agrarian question has been solved for once and for all. On the basis of their land deeds, the various villages in the state have taken possession of the land in question." While Mexico City verged on starvation, people in Morelos were evidently eating more food than in 1910—and paying less for it. This resulted from shifting land from sugar production to food crops that supplied not only villages but guerrilla forces.[92]

By 1916, the contrast between Morelos and the rest of Mexico was too glaring for the Constitutionalists to ignore. With Villa's forces defeated and scattered, Carranza ordered his forces into Morelos, with the support of the organized working class, industrialists, the middle class, and *hacendados* who wanted to reclaim their land. In April 1916, the Constitutionalist advance began. The 30,000-man army advancing into Morelos differed little from Díaz's army of the previous decade. Its troops came not to liberate, but to conquer the local population, which at best were treated as prisoners of war.[93]

By July 1916, all towns in Morelos were occupied, and the Constitutionalist commander reported the campaign concluded. Once they had assumed control, the Constitutionalist officers systematically looted Morelos. They took everything they could possibly move to be sold on the black market in Mexico City, including bathtubs from hotels in Cuernavaca and sugar mill equipment to be sold as scrap iron.[94]

Due to their lack of preparation, the Zapatistas could offer little resistance during the first half of 1916. However, later in the year they regrouped and again waged effective guerrilla warfare, despite their constant currency and ammunition shortages. The Zapatistas fought with the aid of the entire population, who served as observers, informers, and suppliers of food and shelter, as well as combatants who would take up arms for a battle and then return to their farms.

The government responded with mass assassination. Guerrillas in turn stepped up attacks on railroads, sugar mills, factories, and the southern limits of the Federal District itself. By December, the 30,000-man Constitutionalist army that had occupied Morelos was demoralized and disintegrating. By year's end, Carranza's army had been forced to evacuate Morelos.[95]

Even though the Zapatistas continued to control Morelos, after Villa's defeat Carranza was without political commitments and free of opponents who threatened his regime. The Constitutionalist leader differed from Madero in that he felt that Mexico would not progress until it modernized economically. This was a major departure from Madero's call for "Effective suffrage" and "No re-election." In order to overcome backwardness, Carranza sought to eliminate those opposing change. Despite his being ambitious, there is no doubt that he sincerely felt his government would lead to progress for Mexico and a better life for its people.[96]

The year 1916 saw the end of major combat and the implantation of a coherent national policy by the triumphant Constitutionalists. Once he no longer faced military threats, Carranza halted his reforms. He returned confiscated property to the Porfirian elite (with the exception of very visible enemies such as Huerta's widow, Félix Díaz, and former president De la Barra, who had served as Huerta's foreign minister). The Constitutionalists crushed strikes and allowed land reform to endure only in those states where governors had already committed themselves to such policies, certainly a tiny minority nationwide. In 1916, General Francisco Múgica wrote, "When I was in the capital of Mexico in February of this year, I saw that the Villistas, Zapatistas, and members of the Convention were persecuted far more than the supporters of Huerta . . ."[97]

The new Constitutionalist administration began to rebuild a centralized state—a task that required decades. Mexico City seethed with dissatisfaction, and services were interrupted. Elsewhere in the country, crop failures led to widespread food scarcity. Transportation was uncertain, and, in many areas, government authority was lacking. Bands of disgruntled, leaderless revolutionaries marauded the countryside.[98]

To implement Carranza's policies, Constitutionalist officers, who overwhelmingly came from northern Mexico, assumed governorships and other top posts throughout central and southern Mexico. Often these northern officers were viewed not as liberators but as carpetbaggers attempting to impose unwanted, alien values. Anyone who opposed or openly questioned them was branded a "reactionary." Carranza's northern officers so widely abused their positions that a new term was coined, *carrancear,* meaning to sack, pillage, confiscate, and rob. Unfortunately, such personal enrichment was also prevalent among the officers of other revolutionary groups, including the Zapatistas.[99]

Historian Luis González y González described how these raids played out in San José de Gracia:

> Parties of rebels often came to visit their friends in San José, either to rescue the girls from virginity, or to feast happily on the delicious local cheeses and meats, or to add the fine horses of the region to their own . . . They summoned all the rich residents and told them how much money in gold coin each was to contribute to the cause. In view of the rifles, no one protested.[100]

To consolidate and legitimize his power, in September 1916 Carranza called for a constitutional convention to provide a legal foundation for his government. The convention met and promulgated a new constitution on February 5, 1917. In March 1917, elections were held to select Carranza as president.

THE OUTCOME

> The 1910 Revolution occurred because a political crisis—associated with the Porfirian regime's failure to institutionalise itself and the mounting opposition of (loosely) middle class reformism—opened the door to popular protest, especially peasant protest.
>
> Alan Knight, 1992[101]

The Constitutionalists won because they planned on a national level and used populist tactics to broaden their support. Their control of Tampico, Veracruz, and Yucatán, all of which generated substantial export revenue, allowed the purchase of arms from abroad. The Plan of Ayala did not address the needs of the more heterogeneous population, including artisans, laborers, itinerant merchants, and others with an urban orientation, outside the state of Morelos. Finally, along with the rest of the Western world of the period, the Constitutionalists adopted mass war as a means to power. By 1917, Carranza's army alone totaled 147,000, seven times the number who served in the army at the end of the Porfiriato.[102]

The fact that the Revolution had been initiated by a section of the elite with little interest in social reform limited revolutionary potential. It was further limited by its being led in Coahuila by Carranza, a conservative *hacendado*. In Chihuahua, the Revolution was largely directed against one family, the Terrazas. In Sonora, it was led by upwardly mobile members of the middle class who would become the next generation's elite. In tiny Morelos, with its broad revolutionary base, the goal was an idealized past of communally held village land. As historian John Womack noted, the Zapatistas were "peasants who did not want to change and thus made a revolution."[103]

Many opposing the Constitutionalists were willing to fight for a better Mexico, but these opponents lacked leadership, ideology, and the sophistication to play national and international politics. Many rebel leaders operated independently and were more interested in power than reform. Félix Díaz, who led a second revolt in Oaxaca in 1916, is a prime example. No ideological bridge linked the interests of peasants and city dwellers.

The Zapatistas failed to achieve victory largely because they were unable to attract support from non-peasants or unify the peasantry on a national basis. Peasants were overwhelmingly illiterate and were often poorly informed politically. Many peasants had more allegiance to a local general, fighting for his own interests, than to their logical allies, Villa and Zapata, fighting in some distant state.[104]

Despite their willingness to fight, peasants often lacked clarity concerning just what they were fighting for, as this incident from the biography of Juan Pérez Jolote, a Chiapas Indian, illustrates:

> We returned to Pachuca again and went out to another village, where the Villistas attacked us . . . They asked us why we'd become Carrancistas, and I said: "The Huertistas made us go with them, and when Carranza started winning we had to change sides . . ." An old man with a big moustache said, "Well, what do you want to do now?" I said, "I just want to be on your side . . ." They signed us up and gave us weapons and five pesos each, and that made us Villistas.[105]

Switching of allegiance, based on personal decisions of leaders or on the perception of who would finally win, occurred frequently.[106]

The very concept of "Mexican Revolution" only developed after the fact. There were various revolutions and movements. Some lost, some won. Before 1920, people spoke of the Madero Revolution, the Constitutionalist Revolution, and Zapata's Southern Revolution. Only after 1920 did the term "Mexican Revolution" gain acceptance.[107]

The Revolution dramatically increased the power of the state. This is ironic, since one of the principal causes of the rebellion, especially in the north, was the desire for more local autonomy. Post-revolutionary governments accepted responsibility for some of the social costs of development, such as education and health care, and assumed new roles, such as implementing land reform and arbitrating labor disputes. The Revolution also laid the ground for the creation of mass organizations, especially for workers and peasants, that the state would control.[108]

The Revolution produced a change in political style. Gone was the old elitist, often racist rhetoric, such as this statement by Joaquín García Pimentel of an elite family in Morelos. In 1916, he declared, "The Indian . . . has many defects as a laborer, being as he is, lazy, sottish, and thieving." Politicians adopted a new style, portraying themselves as frank, open, honest, and even plebeian.[109]

The *soldadera* forms the most enduring image of women in the Mexican Revolution. As in the nineteenth century, the revolutionary armies generally did not have troops assigned to tend the wounded and secure and prepare food. These tasks fell on female auxiliaries who accompanied the forces, usually linked to a husband or lover. *Soldaderas* not only provided essential services but also induced men to fight. A Villista major once commented, "We had to have soldaderas if we want to have soldiers."[110]

Soldaderas served for a variety of reasons. Often service provided a way to keep a family intact or to avoid being left alone and unprotected in perilous times. Some became *soldaderas* to earn a

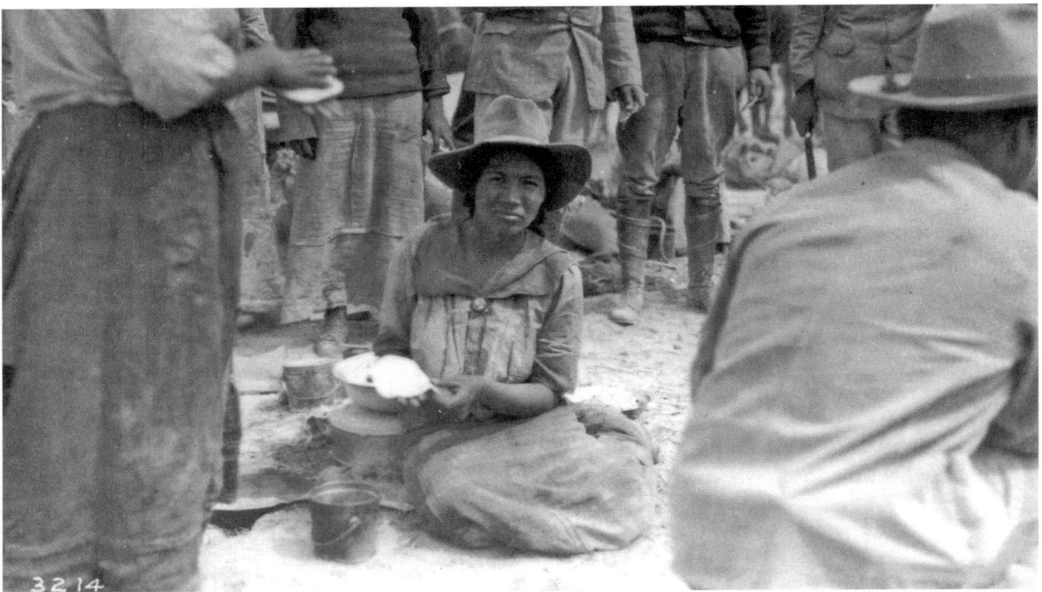

Figure 15.4 *Tortilla maker with army*
Source: El Paso Public Library, Aultman Collection, photo #A 3214

living, given the prevailing economic hardship of the time. When a *soldadera* served, she and her children simply accompanied her man. In his classic account of Villa's forces, *Insurgent Mexico*, John Reed asked a *soldadera* why she fought. She responded by pointing to a nearby figure and replying, "Because he is."[111]

In addition to serving as *soldaderas*, women were active in a variety of revolutionary activities. Some served full-time as combatants, while others smuggled arms and ammunition across the U.S.–Mexico border. In Mexico City, women denounced merchants for hoarding food and occupied markets and bakeries to press their demands for just food prices. They seized government buildings to pressure the government into providing food and services. Upper-class women often volunteered to serve in organizations such as the Red Cross. Still others served as couriers, spies, and political organizers, building support for the revolutionary leaders they supported.[112]

On January 15, 1915, Carranza issued his one significant decree affecting women. For the first time in Mexico, it allowed divorce, in the modern sense of the word. Carranza explained the measure as one that would increase marriage, since, he claimed, those legally married to others could divorce and marry those with whom they were actually living. Carranza also claimed the poor would marry more often if they know they could dissolve a bad relationship. This decree reflected not grass-roots pressure but the anti-clerical sentiments of the revolutionary elite. It was not popular with the mass of Mexican women.[113]

The lack of other action concerning women's rights was not due to women remaining passive. In Mexico, just as in the United States and Great Britain, women's suffrage became an issue. Women petitioned President de la Barra for the right to vote in upcoming elections. Neither De la Barra nor Madero acted on the petition.[114]

Yucatán provides a glaring exception to inaction on women's issues. Change in Yucatán was driven from above by the presence of Salvador Alvarado, who was sent by the Constitutionalists to serve as a virtual proconsul from 1915 to 1918. Only a few of the revolutionary leaders, such as Alvarado, considered women's emancipation to be an integral part of the elevation of Mexico's oppressed peoples. He opened positions in the state government—such as office worker, clerk, cashier, and accountant—to women for the first time and urged women to apply for these jobs. He greatly expanded women's access to education and urged women to study medicine, dentistry, and pharmacy. Minimum wages and maximum hours were established for domestics. Alvarado required *hacendados* to pay the salary of teachers as well as the cost of school equipment. During Alvarado's administration, 1,000 rural schools were created, which led to the hiring of so many teachers that their number rivaled that of soldiers.[115]

In 1916, Alvarado called two feminist Congresses, which he instructed to consider: the best means of freeing women from the yoke of tradition; the role women should play in public life; and the role of primary education in elevating the position of women. Even though those attending were predominantly urban, educated women, Alvarado encountered strong resistance among women themselves to changing their role. Some delegates lamented that more women were going beyond primary school and felt that so much education would prove to be an impediment to marriage. Others favored only gradual change, claiming that women needed to be better prepared before exercising political rights. At the second Congress, attended mainly by middle-class schoolteachers, delegates passed a resolution favoring women's suffrage at the municipal level by a vote of 147 to eighty-three, but rejected the right of women to seek municipal office by a vote of sixty to thirty. Despite the reluctance of even educated women to accelerate the rate of change, the Congresses did put women's issues before the public and thus represented an enormous step forward for the advancement of Mexican women.[116]

As historian Alan Knight noted, "Out of the maelstrom of revolution . . . emerged a society which, compared with pre-1910, was more open, fluid, mobile, innovative and market-oriented." Society opened more fully to mestizos, who jettisoned their alliances with the pre-Revolutionary dominant classes and looked for new allegiances. Those with battlefield experience and a working-class background assumed leadership positions that previously had been reserved for those with a college education and civilian institutional experience.[117]

Between 1910 and 1921, Mexico's population declined from 15.1 million to 14.3 million, thus providing a measure of the Revolution's impact. This population decline only in part resulted from battlefield fatalities, the execution of prisoners, and wounds that often proved fatal due to poor medical care. This decline also resulted from a lowered birth rate, increased emigration, and a lower living standard, which made people more susceptible to diseases such as typhus and the 1918 "Spanish flu" epidemic, which killed as many as 400,000. The 1920 U.S. census enumerated 486,418 U.S. residents born in Mexico, compared to 221,915 in 1910. Living conditions in Mexico cannot be measured with precision, but a decline in nutrition is indicated by corn production plummeting from an average of 3.22 million metric tons between 1906 and 1910 to 1.96 million in 1914.[118]

As a result of the Revolution, Mexico became a haven for refugees whose politics were too radical for them to safely remain in their home country. In the 1920s alone, Peruvian Víctor Raúl Haya de la Torre, Nicaraguan César Augusto Sandino, and Cuban Julio Antonio Mella found refuge in Mexico. In subsequent decades, Mexico continued to accept refugees.[119]

These changes resulted not from the poor dominating the outcome of the Revolution but from their holding on long enough to force the elite to make concessions. This contrasted sharply with Mexico's War for Independence, in which the poor were defeated, leaving the elite to shape independent Mexico's first government to suit its own interests.[120]

During the period of the armed struggle, 1910–1917, the goals of the Revolution lacked clarity since there was no overall coordination of combatants, some of whom fought for opposing goals. In the aftermath of the Revolution, a consensus emerged concerning what the Revolution stood for. These goals, some of which were only inserted into the revolutionary portfolio well after the last battle, included: 1) replacing the Díaz dictatorship with democracy; 2) supplying land to the tiller; 3) the creation of a new government with a strong executive; 4) nationalism; 5) uplifting labor; 6) a coherent state-led development strategy; 7) mass education; and 8) support for Mexico's indigenous population.[121]

WHAT WAS THE REVOLUTION ALL ABOUT?

> It has become clear that what we refer to as the Mexican Revolution was not a linear, homogenous process. Rather it was a variegated mosaic in which diverse social groups with various political agendas converged. Often these groups had markedly different, antagonistic goals. There were sharp regional contrasts and different levels of mobilization.
>
> Felipe Arturo Ávila Espinosa, 2007[122]

Just as was the case with the Conquest of Mexico, the first accounts of the Revolution were written by its victorious participants. These Constitutionalist narrators portrayed the Revolution as a broad, popular movement, strongly agrarian in terms of both social composition and political agenda. They justified the Revolution as a movement that replaced an elitist, authoritarian, inegalitarian, xenophile Porfiriato with a progressive, egalitarian, nationalist society.

By the 1930s, the historiography of the Revolution reflected the structure of the official party. This view stressed the unity of the Revolution, not its various factions. The thesis of the Revolution being a popular, progressive, nationalist revolution against an exploitative regime remained dominant through the 1950s.[123]

This Mexican view of the Revolution was closely mirrored in the United States, the principal source of early foreign studies of the Revolution. Two books written by Americans, Ernest Gruening's *Mexico and its Heritage* (1928) and Frank Tannenbaum's *The Mexican Agrarian Revolution* (1929) presented U.S. readers with the image of a nationalist, populist revolution carrying out agrarian reform. The following generation of American historians, such as Stanley R. Ross and Charles C. Cumberland presented much the same view to American readers.[124]

During the 1950s and 1960s, this consensus on the Mexican Revolution began to dissolve. Critiques of the Mexican government, such as Daniel Cosío Villegas' 1947 article "*La crisis de México*" raised the question "How could a society with so much injustice emerge from one that only a generation earlier represented social justice?"

Regional studies also undermined the old consensus. These studies of the Revolution as it occurred within a single state or region found that disputes among land owners and the rise of new caciques were the dominant events. It raised the question "If the Revolution did not occur in this region, just where did it occur?"[125]

The Cuban Revolution also led to a reevaluation of the Mexican one. The rapid dispossession of the old elite in Cuba caused many to view the Mexican Revolution as being far less revolutionary than it had been portrayed. Similarly, the massacre during the 1968 student movement raised the question "How could a government born out of a popular revolution murder its own children?" The 1968 student movement also launched a generation of scholars who reappraised the Revolution, not as citizens who trusted government but as citizens who distrusted it. The 1960s also had an impact on U.S. scholarship. John Womack's now classic book on Zapata, published in 1969, was the first to emphasize division and conflict among the revolutionary elite.[126]

These events produced a new vision of the Revolution. The revisionists interpret it as a struggle in which the middle class, marginalized by the Porfirian oligarchy, allied with workers and peasants to topple a personalistic, ossified, regime. These revisionists claim the regime emerging from the Revolution crushed local autonomy and established a centralist, elitist state, à la Porfiriato. The similarities between pre- and post-Revolutionary society led essayist José Emilio Pacheco to write, "Our Revolution was the longest, most painful road leading from the Porfiriato to the Porfiriato."[127]

This shifting perception of the Revolution has not been unanimous. Some historians, such as Alan Knight, continue to emphasize the agrarian character of a genuine social revolution that changed the mentality and increased the autonomy of the masses, thereby altering the balance of power in Mexican society.[128]

Chapter 16

Destruction and Development, 1910–1916

The economic impact of the Revolution varied widely by place, year, and type of industry. As a whole, the economy performed well through 1914, after which militarization and destruction took their toll. Destruction associated with the Revolution was highly regionalized, with the north-central and south-central regions being especially hard hit. Coastal areas, the far south, and Mexico City suffered far less. Industries closely tied to the railroad, such as mining, were devastated, while producers of commodities exported by ship, such as oil, bananas, and henequen, prospered.[1]

The Revolution left its mark on virtually all economic activity. As other sectors languished, the proportion of the labor force in agriculture increased. Population and, therefore, the labor supply shifted to the northwest and the Gulf Coast. Many small American-owned firms, which lacked cash reserves, sold their holdings to large American companies, which gained dominance over the economy to a far greater degree than ever before.[2]

ECONOMIC DECLINE, 1911–1916

The Revolution brought an end to the Profirian economic boom. The 2.6 percent average economic growth rate that Mexico enjoyed between 1901 and 1910 would not be achieved again until after 1936. Economist Raymond Vernon calculated that as a result of the Revolution, economic development was retarded by a decade.[3]

The departure of Díaz did not immediately result in economic decline. U.S. tourist investors continued to appear in Mexico and to be met by interim President León de la Barra and then by Madero, just as they had been met by Díaz.[4]

However, as security conditions deteriorated, a decline in new investment halted economic growth. Long-term investment was discouraged by the very real possibility that assets would be destroyed and by the inability to predict future markets and government policy. Beginning in 1912, many U.S. investors curtailed and, if possible, repatriated their investments in railroads, mining, land, and utilities. By 1914, only the oil industry was attracting new investment, and Canada had surpassed Mexico as the largest recipient of U.S. direct foreign investment.[5]

Destruction of productive assets was widespread. Armed bands frequently sacked haciendas. This description of Ciudad Juárez reflected conditions in countless locations from Chihuahua to Morelos:

> At every turn you come upon ruins—houses riddled with bullet holes or breached with shot and shell; a public library razed to the ground, a mere heap of stones; a post office badly damaged; and, opposite the Juárez monument, a brick building, roofless, with gaping windows and walls . . .[6]

As a result of the Revolution, rail service was severely curtailed. To prevent the advance of opposing troops, bridges were destroyed, rails bent, and ties burned. Between 1910 and 1914, the Mexico North Western Railway alone reported 850 bridges burned. All factions seized rolling stock, which was diverted from passenger and freight service to military uses. Shipping costs soared as security needs meant that scout trains had to be sent out, soldiers and armored cars had to be placed on runs, schedules and routes had to be varied, night shipments had to be canceled, and guardhouses had to be maintained along the most vulnerable sections. Carrancista military officers who controlled rail shipments demanded payments, which they pocketed, to free rolling stock for transporting non-military goods. In the fall of 1915, businessmen were paying as much as 3,000 pesos in bribes per freight car or locomotive. Given the interruption of fuel supplies, locomotives were converted to use wood as a fuel. To meet immediate fuel needs, stations were sometimes dismantled and burned as fuel. The decline in rail service allowed the mule and the donkey to stage a comeback and hastened the introduction of truck transport.[7]

The collapse of rail service seriously affected mining. Mines relied on railroads to remove ore and obtain supplies and fuel for their on-site electrical power plants. Some smelters closed due to fuel shortages. As a result of U.S.-imposed embargoes, miners were sometimes unable to purchase dynamite from the United States. As the rule of law receded, revolutionaries and bandits would plunder mine installations. To prevent theft by bandits, who almost invariably arrived by horse, silver was sometimes cast in 400-pound ingots. Revolutionaries, who knew that large mines had access to company funds from the United States, would levy special war taxes. Given the prevailing turmoil, skilled laborers abandoned isolated, vulnerable mine sites. By the beginning of 1914, an estimated 80 percent of the Americans in Mexico had left the country.[8]

Villa did his best to persuade mine owners to continue operations, since mines provided employment and could be taxed. He even prevented members of the militant Industrial Workers of the World (commonly known as IWW or "wobblies") from entering Mexico to organize miners. In February 1915, mine managers in Chihuahua reported that Villa "wanted us to do our very best in the way of working our mills and railroads and that if we required any more help . . . to come and see him."[9]

Of the 110 American mining companies in Mexico, only fourteen worked steadily from 1914 to 1919. In 1915 and 1916, the American Smelting and Refining Company declared no earnings in Mexico, the number of its employees declined from 12,000 to 6,000, and its production declined by 75 percent. Between 1914 and 1916, innumerable small mining firms suffered bankruptcy. In a three-year period, 1912 to 1915, silver production declined from 2,526,715 kilograms to 712,599. The mining sector recovered slowly from the effects of the Revolution. As late as 1921, mine output remained 40 percent below the 1910 level.[10]

Agriculture also suffered a prolonged decrease in production. Buildings were destroyed, and *hacendados* and managers fled, leaving workers without supervision, capital, or tools. So many workers left rural areas to participate in the insurrection that harvests were jeopardized. Cattle were stolen or seized by revolutionary armies to be used as a food source or to be sold in the United States to raise money for arms purchases. The seizure of crops by revolutionary armies discouraged planting. After the land-owning elite fled, Patrick O'Hea, the British vice-consul in Torreón, wrote, "The organization necessary in many cases in this republic for successful agriculture, particularly in regard to irrigation, has been destroyed and production under the changed conditions has been very much reduced."[11]

Between 1910 and 1915, the volume of agricultural production fell by 24 percent. Between 1910 and 1921, the number of cattle in Chihuahua declined from roughly 1.2 million to 60,000.[12]

Various trends—none planned—could be observed in the agricultural sector. In August 1915, as the national transportation system ceased to function, price disparities for corn reached levels of ten-to-one from one region to another. The rural share of national income declined considerably.

While many haciendas were ravished, agriculture in the northwest boomed, since its rail links to the United States remained intact. Despite Carranza's proclaimed agrarian reform, land holdings became increasingly concentrated. Between 1910 and 1921, estates of 1,000 hectares (2,470 acres) or more increased their share of privately held land from 71.8 percent to 77.9 percent.[13]

Few factories and cotton mills were destroyed during the Revolution, since most were located in Monterrey, Mexico City, and the Veracruz–Puebla corridor—areas that saw little combat. All factions considered factories as economic assets to be taxed and thus spared them from attack. In Puebla, mill hands joined their employers to protect their workplaces (and jobs) from attacks by anti-regime elements. Factory production plummeted, though, as rail service declined, making it difficult to market goods or obtain spare parts and raw materials. Monetary collapse provided a further impediment to sustained industrial production. In 1912, 126 cotton textile mills were in operation, but by 1915, only eighty-four were.[14]

The lack of a stable currency added to Mexico's economic woes. To finance his struggle against the Constitutionalists, Huerta forced banks to lend to his administration. To facilitate the massive loans required, the banks' reserve requirements were lowered, thus undermining the credibility of paper currency. As holders of paper currency increasingly turned in bank notes for gold and silver coins, Huerta allowed banks to refuse to convert paper currency to coins. Monetary confusion reigned as Huerta's opponents, military chiefs, and banks each emitted their own paper money.[15]

In 1914, Huerta suspended payment on Mexico's foreign debt. Creditors called for military intervention to force payment. Having learned their lesson in the 1860s, none of the major powers was willing to rescue the lenders. This suspension of payments caused foreign lenders to deny Mexico credits until 1942.[16]

To finance their war efforts, both Villa and Carranza turned to the printing press. Since victors were expected to repudiate the currency of the vanquished, sellers had to make political judgments as to which currency they would accept and at what rate of discount. The paymaster at El Cubo mine in Guanajuato offered miners the choice of receiving their salaries in Villista currency or Carrancista currency. Given the decline in Villa's military fortunes, by the fall of 1915, 20,000 Villista pesos would not buy a tortilla in the Laguna. Since much of the printing was of poor quality, counterfeiters could produce currency that looked as good as, if not better than, the real thing.[17]

By mid-1915, the Constitutionalists had printed 672 million pesos, compared to the 193.2 million pesos that were in circulation in 1910. In keeping with Gresham's Law, the proliferation of paper currency drove silver coins out of circulation. A 1916 government decree referred to twenty-one types of paper money, all of them legal tender. During that year, as a result of runaway inflation, the peso–dollar exchange rate shifted from 22.72 to 1 to 217.39 to 1. The Constitutionalists even began to demand partial payment of taxes, not in their own currency, but in gold. There was widespread reversion to a barter economy, except in export enclaves and border areas where foreign currency circulated.[18]

The lack of a stable currency caused producers to stockpile goods rather than selling them for increasingly depreciated currency. It also disrupted the government's ability to collect taxes and led to massive capital flight. The lack of any acceptable means of payment even prevented many from boarding Mexico City streetcars. Labor's already precarious share of national income declined as wages failed to keep up with inflation.[19]

Two factors led to the reestablishment of a stable currency. In 1916, with victory in hand, the Constitutionalists began the massive minting of gold and silver coins. Also, in a reversal of Gresham's Law, as paper currency ("bad money") fell to near zero value, hoarded coins ("good money") went back into circulation to provide a medium of exchange, bypassing the official currency. This shift occurred within a matter of days, and paper money would not circulate again in large amounts until the end of 1931.[20]

REVOLUTIONARY DEVELOPMENT, 1911–1916

While rail service was interrupted, marine commerce was largely unaffected by the Revolution. Even during 1915 and 1916, the American-owned Ward Line provided almost uninterrupted passenger and cargo service between New York, Havana, Veracruz, Tampico, and Progreso, Yucatán. Thanks largely to maritime commerce, U.S. imports from Mexico, which totaled $57 million in 1911, increased through 1916, when they reached $105 million. Even though U.S. exports to Mexico declined at mid-decade, they quickly rebounded.[21]

After 1911, the oil industry boomed, the Revolution not withstanding. By 1915, Mexico had become the world's second largest oil producer, behind only the United States. The following year, production reached 40.5 million barrels, up from 12.6 million in 1911. Between 1910 and 1921, the population of Tampico, the major oil center, increased from 23,310 to 94,667. With soaring production levels, the weak Mexican market was soon saturated, causing oilmen to turn to exports. All the revolutionary leaders refrained from damaging oil production facilities because they hoped to tax petroleum. Also, since production remained largely in the hands of American and British companies, no revolutionary leader wanted to offend the U.S. and British governments by attacking property of their citizens.[22]

The problem for oilmen operating in Mexico shifted from locating fields and securing leases to finding foreign markets and ships to deliver the oil. Beginning in 1912, Doheny began to order tankers to meet his transport needs. Fortunately for these oil producers, world demand soared, spurred by increases in heating, shipping, paving, industry, auto use, and the conversion of the world's naval fleets from coal to oil. Since the oil industry had few ties to the rest of the economy, producers were largely unaffected by interruptions in the delivery of Mexican-supplied goods. Jobs were so scarce that workers would appear on their own, seeking oil-field employment, sparing companies the effort of recruiting.[23]

Spectacular oil strikes continued, most notably at a well known as Cerro Azul No. 4, seventy-five miles south of Tampico. When the well blew in on February 10, 1916, the 4,000-pound string of drilling tools shot straight out of the hole and landed 125 feet away. Cerro Azul spewed a 260,000 barrel-a-day jet of crude a thousand feet into the air—the largest gusher in the history of the industry. The well ran wild for nine days, saturating the ground for two miles around. When the flow was finally shut in, 150,000 barrels a day flowed from the well without pumping, making it the most productive shallow well ever. By 1932, it had produced 80 million barrels.[24]

The weak central governments of the revolutionary period exercised little control over the oil industry. The advantages provided by the absence of government regulation were offset by armed rebels who would enter oil camps and demand supplies, including food, livestock, and fodder. Oil companies often paid "taxes" to competing revolutionary bands so they might operate in peace.

Between 1914 and 1920, a former Huertista general, Manuel Peláez, requested large "loans" from oil companies. These funds allowed him to assemble the best-paid, best-fed, best-outfitted armed force in Mexico. He exercised control over substantial oil properties along the Gulf Coast and operated virtually independently of other leaders. The presence of Peláez, who was variously characterized as an extortionist, a cacique, and the champion of local *hacendados*, was key to the sustained growth of the oil industry during the Revolution.[25]

Changes in the Mexican oil business occurring at this time reflected changes in the world oil business. Increasingly, production was dominated not by larger-than-life pioneers such as Doheny and Pearson but by huge, impersonal, vertically integrated corporations. Pearson sold his oil properties to Royal Dutch-Shell. Standard Oil of New Jersey began to buy massive amounts of Mexican oil. Thanks to the oil boom, U.S. and British investment in Mexico increased substantially during the Revolution.[26]

As a result of oil, Mexico became more closely linked than ever to the United States. In 1911, Mexico only supplied 1 percent of U.S. petroleum needs. By 1919, Mexico supplied 14 percent of the greatly increased U.S. demand. More than two-thirds of the petroleum was exported as crude oil, with little value added.[27]

Given its isolation from combat zones, henequen production was not interrupted. The United States had become so dependent on henequen twine for its wheat harvest that when unrest threatened to interrupt supply, President Wilson ordered U.S. navy ships to Yucatán to assure delivery of the fiber. These vessels brought the gold used to pay for the henequen to Yucatán and then returned to U.S. soil with the fiber. As historian Gilbert Joseph commented, "While the rest of the Republic made war, Yucatán made money."[28]

As soon as Villa was driven back to Chihuahua, the Constitutionalists turned their attention to economic recovery. They welcomed industrial magnates, foreign and domestic, back into Mexico. Relying on an established industrial elite facilitated economic recovery. Beginning in 1916, to increase agricultural production for both export and domestic use, Carranza began to return seized estates to their former owners, including such arch-enemies of the Revolution as the Terrazas and the Creels. He believed that the elite could best restore agricultural production. Such a return of land also allowed Carranza to build a political base among members of this group.[29]

Given the disruption of the war years, Mexico did not carry out a census until 1921. Based on this census data, economist Leopoldo Solís calculated that between 1910 and 1921, the economy shrank from 11,650 to 11,273 million 1950 pesos.[30]

Chapter 17

Trying to Pick a Winner, 1910–1916

U.S. efforts to interfere notwithstanding, the Revolution was started by Mexicans, conducted by Mexicans, and resolved in a wholly Mexican fashion.

John S. D. Eisenhower, 1993[1]

TAFT AND THE FALL OF DÍAZ, 1909–1911

By the end of the Porfiriato, the United States and Mexico were inexorably linked. Henry Lane Wilson, who presented his credentials as ambassador in March 1910, reported that the U.S. embassy in Mexico City generated 33 percent of all State Department correspondence, which was handled by "as many as six clerks."[2]

The embassy served the needs of some 70,000 Americans living in Mexico and of U.S. investors who had roughly $800,000,000 invested there. With this large stake in Mexico, it became clear that the United States could never again be truly neutral in matters concerning Mexico. Recognizing Mexican governments put the U.S. stamp of approval on them and discouraged rebels. Non-recognition encouraged rebels. The U.S. also exerted influence over Mexico by making or withholding investments and loans, by raising or lowering tariffs, and by selling or embargoing arms.[3]

Throughout the Revolution, the crucial question for U.S. policy makers was not neutrality but whether or not to intervene militarily. During the twenty-five-year period after the Spanish–American War, the United States intervened thirty-five times in Central America and the Caribbean.[4]

Near the end of the Porfiriato, the United States might have seized on any of a number of reasons to oppose Díaz. These included the possible leasing of Magdalena Bay in Baja California to the Japanese, Díaz's favoring of British investors, and his support for Nicaraguan President José Santos Zelaya (ousted by a U.S.-supported rebellion), In addition, the Mexican government began taxing oil imports, angering Standard Oil Company officials, since one of its subsidiaries was Mexico's sole oil importer. Finally, U.S. officials became concerned that Díaz would be unable to quell unrest.[5]

Despite having reasons to do so, President Taft did not attempt to oust Díaz. Taft's sympathies lay with his dictatorial Mexican counterpart, and he hoped his 1909 meeting with Díaz in Ciudad Juárez would strengthen Díaz's hold on the presidency. Taft had a well-founded fear that Díaz's downfall would, as Henry Lane Wilson expressed it, "result in a long period of disorder and anarchy."[6]

In 1910, after issuing his Plan of San Luis Potosí, Madero and his associates printed and distributed their literature throughout the U.S. southwest and freely exported arms to Mexico for their insurrection. Even if Taft had attempted it, suppressing arms smuggling into Mexico through isolated border areas would have been difficult, since the population on the border generally sympathized with Madero.[7]

Taft, the former colonial governor of the Philippines, never ruled out the possibility of intervention. He wrote his wife in October 1909, ". . . it is inevitable that in case of a revolution or internecine strife we should interfere, and I sincerely hope the old man's official life will extend beyond mine, for that trouble would present a problem of the utmost difficulty."[8]

With the exception of Standard Oil Company officials, most American businessmen remained pro-Díaz. U.S. journalist John Kenneth Turner observed that due to the availability of cheap labor in Mexico, "American capitalists support Díaz with a great deal more unanimity than they support Taft."[9]

U.S. tolerance of Madero's insurrectionary activities contributed to his victory. As would be the case throughout the Revolution, the U.S. government did not act with a single mind. Officials on the border tolerated arms smuggling into Mexico, Ambassador Wilson felt keeping Díaz in power was the key to Mexican stability, and Taft professed neutrality. As Díaz was going into exile, President Taft sent him a hand-written letter stating:

> I write to express my feeling of warm friendship and admiration for you as a man, a statesman, and as a patriot. After your long and faithful service to Mexico and the Mexican people, it arouses in me the profoundest feeling of sympathy and sorrow to see what you have done temporarily forgotten.[10]

THE UNITED STATES AND MADERO, 1911–1913

The Taft administration felt that Madero would reverse Díaz's pro-British policy and thus quickly extended recognition to his government. When the Orozco revolt broke out, Taft offered to let Madero transport troops across Texas by rail. On March 14, 1912, to cut off the supply of arms to Orozco, Taft embargoed the shipment of arms to Mexico. Two weeks later, when it became obvious that this hurt Madero, Taft exempted Madero's government from the embargo. Madero took advantage of this exemption to buy guns, ammunition, and two observation planes for General Huerta to use against Orozco. This U.S. support for Madero, which reflected a fear of generalized violence in Mexico, forced Orozco to shift from fielding a regular army that threatened Mexico City to guerrilla warfare.[11]

The honeymoon between the United States and Madero ended after it became apparent that Madero could not quickly suppress the Orozco and Zapata uprisings. This called into question Madero's ability to maintain law and order. Ambassador Wilson was especially shrill in his condemnation of Madero, since he felt not only that Madero was unable to maintain order but also that he was a naive dreamer. Wilson felt Madero's advocacy of democracy demonstrated naiveté in a country where, as he noted, "80 per cent. of the population is Indian, unable to read or write, with no ideas of citizenship or notions of constitutional government."[12]

In June 1912, when Madero instituted a $0.015 per barrel tax on oil produced in Mexico, U.S.–Mexican relations took a turn for the worse. When Madero announced the new tax to finance the military effort against Orozco, oilmen became furious. They clamed the tax was confiscatory and equaled 17 percent of their profits. This was an outrageous lie, but it made good newspaper copy. The oil companies finally negotiated a lower tax rate.[13]

Madero also ordered the dismissal of U.S. railroad employees who did not speak Spanish. This, the oil tax, and Madero's permitting trade union organization turned U.S. businessmen against him. After decades of Díaz's accommodating attitude, the U.S. business community refused to accept any tinge of nationalism. This became self-defeating. As successive revolutionary leaders emerged, the United States came into conflict with each of them as they adopted nationalist policies.[14]

Late in 1912, the Taft administration, fearing that Madero would be unable to protect U.S. lives and property, sent warships to Mexican ports to protect American interests. Once the Mexican people saw the ships, they concluded that the U.S. government had given up on Madero.[15]

When Félix Díaz and Bernardo Reyes revolted against Madero, Ambassador Wilson's actions reflected not U.S. policy but his personal opinion of Mexico's president. During the stalemate between Félix Díaz and Madero's forces, Ambassador Wilson did his best to discredit Madero and to turn the diplomatic corps and the U.S. government against him.[16]

On his own initiative, Ambassador Wilson arranged for General Huerta, still ostensibly fighting to preserve Madero's presidency, to meet secretly with Félix Díaz in the U.S. embassy. There they signed the Pact of the Embassy, the agreement that Huerta would betray Madero, join Díaz, and become the provisional president.[17]

After helping arrange this unholy transfer of power, Ambassador Wilson informed Washington, "Our position here is stronger than ever." He did not realize that, rather than restoring order, the coup he was involved in would lead to even more massive bloodshed.[18]

Wilson bragged of his intimate knowledge of the coup. He toasted to its success with Félix Díaz and declared: "This is the salvation of Mexico. From now on there will be peace, progress and wealth." The day Madero and his vice-president were arrested, Wilson hosted a reception at the U.S. embassy attended by both Huerta and Díaz.[19]

While Huerta still held her husband prisoner, Sara Pérez de Madero pleaded with Ambassador Wilson to intervene on her husband's behalf. In his memoirs, Wilson noted that after meeting with Madero's wife, he had told Huerta of his concern for Madero's safety. However, in the cable Wilson sent to Secretary of State Philander Knox on February 19, 1913, he stated:

> My advice as to whether it was best to send the ex-President out of the country or place him in a lunatic asylum was asked by General Huerta, to which I replied that that which was best for the peace of the country ought to be done by him.

Since Madero's death, this response has been generally viewed as assent for his murder.[20]

Ambassador Wilson was one of the few to publicly accept the official version of Madero's murder. He cabled the State Department two days after the killing, "I am disposed to accept the Government's version of the affair and consider it a closed incident."[21]

Despite the ensuing civil strife that cost hundreds of thousands of lives, Ambassador Wilson never had second thoughts. In his memoirs, he justified his role, claiming the coup "stopped further effusion of blood, allowed the population of the city to resume its usual peaceful occupations, and led finally to the creation of a provisional government which rapidly restored peace throughout the republic."[22]

Mexicans do not remember Ambassador Wilson that way. Author Carlos Fuentes expressed the widely held Mexican view: "Madero respected free elections, a free press, and an uncontrolled Congress. Significantly, he was promptly overthrown by a conspiracy of the American ambassador, Henry Lane Wilson, and a group of reactionary generals."[23]

THE UNITED STATES AND HUERTA, 1913–1914

Huerta, realizing that a positive response from the United States was crucial to his long-term survival, cabled Taft on February 18, 1913, "I have the honor to inform you that I have overthrown this government, the forces are with me and from now on peace and prosperity will reign." Huerta assumed that since the United States had embraced Díaz, it would embrace him.[24]

The U.S. business community in Mexico welcomed Huerta, feeling the country needed a new strongman and that Huerta would fill that role. The U.S.-owned *Mexican Herald,* the newspaper catering to the English-language community, made the following front-page comment after the coup: "Viva Díaz! Viva Huerta! After a year of near anarchy a military dictatorship looks good to Mexico." Ambassador Wilson recommended the recognition of Huerta. However the State

Department, rather than following its usual policy of recognizing de facto governments, made recognition dependent on Huerta making concessions and demonstrating his ability to protect U.S. lives and property.[25]

Unfortunately for Huerta, his government had not received U.S. recognition by March 4, 1913, when Woodrow Wilson, a former political science professor at Princeton, assumed the presidency. He believed that Christian virtues were as applicable to the conduct of foreign affairs as to personal conduct. This led him to remove Ambassador Wilson (no relation to the president) whom he felt was morally implicated in Madero's murder.[26]

President Wilson's efforts to apply what in the abstract were noble principles produced contradictory and often unexpected results. On the one hand, Wilson believed that each nation should determine its own destiny. At the same time, he had a strong desire to shape Mexico so that it met his standards of decency and democracy. In November 1913, when he was asked to explain his Mexican policy, Wilson replied, "I am going to teach the Spanish American republics to elect good men."[27]

In applying his interpretation of morality, Wilson refused to recognize Huerta's government. In his 1913 State of the Union Address, Wilson explained this refusal:

> There can be no certain prospect of peace in America until Gen. Huerta has surrendered his usurped authority in Mexico; until it is understood on all hands, indeed, that such pretended governments will not be countenanced or dealt with by the Government of the United States.[28]

In addition to non-recognition, President Wilson used his control over arms sales to undermine Huerta. Initially, under the policy inherited from Taft, arms could legally be sold only to the Mexican government, thus preventing arms sales to rebels. To end the supply of arms to Huerta, on August 17, 1913, Wilson decreed an embargo on all arms sales to Mexico. This, however, had an unanticipated effect. Huerta, who controlled several ports, could buy arms on the international market. The Constitutionalists trying to oust him controlled no ports and therefore suffered because of the embargo, despite sympathetic U.S. citizens smuggling arms across the border.[29]

After Huerta dissolved the Mexican Congress in October 1913, Wilson threw his full support to the Constitutionalists. Huerta's subsequent actions further soured relations with the Wilson administration. He substantially increased the oil tax imposed by Madero. This reflected financial necessity more than nationalism. Given the U.S. failure to recognize his government, Huerta increasingly turned to Europe, and especially Britain, for loans and investment capital, which further estranged him from the United States.

In November 1913, Wilson announced, "If General Huerta does not retire by force of circumstances it will become the duty of the United States to use less peaceable means to put him out." To further undermine Huerta, Wilson applied pressure on the European powers that had recognized Huerta to suspend loans and arms sales to Mexico.[30]

When it became apparent that the arms embargo was benefiting Huerta, Wilson complained that it "hinders and delays the very thing that the government of the United States is now insisting upon, namely, that Mexico shall be left free to settle her own affairs and as soon as possible put them on a constitutional footing." On February 3, 1914, Wilson ended the embargo on arms sales to Mexico, and the Constitutionalists began to buy copious amounts of arms and ammunition from the United States.[31]

Throughout his presidency, Wilson came under intense pressure from railroaders, oilmen, and cattle barons such as William Randolph Hearst to intervene directly in Mexico to restore peace, order, and security. Wilson would decline, noting, "I have to pause and remind myself that I am the President of the United States and not of a small group of Americans with vested interests in

Mexico." Some of the factors making direct intervention unattractive were: 1) its high financial cost; 2) the worsening of diplomatic relations throughout Latin America that interventions produced; 3) the diplomatic embarrassment created outside of Latin America; and 4) the inability to guarantee that direct intervention would achieve even short-term objectives.[32]

The major U.S. oil producers joined the effort to oust Huerta. At this point, they preferred Carranza, whom they considered more pro-American than Huerta. The oil companies refused to pay taxes to Huerta and paid them to Carranza. Such "taxes" would be paid to Carranza even before his troops occupied the area where the oil wells being taxed were located. Doheny's company alone apparently gave Carranza $685,000.[33]

Wilson took concrete action to oust Huerta in the spring of 1914. This action followed the arrest on April 9 of eight U.S. sailors from the U.S.S. *Dolphin* who were attempting to buy gasoline. They had unwittingly landed their small boat in a restricted zone in Tampico, a port under Huerta's control but besieged by Constitutionalists. The arrested sailors were released unharmed after ninety minutes, with apologies from the port commander and an expression of regret by General Huerta himself.[34]

In response, Rear Admiral Henry Mayo, the commander of the U.S. naval squadron at Tampico, demanded that the Mexicans hoist the U.S. flag on shore and salute it with twenty-one guns. The matter was referred to General Huerta, who replied that the U.S. flag would be saluted if U.S. forces would then salute the Mexican flag. At the time, he wryly commented that it was odd that the United States should demand a salute from a government it did not even recognize.[35]

The U.S. flag had yet to be saluted by April 21, 1914, when U.S. troops landed in Veracruz. Although the landing has generally been associated with the arrest of the sailors in Tampico, as Secretary of Navy Josephus Daniels later wrote, "The purpose of the landing was accomplished in the weakening and the undoing of Huerta's reign of terror."[36]

The landing was timed to prevent the German steamer *Ypiranga* from unloading a shipment of 200 machine guns and 15 million cartridges destined for Huerta. The Wilson administration felt that if Huerta obtained the arms, it would prolong the killing of Mexicans and that if the United States ever intervened, the arms would be used against Americans. Secretary of Navy Daniels' message to Rear Admiral Frank Fletcher, anchored off Veracruz, was brief and to the point. It stated: "Seize the custom house. Do not permit war supplies to be delivered to Huerta government or any other party."[37]

Even though the Mexican commander at Veracruz ordered Mexican troops not to oppose the landing, volunteers and cadets at the naval academy resisted the Americans. Cannons on U.S. ships were used to silence the Mexican defenders. Before the U.S. forces took control of the port, seventeen Americans and 126 Mexicans had been killed. The intensity of the fighting is indicated by the awarding of fifty-five Medals of Honor to members of the landing force—the most ever awarded for a single engagement.[38]

The Veracruz landing had several unintended effects. Huerta played the anti-gringo game, declaring, in effect, "Either you support me or you are pro-gringo." The *Ypiranga* landed at Puerto México (today Coatzacoalcos) and delivered the arms to Huerta. The landing inflamed anti-American feelings and led to the stoning of the *Mexican Herald* and the U.S. consulate in Mexico City. Elsewhere in Mexico, U.S. flags were burned. Thousands of U.S. citizens, including many who had established small farms, left Mexico fearing an outbreak of anti-American violence.[39]

Carranza, in a display of the nationalism that would bedevil Wilson for the rest of the decade, denounced the landing as a violation of Mexican sovereignty. On April 23, 1914, in response to this criticism, the Wilson administration imposed an arms embargo on the Constitutionalists. On May 16, after Carranza moderated his anti-American rhetoric, Wilson allowed the shipment of arms to ports such as Tampico that by this time was in Constitutionalist hands. Allowing arms shipments to ports, but not across the U.S.–Mexico border, clearly favored Carranza, who controlled Tampico, over Villa. Wilson never explained his decision, which has been attributed to the influence of John Lind, Wilson's special representative to Mexico, who favored Carranza. Also, historian Friedrich Katz has suggested that Wilson may have been trying to maintain rough parity between Carranza and Villa so he could play them off against each other and influence the outcome of the Revolution.[40]

While the landing at Veracruz failed to deny Huerta the arms on the *Ypiranga*, it did have its intended effect. The U.S. occupation of the port denied the Huerta administration customs revenue, hastening its collapse. The United States collected and retained customs duties while it occupied the port.

Eventually Wilson concluded that Huerta would not call democratic elections, so he convened an international conference to facilitate regime change. From April 22 to July 5, 1914, the conference met at Niagara Falls, Ontario. Delegates sent by Wilson and Huerta met with the ambassadors of Argentina, Brazil, and Chile. These countries offered their good offices to help resolve the conflict. Wilson had hoped to use the conference to remove Huerta and to provide an alternative to the Constitutionalists, whom he viewed as too nationalistic.[41]

Once again, Carranza's nationalism confronted Wilson. The Mexican leader refused to participate in the Niagara Falls conference, declaring he would "never be made a party to proceedings which place the election of a President of Mexico in the hands of the Washington government." On June 1, Wilson embargoed arms shipments to Carranza to pressure him into allowing the conference to choose a provisional president for Mexico. The conference was finally halted when it became obvious that Constitutionalists would achieve a military victory over Huerta, despite the arms embargo.[42]

WILSON AND THE CONSTITUTIONALISTS, 1914–1916

The question facing the United States after the collapse of the Convention government was whether to favor Villa or Carranza. On September 9, 1914, in a display of evenhandedness, all restrictions were removed on arms shipments from the United States to Mexico. Both Villa and Carranza realized that they could not stay in power if the United States was openly hostile to them, so they attempted to generate favorable publicity for their respective factions.[43]

At the time of Huerta's resignation, Villa appeared to have a better chance of securing U.S. backing, since he was viewed as more pro-American. His preventing looting after capturing Torreón in October 1913 impressed U.S. observers. Subsequently he protected U.S. commercial interests not only from true bandits but also from other revolutionaries who were called bandits by foreign firms. He so scrupulously respected U.S.-owned properties that opportunistic Americans would buy Mexican-owned land in order to protect it from expropriation. The Mexican owners preferred the meager prices offered by the Americans to having their properties seized by Villistas without compensation.[44]

To bolster his pro-American image, Villa even ordered his troops to protect the property of cattle baron William Randolph Hearst and that of the American Smelting and Refining Company. He pledged to a U.S. agent that he would respect U.S. interests and that he would not adopt anti-American positions. Villa's stand on foreign investment was that it would be "religiously respected." For a time, Villa was the ideal revolutionary from the U.S. point of view in that he defused the potential for violent upheaval by implementing reforms, but only seized Mexican properties.[45]

Many U.S. businessmen favored Villa since he was seen as a strong leader, Díaz style, who could rule Mexico with an iron hand. They felt that the proper solution to Mexico's problems was control, not democracy. After the landing at Veracruz, even though nominally Carranza's subordinate, Villa ingratiated himself to Wilson by publicly declaring that he had no objection to the landing since its goal was to oust Huerta. Wilson indicated his pro-Villa position in a December 1914 conversation with a French military attaché in Washington. He stated: "Villa today represents the only instrument of civilization in Mexico. His firm authority allows him to create order, and to educate the turbulent masses of peons so prone to pillage."[46]

Carranza, a *hacendado* himself, was loath to seize haciendas and so raised money by taxing U.S. interests. This initially turned the United States against him, as did his comments concerning the landing at Veracruz and the Niagara conference. Carranza's unwillingness to accept policy favored by the United States led President Wilson to state in a July 1915 memo to Secretary of State Robert Lansing, "I think I have never known of a man more impossible to deal with on human principles than this man Carranza."[47]

With Huerta gone, the Wilson administration no longer had a rationale for occupying Veracruz. As a result, U.S. troops withdrew on November 23, 1914, after having made substantial sanitary improvements. As U.S. troops departed, they turned over to Carranza war matériel seized when U.S. troops landed, other arms intended for Huerta that had arrived after the U.S. landing, and arms brought by U.S. troops and not removed. This matériel, which included cars, trucks, radios, artillery, machine guns, 12,000 rifles and carbines, 3,375,000 rounds of ammunition, and 632 rolls of barbed wire, was used by Obregón to rout Villa's forces. The United States also turned over to Carranza the 2,604,051.20 pesos that it had collected in customs revenues while it occupied the port. As historian John Hart declared, "The Americans' transfer of arms stored at Veracruz to the Constitutionalists in November 1914 turned the tide of the revolution." No official explanation was given as to why these arms were delivered to Carranza. Perhaps it was simply a matter of expediency—Carranza's forces controlled the area and no Convention forces were nearby.[48]

By 1915, economic pressures had forced Villa to change his policy. He had exhausted his supply of cattle, so he began to tax American-owned haciendas and mining companies. He also began seizing from foreigners whatever goods he needed and threatened mining companies with seizure if they did not resume operations. The U.S.-owned Cananea Copper Company was subjected to forced loans. Since Carranza could also rely on oil revenue and customs duties, soon taxes levied by Villa exceeded those of Carranza.[49]

Villa's image in the United States also suffered due to his association with Gutiérrez and the Convention government. Gutiérrez had led guerrilla attacks on American-owned mines in San Luis Potosí. As provisional governor of that state he had abolished debt peonage, established minimum wages, and threatened nationalization of foreign-owned property. Not only was Gutiérrez seen as too radical but the Convention was linked with Zapata, who was in disfavor in Washington.[50]

In contrast to Villa, Carranza was the only viable elite leader left in Mexico. Carranza's return of confiscated estates to their former owners and his lack of close ties to Europeans contributed to his becoming an increasingly attractive option for the United States. Beginning soon after his issuance of the Plan of Guadalupe, Carranza sent agents to the United States to promote the Constitutionalist cause and to pay for favorable publicity. This propaganda campaign intensified after Huerta's fall as Mexican consuls in the United States promoted Carranza and subsidized pro-Carranza newspapers. Beginning in 1916, an attractively designed magazine, the *Mexican Review*, was mailed to a target list of 15,000 influential Americans. At the same time, Carranza's spinmeisters portrayed Villa as a common bandit who served as a tool of reactionaries. All these factors led the United States to cast its lot with Carranza.

The impending Great War began to dominate U.S. thinking, leading policy makers to seek a rapid end to hostilities in Mexico. Early in his administration, Wilson had sought to maintain parity among revolutionary groups, thus allowing the United States to force them into compromise. However, as war began to loom in Europe, the United States decided to pick a winner, propel him to a rapid victory, and thus prevent Germany from taking advantage of on-going conflict to meddle in Mexican affairs. On October 10, 1915, Secretary of State Lansing wrote in his diary, "Our possible relations with Germany must be our first consideration; and all our intercourse with Mexico must be regulated accordingly."[51]

As a result of Villa's taxes, effective pro-Carranza propaganda, and the threat posed by Germany, on October 19, 1915, the Wilson administration granted Carranza de facto recognition. That same day, he placed an embargo on the sale of arms to all other factions.[52]

THE COLUMBUS RAID AND WILSON'S RESPONSE

On March 9, 1916, about 500 Villistas raided Columbus, New Mexico, four miles north of the U.S.–Mexican border. Villa remained with a small reserve on the Mexican side of the border, while his main force stormed the small town at 4:45 a.m. In the raid, the Villistas obtained a small amount of loot and a few horses. Eight U.S. soldiers and nine civilians died. Roughly sixty Villistas were killed in Columbus and about seventy more died as they were chased back to Mexico.

Ever since the raid, which was the first foreign attack on U.S. territory since the war of 1812, historians have debated Villa's motive. Several reasons have been suggested, including Villa being incensed at the U.S. recognition of Carranza and the turning over to him of the arms and customs revenues at Veracruz. Villa believed that Carranza had signed a pact with the United States that compromised Mexican sovereignty. This belief turned out to be false, but Villa's mistaken notion could have led to the attack. Villa could also have been hoping to draw the United States and Mexico into war, an event that could have produced the collapse of the Carranza government.[53]

Another suggested cause for Villa's attack was revenge for his November 1915 defeat at Agua Prieta. Villa attacked Carranza's forces in this border town, located across from Douglas, Arizona. Unbeknown to Villa, the Wilson administration had allowed 3,500 of Carranza's troops to leave Mexico at Piedras Negras, travel by rail across U.S. territory, and then cross back into Mexican territory to reinforce Agua Prieta. The Carrancistas defended Agua Prieta with barbed wire and machine guns supplied by the United States. As a result, when Villa attacked, his forces were decimated.[54]

Regardless of Villa's motives for the attack on Columbus, from then on he remained bitterly anti-American. In a 1922 interview, Villa stated he would like to send his children abroad for an education. When asked if he would consider sending them to the United States, he replied: "No, not to the United States. The first thing I'm going to teach my children is to hate the enemy of my race."[55]

The U.S. response to Villa's raid was one of outrage. President Wilson ordered an embargo on all arms shipments to Mexico. Ironically, this hurt Carranza, who could afford to buy U.S. arms, and favored his two major opponents, Villa and Zapata, who could not afford such purchases.[56]

Wilson, facing reelection in 1916, was conscious that he could not look "weak" to the electorate. Given this political imperative, he ordered General John "Black Jack" Pershing into Mexico "for the sole purpose of capturing the bandit Villa." Pershing's force crossed the border with 5,000 men, including cavalry, infantry, engineers, artillery units, and the entire U.S. Air Force—eight Curtiss Jenny biplanes—for reconnaissance. Later, the strength of his force was increased to 10,000 men. Pershing's search for Villa relied on the tactics used to pursue Apaches. He deployed small, highly maneuverable units that could live off the land for days. These mounted troops made several indecisive contacts with the Villistas, who broke and scattered.[57]

Even though Villa's attack on Columbus was the initial rationale for the Pershing expedition, after Pershing entered Mexico his withdrawal was used as a bargaining chip. The Wilson administration indicated that Pershing would remain until Carranza provided a written guarantee that his forces would protect Americans and their property. That the expedition was used for purposes other than chasing Villa was not surprising. Many questioned its purpose from the start, noting the heavy presence of infantry and artillery, neither of which was suitable for chasing mounted Villistas.[58]

Given Carranza's reaction to the landing at Veracruz, it is not surprising that he also criticized the Pershing expedition as a violation of Mexican sovereignty. He refused to let Pershing's forces

Figure 17.1 *Pershing's supply wagons*
Source: El Paso Public Library, Aultman Collection, photo #B 692

use the Mexican rail system for supply, so Pershing monopolized the production of the infant American truck industry. Eventually, his expedition acquired more than 500 trucks.

As Carranza grew stronger, he directly challenged Pershing. On June 16, he informed Pershing that movement of U.S. troops in any direction but north would be met by armed resistance. Five days later, Carrancistas attacked an eastbound American cavalry patrol at Carrizal, Chihuahua. The resulting combat resulted in the death of ten Americans and the capture of twenty-three.

In response to the Carrizal incident, Wilson mobilized the National Guard. Once again, war between the United States and Mexico seemed likely. By the end of July, 112,000 troops had been positioned at four assembly points—San Antonio, Brownsville, El Paso, and Douglas, Arizona.[59]

Whether war with Mexico would have broken out if Wilson had had a free hand is unclear. In any case, as the First World War loomed, U.S. concerns in Europe prevailed over those in Mexico. Wilson was aware that intervention in Mexico would turn the rest of Latin America against the United States. As a result, Wilson recalled Pershing's force, which, although it did not capture Villa, did disperse his major troop concentrations. The last U.S. soldier departed Mexico on February 5, 1917, accompanied by some 500 Chinese and 1,500 Mexicans who had assisted Pershing and who claimed that if they remained in Mexico, they would face reprisals from Villa.[60]

Villa benefited from his attack on Columbus in that it led to a serious deterioration in relations between Carranza and the Wilson administration. Even after Pershing's force had returned to the United States, Wilson left the arms embargo in place. American banks refused Carranza loans. This weakened Carranza militarily and thus allowed the survival of both Villa's and Zapata's irregular forces past the end of Carranza's presidency, when they could obtain concessions. The raid also enhanced Villa's stature by pitting him against the United States.[61]

THE 1916 U.S. ELECTIONS

During the 1916 U.S. presidential elections, Mexico became a major policy issue. Republican Senator Albert B. Fall of New Mexico criticized the Wilson administration for not converting the Pershing expedition into a full-scale invasion and warned that if the United States did not take sterner measures it would lose control of "the richest, underdeveloped country not only upon this continent, but in the world." The desire for armed intervention created some rather unusual political bedfellows. Pro-intervention factions included oil and mining interests and U.S. Catholics opposed to Carranza's anti-clericalism.[62]

The Democrats adopted a less belligerent position. Their platform stated, "Intervention, implying as it does, military subjugation, is revolting to the United States, notwithstanding that the provocation to that course has been great, and it should be resorted to, if at all, only as a last resort." The Republicans' bellicosity backfired, and anti-war sentiment helped get Wilson reelected.[63]

NATIONALISM AND ANTI-AMERICANISM

> At every decisive moment of the lengthy and complex Mexican civil struggle, U.S. influence was exerted.
>
> Lorenzo Meyer, 1985[64]

Although direct U.S. military intervention was limited to the Veracruz landing and the Pershing expedition, there was widespread fear in Mexico of a full-scale invasion. Carranza claimed the reason he began to act more conservatively was his fear of U.S. intervention. Similarly, if Villa had carried out a radical land reform, he might have alienated the Wilson administration and the American business community earlier than he did.[65]

All in all, the Mexican Revolution was neither pro- nor anti-American. The United States as a nation and U.S. citizens were simply judged by what they did. For example, when American agricultural colonies were attacked, it was often due to their owners having appropriated land without having provided jobs. American *hacendados* often protected themselves from anti-American outbursts by paying their employees higher wages than those paid on Mexican-owned estates. In general, American businesses were not attacked since they were a prized source of well-paying jobs. In the free-ranging debate at the Aguascalientes Convention, the occasional references to the United States were generally favorable.[66]

EMIGRATION

Throughout the armed phase of the Revolution, violence and declining employment in Mexico and continued U.S. economic prosperity led to a sharp increase in emigration. Mexicans easily found employment in the United States, since the outbreak of the First World War in late 1914 halted European emigration. In the decade 1911–1920, 219,004 legal immigrants entered the United States from Mexico. Another 628,000 Mexicans came as temporary workers, and countless others came as refugees or undocumented workers.[67]

At the time, Americans simply regarded Mexican workers as a needed source of labor for agriculture, mining, railroads, and smelting, and their presence produced little controversy. For the first time, a sizable number of *hacendados*, middle-class professionals, and intellectuals emigrated north along with the rural poor. They abandoned Mexico because they feared for their safety at the hands of revolutionaries due to their wealth or their having supported a losing political faction.[68]

Part Six

After the Revolution, 1917–1940

Chapter 18

Institutionalizing the New Regime, 1917–1940

> The revolutionary campaign destroyed the old regime of Porfirio Díaz, liquidated the Porfirian army, and brought to power a coalition that was heterogeneous yet strongly influenced by forces from the north and broadly committed to a project of state-building and capitalist development.
>
> Alan Knight, 1990[1]

THE CARRANZA ADMINISTRATION, 1917–1920

In October 1916, Mexicans elected delegates to the Constitutional Convention that Carranza had convoked the previous month. Even though there was only one candidate in some districts, in others there was real competition between would-be delegates. Carranza stipulated that those who had aided any other faction in the Revolution or who had served Huerta in a civil or a military capacity would be ineligible to become a delegate. This provision prevented any delegates from representing Villa or Zapata. Also largely excluded from the Convention were agrarian and working class interests as well as representatives of the two main conservative institutions—the old federal army and the Church. The turnout for the election, which did not exceed 30 percent, reflected the lack of interest in the technical issues involved in what was widely billed as a rewriting of the 1857 Constitution. It also indicated a willingness to give the Carrancista leadership a free hand in a process that seemingly had little direct local relevance.[2]

The delegates to the Convention reflected the youth and middle-class origins of the Constitutionalist leadership. Of the 138 whose age is known, twenty-nine were in their twenties, sixty-two were in their thirties, and thirty-one were in their forties. An estimated 85 percent of the delegates were white-collar professionals, including sixty-two lawyers, eighteen teachers, sixteen engineers, sixteen physicians, and fourteen journalists.[3]

Carranza presented the Convention delegates, who assembled in Querétaro, with a draft of a new constitution. Delegates could then approve or modify the draft on an article-by-article basis. The draft Carranza presented was very close to the 1857 constitution and did not greatly increase government power. It left largely unaddressed the needs of the landless and workers. It reflected not only the low priority Carranza placed on social reform, as opposed to political reform, but also his belief that social reform could be best addressed by legislation, not a constitution.[4]

Despite having dictated the process for selecting Convention delegates, Carranza proved unable to dominate the Convention once it convened. A radical majority emerged that sought a strong federal government that could challenge the Church and implement social reform. Two figures dominated this reformist wing of the Convention. One, Francisco Múgica, a thirty-two-year old general from Michoacán, represented the reformist elements of the Constitutionalist army and considered redistribution of wealth as a worthy goal in its own right. The other was Obregón, who saw social reforms as necessary for building a solid base of political support. Although he was not a delegate, Obregón promoted more radical positions and established friendships at the Querétaro Convention that would later prove invaluable to him.[5]

Article 3 of the completed constitution decreed education would be compulsory and without charge. As with other articles, it was out of touch with Mexican reality. With just over 1 percent of the budget earmarked for education, for most Mexican children school attendance was only wishful thinking. The article left education in the hands of states and municipalities, the entities least able or willing to implement it.[6]

Article 27 granted the government the power to control land use for "public utility," thus providing the legal basis for Mexico's far-reaching land reform. This article also declared the government owned "all minerals . . . such as . . . petroleum. . . ." It reflected the thinking of Andrés Molina Enríquez, the author of *Los grandes problemas nacionales*. He rebutted charges that the article was "communistic," noting that it merely represented a return to the colonial model. In that model, the Crown, or its successor, the state, could never relinquish ultimate ownership of land. According to Molina Enríquez's thinking, even if individuals were allowed to use land, the Crown and later the state at all times had the power to transfer that land to a new owner for what it considered a better use.[7]

Article 123 contained a rich lode of labor rights, including the right to unionize and strike, the eight-hour day, and equal pay for equal work regardless of one's gender or nationality. This article also ignored Mexican reality. It prohibited child labor in an economy where such labor was essential for the survival of many families.[8]

It was clear to all that the provisions of Article 123 would not be implemented immediately. Rather, they formed a statement of intent—a promise of better things to come. Miner Nicolás Cano, one of the few workers at the Convention, was prescient in noting that by protecting only "legal" strikes, Article 123 left the door open for business and government to jointly declare strikes illegal and oppress labor. The immediate impact of Article 123 was to convince the labor and peasant movements that they did not need a Villa or a Zapata to be included in the new order.[9]

To correct what was perceived as an excessively weak presidency created by the 1857 constitution, the 1917 document created a strong presidency. Article 76 granted the Senate—which became subservient to the president—the right to remove state governors. Article 71 allowed the president to introduce legislation. As a result of this provision, most of the legislation passed for the rest of the century was in the form of presidential initiative. Article 72 allowed the president to veto legislation, but permitted Congress to override the veto with a two-thirds majority.[10]

The constitution placed one crucial limit on this strong presidency. Article 83 prohibited both immediate presidential reelection and a later return to the presidency à la Porfirio Díaz in 1884. This reflected the belief that the ills of the Porfiriato resulted from Díaz's repeated reelection. With the single exception of 1928, this prohibition remained for the rest of the century. In addition, the immediate reelection of mayors and governors was prohibited. These prohibitions remain a cardinal principle of Mexican politics and have had a major impact on shaping the political system.[11]

The 1917 constitution laid the foundation for an activist federal government that could defend the interests of poor Mexicans vis-à-vis *hacendados* and foreign capitalists. However, this activism took an unexpected form. Carranza and his successors not only wielded the power granted them in the constitution but also viewed it as a document that they could review, amend, or ignore to suit their generally conservative purposes. Despite its spotty application, the 1917 constitution did shape government action, and it remains in force to this day. It significantly influenced social thinking throughout Latin America, and its progressive provisions were widely adopted in legislation and constitutions elsewhere in the region.[12]

In March 1917, elections were held to legitimize Carranza's presidency. There was no organized opposition, and Carranza received more than 97 percent of the vote. Apparently the only ones to take the election seriously were foreigners. The British minister reported, "My chauffeur could not conceal his amusement when I told him that I wished to go and see the elections."[13]

Carranza faced a number of challenges once he assumed the presidency. He had to establish control vis-à-vis his rivals, especially Villa and Zapata, who still led irregular forces. Peasants and workers, having been mobilized by the Revolution, demanded that the government take measures to meet their aspirations. At the local level, entrenched warlords and active-duty generals, many of whom obtained power through the Revolution, defended their prerogatives. Implementing any sort of change required undercutting local interests and rebuilding loyalties to the national government. Given Mexico's economic disarray, merely feeding the population presented a major challenge.[14]

A fusion of Sonoran and Coahuilan groups formed Carranza's ruling coalition. This leadership, with its northern middle-class roots, prioritized nationalism, not social reform. Just as with Madero before him, Carranza felt the Revolution was over. In June 1917, one of oilman Weetman Pearson's representatives wrote:

> A tendency to conservatism is observable now that the government is well established and is not so dependent on the radical military element. Undoubtedly Carranza is doing his utmost to free himself from the extremists, and the most hopeful sign is, that he is commencing to take into the government offices, some of the old regime.[15]

Carranza shared the conviction of the Porfirian elite that land reform would be a disaster for the Mexican economy and that it would sharply reduce agricultural production. In keeping with this notion, he returned many seized estates to their pre-Revolutionary owners. He felt this would increase tax collection and food production and win the political support of those who recouped their land.[16]

Carranza not only restored large estates to their pre-Revolutionary owners but also declared that he did not think "the agrarian problem important." During the five years he exercised power, Carranza distributed only 988,000 acres—roughly the size of a large northern hacienda—to 67,193 beneficiaries.[17]

Resistance to the Constitutionalists continued in Morelos, even though Carranza's army returned to occupy the state in 1917. By 1919, Zapata's dream had vanished as all the cities and haciendas were reoccupied and lands were returned to their former owners. The remaining Zapatistas were forced into the mountains. They no longer had a clear position. Some made overtures to the government while others spoke highly of the Russian Revolution.

Early in 1919, Zapata contacted Jesús Guajardo, a Carrancista colonel whom Zapata had heard was at odds with his commander. Zapata, desperate for men and supplies, suggested that Guajardo defect. Guajardo pretended he was deserting, along with his troops and their weapons. To convince Zapata of his sincerity, Guajardo even had his troops shoot men who had deserted Zapata and joined his force.

Guajardo met Zapata at Chinameca hacienda in Morelos. Upon entering the hacienda courtyard on April 10, 1919, Zapata was cut down by gunfire from an ambush that Guajardo had laid for him. For his part in the ambush, Guajardo was given 50,000 pesos and promoted to general. After Zapata's death, the Zapatistas ceased to be a major political force. However, some Zapatistas did remain in the hills until 1920, when the political climate became more favorable.

Many of Carranza's civil servants, especially at the municipal level, had served under Díaz. He purged progressives from the government and the army and replaced them with politicians and unprincipled militarists. Carranza's civilian appointees began a trend toward personal enrichment through public office on a scale previously unmatched. Such enrichment not only satisfied the desires of those holding power but also bought off challengers. Although Carranza was personally honest, corruption became widespread during his administration. The tone of government changed so radically that by 1920 it was difficult to see any relation between government action and the 1917 constitution. After serving as a senator and governor under Díaz, Carranza, like Madero before him, had no desire to implement sweeping changes.[18]

While Carranza failed to use the promise of social reform to consolidate power, there was someone who was a master at it—his old comrade-in-arms, Álvaro Obregón. After the 1917 Constitutional Convention, amid reports of growing rivalry between the two revolutionary leaders, Obregón resigned his position as secretary of war and "retired" to his estate in Sonora. While there, he profited greatly from brokering Sonora's chickpea trade. Obregón kept abreast of political events and traveled to the United States, where he met with Secretary of State Robert Lansing.[19]

By 1920, Obregón had allied himself with middle-class military men who were dissatisfied with the tenor of Carranza's government. His new allies resented the unfulfilled promises of the Revolution and the increasing power of *hacendados*. The enrichment of Carrancista officials, widespread repression, and Carranza's authorization of the assassination of Zapata only served to increase their dissatisfaction.[20]

In 1919, Carranza attempted to impose his ambassador in Washington, Ignacio Bonillas, as his successor. Bonillas, a virtually unknown engineer who had trained at the Massachusetts Institute of Technology, had such close ties to the United States that he was disparagingly referred to as "Meester Bonillas." Carranza thought he could control Bonillas even after his term was over and thus maintain de facto power. He knew he could not control the outstanding general of the Revolution, Obregón.

In June 1919, Obregón announced his own presidential candidacy. His whistle-stop tours around the country drew enthusiastic crowds. Obregón was already experienced in mass politics, having promised the Yaqui land in exchange for their fighting in the Revolution and having promised workers labor rights in exchange for their formation of battalions during the Revolution. To bolster his presidential candidacy, he turned to organized labor for support. The response Obregón received in Tampico was typical of the labor support he received nationwide. There, a workers convention, responding to his charisma, his military record, and his promises of reform, endorsed Obregón over Bonillas by a vote of 1,082 to three in a straw poll.[21]

While Obregón was campaigning, Carranza subpoenaed him to testify in a case involving an officer charged with rebellion. After arriving in Mexico City, Obregón, fearing arrest or assassination, fled to Guerrero disguised as a rail worker. There he formed an alliance with remnants of the Zapatista movement and called for revolt against Carranza. Obregón had the backing of reform-minded military men, peasants, and workers, who saw in him the hope for change. He also had strong backing in his home state of Sonora, where on April 23, 1920, two generals, Plutarco Calles and Adolfo de la Huerta, issued the Plan of Agua Prieta, which repudiated Carranza's government. As was the case with Carranza's Plan of Guadalupe, it lacked specific provisions for social reform.[22]

Carranza failed to end rural violence, to fulfill the promises of the 1917 constitution, or to resolve the considerable economic problems the Revolution had created. He had little to offer the middle class, which had emerged as a major political force in the revolutionary army and at the Querétaro convention. The army was alienated by his having reduced military spending. The world recession following the end of the First World War exacerbated poverty in Mexico, making a mockery of the revolutionary slogans that had stoked the hopes of ordinary Mexicans.[23]

On May 7, 1920, realizing that he had little political or military support, Carranza filled sixty rail cars with his backers and their weapons, files, and possessions, as well as gold bars from the national treasury. He set out along the traditional path of Mexico's fallen leaders, down from the highlands toward Veracruz. He planned to reestablish his government there and launch a counter-offensive from the coast, just as he had successfully done in 1915. However, Carranza found the rail line had been blocked by rebels well before he reached Veracruz. He abandoned the train and reached the village of Tlaxcalantongo, Puebla, on horseback. There, troops under the command of Rodolfo Herrero assassinated the president in the hut where he was sleeping. Herrero, who had ties to Generals Manuel Paláez and Félix Díaz, held a grudge since Carranza and Carranza's appointee as governor of Puebla had ordered his father killed.[24]

Obregón's rapid victory in Mexico's last successful armed revolt reflected the erosion of Carranza's support. At the same time, given his military record, Obregón attracted broad military support as well as the backing of many workers and peasants who felt he would carry out the reforms promised in the constitution.[25]

Given his background, it is not surprising that Carranza largely ignored the powerful social demands that emerged during the Revolution. Little progress was made at instilling democracy, as the elections that were held during Carranza's term were generally considered a farce. Members of opposing factions were not allowed to nominate candidates and there were widespread accusations of fraud. Finally, as became obvious with the Plan of Agua Prieta, no means of presidential succession had been instituted.[26]

Carranza's strongest legacy is providing an institutional framework—the 1917 constitution—which his successors could build on. Carranza's nationalism forms another part of his legacy. He increased the taxes on oil companies seven-fold between 1917 and 1920. He was not afraid to challenge foreigners' property rights and existing contracts to further his nationalistic goals. He was not anti-capitalist or even anti-foreign and did not seek to eliminate foreign investment, but to control it. Carranza unsuccessfully attempted to force foreign oil companies to accept that the Mexican government, by virtue of Article 27, could radically redefine their oil rights.[27]

THE OBREGÓN ADMINISTRATION, 1920–1924

> Led by the most talented general to emerge from the civil wars, Álvaro Obregón, the Sonorans set out to modernize the country along classical capitalist lines, while at the same time realizing personal ambitions that had been frustrated in the stifling atmosphere of the late Porfiriato.
>
> Dudley Ankerson, 1984[28]

Following Carranza's death, Congress selected Adolfo de la Huerta, a former governor of Sonora, as provisional president to serve the remainder of Carranza's term. Since De la Huerta had not been a military rival of Villa as Carranza had been, he was able to persuade Villa to surrender. In exchange for his surrender, Villa was given Canutillo Hacienda, a 163,000-acre spread situated at the headwaters of the Río Conchos in Durango. Villa was to be defended by a fifty-man guard of his choosing, whose salary was paid by the government. Villa felt such an arrangement would protect him from his many enemies. In fact, he selected Canutillo because it was easily defendable.[29]

While at Canutillo, Villa created a semi-autonomous military colony, the model he had hoped to implement throughout northern Mexico. He showed his concern for education by establishing a school on the premises. He later commented, "When the day comes that a school teacher earns more than an army general, Mexico will be saved."[30]

Other rebels laid down their arms during De la Huerta's presidency. Félix Díaz, who had revolted once again in southern Mexico, was allowed to sail to exile in the United States. Many Zapatistas were incorporated into the regular army. De la Huerta not only left Mexico a more peaceful country after his six-month presidency but also substantially reduced the size of the bloated military.[31]

On September 5, 1920, Obregón, facing only nominal opposition, received 95 percent of the votes for president. Since Bonillas had withdrawn his candidacy and Obregón's backers controlled nearly all the polling places, once again the election served not to select a president but to legitimize a military victor.[32]

On December 1, 1920, Obregón took the oath of office as president. He formed an administration independent of any one sector. Porfirian *hacendados* were played off against peasants, workers, and emerging industrialists, all of whom were overshadowed by foreign interests and the government.

Local military leaders who had supported Obregón in his showdown with Carranza were rewarded with considerable freedom of action as well as government support. Many of these generals controlled their states and regions like oriental despots.[33]

While accepting the reality of local warlords, Obregón did begin the long process of political centralization. Many local figures were bought off with government jobs or forced into exile. Cabinet members and military commanders were amply rewarded for their support with promotions and the possibility of using their position for personal enrichment. To further extend his power base, Obregón formally allied with the major labor federation, the Regional Federation of Mexican Workers (CROM).[34]

During the Obregón administration, the number and diversity of new organizations was unprecedented. Labor unions, peasant leagues, union federations, and political parties all sought to shape post-revolutionary society to their preferences. Their being organized around regional power centers rather than at the national level limited the effectiveness of these groups. Their sheer numbers and their diverse demands also diminished their impact on policy.[35]

Obregón did not attempt to contain the masses through repression as Huerta had. Rather, reform—or the promise of reform—was used as a means of political control. Obregón's indulging in radical rhetoric served to whet appetites and make the impoverished look to his administration for change. The terms "class struggle," "socialism," and "anti-imperialism" flowed easily from officials' tongues.[36]

Land reform became a political tool. By the time Obregón left office in 1924, 2.7 million acres, or 3.5 percent of agrarian land, had been distributed. In contrast, as late as 1925, some 79 million acres were foreign owned. His lack of enthusiasm for land reform is understandable, since his personal estate covered 8,645 acres and employed 1,500 workers. Obregón was aware that a sweeping land reform would alienate his most important base of support, the army, many of whose officers had recently acquired haciendas. Obregón stated that subdividing estates would reduce production. He felt that if haciendas were subdivided, "We would put to flight foreign capital, which at this moment we need more than ever."[37]

Land reform did permit Obregón to consolidate power. In Morelos, where surviving Zapatistas had helped him oust Carranza, Obregón promoted extensive land reform. By 1923, 115 of the 150 towns in the state had received land. Similarly, given the degree of peasant mobilization in Chihuahua, Obregón felt he had no choice but to expropriate the estates of the Terrazas and the Creels and redistribute a large part of them to Chihuahua's landless.[38]

During the 1920s, given the weakness of the central government, state governors had the leeway to experiment with radical social change. Such change often involved the position of women, land holding, and the role of the Church. These state governments dealt with the major issues incorporated in the 1917 constitution, and their projects were known as laboratories of the Revolution.[39]

Conservatives furthered their interests, with or without the blessing of the central government. Landowners in Yucatán assassinated progressive governor Felipe Carrillo Puerto in 1924, thus ending his "socialist" experiment. In Chiapas, the governor used all of his power to obstruct the work of the local Agrarian Commissions and to destroy the agrarian movement. In many areas, agrarian leaders who formed peasant leagues to push for their rights under land reform laws were declared "bandits" and murdered. Generals cooperated with local *hacendados* and state governors to drive off land reform beneficiaries. They used the army as a rural police force, and it sometimes turned its weapons on peasants to maintain the status quo.[40]

Obregón increased social mobility for the middle class. Its members enriched themselves quickly, taking advantage of the power the government gave them. During the 1920s, they became virtually indistinguishable from those whom they had fought during the Revolution. Often their wealth was based on public works contracts or simply on pillaging the public treasury.[41]

By 1922, speculation had begun on who Mexico's next president would be and how he would be selected. Pancho Villa told an interviewer at Canutillo that he was considering getting back into politics. Villa was not at all discreet, stating, "I have told all my friends the same thing, just wait, when they least expect it, the opportunity will come . . ."[42] He bragged that he could "mobilize 40,000 men in 40 minutes."[43] Villa also volunteered this statement concerning Adolfo de la Huerta, who had fallen out with Obregón, "Adolfo is a very fine person and very intelligent, he wouldn't make a bad president."[44]

It is not known if this 1922 interview contributed to Villa's death or not. In any case, on July 20, 1923, as De la Huerta's presidential ambitions began to pose a serious threat to the government, gunfire riddled Villa's car as he drove into town from Canutillo, killing him instantly.

In his magisterial biography of Villa, historian Friedrich Katz concluded, "There can, on the whole, be little doubt that the Mexican government was not only implicated in but probably also organized the assassination of Villa." Likely Obregón took seriously Villa's boast that he could mobilize 40,000 men in forty minutes and feared that they would be mobilized in favor of De la Huerta. He also felt that Villa would rally nationalist sentiment by criticizing a pact, known as the Bucareli Accords, which he had made with the United States.[45]

During his term, Obregón personally chose those who would serve as congressmen, senators, and governors. His departure from the presidency began another Mexican political tradition—the out-going president selecting his successor without popular control or even popular involvement.[46]

Obregón chose Plutarco Elías Calles, another general from Sonora, to succeed him. When Calles's nomination was announced in 1923, General Adolfo de la Huerta, who had served as Obregón's secretary of finance, attempted a coup. He followed the example set in 1920 by Obregón, who had revolted when he was not selected to succeed Carranza.

De la Huerta's revolt drew some 50,000 followers, mainly in the north, and had the backing of conservatives, *hacendados*, and Catholic leaders. Cuts in military spending had once again alienated the army, so half the generals and 40 percent of the troops joined him. The revolt drew support from independent labor, those fearing Calles's radicalism, and nationalists who resented Obregón's compromising of Mexican sovereignty by signing the Bucareli Accords.[47]

Obregón's alliance with peasants, a product of his populist style, served him well. Feeling that Calles offered the best hope of land distribution, 120,000 peasants attacked De la Huerta's lines of communication, sabotaged supplies, and formed small military units. In addition, U.S.-supplied arms, ammunition, and airplanes, as well as support from organized labor, contributed to De la Huerta's defeat.[48]

The revolt lasted three months and cost about 7,000 lives. After personally leading the campaign against the rebels, Obregón had fifty-four of its leaders, his former comrades-in-arms, shot. The De la Huerta revolt permanently weakened the military as an institution, since so many generals died or fled into exile. De la Huerta took refuge in Los Angeles, where he gave voice lessons.[49]

When elections were finally held, Calles received almost 90 percent of the vote. Most Mexicans showed little interest and abstained. It was hard to excite potential voters, since opposition was token at best.[50]

Assassinating Villa and creating schools were exceptions to what was generally a non-activist presidency. Most of the large estates that existed during the Porfiriato were intact at the end of Obregón's term, although ownership of many of them had passed to generals. It was only in 1922 that industrial production surpassed the level of the late Porfiriato. In 1924, Mexicans probably ate less, had fewer jobs, and enjoyed no greater political rights than they had before the Revolution.[51]

Although the Obregonistas took power under the mantle of Revolution, there was little change. Rather, they destroyed Porfirian privilege, such as monopolies and special tax concessions, and opened opportunity for themselves. These reforms were not addressed to the masses. Obregón, like Madero and Carranza before him, was basically a nineteenth-century liberal whose main goal was to update and streamline Mexican capitalism. Obregón did have the distinction of being the first Mexican president in generations to complete his term and leave office.[52]

THE CALLES ADMINISTRATION, 1924–1928

> The victorious revolution, after settling its internal differences, created a dominant party system that resulted in a new authoritarianism, which was very careful to preserve the democratic forms while emptying them of content.
>
> Lorenzo Meyer, 1991[53]

Calles was born in Guaymas, Sonora in 1877 and became a school teacher at age seventeen. Later he worked as a journalist and hotel manager and served as police chief in Agua Prieta, Sonora. He reflected the restlessness of northern Mexico in that he had worked at nine different occupations before entering the military.

In 1915, Carranza appointed him as interim governor of Sonora. While serving as governor (1915–1916, 1917–1919), Calles opened 127 primary schools, organized a Congress on education, and inaugurated a teachers' training school. He introduced a minimum wage and compelled industries and mining companies to establish schools for the children of their employees.[54]

Although Calles was an army general, Obregón described him as "the least militaristic of all the generals." The key to his rapid advancement was his early loyalty to Carranza and his switching to Obregón when his fellow Sonorans challenged Carranza. He served as Carranza's secretary of industry, commerce, and labor and later as Obregón's interior secretary.[55]

Calles campaigned for the 1924 presidential election affirming support for Article 27 and other reformist provisions of the 1917 constitution. He also portrayed himself as an advocate for the "landless classes." In October 1924, as president-elect, Calles muted his populism when he spoke at New York City's Waldorf-Astoria Hotel. He declared the goal of the Revolution was "to secure the social and economic elevation of 12 million submerged Mexicans, but at the same time invite the cooperation of capitalists and industrialists of good will."[56]

Obregón had administered as if the Revolution had ended. Calles, however, resurrected the concept of "the Revolution" and used it as a political tool. He alone would decide what constituted the "Revolution." Calles defined himself and his followers as true "revolutionaries" and labeled opponents as "conservatives" and "counterrevolutionaries."

Calles, who took office with a radical reputation, was most progressive with regard to land reform. From 1924 to 1928, he distributed 7.34 million acres of land. This was more than twice the amount distributed between 1915 and 1924. Early in his term he used the land reform to build a power base among those who received land. Once he had consolidated his power, land distribution slowed dramatically.

Even though Calles substantially increased the amount of land distributed, he viewed the ejido (the communal farm formed by those receiving land) as a transitory institution incapable of meeting Mexico's agricultural needs. Land reform was viewed as a means to correct past injustices or simply as a political necessity in regions where peasants were militant and mobilized. The Sonorans placed their faith in privately owned farms—the dominant agricultural model in their home state. They increasingly turned their attention to making the land more productive, not distributing it. To bolster private agriculture, most of the funds from the National Agricultural Credit Bank, established in 1926, were absorbed by large farms in northern Mexico.[57]

By the end of his term, Calles had become quite conservative. In 1927, he announced, "The Government will do everything in its power to safeguard the interests of foreign capitalists who invest in Mexico." This conservative shift reflected not only the increasing wealth of Calles and his followers but also the close ties the president had developed with U.S. Ambassador Dwight

Morrow. The "ham-and-egg" breakfasts Calles regularly shared with Morrow became a prominent feature of the political landscape. A fall in oil and silver prices and in the volume of oil exports also caused Calles to scale down his attempts to effect change. Efforts to suppress a religious-based revolt known as the Cristiada sapped further energy for reform. Finally, low levels of production on land already transferred to peasants as part of the land reform led Calles to bring the program to a near halt.[58]

Many provisions of the 1917 Constitution remained only as good intentions. On the government-owned rail system workers put in a twelve-hour day, despite the constitution guaranteeing them an eight-hour day. In 1928, Porfirian economic and social structures remained largely intact.[59]

The members of the Sonoran dynasty—De la Huerta, Obregón, and Calles—rebuilt the government bureaucracy and returned power to Mexico City. During this recentralization, revolutionary leaders gained power, the military lost it, and peasants became marginalized. Many supported this recentralization of power since they felt it would lessen anarchy and political violence. Between 1921 and 1930, government employment increased from 1.4 percent of the labor force to 2.9 percent.[60]

When viewed from the top, the political system appeared to have stabilized, with both Obregón and Calles finishing their terms and leaving office as scheduled. However, at lower levels of government the diverse political forces seeking political control produced tumult. Between 1920 and 1930, Puebla had nineteen governors. In June 1930, after a two-hour gun battle in which one legislator and the chief of police were killed, discontented members of the Chihuahua legislature overthrew the provisional governor. The federal government refused to recognize the coup and reimposed the provisional governor. During his term, Calles deposed twenty-five state governors and replaced them with those whose loyalty he could count on. Similar instability existed at the local level. In the two decades after 1920, forty-two men served as mayor of Ciudad Juárez, Chihuahua.[61]

The generals forming the Sonoran dynasty brought to the presidency a set of values alien to central Mexico. The north never had a village-oriented society. The Catholic Church in Sonora was not the major institution it was in central Mexico. Agricultural development in northern Mexico was the forerunner of today's agribusiness and often involved irrigation and other government-financed projects. While Zapata had looked to the Indian village with its communal lands as his model, the Sonorans, who were largely removed from the radical ideological influences of central Mexico, saw Californian agriculture as their model. They felt that the Mexican government had to assume an active role in promoting economic development.[62]

As the end of Calles's term approached, it became clear that Obregón wished to return to the presidency. Calles backed Obregón's reelection, likely feeling that Obregón would return the favor at the end of the 1928–1934 term. The constitution was amended to permit non-consecutive reelection. Another amendment extended the presidential term from four to six years—its current length. (The amendment permitting reelection was repealed in 1933.)[63]

General Arnulfo Gómez and General Francisco Serrano, who had served as Obregón's secretary of war, had each hoped to serve as president. When they learned Calles was backing Obregón, they concluded the election would be stacked against them and rebelled. However, before the rebellion began, plans for the revolt were discovered. In October 1927, Serrano and thirteen of his followers were shot without trial in Huitzilac, just south of Mexico City. A month later, Gómez was shot. A total of twenty-seven generals were placed before firing squads for their participation in the uprising.[64]

Some of the rebellious generals of this period, such as Francisco Serrano, had impeccable democratic credentials dating back to Madero's struggle against Díaz. However, it was military strength, not commitment to democracy, that determined presidential succession during this period.[65]

Obregón campaigned on a platform of fulfilling revolutionary promises and uniting the forces of the Revolution. He faced no opposition candidate, even though labor leader Luis Morones and a broad range of public opinion opposed Obregón—or anyone else—being reelected president. Those who objected to reelection as a matter of principle were denounced as conservatives. On election day, Obregón received all of the 1,670,453 votes cast.[66]

Before Obregón's reelection, labor leader Luis Morones, whose own presidential aspirations were apparent, had launched a virulent anti-Obregón campaign. Serrano and Gómez had also inflamed anti-Obregón passions, denouncing the Sonoran for violating the political taboo against reelection. In addition, during Calles's term, Catholics had taken up arms in opposition to his anticlericalism. In this atmosphere, just after his election president-elect Obregón was assassinated by José de León Toral, a person generally described as a Catholic fanatic.[67]

The assassination placed Calles in a difficult position. Some of his backers wanted him to extend his term to prevent the chaos resulting from not having a president. Others wanted him to leave the presidency on schedule, since they feared members of the Obregón faction would revolt if denied power.

Calles's political ability prevented frustrated Obregón backers from taking up arms to gain the power they considered rightfully theirs. His first step was to appoint well known Obregón supporter General Juan José Ríos Zertuche to investigate the murder of the president-elect.[68]

On September 1, 1928, in his last annual address, Calles announced not only that he would leave the presidency as scheduled but that it was time to make presidential succession an orderly process. He declared:

> Perhaps, for the first time in its history, Mexico faces a situation whose outstanding characteristic is the lack of *caudillos*. This should, and will, permit us, once and for all, to direct the national political process toward institutional rule. Mexico will forever cease to be, as it has been historically, a nation led by a "strongman," and will become a nation of institutions and laws.[69]

With Calles's blessing, Congress designated his Interior Minister, Emilio Portes Gil, as provisional president. Portes Gil was ideal for defusing the political crisis generated by Obregón's assassination. He had close ties to both Obregón and Calles, and as a civilian, his temporary presence in the seat of power ameliorated rivalries between numerous generals, each of whom felt they should replace Obregón. Portes Gil took office at the end of Calles's term and remained until a special election could be called to fill the remainder of the 1928–1934 term to which Obregón had been elected.[70]

The choice of Portes Gil made Obregón loyalists feel that the way was still open for them to assume power. The new president had a progressive reputation, since as governor of Tamaulipas he had distributed more than 494,000 acres of land to peasants on his own initiative. On December 1, 1928, given his acceptability to all major factions, Portes Gil peacefully assumed the presidency.

Shortly before the end of his term, Calles called for the creation of a national political party. This party, the National Revolutionary Party (PNR), served to dominate ambitious caudillos, each striving for national power. The PNR differed from conventional political parties in that it was created to conserve power, not contest it. The creation of the party ten years after the Constitutionalists' victory in the armed struggle highlights the differences between the Mexican Revolution and the revolutions in Russia and China, where preexisting parties guided the post-triumph course of development.[71]

There was no grass-roots participation in choosing representatives to the party's 1929 founding convention in Querétaro. If its founding had occurred in the United States, its organizers would have been referred to as a bunch of good old boys in a smoke-filled room. As political scientist Luis Javier Garrido observed, "The reason that a record of the public debates occurring at the founding cannot be located is simply that no debate occurred."[72]

The regionally based caudillos who formed the initial base of the party were guaranteed control over their local fiefdoms if they backed the party's presidential nominees. Most of these caudillos, aging and quite wealthy, were more than ready to accept mediation by the new party, since they had too much personal wealth to risk losing it in an unsuccessful coup attempt.

In addition to bringing together generals and caciques, the PNR incorporated all the political parties claiming their origins in the Revolution. In 1929, these parties, which numbered more than 1,000, were mostly regional and generally were linked to one political figure. Existing parties were allowed to preserve their local and regional autonomy if they adhered to decisions of the PNR executive committee on national matters. Thanks to its building on existing parties, within a few months the PNR had a functioning nationwide network in place.[73]

Calles selected officials to lead the PNR, which remained an extension of his personal power. Both state and federal governments provided funds to the party, while opposition parties were forced to rely on private funds. The rough-and-tumble battles to decide who would exercise power at the local level soon shifted from independent groups to struggles for power within the PNR. In 1933 Calles pushed through a constitutional amendment to prohibit immediate congressional reelection. This made those wishing to serve in Congress dependent not on constituents they had served but on Calles approving their nomination. Left outside the party were workers, peasants, and members of the middle class. Politics became a game played exclusively by the closed circle around Calles.[74]

As political scientist Judith Hellman noted, "Few people observing the motley conglomeration of semi-independent parties, movements, interest groups, and political cliques that was the PNR in 1929 could have believed that it would develop into a unified and enormously powerful organization."[75]

THE PRESIDENTIAL PUPPETS, 1928–1934

Calles continued to govern as the power behind the throne during Portes Gil's interim presidency, which extended from December 1928 to February 1930. He orchestrated the nomination of Pascual Ortiz Rubio as presidential candidate for the remainder of the term to which Obregón had been elected. In 1926, Ortiz Rubio had been appointed as Mexican ambassador to Brazil. He was attractive to Calles since by virtue of his having been abroad he had no power base and was totally dependent on Calles.

The designation of Ortiz Rubio triggered Mexico's last widespread revolt, led by generals Jesús Aguirre and José Gonzalo Escobar, who had their own presidential aspirations. They had hoped to attract the broad coalition that had been held together by Obregón's strong personality. Without its leader, however, the coalition had disintegrated. Thus they were soon defeated by Calles, who stepped in as secretary of war. Irregular rural forces, whose members had either received land in the land reform or hoped to in the future, contributed significantly to Calles's victory, as did the U.S. government, which supplied the Mexican government with arms. As a result of the revolt, forty-seven generals were shot or exiled and 2,000 combatants died. The failure of the revolt delivered a clear message—from then on, the route to power was through official channels, not through toppling the by-then-entrenched government.[76]

While the Escobar revolt eliminated Ortiz Rubio's military challengers, he did face an electoral challenge by educator José Vasconcelos, who had served as rector of the National University and as secretary of public education under Obregón. Vasconcelos ran as a reformist, criticizing public office being used for private gain. He advocated a literacy program and an expansion of the educational system. Many saw Vasconcelos, who stressed the need for democracy, as a new Madero. Another plank of Vasconcelos's platform called for granting the vote to women. In contrast to Madero, Vasconcelos advocated accelerating land reform.[77]

During his campaign, Vasconcelos, who enjoyed strong urban support, drew large crowds. He was hampered by having to rely on private funds while the PNR enjoyed access to public funds. Pro-government goons repeatedly attacked his rallies. This violence continued through election day, when nine died and nineteen were wounded in Mexico City alone.[78]

Another feature of the PNR became apparent on election day. The party counted the votes. Despite Ortiz Rubio being virtually unknown, Vasconcelos was credited with only 105,655 votes nationwide compared to Ortiz Rubio's 1,825,732. Some individual Vasconcelos rallies in Mexico City had attracted more than 100,000 supporters. It was clear that Calles and the generals supporting him were unwilling to lose at the ballot box what they had won by force of arms. As historian Jean Meyer commented, the elections were "quite manifestly fraudulent."[79]

Vasconcelos denounced the official results, threatened revolt, and took refuge in the United States. However, it was clear that as Ortiz Rubio had the backing of the army, Calles, and both the U.S. and Mexican governments, rebellion would be futile. The main result of the election was increased cynicism about democracy among an entire generation of middle-class Mexicans.[80]

Ortiz Rubio served as a figurehead president from February 1930 to September 1932. His dependency on Calles—who lived directly in front of the presidential residence in Chapultepec Castle—was so great that Mexicans would point to the castle and proclaim, "*Aquí vive el presidente, él que manda vive enfrente*" ("Here lives the president, the boss lives in front").

Calles ousted his own choice as president when Ortiz Rubio disagreed with him on policy and choice of cabinet members. Ortiz Rubio left without a fight, admitting that he "had arrived at the presidency by the aid and will of the General [Calles] and not through my own popularity or personal strength . . ."[81]

To finish the presidential term ending in 1934, Calles selected Abelardo Rodríguez, a typical millionaire general. From 1923 to 1929, as governor of Baja California Norte, Rodríguez had loyally served Obregón and Calles and had enriched himself by promoting gambling and prostitution. During Rodríguez's presidency, which lasted from September 1932 through November 1934, reforms were put on hold and government emphasis shifted to promoting economic development, protecting private enterprise and attracting foreign capital. As president, Rodríguez continued to add banks and casinos to his personal holdings. To maintain the delicate balance between appearing foolish and threatening Calles, the president instructed his cabinet members to consult him, not Calles, unless Calles initiated the contact.[82]

Calles's role as the central figure with the final word on political matters earned him the title of Jefe Máximo (top chief). In 1929, he stated that in the future any land taken for land reform would be paid for in cash. Given the lack of funds in the Depression-wracked treasury, Mexicans generally viewed that statement as signaling the end of land reform. After that date, agricultural production, not distributing land to the landless, was emphasized. This reflected Calles's view that agriculture should be left to commercial farmers receiving government guarantees and incentives.[83]

Agricultural workers were eating less than in 1896, and the low wages paid them in 1910 would have looked magnificent in 1934. Given this situation, it was hardly surprising that as the 1934 elections approached, the political situation in Mexico was threatening to escape from Calles's control. The country was still suffering from the Depression. Labor unrest was increasing, and foreign observers spoke of the likelihood of new peasant wars.[84]

In response to these conditions, a faction opposing Calles formed inside the PNR. Its members were of middle-class origin, felt dispossessed, and were in disagreement with the ruling faction. Weak in itself, this faction found support in workers and peasants, whose aspirations it had raised.[85]

The leader of this faction was a general of humble origins, Lázaro Cárdenas. His ancestry was mixed at a time when other leading political figures were of higher social status and had lighter skins. He joined the Revolution as a teenager after only four years of formal education. Cárdenas advanced rapidly through the ranks of the army and was promoted to general at age twenty-five.

Between 1925 and 1928, he served as a military zone commander on the oil-rich Gulf Coast, where he witnessed firsthand the squalor and inequality of oil camps and the companies' cynical disregard of the host population. Such abuses would later come back to haunt these firms.

In 1928, Cárdenas became governor of his native state of Michoacán, where he promoted rural education and carried out land reform on his own initiative. There he faced a conservative backlash. *Hacendados* and even some conservative Indian communities felt threatened by teachers introducing not only literacy but also modern ways and anti-clerical views. Teachers frequently came to school armed to protect themselves and their schools. As governor, Cárdenas set a pattern that he would follow as president—his door was open to peasants and workers with a complaint.[86]

In 1933, the dissident faction led by Cárdenas dominated the drafting of the PNR's Six-Year Plan for the 1934–1940 presidential term. The Plan called for an increased state role in agriculture, industry, and infrastructure, as well as social development. It reflected the skepticism in the free market produced by the 1929 Depression. It was markedly pro-labor and nationalistic and emphasized the need to provide land to all agrarian communities that did not have sufficient acreage to support themselves. The Plan, which reflected the views of a rising generation of politicians, technocrats, and intellectuals, became Cárdenas's de facto political platform. Few, however, believed that Cárdenas would be able to implement it, since Calles remained as Jefe Máximo.[87]

As the 1934 presidential elections approached, Cárdenas openly sought the PNR nomination. As a result of the reforms he had carried out as governor, he enjoyed widespread support within the PNR and from the army and peasants. Calles was virtually forced to nominate Cárdenas, despite his preferring a more conservative aspirant, PNR President Manuel Pérez Treviño. To have nominated his favorite not only would have alienated important sectors of the ruling coalition but would have also risked rebellion by peasants and workers whose salaries had declined due to the Depression.

Calles, taking into consideration the broad support for Cárdenas, approved his candidacy for the 1934–1940 term. The Jefe Máximo assumed Cárdenas would distribute enough land to quiet the most radical peasants but not enough to upset the existing social order. He felt he could control Cárdenas, as he had controlled his immediate predecessors, and that power would inevitably make Cárdenas more conservative. Calles assumed that since Cárdenas was not only his friend but had also served as: 1) head of the PNR, 2) a revolutionary general, 3) interior minister, 4) and governor of Michoacán, he was as much a part of his system as one could be. Also, Cárdenas's record was not uniformly progressive since he had participated in a campaign against the Yaqui in Sonora and in 1932 as minister of war he had overseen the disarming of agrarian radicals in Veracruz led by Adalberto Tejeda.[88]

Even though he lacked significant opposition, Cárdenas undertook a marathon campaign, traveling more than 17,000 miles by car, rail, airplane, boat, and horse. This served not to convince voters—his election was assured—but to give him the opportunity to learn about Mexico's problems, to familiarize people with his ideas, and to build a base of support.[89]

As a candidate, Cárdenas stressed the need for better distribution of wealth, a greatly expanded role for peasant and worker groups, and a larger government role in social and economic matters. He alluded to the inevitable conservative backlash such actions would produce in a May 1934 speech, "I shall give to the campesinos the Mausers [rifles] with which they fought the Revolution so they can defend themselves, the *ejido*, and the rural school." In declaring that the solution to Mexico's economic problems would require massive state intervention, Cárdenas was the first major political figure to explicitly repudiate the liberal, laissez-faire model that had been in vogue among Mexican policymakers since the nineteenth century.[90]

The election, in which Cárdenas ran virtually unopposed, aroused little interest. Only 14 percent of the electorate bothered to cast a ballot to select Cárdenas for the 1934–1940 term.[91]

During the Maximato, the PNR simply incorporated caudillos into its ranks. Its goal was to maintain consensus and eliminate violence as a way to settle disputes among the elite. The PNR regularly won elections since it had the backing not only of caudillos but also of government arms and financing. Thanks to this, membership in the PNR became an indispensable requirement for political success. No one from the outside could be elected to or volunteer for PNR leadership. In its attempt to satisfy the contradictory demands of labor, business, and peasants, the party called upon these groups to oppose "reactionary forces," whose identity was never precisely spelled out.[92]

THE CÁRDENAS ADMINISTRATION, 1934–1940

> When Cárdenas took office on December 1, 1934, it appeared that the revolution had lost momentum. Millions of campesinos remained without land of their own. With the labor movement splintered into thousands of small local and regional organizations, the Maximato had kept tight hold on labor activism, outlawing strikes that threatened economic growth in the Jefe Máximo's opinion.
>
> Jürgen Buchenau, 2007[93]

Cárdenas refused to accept the role of puppet that Calles had assumed he would. He immediately began to build a broad coalition to challenge Calles's power. By the end of 1935, the government had distributed more than 6.7 million acres of land to more than 100,000 families. This land transfer not only won support for Cárdenas but also undermined the power of Calles's wealthy backers. The provision of increased agricultural credit and extension services further cemented peasant loyalty.[94]

On June 14, 1935, Cárdenas had his entire cabinet resign. He then replaced Calles's supporters with those whose loyalty he could count on. During 1935 and 1936, fourteen governors whose loyalty to Cárdenas was suspect had their powers declared void, had elections annulled, or were forced "to go on leave." Most dramatically, he declared void the election of Plutarco Elías Calles, Jr., the Jefe Máximo's son, as governor of Nuevo León. Cárdenas's style contrasted with that of the ruling clique from Sonora. Its members relied on force of arms to obtain power, while Cárdenas relied on more subtle political maneuvering.[95]

Cárdenas shuffled army commands to get his loyalists in key positions and moved pro-Calles generals to positions of less power. Military men who had fallen out with Calles, including Zapatistas, Carrancistas, and Villistas, were rehabilitated. Cárdenas further bolstered his support by offering loyal officers seats in Congress.[96]

Few key institutions escaped Cárdenas's base-building. Following a September 1935 shooting incident in the congressional chambers, eighteen of the most prominent Callista deputies were expelled. Cárdenas also sought support from the two strongest remaining caudillos, Saturnino Cedillo in San Luis Potosí and Juan Andreu Almazán in Nuevo León, both of whom enjoyed the personal loyalty of the troops they commanded. These caudillos viewed weakening Calles as an opportunity to increase their political power without realizing that using Cárdenas to weaken Calles might enable Cárdenas to become even more powerful than Calles had been.[97]

In January 1936, Monterrey steelworkers, emboldened by government support for labor, voted to join the Miners and Metalworkers Union. On February 1, after a labor court ruled in their favor, other workers voted to join a union at the Monterrey Glassworks.[98]

In response to organized labor's successful establishment in Monterrey, the closely knit, conservative businessmen who dominated the city staged a two-day lock-out, closing industry and commerce. They adroitly framed the issue not as business versus labor but as the defense of the Mexican nation versus imported Soviet communism. On February 5, 60,000, including Catholic women, merchants, professionals, and members of forty-two company unions, attended an anti-government rally—the largest post-revolutionary protest to date. They built support by using the radio, a medium that was just emerging as a major force. Their radio spots denounced "the communist government of Mexico" and called for "the defense of our holy religion."[99]

Figure 18.1
Lázaro Cárdenas

Source: Reproduced courtesy of the Benson Latin American Collection, the University of Texas at Austin

Cárdenas considered the lock-out as a challenge to his authority. In response, he made an unscheduled seven-day appearance in Monterrey. Thousands of steel, rail, and smelter workers celebrated his presence with daily parades and labor rallies.[100]

While in Monterrey, Cárdenas declared that, in the future, fourteen points would regulate labor-management relations. The principal point was that government was to be the arbiter of labor conflicts. He proclaimed that wages should not be fixed by the law of supply and demand but by the ability of each enterprise to operate without losses. He responded to the charge that labor unrest resulted from communist agitators. Unrest resulted not from the insignificant communist movement, he stated, but from unmet aspirations of workers and non-compliance with labor regulations. Cárdenas stated that if businessmen were tired of social conflict they could turn their firms over to workers or the government. He told them such a transfer, not suspending production, would be the patriotic course. Cárdenas warned the industrialists, "Oppression, industrial tyranny, unmet needs, and obstinacy can at any moment touch off the violent disturbances which you fear so much."[101]

When Cárdenas learned Calles was trying to organize a new political party, he acted. By this time, Cárdenas had the backing of the military, workers, peasants, and some churchmen. In April 1936, he ordered Calles onto a chartered Ford Trimotor, which flew him to exile in the United States. Upon arriving in Dallas, Calles told reporters, "I was expelled from Mexico for fighting Communism."[102]

Removing Calles from the political scene united party and government authority under one individual—a pattern that was to endure for the rest of the century. Despite his vastly increased power, Cárdenas set a less imperial tone for the presidency, moving the official residence from Chapultepec Castle to nearby Los Pinos— the current presidential residence. He also accelerated his reforms.[103]

Cárdenas's reforms, in contrast to the "revolutionary" rhetoric of the previous regimes, had a profound impact throughout the country. During the Depression he did not have to worry about foreign business concerns, since exports had plummeted and no foreign capital was entering Mexico. His reforms relied on state intervention in labor relations and land reform. Cárdenas explained the rationale for these reforms: "The modern view of the state and of labor legislation requires that doubtful cases be resolved in favor of the weaker party. To grant equal treatment to unequal parties is not justice, nor is it equitable."[104]

Land reform, for which he is still remembered, was Cárdenas's most ambitious program. From 1910 to 1930, only 3.9 percent of Mexico's land surface was distributed to the landless, two-thirds of the large holdings were untouched, and only 780,000 of Mexico's 3.6 million peasants were in permanent possession of any land. Before 1934, most beneficiaries of land reform received little technical aid or credit and did not have enough acreage to support a family.[105]

Cárdenas began the rapid transfer of land to peasants. Land was not only taken from traditional haciendas whose operations harkened back to colonial days but also from well-run, profitable commercial operations. Those receiving land benefited from larger plots than had previously been distributed and from new schools, improved social services, and the increased availability of credit. Rather than viewing the ejido as a transitional stage towards privately owned farms, as his predecessors had, Cárdenas believed the ejido should form the basic unit for rural development.[106]

The official party, the PNR, was still closely associated with Calles and remained in the hands of the political elite. In yet another of his sweeping reforms, Cárdenas transformed the party, which was renamed the Mexican Revolutionary Party (PRM), dividing it into four major sectors—peasants, the military, organized labor, and a "popular sector." Initially most members of the popular sector were civil servants. In adopting the corporate model, the PRM followed a model ascendant internationally, most notably in fascist Italy, Spain, and Germany but also in non-fascist countries such as Brazil. Thanks to its corporate structure, one joined the party not as an individual but as a member of an organized, recognized group.[107]

This reorganization came just twelve days after the nationalization of the oil industry and allowed Cárdenas to mobilize mass support against external political and economic pressure. By virtue of these sectors, which automatically incorporated soldiers, government workers, trade union members, and land-reform beneficiaries, the party could claim more than 4 million members, out of a total population of slightly less than 19 million.[108]

The PRM provided each major constituency (except business and the Church) a communication channel to the government—and, at the same time, enabled the government to control party members. The creation of peasant and labor sectors of the PRM not only increased the influence of these constituencies but also made the president less dependent on professional politicians, government employees, and the military.[109]

Despite the party being renamed and given a new slogan, "For a workers' democracy," it remained an undemocratic institution. The restructuring of the official party shifted power from caciques and other regional interests to Mexico City. As was the case when the PNR was founded, there was no public debate about restructuring the party. Cárdenas simply decreed the change was to occur. Also, as with the PNR, the citizenry was excluded from selecting candidates for public office. Mexico's national leaders, from Carranza to Cárdenas, all rejected Madero-style democracy as a source of instability and as the preamble to being overthrown. Madero had become a figure who was revered but not imitated.[110]

After the March 1938 nationalization of the oil industry, there was a sharp decline in oil and silver sales to the United States and thus less income for the government. An increase in U.S. tariffs and war in Europe also reduced export income. Mexican businessmen, who feared Cárdenas's radicalism and further nationalizations, not only refused to invest but sent their money out of the country. The 1937 recession in the United States also caused a slowdown in the Mexican economy.[111]

In 1938, as a result of these economic factors, government spending exceeded income by 15 percent. To meet this shortfall, the government printed paper money, producing serious inflation. Late in the Cárdenas administration, this inflation led to a decline in the buying power of wages. As the end of Cárdenas's term approached, money to finance additional restructuring was lacking.[112]

Domestic opposition to his reforms presented Cárdenas with yet another challenge. His opponents included Catholic traditionalists, rural people rejecting land reform and an activist state, and *hacendados* (both those retaining land and those recently deprived of it). The middle class and agricultural laborers who had not benefited from reform also swelled opposition ranks. Many, such as foreign investors, provincial elites, Monterrey industrialists, bankers, and merchants, feared Mexico was careening hell-bent down the road to socialism. Literature from opposition groups claimed Cárdenas's government was "communist" and subversive to the ideals of motherhood, patriotism, and family, and portrayed the land reform as a reckless attack on private property.[113]

In January 1938, the British minister commented on opposition to Cárdenas's reforms:

> A large body of public opinion heartily dislikes the present trend of events; indeed the army, the middle classes, the more conservative and religious peasantry are all equally opposed to it. But thanks to the lack of a strong personality round whom they can rally, to their inertia, and to the shrewd way in which the Government has tied their hands, they lack any means of making their views felt.[114]

Given financial constraints and mounting domestic opposition, reforms largely ceased. Despite the urgings of radical elements, after the nationalization of the oil industry, Cárdenas showed no interest in nationalizing any other industries.[115] As Table 18.1 indicates, the pace of land reform drastically slowed.

Cárdenas ceased supporting strikers, who bolstered his detractors' claims that there was insufficient "order" for economic development. In response to this shift, the Mexican Workers Federation (CTM), the main labor organization, promised to reduce the number of strikes. By 1940, the number of strikes had declined by 50 percent and the number of workers involved in strikes had declined by 80 percent.[116]

As the end of Cárdenas's 1934–1940 term approached, he faced the prospect of either selecting a PRM presidential candidate who would implement further change or one who would guarantee the reforms he had carried out would not be reversed. Cárdenas and his backers had little maneuvering room since conservatives were launching a strong electoral challenge. In addition, the international scene was most discouraging, with Republican Spain defeated, fascism spreading, and the Second World War on the horizon. As Cárdenas later commented, presidential succession was complicated by "problems of an international character."[117]

There were two viable PRM candidates. One was Francisco Múgica, a dedicated reformer who once wrote for *Regeneración*. As leader of the radical wing of the 1917 constitutional convention,

Table 18.1 *Land distribution, 1935–1940*

Year	Acres distributed (millions)
1935	4.7
1936	9.6
1937	13.3
1938	37.9
1939	4.9
1940	3.2

Source: Ruiz (1992: 399)

he was largely responsible for the 1917 constitution's anti-clerical and pro-labor provisions. In 1920, after taking office as governor of Michoacán, he promoted land reform and implemented labor legislation. Sixteen months later, he was ousted in a state-level coup and replaced by a conservative governor. Múgica later served as Cárdenas's secretary of communications and public works. His presidential candidacy was opposed by conservatives who felt him to be too radical and by opportunists and professional politicians who felt he would not tolerate their self-enrichment.[118]

The other main contender for the PRM presidential nomination was General Manuel Ávila Camacho, Cárdenas's secretary of defense. Ávila Camacho at most stood for maintaining intact the reforms that Cárdenas had instituted. He had studied accounting and joined the Constitutionalists in 1914 as a paymaster. His military record was so undistinguished that he was referred to as the "unknown soldier" and the "virgin sword." By the end of Cárdenas's term, Ávila Camacho was known as an honest functionary and as a middle-of-the-roader. The political establishment backed him and no group strongly opposed him. By virtue of his having served as secretary of defense, he could hold the army within the PRM coalition.[119]

Cárdenas finally selected Ávila Camacho as his successor. The designation of Múgica might have produced a conservative-led coup and a roll-back of reforms, such as the nationalization of the oil industry. Cárdenas's choice reflected the conservatives' strength and his desire for peace and stability. Mexico's president realized that he had bumped up against what political scientist Nora Hamilton termed the "limits of autonomy," that is, he had instituted as much change as the international capitalist system was willing to accommodate.[120]

Once Cárdenas let it be known he had decided to support Ávila Camacho, Múgica withdrew his candidacy. In his July 1939 withdrawal speech, he warned that peasant and labor leaders had become more inclined to side with professional politicians and the government than with their own constituencies.[121]

For the 1940 elections, conservatives rallied around General Juan Andreu Almazán, the military zone commander of Nuevo León. In the early stages of the Revolution, Almazán became Mexico's youngest brigadier general. During his military service, he grew wealthy as his construction company received numerous government contracts. While commander in Nuevo León, he established close ties with Monterrey businessmen and drove out labor and peasant organizers, charging them with being communists.[122]

Almazán enjoyed the support of surviving *hacendados*, oil interests, high clergy, and even some dissident PRM members. Many in the middle class, who had largely been ignored by Cárdenas and who resented official anti-clericalism, supported Almazán. His supporters were hard to pigeonhole ideologically. They included workers and peasants resenting corruption, high inflation, and having their leaders imposed on them by the PRM. The revolutionary muralist Diego Rivera supported Almazán, characterizing the PRM as "fascism with a socialist mask."[123]

Even though Ávila Camacho failed to excite any constituency, his conservative, Catholic family background tended to lessen opposition to his candidacy. Regional political machines tied to the PRM backed him, as did the party's peasant sector. To strike a conciliatory stance, the official labor organization, the CTM, which also supported him, replaced its "class struggle" slogan with one of "national unity."[124]

Almazán, in contrast, drew enthusiastic crowds, especially in the north and in middle-class urban districts. In Mexico City, 200,000 attended one of his rallies. He received most of his financial support from northern businessmen. One of his campaign slogans was, "Mexicans must embrace Almazán and God or they will be dominated by the USSR."[125]

During the campaign, Ávila Camacho moved to the political right while Almazán moved left. The campaign rhetoric of the two candidates became virtually indistinguishable. Both stressed class harmony, protecting foreign investment, and national unity, and declared they preferred the privately owned farm to the ejido.[126] In February 1940, Ávila Camacho pledged that he would "give all possible guarantees to foreign investment."[127] The next month, Almazán complained Ávila Camacho was stealing his program:

> They no longer speak of radicalism, they speak no more of socialist education. They are no longer proclaiming the dictatorship of the proletariat. Now they are very respectful of society, they predict harmony, they abominate violence, and they pretend to be the defenders of the family, of the small property owners, of the freedom of worship, and they repudiate communism.[128]

The election was the most violent in recent history. Operating under Ávila Camacho's direct orders, Gonzalo Santos, a leading political figure, and some 300 armed men ransacked polling places and stole ballot boxes in Mexico City. By Santos's own admission, voters there overwhelmingly supported Almazán. Some Mexico City polling places were defended by armed Almazán supporters. However, since Santos's group—mainly military men—was armed with Thompson submachine guns, they quickly overcame resistance. In Mexico City alone, twenty-seven died on election day and roughly 150 were wounded.[129]

According to official returns, Ávila Camacho received 2,476,641 votes. Almazán was credited with only 151,101 votes nationwide—fewer than the number attending his Mexico City rallies. It was clear in 1940—as it had been when Vasconcelos was a candidate—that the official party was unwilling to let elections be used to oust the political elite from power and that the common citizen had very little to do with choosing leaders. Political scientist Luis Javier Garrido characterized the whole process "as a grotesque electoral fraud."[130]

Almazán departed for the United States shortly after the election. When he was safely north of the Rio Grande, he proclaimed, "At the proper time, I will return to Mexico and claim the high office to which I am entitled by an overwhelming vote of the people." Almazán soon realized that with the majority of the Mexican army, official labor organizations, and the U.S. government supporting Ávila Camacho, a revolt would be futile.[131]

After Ávila Camacho's inauguration, Cárdenas remained a public figure, but in no way attempted to maintain political power as Calles had. He overcame the legacy of the fraudulent 1940 elections and became a symbol of Mexico's hopes for electoral democracy and civil liberties. His leaving of both the presidency and power completed the institutionalization of the Revolution and is one of the central elements of Cárdenas's legacy. For more than half a century, Cárdenas's successors would follow his example of selecting a successor and then relinquishing power.[132]

While Cárdenas failed to make progress at instituting political democracy, he made huge strides in promoting "social democracy." This concept was defined in Article 3 of the 1917 constitution: "Democracy shall be considered, not just in juridical and political terms, but as a social system based on constant economic, social, and cultural improvement." A variety of statistics indicate Cárdenas's success at promoting social democracy. In addition to distributing land, during his term 3,000 schools were constructed and 100,000 teachers trained. In 1930, 5.5 percent of the labor force was unionized, while by 1940, 14.5 percent was. During Cárdenas's term the buying power of salaries increased by 43 percent. Social spending, which included health and education, reached an unprecedented 18 percent of the federal budget. As political scientist Lorenzo Meyer observed, "The Mexico Cárdenas left in 1940 was doubtlessly more just than the one he received in 1934."[133]

The Cárdenas administration produced a state much more powerful than the one destroyed by the Revolution. During his term the ideology of the Revolution crystallized into a belief system supported by the majority of Mexicans. Even after adjusting for inflation, per capita federal spending under Cárdenas was more than twice the level it was under Díaz. Cárdenas's reforms reflect the impact of the Revolution and the Depression as well as his own value system, which was formed in central Mexico with its strong village base. They also reflect foreign influences of the time. Both the reforms being carried out by U.S. President Franklin D. Roosevelt (FDR) and the favorable publicity emanating from the Soviet Union made state intervention in the economy appear attractive. The Mexican experience was typical of post-Depression Latin America, as governments throughout the region increased social services and promoted economic development.[134]

After the fall of the Spanish Republic, more than 200,000 Spaniards came to Mexico, where they were offered citizenship and asylum. To defuse conservative opposition to the arrival of the Loyalist refugees, the first group admitted was composed of orphans with whom Cárdenas prominently posed. Not only was allowing this influx an act of mercy but it also brought tremendous cultural and economic capital to Mexico. Spanish refugees revitalized Mexican intellectual life and formed the Casa de España en México, which became the Colegio de México—one of Mexico's foremost centers of higher education.[135]

As was the case with his U.S. counterpart, FDR, Cárdenas made conservation one of his priorities. During his administration, 6 million trees were planted, a third of which were in the Valley of Mexico. Cárdenas also created forty national parks, three-quarters of the current system. These parks range in size up to the 168,000-acre Popocatépetl–Iztaccíhuatl Park, which surrounds the two volcanoes southeast of Mexico City.[136]

Despite the vigorous efforts of Miguel Ángel de Quevedo, whom Cárdenas appointed to head the Autonomous Forestry Department, environmental protection was undermined by many of the same factors hampering present-day conservation efforts. Peasants, who were not consulted on drafting regulations, felt that the measures were too draconian. Since fossil fuels cost more than the readily available timber, unauthorized cutting of trees continued apace to provide fuel. Finally, the forest service was not well enough staffed nor was it well enough paid to ensure compliance with forestry legislation.[137]

Cárdenas retained immense moral influence up until his death in 1970.[138] Writer Carlos Fuentes commented on his presidency:

> I have known all of the presidents of Mexico from 1934 to the present. Some have been more intelligent than others, some more politically astute, some more cultivated; but only one has attained true greatness: Lázaro Cárdenas. By greatness I mean, over and beyond tactical skill, energy, and determination, the concept of nationhood, the lofty vision that Cárdenas had of Mexico, its people, its history and culture, its destiny. He never thought small; he never belittled Mexico or its people.[139]

THE MILITARY

Carranza had difficulty controlling the large standing army that had emerged from the Revolution and the regionally based caudillos who led it. This force, which lacked an effective internal command structure, was composed of groups of armed men who were loyal to their immediate chief, not the central government. The military received two-thirds of the federal budget, which hampered Carranza's efforts at both social reform and economic restoration. As had been the case after previous wars, the military was reluctant to disband. Military officers, who occupied 46 percent of top government positions between 1914 and 1920, were permitted to enrich themselves through their positions, since Carranza felt that if they were getting rich, they would not be plotting coups.[140]

During the Obregón administration, many of the newly rich generals became petty rural tyrants upon whom Obregón relied to control their respective turfs. As Obregón noted, his military officers thought the land tenure problem was solved as soon as they owned the best haciendas.[141]

Obregón initiated the decades-long task of converting the military from the destroyer of governments to their protector. He increased military pay scales and founded a national military

Table 18.2 *Military share of federal expenditure, 1921–1940*

Years	President	Military share (%)
1921–1924	Obregón	44
1925–1928	Calles	31
1929–1930	Portes Gil	34
1930–1932	Ortiz Rubio	29
1933–1934	Rodríguez	24
1935–1940	Cárdenas	18

Source: Cothran (1994: 37)

academy that stressed military subordination to civilian government. The academy's graduates owed their loyalty to the military institution, not to locally based caudillos. New graduates slowly weaned power from the generals, who numbered one per 200 soldiers in 1920. During the first three years of the Obregón administration, the size of the army declined from more than 100,000 soldiers to 40,000, and military spending declined from 61 percent to 36 percent of the federal budget. Commanders were regularly rotated so their troops would be loyal to the military institution, not to their commanding officer.[142]

Calles continued Obregón's efforts to bring the army under tighter government control. In 1926, the military accounted for 33.5 percent of government spending and education for only 9.3 percent. In non-revolutionary Argentina, the military only took 17.5 percent of the budget while 20.8 percent was earmarked for education. Calles continued to rotate zone commanders so they would not develop personal ties to the troops they commanded, and he retired roughly sixty army generals, many of whom were given governorships as a reward for their leaving quietly.[143]

Calles's founding of the PNR definitively defanged the military establishment. He assembled leading generals and had them each promise that for the good of the country none of them would aspire to the presidency. Calles made a similar promise. Since the party's founding the military has not mounted a serious armed challenge to the incumbent administration.[144]

When Cárdenas assumed office, the military still wielded substantial power. Eleven state governors were military men, and generals governed three federal territories. To continue the process of shifting troop loyalty from caudillos to the government, Cárdenas raised military salaries, improved army education, and promoted junior officers who then owed their position to the president. Increasingly Cárdenas used the army to construct public works, such as hospitals, ports, and irrigation canals. He lowered the military retirement age, shoving out revolutionary generals and making room for a more loyal generation. The share of top government positions held by military men declined to 27 percent during the Cárdenas administration.[145]

In response to those who criticized Cárdenas for formally including the military in the newly organized PRM, Cárdenas noted: "We did not put the army in politics. It was already there. In fact it has been dominating the situation, and we did well to reduce its influence to one vote out of four."[146]

THE POLITICAL OPPOSITION

Just as was the case after Mexican independence, after the Revolution charismatic leaders were the backbone of politics. As the end of a presidential term approached, old organizations would be revived and new ones created to support the contenders. These ephemeral political parties were based on ideology and regional, economic, and, especially, personal interests. Obregón, a sure winner in 1920, received support from four national parties and innumerable state organizations.[147]

Once the PNR was formed, most existing parties became a part of its national structure, thus further centralizing political power at the national level. In 1932, this centralization was formalized as Congress dissolved all the parties that had joined the PNR.[148]

Elections and political parties were not the key to change between 1917 and 1940, since: 1) Mexico lacked a democratic tradition; 2) the incumbents' taking of power by military means destroyed the existing party structure; and 3) the revolutionaries' almost total dominance of the political space left the opposition little room in which to maneuver.[149]

The National Action Party

Several events led to the 1939 founding of the National Action Party (PAN). The failure of Vasconcelos to create an enduring political party caused many who had supported him to feel a party reflecting their views was needed. In addition, the Church-state conflict of the 1920s caused many to conflate Bolshevism and Mexico's revolutionary government. In the 1930s, this desire to create a new political party intensified after the constitution was amended to mandate "socialist education" and Cárdenas had accelerated the land reform, which many regarded as an unwarranted attack on private property. The new party protested what its founders felt was the exercise of power by a small group acting without institutional limits.[150]

Manuel Gómez Morín, who had served as the unofficial treasurer of the Vasconcelos campaign, spearheaded the organization of the new party. By 1939, Gómez Morín had already had a distinguished career in the public sector, having served as Obregón's undersecretary of finance, as a financial advisor to the Calles administration, and as president of the first Central Bank Board. He had taught in the National University law school and later served as rector of the university. In addition he had developed close ties to the private financial sector. His achievements in the public sector were unusual for someone not sharing the military background of the political elite.[151]

Late in 1938, Gómez Morín began contacting friends concerning the founding of a new political party that would be based on Mexico's Catholic tradition. Gómez Morín's goal was not only to provide an alternative for the upcoming 1940 elections but also to create a political party that would guide Mexico into the future.[152]

In September 1939, Gómez Morín's organizational efforts came to fruition as roughly 1,000 delegates founded the PAN. He told the delegates at the convention:

> The group of men who have seized control of the national government is increasingly removed from the interests of the nation. Their exclusive preoccupation is keeping power through corruption, deceit, violent means, bribery and the illegal use of state power.[153]

Convention delegates were united by their fear that the PRM was leading Mexico to socialism. Some of the delegates came from the Catholic middle and upper classes and sought to promote religious values. Others had worked with Gómez Morín at the National University. Business and financial leaders formed a third group, whose members sought to protect their assets from government reformers. In educational terms, PAN leaders were very much an elite group, as 73 percent of the PAN's initial National Council were professionals. Bankers composed 24 percent of the party's National Executive Committee, which also included three ex-rectors of the National University. This intellectual background, as much as ideology, contrasted with the PRM, a party that political scientist Soledad Loaeza characterized as "still reeking of gunpowder."[154]

The party's basic beliefs were enunciated in its Doctrinal Principles, drafted at its founding convention. They declared the state should concern itself with social justice, not class struggle. While Catholicism was not specifically mentioned, the Principles did declare that religious liberty should always be upheld and that all laws that directly or indirectly opposed it should be repealed. Private property was declared "the best means to assure national production and guarantee human dignity." The Principles stated that the municipality should serve as the basis of Mexico's political structure. The document declared the ejido should be converted into private property and that the government should extend irrigation and supply rural producers with training and credit. One of the unifying themes of the PAN was the belief that it was possible to create a society based on a third way, distinct from both capitalism and "statism."[155]

Some party members advocated abstaining from the 1940 elections, since it was obvious that any PAN candidate would lose, even if votes were counted honestly. In addition, a PAN candidate would only draw support from Almazán, whose belief in the sanctity of rural property, distrust of the labor movement, and desire to reestablish relations between Church and state were shared by most PAN members.[156]

The PAN finessed the issue of electoral participation by declaring that while it would not nominate Almazán as an official candidate, it would support him as long as he accepted its principles. This decision reflected the desire of many PAN members to plunge into the political fray as well as the realization that Almazán would be the only serious opposition candidate. The party did explicitly abstain from the 1940 congressional elections, stating that it needed time to recruit members and familiarize the citizenry with its views. Once the 1940 elections had passed, the party turned to the ideological preparation of its members and the dissemination of its ideology.[157]

SOCIETY, 1917–1940

> What the villagers of Morelos had always feared gradually came to pass: the city expropriated the revolution. It was there, in the city, that the increasingly powerful revolutionary state was centered and, in the name of progress, it was the city that this state favored when it distributed resources, for the new ruling class progress meant industrialization and urbanization.
>
> Samuel Brunk, 1995[158]

Upward mobility based on the Revolution came in waves. Under Madero, the dissident elite assumed power. Then, as Villa and Zapata dominated the political scene, the lower class became upwardly mobile. From the Constitutionalist victory through 1940, the middle class harnessed the Revolution for its own enrichment. Finally, as Mexico stabilized, technical and administrative expertise became more important, and the political elite was increasingly drawn from the university-educated professional classes. This tendency intensified after the Second World War. Upward mobility often resulted from seizing haciendas, marrying daughters of the Porfirian aristocracy, selling influence in government circles, embezzling government funds, selling food allocated to feed soldiers, or obtaining sweetheart loans from government banks.[159]

Changes in leadership were much more dramatic than changes in living standards. The year 1917 was not the year of the constitution for most Mexicans, but rather one of hunger. The government, burdened with enormous debt and without access to internal or external credit, had difficulty buying grain to feed the population. Unemployment was rising, and the country lay in ruins. Just as the Mexican population was beginning to benefit from economic recovery, the Depression halted progress in health and education. Annual per capita consumption of corn, the mainstay of the popular diet, fell from 300 pounds in 1928 to 194 in 1930.[160]

At the time of Cárdenas's inauguration, rural life had changed little. Many small towns, accessible only by mule trail, lacked schools, churches, and running water. In his classical study of Tepoztlán, Morelos, anthropologist Robert Redfield observed that in the late 1920s the town lacked electricity and power tools. Even though the village was only fifty miles from Mexico City, because of the rough, rocky roads, humans and a variety of quadrupeds carried all the cargo coming to town.[161]

In contrast to the Sonora dynasty, which focused on economic progress promoted by the state, Cárdenas used the state to promote social justice. The major agents of change were education and land reform. Improved communications also facilitated change, as Cárdenas donated radios so residents of every agricultural and workers community in Mexico could listen to three state radio stations—one belonging to the education ministry and two to the official party. By 1940, Mexicans were benefiting from thousands of new schools, innumerable public services, and extensive new irrigation projects. Government-run stores opened in urban areas, selling food at reduced prices. As Carlos Fuentes noted, "Even if the upper and middle classes were favored, the working and peasant classes received larger slices of the national pie than they had before or ever have had since."[162]

As the Revolution faded into history, it became increasingly difficult to isolate what emanated from the Revolution and what was attributable to change sweeping all of Latin America. Motor vehicles, for example, had an impact far more diffuse than that of the railroad, which left the vast majority of Mexico's villages just as isolated as they had been in colonial times. As naturalist Aldous Huxley noted:

> Over and above their material freight, the Fords will carry an invisible cargo of new ideas, of alien, urban ways of thought and feeling . . . Along the metalled roads the Fords will bring, not only reading matter, but also notions that will make the printed words fully comprehensible . . . The metalled roads and the Fords will have the effect of making large-scale urban vulgarity accessible to almost all.[163]

Rustic village shops increasingly stocked such city-made goods as matches, candles, beer, and even canned foods. Other changes included increased state bureaucracy, extension of tax powers, and more mass participation in politics. These changes were occurring not only in revolutionary Mexico but also in non-revolutionary Argentina, Brazil, and Chile.[164]

While change was indeed occurring, the Mexico of 1940 in many ways had more in common with the Mexico of the late nineteenth century than that of the late twentieth. The population remained small, rural, and agricultural. Although there was steady population increase and migration from rural to urban areas, the rate of change was quite low compared to the rate later in the century. In 1921, 68.8 percent of the population was rural, and by 1940, 64.9 remained so.[165]

The Elite

Historian Frank Tannenbaum described the process by which dedicated revolutionaries became opponents of social change:

> Their difficulty lay in the fact that they had come to power suddenly and without preparation, either morally, psychologically, politically, or even administratively. They were taken from their villages as barefooted youngsters who had slept on the floor and could barely read, and after a few years spent on the battlefields found themselves tossed into high office and great responsibility. This new world was filled with a thousand temptations they had not dreamed of: gold, women, houses, carpets, diamonds, champagne . . . Here, at no price at all, just for a nod, all their hearts desired was offered them in return for a favor, a signature, a gesture, a word.[166]

Historian Ernest Gruening noted that Nuevo León had

> [the] distinction of having had probably the most dishonest governor in all the twenty-eight states, General Porfirio González, who, not content to confine his thieving to state taxes collected in advance, defrauded the federal treasury by organizing wholesale smuggling from the United States.

The flagrant enrichment of officials did not escape popular notice. The street in Cuernavaca where Calles and his cronies built their lavish mansions was known as the street of "Ali Baba and the Forty Thieves."[167]

Those holding political power manipulated state policy to facilitate their own enrichment. Revolutionary officers so thoroughly converted the Agricultural Credit Bank into their private treasury that its founder (and later PAN leader) Manuel Gómez Morín resigned in disgust, declaring that it "had become a whorehouse." The unchecked enrichment of revolutionaries created such a problem that Obregón lamented that it was becoming difficult for Mexico to "liberate itself from its liberators."[168]

Even though the economic elite was never incorporated into the official political party, it was always active, well organized, and influential. The government sought the cooperation of businessmen to rebuild the economy, the radical tone of the constitution notwithstanding. In 1917, to encourage this cooperation, the Carranza administration invited businessmen to create the National Federation of Chambers of Commerce (CONCANACO) and the National Federation of Industrial Chambers (CONCAMIN). These groups were followed by the Businessmen's Federation of the Mexican Republic (COPARMEX), organized in 1929 to oppose the proposed federal labor law. Representatives of these groups became the spokesmen for business. During the Cárdenas administration, COPARMEX representatives lobbied against diverting capital away from investment to promote social justice, claiming that such a diversion would deplete capital and lower production.[169]

Profirian office holders and *científicos* vanished from power early on. The *hacendado* class was much more tenacious. Except in Morelos and Chihuahua, most *hacendados* survived into the 1930s with their economic positions relatively intact. Even in Chihuahua, families such as the Terrazas maintained enormous wealth and power through kinship ties and diversified holdings. In 1922, when Obregón finally expropriated all their holdings not under cultivation, the Terrazas received 13.5 millions pesos compensation for their land.[170]

The old *hacendado* class was anything but fatalistic in accepting its displacement. Some sold their land to Mexicans in small parcels before the agents of land reform arrived and moved their capital into industry and urban commerce. Others sold land to foreigners whose nationality made authorities reluctant to question the sale. In other instances, they bribed local land reform officials to exempt their properties. In some cases, landowners would rent land to military officers to deter agrarian takeover. *Hacendados* repeatedly resorted to the courts, using shrewd lawyers and their financial resources to outlast the financially strapped peasants. By forming alliances with local military leaders, the elite could use troops to block land reform. They also engaged in subterfuge, dividing their estates into many small units among family and friends. If government forces were unavailable or unwilling to do their dirty work, landowners hired private armies variously called militias, *rurales*, *guardias blancas,* and *guardias municipales*, which murdered agrarian leaders and terrorized rural populations.[171]

Though vastly diminished in power, even after Cárdenas's massive land reform many members of the agrarian elite remained wealthy. Those who had been unable to convert their land to cash and invest elsewhere were allowed to retain 370 acres of irrigated land or its equivalent in dry land. Often they controlled milling, credit, agricultural inputs, and marketing outlets and, through these channels, profited from dealings with the direct beneficiaries of land reform.[172]

At the end of Cárdenas's presidency, the industrial elite was in an advantageous position. Cárdenas's support for labor had its greatest impact on foreign capitalists, not Mexican ones. The state had financed infrastructure with internal and external debt, not higher taxes. The oil nationalization held the promise of an inexpensive fuel supply. With the government having vastly enlarged the domestic market with land reform, rosy days lay ahead for businessmen, especially during the Second World War-induced boom.[173]

Workers

> Organized labor's entry into national politics was among the most significant consequences of Mexico's 1910–1920 social revolution.
>
> Kevin Middlebrook, 1995[174]

Mexico adheres to the Hispanic tradition in relying on statutory laws to implement constitutional provisions. Until such legislation is enacted, constitutional guarantees are unenforceable. Given the absence of prompt federal action following the promulgation of the 1917 Constitution, individual states passed labor legislation concerning safety, union contracts, and workplace conditions. Legislation in states with a strong labor tradition, such as Veracruz and Puebla, was decidedly pro-labor, while other states lacked any labor legislation.[175]

Even when it was protected by state legislation, labor organizing was fraught with difficulties. In 1921, Mexico remained a largely rural society, with 71.4 percent of its work force in agriculture, forestry, hunting, and fishing. Organizing was also complicated by the dispersal of the labor force into many small work sites. Few large concentrations of workers existed outside mining, railroads, oil, textiles, and the public sector.[176]

With Carranza's backing, the governor of Coahuila sponsored the organization of a national labor federation in an effort to preempt an anticipated independent labor federation. The group's founding convention, which convened on May 1, 1918, drew a wide variety of labor leaders representing 113 organizations.[177]

The anarchist faction at the convention advocated "direct action," their term for confronting business without involving government. Another faction, led by Luis Morones, advocated "multiple action," which combined strikes and working with government to formulate policies favorable to labor. Morones's faction predominated, and he was selected as secretary general of the new organization, the CROM. The CROM's initial goals included conciliation with the state and ensuring the labor provisions of the 1917 constitution were enforced. Morones urged that workers take a moderate stance since labor was too weak to win radical demands and such demands could provide the United States with a pretext to intervene in Mexico.[178]

Carranza viewed strikes as a direct challenge to his effort to reinvigorate the economy, so he often repressed them. Court decisions rarely favored workers. To make matters worse, the labor market was glutted, and the First World War-induced inflation eroded the buying power of wages. Before 1920, labor saw little benefit from the Revolution. Wages remained low, hours were long, working conditions were deplorable, and workers were subject to arbitrary treatment by management.[179]

Given Carranza's lack of support for labor, CROM leaders sought other leadership, which they found in Obregón, who was viewed as a friend of labor for his having championed the inclusion of pro-labor provisions in the 1917 Constitution. In August 1919, the CROM signed a secret pact with Obregón, in which it agreed to mobilize support for Obregón in the 1920 presidential election. In exchange it was to receive privileged political access, the creation of a separate labor ministry with CROM influence over it, and presidential support for statutory law implementing the provisions of Article 123.[180]

The CROM was amply rewarded for its support of Obregón. Under his administration, the CROM could organize freely. In 1921, there were more than 300 strikes involving 100,000 workers. The government began to impose settlements favorable to labor, thus permitting the CROM to win the majority of its industrial disputes between 1920 and 1924. In many cases, as a result of government pressure management made concessions even before strikes occurred. This provided tangible benefits for the small industrial working class. Celestino Gasca, an ex-cobbler and prominent member of the CROM, was named governor of the Federal District, a relatively unimportant position but one that would have been unthinkable for a worker a few years before. As it became obvious that joining the CROM provided material rewards, its membership soared from 300,000 in 1920 to 1.2 million by 1924.[181]

With the benefit of hindsight, many have criticized CROM leaders for having allowed themselves to fall under state control. At the time, however, there were numerous reasons for welcoming an alliance with the state. Labor justified cooperation with the government by declaring that the main enemy of the Mexican working class was international capital, which both the government and labor should confront. It was also obvious that labor was weak numerically and organizationally and that it needed to build alliances to meet its goals. Collaboration with the government yielded government subsidies for labor organizations. Labor also cooperated with industrialists since both constituencies supported high tariffs, the former to protect their jobs and the latter to protect their profits.[182]

In 1924, the CROM backed Calles's presidential candidacy, a move for which it once again received ample reward. Between 1924 and 1928, Morones served as minister of industry, commerce, and labor and became one of the most powerful politicians in Mexico. Other CROM members received congressional seats. The CROM repeatedly won enforcement of legally mandated seniority rights, minimum wages, and severance pay and gained control over labor conciliation and arbitration boards through which it could force settlements favorable to labor. Workers affiliated with the CROM enjoyed higher wages and had more rights than did members of independent unions. By virtue of its obvious government support, the CROM could claim 2 million members in 1928, indicating organizing well beyond the roughly 30,000 textile workers.[183]

The CROM-government alliance served Calles well since this workers group became his major non-military power base. His alliance with the CROM allowed him to influence its demands. Urban workers were told they should moderate their demands to attract foreign capital and to ensure economic stability and capital accumulation—arguments similar to those used under Díaz.[184]

Obregón's assassination shattered the cozy relationship between Morones and the government. Obregón supporters widely believed Morones had masterminded the assassination since he had his own presidential ambitions. For self-preservation, Calles distanced himself from Morones, forced him from his cabinet, and withdrew government support from the CROM. By distancing the government from the Morones-led labor federation, Calles calmed the political waters.[185]

Once it became apparent that the CROM no longer enjoyed government support, trade unions began to desert en masse. The number of affiliated organizations declined from 1,172 in 1928 to 349 in 1932. Portes Gil's becoming president only compounded the CROM's difficulties, since he had become a bitter enemy of the CROM during his days as governor of Tamaulipas, when the CROM vied with him for control of the state. Calles's successor removed CROM members from the government and used army troops against CROM unions.[186]

In 1931, in response to Calles seeking to draw labor into the PNR and due to worsening labor conditions resulting from the Depression, a Federal Labor Law was passed. The law implemented the pro-labor provisions contained in Article 123 of the 1917 constitution and reaffirmed workers' right to organize unions and strike. It required the government to certify whether unions were legally constituted, thus allowing the government to deny the registration of radical unions and giving the state detailed knowledge of labor organizations. In addition, the law provided for a closed shop, which allowed unions to force the dismissal of any worker engaging in anti-union activity.[187]

The void produced by the withdrawal of state support for the CROM was filled in 1933 with the founding of the General Federation of Mexican Workers and Peasants (CGOCM), which declared that its ultimate goal was the elimination of capitalism. However its short-term goals focused on improving the living conditions of workers. By the end of 1934, the combative, politically independent CGOCM claimed 890,000 members, making it the largest labor federation in Mexico.[188]

During the Depression, the number of strikes declined, since workers were afraid of losing their jobs and the government discouraged strike activity. In June 1932, Secretary of Industry, Commerce, and Labor Abelardo Rodríguez declared: "At this time, strikes are inopportune and unpatriotic. The cooperation of everyone is needed and especially that of workers, since there is a revolutionary government, dedicated to rebuilding the country."[189]

Labor became polarized, with the CROM and Morones siding with Calles. However the CGOCM, after deciding that Cárdenas did in fact support labor, organized the National Committee of Proletarian Defense (CNDP) to back Cárdenas in his confrontation with Calles. The CNDP, which organized both peasants and workers, announced that if necessary it would call a general strike to defend the freedom to strike, associate, and assemble.[190]

In 1936, the CNDP called for a convention to found a new labor organization. More than 3,000 labor representatives met and created the CTM, which included the CGOCM, the Mexican Labor Federation (CSUM), and many other groups. The CTM soon claimed 3,594 affiliates and 946,000 members, dwarfing the remaining labor groups. Reflecting the radical thinking of the period, the CTM statutes declared, "The working class of Mexico must never forget that the final aim of its struggles is the abolition of the capitalist regime."[191]

Membership in the CTM continued to increase, since the federation was successful at gaining increased wages, collective contracts, and compliance with federal labor law. The CTM enjoyed obvious government support in the form of a cash subsidy, protection for CTM activities, and the persecution of the CTM's enemies. The CTM's close relationship with the government was formalized in 1938, as the CTM voted to become part of the Partido Nacional Revolucionario (PNR). At the time, CTM leaders felt they could maintain their autonomy.[192]

As historian Joe Ashby noted, "Under the Cárdenas regime, the Mexican labor movement attained its highest form of organization, prestige, and influence in national economic policy." The number of officially recognized strikes rose from thirteen in 1933 to 833 in 1937. Since such labor actions had government support, during Cárdenas's term, there was a 43 percent increase in real wages and an improvement in working conditions. Nearly 15 percent of the non-agricultural labor force was organized, a marked increase over previous administrations. Pressure from labor unions, constant strikes, workers demands, and the presence of pro-labor authorities undermined the patriarchal style in which businessmen had traditionally treated their employees.[193]

Rural Mexico

> Popular groups can hardly be said to have won the war, but they certainly succeeded in shaping the state, in so far as elites were forced to accommodate values, practices, and institutions that ran contrary to their understandings of a modern, secular, capitalist society.
>
> Jennie Purnell, 1999[194]

After the Revolution, three competing notions of land ownership emerged. One—similar to that then prevailing (and still doing so) in the United States—held that individuals were entitled to own as much land as they wanted (and could afford). The second view, adopted by the Zapatistas, was that justice demanded that peasants have land to sow and that the peasants themselves, guns in hand if necessary, should transfer land from large estates to the tillers. The third view agreed with the second in its belief that justice demanded that peasants be given land to sow, but held that the government should determine which land was transferred to peasants, when it was transferred, and which peasants would receive it.

The first view was supported, not surprisingly, by *hacendados*. In addition, it was shared by a wide variety of others, including many priests who identified with *hacendados*' interests. A surprising number of poor people also supported it because they believed people should earn their property, or because they had been convinced by priests that it was morally wrong to accept the property of others, or because they concluded that changing the system would not improve their lot in life.

Even though Zapatismo disappeared as a movement after 1920, many still accepted the premise that peasants should claim land on their own. The General Federation of Workers (CGT), an anarchist labor federation, openly advocated peasants taking land on their own initiative. This approach to land reform remained a potent force for decades, especially as peasants saw that government-sanctioned land reform was agonizingly slow and corrupt, or excluded them for a variety of reasons.[195]

The third view was accepted by government policymakers as a way to control peasant movements and as an orderly way to transfer land to the rural poor. It gained widespread acceptance among peasants since when they attempted to claim land on their own violent clashes frequently ensued. It also became widely popular among a whole class of intermediaries who found that by involving themselves in the land distribution process they could influence it to further their personal interests.

To implement land reform, the government created a new institution known as the ejido. To establish an ejido, the government would designate a certain extension of land as having surpassed the legal ownership limit. Typically, land would be transferred from private ownership to the ejido and then would be divided into plots that would be distributed to male heads of families included in the ejido. The plot could be farmed by the family, but not legally sold, rented, or mortgaged. This provision prevented the reconcentration of land into large estates. Ejido land could be inherited by family members, thus keeping the institution viable for generations. This government-mandated transfer of land often involved the use of force or the threat of force against both recalcitrant *hacendados* and militant peasants.

Before land was transferred to a specific ejido, villagers had to demonstrate an economic need for land and that land existed within four miles of their village that surpassed the legal limit for one owner. Even though the details of eligibility were spelled out in great detail, politics rather than technical criteria often determined who would receive land. Many *hacendados* attempted to force claimants or potential claimants to move before their claims had been processed. If the *hacendados* were successful, the claims became invalid since the claimants would no longer live within four miles of the land claimed.[196]

During the 1920s, the rate of land distribution reflected political priorities. Early in his administration, Obregón sharply increased the rate of land distribution, since he needed to build a political base. By 1922, he had become firmly entrenched, and the pace of distribution slowed. In 1927, since it faced widespread revolt, the government once again felt compelled to court peasant loyalty by accelerating land distribution. Secretary of Agriculture Luis León acknowledged the motivation for this measure, "In order to isolate reactionary groups and diminish the veiled influence of priestly propaganda, the government has been forced to promise the campesinos an acceleration of land reform." In addition, regions where peasants were highly mobilized were more likely to see land distribution than those where peasants were more passive.[197]

Various institutional obstacles slowed land distribution. Members of the Sonora dynasty viewed land reform as a means to calm peasant militancy, not as the basis of a sound agricultural economy. The Church spoke out against land reform. A 1920 pastoral letter stated, "As men are naturally unequal in strength and intelligence, so they must be unequal in terms of what they own; the church commands that property rights, rooted in nature, are inviolable." The army often favored *hacendados*' interests, not peasants'. Soldiers, whatever their original motivation for joining revolutionary armies might have been, had usually been away from their home region for years and had become members of what anthropologist Arturo Warman described as "a plundering, adventurers' legion." *Hacendados* had much more to offer both officers and men in this "legion" than did the landless peasants pressing their claims.[198]

Before the Cárdenas administration, those receiving ejido land usually did so only after large-scale mobilizations to pressure authorities. These mobilizations were subject to violent repression by *hacendados*. Leaders of such movements were often rendered ineffective by providing them with employment in state peasant organizations. In other cases, leaders were simply murdered. The most effective peasant leader in 1920s Michoacán was Primo Tapia, who had worked for thirteen years in the United States, where he had been influenced by the Flores Magón brothers. He became so successful at leading peasants demanding land that Calles, fearful of Tapia building an independent power base, ordered the army to murder him.[199]

Even after those soliciting land had received it, *hacendados* continued to resort to violence in an attempt to drive them off and deter others. Authors Nathaniel and Sylvia Weyl describe one such effort in Michoacán:

> After the distribution of lands in Langostura, the "white guards" of the *hacendados* attacked the *ejidatarios* in the fields. The men and women of the village repelled the invasion. Mauser [rifle] in hand, the members of the feminine league stood guard over the fields while their husbands worked.[200]

By 1930, as a result of these factors, little progress had been made toward addressing the inequality in land tenure. In that year, of 3.5 million agricultural workers, 2.5 million had no land. Haciendas with more than 2,470 acres of land, 0.8 percent of all holdings, controlled 79.5 percent of the land.[201]

Unlike his predecessors, Cárdenas felt the ejido was both morally and economically superior to the hacienda. Prior to the Cárdenas administration, ejido plots were small and lacked government support. They mainly served to maintain peasants between stints when they performed wage labor on nearby haciendas. In contrast Cárdenas felt the ejido could and should be the major unit of agricultural production for the market. He made this clear when he spoke at the Laguna:

> As an institution, it [the ejido] shoulders a double responsibility; as a social system it must make the country worker free from the exploitation to which he was subject under the feudal as well as under the individualist system; and as a system of agricultural production it must render such a yield as to provide the country at large with food . . .[202]

Just as earlier attempts at land distribution had met with armed force, Cárdenas's efforts were opposed by *hacendados*' hired gunmen. In a three-month period in 1936, 500 peasants were killed in land disputes. However, rather than backing down to the show of force by landowners, Cárdenas armed some 60,000 peasants.[203]

To organize peasants, Cárdenas created the National Peasant Confederation (CNC), which incorporated existing state-level agrarian leagues. Spontaneous land seizures were suppressed, leaving the CNC as the only channel through which land was available. Guns to defend newly granted lands also were channeled through the CNC. Those receiving ejido lands automatically became members of the CNC, and through that membership, they became PRM members. Although Cárdenas used the CNC to channel land and resources to peasants, subsequent presidents used this run-from-the-top-down organization to dominate peasant movements and to prevent protests not sanctioned by the government.[204]

During the Cárdenas administration, land was distributed to 728,847 peasants. As a result, in 1940, *ejidatarios* cultivated 17.3 million acres, while private farmers cultivated only 16.8 million. Since corn required relatively little capital to grow and techniques for growing it were familiar to many, *ejidatarios* concentrated on producing it. Between 1930 and 1940, Mexico's corn production increased by almost 50 percent. During that same period, the volume of all agricultural production increased by 29 percent.[205]

The land reform increased the standard of living of its beneficiaries, weakened the *hacendado* class, preserved rural political stability, and increased peasant self-esteem. American hacienda owner Rosalie Evans commented on the psychological impact land reform had had on her hacienda workers, "The Indians are in appearance as you know them, but are no longer apathetic, they are insolent and aggressive."[206]

Given that land tenure was only part of Mexico's agricultural problem and that Cárdenas's efforts were thwarted by resource limitations and by domestic and foreign opposition to land reform, in 1940 numerous problems remained in rural Mexico. One of the most significant of these problems was an excess of rural labor. Some 50 percent of the agricultural work force remained landless when Cárdenas left office.[207]

Substantial inequality remained in rural Mexico. Those who lost land to land reform were allowed to retain 370 irrigated acres or its equivalent in dry land. Large extensions of commercial crops, such as coffee, cacao, and rubber, were exempt from expropriation. The land reform law allowed owners facing expropriation to choose which piece of land they wished to retain, along with their installations, equipment, and livestock.[208]

With the hacienda largely out of the picture and with the countryside more peaceful that it had been for generations, by 1940 life in rural Mexico had indeed changed. However the ejido only addressed the concentration of land ownership. Rural Mexico continued to face numerous other problems, such as a lack of credit, the lack of competitive advantage in basic grain production, an underdeveloped market, and the poor quality of much cultivated land. Even in relatively modern areas, such as the Laguna, 73 percent of agricultural workers were illiterate. The Weyls described the farm technology used in the late 1930s as "contemporary with the Egyptian pharaohs."[209] They also observed:

> Fourteen and half of Mexico's twenty millions live in villages, separated from each other by high mountain ranges and deep forests. Winding paths worn by the plodding feet of burros and gullied by the torrential floods of the rainy season are often the sole means of communication.[210]

While traveling through Oaxaca in 1933, Aldous Huxley described what happened as land-hungry peasants cleared steeply sloping land: "With the disappearance of the trees, erosion sets in. The soil disappears altogether from the slopes; the level ground is scored with ever-deepening gullies. The land becomes either sterile or unworkable."[211]

The Indigenous Population

Except for its effect on those who actually fought in the revolutionary armies, the Revolution was slow to impact indigenous communities. The delegates to the 1917 Constitutional Convention did not debate indigenous rights, and there is no indication that Indians concerned them. No specific rights were granted indigenous people based on their identity. At the time, the indigenous population remained reliant on craft production, poorly remunerated labor on haciendas, and the use of low-yield agricultural techniques on poor land. This use of poor land reflected the process by which non-Indians, beginning in colonial times, had inexorably appropriated the best Indian lands.[212]

During the 1920s, government policy makers sought to improve the lot of Mexico's indigenous population. Unlike land reform, the government was not responding to popular pressure from below. Rather, the non-Indian intelligentsia imposed reform from the outside. Advocates of new government policies, known collectively as *indigenismo*, rejected nineteenth-century notions that Indians were biologically inferior. Such beliefs were replaced by the notion that Indian poverty resulted from their cultural values, the social structure of the Indian community, and the domination, exploitation, and oppression embedded in relations between Indians and non-Indians.[213]

Indigenismo advocated the voluntary integration of the Indian into Mexican society, especially through education. Its supporters claimed that Indians could become educated, bilingual, and politically mobilized and, at the same time, sustain their distinctive language, dress, religion, and mores.

While it was designed specifically to address what non-Indians perceived as the "Indian problem," as historian Alan Knight observed, "Indians themselves were the objects, not the authors, of indigenismo."[214]

The person most responsible for the development of *indigenismo* during the 1920s and 1930s was Manuel Gamio, who received the best anthropological training available at the time, having obtained a Ph.D. from Columbia University. He was a public intellectual committed to the success of the Revolution and the building of the nation. In addition to his contributions to *indigenismo*, he directed the restoration of Teotihuacan, where he studied not only the ancient civilization found there but also the modern inhabitants of the region.[215]

Gamio felt society, not genetics, shaped indigenous communities. He defined "Indianness" in cultural terms and even declared that Juárez was not an Indian since he had totally assimilated Mexican culture and thus lost his Indian status.

Gamio also believed the indigenous should be acculturated, not because their culture was inferior but because until Mexicans had a common culture they would not form a true nation. On a more practical level, Gamio initiated a program to revive the production of Indian textiles, ceramics, lacquerware, porcelain, and metalwork, whose production had declined during the nineteenth century as industrial production displaced them.[216]

Indigenismo was formulated without the participation or even awareness of most Indians. Its implementation involved establishing schools in isolated Indian villages. The primary goals of these schools were teaching Spanish and incorporating Indians into the national culture. In addition to being woefully underfunded in relation to the large indigenous population, the program had limited impact since its monolingual Spanish curriculum was detached from Indian reality.[217]

Rather than rushing to join the Mexican nation, many Indians consciously withdrew from it, since they felt they generally came out the worse when they worked for or sold goods to non-Indians. The indigenous community of Chamula, in Chiapas, even prohibited the selection of a mayor who spoke Spanish. Chamulans felt that mayors who spoke only the village language, Tzotzil, would be unable to sell out village interests to non-Indians.[218]

Cárdenas, following the tenor of *indigenismo*, viewed Indians' problems as resulting from their economic relationship with non-Indians. In 1940, he declared:

> That which Indians have in common, more than the color of their skin, their forms of political organization, or their artistic creations, is their condition as an oppressed class, destined to perform the most unhealthy tasks in mines or to subsist on the hardest labor in agriculture, in the oil fields, and in the forests, anywhere that cheap labor is needed by exploitative corporations.[219]

To address these problems, Cárdenas proposed changing Indians' economic relations with non-Indians. He noted, "The program of Indian liberation is essentially that of the emancipation of any country's proletariat." In addition he declared the solution to Indians' problems required new technology: "Irrigation, interstate highways, feeder roads, hydroelectric plants, animal husbandry centers, plant nurseries, orchards, improved seeds, trade schools, and sanitary services will rapidly restore the landscape of Indian regions."[220]

During the Cárdenas administration, the programs that had the greatest impact on Indians were those that affected all Mexicans. Land reform increased access to land for Indian as well as non-Indian. Similarly, both Indians and non-Indians enjoyed increased access to water, credit, and technical aid. Such programs also lessened local autonomy as they tied Indians more closely to state and federal governments through labor unions, land-reform offices, and local branches of the PRM and its peasant sector, the CNC.[221]

While Indian incorporation was the mantra of *indigenismo*, there were dissenting views. In 1936, labor leader Vicente Lombardo Toledano proposed: 1) the creation of new territorial divisions that would be homogeneously Indian; 2) "absolute" political autonomy for these units: 3) the promotion of Indian languages; 4) locating production in areas inhabited by Indians; and 5) collectivizing and industrializing Indian agriculture.[222]

During the Carranza administration, the Yaqui continued to resist outside control and raided Mexican settlements that had sprung up on land that had been usurped from them. In response, in December 1917, 1,500 Yaqui were deported to other parts of Mexico and were eventually sent to the Islas Marías penal colony. Yaquis would work in the United States to earn money so they could buy arms to attack Mexicans. From October 1926 to April 1927 Obregón took to the field, commanding 15,000 men to subjugate the Yaqui in an offensive that involved the aerial bombardment of Yaqui towns.[223]

In 1937, rather than mobilize yet another army to impose outside control on the Yaqui, Cárdenas restored to them 1.2 million acres of land and provided credit, irrigation water, trucks, tractors, tools, livestock and organized schools, health programs, and co-ops. These measures ended the two-century-long struggle to dominate the Yaqui. From the point of view of both the Yaqui and the government, the measure was a success. Conflict ceased, and the Yaqui became Cárdenas's staunch supporters.[224]

On the abstract level, Indian "integration" remained a goal during the Cárdenas administration. However, at the more practical level, it became apparent that programs tailored for the non-Indian population were not addressing the needs of Indians. This led to the 1936 creation of the Department of Indian Affairs. Its agents represented Indians in matters involving land, taxes, and labor rights. It managed vocational schools for Indians that taught agricultural techniques to boys and homemaking to girls. The agency gave free legal advice to indigenous communities and sought to guarantee labor rights for Indians employed on plantations. It organized co-ops, taught Spanish, and promoted government construction of roads, reservoirs, and schools. The agency also coordinated its work with that of other government agencies, such as the Education Ministry, whose work affected Indians.[225]

After the Revolution, Indians were indeed integrated with the rest of Mexico, but as proletarians and peasants, official clients, and (occasionally) as official caciques. The forces of the market overwhelmed the meager funds that the government set aside to address Indians' concerns. A 1936 Department of Indian Affairs report declared that "conditions of virtual slavery exist in Chiapas."[226]

Between 1921 and 1940, the proportion of the population over five years of age that spoke an indigenous language only varied slightly, declining from 15.1 percent to 14.8 percent. In 1929, using physical anthropological criteria, 29.2 percent of Mexico's population was declared to be Indian. Precise figures on the number of Indians are lacking since enumeration was so subjective. There was no agreement on what physical or cultural characteristics marked one as an Indian. Speaking an Indian language was also subjective since it was never clear how much of a language one had to speak to be considered as Indian. Often enumerators simply asked subjects if they could speak an indigenous language. To further complicate the quantification of Mexico's Indian population, beginning in 1930 racial categories were removed from the census since officials felt that the important social divisions were no longer ethnic or racial but socioeconomic.[227]

Women

In 1917, Hermila Galindo, the editor of *La Mujer Moderna,* and several other women presented demands for women suffrage to the all-male Constitutional Convention. The committee on citizenship reviewed their demand based on the citizenship section included in the draft constitution, which had been brought forward unchanged from the 1857 constitution. The earlier document did not explicitly deny the vote to women; instead, it merely stated (using a gender-ambiguous term) that *mexicanos* could vote. The 1917 committee reviewed the text and declared women would not be allowed to vote, since: "The fact that some exceptional women have the qualifications necessary to exercise political rights satisfactorily does not justify the conclusion that these should be conceded to women as a class. The difficulty of making the selection authorizes the negative." The committee also noted that Mexican women "do not understand the necessity of participating in public affairs, which is demonstrated by the lack of any collective movement for this purpose."[228]

While the 1917 constitution did not enfranchise women, it did contain special provisions relating to them. Article 123, which concerned labor rights, prohibited women from engaging in "unhealthy or dangerous work" and from working industrial night shifts. The same article granted women the right to take one month maternity leave at full pay and then reclaim their job and take lactation breaks. Finally, it guaranteed women equal pay for equal work.

The legal status of women was further elaborated in the 1917 Law of Family Relations, which guaranteed husband and wife equal rights with respect to guardianship and child custody, entering litigation, and drafting contracts. Women received equal authority with husbands concerning their children's education and the expenditure of family funds and were granted the right to receive alimony and manage their own property. The law granted divorcées the right to remarry. [229]

During the 1920s and early 1930s, little official attention was paid to women's rights, since few male leaders were concerned with the issue and they were burdened with what for them were more pressing issues. During this period, Mexican women more than made up for their male leaders' inactivity by plunging into a plethora of organizing efforts. In fact, the multiplicity of groups and issues addressed, as well as divisions along class, ethnic, religious, and ideological lines, limited their ability to achieve their goals. Women's groups promoted temperance, addressed labor and agrarian issues, and formed mothers clubs, consumption cooperatives and labor unions. While lay groups demanded recognition of women as wage earners, the largest Catholic women's organization defined them as "the paradigm of purity, abnegation, and sublimity."[230]

During the 1920s, the issue of women suffrage shifted to the state level. During his 1922–1924 administration, Yucatán Governor Felipe Carrillo Puerto granted women the right to vote and to be elected to public office at the municipal and state level. By 1934, three more states would follow this path. Some of these gains proved to be fleeting. After Carrillo Puerto was assassinated and conservatives regained control over the state, Yucatecan women lost their vote. The three women who had been elected to, and seated in, the state legislature were removed.[231]

During the late 1920s and early 1930s, while systematically denying them leadership roles, both the revolutionary state and the Catholic Church sought to enlist women to support their respective causes. The males leading the government assumed that women would overwhelmingly support the very clerical elements they were seeking to control and thus denied them suffrage. The males leading the Church, acting on the same assumption, favored women suffrage.[232]

Even though the political elite was unwilling to grant women the vote, it sought to mobilize them to implement reforms and in its struggle with the Church. In 1932, the PNR attempted to finesse the suffrage issue by declaring, "The Constitution does not deny a woman's right to vote, but considering that the State wants to introduce women gradually to civic life, it is not advisable to precipitate this matter." PNR leaders did allow women to vote in party plebiscites.[233]

While on the campaign trail, in contrast to his forthright support for labor and peasant struggles, PNR presidential candidate Cárdenas clung to standard party platitudes concerning women. In a December 1933 speech, he declared:

> It is necessary to invigorate and promote the effort which Mexican women have made to integrate themselves in the public life of the nation. This must be done in a balanced and progressive manner in order to employ their great energies and virtues for the general welfare, since women are beings eminently aware of human problems and sufficiently generous to seek the general interest.[234]

Cárdenas's position had shifted by the time of his 1935 State of the Nation address in which he declared that the PNR had recognized that "working women have the right to participate in elections." Cárdenas soon began organizing women to build a mass base, just as he had done with other groups. In the spring of 1936, the PNR granted women the right to vote in party primaries.[235]

Cárdenas's open support for women suffrage galvanized the United Front for Women's Rights (FUPDM), organized in 1935. This group served as an umbrella organization including some 800 feminist organizations that claimed 50,000 members. The front embraced women from a broad political spectrum, ranging from the Mexican Communist Party to the official PNR and included rural and urban women, professionals, and workers. In addition to promoting its central issue—women suffrage—the Front pressed for expanded employment opportunities, lower rents, lower electric rates, lower taxes for women market vendors, the establishment of day-care centers, and the granting of the same rights to ejido land to women as to men.[236]

In his September 1937 State of the Nation address, Cárdenas declared there was a "need to reform the nation's Code so that the rights of women, who form an integral half of Mexican society and the citizenry, may be redressed as befits the dignity of a people."[237]

The following November, Cárdenas's secretary of the interior sent Congress a draft amendment to the constitution that provided for women suffrage, along with a message stating that women would be more subject to Church influence if they remained outside the electoral process than if they were included.

Both houses of Congress soon approved a constitutional amendment enfranchising women. By May 1939, the legislatures of all twenty-eight states had ratified the amendment. However, as Article 135 of the 1917 constitution stipulated, one step remained—Congress had to tabulate the votes of the legislatures and declare the amendment to be in effect.

At this point, the political momentum toward enfranchising women faltered. Politicians considered women to be overly influenced by the Church. The sight of women marching from churches to polling places in bitterly divided Spain reinforced this belief. As one functionary commented, "If we granted women the right to vote, the Archbishop of Mexico would be the next president of Mexico." As Almazán's candidacy gained strength, PRM leaders felt that if women were enfranchised, they would back Almazán. Although they were a decidedly small minority, public demonstrations by well-dressed, well-organized women who supported Almazán reinforced this perception.[238]

Congress adjourned in July of 1939 without having declared the Constitution amended to permit women suffrage. In his September 1939 address to Congress, Cárdenas stated, "Suffrage in Mexico should be perfected by extending the vote to women, since otherwise, the electoral process will be incomplete."[239]

On March 24, 1940, realizing that the clock was running out on the women suffrage amendment, the Feminine Action Section of the PRM sent Cárdenas a telegram urging him to call a special session of Congress for the sole purpose of officially proclaiming the passage of the women suffrage amendment. Cárdenas failed to call the session, raising the question of whether, as his term wound down, he still favored enfranchising women. Since Cárdenas, on his own initiative, had accelerated land reform, transformed the PNR, and nationalized the oil industry, he could presumably have pushed though women suffrage if he had still supported it. At the end of Cárdenas's term, feminists Adelina Zendejas and Concha Michel concluded: "Cárdenas felt that women were controlled by the clergy, and said, 'If they have the vote, then we'll be beaten, because they are a majority.' That's why they never declared the passage of the suffrage amendment."[240]

The failure of the PRM leadership to enfranchise women by no means brought to a halt the social forces that were, willy-nilly, changing women's role in Mexican society. Women not only received more education but increasingly imparted it. The opportunity to become a rural schoolteacher provided many young women with professional identities and modest incomes. However, women were still denied equal access to education, due to the widespread belief that highly educated women would not be able to find males willing to marry them and due to families with limited income only investing in educating male children. Such families felt investments in female education would never be recouped since after marriage women would become full-time homemakers regardless of their educational level.[241]

After the Revolution, female employment increased rapidly in the state sector, especially in agencies concerned with social welfare, such as health and education. During the early 1920s, an unprecedented number of careers opened to women. They worked in medicine, law, accounting, and real estate, and served as stenographers and telephone operators. The operators' union, El Sindicato de Telefonistas de la República Mexicana, represented the largest group of women in the formal economy.[242]

Even though new areas of employment were opening for women, between 1921 and 1930 female employment declined from 6.7 percent of the workforce to 4.6 percent as women were disproportionately laid off during the Depression and as demobilized revolutionary veterans rejoined the labor force. By 1940, as Mexico began to urbanize and recover from the Depression, female employment increased to 7.4 percent of the labor force.[243]

Perhaps the biggest change of all in the lives of women resulted from the widespread introduction of *molinos de nixtamal* (corn mills) powered by internal combustion engines. Since pre-historic times, grinding the corn kernels used to make tortillas had been culturally defined as women's work. Mechanical mills, which began to appear in the 1920s, freed women from rising before dawn and spending tedious hours on their knees grinding corn. In petitions listing a community's needs, women often placed a mill above schools, clinics, and water rights. In some cases, mills even produced a male backlash, since they dramatically changed women's daily routine. Men in Tepoztlán commented that the flavor of tortillas coming from the mechanical mill was inferior, and repeatedly opposed the mills on the grounds that women would use their increased free time for gossip, idleness, and—so it was believed—infidelity.[244]

Population

Death rates remained high, especially for children, well into the post-Revolutionary period. In 1930, more than half the population still lacked safe drinking water sources. Medical care remained beyond the reach of most Mexicans. Between 1932 and 1936, 86 percent of deaths in villages with less than 10,000 population were without medical attention. Mexico City had one doctor for every 679 inhabitants, while the predominantly indigenous state of Oaxaca had one for each 18,107.[245]

The government sought to accelerate the rate of population increase, reflecting its long-standing pro-natal views that resulted from the teachings of the Catholic Church, from the lesson drawn from the Mexican–American War, and from the desire to compensate for population loss resulting from the Revolution. The PNR's 1934–1940 Six-Year Plan called for "an increase in, the improvement of, and better distribution of our population." To accelerate population increase, the government banned ads for contraceptives and abortions and offered prizes for having large families. In 1931, abortion was made illegal.[246]

Table 18.3 *Mexican population, 1921–1940*

	1921	1930	1940
Total population (in millions)	14.3	16.6	19.7
Percent urban* (%)	31.2	33.5	35.1
Average annual growth rate in previous decade (%)	−0.51	1.71	1.76

*Defined as people living in a population center of 2,500 or more

Source: INEGI (1994: 14, 42) and Ordorica & Lezama (1993: 51, Table 8)

In demographic terms, late 1920s Mexico closely resembled turn-of-the-century Mexico. Between 1925 and 1929, the birth rate was 44.3 per thousand, while the death rate was 26.7 per thousand. The annual rate of population increase between 1921 and 1930 was 1.6 percent. (Between 1900 and 1910, it had been 1.1 percent.)[247]

In 1940, the birth rate remained at 44.3 per thousand, while the death rate had declined to 22.8 per thousand. This resulted in an annual population increase of 1.76 percent.[248]

EDUCATION

> Revolutionary educators shared a commitment to the incorporation of Mexico into the world of Western nations on a footing more equitable and competitive than had prevailed in the past. Such incorporation required education to transform the behavior, loyalties and identity of rural Mexicans.
>
> Mary Kay Vaughn, 1997[249]

Along with land reform, education was one of the great transforming forces of the post-revolutionary period. Article 3 of the 1917 constitution guaranteed free public education. However, just as was the case with land reform, this constitutional mandate was not immediately implemented.

Carranza, claiming he was deferring to local authority, abolished the Ministry of Public Instruction. Shifting the responsibility for education to chronically underfunded states and municipalities resulted in hundreds of school closures. The federal government offered little assistance, as is indicated by Carranza devoting only 1.2 percent of the federal budget to education.[250]

By the time Obregón took office in 1920, it had become obvious that Mexico was failing to meet its educational goals. In many cases, school attendance was below the rates of the Porfiriato. In Tlaxcala, 47 percent of the school-age population attended school in 1907, while by 1920, only 15 percent did. The reason for this backsliding was clear—municipalities had neither the resources nor the will to promote education.[251]

To fill this gap, Obregón pushed through an amendment to Article 73 of the constitution that granted the federal government the right to build and administer schools. In 1921, he established a new cabinet post, the secretary of public education, which oversaw federal schools, libraries, and the fine arts. By 1928, 34 percent of primary students were in federally run schools, a figure that had increased to 40 percent by 1940.[252]

Obregón's appointment as the first secretary of public education was José Vasconcelos, who as a youth had belonged to the Ateneo de la Juventud, a group of young intellectuals who rejected the positivism in vogue during the Porfiriato for its having omitted artistic aspects of life. While most of its members later avoided politics and engaged in cultural pursuits, Vasconcelos took an active part in the Madero movement of 1910 and the Aguascalientes convention of 1914–1915.

As education secretary, Vasconcelos vigorously promoted education, and by 1923, educational spending had risen to a record 9.3 percent of the federal budget. Between 1921 and 1924, more schools were built than had been built during the previous fifty years. More than 1,000 of these schools were in rural areas. Teachers sometimes rode by horseback for days from the nearest railroad station to their assignment.[253]

Rather than accepting the Porfirian educational model, educators consciously created a new educational model that drew heavily on John Dewey, the U.S. educator who stressed learning by doing. The new schools sought to integrate the rural masses–thought to be backward and technologically primitive—into a secular, urban, culturally homogeneous state. Porfirian notions of liberal education were cast aside, and practicality was emphasized. Moisés Sáenz, who later served as secretary of education declared, "The vocational principle wished to say that all men ought to be agents of production within the group in which they live and that education ought to train them to fulfill this vision."[254]

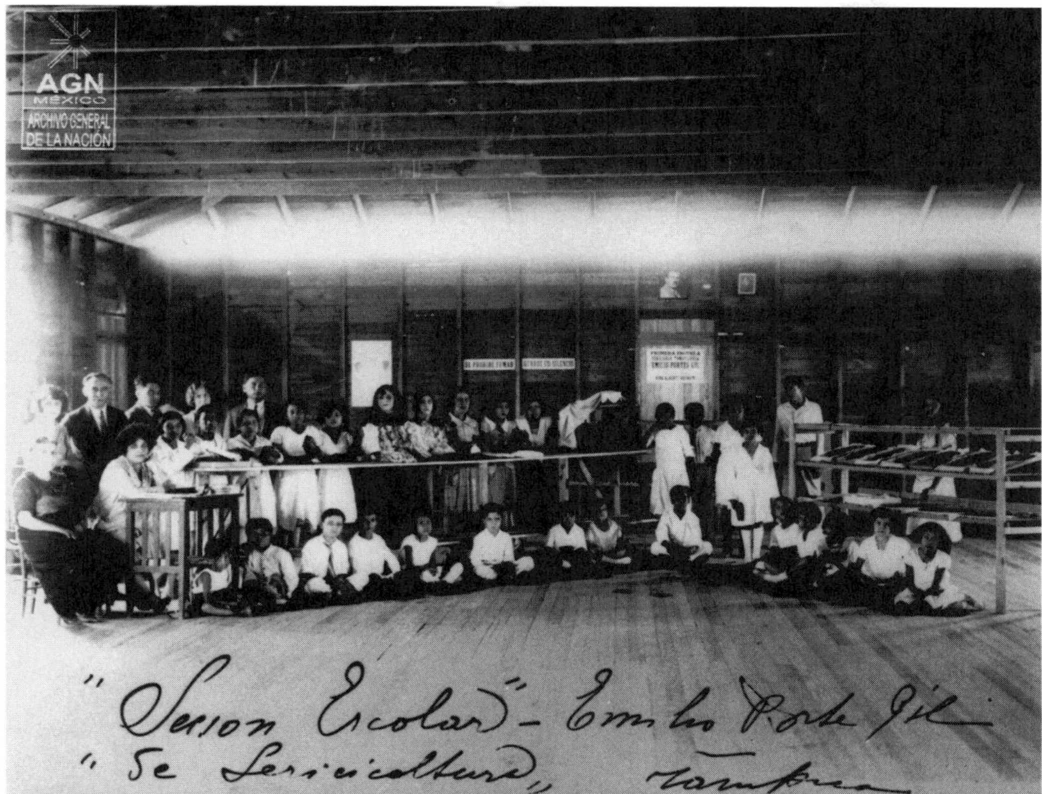

Figure 18.2 *School scene*

Source: Reproduced courtesy of the Archivo General de la Nación

Like their later Cuban counterparts, the Mexican revolutionaries sought to create a new man (and with less emphasis, a new woman) who would be sober, industrious, literate, and patriotic. Teachers were instructed to organize festivals commemorating patriotic holidays such as the Cinco de Mayo and the births and deaths of such figures as Hidalgo, Juárez, Morelos, and Madero. Educators felt these holidays offered attractive alternatives to religious festivals. Teachers were instructed to change the way people farmed, marketed, consumed, and organized their households. They were to do this by visiting mothers in homes and forming co-operatives and hygiene brigades.[255]

Under Calles, teachers were, willy-nilly, drawn into the Church-state conflict, which turned violent in the late 1920s. Even if they were not anti-clerical themselves, teachers presented an easy target since they were often the only identifiable federal presence. As a result, schools were burned and teachers harassed and even murdered.[256]

During the 1920s, education was one mandate of the Revolution that most Mexicans agreed upon, since it did not challenge existing property relationships. Between 1921 and 1931, the educational budget increased from 4 percent of government spending to 14 percent. Between 1920 and 1928 the number of primary school teachers increased from 19,542 to 32,657, and primary school enrollment increased from 743,896 to 2,402,731. As a result of this effort, in 1928, 46 percent of school-aged children attended school. For all but a privileged few, education stopped with the elementary school. In 1928, there were only 16,024 at the secondary-preparatory level and 9,763 in professional schools.[257]

Further increases in enrollment were limited by the large number of children who could not afford to defer earning an income while in school. Also, even though education was nominally free, remaining fees and the need for presentable clothing remained as an obstacle for many. While school attendance was reasonably comprehensive in Mexico City—where 90 percent attended school in 1928—it remained low in rural areas. In Chiapas, only 10 percent of school-age children were in school that year—a 3 percent decrease from the 1907 level.[258]

The next wave of educational reform came during the Cárdenas administration. The six-year plan for 1934–1940 called for educational spending to constitute between 15 and 30 percent of the federal budget. The month Cárdenas took office, Article 3 of the constitution was amended to read:

> Education imparted by the State will be socialist, and, in addition to excluding all religious doctrine, it will combat fanaticism and prejudice, to which ends the school will organize teaching and activities to permit the formation in the youth of a rational and exact concept of the universe and of social life.

The official adoption of socialist education reflected the views of PNR radicals who saw religion as the ideological arm of an unjust economic system. They felt mandating socialist education would eliminate the pernicious influence of religion from schools. This educational policy became the main source of friction between the Church and government in the 1930s.[259]

This amendment led to a debate about what the term "socialist education" actually meant. Some thought it required praising the Soviet Union and singing a communist anthem known as the "Internationale." This presented a problem, since as Education Secretary Ignacio García Téllez noted, 60 percent of teachers were conservative women who were "almost totally ignorant of socialist philosophy." In practice, socialist education embodied new textbooks promoting land reform, the dignity of labor, a materialist approach to history, and the Mexican national identity.[260]

At the same time as the content of education became more controversial, teachers were given a broader mandate. Not only were they, as in the 1920s, expected to teach the three Rs and raise the cultural level of the communities where they taught but they were also charged with organizing peasants in their communities to facilitate land reform. Teachers would not only impart socialist education, which was designed to prepare peasants for receiving land, but they would also draft the official document requesting land be transferred to community residents and then impart advice on how to organize production. This included giving advice relating to crop rotation, the use of improved seeds, and how to obtain credit and market produce. Often the newly built school building, known as the Casa del Pueblo (Town House), served as a school by day and a village meeting hall by night. It became a symbol of the government effort to wrench the countryside from the grasp of the Church and the *hacendado*.[261]

This frontal challenge to local interests, including the Church, *hacendados*, and local authorities, led to bitter conflict. During the Cárdenas administration, between 200 and 300 teachers were killed and many schools were burned. Some teachers began carrying guns. Rather than exposing their children to socialist precepts, many parents simply kept their children home. In 1935, the mayor of Zamora, Michoacán, lamented that due to the anti-clerical content of instruction, only 391 of the municipality's 5,000 children remained in school.[262]

The key to educational success in the 1920s and 1930s was the willingness of teachers to accept low pay and difficult living conditions. Parallels were often drawn between the missionary task of rural teachers and the efforts of the Franciscan missionaries in the sixteenth century. Teachers persisted despite the violent opposition of local landowners and political bosses who did not want their workforce educated, literate, and informed about new revolutionary laws. Often teachers' salaries were in arrears, and always resources were insufficient. The teacher in the Nahua community of San Miguel Tzinacapan, Puebla, noted that he alone was charged with educating 120 students.[263]

This dedication not withstanding, teachers' actions often interfered with education. This resulted from teachers, many of whom had not completed primary school themselves, being expected to simultaneously embody the virtues of educator John Dewey, social worker Jane Addams, community organizer Saul Alinsky, and agronomist Norman Borlaug. Teachers failed to realize that religious festivals and church maintenance, which they branded as a waste of time and money, were as vital to community substance as productive work. In doing so, they offended religious elders who controlled both secular and religious dimensions of the community. Although they were charged with improving agriculture, in many cases, it was apparent that the teachers knew far less about farming than the parents of the children they taught. Teachers often carried their mission of spreading hygiene and vaccination into students' homes, where the notions were ill received not so much because of the nature of the message but because it was a violation of the parents' personal space.[264]

The revolutionary educational efforts were most successful in areas such as the Laguna where they were accompanied by reforms wrought by other government agencies. In other areas, local communities accepted, discarded, and altered aspects of the state's project. The revolutionary educational effort was a success in that it did extend literacy to rural areas. It failed in that it did not alter the old ways—such as burning candles for saints, enjoying liquor, and farming in age-old ways—as it had sought.[265]

From 1935 to 1940, the number of children enrolled in primary school increased from 1.7 million to 2.2 million, and educational spending accounted for between 12 and 14 percent of the federal budget. Between 1910 and 1940, male literacy increased from 32 to 50 percent, while female literacy increased from 24 to 42 percent.[266]

THE CHURCH

> Differences between pro-clerical and anti-clerical Mexican Catholics was one of the most profound lines of social cleavage during and after the revolutionary era.
>
> Diane Bush and Stephen Mumme, 1994[267]

At the 1917 Constitutional Convention, the Church siding with Huerta remained a vivid memory for delegates. Assuming the role of modernizers, delegates felt it their duty to lead the Mexican people away from the conservatism, ignorance, intolerance, superstition, and fanaticism they associated with the Church. Delegates also felt that if they did not defeat clerical forces at the Convention, Church-backed conservatives would launch other revolutions that would put the country in danger.[268]

While there was consensus on opposing the Church, the moderate faction at the Convention claimed that denying the Church access to various roles—such as education—denied the people freedom and democracy. Múgica expressed the radical view:

> If we allow absolute freedom of education so that the clergy can participate in it with their antiquated and backward ideas, we will not create new generations of thinking, sensible people; rather our posterity will receive from us the inheritance of fanaticism, of insane principles.[269]

The radical views triumphed on religious matters, resulting in a constitution laden with anti-clerical provisions. Article 3 prohibited the Church from imparting primary education. Article 5 prohibited any pacts or contracts that irreversibly deprived one of liberty. Since monastic orders were seen as irrevocably committing one to remain in the order, such orders were specifically prohibited. Article 24 outlawed outdoor religious services. Article 27 prohibited the Church from owning any property, even if it was dedicated to worship. The state claimed everything that had been considered Church property. Article 130 provided for extensive regulation of the Church. It declared marriage a civil contact and denied the Church standing as a legal entity. Priests and ministers were declared to be professionals subject to regulation, just as physicians and lawyers were. State legislatures were granted the power to limit the number of priests in their respective states. Article 130 also required priests and ministers to be Mexicans by birth. Priests were denied the right to vote, hold office, or criticize laws or government officials. Religious publications were forbidden to comment on national politics or national political figures. Finally, religious-based political parties were prohibited.

Both Carranza and Obregón, intent on consolidating their regimes, looked the other way as the Church hierarchy ignored the restrictions the 1917 constitution had placed on religious activities. By 1925, five new dioceses had been created, missionary activities had expanded, and religious orders—particularly congregations of women—were growing rapidly. Since there was no feasible alternative to religious education, the Church continued to administer a fifth of Mexico's schools.[270]

While the federal government adopted a live-and-let-live attitude toward the Church, some state governments, operating with a great deal of independence from the federal government, set limits on the number of priests. In 1918, Jalisco limited the number of priests to one for every 5,000 residents of the state. In Veracruz, Governor Adalberto Tejeda systematically changed the names of towns named after saints and closed and expropriated Church property.[271]

State autonomy on religious matters was most conspicuous in Tabasco. The state remained under the control of Tomás Garrido Canabal from 1920 to 1935. The virulent anti-clericalism of Garrido Canabal, the son of a *hacendado*, has never been explained, although it was presumably in part due to the influence of Múgica, who served as governor of Tabasco in 1915 and 1916. Garrido Canabal, who served two terms as governor, closed all churches in the state, required all priests to be married, and prohibited the display of religious images. Not content with merely closing churches, he ordered some church buildings demolished and converted others into schools. Garrido Canabal introduced anti-clericalism into schools through the use of slogans such as "The priests and the capitalists take bread from our mouths." Garrido Canabal even banned the use of the word "*adios*," since it contained the word "*dios* (god)." It was to be replaced with "*salud*." Garrido Canabal's efforts were so extreme, even in the context of Mexican anti-clericalism, that they inspired Graham Greene's novel *The Power and the Glory*.[272]

In contrast to Carranza and Obregón, Calles came to the presidency with a well-deserved reputation for being militantly anti-clerical. In 1916, while governor of Sonora, Calles referred to priests as "inciters of illiterates and fanatics." Calles had the simplistic notion that Church-state conflict resulted from the "great chiefs" of the Catholic Church ignoring Mexican law.[273]

By the beginning of 1926, Church and state were engaged in low-intensity conflict. The Church prohibited its members from joining the CROM. Early in 1926, the state of Hidalgo limited the number of priests in the state to sixty. Some of the Catholic hierarchy publicly (and according to the 1917 constitution, illegally) criticized this limit. In January, the bishops stated, "We must collectively declare that these measures and any others that violate religious freedom cannot be respected by the prelates and the clergy."[274]

Early in 1926, the government seized on the incident to unleash an anti-clerical offensive. On February 10, many Spanish-born priests were rounded up and sent to Veracruz for deportation. During the last week of February 1926, Calles urged state governors to take immediate steps to enforce the constitutional articles relating to religion that had remained largely a dead letter. By September, 183 clergymen had been expelled, and seventy-three convents, 129 schools attached to convents, and 118 orphan asylums under religious control had been closed.[275]

On June 14, Calles signed a decree known as the "Calles Law," which prohibited foreign priests, monasteries, convents, religious instruction in primary schools, priests criticizing existing laws, and the wearing of religious garb outside church buildings. Article 19 of the Law was the most inflammatory of the provisions, since it required that priests register with officials before they could exercise their ministry. Both the hierarchy and lay Catholics felt registration was an attempt to take effective appointment of priests out of the Episcopate's hands.[276]

Calles's obtuse anti-clericalism soon led the nation to civil war. Historian Jean Meyer suggests that Calles rejected his predecessors' peaceful co-existence with the Church because he felt the Church posed a threat to his power. Meyer himself admits puzzlement, noting: "It is difficult to understand how the president, with all his qualities, could allow himself to become bogged down [in religious strife]."[277]

On July 25, the Mexican Episcopate, with Papal authority, ordered that all Catholic churches be closed and public worship suspended to protest Calles's anti-clerical measures. Calles remained unmoved and referred to his dispute with the Church as "the struggle of darkness against light." In fact, Calles welcomed the suspension of religious services, which began on July 31, since he assumed that if religious practice was suspended, people would gradually forget about the Church and become non-religious.[278]

The response of Mexico's devoutly Catholic peasantry caught the government, the army, and the Church completely off guard. By the end of February 1927, U.S. Consul Dudley Dwyre reported that the entire population of the state of Jalisco supported rural uprisings except for the "federal and state governments, police, and radical labor and agrarian groups." By the spring of 1927, sustained rebellion was occurring not only in Jalisco but also in Michoacán, Colima, Guanajuato, and southern Zacatecas. Since the rebels used the battle cry of "*¡Viva Cristo Rey!*" ("Long Live Christ the King!"), they became known as Cristeros, and the uprising as the Cristiada.[279]

Although Mexican peasants were Catholic throughout the nation, the Cristiada was strongest in west-central Mexico where villages: 1) had survived the liberal reforms with a relatively intact land base, 2) had a dense network of Catholic organizations at the local level, and 3) associated the centralized power of the state with land reform and state-sponsored anti-clericalism. Rather than viewing land reform as a measure aimed at social justice, the Cristeros were predominantly small landholders for whom the reform was either irrelevant or an active threat to their holdings.[280]

The composition of Cristero forces varied widely from place to place due to differing local histories and interests. In general, though, they included the landless, smallholders, sharecroppers, tenants, and members of corporate Indian communities. Some former Zapatistas participated in the Cristiada, viewing themselves as simply continuing their struggle for justice and religious liberty. Generally, priests did not participate in, or even actively support, the Cristiada. There were some exceptions, such as Father Vega, who became such an effective rebel leader that he was known as "Pancho Villa in a cassock." Cristeros were united in wanting to overthrow the government and eliminate any semblance of official anti-clericalism and socialism.[281] In 1969, Francisco Campos, a former Cristero from Durango, eloquently commented on Cristero motivations:

> On July 31, 1926, some men forced God Our Lord away from His churches and out of Catholic homes. However, some other men did what they could to bring Him back. These men did not think about the innumerable troops and incalculable amounts of money and arms the government had. They ignored all that. What they did think about was the defense of their God, of their religion, and of the Holy Church. This is what they thought about. These men were willing to leave their parents, their children, their wives, and all their worldly goods. They marched off to the battlefield to seek God Our Lord.[282]

The Cristiada lasted for three years as mounted guerrilla forces dodged more than 70,000 federal troops. The federal army adopted tactics resembling those of the Spanish during the war for independence. It established concentration camps and declared that anyone found outside them would be subject to summary execution. Rather than reducing support for the Cristeros, the brutality of this policy generated yet further resistance to the state, and rebel ranks swelled accordingly. After three years, federal forces had made little progress at suppressing the rebellion. They would leave their barracks, travel down rail lines and highways, and launch futile attacks against an enemy whose high degree of mobility allowed him to avoid superior federal forces.[283]

Cristero control was so thoroughly established in broad areas that they could establish a civil government that operated print shops, delivered mail, managed schools, and collected taxes. Since so many men had joined Cristero forces, women assumed many traditionally masculine roles. They worked the land to ensure a food supply and directly contributed to the war effort by carrying messages, bringing food to Cristero forces, smuggling in ammunition, and caring for the wounded.[284]

While the Cristiada raged in west-central Mexico, urban Catholics also resisted the government. In November 1927, members of a Catholic group attempted to assassinate Obregón by throwing a bomb at his car. The assassins failed in their attempt to kill Obregón, but did provide the government with an opportunity to strike a blow at urban Catholics opposing government anti-clerical measures. Four people were shot for their supposed role in the assassination attempt, including one of the most effective urban organizers, Miguel Agustín Pro, a Jesuit priest. Those executed were never placed on trial nor was any evidence presented to demonstrate their guilt.[285]

The execution of the four, and especially of Father Pro, deeply troubled an introverted mystic, José de León Toral, and led him to another attempt on Obregón's life. This time the attempt was successful. However, rather than striking a blow for the Church, as he intended, he only succeeded in prolonging strife. Unbeknown to Toral, Obregón had planned to meet with U.S. Ambassador Dwight Morrow to bring an end to the Cristiada. The cession of hostility they were to arrange had already received Papal approval as well as that of Calles. However Obregón's assassination plunged the nation into political crisis, forcing Calles to focus his attention on more pressing matters. As historian Jean Meyer noted, by delaying the end of the Cristiada, Toral's action led to the loss of tens of thousands of additional lives. Meyer also noted that in any case Toral's action was misdirected since Obregón was not responsible for Calles's anti-clericalism and had warned him not to become bogged down in a struggle with the Church.[286]

By mid-1929, it was obvious to the Mexican government, the Episcopate, and the Vatican that the Cristiada had turned into a hopeless stalemate. Through the good offices of U.S. Ambassador Morrow, who feared Mexico would plunge into chaos, an agreement was reached between the Episcopate and the government. On June 21, 1929, President Portes Gil announced that the government would pardon all Cristeros, return church buildings to the Church, and allow Catholics to engage in educational and social welfare activities, and that persecution of the Church would cease. In short, even though the Calles Law was to remain on the books, it would not be enforced. The Episcopate agreed to allow Church services to resume and condemned rebellion against the government in an effort to persuade Cristeros to lay down their arms.[287]

With churches reopened and in the face of episcopal condemnation, the Cristero movement soon dissipated. Many hard-liners who wanted to topple the government felt betrayed, and some even continued to fight. However, for the vast majority of Cristeros, the war was over. A third accepted government-issued safe-conducts, turned in their weapons, and went home. The rest, distrusting the government, kept their weapons and simply went home. The total number of deaths resulting from the Cristiada, including both civilians and the military, reached almost 200,000. In addition, since the rebellion occurred in the heart of Mexico's granary, cereal production plummeted by almost 40 percent between 1926 and 1929. Even though the Cristiada is less well known than the Revolution, as historian Jean Meyer noted, "No other popular uprising in the twentieth century led so many from such diverse backgrounds to take up arms over such a large area." The number of insurgents reached 50,000, spread over seventeen states.[288]

The Church-state cooperation that began in 1929 set the tone for the following decade. During the Cárdenas administration, Church–state relations further improved, since Cárdenas wanted Mexico to be undivided by religious issues so Catholics would rally around him when his reforms were challenged. With moderate leaders at the helm of both the government and the Church, an officially acknowledged modus vivendi was established.[289]

Cárdenas's overtures to the Church yielded results, as the hierarchy supported his land reform and the oil nationalization. After the oil nationalization, Archbishop of Mexico Luis María Martínez stated: "There is no reason why Catholics should not cooperate with the government effort to pay the indemnification to the oil companies. This is not a political issue, in which we would not become involved, but an issue of patriotism." In 1940, the Episcopate dissociated itself from Almazán's conservative presidential candidacy.[290]

MEXICO CITY

> Mexico is a country of peasants and handicraftsmen; Mexico City, an oasis—or, if you prefer it, a small desert—of urbanism and industrialism.
>
> Aldous Huxley, 1934[291]

Between 1920 and 1940, the area of Mexico City expanded from eighteen square miles to forty-five. As the city expanded laterally, it engulfed what had been geographically separate, centuries-old towns. In 1929, Mixcoac, Popotla, Tacuba, and Tacubaya were officially incorporated into Mexico City. Tram lines linked these communities, the downtown, and new subdivisions. In 1918, horse-drawn carriages were more common than automobiles. In 1928, the use of carriages was outlawed.[292]

Through 1934, Mexico City benefited from the decision of the national political leadership to prioritize economic development and political stability in Mexico City at the expense of most other regions. This decision ensured that the capital city would receive a disproportionate share of national resources and that its principal resident populations—bureaucrats, middle classes, and urban-based industrial laborers—would hold disproportionate say in determining national policies.[293]

The wealth resulting from the Revolution was reflected in new subdivisions to the west of the town center—Anzures, Lomas de Chapultepec, and Polanco. The preferred architectural style was baptized "California colonial," since wealthy Mexicans built homes that imitated the homes of wealthy Californians who favored stucco and tile—homes that they had built in imitation of Mexican architecture.

The city financed the extension of Insurgentes Avenue, the city's main north–south thoroughfare, south to San Ángel. Developers, who enjoyed privileged access to city officials, lobbied to influence such investment decisions. In addition, the municipal government preferred to finance middle- and upper-class subdivisions, since they increased the tax base and allowed the government to recoup its investment. Providing infrastructure to the populous, impoverished east side was seen as the equivalent of dropping money into a black hole since the poor, with or without services, were unlikely to generate significant tax revenue.[294]

As the city segregated itself according to wealth, less affluent areas developed community and class consciousness, as is indicated by a rent strike in 1922. Housing for the poor remained—as in the nineteenth century—unhealthy. Naturalist Aldous Huxley, visiting the city in the 1930s, declared: "I never saw so many thin, sickly and deformed people as in the poorer quarters of the metropolis; never such filth and raggedness, such signs of hopeless poverty. As an argument against our present economic system, Mexico City is unanswerable."[295]

In the 1920s, a problem that would plague the city for the rest of the century became apparent—subsidence. As a combined result of increased water usage and drainage projects completed late in the Porfiriato, the water table descended. As the overlying sediments dried up, they contracted. Since the subsidence was uneven, buildings began to tilt, and sewers stopped flowing in some places. This occurred as expanded ground cover increased run-off into the sewer system. Sewage frequently overflowed after heavy rains, since sewage and storm run-off were (and are) channeled into the same system.[296]

During the Cárdenas administration, Mexico City lost its privileged status. As organized labor and peasants enjoyed unprecedented government support, Mexico City lost out. Given increasingly tight federal budgets, the government was financially unable to shower benefits on all sectors. Fewer resources were allocated for developing the city's markets, drainage, water supply, street paving, public lighting, and health services, which had been the principal demand of non-unionized,

Table 18.4 *Population of Mexico City, 1921–1940*

Year	Mexico City population	Percentage of national population
1921	615,367	4.3
1930	1,029,068	6.2
1940	1,802,679	9.2

Source: INEGI (1994: 13, 31)

middle-class residents, especially shopkeepers and small industrialists who relied on these services. In 1939, a severe flood highlighted the lack of investment in drainage.[297]

A combination of continued growth and the Cárdenas administration having transferred much of the land adjacent to the city into the ejido sector, thus preventing its legal sale, drove up prices for accessible land. Between 1935 and 1940, land prices in the Federal District increased between 50 and 200 percent. This led to soaring rents, which in turn produced demands for rent control—demands that were backed with marches and rent strikes. Between 1935 and 1940, an estimated 73,274 were involved in illegal land invasions, pitting speculators holding land for later sale and development against the urban poor, who adopted the Zapatista view that social needs should determine the use of land, not legal titles.[298]

Cárdenas's policies came back to haunt the PRM. By 1940, the PRM's legitimacy was nearing bottom in the capital, since its residents felt neglected as government-provided services declined. They also felt disenfranchised, since the mayor was appointed by the president, and small merchants, artisans, and the unemployed had no organization they could rely upon to press their demands. Despite electoral fraud in 1940, Almazán carried the Federal District.[299]

In the 1930s, contrasting visions of the city emerged that would persist for the rest of the century. One group argued strongly for protection and restoration of the colonial architectural beauty of downtown areas, as well as for keeping central city streets uncluttered by vendors and clear for urban transport vehicles. In contrast, small merchants, street vendors, and renters, many of whom lived in old dilapidated buildings in the center, saw this campaign as posing a serious threat to their livelihood. They lived in housing stock passed down from one artisan-worker family to another for generations. To be displaced from these locations, particularly at a time when large industries and commerce were beginning to dominate the urban economy, would be a fatal blow to these small, central-city businesses.[300]

A number of factors led to population increase in Mexico City. As Mexico's largely rural population increased, it found few rural job opportunities. Many rural areas remained insecure well after the major armies had ceased to fight. As haciendas went bankrupt or were converted into ejidos, many lost jobs. These factors resulted in migration to the capital. Also, high government spending, at least until 1934, generated jobs in Mexico City and made it a more pleasant place to live in. Even after 1934, the federal government increased its role, adding additional employment in the bureaucracy. Finally, as industrialization increased, new jobs were generated, which, given government support of unions, were relatively high paying.

THE INTELLECTUAL SCENE

> A unique feature of the Mexican Revolution has been the way in which artists, rather than writers, emerged as the intellectual vanguard in the 1920s.
>
> Alistair Hennessy, 1991[301]

Mexico's first Secretary of Public Education, José Vasconcelos, conceived of education and culture as instruments of nation building—the means of incorporating the peasantry and urban workers into the reconstruction of Mexico. Under Vasconcelos (1921–1924), painters were assigned a central role in the process of national regeneration, legitimizing revolutionary politics by fusing the myths of the national past with visions of the revolutionary future. Under Vasconcelos's patronage, three artists—Diego Rivera, José Clemente Orozco, and David Alfaro Siqueiros, who became known simply as the Big Three—were put on government salary to paint murals.[302]

The Big Three began their work at the National Preparatory School and in the process launched an artistic movement that would dominate Mexico for a generation. The muralists, who would embellish dozens of public buildings in Mexico, celebrated the mestizo, Mexico's Indian roots, and the long struggle for social justice against rich Mexicans and foreign imperialists. Not only were their murals politically charged but, unlike Mexico's previous Eurocentric artistic creation, they depicted people who looked like most Mexicans—brown-skinned peasants—rather than idealized Greek figures. Their murals incorporated scenes from everyday life, landscapes, the Revolution, patriotic heroes, and religious celebrations. A final element of the mural movement was a faith in progress. Rivera's biographer Bertram Wolfe commented on government art policy, "It spread out magnificent frescoes before the gaze of a people to which it could not offer sufficient books or literacy, nor guarantee a wage sufficient for the purchase of a daily newspaper."[303]

As with most sweeping changes, controversy swirled around the shift from reproducing European fashions in easel art to depicting Mexican-looking figures in murals while at the same time attacking the economic status quo. Egged on by a conservative press, students at the National Preparatory School defaced some of the murals and demanded that the work at the school cease. The writer Salvador Novo called the murals repulsive and designed to awaken in the viewer not an aesthetic emotion but "an anarchistic fury if he is penniless or, if wealthy, to make his knees buckle with fright." The vilification of mural art only ceased after critics in Paris and New York began to praise the murals. By the end of the 1920s, the muralists had emerged as cultural heroes, much as movie stars of a later generation, and just as with movie stars, their turbulent private lives became highly public.[304]

After Obregón and Vasconcelos left office in 1924, official sponsorship of the muralists ended and each of the Big Three went their separate ways. Only Rivera remained in government employment, painting 235 panels in the building of the Secretary of Education. These murals form only a small part of his enormous artistic legacy, which despite his focusing on Mexican themes, brought in the latest European influences.[305]

Rivera's legacy includes murals at the National Agriculture School at Chapingo and scathing visual representations of the new political class in his mid-1930s frescos in the National Palace. Rivera left behind not only a wealth of great paintings but also the very idea of a people's art, inspiring others to paint with a social consciousness. Rivera's biographer commented, "It was Diego's hope that an illiterate people who had been told the stories of the saints through the painted image would respond to this new secular myth of the Revolution and its promises for man's life on earth."[306]

During the 1920s, the mural renaissance, with its static visual imagery, could still exercise a compelling effect on Mexico's population, since both cinema and radio were in their infancy. By the 1930s, radio and cinema were the harbingers of mass media. Their impact during the Cárdenas administration far outstripped the static visual didactics of the revolutionary muralists, whose work was seen only by a relatively small fraction of the population.[307]

Despite their critiques of capitalism in general (both Rivera and Siqueiros were members of the Mexican Communist Party) and of the revolutionary nouveau riche in particular, by the end of their careers the Big Three had been firmly embraced by the political establishment. In 1949, a fifty-year retrospective of more than 1,000 Rivera art works opened at the Palace of Fine Arts. At its inauguration, Mexican President Miguel Alemán referred to Rivera as a national treasure. In 1956, the government declared Rivera's seventieth birthday as a day of national homage. When Rivera died the following year, he was buried in the Rotunda of Illustrious Men in Mexico City's Dolores Pantheon. Upon his death in 1949, Orozco was also accorded high honors. Siqueiros was the last of the Big Three to be embraced by the establishment. He was jailed from 1960 to 1964 for his efforts on behalf of political prisoners and his criticism of the government. His fate shifted between 1967 and 1971 when he was commissioned to decorate the massive exterior panels and the interior dome of the Polyforum, part of a privately owned development project—today's World Trade Center in Mexico City. At the 1971 inauguration of the Polyforum, President Luis Echeverría hailed Siqueiros's work as a fitting monument to fifty years of muralism in Mexico.[308]

The literary depiction of the Revolution began later than the artistic one, only gaining ground in 1924 with the "discovery" of *Los de Abajo*, which had been originally published in 1915. This novel by Mariano Azuela, a physician who served with Pancho Villa, described the suffering and killing of the Revolution by depicting the exploits of a band of peasant revolutionaries led by Demetrio Macías. In *Los de Abajo*, which was translated in 1929 as *The Underdogs*, one of the rebels declares, "The revolution is the hurricane, and the man who surrenders to it is no longer a man, he's a poor dead leaf tossed about in the gale . . ." In addition to emphasizing the lack of clear motives behind the Revolution, Azuela focused on its cruelty, plunder, and betrayal of popular ideals. Some of Azuela's later novels dealt with the middle and upper classes, of which he was also critical for their cynicism and venality.[309]

The other great novelist of the Revolution was Martín Luis Guzmán, a journalist and one-time secretary to Pancho Villa. His 1928 novel *El Águila y la Serpiente*, translated in 1930 as *The Eagle and the Serpent,* is a memoir of the author's experiences with Villa. Guzmán's other major literary work *La sombra del caudillo* was not published in Mexico until 1938. Unlike previous novels of the Revolution, it deals with events after 1920, depicting an unnamed caudillo who employed treachery and murder to install his chosen candidate as his successor.[310]

There are two striking contrasts between the Revolution as depicted by the muralists and by novelists. The muralists, excepting Orozco, portrayed the Revolution as the dawn of a better tomorrow, made possible by harnessing machines in a new social order. In contrast, the novelists' view of the Revolution was much more pessimistic. The other contrast is the impact of the two mediums. While the murals and the muralists became known internationally, the novels of the Revolution had a much more restricted audience.[311]

In addition to supporting the mural movement, Vasconcelos broadened the dissemination of books. Reflecting his admiration for the U.S. public library system, he charged the Public Education Ministry with the creation of public libraries. As a result, in the 1920s, thousands of small libraries were stocked with inexpensive editions of European and Mexican literature and works of social science. Rural school libraries stocked some fifty books, packed into specially designed crates that could be transported on the back of a mule. Under Cárdenas, the founding of the Fondo de Cultura Económica further stimulated book publishing. This government-sponsored publisher made available books concerning a wide variety of subjects.[312]

Unlike many revolutions, the Mexican Revolution did not lead to a loss of press freedom, although the press had restrictions placed on it in the post-revolutionary period. The 1917 Press Law specifically prohibited criticizing the military—the largest government institution. When *El Nacional* published an editorial critical of militarism in the abstract, the paper was temporarily closed and its editor jailed.[313]

Despite restraints, papers such as *El Universal*, which began publishing in 1916, and *Excélsior*, which began publishing the following year, offered views independent of the government. Generally these papers were more conservative than the government and criticized what were perceived as its leftist excesses. However *El Machete*, the official organ of the Mexican Communist Party, criticized government conservatism.

Newspapers flourished during the Cárdenas administration as is indicated by their annual sales rising from 140 million in 1935 to almost 200 million in 1937. Even though the Cárdenas administration faced significant opposition, it preserved press freedom, which allowed many papers and columnists to endorse Almazán's presidential candidacy.[314]

While post-Revolutionary papers were freer than they had been under Díaz, they were not demonstrably less venal. In 1940, German Minister to Mexico Baron Rüdt von Collenberg-Bödigheim lamented that a lack of funds prevented him from getting Axis views aired in the Mexican press. He observed, "In this country all newspapers and most journalists expect cash for cooperation, as obviously the other side is offering plentiful."[315]

RADIO

In the nineteenth century and early twentieth century, newspapers circulated among the literate elite, leaving it to radio to become Mexico's first mass media. It could fill this role since it was free (except for the set) and it did not require literacy or the land distribution channels that newspapers used.[316]

Commercial radio first appeared in Mexico in the 1920s. Early on, the government decided to follow the U.S. model, that is, to have programming paid for by selling ads. Some of the early stations were owned by the companies that sought to market their products. El Buen Tono, a cigarette manufacturer, owned a station and then created a cigarette brand, El Radio, to market on the air. Radio came of age in 1930 with the inauguration of XEW, a 200-kilowatt station, the most powerful in the western hemisphere. This station, owned by Emilio Azcárraga Vidaurreta, was known as "The Voice of Latin America." Azcárraga used his business talents and his marriage into the Monterrey industrial elite, which gave him access to capital, to build a radio-based media empire.[317]

During the 1930s, radio became increasingly influential. By 1935, there were eighty radio stations and 250,000 sets. In 1937, the government began to produce a weekly program, which it mandated that all stations play at the same time. This program, known as *"La Hora Nacional"* ("The National Hour"), combined government messages and, to attract listeners, music. It was one of the first cultural phenomena to link the entire nation. Cárdenas effectively used radio to broadcast his speeches and rallies and even announced the nationalization of the oil industry on the radio.[318]

Chapter 19

Picking up the Pieces, 1917–1940

> The revolution slowed growth for almost thirty years, but reshaped the Mexican social structure and the opportunities for social mobility in a manner very favorable to the post-1940 economic boom.
>
> Roger Hansen, 1974[1]

THE ECONOMY, 1917–1929

Between 1916 and 1918, the Mexican economy passed its nadir and began a slow recovery. Carranza relied on *hacendados* to resume agricultural production, feeling that was the surest way to alleviate the disastrous agricultural scarcity. The 1918 corn crop was only a third or a quarter of the usual 150 million bushels.[2]

The commodity boom induced by the First World War favored the Mexican economy. As a result of increased prices for metals, oil, and henequen, exports nearly doubled in value between 1916 and 1920. Once the war was over, the received wisdom in the United States and Great Britain was that it would be best for the world to simply return to the old economic system. Carranza's Secretary of Industry and Commerce Alberto Pani shared this view, advocating a continued reliance on raw material exports, albeit with further processing in Mexico.[3]

Financing economic recovery presented Carranza with a dilemma. He wished to exert control over exports and the rural economy—two sectors dominated by foreigners. At the same time, he desperately needed foreign investment. Wealthy Mexicans shied away from new investments, deterred by continued political instability, the radical tone of the 1917 constitution, and the increased strength of labor organizations. Since Mexico was already in default on its foreign loans, there was little likelihood of obtaining loans outside Mexico. Given the lack of other sources, there was general agreement, even among Mexican industrialists, that Mexico would have to rely on private foreign investors to rebuild the economy. With their enormous increases in efficiency and output, American companies seemly held the promise of endless improvements in material well-being.[4]

A few days after he took office in 1924, Calles declared, "The revolutionary movement has entered its constructive phase." This "constructive phase" was based on private enterprise and a continued reliance on exports and foreign investment. A central bank, modeled on the U.S. Federal Reserve Bank, was created in 1925. Until its creation, private corporations, many of them foreign, dominated the Mexican banking system. As a result, there was little the government could do to insure that banking activity conformed to its economic goals. To entice Mexican bankers back into the market, they were virtually allowed to write banking regulations themselves.[5]

During the Calles administration (1924–1928), Mexico began to shift away from its reliance on mining, oil, and subsistence agriculture towards manufacturing and commercial agriculture—the sectors that would undergird the economy in the latter half of the twentieth century. Calles felt that, in the absence of other sources of investment, the state should create banks, reservoirs, and roads. Officials frequently used the term "businesslike" untranslated in Spanish documents.[6]

The combination of political order, a revamped banking system, and government austerity began to attract foreign investors. Such investment was welcomed since the political elite felt that if the country relied exclusively on domestic investment, development would be postponed indefinitely. Mexico's wealthy also became confident enough to begin investing. Calles's Treasury Minister Alberto Pani referred to Mexicans who invested productively as "revolutionary capitalists."[7]

Pani's phrase notwithstanding, there was little one could call revolutionary about the Mexican economy. Mexico was tied more closely than ever to the United States by trade. Many members of the old Porfirian business community had survived and even prospered, working in cooperation with the state. Oil, silver, and industrial minerals accounted for up to 80 percent of exports. Large estates remained intact. Between 1919 and 1929, U.S. direct investment in Mexico increased from $644 million to $709 million. In 1935, foreigners controlled 98 percent of mining, 99 percent of the oil industry, 79 percent of the railroad and trolley system, and 100 percent of electrical power generation. Manuel Gómez Morín, who later founded the National Action Party (PAN), commented, "Despite the nationalism which our laws proclaim, we are losing control day by day of our economy and, with it, all hope that one day we may fully control it."[8]

Export industries created little consumer demand, since in 1930 mining and oil together employed only 1 percent of the work force. Labor was distributed in much the same way it had been thirty-five years earlier. In 1930, agriculture employed 68.7 per cent of workers, compared to 66.5 per cent in 1895. Manufacturing employed 9.9 per cent of workers, down from 11.5 per cent in 1895.[9]

Between 1921 and 1929, the economy grew at 1.7 percent a year. This growth largely resulted from raw material exports. In 1929, exports were 265 percent above the 1909–1910 level. Mineral exports had increased by 336 percent and agricultural exports by 190 percent. As had been the case under Díaz, exports did little for the economy as a whole. Wages in the export sector and export taxes remained low, and ties to the rest of the economy were limited.[10]

THE DEPRESSION, 1929–1934

Between 1929 and 1932, as the international demand for raw materials plummeted during the Depression, the value of Mexican exports declined from $274 million to $96.5 million. Since the government was heavily reliant on export taxes, tax receipts fell from 231 million pesos to 155 million during the same period. In 1932, Mexico's gross domestic product (GDP) was 24 percent below its 1926 peak.[11]

The Depression resulted in massive job loss, plus the return of hundreds of thousands of Mexicans who had been working in the United States. However, the impact of the Depression was limited since only 3 percent of the non-rural labor force worked in oil and mining, the sectors that produced 65 percent of exports. The Depression also had limited impact on the large number of people engaged in subsistence agriculture.[12]

Beginning in 1931, to stimulate the economy the government sharply increased its spending and the money supply. To fill the void left by the lack of foreign credit and investment, in 1934 the Nacional Financiera, a government investment bank, began issuing bonds to finance agricultural and industrial projects.[13]

Higher government spending and an increase in oil and silver prices aided Mexico's recovery from the Depression. In addition, 1933 was a good crop year. Between 1932 and 1935, as traditional foreign markets recovered from the Depression, Mexico's exports doubled in value.[14]

Throughout Latin America, as a result of the Depression, the volume and price of exports declined and the large influx of foreign investment ceased. The new development strategies created in response to the Depression emphasized greater state intervention in the economy and a focus on the domestic market.[15]

THE CÁRDENAS YEARS, 1934–1940

Cárdenas faced a dual challenge—rebuilding the Depression-ravaged economy and making it responsive to Mexican needs rather than foreign ones. During his administration (1934–1940), the share of the federal budget devoted to economic development increased from 22 to 38 percent. Unlike his predecessors, Cárdenas felt that social justice would facilitate economic development rather than retard it. Reflecting this, during the Cárdenas administration, social welfare expenditure rose to a record 18 percent of government spending.[16] Cárdenas stated he wanted

> the state to intervene to determine what the nation should produce and to organize commercial distribution. This will undoubtedly benefit the country enormously. Thus the state will determine the income share received by capital, the share received by labor, and the share received by the government.[17]

Cárdenas nationalized the rail lines in 1937 and set low rail rates to stimulate development. After the 1938 oil nationalization, he set low domestic oil prices as a subsidy to industry. Since the Depression interrupted foreign and domestic credit, he established government-run banks to supply the credit necessary for development. Allowing the peso to decline in value relative to the dollar increased the cost of imports, thus making domestic production more attractive. Eduardo Suárez, his Finance Minister, was an admirer of British economist John Maynard Keynes, so not surprisingly the government relied heavily on deficit spending. Unlike his successors, Cárdenas directed capital to both the "traditional" and the "modern" sectors.[18]

During the Cárdenas administration, there was a sharp drop in foreign investment as the oil industry and railroads were nationalized. Cárdenas's nationalism deterred new foreign investment. In 1940, U.S. investment totaled only $300 million, down from more than $1 billion in the 1920s. In 1939, the principal investors were the state, which accounted for 39 percent of new investment, and Mexican citizens, who accounted for 46 percent. Foreigners accounted for only 15 percent of investment. In 1940, 47 percent of the U.S. investment remaining in Mexico was in mining, while the remaining investment was mostly in transportation, communications, and utilities.[19]

Even though he was a nationalist, Cárdenas did not oppose foreign investment. As long as investors did not expect special privileges, they were welcome. In May 1938, just after the nationalization of the oil industry, Cárdenas stated:

> Mexico, underpopulated and extensive, has opened its doors to all foreigners who come to our land without humiliating superiority complexes and without seeking special privileges to promote agriculture, industry, science, and the arts with their labor, their capital, and their scientific knowledge.[20]

Rather than relying on exports, as Mexico had for the previous half century, economic recovery resulted from increased internal demand, stimulated by the land reform and wage increases. Between 1932 and 1939, annual economic growth averaged 6.2 percent. During the Cárdenas administration, manufacturing increased by 51 percent, commerce by 41 percent, and construction by 40 percent.[21]

By 1940, the state had emerged as an important economic actor, with a major if not exclusive role in finance, railways, petroleum, electrical energy production, road building, and the expansion of irrigation works. Public expenditure per capita during the Cárdenas administration was 41 percent above the previous six-year period.[22]

Cárdenas's policies set the stage for unprecedented subsequent expansion. Hacienda labor became more mobile. With land reform, the old order crumbled, and rural people began to examine their options. Some farmed for themselves, others decided the city had more to offer and sought industrial jobs. Increased investment in education and health care, although slow to pay economic dividends, was crucial to subsequent development.[23] As anthropologist Oscar Lewis observed, consumption patterns shifted:

> More and more people sleep on beds instead of on the ground, wear shoes instead of huaraches or going barefoot, use store-made pants instead of home-made white cotton calzones, eat bread in addition to tortillas, grind their corn in the mill instead of by hand, drink beer instead of pulque, use doctors instead of curanderos, and travel by bus or train instead of on foot or by burro.[24]

MINING

To encourage mine operations, the Carranza administration allowed mining machinery to enter Mexico duty-free. The mining sector quickly recovered from the Revolution, spurred by the First World War-induced commodities boom and substantial investment in mines, smelters, and chemical refining plants. In 1920, Mexico's 100,000 miners produced 9 percent of Mexico's gross domestic product and 60 percent of its exports.[25]

Mining remained vibrant during the 1920s, aided by new refining technology, peaceful conditions in Mexico, improved rail service, and a booming U.S. economy, which increased the demand for silver, lead, zinc, and copper. Through the 1920s, investment in new mining equipment continued at record rates. As was the case before the Revolution, foreign investment in mines was welcomed, since Mexico needed foreign capital, technology, and access to export markets. By the end of the decade, Mexico was producing more copper, silver, and lead—its three main mineral exports—than it had before 1911.[26]

The mining industry was 95 percent foreign controlled. During the Revolution, many smaller firms either were forced to sell out or went out of business, leaving the industry increasingly dominated by a few large American firms. Between 1919 and 1929, U.S. mine investment increased from $222 million to $248 million. The American Smelting and Refining Company expanded its Chihuahua smelter, making it the largest lead smelter in the world. Mining, which in 1930 accounted for 6 percent of Mexico's gross domestic product, remained an enclave industry. Its main link to the rest of the economy was through taxes.

During the late 1920s, many Mexican mines were facing depletion. As a combined result of depletion and reduced foreign demand during the Depression, the value of mine production fell by 50 percent. By 1932, half of Mexico's 90,000 miners were unemployed. As government control over mining increased, foreign capital was withdrawn.[27]

During the Cárdenas administration, mining began to recover and the life of miners improved dramatically. With administrative and judicial support, miners' strikes in 1934 and 1935 resulted in a 40 percent wage increase. Cárdenas also required mine operators to hire Mexican professionals to fill the mine jobs U.S. professionals had performed. As a result of ore depletion, potential investors' fear of Mexican nationalism, and the increased importance of other sectors, mining would never again play the key role it had in the past. By 1940, its contribution to Mexico's gross domestic product had declined to 3.7 percent.[28]

ROADS AND TOURISM

Before the Revolution, the railroad led to a transportation revolution. However, even the great nineteenth-century railroad building boom left most areas isolated. In the early 1920s, France had eight times as many kilometers of railroad per square kilometer as Mexico did, while the United States had five times as many.[29]

After the Revolution, road building created another transportation revolution. Calles initiated a massive road-building program that integrated isolated rural areas into the national economy and facilitated sanitation and health programs. A variety of interests—including construction companies, auto manufacturers, and auto dealers—lobbied for increased highway construction.[30]

Mexico's first highway, from Mexico City to Puebla, was completed in 1926. That same year work started on the Pan American Highway, which would link Mexico City to the United States. However, it would be decades before roads posed a serious challenge to the railroad. As late as 1930, Mexico only had 868 miles of paved road, probably less than the City of Los Angeles.[31]

During the 1930s, agrarian expert Eyler Simpson described Mexican goals and needs as "roads and schools, Fords and books." Cárdenas shared this view, devoting 26.6 percent of government investment to road building, literally paving the way for subsequent development. Between 1930 and 1940, road mileage increased from 884 miles to 6,156. During this same period, the number of motor vehicles increased from 85,535 to 149,455. By 1940, highways linked eleven of Mexico's twelve largest cities. Of the twelve, only Mérida remained isolated.[32]

By reducing transportation costs, new roads facilitated a consumer invasion that included Frigidaires and Palmolive products. They also increased personal mobility, taking villagers to the city. Many, especially the better educated, never returned.[33]

Road building facilitated an expansion of tourism. In 1920, only 8,000 foreign tourists, almost all from the United States, entered Mexico. To increase this number, in 1928 the Mexican government formed a commission to promote tourism. The commission placed ads in U.S. media and worked diligently to generate favorable stories concerning Mexican tourism. A flood of U.S. tourists ensued. The number of visitors further increased as auto ownership in the United States became widespread and Europe was closed to tourism due to war. In 1939, 139,010 foreign tourists, of whom 86.1 percent came by car, visited Mexico. That year U.S. tourists spent $52 million. This increase in tourism led to a boom in hotel and service-related construction.[34]

Elaborate celebrations marked the opening of new highways, just as they had marked the opening of new rail lines in the nineteenth century. To celebrate the completion in 1939 of the Pan American Highway from Laredo, Texas, to Mexico City, a celebrity motorcade wended its way from the border to the capital.[35]

AGRICULTURE

> The leaders of the Mexican Revolution were seldom economic or political theorists and left no clear statement of the ultimate ends they sought to gain via land reform. In fact, the objectives were constantly changing, sometimes without a recognition that such a change was occurring.
>
> Robert Edminster, 1961[36]

For Obregón and Calles, land reform was a political instrument for maintaining the loyalty of peasant groups, manipulating and subordinating them. The Sonorans' aim was to encourage the kind of entrepreneurial, market-orientated, and mechanized farming that Obregón had engaged in personally. They placed more emphasis on irrigation works and the promotion of commercial agriculture than on changing land tenure.[37]

One of Calles's main concerns was agricultural production. Between 1907 and 1929, corn production had declined 40 percent and bean production by 31 percent as producers either ceased farming or switched to more lucrative crops. Meanwhile, the population had increased by 9 per cent. Given the desperate need to increase food production, by the end of his term, Calles, like Carranza, favored reliance on the hacienda. In March 1930, he informed President Ortiz Rubio and his cabinet that he felt that the distribution of more land would damage the national economy and that land reform should end. At that point, many felt that no more land would be transferred to ejidos.[38]

Between 1907 and 1929, land ownership became more concentrated, with a mere 1.5 percent of landowners owning 83 percent of private farmland. Agriculture also became polarized geographically, with production in the north increasing by 430 per cent. Northern agriculture was in the hands of aggressive entrepreneurs who employed modern technology to produce high-value crops for distant markets. The problem in the north was distributing everything that was produced.

In central Mexico, agriculture—which was at the subsistence level and relied on traditional, labor-intensive methods—declined by 38 per cent between 1907 and 1929. There was little investment in producing corn—the main staple. The government imported food to make up for the decline in food production there.[39]

Despite the promises of land reform made in the heat of battle, the main trend in the 1920s was not a radical land reform but a mixed economy based on small and medium-sized plots in addition to the hacienda. In part, this backtracking occurred due to revolutionary military leaders allying with *hacendados* and their appropriating some haciendas themselves. Landed interests sought to prevent land distribution and to have the federal government provide them with roads, subsidized credit, and irrigation works. Except in the area dominated by the former Zapatista leaders, during the 1920s the federal army did more to block land reform than further it. By 1928, only 4 percent of all agricultural land had been distributed as part of the land reform.[40]

Several factors affected agricultural production between 1920 and 1934. Some large owners deferred agricultural investment because they feared their land would be taken for land reform. This was in part offset by massive road building and irrigation works in northern Mexico. In both the ejido and private sectors, worker productivity was low. In 1930, almost 70 percent of the labor force worked in agriculture, but generated only 22 percent of national income.[41]

Due to the vagaries of weather, politics, and the international economy, there were sharp variations in the volume of agricultural production. Henequen production plummeted due to the introduction of combines (which needed no twine), competition from other nations, and the increased use of synthetic fibers after the Second World War.[42]

Cárdenas differed from his Sonoran predecessors in that he viewed the ejido as the key to social justice *and* as a viable form of rural production. He realized that to be successful ejidos would require improvements such as electricity, roads, potable water, and schools, just as large commercial farms required them. The January 1, 1934 entry into his diary stated it was the responsibility of the present generation to distribute land to villages that lacked it and provide them with the necessary credit to cultivate it: "The Revolution requires *ejidos* and the subdivision of great estates. This will expand production, increase the purchasing power of the rural masses, and benefit the economy as a whole."[43]

Table 19.1 *Land reform, 1917–1940*

President	Area distributed (in acres)
Carranza	414,801
De la Huerta	83,229
Obregón	2,717,288
Calles	7,343,003
Portes Gil	4,218.142
Ortiz Rubio	2,333,008
Rodríguez	1,953,014
Cárdenas	46,401,743

Source: INEGI (1994: 381)

Cárdenas addressed this responsibility by distributing almost 10 percent of Mexico's total land area to 723,000 families. As a result, in 1940 *ejidatarios* cultivated 17.3 million acres, while private farmers only cultivated 16.8 million. In 1930, only 13.1 percent of irrigated land was included in the ejido sector, while by 1940, 57.4 percent was. In addition to land, during Cárdenas's term ejidos received credit, machinery, marketing assistance, and agricultural extension services.[44]

Since the beginning of the land reform, the ejido has been subjected to criticism for being "inefficient." However, it was well suited to the times in that it utilized what was in abundance—land and labor—and required relatively little scarce capital. In addition, it increased security for larger producers whose fears of peasant takeovers were quieted. Cárdenas's efforts not withstanding, ejidos suffered from having less water, fertilizer, fixed capital, and financing than privately owned farms.[45]

Beneficiaries of land reform saw an immediate improvement in their standard of living and broke out of their fatalism. Ejidos benefited the economy as a whole by producing lasting rural peace and by adding nearly three-quarters of a million families to the market. After the land reform, the old landowning class abandoned its passive *rentier* role and became actively involved in new financial and industrial undertakings. Many of its members shifted from direct ownership of land to processing and marketing the production of ejidos. Agribusiness established profitable ties to ejidos. Anderson Clayton purchased cotton produced on ejidos in the Laguna. The highly productive ejidos of the Yaqui Valley became appendages of the U.S. agricultural economy.[46]

INDUSTRY

> Within the revolutionary leadership, political factions oriented toward a broad variety of urban populations prevailed, to the exclusion of campesinos, such that the development policy of choice in those critical early years after the Revolution was urbanization-led industrialization, not rural development.
>
> Diane Davis, 1994 [47]

The destructive effects of the Revolution on Mexican industry were so short and mild that Porfirian industrial growth largely merged with post-revolutionary growth. Unlike the landed elite, the barons of industry remained wealthy and powerful after peace returned.[48]

Mexico did not take advantage of the First World War to industrialize, as other Latin American nations did, since raw material exports were booming and attention was devoted to restoring damage wrought by the Revolution. Industrialization was also delayed by the need to reestablish effective rail and banking services. Finally, even though their properties had been largely unaffected by the Revolution, industrialists remained reluctant to invest in new areas. As a result, the government stepped in as an investor of last resort to stimulate industrialization.[49]

To promote industry, during the 1920s the government sharply increased tariffs. Tariffs on clothing and textiles, which ranged between 40 and 100 percent, were the highest. Government-mandated subsidies for the cotton used to produce textiles provided a further incentive for production. These measures greatly increased mill owners' profits, some of which were passed on to labor, causing the number of strikes to decline.[50]

During the 1920s, foreign corporate investment began to supplement domestic investment in industry. By 1929, U.S. corporations had invested $6 million in manufacturing. Such investment was favored by the U.S. State Department, which felt it would benefit the United States by permanently linking the two countries. Calles was also a strong advocate of foreign direct investment (FDI).[51]

One of the pioneers in Mexican industrial investment was the Ford Motor Company, which began assembling autos in 1926. Ford's Mexico "plant" was essentially a warehouse where a few mechanics bolted together knocked-down kits. Many of the potential benefits that Mexico might have reaped from such an operation were signed away by Calles. He agreed to lower freight rates, customs duties, and tax rates for Ford and indicated that the company would have no labor problems.[52]

During Calles's term, British American Tobacco and the International Match Company also began operations in Mexico. However, throughout Latin America, most U.S. firms found it easier to manufacture in the United States and supply the still minuscule Latin American market from there. As a result, in 1929, manufacturing accounted for only 8 percent of U.S. capital invested in Latin America.[53]

The presence of foreign manufacturers became highly controversial. Critics called such investment a "menace" to Mexico that would lead to foreign domination and corrupt Mexican culture. They felt it would be better to forgo such investment and grow more slowly, but on a sounder basis. Advocates of foreign investment felt foreign capital would create more jobs and increase wages. They felt American companies, with their enormous increases in efficiency and output, held the promise of seemingly endless improvements in material well-being.[54]

Up until the Depression, industrialization continued at about the same rate it had under Díaz. From 1901 to 1910, manufacturing had increased by 3.1 percent a year. From 1922 to 1935, it grew at 3.8 percent a year. Traditional industries continued to dominate. In 1926, only 0.8 percent of manufactured products were exported. Most industry remained in the hands of artisans. The average number of workers per industrial establishment was only six. As had been the case under Díaz, the government protected industry from foreign competition. With the exception of the well-organized textile industry, the government also protected industry from the unwelcome demands of labor. Industry continued to be stymied by the export-dominated economy not producing a dynamic consumer market.[55]

By drastically reducing the amount of foreign currency Mexico received from its exports, the Depression forced Mexico to produce what it could no longer afford to import. In addition, as President Ortiz Rubio noted in his 1930 Annual Address, he increased tariffs "to stimulate various sectors of the national economy." The Depression shocked Mexican leaders out of thinking they could rely on raw material exports forever. To secure a reliable supply of manufactured goods, they decided they would have to produce them domestically. The fatalistic notion of "natural comparative advantage" was rejected. It became official dogma that it was not the Creator's design that Mexico produce raw materials while other countries industrialized. Policy makers felt that with modern technology and transportation systems, Mexico could manufacture what it needed.[56]

One of the declared goals of the Six-Year Economic Plan for 1934–1940 was "stimulating the creation of new industries which will serve as a profitable substitute for imports, or which will permit the use of resources which are not currently used or which are being poorly exploited." A variety of government polices stimulated Mexico's still-weak industries. Between 1929 and 1933, the peso was devalued by 64 percent, making it much more expensive to import manufactured goods. The 1936 Law of Industrial Saturation closed entry to branches of industry with excess capacity. In 1937, there was a 26 percent tariff increase. After the 1938 oil nationalization, there was further devaluation of the peso. Government deficit spending increased the demand for industrial goods. Cárdenas also granted new industries a five-year tax exemption.[57]

During the 1930s, other changes made investing in industry more attractive. As income became more evenly distributed, the market for locally produced goods increased. The prices of industrial goods rose more rapidly than those of agricultural goods, so landowners invested not in increasing their agricultural production but in industry.[58]

Between 1932 and 1940, as a result of both policy shifts and changed conditions in Mexico, industrial output increased by 6.1 percent a year, with industry for the first time becoming the most dynamic sector of the economy. With profits soaring, Mexican industrialists began to update their facilities. Output per industrial worker increased 37 percent in the 1930s. Between 1929 and 1940, manufacturing increased from 11.9 percent of gross domestic product to 24.2 percent, while agriculture declined from 23.7 percent to 14.6 percent.[59]

Almost all of this industrialization was financed domestically. Both the old landed classes and the new political class invested their wealth in industry. Most foreign investors remained on the sidelines while Cárdenas was in office. However, General Motors and Chrysler did open plants during his term.[60]

OIL

During the Carranza administration (1917–1920), the oil industry boomed. In 1918, Mexico became the world's largest oil exporter and its second largest oil producer, behind only the United States. The success of Pearson and Doheny drew in swarms of foreign investors. In 1920, Mexico pumped 25 percent of world production. At their peak, oil taxes accounted for a third of government income.[61]

Several features of the Mexican oil industry remained constant through the 1920s. Most of the production was exported, mainly to the United States and Britain. In 1926, only 10.5 percent was retained for Mexican use. Ownership of the industry also remained overwhelmingly foreign. As before the Revolution, the oil industry imported almost all the equipment it needed.[62]

At its peak, the oil industry provided 40,000 jobs to unskilled and semi-skilled Mexican workers, who found better pay than otherwise available. The oil labor force was highly stratified, with the best jobs, housing, and salaries reserved for foreign employees who were not interested in learning Spanish or in sharing their technical know-how with Mexicans.[63]

During the 1920s, Mexico's oil boom turned to bust. Annual production fell from 193.4 million barrels in 1921 to 44.7 million in 1929. Previously productive wells filled with salt water as oil was exhausted. In 1927, the average production per well was one-eighth what it had been in 1920. Few new wells were found to replace exhausted ones, despite extensive exploration efforts. Between 1921 and 1929, oil declined from 76 percent of Mexican exports to 15 percent. By 1935 oilfield employment had declined to 15,000. Although the oil companies were often accused of reducing production in response to Mexican nationalism, it was geology, not politics, that caused production to decline.[64]

After 1921, as production began to decline, foreign oil companies came to be regarded as despoilers of the land rather than as agents of progress. Increasingly, attention focused on polluted streams and large areas of deforested land blanketed in oil. Along the coast, there were oil-fouled oyster beds, shrimping grounds, and mangrove swamps. Roads, telegraph lines, and some 2,589 miles of pipeline, which ruptured with regularity, cut though what had been tropical forest. Rivers were so polluted that they sometimes caught fire.[65]

As Mexican nationalism increased and production declined, the Mexican vision of the oil industry became increasingly skeptical if not hostile. In 1926, Múgica penned this image of Tampico, the major oil port:

> The mushrooming city appears to have sprung from the sea. The sea and oil breathe life into it. It is a city of marshes, which lives like the oyster, clinging to the river and the rich lagoons. Perched high on the sand dunes are elegant homes. The unhealthy lowlands are cluttered with shacks. The river banks rumble with industry . . . There machines pump the country's wealth, and load it on ships which carry it away. The old city is mutating, with the humble tile-roofed adobe house giving way to reinforced concrete. As in all cities, there are people of every race. But what is modern, healthy, and beautiful belongs to foreigners.[66]

After 1933, Mexican oil production began to increase again, but it never regained its influence on the world market since both Venezuela and the Middle East would continue to out-produce it. This rebound was driven by an increase in oil prices and the discovery of the large Poza Rica field.[67]

Chapter 20

Uncle Sam Confronts Revolutionary Nationalism, 1917–1940

CARRANZA AND THE UNITED STATES, 1917–1920

Even before the promulgation of the 1917 Constitution, the United States made it clear that it would not accept Mexico's desire to restructure its society as justification for overriding the rights the United States claimed under international law. In 1916, Secretary of State Robert Lansing warned that Carranza's refusal to guarantee U.S. investment would lead to "the gravest consequences." Such statements indicated a contradiction in U.S. foreign policy. President Wilson publicly urged redistribution of wealth in Mexico but would not countenance any change involving wealth belonging to Americans.[1]

The Americans viewed Article 27, which governed subsoil rights, as the first of many such challenges U.S. interests would face in Latin America, and, as such, they viewed it as a test case for U.S. policy. Policy makers felt that if Mexicans changed the rules governing foreign investment after the investment had been made, other nations might do likewise. In 1916, the president of the Maritime Oil Company warned, "If our government shall permit the Mexican government arbitrarily to repudiate these contracts, it will cast a cloud upon the title to all American investments, not only in Mexico, but in Central and South America."[2]

Mexican leaders never foresaw their country developing in isolation from the United States. Rather, they wanted to redefine Mexico's relations with the Colossus of the North. Mexican policy makers sought to: 1) protect and regulate the exploitation of Mexican natural resources, 2) regulate the activities of foreign businesses and investors, and 3) increase the government's economic role. Carranza did not oppose U.S. investment as long as investors did not demand special privileges. In 1917, he pledged "all the security and guarantees granted by Mexico's laws" to U.S. investors.[3]

State Department goals during the First World War were to maintain stability in Mexico, keep oil shipments flowing to allied fleets, and postpone conflict about property rights until after the war, when the United States would be in a much stronger position. Henry Fletcher, who served as U.S. ambassador to Mexico between 1917 and 1920, stated, "During the war my job was to keep Mexico quiet, and it was done."[4]

During the war, President Wilson attempted to safeguard U.S. investments in Mexico without driving Mexico into the hands of Germany. At the same time, Carranza remained neutral in the First World War, demonstrating his independence from the United States.[5]

The seriousness of the German threat to the United States was emphasized by the Zimmermann telegram, sent to Mexico in February 1917 by German Foreign Minister Arthur Zimmermann. This coded message proposed that Mexico join the war on the German side and fight the United States. In exchange, Mexico would be allowed to regain Texas, New Mexico, and Arizona from the United States. Carranza, realizing that Germany was distant and thus unable to provide effective support, did not accept the proposal.

The Zimmermann telegram backfired after the German code was cracked by British intelligence, which passed the contents of the telegram to the U.S. government. When the message was published in the United States, it turned public opinion strongly against Germany and influenced Wilson's decision to declare war.[6]

It was U.S. investment in Mexico, not German-Mexican relations, that produced conflict with the United States during Carranza's 1917–1920 term. U.S. investors controlled 78 percent of the mining industry, 72 percent of smelting, 68 percent of rubber production, and 58 percent of the oil industry. Their investments were worth more than the combined total of all other foreign investments.[7]

In April 1917, Carranza increased the tax on oil to 10 percent of the value of oil exported. U.S. companies denounced the tax as illegal, since their concessions acquired before 1910 specifically granted them relief from such taxes. Furthermore, they claimed that the tax was "excessive beyond the point of being confiscatory."[8]

After the end of the First World War, U.S. ownership of land increased, as did investment in oil, mining, and banking. Mexican wartime neutrality as well as new taxes on these investments soured relations with the Wilson administration. A vociferous minority in the United States demanded armed intervention in Mexico and attacked President Wilson for not more vigorously defending U.S. lives and property there. Oilmen enjoyed the full support of powerful political figures such as New Mexico Senator Albert B. Fall.

In 1920, as a result of intense U.S. and British pressure, Carranza agreed not to enforce a decree requiring drilling permits until the matter was settled by Mexican courts—a face-saving way to avoid conflict. He took a moderate stance since: 1) the end of his term was approaching and he did not want to provide his opposition with a pretext to seek foreign support to oust him; 2) without new oil wells being drilled, production would decline; and 3) he needed the revenue the oil wells provided. The issue still had not been resolved when Carranza was overthrown.[9]

In his dealings with foreign oilmen, Carranza clearly came out a winner concerning taxation. Between 1914 and January 1, 1920, he vastly increased the share of oil wealth remaining in Mexico by raising the oil tax from an almost trivial 60 centavos per ton to 10 percent of the value of the oil.[10]

Carranza's ability to make such increases resulted from the U.S. preoccupation with the First World War. President Wilson also contributed to Carranza's success in that, even though Wilson ordered the landing at Veracruz and the Pershing expedition, he was not as pro-intervention as many of his U.S. contemporaries. While the First World War gave Carranza some latitude vis-a-vis U.S. interests, the presence of a powerful, foreign entrepreneurial sector did form one of the real limits on the alternatives open to the Mexican Revolution.[11]

OBREGÓN AND UNITED STATES, 1920–1924

After the First World War, the United States definitively replaced Great Britain as the major economic power throughout Latin America. As in the rest of Latin America, the United States increased its dominance over Mexico's foreign trade. By 1922, the United States was selling ten times as much to Mexico as Great Britain and buying four times as much from Mexico as Great Britain.[12]

The United States also replaced Great Britain as the main source of foreign investment. In 1913, the United States and Great Britain were virtually tied with $800 million each in direct investment in Mexico. By 1926, British investment had risen to $1 billion, while U.S. investment had increased to $1.5 billion. In 1928, U.S. investments in the oil industry totaled $408 million, followed by $391 million in mining and smelting, and $300 million in railroads. As these figures indicate, U.S. investment was still overwhelmingly involved in producing raw materials and shipping them out of the country, not in producing for the Mexican market.[13]

The May 1920 coup that deposed Carranza defused the mounting tension caused by the clash between Carranza's nationalism and U.S. unwillingness to change its ways of doing business.

In response to the coup, the United States suspended diplomatic relations with De la Huerta's interim government, claiming that it had been formed unconstitutionally. This allowed the reestablishment of diplomatic relations to be used as a bargaining chip to gain concessions from Mexico.[14]

When he took office in December 1920, Obregón sought to normalize relations with the United States. However, before extending recognition, U.S. President Warren Harding, who took office only three months after Obregón, demanded guarantees for foreign property rights—in effect, the abandonment of Article 27. Charles Evans Hughes, Harding's Secretary of State, declared that to gain recognition Mexico had to promise not to "cancel, destroy or impair any right, title, or interest in any property" held by Americans in Mexico. The U.S.'s refusal to recognize Obregón stood in sharp contrast to its quickly recognizing the Orellana government in Guatemala after it came to power in a 1921 coup.[15]

Obregón faced a formidable array of forces demanding that he abandon nationalistic investment rules. Harding was much more responsive to oil interests than his predecessor. The U.S. president's attempt to maintain control over Mexican oil reflected early 1920s predictions that foresaw the exhaustion of U.S. oil supplies in about a decade. Harding supported the oil companies' demand that Mexico explicitly repudiate all revolutionary legislation concerning oil. U.S. oil companies attempted to discredit Obregón with tales of a rising tide of Bolshevism in Mexico. The Catholic lobby also opposed recognition due to the Sonoran dynasty's anti-clerical policies. The United States held out the prospect of recognition to pressure Mexico into settling damage claims by U.S. citizens, leaving intact existing oil concessions, making debt payments, and ending the seizure of U.S.-owned properties for land reform.[16]

In 1921, progress began on breaking the impasse on recognition. In August, the Mexican Supreme Court, following Obregón's wishes, ruled that oil lands acquired before 1917 could remain in oil company hands if improvements, known as "positive acts," had been made on them. The most common such act was drilling a well.[17]

The United States made it clear to Mexico that any discussion of future loans required settlement of existing Mexican debts. As much as the government might wish it, it could not just walk away from debt incurred by its pre-Revolutionary predecessor. This debt, which Huerta had defaulted on in 1914, included a public debt of $300 million and another $300 million in bonds that the Díaz administration had issued to finance the purchase of foreign-owned railroads.

In response to U.S. pressure, in 1922 Mexico agreed to a meeting to resolve the debt question. The Mexican negotiator was Adolfo de la Huerta, then Obregón's Secretary of Finance. De la Huerta emphasized that Mexico was willing to recognize its pre-Revolutionary debts, but that the government would not sacrifice the well-being of the Mexican people to make immediate payments.

The negotiator for the International Committee of Bankers, representing U.S. and British interests, was Thomas Lamont, of J. P. Morgan Company, the most powerful American financial house. The Committee's leaders met frequently with the U.S. State Department and had its blessing in dealing with Mexico.[18]

De la Huerta's arguments did not persuade Lamont. As a result, there was no compromise on the debt. The negotiated result, known as the Lamont-De la Huerta Agreement, committed Mexico to pay the entire debt contracted by Obregón's predecessors, as well as a considerable part of the interest accrued. This included paying full face value on bonds worth only half that on the market. The Lamont–De la Huerta Agreement stood in marked contrast to the example of the Soviets who had recently repudiated Czarist bonds.[19]

Signing the Lamont–De la Huerta Agreement led bankers to support diplomatic recognition of Obregón. They felt that if Obregón fell, the agreement would be rejected and debt payments would cease. The agreement drove a wedge between oilmen and bankers in that it guaranteed payment of past debts with future taxes on oil exports.[20]

Obregón's seeking U.S. recognition was sound from both the economic and political point of view. With recognition would come—Obregón hoped—loans and protection from being toppled by revolts organized in the United States. U.S. Undersecretary of State Robert Olds commented on the importance of U.S. recognition, "Central America has always understood that governments which we recognize and support stay in power, while those we do not recognize and support fall."[21]

In 1923, Obregón, still unrecognized, agreed to hold talks with the United States. Not only was he in urgent need of loans but he also faced the threat of revolt posed by his former ally De la Huerta. Recognition by the United States was vital, since it would not only preempt U.S. support of De la Huerta but also allow the purchase of U.S. arms.

From May to August 1923, U.S. and Mexican representatives met in downtown Mexico City at No. 85 Bucareli Street, the former home of Porfirio Díaz's finance minister. Given the relative strength of the two parties, not surprisingly, virtually all U.S. demands were met. In an understanding known as the Bucareli Accords, Obregón reaffirmed the Supreme Court decision on positive acts to property acquired before 1917. Its practical effect was to grant in perpetuity oil concessions made between 1876 and 1917. Mexico agreed to the formation of a claims commission to settle damage claims by U.S. citizens against Mexico. Finally, Mexico agreed to pay cash at market values for estates larger than 4,385 acres taken from U.S. citizens as part of the land reform. Since the Mexican government lacked cash to pay for such estates, the Bucareli Accords in effect guaranteed the tenancy of large, but not small, American landowners.[22]

About all that Mexico salvaged from the Bucareli negotiations was the stipulation that bonds, rather than cash, were acceptable as payment for estates of less than 4,385 acres taken for the land reform. Mexican surrender on oil issues was virtually total. Oil companies were unhappy that Mexico did not formally repudiate Article 27. The effect, though, was the same. Oil interests might have pushed through a formal repudiation if they had not been discredited by the Teapot Dome Scandal—a scandal that resulted in Senator Fall's conviction for bribery.[23]

The Lamont–De la Huerta and Bucareli Accords led to U.S. recognition of the Obregón administration on August 31, 1923. In their 1924 platform, the formerly bellicose Republicans stated that "our difficulties with Mexico have happily yielded to a most friendly adjustment." From then on, the United States would back incumbent Mexican governments when they were threatened by coups, since it feared instability would damage U.S. interests.[24]

For Obregón, the most immediate benefit of recognition was access to U.S. arms. When De la Huerta revolted, the United States supplied the Mexican government with sixteen aircraft, rifles, ammunition, and permission to move Mexican troops through Texas. The *New York Times* commented on the significance of these arms sales, "The State Department, acting with the support of President Coolidge, is opposed to the success of the De la Huerta revolutionary movement and hopeful that the Obregón government will succeed in putting down the present revolt."[25]

As a result of declining oil exports and the costs incurred in suppressing the De la Huerta uprising, foreign debt payments were suspended. Mexico was unable to obtain loans and investment to revive the economy. The United States limited Mexico's ability to service its debts by restricting imports from Mexico. This denied Mexico a source of foreign currency that could be used for debt service. As with its loan default in the 1820s, the 1924 default resulted not from Mexican unwillingness to pay but from a lack of foreign currency to pay with.[26]

CALLES AND THE UNITED STATES, 1924–1934

> National sovereignty over natural resources was a beautiful constitutional provision which was totally removed from reality.
>
> Arnaldo Córdova, 2007[27]

Shortly after Calles took office in 1924, U.S.–Mexican relations began another downward spiral. Calles declared that the Bucareli Accords had been merely informal arrangements between Obregón and the United States and therefore were not binding on Obregón's successors.[28]

Once again the dispute revolved around oil. Rather than abandoning the goal of Mexican control of oil, in 1925, Calles promulgated a law that limited concessions acquired before 1917 to fifty years, even if positive acts had been performed. This posed little threat to the oil companies, since as experience would demonstrate, fifty-year concessions could be pumped dry in much less than fifty years. Once again, oil companies—afraid of the precedent that might be set for other areas—refused to accept the new legislation, which also held oil companies responsible for damages to fishing and agriculture.[29]

U.S. President Calvin Coolidge, who took office in 1923, firmly supported the status quo.[30] In the summer of 1925, Secretary of State Frank Kellogg stated:

> It should be made clear that this Government will continue to support the Government in Mexico only so long as it protects American lives and American rights and complies with international engagements and obligations. The Government of Mexico is now on trial before the world.[31]

The continued seizure of American-owned property for land reform further strained relations. Of the 6.2 million acres expropriated by 1925, 494,000 had belonged to Americans. The bonds agreed to as a form of payment for small properties in the Bucareli Accords were clearly inadequate as a means of payment since Mexico was unable to service the bond debt.[32]

The oil issue dragged on into 1927, with both sides refusing to give ground. Mexicans viewed Calles as a dedicated nationalist. Americans considered him as anti-capitalist. Mexicans viewed oilmen as foreigners exploiting non-renewable resources and leaving behind only ruined land. Oil companies portrayed themselves as creators of jobs and as taxpayers.[33]

Tensions continued to rise during the first half of 1927. Oil companies were drilling without the permits they were legally required to have, apparently in hopes of provoking a confrontation. In response, the government would seal wells, and the companies would break the seals. Calles would then order troops to close the valves. In response to the imminent threat of military intervention, Calles ordered the military commander in the oil-producing area, General Lázaro Cárdenas, to set the wells on fire in the case of a U.S. landing.[34]

Fortunately for both nations, the U.S. Senate passed a resolution calling for arbitration of all outstanding issues with Mexico. This resolution was spearheaded by the chairman of the Senate Foreign Relations Committee, Senator William Borah of Idaho. Borah felt that in the long run, continued armed intervention in Latin America was counterproductive. His views later became the accepted wisdom in Washington and would be incorporated into FDR's Good Neighbor Policy (see later in the chapter).[35]

A definitive shift in the tone of U.S.–Mexican relations came with the mid-1927 appointment of Dwight Morrow as U.S. ambassador. Morrow, an Amherst College classmate of Coolidge, had served as a corporate lawyer and partner in the banking firm of J. P. Morgan. At the time of Morrow's arrival, U.S.–Mexican relations had sunk so low that a Mexican newspaper ran the headline, "After Morrow come the marines."[36]

Morrow's instructions from Coolidge were short and to the point: "Keep us out of war with Mexico!" As a friend of Coolidge's, Morrow had more leeway than most diplomats. He also had a knack that was rare for diplomats of the time—he could see both sides of an issue.[37]

Morrow's appointment reflected the shift that was occurring in U.S. Latin American policy. Before arriving in Mexico City, Morrow had stated unequivocally that private debts ought not to be collected by government coercion. None of his predecessors had made such a statement publicly. Morrow's strength lay in persuading, not threatening.[38]

Morrow soon began traveling around Mexico with Calles as a friend and advisor, and he became a major influence on the Mexican president. His greatest success at persuasion was ending the impasse created by the 1925 oil law. Morrow suggested that a face-saving solution could be arrived at if the Mexican Supreme Court would declare the law to be ex post facto and therefore illegal. Such a ruling would defuse the situation, without Mexico recognizing a U.S. veto power over Mexican legislation.

Calles passed Morrow's suggestion on to the Supreme Court, which was not noted for its independence. Within a month, Calles had the ruling he wanted. The following month, January 1928, a new oil law took effect that reflected this decision, thus ending the oil crisis. The 1928 law declared that lands improved before 1917 would remain in oil company hands.[39]

Similarly, the problem raised by taking land owned by Americans for land reform was defused as Morrow persuaded Calles that providing land to illiterate peasants was counterproductive. Morrow's influence extended not only to Calles but to his cabinet as well. Colonel Alexander Macnab, who served under Morrow as military attaché in the Mexico City embassy, commented on this influence: "There is no department of government in Mexico which he has not advised and directed. He took the Secretary of Finance under his wing and taught him finance."[40]

Morrow caught the Mexican public's imagination as few U.S. ambassadors ever have. He had a genuine interest in Mexican culture, studied Spanish, and decorated his home with Mexican handicrafts. His biggest public relations coup was inviting Charles Lindbergh to Mexico. Lindbergh flew his plane non-stop from New York City to Mexico City. Morrow's biographer described the effect of Lindbergh's visit: "During the next week Mexico City abandoned itself to the cult of Colonel Lindbergh. Ambassador Sheffield [Morrow's unpopular predecessor], the oil magnates, Porfirio Díaz, and even the Treaty of Guadalupe Hidalgo, were forgotten." The trip had a lasting effect on Lindbergh. While in Mexico he met ambassador Morrow's daughter Anne, whom he later married.[41]

Morrow did not betray U.S. interests, even though his detractors often accused him of that. He only defended a broader set of interests than oil. He commented on his surprise at the "extent to which responsible oil companies seem to believe it is the duty of the State Department to run their businesses in foreign lands." He balanced the interests of oilmen, bondholders, and those who had lost land to the land reform while exacting payment of as much of Mexico's foreign debt as its weak economy could bear. Unlike his predecessors who had ignored Mexican interests, he observed,

Figure 20.1 *Dwight Morrow inspecting pottery in Oaxaca*
Source: Courtesy Amherst College Archives and Special Collections

"It would be short-sighted policy for the creditors to insist that they be paid at whatever the cost to the people of Mexico."[42]

In his last annual address, Calles stated that the Mexican government was "free of all vexatious difficulties with the neighbor republic of the north." Between 1928 and 1934, relations between the two countries remained cordial due to Calles's increasing conservatism and the settlement of conflicts to both U.S. and Mexican satisfaction.[43]

Once the oil question had been dealt with, stability in Mexico became the primary U.S. concern. Rather than risking a change in government, when Escobar rebelled in 1929, the United States supplied 10,000 Enfield rifles, 10 million rounds of ammunition, airplanes, and pilots to suppress the rebellion. The United States also allowed outnumbered troops loyal to Calles to leave Ciudad Juárez, pass through U.S. territory, and then return to Mexico through Eagle Pass, Texas.[44]

Throughout the 1920s, U.S. influence continued to increase. In 1928, trade between Mexico and the United States totaled $241 million. That year the United States accounted for 68 percent of both Mexican exports and imports. In addition, the Mexican elite increasingly sent their children to college in the United States. This trend was decried by nationalists and Hispanophiles alike—former Education Secretary José Vasconcelos commented that children of the elite were sent to study in the United States "so they might become lackeys of imperialism."[45]

FDR AND THE GOOD NEIGHBOR POLICY

> In the field of world policy I would dedicate this nation to the policy of the good neighbor—the neighbor who resolutely respects himself and, because he does so, respects the rights of others—the neighbor who respects his obligations and respects the sanctity of his agreements in and with a world of neighbors.
>
> Franklin D. Roosevelt's inaugural address, 1933[46]

Thanks to the warm relationship established between Morrow and Calles, no serious problems clouded U.S.–Mexican relations when FDR took office in March 1933. Relations with the oil companies were so amicable that when the Mexican government was strapped for cash during the Depression, oil companies voluntarily paid taxes in advance. Americans continued to demand settlement of debt claims and payment for property taken for land reform. However, neither of these issues was critical. Throughout Latin America, relations with the United States were improving as FDR avoided military intervention and adopted a more conciliatory approach known as the Good Neighbor Policy.[47]

After FDR took office, U.S. policy in Latin America shifted from the defense of U.S. investment in extractive industries to promoting trade. Also, as the Second World War approached, hemispheric defense became an increasingly important concern. At this time, the United States switched from defending its interests in Latin America with armed force to using its economic power, such as withholding loans from the Export-Import Bank.[48]

In 1933, to implement his Good Neighbor policy, Roosevelt appointed Josephus Daniels as ambassador to Mexico. Daniels, a North Carolina newspaper editor, had served as secretary of navy under President Wilson. The then relatively unknown FDR served under Daniels as assistant secretary. As ambassador, Daniels attempted to implement Roosevelt's Good Neighbor Policy, which often produced conflict with the more traditional State Department. Daniels felt U.S. interests in Mexico could be reconciled with Mexican interests. He was not anti-business but saw reforms as a way to provide Mexicans with greater purchasing power, which would make them more stable neighbors and greater consumers of U.S.-made goods.[49]

Conflict soon arose between New Dealer Daniels and State Department officials. In 1935, the State Department instructed Daniels to inquire about increases in Mexican oil taxes. Daniels responded that taxes were "purely a domestic question" and that the United States had no more right to inquire about Mexican taxes than Mexico had to inquire about U.S. taxes.[50]

Daniels's position on the land issue more closely resembled Mexico's position than that of the State Department. He noted that the Mexican government did not have enough cash to pay for all the land needed for land reform. To pay Americans and not Mexicans would be to treat Mexicans worse than U.S. citizens in their own country. Furthermore, he felt land reform was crucial to the survival of Cárdenas's government. Daniels claimed that no government in Mexico "could long endure if it did not give the lands to the people who have long tilled them."[51]

The stage was set for more severe conflict between Mexico and the United States in early 1936 when the national oil workers union demanded a 30-million peso ($8.3 million) wage increase and increased control over the workplace similar to the control that textile workers were already exercising.[52]

Negotiations between the oil workers and oil companies began in July 1936. The companies claimed that since they were paying among the highest wages in Mexico, further wage increases were unwarranted. Oil companies also claimed that wage increases would make them non-competitive internationally and thus would ruin the industry. Labor claimed that their high profits justified the workers' demand for increased wages and benefits.

Negotiations dragged on until May 1937. The oil companies offered only a 14-million peso increase, so oil workers throughout the industry went out on strike. Given the impact of the strike on the Mexican economy, the Federal Board of Conciliation and Arbitration declared a national emergency and ordered the strikers back to work. At the same time, it ordered oil companies to submit their books to the Board so it could determine if they were financially able to meet the workers' demands.[53]

Before weighing in on the wage increase, the Board appointed a panel of Mexican experts to review oil industry operations. In August 1937, the experts issued a 2,700-page report that recommended that oil workers be granted a wage-and-benefit package worth 26 million pesos. The panel of experts based the 26-million-peso figure on its finding that annual oil company profits amounted to 79 million pesos. The experts noted that Mexican workers received a third or a quarter of what U.S. oil workers received but produced twelve times as much oil per worker.[54]

Once again Ambassador Daniels assumed a position closer to the Mexican one than to that of the State Department. In September 1937, he noted:

> Having made big money on absurdly low wages from the time the oil gushers made Doheny and Pearson rich, all oil producers oppose any change in taxes and wages, and resent it if their Governments do not take their point of view. Mexico can never prosper on low wages and we must be in sympathy with every just demand . . .[55]

To increase the pressure on the Mexican government for a favorable ruling, in November 1937, the oil companies declared that if the government ordered the 26-million-peso increase, they would suspend oil production. Company spokesman Lawrence Anderson declared, "*We cannot and will not pay*."[56]

On December 18, 1937, the Arbitration Board followed the recommendation of the experts and awarded oil workers a 26-million-peso wage-and-benefit package. The oil companies immediately appealed the ruling to the Mexican Supreme Court, hoping the Court would provide the government with a face-saving way to yield to the oil companies, as it had under Calles.

However, on March 1, 1938, the Supreme Court ruled that the decision of the Board was binding on the oil companies. On March 15, oilmen announced: "The companies are unable to put the award into effect. It would ruin their businesses."[57]

Rather than accepting the rule of Mexican law, the oil companies considered themselves above it. They thought their power would permit open defiance of the nascent revolutionary state. Their ability to apply economic pressure and their belief that Mexicans could not operate the oil industry also emboldened them. Finally, since their operations had largely shifted to Venezuela, oil companies were prepared to risk their reduced holdings in Mexico to preserve traditional employer prerogatives.[58]

On the night of March 18, 1938, in a nationwide radio address, Cárdenas announced the nationalization of the oil industry:

> This is a clear-cut case which forces the government to apply the existing Expropriation Act, not only to force the oil companies to obey and submit, but due to the labor authorities' having declared void the contracts between the companies and the workers. An immediate paralysis of the oil industry is imminent. This would cause incalculable damage to the industry and to the rest of the economy.[59]

Cárdenas felt he was in a good position to act due to his widespread domestic support and the U.S. awareness that a strong response might push Mexico into the embrace of the Axis powers. His action was unquestionably the most popular of his government and probably of any government since the Mexican Revolution.[60]

The popularity of the move resulted not from abstract nationalism but from the sordid reputation of the oil companies in Mexico. During Carranza's presidency, oil companies had avoided government control by supporting Manuel Peláez. A long litany of abuses followed. In the 1920s, when Cárdenas was stationed in the oil-producing area, he observed that oil companies acted as if they were operating in "conquered territory." Oilmen formed company unions, dismissed union organizers, and hired goons to harass and assassinate independent labor leaders. The 1920s decline in oil production was considered oil company skullduggery.[61]

Cárdenas justified the nationalization of the oil companies on the basis that they had violated the labor provisions of Article 123. He promised compensation for nationalized property, but not payment for oil in the ground. By the Mexican interpretation of Article 27, such oil had always belonged to the Mexican government.[62]

Massive demonstrations in support of the nationalization sent a clear message to the United States—an attack on Cárdenas would be an attack on the nation as a whole. Historian Frank Tannenbaum commented on the psychological effect of the nationalization, "If one is to mark a date in Mexico when the nation felt itself in possession of its own house at last, it was the day of the expropriation of the oil wells."[63]

Throughout the oil crisis, U.S. policy was never unified. Some officials thought in terms of the Good Neighbor Policy, others in terms of the Big Stick. The former group considered trade ties and good hemispheric relations paramount. In the summer of 1938, the U.S. National Foreign Trade Council called for an "early settlement of the present controversy between the two governments because of the unsettling effects present differences have upon trade . . . ." More bellicose observers saw the nationalization as a threat to American investments around the world and to U.S. access to raw materials.[64]

The State Department demanded the return of oil properties or immediate payment for improvements and oil in the ground. It attempted to force Mexico to rescind the nationalization by pressuring other Latin American governments not to buy Mexican oil. Most of Mexico's customers continued purchasing Mexican oil, since Mexico cut its prices to keep its markets. However, some loyal U.S. allies such as Anastasio Somoza of Nicaragua agreed not to buy Mexican oil.[65]

Conflict within the U.S. government became evident when the State Department began pressuring the Treasury Department to suspend silver purchases from Mexico. Treasury Secretary Henry Morgenthau, Jr., responded that silver purchases were a monetary, not a political matter. The Treasury Department suspended purchases only when formally requested to do so by the State Department. This, however, dealt a potentially fatal blow to U.S. mining companies in Mexico, which produced 90 percent of Mexico's silver. They bitterly complained to Washington that they were "suffering for the sins of the oilmen." After a three-day hiatus, the Treasury Department resumed silver purchases at a slightly lower price.[66]

FDR assumed a more moderate position than did the State Department. He encouraged oil companies not to try to recover their property but to negotiate terms for compensation. He felt that American companies were only entitled to payment for total investment less depreciation. Such a figure would not include prospective profits from oil in the ground.[67]

Ambassador Daniels was even more moderate, and in the eyes of many, actually pro-Mexican. He later commented:

> President Cárdenas was acting under clear and well-understood Mexican law. The Constitution of Mexico, for many years prior to the expropriation, had required . . . the full submission by foreigners to the laws of Mexico without recourse to their own governments.

Daniels in effect created his own foreign policy. Rather than seeking to regain control over the oil fields, he sought to prevent a break in relations between Mexico and the United States.[68]

State Department officials knew that Daniels was formulating his own policy. Secretary of State Cordell Hull complained, "Daniels is down there taking sides with the Mexican government [giving] the impression that they can go right ahead and flaunt everything in our face." Like Morrow before him, Daniels's close ties to the president gave him unusual diplomatic latitude.[69]

A number of factors restricted U.S. government action. A week before the nationalization, Hitler had invaded Austria, so war in Europe shaped the U.S. response. FDR, when forced to choose between maintaining the Good Neighbor Policy throughout Latin America and taking a hard line on Mexico, chose the former. Since most of the expropriated oil belonged to Holland and Britain, the U.S. response was more moderate. The United States realized that if too much pressure was placed on Cárdenas, his government might fall. If Cárdenas had fallen, he would likely have been replaced by a pro-fascist regime.[70]

The U.S. business community was divided on the oil question, just as the U.S. government was. Big oil companies tried to block Mexican oil exports, while small U.S. companies with no property in Mexico bought Mexican oil and shipped it to Europe. U.S. hotel owners in Mexico complained that oil company disinformation was scaring tourists away. Bondholders favored the oil nationalization, since that would provide the Mexican government with increased revenue to service its bonds.

The British assumed a more obdurate position than the United States. Mexican oil was much more important to Britain than to the United States. The entire British empire produced only 5 percent of the world's oil, while U.S. domestic production accounted for 61 percent. British investment in Mexico was concentrated in oil, so oilmen shaped the British response. U.S. investors represented a wider range of interests, so oilmen could not call the shots alone.[71]

While various U.S. interests vied to have their preferred policy implemented, Mexican policy makers masterfully averted a confrontation with Washington by emphasizing that they would provide compensation for land taken for the agrarian reform as well as oil company assets as soon as possible. They effectively stalled for three years, all the while telling the Roosevelt administration what it wanted to hear concerning land reform, bilateral trade, and the fight against international fascism.[72]

While pressure was being exerted from abroad, Mexico faced the problem of managing the oil industry. Foreign technicians had been withdrawn. Mexico could not replace aging oil field equipment and lacked workers trained in technical roles. Nevertheless, to the oil companies' astonishment and dismay, Mexicans were able to resume production. Within three months, production reached 65 percent of the pre-nationalization level.[73]

The Mexican oil industry had changed since the 1920s. By 1938, domestic use accounted for 57 percent of hydrocarbon production, so the government did not need to find markets for as much oil as it would have if nationalization had occurred in the 1920s. In any case, the loss of exports still hurt. Petroleum exports, which were worth 112 million pesos in 1937, declined to 52 million pesos in 1938.[74]

The oil companies were unable to prevent increased trade between Mexico and the United States. In 1938, 67 percent of Mexico's foreign trade was with the United States. The following year, as war closed European markets, the figure was 74 percent. As trade increased, the pressure to normalize relations rose.[75]

As a result of the Second World War, the U.S. government intervened to resolve the oil dispute and thus eliminate a potential source of conflict with its southern neighbor. In November 1941, the U.S. and Mexican governments, acting without the oil companies' consent, appointed experts to evaluate the expropriated properties. The experts placed the value of the oil holdings, which the oilmen claimed to be worth more than $260 million, at just over $29 million. This value took into consideration the obsolescence of the twenty-five-year-old equipment. The two nations accepted this value on April 17, 1942, four months after Pearl Harbor.[76]

The agreement stipulated that Mexico was to pay $9 million immediately, with the rest to be paid in installments. The oil companies were not actually forced to accept the settlement. However, they had little choice. The United States announced that it would no longer support oil company claims. Their only other recourse was to seek redress in the Mexican court system.[77]

Mexican writer Carlos Fuentes commented on FDR's role in the settlement: "Instead of menacing, sanctioning or invading, Roosevelt negotiated. He did not try to beat history. He joined it . . ."[78]

Given wartime imperatives, the U.S. government also pushed through a settlement on debt claims. In 1941, debt claims totaling as much as $1.07 billion, depending who was doing the counting, were settled for $116.9 million. Of this amount, $22 million compensated U.S. landowners, who lost holdings ranging in size from six to 412,000 acres. Bondholders suffered the heaviest losses. A 1942 agreement signed by U.S. financier Lamont and Mexican Finance Minister Eduardo Suárez obliged bondholders to accept cancellation of roughly 90 percent of the nominal value of their bonds. FDR instructed Lamont to inform bondholders to take the deal or get nothing. Historian E. David Cronon commented, "The agreements showed that Washington was now willing to pay a considerable price for a *rapprochement* with Mexico, for it was plain that the United States would be underwriting the Mexican payments."[79]

Ironically, the oil nationalization resulted in Mexico becoming more conservative. The economic crisis produced by the nationalization left the government unable to meets its payrolls, much less carry out reforms. Government projects such as road building and land reform were curtailed. The interests of government and labor diverged. Previously, the government had supported workers demanding higher wages from foreign corporations. After March 1938, the government sought higher production levels, but wanted wages to remain low to husband scarce cash reserves. Oil workers received neither the increased wages nor the administrative prerogatives they had demanded from foreign oil companies. Miners, who greatly outnumbered oil workers, were told to moderate their wage demands so as not to interrupt vital mineral exports. As the government withdrew its support and began to emphasize production, the labor movement lost momentum.[80]

Cárdenas became more conciliatory toward conservatives in Mexico. He feared that otherwise oil interests might split Mexico along class lines. National unity, not class conflict, became the dominant theme. In March 1939, in response to the conservative shift in Mexico, the U.S. embassy informed Washington that regardless of who won the 1940 presidential elections, the radical stage of the revolution had ended.[81]

Even before the oil settlement, U.S.–Mexican relations were improving. In 1940, American policy makers favored Ávila Camacho over Almazán, who would have moved Mexico sharply to the right. They felt such a change would likely produce instability. To thwart Almazán's post-election maneuvers, the FBI, U.S. military intelligence, and Mexican agents systematically monitored and disrupted activities of Almazán's agents in the United States, along the border, and inside Mexico.[82]

The announcement that U.S. Vice-President Henry Wallace would attend Ávila Camacho's inauguration provided a clear sign of improved relations. It also ended Almazán's hopes, since he had no chance of attaining the presidency without U.S. backing. This was not unnoticed by Almazán partisans, who staged a violent demonstration at the U.S. embassy when Wallace arrived. Wallace and Daniels received a standing ovation at the inauguration.[83]

IMMIGRATION, 1917–1940

The Immigration Act of 1917 restricted the flow of Mexican workers coming to the United States by adding a literacy requirement and a head tax of $8.00. These requirements could be waived in case of emergency.[84]

The First World War justified the emergency waiving of the literacy requirement and the $8.00 head tax. This allowed Mexican agricultural workers to fill jobs vacated by Americans who were fighting or who had gone north to work in well-paying industrial jobs. Rail and mine workers as well as other industrial workers were later admitted on similar emergency exemptions. From 1917 through 1921, 72,862 Mexicans took advantage of these exemptions to enter the United States. Given the cumbersome paperwork required to hire workers under these emergency measures, many growers preferred to hire workers who had entered the United States illegally. As a result, illegal entrants likely outnumbered legal ones during this period.[85]

During the First World War, migration to the United States, which was accepted and encouraged on both sides of the border, formed a positive element in U.S.–Mexican relations. Given the poor state of the Mexican economy, the lack of access to tillable land prior to 1934, and demographic pressure in north-central Mexico, jobs in the United States were extremely attractive. In 1918, the Mexican government even offered train fares to the border and provided personnel who facilitated job seeking in the United States. While the national government supported those seeking jobs in the United States, the state governors of Jalisco and Tamaulipas complained that their states were losing their labor force.[86]

After the First World War, given the poor economic situation in Mexico and the reluctance of Americans to perform unskilled, backbreaking jobs at the wages offered, the northward flow of Mexicans continued. From 1919 to 1921, 112,937 Mexican immigrants legally entered the United States. Except in New Mexico with its long-established Hispanic population, new arrivals soon outnumbered long-established Spanish or Mexican residents.[87]

As a result of the U.S. recession of 1921, the demand for labor declined throughout the southwest, and Mexican workers suddenly found themselves unwelcome. In 1921, roughly 100,000 Mexicans were either deported or voluntarily returned to Mexico. Many who returned "voluntarily" had little choice since once they lost their jobs, they found that public and private charities had limited resources and considered caring for U.S. citizens as their first priority.[88]

The Immigration Act of 1921 established quotas for European immigrants based on the number of persons of a given national origin who were reported in the 1910 U.S. census. As a result of this law, the number of legal immigrants entering the United States declined from 805,228 in 1921 to 309,556 in 1922. The rapid recovery of the U.S. economy from the 1921 recession, the reduction of European immigration, and the near stagnation of the Mexican economy resulted in soaring emigration from Mexico to the United States.[89]

Mexicans were not included in the country quotas established by the Immigration Act of 1924 since: 1) potential border-state employers lobbied for an exemption to quotas for residents of the western hemisphere in order to gain access to cheap labor; 2) the State Department felt quotas would damage Pan-American solidarity; 3) legislators felt Mexicans who came would only stay temporarily; and 4) the perceived problems resulting from massive European immigration occurred in eastern and mid-western cities, while Mexican immigrants were largely employed in southwestern agriculture, removed from the scrutiny of most congressmen.[90]

In 1924, the Border Patrol was established to enforce immigration laws. Prior to 1924, those who had successfully entered illegally faced little chance of deportation unless they were involved in a legal infraction. After that date, undocumented workers were driven into clandestinity. The number of Mexicans deported in the four years prior to the founding of the Border Patrol was 5,096, compared to 15,434 in the following four years. These numbers represent only a small fraction of those who entered illegally and found employment. Both U.S. officials and Mexican workers understood that it was the demand for labor in the southwest, not laws drawn up in Washington, that defined Mexican immigration to the United States.[91]

During the 1920s, given the cost of legal immigration and the reluctance of some U.S. officials to issue visas to Mexicans, an estimated five Mexicans entered the United States illegally for each one who entered legally. By making unauthorized entry illegal, without making it illegal to hire undocumented immigrants, the U.S. government shifted power even further in favor of U.S. employers to the detriment of Mexican workers. Strike leaders and labor organizers could be targeted for deportation. Growers could report Mexican workers to the Border Patrol if they pressed demands concerning wages or working conditions. Some growers would simply inform the Border Patrol where it could find their undocumented employees rather than paying them. This ambiguous status was used at the local level to lower wages. At the national level, it served as a valve. When the demand for labor rose, enforcement declined. When there was an oversupply of labor, enforcement increased.[92]

From the employers' point of view, Mexican labor was ideal. Workers were young and healthy, and growers did not have to pay taxes for schools to educate their children. They would accept undesirable jobs, permitting the pay for those jobs to remain low. It was difficult for Mexicans to organize unions, especially if they were in the United States illegally. They could be sent home in times of recession, minimizing both the cost of unemployment payments and the political fall-out from a large number of unemployed.[93]

Between 1921 and 1930, 459,287 Mexicans, 11.2 percent of all legal U.S. immigrants, came from Mexico. The rate at which Mexicans entered the United States during the late 1920s would not be equaled again until the 1990s. The 1930 census reported 1,422,533 persons who were Mexican-born or of Mexican ancestry, compared to 700,541 in 1920. Texas had the highest concentration with 683,681, followed by California with 168,013. The cities with the most Mexican-born residents were Los Angeles with 97,116 and San Antonio with 82,373.[94]

In the 1920s, as Mexicans became an increasingly important part of the U.S. labor force, Americans began debating the desirability of relying on Mexican labor. Organized labor opposed the presence of Mexican workers, claiming they cost U.S. citizens jobs and lowered the wage level. Other groups characterized Mexicans as being "inferior," just as earlier waves of German, Irish, East European, and Asian immigrants had been branded as inferior.[95]

New York Congressman La Guardia was very candid when asked why, if Mexicans caused problems, they were not excluded. He replied, "Because the influence of the sugar-beet growers and railroads is too strong."[96]

Mexican government officials viewed workers coming to the United States as a safety valve to defuse rural tension. They also shared anthropologist Manuel Gamio's view that working in the United States served to instill good work habits, as well as agricultural and industrial skills. Mexicans in the United States aided the Mexican economy by sending millions of dollars to their families in Mexico. Finally, the labor loss was rationalized as being only temporary. However, as the 1930 U.S. census indicated, many Mexicans did not return. Rather, they remained and brought their families from Mexico or started new ones in the United States.[97]

In 1930, most of the population that was Mexican by birth or ancestry had arrived recently. Only 18.6 percent were U.S.-born of U.S.-born parents. That year, 58.8 percent of the Mexican population lived in urban areas, indicating a move away from agricultural employment. Mexicans were slowly moving away from Colorado and the four U.S. states bordering Mexico. By 1930, about 15 percent were in the other forty-three states. Many took jobs in the midwest—harvesting sugar beets, laying railroad track, and in meat packing plants. More than 3,000 Mexicans worked in Ford auto plants, as Henry Ford deliberately created an ethnically divided labor force.[98]

When the Depression hit, Mexican workers in the United States again found themselves unwelcome. By January 1930, there were more than 6 million unemployed Americans. Not only did many of the jobs held by Mexicans vanish but the unattractive jobs they still held were being sought by Americans, desperate for work. Generally, Mexican workers were the first laid off. To add insult to injury, Mexicans found themselves blamed for U.S. joblessness.[99]

At the onset of the Depression, many Mexicans who were working in the United States not only lost their jobs but were denied relief funds unless they could prove legal residence in their community. Many communities used selective allocation of relief funds to reduce the number of Mexicans as well as poor whites and blacks from the U.S. South. Facing joblessness and hunger and with the Mexican government encouraging Mexicans to return, the tide of immigration reversed.

Between 1929 and 1931, many returning Mexicans arrived with their own cars or trucks piled high with their belongings. Others boarded special trains to the border at collection centers such as Detroit, Chicago, St. Louis, Denver, Phoenix, Oklahoma City, and Los Angeles. Ships carried additional repatriates from New York and California.[100]

After 1931, it became obvious that the Depression was not just a temporary recession. This resulted in a more concerted effort to drive Mexican workers out of the United States. Secretary of Labor William Doak, who took office in 1930, spearheaded this effort, promising to provide jobs for Americans by deporting illegal aliens. The campaign to expel Mexicans drew widespread support in the United States.

Acting under Doak's orders, agents began to raid private homes and workplaces in a search that extended from Los Angeles to New York. For the first time, immigration agents operated throughout the country, rather than just along the border. Some of the raids involved complex logistics and resembled full-scale paramilitary operations. Enforcement of immigration ceased to be an ordinary bureaucratic process and became sensationalized in the press. The Los Angeles Bar Association condemned these deportations as a wholesale violation basic human rights.[101]

Most Mexicans were not deported in the legal sense of the word. In addition to being denied relief benefits, they were told that if they did not leave voluntarily, they would be deported and thus ineligible to ever return to the United States.

Since many of the Mexicans being forced out had lived in the United States for years, their children had often been born in the United States, making them U.S. citizens. In some cases older, U.S.-born children elected to remain north of the border, thus splitting families.[102]

Many groups, including social welfare agencies, church charities, and the Red Cross, provided financial aid and basic necessities to the deportees. Some were also aided financially by Mexican consular officials and Mexican mutual aid societies.[103]

Special trains carried returnees from the border into interior Mexico without charge. Most of those deported returned to their place of origin. However, in some cases, the Mexican government established agrarian colonies and provided the returnees land to farm.[104]

By 1934, the massive expulsions were largely over. The grapevine spread the word in Mexico that there were no jobs in the United States and that Mexicans were unwelcome, so Mexicans largely stopped going. As the U.S. government assumed an increased share of relief efforts, there was less pressure at the local level to force out remaining Mexicans. Business groups led by the Bank of America and the Chamber of Commerce of Los Angeles realized that deportations were reducing the demand for goods and services, so they lobbied for deportation to be restricted to those who voluntarily returned to Mexico. Finally, the government outlook changed with the New

Deal. Daniel MacCormack, FDR's Immigration Service Commissioner, announced that authorities would have to obtain arrest warrants before detaining suspected aliens—not after, as had been the case. He also announced that there would be no more mass round-ups.[105]

By 1937, the often contradictory nature of Mexican employment in the United States was manifest. Some Mexicans were still returning to Mexico in desperation. Other Mexicans, just as desperate, were leaving Mexico to find work in the United States. Between 1931 and 1941, only 22,319 Mexicans legally entered the United States.[106]

The total number of Mexican returnees in the 1930s has been placed at between half a million and 1 million. These figures include some returnees who had intended to return to Mexico even before the onset of the Depression, as Mexicans had been doing for generations. Most returnees came from Texas and southern California. The effect of the Depression is clear from U.S. census data. While the 1930 census showed 639,107 Mexican-born people in the United States, the 1940 census found only 377,433.[107]

THE BORDER

As a result of the Revolution, development on the Mexican side of the border largely came to a halt while the U.S. border area boomed. Because of communications and transportation bottlenecks, Mexican border cities found themselves cut off from the rest of Mexico. As a result, they became commercially, economically, and socially dependent on the U.S. side of the border. In 1921, the largest Mexican border city was Ciudad Juárez, with a population of 19,457.[108]

Prohibition in the United States, which lasted from 1920 to 1933, led to an explosion of tourism in the border cities. During the 1920s, the population of Juárez more than doubled while Tijuana's more than octupled. Juárez benefited from El Paso being a stopping point on a major transcontinental rail passenger route, while Tijuana was within easy reach of San Diego and Los Angeles residents. Along with liquor for thirsty U.S. tourists came gambling, drug smuggling, and prostitution. American celebrities frequented Tijuana's horse and dog race tracks.[109]

Tourism brought the impoverished border cities economic prosperity and an unsavory reputation. Gambling in Juárez became the main source of revenue for the state of Chihuahua, yielding 700,000 pesos in 1932. Prohibition-era tourism financed a wide range of urban services there, including sewage, electricity, pavement, trolleys, and water distribution.[110]

The end of Prohibition and the onset of the Depression dealt a severe blow to border tourism. Within a single month after the repeal of Prohibition, 150 commercial establishments related to liquor ceased operation in Tijuana. President Cárdenas (1934–1940) further undermined tourism

Table 20.1 *Border state populations, 1921–1940*

State	1921	1940	Percent change
Baja California	23,537	78,907	235
Sonora	275,127	364,176	32
Chihuahua	401,622	623,944	55
Coahuila	393,840	550,717	40
Nuevo León	336,412	541,147	61
Tamaulipas	286,904	458,832	60
Total	1,717,442	2,617,723	52
Percent of Mexican population	12.0	13.0	

Source: INEGI (1994: 15–24)

by cracking down on vice, especially gambling, in border cities. The number of border crossings declined from 27.1 million in 1928 to 21.1 million in 1934.[111]

During the 1920s, the population of the Mexican border states increased slightly faster than that of Mexico as a whole. These states benefited from both increased tourism and massive government-funded irrigation works. During the 1930s, population growth in the border states continued to outpace that of Mexico as a whole as government-funded reclamation projects continued. Many Mexicans who left the United States during the Depression either could not afford transport south or remained in the border area with the intention of returning north. Finally, Tijuana was declared a duty-free area, which stimulated commerce there.[112]

Part Seven

The Rise of the "Perfect Dictatorship," 1941–1970

Chapter 21

After Cárdenas, 1941–1970

> The moment always arrives when revolutions lose currency and cease to be because they exhaust their creative vitality, because they realize their task in history, or because there are new forces which restrain or overcome them.
>
> Jesús Silva Herzog, 1949[1]

THE ÁVILA CAMACHO ADMINISTRATION, 1940–1946

In his inaugural address, Ávila Camacho stated that entrepreneurs would find "institutional guarantees." Rather than extolling land reform, he pledged protection for private landowners "not only to protect those holdings which now exist, but to stimulate the formation of new private holdings on vast uncultivated expanses."[2]

During the Cristero Rebellion, Ávila Camacho had developed a reputation for negotiating the surrender of Cristeros rather than annihilating them as his colleagues had attempted. He now brought these same conciliatory talents into the presidency. He praised Monterrey industrialists, Cárdenas's staunchest foes, and won their loyalty. Teófilo Oléa y Leyva, a founder of the National Action Party (PAN), received a Supreme Court appointment. At the same time, some Cardenistas, such as Eduardo Suárez, who had served as Cárdenas's treasury secretary, were included in his cabinet. The middle class, much of which had supported Almazán, was successfully courted. Old grudges were forgotten and backers of Calles and Almazán received positions in the Ávila Camacho administration.[3]

As president-elect, Ávila Camacho pledged that Mexico would remain neutral in the Second World War. He declared: "The current war is only a war for markets. All we should do is ensure that we cannot be conquered."[4]

In less than two years, U.S. pressure and German submarine warfare changed Ávila Camacho's view on the war. A German submarine sank the Mexican tanker *Potrero del Llano* in May 1942. Even after the sinking, obtaining support for a declaration of war was difficult, since Britain and the United States were widely seen as enemies of Mexico, while Germany, Italy, and Japan were not. A strong pro-Axis movement in Mexico attempted to block a declaration of war. Later the same month, after the sinking of a second tanker, the *Faja del Oro*, public opinion turned against Germany, and Mexico declared war.[5]

On September 15, 1942, all six living ex-presidents, including Calles back from exile, appeared with Ávila Camacho to demonstrate their commitment to national unity and the war effort. The president told the crowd gathered in front of the National Palace, "When what is at stake is the continued existence our nation, personal differences and partisan desires have no place."[6]

In 1943, to provide political space for the increasingly important middle class and to blunt the appeal of the PAN and other conservative groups, the National Federation of Popular Organizations (CNOP) was founded as an officially sanctioned group within the Mexican Revolutionary Party

(PRM). The CNOP became something of a catch-all, serving to organize public employees, youth groups, professionals, non-unionized artisans, shopkeepers, women, street vendors, and others who did not belong to the peasant or labor sectors.[7]

The CNOP courted the middle class by favoring such policies as women's rights, limiting foreign capital, and public housing for federal employees. Its members had greater political skills, more training, and were wealthier than members of the labor and peasant sectors. As years passed, the CNOP increasingly dominated the official party, and its members were disproportionately selected to hold office, especially in the Chamber of Deputies.[8]

A number of factors permitted Ávila Camacho to shift to the political right without facing strong opposition. Since Cárdenas had moderated his policies at the end of his term, the shift in government policy was not as sharp as it would have been had Ávila Camacho initiated the shift. Mexican participation in the Second World War also facilitated the rightward shift. During the war, former president Cárdenas was placed on active military duty, so he was under military discipline and thus was not in a position to challenge Ávila Camacho's move the right. The pro-Soviet left was neutralized as it urged war production to aid the Soviet Union, even at the cost of a lowered standard of living for Mexican workers. The presence of pro-Axis elements in Mexico allowed Ávila Camacho to be viewed as a moderate between the left and right. Within the PRM, he held the middle ground between the conservative caudillos of the Revolution and backers of Cárdenas and labor leader Vicente Lombardo Toledano. The Fascist victory in the Spanish Civil War caused broader acceptance of a government move to the political center to preempt a repeat of the Spanish experience.

Ávila Camacho's ability to withdraw support from labor and peasants without entailing any organized resistance was a testimony to the control established over these groups during the Cárdenas administration. Labor was immobilized as Fidel Velázquez, a pliant ally of the government, was installed to head the official labor federation, the Mexican Workers Federation (CTM).[9]

Under Ávila Camacho, corruption reached the highest levels of government. Maximino Ávila Camacho, who served as secretary of communications and public works during his brother's presidency, so routinely took a cut from public contracts that he became known as "Mr. Fifteen Percent." After being sworn in, he even canceled existing contracts so new ones that would include his 15 percent could be signed.[10]

In early 1946, his last year in office, Ávila Camacho presided over the reorganization of the official party, which was renamed the Revolutionary Institutional Party (PRI). The reorganization resulted in the labor, peasant, and popular sectors having a reduced role. Power was further concentrated in the hands of the president and the party's National Executive Committee. As occurred with the founding of the National Revolutionary Party (PNR) and the PRM, decisions concerning the formation of the PRI were made from the top down. In one day, the party's convention agreed on an already-drafted declaration of principles, program of action, and statutes. *Ejidatarios* and trade union members continued to become automatic party members.

A new election law, approved in January 1946, greatly increased the power of the federal government in electoral matters. Before that date, elections were organized under the 1918 election law, which charged municipal authorities with drawing up voter lists and organizing elections. The 1918 law allowed candidates to run without the backing of a political party and made it very easy to organize a political party. Only a hundred members were required at a party's founding assembly. The 1918 law, drafted in response to Díaz's centralized political manipulation, made it difficult for the weak post-revolutionary governments to impose candidates. However, it did give local strongmen the opportunity to do so.[11]

The 1946 election law strengthened central government control and presidential influence over elections. Individuals were required to run as the candidate of a recognized political party. It became much more difficult to receive official recognition, since to be recognized as a political party a group was required to have 30,000 members nationwide and at least 1,000 members per state in two-thirds of the states. The law granted the secretary of the interior the power to recognize parties and cancel their registration. Through this control, anti-establishment candidates and parties could be ruled off the ballot. A new agency, the Federal Election Oversight Commission, was charged with preparing the voter list and organizing elections. At the time, this was hailed as a way to prevent local bosses with no commitment to democracy from perpetuating fraud. What was not mentioned was that this centralization of authority simply nationalized fraud management. As was intended by its drafters, this legislation discouraged electoral opposition. In 1946 the average number of congressional candidates per district was 5.3, while by 1949 it had declined to 2.0.[12]

Ávila Camacho's choice of his Interior Secretary Miguel Alemán to be the first PRI presidential candidate signaled a continuation of the conservative trend in government. Alemán had resigned his governorship of Veracruz to manage Ávila Camacho's presidential campaign. In his speech accepting the PRI nomination, Alemán emphasized agricultural and industrial development. Alemán, a career civilian bureaucrat, was the first of a string of professional politicians who would dominate Mexican political life for the rest of the century.[13]

The outlines of a new Mexican political system were clearly visible by the end of Ávila Camacho's term. He established cordial relations with the Church and the United States. Presidential power had greatly increased, accumulated on the pretext of war emergency but retained after the end of the war. The government and business began a close alliance that over the course of the next thirty years was to transform Mexico socially and economically. Foreign business interests became active participants in this alliance. Workers and peasants were left leaderless as their nominal leaders looked increasingly to the government rather than their base. Ávila Camacho and his successors, rather than admitting a change in direction, extolled economic nationalism and industrialization, all of which was cloaked in the symbolism of the Mexican Revolution.[14]

MIGUEL ALEMÁN, 1946–1952

> Alemán is arguably the most important president in 20th-century Mexican history. He profoundly changed the nation's course by allying the state with moneyed interests, wooing foreign capital, accelerating industrialization, and undoing or mitigating many of the reforms promulgated by Cárdenas.
>
> John W. Sherman, 2000[15]

Many welcomed Alemán as a charismatic young leader with something of a playboy image. The average age of his cabinet members, who were largely civilian university graduates like the president himself, was forty-four—the first cabinet formed by the generation that had grown up under the Revolution. Military men headed only the secretaries of national defense and navy. Alemán's rise to the presidency made it clear that the military no longer provided entry into the political establishment. Graduation from the National University and a career in government had become the route to the presidency.[16]

The month after he was inaugurated, Alemán declared in a widely publicized speech: "Each Mexican should be a soldier in the great battle for the industrial growth of Mexico. That is the only way we can combat the high cost of living and strengthen our economic independence."[17]

By 1950, the PRI had become a smoothly functioning political machine. That year the party adopted new statutes, a declaration of principles, and a plan of action. The 1,066 delegates at the PRI convention unanimously approved drafts of these documents in two days of sessions. The degree to which the PRI had become subordinated to the president was indicated by this overblown resolution passed by the 1951 General Assembly of the PRI:

> We consider the political ideas expressed by President Alemán to be doctrine of such congruence, profundity, and precision that it can serve as an official source to stimulate our thinking and our

will . . . This Assembly resolves to increase its reliance on the political thinking of MIGUEL ALEMÁN and the Party's Declaration of Principles so that they may constantly guide the Party's actions.[18]

Alemán forced all elements of the government to accept his ideological position. Alemán-like political clones replaced the center-left to center-right coalition that had existed under Cárdenas. During his first eight months in office, Alemán removed ten governors who were unwilling to follow his policies or who were closely associated with other strong political figures. Alemán further marginalized the military, which for the first time since the Revolution was allocated less than 10 percent of the federal budget.[19]

Even though Alemán began his administration with a pledge to fight corruption, graft became more firmly entrenched than ever in the Mexican political system. By one estimate, during his term Alemán and his associates "plundered" $800,000,000. Lesser officials followed Alemán's example, noting: "Alemán led and we followed."[20]

Corruption took several forms:

- In some cases, money was illegally transferred from municipal, state, or federal coffers to private accounts.[21]
- Politicians funneled government contracts to themselves or their associates.
- A bribe, known as a *mordida*, would expedite legal activity or prevent prosecution for illegal activity. During the Second World War, when he was serving as interior secretary, Alemán, for a fee, arranged to protect citizens of Axis nations and prevent foreclosure of their property. A 1951 CIA report commented on the social impact of the *mordida*, "The *mordida*, because it gives the moneyed class an advantage over the poor, is a serious obstacle to the democratic functioning of government in Mexico . . ."[22]
- Public office was used to engage in lucrative but illegal activity. The CIA commented on Carlos I. Serrano, the head of the Federal Security Directorate: "Serrano, an unscrupulous man, is actively engaged in various illegal enterprises, such as narcotics traffic. He is considered astute, intelligent, and personable, although his methods violate every principle of established government administration."[23]
- Insider trading took place. Just before a devaluation, those in the know would change their pesos to dollars. They bought land at low prices when they knew government-financed irrigation projects would make it valuable. Alemán purchased extensive tracts in Acapulco at low prices and then saw his property soar in value as the government built a new airport, an oceanfront boulevard, and a highway connecting Acapulco with Mexico City.[24]

Historian Daniel Cosío Villegas observed, "It has been the dishonesty of the revolutionary governments, more than anything else, which has cut off the life of the Mexican Revolution . . ."[25]

Alemán furthered rapid industrialization and increased agricultural production by promoting an alliance between the state and foreign and domestic capital. If he felt the left or independent trade unions stood in the way of achieving these goals, they would be violently suppressed. As writer Octavio Paz noted, this emphasis on development was not irrational since one of the contradictions of revolutions in underdeveloped countries is that they have no base to finance reform. For this reason, Paz believed development was tied to, not antithetical to, social reform. Industrialists and most of the rising middle class felt authoritarianism and increasing social inequality were an acceptable price to pay for achieving these goals.[26]

In October 1951, it was announced that the PRI presidential candidate would be Adolfo Ruiz Cortines, Alemán's colorless interior secretary. As governor of Veracruz, Ruiz Cortines had administered his state efficiently and eliminated widespread graft and waste. Since he exuded honesty and austerity, he was an ideal candidate to offset Alemán's corruption and profligate spending.[27]

Ruiz Cortines faced an electoral challenge by General Miguel Henríquez Guzmán, a wealthy contractor with impeccable establishment credentials. Henríquez Guzmán had been a close associate of Cárdenas while serving as an army officer. After unsuccessfully seeking the 1952 PRI presidential nomination, he left the party to challenge the official candidate. Henríquez Guzmán drew a substantial following including Cardenistas excluded from the Alemán coalition, military men who resented being replaced by younger civilians, members of the middle class wanting multi-party democracy, and peasants resenting government aid going to landowners with political ties rather than to poor farmers. Most of Henríquez Guzmán's support was concentrated in urban areas—a harbinger of the long-term decline in the PRI's urban strength.[28]

Henríquez Guzmán directly criticized the lack of social justice. He noted that rising living costs had hurt the majority, that government agricultural policy had left peasants in misery, and that there was no democracy. He also criticized government control over organized labor and Mexico's increasing dependence on the United States.[29]

Henríquez Guzmán supporters called for a victory rally in the Alameda, a park in downtown Mexico City. The day after the election, thousands gathered there to celebrate the "victory," even though official election returns had not yet been released. Police and army troops attacked the crowd of Henríquez Guzmán supporters, leaving dozens dead and wounded and as many as 500 arrested. The message was clear—the government was unwilling to tolerate independent political activity.[30]

Official election returns attributed 74 percent of the vote to Ruiz Cortines and 16 percent to Henríquez Guzmán. The challenger's poor showing was not surprising, since his party, the Federation of Parties of the People, had been created specifically to back his candidacy. He lacked a political machine comparable to the PRI's, the means to prevent the rampant vote fraud that occurred, and an endorsement by the one Mexican who might have propelled him into the presidency—Lázaro Cárdenas. In 1978, historian Olga Pellicer de Brody commented on the legacy of Henríquez Guzmán's candidacy: "Since then, members of the political bureaucracy have accepted that the only way to reach the peak of power is to submit to decisions of the incumbent president."[31]

ADOLFO RUIZ CORTINES, 1952–1958

By the time Ruiz Cortines took office, the task of the president had become maintaining the political system, not innovating. As with other incoming presidents, Ruiz Cortines was presented to the Mexican people as the solution to his predecessor's excesses. The fact that the new president belonged to the same party as the incumbent and was chosen by him was not stressed. Rather, he was assumed to be capable of remedying the problems his predecessor was unable to solve or had in fact created.[32]

To a large extent, Ruiz Cortines's policies were a response to the increasing unpopularity of the ruling elite. His most dramatic move was a vigorous attack on corruption. The *New York Times* noted that Ruiz Cortines's biggest asset was that he could be believed when he said, "I was poor as a boy and I still am; I have always lived on my salary." In an effort to limit illicit gain, legislation passed during Ruiz Cortines's term required government officials to register their assets upon taking office and again when leaving office. Despite this law and the dismissal of corrupt police officials, by 1954 widespread reports of official corruption were once again being heard. After the Ruiz Cortines administration, anti-corruption declarations became standard fare for newly inaugurated presidents, who often left the presidency as millionaires, despite their having spent their entire adult life in government service.[33]

Ruiz Cortines had more success achieving his second goal, limiting government spending. He inherited several of Alemán's spectacular semi-finished projects, such as a new campus for the National University and the Papaloapan River Basin Project, which resembled the U.S. Tennessee

Valley Authority. He limited new projects until old ones could be finished, thus keeping the budget within reasonable limits.

After 1955, there was a shift in public policy. Along with economic development and retaining power, a major goal of PRI administrations was stability and social peace. In the face of rising criticism and social unrest, social spending rose from 13.3 percent of the federal budget under Alemán to 14.4 percent under Ruiz Cortines. During Ruiz Cortines's term, the government expanded the social security program and constructed rural clinics and hospitals. To combat inflation, price controls were placed on basic necessities. After 1955, the government ensured that the buying power of organized labor would increase. This met little opposition, since the Mexican economy was growing rapidly at the time.[34]

On November 4, 1957, the Secretary General of the National Peasant Confederation (CNC) announced that Labor Secretary Adolfo López Mateos would be the PRI presidential candidate, since "the absolute majority of *ejido* committees, agrarian executive committees, regional committees, leagues of agrarian committees, and other agricultural groups have chosen him." No one was impolitic enough to inquire just when representatives of these groups had made such a momentous decision.[35]

Presumably López Mateos's negotiating skills led to his selection. While serving in Ruiz Cortines's cabinet, López Mateos faced the threat of 5,000 strikes by workers seeking wage increases to offset their inflation-induced loss of buying power. He negotiated settlements limiting wage increases to 16 percent, well below what workers were asking, thus avoiding a surge of inflation and an economically damaging wave of strikes.[36]

On November 15 and 16, 1957, there was a PRI convention to ratify the president's choice and make López Mateos the official PRI candidate. In eighteen minutes, the nearly 5,000 delegates meeting in the Cine Colonial in Mexico City voted unanimously for López Mateos. The result was such a foregone conclusion that banners extolling López Mateos had been hung even before the meeting began.[37]

Then, as happened every six years, a massive government-financed public relations campaign began to sell the candidate to the public. As an American observer noted, "Half the stone walls are painted with giant signs of public support; all the mass media are alive with eulogies." Before television came to dominate the political scene, so many walls were painted to promote PRI candidates that it was said that U.S. paint manufacturer Sherwin Williams was the main beneficiary of Mexican elections.[38]

The 1958 election proceeded smoothly. Henríquez Guzmán's potentially divisive Federation of Parties of the People had been ruled off the ballot. In 1954, to ensure that no challenger to the president's designated successor would emerge, new legislation increased the number of members required to form a political party to 75,000, which had to include at least 2,500 members per state in two-thirds of the states.[39]

Between 1958 and 1994, there was relatively little change in PRI candidate selection. Presidential aspirants were expected to give the public appearance of meekly awaiting the president's designation of his successor. The president would decide who would be the PRI candidate, a choice known as the *dedazo* (finger pointing). A trusted functionary then revealed the choice—an announcement known as the *destape* (the unveiling). Once this occurred, the PRI establishment would jump on the bandwagon. Even bitter rivals of the nominee, the *destapado* (the unveiled), were expected to swallow their pride and affirm that the president's choice was the best man for the job. To do otherwise would be to fall out of favor and lose the chance for a desirable position during the next presidential term.

The PRI continued to maintain that the choice of its candidates at all levels reflected the popular will. Braulio Maldonado, who served as governor of the newly created state of Baja California, was one of the first to break the taboo and openly declare that in fact the president, not the citizenry, chose PRI candidates. He stated: "I was designated by the President of the Republic, who at that time was my distinguished friend, don Adolfo Ruiz Cortines. In our country, all the officials, high and low, have been designated that way since 1928."[40]

Mexicans, rather than selecting the PRI's next candidate, engaged in a spirited game of guessing who would be the president's choice. They looked to signs, observing who was seen talking to whom, much as Kremlin watchers of the Cold War era attempted to divine Soviet policy.

ADOLFO LÓPEZ MATEOS, 1958–1964

More than any other president before him, López Mateos brought Mexico onto the international stage. During his term, Mexico received visits from eighteen heads of state, including Dwight Eisenhower, John F. Kennedy, Charles de Gaulle, Jawaharial Nehru, and Marshal Tito. López Mateos's travels took him to sixteen nations in Asia, Europe, and the western hemisphere. These trips provided him with the opportunity to proclaim Mexico's non-alignment in the Cold War and his country's adherence to the policies of self-determination and non-intervention. In addition to generating favorable press coverage, such travels attempted to dilute U.S. influence over Mexico. Mexico's president traveled so widely that he was nicknamed "*López paseos*" ("López's promenades").[41]

López Mateos instituted reforms, but always on his own terms. Between 1958 and 1964, social security coverage (which included health care) increased from 7.7 percent of the population to 15.9 percent. After a rail strike was crushed, the government increased wages, not only for rail workers but also for teachers, electrical workers, and oil workers. Social spending under López Mateos increased to 19.2 percent of the federal budget.[42]

The reform measures chosen by López Mateos reflected a major change in Mexico. For the first time, the 1960 census indicated that a majority of Mexicans lived in urban areas. After 1960, the promise of land reform would mean little to the majority.

López Mateos's designated successor was his Interior Secretary Gustavo Díaz Ordaz, who had the reputation of being an anti-Communist hard-liner. His candidacy received support from the Church and former President Alemán, the leader of the conservative faction in government.[43]

López Mateos left office a popular man. He was the last president to do so for decades. Economic growth and government benefits provided during his term created optimism for the future. His public support for Cuba was well received, since it was viewed as a sign of his standing up to the United States.

GUSTAVO DÍAZ ORDAZ AND THE 1968 STUDENT MOVEMENT

Díaz Ordaz brought considerable experience to his position, having served as a judge, law professor, vice-rector of the University of Puebla, deputy, senator, and interior secretary. A 1964 CIA report observed, "Diaz Ordaz most nearly represents the PRI's middle-class managerial and technical groups."[44]

When Díaz Ordaz took office in 1964, few anticipated significant social strife during his term. In a book published the year before he became president, U.S. historian Howard F. Cline noted, "The PRI is now so secure that it can afford to relax and does not need many of the repressive measures it earlier took in dealing with the opposition."[45]

The chain of events for which Díaz Ordaz will always be remembered began in the summer of 1968. On July 23, there was a street fight between students from two high schools in Mexico City. Police broke up the fighting and chased the students into a school building, clubbing everyone in sight, including students and teachers who had nothing to do with the fighting. This produced a typical response—a march three days later to protest police brutality. Police, rather than ignoring the protestors, again waded in with clubs.

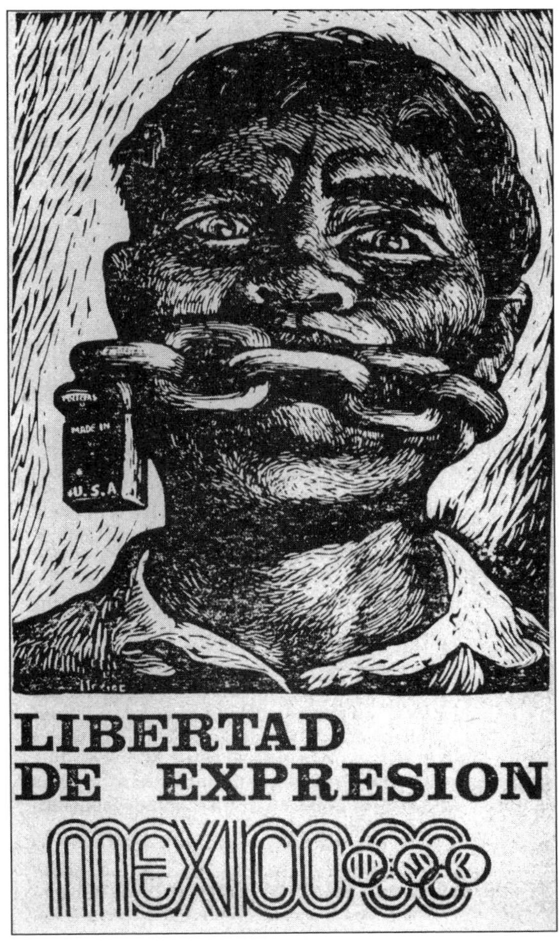

Figure 21.1
Poster from 1968 student movement
Source: Russell (1977: 133)

Before the day was over, students seized several city busses and occupied some high schools in protest. On July 30, police forcibly removed protestors from four high schools affiliated with the National University and one affiliated with the National Polytechnic Institute. At Preparatory School Number One, a bazooka was used to blow down the school's 200-year-old wooden doors. On that day, 400 were injured and more than 1,000 were arrested. This repression resulted in still more protest.[46]

The National University, the National Polytechnic Institute, and their affiliated high schools went out on strike. On August 5, strikers issued six demands that reflected a belief that somehow, somewhere, democracy and social justice were still a part of the Revolution. Their demands were: 1) freedom for political prisoners; 2) the disbanding of the *granaderos*, Mexico City's despised police riot squad; 3) the dismissal of Mexico City's police chief; 4) the repeal of the statute making "social dissolution" a crime; 5) compensation for those wounded and for the families of those who had been killed by the police; and 6) the arrest and trial of public officials guilty of abuse.

On August 1, Javier Barros Sierra, the rector of the National University, led a 100,000-person demonstration that protested the occupation of the University-affiliated schools as a violation of university autonomy. A second demonstration on August 13 saw 150,000 march and chant insults to the press, the police, and the president. At a third demonstration on August 27, there were 200,000, including many non-students.

The vast majority of the activists were political neophytes with no ties to any political organization. They were largely sons and daughters of the middle class that had arisen in the previous decades. Operating through a National Strike Council (CNH), the movement functioned in each school or university faculty. As historian Enrique Krauze noted, "In total contrast to the usual methods of the PRI, everything was discussed between equals within the Movement, and everything was subject to a vote."[47]

On September 13, 100,000 marched in complete silence to demonstrate that the movement was disciplined. To counter charges that they were unwitting stooges of international communism, the marchers left behind their Che Guevara posters and carried images of Hidalgo, Morelos, Zapata, Juárez, and Villa.[48]

Rather than making concessions to end the movement, the government continued to respond with force. Houses were searched without warrants, phones were tapped, and students were arrested without charge. Police smashed store windows during demonstrations to make the movement look irresponsible.[49]

On September 18, in a flagrant violation of its autonomy, 10,000 troops occupied the National University campus to prevent it from being used as the movement headquarters. On September 23, in a pitched battle, government forces occupied the National Polytechnic Institute, which had been fortified by dozens of hijacked city busses and felled telephone posts. By then, the movement had changed. It was no longer idealistic students questioning authority, but Molotov cocktails versus army tanks. In that confrontation, several were killed by police.[50]

By September 25, between ten and twenty students had been killed. Not surprisingly, the repression and the government's refusal to negotiate changed the strikers' views. They began to question the basic values of a system they had implicitly believed in only shortly before. For the first time in living memory, direct criticism was launched at an incumbent president, who was mercilessly caricatured. At the same time, students began to fan out into working-class neighborhoods, distributing leaflets, giving quick speeches, and fleeing before the police arrived. As the students' radicalism increased, they added political rights, economic justice, and lessened dependency on the United States to the original six demands. The military's continued occupation of university facilities aroused further outrage.[51]

Artists, writers, and intellectuals often met with the students and lent support. Not surprisingly, though, most of the establishment turned its back on the students. Official labor and peasant leaders as well as opposition political parties denounced the movement.[52]

A march scheduled for October 2 had been prohibited by the government, so strikers decided to hold a rally near the center of Mexico City "to avoid violence." As 5,000 to 10,000 were peacefully listening to speakers in the Plaza of Three Cultures at the Tlatelolco housing project, 5,000 soldiers surrounded them. Then heavy gunfire broke out. As people tried to flee, they were cut down by bullets.

Estimates of the number killed at Tlatelolco run into the hundreds. Bodies were burned to avoid a politically embarrassing string of funerals just before the Olympics. Military Camp Number One, the main military base in Mexico City, became a virtual prison as hundreds of student activists were detained there. Ironically the 1968 Olympics—the first held in the underdeveloped world—were to have shown the great progress Mexico had made. The desire to establish peace before the opening of the Olympics, even if it were the peace of Porfirio Díaz, partially explains the brutal actions at Tlatelolco.[53]

In the aftermath of the massacre, the military claimed to have fired their weapons in response to incoming sniper fire. The military assumed the students were the only possible source of the incoming bullets. Student activists and the public in general assumed that the "sniper fire" was a lame excuse to shift blame from the military to students. However, documents drawn up by then-Secretary of Defense Marcelino García Barragán and only made public after his death paint a very different picture.

The documents indicate that during the rally marksmen from the presidential guards stationed in adjacent apartment buildings fired on regular army troops monitoring the rally. This caused the regular army troops to fire on the students in what they considered to be self-defense, thus creating plausible deniability for military authorities while smashing the student movement. Forces from the Interior Ministry, the military, and the presidential guards were present. In theory, the chain of command for all three forces led back to the president. It remains unclear if Díaz Ordaz knew in advance of the positioning of the presidential guards to fire on the regular army or if rogue elements orchestrated the operation. Declassified U.S. Defense Department documents state that the firing by the marksmen resulted from military insubordination, with officers ordering the shooting without the knowledge or consent of the president or the secretary of defense.[54]

The attack at Tlatelolco marked the end of the student movement. According to a then-secret government security report, by the afternoon of October 3, 1,043 had been arrested. Arrests of activists continued for weeks. Students who only weeks before had believed in a democratic Mexico had no response.[55]

The 1968 student movement reflected the government's inability to respond to the needs of the middle class. Protests also reflected dissatisfaction with Mexico's skewed distribution of wealth, at a time millions were being spent on the Olympics. University budgets were declining as enrollments were burgeoning. By 1967, spending per university student had fallen to the 1959 level.[56]

In his state of the nation address following Tlatelolco, Díaz Ordaz thanked workers and peasants "who would not listen to sedition." He also commented that the student movement had operated "without ideology or program, using disorder, violence, rancor, frightening symbols, and an alarming spontaneity. It tried to overthrow our society . . ." He also stated, "I fully assume personal, ethical, social, juridical, political, and historical responsibility for the decisions taken by the government in relation to last year's events."[57]

Octavio Paz commented on the impact of the Tlatelolco massacre:

> At the very moment in which the Mexican government was receiving international recognition for forty years of political stability and economic progress, a swash of blood dispelled the official optimism and caused every citizen to doubt the meaning of that progress.[58]

While the students' demands remained unmet, many participants in the movement later played leading roles in urban, peasant, and trade union movements that contributed to eventual democratic change.[59]

The economy grew at an annual rate of more than 6 percent during Díaz Ordaz's term. This insulated the president from much of the criticism by students. In addition, government social spending increased under Díaz Ordaz, as it had during the previous two administrations. Social welfare spending and economic growth continued to be portrayed as the fruits of the more just, nationalistic order ushered in by the 1910–1917 Revolution.[60]

THE MILITARY

> I belong to the army, and I love it very much. But for Mexico, the era of the generals is over now. I am sure that the civilians will successfully do their duty.
>
> President Ávila Camacho, 1946[61]

By the end of 1940, the danger of the military staging a coup in support of Almazán had passed. As a result, during his first week in office, Ávila Camacho disbanded the military sector within the official party. Military men were allowed to continue in politics, but had to do so as members of the popular sector. Most military men accepted this willingly, since they had never been sure exactly what their role within the party had been. At the same time, Ávila Camacho ordered the retirement of 550 generals and 550 colonels, most of the revolutionary commanders still on active duty, thus wresting additional political influence from the army.[62]

During the Second World War, the main role assigned to the Mexican military was to contain a Japanese invasion until U.S. troops could arrive. In 1940, Cárdenas decided the Mexican military should defend its own territory without the United States establishing bases on Mexican soil. Ávila Camacho maintained this policy through the end of the war.

Given its new role, the Mexican army's state of readiness became a matter of national concern to the United States. To increase Mexican military capabilities, the United States provided Mexico with arms, including coastal artillery and 305 aircraft, and sent officers to teach in Mexican military schools. Select military officers came to the United States for advanced training.[63]

Squadron 201 of the Mexican air force did see combat in the Pacific theater. This unit, which flew P-47 Thunderbolts, trained in the United States, flew fifty-nine combat mission in Luzon and Formosa (Taiwan), and won General Douglas MacArthur's thanks. After the war, the unit, which suffered five casualties, returned to a hero's welcome in Mexico.[64]

The ties established between the Mexican military and the U.S. military during the Second World War remained after the war. These ties were, however, quite weak compared with the ties between the United States and other Latin American militaries. Between 1950 and 1972, 427 Mexican military men, 1.7 percent of the Latin American total, trained in the United States. Between 1946 and 1971, U.S. military aid to Mexico totaled $17.6 million, less than 1 percent of the Latin American total.[65]

As the economic and social role of the Mexican government increased, the percentage of the budget devoted to the military declined. Under Ávila Camacho (1940–1946) military spending accounted for 18.85 percent of the federal budget. By the time of Díaz Ordaz's term (1964–1970), it had declined to 2.63 percent.[66]

Between 1940 and 1970, the Mexican military steadily expanded, from 50,000 to 67,100 troops. However, this expansion was slower than population growth. As a result, the ratio of soldiers per Mexican shifted from 1 to 393 in 1940 to 1 to 718 in 1970. Mexico spent less for the military as a percent of gross domestic product (GDP) and had a lower percentage of its population under arms than any other major Latin American nation.[67]

After the Second World War, the number of military officers holding important civilian positions declined. Beginning in 1946, each president was a civilian. Military men regularly headed the PRI until 1964, when civilian Carlos Madrazo assumed that position. In 1940, fifteen governors were military men, while between 1964 and 1985 only one was. Similarly, with the exceptions of the secretaries of defense and navy, civilians held all cabinet positions. By 1970, the control of politics had definitively shifted to civilians.[68]

THE OPPOSITION

Political scientist Álvaro Arreola Ayala commented on how, just as in the times of Porfirio Díaz, the political elite placed great importance on staging elections:

> One of the distinguishing characteristics of the post-revolutionary Mexican state has been an obsessive desire to exhibit, both domestically and abroad, a formal political structure which is similar to or at least comparable to those of the western capitalist democracies.[69]

Through 1970, the opposition parties served more as pressure groups than as real alternatives to the official party. PRI presidential candidates won by overwhelming majorities—90.5 percent in 1958, 89.0 percent in 1964, and 85.8 percent in 1970. PRI candidates for lower offices usually won by similar margins.[70]

Since it was clear that elections did not lead to a change in government, the opposition parties constantly faced the question of what their role was. Many felt the primary purpose of the opposition parties was legitimizing the PRI. The raison d'être of the opposition political parties was further clouded by some of them regularly backing the presidential candidates of the PRI.[71]

A variety of motives prompted the recognized opposition parties to continue to present candidates. Election campaigns allowed opposition parties to enunciate their views and lobby for concessions. A few opposition victories at the mayoral and congressional level whetted the political appetites of would-be challengers to the PRI. Finally, even if the opposition parties could do little for the average Mexican, they did benefit party officials and the handful of opposition party candidates who held office. This select group received recognition, contracts, loans, services, and political training for a more auspicious political future. Sociologist Pablo González Casanova observed that the masses "learn that the opposition parties solve the problems of opposition politicians, not those of the masses."[72]

In 1963, the government enacted a political reform in order to enhance the image of democracy, decrease domestic dissidence, and undercut sympathy for the Cuban Revolution, which caused the political elite to run scared throughout Latin America. The reform legislation provided that any opposition party receiving 2.5 percent of the vote nationwide would automatically be awarded five seats in the Chamber of Deputies, regardless of whether its candidates had won a plurality in any single congressional district. (There are no run-off elections in Mexico, so all that is needed for victory is a plurality.) For each additional half percentage point of the vote nationwide, the party would receive another seat, up to a maximum of twenty. This law was clearly not designed to undermine PRI power. Even if the four recognized opposition parties received the maximum of twenty seats, the PRI would continue to control the Chamber of Deputies. The law denied proportional representation to any party winning more than twenty single-member congressional districts.[73]

The 1963 political reform did produce change. The number of opposition deputies in the Chamber of Deputies increased from six after the 1961 election to thirty-five after the 1964 election. A wider variety of views—left and right—were expressed in the Chamber and, to the extent that they were covered in the press, these views were made available to the public. However, the reform did not entice voters back to the polls. In the first mid-term elections after the reform, voter participation declined by five percentage points compared to the previous mid-term elections. Through the late 1960s, two recognized opposition parties even failed to receive the 2.5 percent of the vote necessary to receive deputies. The government, wishing to enhance the image of democracy, granted them some deputies anyway, claiming that was in the "spirit" of the law.[74]

The 1963 political reform did breathe a little life into the Chamber of Deputies, but had no impact whatsoever on the rest of the electoral process. Thus for example, between 1946 and 1970, more than 27,000 municipal elections occurred. Of these, the opposition, left and right, only won forty.[75]

The Political Left

> The Mexican security services are so effective in stamping out the extreme left that we don't have to worry. If the government were less effective we would, of course, get going to promote repression.
>
> Former CIA agent Philip Agee, 1975[76]

Mexico's very small Communist Party, which had worked closely with the Cárdenas administration, continued to support the official party until 1949. A number of factors prevented it from playing a major role before or after that date. It often was perceived as serving the interests not of Mexico but of Moscow. It expelled many of its members for perceived ideological transgressions. As Mexico found itself caught up in the Cold War, communists were purged from government, Congress, and labor unions. The party could not even decide whether the United States or Mexican business was the main enemy.

Though hamstrung by repression, purges, and ideological splits, the party did play a significant role in some of the social movements of the day. Many of the leaders of a bitter 1959 rail workers strike were party members. In the early 1960s, the party lent support to agricultural wage laborers and peasants soliciting land. In the late 1960s, the party developed a strong presence among university workers, professors, and students. The party supported the 1968 student movement, an action that resulted in dozens of communists being jailed.[77]

The CIA estimated that the party's membership had declined to 15,000 in 1951 and to 5,000 in 1964. By that time, as the CIA noted, the party was weakened by "internal dissension, poor leadership, and inadequate resources." The remaining party members did become more independent of the Soviet Union, and, in 1968, the party denounced the Soviet invasion of Czechoslovakia.[78]

The enormous flexibility of what was called the ideology of the Mexican Revolution made it very difficult for the left to present programs that were perceived by their potential followers—peasants and workers—as something strikingly different from what the progressive wing of incumbent administrations espoused. Much of the economy was already under state control. Incumbents would frequently advocate land reform, labor rights, and the struggle against imperialism. Since incumbents had the power to implement the changes they spoke of, their positions appeared more credible than those of the left. In addition, the PRI and the government so predictably hired talented Communist Party members that PRI functionary Guillermo Martínez Domínguez declared the party to be the training school for PRI staffers.[79]

The Political Right

In 1940, the PAN was hardly more than a will-o'-the-wisp. Given the ephemeral existence of many parties formed at election time, mere survival presented the PAN with a serious challenge. In addition, the PAN had to face numerous unfavorable (for the party) trends. As the government became increasingly pro-business, entrepreneurs abandoned the PAN. Similarly, as government anti-clericalism declined, fewer were drawn to the PAN for religious reasons. The PRI's CNOP attracted middle-class support from the PAN, as did the government's hiring of many university graduates. The PAN had to live down its initial enthusiasm for Spanish dictator Francisco Franco and its initial lack of support for the Second World War.[80]

When Ávila Camacho was inaugurated, no PAN members held public office and elections were three years away. Between 1940 and 1943, the PAN, which relied on its poorly funded volunteer base, built its organization, presented conferences around the nation, and organized local groups. The party saw its goal as long-term education, not the immediate assumption of power through electoral victory.[81]

The initial issues upon which the PAN had recruited—government anti-clericalism and what was perceived as government opposition to capitalism—were largely preempted by the conservative shift under Presidents Ávila Camacho and Alemán. This forced the PAN to find issues that would resonate with the public. In 1943, the PAN called for allowing outdoor worship services, eliminating socialist education, and a vastly decreased government role in the economy. After 1946, the party made municipal independence from central control a major issue. In 1949, the PAN issued a call for the enfranchisement of women at the federal level. The party became a moral crusade, attacking the legitimacy of the ruling group, which it branded as undemocratic and corrupt.[82]

As businessmen left the party, drawn by the government's pro-business stance, Catholic influence inside the party increased. This Catholicism gave the party backbone in a hostile environment. In fact, the party embraced the Church with much more fervor than the Church embraced the PAN. The Church was reestablishing a modus vivendi with the government and did not want this to be complicated by its backing an opposition party.[83]

During the 1940s, the meager results produced by participating in elections presented the party with a dilemma—it was far removed from power, yet its participating in elections made the PRI look democratic. Many within the party felt the PAN should abstain from elections to protest election fraud. The PAN in the 1940s had more influence than its small vote totals would indicate, since many of its leaders were or had been prominent intellectuals, capitalists, and politicians.[84]

Historian Daniel Cosío Villegas commented on the poor showing of early PAN candidates:

> As far as Mexicans are concerned, the PAN candidates don't have any sex appeal. None of their leaders are common citizens. They do not come from rural areas or small towns. They are from the upper middle class and their interests and experience are confined to the walls of their offices and the temples of the Church.[85]

By the end of the 1940s, the PAN had emerged as an independent, loyal Mexican political alternative to the Revolution. The PAN closely followed Church social views, since both institutions saw the future of the world as a stark choice between Catholic social justice and communism. Catholic faith replaced a professional degree as the salient characteristic of PAN members, especially after women received the vote in 1953 and increased their role in the party. All the party's presidents through 1972 had their initial political formation in openly Catholic organizations, such as the National Catholic Student Union, and then moved into the PAN. The party's very existence remained in question, as Soledad Loaeza noted in her magisterial history of the party, "For the PAN, the decade of the 1950s was a long crossing of the desert, during which time it was barely able to make its presence felt at election time."[86]

In the early 1960s, various tendencies existed within the PAN. Leftwing Christian Democrats and Social Christians demanded massive redistribution of income and socialization of property. Secular PANistas opposed what they viewed as an overly intrusive government, but did not ground their views in Catholicism. More conservative PANistas were primarily concerned with defending property rights.[87]

In 1963, the conclusions of the Catholic Church council known as Vatican II were published. After these conclusions were released, the PAN abandoned its traditional defense of the status quo and became a champion of human rights, promoted a more active social role for the government, and was influenced by liberation theology. Vatican II served to invigorate party members and recruit newcomers. In 1969, the party advocated a third path of development between capitalism and socialism, called "*solidarismo*," which has been described as "political humanism." The PAN's reformist orientation was evident in a 1970 speech by its presidential candidate, Efraín González Morfín:

> If workers organizations are subject to unjustified political control which seeks to subordinate them to the government and the official party, workers should struggle for true independence—independence from the government, from the official party, and from employers.[88]

By 1970, the PAN had established a significant electoral base. However, the party remained unable to force the PRI to acknowledge its electoral victories. It was widely believed to have won the mayoralties of Tijuana and Mexicali in 1968 and the 1969 gubernatorial election in Yucatán. After the 1958 elections, the government declared six PAN candidates had won seats in the Chamber of Deputies. The PAN felt that this number was well below the number of deputy candidates who would have won had the election been honest. As a form of protest, the party instructed the six declared winners not to take their seats. Two of the six obeyed, the remaining four took their seats and were expelled from the party. The PRI responded not by cleaning up elections but by passing legislation that declared it a criminal offense to be elected to a public post and then not occupy it. The law also mandated canceling the registration of any political party condoning such an act.[89]

Despite its repeatedly charging vote fraud, the PAN kept fielding candidates. In 1963 and 1966, PAN mayoral victories were recognized in San Pedro Garza García, an affluent suburb of Monterrey. As these victories reflect, after 1958 the PAN picked up increased strength in northern Mexico. Vote totals credited to PAN presidential candidates increased steadily from 7.8 percent in 1952 to 14.0 percent in 1970. PAN members soldiered on, viewing their central mission not as obtaining power via elections but as inserting morality into politics, educating the people, and inculcating them with a set of principles that would guide their political actions.[90]

From the outside, such goals appeared to be illusory. The PAN suffered constant financial problems since even though some businessmen sympathized with the party, they did not want to be publicly associated with it for fear of losing government contracts vital to their survival. After the 1970 elections, historian Daniel Cosío Villegas wrote, "Since the PAN is not gaining strength, it is hard to believe that in the foreseeable future the party will be able to serve as a restraining wall for the overwhelming power of the government and its party."[91]

THE "PERFECT DICTATORSHIP"

Mexico stands out as a paragon of political stability within contemporary Latin America.
Peter Smith, 1990[92]

After the collapse of the Soviet Union, the PRI became the world's longest-running political act. Since 1934, all its presidents had come and gone every six years as scheduled. In 1991, Peruvian novelist Mario Vargas Llosa visited Mexico and observed that Mexico was a "perfect dictatorship." He noted that the PRI political machine had overcome the fatal flaw of Porfirio Díaz's earlier political machine—the lack of a succession mechanism. By choosing a new president every six years, in theory the PRI machine could last forever.[93]

One of the keys to Mexican political stability was rigid adherence to the "no reelection" rule for the president. The forced retirement of the president every six years kept the politically ambitious in check by providing them with a chance at power six years later. They remained in the PRI since that party was correctly perceived as the only route to high public office. The regular changing of administrations provided a chance for the talented to move up to higher positions in the public sector and for the incompetent to be winnowed out.[94]

Another key to Mexico's long-term political stability was the concentration of power in the president. The Mexican president exercised the powers normally associated with the president of a constitutional democracy, such as being commander-in-chief of the armed forces. In addition, he exercised a wide variety of other powers, referred to as "metaconstitutional" powers. Given the lack of checks and balances, no person, group, or institution could challenge the president when he exercised these powers. In addition to choosing his successor, an outstanding metaconstitutional power was the president's control of the ruling political party, the PRI. Exercising his metaconstitutional power, the president would name the president of the PRI. This enabled him to make crucial decisions on PRI nominees for senators, federal deputies, governors, and sometimes mayors.[95]

Political scientist Lorenzo Meyer described Mexico's Congress as "an assembly of unconditional supporters of the executive who approved almost everything the president sent it and never questioned him effectively nor called to account those responsible for political actions." As late as 1974, Congress had yet to reject a federal legislative initiative. Most legislation was submitted to Congress by the president and passed by acclamation.[96]

The key to presidential dominance over Congress was the legal prohibition against the immediate reelection of congresspersons. This meant that congressional representatives had to look to the president for their next position in the public sector. Having served one's constituency admirably had nothing to do with a congressperson's ability to continue in public service.

Rather than being selected to formulate policy, congresspersons were selected as a reward for faithful service or as a possible first step up the political ladder for a talented neophyte. The allocation of seats in the Chamber of Deputies maintained the loyalty of PRI sector leaders. In 1970, forty-one deputies came from the peasant sector, seventy-two from the popular sector, and twenty-two from the labor sector.[97]

Since Mexico lacked a tradition of an independent judiciary, presidentially appointed judges, who were approved by the presidentially controlled Congress, lacked independence. Legislation passed in 1949 prevented the Supreme Court from hearing disputes involving elections. This prevented aggrieved candidates from raising legal challenges to electoral fraud, as had happened earlier in the 1940s.[98]

Another factor contributing to the durability of the "perfect dictatorship" was sustained economic growth. Between 1950 and 1970, Mexico's per capita GDP increased at an average annual rate of 3.35 percent—well above the Latin American average of 2.40 percent.[99]

While the fruits of this growth were inequitably distributed, economic development between 1940 and 1970 did result in increased income for a substantial majority of Mexicans. As a result the PRI enjoyed genuine support. Journalist Alma Guillermoprieto commented:

> For all its inefficiencies and other faults, the patrimonial system worked well enough to pull a largely rural and illiterate population into the twentieth century, insuring levels of education, health care, public services, and social mobility which comparable societies (Peru, Brazil, and Colombia, say) never achieved.[100]

Even though the PRI was not involved in choosing its own presidential candidates, it performed a number of functions that maintained the system. Its sectors gave average citizens, such as street vendors, factory workers, or *ejidatarios*, at least the perception that there was an official channel that would respond to their complaints. The PRI also recruited political cadres, controlled mass organizations, carried out social and welfare roles, and organized elections to legitimate the regime. The party was so effective at organizing elections that, through 1970, it never lost a presidential, gubernatorial, or senatorial election. A 1964 CIA report observed: "The party-government complex has become so large and intricate in the attempt to be all things to Mexicans of all political views, that its orientation defies conventional definition."[101]

The PRI could tap government personnel, resources, and finances on an overwhelming scale unavailable to other parties. In the absence of open accounting, office size can serve as a proxy for budget size. The floor space of the headquarters of the popular sector of the PRI exceeded the combined floor space of the national headquarters of all the opposition parties. The popular sector headquarters in turn paled in comparison with the PRI national headquarters in Mexico City, which resembled a small college campus.[102]

The PRI worked closely with the government to keep the peace and stage elections. The PRI enjoyed a multiplicity of resources to ensure its candidates won. If one tactic failed or seemed imprudent, it had many alternatives.

In shantytowns, PRI municipal governments provided clinics, schools, lighting, water, land titles, and street paving on a discretional basis. Residents were expected to show support for PRI candidates and attend rallies in an implicit quid pro quo for obtaining these services. To petition for any of these services, one had to be a member of a recognized residents *(colonos)* association. Such associations became a source of political control since they were automatically incorporated

Figure 21.2 *PRI-organized rally of its peasant sector, with Mexico City cathedral in background*
Source: Reproduced courtesy of Archivo General de la Nación

into the PRI. Residents would work through the officially sanctioned associations, since the government was the only source of land titles and needed services. However, just in case they decided to bypass official channels, the law providing the framework for residents associations stipulated that any unrecognized neighborhood group would be "immediately dissolved."[103]

Co-opting members of opposition parties and movements served to maintain PRI control. This was an effective tactic since collaboration with the PRI was one of the few avenues of social and economic mobility open to many Mexicans, especially those in the lower classes. Co-opted leaders would sell out their constituencies for cash or a cushy job. The co-opted leaders claimed, or may even have believed, that their constituencies would be better served if they worked within the system. Many veterans of the 1968 student movement soon became upwardly mobile by working in technocratic government posts. Co-optation became so predictable that one of the best ways for a college student to assure himself an attractive job offer after graduation was to build a reputation as a militant leftist student leader. Many of the choicest plums in the state and party hierarchy were reserved for the most articulate, charismatic, and, hence, politically dangerous leftist students.[104]

Once important decisions had been made and personnel selected to fill public offices, elections were staged with great fanfare. Millions would be spent to hold campaign rallies, often using rented trucks and busses to haul in people to create the appearance of widespread support for the PRI. A single 1961 PRI rally in San Luis Potosí cost $74,520 to stage. The largest single cost was $2 paid to each of the 15,000 attendees. In 1970, a peasant at a PRI rally told political scientist Judith Hellman:

> I go to the demonstrations and shout "vivas" along with everyone else, because they give you five, sometimes ten pesos and a meal. Besides, if you refuse to go when the truck comes to the *ejido* to pick you up, you only make enemies in the CNC and trouble for yourself.[105]

The official party carried out a wide range of activities that could be termed "dirty tricks." These ranged from the benign to the lethal. At a 1946 opposition rally in Mexico City, PRI sympathizers passed out free movie tickets to lure attendees away, if in fact they arrived at all, since public transportation had been halted to lower attendance. In Zacatecas, the PRI used loudspeakers to drown out PAN speakers at a rally staged to support its 1958 presidential candidate, Luis H. Álvarez. In 1951, in Tlacotepec, Puebla, a Henríquez Guzmán campaign convoy was not only denied passage through town but also fired on, leaving five dead.[106]

If the outcome of an election was in the slightest doubt, the PRI had a multi-layered defense to guarantee victory. Through its control of election machinery, polling places could be established far from areas known to favor the opposition or such polling places could be given insufficient ballots or opened late and closed early. After the polls opened, the PRI had several colorfully named methods of enhancing its vote count. A "taco" was simply a wad of ballots already marked for the PRI that a single voter would deposit in the ballot box. A "pregnant ballot box" was one filled with ballots marked for the PRI before the voting started. "Flying squads" went from polling place to polling place to repeatedly vote for the PRI. Little ingenuity was needed for such scams, since election judges were under PRI control.[107]

If, due to some oversight, after polls closed the outcome of the election was still in doubt, it was not too late to snatch victory from the jaws of defeat. In Baja California, PAN candidate Salvador Rosas Magallón noted that after polls closed in his 1959 gubernatorial race, soldiers appeared and carried the ballot boxes back to their barracks. A PRI victory was later announced without PAN members having any idea of how the announced vote totals were determined. If all else failed, elections could be annulled, as occurred in 1968 when the PRI-controlled Baja California state legislature annulled municipal elections in Tijuana and Mexicali, where PAN candidates presumably won.[108]

Dissidents could be charged with "social dissolution," the crime that members of the 1968 student movement demanded be removed from the books. The statute defining social dissolution, Article 145 of the penal code, declared:

> Any foreigner or Mexican, who orally, in writing, or by any other medium, spreads political propaganda among foreigners or Mexicans or disseminates ideas, propaganda, or courses of action of any foreign government, which disturb public order or affect the sovereignty of the Mexican state, shall be imprisoned for from two to six years.[109]

One of those charged this offense was muralist David Alfaro Siqueiros. He was imprisoned for paraphrasing President López Mateos's statement that he was administering "on the left within the constitution." Siqueiros described López Mateos's administration as being "on the extreme right and outside the constitution."[110]

If attempts at co-opting regime opponents failed, the result was frequently violence. Small-scale violence was especially common in rural areas as a repressive tool. At least twenty-two members of Henríquez Guzmán's party were murdered during his presidential campaign. The mass repression of the 1968 student movement reflected the government's inability to either co-opt or repress individual leaders, whom the students frequently rotated in their positions to prevent just that.[111]

Those firing on political protestors, those running election-day scams, and those engaged in the massive transfer of wealth from the public sector into the hands of well-connected individuals all relied on one factor—impunity. Since the government, the PRI, the Congress, the president, and the judicial system formed a seamless whole, political control and loyalty to the system could be maintained. Spanish human rights activist Carlos Castresana commented, "It is useless to pretend that democracy can take root in nations, such as Mexico, where there is systematic impunity with respect to the most serious, repeated violations of human rights."[112]

A final key to regime survival was ideological flexibility. As historian Jesús Silva Herzog noted, even the president considered to be the most conservative, Miguel Alemán, would "oscillate to the right or left, according to both international events and to the internal pressure of the most active political parties and social organizations . . ." Examples of major policy shifts include Ávila Camacho's decision to ally with the United States during the Second World War and Alemán's decision to emphasize industrialization. Essayist Jorge Castañeda commented on Mexican presidents, "Conventional wisdom notwithstanding, they have proved remarkably successful at changing just as much as necessary to ensure the system's survival."[113]

MEXICAN SOCIETY

> Rural emigration—which is a continuous flow—has simply transferred poverty and underemployment from the countryside into the cities.
>
> Rodolfo Stavenhagen, 1975[114]

The pervasive social and economic forces unleashed during the 1940s produced more change in Mexico than the earlier revolutionary programs that had social change as their object. Change resulted from the Second World War, population growth, rural-to-urban migration, and decisions made by private investors. Between 1940 and 1970, Mexico's population increased by 145 percent, its urban population increased by 296 percent, and the share of total production contributed by industry rose from 25 to 34 percent.[115]

Gone were the days when revolutionary leaders sought to modify the economic and political structures to improve the lives of poor Mexicans. The growth of industry and commercial agriculture replaced full employment, higher wages, social welfare, and more equitable income distribution as top government priorities.[116]

Rural-to-urban migration in search of jobs and education caused millions to pack their meager belongings and move to the city. The grapevine told of many newly created industrial jobs. The locus of government investment shifted from rural areas to the city. In addition, most of the new jobs in the burgeoning government bureaucracy and in commerce were added in cities. City life appeared especially attractive since urban residents received almost six times the per capita income of rural people.[117]

During the 1940s, 57 percent of urban population growth resulted from rural-to-urban migration. After 1950, the number of births in urban areas exceeded the number who migrated from rural areas. By the 1960s, only 33 percent of urban population increase resulted from migration.[118]

Between 1940 and 1970, the large cities—Mexico City, Monterrey, and Guadalajara—absorbed more than 60 percent of rural-to-urban migration. In 1950, 4.9 million Mexicans held agricultural jobs, while 3.4 million worked in urban jobs. Twenty years later, the number of agricultural jobs had only increased by 0.2 million, while the number of urban jobs had increased by 4.6 million.[119]

During the 1960s, the number of urban workers increased by 2.673 million, but the number of industrial jobs increased by only 600,000. This imbalance between the increase in the urban work force and the number of industrial jobs forced many into commerce and other services, where they were underemployed and impoverished.[120]

Often newly established industries exacerbated employment problems since the number of artisans they displaced exceeded the number of new jobs created in capital-intensive factories. To cite one example, in 1949 there were 290 factories and workshops producing soap. Colgate Palmolive, which had a national distribution system and a nationwide advertising campaign, soon forced all but a handful out of business.[121]

Massive urban migration, natural population increase in cities, and a continuing scarcity of well-paying jobs led to rings of owner-built housing surrounding major population areas, inhabited by those who could not afford other accommodation. Such settlements, often referred to as shantytowns, lack a good English term of reference. In Brazil, they are known as *favelas*, in Peru as *barriadas*, in Chile as *callampas*, and in Mexico as *colonias proletarias*.[122]

Colonias proletarias had several common characteristics. They were almost always established illegally. Depending on the political climate, would-be residents sometimes staged a land invasion, just as peasants did, and occupied vacant land without the owner's permission. Others, to avoid the risk of eviction, preferred to either rent or buy illegally subdivided plots. They were aware that once thousands moved onto the land, there was little likelihood the government would remove them. A second characteristic of such residential areas is that they initially lacked paved streets and services such as water and electricity. Finally, the residents gradually replaced the initial shanties with solidly built one- or two-story concrete-block homes, giving the neighborhood a completely different appearance within fifteen or twenty years of its initial occupation.[123]

Such housing provided those who otherwise could not afford to do so an opportunity to escape either rural poverty or an inner-city landlord. Since most investment was made after moving in, residents did not have to make large initial payments. Given the absence of rent, if an economic crisis resulted in job losses, residents would not be forced out.[124]

After visiting many shantytowns in several Latin American countries, sociologist Alejandro Portes observed:

> Far from being the menacing belt of misery which the upper and middle classes imagine, these peripheral populations could be defined more accurately as a belt of social security. These areas certainly house the newly arrived poor. However they are not the poor at the end of a downward spiral, the most miserable, apathetic, and frustrated who have moved into these areas. Rather, it is the most upwardly mobile who have moved there in search of the minimum of security which their own home represents.[125]

Distribution of Wealth

> Cárdenas' commitment to the social welfare of the less well off has not been shared by most of his successors, who have responded to other concerns and groups.
>
> Roderic Camp, 2003[126]

Since at least the time of Humboldt, it was evident that there was widespread poverty in Mexico. However, it was only at the middle of the twentieth century that sufficient data became available to measure the distribution of income statistically. This data indicates that while income remained highly concentrated, middle-income earners were gradually increasing their share of income at the expense of both of the poorest and wealthiest sectors of society.

The obvious reason for the maldistribution of income is the maldistribution of wealth. In each sector of the economy, ownership was not only highly concentrated but also becoming more concentrated as years passed. The 1965 industrial census indicated that the largest 1.5 percent of industrial firms accounted for 77.2 percent of capital and 75 percent of industrial production.

Table 21.1 *Distribution of family income as a percentage of total income, 1950–1970*

	1950 (%)	1970 (%)
Bottom 30% of families	8.2	7.2
Middle 40% of families	22.9	26.3
Top 30% of families	68.6	66.2

Source: Weintraub (1990: 35, Table 2.3)

Note: Totals do not equal 100% due to rounding

In 1960, the largest 0.6 percent of commercial establishments controlled 47 percent of capital and generated 50 percent of income from sales. In 1960, the top 0.65 percent of producers held 30 percent of the cultivated land, while the bottom 50 percent only cultivated 12 percent.[127]

Inflation, which soared due to the Second World War shortages, continued to ravage wages through the mid-1950s as the government relied on deficit spending to stimulate the economy. By 1952, the value of industrial wages in Mexico City had declined to 60 percent of their 1940 level. After the mid-1950s, as inflation declined, the buying power of industrial wages began to rise again, reaching 108 percent of their 1940 level by 1970. During the Díaz Ordaz administration, the purchasing power of wages increased by 6 percent a year, an increase that kept the working class loyal to the regime.[128]

Increases in productivity per worker were largely captured by business owners, further concentrating income. Between 1940 and 1970, the productivity of industrial workers increased by 200 percent, while the buying power of their wages increased by only 8 percent. [129]

As a result of population growth, the supply of labor in both rural and urban areas exceeded demand, which was an additional factor concentrating income. By the 1960s, 400,000 new workers a year were coming into the labor force—an influx that depressed wages, as most employees signed on not with union contracts but as individuals, leaving them at the mercy of their employers. As capital was replacing labor throughout the economy, employers prospered, some workers earned a steady wage, and millions of others joined the marginal population.[130]

Regardless of whether the income of the poorest was rising or falling, it was clear that many millions of Mexicans, often referred to as the marginal population, were mired in poverty. Political scientist Lorenzo Meyer observed:

> Marginality, that is, the low productivity which results from underemployment, was a phenomenon found both in rural areas and in the city. The enormous slums surrounding the major cities indicate that population growth long ago surpassed the capacity of the urban economy to absorb the available labor, a product of births in the cities and of migration from rural areas to the city.[131]

It was clear that given low educational levels, malnutrition, and the resulting low productivity of marginalized workers, there was no quick fix for these millions of Mexicans. In 1970, sociologist Pablo González Casanova, evoking the Cárdenas administration, suggested, "There must be legislative, political, and economic reforms in order to ensure the integration of the marginal strata into full economic and political citizenship."[132]

The Elite

> The primary fact of life in contemporary Mexico is that although the government has a political monopoly it does not control the economy. Seven banking groups in Mexico are as strong in the economic life of the nation as the PRI is in the political life.
>
> Stephen Niblo, 1975[133]

The Mexican elite that emerged after 1940 contained two groups—one controlling the reins of political power and the other the reins of economic power. As the Mexican economy grew, the political elite increasingly shared power with domestic and foreign business interests. The public-sector elite of necessity maintained dialogue with the private-sector elite since the government was a major economic player. The two groups existed symbiotically—in exchange for relative impunity in business operations, including tax evasion, the business elite supported the PRI. Antonio Ortiz Mena, finance minister from 1958 to 1970, commented: "Our contact with the private sector leaders was constant when I was in government. We would call them, give them our ideas about a policy, wait for their reactions, take them into account, and incorporate them into our final policies."[134]

After 1940, the political elite promoted development policies that clearly reflected the interests of national business and its foreign partners. Policy makers justified their pro-business stance by stating that it: 1) contributed to national development, 2) safeguarded national security, and 3) created the wealth necessary to raise the general standard of living.[135]

After 1940, the business elite grew more powerful, reflecting the increased wealth of its members, who diverted substantial human resources from production to lobbying for government favors, making personal contacts with the political elite, and to maintaining such business organizations as the National Federation of Industrial Chambers (CONCAMIN). Political discourse pointedly ignored the intimate links between the PRI and big business. Government subsidies, trade protection, and other government benefits became the key to success, not lower production costs and higher quality goods.[136]

Membership in a business group increased an individual's political clout, which was key to prospering in Mexico's highly regulated economic atmosphere. Business groups had enough power to prevent the implementation of a progressive tax scheme, which could have laid the groundwork, via investing in education, for higher future economic growth. The failure to implement substantial tax reforms in the early 1960s would have far-reaching consequences since it forced the government to finance later efforts to increase its social and infrastructural spending by borrowing abroad. This would contribute to the debt crisis of the 1980s.[137]

Through the 1960s, the political and economic elites existed harmoniously since, as political scientist Lorenzo Meyer observed:

> For the private sector, regime legitimacy depended not on its democratic merits, which it never had, but on its capacity to maintain workers under its control, as well as to develop a system of tariff protection, with fiscal incentives, subsidies, and the construction of infrastructure, which permitted investors an acceptable profit rate.[138]

The Middle Class

By one estimate, between 1940 and 1970, membership in the middle class increased from 16 to 34 percent of Mexico's population. The increased size of the middle class was closely tied to increased industrialization and expanded access to education. The middle class, whose earnings were well above the national average, was largely made up of professionals, managers, office workers, small-scale entrepreneurs, and some unionized workers in strategic industries.[139]

During the prolonged economic growth of the 1950s and 1960s, upward social mobility was a reality. In 1962, sociologist Pablo González Casanova commented: "In Mexico, which is industrializing and urbanizing, there is permanent social mobility. Yesterday's peasants are today's workers, whose children can become professionals."[140]

For the first time, large numbers of government bureaucrats, university professors, and shopkeepers could buy cars, study abroad, acquire homes of their own, take vacations in Acapulco, travel to the United States, and buy home appliances on credit at Sears.[141]

The burgeoning middle class reaped material rewards offered by the system and returned the favor by backing the PRI. For them, upward mobility was more important than multi-party democracy. This support was rewarded by actions favoring the middle class, which further cemented their loyalty. To cite one example, in 1947 Alemán announced a $10-million program to construct subsidized housing for the middle class and federal employees.[142]

During the 1960s, as a college education became accepted as a prerequisite for high political office, top state and federal officeholders, as well as the leadership of the PAN, increasingly came from the middle class.[143]

During the 1960s, the very success of the middle class produced contradictions that would lead to change. The political system, which had been structured in the 1930s to accommodate workers and peasants, failed to provide a political role for members of the middle class, aside from those actually holding office. Also, by the 1960s, the number of aspirants to higher education exceeded capacity. To add insult to injury, there were not enough jobs being created to give professional employment to the soaring numbers of university graduates. These tensions formed the backdrop for the 1968 student movement, which cost the political loyalty of middle class members whose parents had strongly supported the system that had provided them with upward mobility.[144]

Labor

> The history of Mexican trade unionism has oscillated between two extremes: the submission of trade unions to the state and the repression of the independent movements which have tried to extricate themselves from that situation.
>
> Raúl Trejo Delarbre, 1976[145]

After the Cárdenas administration, policymakers felt control over labor was necessary for capital accumulation, which is a prerequisite of industrialization. The government adroitly combined legal, financial, and political controls in its effort to provide a cheap, docile labor force to industrialists.[146]

In 1931, the Mexican private sector, the U.S. government, and U.S. business interests in Mexico vigorously opposed passage of the Federal Labor Law. Henry Ford threatened to remove his auto plant from Mexico if the proposed legislation became law.[147]

The fears of businessmen were ill founded, and it soon became apparent that the law could be used to control, not uplift, labor. Minimum wage regulations often harmed labor. In many cases, those who were receiving more than the minimum had their wages reduced to the minimum, and those who received less than the legally established minimum found that there was no effective means to force compliance with minimum wage legislation.[148]

Government control over labor made it attractive for entrepreneurs to invest in industry. This control also enabled the PRI to mobilize labor at election time, to receive its support in times of crisis, and to control inflation by keeping wage demands in check during periods of economic instability.[149]

A key element to government control over labor was Fidel Velázquez. In 1941, President Ávila Camacho supported Velázquez, a former milkman, to head the main labor federation, the CTM. The new CTM head slavishly allied himself with incumbent presidents to suppress rival leaders and labor organizations. He remained in this position until his death in 1997.[150]

The government had a wide variety of tools at its disposal to maintain its control over labor:

- The Labor Department had the legal power to deny registration to any labor union. If unions were not registered, they could not call legal strikes, enter into arbitration proceedings on behalf of their members, negotiate labor contracts, or appoint members to positions on government wage commissions. In addition to rejecting an application outright, the government could indicate its attitude toward a union by either expediting or delaying its registration. Political scientist Kevin Middlebrook found that the time that elapsed between the application for union registration and its acceptance ranged from one day to 24.9 years.[151]
- Legal strikes could only be called by legally registered unions. In addition, the legality of each strike had to be recognized on a case-by-case basis. If a strike was not declared legal, workers were subject to firing and replacement by strikebreakers.[152]
- Union elections were as undemocratic as those for political office. Through his power to recognize union elections as legitimate, the secretary of labor could deny membership in union executive committees to those who challenged government labor policy. Once in power, union officials would rely on the lack of effective trade union democracy to retain their jobs, often for decades. During their tenure in office, trade union officials used their positions to amass considerable personal wealth. Investigative journalist Manuel Buendía estimated that leaders of

the oil workers union netted $750 million annually from their legal and illegal activities. Sometimes employers would bribe labor leaders to suppress their employees' wage demands, since that cost less than increasing wages.[153]

- So long as labor leaders followed the PRI party line and kept their rank-and-file in line, the official party would ensure their tenure in office. Such leaders could aspire to PRI posts and elective office at the local, state, and federal level. Dozens of seats were reserved for labor in the Senate and Chamber of Deputies. As they became a moneyed elite in their own right, labor leaders came to share interests not with the workers they nominally represented but with management.[154]
- Labor leaders could eliminate dissidents who were merely minor irritants by resorting to the exclusion clause, a provision of the labor code that enabled union officials to legally expel from the union anyone they deemed a troublemaker. Since Mexico's "progressive" labor legislation provided the closed shop, dissidents who lost union membership via the exclusion clause automatically lost their jobs. More serious labor dissidents would be charged with the same offense—social dissolution—used to silence political dissidents. The already broad definition of that offense was extended to include obstructing "the path of legitimate government aims."[155]
- Union federations such as the CTM received massive government subsidies, thus permitting them to hire staff at salaries well above a laborer's pay. This led workers to kowtow to the CTM in hopes of gaining employment in the labor bureaucracy. To limit labor's power, the more conservative Regional Federation of Mexican Workers (CROM) was played off against the CTM. In 1950, to further fragment labor's power, the Alemán administration facilitated the formation of the Revolutionary Federation of Workers and Peasants (CROC), a new group that was loyal to the PRI and hostile to the CTM. Individual unions within these federations had limited power due to their small size. In 1960, the average membership was 134 per union.[156]
- During the Cold War era, labor insurgency was frequently labeled "Communist," thus delegitimizing workers' demands and making repression more politically acceptable.[157]
- Unions were heavily subsidized by government. In 1950, 62 percent of the CTM's monthly receipts came from the government.[158]
- Relatively few workers were unionized at all. In 1970, only 14.8 percent of the labor force belonged to a union. In the most unionized sector, industry, 37.2 percent belonged to unions, while only 12.9 percent of service workers were unionized. Union members received higher wages than non-union workers. In addition, they had written contracts and benefited from social security (which included health care) and subsided commodities and housing. Non-unionized workers often received below the legally mandated minimum wage and lacked such benefits as social security health care.[159]
- The PRI's protectionist polices shielded Mexican manufacturers from foreign competition. This allowed manufacturers to pay relatively high wages and pass the cost on to consumers. Since the PRI was strongly identified with industrial protectionism, labor had good reason to support that party. Auto workers, for example, received wages five times the average, generous welfare benefits, and scholarships for their children. Similarly, public-sector workers received above-average wages and benefits, so they backed the official party.[160]

In his 1946 inaugural address, President Alemán set the tone for post-war labor relations by declaring, "There must be no illegal work stoppages." When oil workers attempted a twenty-four-hour work stoppage a few weeks later, the army occupied refineries, oil wells, gas stations, and pipeline pumping stations. Many union leaders were jailed and beaten.[161]

During Alemán's presidency (1946–1952), union leaders who were identified with the Communist Party or who promoted Cárdenas's development model were replaced by more pliant labor leaders. Alemán's policy of freezing wages during a period of rapid inflation made the weakest people contribute the most to the process of capital accumulation. A 1956 article in *Fortune* magazine commented:

> Indeed it might be correctly said that the true hero of the Mexican investment boom is the ordinary Mexican worker, whose acceptance of a declining real income has in effect "subsidized" much of the nation's building . . . It is a token of Mexico's political stability that this program of inflation has been accompanied by no political disorders or even by any notable diminution of the party in power.[162]

After a bitter confrontation with the rail workers, which occurred during the first months of his term, López Mateos (1958–1964) was more lenient with strikers, and a number of them won raises, which the government accepted as necessary to maintain labor peace. The Labor Ministry began to use its extensive powers to pressure employers to increase wages and benefits granted workers. Wage increases, especially in strategic sectors of the economy, and tame leadership contributed to a period of labor peace that extended through the end of the 1960s. In 1970, wages totaled 35.3 percent of the GDP, up from 23.4 percent in 1951. Not only did labor's share of national product increase but the national product itself was increasing. As a result, the buying power of wages quadrupled between 1952 and 1976.[163]

Workers in nationalized industries were especially favored, since the government was willing to pay the price for their loyalty and support, even though it was unwilling to mandate such benefits for the working class as a whole. In 1962, when Joaquín Hernández Galicia became secretary general of the oil workers union, he rained down so many benefits on oil workers that the cost became a national scandal. As historian Enrique Krauze commented, with a few exceptions, workers accepted the labor leadership since they "knew that their situation was better than the great majority of Mexicans."[164]

Rural Mexico

> With the one major exception of Lázaro Cárdenas (1934–40), Mexican presidents regarded land distribution more as a way to pacify the peasantry and ensure their support rather than as a central component in an integrated rural development program.
>
> Tom Barry, 1995[165]

After the Second World War, rural Mexico saw a communications revolution. The village of Tepoztlán in Morelos was typical. In 1943, only four villagers there had a radio. By 1958, there were 80 battery-powered sets, and, by 1964, after electricity was introduced, only the very poor lacked radios. In 1944, movies came to San José de Gracia, Michoacán. The priests forbade attendance on the grounds that films introduced immorality. That warning notwithstanding, parishioners gradually began to attend the twice weekly showings. During the same period, rural transportation was shifting from muscle power to fossil fuels. In 1940, people overwhelmingly walked or rode carriages, horses, or burros. During the next decades, there was a massive shift to cars and busses as new roads made this alternative feasible. Between 1929 and 1933, when anthropologist Elsie C. Parsons studied the village of Mitla, Oaxaca, there was one bicycle, one truck, and one automobile in town. By 1964, there were thirty-two motor vehicles and an estimated 200 bikes.[166]

As anthropologist Oscar Lewis observed in Tepoztlán, the road was key to the entrance of both new goods and ideas:

> There were the new asphalt road, the buses, the tourist cars, the Coca-Cola and aspirin signs, the Sinarquista placards on a roadside wall, the queue of women and children waiting to have their corn ground at the mills, the new stores and poolrooms in the plaza, and a few women with bobbed hair and high-heeled shoes.[167]

Rural Mexicans suffered from the combined effects of soaring population, government neglect, and low productivity. In 1969, the value added per agricultural worker was only 30 percent of the average for all Mexican workers. Population growth overwhelmed the tepid efforts at land reform. Between 1940 and 1970, the number of agricultural workers increased from 3.8 million to 7.8 million, while the number of land reform beneficiaries only rose from 1.5 million to 2.1 million. During this same period, the cultivatable area per agricultural worker declined from 3.0 to 1.5 acres. As farm income was spread among an ever increasing number of families, anything beyond a rudimentary education became an unaffordable luxury. In 1970, 49 percent of rural households were below the poverty line.[168]

The poorest and the most numerous of the agricultural workers were the wage laborers who often joined the migratory circuits that criss-crossed Mexico and extended into the United States. Rural wage laborers were generally unorganized, rarely worked for one employer for extended periods, and were little affected by labor legislation, including the minimum wage law. Between 1940 and 1970, the number of landless agricultural workers increased from 2.5 to 4 million. Not surprisingly, the wages of agricultural workers decreased by 41 percent between 1950 and 1969. In 1950 agricultural wage laborers averaged 194 days of work per year, while in 1970 they only averaged 75.[169]

According to 1960 census data, 83 percent of farms were less than self-sufficient, meaning that farmers had to find sources of supplementary income to buy food. Members of this group, numbering some 2 million, resorted to a variety of strategies to increase their income. Supplementary income sources included wage labor on other farms, temporary migration to Mexican cities or to the United States to work, and home production of non-agricultural goods.[170]

A definitive result of Cárdenas's land reform in the 1930s was the breaking up of the traditional patriarchal hacienda with its large resident population. Cárdenas's actions only hastened the decline of the hacienda—a process that was occurring throughout Latin America. *Hacendados* were replaced by people who, in the 1950s, were called nylon farmers, a reference to both their newness and their synthetic nature. These nylon farmers lacked the aristocratic pretensions of the *hacendado*—they just wanted to make money and often used their political contacts to do so. They rented land and labor and often moved from place to place. To the extent possible, they relied not on their own wealth but on government credit. Often they invested agricultural profits in cities. As anthropologist Arturo Warman remarked, "In the countryside, they left neither capital, mansions, nor towns with their names attached, nothing, not even a memory."[171]

Others formed long-lasting commercial farms—sometimes on land that they retained after the land reform, sometimes on land irrigated at government expense. These farms benefited from roads built by the government, government-supplied credit and crop insurance, and government-funded research. The government also subsidized the costs of fertilizer and provided highly lucrative price supports. The owners of these large units, given their access to credit, could employ the latest agricultural technology and could warehouse and market their corps efficiently. As a result, their profit per ton was higher than the profit small farmers received for producing the same crop.[172]

The largest 3 percent of farms produced 54 percent of Mexico's food and fiber. In 1968, the top 7.1 percent of farms produced four times the output per acre and twenty times as much per worker as the 52 percent of farms classified as subsistence. Such large farms produced export crops, industrial raw materials, and animal feed, and supplied the Mexican market with wheat, fresh fruits, and vegetables.[173]

Landholders with close ties to government officials and with access to a virtually unlimited pool of cheap labor accumulated large amounts of land without facing the threat of expropriation. Some held the large estates cattlemen were legally allowed. Others skirted the limits on farm size the land reform law imposed by registering properties in the names of friends and relatives.[174]

Increasingly, those profiting from agriculture did not own land or raise crops. They profited instead from their control of financial services, selling pesticide, fertilizer, and farm machinery, as well as the buying and processing of crops. As this occurred, the locus of rural power, which had been the hacienda, shifted to provincial cities and towns.[175]

Beginning in the 1940s, successive Mexican governments favored privately owned agricultural properties, not the ejido. Each new government would reaffirm that land reform was a "major goal" of the Revolution and then lavish benefits on commercial farmers. The rate at which the government processed petitions for land provided an indicator of its waning interest in land reform. Such petitions would often languish in government offices for years, if not decades. Sociologist Rodolfo Stavenhagen found that the time that elapsed between the filing of a petition for land and receiving final title averaged thirteen years.[176]

After the Second World War, it became obvious that land distribution per se was not producing equality in the countryside. *Ejidatarios* and small farmers found themselves caught in a vicious cycle. They had low educational levels, small plots, and little access to capital. As a result of using antiquated technology on land that was often poor to begin with, yields per acre were low. Their meager income was further reduced by their relying on others to transport and warehouse crops. While the rural population was rapidly increasing, job loss occurred as capital-intensive agricultural technology was transferred from developed countries to rural Mexico and land was shifted from labor-intensive crops to raising cattle.[177]

Ejidatarios and other smallholders faced a huge hurdle in obtaining credit. The Ejido Credit Bank became increasingly bureaucratic and corrupt. Those lacking credit from the government often turned to loan sharks.[178]

Rural bosses, known as caciques, drained wealth from small producers. In the areas they dominated, caciques, who functioned with PRI and government acquiescence, would often profit from marketing locally grown crops, selling manufactured goods, collecting bribes, and supplying credit at usurious interest rates. They controlled police and public investment within the areas they dominated. In many ways, caciques functioned as an old fashioned political machine, distributing jobs and favors to sympathizers and resorting to violence if anyone challenged their economic and political control.[179]

In the 1930s, the ejido provided a quick response to the Depression, combining land and labor, both of which Mexico had in abundance. Transferring land to the ejido alleviated immediate employment problems, but in the process created obstacles to increased agricultural production. Corruption undermined the efficiency of many ejidos. Article 27 of the constitution provided the legal basis for the ejido, but prohibited corporate investment in land, thus limiting capital available for both private and ejido land. Even in areas such as Morelos where ejidos enjoyed widespread support, they failed to lift many out of poverty since they lacked credit and few draft animals were available to plow. Over the years, the division of land among many children led to plots so small that it was impossible to achieve economies of scale and apply modern technology. Given differences in plot size, soil fertility, and water availability, some *ejidatarios* did well and escaped poverty, but many did not.[180]

Despite the numerous grievances of the rural population, the government effectively headed off rural unrest. One factor enabling the government to contain peasant unrest was the lack of effective rural organization. From its inception under President Cárdenas, the CNC relied on patron-client relationships with those it organized. Under Cárdenas, the CNC offset the power of the landed elite and channeled goods, services, and land to the peasantry. However, after 1940, as the government's commitment to land reform waned, the CNC maintained the rural status quo rather than promoting land reform or redressing the imbalance of power between peasant producers and the small elite of commercial farmers. Credit and infrastructure projects were allocated on a discretional basis, leading most peasants to continue looking to the CNC to improve their lot in life.[181]

The secretary general of the CNC was selected by the president and then publicly "elected" at a national CNC assembly. Those selected to lead the CNC were usually from the urban middle class. CNC staffers found that employment in that agency was a splendid form of upward mobility. With each step up the CNC ladder, salaries increased and there were opportunities for kick-backs, payoffs, and other illicit gains. Top officials often amassed personal fortunes and became large landowners. Career advancement was based on docility toward those above and control of those below.[182]

The CNC retained its influence by channeling government resources to ejidos. It remained as the only channel available for receiving land via the land reform. If peasants went outside the CNC to make demands, they were ignored or repressed. The CNC depended on the PRI and various government agencies for its operating expenses. In exchange for this subsidy, the CNC faithfully delivered the peasant vote for the PRI. As one former secretary of agriculture commented, "Mexican peasants are organized to vote, not to produce."[183]

With the official peasant organization intent on maintaining the status quo, landless peasants repeatedly turned to extralegal methods in their quest for land ownership. Their most frequent tactic was moving onto land they felt exceeded the limits imposed by the land reform law and laying claim to it—a process knows as a land invasion. By doing so, they kept alive Zapata's notion that land reform should be carried out by peasants without state intervention.

The Indigenous Population

Based on the number of people speaking an Indian language, census authorities reported that the Indian population increased from 2.5 million in 1940 to 3.1 million in 1970. In 1970, the Indian language with the greatest number of speakers was Nahuatl, with 799,394 speakers, and the state with the most Indians was Oaxaca, with 677,347. Calculating the number of Indians by counting the number of people speaking an indigenous language was notoriously subjective. Guidelines for deciding if an individual spoke an Indian language were in constant flux. Non-linguistic methods were also used to determine Indian identity. Sociologist Pablo González Casanova defined an Indian as an individual with an "awareness of belonging to a community which is different and isolated from the national culture . . ." By applying that definition, he calculated that in 1960 the number of Indians was between 6 million and 7.5 million, or 20 to 25 percent of the national population.[184]

From the end of Cárdenas's term until 1988, the Indian faded from official discourse and party platforms. Intellectual discourse concerning the Indian increasingly focused on how the poverty of the Indian community resulted not from Indians' biological endowments or their social organization, as had been often argued in the past, but from mistreatment and neglect by the rest of Mexican society. Closer integration to the Mexican nation was viewed as the solution to the Indian problem. In 1967, influential anthropologist Gonzalo Aguirre Beltrán voiced this view of *indigenismo*, the term used to describe the government's Indian policy:

> The ultimate goal of indigenismo is not to capture the attention of the Indians and improve their lot, but to achieve a much loftier goal: the integration of the Indian, under socially just conditions, so that Indian and non-Indian are really free and equal citizens.[185]

Government programs dealing with the Indian were coordinated by the National Indigenous Institute (INI), which was founded in 1948. In regions with a high indigenous population, the INI established "coordinating centers." These centers drew on the services of physicians, agronomists, veterinarians, engineers, and lawyers. Complementing the efforts of the non-Indian professional was the bilingual teacher, or "promotor." The promotor was a member of the indigenous community who could speak the local Indian language as well as Spanish and who was trained as a bilingual teacher.

In 1951, the first coordinating center was established in San Cristóbal de las Casas, Chiapas. By 1970, there were eleven such centers. They took a gradual approach and did not seek to overturn either local Indian governments or the inegalitarian land tenure system. Rather, they provided roads, schools, health care, legal assistance, drinking-water systems, and other services. They also sought to stimulate handicraft production.[186]

While these efforts were a well-meaning attempt to end the poverty in which most Indians found themselves, they never addressed the question of whether Indian cultures could be preserved while at the same time being integrated more closely to the national culture. It also remained unclear just who received the most benefits from the increased integration of the Indian with the national economy. As anthropologist Cynthia Hewitt de Alcántara noted:

> Rural roads ran in two directions, and the greater experience and economic power of many inhabitants of the urban terminal gave the latter a definitive advantage over the peasantry in putting the new means of communication to profitable use.

Indians did not have a role in the design of INI programs at the national level or even in managing the coordinating centers, which implemented INI policy at the regional level.[187]

Literary critic Anne Doremus commented on the Indians' lot in 1940: "Most lived in abject poverty, isolated from the rest of Mexican society and lacking any sense of citizenship." The efforts of the INI did little to change that reality since in 1970 the INI budget only totaled $2.2 million. Assuming there were 3 million Indians at the time, this was less than one dollar per Indian per year. The INI spent much of that budget to hire its non-Indian professional staff, to maintain a headquarters in Mexico City, and to acquire vehicles and supplies.[188]

Between 1940 and 1970, Indian communities throughout Mexico were remarkably quiescent, given not only their poverty but also ethnic discrimination and their often criminal treatment by outsiders, which included robbery, murder, and usurpation of their lands.[189]

Women

Congress's failure to implement the women's suffrage amendment at the end of the Cárdenas administration caused women's organizations to shift their attention to other goals, such as providing for child care, the establishment of cooperatives for indigenous women, guaranteeing maternity leave, and passing legislation to protect domestic servants. The United Front for Women's Rights (FUPDM) changed its name to the Women's Committee for the Defense of the Nation and turned its attention to organizing women to support the war effort.[190]

Having lost their organizational momentum during the war, women were unable to regain it after the war. This was in part due to Mexico being essentially a one-party state in which the PRI absorbed many politically active women and channeled them into positions in the official bureaucracy.[191]

During his 1946 presidential campaign, Miguel Alemán promised to grant the vote to women in municipal elections. To avoid a conservative backlash, he offset this tepid step forward by including in his platform a statement that declared that women were "by tradition immemorial incomparable mothers, abnegated and industrious wives, loyal sisters, and chaste daughters." Alemán justified granting women the right to vote in municipal elections by declaring, "Women understand municipal problems exceptionally well, since these problems concern schools, public health, the prices of basic commodities such as water and milk, and other matters relating to the well-being of the home and family."[192]

Alemán made good on his campaign promise. In 1947, Article 115 the constitution was amended to read: "In municipal elections, women shall have the same rights to participate as men, including the right to cast a vote and to be a candidate."

Even though women's organizations lost momentum during the 1940s, the suffrage issue was not forgotten. In 1952, suffragist Amalia Caballero de Castillo Ledón interviewed PRI presidential candidate Adolfo Ruiz Cortines. He promised her that if she could gather the signatures of half a million women (out of a population of 30 million), he would grant women the right to vote. She launched a successful petition drive, and Ruiz Cortines pushed though an amendment to Article 34 of the constitution. That article was revised to state that both men and women (*los varones y las mujeres*) had the right to vote in national elections.

Ruiz Cortines's decision to grant women the vote was not triggered by a massive groundswell in favor of women's suffrage. Rather, changes in Mexican society paved the way for the enfranchisement of women. By the 1950s, the PRI was so well entrenched that it no longer needed to worry about the supposed pro-Catholic tendency of women voters. Instead, the ruling party regarded women as an enormous voting block it could co-opt. As Mexico urbanized and industrialized, values changed. Women were attending the university in greater numbers, providing ready examples of individuals qualified to assume public office. Finally, there was a generational shift among the political elite. From 1920 through the Ávila Camacho administration (1940–1946), the political elite was based on revolutionary ties—the ultimate good-old-boy network, no girls allowed. Only when that generation retired did the path open for women's suffrage.[193]

In the 1958 presidential election, 7,845,400 votes were cast. This was more than twice the total cast in 1952, reflecting not only population increase but also the enfranchisement of women. Contrary to the predictions made by opponents of women suffrage, there was not a marked increase in the vote for the PAN. By and large, women voted for the PRI, just as men did. In response to the enfranchisement of women, official party organizations began to devote increased attention to women's interests.[194]

During the 1950s and 1960s, women gradually made their presence felt at the top levels of government. In 1961, María Cristina Salmorán de Tamayo became the first woman to sit on the

Figure 21.3 *Woman voting for the first time, 1958*

Source: Reproduced courtesy of Archivo General de la Nación

Supreme Court. During the 1967–1970 term, there were twelve women serving in the Chamber of Deputies. Often women who served in top posts were kin or lovers of powerful men. These women reflected the racial and social hierarchy of Mexico in that they appeared very European, came from families with high socioeconomic status, and were not overly concerned with the plight of Mexican women of lower status. In Congress, their voting patterns were similar to those of males.[195]

Even though women failed to have a major impact on the political system in the 1950s and 1960s, they did reshape the Mexican labor force. As Mexico urbanized and industrialized, the percentage of women in the labor force increased from 7.4 in 1940 to 19.0 in 1970. In 1970, within the highly urbanized Federal District, women comprised 29.7 percent of the workforce, while in more traditional Zacatecas they comprised only 9.1 percent. Women's participation in the labor force also varied by age. Only 17 percent of those aged forty to forty-four were in the labor force, while 25 percent of those aged twenty to twenty-four were. Many of those joining the labor force had migrated from rural areas. Women migrants, drawn by jobs in education, commerce, and domestic service, outnumbered men, as was the case throughout Latin America.[196]

Generally women found employment in jobs that were an extension of their traditional roles in the home. They worked as domestics (cleaning and cooking) and in food service (cooking), the garment industry (sewing), hospitals (caring for the sick), and schools (caring for children). In 1970, 69.6 percent of the 2.5 million women in the formal labor force worked in the service sector. Of these, 488,344 were domestics.[197]

Population

> Mexico has been a country of deeply rooted pro-natality views. Generally, governments during this period did not perceive a conflict between individuals' reproductive behavior and the fulfillment of government responsibilities. On the contrary, this behavior was encouraged, since it was felt to further the goals of territorial integration, national survival, and industrialization.
>
> Francisco Alba, 1993[198]

As the North Atlantic nations modernized, they underwent what is known as the demographic transition. Before the industrial revolution, as with the rest of the world, these nations had high birth rates almost matched by high death rates. With the introduction of improved medical care, higher standards of living, and public heath measures, such as clean water and vaccination, the death rate plummeted. This led to a sudden increase in population as birth rates remained high and death rates declined. In nations undergoing the demographic transition, the realization sank in that numerous children were no longer needed to guarantee the survival of some to support adults in old age. Also, pensions and social security made parents less reliant on children for support in old age. As populations urbanized, children ceased to be an economic asset. These factors eventually led to a sharp decrease in the birth rate. In some European nations, such as Spain, Italy, and Greece, the fertility rate eventually fell to between 1.1 and 1.3 children per woman—well below the rate needed to maintain a constant population.[199]

As the population of the North Atlantic nations was rapidly increasing, they were industrializing, so many found jobs in labor-intensive industries. Also, there were wide-open spaces in North and South America and elsewhere to which millions of Europeans emigrated.

Mexico plunged into its demographic transition more than a century after the North Atlantic nations. As late as 1940, both birth rates and death rates remained high compared to the levels found in the North Atlantic nations. After 1940, Mexico entered into the high-population-growth phase of the demographic transition. Immigration had scant impact on Mexico's population between 1940 and 1970—the surge in population resulted from births far exceeding the number of deaths.

Table 21.2 Mexican population, 1940–1970

	1940	1950	1960	1970
Total population (millions)	19.7	25.8	34.9	47.2
Percent urban* (%)	35.1	42.6	50.7	57.8
Average annual growth rate in previous decade (%)	1.8	2.7	3.1	3.4

*Defined as people living in a population centers of 2,500 or more

Source INEGI (1994: 42) and Ordorica & Lezama (1993: 51, Table 8)

Between 1940 and 1944, the birth rate was 44.6 per thousand population. This rate remained virtually unchanged, averaging 44.3 per thousand between 1965 and 1969.[200]

Continuing a trend begun in the 1930s, between 1940 and 1970 the death rate plummeted from twenty-three per thousand population to eleven per thousand. During this period, the government built rural and urban health centers, provided drinking water systems and sewage treatment plants, and made more than a few applications of DDT to eradicate malaria. A higher standard of living, increased access to markets, and improved diets further reduced mortality. Mexico acquired the technology to prevent and treat infectious and parasitic diseases that had caused a large proportion of deaths, especially in children. The introduction of antibiotics reduced deaths from tuberculosis, pneumonia, tetanus, and typhoid. The proportion of deaths attributable to infectious and parasitic diseases declined from 42.6 percent of total deaths in 1930 to 23.1 percent in 1970.[201]

During the late 1960s, as a result of the imbalance between births and deaths, Mexico's annual population growth rate reached 3.6 percent, one of the highest in the world. Within a thirty-five-year period—1940–1975—Mexico's population tripled. The previous tripling, between 1820 and 1940, had required 120 years.[202]

The changes in economic and social welfare that occurred between 1940 and 1970 had a much greater impact on mortality than they did on the birth rate. Most families clung to attitudes concerning desirable family size formed when infant mortality rates were appallingly high and children could help on the farm. In 1966, a national survey found that only 17.7 percent of men and women felt that an ideal family would have fewer than four children. For 23.8 percent, more than six children was the ideal.[203]

Much to virtually everyone's surprise, population increase began to affect almost every aspect of Mexican life. By 1970, 46 percent of Mexico's population was below age fifteen. This required increased educational budgets—capital that might otherwise have resulted in new investments or in educating a smaller number of children longer, thus making them more productive. In 1958, President López Mateos noted that 300,000 new jobs were needed annually to accommodate job seekers who were born in the 1940s. Eventually the number of new job seekers entering the labor force annually would exceed 1 million.[204]

EDUCATION

After 1940, the educational system was increasingly seen as the key to economic development, not as a vehicle for instilling new values in students. In 1946, Article 3 of the constitution was amended to state that education should stimulate "love of country and international solidarity." The reference to "socialism" was deleted from the article.[205]

Even though the overt political messages were dropped, schools continued to foster change. This was especially true of female students. As corn-grinding mills, sewing machines, store-bought utensils, and water sources close to home were introduced, girls had more time to attend school.

As it became apparent that schooling increased the productive capacity of family members both on and off the farm, parents became increasingly willing to permit rural girls to attend school. Anthropologist Robert Redfield felt education was the key to the changes he observed after 1931 in the village of Chan Kom, Yucatán. He commented on the young women who had attended school there: "She speaks up when spoken to and has not the shy, almost voiceless and completely unassertive manner which prevailed among young women in former generations."[206]

After 1950, due to population increase, a tidal wave hit the educational system. The number of Mexican children attending elementary school increased from 2.7 million in 1950 to 4.9 million in 1960 and then to 8.5 million in 1970. At the same time, with increased prosperity, many children could afford to stay in school longer. As a result, while primary enrollment increased by 3.7 percent a year between 1950 and 1970, secondary enrollment increased by 16.9 percent a year. In response to increased enrollments, the education budget rose from 7.8 percent of federal spending under Alemán (1946–1952) to 13.2 percent under Díaz Ordaz (1964–1970). Even with increased budgets, new enrollments strained the system. The average number of children per classroom increased from forty-five during the Díaz Ordaz administration (1964–1970) to fifty-three during the Echeverría administration (1970–1976).[207]

Between 1940 and 1970, as a result of both adult literacy programs and the increased education of children, the percentage of illiterates in the population decreased from 58 to 28. However, given the huge population increase, the number of illiterates rose from 9.5 million to 10.9 million during this same period. The workforce continued to reflect past limitations on educational opportunity. In 1970, 67 percent of the population over twenty-four had three years or less of formal education and only 9 percent had attended secondary school.[208]

Despite prodigious efforts to educate all children, many left the school system at each level. The following enrollment figures indicate how enrollment declined at each successive level:

1,823,765 students entered primary school in 1958, of whom

387,533 passed sixth grade in 1963, of whom
146,058 passed ninth grade in 1966, of whom
58,332 enrolled in college in 1969.[209]

In many ways, the educational system reinforced existing social inequality. In 1970, rural Mexico, home to the majority of Mexico's poor, accounted for 42 percent of the school-age population but only 9 percent of those finishing primary school. Government allocation of resources reinforced rural poverty. In rural areas, 74 percent of schools offered only grades one to four. Money and the best teachers flowed to areas that already had above average income.[210]

There was a very close, circular relation between education and poverty. In families classified as poor, 47.7 percent of family heads had no formal education and only 2.8 percent had continued beyond elementary school. Since children in these families could not afford to remain in school for long, they formed another poorly educated generation on its way to poverty.[211]

In the early 1950s, the National University moved to a new campus on the southern fringes of Mexico City. The new campus, whose buildings were decorated with mosaics and frescos by David Alfaro Siqueiros, Diego Rivera, and Juan O'Gorman, boasted some of the finest examples of modern architecture anywhere. An imposing statue of President Alemán towered over the grounds of the campus whose creation he had ordered.[212]

The National University entered its golden age after moving to the new campus. Its graduates dominated Mexico's cultural, political, and entrepreneurial elite. Alliances made while on campus served politicians and bureaucrats as they moved up the political ladder. All Mexican presidents from Alemán (1946–1952) through Salinas (1988–1994) were graduates of the National University.[213]

Figure 21.4 *National University Library, with mural by Juan O'Gorman. Statue of President Alemán stands to left*

Source: Reproduced courtesy of the Benson Latin American Collection, the University of Texas at Austin

The National University experienced the same accelerated growth that lower levels of the educational system did. Between 1950 and 1970 its enrollment increased from 24,929 students to 106,038.[214]

While the National University continued to dominate higher education, other institutions were founded, laying the groundwork for the diversification of higher education. The Colegio de México, which was formalized in 1940, specialized in the social sciences and history and benefited from Spanish refugees on its faculty and funds from the Rockefeller Foundation. To this day this unique public-private hybrid produces outstanding works on Mexico (including sixty-one cited in this book). In 1943, to ensure a continued supply of technicians for Garza-Sada enterprises, Eugenio Garza Sada, a second-generation member of the Monterrey elite, spearheaded the creation of the Monterrey Institute of Technology. It became a highly regarded technical training center modeled on MIT, of which Garza Sada was an alumnus.

By 1960, twenty-two state universities had been established. As a result of these new campuses, total enrollment in higher education rose from 29,892 in 1950 to 252,200 in 1970–71. Between 1960 and 1970, the number of degrees granted by universities rose by 12.4 percent a year. A college degree, which had been the key to upward mobility in the 1950s, became a source of discontent in the 1960s, as the number of college graduates exceeded the number of professional jobs being created.[215]

Even though university enrollment was increasing faster than the population as a whole, access to higher education remained sharply tilted toward economically and geographically privileged males.

The average family income of National University students was 3.2 times the national average. In 1963, only 17 percent of those enrolled in higher education were women. The next year, a survey found that only 18 percent of National University students had a worker or peasant background. As was the case with so many aspects of Mexican life, the Federal District was over-represented. The National University and the National Polytechnic Institute, founded in Mexico City by Cárdenas to provide technicians sympathetic to his development goals, together accounted for 49 percent of the university students in Mexico. As political scientist Soledad Loaeza commented in 1984, "Despite the undeniable expansion of educational services during the last 40 years, access to secondary and higher education continues to be reserved for a very small fraction of Mexican society."[216]

RELIGION

> Beginning in 1940, the government and the Church sought to maintain relations of mutual tolerance and avoid invading each other's turf since both had learned that in direct confrontations each had much to lose and little to gain.
>
> Lorenzo Meyer, 2000[217]

The situation of the Church after 1940 resembled that of the Church during the Porfiriato. In both cases, anti-clerical legislation remained on the books, but was unenforced. Mexico remained staunchly Catholic. In the 1970 census, 96 percent of the population identified themselves as Catholic. The Church faced the same demographic pressures faced by the educational system. In 1940, there were 3,863 priests, or one per 5,088 Mexicans. In 1967, there were 7,922 priests, or one per 5,765 Mexicans.[218]

In 1940, presidential candidate Ávila Camacho stated in the journal *Hoy*, "I am a believer."[219] This break with officially sanctioned anti-clericalism paved the way for cordial Church-state relations during the 1940s. The Church responded to Ávila Camacho's declaration of faith by backing the war effort. After Mexico declared war on Germany, Archbishop of Mexico Luis M. Martínez stated:

> According to Christian doctrine, it is the duty of the civil government to set foreign policy, especially in regards to international conflict. When the civil authority has legally established such policy, it is the duty of Catholics to support it unless it is *clearly against* their conscience.[220]

During the 1940s, Church-state collaboration ceased to be covert as presidents and bishops openly participated in joint ceremonies. The Church increased its influence by controlling important centers of secondary and higher education that were attended by middle- and upper-class students. The Church lobbied the government, especially on matters concerning private education. It used a wide variety of magazines, books, and other publications to disseminate its views. In both the number of people organized and in the volume of its publications, the Church was second only to the government.[221]

During the 1950s, the Church remained the non-governmental entity with the largest organizational base. In 1953, an assembly of Catholic leaders drew representatives from forty-four Catholic groups with a membership of 4,530,000. In 1955, Archbishop Martínez could find little to complain about concerning Church-state relations, noting: "The only thing that remains now is to change the constitution. But this is not yet possible."[222]

The Church became more critical of social conditions and began to use the social sciences to critique the Mexican development model. It did not challenge capitalism as an institution—only its excesses. Church officials spoke out against corruption in government and the inequitable distribution of income. In addition to criticizing the government and the economic system, the clergy attempted to influence attitudes towards such innovations as movies, the mambo, and women's sleeveless dresses—all of which were denounced.[223]

During the 1960s, events outside Mexico exercised an increasing influence on the Church. In response to the Cuban Revolution and the widespread sympathy for it in Mexico, the Church launched a vigorous anti-Communist campaign that used the slogan, "Christianity Yes, Communism No." This was in part self-defense, since the hierarchy felt that there was a definite likelihood that the rest of Latin America would follow the Cuban model. The campaign varied widely from place to place. In Puebla, priests read a pastoral letter that called on the faithful to "pray to the Virgin of Guadalupe to protect Mexico against communism" and warned that "those who profess the anti-Christian, materialist communist doctrine and especially those who defend and propagate it, will be *ipso facto* excommunicated."[224]

In 1959, Pope John XXIII called for a Second Vatican Council to modernize the Church. The council, which was convened in 1962, issued statements defining Church responsibility concerning education, land reform, social problems, and poverty. The notion of sin was expanded and became "viewed as a social problem resulting from oppression and injustice and not simply as failings of personal behavior and morality." As a result of this council, usually referred to simply as Vatican II, the Mexican Church became increasingly involved in political and developmental issues.[225]

In 1968, the religious status quo was further challenged by the General Latin American Episcopal Conference, held in Medellín, Colombia. Bishops there considered how Vatican II could be applied to Latin America. The conference concluded that Latin America was on the verge of revolution and that "audacious, urgent, global, and profound reforms were needed." While this conference led much of the South American Church into unprecedented social and political activism, the Mexican Church distanced itself from the conclusions of the conference, which were viewed as reflecting South American, not Mexican, reality. However, the ideas discussed at Medellín were quite influential in a few Mexican dioceses where bishops were receptive to them. Their strongest influence was in Chiapas where they were embraced by Bishop Samuel Ruiz.[226]

The divergence of opinion within the Church was evident during the 1968 student movement. In September 1968, Bishop of Cuernavaca Sergio Méndez Arceo and thirty-seven other priests published a letter that downplayed the alleged communist threat posed by the students and justified some of their demands. Méndez Arceo was the only bishop to protest the killings of October 2. The rest of the hierarchy did not accept his view. The archdiocesan curia issued a statement declaring the September declaration was unrepresentative of the Church's position. The episcopal hierarchy staunchly defended the government response to the 1968 student movement.[227]

Between 1940 and 1970, the number of Protestants in Mexico rose from 177,954 to 876,879. Membership in Protestant groups increased at twice the rate of the population during this period. Their membership rose in part due to an influx of U.S. Protestant missionaries, many of whom had been displaced from Asia by the Second World War. In other cases, Mexicans working in the United States during the war underwent conversion to Protestantism and then returned to Mexico.[228]

In 1940, Protestants in Mexico mainly belonged to "mainstream" U.S. denominations. Later, such groups as the Assembly of God and the Light of the World had the largest increase in membership. New members largely came from rural areas and urban slums. Increasingly, Mexican Protestantism moved away from its original U.S. and British origins and adopted Latin American values. Often a single individual embodied a church. For example, the Church of the Light of the World was founded in 1926 by an agricultural worker in Guadalajara. Its founder adopted the name Aaron and became the uncontested leader of the movement. Upon Aaron's death in 1984, he was succeeded by his son who used the name Samuel. The influence of these groups varied widely. In traditionally Catholic west-central Mexico (home to the Cristeros), there were fewer Protestants. Protestants in Querétaro, for example, accounted for only 0.3 percent of its population in 1970. In contrast, in Tabasco, where the Catholic Church was traditionally weaker, 8.3 percent of the population was Protestant.[229]

MEXICO CITY

> The capital came to be synonymous with seemingly unlimited employment opportunities, wealth, and urban and economic development.
>
> Diane Davis, 1994[230]

Between 1940 and 1970, Mexico City's population increased from 1.8 million to 8.8 million due to rural-to-urban migration and the high birth rate of its residents. During the 1940s, 612,000 migrated to Mexico City. The number of migrants increased to 800,000 during the 1950s and 2.8 million during the 1960s. The built-up area increased from forty-seven square miles to 298 square miles between 1940 and 1970. In the 1960s, a major attraction of the Federal District was an income level 185 percent above the national average, which translated not only into more spending money but also into access to education, health care, clean water, sewers, and electricity.[231]

Several factors caused urban growth and industrialization to be concentrated in Mexico City. Between 1940 and 1970, the federal bureaucracy expanded, thus increasing the number of government employees living in the capital. Given the major role the government played in the economy, industrialists wanted to be close to the seat of power. The government subsidized the cost of gasoline, transport, education, and water in the capital. As affluent Mexicans became concentrated in the capital, locating industry there reduced the costs of transporting goods to consumers. Excellent transportation allowed the low-cost shipment of goods to other markets. The availability of professional and financial services also made locating industry in Mexico City attractive. The political elite favored Mexico City as a site for industry since it felt that industrialists locating in the capital, unlike the Monterrey elite, would accept government social objectives. Policy makers viewed rapid urbanization as providing a market for industry as well as a labor force for it.[232]

By 1965, 46 percent of Mexico's industrial employment and 51.3 percent of industrial production were in the Mexico City metropolitan zone. Between 1950 and 1970, the number of manufacturing jobs in Mexico City increased from 156,697 to 672,446. This increase in the number of manufacturing jobs fell far short of the number of new job seekers, leaving the city with millions of poorly paid, underemployed residents.[233]

Mexico City, which had been neglected during the Cárdenas administration, rebounded during the 1940s. The federal government began massive investment in infrastructure projects to attract manufacturing to the capital. During the Alemán administration (1946–1952), to win the loyalty of industrial workers, large-scale public housing projects were created for trade union members. During the 1940s, the city's population increased by more than 6 percent a year. To house new residents, the city spread south along two major streets, the Calzada de Tlalpan and Insurgentes Avenue. Commercial decentralization began with the opening of a Sears store south of the traditional commercial center.[234]

As it expanded south, the built-up area enveloped centuries-old villages. Due to the envelopment of one such village, Mixcoac, one could travel along streets lined with modern buildings and then suddenly encounter

> churches, plazas, gardens, and old parks . . . Old houses, which are still standing, date from the late nineteenth century and the beginning of the twentieth and mark the transition from one epoch to another. The walls separating the lots are noteworthy due to their style and their being made of adobe bricks, reminding us that the area has rural roots.[235]

In 1951, rather than accepting that Mexico City had natural growth limits, the government began to pump water thirty-six miles from the Lerma River Basin into the Valley of Mexico. Later, pipes were extended sixty miles to the Cutzamala River Basin. By 1970, ten cubic meters a second were being pumped east to Mexico City. Pumping the water up as much as 3,600 feet would

Table 21.3 *Mexico City population, 1940–1970*

Year	Population (millions)	Percentage of national population	Percentage born in Federal District
1940	1.8	9	51
1950	3.1	12	52
1960	5.3	21	58
1970	8.8	18	66

Source: INEGI (1994: 31) and decennial censuses

permanently saddle the government with a huge energy bill. In addition, diverting the water out of the Lerma destroyed traditional indigenous cultures in the area that relied on the water.[236]

During the 1950s, the city crossed the boundaries of the Federal District and sprawled into the State of Mexico, which bounds the District to its east, north, and west. This made planning much more difficult since plans had to be formulated by the appointed mayor of Mexico City and by the governor of the State of Mexico and the mayors of the municipalities adjoining the Federal District.[237]

During the 1960s, Mexico City boasted Latin America's first skyscraper, a rising standard of living, a sophisticated cultural life, and some of the developing world's most modern urban amenities, such as parks, gardens, and boulevards. In the Federal District, the government spent twice the national average on education and four times the national average on secondary education. Mexico's capital was seen as a symbol of Mexico's success at modernization.[238]

During the 1960s, central Mexico City's population increased at only 0.3 percent a year. At the same time, some of the municipalities in the State of Mexico that adjoined the Federal District had annual population growth rates as high as 18 percent for more than a decade. By 1970, only 38.2 percent of the city's population growth resulted from migration. Births in the city accounted for the rest.[239]

The spatial separation by income that had begun during the late Porfiriato accelerated in the 1950s. Generally, the middle and upper classes moved northwest, west, and south to more desirable areas with hills, woodlands, fresh water, and less contamination and congestion. Between 1960 and 1977, 150 subdivisions (*fraccionamientos*) were laid out in the State of Mexico alone. The existence of freeways, which cut travel time to downtown, was explicitly used in the ads that sold homes in these new subdivisions.[240]

The housing in such planned, built-for-profit subdivisions was far too expensive for the majority of those wishing to establish households. This led to the creation of irregular settlements, or *colonias proletarias*, which in 1970 housed slightly more than half of Mexico City's population and which covered between 40 and 50 percent of its area.[241]

One of these *colonias proletarias*, Nezahualcóyotl, become something of a celebrity slum in that it was close to downtown and grew from virtually nothing so quickly. The 1960 census reported that Nezahualcóyotl, on the dry lake bed of Lake Texcoco just to the east of the Mexico City airport, was a *ranchería* with a population of 306. By 1970, Nezahualcóyotl had been elevated to the status of municipality and had a population of 580,436. Ten years later, its population reached 1,341,230.[242]

The first residents of Nezahualcóyotl lacked electricity, water pipes, a sewage system, and even plants, since the soil of the dry lakebed was too saline to support life. The more fortunate residents faced a one- to two-hour commute each way to factories north of the city. Others eked out a living as street vendors or service workers. As late as 1975, fewer than a dozen streets in the thirty-two square-mile community were paved, leaving the rest to turn into mud holes after rains. That year, the average family size was six, and the average daily family income was $5.00. Services came slowly. As late as 1977, there was only one telephone per 40,000 residents.[243]

THE INTELLECTUAL SCENE

Painting

> From the 1940s onward, muralists increasingly began to appear as part of the revolutionary establishment, with the role of legitimizing the institutionalized revolution . . . Muralism seemed to succumb to the iron law of co-optation of Mexican politics.
>
> Alistair Hennessy, 1991[244]

In 1940, the Revolution remained the dominant theme of public art, reflecting the state's willingness to subsidize muralists in an effort to keep alive the image of the Revolution. By 1950, mural art had become an obstacle to Mexican artistic development. As Octavio Paz commented: "Muralism died of an ideological infection. It began as a search and ended as a catechism."[245]

Younger artists rebelled against muralism. Rufino Tamayo, a member of the new generation of artists, commented, "Mexican peasants triumphed only in the murals." In the most publicized criticism of muralism, painter José Luis Cuevas charged in a 1956 essay, "The Cactus Curtain," that the continued ascendancy of the Mexican mural school stifled creative freedom and kept the nation isolated from artistic developments in other countries. Cuevas declared, "What I want in my country's art are broad highways leading out to the rest of the world, rather than narrow trails connecting one adobe village with another."[246]

Eventually Mexican artists did break away from the muralist school. This was formally acknowledged when the works of a new generation of artists were included in a 1966 exposition at the Palace of Fine Arts entitled "Confrontación '66." This exhibit was later sent to Montreal to be exhibited at the 1967 world's fair. Unlike the mural movement, there was little to unite the post-mural generation. Its members worked in a variety of individual, almost isolated styles.[247]

Of the artists in this post-mural movement, Frida Kahlo became the most widely recognized in the United States. Her father, Guillermo Kahlo, was a German-Jewish expatriate of Hungarian descent who was commissioned by Porfirio Díaz to photograph major architectural monuments for the 1910 centennial celebration. Her mother was of mixed Spanish and Indian heritage.[248]

When she was six, Kahlo contracted polio, which left her right leg shorter than her left. Then, at age eighteen, she was involved in a near-fatal bus-trolley accident that crushed her spine and pelvis, leaving her with pain for the rest of her life. She began painting while convalescing.

In 1929, Kahlo married muralist Diego Rivera, who was twenty-one years her senior. Her parents described the marriage between the expansive Rivera and the diminutive Kahlo as a "marriage between an elephant and a dove." During their marriage, Rivera and Kahlo each took many lovers and she became involved with both men and women, thus providing ample fodder for the press.[249]

Politically, Frida (as she is almost universally known) was influenced by her celebrity husband, and she joined the Mexican Communist Party, in which Rivera was active. Significantly, though, she did not adopt a single element of Rivera's artistic style. In her self-portraits, which introduce Catholic symbolism, pre-Columbian imagery, and fantasy, she typically appears wearing the headdress of the indigenous women of Tehuantepec.[250]

Given her husband's celebrity status, Kahlo had difficulty emerging as an artist in her own right. She produced her best work in the 1940s. However, during her lifetime Frida had only two one-woman gallery shows, and her work was mainly bought by her friends.[251]

After her death in 1954, her casket lay in state in the rotunda of the Place of Fine Arts. Many prominent figures attended her funeral, including Lázaro Cárdenas. Even in death she could not escape from the shadow of her husband. When Cárdenas commented on her death, he referred to her simply as "the wife of my friend, the excellent painter Diego Rivera, whose art has given such glory to Mexico."[252]

In contrast to Rivera, whose artistic legacy came to be viewed with less enthusiasm in the late twentieth century, Kahlo became an icon for feminists as well as for art lovers everywhere. A single 1997 review essay considered nine works concerning her that were published in the United

States between 1991 and 1996. At least six films have been made on her life, including the 2002 release *Frida*, starring Salma Hayek.[253]

The Golden Age of Mexican Cinema

During the 1930s, Mexico developed a robust film industry. In 1938, fifty-seven films were produced. The 1936 film *Allá en el rancho grande* (*Out on the Big Ranch*) won international acclaim and made the singing cowboy, the *charro,* an internationally recognized symbol of Mexico. From its beginnings, the Mexican film industry was highly nationalistic in that it almost exclusively dwelt on Mexican landscapes, customs, and events.[254]

After the 1938 nationalization of the oil industry, film production slumped due to the ensuing economic crisis. In addition, the fledgling Mexican film industry had to face Hollywood competition. At the end of the 1930s, Hollywood's share of the Mexican market was 78.9 percent. The showing of other foreign films left Mexican film producers with a mere 6.5 percent of their domestic market. The lack of theaters also held back the film industry. In 1940, only 446 licensed movie theaters operated in Mexico. That year, Mexico produced only twenty-nine films.[255]

The Second World War snapped the Mexican film industry out of its doldrums. Hollywood shifted to propaganda films, lessening the competition Mexican films faced both domestically and in the rest of the Spanish-speaking world. At the same time, U.S. wartime planners became concerned that the Spanish-speaking world would be viewing movies made in fascist Spain or neutral Argentina. As a result, the U.S. government's wartime Office of Coordination of Inter-American Affairs came to the aid of Mexican film producers. Beginning in 1942, the United States supplied capital, equipment, and technical support to the Mexican film industry. Twentieth-Century Fox donated sound equipment. In 1944, RKO supported the creation of Churubusco Studios, which became the most important studio in post-war Latin America. U.S. planners allocated scarce raw film stock to Mexico and denied it to Argentina.[256]

The Mexican government provided support for Mexican filmmaking by heavily subsidizing ticket prices and by removing import taxes on material used for filmmaking. In 1942, the Banco de México, with the support of the Mexican government, organized the Banco Cinematográfico, thus largely resolving the biggest problem faced by Mexican producers—the lack of capital.[257]

As a result of both U.S. and Mexican government support and lessened competition, feature film production soared from twenty-nine in 1940 to eighty-five in 1944. By 1943, the quality of Mexican films had risen so much that *Variety* suggested they could be thought of as "arty" replacements for French films, which were unavailable due to the war. Between 1940 and 1946, the number of motion-picture theaters grew to almost 1,000, more than double their number in 1940. Film had a much greater cultural impact than the static revolutionary murals.[258]

The Second World War ushered in what is known as the Golden Age of Mexican cinema. Film momentum continued after the war, and by 1947 four studios employed 32,000 people to produce films. In the early 1940s, the *comedia ranchera,* set in rural areas, was a dominant theme. Singing cowboys Jorge Negrete and Pedro Infante invoked a safely romanticized rural past as millions were moving to the cities. Other films, especially those directed by Emilio "El Indio" Fernández, romanticized and attempted to dignify the life of the Indian. Even films sympathetic to the Indian created a false image of a simple, unspoiled life. In *María Candelaria*, the star, Dolores del Río, who portrays a poor Indian, always emerges from her hut with dress and coiffure immaculate. Nonetheless, this film did accurately portray how Indians lived at the mercy of non-Indians.[259]

In the late 1940s, as Mexico continued to urbanize, directors increasingly chose urban settings. In both life and film, Mexico City sparkled as the shining star on Mexico's horizon. A genre known as the cabaret film dealt with the tragic life of the naïve country girl who went astray and ended up in a brothel. If the *comedia ranchera* stood for traditional values, the cabaret film dramatized the breakdown of these values as Mexico urbanized and corruption flourished.[260]

A common characteristic of 1940s films was their dealing with politically safe themes. The most powerful national institutions—the local and national governments, the police, the Church, and the wealthy—were portrayed as benign if not altogether above reproach. Politicians, extreme poverty, social criticism, and open sexuality were excluded.[261]

After the Second World War, Hollywood films began to flood the Mexican market again. In 1953, 226 U.S. films premiered in Mexico, while only eighty-seven Mexican ones did. The inescapable U.S. film presence in Mexico led journalist Paulo Antonio Paranaguá to comment, "Poor Mexico, so far from God and so close to Hollywood." Mexico attempted to protect its domestic market by taxing the exhibition of foreign films. In response, the United States slapped a retaliatory tax on Mexican films, depriving Mexico of the lucrative U.S. market. Hollywood filmmakers not only had much larger budgets than their Mexican counterparts but also had the active support of the U.S. State Department to regain export markets. In order to receive allocations of still-scarce raw film for its domestic film industry, Spain had to grant U.S. film exports privileged access to its domestic market. This effectively shut out Mexican exports.[262]

Films remained politically bland since the government had the legal right to prohibit the production or exhibition of any film. Julio Bracho's 1960 film, *La sombra del caudillo*, a lightly fictionalized account of the ugly power struggle among ex-revolutionaries, was immediately censored and remained unseen for thirty years.[263]

During the 1960s, the immense popularity of the TV soap opera undermined the film industry as resources were shifted from local film production toward TV, which, since it was not competing directly with Hollywood, was more profitable.[264]

The Literary Boom

During the 1960s, Mexico became caught up in what is known as the Latin American literary boom. Essayist Carlos Monsiváis commented on it:

> As never before, Spanish-language readers were confronted by the intense and complementary correspondence between literature and reality. In the midst of every sort of transition (towards fascism, towards revolutionary nationalism, towards the incongruous practices of Third Worlders), readers clung to these books as a means of escaping, not a cultural tradition, but the oppression of underdevelopment.[265]

The boom transcended the boundaries of Latin America, and reading Latin American fiction soon became fashionable among the cultural elite of the United States and Europe.[266]

Carlos Fuentes's 1958 novel *La región más transparente* (*Where the Air is Clear*, 1960) is one of the novels that launched the boom. It brought instant recognition to Fuentes, the son of a Mexican diplomat, who attended school in Argentina, Chile, and Washington DC. His novel evoked the Mexico City of the 1940s and 1950s, where the aggressive capitalism of Ávila Camacho and Alemán clashed with the idealist revolutionary rhetoric of an earlier period. Fuentes set his story in urban surroundings, as was characteristic of boom writers, whose primary reality was the city and its inhabitants.[267]

Fuentes's next novel, *La muerte de Artemio Cruz* (1962; *The Death of Artemio Cruz,* 1964), was not only one of the most celebrated indictments of the Revolution and the society it created but also one of the most popular boom novels. In it, Fuentes depicted a revolutionary veteran on his deathbed recalling his rise to power and wealth through betrayal and opportunism. One flashback recounted how the veteran gained control of a hacienda and then betrayed the peasants living there by providing them with near worthless land as part of the "land reform" while keeping the best land for himself.

In 1971, Fuentes published *Tiempo Mexicano*, a collection of his best essays and reporting from the previous decade. He described the Revolution not as a historical event but as a myth. He stated,

"We are a dependent nation, semicolonial, we have no more room to maneuver than Poland." Fuentes also noted that Mexico was saddled with what for the times was an enormous foreign debt of $3 billion. In *Tiempo Mexicano*, Fuentes criticized "development for the sake of development." As with many intellectuals of his generation, he felt the solution to Mexico's problems was "an energetic intervention by the state in Mexico's economic life."[268]

The 1950s were one of the most productive periods for Mexico's great man of letters, Octavio Paz. Paz, the son and grandson of revolutionary intellectuals, is best known in the United States for his *El laberinto de la soledad* (1950; *The Labyrinth of Solitude*, 1961), the definitive study of what it meant to be a Mexican. In it, he delved into what he felt were Mexicans' feelings of inferiority and resignation. Paz also published poetry and essays, lectured on and presented new poets and painters, and founded journals and a theater group. Later, he joined the diplomatic corps, and in 1962 he was appointed ambassador to India.[269]

When Paz learned of the 1968 student massacre, he resigned his ambassadorship in protest. The next month, he commented on the massacre in a *Le Monde* interview: "If there were any hopes the PRI could be reformed, they have become absurd after the events of October 2. The only solution is to criticize it from the outside and remove it from power." In 1970, Paz published *Posdata* (*The Other Mexico*, 1972), a revaluation of Mexican reality in light of the 1968 student movement. In this book, Paz described two Mexicos, one modern and one underdeveloped. He felt this duality was "the result of the Revolution and the development that followed it: thus, it is the source of many hopes and, at the same time, of future threats."[270]

Paz was one of the few lucky intellectuals who could, due to his stature, exist without drawing a government salary. The vast majority of Mexican intellectuals, one way or another, had to work for the government. Most universities were public, and the private ones tended to be conservative Catholic institutions that were inhospitable to the left-leaning intelligentsia. Intellectuals often held positions in the PRI, a government ministry, or a government-funded research center. As political scientist Judith Hellman noted, "Sooner or later all intellectuals who are not independently wealthy must deal with the dilemma of how to earn a living in Mexico and still retain political independence."[271]

Print Media

> The regime permits freedom and dissent up to the point at which tolerance causes it less trouble than repression, and that point is different for different freedoms. Moreover, different officials see different dividing points.
>
> Daniel Levy & Gabriel Székely, 1983[272]

After the middle of the century, the newspaper industry boomed, driven by cheaper printing technology, government-subsidized newsprint, greater affluence, and a thriving ad industry tied to mass-produced consumer goods. In 1970, 7.7 million newspapers were printed daily in Mexico, or one paper for every 4.2 Mexicans over age ten. In the Federal District, 4.5 million newspapers were printed daily, almost one paper for each of the District's 4.9 million residents over age ten. In contrast, to cite the extreme, in Morelos, only one newspaper was printed daily for every forty-five residents over age ten.[273]

Despite the large number of papers published, as historian Enrique Krauze noted, "It was a given that the press did not honestly, thoughtfully, or independently report on political events or politicians." Even though the government lacked the formal legal power to censor print media, it had numerous more subtle means of control.[274]

From 1960 to 1970, the government placed 20 to 30 percent of all advertisements. By simply withholding its ads, the government could exert pressure on publishers. Papers providing favorable coverage would receive sufficient ad revenue to wipe out debts resulting from unpaid contributions to the government-run social security system. Often government ads made the financial survival of a publication possible. After Carlos Fuentes published a detailed account of the government murder of peasant leader Rubén Jaramillo in *Siempre!*, the government ceased buying ads in that magazine.[275]

Many papers depended on financing from the government-owned development bank Nacional Financiera and on credit to buy newsprint from the government newsprint monopoly PIPSA. PIPSA would supply newsprint on credit to papers that did not rock the boat. Slight government displeasure could be shown by PIPSA demanding immediate payment for past due accounts. On rare occasions, PIPSA denied a publication newsprint, as happened when the left-wing magazine *Política* planned to publish an issue attacking President Kennedy just before his visit to Mexico.[276]

Another form of control was the *iguala*, a payment of up to $2,000 a mouth to reporters in exchange for favorable treatment of the agency or politician making the payment. It was hard for journalists to turn down such payments since publishers paid them virtually nothing on the assumption they would receive *igualas*. Politicians wanting to fine-tune the favorable coverage could purchase a *gacetilla*, which appeared, not as a political ad, but as an ordinary newspaper story. However its content was written by the subject of the *gacetilla*, who, if the payment was sufficient, could even get the *gacetilla* on the front page. The price of a front-page *gacetilla* in *Excélsior,* one of the more respected newspapers, was $8,000. In other cases, the government directly subsidized publications. In 1943, Guy W. Ray, the first secretary at the U.S. embassy, commented on the magazine *Así: "Así* is generally supposed in newspaper circles to be subsidized by the President principally for the purpose of making public attacks on persons who have become prominent or who are out of line with his policies."[277]

There was little economic incentive for publishers to criticize the government and run the risk of losing *gacetillas*, government ads, and credit to purchase newsprint. Instead of challenging the system, the media generally resorted to self-censorship.[278]

The degree of U.S. influence on the press was a source of concern among the intelligentsia. Three of the major magazines covering politics, *Life en español, Visión*, and the Spanish-language edition of *Reader's Digest*, were produced by U.S. firms. In 1964, their combined circulation was 546,000, more than 200,000 above the combined circulation of the top ten Mexican magazines. The Associated Press and United Press International were practically the only sources of international news.[279] Political scientist José González Pedrero commented on the impact U.S. media had on Mexican children:

> The children of our country probably know more about the virtues of the marines, the works of Walt Disney, Jefferson's advanced ideas, and the acts of Superman than of the history of Mexico, the life of Benito Juárez, the political significance of Emiliano Zapata, or the needs of our country.[280]

Due to their high costs, books only circulated among a relatively elite audience. Press runs for many social science works were often only 3,000. There was little government control over book content, and those who could afford them were free to buy books by authors ranging from Karl Marx to Milton Freedman.[281]

In the 1940s, the government-owned Fondo de Cultura Económica became the most prestigious publishing house in Latin America. It published works of exiled Spanish intellectuals and made available the most important works in contemporary economic theory. In the series "Letras Mexicanas," it published Fuentes's *La región más transparente* as well as *El llano en llamas* and *Pedro Páramo* by acclaimed novelist Juan Rulfo. By 1979, the Fondo had published 2,992 titles and had come to occupy a niche similar to that occupied by university presses in the United States.[282]

Even though the mass media was almost uniformly uncritical, decades before vote totals began to show the PRI was losing its grip, academics were undermining its foundations. In 1943, economist Jesús Silva Herzog wrote an article entitled "The Mexican Revolution in Crisis." In it, he criticized the failure of the government's economic model to improve the lives of broad sectors of the population. He recommended a continuation of the agrarian reform, denounced corrupt labor officials, and advocated an increased emphasis on education.[283]

In 1947, historian and economist Daniel Cosío Villegas provided another critique, which directly targeted the political establishment. In an article entitled "Mexico's Crisis," he stated, "The men of the Revolution can be judged now with certainty—they were magnificent destroyers, but nothing they created to replace what had been destroyed has proven indisputably better." He noted that the political system was rife with corruption, that crimes were committed with impunity, and that the population was so accustomed to the press mouthing the government line that readers instinctively assumed to be true the opposite of what the press claimed. Finally, he concluded, "The men of the Revolution have exhausted their moral and political authority."[284]

During the 1950s, the journal *Problemas Agrícolas e Industriales de México* published broad-ranging debates about the direction of Mexican economic development. This journal featured extensive reports on a variety of economic issues and served as a forum for U.S. scholar Frank Tannenbaum, who felt Mexico should base its development on agriculture and mining, a view that was largely abandoned in official circles after the Cárdenas administration. He deplored the creation of a few capital-intensive industries that increased the gross national product and made owners rich but created jobs for only a few. Tannenbaum felt that rather than trying to imitate the U.S. industrial model, Mexico should follow a path more like those of Denmark and Switzerland.[285]

In 1965, sociologist Pablo González Casanova published *Democracy in Mexico* (cited twelve times in this work), the most devastating critique yet of the direction the Revolution had taken. In his work, he applied sociological methodology to official statistics and concluded that after the Second World War Mexico had generated substantial economic growth but had not lessened dependency, underdevelopment, or inequality.[286]

In general, scholars were free to publish their works, given that limited distribution minimized their impact. Occasionally they would cross the poorly defined line between what was tolerable and what was beyond the pale (as defined by the political establishment). In 1965, Arnaldo Orfila Reynal, the director of the Fondo de Cultura Económica, crossed this line by publishing the *Children of Sánchez*, a book by U.S. anthropologist Oscar Lewis, which graphically described the life of a family in Tepito, a Mexico City slum. By publishing this book in Mexico, Orfila Reynal laid bare the degree to which economic development had failed the poor. President Díaz Ordaz asked Orfila Reynal to resign for having published what the president regarded as an insult to Mexico. The director refused to resign, stating he had done nothing wrong and that if Díaz Ordaz wanted to get rid of him, he would have to fire him. Díaz Ordaz promptly did so.

Orfila Reynal then used his severance pay and the financial support of other Mexican writers to found the publishing house Siglo XXI, which became what historian Enrique Krauze described as "the indisputable vanguard of publishing in Mexico and Latin America." Many of the works Siglo XXI published were Marxist in outlook and were much more critical of the system than was the *Children of Sánchez*. Not only did Siglo XXI publish numerous critiques of the government but the publisher Joaquín Mortiz reprinted the *Children of Sánchez*, which became a best-seller.[287]

Broadcast Media

In 1940, Mexico had ninety commercial and twelve government radio stations and an estimated 450,000 radio sets. Radio had a nationwide cultural influence and served to popularize dances such as the samba and the rumba that had become popular in Mexico City. By 1960, there were more than 3 million radios, five or six times the number of TV sets. In 1961, radio accounted for 36 percent of the $120 million spent on advertising in Mexico, while television accounted for only 6 percent.[288]

Radio reached its zenith about 1970, when there were 17 million sets. Station ownership was highly concentrated, as nine groups controlled 70 percent of the stations. Even though the law restricted station ownership to Mexicans, radio paved the way for increased foreign influence. A 1971 study found that 84 percent of the products advertised on XEW, one of the most influential radio stations, were produced by foreign-controlled firms.[289]

In 1948, before television broadcasting began in Mexico, President Alemán decided that Mexican TV would be privately owned and financed by ad sales, as in the United States, rather than being publicly financed as was the British Broadcasting Company. In 1950, he awarded the first broadcast license to his close confidant Rómulo O'Farrill. The newly licensed station, XHTV, which was the first full-time TV station in Latin America, began its initial broadcast with Alemán's 1950 state of the nation speech.[290]

The next year radio tycoon Emilio Azcárraga Vidaurreta launched another station, XEW-TV. Four years later, O'Farril and Azcárraga concluded that the middle class was still not large enough to support competing television networks, so they merged their two fledgling networks with the one other private station, forming a monopoly, despite the prohibition on monopolies contained in Article 28 of the Mexican constitution.[291]

The merger created Telesistema Mexicano, which, by 1959, was operating twenty stations. This monopoly faithfully served presidents Ruiz Cortines, López Mateos, and Díaz Ordaz by supporting the government. These presidents in turn favored the existing TV monopoly.[292]

By 1968, television had replaced radio as the main source of home entertainment and had surpassed radio in ad sales. Telesistema Mexicano kept its profits high by establishing a company union that depressed wages. The absence of a rival network that might compete with Telesistema for talent also contributed to its profitability. The medium proved to be so lucrative that Azcárraga was able to purchase a TV station in San Antonio, Texas, that developed into the Spanish-language U.S. network, Univisión.[293]

Under Azcárraga's direction, Telesistema pioneered live intercontinental transmission of sporting events. The program "Siempre en Domingo" became the most influential music show in the Spanish-speaking world. Mexico City, the nerve center of Telesistema operations, drew actors from throughout Latin America seeking jobs and the opportunity to work with the latest technology. As Claudia Fernández and Andrew Paxman observed in their book on Azcárraga: "By the end of the 1960s, Mexico City was without a doubt the capital of Spanish-language television. It was the most prolific producer, the biggest exporter of programs, and the Mecca for talent."[294]

Just as with radio, the law restricted the ownership of TV stations to Mexican citizens. However, in 1976, foreign ad agencies, mainly U.S.-owned, handled 70 percent of the value of all advertising. Even ad agencies not owned by foreigners largely produced ads for products made by foreign corporations. U.S. corporations dominated the production of such heavily advertised products as autos, detergents, food, cosmetics, tobacco, pharmaceuticals, chemicals, and soft drinks. TV commercials promoted cigarettes, perfumes, alcoholic beverages, luxury cars, and shopping trips to San Antonio, Texas. As they were designed to do, they shaped tastes. White bread and soft drinks became a high priority even in the poorest villages since they were believed to be a key to good health.[295]

Even though there was no formal mechanism of censorship, as there was with movies, concentrated media ownership stifled diversity of opinion. Advertisers' opinions and interests shaped content. The government—upon which stations relied for licenses and ads—openly pressured Telesistema Mexicano to minimize coverage of the 1968 student movement. As a result, as Octavio Paz observed in 1975:

> Freedom of the press is more a formality than a reality; radio and television are in the hands of two or three families who are more interested in earning money by brutalizing the audience than in analyzing the country's problems honestly and objectively.[296]

Chapter 22

The Mexican Economic Miracle, 1941–1970

> Between 1940 and 1970, there occurred an industrial revolution as well as an urban revolution, without first having resolved the worst problems of rural Mexico. Under the leadership of a coalition of industrial, commercial, and anti-agrarian interests, the federal government abandoned Cárdenas' strategy of development based on the participation of small rural producers and urban workers and replaced it with one based on rapid industrial expansion regardless of the social cost.
>
> Cynthia Hewitt de Alcántara, 1977[1]

THE WAR YEARS, 1940–1945

While Mexico was only marginally involved in the Second World War militarily, it was heavily involved economically. The Mexican and U.S. governments worked closely to coordinate Mexican production for Allied war needs. Production rapidly increased as lead, iron, zinc, and copper mines operated twenty-four hours a day. Many non-working mines were reopened to meet soaring demand. Since mining was already largely under the control of U.S. corporations, it was easy to integrate mining into the U.S. war effort.[2]

The U.S. agricultural attaché and the Mexican secretary of agriculture worked closely together to increase the production of fibers, vegetable oils, and other crops needed for military use. Between 1942 and 1943, 1.7 million acres were shifted from producing corn to crops such as cotton, henequen, and sesame. Corn production fell 23 percent. There was a concomitant shift in labor as agricultural workers accepted job openings in Mexican industry or departed for the United States. As a result of the decline in food-crop acreage and in the labor supply, there were severe food shortages.[3]

Wartime expansion of Mexican industry was limited not by a lack of demand or capital but by the lack of U.S.-produced machinery. Mexican industry was considered "low priority" by American war planners and thus it received limited allocations of scarce manufacturing equipment. Especially favored was industry that would aid the Allied war effort. In 1942, for example, the U.S. Export-Import Bank approved a $6 million loan for the construction of a steel mill in Monclova, Coahuila.[4]

A by-product of the war economy was inflation. Since production was directed to Allied military needs, consumers had less to buy. Even before Pearl Harbor, capital seeking a safe haven was flowing into Mexico at a rate of $40 million a year. Mexicans repatriated funds from the United States to escape war-time restrictions. Additional funds came from exports, U.S. tourists, Spaniards fleeing their civil war, and Mexicans working in the United States. As more money chased fewer goods, an inflationary spiral resulted. In 1944, inflation reached 33 percent.[5]

During the war, the government increased its role in the economy and changed economic priorities. An emphasis on industrialization regardless of social cost replaced Cárdenas's vision of prosperous peasants working their own land. To promote industrialization, the government tightened its control over labor, provided favored entrepreneurs with credits and other financial incentives, kept taxes low, and increased investment in infrastructure. Between 1941 and 1945, the government was responsible for 58 percent of all investment. Road building and irrigation projects absorbed 44 percent of this investment. Between 1940 and 1946, as a result of federal investment, the area irrigated increased from 293,200 acres to 882,300.[6]

Between 1940 and 1945, as a result of wartime demand and increased government economic support, the Mexican per capita gross national product increased by 4.6 percent a year, and exports increased at an annual rate of 11.7 percent. During the war years, there was an 850 percent increase in manufactured exports as Mexican textiles, chemicals, and processed food replaced production by the great powers, whose industrial capacity was diverted to military needs.[7]

Between 1940 and 1945, manufacturing production increased at an annual rate of 10 percent. Most of this expansion came from full utilization of installed industrial capacity rather than from new equipment. As additional shifts began working at existing plants, the number of manufacturing workers increased from 568,000 in 1940 to 938,000 in 1945.[8]

While these statistics pleased Mexican economists, the effect of these changes on the average Mexican was anything but pleasant. As agricultural production shifted to non-food crops, nutritional standards plummeted. Recognizing Mexico's contribution to the war effort, the Allies supplied Mexico with what food they could. Military needs and transport shortages made this difficult. Grain was even shipped to Mexico from Australia, since it could be loaded on U.S. cargo ships that otherwise would have returned empty from the Pacific theater.[9]

High inflation, weak labor leadership, and a lack of government support for labor resulted in a 37 percent decline in workers' buying power between 1940 and 1944. Wealth was quickly shifted to business owners.[10]

In 1943, a commentator noted:

> To the great bulk of the Mexican people the world conflict is evident mainly in terms of eggs costing more this week than they did when laid by the same hen last week; of corn, the traditional mainstay of their simple lives, suddenly disappearing from the market and reappearing days later at undreamed-of prices . . . Banks, business firms, and industries are enjoying unprecedented prosperity, and speculators are thriving. Meanwhile the conditions of the masses steadily deteriorates, causing unrest and resentment.[11]

IMPORT SUBSTITUTION INDUSTRIALIZATION, 1946–1954

> For the young group of civilians that came to power with President Alemán, the obsession was first to create wealth by means of industrial substitution of traditional imports, and then distribute it according to the demands of social justice. Nobody set a date for this second stage, and the public and private leaders of the country seemed interested only in the first stage: to accumulate capital.
>
> Héctor Aguilar Camín and Lorenzo Meyer, 1993[12]

Even as Mexico rode the Korean War (1950–1953) raw material export boom, the government officially embraced an economic development strategy known as import substitution. Its proponents believed that the traditional strategy of underdeveloped countries—exporting raw materials and importing manufactured goods—led to an economic dead end. Planners also noted that the failure to develop local industry limited job creation. Import substitution shifted the central focus of development policy from the international market to the domestic market.

Various social groups favored this emphasis on industrialization. They included government policy makers, an urban population little interested in land reform, workers in industries protected from foreign competition, and owners of industry, who had emerged during the Second World War as a major interest group.

The views of government policy makers were shaped by the experience of the Depression (when Mexico could not afford manufactured imports due to a decline in its raw material exports) and the Second World War (when the Allies limited the export of manufactured goods due to wartime priorities). To Mexican planners, industry was the key to both economic autonomy and the new technology needed to increase productivity. Industrialization was made almost synonymous with national sovereignty and economic development. U.S. historian Lesley Byrd Simpson compared the zeal of industrial planners to that of the sixteenth-century missionaries. Simpson noted that both groups felt that they had the solution to Mexico's problems in hand.[13]

For the industrialists who had emerged during the Second World War, import substitution industrialization seemed to offer a way to avoid competing with U.S. industry. Such competition appeared especially daunting because after The Second World War the United States produced more than half of the world's manufactured goods and owned half of the world's shipping.[14]

The rapidly expanding and increasingly influential urban population craved industrial products. Even those not having a direct stake in an industrial project felt that industry would enable Mexico to escape from its impoverished rural past.[15]

In 1947, the opening of Mexico's first Sears, Roebuck store indicated the tremendous appeal of consumer goods. An estimated 15,000–18,000 customers visited the store in its first three days and another 10,000–25,000 were turned away daily. By the mid-1950s, Sears had seventeen stores in Mexico. Only sixteen of Sears' 3,200 employees were U.S. citizens. What the parent company did supply was marketing know-how, which was reflected not only in U.S.-style home appliances but in single prices, merchandise guarantees, cash registers, credit-card installment buying, and large-scale display advertising in newspapers.[16]

The existing pro-industry views of Mexican manufacturers, government planners, and urban residents were reinforced by an emerging Latin American consensus on development. Argentine economist Raúl Prebisch, who served as executive secretary of the U.N. Economic Commission for Latin America (ECLA) between 1949 and 1963, forcefully articulated this consensus. Prebisch observed that the already developed nations were extracting wealth from Latin America by buying inexpensive raw materials and then supplying the region with costly manufactured goods. He also believed that the prices of raw materials were rising more slowly than those of manufactured goods. Finally, he felt that increases in industrial efficiency in the developed world were reflected in increased wages there—not in higher wages for Latin American workers producing raw materials. ECLA doctrine formally abandoned the nineteenth-century notion of free markets and replaced it with the notion that governments should ensure sound development practice.[17]

Mexican government officials, following Prebisch's reasoning, encouraged the production of manufactured items that had been previously imported. A 1946 law empowered officials to decree certain industries "new and necessary." Tariffs would then be levied on the type of goods these industries produced. In some cases, the government would prohibit the importation of an item or impose an import quota. As each item appeared on the "new and necessary" list, Mexican entrepreneurs would begin production, often taking advantage of low-interest loans from the government development bank, Nacional Financiera. Thanks to tariffs and import prohibitions, they would not have to worry about foreign competition. New industries received a five-to-ten-year exemption on taxes and a duty-waiver to import manufacturing machinery. In the Federal District, the government expropriated land and constructed industrial parks for new industries. Autos, refrigerators, and electrical products were among the items whose import was restricted in an attempt to stimulate their domestic production.[18]

Even though President Alemán was a staunch advocate of private enterprise, he felt government should make key investments to further the development process. The areas targeted for such investment were those deemed too large or risky, or with too long a payback period to attract the private sector. Thus the government maintained or increased its role in irrigation, banking, railroads, communications, road building, and oil production. It also sought to eliminate economic bottlenecks by increasing the production of steel, chemicals, fertilizer, and railroad cars. The private sector, having seen how the government favored it during the war, welcomed such investment, especially in energy production. During Alemán's 1946–1952 term, 52 percent of the federal budget was allocated to economic development, compared to 39 percent under Ávila Camacho and 38 percent under Cárdenas. The eleven largest corporations in the nation, which included those producing oil and electricity and providing rail and phone service, were government-owned.[19]

The emphasis on economic growth affected the entire society, as spending for economic development became a higher priority than social spending. By the end of the 1950s, the government was spending only 1.4 percent of the national product on education, while Argentina was spending 2.5 percent and Brazil 2.6 percent.[20]

Thanks to pent-up consumer demand, protection from imports, high public spending, and $372 million of export income accumulated during the Second World War, economic growth during Alemán's term averaged 5.8 percent a year. In a testimony to the success of import-substitution industrialization, by 1955, 90 percent of the sales in Sears stores were of domestically manufactured products.[21]

Mexican businessmen poured their profits back into the economy. During Alemán's term, the government, relying on taxes, monetary expansion, and income from state-owned enterprises, financed additional investment. During the 1940s, 99.1 percent of industrialization was domestically financed.[22]

Amidst the euphoria surrounding this development, few paused to notice some not so welcome trends. To entice investors, the government ensured that profits remained high by keeping salaries low. Salaries remained low and even decreased as the government allowed a high rate of inflation. Workers could survive on low salaries since the government deliberately kept food prices low. This allowed handsome industrial profits but ultimately stymied agricultural development. Industrial workers were all too aware that there was a widening gap between wages and profits, but thanks to PRI-controlled labor unions, PRI-imposed union leaders, and the repression of movements not directly controlled by the PRI, they could do little about this disparity. Finally, consumers were saddled with expensive goods due to the non-competitive nature of the factories that arose behind tariff barriers. However, they had no means to reject existing policies, which were set by PRI functionaries.[23]

THE BOOM YEARS, 1954–1970

> Mexican industry grew behind high tariff walls, companies were cosseted and subsidized (e.g., by cheap fuel), and favored workers won featherbedded security. But even if aggregate output was thereby depressed (and consumers were ripped off), the system embodied elements of stability, reciprocity, and manageability.
>
> Alan Knight, 2007[24]

The 1953 armistice in Korea brought an end to the boom in exporting lead, zinc, cotton, and sulfur to the United States. In 1954, to snap Mexico out of the ensuing economic slump, the peso was devalued. For Mexican buyers who paid for imports in pesos, prices increased, thus stimulating the sale of Mexican-produced goods. To maintain the momentum of import substitution, in 1965, there was a 6 percent increase in tariffs. By 1970, import quotas had been placed on nearly 13,000 categories of goods.[25]

Given the memory of the 1938 oil nationalization and competing opportunities for investment, foreign capital was slow to return to Mexico. Revenue from food and fiber exports underwrote much new investment. However, as potential investors saw that Mexico provided a safe investment climate, the rate of private foreign investment accelerated. By 1956, U.S. corporations had invested $600 million, of which $240 million was in industry. Of the other Latin American countries, only Brazil had attracted more U.S. manufacturing investment. This investment notwithstanding, as late as 1959 Americans were financing only 9 percent of manufacturing investment.[26]

A 1956 article in *Fortune* magazine described the visual impact of U.S. investment:

> The signs surmounting the new plants proclaim one U.S. company name after another. General Motors, Singer, Goodrich, Studebaker, R.C.A., Eastman Kodak—only the corporate suffix "S.A." (for Sociedad Anónima, i.e., anonymous society) attests plainly that the locale is other than Rahway, New Jersey.[27]

Government investment decisions were not formulated in isolation. The increasingly powerful business sector did its best to influence the type of investment and who would receive lucrative government building and supply contracts. Import licenses were often crucial to a business's success. Businessmen threw lavish parties, paid the travel expenses of government officials, and presented them with gifts in hopes of receiving favorable treatment.[28]

Between 1955 and 1970, Mexico adopted an economic development strategy known as "stabilizing development." This policy was based on: 1) price stability, 2) maintaining a fixed exchange rate between the peso and the dollar, 3) providing energy and government services to industry at low prices, 4) heavy government investment in roads and irrigation works, and 5) the use of foreign credit and foreign investment to complement domestic savings.[29]

After the government erected tariff barriers, foreign corporations felt that if they did not begin manufacturing in Mexico, they would lose that market. Previously it had been more attractive to manufacture in the United States, taking advantage of economies of scale, and then ship to Mexico. Low taxes and a minimum daily wage of $0.75 made investing in Mexico attractive. Corporations also welcomed the government's low prices for oil, electricity, and rail services. By the end of the 1960s, such low prices had transferred an estimated $2 billion to the private sector.[30]

Along with U.S. manufacturing investment, which totaled $1.2 billion in 1970, came new technology and marketing innovations. During the 1960s, the rate of investment reached 20 percent of the GDP. Investment was attractive because Mexico had a consistent economic policy, as well as political stability. This policy consistency stood in sharp contrast to the repeated economic policy shifts elsewhere in Latin America.[31]

In contrast to the nineteenth century when exports financed much of Porfirian industrialization, after the end of the Korean War-induced commodities boom, Mexican exports were unable to finance the imports needed to industrialize. To finance such imports, Mexico increasingly turned to foreign direct investment (FDI). By 1970, this investment, 79 percent of which came from the United States, totaled $2.8 billion. Even though foreign investment was increasing rapidly, in 1970, 65 percent of Mexican industrial production remained in Mexican hands, largely financed by reinvesting the high profits resulting from tariff protection and low-cost labor.

In the 1950s Mexico also turned to foreign loans to finance its development. Between 1949 and 1959 the World Bank loaned Mexico $190 million for electrification, railroads, and industrial development. In 1958 and 1959, Mexico borrowed almost $200 million to cover its balance of trade deficit and borrowed an additional $200 million to indemnify foreign owners of the electrical generating companies nationalized by López Mateos.[32]

In the 1960s, Mexico increasingly relied on foreign borrowing. During this decade, Mexico borrowed $2 billion from the World Bank, the Export-Import Bank, and Inter-American Development Bank to buy capital goods and for electrification, road building, and irrigation. Private foreign banks also began lending substantial sums to finance development in the 1960s. Between 1960 and 1970, U.S. bank loans to Mexico rose from $385 million to $3.3 billion.[33]

Table 22.1 *Annual increase in gross domestic product, 1953–1970*

	GDP	GDP per capita
Ruiz Cortines, 1953–1958	6.8	3.7
López Mateos, 1959–1964	6.7	3.4
Díaz Ordaz, 1965–1970	6.8	3.4

Source: Ramírez (1989: 46)

As financial expert Edmundo Sánchez Aguilar commented at the time, "for every year of 1957–72 Mexico has paid its external debts not from real earnings of foreign exchange income from its foreign trade and tourism, but from new borrowings in foreign currencies." This perfectly described a Ponzi scheme. From 1957 to 1971, interest payments on previous loans totaled $1.14 billion. The 1970s oil boom delayed the inevitable crash until the 1980s.[34]

By the 1960s, observers inside and outside Mexico were referring to Mexico's economic growth as the "Mexican miracle." Mexicans felt that they had finally found the path to prosperity. In 1964, Antonio Ortiz Mena, who served as treasury secretary from 1958 to 1970, commented: "The foremost concern of the Chief of the Executive was to transmit the conviction to the people that economic development would be continued and abundance would be procured with monetary stability."[35]

ROADS AND CARS

The extension of the road system formed a key ingredient of the Mexican economic miracle. Highways allowed the rapid transport of goods between major cities and extended sales into areas not reached by rail. Road construction facilitated Mexico's superb bus service, which to this day is light years ahead of its U.S. counterpart.

A wide variety of interests favored building roads. Mexican manufacturers sought roads to get their products to market and to lower the cost of bringing food to their workers. The U.S. auto industry, Mexican auto dealers, and Mexican construction companies also favored road construction. In 1947, U.S. Ambassador to Mexico Walter Thurston commented on how the Mexican auto industry benefited the United States when advocating a loan to Mexico for road building:

> American export trade will be benefited in many ways by the augmentation of these communications facilities between the two counties, in addition to the direct benefit deriving from the sale of additional road construction machinery, filling station equipment, et cetera. Additional sales to Mexico of automobiles, trucks, parts and accessories are only some of the items which are bound eventually to enter in larger volume by reason of the additional mileage added to the highway system.[36]

The extension of roads stimulated the Mexican automobile industry. In 1961, twelve companies assembled 40,000 autos, compared to only four companies in the far larger U.S. market. Auto dealers distributed forty-three brands and 117 models. Auto assembly involved very little actual manufacturing. Rather, parts were imported and assembled in Mexico. Imports were so pervasive that assemblers joked that they even imported air to inflate tires.[37]

In 1962, the Mexican government decided to restructure the auto industry since it considered there were too many models for the small Mexican market and that importing parts, rather than manufacturing them in Mexico, cost jobs. The auto sector alone accounted for 10 percent of imports. The government announced it would limit to seven the number of auto manufacturers and require

Table 22.2 *The automobile revolution, 1940–1970*

Year	Miles of paved roads	Number of automobiles
1940	2,964	93,632
1950	8,428	173,080
1960	16,726	483,101
1970	26,007	1,233,824

Source: INEGI (1994: 692, 694)

that 60 percent of the value of each car be manufactured in Mexico. The government also sought to eliminate costly annual model changes, limit the number of models sold in Mexico, and produce standardized parts through the entire Mexican auto industry.[38]

Mexico immediately came up against the power of not only the multinationals but also their home governments. Nissan was allowed into the Mexican market after the Japanese government threatened to cease buying Mexico's number one export, cotton, if Nissan was excluded from the Mexican market. U.S. Ambassador Thomas Mann informed the Mexican government that the exclusion of any U.S. auto firm that had been operating in Mexico would be viewed unfavorably by the United States, so the U.S. Big Three were allowed in. Auto manufacturers mobilized domestic auto dealers and parts vendors, threatening to pull out of Mexico entirely if they were not allowed to make their own manufacturing decisions.[39]

Due to pressure from corporations and foreign governments, Mexico backed down on standardizing parts and limiting the number of auto makers, the number of models, and annual model changes. The Mexican government did achieve its goal of 60 percent local content. The content rule alone produced major changes. Between 1962 and 1966, the number of workers in the auto parts industry increased from 29,000 to 52,000, and investment rose from $160 million to $448 million. Increased auto parts manufacturing stimulated glass, steel, aluminum, paint, plastics, and machine-tool production.[40]

THE OIL INDUSTRY

After the 1938 oil nationalization, the Mexican petroleum industry, which had been almost entirely export orientated, became closely linked to increased domestic motor vehicle use. Mexican oil production began a steady increase. In 1940, oil production only totaled 44.0 million barrels. By 1970, production had reached 156.6 million barrels.[41]

In 1938, the government established a public enterprise, Petróleos Mexicanos, generally known as Pemex, that held a monopoly on oil drilling, refining, and fuel distribution. The oil industry had suffered from years of neglect and had become badly worn, inefficient, and obsolescent. Compounding this neglect was the closure of foreign markets to Mexican oil and the refusal of suppliers to sell chemicals or equipment necessary for refining. Senior technicians and administrators departed at the time of the nationalization, taking with them geological reports. During the early 1940s, the industry continued to have difficulty buying equipment due to wartime shortages. In 1946, Pemex surprised many observers by not only surviving but surpassing the 1937 level of oil production.[42]

After the oil nationalization, exports largely ceased while demand within Mexico was soaring. To meet this demand Pemex reoriented its distribution system, which previously had consisted of pipelines from wells to ports on the Gulf of Mexico. After 1938 it was necessary not only to expand refining capacity but also to deliver fuel to users throughout Mexico.[43]

With the oil industry in government hands, oil workers sought both the material benefits of oil wealth and effective control over the industry. Not surprisingly, this conflicted with the government's desire to direct the oil industry in furtherance of its own goals. After the end of the Second World War, this conflict broke into the open.[44]

In 1946, to assert government control over the industry, President Alemán appointed as director of Pemex Antonio Bermúdez, an energetic, wealthy, businessman-turned-politician. In December 1946, when oil workers went out on strike, the military occupied oil installations. Within twenty-four hours the strike collapsed, and the union leadership was fired. The crackdown on labor drew mixed reviews since many resented oil workers for having used their status as heroes in the "battle against imperialism" to obtain an average wage of twenty-four pesos a day, ten to twelve times the national average.[45]

Given increased Middle Eastern oil production, the export market was weak in the 1950s. At that time, crude oil marketing was a virtual monopoly of big oil companies, which were not keen on lending Pemex a hand. This led Bermúdez—who headed Pemex until 1958—to concentrate on supplying the domestic market. He observed:

> Mexico is not and never shall be a large exporter of oil. It is illusory—and it would be very damaging—to expect oil, exported in large quantities, to become the workhorse of our economy or the panacea of our economic ills.

In addition to meeting soaring domestic oil demand, Bermúdez encouraged Mexicans to supply Pemex with equipment. As late as 1947, 100 percent of Pemex equipment was imported. By 1957, domestic producers supplied half of its equipment. A 1952 *New York Times* article commented on how Bermúdez had expanded exploration, reserves, production, consumption, and the distribution network:

> Senator Bermúdez' role in building up Pemex to the status of a modern, progressive industry is one of the few things about Pemex that no one disputes whether they are for or against the nationalized oil company.[46]

From the 1940s through the 1960s, Pemex maintained low prices in an effort to stimulate economic development. President Ávila Camacho stated that since the oil industry was nationalized, it "could operate without worrying about the profit motive, only taking into account the general interest." The availability of cheap energy did spur industrial growth. However, the policy had several drawbacks. Its effect was regressive, since it disproportionately benefited the wealthiest areas of the country, where the most fuel was used. It also lowered the revenue Pemex generated, so little money was available for oil exploration. Pemex's low prices and excessive hiring, which inflated costs, led the company to rely on foreign loans, which financed the majority of the company's investment by 1958. Finally, its low prices encouraged the profligate use of energy, which, beginning in the 1960s, forced Mexico to import oil to meet demand.[47]

Bermúdez and his successors achieved labor peace in the oil industry by tolerating widespread corruption. Union leaders were allowed to enrich themselves if they ensured that the industry did not face serious labor problems. Such leaders regularly received contracts to supply Pemex with goods and services and then farmed the work out to others for a percentage of the profits. They sold Pemex jobs for between $450 and $1,200. This was especially lucrative since management allowed them to hire excess workers. Employees engaged in widespread theft of gasoline. Dissident workers were greeted with job loss and violence. This corruption extended up to the very top of the corporation. When President López Mateos chided his Pemex director, Pascual Gutiérrez Roldán, for distributing Pemex contracts to his friends and business partners, the director replied, "Do you expect me to give them to my enemies!"[48]

Despite its being hobbled by corruption and its low-price policy, Pemex retained its status as a national icon—a symbol of victorious Mexican nationalism. In 1964, President Díaz Ordaz's appointing of Jesús Reyes Heroles as Pemex director further enhanced Pemex's reputation. Reyes Heroles improved the company's efficiency and launched an ambitious exploration effort that was to pay dividends in the 1970s.

As a 1967 *Wall Street Journal* article noted, Pemex's positive image caused foreign oil companies to worry that it might attract imitators:

> Private oil company executives are worried about the impact an increasingly efficient Pemex might have on private oil operations in the rest of Latin America and in the Mideast. "As a successful government venture, Pemex is the model for other countries wanting to nationalize their oil," says an apprehensive vice president of a U.S.-based international petroleum concern.[49]

TOURISM

Several events set the stage for modern Mexican tourism. U.S. tourists eventually realized that Mexico was no longer under the sway of bandoleer-clad revolutionaries or Marxist presidents who expropriated U.S. property. The Second World War favored Mexican tourism, since the war closed Europe to those with travel lust, and Mexico provided Americans with an opportunity to escape ration books.[50]

After the Second World War, increased highway mileage, the elimination of malaria, and U.S. affluence led large numbers of students, teachers, artists, and retirees to visit Mexico. The number of hotel rooms in Mexico doubled between 1954 and 1962. After 1959, the Cuban Revolution caused many who would have otherwise have visited Cuba to divert to Mexico. In the 1960s, improved communications and the availability of cheap airfares on jet aircraft led to the arrival of still more tourists.[51]

Heritage sites, both pre-Columbian and colonial, were specifically prepared to attract tourists. Pre-Columbian sites included Monte Alban in Oaxaca, Teotihuacan near Mexico City, and various Mayan sites in Yucatán. Colonial sites included Taxco, Guanajuato, and Mexico City's central historical distinct. Handicraft production and Mexico's world-renowned Ballet Folklórico linked tourism with Mexico's contemporary indigenous cultures. In 1964, to highlight both Mexico's pre-Columbian heritage as well as contemporary ethnographic material, the National Anthropological Museum opened in Mexico City's Chapultepec Park. Historian Brian Hamnett described the museum as "so magnificent in its contemporary form and location that it could be described as a wonder of the modern world."[52]

Tourism was one of the Mexican government's greatest postwar development successes. The individual most closely associated with developing tourism is Miguel Alemán, who not only promoted tourism as president, 1946–1952, but served as director general of the National Tourism Commission between 1958 and 1983. In 1961, the Department of Tourism was established as an autonomous government agency to promote tourism. In 1971, it had a budget of just over $7.4 million dollars. Government tourism development faced a twin challenge—continuing infrastructure development to handle the ever increasing number of foreign tourists and making Mexican tourism attractive to Mexicans so they would not deplete scarce foreign exchange by traveling abroad.[53]

Between 1950 and 1972, foreign tourism increased at an annual rate of 12 percent, roughly double that of the economy as a whole. In 1972, receipts from foreign tourism totaled $1.7 billion, more than total merchandise exports. That year Mexico received almost 2 million tourists, nearly half the Latin American total. In 1965, 208,000 were employed directly in providing services to foreign tourists and in addition an estimated 1 million families were at least partially employed in supplying handicrafts for sale to tourists.[54]

AGRICULTURE

> During the period of ISI [import-substitution industrialization], Mexican agriculture, rural environment, and peasantry provided the cheap food, abundant labor, raw materials, and capital crucial to the development of industry.
>
> David A. Sonnenfeld, 1992[55]

In response to wartime needs, Ávila Camacho shifted the focus from land reform to agricultural production. Thanks to increased agricultural prices, more government credit, and government spending on highways and irrigation, agricultural production increased by 52 percent between 1940 and 1944. Wartime agriculture was tailored toward meeting Allied industrial needs, not feeding Mexico's population.[56]

In response to wartime food shortages and the generally low yields throughout Mexican agriculture, the government invited the Rockefeller Foundation to establish an agricultural research program in Mexico. Rockefeller researchers accepted the offer and developed a package of new technology, often referred to as the Green Revolution. It combined agricultural mechanization, extensive irrigation, and the use of hybrid seeds, inorganic fertilizers, and pesticides. Production of wheat, the crop to benefit most from the Green Revolution, increased from nearly 400,000 tons in 1940 to 2.1 million tons in 1970. The Rockefeller effort was so successful at raising yields that one of its chief scientists, Norman Borlaug, received the Nobel Peace Prize in recognition of his plant breeding efforts.[57]

Due to limitations imposed by climate, soil, and topography, few existing farms could profit from Green Revolution technology. This technology was most widely applied on newly irrigated land in northwestern Mexico where the government attempted to emulate the success of the Tennessee Valley Authority. Agricultural investment increased from 13.3 percent of total investment in 1939 to 19.5 percent in 1950. Between 1945 and 1955, agricultural production increased by 5.8 percent a year, and in the following decade it increased by 4 percent a year.[58]

A commercial revolution accompanied the Green Revolution as increasing amounts of machinery and other inputs were required to maintain production. Fertilizer use rose from 1,800 metric tons in 1940 to 533,700 in 1970. By 1960, Mexico had 39,000 farm tractors, more than any other Latin American country, including Argentina, which had roughly twice as much agricultural land as Mexico. In 1947, to tap into this market, International Harvester opened an implement manufacturing plant in Saltillo.[59]

During the immediate postwar period, Mexican agriculture fed a rapidly increasing and urbanizing population and provided exports that financed the import of industrial machinery. The government established low corn prices so that industrial wages would not have to be raised to cover food costs.[60]

Mexico's success at feeding its urban population and exporting agricultural products to finance industry came at the expense of the environment. Increased irrigation led to soil salinization as the salt carried in by irrigation water remained in the soil when the water evaporated. Eventually, more than a million irrigated acres were lost due to such salinity. Insecticides killed not only pests but predators that preyed on them. Pests soon developed immunity to the insecticides used to control them. Farmers responded to this immunity by making as many as twelve insecticide applications a season. They also shifted from older pesticides such as DDT to newly developed compounds. As farmers increased the volume of insecticides applied and switched to more costly compounds, insecticide purchase and application became the largest single cost of cotton production. Farmers found themselves on what has been called the "pesticide treadmill," involving ever increasing pesticide costs. Once the process began, farmers could not simply quit applying pesticides, since with insect predators eliminated by the pesticide, pervasive pests would wreak havoc. Finally, while yields rose, the Green Revolution led to a sharp decline in energy efficiency. Crops produced with the new technology required enormous amounts of energy to manufacture and power farm equipment and to produce pesticides and fertilizer.[61]

Agricultural policies after the Cárdenas administration consistently favored large growers. Only two days after his inauguration, Alemán expanded the maximum legal size of land holdings to 100 hectares (247 acres) of irrigated land or 200 hectares of seasonal rain-fed land. Between 1940 and 1950, the area of privately owned, irrigated land nearly doubled, while there was only a 23 percent increase in irrigated ejido land. To encourage mechanization, which only larger farms could afford, the government exempted agricultural equipment from import duties and provided ample financing to facilitate its purchase. Water supplied by government irrigation projects was so heavily subsidized that water payments failed to recover distribution costs, let alone the initial cost of the dams and canals. Special subsidies reflected wheat farmers' political influence. Not only did the government subsidize the cost of shipping wheat to markets in central Mexico but it set a domestic wheat price above the international price, resulting in the transfer of some $20 million a year to wheat growers.[62]

The farmers who benefited most from the Green Revolution were the ones who most closely resembled U.S. farmers. They owned large farms, were better educated, had access to credit, and sought out new technology on their own. The marketing of cotton, Mexico's leading export between 1949 and 1969, was controlled by the U.S. agribusiness giant Anderson Clayton, which provided more credit for cotton than did the National Ejido Bank for all *ejidatarios*. In 1969 these large farms produced the bulk of Mexico's main agricultural exports—cotton, tomatoes, sugar, and melons. By 1970, 2 percent of Mexican farmers produced half of the value of agricultural and forest products.[63]

Ejidatarios and small private farmers were unable to plunge into the lucrative agricultural export market, so they concentrated on producing crops such as corn and beans whose price was deliberately kept low as a favor to urban interests. "Guaranteed" agricultural prices frequently became maximum prices, which benefited urban consumers at the expense of farmers. The reduced farm size, isolation, poverty, and frequent illiteracy of the small farmer formed an insurmountable obstacle to Green Revolution technology.[64]

Despite its post-1940 neglect by policy makers, the ejido remained an important element of Mexican agriculture. In 1960, 34 percent of agricultural production, as measured by value, came from the ejido. Yield per acre for corn and beans produced on ejidos was virtually the same as the yield on large private farms.[65]

Ejidatarios and small private farmers paid a high price for the success of postwar Mexican agriculture. They remained dependent on government credit, which corrupt officials often delayed. Excessive staffing at the government agricultural credit agency led historian Stephen Niblo to comment, "It is very difficult to avoid the conclusion that the agricultural bureaucracy was, in effect, an employment-generating scheme for the urban middle class." Ejidos became a captive market for government agencies whose administrators could dictate the prices *ejidatarios* paid for fertilizer, insecticides, seeds, and other inputs. Adjusting for inflation, the 1971 corn price was below that of 1940. In response to low prices, corn growers shifted land from producing corn to cattle, which required less labor, thus exacerbating unemployment. As early as the 1950s, some were simply abandoning their ejidos seeking employment in the United States.[66]

In terms of output, Mexican agriculture after the Cárdenas administration was quite successful. By 1965, Mexico had become self-sufficient in basic foods. Between 1950 and 1966, agricultural exports almost tripled in value. In large part, this success was due to high levels of government support for commercial agro-exporters. Thanks to government investment in irrigation, especially in northern Mexico, the area cultivated increased by 1.5 percent a year between 1940 and 1970.[67]

The generally positive results from the Mexican agricultural sector masked a dual system of large highly capitalized private farms with high productivity per worker and small farms with limited capital and low productivity per worker. As a result, average agricultural productivity was well below that of workers in other sectors. In 1940, almost two-thirds of the population worked in agriculture, but they produced only 18 percent of GDP. In 1970, the 30 percent of the population working in agriculture produced only 11 percent of GDP. Productivity per worker on many small farms declined due to reduced government support and large families whose children inherited ever smaller, less efficient plots.[68]

MINING

Foreign investment in mining declined after the Ruiz Cortines administration granted substantial tax advantages to small mining enterprises, making it difficult for large foreign-owned mines to compete. Early 1960s legislation forced foreign mining companies to sell 51 percent of their capital to Mexicans and stipulated that new mining concessions would only be granted to firms with at least 66 percent Mexican capital. These measures, as well as labor unrest, ore depletion, high taxes, low export prices, and poor transport discouraged new investment in mining.[69]

By the end of the 1960s, Mexicans had successfully assumed control of the mining sector. However, the mining sector did not maintain its previous dynamism. From 1910 through 1960, mining volume remained roughly the same, while the rest of economy boomed. Between 1940 and 1970, mining declined from 3.7 percent to 1.0 percent of the GDP.[70]

THE GOOD OLD DAYS?

Between 1940 and 1970, consumer goods declined from 25 to 15 percent of Mexico's imports. This was accompanied by an expansion of industry, job creation, an increased standard of living for broad sectors of the population, and transfer of technology into Mexico. Between 1940 and 1970, manufacturing increased from 16.6 to 23.3 percent of GDP.[71]

Between 1940 and 1970, Mexican per capita gross domestic product increased more rapidly than that of the rest of Latin America, that of the United States, and that of the world. During this thirty-year period, Mexican per capita income rose from 16 percent of U.S. per capita income to 22 percent. Factors permitting this rapid growth included political stability resulting from Cárdenas's land reform and PRI political domination, as well as ample access to credit from both private and public sources.[72]

A number of drawbacks to the postwar Mexican development model offset these achievements. Even though these drawbacks became increasingly evident in the 1960s, it was difficult to change the development strategy since so many had a vested interest in maintaining the status quo. The private sector resisted any changes since, as economist Roger Hansen noted in 1971, "It is hard to imagine a set of policies to reward private entrepreneurial activity more than those of the Mexican government since 1940." The government was reluctant to modify the system since that would deny it the ability to control the private sector through the favors it dispensed. Organized labor also backed the system, since it felt tariffs and import quotas were key to retaining industrial jobs. Finally, there existed a general consensus among Mexican economic policy makers that the state needed to protect domestic industries from foreign competition.[73]

The most obvious economic problem resulting from the postwar development model was a growing balance of payments deficit. Mexican-made consumer goods, such as cars and refrigerators, were generally produced with imported machinery and contained imported materials and components. Multinational corporations (MNCs) were reluctant to substitute Mexican-made parts for imports from their own plants abroad. As a result, when production increased, imports increased. To cite an example, in 1964, when the Mexican economy grew at the phenomenal rate of 10 percent, imports of raw materials and intermediate goods rose by 15 percent and that of capital goods by 31 percent. Even with the 60 percent local-content rule in place, in 1970 each new car contained well above $1,000 of imported parts and materials. Largely as a result of increased production, between 1960 and 1970 Mexico's annual trade deficit rose from $457 million to $1.038 billion. This mounting trade deficit was compounded by foreign corporations taking profits, royalties, and other payments out of Mexico. Between 1960 and 1971 such payments totaled $3.48 billion—more than the total value of FDI during that period.[74]

In theory, Mexican exports could have paid for the imports used in manufacturing. However, there was limited foreign demand for Mexican manufactured goods since there was no outside competition to stimulate quality control or the adoption of new technologies. Mexican-made goods were costly to produce due to small production runs. The entire Mexican production of cars, for example, was well below that of a single integrated auto plant in the United States. As various auto manufacturers each maintained small assembly plants, the cars produced cost roughly 50 percent more than they did in the country where they were designed.[75]

Several other factors impeded exports. Even though Mexican inflation was higher than U.S. inflation, a fixed exchange rate was maintained between the peso and the dollar between 1954 and 1976. This resulted in an overvalued peso that discouraged exports. Since exporters were forced to rely on expensive Mexican-made inputs, their costs were higher than those of their foreign competitors, who could use the cheapest inputs available. Domestic industry, protected by tariffs, often failed to modernize. The textile industry provides an extreme case of this failure to modernize. In 1957, 33 percent of the looms and 34.4 percent of the spindles operating had been built before 1910.[76]

Another flaw of import substitution industrialization was that production tended to simply reproduce what had been imported previously. Since luxury cars were imported before import substitution began, production of them began in Mexico. Luxury cars were produced, even though cars themselves constituted a luxury. In 1970, only one Mexican per 41.1 citizens owned a car at all. Public utility would have been better served by restricting vehicle manufacture to buses or to a single inexpensive model, such as the Volkswagen Beetle (which was produced in Mexico).[77]

Import substitution led to other economic problems. The government kept wages low to encourage investment in industry. Economist Victor Urquidi commented on the resulting poor income distribution: "Unless income distribution is improved, consumer-goods industries will gradually saturate their limited, and at times luxury, urban markets . . ." As industry increasingly relied on capital-intensive machines designed in nations with high labor costs, job creation lagged. In 1970, 43.1 percent of the labor force was underemployed. MNCs exacerbated employment problems since in 1969, for example, they accounted for 27.7 percent of manufacturing production but only 13.6 percent of manufacturing employment.[78]

Import substitution clearly failed to end dependence on foreigners. In the early 1970s, the Coca-Cola Company controlled 42 percent of the Mexican soft drink market. It supplied local bottlers with syrup, advertising copy, promotional materials, and technical assistance. A similar pattern existed in many industries. A 1975 U.S. Senate report commented "Through their control over vital industries, leading firms, and a substantial share of the national market, MNCs [multinational corporations] exercise a great deal of influence in the Mexican economy, and their conduct is crucial to its performance." Ironically, ending dependence on foreigners had been one of the initial justifications for import substitution.[79]

Chapter 23

The New Partnership, 1941–1970

THE WAR YEARS, 1941–1945

> The second world war was favourable to Mexico in many ways, mainly because it brought a great and lasting improvement in relations with the United States.
>
> Angus Maddison, 1985[1]

A rapprochement with the United States accompanied Mexico's early 1940s shift to the political right. The Second World War gave Mexico a certain leverage in dealings with its northern neighbor. Mexico's leaders took advantage of this leverage to modernize the Mexican army at U.S. expense, to settle on-going bi-national disputes, and to reap economic benefits from wartime trade with the United States.[2]

In response to Pearl Harbor, the Mexican government broke relations with Axis powers. Soon thereafter, the government seized assets of Axis nationals as well as those of Mexicans who still traded with the Axis powers. In the words of the British minister, this created an "unlimited opportunity for graft."[3]

The Mexican government granted U.S. military aircraft the right to fly through Mexican airspace and land at Mexican airports en route to the Panama Canal. Cozumel became a base for U.S. anti-submarine warfare after it became apparent that German submarines operating in the Gulf of Mexico posed a greater threat than did Japanese invasion. While Squadron 201 was the only military unit that went into combat, 15,530 Mexicans joined the U.S. army and suffered 1,492 casualties.[4]

In July 1941, the U.S. government agreed to buy the entire surplus of eleven Mexican strategic minerals. The next year, it provided a $40 million Export-Import Bank Loan for road construction, made available $40 million to stabilize the peso, and pledged to purchase up to $25 million of Mexican silver annually. A $6-million loan financed the construction of a rayon plant built in cooperation with the Celanese Corporation of America. Animosity resulting from the 1938 oil nationalization was set aside as the U.S. government paid Bechtel Corporation $20.8 million to build a refinery and pipeline in Mexico. The Mexican government used U.S. funds to upgrade highways and rebuild the Mexican rail system, thus expediting shipments north. U.S. war planners diverted scarce parts, rolling stock, and repair machinery to sustain Mexican railroads.[5]

Conciliatory discourse replaced the strident diplomatic language of the late 1930s. In 1942, U.S. Ambassador George Messersmith, who had replaced the aging Josephus Daniels, declared, "President Ávila Camacho believes that we must live in the present and look forward into the future and forget, so far as is possible, the past." That same year, Mexican Foreign Secretary Ezequiel Padilla declared that the border was "a line that unites us rather than divides us." In 1943, to emphasize the cordiality and importance of U.S.–Mexican relations, President Roosevelt visited Monterrey, Nuevo León—the first time a U.S. president had ventured beyond the border. Ávila Camacho responded with a visit to Franklin D. Roosevelt (FDR) in Corpus Christi, Texas.[6]

Mexico's Second World War experience shaped the nation for decades to come. In 1937–1938, only 56 percent of Mexico's trade was with the United States. By 1940, as the Second World War closed European markets, the United States accounted for 90 percent of Mexico's foreign trade. This overwhelming U.S. dominance of Mexican foreign trade continued after the war. By 1946, some 350 new foreign companies, mostly American, had begun operations in Mexico. This was only the beginning of a decades-long increase in U.S. investment. Mexico's wartime ability to settle debt disputes opened the way for Mexico's postwar reintegration into international capital markets. The U.S. embassy, whose staff increased from 400 to a wartime peak of 800, remained as a major presence after the war.[7]

THE COLD WAR YEARS, 1945–1970

The end of the Second World War marked a shift in U.S.–Mexican relations. The death of President Roosevelt in April 1945 deprived the Good Neighbor Policy of its key backer. By mid-1945, most of the senior officials who had helped develop the Good Neighbor Policy had left the State Department. FDR's successor, Harry Truman, possessed none of the skills and sensitivities needed to maintain the policy. After the Second World War ended, the United States no longer needed huge quantities of strategic materials. Finally, with the advent of the Cold War, as historian Stephen Niblo observed, interest in Mexico dwindled:

> The Great Power rivalry between the United States and the USSR shifted attention to the perimeter of the Soviet Union. Mexico, formerly valued as a frontline state against fascist expansion and an economic ally during the war, soon became marginalized.[8]

In February 1945, to lay the groundwork for postwar cooperation with Latin America, the United States sponsored a Pan American conference at Chapultepec Castle in Mexico City. For the Latin Americans who attended, the most pressing concern was postwar economic development. They felt that the United States had an obligation to repay Latin American wartime cooperation with aid. Mexican Foreign Secretary Padilla proclaimed that Latin Americans should "do more than produce raw materials and live in a state of semi-colonialism." Mexico joined the other Latin American nations in advocating tariffs to protect still vulnerable new industries, controls on foreign (meaning U.S.) investment to ensure that it was in the "public interest," and the stabilization of commodity prices. As historian Frank Niess observed, "All in all, the Latins' objective at Chapultepec was nothing less than a more equitable distribution of the profits of the inter-American division of labour."[9]

At the Chapultepec Conference, the United States presented a very different economic vision for postwar Latin America. U.S. planners felt the ideal was the unimpeded flow of capital, the elimination of trade barriers within the hemisphere, and free access to each country's markets and raw materials. The American delegates advocated the use of private capital, not foreign aid, to finance Latin American development.[10]

As it enunciated its economic preferences, the United States touted its own free-market development model as the only viable path of development and dismissed models that strayed too far from it. The U.S. version of its own economic history conveniently omitted any mention of how in the nineteenth century the United States was the most tariff-protected nation in the world and how various nineteenth-century U.S. administrations had promoted economic development.[11]

A 1947 exchange of visits between Presidents Harry Truman and Miguel Alemán indicated the cordiality in relations between the two nations. In 1947, Truman visited Mexico City—a first for a U.S. president. While there, Truman made the dramatic gesture of laying a wreath at the monument to the Mexican cadets, known as the Niños Héroes, who died during the

Mexican–American War. Foreign Secretary Jaime Torres Bodet rose to the occasion and proclaimed that Truman "threw a bridge across the chasm of the past." Alemán responded to Truman's visit with another first—a visit to the U.S. capital by a Mexican president. Alemán devoted a chapter in his memoirs to the exchange. As an indication of the asymmetry of relations between the two nations, Truman's much longer memoirs contained only three lines concerning his Mexico City visit and failed to even mention Alemán.[12]

In 1948, the Ninth Conference of American States, held in Bogotá, Colombia, laid the groundwork for the Organization of American States (OAS). At this conference, U.S. Secretary of State George Marshall quashed any remaining hopes that a Marshall Plan for Latin America would be forthcoming. Rather, he informed the representatives of the twenty-one Latin American republics gathered there that the United States would not supply Latin America with aid on a scale similar to the aid being offered Europe since "it is beyond the capacity of the United States government to finance more than a small portion of the vast development needed. The capital required through the years must come from private sources, both domestic and foreign . . . ."[13]

Harmonious U.S.–Mexican relations continued into the early 1950s. A 1951 CIA report observed, "Mexico supports US views in major international issues, and relations with this country have been increasingly friendly and mutually cooperative."[14]

With the exception of the regime change in Guatemala, by the early 1950s Latin America had ceased to be a major focus of U.S. attention. The 1949 U.S. Mutual Defense Act provided for the expenditure of $1.3 billion to bolster friendly militaries around the world. Not a cent went to Latin America. Between 1945 and 1952, Belgium and Luxembourg, with an area less than the Mexican state of Puebla, received more direct aid than all of Latin America combined. As with the rest of Latin America, Mexico drew little attention from its northern neighbor, and U.S.–Mexican relations entered into what historian Alan Knight has described as "their long period of somnolence."[15]

The Mexican government under President López Mateos (1958–1964) maintained a delicate balance. To have fully supported the Cuban Revolution would have alienated the Church, the United States, and Mexican business interests. To have supported U.S. actions relating to Cuba, and especially the U.S.-sponsored Bay of Pigs invasion, would have alienated the Cuban government, Mexican intellectuals, and the Mexican left, which might have become even more radical.[16]

López Mateos's initial reaction to Castro's 1959 triumph was to welcome the victory and affirm Cuba's right to self-determination. In June 1960, when Cuban President Oswaldo Dorticós visited Mexico, López Mateos declared, "We who have passed through a similar process, understand and value the changes which Cuba is carrying out . . . We are confident that the Cuban Revolution will, as ours has, contribute to the greatness of the Americas." The Mexican government condemned the U.S.-organized Bay of Pigs invasion. At the time of the October 1962 Cuban Missile Crisis, Mexico supported the United States by joining in the OAS's resolution calling for the withdrawal of nuclear missiles from Cuba. However, Mexico qualified its support by declaring that the United States should not use the incident as a pretext for invading Cuba. In 1964, Mexico alone rejected U.S. demands at the OAS that Latin America break diplomatic and trade relations with Cuba.[17]

The principle of non-intervention became the cornerstone of Mexican foreign policy and an integral part of Mexico's national identity. The PRI benefited from the broad approval of this stance.[18]

While Mexico maintained a public stance of support for the Castro regime, it secretly yielded to U.S. pressure. Prior to each Cubana Airlines departure from Mexico City to Havana, Mexican authorities supplied the Mexico City CIA station with a passenger list so that names could be checked. In the case of U.S. citizens, the Mexican authorities would prevent the departure of someone if the station requested them to do so. These authorities would also supply personal data and mug shots—taken of all passengers departing for Cuba—to U.S. intelligence services.[19]

It is evident from declassified documents that Mexico's ambassadors to Havana regularly supplied U.S. intelligence services with information on Cuba's internal political, economic, and social developments. For example, on June 2, 1967, Mexico's ambassador to Cuba, Fernando Pámanes Escobedo, used a visit to Mexico City to meet with U.S. embassy officer Francis S. Sherry III. Pámanes briefed Sherry on a wide range of highly sensitive topics including the impact of Cuban economic woes on its citizens, popular discontent, military matters, Cuban–Soviet relations, and Cubans seeking asylum at the Mexican embassy in Havana.[20]

As a result of their carefully hidden cooperation on the Cuba issue and other shared interests, relations between Mexico and the United States remained cordial. In 1963, Presidents López Mateos and Kennedy further improved relations by finally laying to rest the Chamizal dispute. The dispute had arisen when an 1864 flood caused the Rio Grande to cut off a bend, leaving almost a square mile of Mexican territory on the north side of the river at El Paso. Mexicans continued to claim the land—named the Chamizal for a bush growing there—as their territory. At the same time, El Paso residents treated it as de facto U.S. territory. As a result of the 1963 settlement, 439 acres were returned to Mexico. A concrete channel for the Rio Grande separated this land from 193 acres that remained on the north side and that became U.S. territory. Although the settlement made poor geography, putting a bend back where the river had straightened its course, it was good politics. By sacrificing a few acres, which were of little use since land titles were at best shaky, the United States removed a long-time irritant in U.S.–Mexican relations. To the Mexicans, the settlement was a source of national pride, and the ceremony marking the formal transfer of territory was carried live on Mexican television.[21]

The presidency of Lyndon Baines Johnson, who served between 1963 and 1968, marked the end of a simpler era. Problems such as the Chamizal were often localized and relatively easy to solve. Johnson relied on personal contacts with Díaz Ordaz to maintain cordial relations between their two nations. During his administration, he met with Díaz Ordaz as president-elect and as president on seven separate occasions. As president, Johnson devoted more attention to Mexico than to any other Latin American nation. Before a scheduled 1967 meeting between Johnson and Díaz Ordaz, a U.S. intelligence report stated, "Relations between the Mexican and US governments are extremely friendly, and President Johnson is personally popular in Mexico."[22]

The United States tolerated Mexico's foreign policy deviations since the main American goal in Mexico was political stability. U.S. policy makers correctly viewed Mexico's foreign policy independence as giving the Mexican government legitimacy, thus contributing to stability. In 1964, the CIA reported that one could overlook Mexican declarations on non-intervention and Cuba's right to self-determination and find that "The government is basically pro-Western, friendly toward the United States, and fully aware that its economic and political interests are closely tied to this country."[23]

These shared interests paved the way for increasingly close ties with the United States. By 1970, the United States accounted for 79 percent of the $2.8 billion of direct foreign investment in Mexico. The volume of Mexico's trade with the United States steadily increased, although as Mexico's trading links diversified, the U.S. share of Mexico's foreign trade decreased from 72.1 percent in 1960 to 63.7 percent in 1970. Historian Daniel Cosío Villegas commented on the steadily increasing U.S. economic and cultural influence, noting that like "that of the Christian god, it is all powerful and omnipresent."[24]

The Mexico City CIA station, with fifty employees and a $5.5 million annual budget, became the largest in the western hemisphere. Former CIA agent Philip Agee reported that Gustavo Díaz Ordaz, who was appointed interior secretary in 1958, worked "extremely closely" with the CIA. Its agents would pass their findings to Mexican government agents, who used the information to plan "raids, arrests and other repressive action." The importance of the CIA was such that when station chief William Scott married in Mexico, President López Mateos and Interior Secretary (and future president) Díaz Ordaz served as official witnesses.[25]

BRACEROS, WETBACKS, AND IMMIGRANTS

Migration to the United States, which had largely ceased during the Depression, once again surged due to the Second World War labor demands. In the United States, the anti-Mexican feelings of the 1930s were replaced by the perception that Mexicans were a "hard working people."

The flow of workers out of rural Mexico to the United States formed part of the much larger migration that departed for Mexico City and other Mexican urban areas. Although by U.S. standards Mexicans working in the United States were exploited, for many Mexicans, crossing the border provided a unique opportunity to earn money to support a family, buy land, start a small business, or make an ejido plot more productive.[26]

The U.S. government, facing a war-induced labor shortage, formally requested a program to bring Mexican labor into the United States. Under the program agreed to by the two nations, Mexican workers known as *braceros* (from the Spanish word *brazo*, meaning "arm") would be contracted to work in the United States for periods of up to six months. The U.S. Department of Agriculture administered the program, contracting workers at recruitment centers in central Mexico and placing them with private U.S. employers, guaranteeing, in theory, adequate wages and working conditions.[27]

In September 1942, the first *braceros* began work, harvesting California sugar beets. By July 1945, there were 58,000 *braceros* working in agriculture and another 62,000 maintaining U.S. railroads. More than 300,000 *braceros* came north to work during the war. The *bracero* program benefited the United States by providing low-cost labor. It also benefited growers by lowering U.S. agricultural wages. Mexico gained by exporting surplus labor and receiving remittances. Individual Mexicans, despite their housing, food, and wages often falling below agreed-upon standards, earned far more than they could have had they remained in Mexico.[28]

After the war, lobbyists for U.S. agricultural interests declared that *braceros* would still be needed since U.S. citizens would not perform stoop labor. They failed to mention that California's crops had been harvested by U.S. citizens during the 1930s. In response to the lobbyists' pleading, Congress extended the *bracero* program, thus allowing growers to pay wages so low that jobs on their farms would not be attractive to U.S. workers.[29]

The number of *braceros* continued to increase until 1959, when it reached a peak of 447,000. After that date, the number of *braceros* declined due to the mechanization of U.S. agriculture.[30]

After the Second World War, the *bracero* program and the presence of undocumented Mexican farm workers came under increased political attack in the United States. The U.S. labor movement viewed *braceros* and undocumented immigrants as an unmitigated evil—a flooding of the domestic labor market with low-wage workers. The National Agricultural Workers Union (NAWU), a member of the American Federation of Labor (AFL) called on the Immigration and Naturalization Service (INS) to round up and deport all illegal aliens and declared that *braceros* and undocumented workers "doomed in advance" any effort to organize farm workers. It therefore lobbied to end the *bracero* program.[31]

Civil rights, religious, social-activist, and Mexican–American groups such as the G.I. Forum (a veterans' group) and the League of United Latin American Citizens (LULAC) joined in the chorus demanding an end to *bracero* labor. Mexican–Americans invoked their citizenship to distinguish themselves from undocumented workers and *braceros*. They particularly resented *braceros* enjoying certain privileges that eluded domestic workers. LULAC criticized the INS for "allowing an avalanche of illegal Mexican labor." In 1948 it sent telegrams to President Truman alleging that the illegal entry of laborers from Mexico constituted "a direct danger to our own citizens" and called for law enforcement to deport them.[32]

In 1956, NAWU organizer Ernesto Galarza published an influential critique of the *bracero* program entitled *Strangers in our Fields*. It was so critical of conditions in the Di Giorgio Fruit Corporation's grape fields that the company sued Galarza for libel, thus further publicizing the

Figure 23.1 *Braceros*

Source: University of Texas at El Paso Library, Special Collections Department, Julian Strauss "The Bracero" (M.A. Thesis, UTEP, 44)

study. Public support for the *bracero* program was further eroded by the 1960 airing of Edward R. Murrow's CBS-TV show entitled "Harvest of Shame." The documentary depicted the physical toil of stoop labor and exposed abuses by growers, including unpaid wages and poor housing.[33]

U.S. agribusiness, which sought to maintain its access to cheap labor, favored the program's extension. The other principal advocate of extending the program was the Mexican government. In 1964, Mexico's Ambassador to the United States Antonio Carrillo Flores accurately predicted that the absence of a *bracero* agreement

> would not end the problem but rather would give rise to a de facto situation: the illegal introduction of Mexican workers into the United States, which would be extremely prejudicial to the illegal workers and, as experience has shown, would also unfavorably affect American workers, which is precisely what the legislators of the United States are tying to prevent.[34]

After 1961, with a Democrat in the White House, opponents of the *bracero* program received a more sympathetic hearing. American liberals, in a time of postwar prosperity, associated Mexican farm laborers with the impoverishment of migratory U.S.-born farm workers and therefore opposed their presence. Given mounting criticism, the U.S. Congress voted not to extend the program beyond December 1964.[35]

During its twenty-two-year-long history, roughly 4.6 million *bracero* contracts were signed. This figure overstates the number of individuals involved since many individuals signed on as *braceros* more than once. In part, the end of the program represented a victory for progressive forces in the United States. However, it also indicated the impact of mechanization on U.S. agriculture. Due to decreased labor demands, agribusiness interests were unwilling to spend their political capital on maintaining the program. Many *braceros* returned to the same employer as undocumented workers after the program ended. In other cases, employers arranged legal permanent residence for some of their former *bracero* employees.[36]

Between 1942 and 1964, even though the *bracero* program provided legal access to the United States, many Mexicans came to the United States to work illegally. They chose to come illegally so that they could avoid passing through a recruitment center and perhaps having to bribe a Mexican official to be considered for hiring. Undocumented workers could also work outside agriculture and railroads, the areas of employment to which *braceros* were legally restricted. Many U.S. employers preferred undocumented workers since they did not have to pay transportation costs to the job site, which they had to pay if they hired *braceros*. There was less monitoring of wages and working conditions if workers worked illegally. Finally, the hiring of undocumented workers could exceed the numerical limits set by the *bracero* treaty.[37]

Well before the end of the *bracero* program, undocumented labor had become a vital part of U.S. agriculture. As Ernesto Galarza observed in *Merchants of Labor*, his classic book on Mexican agricultural workers in the United States, "In 1952, had every Wetback been suddenly removed from California, commercial agriculture would have been in a serious predicament." During the twenty-two years the *bracero* program was in effect, there were 5.3 million apprehensions of undocumented Mexican workers. Since it is generally assumed that less than half of the undocumented workers were apprehended, the number of illegal workers presumably exceeded the number of legally admitted *braceros*.[38]

As Ambassador Carrillo Flores had predicted, the expiration of a formal *bracero* treaty did not halt the flow of Mexican workers into the United States. It simply drove the flow into illegality. Between 1961 and 1965, 222,827 undocumented Mexicans were apprehended and deported. Between 1966 and 1970, after the end of the *bracero* agreement, 794,964 were deported. During the following five-year period, deportations totaled 2,865,173. Even though the number of undocumented Mexican workers in the United States increased rapidly after the expiration of the *bracero* agreement, their presence received limited attention since most who came illegally were concentrated in the rural southwest and only stayed a short while before returning to Mexico. Their numbers peaked seasonally when the need for agricultural labor was at a maximum and then decreased in winter when the demand for agricultural labor declined and many returned to celebrate Christmas with their families.[39]

Braceros and those who entered the United States illegally formed the two main streams of Mexicans coming to work in the United States. Legal immigrants, who numbered 61,000 during the 1940s, formed a third group. During the 1950s, the number of legal immigrants swelled to 300,000. In that decade, Mexico became the third largest source of legal immigrants to the United States, after Canada and Germany. During the 1960s, legal immigrants from Mexico totaled 454,000. Between 1940 and 1970 the number of U.S. residents who were born in Mexico increased from 377,433 to 759,711. This number includes *braceros* and undocumented workers who had simply remained in the United States, as well as legal immigrants.[40]

During the Second World War, there was a broad consensus favoring the *bracero* program. Mexican Foreign Secretary Padilla commented that the program provided Mexicans with "an opportunity to earn high wages, a noble adventure for our youth and above all, proof of our cooperation in the victory of our cause."[41]

After the Second World War, Mexican attitudes toward labor migration were mixed. Many Mexicans were embarrassed that their fellow countrymen had to go north to support their families. Mexican trade unions, industrialists, and agricultural interests lamented the loss of labor needed to develop Mexico. The Catholic Church in Mexico opposed the *bracero* program due to its negative impact on the morals and family life of those who left their families for months at a time. Most

Mexican government officials considered short-term employment in the United States as an "escape valve" that provided Mexico with badly needed foreign exchange. In his 1954 state of the nation address, President Ruiz Cortines optimistically declared, "The difficult problem presented by the departure of Mexican workers to the United States will improve as U.S. authorities adopt more efficient methods of preventing the attraction and hiring of illegal workers."[42]

Due to the variety of interests affected and the ups and downs of the economic cycle, the United States had difficulty formulating a coherent policy concerning labor migration from Mexico. Illustrating this cloud of confusion, Roy Rubottom, who occupied the Mexico desk of the State Department in 1950, declared:

> Legalization of wetbacks is the most practical method of extricating ourselves from this situation. This approach will make no difference in the Lower Valley [of Texas] . . . since the wetbacks are already there by the thousands and are still flooding in . . . INS has insufficient personnel to carry out its program of rounding up wetbacks . . .[43]

Due to the recession that followed the end of the Korean War in 1953, the live-and-let-live attitude toward Mexican laborers turned to hostility. Mexican workers were widely proclaimed to be the cause of economic problems, just as Irish and Japanese immigrants had been scapegoated during previous recessions. To remove what was widely felt to be the cause of the recession, Immigration and Naturalization Commissioner Joseph Swing, a retired army general, oversaw the massive deportation of undocumented Mexicans—an undertaking officially known as "Operation Wetback." The U.S. Border Patrol, assisted by the FBI, the Army, the Navy, customs officials, and federal, state, and county authorities, established roadblocks, boarded trains, deployed spotter aircraft, and cordoned off neighborhoods to detain undocumented workers. Although most apprehensions occurred near the border, workers as far north as Spokane and Chicago were apprehended. General Swing commented, "Operation Wetback was pursued with military efficiency and the result was that over a million wetbacks were expelled from the country in 1954." Most of those who were included in the "million" were Mexicans who departed voluntarily to avoid detention during the well-publicized operation. The number of voluntary departures was only estimated and likely was inflated to justify increased appropriations for the Immigration and Naturalization Service. Operation Wetback transferred to the Mexican side of the border the social dislocations caused by the economic slowdown in U.S. agriculture after the end of the Korean War.[44]

Once the recession passed, public concern about Mexican labor declined, and the Border Patrol once again relaxed enforcement so that the needs of southwest agribusiness could be met. Those hiring undocumented workers did not face legal sanction thanks to the so-called "Texas clause." This legislative provision, passed at the urging of the Texas congressional delegation, allowed employers to legally hire workers who had entered the country illegally. During the 1950s, with the exception of the 1953 recession, few even thought about limiting the number of Mexican workers. As U.S. historian Lesley Byrd Simpson commented: "So long as the present factors continue to operate, I don't think the wetbacks can be stopped. In one way or another the labor vacuum will be filled."[45]

The communities in Mexico whose residents worked in the United States benefited from the earnings these workers sent home. In 1957, *bracero* remittances ranked third, after tourism and cotton, as a foreign exchange earner. Money sent home paid for fertilizer, tractors, plow rental, and family consumption. Returning workers brought new skills and values.

There were also negative aspects to labor migration, such as the tendency of workers with above average educational levels to leave. The loss of workers to the United States produced widespread complaints of labor shortages. In 1944, the governor of Durango lamented that half the schools could not open since teachers had departed to work in the United States. By the 1950s, half the population of ejidos near Ciudad Juárez had crossed the border to work.[46]

The impact Mexican workers had on U.S. communities where they worked was minimized since most of them stayed in the United States for less than a year and then returned to Mexico. Since many such workers were young and unmarried, they placed few demands for services on the communities in which they worked. Employers grew wealthy as they paid as little as $2.50 for a twelve-hour day in 1950. After factoring in inflation, there had been no increase in agricultural wages in a quarter century. As Julian Samora noted in *Los Mojados*, his ground-breaking study of undocumented workers, "It goes without saying that growers set the wages, managed the labor supply, encouraged an oversupply of labor, and, with the help of law-enforcement officers, suppressed any attempts at strikes." In some cases, at the end of the harvest growers would notify the Border Patrol that there were undocumented workers on their land and thus avoid having to pay wages to their labor force.[47]

The reliance on Mexican workers produced other losers. The presence of Mexican agricultural workers in the United States helped defeat the effort of Mexican–American farm workers to unionize and improve their working conditions. In the border region, both Mexican–Americans and legal resident alien Mexicans often had to compete with undocumented workers for the unskilled employment available. During the debate on whether the *bracero* program should be extended, Dr. Paul O'Rourke, the director of California's anti-poverty program, commented that any anti-poverty program in his state was meaningless unless *bracero* labor was ended. In 1965, after the *bracero* program was ended, United Farm Workers leader César Chávez commented on growers' efforts to reinstate the *bracero* program, "For the 500,000 farm workers in California, this would be a catastrophe."[48]

THE BORDER

> There is no frontier anywhere in the world quite like it. It is as if Algeria were to border directly upon the South of France, or West Germany upon Zaire. To enter Mexico overland from the United States is to travel, in a matter of a few miles, the vast distance between those who have and those who have not . . .
>
> Gene Lyons, 1977[49]

During the Second World War, the northward movement of goods and workers initiated a period of unprecedented growth along the Mexican side of the border. Reference to the Mexican "border" (or *frontera*) became commonplace, referring not only to the 1,600-mile-long dividing line but also to the communities and even states that abutted the United States. Even though the border was often mentioned as a single entity, little united it except its proximity to the United States, its desert or semi-desert climate, and its extremely rapid population growth. As in colonial times, there was little direct east–west communication between the different regions that eventually constituted the Mexican border region. Economic links to the rest of Mexico were tenuous since central Mexican factories were distant, roads were poor, shopping centers were lacking, and many border residents preferred imports to Mexican goods.[50]

Border population growth was closely linked to labor migration to the United States. Many Mexicans on their way to the United States would pause and work for a period to earn money before continuing northward. *Braceros* would move their families north from the interior to be close to them during the off-season. Deported Mexicans were often simply dropped at the border, and many remained there permanently. The use of the border as a staging area for entry to the United States was especially evident in Tijuana, since it was close to the huge California labor market.[51]

Between 1940 and 1960, the irrigated area in the border states more than doubled. During the Second World War, border cities near major U.S. military posts, such as Tijuana and Ciudad Juárez, gained notoriety for cheap liquor, drugs, and prostitution. After the war, tourism became

Table 23.1 *Border state populations, 1940–1970*

State	1940	1970	Percentage change
Baja California	78,907	870,421	1,003
Sonora	364,176	1,098,720	202
Chihuahua	623,944	1,612,525	158
Coahuila	550,717	1,114,956	125
Nuevo León	541,147	1,694,689	213
Tamaulipas	458,832	1,456,858	218
Total	2,617,723	7,848,169	200
Percentage of total Mexican population	13.3	16.3	

Source: INEGI (1994: 15–24)

tamer, with many visiting border cities to buy curios, eat, and drink. Catering to the increasing number of tourists visiting border cities and driving into the Mexican interior fueled job growth on the border. In 1970, the border zone received 58 million visitors who spent an average of $15 per visit.[52]

Reclamation projects continued to stimulate economic and population growth. Agricultural development, facilitated by irrigation, brought still more people to the border region. The Mexicali area, with its close ties to the U.S. market, became one of Mexico's most productive agricultural regions. By 1960, Mexico's northern region was producing 44 percent of the gross value of Mexico's agricultural, livestock, fishery, and forestry products.[53]

A mushrooming population on the U.S. side of the border stimulated the demand for services on the Mexican side. The number of border crossings increased from 23 million in 1940 to 144 million in 1970, as people increasingly chose to work, shop, and relax on the other side of the border. Between 1950 and 1970, in Mexican border communities, those employed in trade and services increased from 25 to 46 percent of the labor force, figures that were remarkably higher than the national figures of 21 and 32 percent, respectively.[54]

A birthrate that was slightly higher than that of Mexico as a whole further contributed to population growth. By 1970, despite Tijuana's population having increased from 16,486 in 1940 to 340,583 in 1970, 49 percent of its population had been born in the city.[55]

Due to the economic boom along the border, many came from central Mexico seeking employment. As his term ended in 1959, Ciudad Juárez Mayor René Mascareñas Miranda commented, "Migrants arrive in the northern ports in search of a better way of life, thinking that extraordinary employment opportunities exist in these border cities or having high hopes of earning dollars in the United States."[56]

In sharp contrast to its earlier history, the border became the most urban region in Mexico. By 1970, 85 percent of the Mexican border population lived in urban areas, a figure that was 25 percent above the national average. In 1970, three of the border cites—Ciudad Juárez, Tijuana, and Mexicali, which had populations of 424,135, 340,583, and 396,324, respectively—were among the ten largest cities in Mexico.[57]

The meteoric population growth of border cities far outpaced their ability to provide public services—a problem that would remain acute through the end of the century. In Ciudad Juárez, as in other municipalities, city officials, who sought, but failed, to stop a flood of squatters from occupying public and private land, accepted unsightly shantytowns as a permanent feature of border life. In 1953, *El Fronterizo*, a Ciudad Juárez newspaper, commented on the result of rapid population growth:

> Thousands live under incredible conditions, in shacks . . . built on public lands . . . having no public services. The residents lack sufficient elements to maintain their health and are in need of adequate food. In those areas where conditions are the worst, an alarming rate of infant mortality has been recorded.[58]

In 1959–1960, commerce between border municipalities and the rest of Mexico totaled only 4.9 billion pesos, while their commerce with the United States reached 9.6 billion pesos. U.S. retailers did their best to maintain this imbalance, bombarding residents on the Mexican side of the border with TV, radio, and newspaper ads announcing bargains on the American side of the border.[59]

In 1961, the Mexican government responded to the border's commercial dependency on the United States with the National Border Program (PRONAF). It sought to substitute Mexican manufactured goods for imports along the border, increase the sale of Mexican manufactures to foreign consumers, stimulate border tourism, and improve living conditions along the border. To implement the program, the government financed the construction of shopping centers, which featured arts and crafts as well as goods produced by U.S. and Mexican factories. Despite PRONAF's provision of tax breaks and subsidies for shipping goods from central Mexico to the border, Mexican merchants in the 1960s were never able to compete with their U.S. counterparts who offered a greater selection of goods at lower prices.[60]

Part Eight

The Fall of the "Perfect Dictatorship," 1971–2000

Chapter 24

Politics in Times of Crisis, 1971–2000

THE ECHEVERRÍA YEARS, 1970–1976

On October 21, 1969, a spokesman for the National Peasant Confederation (CNC) declared that the group supported forty-seven-year-old Interior Secretary Luis Echeverría for the PRI's presidential nomination, thus signaling that Díaz Ordaz had chosen his successor. Never before had there been a PRI presidential nominee who had been born and raised in Mexico City. He was also the first of a generation of Mexican presidents who had never held elective office, so he had had less contact with the variety of interest groups that elected officials routinely deal with. Since their forte was the technical aspects of public administration, these presidents became known as the technocrats.[1]

On the campaign trail, Echeverría, a previously taciturn lawyer who had been viewed as a hard-line conservative, metamorphosed into an extrovert who began criticizing the government that he had so loyally served. He repeatedly emphasized that poverty had become a national problem and stressed the need to change Mexico's economic development model. Even though his election was assured, Echeverría traveled a record-breaking 33,000 miles during his campaign, which has often been compared to Lázaro Cárdenas's 1934 campaign.[2]

As expected, Echeverría breezed through the election with 85 percent of the vote, only 4 percent less than Díaz Ordaz had received in 1964. PRI (Revolutionary Institutional Party) candidates for the Chamber of Deputies won every single-member district, indicating the party's continued dominance of the political scene.[3]

The Echeverría administration attempted to address a variety of problems, such as high unemployment, low wages, income concentration, and increasing rural poverty. Policy makers felt that increased government spending would lead, in Keynesian fashion, to higher economic growth. Such high growth would make it economically feasible to provide food subsidies and a massive expansion of services to the poor. Planners felt increased government spending and expanded services would ensure the stability of the regime by recapturing the loyalty of disaffected sectors of society.[4]

Echeverría's economic policy, known as "shared development," involved massive state intervention to stimulate the economy. The economic emphasis shifted from increasing gross national product to job creation and the redistribution of income. Echeverría financed government spending, which almost quadrupled between 1971 and 1975, by printing money and borrowing from aboard. Historian Enrique Krauze commented on Echeverría's profligate spending: "With the money (printed or borrowed) raining down from his hands, he would wash away the responsibility for 1968."[5]

Echeverría sought to break Mexico's commercial dependence on the United States by signing foreign trade agreements with Western and Eastern European and Central and South American nations. In pursuit of these goals, he traveled to thirty-six nations, usually with an immense retinue. He even brought along mariachis and Indians to make tortillas and Mexican food so that the heads of state he visited could savor authentic Mexican cuisine. In 1970, Mexico maintained diplomatic relations with sixty-seven nations, while six years later the number had increased to 131. Echeverría's international junkets were attacked by his critics who viewed them as too expensive and as distracting the president from solving Mexico's problems. His supporters claimed the trips were necessary to overcome Mexico's psychological and economic dependence on the United States.[6]

By the beginning of 1976, Echeverría had lost control over public expenditures. Inflation surged, resulting in an overvalued peso, which discouraged exports. Echeverría committed the same error his successors would repeat later in the century—he kept the peso stable relative to the dollar rather than devaluing to stimulate exports. The financial elite, already alienated by Echeverría's leftist rhetoric and high government spending, responded to increased government indebtedness by sending their money out of Mexico. Capital flight in 1976 alone totaled an estimated $4 billion. At the same time, increased government investment resulted in massive imports, which worsened Mexico's trade deficit. Between 1970 and 1975, this deficit increased from $1.0 billion to $3.7 billion.[7]

Eventually, Echeverría was forced to face the obvious—the exchange rate could no longer be maintained. On August 31, 1976, for the first time since 1954, the peso was devalued. The government allowed the peso to float—"like a rock" as Mexicans wryly noted—and it declined from 12.5 to the dollar to 28.5 before the end of the year.[8]

Unlike the 1954 devaluation, which was well timed, the 1976 devaluation was far too late in coming. This allowed speculators to drain financial reserves and ruined the incumbents' reputation for sound financial management. It also left the government financially prostrate, so that it was forced to turn to the U.S. Treasury Department and the International Monetary Fund (IMF) for a bailout, thus sacrificing the nationalistic principles that Echeverría had proclaimed.[9]

Peasant unrest also caught up with Echeverría before he left office. During his term, peasants repeatedly staged land invasions in various states. Some had turned violent, and the army had intervened in many. In 1976, security forces killed fifty-eight in Chiapas after peasants there had killed three landowners.[10]

In November 1976, the landless invaded farms in northwestern Mexico, hoping that the relative power vacuum associated with the presidential transition would favor them. In Sinaloa, according to landowners, 200 landholdings were invaded. In Sonora, armed peasants occupied twelve properties in the Yaqui Valley. Seven of the invaders were killed in a bloody effort by police to oust them. To defuse the situation, Echeverría ordered that 247,000 acres be expropriated in Sonora and Sinaloa and given to 8,037 landless families. Six of the expropriated farms covered at least 2,470 acres—ten times the legal limit imposed by land reform legislation. Sonoran landowners, the group most politically hostile to Echeverría, were offered no compensation on the grounds that the land was illegally held. This act, coming only days before the end of the presidential term, further poisoned relations between the Echeverría administration and the business community.[11]

Echeverría expanded social security coverage (which included health care) from 12 million to 22 million and increased government spending for social programs to almost 24 percent of the budget, its highest level ever. Under Echeverría, the economy, which grew at an average rate of 5.6 percent, continued to outpace population growth.[12]

Such accomplishments are offset by the many negative aspects of the Echeverría administration. By greatly increasing the government's role in the economy, Echeverría made Mexico's fundamental economic flaws even worse. Between 1970 and 1976, as the state addressed myriad problems, public-sector employment increased from 600,000 to 2.2 million. During his term, foreign public debt over one year increased from $3.8 billion to $15.9 billion. Rather than decreasing Mexico's economic dependence on the United States, that dependence increased as America exported food to Mexico, increased lending and investment, remained the major source of tourists, and employed Mexican immigrants who sent remittances home. At the time of the devaluation, the government signed an agreement with the IMF—where the United States held decisive power—further increasing U.S. influence.[13]

Not surprisingly, Echeverría was extremely unpopular when he left office, and his presidency was widely regarded as a failure. The 1976 devaluation shattered the illusion of progress associated with Mexico's "economic miracle." That year inflation hit 40 percent and economic growth slowed to 2 percent of gross national product—well below the rate of population increase. In the final tense months of his administration, rumors of a military coup circulated widely.[14]

THE JOSÉ LÓPEZ PORTILLO YEARS, 1976–1982

On September 22, Mexicans learned that Treasury Secretary López Portillo would be their next president. As was the case with Echeverría, the candidate had been born in Mexico City and had received a law degree from the National University. Also like Echeverría, he had never held elective office. López Portillo had practiced law until age forty and then had begun a career in public service.

López Portillo's presidential campaign was unique in that he faced no opposition. Two of the recognized opposition political parties supported the PRI presidential candidate, as they usually did. The only other registered opposition party, the PAN, became deadlocked and did not present a presidential candidate.

On December 1, 1976, López Portillo took office in the midst of uncertainty, capital flight, inflation, and political and economic crisis. In his inaugural address, the new president announced that Mexico had to unite, heal its wounds, and move on as one. Absent from the speech was Echeverría's reformist rhetoric. Rather, López Portillo attempted to regain the support of the business community by announcing an "alliance for production" between the public and private sectors. The president of the American Chamber of Commerce in Mexico declared the inaugural address reflected "the kind of philosophy that businessmen can understand."[15]

López Portillo drastically cut government spending, thus winning the approval not only of domestic businessmen but also of international financiers. A 1979 article in *Fortune* declared:

> Many financial experts in the U.S. and Mexico are so impressed by the way he has restored confidence that they believe Mexico could have come out of the 1976 crisis even without oil, though the climb would have been slower and more halting.[16]

Early in the López Portillo administration, it was becoming increasingly apparent that absolute political control and political legitimacy were incompatible. Several factors, such as the economic crisis under Echeverría, the lack of an opposition presidential candidate in 1976, and the lingering memory of 1968 tarnished the regime's legitimacy. In response, in 1977, there was an another political reform.[17]

The number of electoral districts was increased to 300, each of which would be represented by a member of the Chamber of Deputies, elected much as members of the U.S. House of Representatives are elected. One hundred additional seats in the Chamber were allocated to opposition parties, even if they did not win a plurality in any single electoral district. Rather, the one hundred seats were allocated among the opposition parties based on the proportion of the vote they received nationwide.

Since the law was directed at image building, not democracy, it had many flaws that observers were quick to point out. The opposition was only guaranteed one hundred seats in the 400-member Chamber of Deputies, leaving the PRI firmly in control of that body. Elections to select senators and state and municipal officials remained unaffected. The PRI continued to dominate the Federal Election Commission—which organized elections—and to receive overwhelming financial support from the government that was unavailable to other parties. Finally, Congress was not the arena where major political decisions were made.[18]

By mid-term, López Portillo found himself free of the IMF-mandated belt-tightening that had characterizing his first years in office. Early in his term, it became apparent that Mexico's oil reserves were among the largest in the world. Rather than waiting for increased oil sales to produce revenue that could finance an expansion of production capacity, Mexico began to borrow abroad. International commercial banks, bulging with Arab petrodollars, were only too glad to finance this accelerated oil development. As billions of dollars were loaned, it appeared that at long last Mexico could have it all—rapid economic growth and general social programs. López Portillo used oil revenue (or money borrowed in anticipation of oil revenue) to build new refineries, pipelines, tanker facilities, and petrochemical plants. The government undertook an ambitious program to stimulate food production and extended superhighways and Mexico City's subway system. A nuclear power plant, power lines to rural areas, and rural health centers were also built. Airports, tourist facilities, and the steel industry were expanded. As historian Enrique Krauze noted, "Everything was to be modernized by the end of the *sexenio* [presidential term]." López Portillo's borrowing to increase oil production capacity and to stimulate economic growth is understandable since so many Mexicans were poor and in need of jobs. Future income seemed unlimited as oil prices increased from $14.30 a barrel in 1979 to $33.60 in 1981.[19]

Between 1978 and 1981, economic growth averaged 8.4 percent a year. Massive government investment led to rapid economic growth, which induced foreign and domestic corporations to invest. Increased employment, investment, and demand had a ripple effect throughout the economy. The whole nation was caught up in what can only be described as "oil fever." López Portillo declared that in the future Mexico's biggest economic problem would be the "management of abundance." Even normally skeptical essayist and novelist Carlos Fuentes fell victim to oil fever and in 1980 declared oil exports would "give to Mexico, for the first time in its history, something precious—international financial independence."[20]

In 1980, with the political reform accomplished and an oil-induced economic boom under way, pundits were proclaiming López Portillo's presidency to be the most successful in decades. Then, almost overnight, that illusion vanished.

Beginning in mid-1981, world oil prices plummeted due to a combination of energy conservation in the developed world, OPEC members cheating on production quotas, and a worldwide recession. As a result of the recession, prices for Mexico's other major exports, such as silver, cotton, lead, coffee, and shrimp, also fell. In response to the fall in commodity prices, foreign lending ceased. Unfortunately for Mexico, just as world commodity prices were plummeting, the United States raised interest rates to combat inflation at home. This increased the interest Mexico paid on its variable-rate loans, costing it $2 billion in 1982 alone. As individuals and businesses observed the plunge in oil prices and the increase in U.S. interest rates, they began move their money out of Mexico in anticipation of an economic crisis. This produced a self-fulfilling prophecy—private actors sent money out of Mexico, producing a shortage of dollars. To address this shortage, the government borrowed at ever higher interest rates, thus increasing the risk of financial crisis. As the risk of financial crisis rose, more capital left Mexico. In 1981 and 1982, capital flight totaled $20 billion.[21]

Even though orthodox economic doctrine would have indicated a devaluation of the peso, López Portillo viewed such a move as surrendering to his enemies. In a speech on February 5, 1982, he said he would "defend the peso like a dog." Thirteen days later the peso was devalued, and its value plunged from twenty-seven to thirty-seven to the dollar. Rather than solving the economic crisis, the devaluation led to increased capital flight because speculators felt that the peso had not been devalued enough and they no longer trusted those formulating financial policy. As the government was running out of dollars, it decreed that deposits in dollar accounts in Mexican banks would only be repaid in pesos at a below-market rate. This thinly veiled confiscation hit the middle class especially hard. (The truly wealthy deposited their dollars in foreign accounts.) A second devaluation in August lowered the value of the peso by another 50 percent. By the end of 1982, the Mexican currency was trading at 157 to the dollar.[22]

In August, Mexico grabbed headlines around the world when it announced that it could not service its $80 billion foreign debt, the largest among the developing countries. Loans to Mexico by the nine largest U.S. banks equaled 44 percent of their capital. The U.S. government, loath to see its own banks and the Mexican economy go under, stepped in. Paul Volcker, chairman of the U.S. Federal Reserve, cobbled together a rescue package to avoid the damage to the international monetary system that an outright default by a major debtor nation would produce. The complex rescue package involved an immediate $2.5 billion payment by the U.S. government, followed by an additional $1.85 billion from the U.S. Federal Reserve and European central banks. This tided Mexico over until November, when the IMF reached an agreement with Mexico on a $4 billion loan.[23]

In his September 1982 state of the nation address, López Portillo stunned the nation by announcing the nationalization of Mexico's private banks. He justified this unprecedented move by declaring:

> A group of Mexicans, led, counseled, and supported by the private banks, has taken more money out of the country than all the empires that have exploited us since the beginning of our history . . . We have to organize to save our productive structure and provide it with financial resources to move forward. We have to end the unjust, pernicious cycle of capital flight, devaluation, and inflation that especially harms workers, jobs, and the firms which create employment.[24]

The bank nationalization was a desperate attempt to deflect criticism from the economic crisis, neutralize the restless left, and reassert the PRI's revolutionary credentials. Architects of the nationalization sought to break the power of financial-industrial conglomerates, increase state control over investment, improve the state's financial position, and reduce capital flight. While the nationalization failed to meet its intended goals, it did greatly increase the economic role of government, which began to allocate credit and manage the numerous industrial and commercial firms that the banks had owned.[25]

López Portillo's 1982 bank nationalization produced a qualitative change in relations between business and government. For the first time since the Revolution, owners of capital abandoned closed-door negotiations with the political elite and sought political power for themselves. Owners of small and medium-sized businesses, especially in the north, felt that the bank nationalization indicated the danger of a presidency whose powers were unchecked by the political system—constrained neither by opposition political parties nor by Congress.[26]

The Mexican public soon concluded that debt default, bank nationalization, and the devaluation—which led to 98.9 percent inflation in 1982—constituted a prima facie case of government economic incompetence. That year the economy shrank by 0.5 percent, the first such decline since the Great Depression of the 1930s.[27]

Inflation reduced buying power, the lack of credit halted job creation, and the budget crisis lowered social spending, including subsidies for bread, corn, electricity, and gasoline. The PAN, the Catholic Church, and private media joined the business elite in attacking the bank nationalization. The López Portillo administration was the swan song of the activist post-revolutionary state—a final, gigantic effort that left it exhausted and from which it never recovered.[28]

While López Portillo bears the blame for economic mismanagement, it should be noted that the private sector, the middle class, Mexican labor, and foreign bankers strongly supported his policies until near the end of his term. Also, when it comes to poor countries dealing with sudden oil wealth success stories are few—consider Iran, Nigeria, and Venezuela.

Further undermining the image of the government during López Portillo's term was an explosion of corruption, facilitated by billions of poorly audited petrodollars flowing through state coffers. According to some estimates, López Portillo himself accumulated more than $1 billion during his presidency. The lavish five-mansion estate he built on a hill overlooking Mexico City was dubbed "Dog Hill" by enraged citizens who never forgot his pledge to defend the peso "like a dog."[29]

MIGUEL DE LA MADRID, 1982–1988

On September 25, 1981, labor leader Fidel Velázquez announced that the 1982 PRI presidential candidate would be López Portillo's friend and disciple Budget and Planning Minister Miguel De la Madrid. As was the case with his two immediate predecessors, De la Madrid had received a law degree from the National University and had never been elected to public office. As would be the case with his two immediate successors, he had received an advanced degree from an Ivy League university (a master's in public administration from Harvard).[30]

De la Madrid, an uninspiring speaker lacking the faintest glimmer of charisma, set out on a conventional PRI-style campaign. On the campaign trail, he emphasized that his administration would eliminate public corruption and modernize, but offered few specific solutions to Mexico's pressing economic problems. His was the first Mexican presidential campaign to rely heavily on television, a medium that repeatedly broadcast his interviews.[31]

As a result of the 1977 political reform, which made it easier to register new political parties, seven parties fielded presidential candidates in 1982. However, this reform did little to redress the imbalance between the PRI and the political opposition. While the government distributed $20 million to opposition political campaigns, the PRI spent an estimated $300 million on its own campaign.[32]

The 1982 economic collapse tainted both De la Madrid and the political system. The PRI candidate received only 70 percent of the vote, the lowest the official party had received in its history. Despite this decline, the PRI remained firmly in control of the electoral scene. Its candidates for the Chamber of Deputes won 299 of the 300 directly elected seats. To increase voter turnout, television broadcasts of World Cup soccer games were suspended during the election to prevent voters from watching the games rather than voting.[33]

Upon taking office, De la Madrid faced rampant inflation, a huge budget deficit, massive foreign debt, collapsing oil prices, a shrinking economy, and growing labor unrest. He had little leeway in dealing with these problems since at the time of the 1982 economic crash, the Mexican government, in exchange for its IMF loan, had agreed to raise taxes, lower subsidies, reduce the budget deficit, cap wage increases, and limit public-sector borrowing.[34]

De la Madrid reduced public investment and lowered subsidies for a wide range of goods and services, including foodstuffs, electricity, health care, and the Mexico City subway. As a result of decreased subsidies, between May 1984 and December 1985, the price of bread increased by 60 percent, that of tortillas by 48 percent, and that of sugar by 61 percent. Finally, in a measure supported by the government-dominated trade union federation, the Mexican Workers Federation (CTM), 1983 wage "increases" were limited to 40 percent while the rate of inflation reached nearly 81 percent. This last measure was aimed not at deficit reduction but rather at regaining business support.[35]

De la Madrid's recovery program notwithstanding, the overriding economic issue became paying interest on Mexico's huge foreign debt, even if that meant sacrificing domestic consumption and investment to stimulate exports. The sale of these exports provided the wherewithal to make annual interest payments of $13 billion. Reduction of debt principal was a financial impossibility.

The economy shrank by 4.7 percent in 1983. On a per capita basis, it decreased 6.9 percent. An estimated 1 million Mexicans lost their jobs, many businesses closed, and most construction was suspended. The optimism of the 1950s and 1960s was replaced by despair.[36]

As if the economy were not enough to tax De la Madrid, his economic problems soon became political problems. Owners of small and medium-sized businesses began to defect to the PAN, and austerity undermined the PRI's traditional labor and peasant base. To make matters worse, Mexicans quit blaming problems on presidents who as individuals made mistakes and began to question a system that put such power in the hands of a single individual. Despite difficult economic times and declining faith in the system, De la Madrid pledged to respect election results. This pledge, made at the beginning of his term, was a way to gain political legitimacy. As political scientist

Soledad Loaeza commented, "Since they lacked economic growth, they offered electoral democracy instead."[37]

By the end of 1983, the PRI had lost mayoral races in the capitals of San Luis Potosí, Durango, Guanajuato, Sonora, and Chihuahua, as well the race in Ciudad Juárez, the sixth largest city in the country. These elections made it apparent that Mexico was becoming polarized regionally. On the same day that the PAN won the mayoral races in Chihuahua and Durango, the PRI won all fifty-two elections for legislative seats further south in the states of Campeche, Michoacán, and Zacatecas.[38]

The PAN's sudden electoral strength in the north reflected the unity of the economic, political, and religious right. In response to the bank nationalization, business interests began to finance the PAN in the north while Catholic prelates criticized the PRI's management of the country from their pulpits. The declining PRI vote also reflected the centuries-old antagonism between Mexico's northern regions and what their residents perceived as smothering control by the highly centralized political system based in Mexico City.[39]

Under pressure from local PRI cadres and an embarrassing string of electoral defeats, De la Madrid returned to the PRI's roots—election fraud. Labor leader Fidel Velázquez supported this shift, as did many traditional PRI stalwarts, noting: "We revolutionaries got where we are by bullets. Anyone wanting to remove us can't do it with the ballot, they'll have to use bullets too."[40]

Beginning with the September 1983 elections in Baja California through the November 1984 elections in Yucatán, systematic government-managed electoral fraud became the standard operating procedure. In 1984, the PRI claimed victory in thirty-five of the thirty-eight municipalities in the northern border state of Coahuila.[41]

These electoral "victories" came at a high cost for the PRI. PAN members refused to play by the traditional rules of the game, which called for them to verbally protest PRI electoral fraud and then meekly wait until the next election when their participation would once again validate the process. Rather, a new generation of aggressive, militant PANistas raised the political ante. PAN protestors in Coahuila rioted and burned city halls in two of the cities where they claimed election fraud. Local police responded by firing into the crowds, killing at least two and wounding thirty-five. Army troops were sent in to control the situation. To maximize their coverage in both domestic and foreign media, PANistas would seize bridges across the Rio Grande to publicize their fraud charges.[42]

The 1985 mid-term congressional elections were vigorously contested. The PAN campaigned under the slogan, "We are the new majority." Despite the presence of several dynamic opposition candidates, money and media overwhelmingly focused on the PRI candidates. The official vote count credited the PRI with 68.2 percent of the vote, down from 74.2 percent in the previous mid-term elections. Returns indicated that PRI candidates won in 289 of the 300 single-member congressional districts. The PRI remained strongest in rural areas, where it surpassed its national average by fifteen percentage points.[43]

These "victories" came at the cost of a further decline in PRI prestige. Going into the election, 55 percent of the voters felt the elections would be fraudulent. The many denunciations of fraud after the election only reinforced such skepticism. A *Wall Street Journal* article entitled "Mexico's rigging elections hurts its image and its credit rating" reflected the tenor of the international coverage Mexico received.[44]

By 1986, rather than legitimizing the PRI, elections delegitimized it. This created a negative feedback loop since non-presidential elections increasingly attracted national and international attention, which increasingly exposed fraud, which increasingly delegitimized the PRI. This attention on PRI politicians, as essayist Carlos Monsiváis observed, only highlighted their being "isolated and lacking in verbal, ideological, and cultural substance."[45]

In response to the emergence of democratic regimes in South America and increasing media scrutiny during Mexican elections, in late 1986, Congress legislated yet another electoral reform in an attempt to enhance the regime's badly tarnished democratic credentials. The new electoral law maintained the 300 single-member districts provided by the 1977 reform law, but increased to 200 the number of seats that would be allocated indirectly. The increased number of seats served one of the intended purposes of the law—image building.[46]

Another intended purpose of the law was guaranteeing continued PRI political control despite massive voter disaffection. The political elite realized the PRI might lose control of the Federal Electoral Commission, since each recognized political party was entitled to one seat on the Commission. As the number of parties increased, PRI control became more tenuous. To ensure PRI control of the Commission, the rules were changed to make the number of representatives a party had on the Commission proportional to its previous vote total. This rule change resulted in the PRI receiving sixteen representatives on the Commission, compared to the twelve received by all of the opposition parties combined.[47]

To ensure that the PRI would maintain control of the Chamber of Deputies, even if its vote total fell below 50 percent, the reform included a "governability clause." This clause provided that if any party received less than 50 percent of the vote, but still received a plurality, it would be awarded sufficient seats from the 200-seat proportional representative pool to increase its representation in the Chamber to 50 percent plus one. Once the party winning the plurality (assumed by the drafters of the law to be the PRI) was guaranteed a majority, the remaining seats would be awarded to opposition parties according to the percentage of the vote they received nationwide. This brazen move to cling to power was opposed by both the political left and right.[48]

The shift in the allocation of proportional representation seats during the nine-year period between the 1977 reform and the 1986 reform highlights declining PRI fortunes. In 1977, seats allocated on the basis of proportional representation served to make opposition parties visible and ensure their continued participation in the electoral process. By 1986, such seats served to guarantee the PRI a majority in the Chamber of Deputies, even if its vote total fell below 50 percent.

De la Madrid's orchestrating, or at least tolerating, of electoral fraud tarnished his image, as did a stagnant economy. Between 1983 and 1986, the number of job seekers increased by almost 3.7 million, while the number of jobs increased by less than 1 million. During De la Madrid's term, the peso declined from 157 to the dollar to 2,280 as inflation ravaged the country. As a result of near-zero economic growth, between 1982 and 1988 per capita gross domestic product (GDP) declined by 15 percent. Not surprisingly, De la Madrid's opening remarks at the 1986 World Cup soccer championship in Mexico City were drowned out by boos and whistles.[49]

Several factors—in addition to massive debt payments—retarded economic growth during De la Madrid's term. Between 1982 and 1988, public investment declined by 50 percent while private investment declined by 15 percent. Decreased private investment resulted from a lack of confidence in government and excess production capacity. Despite receiving favorable treatment from the government, the business elite failed to return much of the capital that had fled Mexico during the last years of the López Portillo administration. Rather, between 1983 and 1985, additional capital flight totaled $16 billion.[50]

De la Madrid shifted the fundamental economic assumptions concerning the Mexican economy. His administration abandoned the model of an economy oriented toward the internal market with the state stimulating production in a Keynesian fashion and protecting industry from foreign competition. Replacing the old model was the notion that Mexico should create an internationally competitive export-oriented economy. Foreign investment was to become the engine of growth. Such a model, often referred to as "neoliberal," foresaw the government ceasing to direct energies and initiatives of society and instead simply regulating and overseeing growth. Allowing business to make most investment decisions represented a major shift in power from government to the private sector.[51]

Shifting the economic role of government was a substantial legacy in itself since it set Mexico's economic agenda into the twenty-first century. De la Madrid's successors implemented most of the changes required by the new economic model. Before he left office, De la Madrid did make significant progress at shrinking the federal government's role in the economy. Public investment declined from 11 percent of GDP in 1981 to 3.4 percent in 1986. Between 1982 and 1988, privatization reduced the number of government-owned corporations from 1,100 to 412. However, since the large corporations, such as Pemex, were retained, the size of the government sector declined by only 25 percent during De la Madrid's term.[52]

THE SALINAS ADMINISTRATION, 1988–1994

> Carlos Salinas de Gortari brought more fundamental change to Mexico than any president since Lázaro Cárdenas in the 1930s.
>
> Joseph Klesner, 1994[53]

Early in 1986, the first indications came that the 1988 presidential succession would not lead to a normal transfer of power. Several prominent PRI members began to meet informally to question the party's policies. Perhaps the best known member of the group was Porfirio Muñoz Ledo, who had served as president of the PRI, as Mexico's ambassador to the United Nations, and as secretary of labor and secretary of education. Another outstanding member of the group was Cuauhtémoc Cárdenas, who in addition to being the son of Lázaro Cárdenas, had served as a senator, as subsecretary of forestry and fauna, and then, from 1980 to 1986, as governor of Michoacán.

This informal group, which eventually became known as the Democratic Current, raised the issue of democratic candidate selection and questioned De la Madrid's economic and social policies. It also highlighted the uncomfortable fact that the PRI served to implement presidential decisions and promote presidentially selected candidates, not to discuss issues.[54]

During the spring of 1987, Democratic Current leaders traveled around Mexico stating their case and recruiting supporters. In July 1987, the Democratic Current offered Cuauhtémoc Cárdenas as a potential PRI presidential candidate. Its members regularly spoke out in the press, criticizing the social and economic policies of the De la Madrid administration. Criticism focused on the administration continuing to service the foreign debt at the cost of Mexico's own social and economic development.[55] Another target was the increased reliance on foreign investment. Cárdenas declared:

> We feel that foreign investment can, perhaps, in the short run, help resolve the employment problem and supply needed resources, but if not in the short or medium run, certainly in the long run, foreign investment of necessity decapitalizes the country.[56]

On the morning of October 4, 1987, the PRI brought in a compliant crowd to support its presidential candidate, whose name they were not yet aware of. Just as they were expected to do, its members cheered when they were informed that Carlos Salinas de Gortari, De la Madrid's secretary of budget and planning, would be the PRI candidate. Essayist Jorge Castañeda commented on Salinas's selection, "If Mr. Salinas owes his designation to one factor, it is probably his commitment to pursue most of Mr. de la Madrid's economic policies: trade liberalization, austerity, cutbacks in the public sector and consumer subsidies."[57]

On October 14, 1987, Cuauhtémoc Cárdenas accepted the nomination of the Authentic Party of the Mexican Revolution, a small political party that had backed PRI presidential candidates since 1952. Subsequently, two other small parties, which in the past had backed PRI presidential candidates, also nominated Cárdenas, who launched his presidential campaign on November 29, 1987. This joint campaign, which became known as the Democratic National Front (FDN), soon incorporated a variety of social movements that were not recognized as political parties. Later in the campaign, the candidate of the Mexican Socialist Party, Heberto Castillo, withdrew his candidacy in favor of Cárdenas, his former engineering student at the National University.

Despite his lack of financial backing and organization, several factors favored Cárdenas. As the son of one of Mexico's most revered presidents, he inherited a deep well of popularity and good will. Though he lacked traditional political charisma, his somber style attracted many who were repelled by PRI demagogy. Another plus was his bronze skin and Indian features in a nation with a mestizo majority that had long been ruled by those of largely European ethnic and cultural backgrounds. Finally, Cárdenas could appeal to broad sectors of the population that had suffered as a result of the economic crisis of the 1980s.[58]

The FDN platform declared De la Madrid's economic policies were impoverishing the majority and called for limiting foreign investment and prioritizing economic growth over foreign debt payments. Cárdenas argued: "I think that this administration has been letting foreigners take over our fundamental decisions. It has acted not in the interest of the country but of foreigners who are against Mexico."[59]

The dominant theme of Salinas's campaign, which cost an estimated $800 million, was "modernization." Such "modernization" included a continuation of De la Madrid's opening the Mexican market to imports, export promotion, continued debt service, and the welcoming of foreign capital.[60]

The PRI campaign had far more resources at its disposal than did the other campaigns. Salinas's enormous entourage flew from campaign stop to campaign stop in a fleet of jets and helicopters, accompanied by a 727-load of journalists traveling at government expense. In contrast, Cárdenas and his campaign staff traveled to major cities on commercial flights and then rode in cars belonging to local supporters. The media overwhelmingly focused on Salinas.[61]

The PRI proudly proclaimed that "modernization" would be visible on election day. Returns would be tabulated on a central government computer and made available to the public real time. However, on the evening of election day, July 6, 1988, just as the returns began coming in, the computer crashed. Early returns from urban boxes had favored Cárdenas, and the PRI was apparently afraid its traditional rural base would be incapable of overcoming Cárdenas's lead.[62]

A week after the election, the official results declared Salinas a winner with 50.7 percent of the vote. The returns credited Cárdenas with 31.1 percent and Manuel Clouthier, the PAN candidate, with 16.8 percent. Two other small parties received the remainder of the vote. In the bellwether Federal District, the PRI claimed only 27.3 percent of the vote.

The official returns can be interpreted in three ways. First, they accurately reflected the vote. Second, Salinas won with only a plurality, and the official total was inflated to enhance his mandate. A Cárdenas victory is a third possibility.[63]

An August 1989 *Los Angeles Times* poll found that only 24 percent of Mexicans believed that Salinas had won. Partially burned ballots marked for Cárdenas were found in many locations. Statistical anomalies abounded. In some precincts, by official count, Salinas received 100 percent of the vote, while in adjacent precincts with the same socioeconomic make-up, he only received 30 percent. Far more than 10 percent of the PRI ballot box totals ended in zero, indicating not random distribution but election officials adding a zero to the PRI vote total on the assumption that no one would notice a zero.[64]

Subsequent declarations have confirmed the fraud that most Mexicans assumed at the time. In June 1994, Arturo Núñez, the director general of the Federal Electoral Institute (IFE), admitted that the computer system had been forced to fail in 1988. His admission, however, did not adequately describe the scope of the fraud. Political scientists Alberto Aziz Nassif and Juan Molinar Horcasitas did that:

> It can be stated that the election fraud of July 6, 1988 was massive and was coordinated at the national level. It did not result from errors committed by isolated individuals, but from manipulating the results to subvert the voters' will. This massive fraud occurred in rural areas where there were practically no opposition poll watchers.[65]

Cárdenas claimed that he had won the presidency, but fearing uncontrollable escalation, he did not call for his followers to engage in illegal acts, such as seizing buildings, to press his claim. He concluded he could not overturn the official results by creating disorder. Historian Enrique Krauze commented on Cárdenas' restraint:

> An order from him [Cárdenas] would have sent Mexico up in flames. But perhaps in memory of his father, the missionary general, a man of strong convictions but not a man of violence, he did the country a great service by sparing it a possible civil war.[66]

The 1988 elections were significant because for the first time they clearly indicated that opposition parties were strong enough to win, shattering the assumption that PRI victories were inevitable. The departure of Cuauhtémoc Cárdenas and the Democratic Current from the PRI left the party more conservative, since it removed the political heirs of Lázaro Cárdenas from inside the PRI. As a result of the elections, the opposition acquired sufficient strength in the Chamber of Deputies to prevent the PRI from amending the constitution on its own, since a two-thirds vote is required for amendments. Political scientist Lorenzo Meyer commented: "The presidential elections of July 6, 1988 represent a watershed in the political history of post-revolutionary Mexico. They opened the door to a difficult transition, from state authoritarianism to democracy."[67]

Salinas quickly confounded his critics by making several bold moves that established him as a decisive leader. On January 10, 1989, he sent the army to arrest Joaquín Hernández Galicia who, as head of the oil workers, presided over Mexico's most powerful and corrupt labor union. The removal of Hernández Galicia repaid him for his support for Cárdenas in the 1988 elections. Soon after that, Salinas forced the retirement of Carlos Jonguitud Barrios, the long-entrenched leader of the national teachers union, who had proved unable to quell dissident teachers who favored union democracy. In April 1989, the formerly untouchable Miguel Ángel Félix Gallardo, whom the U.S. Drug Enforcement Agency (DEA) claimed shipped as much as two tons of cocaine a month into the United States, was arrested. In June of 1989, José Antonio Zorrilla, the former head of the Federal Security Directorate, was arrested on charges of having planned the murder of well known investigative reporter Manuel Buendía. All these moves established that, the dubious election notwithstanding, Salinas was very much the man in charge.[68]

After the 1988 elections, the PAN and Cárdenas's FDN formed a de facto alliance to protest electoral fraud. Once in office, Salinas adroitly split this alliance, creating his own de facto alliance with the PAN leadership, while isolating the Cárdenas-led faction. This led the PAN to shift from Clouthier's denunciation of the Salinas administration as "illegal and illegitimate" to the party's president announcing that the Salinas administration could "legitimize itself through the exercising power well."[69]

In October 1988, Cárdenas called for the replacement of the FDN—an unwieldy four-party alliance that was already disintegrating—with a new center-left party, the Party of the Democratic Revolution (PRD). The PRD, which proclaimed itself to uphold the values of the Mexican Revolution, refused to cooperate with what it branded the "usurper" administration.[70]

Salinas did his best to prevent the growth of the PRD and to convince the electorate that PRD election victories would destabilize the country. In the central Mexican states where Cárdenas had strong backing, such as Michoacán, Guerrero, Morelos, and the State of Mexico, elections were marred by violence, and the results were widely rejected as fraudulent. PRI-controlled state and federal governments denied funds to the handful of PRD members whose mayoral election victories were recognized. Finally, often in the aftermath of disputed elections, the government unleashed deadly force on PRD followers. Between 1989 and 1993, roughly 400 PRD members were killed for political reasons.[71]

Salinas's effort to split the post-election alliance between Cárdenas and the PAN dovetailed with the PAN's own perception that it would gain stature and power by working with the PRI and refashioning its image as that of a party that could govern. This emerging PAN-PRI alliance saw Salinas recognizing some PAN electoral victories and the PAN embracing flawed PRI political reforms that the PRI did not have enough votes to pass on its own in the Chamber of Deputies. Salinas felt comfortable working with the PAN since, after the PRI's switch to neoliberal policies, the PRI and the PAN were close ideologically.[72]

Salinas's favoring of the PAN became apparent when, after repeated protests charging stolen gubernatorial elections, a PAN victory was recognized in the 1989 gubernatorial election in Baja California. The PRI's loss to PAN candidate Ernesto Ruffo resulted from: 1) local resentment at Salinas imposing a political outsider as the PRI candidate, 2) the unusually high level of corruption during recent PRI administrations in Baja California, 3) major splits in the state PRI organization, 4) the attractiveness of the PAN candidate, a successful fishing company executive who had served as mayor of Ensenada, 5) the effective mobilization of 10,000 PAN election monitors who thwarted PRI attempts to steal the election, 6) the presence of 600 Mexican and foreign journalists who increased the political cost of stealing the election, and 7) the lack of a substantial rural population—the PRI's traditional base. Even though the PRI candidate carried all the rural districts in Baja California, Ruffo won, since 90 percent of the state's population was urban.[73]

In 1990, Salinas pushed through yet another political reform, which was known as the Federal Code of Electoral Institutions and Procedures (COFIPE). It was passed with PAN support, but over the strenuous objection of the PRD. The most dramatic aspect of the reform was the creation of the IFE, a fourth branch of government to organize elections.

Given the COFIPE's dual purpose of building regime credibility and at the same time maintaining PRI control, it was flawed in several ways. It retained the "governability clause," which guaranteed PRI control of the Chamber of Deputies even if its vote total fell below 50 percent. Control of the IFE itself remained under the interior secretary and representatives of the PRI.[74]

Salinas launched a massive new anti-poverty program, which cost more than $15 billion during his term. This program, known as Solidarity, funded a wide variety of projects such as electrification, street paving, medical centers, rural credit, sewage treatment plants, and drinking water systems. Projects often combined federal funding with community labor and planning. Salinas's control of Solidarity funding enabled him to increase his personal power at the expense of both the PRI and the government agencies that had traditionally supplied the services Solidarity offered.

The PRI staged a remarkable comeback in the 1991 mid-term congressional races. Its vote total rose to 61.4 percent, compared to the 50.4 percent its candidates for deputy had been credited with in 1988. Its candidates won 290 of the 300 single-member congressional districts. In large part, the PRI victory reflected Salinas being seen as a strong, efficient president. In 1991, he enjoyed a 62 percent popularity rating. The PRI recovery also reflected the large number of people who expected Salinas's economic policies to provide a better future and who had benefited from the Solidarity program.[75]

Other factors leading to the PRI recovery included vastly better grass-roots organization made possible by funds unavailable to other parties. The Mexican Institute of Public Opinion estimated that the PRI purchased 97 percent of the political ads on television, 86 percent of those on radio, and 72 percent of the print ads.[76]

Salinas's approval rating was largely based on the expectation of a better future, not strong economic growth. During his term, the increase in GDP averaged only 3.9 percent, well below the rate during the glory days of the Mexican economic miracle. Salinas's having increased tax collection and reduced inflation from triple digits to one digit added to his luster. Both the domestic and international press provided Salinas with adulatory coverage. In 1993, the *Economist* declared, "Mr Salinas has a claim to be hailed as one of the great men of the 20th century."[77]

Given electoral fraud charges resulting from the 1991 election and the upcoming U.S. congressional vote on the North American Free Trade Agreement (NAFTA), Salinas decided to burnish

Mexico's democratic image with further political reform. In 1993, a reform law eliminated the governability clause and included candidate spending limits. With this reform, Congress legislated away many of the tools that the PRI had previously used to fix elections. Salinas assumed his popularity would enable the PRI to win elections without its having to resort to its traditional election-fixing techniques.[78]

Salinas undercut the three major pillars of the revolution—state enterprises, an independent foreign policy, and the ejido (whose sale he allowed). He welcomed the pope and privatized the Cananea copper mine—a revolutionary icon. The popularity of his moves was such that, at the time of his last state of the nation address, he was widely applauded for his accomplishments, both inside and outside Mexico.[79]

Salinas continued with the neoliberal economic model he had helped introduce during the De la Madrid administration, adding a renegotiation of the foreign debt, NAFTA, and increased privatization. He deregulated the economy to attract foreign investment and reestablished amicable relations with the business sector, which led to increased domestic investment.[80]

Mexico was so restructured under Salinas that *Washington Post* writer Edward Cody commented that the president "has proved to be as radical in his own way as the revolutionaries who galloped over Mexico at the beginning of the century with bandoleers across their chests."[81]

The Indian uprising in Chiapas on New Years Day 1994 raised the likelihood that the political arena would shift from elections to armed force. This produced yet another political reform in hopes of keeping politics focused on the ballot box. With the exception of one small party, all the candidates and parties in the 1994 election signed an "Agreement for Peace, Democracy, and Justice." This agreement led the parties, including the PRD, to negotiate a reform package designed to appeal to those who might be tempted to employ armed force as a means of political change. The resulting reform increased the independence of the IFE by providing that ten of the eleven seats on its governing council be selected without presidential intervention.[82]

At the end of his term in November 1994, Salinas enjoyed a 66 percent approval rating. By February of 1995, 77 percent of those queried felt that Salinas should be put on trial. Rarely in history has any president's popularity fallen so precipitously so soon after leaving office.[83]

A few weeks after Salinas left office, Mexico suffered its worst economic downturn since the Depression. The peso had become seriously overvalued and, rather than devaluing it before he left office, Salinas left the devaluation for his successor. The blame he received for this was intensified by the widespread belief that his failure to devalue resulted from his aspiring to become executive director of the newly created World Trade Organization, a post he would be unlikely to receive if he were perceived as having bungled the economy. As essayist Carlos Fuentes commented: "Salinas made a mistake. A timely, well-ordered devaluation without panic would have benefited not only the national currency but also Salinas himself, and now he is berated for the difficult situation he left behind."[84]

THE ZEDILLO ADMINISTRATION, 1994–2000

Given the PRI's 1991 electoral rebound and Salinas's popularity, it appeared that the 1994 transfer of power to Salinas's successor would be routine. On November 28, 1993, Salinas named Secretary of Social Development Luis Donaldo Colosio as the PRI's presidential candidate. Before joining Salinas's cabinet, Colosio had served as president of the PRI and as a senator.

The indigenous rebellion in Chiapas on New Year's Day 1994 upset the carefully laid plans for Colosio's campaign. The Mexican public's attention was so firmly riveted on Chiapas that the first two months of Colosio's ill-fated campaign passed almost unnoticed.[85]

Only in March did the Colosio campaign finally begin to gather political momentum. At the ceremony commemorating the sixty-fifth anniversary of the PRI on March 6, Colosio was the sole speaker. There he promised to make "the PRI independent with respect to the government" and to admit foreign election observers. He also vowed to trim presidential power to "strictly constitutional limits." The PRI candidate declared that many of Mexico's ills were due to the excessive power assumed by past presidents.[86]

On March 23, as he was leaving a campaign rally in the border city of Tijuana, Colosio was gunned down. A twenty-three-year old factory worker, Mario Aburto, was arrested on the spot and charged with assassinating Colosio. The government declared that Aburto was a "lone nut" (à la Lee Harvey Oswald). Aburto, who was sentenced to forty-two years in prison, variously claimed that he was a "pacifist," a political militant, or that he had pulled the trigger by accident after being pushed by the crowd (even though two shots hit Colosio!).[87]

Conspiracy theories to explain the assassination abounded. Blame was most commonly laid at the feet of hard-liners at the national level of the PRI. None of the various explanations officially offered for the Colosio assassination have satisfied Mexican public opinion, which interpreted the event as a violent settling of scores among the PRI political elite.[88]

It will never be known if Colosio became a convert to democracy sometime between his leaving the presidency of the PRI and his speech on March 6. Columnist Carlos Ramírez summarized Colosio's democratic legacy as of 1991—his last full year as PRI president:

> Colosio was one of the national presidents of the PRI who made speeches most strongly promoting internal democracy, but who was most inclined to impose PRI candidates . . . The new PRI is the old PRI, and Colosio emerged as a dinosaur disguised as a democrat.[89]

On March 29, six days after Colosio's assassination, Salinas assembled a group of state governors and PRI officials in the presidential residence and informed them that the replacement presidential candidate would be Ernesto Zedillo, who had served in his cabinet secretary of budget and planning and as secretary of education. Zedillo had resigned from the latter post more than six months before the election to manage Colosio's campaign.[90]

Zedillo, unlike his four immediate predecessors who were National University graduates, had graduated from the National Polytechnic Institute. He had then earned a doctorate in economics from Yale and returned home to work in the Banco de México, Mexico's central bank. Upon learning of Zedillo's candidacy, political scientist Roderic Camp commented, "Zedillo is a continuation of the De la Madrid and Salinas mold of the narrowly formed technocrat, and he is particularly narrow."[91]

The August 21, 1994 presidential election featured a number of innovations that were clearly an improvement over elections past. The IFE, headed by Jorge Carpizo, the widely respected former director of the National Human Rights Commission (CNDH), organized the election. Under IFE auspices, officials staffing polling stations were selected from a random sample of voters, as opposed to letting PRI and government officials select PRI sympathizers, as had occurred in the past. The IFE spent $730 million preparing the voter registry and providing photo IDs. Fourteen groups, including the Alianza Cívica (Civic Alliance), a coalition of more than 400 Mexican non-governmental organizations (NGOs), coordinated election monitoring by 50,000 Mexican and 950 foreign election observers. Significantly, public funding paid for 90 percent of campaign spending, thus minimizing the influence of private donors.[92]

The final vote totals only confirmed what polling data had indicated. Zedillo received 50.18 percent of the valid votes, PAN candidate Diego Fernández de Cevallos 26.69 percent, and Cárdenas, who was the PRD candidate, 17.08 percent. The PRI won 275 of the 300 single-member congressional districts. In an apparent validation of the democratic process, voter turn-out was a near record 77.7 percent.[93]

Several factors explain why Cárdenas lost his 1988 political momentum. As a result of five years of Salinas's spin control and hostile media, broad sectors of the population felt threatened by

Cárdenas's party and its social policies. As had occurred in 1988, those with the least education—Cárdenas's logical base of support—voted for the PRI. Cárdenas was not telegenic, and as Adolfo Aguilar Zínser, his campaign spokesman, lamented, "Cárdenas never accepted the premise that this campaign would be won or lost in large part on television."[94]

As soon as the returns were reported, the struggle shifted from the ballot box to public opinion. Alianza Cívica reported that even though it did not change the outcome of the presidential election, there was widespread illegality, especially in rural areas. Its report on the elections concluded:

> It is difficult to characterize in a single word or phrase the voting process that is so complicated and contradictory. One cannot simply reject the entire election, but neither can one accept the victors' triumphalism or consider it an example of fairness and honesty.[95]

As had been the case in previous elections, the PRI had far more resources at its disposal than did other parties. A study by the IFE reported that the PRI accounted for 71.4 percent of campaign spending, leaving the other eight parties with 28.6 percent. The PRI benefited from its close linkage to the government. One of the foreign election observers noted:

> When we were in Pátzcuaro a couple of days before the election, you could see lines of peasants standing outside the bank, because they had just received money from the government support program, PROCAMPO. This was a not very well disguised attempt to buy their vote.[96]

On December 19, 1994, rebels in Chiapas announced that their troops had taken up positions throughout the state and that they had occupied several city halls. This was the straw that broke the camel's or, rather, the peso's back. However, the rebels were by no means the cause of the economic crisis, despite Zedillo's lame attempts to blame the crisis on them.

The crisis resulted from the combination of:

- the increasing outflow of dollars resulting from trade deficits and debt payments.;
- the increasing use of short-term treasury bonds (*tesobonos*) to finance this outflow;
- the increasing overvaluation of the peso.

The outflow of dollars largely resulted from Mexico spending $32.8 billion to service its foreign debt in 1994. Another $21.2 billion left the country as a result of the deficit in trade and services.[97]

The overvaluation of the peso underlay the crisis. Salinas had done a magnificent job of slowing inflation, which declined from well over 100 percent when he took office to 10 percent in 1993. However, the Mexican inflation rate was still well above the U.S. inflation rate, while the value of the peso was kept at roughly three to the dollar. The Salinas administration claimed that maintaining this exchange rate was vital for investor confidence and fighting inflation. Rather than devaluing the peso in 1994, the government implemented an expansionary fiscal and monetary policy to stimulate the economy, thus enhancing the PRI's luster before the presidential election.[98]

The combination of the Chiapas rebellion in January 1994 and the assassination of Colosio in March caused many investors to question the security of their Mexican investments. As a result of these events, during the six weeks following Colosio's assassination, Mexico lost more than $10 billion of its $28 billion in foreign reserves as investors, both domestic and foreign, moved their assets elsewhere.[99]

To entice investors to keep their capital in Mexico, the Mexican government increasingly relied on short-term, high-interest *tesobonos*. These bonds provided a measure of assurance to investors, since if a devaluation of the peso occurred, they would lose nothing as their return was payable in dollars.[100]

Investors flocked to the *tesobonos* since Mexico was regarded as creditworthy. This investment influx caused the value of the peso relative to the dollar to increase, which kept inflation low and facilitated imports. Imports also increased as economic recovery and easy credit fueled the demand for imported capital equipment, intermediate goods, cars, home computers, and big-screen TVs.[101]

As imports flooded in, exports declined, since the high value of the peso made them prohibitively expensive on the world market. The resulting deficits were sustainable only as long as Mexico could rely on new investments or foreign currency reserves. Through the summer of 1994, this latter remedy was applied. The September assassination of PRI Secretary General Ruiz Massieu once again called into question Mexico's stability. After that, investors became increasingly reluctant to keep their funds in Mexico. The U.S. Federal Reserve raised interest rates by a surprisingly large three-quarters of a percentage point in November, which siphoned off investment that might otherwise have gone to Mexico. As a result, Mexico's foreign currency reserves had declined to $11 billion by early December. At the same time, Mexico's short-term public debt (mainly *tesobonos*) totaled $27 billion.[102]

The government continued to repay *tesobono* holders as the twenty-eight-day notes came due, but few were stepping up to buy new ones. By late December, Mexico's reserves had declined to $6 billion. This decline was so precipitous that the government decided to devalue the peso by 15 percent to stave off financial crisis.

Soon a chain reaction began. Investors lost confidence, dumped pesos, and caused others to dump their peso holdings. Treasury Secretary Jaime Serra Puche flew to New York to plead with seventy money managers and top bank executives to keep their funds in Mexico. In two days, the value of the peso declined from 3.5 to 7.5 to the dollar. During the next three months, the Mexican stock exchange lost 50 percent of its value.[103]

To prevent a massive decline of U.S. exports to Mexico and a possible refugee crisis, as well as to protect the image of neoliberalism, later in January U.S. President Bill Clinton provided Mexico with $20 billion in loan guarantees from the Treasury Department's Exchange Stabilization Fund. This was accompanied by loans of $17.8 billion from the IMF and $10 billion from the Bank of International Settlements. Clinton and the international financiers felt it was necessary to intervene to: 1) protect U.S. investors who otherwise would have lost their capital, 2) restore calm in international financial markets, 3) support Zedillo and the PRI, and 4) to maintain confidence in NAFTA.[104]

On March 9, 1995, Zedillo offered an austerity plan designed to restart the economy and restore investor confidence. It included further decreases in government expenditures, increases in the price of gasoline and electricity, and an increase in value-added tax (VAT) from 10 percent to 15 percent.[105]

The impact of lower government spending, higher government fees and taxes, and higher interest rates (to keep even more investors from fleeing Mexico) threw the economy into reverse. In 1995, the GDP fell by 6.6 percent. That year, as more than one million Mexicans reached working age, there were 750,000 layoffs. Per capita income fell below the 1980 level. The annual interest on loans, mortgages, and credit cards reached 100 percent, causing massive defaults among middle-class debtors. Banks, businesses, producers, and consumers all suffered as a result of the crisis.[106]

Zedillo himself was stigmatized with the image of incompetence. Voters took out their wrath on the PRI, which in early 1995 lost gubernatorial races in Jalisco, Guanajuato, and, for an unprecedented second time, Baja California. By mid-1995, the two major opposition parties governed nearly a third of the Mexican population at the state or local levels. As Paige Bierma noted:

> Gone were the low inflation rates Mexicans had voted for; gone were the dreams of being able to inch closer to U.S. standards of living; gone were many of the Solidarity checks the rural and urban poor had depended on; and gone were the illusions that many had had of the PRI.[107]

After the peso crash and the Chiapas uprising threatened to further diminish the government's credibility, the Zedillo administration legislated yet another political reform in hopes of reversing a spate of PRI electoral defeats. This reform, the last of the twentieth century, had special significance since it set the ground rules for the 2000 presidential race.[108]

The 1996 political reform granted Congress the power to select nine general council members who would head the IFE. The nine would then select one of their number to serve as the IFE president. This provided the IFE with complete autonomy from political parties and the executive branch of government. The reform provided that the mayor of Mexico City be elected, rather than being appointed by the president as had occurred in the past. Campaign financing was greatly increased and made more equitable. The legislation prohibited campaign donations by governments, foreigners, churches, and corporations. Finally, the reform limited private campaign contributions to 10 percent of the amount received from public funds.[109]

In 1997, the IFE spent $264 million on organizing truly competitive congressional elections. Clear limits on campaign spending, more access to radio and TV for opposition parties, and more balanced coverage of the opposition on TV newscasts contributed to electoral fairness. For the first time, the distribution of public campaign financing roughly matched the proportion of the vote the major parties received.[110]

The PRI received only 39.1 percent of the vote in the 1997 elections, and this cost it its majority in the Chamber of Deputies. Almost as remarkable as the PRI losing its control over Congress was the broad range of opinion that characterized the elections as fair. Historian Enrique Krauze declared, "True democracy finally came to Mexico." By 1997, as a result of numerous political reforms, the political playing field in Mexico was as close to level at those in many established democracies.[111]

The reasons for the PRI's record low vote include: 1) corruption, which was highlighted by but by no means limited to former president Salinas's jailed brother Raúl; 2) resentment resulting from mishandling the 1994–1995 peso crash; and 3) the unpopularity of the PRI-imposed neoliberal economic model, which 64 percent of Mexicans opposed in a 1996 poll. Even though the PRI lost its majority in the Chamber of Deputies, it was still far from routed politically. In separate ballots on the same day, in senate races, the PRI won a plurality in all thirty-one states and the Federal District.

Reinvigorating Mexico's economy forms a lasting part of Zedillo's legacy. Between 1996 and 2000, buoyed by high oil prices and exports to its booming NAFTA partner to the north, Mexico's GDP averaged 5.4 percent growth. By the end of Zedillo's term, inflation had declined to a single digit. In 2000, the Mexican economy was deemed so sound that, for the first time, Moody's Investment Service rated Mexico as investment grade.[112]

The improved economy allowed Mexico to avoid an economic crisis as power shifted from Zedillo to his successor. Mexico's accumulation of $33 billion in foreign exchange reserves and a current account deficit that was only half that of 1994 made a run on the peso uninviting.[113]

Democratization, as well as economic recovery, enhanced Zedillo's legacy. His handling of the 2000 presidential election further bolstered his standing. The week before the election, *Wall Street Journal* writers Peter Fritsch and José de Córdoba commented, "The victor in Mexico's hotly contested presidential election this Sunday is clear: Ernesto Zedillo Ponce de León." Not surprisingly, at the end of his term, Zedillo enjoyed a 69 percent approval rating, up from 31 percent five years earlier.[114]

THE MILITARY

> The Mexican military that is emerging from the Cold War is primarily charged with the armed management of social conflict and execution of U.S. designed counter-narcotics strategies.
>
> Global Exchange, 2000[115]

As the military suppressed the urban and rural guerrilla groups that sprang up after the 1968 student movement, its influence in governing circles increased. During the Echeverría administration (1970–1976), a new 900-acre military academy was built on the southern outskirts of Mexico City—its cost a military secret. Large sums were spent on modernizing equipment. Beginning in 1977, cavalry units began to receive motor vehicles to replace their horses. As late as the 1970s, some of Mexico's combat aircraft dated from the Second World War. During the López Portillo administration (1976–1982), the military shared in the oil wealth as Mexico acquired supersonic F-5 jet fighters.[116]

Military involvement with Chiapas increased after the indigenous rebellion there in 1994. After its initial ten-day counteroffensive, the military was assigned the role of cordoning off, but not crushing, the rebel force. Tens of thousands of troops were permanently stationed around rebel-occupied areas.[117]

The military assumed a greatly increased role in fighting illegal drug production. By 2000, 36,000 troops, a fifth of the total, were involved in drug eradication. In parts of Oaxaca, Sinaloa, Jalisco, and Guerrero, where the military concentrated its forces to fight drugs, the army became de facto the supreme authority. The military's role in drug enforcement inevitably opened the door to corruption. It also led to widespread human rights abuse. In 1990, Americas Watch reported that "torture and political killings are still institutionalized techniques in the military."[118]

During the crime wave that gripped Mexico City after the 1994 peso crisis, President Zedillo lost confidence in Mexico's notoriously corrupt and venal police and appointed army General Enrique Tomás Salgado Cordero as the top public security chief in the city. He also named generals and colonels to the city's top public safety posts.[119]

The military replaced police elsewhere in Mexico. Thousands of soldiers substituted for police in Baja California. Some twenty states recruited active or retired military officers for key police posts, and military officers commanded most anti-drug agencies. Political scientist Roderic Camp commented on the military's performing police work: "It's misguided to think that military officers are going to meet success where the police and political institutions have failed. The major danger is that it will further compromise the military as an institution by exposing it to all these sources of corruption."[120]

As Mexico opened its economy to the rest of the world, the Mexican military also opened itself to the outside world, which, given the reality of geopolitics, meant the U.S. military. U.S. arms sales to Mexico, which had totaled only $32.3 million dollars between 1950 and 1979, soared to $508.4 million between 1980 and 1988.[121]

During the 1990s, U.S.–Mexican military cooperation increased still further. In 1995, to discuss security issues, U.S. Secretary of Defense William J. Perry made an official visit to Mexico—a first for a U.S. secretary of defense. This unprecedented visit symbolized the increasingly close relationship between the two militaries. In 1997, Mexico supplied 305 students, more than any other Latin American country, to the School of the Americas located at Fort Benning, Georgia. This school has been frequently criticized for training personnel who later return to their home countries and commit human rights abuses. In 1999, Mexico was the second largest recipient (after Colombia) of U.S. military aid in Latin America.[122]

Links between the two militaries reflect the expanded mission of the Mexican military. Between 1996 and 1997, U.S. security assistance to Mexico increased from $5.33 million to $74.25 million as the Mexican army plunged into the war against drugs. Similarly, the number of Mexican military officers trained in the United States increased from 300 to 1,500. After the September 11, 2001 terrorist attacks, the Mexican military mission expanded to include counterterrorism. Between 2001 and 2005, U.S. security assistance to Mexico averaged $41.7 million, while the number of Mexican military personnel trained averaged 717.[123]

Mexican military spending soared as the pace of the anti-drug effort increased and as the military deployed to Chiapas and elsewhere to contain rebels. Such spending increased from $678 million in 1990 to $3.22 billion in 2006.[124]

THE POLITICAL OPPOSITION

The Party of the Democratic Revolution (PRD)

The broad goals of the new party, the PRD, were democratization, social justice, an independent foreign policy, a role for the state in the economy, and defense of the revolutionary heritage, which included Pemex. Even though the PRI tarred the PRD as forming a part of the radical left, it would have been considered a moderate social democratic party if it had been in Europe.

As Lorenzo Meyer observed in 1991, in its early years the PRD was far too dependent on its outstanding figure, Cuauhtémoc Cárdenas, "The PRD continues without congealing as a party and as alternative project, as it remains absolutely dependent on one factor to mobilize the electorate: the person of engineer Cuauhtémoc Cárdenas . . ." Cárdenas became the court of last resort for those who lost in party committees. When he tried to stay out of internal conflicts, critics accused him of ducking responsibility and letting the party drift. When he stepped in to resolve them, he was accused of authoritarianism.[125]

The fortunes of the PRD improved after the 1994 elections. The factional disputes that had bedeviled the party lessened. The PRD's public image improved as President Zedillo involved the party in the political process, including negotiating the 1996 political reform. Also, as the Zedillo administration recognized PRD electoral victories, the PRD was no longer cast in the role of the violent protestor. Finally, the election of Andrés Manuel López Obrador as president of the PRD for the 1996–1999 term improved the party's fortunes. The election itself showcased the PRD's increasing maturity, as 360,000 voters nationwide cast a vote without violence or significant charges of fraud. Unlike Cárdenas and Porfirio Muñoz Ledo, his predecessors as president of the PRD, López Obrador was not a notable at the time of the PRD's founding. Rather, López Obrador rose to his leadership position within the party combating election fraud and Pemex contamination in his home state of Tabasco. López Obrador won the PRD presidency on the basis of successfully weathering crises, which involved PRD-led mobilizations and negotiated solutions.[126]

After becoming party president, López Obrador offered PRD congressional and gubernatorial nominations to many individuals not affiliated with the PRD, including members of the PRI and PAN, if they renounced their previous political affiliations. This brought new constituencies into the party. Under López Obrador's leadership, the party began to organize Sun Brigades, groups of party workers named for the party's Aztec sun logo. Thousands of these brigade members went house-to-house explaining the PRD's program and dispelling doubts voters might have had about the party.[127]

The party's improved fortunes were apparent in 1997, as Cárdenas, the PRD candidate for mayor of Mexico City, won with 46 percent of the vote, the same percentage of the vote he had won there in 1988. This impressive comeback was facilitated by Cárdenas using the vastly increased financial resources provided by the 1996 political reform to produce sophisticated, clever TV commercials that enhanced his public image. In addition, Cárdenas benefited from the intense animosity most Mexican felt toward Salinas after 1994, since he was associated with having adamantly rejected the Salinas presidency.[128]

In 1997, Cárdenas's high polling numbers before the Mexico City election energized the PRD nationwide. This was reflected in the party winning 25.7 percent of the vote and receiving 125 deputies, 25 percent of the total. This increased vote percentage also reflected the party's emphasis on the defense of democratic rights and the living standards of the poor as well as the toning down of its leftist rhetoric. Journalist Antonio Jáquez commented on this rhetorical shift: "The left of the PRD is increasingly afraid to use the word 'left'. It's a left in which the former '-isms' that were its ideological base—socialism, communism, Maoism, Trotskyism—have been replaced by a new -ism: pragmatism." This formula led to a sharp increase in PRD officeholders. Just before the 2000 presidential elections, 116 deputies and fourteen senators represented the party in Congress. PRD mayors and governors presided over a quarter of the population, and the party was either the first or second strongest political force in fourteen states.[129]

The National Action Party (PAN)

> The forces leading the Mexican Revolution to victory came from the North. This same region is now home to forces that propose to bury the Revolution.
>
> Abraham Nuncio, 1986[130]

José Ángel Conchello's 1972–1975 term as PAN president marked a turning point in the history of the party. Conchello, a Nuevo León businessman, considered that Echeverría's fiscal policies were irresponsible and that the increasing economic role of the state was detrimental to the market and to private property. This emphasis on economic policy soon drew the wrath of traditionalists under the leadership of 1970 PAN presidential candidate Efraín González Morfín. Traditionalists argued that the political upstarts, led by Conchello, were threatening to undermine the party's identity and open the way into the party for political opportunists who had no interest in the party's doctrine. The heated debate over the direction the party should take went on almost unnoticed by the public. The lack of public interest in the PAN is indicated by the fact that the party won only nineteen mayoral elections between 1970 and 1976.[131]

The party remained divided as it convened to nominate a candidate for the 1976 presidential race. One faction in the party advocated an aggressive electoral campaign to seek out new supporters. The other felt the party should maintain its more traditional position, prioritizing civic indoctrination, even if that meant losing elections. PAN party statutes required that a presidential nominee receive 80 percent of the votes at the convention. Neither the traditionalists nor the modernizers, who soon became known as neo-PANistas, could muster 80 percent of the convention delegates, so the party did not nominate a candidate.[132]

In the 1979 mid-term elections, given the general ineffectiveness of electoral opposition to the PRI, the PAN remained as the principal opposition party, winning four single-member congressional districts. None of the other seven opposition parties participating won a single-member district. These elections also marked the beginning of a shift of the PAN vote to northern Mexico. As a result of this shift, which became more pronounced in the 1980s, the northern border states displaced the Federal District as the party's center of gravity.[133]

Three events moved the PAN from civic education to contending for power, especially in northern Mexico. The first was President Echeverría's massive 1976 land expropriation in northwestern Mexico. The second was the 1982 bank nationalization ordered by President López Portillo. The third was the economic crisis of the 1980s. These events convinced many, including large numbers of small and medium-sized business owners, that the PRI could no longer be trusted with the reins of power and that the PAN was the logical alternative. Early in De la Madrid's 1982–1988 term, these three events, plus the welcoming of those bearing free market ideology, led to a wave of electoral victories in northern Mexico.

While there is no evidence that the PRI as a party was responsible for the 1982 bank nationalization, it was the PRI as a party that bore the brunt of electoral punishment for that unpopular decision. Up until 1988, discontent with the PRI resulted in increased support for the PAN, rather than for the increasingly marginalized left. The PAN's image as a consistent, dependable opposition party enabled it to pick up the bulk of the protest vote. The 1977 electoral reform made it possible for increased support for the PAN to be quickly reflected in an increased number of PANista deputies in the lower house of Congress.[134]

As the old political and economic model was collapsing in the 1980s, the PAN successfully capitalized on discontent based on: 1) its long-term opposition to an overarching state, 2) opposition to an all-powerful presidency, 3) its advocacy of private enterprise, and 4) its promotion of municipal and states rights. The party de-emphasized its earlier adherence to Christian doctrine. Instead it became a vehicle for middle-class protest. Critiques of the incumbent government dominated its campaigns. The party increasingly emphasized individual merit and the notion that the state had very limited social responsibility. The PAN, which had been considered as an anachronism during the Mexican economic miracle of the 1960s, emerged as the standard-bearer of modernity. By the 1980s, as the PAN rode a wave of democracy and free-market economics, the authoritarian PRI increasingly appeared to be the anachronism.[135]

Despite the influx of northern businessmen and members of the middle class, during the 1980s, the PAN remained very much a minority opposition party. In 1987, only eighteen of Mexico's 2,400 mayors came from the PAN. PAN mayors together administered less than 1 percent of the population.[136]

For the PAN, the 1988 elections were a disappointment, as the party's vote total lagged behind both Cárdenas's and Salinas's. Rather than supporting PAN candidate Manuel Clouthier, those who sought to either replace or at least severely punish the PRI voted for Cárdenas. Systematic vote fraud during the Salinas administration (1988–1994) caused those opposing the PRI to shift their protest votes back to the PAN, since they felt that PRD election victories were unlikely to be recognized.[137]

During the 1980s, the primary goal of the PAN remained "democracy," which meant free elections, a true multiparty system, and freedom of expression and assembly. The party also favored transferring as much governance as possible to the state and municipal level. As political scientist Soledad Loaeza observed:

> PAN members feel threatened, not by the marching proletariat, nor by an armed peasantry, not by a closed and distant bourgeoisie, nor by a leftist government, but by a State which it considered inefficient and corrupt, incapable of creating a more egalitarian country . . .[138]

During the Salinas administration, dealing with a regime of dubious legitimacy presented the PAN with a dilemma. Luis H. Álvarez, who served as president of the party between 1987 and 1993, decided the best interests of the party would be served by positioning the PAN as an alternative governing party. Salinas needed the PAN to enhance his own democratic image. Álvarez used the threat of breaking off contact with Salinas to ensure the recognition of PAN electoral victories and to leverage political and economic reforms to his party's liking.[139]

Regardless of whether they were compatible with traditional PAN doctrine, the policies adopted by the party during the Salinas administration were an enormous success electorally. The PAN's vote increased from 3.2 million in 1988 to 9.0 million in 1994. In 1987, fewer than one million Mexicans lived under a PAN municipal or state administration, while by November 1995, more than 30 million did.[140]

In 1994, much of the PAN's strength lay in the rapidly increasing youth vote. A surprisingly large 45 percent of all PAN voters were under twenty-nine. By comparison, only 38 percent of PRI voters were that age or younger and only 37 percent of PRD voters were. By 1994, the PAN had become a party with a nationwide base. That year it was placed second in twenty-three states and the Federal District. This was especially significant since, according to new proportional representation rules, it received a senate seat to represent each state where it came in second.[141]

The party's momentum continued into the Zedillo administration (1994–2000) since: 1) after Ruffo won the governorship of Baja California, the PRI was seen as vulnerable, 2) the party was considered to be a peaceful path to change, as opposed (especially) to the Indian rebels in Chiapas, 3) existing PAN governments were considered more efficient and honest than their PRI predecessors, 4) the PAN had developed the image as a stable, well-established party, and 5) the party made effective use of radio and TV. As columnist Arturo Martínez Nateras noted in 1995, "Today, the PAN is the only party which is growing and whose vote in increasing." That year the PAN held four governorships and the mayoralties of eleven state capitals and governed thirteen of the twenty largest municipalities.[142]

The 1990s saw the party extend from its power base in the north into central Mexico. After winning its first two gubernatorial elections in border states, it won several gubernatorial elections in the center, including Jalisco (1992 and 1998), Guanajuato (1994 and 2000), Querétaro (1997), and Morelos (2000). After the 1994 peso crash, the PAN moved into more open opposition to the PRI, leaving behind the conciliatory posture it had adopted during the Salinas administration. In 1997, this conciliatory stance came back to haunt the party as protest voters associated the PAN with the by then unpopular Salinas and cast fewer votes for the PAN than for the PRD. This dip in the PAN's voting strength proved to be temporary. As of June 1999, there were six PAN governors and 215 mayors. The party held 24 percent of the seats in both the Chamber of Deputies and the Senate and administered 33.1 percent of the population at the state or municipal level (almost three times the percentage under PRD administration).[143]

At the end of the century, the neo-PANistas held sway in the party. They brought the PAN much needed financial resources, leadership styles, organizational capabilities, and new advertising techniques drawn from their own private-sector experience. They often emphasized the link between leader and voter, ignoring the party and the government. They envisioned a sharp reduction in the state's role in Mexican society and were guided by an aggressive individualism and the notion that the best government was the least government.[144]

ARMED OPPOSITION

Chiapas

> The Zapatistas have pulled back the curtain that covered up the other Mexico. It is not the Mexico of eager entrepreneurs lined up to open Pizza Hut franchises or consumers eager to shop at Wal-Mart, but rather the Mexico of malnourished children, illiteracy, landlessness, poor roads, lack of health clinics, and life as a permanent struggle.
>
> Lynn Stephen, 1994[145]

The social conditions under which Indians lived underlay the 1994 uprising in Chiapas by a group known as the Zapatista Army of National Liberation (EZLN). The state had the highest number of illiterates, the highest number of those over fifteen who had not finished elementary school, and the highest percentage of the population lacking electricity of any state.[146]

In the late 1960s, Maoist political organizers began arriving in Chiapas. Following the notion of "insertion among the masses," the organizers maintained a low profile, worked directly with peasants, and remained for years. This diaspora into the hinterlands of Chiapas was typical of the

Mexican left after the massacre of students in 1968 and the subsequent decimation of urban guerrilla groups. The arrival in Chiapas of organizers with a political agenda continued into the 1980s.[147]

The Catholic Church also had plans for change in the state. The key figure behind this effort was Samuel Ruiz, who became bishop of San Cristóbal in 1960. He arrived in Chiapas as a conservative, but became an advocate for the poor after witnessing the conditions under which Indians lived. The Medellín bishops conference, where liberation theology offered hope for peaceful change, also influenced Ruiz's thinking.[148]

Under Ruiz's guidance, the Church trained 8,000 catechists and 400 deacons and dispatched them to more than 2,500 indigenous communities, where they drew the local population into discussing the causes of their poverty. Many catechists became community leaders since they had ties to the Church and spoke Spanish, which made them ideal intermediaries with the outside world. In 1990, Ruiz commented on his role in Chiapas: "I illuminated the way for the Indians, using their faith. This enabled them to see the problems they faced, and they chose the way to solve them."[149]

On New Year's Day 1994, residents and tourists alike were totally surprised when they awoke in San Cristóbal, the main city in highland Chiapas, to find ski-masked rebels huddled around small bonfires. All that day rebels and especially their apparent leader, who became known to the world as "Marcos," not only chatted with the curious but declared war on the Mexican army and promulgated a series of revolutionary laws.[150]

Rebels also occupied the municipal seats in Ocosingo, Las Margaritas and Altamirano, the local power centers for eastern Chiapas. The rebels soon withdrew from these towns rather than facing the overwhelming firepower of the Mexican army. Between January 1 and January 11, 1994, roughly 152 were killed. Most of the dead were rebel combatants and civilians.[151]

Figure 24.1 *EZLN rebels in Chiapas*

Source: Benjamín Flores/*Proceso*

To coincide with their offensive, the rebels published a declaration of war. It concluded:

> To the Mexican People:
>
> We honest, free men and women, believe that the war we are declaring is our last hope and that it is just and necessary. For many years dictators have been engaged in an undeclared genocidal war against our people. For this reason, we ask for your participation and support in our struggle for *jobs, land, housing, food, health, education, independence, liberty, democracy, justice and peace*. We will not stop fighting until these basic demands are met and a free and democratic government rules in Mexico.[152]

The date of the rebellion, the same day as the NAFTA entered into effect, symbolized the Zapatistas' opposition to NAFTA and neoliberal economic policies. Bishop Ruiz commented on another aspect of the movement:

> The Zapatistas never tried to gain power as the other guerrilla movements did. What they were trying to do was to shake up the sociopolitical conscience of the citizens of this country and ask them to participate in creating a transitional government until a more democratic government was in place.[153]

On January 12, Salinas offered the rebels a ceasefire since he was concerned with his image as TV sets around the world showed the government carrying out indiscriminate aerial attacks. As historian Lorenzo Meyer observed at the time, "To build popular support for a prolonged war against the EZLN, the government needs consensus and, above all, legitimacy, both of which have been lacking for some time."[154]

Salinas's offer of a ceasefire and a pardon for participants in the uprising led Marcos to reply:

> Today, January 18, 1994, we learned of the formal "pardon" which the federal government offers us. For what should we ask pardons? For what are they pardoning us? For not dying of hunger? For not quietly accepting our misery? For not humbly accepting the gigantic historical burden of scorn and neglect? For having risen up in arms when we found all other paths closed?[155]

The internet soon came to play a crucial role in the Zapatista movement. In early 1994, the Zapatistas had no links to the internet and relied on sympathizers posting their declarations after they appeared in print. They soon acquired computers and satellite uplinks so they could post their own material. This internet information initially flowed through channels developed in organizing opposition to the North American Free Trade Agreement. The internet allowed the rebels to: 1) counter pro-government media, 2) mobilize Mexican and foreign supporters to halt the January 1994 offensive as well as a February 1995 government offensive, 3) circulate Zapatista demands that the print media declined to publish, 4) describe how the government was carrying out low-intensity warfare in Chiapas, 5) discuss rebel plans and those of others to democratize Mexico, and 6) organize mass mobilizations.[156]

In January 1996, a Mexican government congressional negotiating team reached an agreement with the EZLN. This agreement—often referred to as the Accords of San Andrés for the town in which it was negotiated—was ratified by the EZLN. It called for amending the Mexican constitution to permit indigenous autonomy and to recognize the right of indigenous people to compete for office independently of political parties. Other reforms were to be implemented at the state and national level to guarantee indigenous people increased political representation.[157]

The Accords of San Andrés marked the final attempt by Zedillo and the EZLN to peacefully resolve the standoff in Chiapas. This led the Zapatistas to declare that the failure to implement the

Accords indicated bad faith by the government. They declined further negotiations, producing a standoff lasting through the end of the Zedillo administration.

Rather than coming to a negotiated agreement with the rebels or launching an all-out assault on the area under rebel control, the Mexican government early on choose a half-way course—low intensity warfare. This decision was made crystal clear in a leaked government document entitled "1994 Campaign Plan." The document stated that one of the aims of the Defense Department counter-insurgency strategy was to "break the relations of support that exist between the population and the violators of the law [i.e. the EZLN]." Military instructors were charged with "training and support of the self-defense and other paramilitary organizations." Finally the document stated, "In case such groups do not exist, it will be necessary to create them."[158]

A key element in the low-intensity warfare strategy was wearing down communities and groups identified as supporting the EZLN. Paramilitary forces assumed a key role in this task. Their members were recruited from the unemployed landless and allowed to carry guns and use them for personal enrichment. During 1996 and 1997, an estimated 1,500 were killed by paramilitaries and perhaps ten times as many fled their homes in fear of them.[159]

The most horrific action by paramilitary forces occurred in December 1997 at Acteal, in the municipality of Chenalhó. There, an estimated sixty paramilitaries attacked a makeshift refugee camp housing those who had fled from PRI-dominated areas. After four hours of firing, they had killed seven men, nineteen women, and nineteen children.[160]

Political killings in Chiapas have been carried out by police, the military, paramilitaries and Zapatista supporters. In an attempt to end such brutality, various human rights groups sent representatives. In 1999 and 2000 alone, Chiapas was visited by Asma Jahangir, UN Special Reporter on Extra-Judicial Executions, Mary Robinson, UN High Commissioner for Human Rights, and Erika Des, President of the UN's Special Working Group on Indigenous Peoples. They all filed reports highly critical of abuses by the government and those acting under its aegis. Rather than addressing human rights in Chiapas, the government engaged in the massive deportation of foreign human rights observers. In 1998 and 1999 alone, 175 were deported.[161]

One of the great successes of the EZLN was stimulating Indian activism throughout Mexico. After he retired, Bishop Samuel Ruiz commented: "Overall something which is irreversible is raising the level of Indian consciousness continent-wide. They are taking control of their own history."[162]

The 1994 uprising dramatically changed land tenure in Chiapas. Zapatista sympathizers, PRI sympathizers, and independent groups occupied vast amounts of land, much of which was converted into ejidos. In the eighty years before 1994, an average of twenty-four ejidos were created annually in Chiapas. During the following six years, the annual average jumped to 200. However, rather than representing a belated commitment to social justice, land allocation formed part of government counterinsurgency strategy. Most land was allocated to government sympathizers in an attempt to wean support away from Zapatistas.[163]

The rebellion was an impetus to democracy. As late as 1988, the PRI won 90 percent of the vote in Chiapas. By 1997 its vote had fallen to 50.6 percent, since other parties could compete effectively. At the national level, the rebellion galvanized the political establishment into passing the 1994 political reform, in hopes that such reform would forestall more widespread rebellion.[164]

HUMAN RIGHTS

> Mexico historically has opted for form over substance in the promotion and protection of human rights. If Mexico rigorously adhered to the provisions of its Constitution and statutes, Mexico's human rights recorded would be exemplary.
>
> Human Rights Watch, 1990[165]

Throughout Latin America in the 1950s and the 1960s, authoritarian governments abused human rights in the name of the crusade against communism. Similarly the left violated human rights with impunity in the name of carrying out a radical transformation of an inherently inhuman social order while denigrating the very concept of human rights as a façade to mask fundamental social inequalities. As political scientist Francisco Panizza noted, "Double standards on both sides of the great ideological divide of that time risked emptying the concept of human rights of its meaning."[166]

During the 1970s, human rights issues assumed unprecedented centrality. The Carter administration (1977–1981) in the United States attributed new importance to the issue. At the same time, the opposition in Latin America sought to find a new language that would be more difficult to silence and began to accept the importance of formal democracy. A new global culture and the rise of international public opinion increased the attention focused on human rights. Satellite TV made it increasingly difficult for governments to conceal their crimes.[167]

The notion of human rights only entered Mexican political discourse in the relatively recent past. None of those protesting government suppression of the 1968 student movement invoked the notion of "human rights." Rather, condemnation of government action revolved round such notions as repression and violations of university autonomy.[168]

Between 1970 and 1976, just as human rights issues were taking on increased significance throughout the Americas, Mexico went though a largely secret version of the same "Dirty War" that flared up in other Latin American countries. In Mexico, a part of the generation of 1968 clashed with the power of the government and the army. During this period, political arrests, torture, disappearances, and murder by security forces increased markedly. The government itself later identified more than 700 cases of enforced disappearances and more than a hundred extrajudicial executions during the Dirty War.[169]

In an effort to improve his image, in 1977 President López Portillo freed 552 political prisoners. At the time, Amnesty International estimated that an additional 100 to 200 political prisoners might have remained in government custody. While freeing prisoners was a positive gesture, it did not indicate a significant improvement in human rights. Amnesty International commented on the human rights situation during 1981, López Portillo's last full year in office, noting that it "continued to receive reports of arbitrary detentions, torture, and killings by regular army units, acting in conjunction with local landowners and unofficial paramilitary units."[170]

The 1985 earthquake in Mexico City, which caused the headquarters of the Attorney General of the Federal District to collapse, dramatically illustrated Mexico's continuing abuse of human rights. Rescue workers there found bodies bearing unmistakable signs of torture. This, of course, was just one indicator of systematic human rights abuse during the De la Madrid administration (1982–1988). A 1987 Amnesty International report noted that it continued to receive "reports of political killing, torture, arbitrary arrest of political opponents and the use in evidence of confessions obtained under duress."[171]

In 1984, sociologist Sergio Aguayo founded the Mexican Academy for Human Rights, which investigated individual violations of human rights and educated the public about their rights. Among the Academy's board members were intellectual luminaries such as Carlos Fuentes and Elena Poniatowska. The Catholic Church organized several human rights groups, including the Centro Vitoria, which initially addressed Central American human rights violations but later focused on Mexican ones. In 1988, Miguel Concha Malo, of the Centro Vitoria, published a detailed tabulation of some 6,813 human rights violations that occurred between 1971 and 1986. Of these, 2,982 were against peasants, 449 against students, and 316 against workers. More than a third of the violations—2,440—were in Chiapas. By the mid-1980s, there were at least fifteen human rights groups functioning in Mexico.[172]

In 1989, shortly before NAFTA negotiations were to begin and just after the release of a scathing Americas Watch report, *Human Rights in Mexico: a Policy of Impunity*, Salinas founded the CNDH. Jorge Carpizo, a Supreme Court justice and former rector of the National University, was chosen to head the CNDH, thus lending credibility to this new government agency. The CNDH's mandate included the investigation of human rights abuses by government agents and the forwarding of its findings to the agency responsible for such action. The CNDH lacked authority to enforce its recommendations, which all too often were ignored by the government agencies responsible for human rights abuses. Statutes explicitly prohibited it from investigating violations of political and labor rights. As Aguayo noted, Salinas "created the commission in 48 hours because he wanted to create a card for his trip to Washington."[173]

Despite its statutory limitations, the CNDH unquestionably played an important role in promoting human rights in Mexico. It released hard-hitting reports on torture and "disappearances" committed by the army and strongly criticized government actions against supporters of the EZLN. It sent its own medical staff to examine torture victims and carry out exhumations, thus providing important human rights documentation. It also sponsored many studies and symposia and published a wide range of documents concerning human rights.[174]

By 1994, Salinas's last year in office, there were no signs of his "modernization" when it came to human rights. An Amnesty International account of events that year reported:

> Scores of prisoners of conscience, mostly indigenous peasants, were detained. The widespread use of torture and ill-treatment by law enforcement agents continued to be reported. At least twenty people "disappeared" and the whereabouts of hundreds who "disappeared" in previous years remained unknown. Dozens of people were extrajudicially executed. Those responsible for human rights violations continued to benefit from impunity.[175]

In general, as long-time human rights activist Mariclaire Acosta observed, the human rights situation worsened under President Zedillo (1994–2000) as:

- rampant human rights violations occurred in Chiapas;
- the institutionalized presence of the military in many rural areas produced serious human rights abuses;
- those responsible for various massacres, especially in the state of Guerrero, remained unpunished.[176]

Amnesty International Secretary General Pierre Sane observed in 1997: "There is a human rights crisis in Mexico today. The threats, attacks and other violations against human rights defenders, as well as journalists, have rocketed to unprecedented proportions." Sane charged that Zedillo lacked the political will to curb human rights abuses, especially in cases involving the armed forces, and noted that Zedillo's use of the military to run key police agencies was "fueling the crisis."[177]

In 2000, Vicente Fox's new administration seemed to bode well for human rights. As he had promised during his campaign, he named a special prosecutor for crimes committed during the Dirty War. He also appointed human rights activist Mariclaire Acosta as Under Secretary of Foreign Affairs for Human Rights and Democracy.[178]

By 2006, those who had pinned their hopes on Fox were sorely disappointed. Acosta found herself in a turf battle with the government's National Commission on Human Rights, which she described as having spent "15 years covering up the truth about human rights in Mexico." Later she was essentially fired when Foreign Minister Ernesto Derbez abolished her position. The special prosecutor appointed to investigate the Dirty War never won a single conviction as his office was pressured by the PRI and the armed forces not to delve into sensitive matters. As Amnesty International reported in 2007, "President Vicente Fox completed his mandate without fulfilling the administration's commitment to end human rights violations and impunity, which remained widespread." Nor did the 2006 presidential campaign seem to offer a better future, since as Amnesty International investigator Rupert Knox noted, there was a total absence of human rights discussion during the campaign.[179]

Of the various human rights problems inherited by the Fox administration, the murder of women in Ciudad Juárez received the most publicity. Up until the 1990s, roughly three women a year were murdered in the city. Then in the early 1990s, corpses, mostly of young women, many who had been raped and mutilated, began turning up in fields. By 2007, more than 400 victims had been found. The killings have been widely linked to the rapid change in gender roles in a city where so many women work in maquiladoras and where narco-trafficking, the sex trade, and globalization have eaten away at the social fabric. The Ciudad Juárez police department was woefully inadequate in investigating these crimes due to budget limitations. The city, with twice the population of its neighbor El Paso, had less than an eighth of El Paso's budget. Compounding the lack of resources was incompetence and corruption, leading to botched investigations. As Human Rights Watch noted in 2007, "The failure over a decade to resolve the murders of hundreds of young women and girls in Ciudad Juárez, in Chihuahua state, offers a paradigmatic example of impunity in Mexico."[180]

Oaxaca also illustrated the scant attention paid to human rights. In May 2006, 70,000 of the state's teachers, who earned only $400 to $600 a month, struck for higher wages and better working conditions in what was almost an annual ritual. To ensure that their demands were not ignored, striking teachers formed an encampment in the colonial center of Oaxaca City. In a sharp departure from past practice, in June the governor ordered the violent removal of the teachers using police and tear gas. This enraged teachers and led to a broadening of the movement that became known as the Popular Assembly of the Peoples of Oaxaca (APPO). APPO raised a new demand—that Governor Ulíses Ruiz be removed from office. Through October the demonstrators occupied the town center, shutting down the lucrative tourist trade and seizing state-owned radio and TV stations. On October 27, 2006, parties loyal to Ruiz attacked the demonstrators in the city, killing three, including an American journalist. This led the Fox administration to send some 4,000 police, backed by tear gas, water cannons, and helicopters. The force made its way through the protestors' barricades and restored an uneasy calm to the city. Hundreds were arrested in the police crackdown, many of whom had not violated the law. The National Commission of Human Rights reported that by January 31, 2007, as a result of the conflict, twenty had been killed, 381 injured, and 366 arrested. There were fifteen documented cases of torture, of which thirteen were committed by the Federal Preventive Police and two by Oaxaca State police.[181]

Human rights reports published during the Calderón administration made it clear that rather than bringing an improvement in human rights, having a PAN president in Los Pinos simply meant violations as usual. Amnesty International documented the continued use of torture and linked continued human rights abuse to the widespread use of the military in the fight against drugs. In 2008, Liliana Velázquez, president of Amnesty International in Mexico, declared that authorities in Oaxaca, Chihuahua, and the State of Mexico "owe their citizens an apology for the reigning impunity related to police abuse and the murder of women."[182]

Human rights abuses continue despite laws and the dedicated efforts of countless human rights activists since:

- Violators of human rights are rarely punished. A 2007 report by Amnesty International concluded:

  > Impunity for human rights violations remains the rule. The lack of accountability for public security and criminal justice officials means that they are free to resort to abusive practices when carrying out their duties, in the knowledge that they will not be sanctioned.[183]

- The war on drugs invites abuse when anti-narcotics operations occur in rural areas, since praise and promotions result from obtaining convictions on drug charges. As a 2009 Americas Watch report noted, while carrying out its drug-enforcement duties, the armed forces have "committed serious human rights violations, including enforced disappearances, killings, torture, rapes, and arbitrary detentions." The report noted that no member of the military had been convicted for such abuses by the military courts that try such offences.[184]

- Human rights violations are seen as key to maintaining the status quo. As journalist John Ross wrote in 2007, "The criminalization of social protest is filling the nation's jails and prisons with political prisoners."[185]
- Law enforcement is heavily reliant on the use of torture to obtain confessions that judges then use to convict even if the accused retracts the confession. Shifting to conventional investigative work to obtain convictions would require large expenditures and extensive training of police.

MEXICAN SOCIETY

> Income distribution in Mexico approaches the most unequal in the world: while the wealthiest quintile (20 percent) of the population owns roughly 60 percent of the country's resources, the poorest quintile claims a paltry 3 percent of national income.
>
> Emily Edmonds-Poli and David Shirk, 2009[186]

The Social Impact of "Free Trade"

Through the 1970s, the lot of the average Mexican continued to improve. The buying power of wages increased by 2.4 percent annually between 1971 and 1979. The government set guarantee prices for crops, subsidized agricultural credit, food for urban dwellers, and farm inputs such as fertilizer. Between 1970 and 1981, there was a 4.8 percent annual increase in job creation. The combination of rapid job growth, social programs, and government support for labor resulted in wealth becoming more evenly distributed during the 1970s. Those living in poverty declined from 75 percent of the population in 1960 to 48 percent in 1981.[187]

As a result of the 1982 debt crisis and the decision to adopt neoliberal economic policies, per capita government social spending declined by 32.7 percent between 1982 and 1988. To reduce imports, the peso was devalued and as a result inflation soared. Since wage increases lagged far behind inflation, the buying power of wages declined by more than 7 percent annually between 1983 and 1988. Rather than intervening to distribute the costs of the crisis, the government welcomed the decline in wages, since that lowered the cost of labor and made Mexico more attractive to foreign investors, whom the government expected to finance Mexican development.[188]

During the 1980s, 400,000 jobs disappeared, while at the same time the labor force increased by 8 million. Few jobs replaced those lost since both public and private investment declined. Those living on wages fared worse than those living on rents and property, thus worsening income distribution. Not only did income become less evenly distributed but there was also less to distribute as the per capita GDP declined by 10 percent between 1982 and 1987. The proportion of the Mexican population living in poverty increased from 68.5 percent in 1984 to 73.4 percent in 1989. By 1990, the average Mexican's calorie intake approached half that recommended by the World Health Organization.[189]

In the wake of the 1994–1995 economic crisis, which led to a sharp increase in poverty, President Zedillo launched a new anti-poverty program known as Progresa. This program, which targeted the poorest rural families, was designed to break the intergenerational transmission of poverty. Benefits for those in the program included cash to buy food and scholarships of up to $25 a month awarded to children if they stayed in school. In addition, pregnant and nursing women, and children from four to twenty-four months of age received nutritional supplements. By the end of the Zedillo administration, some 2.6 million families, 40 percent of all rural families, had been included in the program. However, due to its not providing benefits to the urban poor, Progresa served only a quarter of the households in poverty. While Zedillo's administration spent $93 billion to bail out the banking system, in 1999, it only allocated $540 million to Progresa, arguing that no more funds were available.[190]

Progresa was successful in that it resulted in longer school attendance, greater stature among children as a result of improved nutrition, and fewer illnesses in families covered by the program.

However, the program failed to substantially reduce poverty. At the end of the Zedillo administration, an estimated 54 million Mexicans lived in poverty.[191]

Based on its record under Zedillo, President Fox continued the Progresa program, although he changed its name to Oportunidades. He expanded its reach, targeting the urban as well as the rural poor. As a result of this expansion, by 2006 Oportunidades had a budget of $2.5 billion and covered 5 million households, slightly more than the entire population estimated to be living in poverty.[192]

The lack of jobs the poor can aspire to appears to doom the Oportunidades program to failure since it was founded on the notion that poverty results from insufficient education. However, given that Oportunidades does nothing to increase the number or quality of jobs being offered, as more beneficiaries of Oportunidades appear on the labor market employers will increase the educational requirement. Thus they might require waiters to have a secondary education not because it is necessary for the job but simply to reduce the number of job applications they must process. The number of jobs and income remain constant, despite workers having more years of education.[193]

The lack of progress in combating poverty indicates the importance of establishing coherence between poverty alleviation programs and economic reform. No poverty program can substitute for development policies that effectively incorporate the poor into growth-oriented sectors of the economy. Nor can poverty programs compensate for the loss of productive employment, the drastic reduction in wages, and lack of investment in productive and human assets. Similarly they cannot counteract the adverse impact of economic instability and the contraction of sectors from which the poor obtain their income.[194]

Trends

Several trends continued from mid–twentieth century through the end of the century. They include population increase, migration to the United States, and rural-to-urban migration.

This last trend, rural-to-urban migration, dates back to the nineteenth century. It has been driven by population increase, rural job loss, and higher wages and better employment opportunities in urban areas. Between 1970 and 2000, the rural population fell from 41.3 percent of Mexico's total population to 25.3 percent. During this period, due to increased population, the rural population actually rose from 19.9 million to 24.6 million.[195]

Another long-term trend is an increase in the percentage of the workforce in the service sector, which includes commerce. In 1910, only 14.2 per cent of the workforce was employed in the service sector. By 2008, this figure had increased to 56.4 percent.[196]

Another trend is the massive expansion of the informal sector. The informal sector includes a wide variety of employment, such as ambulatory vendors, domestics, and street-corner services (shoe-shiners, for example). The defining characteristic of the informal sector is that it produces goods (such as tamales for sale on the street) or services (such as washing windshields at traffic lights) that are legal. However, it is distinct from what is often called the formal sector in that some or all regulations governing trade unions, the minimum wage, social security, taxes, and health and safety regulations are not observed.[197]

Four factors have driven millions into the informal sector. As Mexicans come of age, their number far exceeds the number of jobs created in the formal sector. As wages declined in the 1980s, there was little monetary incentive to obtain a factory job rather than a job in the informal sector. High social security taxes deter the hiring of low-skilled labor with formal contracts. Instead, such workers obtain informal employment. Finally, the cost and time required to obtain the legally required licenses to operate a business have led many to bypass these requirements.[198]

During the boom years, 1950 to 1980, the informal sector shrank from 37.4 percent to 35 percent of the workforce as formal job creation exceeded new entrants to the labor force. Between

1980 and 1994 this trend was reversed as only 3.7 million formal-sector jobs were created in that time, but almost 1 million young people entered the labor force annually. Between 1989 and 2005, more than 70 percent of new job creation was in the informal sector.[199]

Since 1978, it has been government policy to encourage growth in mid-sized cities rather than the traditional big three—Mexico City, Monterrey, and Guadalajara. Government policy and the increasing dysfunctionality of these three cities led to the growth of mid-sized cities. Also, as factories moved north to be close to the U.S. market, industrial administration, which frequently remained in Mexico City, became spatially separated from industrial production. In 1970, 3.1 percent of Mexico's urban population lived in the one city in the 500,000 to 999,999 range, while by 2000, 17.1 percent of the population lived in the seventeen cities in that range. In 2000, there were sixty cities in the 100,000 to 999,999 population range. During the 1990s, they grew at 2.6 percent annually—faster than the three largest cities or the nation as a whole.[200]

As has occurred throughout Latin America, criminality in Mexico has been increasing. A 2007 poll found "delinquency and insecurity" was considered to be the greatest problem facing Mexico. As increasing numbers of young males from impoverished families have no prospect of improving their station in life, they engage in illegal and often violent acts to redistribute wealth and income. High crime rates have led to a proliferation of private security forces and gated communities, especially in the Federal District.[201]

The Social Impact of Neoliberal Development

> Mexico's rulers—under internal and external pressures—turned to globalization and neoliberalism, culminating in the promises of NAFTA and democratization. For Mexico's majority, the social consequences, to date, have been declining incomes, widespread insecurities, the end of land reform, and accelerating migration to labor, seasonally or permanently, in the United States.
>
> Leticia Reina, Elsa Servín & John Tutino, 2007[202]

The stagnation of Mexico's GDP per capita is key to understanding the impact of neo-liberalism. In 1980, per capita GDP was $3,424. After remaining below that level until the late 1990s, per capita GDP reached $3,537 in 2000. Between 1983 and 2004, per capita GDP increased at an annual rate of only 0.3 percent. The lack of significant variation in per capita GDP could lead to increased social welfare if income distribution improved. However, just opposite has occurred, exacerbating social problems.[203]

Between 1984 and 1992, the share of income received by the top 10 percent of income earners increased from 34.2 percent of income to 40.5 percent. Income concentration remained largely unchanged during the 1990s. Between 1994 and 2003, non-maquiladora manufacturing wages declined, while productivity was up 24.7 percent. The owners of many mom-and–pop stores lost income as they were displaced by large-scale retail establishments such as Wal-Mart. The declining income of the rural poor, forced to compete with low-cost agricultural imports, also contributed to income concentration.[204]

The rapid expansion of the export sector further concentrated wealth. Some 700 firms, representing only 2 percent of all export-oriented firms, generated 80 percent of exports. Technologically sophisticated plants producing goods for export required an increasingly skilled labor force. As a result, between 1984 and 1995, the buying power of skilled workers increased by 8 percent, while that of unskilled workers decreased by 22 percent. Between 1991 and 2001, exports increased by more than 300 percent, but formal employment in the export sector increased by less than 50 percent.[205]

Employers in manufacturing, and especially the export sector, benefited as the value of wages declined thanks to the high rates of inflation and because increases in productivity were not matched by increased compensation to workers whose productivity was rising. These factors contributed to the amount of wages in the economy falling from 35.7 percent of GDP in 1970 to 29.1 percent in 1996.[206]

By 2005, income distribution had only marginally improved, as the share of income going to the wealthiest 10 percent had declined to 36.5 percent. The next wealthiest 30 percent of the population received 36.8 percent of income, leaving the bottom 60 percent with only 26.7 percent. This maldistribution of wealth is reflected in the millions of young people joining the informal economy, resorting to crime, or emigrating. Economist Rosa Albina Garavito commented on how wealth came to be so poorly distributed:

> Since salaries increased more slowly than prices, wealth has been concentrated. Similarly national wealth was transferred to private hands by privatizing public enterprises. Financial speculation has also concentrated wealth. As a result, Mexico is one of the world's principal producers of personal fortunes, while at the same time it occupies some of the lowest positions in competitiveness, prosperity, and social welfare.[207]

As a result of these social and economic forces, whose impact far outweighed the government's efforts to reduce poverty, Mexico is one of the most unequal countries in the world. According to a United Nations study on equality, Mexico only ranked 103rd of 126 nations in terms of equality.[208]

The Elite

Roughly 3 percent of Mexico's population belongs to the elite. Its members include top government officials, owners of large firms, managers of foreign corporations operating in Mexico, and administrators of public-sector firms such as Pemex.[209]

The Mexican experience with globalization and neoliberal economics resulted in an especially sharp concentration of wealth since highly profitable corporations were transferred to the hands of a favored few. In 1994, *Forbes* magazine found that the number of Mexican billionaires (as measured in U.S. dollars) had reached twenty-four, up from only one in 1990—a 2,400 percent increase. In the same four-year period, 1990 to 1994, per capita GDP increased by only 4 percent. At the time, the magazine commented, "Of the 358 people identified as billionaires in the latest *Forbes* world survey, 24 were Mexican—a percentage out of all proportion to Mexico's place in the world economy."[210]

PAN presidential candidate Vicente Fox received substantial support from business interests. Not surprisingly, once Fox took office, the influence of the business elite increased, along with that of the Church, to the detriment of the middle class, labor, and the peasants. Political scientist Denise Dresser commented on this influence:

> Mexico has a dense, intricate web of connections and personal ties between the government and the business class. This ends up creating a government that doesn't defend the public interest, that isn't willing to go out and regulate in the name of the consumer. But it is rather willing to help its friends, its allies, and, in some case its business partners who thrive at the expense of the Mexican people.[211]

While the government institutes programs such as Oportunidades, many of its policies serve to concentrate wealth. It tolerates monopolies and duopolies, especially in telecommunications, which benefit a handful of owners. Its massive electric rate subsidy disproportionally benefits affluent owners of appliances and air conditioners. In 2002, the government spent five times as much on its electricity subsidy as it did on poverty eradication programs. Similarly, subsidies for gasoline and higher education mainly benefit the already affluent.[212]

Mexico never regained the share of the world's billionaires that it enjoyed in 1994. Between 1994 and 2008, Mexico's share of billionaires declined from 7 percent to 1 percent, not due to Mexico becoming more egalitarian but due to the rest of the world generating wealth more rapidly than Mexico. In 2008, of the world's 1,125 billionaires, ten were Mexican.[213]

The Middle Class

Mexico's middle class emerged as a result of: 1) urbanization, 2) education, and 3) government jobs. Due to these factors, by the 1970s, the middle class encompassed roughly 30 percent of Mexico's population. This figure declined by a quarter after 1980 due to the economic crisis.[214]

At one point, Mexico's middle class was dominated by professionals and small independent businessmen. Then, as the economy grew, an increasingly large percentage of the middle class was composed of salaried workers, especially in government. There is considerable variation in income and social status of those within the middle class. Since it is never clear just who should be included in the middle class, estimates of its size vary substantially.[215]

At one time Roman Catholicism was a major influence on the middle class. However, in the latter part of the twentieth century, universities, consumerism, mass media, and the state bureaucracy exercised an increasing influence. Values generally espoused by members of the middle class include individualism, private property rights, personal merit, family authority, order, and (until the end of the Cold War) anti-communism.[216]

The early 1980s economic bust and bank nationalization turned the middle class against the system. Its members were especially hard hit, since they were highly reliant on salaried income, which declined by 36 percent between 1981 and 1985. Fewer middle-class jobs were created, and many were eliminated, especially in government.[217]

The middle class joined the economic elite in blaming their plight on an inefficient and corrupt state. The sudden switch to viewing the state as an obstacle, not a solution, dovetailed nicely with the PAN position, so many members of the middle class began to actively support the PAN. As crime increased after 1982, the middle class shared the upper class's security concerns. By 1990, democracy had become the principal demand of the middle class.[218]

By the 1990s, the cumulative effects of the 1968 student movement, repeated economic crises, and the fraudulent 1988 presidential elections had cost the PRI middle-class support. As Dennis Gilbert noted in his study of the middle class, "By the late 1990s, middle-class Mexicans had little faith in the dual myths of the revolution and the Mexican economic miracle." Not surprisingly, in the 2000 election, PAN presidential candidate Vicente Fox received 58 percent of the middle class vote.[219]

After the 1994–1995 economic crisis, neoliberal economic policies favored the middle class as well as the elite. The number of families with monthly incomes in the $600 to $1,500 range rose from just over 5 million in 1992 to more than 9 million in 2004. As has been the case throughout Latin America, this newly emerging middle class is increasingly linked to the market, not the state. Gilbert noted that in 2000 the middle class was "bigger, better educated and more affluent than it was in the early 1980s."[220]

During the Fox administration (2000–2006), members of the middle class enjoyed increased access to consumer credit. This enabled them to purchase such middle class trappings as refrigerators and washing machines. Lower interest rates resulted in a housing boom as mortgage rates tumbled and twenty-five-year mortgages became available. Previously lenders offered only ten-year mortgages. In the first five years of the Fox administration, 2,355,000 housing loans were issued, more than twice the number issued under Zedillo.[221]

Together the elite and the middle class constitute roughly a third of Mexico's population. They, along with another 10 percent of the population, skilled workers who disproportionally work in export-oriented industries, have been the beneficiaries of the neoliberal policies adopted in the 1980s. These three groups—the elite, the middle class, and skilled labor—constitute just under half the population.[222]

Labor

> In small- and medium-sized industries producing textiles, shoes, and toys, union representatives blackmail and extort workers. In the big national unions, they protect inefficiency and low productivity and are cesspools of corruption.
>
> Sara Sefchovich, 2008[223]

Through the 1970s, labor remained a major part of the ruling PRI coalition, and government consulted union leadership concerning economic, labor, and electoral issues. Leaders of the CTM, the main labor federation, received lucrative government posts. Labor leaders supported the import-substitution development model since: 1) it advocated a strong government role in the economy—a role that was in tune with their nationalist ideology, 2) it created a large public sector that was union friendly, and 3) private industry was protected from foreign competition, allowing labor costs to be passed on to the consumer. Labor also supported government investment that created jobs, and the government's distribution of wealth in the form of education, health care, housing, and subsidized prices for basic goods.[224]

Through the 1970s, unions guaranteed labor stability—a key element for economic development. The union structure mirrored the political structure in that most unionized workers were in PRI-controlled labor federations. However, there were a few feisty, independent unions, just as there were small independent political parties. In 1978, 27 percent of the workforce of 18.8 million were unionized. These 5 million unionized workers were, by and large, protected by labor laws and enjoyed legally mandated health care, disability, and retirement benefits. Policy makers viewed wage increases as necessary for maintaining labor peace and as a key ingredient to enlarging the market for domestically produced goods. Between 1970 and 1981, the number of paid workers increased from 13 million to 21.5 million, as both population and the economy grew, and as the number of working women increased.[225]

During the early 1980s, policymakers began to favor sharply decreased wages in an effort to make Mexico more attractive to foreign investors and to make the country more competitive in international markets. Inflation, which averaged 93 percent annually between 1983 and 1987, presented the government with the perfect opportunity to lower the value of wages. The government only had to ensure that the rate of wage increase fell behind the rate of inflation. The desired reduction in wages occurred, as workers' buying power declined by 61 percent between 1983 and 1988.[226]

During the 1980s the PRI maintained a delicate balancing act. It promoted policies that lowered wages and at the same time continued to reward the CTM leadership, thus maintaining the federation's support for government policies. Geriatric CTM leaders—increasingly isolated from their base, which they could no longer reward with increased wages—cast their lot with the PRI. They backed government policies that lowered wages and resulted in massive layoffs, supported PRI candidates at the time of presidential elections, and, in the early 1990s, supported the signing of the NAFTA.[227]

There are several explanations for the government's ability to impose such sharp wage reductions on a workforce with a long tradition of union struggle:

- Leaders of organized labor supported government policy. Based on long experience, they realized that their tenure in office was based on loyalty to the political elite, not to serving their membership.[228]

- During the 1980s and 1990s, the Labor Ministry facilitated defections by workers from the CTM to rival PRI-affiliated confederations when the CTM indicated a reluctance to cooperate with government policy.[229]
- Labor unions were hurt by the shift of industry away from central Mexico, with a strong union tradition, to northern Mexico, where unions were traditionally weak or non-existent.[230]
- The government, official unions, and management would resort to extralegal means to enforce acceptance of lowered wages. In 1992, human rights activists Mariclaire Acosta and Rocío Culebro observed, "Serious violations of individual, social, economic, and political rights of workers occur with impunity in Mexico today."[231]
- One of the rights denied was the right to strike. In 1990, the human rights journal *Christus* commented: "The right to strike which previously was exercised with relative frequency, has been practically denied to unions. Declaring a strike illegal is the typical response of the labor boards and tribunals." Between 1983 and 1988, federal authorities accepted as legal only 1.8 percent of workers' petitions declaring their intention to strike.[232]
- The climate for labor organizing was not propitious. Between 1983 and 1987, only 234,000 jobs were created, while 900,000 entered the labor force annually.[233]
- As foreign imports began to compete with locally produced goods, management could convincingly argue that wages had to decline to protect jobs.
- Plant managers not only threatened to move the plant to lower-wage nations but sometimes they actually did just that. The Sunbeam Corporation plant in Matamoros, just across from Texas, provides a perfect example. In 2000, the company moved production of electrical appliances from its Cleveland, Ohio plant where workers made more than $21 an hour, to Matamoros, where they made $2.36 an hour. Three years later, the company moved production to China where workers received 47 cents an hour.[234]

Much of the new job creation during the 1980s occurred in northern Mexico, where workers would accept wages considerably below those prevalent in central Mexico. Once established, these lower wages served as a benchmark, and wages in central Mexico were reduced, via inflation, to match the northern benchmark. Workers at a new General Motors plant in the border state of Coahuila found that a corrupt union boss had created a bogus union and signed a collective contract before a single worker had been hired.[235]

For having acquiesced to massive wage reduction, labor leaders lost the support they had formerly enjoyed. In 1988, this became glaringly apparent as all labor leaders who ran as PRI candidates for the Chamber of Deputies were defeated. Loss of support for the PRI was especially notable among oil workers, who feared the PRI might privatize the industry. As a result, in 1988, Cárdenas scored electoral victories in oil towns such as Poza Rica and Minatitlán.[236]

Under Salinas, the influence of organized labor waned as many companies restructured or were privatized. Labor's presence in the PRI declined, as did the role of unions in such formal institutions as the Minimum Wage Commission. By 1994, the number of manufacturing workers, who were traditionally highly unionized, was 25 percent below the 1980 level. Finally, as political scientist Kevin Middlebrook observed, "Organized labor could not prevent the Salinas administration from interpreting and applying existing law in such a way as to provide employers in practice with the flexibility to redefine workplace industrial relations . . ."[237]

During the Zedillo administration (1994–2000), May Day celebrations, which had long served as a ritual to reaffirm the bonds between labor and the ruling party, became symbols of the rupture of that relationship. Beginning in 1995, the formal May Day marches were repeatedly canceled, since official labor leaders were afraid they would become uncontrollable anti-government protests. In 1995, tens of thousands marched in independent May Day parades. Many wore ski-masks to signal their support for Chiapas rebels, who characteristically wore ski-masks to hide their identity.

On May Day 1997, between 60,000 and 250,000 joined the unofficial parades, which called for wage increases, an end to undemocratic control of labor, and a change in government economic policies.[238]

At the turn of the century, the outlook for labor was discouraging. Union membership had declined to 9.8 percent of the labor force. In 1999, labor activist Berta Luján found that the greatest obstacles to union freedom were: 1) the proliferation of contracts signed between management and union leaders, without the knowledge or consent of the workers affected, 2) the declaration that strikes were illegal, 3) the government taking over firms to break strikes, 3) the lack of a secret ballot in union certification elections, and 4) the widespread use of subcontractors and temporary workers. Harley Shaiken, director of the Center for Latin American studies at the University of California in Berkley, observed:

> The Mexican government has created an investment climate which depends on a vast number of low wage earners. This climate gets all the government's attention, while the consumer climate—the ability of people to buy what they produce—is sacrificed.[239]

The death in 1997 of Fidel Velázquez, who had served continuously as the secretary general of the CTM since 1950, highlighted the woeful state of organized labor. He had backed the fifteen Mexican presidents he had dealt with as a labor leader. In 1959 he had supported the army as it suppressed rail workers, and he had backed the suppression of the 1968 student movement. Later he had supported Mexico's entry into NAFTA and the suppression of wages that had accompanied it. Given this unwavering support and the contacts he had built up over decades, Velázquez could deliver more than any other labor leader. He brokered wage hikes and other concessions from PRI governments, especially at election time.[240]

In 1989, Kevin Middlebrook wrote, "Velázquez symbolizes the social pact forged between organized labor and the post-revolutionary Mexican state in the 1930s and 1940s." That same year, political scientist Lorenzo Meyer commented, "Having such an old man at the front of the labor sector objectively helped to dismantle it."[241]

President Zedillo appointed a relatively spry seventy-eight-year old, Leonardo Rodríguez Alcaine, to replace Velázquez. Rodríguez Alcaine had risen to prominence when he took control of the electrical workers union in the 1970s and suppressed attempts to democratize the union. Soon after his appointment, Rodríguez Alcaine promised to maintain the "historical alliance" between the CTM and the PRI.[242]

After the passage of NAFTA, employers declared that the existing Federal Labor Law made them non-competitive and lobbied to have it reformed. Changes they sought included the right to hire workers on a temporary and part-time basis, pay by the hour (not day), reduce the costs of dismissing workers, introduce probationary periods in employment, and promote employees according to performance rather than by seniority. Even though the Federal Labor Law remained unchanged, employers achieved almost everything they sought via contract revisions. Such changes were facilitated by the signing of protection contracts behind workers' backs. By one estimate, in 2000 about 90 percent of all union contracts were protection contracts.[243]

As PRI control over society was weakening and as traditional labor leaders delivered less to the union members, there was an upsurge in independent labor groups. The most prominent of these was the National Workers Union (UNT), which was founded in 1997. The UNT brought together the National Union of Social Security Workers, the Union of National Autonomous University Workers, and the Mexican Telephone Workers Union, as well as the Authentic Labor Front (FAT), a small independent labor organizing group dating back to the 1960s. The UNT opposed reform of labor law called for by business and instead called for respecting the right to strike and for the open registry of unions and contacts. While facing many of the obstacles other independent unions faced, the UNT did have some successes, such as the recognition of an independent union at the Siemens auto parts plant in Puebla. By 2000, the UNT claimed 1.5 million members.[244]

Rather than bringing sweeping change to the traditional union structure, Fox left the same labor leaders in place. Mexico's often long-entrenched labor leaders received backing from Fox due to his fear that radicals would dominate labor if there was a leadership change and due to the feeling that incumbents could be used to ensure the passage of legislation waiving rights that had long been guaranteed to labor, at least on paper. In 2005, CTM head Leonardo Rodríguez Alcaine died in office at age sighty-six, once again indicating the sclerosis of official Mexican labor.[245]

The unions that retained strength and the ability to defend their membership's interests past the end of PRI rule were unions in the public sector, which by definition could not relocate, the mine workers union, which similarly did not face companies relocating, and the rare private-sector union, such as the Volkswagen workers union, which relied on its being prohibitively costly for VW to relocate its sprawling Puebla facility.

At the end of the Fox administration, neither labor nor business was satisfied with the status quo. Labor resented lost status in the ruling coalition, reduced wages, and the inability to democratically select union leaders. At the same time, business found that PRI-era labor legislation denied it the flexibility in employer-employee relations it sought. Late in the Fox administration, an IMF study found that Mexico's labor market was the least flexible in the region.[246]

Rural Mexico

> Perhaps peasant producers are not as efficient as rural entrepreneurs when measured by the standards of private business, but without a doubt they are infinitely more efficient if we consider social, cultural, and environmental impacts, categories where agribusiness clearly flunks the test of sustainability.
>
> Armando Bartra, 2004[247]

Through the 1970s, rural poverty was at least mitigated by government intervention in the rural economy. The government-owned National Bank of Rural Credit (Banrural) supplied credit at subsidized prices. Specialized government agencies such as INMECAFE and TABAMEX purchased coffee and tobacco at guaranteed prices. There were also subsidies for agricultural inputs such as electricity, fuel, and fertilizer. The government grain agency, CONASUPO, became the third largest enterprise in Mexico. It bought and sold twelve different grains, operated a retail chain with more than 20,000 outlets, and maintained a network of grain silos and food-processing plants. Such efforts attempted to shield producers from the vagaries of the market and provide inexpensive food to the poor.[248]

While such government support did transfer wealth to small producers, it also created problems. Caciques and government bureaucrats would often gain control of credit allocation and use this control to their personal advantage. Credit from the Banrural came with so many restrictions concerning the type of crop and production techniques that producers were left with little decision-making power. The government role in peasants' lives became so pervasive that cynics declared that peasants fought for "*tierra y libertad*" ("land and liberty") but instead received "*tierra y el estado*" ("land and the state").[249]

The CNC entered the 1970s as a tightly controlled organization that transmitted government wishes to its members, thus lowering its legitimacy. Since the raison d'être of the CNC was to obtain land for the landless, as land distribution wound down, it had to compete for influence and loyalty with other government agencies, landowners' associations, and independent peasant groups. CNC leaders often collaborated with government and large landowners, even when such collaboration ran counter to the interests of CNC members.[250]

Several different government programs channeled resources to rural Mexico. Under López Portillo (1976–1982), agricultural spending constituted 5.5 percent of the federal budget, compared to only 2.5 percent under Díaz Ordaz (1964–1970). The best known program was the Mexican Food System (SAM), which benefited small producers with higher prices, subsidized inputs, crop insurance, and technical assistance. In 1981, Mexico produced a record 28.6 million tons of grain, and SAM was declared a success. Its being the most expensive grain in the world seemed of little importance. The high cost of grain production did become a concern after oil prices plunged at the end of López Portillo's term. When President De la Madrid took office in 1982, SAM was quietly forgotten.[251]

Given the emphasis on servicing the national debt, under President de la Madrid (1982–1988) there were sharp decreases in government intervention in the agricultural sector. This left small producers without crop insurance, credit, fertilizer subsidies, or marketing facilities. The government dismantled the guarantee prices of twelve food crops. Between 1981 and 1988, government investment in rural development declined from 2.4 percent of GDP to 0.2 percent.[252]

During the 1980s, decreased government support for rural Mexico led to widespread protest movements. Coercion against those opposing the PRI's rural dominance increased as the incentives the party could offer declined. Challenges to the prevailing distribution of rural wealth were also repressed. More than 800 peasants, many of whom were members of organizations not affiliated with the PRI, were killed in land-related disputes between 1981 and 1987. Many others were imprisoned for political activity in support of landless groups.[253]

Institutional changes continued to impact rural Mexico through the 1990s. Salinas amended Article 27 of the constitution to end the land reform. Then, in 1994 the NAFTA allowed (after a grace period in some cases) the tariff-free importation of food from the United States. In 1998, the government dissolved CONASUPO, the system of state-run stores that had sold basic foods, such as tortillas and milk, at subsidized low prices. In 1999, the government ended its guarantee prices on corn and beans. This reflected its policy of letting Mexican food prices adjust to international levels, even if it forced some domestic producers out of business.[254]

Public investment in rural development declined 74.2 percent between 1991–1993 and 2000–2002. The remaining federal support was directed to farms, such as those producing fresh fruit and vegetables, that were competitive in the export market. Smaller producers on rain-fed land were considered as a social welfare concern rather than as an economic policy matter.[255]

Neoliberal policies have devastated small rural holdings by eliminating subsidies and pushing farmers, sink or swim, into global commodity markets dominated by First World agribusiness. Few producers can break into the export market—in addition to physical endowments, such as good land and water, it requires processing, storage, and transport facilities as well as sophisticated managerial skills. During the 1990s, the rapidly increasing dominance of retail food distribution by supermarkets such as Wal-Mart further marginalized small producers. Small farmers are generally unable to meet large retailers' demands for uniform quality, reliable delivery, and large quantities.[256]

Population increase, a multiplicity of very small farms, soil degradation, declining government support, and competition from imports has left rural Mexico mired in endemic poverty. Roughly a quarter of Mexico's population live in rural areas, but only contribute 5 percent of GDP. Only 38 percent of rural households own any land at all, and of those with land, more than two-thirds have less than five acres. Agricultural income is poorly distributed, as the 77 percent of farms relying on rainfall receive only 44 percent of agricultural income. Some 4 million rural residents are landless wage laborers, who usually work as migrants. In 2004, 56.9 percent of the rural population was living in poverty.[257]

NAFTA and neoliberal policies are frequently blamed for impoverishing Mexico's rural population. That charge is unjust in that there was endemic rural poverty before neoliberal policies were adopted in the 1980s. What neoliberal policies failed to do was to provide rural residents either with sufficient income or with urban jobs to which they could move and thus escape poverty. In 2003, as economist Kirsten Appendini commented:

> After more than a decade of reform . . . agricultural performance has not realized the expectations set by the neoliberal agenda of the administrations of Carlos Salinas de Gortari or Ernesto Zedillo; neither have peasants and the rural population in general seen any improvement in their livelihoods.[258]

Given rising population, declining farm income, and physical limitations (lack of access to water and good land), rural people increasingly turned to non-agricultural sources of income. As early as 1975 anthropologist Ralph Beals found that for rural Oaxacans "farming is neither their primary occupation nor is it the main source of income . . . Their ways of making a living hence are numerous and varied." During the 1990s, as the government reduced its role in the agricultural economy and population continued to increase, reliance on sales of one's crops continued to decline, and survival was based increasingly on consuming one's own crop production, day labor, government subsidies, and remittances from relatives in the United States.[259]

One response to rural problems is out-migration. Such moves reflect the lack of job creation, the persistent poverty, and the fact that rural people are becoming increasingly aware that there are better alternatives. As anthropologist Pierre Beaucage noted, "After twenty-five years of intense exposure to modernity, nobody wants to return to the old days, where you worked from dawn to dusk and were happy to have enough corn to eat and a few pesos to spend at the fiesta."[260]

Massive out-migration has had varied effects. In some cases, remittances sent by migrants have revitalized communities, providing sustenance for family members and permitting new construction, the opening of businesses, continued education, and the maintenance of traditional village festivals. However, increasingly emigration has simply hollowed out communities. Ventura Vega, of Huacao, Michoacán commented: "Just look in all the houses and you see that there's no one. Once we had a group of musicians that performed in the plaza. Even they have gone. And now we are left with no music." All of Vega's eleven children and their families moved to California.[261]

The majority of those working in the United States continue to maintain ties to their community, either personally or through close relatives. However the ejido is no longer seen as the road to the future. Half the *ejidatarios* are over age fifty. Newly wed couples migrate out, and more children are being born or raised in the United States and do not speak Spanish well. Visits back to the sending community inevitably became less frequent and shorter.[262]

The Indigenous Population

> Most of the indigenous population lives in municipalities in poor states which have low indices of social and human development. In these regions, families frequently rely on subsistence agriculture amid unforgiving surroundings, where the land does not feed the family, forcing people increasingly to emigrate, including to foreign counties, to meet their necessities.
>
> Rodolfo Stavenhagen, 2003[263]

Indigenous people in Mexico speak sixty-two different languages, which places the country second in linguistic diversity behind India, with its sixty-five languages. In 1970, 3.11 million Mexicans over age four spoke one of these indigenous languages. By 2000, that number had reached 6.04 million, a 94 percent increase. This was very close to Mexico's total population increase of 102 percent during these same years and far greater than the 24 percent increase in the rural population. At more than 10 million, Mexico's indigenous population is the largest in Latin America.[264]

Mexico's Indian population is in the population growth phase of the demographic transition with its high birth rate and sharply declining death rate. The completed fertility rate for indigenous women is 7.5 children, well above the national rate. The Indian population would have grown even more rapidly if out-migration and assimilation to outside society had not reduced its size.[265]

The indigenous population has migrated from their communities more rapidly, in percentage terms, than the rural population as a whole due to a combination of environmental degradation (especially soil loss), poverty, and population increase. More than 1 million of these migrants have settled in Mexico City, where they are among the poorest residents. Seasonal migrants harvest sugar cane in Morelos and raise commercial crops in northern Mexico. A politically active community of Mixtec agricultural workers has formed in the San Quintín Valley of Baja California. Still other indigenous workers continue on to the United States, where they receive lower pay and less desirable jobs than mestizos. In California, radio programs in Mixtec and Triqui address the sizable population of Mexican migrants speaking those languages.[266]

Extensive work experience outside one's community, more years of schooling, and television have increased knowledge of Spanish and urban ways. The indigenous population has converted to non-Catholic Christian faiths more rapidly, in percentage terms, than the Mexican population as a whole.[267]

Between 1970 and 1976, to further its *indigenista* goals, the National Indigenous Institute (INI) expanded its network of coordination centers in Indian areas from twelve to sixty-four. The INI budget increased by more than 700 percent during this period. Another twenty-one centers were opened during the López Portillo (1976–1982) administration. As part of this effort, schools and clinics were built and roads were extended into Indian areas.[268]

During the 1970s and 1980s, indigenous leaders began to demand a much greater role in the design and implementation of policy affecting Indians. The number of Indian protests rose dramatically in the 1970s and was still higher during the 1980s. Beginning in the 1980s, Indian demands were two-pronged. Some concerned solutions to concrete problems such as the freeing of political prisoners, the removal of abusive municipal authorities, and an end of repression by caciques, landowners, and government officials. A second set of demands concerned modifying the institutional relations between the nation and the Indian population.[269]

Indigenous organizing efforts were bolstered by NGOs, progressive elements of the Catholic Church, and critical anthropologists who denounced the injustices Indians suffered and the ethnocidal consequences of the government's assimilationist policy. During the 1980s, Indians not only formed their own groups but integrated them into such national organizations as the National Union of Autonomous Regional Peasant Organizations (UNORCA), where they gained valuable experience organizing at the regional and national level.[270]

Factors leading to this increased Indian politicization include the impact of neoliberal economic policies on rural areas, increased population, Guatemalan indigenous activist Rigoberta Menchú's winning of the Nobel Peace Prize, and indigenous activism in other Latin American nations such as Nicaragua. Finally, the commemoration of the five-hundredth anniversary of Columbus's arrival in the New World brought to the forefront questions such as the role of Europeans in New World and the current status of the Indian.[271]

During the 1980s and early 1990s, old assumptions concerning assimilation vanished as the government decided it was better to accept ethnic differences than to suppress them. While the nature of government discourse shifted, Indians suffered the same hardship as other rural people when the government, in its effort to service its foreign debt, reduced programs in rural areas. Indians also suffered because there was a 51 percent reduction in spending by the INI.[272]

The Salinas administration (1988–1994) responded to increased indigenous activism by once again increasing the INI budget. Through the Solidarity program, his administration also distributed funds to a wide variety of projects run by and benefiting indigenous people. Finally, during his administration Article 4 of the Mexican constitution was amended to include the following:

> The Mexican nation has a multicultural composition originally based on its indigenous peoples. The law will protect and promote the development of their languages, cultures, uses, customs, resources, and forms of social organization and will guarantee them effective access to the jurisdiction of the state.

This amendment to Article 4 represented an explicit reversal of the post-revolutionary goal of creating a culturally homogenous nation.[273]

The 1994 rebellion in Chiapas made it clear to the world that past policy had failed to meet the material needs of indigenous people or to guarantee them the rule of law. The rebellion led to unprecedented Indian activism and protests throughout Mexico. Finally, even though Indians had been discussing autonomy among themselves, the rebellion brought that notion to the forefront of discussion concerning Indian rights.[274]

The key elements to autonomy are: 1) a defined territorial base for each indigenous group, 2) Indians exercising judicial and administrative power within the territorial base, 3) national unity (autonomy does not imply separation from Mexico), 4) equal treatment for all individuals, 5) equality of social groups within the autonomous unit (some groups such as the Zapotecs are perceived to have had a privileged position over other indigenous groups, just as the Sunni received preferential treatment in twentieth-century Iraq), 6) Indians deciding which groups have a population mass sufficient to warrant the creation of an autonomous region, and 7) solidarity and fraternity among various ethnic groups in the nation (meaning the wealthy part of the nation cannot simply ignore the poor but has a positive duty to assist their development). Proponents of autonomy in Mexico seek structures analogous to those created for the Inuit in Greenland and northern Canada. Most advocates of Indian autonomy foresee the creation of a fourth layer of government, between the state and the municipality, which would administer Indian autonomous regions. Such regions under one autonomous administration would roughly parallel the regional pre-Conquest Aztec administrative entity known as the *altepetl*.[275]

Even though the notion of autonomy was embraced by almost all indigenous groups, many anthropologists, and most political progressives, it generated widespread opposition. Many consider drawing workable boundary lines around indigenous areas as an insurmountable problem. There are, for example, major concentrations of Nahua, the most numerous indigenous group, in eight different states. An acceptance of autonomy can be seen as coming at the expense of respecting individual rights. Others feel that autonomy is a step to succession or that it undermines the nation state, already assailed by globalization. Historian Héctor Aguilar Camín noted, "The Indians who have done the best are the ones with the most, not the least, contact with the rest of society." He also noted that the million Indians living in Mexico City had more access to electricity, running water, and hospitals than Indians in isolated areas.[276]

One of the reasons that autonomy has received widespread support is that past experience indicates that policy made for Indians rather than by Indians has yielded such unsatisfactory results. Indigenous people constitute roughly 10 percent of the population, but 35 percent of those in extreme poverty. A third of those who speak Indian languages are illiterate, more than three times the national average. Finally, Indians have been marginalized politically. At the close of the twentieth century, there were only fourteen indigenous members of the Chamber of Deputies, a fifth of what there would have been if Indians had been represented in proportion to their population.[277]

For a fleeting moment, the twenty-first century seemed to offer the promise of autonomy for indigenous peoples and a peaceful settlement to the stand off in Chiapas, where Zapatista rebels had remained since the 1994 uprising. On the day he took office, December 1, 2000, President Fox ordered a troop withdrawal from more than fifty positions the military held around the rebel-controlled area. On December 5, he sent to Congress the agreements concerning autonomy for Indian areas that had been negotiated with the rebels during the Zedillo administration.[278]

In response to Fox's overtures, the Zapatista rebels made a dramatic 3,000-mile march to Mexico City in 2001 to present their case to the Mexican nation. The march, nicknamed the Zapatour, traveled through twelve states and arrived in Mexico City where more than 100,000 provided a tumultuous welcome. Zapatista Comandante Ester, a small, frail indigenous woman, presented the Zapatistas' case to Congress in broken Spanish, in full view of the national media.[279]

Once the Indians went home and the issue was no longer on the front pages, momentum on the proposed Indian law was lost. Even though Fox presented the proposed autonomy law to Congress, as had been agreed in negotiations with rebels during the Zedillo administration, members of Fox's own party felt the agreement ceded too much federal power and so watered it down. When finally passed, the reform lacked several key provisions that Indians had hoped for. Autonomy for indigenous people was defined at the municipal level, not the regional level. Soil, subsoil, and water rights remained vested in private interests, upon which autonomous indigenous communities would have little leverage. Individual states, whose commitment to indigenous autonomy was often questionable, were charged with interpreting and implementing much of the legislation. The revised legislation, which was passed by Congress and incorporated into the constitution, did recognize Indian communities had the right to form autonomous municipal governments.[280]

The Fox administration disbanded the INI, which had facilitated government efforts on behalf of the Indian. It was replaced with the National Commission for the Development of Indigenous People (CDI), headed by a successful Otomí businesswomen Xóchitl Gálvez. Rather than implementing programs, as the INI had, the CDI focused on coordinating programs administered by health, education, and other government departments. Not only was the Commission headed by an indigenous woman but indigenous representatives were given a greater role in program design. There was a change in emphasis, with more effort directed toward cultural development and elevating the status of women within the indigenous community.[281]

The creation of the CDI inevitably was questioned by those who felt that its programs did not differ substantially from those of its predecessor, since it involved the government providing top-down assistance to Indian communities. They also cited the financial limitations of the CDI, even after its budget rose to 19.6 billion pesos in 2004. That resulted in spending roughly $200 per Indian per year, which is neither enough to pull individuals out of extreme poverty nor to offset the negative impact of neoliberal policies on farming communities. Not surprisingly, in late 2005, the former Bishop of Chiapas Samuel Ruiz declared that the situation of the Indian had not changed since the uprising in 1994.[282]

The 1994 Chiapas uprising failed to pave the way for the type of autonomy many Indians and their supporters sought. However, it did pave the way for changing non-Indians' outlook on Indians as political actors. During the five centuries following the Spanish Conquest, non-Indians formulated detailed plans on how to save Indians from heathenism, poverty, malnutrition, and exploitation. However, it was only as the twentieth century wound down that Mexican society accepted Indians as intellectual actors who could, on their own initiative, address these problems.[283]

Women

> It is impossible to speak of Mexican women as a homogenous entity, even though all women in the country bear the weight of different forms of machismo, from the most blatant to the most subtle. Regional heterogeneity, economic differences, rural or urban residence, age, and ethnic identity shape the various ways in which women experience being women, have access to education and paid employment, and engage in politics.
>
> Marta Lamas, 2003[284]

If in the first half of the twentieth century it was the mechanical tortilla mill that changed women's lives, in the second half it was increased access to education. Parents became increasingly willing to make sacrifices for their daughters' education since, with expanded employment opportunities for women, education increased their daughters' economic security in life and their productive capacity in both rural and urban settings.[285]

During the last thirty years of the twentieth century, the average educational level for women increased from 3.2 years to 7.3 years. For the entire age range between six and nineteen years, a higher percentage of females were enrolled as students than males. Women increasingly entered formerly male-dominated fields. For example, they constituted more than 50 percent of medical school enrollment. Education not only increased women's employment opportunities but was the factor most closely correlated with lower infant mortality and lower fecundity.[286]

The three main areas of female employment are services, with 5.5 million workers, commerce with 3.2 million, and industry with 2.6 million. Women now constitute some 40 percent of the 5.4 million professionals working in Mexico. Some 63 percent of teachers are women, as are 54.7 percent of sales workers. The majority of those employed in assembly plants known as maquiladoras are women. They are preferred there since they are willing to work for lower wages than men and are perceived to be less likely to join a union, more manually dexterous, and better able to tolerate the monotony of repetitive assembly work. Women with limited education seek maquiladora employment since such work is better paid than alternatives commonly available to them in farm labor, domestic service, and market vending. An increasing number of jobs opened for women in agriculture since emigration depleted the male labor force and the export of fruit, vegetables, and flowers increased employment opportunities. Such agricultural employment, though, is hardly liberating, since women occupy dead-end positions, receive low wages, and work long hours in poor conditions.[287]

A majority of those working in the informal sector are women. The informal sector offers women a flexible work schedule, low entry cost, and the opportunity to fulfill household obligations while earning an income. Women in the informal sector make clothing, prepare foods, and manage one-person businesses with limited capital. A substantial number of women also work as domestics. Many of the job opportunities of more affluent women are made possible by the availability of inexpensive domestic labor to maintain their households. Writer Rosario Castellanos observed that cheap domestic labor had dampened radical feminism in Mexico. She declared, "When maids . . . disappear, radical feminists will appear."[288]

Paralleling women's increased entry into the formal labor force, women have assumed an increased role in the formal political process, traditionally the domain of a small male elite. The number of women serving in the Chamber of Deputies reflects this. In 1952, its first woman member constituted 0.6 percent of that body. By the 2003–2006 session, women comprised 23 percent of the Chamber. The 2006 election reversed the upward trend in women's representation, as the number of deputies fell from 115 to 113 and the number of senators from twenty-four to twenty-two. In other political arenas, women's progress has not been as great. In early 2007, only one woman, Amalia García in Zacatecas, served as governor. Of the 2,435 municipalities in Mexico, only eighty-six had a woman mayor.[289]

Despite these slow gains, as political scientist Victoria Rodríguez noted, "For the majority of Mexican political women, the playing field is far from level, and there is still considerable negative societal and cultural baggage attached to being a women in politics and to promoting women's causes." Rodríguez also noted that the question was still open as to whether women would change the system or attempt to fit into the old one. In some cases, the presence of women has led to qualitative change. For example, women in Congress pushed through legislation increasing the penalties for sex crimes. In any case, the primary alliance of women voters is not defined by gender. Women voters do not tend to favor women candidates. In 1997, 52 percent of registered voters were women, but only 17 percent of the members of the Chamber of Deputies were.[290]

The single greatest obstacle to legalization of abortion has been the adamant opposition of the Catholic Church. Joining the Church is a well organized group opposing abortion known as

Pro-Vida (Pro-Life), best known for ferreting out and denouncing clandestine abortion clinics. Mexican politicians by and large resist supporting a liberalization of abortion legislation since they do not want to be stigmatized by the Catholic Church.[291]

The first major shift in abortion policy came in 2007, when the PRD-dominated Legislative Assembly of the Federal District voted to legalize abortion during the first three months of pregnancy, a measure that affected only the Federal District. Pope Benedict XVI publicly condemned the bill, as did Felipe Aguirre Franco, archbishop of Acapulco, who declared lawmakers who voted for the bill would be automatically excommunicated. Demonstrators marched in the streets to express their views, pro and con. A marcher opposed to legalization carried a placard with an image of the Virgin of Guadalupe and the slogan: "You killed one of my children! Are you going to kill more?" A supporter countered with a sign declaring, "Keep your rosaries off my ovaries."[292]

Rather than signaling a trend toward legalizing abortion, the Federal District legislation created a backlash. Twelve states passed constitutional amendments declaring that the fertilized human egg is a person and therefore is protected by the constitution. Abortion remained illegal in other Mexican states.[293]

Despite the illegality of abortion up until 2007, between 500,000 and 1 million abortions occurred annually. Roughly 1,500 women died each year from illegal abortions, making abortion the third most common cause of maternal mortality. Providing illegal abortions generated an estimated $100 million a year in revenue. As with so many other aspects of Mexican life, it is poor women who suffer most from the lack of legal abortions. Affluent women are able travel to the United States or find a physician to perform an abortion, while the less affluent face much more risky options when they seek a back-street abortion.[294]

Population

> Here is the dilemma, either the developed Mexico will absorb and integrate the other, or the underdeveloped Mexico, by sheer dead weight of demographic increase, will end up strangling the developed Mexico.
>
> Octavio Paz, 1972[295]

On the campaign trail in 1970, Luis Echeverría boasted of his opposition to population control and presented himself as the proud father of eight. In his inaugural address, he declared, "On various occasions I have stated that population growth is not a danger, but a challenge which tests our creative potential."[296]

A number of factors led Echeverría to make a sharp reversal on population policy. The 1970 census data made it clear that the "Mexican economic miracle," which was running out of steam, could not provide for the rapidly increasing population. This impression was reinforced by the 1971 economic downturn, which resulted in the rate of population increase exceeding the rate of economic growth. Academics produced studies indicating that rapid population growth was putting strong pressure on available resources, such as housing, education, water, and employment, and that it was impossible for any economic system to meet the demands generated by such rapid population growth.[297]

Echeverría's changed views on population growth soon found their way into legislation. The 1973 General Law of Population empowered the federal government "to carry out a program of family planning through the educational and health services of the public sector . . . with the object of regulating rationally and stabilizing the growth of the population." In 1974, the Mexican constitution was amended to state, "Men and women are equal before the law . . . All people have the right to decide in a free, responsible, and informed manner on the number and spacing of their children."[298]

Table 24.1 *Mexican population, 1970–2008*

Year	Total population	Annual percentage increase since previous census
1970	48,225,238	3.0
1980	66,846,833	2.9
1990	81,249,645	2.3
2000	97,014,867	1.8
2008	106,682,518	1.2

Source: CONAPO (2001: 166), Cortés et al. (2005: 227), and Aguayo (2008: 34, Table 1)

Subsequent presidents have adhered to Echeverría's policy of promoting slower population growth. Carlos Salinas, on the campaign trail in 1988, declared:

> The dramatic rise of our population—600 percent in three generations—has been the foremost and unavoidable cause of pressure on services, employment, food, housing, and the use of information. To a large extent, population dynamics have held back the county's social progress and diluted its achievements.[299]

The decades since Echeverría's policy shift have seen a dramatic decline in the rate of population increase. However, even though the rate of population increase declined, between 1970 and 2000 the population increase exceeded the population increase that occurred between the arrival of the first human in Mexico and 1970. Furthermore, the annual number of births only started to decline in 1995.[300]

In 1970, Mexican women averaged 5.7 children, while by 2007 that figure had declined to 2.2. This fertility decline parallels a worldwide decline in fertility. Other Catholic nations, despite the Church's opposition to birth control, also follow this trend. One of these Catholic nations, Brazil, had a fertility decline of more than 50 percent between 1975 and 2000 even though the government did not undertake a program to reduce population growth. All one can say with certainty is that the decline reflects a dramatic change in desired family size.[301]

Some of the causes suggested for Mexico's decline in fertility include:

- an increased awareness of the economic advantages of small family size;[302]
- increased access to and acceptance of contraceptives;[303]
- the cost of raising children, which has skyrocketed since providing them with at least an elementary education is now accepted as a family responsibility;[304]
- the mechanization and proletarianization of agriculture, which has reduced the economic advantages of having children;[305]
- the fact that as women increasingly enter the labor force and obtain better jobs, remaining at home to raise children has become an increasingly costly option. In 1996, working women had an average of 2.0 children, while non-working mothers averaged 3.4.[306]

Emigration to the United States has lowered the rate of population growth. Between 1970 and 2000, Mexico's estimated population loss to its northern neighbor was between 5.97 million and 7.25 million. This emigration accelerated under the Fox administration. Between 2000 and 2005, more Mexicans emigrated to the United States than died. During those years, an average of 577,000 emigrated to the United States annually, while deaths averaged 495,000.[307]

Birth rate and poverty are as inexorably linked as are education and poverty. Of the roughly 110 million Mexicans in 2007, 20 million lived in extreme poverty, an additional 60 million lived in poverty, and 30 million lived above the poverty line. The 18 percent of the population living in extreme poverty accounted for 27 percent of births, and the 55 percent living in poverty accounted for an additional 64 percent of births. The 27 percent above the poverty line accounted for only 9 percent of births.[308]

Finally, even though the rate of population increase is declining, the increase in total population will continue for decades. As a result of the declining birth rate and massive out-migration, annual population growth has declined to 1.4 percent a year, but this addition of roughly 1.5 million people a year to the population continues to put aquifers, food supplies, and the urban environment under ever increasing environmental stress.[309]

EDUCATION

> If our educational system doesn't improve, we won't resolve the immense, painful problem of poverty.
>
> Jorge Castañeda, 2004[310]

Mexico has made steady progress at raising literacy and the educational level of its population. In 1970, 74.2 percent of the population was literate, and the average educational level was 3.4 years. By 2006–2007, 91.9 percent of the population was literate, and the average educational level was 8.2 years. While these statistics indicate substantial progress, the educational levels of other Latin American nations such as Chile, Argentina, and Columbia surpass that of Mexico. Mexico is even further behind the educational levels of economic rivals such as South Korea.[311]

Elementary school enrollment increased from 9.2 million in 1970–1971 to 15.4 million in 1983–1984, and then began to decline, reaching 14.6 million in 2006–2007. The current *decline* in primary school enrollment reflects two trends—fewer children being born and fewer children repeating grades.[312]

Mexico faced three major challenges relating to primary education. The first, providing for all those in the six to twelve age range, has been largely completed—after many decades of Herculean effort, 98 percent of primary-school-age children are in school. A second task was to increase the number of students who continued on to secondary. The third was to increase the quality of education imparted.[313]

While Mexico's current primary enrollment places it at a respectable twenty-first among 125 nations, it will take decades to overcome past educational shortfalls. The 2000 census reported that 32.5 million Mexicans over age fifteen had not finished elementary school. Efforts to decentralize governance to the municipal level are handicapped by 32 percent of Mexico's mayors having only a primary education, or less.[314]

The number of secondary school students (seventh to ninth grade) continues to increase since an increasing percentage of students remain in school after finishing primary. Secondary enrollment increased from 1.1 million in 1970 to 6.0 million in 2006–2007. In 2008, 92 percent of thirteen to fifteen year olds were attending school.[315]

Between 1970 and 2006–2007, enrollment in grades ten through twelve increased from 0.39 million to 3.7 million. By 2008, despite such massive gains, only 52 percent of those in the fifteen to seventeen age range remained in school.[316]

Between 1970 and 2006–2007, college undergraduate enrollment increased from 0.25 million to 2.52 million. Although in percentage terms this is an impressive gain, in 2008, only 21 percent of nineteen to twenty-four year olds remained in school, 7 percent behind the Latin American average.[317]

Problems of low quality are pervasive throughout the public educational system. This decline in quality began in the 1970s as emphasis was placed on increasing the number of students, not maintaining educational quality. Standards further declined in the 1980s as educational budgets were slashed. Teachers' salaries lost 70 percent of their buying power between 1981 and 1989. Even as educational budgets increased in the 1990s, teaching remained one of the poorest paid professions and, as a result, it had difficulty attracting highly qualified individuals. A report found that Mexico was thirty-first among 134 nations in educational expenditure, but 127th in quality of math and science education. Educational quality became an issue in the 2000 presidential election, PAN candidate Vicente Fox declared, "Mexico can't compete when our scholastic level is below the countries we do business with."[318]

As has occurred throughout Latin America, the poor quality of public education has led to the proliferation of private schools, which reinforces the economic gap between those who can pay for a good education and those who cannot. Many members of elite families now attend private schools from kindergarten through college. At the other extreme, public universities annually reject 300,000 applicants—most of whom cannot afford private universities—since there is no space for them.[319]

By 2002–2003, private schools enrolled 32 percent of students in higher education. Private institutions of higher learning were created in three waves. Catholic schools such as the Jesuit Universidad Iberoamericana, formed the first wave. These schools maintain rigorous academic programs and highly selective admission requirements. Elite secular schools formed the second wave. These schools are not only very selective academically, but are socially selective, since most cannot afford their tuition. Monterrey Tec is the best known of these secular schools. It expanded from its original Monterrey base and by 2003, it had 91,000 students enrolled in thirty-three campuses scattered around Mexico. The third wave of institutions was formed to absorb the rapidly increasing demand for alternatives to public higher education. These institutions are profit-driven and often fail to offer higher quality than the less costly public universities.[320]

In the aftermath of a bitter student strike over tuition increases that paralyzed the National University for a year (1999–2000), political scientist Denise Dresser commented on how higher education mirrors Mexican society:

> On the threshold of the millennium there are millions of Mexicans who don't have an entry ticket. They see a bright future for politicians, bilingual bankers, and intellectuals with international reputations. They see an elite that disparages the poor for being disheveled, longhaired, dark-skinned guerrillas who do not speak eloquently. They see an educated, elegant elite for whom the notion of social justice is interesting but irrelevant. The university rebellion reflects a badly divided country . . .[321]

MEXICO CITY

> The seat of the Mexican government is Mexico City, in the Federal District, a jurisdiction with certain similarities to the District of Columbia in the United States. Mexico City, however, unlike Washington, D.C., combines the qualities of New York City, Chicago, and Los Angeles, for Mexico's political capital is also its intellectual and economic capital.
>
> Roderic A. Camp, 2003[322]

In 2004, Mexico City's population reached an estimated 22.1 million, up from 2.9 million in 1950. This growth, however, has been far from uniform. The city's rapid growth, based on the import-substitution economic model, continued through the 1970s. Between 1950 and 1980, the population of the industrial zone north of the Federal District increased by 13.6 percent a year. In 1975, the Federal District and the adjacent State of Mexico provided 44 percent of Mexico's GDP, and the Mexico City metropolitan area generated 46 percent of its industrial employment.[323]

Between 1970 and 1980 the city's population increased by 5.1 million—its fastest growth ever. In part, this growth resulted from migrants seeking jobs created by 1970s prosperity. Industrialists located their facilities in the city to be close to government officials who made myriad decisions upon which the success of their business depended. However, official policy sought to discourage the further growth of the city. The 1978 National Urban Development Plan explicitly set as its goal "discouraging the growth of the Mexico City metropolitan area."[324]

The decision at the national level to emphasize exports had a marked impact on Mexico City. During the 1980s, Mexico City increased in population by only 1.3 million. Between 1980 and 1988, manufacturing employment in the city declined from a little over 1 million to below 750,000 as non-competitive factories closed and new plants were located near the U.S. border. Many who lost or failed to find manufacturing jobs turned to street vending. By the early 1990s, an estimated 149,000 street vendors plied the city's streets, drawing the wrath of established businesses. Shopkeepers complained that street vendors created health problems, caused more affluent customers to shop elsewhere, and competed unfairly since they did not have to pay rent or taxes. In the 1980s, to compound the city's problems, the De la Madrid administration reduced the massive federal subsidies the city relied on as the federal government struggled to meet its foreign debt obligations.[325]

The city, which had been a beacon of hope for the rest of the country, lost its allure. The government estimated that between 1985 and 1990, the city suffered a net population loss of 300,000 as many abandoned its crime, pollution, and congested streets. Those remaining in the city vented their spleen at the ballot box. In the July 1985 elections, the PRI captured only 42.6 percent of the vote in the Federal District, 22 percent below the PRI's national vote.[326]

In September 1985, an earthquake registering 8.1 on the Richter scale hit the city, which was already overwhelmed by uncontrolled growth and industrial decline. The quake hit the central city area hardest, killing 8,000–10,000, causing an estimated $4–5 billion in material damage, leaving 150,000 homeless, and destroying the workplaces of another 150,000.[327]

In the aftermath of the quake, one could see Mexico at its best—and worst. Neighborhood groups quickly organized in response to the quake, rescuing people and providing food and medicine. On their own initiative, college students formed brigades to dig survivors out of collapsed buildings. Residents later formed the Earthquake Victims' Coordinating Committee to press for the rebuilding of old neighborhoods rather than the relocation of those who had lost their homes. The Committee successfully pressured the government into heavily subsidizing the construction of 28,000 housing units, which converted tenants of destroyed buildings into homeowners who could remain in their old neighborhoods.[328]

On the negative side, the government's slow, inept response to the quake caused residents to lose what faith they had in government, as it exposed the inability of local and national politicians to manage the city's basic services in a time of disaster. The quake also provided disturbing snapshots of life in Mexico. The owners of clandestine sweatshops that collapsed were manifestly more interested in salvaging equipment and inventory than in caring for their employees who had toiled off the books with no labor rights. Many of the more than 370 buildings that collapsed fell because corrupt contractors cut corners during construction.[329]

Table 24.2 *Mexico City population, 1970–2005*

Year	Population (millions)	Percentage of national population
1970	8.8	18
1980	13.0	19
1990	15.3	18
2000	18.0	19
2005	18.7	18

Source: United Nations (2008: Table A.11)

During the 1990s, commerce and services emerged as the city's driving economic force, more than making up for the decline in manufacturing. During that decade the city's population increased by 2.8 million. Between 1988 and 1996, the Federal District's share of Mexico's GDP increased from 21 to 23 percent, as the city emerged as one of the chief financial service centers of Latin America. By the turn of the century, the city provided 60 percent of Mexico's banking services. Between 1990 and 1997, the number of top 500 Mexican companies headquartered in the city increased from 145 to 245. In 1998, only 24.9 percent of the city's jobs were in manufacturing, down from 40.4 percent in 1970.[330]

THE INTELLECTUAL SCENE

The Intellectuals

> Intellectuals . . . were always searching for the balance between influencing the state and being used by it.
>
> Julia Preston and Sam Dillon, 2004[331]

The 1968 student movement continued into the 1970s—at least in the printed word. Essayist and social critic Carlos Monsiváis commented that the suppression of that movement led to "the rejection of official mythologies." This was evident in his own work. In 1971, he published *Días de guardar* (*Days to Remember*), a rambling chronicle of Mexico's difficult transition to modernity and the 1968 student movement.[332]

In 1971, Elena Poniatowska published *Noche de Tlatelolco*, a collection of her reports from survivors of the October 2, 1968 killing of students. In this work, which Monsiváis to referred to as an "extraordinary multi-testimony," Poniatowska combined the words of both government officials and survivors with her own reflections. *Noche de Tlatelolco* went through fifty-six printings and was published in English as *Massacre in Mexico* (with a preface by Octavio Paz).[333]

In response to writers such as Monsiváis and Poniatowska, Echeverría sought to woo intellectuals back to the establishment. He found them easy to befriend and disarmed the left-leaning intelligentsia by adopting its rhetoric. He gained further legitimacy by increasing spending on universities and by supporting Cuba, Allende's Chile, and Third World causes in general. Carlos Fuentes, who up until the Echeverría administration had been best known for questioning the effects of Mexican modernization, was one of the many intellectuals embracing the administration. In 1971, he wrote: "Echeverría lifted the veil of fear that Díaz Ordaz threw over the body of Mexico. Many Mexicans felt free to criticize, to express themselves, to organize without fear of repression." Echeverría's supporters, such as Fuentes, were amply rewarded. Echeverría appointed him as ambassador to France and selected writer Rosario Castellanos as ambassador to Israel. In addition, Echeverría courted the intelligentsia by inviting its members to presidential dinners, soliciting their advice, lavishing funds on the arts and research institutes, pledging to steer the state back to the true course of the Mexican Revolution, and inviting them on his frequent Third World junkets. The press plane on such trips was so packed with intellectuals that cartoonist Abel Quezada quipped that if it crashed, Mexican culture would cease to exist.[334]

During the Echeverría administration, the Mexican intelligentsia divided into two groups that would endure for the rest of the century. One was led by Octavio Paz, who after resigning his ambassadorship to India in 1968, remained aboard until 1971. That year he returned to Mexico and founded *Plural*, a cultural supplement to the paper *Excélsior*. After the removal of that paper's editor in 1976, he resigned from *Plural* to protest the removal (see page 528) and founded the independent magazine *Vuelta,* where he was joined by historian Enrique Krauze, many of whose works are cited in this book. *Vuelta* became highly influential even though its circulation never rose above 18,000.[335]

In 1978, as a counterpoint to *Vuelta*, a group of writers founded the magazine *Nexos*, modeled on the *New York Review of Books*. While democracy was the central goal of writers at *Vuelta*, the *Nexos* group saw democracy as one goal among many, including social justice. Its founders brought academic research to bear on public policy and took on topics the mainstream press considered too hot to touch. Writers at *Nexos* generally supported militant, even armed, action to bring equality and justice for the poor.[336]

The fraudulent 1986 elections in Chihuahua brought the intellectual community together again briefly. In response to the fraud, a broad range of writers, including Paz, Krauze, Monsiváis, and Poniatowska, signed a letter of protest that appeared in several daily newspapers. It stated:

> Citizens as well as the national and international press have documented sufficient irregularities to sow reasonable doubts about the legality of the entire process. To clear away these doubts, which touch the very fiber of the credibility of politics in Mexico, we think the authorities, acting in good faith, should reestablish public harmony and annul the Chihuahua elections.[337]

Rather than keeping the intelligentsia united, the 1988 elections split it, with most intellectuals considering the election fraudulent and backing Cárdenas. In response, Salinas surrounded himself with intellectual advisors and offered the intelligentsia dinners in the National Palace and junkets abroad. Paz switched from being anti-regime to being one of the firmest backers of Salinas and his economic polices. He declared: "I applaud the opening with all the world and especially the opening with the United States. It's the first time in my lifetime when I feel there have been important changes in the country." Both Paz, editing *Vuelta*, and Héctor Aguilar Camín, the editor of *Nexos,* were drawn to Salinas, depriving these magazines of critical bite.[338]

The death of Paz in 1997 symbolically marked the end of the era of the intellectual in Mexico. Paz—who received the Nobel prize for literature in 1990—is remembered for his vast oeuvre, which includes almost thirty volumes of poetry and more than thirty volumes of essays, as well as his founding journals and contributing to public discourse. As critic Rafael Pérez Gay noted, Paz was "first and foremost a poet, and wanted to be remembered this way, his works combine contemplation and action, reflection and criticism, the local and the universal. His literary interests were as vast and diverse as his own work."[339]

After Paz's death, *Vuelta* ceased publication, and his intellectual heir Enrique Krauze founded a new magazine, *Letras Libres*. However, neither *Letras Libres* nor *Nexos* would exercise the influence that the *Vuelta* and *Nexos* had in the 1980s. Their influence was diluted by other journals of political analysis. Also, the mainstream press began publishing a wider range of views for an ever-wider audience. Pundits such as Soledad Loaeza and Lorenzo Meyer, who had previously published in highbrow journals such as *Vuelta* and *Nexos,* not only wrote columns in daily newspapers but increasingly used television to reach a broader audience.[340]

Print Media

The Old Order

> At the end of the 1970s, the government strictly controlled information. Daily newspapers, with some notable exceptions, reported what the regime wanted to hear.
>
> José Aguilar Rivera, 2003[341]

The PRI's system of media control maintained a pliant press into the 1980s. In his 1985 classic, *Distant Neighbors,* Alan Riding observed that "hundreds" of Mexico City and provincial newspapers received between 60 and 80 percent of their revenue by publishing government handouts as ads or disguised as new stories. This led to extensive coverage promoting the president and his administration. Under López Portillo, the Mexico City police chief provided dozens of leading editors and columnists with cars and drivers. Discreet calls from the Interior Ministry guaranteed omission or softer treatment of unwelcome news.[342]

The results of government largesse were visible in both the quality (favorable) and quantity (voluminous) of PRI political campaign coverage. Journalists covering PRI campaigns received free transportation, food, and rooms in the best hotels as well as envelopes full of cash. In 1994, millions of dollars were paid to large dailies to publish propaganda disguised as news promoting Ernesto Zedillo's presidential campaign. Government ties were key to financial success in newspaper publishing, while readership was largely incidental. In the mid-1990s, Mexico City's twenty-three daily newspapers had a combined circulation of fewer than 500,000. Government assistance allowed many of these papers to operate without serious regard to circulation or commercial advertising.[343]

Not only did journalists fail to question information received from official sources, but they did not view questioning political authority as their role. They supported the status quo and considered themselves part of the governing system and so defended it against attack. Reporters socialized before 1968 portrayed the Mexican political system as a unique species of democracy suited to post-revolutionary Mexican society. The PRI was considered the only valid representative of Mexican society. Given this perspective, the press focused on incumbents and PRI-affiliated organizations, while largely ignoring independent civil associations and opposition political parties.[344]

The New Order

> In the nineties, television, radio and the newspapers expanded and diversified significantly, reflecting the diversity of Mexican opinion for the first time and reinforcing political pluralism.
>
> Soledad Loaeza, 2006[345]

The press freedom Mexico enjoys today can be traced back to the death in 1968 of the editor of Mexico's flagship newspaper, *Excélsior*. Even though the paper was considered Mexico's outstanding paper, it had more in common with *Pravda* than with the world's outstanding papers.

The appointment of Julio Scherer García as the new editor of *Excélsior* initiated a chain of events that changed Mexican journalism forever. Scherer García, who had worked at the paper since 1946 without attracting much attention, soon introduced investigative reporting on topics such as election fraud, government repression, and environmental damage. His goal was not to topple the government but to make visible the illegal activity of the ruling elite. Scherer García assumed that ending impunity began with informing the public of what was happening. *Excélsior*'s newly empowered reporters also investigated the corruption of union leaders and commented on misguided economic policy. The paper ceased to brand as communist-inspired any effort to promote social justice and no longer repeated as divine revelation everything declared by the PRI and the government. Independent academics such as Daniel Cosío Villegas and Rodolfo Stavenhagen (both cited in this book) were invited to write columns.

Excélsior's independence eventually exceeded President Echeverría's tolerance. He took advantage of *Excélsior*'s unique management structure to bring the paper back into Mexico's sycophantic journalistic chorus. The paper had been organized as a cooperative, which chose its editor, in order to insulate it from outside pressure. With Echeverría's backing, some conservative reporters and printers packed a meeting of the cooperative with goons and voted Scherer García out of the editorship. More than 200 writers, reporters, and photographers then walked out of the paper in protest.[346]

After Scherer García's ouster, those who seized control of *Excélsior* scrambled to hire a new staff—a staff that included Eduardo Borrell, who had served as minister of education under Cuban dictator Fulgencio Batista. The formerly proud paper became a pro-government rag that began a slow descent into insolvency and irrelevance.[347]

Government influence over the media was so strong that Scherer García's ouster was hardly commented on by other newspapers. The following statement did appear in one of the few spaces remaining open to critical comment, *La cultura en México*, a supplement to the magazine *Siempre!* It was signed by a long list of intellectuals including Elena Poniatowska, Eduardo del Río, Carlos Monsiváis, Enrique Krauze, and Lorenzo Meyer:

> The *Excélsior* which Scherer García edited will remain in the annals of Mexican journalism as the richest, most fertile journalist experience of the last decade. It is a triumphal monument to journalistic professionalism and an attempt to report in an informed, uninhibited, free manner.[348]

Rather than remaining silent, Scherer García soon founded a weekly news magazine, *Proceso*, which began to publish outspoken journalism of a quality that Mexico had not seen since the advent of PRI rule. The magazine was so hard-hitting that historian Enrique Krauze commented that it was more effective than the Secretaría de la Contraloría, a cabinet-level agency established to combat corruption. It repeatedly denounced financial impropriety and published proof of its occurrence. Ironically, the coverage provided by *Proceso* on topics such as electoral fraud, repression, environmental damage, and biased media coverage was even more hard-hitting than that provided by *Excélsior* under Scherer García. In 1978, Octavio Paz took advantage of *Proceso*'s openness to observe:

> For almost 30 years, between 1930 and 1960, most Mexicans were sure of the path we were following. Such certainty has now vanished, and many are wondering if we should begin again. . . . Economic problems are severe and have not been resolved. Rather, inflation and unemployment are increasing. It is also clear, that, despite our wealth, poverty has not disappeared.[349]

For decades *Proceso* remained as the most widely circulated, most influential political weekly in Mexico. However, after Scherer García retired in 1996, its circulation declined from 200,000 to 70,000, and it faced increasing competition from other newsmagazines such as *Este País*, *Milenio Semenal*, and *Voz y Voto*. It also faced increased competition from the increasingly independent electronic media.[350]

Eight years after the founding of *Proceso*, a new paper *La Jornada* was founded in Mexico City. The newly founded paper gained stature with its extensive coverage and photos of the 1985 earthquake in Mexico City. Later it became the basic source of information on student movements based at the National University, Cuauhtémoc Cárdenas's 1988 presidential candidacy, the PRD, and the 1994 Chiapas rebellion. As a result of its coverage of the 1988 elections, *La Jornada's* circulation more than doubled to almost 100,000 and then rose again with its extensive coverage of the 1994 Chiapas uprising. Rather than buttressing incumbent regimes, *La Jornada* sought to change them. *La Jornada* director general Carmen Lira commented: "*La Jornada* has believed—and has never ceased believing—in the possibility of a more just, civil country, and in citizens' rights and duty to demand such a country and initiate change. In short, in the possibility of change in our country."[351]

While independent journalism was taking root in Mexico City, 500 miles to the north a parallel process began in Monterrey when, in 1973, twenty-four-year-old Alejandro Junco inherited a sleepy, family-run provincial paper, *El Norte*. He prohibited his reporters from taking bribes or commissions from subjects covered and made this feasible by paying salaries well above those paid reporters at other papers. *El Norte*'s drab appearance was made over through the widespread use of color and attractive layout. Most significantly, *El Norte* began publishing real news. For example, when Monterrey held mayoral elections, observers were posted at each polling place to record the number of voters. When the PRI claimed more votes than there had been voters, *El Norte* published the figures it had gathered.[352]

Given its improved coverage and layout, the paper's circulation increased from 30,000 to 145,000, making it the most important paper in northern Mexico. In the early 1990s, not only had *El Norte*'s circulation increased but its private ad sales were higher than those of any other Mexican newspaper—a fact not lost on other publishers.[353]

Rather than rest on his laurels, Junco plunged into the much more competitive Mexico City market. He invested $50 million of his family's money in a new paper, *Reforma.* The paper embraced the strong elements of *El Norte*, including a jazzy layout splashed with color and sophisticated graphics.

Reforma's coverage, which reflected its link to *El Norte*, included reporting on corruption and election fraud. Management refused to publish government propaganda disguised as news and prohibited reporters from selling ads. *Reforma* emphasized the publication of opinion polls, which indicated if a policy was disliked or if a PRI candidate lacked support and was therefore highly unlikely to win. If it was known that a PRI candidate lacked support, the political cost of rigging elections increased. Since they received some of the highest salaries in the industry, $1,500 to $3,000 a month, *Reforma* reporters were not forced into seeking government funds in exchange for favorable coverage. By 2002, the paper had a circulation of 126,000, despite the PRI-dominated newspaper vendors' union refusing to sell it, and was considered the most influential paper in Mexico.[354]

The success of *El Norte, Reforma, La Jornada*, and *Proceso* paved the way for more independent journalism throughout Mexico. Alejandro Junco founded other newspapers, such as *Mural* in Guadalajara and *Palabra* in Saltillo. By 2000, the Junco chain employed 1,070 reporters and published 460,000 newspapers a day. Other papers, ranging from *El Diario de Yucatán* in Mérida to *Zeta* in Tijuana, also plunged into critical journalism. Various papers in Mexico City began more independent coverage. *El Financiero* published a series of stories on economic policy, drug trafficking, official corruption, and electoral fraud before other papers dared such coverage. Juan Francisco Ealy Ortiz, the owner of *El Universal*, published a paper so drab that it appeared unchanged since its founding in 1916. He admitted that his paper was steeped in "a culture of submission." The example of *Reforma*, however, galvanized Ealy into change. He added color photos and independent coverage and even hired reporters away from other independent papers. Such a shift was not accepted graciously by the existing political order. Ealy was subjected to tax audits and arrested on charges of tax evasion, all but one of which was eventually thrown out in court.[355]

By 2000, Mexico's media had evolved from a closed, corrupt, establishment-oriented press to a reasonably vigorous Fourth Estate. There was regular coverage of official repression, corruption, lying, impunity, and electoral fraud. This independence did not emerge overnight, but was the product of more than two decades of learning and struggle.[356]

Television

> It is difficult to overstate the potential influence of television on Mexican political life. Over two-thirds of Mexicans get their information about politics primarily from the small screen, and even among the most affluent and educated segments of the population, television remains the dominant medium.
>
> Chappell Lawson, 2004[357]

In the early 1970s, both of the early TV networks, Telesistema Mexicano and Televisión Independiente de México, were losing money since they engaged in bidding wars for talent and foreign shows. In addition, competition for ad sales in the still small Mexican TV market forced prices down.[358]

In 1973, the two TV networks merged to form Televisa (which is short for Televisión via Satélite), thus creating what was for all intents and purposes a private television monopoly. The merger created the largest television network in Latin America. Televisa became a far flung conglomerate, broadcasting Spanish-language television in the United States, exporting its soap operas to roughly ninety countries, producing film and print media, and staging sports and artistic events. Eventually Televisa became the world's largest producer of TV programming.[359]

For more than two decades, Televisa and the PRI were deeply intertwined, with the network depending on the regime for broadcast licenses and infrastructure development, and successive PRI regimes depending on Televisa for political marketing. Emilio Azcárraga Milmo, who assumed control of the family broadcast empire after his father's death in 1972, made the network's pro-PRI slant explicit. In January 1988, he stated: "We're from the PRI, we're members of the PRI, we don't believe in any other party. And as members of our party, we will do everything possible to make sure our candidate wins."[360]

Azcárraga's political bias was manifest in Televisa's coverage of political campaigns. PRI candidates received a much greater share of TV coverage than they did of the popular vote. Opposition candidates were presented in an unflattering light, if they were covered at all. In 1988, PRI presidential candidate Carlos Salinas, one of six presidential candidates, was credited with 50.74 percent of the vote, yet received 90.7 percent of TV coverage. To protest the network's bias, PAN presidential candidate Manuel Clouthier called for a boycott of Televisa and its advertisers.[361]

In their 2001 biography of Azcárraga, authors Claudia Fernández and Andrew Paxman proclaimed him to have been "the most powerful businessman Mexico has ever seen." This power came from his enjoying a quasi-monopoly on television. In 1993, Televisa produced all of the twenty top-rated shows in Mexico. In 1994, *Forbes* placed his family's net worth at $5.4 billion. Azcárraga was a famously autocratic leader, a man of vast appetites, and extravagant gestures. His 243-feet long custom-built yacht *Eco* cost an estimated $45 million.[362]

In the 1970s, radio and television surpassed movies and newspapers as shapers of public opinion. By 1984, a third of Mexican homes had a TV set. During the 1980s, fewer than 1 million newspapers circulated daily, while between 15 and 20 million watched TV news every night. The growing impact of TV was revealed by a 1981 poll that found Mexico City children could identify TV characters more readily than national heroes and knew TV schedules better than the dates of religious holidays. This is not surprising, since they spent over 50 percent more time in front of the TV set than in school.[363]

Change came more slowly to television than to print media, since Televisa's quasi-monopolistic nature shielded it from competitive pressure. Serious competition to Televisa only emerged in 1993 when the Salinas administration privatized a little-watched government TV network, selling it to Ricardo Salinas Pliego (no kin to the president) for $642 million dollars.[364]

Salinas Pliego branded his newly acquired network TV Azteca and immediately turned his sights on Televisa. One of his first moves was to air credible newscasts. He began to hire actors away from Televisa, which had so many actors under contact that many failed to get good roles. TV Azteca plunged into the commercially lucrative soap opera market with *Nada Personal* (*Nothing Personal*), which became Mexico's top-rated soap. Rather than the formerly anodyne formula of poor girl marrying rich man, *Nada Personal* dealt with the murder of a politician by drug traffickers. Given its more credible news programming and more socially relevant soap operas, by 2002 Azteca controlled 26 percent of the TV market, compared to Televisa's 71 percent.[365]

A second event that reshaped Televisa was the death of its undisputed patriarch, Emilio Azcárraga Milmo, in 1997. At the time of his death, Televisa owned four separate TV networks totaling 280 stations. During the twenty-five years he headed the company, Televisa's dollar income increased twenty-five-fold and the number of its employees increased from 2,350 to 20,000. He was one of the few children of the rich to actually increase his inherited fortune. While he will probably be best remembered for his allegiance to the PRI, he did serve Mexico in various ways. Under his control, Televisa promoted adult education and broadcast a soap opera favoring family planning. Azcárraga patronized various artistic endeavors, including $2 million donated to the highly acclaimed art exhibit "Mexico: Splendors of 30 Centuries."[366]

Azcárraga Milmo was succeeded by Emilio Azcárraga Jean, his only son. When he assumed control of the Televisa media empire at age twenty-nine, Azcárraga Jean was widely seen as a spoiled rich kid. However, he survived an internal power showdown with other family members, refinanced Telvisa's debt, and laid off more than 6,000 staffers to cut labor costs. He disavowed any allegiance to the PRI and shifted his allegiance to an even more jealous god—the marketplace.[367]

Mounting pressure from the increasingly influential opposition political parties and civic groups also led Televisa to more balanced coverage, as did the loss of market share to TV Azteca. The 1994–1995 economic crash further sullied the image of the incumbents and made criticism of them less risky.[368]

Electoral coverage on television reflected the changes in Mexican TV. By 1994, the airtime dedicated to major parties approximated their share of the national vote. The change was not only in volume, but in tone, in that the opposition was not routinely denigrated. In 2000, the two most watched news shows gave PAN candidate Fox 36 percent of their airtime, while PRI candidate Labastida received 33 percent. Rather than reflecting a new political bias, this imbalance likely resulted from the baritone-voiced Fox being a master at showmanship and the PRI candidate being conspicuously bland.[369]

Remaining Challenges

Despite the undeniable progress made toward more open media over the past decades, a number of challenges remain:

- TV coverage is now yellower than under the old regime, since unrestrained reporting on crime and scandals is used to gain ratings. The simple absence of censorship and repression does not automatically lead to media pluralism or independence in emerging democracies. Private media in emerging democracies tend to be politically conservative, establishment-oriented, and vacuous.[370]
- Television portrays the image of a blond, fair-skinned population quite unlike the physical appearance of most Mexicans. English travel writer Chris Taylor commented on the visual impression generated by Televisa: "Judging by the number of blondes that are on its shows, one could easily conclude that it was the Swedes, not the Spanish, who had colonized Mexico."[371]
- The ownership of companies buying ads is highly concentrated, thus giving a small number of owners undue influence over media content. Telephone magnate Carlos Slim's financial empire is estimated to control 40 percent of Mexico's advertising. Media ownership itself is highly concentrated, with television settling into a duopoly. In 2007, Televisa and TV Azteca controlled 94 percent of the broadcast market.[372]

While the delinking of Televisa from the PRI and the founding of TV Azteca were initially seen as opening the way for critical reporting, it soon became apparent that a narrow range of vested interested interests set policy for the two networks. This became glaringly apparent as they used their media power to influence legislation concerning telecommunications. As media expert Enrique Sánchez Ruiz commented in 2005, "The media no longer contribute to enriching the democratic process in Mexico due to their highly concentrated ownership and control."[373]

At the beginning of the twenty-first century, a wide variety of actors, such as drug traffickers, other organized criminal groups, and the henchmen of crooked politicians, have attempted to silence those whose messages are unwelcome. According to the New York-based Committee to Protect Journalists, at least twenty-one reporters in Mexico were killed between 2000 and 2008. Such violence has made it virtually impossible to report on drug trafficking in northern Mexico. After a 2006 grenade and gunfire attack on the newsroom of *El Mañana* in the border city of Nuevo Laredo, its editor Ramón Cantú lamented:

Even if we find out why, I'm not sure we would print it. We live here under a code of self-censorship, and even under those rules we're vulnerable. Nuevo Laredo continues to be the battleground for drug cartels. And reporters continue to get caught in the crossfire.[374]

RELIGION

> The average Mexican ranks family, work, and religion most important to his life and considers it far more significant than politics.
>
> Roderic Camp, 1997 [375]

In 1974, to strengthen his ties to the Church, Echeverría visited Pope Paul VI in the Vatican. This was the first papal visit by a Mexican president. By visiting the Vatican, Echeverría officially recognized the Church as an organization. His administration also provided financial support for the construction of a new Basilica of Guadalupe in 1976.[376]

In 1979, the government facilitated Pope John Paul II's visit to Mexico to open the Latin American bishops conference in Puebla. The outpouring of enthusiasm for the pope by perhaps 20 million Mexicans served as a reminder of Mexico's deep Catholic roots. The conference issued a statement strongly condemning poverty in Latin America. John Paul II urged the Church to become engaged in social issues so as not to become irrelevant. Yet, at the same time, he attempted to rein in proponents of liberation theology by declaring, "The concept of Christ as a political revolutionary, as a subversive, is not in keeping with the teachings of the Church."[377]

In response to the economic crisis of the 1980s, the Catholic hierarchy recommended to the faithful that they remain calm and aid the government. However, it soon became apparent that no changes were forthcoming from the government in terms of increased morality, economic recovery, or democracy. This led the majority of the Catholic hierarchy to intensify its criticism of electoral fraud and human rights abuses. The Church was in a stronger position to make such criticism since the government was on the defensive and needed allies to maintain the system.[378]

It was no secret that the Church's condemning election fraud favored the PAN, which was strong in the very areas where electoral fraud occurred. After the 1988 presidential elections, when it was the political left that was the victim of fraud, the Church remained conspicuously silent. This silence was rewarded by Salinas inviting two members of the Catholic hierarchy to attend his inauguration—the first time the hierarchy had attended a presidential inauguration since the Cristero rebellion in the 1920s. In his inaugural address, Salinas promised to "modernize" (his favorite word) Church-state relations.[379]

During his administration, several constitutional amendments largely eliminated anti-clericalism, which was so woven into the document that it was necessary to amend five different articles. Article 3 was modified to allow the Church to impart primary education, something that in fact was already occurring. A revised Article 24 allowed religious ceremonies to be staged outside of churches and private homes. Article 130 was changed to recognize the legal existence of religious associations such as the Catholic Church. In addition, priests and ministers were granted the right to vote. After these amendments were passed, the principal remaining vestige of anticlerical legislation was the prohibition on priests holding political office. In 1992, Salinas followed up his reforms by establishing diplomatic relations with the Vatican for the first time since the end of the Maximilian government in 1867.[380]

Since he was not a practicing Catholic, Salinas's reforms did not appear to be religiously motivated. His building bridges to the Catholic Church broadened his political base, since Mexico's largely Catholic population favored the constitutional reforms. In addition, the normalization of Church-state relations made Mexico a better suitor for the upcoming negotiations to establish the NAFTA.[381]

More Mexicans—62 percent—express confidence in the Church than in any other public institution. However, they are increasingly making up their own minds on matters of individual behavior. Even among peasant women, traditionally viewed as more conservative, more than 53 percent practice birth control and one in five has had an abortion. After the Federal District legalized abortion in 2007, an initial sampling of the women choosing a legal abortion found that 81.4 percent were Catholic. Similarly, few Mexicans followed Church counsel concerning the film *The Crime of Father Amaro*, which depicts a priest who has an affair with a parishioner and portrays the Church as being in league with drug traffickers. The Church declared the film blasphemous and announced its support for anyone protesting it. Thanks in large part to the Church's publicizing it extensively, the film was a huge box office success.[382]

Between 1970 and 1990, the number of Protestants increased by 17.6 percent a year, and in southern Mexico, by 24 percent a year. By 2000, the more than 5 million Protestants made up 5 percent of the population. The Protestant churches with the largest following include the Mormons with 783,000 members and Jehovah's Witnesses with 518,000.[383]

The evangelical churches have been especially successfully in obtaining converts in the poor, indigenous states of southern Mexico. In 2000, Protestants made up 14.5 percent of the population of Chiapas, while in traditionally Catholic Guanajuato, they comprised only 1.4 percent. Many Mexicans appear to convert to Protestantism in response to the anomie caused by modernization. For such converts, Protestantism is a mechanism for providing order and meaning in the lives of the dispossessed.[384]

One of the reasons for Protestants having greater success at proselytization compared to Catholics is that the Catholic Church grew complacent with its monopoly status. As a result of this monopoly, which was de jure up until the nineteenth century and de facto well into the twentieth, Catholics provided limited service to poor, outlying communities. Protestants then moved into these underserved communities and gained converts. The Catholic Church has been hard pressed to respond, in part due to its costly, overarching bureaucratic organization that stretches back to Rome. In contrast, the Protestants' low personnel training costs and short lead-time facilitate the ready creation of new churches. Finally, even though the Catholic Church was eloquent in denouncing the undemocratic top-down nature of 1980s PRI administration, it has been unwilling to alter its own structure in response to the more democratic structures in Protestant churches involving elections, pastors, deacons, elders, and women, and where most decisions are made locally with the views of laity taken into account.[385]

Mexican society, as it has for decades, has continued to grow more intellectually independent and secular during the twenty-first century. Indicators of this are the 2007 legalization of abortion in the Federal District as well as the approval of same-sex unions the same year in the District and in the northern state of Coahuila. As journalist Patrick Corcoran commented:

> The recent series of events are simply an affirmation of what has long been true: the Church now, more than ever, is not Mexico's pre-eminent moral guide. It is simply a guide, followed by some, ignored by others. Just as in the United States, the Church in Mexico has been damaged by a series of sex scandals.[386]

Chapter 25

Plunging Back into the International Market, 1971–2000

THE OLD MODEL CRUMBLES

> As ISI [import substitution industrialization] unraveled during the late 1970s and early 1980s, the model of capital accumulation pursued by the larger, more highly industrialized Latin American countries lost vitality and finally collapsed. By the early 1990s the ISI model had largely been rejected, and was being replaced by totally different economic strategies.
>
> Ian Roxborough, 1994[1]

The import-substitution model of economic development that Mexico adopted after 1940 served the country for nearly half a century and produced the Mexican economic miracle—a source of envy throughout much of the developing world. Between 1940 and 1982, Mexico's per capita GDP increased at an average annual rate of 3.6 percent. During that period, per capita income increased by 440 percent, manufacturing by 1460 percent, and agriculture by 420 percent, while population only increased by 240 percent.

By the end of López Portillo's term (1976–1982), the development model was showing signs of disfunctionality. These signs included: 1) 150 percent inflation in 1982, 2) depletion of foreign exchange reserves, 3) virtual collapse of non-oil exports, 4) high foreign indebtedness, and 5) capital flight, which totaled $22 billion between 1980 and 1982.[2]

In retrospect, it is clear the import-substitution model suffered from numerous flaws. These flaws include Mexico's market being too small to permit manufacturing economies of scale. As a result, goods manufactured in Mexico were roughly 50 percent more expensive and of lower quality than their foreign equivalents. Production of consumer durables was mainly for Mexico's upper and middle classes, which were too small to sustain growth. Import substitution placed a constant drain on Mexico foreign currency reserves since factories established under its aegis constantly required foreign purchases of components, intermediate materials, and capital goods. Such purchases resulted in a $28 billion trade deficit between 1970 and 1981. In the early post-Second World War period, agricultural exports financed such purchases. However, after the mid-1960s, agricultural exports declined. Also, just as opponents of massive foreign investment had predicted, foreign investors withdrew $5.3 billion more than they brought into Mexico between 1974 and 1984.[3]

The old economic model exacerbated several existing problems. Most of Mexico's manufacturing was concentrated in the Valley of Mexico, Guadalajara, and Monterrey—leaving little benefit for the rest of the nation. It failed to address Mexico's employment needs since the capital-intensive factories produced few jobs. Direct economic benefits were restricted to plant owners and the relatively small organized industrial working class while the vast majority of the population waited for wealth to trickle down. As economist Manuel Gollás observed, "Industrialization was a very inefficient method of promoting economic justice." Finally, in the late 1960s, labor productivity stagnated, making further wage increases, which had brought social peace, untenable.[4]

By the mid-1980s, economic policy makers deemed these problems to be sufficient cause for adopting a new economic model. While the problems associated with the import substitution are undeniable in retrospect, the question arises as to whether Mexico needed a sudden shift in economic model, as occurred, or whether it could have entered a globalizing economy in a slower, less damaging manner.

THE NEW ECONOMIC MODEL

> The failure of the import substitution model remained hidden for almost ten years as Mexico borrowed abroad and relied on oil sales. It finally burst into the open with the 1982 financial crisis.
>
> Ilán Bizberg, 2003[5]

Early in his administration, President De la Madrid (1982–1988) failed to take decisive action concerning the economy. It took some time for Mexican officials to realize that something was seriously amiss and that the 1982 crisis was not just a momentary concatenation of unfavorable events. Even when the need for change could no longer be denied, De la Madrid's cabinet could not agree upon what measures to take.[6]

By 1985, it had become apparent that the government was unable to restore economic growth using traditional mechanisms. Then, after oil prices plunged from $24 a barrel in December 1985 to $9 a barrel in July 1986, Mexican planners undertook what economist James Cypher characterized as "the most profound shift in economic policymaking that had occurred in 50 years."[7]

Economic policy emphasis shifted from the domestic market to exports. In 1986, Mexico joined the General Agreement on Tariffs and Trade (GATT), a group of nations pledging to reduce barriers to world commerce. Between 1971 and 1980, 74.1 percent of Mexico's imports required a license. By 1989, only 14.2 percent required such a license. Between 1981 and 1988, the average tariff declined from 18.3 percent to 6.1 percent.[8]

The divestiture of government-owned corporations formed another key aspect of De la Madrid's economic policy. In 1982, the government owned 1,155 corporations, while by 1988 only 446 remained public hands. Between 1980 and 1989, as a result of selling corporations and cutting back on investment, the public sector's share of economic activity declined from 24.1 percent of GDP to only 12.5 percent.[9]

Other key elements of De la Madrid's new economic policy, often characterized as neoliberal, were a reduced level of government spending, an end to government social programs, the end of a state industrial policy, and the deregulation of goods, service, labor, and capital markets. This deregulation included lowering (or eliminating) tariffs and welcoming foreign investment. The underlying assumption of De la Madrid's policy was that the market could allocate capital more efficiently than the state, thus accelerating economic growth.[10]

A variety of factors made this shift in economic policy feasible. The 1982 crisis had bankrupted numerous small and medium-sized firms, many of which had supplied the government with goods and services. As a result, they could no longer lobby for maintaining the old economic model. Similarly, labor had lost clout in Mexico's ruling coalition and could not effectively oppose the move. Many assumed economic mismanagement between 1971 and 1982 resulted from a flawed system, not incompetent managers, and so welcomed any change in economic policy.[11]

While the power of those opposed to these changes dwindled, support mushroomed. The PAN, which had long advocated the policies De la Madrid was adopting, threw its rapidly increasing political power behind the changes.[12]

The business elite, which after the bank nationalization, was no longer content to let the politicians formulate economic policy, supported these changes. As De la Madrid noted in his autobiography, Monterrey businessmen demanded that the government adopt U.S. President Ronald Reagan's policy of reducing government economic activity. To disseminate their message, the newly assertive business elite employed: 1) the media, including the magazine *Visión*, the newspaper *El Heraldo*, and especially the TV network Televisa, 2) private institutions of higher learning such as the Universidad Anáhuac and the Autonomous Technological Institute of Mexico, and 3) books and columnists such as Luis Pazos.[13]

There was also strong outside pressure to open the Mexican economy to foreign trade and investment. The World Bank and the IMF advocated such a policy, and, given their ability to condition loans on following their advice, they were listened to. Also, there was strong pressure from the U.S. government. As economist David Félix commented:

> Flushed with the triumphs of Reagonomics, the White House turned the Department of State, the Agency for International Development (AID) and sympathetic foundations and think tanks loose on Latin America in an ideological full-court press to promote privatization, the liberalizing of markets and the unleashing of entrepreneurs.[14]

IMF, World Bank, and U.S. officials found that those in charge of Mexican policy making unabashedly embraced neoliberalism. De la Madrid was the first Mexican president with a graduate degree from the United States. He represented a younger generation than that of Echeverría and López Portillo. Both of De la Madrid's immediate predecessors had witnessed Cárdenas's oil nationalization as students and were steeped in the notion of state intervention to solve economic problems. De la Madrid, however, did not favor a state-led economic strategy. To an unprecedented degree, his cabinet was stacked with people with foreign-trained M.A.s and Ph.D.s. Nearly one in four officials in his administration had studied in the United States. Having been educated north of the border, they sought to capitalize on their neighbor, not keep it at arm's length. Their training in mainstream neoclassical economics predisposed them to look favorably on dismantling the developmentalist state and to identify with the outlook of the foreigners pressuring Mexico.[15]

The advocates of neoliberalism proclaimed that no currently developed nation had developed without foreign trade as a major component of its economy. However, these advocates overlooked an equally important aspect of the currently developed nations—development did not occur simply by opening borders. For example, during the later part of the twentieth century, in the rapidly developing East Asian nations, trade barriers were eventually removed, but only after new jobs were provided in export industries. Infant industries were targeted, protected, and subsidized by East Asian governments in multiple ways. Foreign multinationals were welcomed, but only if their investment involved transfer of technology. Multinationals investing in East Asia were not allowed to take over healthy domestic firms. These nations worked actively to reduce poverty and the growth of inequality, believing that such policies were important for maintaining social cohesion—a precondition for investment and growth.[16]

President Salinas (1988–1994) continued De la Madrid's economic policies, which is not surprising. As secretary of budget and planning under his predecessor, Salinas was one of the main architects of the 1980s changes in economic policy. In 1989, he declared his "fundamental" economic goals were restoring economic growth without inflation and raising Mexicans' standard of living.[17]

Salinas was unabashedly pro-growth. Commenting on the anticipated population increase of 10 million during his term, he emphasized, "For Mexico, growth is not an option to be considered, but an undeniable necessity." Salinas also did something none of his predecessors had done so openly—he admitted that the economic reforms of the Mexican Revolution had ended. In his 1989 state of the nation address, he declared, "Most of the reforms of our Revolution have run their course and no longer guarantee the new development Mexico demands."[18]

Salinas continued De la Madrid's policy of privatizing government-owned corporations so vigorously that the magazine *Euromoney* dubbed him the "Thatcher" of Latin America. Some of Salinas's major privatizations included the steel mill Altos Hornos de México, the Cananea copper mine, Teléfonos de México (Telmex), and the banks that López Portillo had nationalized in 1982.

Salinas's development policy relied heavily on foreign investment. In his 1991 state of the nation address, he explained: "Opening Mexico to foreign investment brings in resources and technology and increases our ability to export." To increase foreign investment, in May 1989 a new investment law allowed 100 percent foreign ownership of firms in Mexico.[19]

Even though he had earlier declared that a free trade agreement with the United States was unwise, the changing world situation caused Salinas to reverse his position. The Mexican people learned of this reversal thanks to a March 27, 1990 *Wall Street Journal* story that reported that the previous month U.S. and Mexican officials had met and agreed to negotiate a free trade agreement.

In a 1991 interview in *Le Figaro*, Salinas declared that Mexico's investment needs prompted him to seek a free trade agreement:

> The decade of the 1990s will be marked by a lack of capital. This lack results from the demand for capital in central Europe and the Soviet Union and for German reconstruction. This will weigh on capital markets. Thus, I took the initiative to negotiate a free trade agreement with the United States and Canada.

Population growth was another factor that influenced his decision. He commented that a free trade agreement was "the only way that I can respond to the interests of the 82 million Mexicans today and the almost two million that are added every year."[20]

Mexican Commerce Secretary Jaime Serra Puche noted another reason for the shift:

> The internationalization of production and the technological and communications revolutions are leading to globalization and increased interdependence. As a result, economic autarky is no longer viable. Now the most promising paths for economic development cross international borders and even continental boundaries.[21]

In August 1992, after fourteen months of haggling, negotiations on a free trade agreement between Mexico, Canada, and the United States were concluded. The final product was a document more than 1,100 pages long. Its drafting required 200 negotiating sessions and seven ministerial sessions.[22]

On December 17, 1992, Bush, Salinas, and Canadian Prime Minister Brian Mulroney signed the full text of the agreement in their respective capitals. Before its implementation, NAFTA also required legislative approval by each of the three signatory nations. While such approval required considerable arm-twisting by President Clinton, who had taken office before its passage, things were much simpler in Mexico. As *Business Week* noted, "With only token opposition in the Mexican Congress, courts, and media, Salinas can steer his country toward free trade with nary a bump."[23]

While NAFTA bears similarities to the treaty that formed the European Community (later to be known as the European Union), it differs in significant ways. The European experience was very slow and deliberate and more democratic in the broad sense, providing each member with time to adjust to one set of changes before undertaking the next. The European treaty did not assume governments of economically weaker members would or could make needed investment. As a result, in nations such as Portugal, Spain, and Greece, the Community supported government budgets, and subsidized improved services and infrastructure, and private companies establishing operations in new member nations. The treaty also allowed workers from any member nation to move freely to other member nations to work. Finally, and most importantly, European Community members saw the common market as an intermediate step to political unity. To facilitate unity, the treaty required that a nation must be a working democracy before entering the community. Critics of the Mexican political system lamented that NAFTA was not used to produce political change when it was available as leverage.[24]

NAFTA provided that tariffs and import quotas between the three member nations would be eliminated over a fifteen-year period. Given special political and economic sensitivities, detailed provisions were spelled out for different products. For example, Mexico was allowed to exclude foreign investment from the oil industry. Agriculture was so sensitive that Mexico negotiated a separate treaty with the United States and another one with Canada.

NAFTA regulates tariffs, non-tariff barriers, and investment. It specifies that goods from any member nation must be treated as well as locally made goods. Thus, for example, one nation cannot ban the import of asbestos insulation on health grounds, while permitting domestic manufacturers to produce it. Similarly, service providers from other NAFTA nations must be treated as well as domestic ones. Investment from other NAFTA nations cannot be discriminated against to favor domestic investment. In 1993, Mexican tariffs averaged about 10 percent while the U.S. level was about 4 percent. Since trade was already nearly tariff-free, NAFTA had its greatest impact on investment rules and intellectual property rights. Mexican analyst (and later U.N. ambassador) Adolfo Aguilar Zínzer acknowledged this when he stated, "This is not a trade agreement, but rather an agreement about investments."[25]

Without NAFTA, subsequent occupants of Los Pinos, the White House, or 24 Sussex Drive could easily erect trade barriers. With NAFTA assuring presumably permanent barrier-free borders, investors could make decisions accordingly. As Salinas noted, "The certainty of access to the U.S. market would be an enormous stimulus to foreign investment in Mexico."[26]

Despite the 1994–1995 economic crash, which might have led him to reevaluate the neoliberal economic model, President Zedillo (1994–2000) maintained Salinas's policies. To attract foreign investment and emphasize his commitment to the neoliberal model, in 1995 he privatized the rail system, satellite communications, and airport and seaport administration.[27]

Zedillo's unwavering support for neoliberalism paid dividends in that the economy grew at an average rate of 4.4 percent from 1997 to 2000 and foreign direct investment (FDI) came in at the highest rate in Mexico's history. During his last year in office, Zedillo wrote:

> What is clear from historical evidence is that in every case where a poor nation has significantly overcome its poverty, this has been achieved while engaging in production for export markets and opening itself to the influx of foreign goods, investment and technology—that is, by participating in globalization.[28]

DEBTS, FOREIGN AND DOMESTIC

> Heavy borrowings by some Western Hemisphere countries to support development have reached the point where annual repayments of interest and amortization absorb a large share of foreign exchange earnings . . . Many of the countries are, in effect, having to make new loans to get the foreign exchange to pay interest and amortization on old loans, and at higher interest rates.
>
> Nelson A. Rockefeller, 1969[29]

In the 1970s, a changed world of global finance presented Latin American policy makers with unprecedented opportunities. Banks were bulging with petrodollars they received from OPEC members. Bankers felt lending this money to Latin America was financially sound since borrowers there paid higher interest than in the United States. From the point of view of the borrowers, the loans were good politics since they satisfied constituencies without incurring the political costs normally associated with redistributive policies. The IMF and the World Bank encouraged such borrowing. Both borrowers and lenders assumed interest rates would remain low, so that debts would not become overly burdensome. Finally, as Citicorp's former chairman Walter Wriston optimistically noted, nations do not go bankrupt, so there was no reason to worry.[30]

As the events of 1968 made clear, Mexico urgently needed to address its social problems. With interest rates often negative after adjusting for inflation, President Echeverría (1970–1976) decided to borrow cheaply, grow the economy, and promote social welfare.[31]

During the latter part of his term, Echeverría became increasingly dependent on foreign loans, since private investment was declining. The old standby—exporting to finance development—no longer functioned since agriculture had been neglected and Mexico's excessively protected industry could not produce the amount of exports needed to finance development. During the last three years of Echeverría's term, the foreign debt increased at an annual rate of 44 percent. By the end of his term, Mexico was borrowing, not only to promote social welfare and finance development projects but to repay old loans and to compensate for capital flight, which totaled an estimated $4 billion in 1976.[32]

President López Portillo (1976–1982) increasingly borrowed from commercial banks, with their enormous deposits of petrodollars, rather than from multilateral agencies such as the World Bank. By the end of López Portillo's term, six large U.S. banking corporations—Citicorp, Bank of America, Manufacturers Hanover, Chase Manhattan, Chemical Bank, and J. P. Morgan—together had loaned Mexico $11.3 billion. Borrowing greatly increased in volume and was increasingly used to finance oil development. By 1982, Mexico's foreign debt was $90 billion, 450 percent above the level a decade earlier. Mexican policy makers felt that petroleum development would permit increased oil exports, which in turn could finance not only the righting of social wrongs but the repayment of loans.[33]

In August 1982, Mexico grabbed headlines around the world when it announced that it would suspend servicing its foreign debt since it did not have the dollars it was scheduled to pay. The underlying cause was again the inability of the classic import substitution model to generate exports needed to pay for imports. Rather than promoting exports, many of the billions borrowed during López Portillo's term were squandered in a non-competitive steel plant, a $6-billion nuclear power plant, new jets for the military, and payoffs to contractors and public officials. Mexico, which since the middle of the century had relied extensively on U.S. capital, found that the United States had begun to import capital to finance its fiscal and trade deficits. Finally, Mexico was increasingly finding itself caught up in the unforgiving world of high finance. Between 1977 and 1982, its foreign debt increased by 21.1 percent a year, while interest paid on the debt increased by 41.6 percent a year. Anyone familiar with geometric progressions or Ponzi schemes could realize such trends would not last long.[34]

The two events that finally ended this lending frenzy were a sharp decline in oil prices and a rise in interest rates as U.S. Federal Reserve Chairman Paul Volcker raised the prime interest rate to dampen inflation. In 1982, $9.182 billion in short-term Mexican debt came due. However, as the value of Mexico's collateral—which largely consisted of oil—declined, banks refused to make new loans.[35]

Rather than following the 1920s model of allowing bankers to form a committee to negotiate with the Mexican government to see what they could salvage, the United States government took the lead in arranging a bailout package for Mexico. Since it shared a long common border with Mexico, the United States did not want to risk destabilizing its southern neighbor. Nor did it want to put its heavily exposed banks at risk. Neither the U.S. nor the Mexican governments wanted to set off generalized financial panic. Thus loan payment schedules were stretched out and new loans were written.[36]

Following López Portillo's bank nationalization, the debt situation worsened since the government absorbed $8 billion of foreign debt owed by the banks. This debt resulted from foreign borrowing by individual banks. In addition, the nationalization caused Mexicans to distrust banks and send their money out of the country for safekeeping. By the end of López Portillo's term, capital flight totaled at least $60 billion.[37]

Under De la Madrid (1982–1988), Mexico adopted a severe IMF-recommended austerity program that included increasing taxes and drastically cutting government services and subsidies. Rather than consuming, Mexico produced goods and exported them to raise money to service the debt. Deferring social programs also provided money for debt services. Mexicans' standard of living plummeted since before the debt crisis Mexico had been consuming more than it produced and using loans to pay for this consumption. After the crisis began, Mexico consumed less than it produced and exported the surplus to pay for debt service.[38]

Between 1982 and 1988, payments on interest and principal exceeded new loans by $48.5 billion. By 1988, debt service absorbed 60 percent of the public-sector budget.[39]

The debt crisis weakened the PRI since the government could no longer afford traditional forms of patronage such as public works, housing, drainage, and water supplies. This decline in support for the PRI became clear to all after the 1988 presidential elections.

Throughout Latin America, nations were beset with debt problems similar to those that Mexico was facing. The result is now termed "the lost decade of the 1980s." During that decade, Latin America transferred more than $200 billion to the developed world. As a result of massive debt payments, the entire area lacked imports to keep factories producing, to build new infrastructure, and to finance social programs. Debt repayment not only pitted rich versus poor but also banks versus manufacturers, since Latin America transferred money to bankers rather than buying U.S. manufactured goods. Former World Bank Executive Director Morris Miller commented on this capital flow: "Not since the conquistadores plundered Latin America has the world experienced a flow in the direction we see today."[40]

At the beginning of the Salinas administration, the debt question cast a pall over Mexico. Even though interest and amortization paid during the De la Madrid administration totaled $60 billion, the foreign debt increased from $92 billion in 1982 to $100 billion in 1988. In 1988, interest payments on the debt totaled 17.7 percent of GDP. As analyst and later foreign minister Jorge G. Castañeda declared, "It isn't possible to make the Mexican economy function when 12 or 13 billion dollars a year are still being sent to service the debt."[41]

To head off a possible unilateral moratorium, to avoid the same violent protest against IMF-designed austerity measures that had racked Venezuela in February 1989, and to restart stalled economies, in March 1989 U.S. Treasury Secretary Nicolas Brady announced a plan to address the Third World debt problem. His proposal, known as the Brady Plan, called for partial forgiveness of debt if debtor nations adopted policies fostering foreign investment. To induce banks to accept "voluntary" reductions in the face value of their loans, the principal of the reduced debt was to be guaranteed by U.S. Treasury Bonds. As Harvard economist Jeffrey Sachs noted, the plan "implicitly recognizes that many debtor countries will be unable to repay their commercial bank debts in full, even if repayment is stretched over time."[42]

The Brady Plan offered banks a choice of reducing principal, reducing interest, or loaning additional funds to Mexico. Few bankers saw Mexico as a place in which to invest, so they accepted a reduction in interest or principal, thus lowering Mexico's indebtedness by $6.6 billion. This was not an act of altruism—more a taking stock of reality. As *Forbes* magazine noted: "Any scaling down of the Mexican debts is no act of sentimental generosity. It is based on a realization that the fates of the U.S. and Mexico are inextricably intermingled. A starving and seething Mexico would threaten U.S. security and would send millions of refugees fleeing across our borders."[43]

Salinas adopted other measures to reduce the foreign debt burden. Receipts from the privatization of government-owned corporations were used to lower the debt. A decline in U.S. interest rates favored Salinas by reducing service costs on Mexico's debt. Despite the Brady Plan, the use of privatization revenue (a one-shot event), and spending $137 billion on debt service between 1988 and 1995, Mexico's public foreign debt remained largely unchanged. In 1988 Mexico's debt stood at $100 billion, while in 1995 it totaled $101 billion. Reduced interests rates did lower debt service costs from 9.4 percent of GDP in 1990 to less than 2.9 percent in 1993, thus allowing an increase in public spending for social services.[44]

Revenue from privatizations, direct foreign investment, remittances from Mexicans working abroad, and oil sales allowed the Zedillo administration (1994–2000) to pay down the debt from $101 billion in 1995 to $85 billion in 2000. As a result of lower interest rates and economic growth, debt service declined from 40.1 percent of export earnings to 20.8 percent during these same years. Nonetheless, service costs—$13.3 billion in 1999 alone—of the still massive foreign debt formed a persisting drag on the economy.[45]

Under President Fox (2000–2006), Mexico's foreign public debt steadily declined. By early 2006, it had reached $53 billion, thanks to repayment based on a favorable combination of low interest rates, high oil prices, direct foreign investment, and soaring remittances from Mexicans working in the United States. In August 2006, the government announced it was reducing the foreign debt by issuing $15.6 billion worth of peso-denominated bonds. The revenue from the bond sale reduced the public foreign debt to only $37.9 billion, or 4.9 percent of GDP. Shifting debt from foreign debt to domestic debt avoided potential problems with interest-rate increases in world markets.[46]

While Mexico has been largely successful in ridding itself of the burden of foreign public debt, it has traded that for another insidious burden—domestic debt. The domestic debt—pesos owed by the government to Mexicans—shot up during the De la Madrid administration since foreign loans to finance government deficits were no longer available. The current fortunes of some of Mexico's richest people, including telephone magnate Carlos Slim, can be traced back to the exorbitant interest rates paid to holders of the domestic debt. The interest rate on this debt reached as much as 56 percent, causing domestic debt service to be more expensive than foreign debt service.[47]

Under President Zedillo (1994–2000), the internal debt rose to almost $70 billion in dollar terms. During the Fox administration, the domestic debt reached the peso equivalent of $198.5 billion, or 25 percent of GDP. While the domestic debt draws much less notice than foreign debt, it is still a powerful force in the Mexican economy. In the first half of 2006, for example, the federal government spent almost 125 billion pesos on internal debt services, a sum that was 138.5 percent greater than what it spent on its twenty major social programs. Increasingly Mexican government finance resembled the early nineteenth century when the *agiotistas* held sway and impoverished the nation. In the nineteenth century, there were few attractive tax sources in a poorly monetized economy. By the twenty-first century, the problem was a lack of political will to raise taxes, not a lack of potential tax sources.[48]

PRIVATIZATION

Privatization came to be seen almost as a cure-all here . . .

Sam Dillon, 1997[49]

During the Golden Age of the Mexican boom, 1954–1973, politicians considered that intervening in markets would assure that benefits of the bonanza would reach broad elements of society and thus keep the incumbents in power. They also felt that the government should retain ownership of some industries, such as the oil industry, to maintain economic sovereignty. Other rationales for government ownership included providing services the private sector was unlikely to provide, such as rural electrification, and services that were highly subsidized, such as Mexico City's subway system.[50]

The decision to privatize many government-owned corporations resulted from foreign pressure and dissatisfaction with the performance of these companies. Although they were initially rationalized as providing economic benefits to society, many government-owned corporations came to be perceived as overly costly, inefficient, and corrupt.[51]

President De la Madrid, who initiated the drive to privatize some 1,156 government-owned corporations, declared, "Public enterprises must be profitable and must not constitute a burden for the people of Mexico who have so many needs which we have not been able to attend to because of a lack of resources." He also felt that transferring enterprises to the private sector would allow the new owners to provide capital, which the government lacked, to modernize the enterprises being sold.[52]

The privatization of the Mexican rail system was one of the most successful transfers of enterprises out of the public sector. The government rail company, Nacionales de México, concentrated on moving coal and minerals and was more noted for paying its bloated workforce overtime than for on-time deliveries. The inefficient service required constant government subsidies. Mexican businesses that were forced to rely on the railroad suffered vis-a-vis their foreign competitors due to the poor quality of service.[53]

Within a decade of privatization, membership in the rail workers union fell from 90,000 to 36,000. After the privatization, the new rail owners diversified into transporting chemicals, autos, auto parts, and steel products. They benefited from the U.S. refusal to honor the NAFTA provisions that would have allowed Mexican trucks into the U.S. interior. The privatized railroads increased their share of Mexican cargo carried from 18 percent in 1997 to 26 percent in 2007. Since the volume of Mexican freight increased during this period, that represented nearly doubling the tonnage hauled. During the Fox administration, private investors facilitated this expansion by plowing $22 billion into upgrading the rail system.[54]

Mexico's experience with privatizing the government-owned phone company Teléfonos de México (Telmex) has not been as positive. Carlos Slim and two associates borrowed money to acquire Telmex. This purchase by Slim raised eyebrows since he was a friend and business associate of Carlos Salinas, during whose presidency Telmex was privatized. Not only was Slim allowed to acquire Telmex at a bargain price but he received a six-year monopoly for fixed-line telephone service after the privatization.[55]

By the time its legal monopoly expired, Telmex controlled such a large portion of telephone communication that it was very difficult for competitors to challenge it. In 2007, Slim's companies controlled 92 percent of fixed-line phones and 73 percent of cell phones. Telmex's annual pre-tax earnings exceeded $6 billion—more than its original acquisition price.[56]

The quasi-monopoly Slim's company enjoys came at a high cost to Mexico. In 2000, Mexican phone rates were nearly twice the OECD average. Telmex uses its enormous financial resources to fend off regulatory orders that would level the playing field for other carriers. The Fox (2000–2006) administration failed to stimulate competition in telecommunications, which is not surprising, since Fox's Telecommunications Minster was Pedro Cerisola, a former Telmex manager. As *Wall Street Journal* columnist Mary Anastasia O'Grady wrote, "Mexican growth has borne the cost of Mr. Slim's privilege."[57]

The Salinas administration decided to grant the private sector $14 billion in road-building concessions, thus lifting much of the infrastructure development burden from the cash-strapped government. Thanks to these concessions some 3,000 miles of toll roads were built during his administration. The most spectacular of these is the Highway of the Sun, which extends 160 miles from Cuernavaca to Acapulco.[58]

The newly built private toll road system immediately ran into trouble since, despite its being in the private sector, many of the crucial decisions, such as location of right of way and length of concession, were determined by the government. Contractors did shoddy work on the assumption that, given the short duration of the concession, someone else would absorb the inevitable repair costs. Since concessions were short in duration, tolls were set well above those in other nations for a similar travel distance. The toll on the Acapulco highway, for example, was $75. When the 1994 economic crisis hit, many of the private road concessionaires tottered on the verge of bankruptcy. To prevent this and keep the roads open, the government assumed $14 billion worth of highway concessionaires' debts. In 2006, to add insult to injury, it became apparent that the Highway of the Sun was so shoddily built that it would require $120 million of reconstruction to keep it in service.[59]

The privatization of the banking system attracted more attention than any other privatization and ultimately cost the government more than the receipts from all other privatizations combined. The government netted $12 billion from the sale of the banks to Mexican financiers and industrialists —foreigners were excluded. This exclusion kept banking in Mexican hands (for a few years), but placed the system in the hands of people without banking experience. As then senator (and later Mexico City mayor) Marcelo Ebrard commented:

> There was very little transparency in the sale of the banks. The purchases were excessively leveraged and the prices too high. In addition, individual buyers and groups—we now know—were allowed to buy even though they had dubious pasts and possessed fortunes of questionable origins.[60]

Once the new bank owners assumed control, they engaged in a sprint to increase market share with little or no risk analysis. After the 1994–1995 economic crisis, when interest rates soared to more than 100 percent, most ordinary debtors were unable to repay loans. To stave off a bank collapse, FOBAPROA (Bank Savings Protection Fund), a government agency analogous to the U.S. Federal Deposit Insurance Corporation (FDIC), stepped in to buy up bad loans and thus keep the banks solvent.[61]

It soon became apparent that the newly privatized banks had operated with virtually no regulatory supervision. In addition to simply loaning money with little risk analysis, Mexico's new bankers made loans to other banks, relatives, phantom businesses, and most audaciously, even to themselves. Carlos Cabal Peniche, who bought two of the privatized banks, later fled the country accused of illegally lending himself $700 million. Financing for the multimillion-dollar campaign to elect Roberto Madrazo as the governor of Tabasco in 1994 came from Cabal Peniche and another banker, Jorge Lankenau.[62]

The cost of the bank bailout eventually reached $150 billion. Since FOBAPROA did not have sufficient resources to take on this debt, in a highly controversial move the bad bank loans were assumed as debt by the federal government. This move, which was widely seen as the government bailing out insider cronies while ignoring pressing needs of the average citizen, was so unpopular that it is often cited as one of the reasons the PRI was voted out of office in 2000.[63]

Mexico continues to be affected by the bank bailout. Mismanagement by inexperienced bankers left the entire banking system weakened. To recapitalize the financial sector, foreigners were allowed to purchase Mexican-owned banks. By 2006, all but one of the eighteen banks privatized by Salinas were in the hands of foreign corporations—a greater degree of foreign control than that found in any other Latin American country. Even then bank lending was far from robust. As a percentage of GDP, banks operating in Mexico provided productive credit at the level of Haitian and Nigerian banks. As Nobel prize-winning economist Joseph Stiglitz commented, "It was very costly for Mexico to have sold banks to foreigners since they focus on large firms, which assures that they will be repaid, and avoid small and medium firms."[64]

Privatized companies that were subject to competition—such as Mexico's railroads—performed the best. Their worst performance was in cosseted sectors, such as banks, telephones, and highways, where there was no direct competition. Mexico also found that privatized companies that enjoyed monopolies, such as Telmex, or duopolies, such as Televisa and TV Azteca, effectively used their economic muscle in the political arena to protect themselves from competition. Economist Ha-Joon Chang summarized the lessons on privatization learned by nations around the world:

> When privatizing, care must be taken to sell the right enterprise at the right price to the right buyer, and to subject the enterprise to the right regulatory regime thereafter—if this is not done, privatization is not likely to work, even in industries that do not naturally favor state ownership.[65]

An undeniable cost of Mexican privatizing has been job loss. Labor need not lose in privatization, particularly if authorities pay attention to easing the social cost of unemployment through adequate severance pay, unemployment benefits, retraining, and job-search assistance. Unfortunately for Mexican workers, most of those who lost jobs due to privatization do not enjoy such benefits.[66]

OIL

> In terms of national identity, oil is, for better or for worse, in Mexico's genes. The mere suggestion of a sell-off provokes a cacophony of vehement public resistance that sends neoliberals scampering for cover. Consensus for privatization is not even on the horizon.
>
> Simon Cahill, 2001[67]

During the Echeverría administration (1970–1976), the "Generation of '38" still remained influential. These engineers, technicians, and managers who answered the call to manage the newly formed Pemex during the Cárdenas administration (1934–1940) felt that Mexican oil should be consumed domestically and provided at low cost to stimulate the economy.[68]

Under the influence of these men, between 1938 and 1973 Mexico nearly ceased exporting oil. Through the 1960s, Pemex continued to rely on fields its private forebears had discovered in the Golden Lane—the string of fields along Mexico's east coast. Up until 1973, low oil prices on the world market provided little incentive to increase production capacity and export. Pemex management never considered the company to be in competition with foreign oil companies, so the high costs associated with meeting domestic energy demand were not viewed with concern.[69]

Two events caused Pemex to abandon its almost static post-Cárdenas operational mode. The first was the first overall petroleum trade deficit registered by Pemex, as Mexico's demand for oil exceeded production in 1970. The second event was the initial OPEC-induced oil price increase of 1973, which caused Mexico's oil import bill to rise to $800 million a year.[70]

As a result of these events, Echeverría launched a $1.4 billion program to locate new oil reserves and thus ensure oil self-sufficiency. This effort resulted in the discovery of the massive Reforma field on the border between Tabasco and Chiapas. An even larger field was located in the Gulf of Campeche, a hundred miles off the Yucatán Peninsula. This field was named for Juan Cantarell, a fisherman who spotted oil slicks around his dinghy and reported them to Pemex.[71]

Echeverría's oil exploration program was so successful that by 1974 Mexico was able to not only meet its domestic needs but to begin exporting oil. The following year Mexican oil production exceeded the record set by foreign firms in 1921. Since it appeared that Pemex had found sufficient oil, exploration was scaled back, as is indicated by the number of exploratory wells decreasing from 143 in 1972 to seventy-nine in 1976.[72]

The technicians managing Pemex were reluctant to publicize the new finds, feeling they would lead to an undesirable emphasis on exports. Echeverría apparently shared the same reservations about exporting oil, noting in his last state of the nation address, "Exhaustive and irresponsible exploitation of our petroleum wealth, essential for the maintenance of Mexico's independent development, is dangerous and unjustified."[73]

President López Portillo (1976–1982) threw caution to the winds and undertook a massive expansion of oil production and export in response to the domestic economic crisis and high prices on the international oil market. He appointed as Pemex's director general Jorge Díaz Serrano, a firm believer in exploring for new fields and expanding Pemex at breakneck speed. Díaz Serrano made the sidelining of the "Generation of '38" crystal clear in a 1977 speech:

> Mexico has oil and Pemex can generate income sufficient to resolve current economic problems . . . It would be folly not to export as long as we have the ability to do so. A failure to export would make integral development more difficult and would trap our economy in a vicious cycle caused by insufficient financial resources.[74]

During the López Portillo administration, Díaz Serrano created a virtual state within a state as he dealt directly with the president on financial matters. He became the second most important person in Mexico, traveling as if he were foreign minister, negotiating trade agreements as if he were commerce minister, and securing international loans as if he were finance minister. During his glory days, Díaz Serrano was frequently mentioned as a possible successor to López Portillo.[75]

International bankers, who felt oil collateralized their loans, willingly financed not only petroleum development but also López Portillo's grandiose development schemes. The oil-induced boom produced enormous profits for Mexican entrepreneurs, including former politicians turned businessmen who contracted with the state. Politicians remaining in government exchanged contracts for commissions. Foreign corporations also shared in the bounty. In 1977, Brown & Root, a division of Halliburton, received a $500 million contract to organize engineering work, purchase production platforms, and build pipelines and shore-based facilities to service oilfields in the Gulf of Campeche. Little attention was paid to rampant corruption and mismanagement, since there appeared to be enough wealth not only to develop the country but also to line pockets.[76]

Increases in oil production exceeded even the ambitious goals set by the López Portillo administration. Between 1977 and 1982, daily production increased from 0.953 million barrels to 2.242 million barrels. To pay for developing oil production facilities and other projects, exports soared from 0.153 million barrels a day to 1.105 million during the same period. In 1981, oil export earnings totaled $15 billion. Petroleum and derivatives constituted only 16.8 percent of Mexico's exports by value in 1976, while by 1981 that figure had leaped to 74.3 percent. In 1981, Mexico became the world's fourth largest oil producer. In his 1978 state of the nation address, the president declared, "For the first time in our history, we will have the opportunity to enjoy financial self-determination."[77]

A few disquieting trends were almost lost in the chorus praising oil development. Given the amount of money invested, relatively few jobs were created in the highly capital-intensive oil industry. Much of the wealth was dissipated, since as oil-industry expert George Grayson noted, oil workers "demonstrated an unusual talent for enriching themselves and their organization from the national patrimony." As had been the case with Venezuela and Nigeria, which had also undergone rapid oil-induced growth, imports flooded in and income distribution worsened. Inflation associated with the boom, as well as government neglect, undermined other exports. Between 1977 and 1981, manufactured goods declined from 43.3 percent to 14.5 percent of exports, and agricultural products similarly declined from 27.9 to 7.5 percent of exports.[78]

Well before the rest of Mexico awoke from its oil-induced stupor, Heberto Castillo, an engineer who had been jailed for his support of the 1968 student movement, emerged as Mexico's foremost critic of rapid oil development. He presciently warned of reserves becoming exhausted within decades. Mexico, he observed, was becoming increasingly dependent on oil exports to the United States and on food imports from that country, which created vulnerability to U.S. political pressure. Castillo declared the decision to rapidly exploit and export oil was a capitulation to U.S. interests that resulted in Mexican natural resources being sold off cheaply for short-term benefit to the detriment of Mexico's long-term needs. Given his numerous books and articles in the newsweekly *Proceso*, his views were widely disseminated, though little heeded.[79]

At the national level, Castillo's was almost a lone voice questioning the course of energy development. At the local level, his solo voice was accompanied by a chorus of aggrieved peasants and fishermen. Pemex drilled wells, built roads, laid pipelines, constructed petrochemical complexes, dredged rivers, and filled lagoons at breakneck speed with little consideration for the environment. Contamination from this activity found its way onto fields and into wells, rivers, and coastal fishing grounds. Thus unlike the United States, where having oil on one's land was a stroke of luck, for Tabasco peasants the presence of oil was a curse.[80]

Environmental damage was not confined to Tabasco. In June 1979, a high-pressure well in the Gulf of Campeche known as Ixtoc-1 blew out and caught fire. Oil spewed into the sea at the rate of 30,000 barrels a day—the worst peacetime oil spill ever. For 281 days, oil gushing into the Gulf contaminated not only the coast of Tabasco but also Texas beaches. It cost Pemex $50 million to extinguish the fire, not to mention the value of the lost oil. Castillo charged, "The accident is characteristic of a wrong-headed policy to produce as much oil as possible as quickly as possible, which is in U.S. rather than Mexican interests."[81]

The year 1982 marked the end of the Golden Age of Mexican oil. After the 1982 debt crisis, oil was no longer viewed as the key to developing the economy—that task was assigned to the private sector. Rather, oil export revenues defrayed the costs of foreign debt service and government operating expenses. The amount of annual government investment in the oil industry declined from $9 billion in 1981 to $2–3 billion annually after the 1982 debt crisis. As manufactured exports increased, oil declined from 74.8 percent of exports in 1983 to 43.0 percent in 1987.[82]

When the question of privatizing Pemex arose, President Salinas (1988–1994) paid homage to Mexican nationalism, declaring: "The constitutional requirements will remain as they are. They have to do with our history, with our sense of being." At the same time, Pemex relied heavily on U.S. suppliers of oil production equipment and exploration and drilling services. The United States also consumed most of Mexico's oil exports. Much of the revenue from these exports never left the United States—it was simply transferred to U.S. banks to service the foreign debt. Historian Lorenzo Meyer commented: "Although the oil is formally ours, half of it goes out just to pay the foreign debt. What is the difference between the situation now and before March 1938?"[83]

The oil workers union typified the worst of Mexican trade unionism in that office holders became extremely wealthy and resorted to violence—including multiple murders—to maintain their positions. Rather than confront the power of the union, between 1981 and 1989 the government allowed the number of Pemex employees to increase from 122,000 to 172,900 even as exploration and production declined. In referring to oil worker head Joaquín Hernández Galicia, Grayson declared, "The crude Machiavellian labour chief and his toadies gripped Pemex with a stranglehold that rivalled eastern Europe's domination by Communist party bosses."[84]

Salinas's spectacular arrest of Hernández Galicia and thirty-four other oil union leaders in January 1989 reduced union power and made possible a reduction in the number of oil workers. By 1992, Pemex employment had declined to 136,000. This produced substantial savings since oil workers enjoyed high wages and a veritable treasure of medical, educational, and housing benefits, as well as lucrative business opportunities. With Hernández Galicia out of power, various costly provisions of the labor contract, such as hiring Pemex union members for all oil-related construction work, were repealed. In addition, for the first time prospective Pemex employees were forced to meet educational standards and pass aptitude tests. A younger generation of technically trained managers was brought in.[85]

The Zedillo (1994–2000) administration sought to increase production and to operate Pemex in a more efficient manner. Adrián Lajous—a British-educated economist whom Zedillo appointed to manage Pemex—declared that the company could best serve Mexico by being an efficient oil producer—not just a job producer. Thanks to increased investment in exploration, oil production increased from 3.07 million barrels a day in 1994 to 3.45 million in 2000. Zedillo was less successful in making Pemex an efficient producer. In 2000, Grayson observed that the company was burdened with "enclaves of corruption, a peso-hemorrhaging petrochemical division, an archaic tax regime, a tangle of red tape, and the huge expense of health, educational and recreational programs provided to its bloated work force."[86]

During the Fox administration, production increased—a result of budgeting between $10 and $12 billion annually for oil and gas exploration and production. These investments paid off as production rose from 3.45 million barrels a day in 2000 to a record 3.89 million barrels a day in 2004.[87]

Despite having reached record production levels during the Fox administration, Mexico is in the same situation as the United States—it is running out of oil. This is not surprising since U.S. production, which began in the late nineteenth century, began its decline in 1970, as its oil fields became exhausted. Mexican oil development, which followed U.S. oil development by roughly thirty-five years, now faces a similar decline. Production started down from its peak in 2004, dropping well below 3.0 million barrels a day in 2009.[88]

At the end of the Fox administration, new discoveries were replacing only 10 percent of oil extraction. A 2008 estimate by independent examiners declared that Mexican reserves were only sufficient for 6.6 years of production.[89]

A possible replacement for Pemex's declining fields is deep-water production in the Gulf of Mexico. Even if such production is feasible, it is a very costly, prolonged process to bring such fields to production. Little consideration has been paid to the possibility that Mexico has passed its oil production peak, and that it should focus not on revitalizing Pemex but on developing alternative energy sources.[90]

Declining Mexican oil production is important for both Mexico and the United States. Not only is oil a major Mexican energy source but it finances roughly a third of government operations. As a major oil supplier Mexico is of strategic importance to the United States. Between 2005 and 2008, reflecting declining production and rising domestic demand, Mexico slipped from being the second most important U.S. oil supplier (behind Canada) to fourth largest (behind not only Canada but also Saudi Arabia and Venezuela). This is especially significant since, as Venezuela becomes less reliable as a supplier, declining Mexican production makes the United States more reliant on Middle Eastern and African oil.[91]

Another problem faced by Pemex is the government's over-reliance on the company as a cash cow. In 2006, Pemex sales exceeded $100 billion while its tax burden was $79 billion. The resulting lack of operating capital forced the company to borrow in order to pay for exploration and construction of new facilities. Energy expert David Shields calculated the total Pemex debt, including large unfunded pension liabilities, at $85.2 billion. Since so much of its income leaves the company in the form of taxes, Pemex has not had sufficient capital to develop refineries. As a result, by 2008 Mexico was importing $12 billion worth of gasoline and $15 billion worth of petrochemicals annually. Due to a lack of funds for maintenance, many Pemex pipelines and other facilities have deteriorated, causing accidents and spills. In 2005, the 700 leaks in Pemex pipelines resulted in $100 million in damages. Pemex was responsible for 57 percent of Mexico's environmental emergencies.[92]

For political reasons, the government has continued to subsidize the cost of gasoline and diesel—a boon to affluent auto owners. In 2008, this subsidy reached $19.2 billion, compared to the $440 million in food subsidies.[93]

A final cloud on Pemex's horizon is its bloated work force. Each Pemex worker produces only eighty-seven barrels of oil a day, compared to 195 for Venezuela's state-owned oil company and 300 for the private Royal Dutch Shell. In addition, theft of gasoline is estimated to cost Pemex more than $1 billion a year. As a result of its high personnel costs, Pemex transfers less wealth to the rest of society.[94]

THE AUTO INDUSTRY

During the 1970s, there were so many companies producing cars for the small Mexican market that they were unable to achieve economies of scale. Much decision-making was by government decree. These decrees limited the amount of imported components that could be included in cars manufactured in Mexico and attempted to force auto manufacturers to export at least as much as they imported. As a result of this pressure to export, by 1980 many "Made in USA" cars contained Mexican-built engines, springs, windshields, and transmissions.[95]

In addition to being highly regulated by government decrees, auto makers were saddled with antiquated machinery, low volume, and erratic quality. In 1981, the production of more than 600,000 vehicles resulted in a trade deficit of $1.548 billion, or 47 percent of Mexico's total trade deficit. That year less than 3 percent of Mexican production was exported.[96]

During the De la Madrid administration (1982–1988), the focus of the automobile industry shifted from the domestic market to the export market. This resulted from: 1) Mexicans by and large being unable to afford new cars after the 1982 economic crisis, 2) sharply increased government pressure to export in order to earn money to service the debt, and 3) U.S. auto makers facing increased foreign competition in their home market and turning to Mexico to lower labor costs.

As a result of this shift, the auto industry decentralized and moved north. Establishing plants in northern Mexico not only lowered the cost of shipping finished vehicles to the United States but also allowed plants to escape the combative unions found in central Mexico. Auto makers typically selected plant locations in areas where they could hire workers without previous factory or union experience. Once the new plants were established, companies went to great pains to prevent horizontal links between workers in the northern plants and workers from the long-established plants in central Mexico.[97]

In the 1980s, while the domestic market languished, auto parts and finished vehicles became the most dynamic export sector. Annual exports of finished vehicles rose to 278,558 by 1990, a 2000 percent increase over 1981. By 1989, largely as a result of exports, auto production surpassed the 1981 level. This increase in exports reflected both high worker productivity and high vehicle quality. These exports were highly profitable as a result of low wages, a well trained, highly motivated workforce, subsidies, tax exemptions, and government-funded infrastructure development. This profitability in turn attracted more investment, which allowed increased exports.[98]

As part of this move to the north, in 1986, Ford opened a $500-million plant in Hermosillo, Sonora. The choice of plant location reflected government financial and infrastructure support as well as its proximity to the U.S. border and the port of Guaymas. The Hermosillo plant employed cutting-edge technology and a high degree of automation, including more than one hundred programmable robots. By 1990, it had attained the highest quality levels of any auto plant in North America. Productivity and profitability remained high due to a flexible work regime, which allowed employee work assignments to be modified according to the plant's needs.[99]

Even before NAFTA came into effect, Mexican auto production was booming. Between 1988 and 1994, domestic car and truck sales increased from 330,965 to 522,350, while exports rose from 174,246 to 575,031.[100]

As a result of NAFTA, parts and new vehicles produced in any NAFTA nation can be shipped to another NAFTA nation without tariffs. Auto plants located in Mexico could specialize in the production of a limited number of models, some of which were sold domestically and some of which were exported. Producers in Mexico could offer Mexican buyers a complete line of their products, since they were free to import from Canada and the United States models not produced in Mexico. As a result of this specialization, models such as VW's New Beetle and the PT Cruiser are made exclusively in Mexico and exported.

Given robust economies in both Mexico and the United States, the Mexican auto sector boomed. New investment was attracted by economic stability, low interest rates, and a growing domestic market. By the late 1990s, the auto industry accounted for more than 22 percent of manufactured exports, and vehicles and auto parts formed the largest single component of NAFTA trade. In 2001, exports of autos and auto parts generated more foreign exchange than either tourism or oil exports.[101]

For decades the U.S. Big Three—Chrysler, Ford, and GM—dominated Mexican auto production. In 2001, they built 1.08 million of the 1.82 million vehicles produced in Mexico. Through 2003, General Motors remained the largest private corporation in Mexico as measured by sales. However, as has occurred in the United States, the Big Three began losing market share to Japanese producers, which in 2007 grabbed a record 35 percent of the Mexican market, up from 23 percent in 2000.[102]

Mexico's domestic auto market changed radically as a result of NAFTA. The number of auto makers in Mexico soared, further expanding consumer choice. The new entrants include Nissan, Honda, and BMW. The 2004 signing of a Japan–Mexico free trade accord facilitated the arrival of Japanese brands such as Mazda and Suzuki, yielding a total of thirty-seven brands being offered in Mexico.[103]

During the early Fox administration (2000–2006), the auto industry went into a slump as both the U.S. and Mexican economies lost dynamism. However, after 2004 the industry rebounded, and in 2006, 2007 and 2008 record numbers of vehicles were produced. Mexico benefited from manufacturers locating much of their capacity to manufacture compacts in Mexico—cars that were suddenly in high demand as U.S. fuel prices increased. In addition, Ford, GM, and Daimler Chrysler shifted production to Mexico to reduce labor costs. Finally, there was increased investment in the auto sector, which responded to Mexico's proximity to the U.S. market, low wages, and a stable peso.[104]

The auto sector plays a crucial role in the Mexican economy, directly employing half a million people. It accounts for roughly 3 percent of GDP, 14 percent of manufacturing output, 23 percent of exports (generating $30 billion in revenue), and 6 percent of FDI.[105]

The auto sector is close to the NAFTA ideal in that auto plants in each of the three signatory nations specialize and achieve economies of scale. Engines and transmissions are often produced in one nation and incorporated into vehicles assembled elsewhere. Ford pickups, for example, were assembled in Cuautitlán, just north of Mexico City, with engines coming from Windsor, Ontario, and transmissions from Livonia, Michigan. Thanks to NAFTA rules of origin for parts, many European and Asian parts manufacturers have relocated to Mexico. In Puebla, seventy parts manufacturers have clustered around the sprawling Volkswagen factory.[106]

There are, however, shortcomings to the auto boom. Despite having productivity as high as or even higher than workers doing the same work in the U.S. and Canada, Mexican auto workers are paid only $8–10 a hour, as opposed to $60 for unionized U.S. auto workers. This limits the amount of stimulus to the domestic market that autoworkers' wages can provide. The huge boom in the auto industry also diverted investment away from other forms of transportation, an important consideration since only 20 percent of Mexicans own a car. Government plans to stimulate the auto industry are apparently oblivious to falling oil production. The minority of car owners produce pollution that all—car owners and the car-free alike—must endure. Relying so heavily on exporting to the U.S. market has left the Mexican auto industry vulnerable to U.S. recession. This was indicated by light vehicle production during the first half of 2009 being 42.9 percent below the 2008 figure.[107]

THE MAQUILADORA

> Mexico remains trapped as a link in the transnational production process which adds little value and which transfers little advanced technology.
>
> David Ibarra, 2008[108]

In recent decades, Mexican manufacturing plants known as maquiladoras have become an integral part of the economy. *Maquila* originally meant the share of flour the mill owner retained for milling a farmer's grain. Unlike, say, the oil or auto industries, maquiladoras produce a wide variety of products including auto parts, computers, electronics, and apparel.

The maquiladora, as originally envisioned, was a plant that would assemble or process elements from another country, typically the United States, and then export them for final finishing and sale. The legal basis of the maquiladora was a 1964 Mexican law that allowed foreign owners to import components and machinery duty-free and to own 100 percent of the production facility. Mexican law also allowed an unlimited number of visas for maquiladora management and technical personal.

Even though the maquiladora was created by Mexican law, its growth depended on a provision of the U.S. tariff code that provided that only the value added in Mexico was subject to duty when assembled components were shipped back to the United States. Typically, this value added consisted of labor costs and overheads. The majority of the value, the original components, was duty-free if the components originated in the United States.

In addition to the provisions of U.S. and Mexican law, the growth of the maquiladora was based on: 1) low wages in Mexico, 2) high-quality labor, 3) Mexican government subsidies to border areas, 4) low transport costs to the United States, 5) U.S. managers being able to live on the U.S. side of the border and work in Mexico, 6) proximity to the home office, 7) low political risk, and 8) lax enforcement of labor and environmental regulations.[109]

Even though the maquiladora was initially rationalized as a source of alternative employment for *bracero* farm labor, it never met this goal since early maquiladora employees were overwhelmingly women. In 1965, there were only twelve maquiladoras with 3,000 employees. The industry expanded slowly through 1982. This slow growth was largely due to the relatively high wages Mexican workers received. In 1982, they received \$1.69 an hour, more than workers in Hong Kong or Taiwan earned.[110]

The key to transforming the maquiladora from relative obscurity to being a major factor in U.S.–Mexican economic relations was the 1982 devaluation of the peso. That drastically reduced the cost of maquiladora labor, as measured in U.S. dollars. Wages sunk as low as \$0.43 an hour in 1987. Manufacturers rushed in, and maquiladora employment increased from 127,048 to 457,000 between 1982 and 1990. The 262.5 percent growth in maquiladora employment between 1980 and 1989 is especially striking when compared to the 10.9 percent decrease in other Mexican manufacturing jobs during this period.[111]

In the early 1990s, maquiladora growth declined as the U.S. economy became sluggish and maquiladora wages rose. However, after the 1994 peso devaluation, maquiladora employment once again soared as the dollar value of wages plummeted and a robust U.S. economy demanded ever more goods. Between 1994 and 2000, maquiladora employment rose from 465,261 to a record 1,338,970. Between 1980 and 2000, exports from maquiladoras increased from 15 percent of all exports to 50 percent.[112]

As managers learned that Mexican workers could perform not only simple assembly but also sophisticated operations, they brought in more capital-intensive production of electronics, computers, and auto parts. During the 1990s, a new generation of maquiladora plants involved transforming components, rather than just assembling them, and required higher skill levels of their workers.[113]

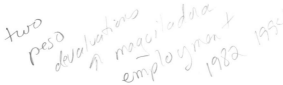

During the early Fox administration, maquiladora employment fell to 1.07 million as China began to flood the U.S. market with exports, the U.S. economy lost dynamism, and more than 600 maquiladora plants relocated to China. From a 2002 low, maquiladora employment rebounded in the latter part of the Fox administration. By 2006, as the U.S. economy expanded, maquiladora plants earned Mexico $16 billion in foreign currency, created 17 percent of industrial jobs, and accounted for more than 65 percent of industrial exports.[114]

Although the maquiladora has provided jobs to hundreds of thousands, it has also created serious problems. These problems largely flow from the combination of low wages, corporations successfully demanding that they remain virtually tax-free, and the mushrooming population on the Mexican side of the border. Historian Richard Sinkin commented on the result: "In some border locations—like Tijuana and Ciudad Juárez—the growth of the maquilas has overwhelmed the ability to provide adequate water, sewage disposal, electricity, roads, adequate housing for workers, and in some cases even workers themselves."[115]

Lax enforcement, or non-enforcement, of environmental regulations has led to a variety of environmental problems. There have been many documented cases of chemical discharges into waterways. Dumping toxics into the sewage system has been deemed Tijuana's primary environmental problem since sewage treatment plants are not equipped to remove such substances. In many cases, toxics have been illegally deposited in the desert outside cities where maquiladoras are located. Finally, massive amounts of toxic materials are sometimes left at abandoned maquiladora sites. Greenpeace México reported that at the abandoned Metales y Derivados site on the Otay Mesa outside Tijuana there were 6,000 to 10,000 tons of lead, cyanide, nickel, cadmium, and zinc. Environmental problems in the border area, where most maquiladoras are located, continued to deteriorate after NAFTA went into effect in 1994.[116]

The financial liberty of maquiladora operators contrasts sharply with tight restrictions on workers' freedom to form unions and choose leaders. Management has the support of the Mexican government in preventing the formation of independent unions. The usual union-busting tools are available to maquiladora managers, including government repression, strikebreakers, and the threat or the reality of relocation. When maquiladoras are established in new areas in central Mexico, they typically hire young women who have never held jobs before and thus are viewed as unlikely to press demands for effective union representation.[117]

While maquiladoras have provided jobs, they have failed to become integrated with the rest of the Mexican economy. Only 3.6 percent of the materials used in production are of Mexican origin. One reason for the small percentage of Mexican inputs, especially compared to Asian inputs in similar Asian operations, is that much long-established Mexican industry is located near the Valley of Mexico and thus cannot easily ship to maquiladoras. Those in charge of purchasing for maquiladoras often work in the United States and so are unaware of what is available in Mexico. Finally, many Mexican producers are unable to meet delivery times and international price and quality standards.[118]

TOURISM

> Forget cheap! That's the old Mexico. The new Mexico has fabulous hotels, great food and those same amazing beaches to sell and the prices are climbing to attract the wealthy tourists who can manage luxury surroundings.
>
> *MB*, 2000[119]

In 1970, roughly 2 million tourists visited Mexico, spending $1.4 billion. Since then Mexican tourism has benefited from the vast expansion of jet travel and from increased world affluence. In this context, Mexico has been able to take advantage of its natural strengths, which include 6,000 miles of coastline, a fine climate, and the world's sixth greatest biodiversity. Its diverse indigenous heritage, which ranges from Zapotec communities in Oaxaca to the Purépecha in Michoacán, forms an additional attraction.[120]

In 2008, tourism generated 2.7 million direct jobs. It is Mexico's third biggest foreign exchange earner, behind only oil and remittances as legal sources of foreign currency. In 2008, 1.96 million worked in the tourist industry and the record 22.6 million foreigners who visited Mexico brought in $10.8 billion.[121]

In contrast to the rest of the economy where the government has largely bowed out, the government plays a major role in promoting tourism. The most prominent example of this government role is Cancún, which in 1970 was an offshore jungle island along the remote coast of Quintana Roo. Fewer than 200 people lived in the lone hamlet in the area, Puerto Juárez, which was so isolated that it lacked electricity, telephone service, and water and sewer systems.[122]

The development of Cancún resulted from Banco de México officials deciding that in order to share in rapidly expanding international tourism by jet, Mexico would have to develop new tourist sites. Planners took an inventory of the Mexican coast and fed data on climate, water temperature, and beach conditions into a computer. The computer selected Cancún as the most desirable site. Government agencies then became in effect the governing power in Cancún. They dredged lagoons, expropriated and cleared land, and erected a complete city, with basic infrastructure, a golf course, and a central market.[123]

In 1975, a year after the first hotel opened, 99,500 tourists visited Cancún. In 1986 Cancún drew more tourists than Acapulco, and in 1989 it surpassed Mexico City to become Mexico's most popular foreign tourist destination. In 2004 2.3 million tourists visited Cancún.[124]

Cancún and its international airport spurred development on the coast south of Cancún down to the Mayan ruins of Tulum and offshore on the island of Cozumel—an area known as the Mayan Riviera. The number of hotel rooms in Cancún and the Mayan Riviera reached 60,000, making it one of the Caribbean's largest destinations. Jamaica, by comparison, has only about 17,000 hotel rooms. The state of Quintana Roo, which includes both Cancún and the Mayan Riviera, accounts for a third of Mexico's annual tourist receipts. Thanks to rapid tourist development, between 2000 and 2005, the state's 4.68 percent annual population growth exceeded that of any other Mexican state.[125]

The government continued to play a strong role in tourist development. Once Cancún was developed, Banco de México officials facilitated the development of four other major tourist destinations, Los Cabos and Loreto on the Baja California peninsula, Bahias de Huatulco in Oaxaca, and Ixtapa on the Pacific Coast near Acapulco. In 1986, Mexican tourism minister Antonio Enríquez Savignac stated the government rationale for developing these centers: "Our goals are threefold. We want to earn more foreign exchange, we want to create more jobs, and we want to develop the more isolated and remote regions of the republic." Los Cabos soon emerged as a major tourist center since it is only two hours by air from Los Angeles and offers a Jack Nicklaus-designed eighteen-hole golf course. In 2006, 2.7 million passengers deplaned at Los Cabos airport.[126]

Even though it was once rather simplistically referred to as the "industry without chimneys," tourism has its downsides, including what might be considered the original sin of Mexican tourism. In many locations such as Cancún and Huatulco, the government expropriated land from the local residents, provided at best meager compensation, and in subsequent development only offered them low-paid wage labor. Infrastructure was developed at government expense, and land was then turned over to large corporations, many of which were foreign.[127]

Since sewage treatment is expensive and provides no quick return on investment, tourists and the workers who serve them have fouled the waters in many locations, especially those located on bay-enclosed beaches such as Huatuclo. In 2003, the Special Federal Prosecutor's Office for Environmental Protection (PROFEPA) released a report that listed twenty-six beaches and coastal areas that it described as highly contaminated. Included in this list were several well-known Pacific resorts such as Acapulco, Zihuatanejo, and Puerto Vallarta.[128]

Relatively little tourist revenue finds its way into the hands of ordinary resort residents. As a result of low wages and intermittent employment, many people have no other choice than to live in the shantytowns that have formed around major destinations such as Acapulco and Cancún. Most tourist dollars flow to airlines and multinational hotel chains, not local service providers. Package travel deals, which include meals, make it difficult for local food providers to tap into the tourist trade. As journalist Marc Cooper observed, "Finding a small family-run Mexican *taquería* or *panadería*—a taco stand or traditional bakery—is much easier in downtown Los Angeles or Chicago than it is in Cancún."[129]

AGRICULTURE

By 1970, the agricultural boom following Mexico's agrarian reform had come to an end. Agriculture, which had accounted for roughly 20 percent of government investment between 1942 and 1956, received only 7 percent by the mid-1960s. Bank lending shifted from agriculture to industry. Declining prices for agricultural products—the result of deliberate government policy—transferred capital from agriculture to urban interests. During the 1970s, increases in grain prices continued to lag behind inflation.[130]

Mexico's agrarian reform, which conservatives continued to resent, was often blamed for the post-1960s stagnation in agriculture. However it was not agrarian reform per se that undermined agriculture. South Korea, Japan, and Taiwan all had post-Second World War agrarian reforms and subsequently enjoyed strong agricultural growth. Mexico's failure was to view agrarian reform as a never-ending process rather than as a single event, as the Asian reforms were. On-going, often demagogic, Mexican land reform measures led to rural unrest and made investors reluctant to invest in agriculture for fear of losing their capital. Due to agrarian reform regulations, extremely small ejido properties could not be consolidated into more productive units.

As Mexico's agricultural growth slowed and its population soared, Mexico lost its food self-sufficiency. During the 1970s, grain imports became so massive that they created costly bottlenecks in the rail system. In 1980, Mexico imported 12 million tons of grain.[131]

Since the 1960s, as is characteristic of nations becoming more affluent, Mexico experienced a sharp rise in cattle, hog, and poultry production as producers catered to the dietary tastes of the rapidly expanding middle class. The soaring demand for meat led to the conversion of cropland from producing wheat and corn to producing animal feed. In 1960, only 5 percent of cropland was used for animal feed, while by 1980, more than 23 percent was. This shift of domestic production to animal feed led to an increase in grain imports to feed people.[132]

Also beginning in the 1960s, winter vegetable exports soared. Between 1961 and 1968, their exports grew from 105,000 tons to 294,000 tons. Much of this export production came from Sinaloa, on the Pacific Coast, which has a comparative advantage over its main competition, south Florida. Florida experiences occasional freezes, while Sinaloa never does. Sinaloa also enjoys low-cost labor, government-financed irrigation works, and good rail transportation.[133]

Rather than being consumed directly, food was increasingly processed. This included long-distance transport and agro-industrial conversion to some product such as packaged breakfast cereal. To the economist, these trends were positive since with each stage of processing—canning, boxing, labeling, and transporting to vendor—more value was added. However, as many of these operations were mechanized, less labor was needed. In the Bajío, between 1960 and 1983, one million jobs were lost as exported fruits, broccoli, cauliflower, and other vegetables replaced corn.[134]

Under President De la Madrid (1982–1988), food self-sufficiency was abandoned as a goal. Policy makers decided to rely on the notion of comparative advantage, producing and exporting what Mexico could produce most efficiently and relying on imports to bridge gaps in food supply. Food henceforth was to be treated simply as another commodity.[135]

As a result, between 1982 and 1990, public spending on agriculture declined by 8 percent a year. This reflected government austerity following the 1982 debt crisis and the desire to bring market forces back into the agricultural sector. There was a abrupt unilateral opening of the Mexican market to agricultural imports. The reduction in government spending also reflected the view of neoliberal planners who felt that most small farmers were redundant due to their inability to compete in the marketplace. Farm policy in the 1980s, following the U.S. model, promoted farm consolidation and capital intensive monoculture. Not surprisingly, as the countryside was starved for funds, agricultural production increased by only 1.1 percent a year between 1980 and 1992, and imports of basic foods rose from 8.5 million tons in 1981 to 10 million tons in 1988. By 1992, per capita agricultural production was below that of 1965.[136]

Salinas further reduced government involvement in the agricultural sector. As a result, the area benefiting from government-subsidized credit declined from 23 million hectares in 1988 to fewer than 5 million by 1995. The Salinas administration also privatized the industries supplying inputs such as fertilizers and improved seeds. Since then, producers have had difficulty in obtaining high quality, competitively priced seeds and fertilizer.[137]

Salinas successfully promoted amending Article 27 of the constitution to allow *ejidatarios* to sell, rent, and mortgage ejido land. After some 250 million acres had been distributed during the course of the land reform, his administration declared there would be no further distribution of land.

Proponents of legalizing the sale of ejido land felt that such sales would allow the creation of larger, more efficient farming units that would attract capital that the ejido was unable to attract. In addition, private owners would be more willing to invest in their own land since they would no longer have to worry about the land being expropriated for the land reform. Salinas himself stated, "The reforms to Article 27 returned to peasants decision-making power in the *ejido* and ended massive state intervention in its internal life." Critics denounced these changes as counter-revolutionary and claimed they would further concentrate land in the hands of a few. In any case, the peasant movement and its intellectual allies were so weak that they were unable to effectively oppose the end of land reform.[138]

Many saw Salinas's reforms as marking the end of the ejido, which at the time of the 1992 reform constituted 52 percent of Mexican territory. Most ejidos, however, continued intact, highlighting their positive aspects. Their biggest success was contributing to eight decades of rural stability. The ejido also proved to be as productive as private farms of the same size, while at the same time giving dignity to generations of participating peasants. As environmental issues now loom larger, it is noteworthy that the ejido is more energy efficient, fosters biodiversity, and uses fewer chemical inputs. Ejidos and privately held small farms, since they rely more on manual labor and animal traction, have a positive energy output (as measured in kilocalories) while large units relying on mechanization and manufactured inputs have negative energy balances.[139]

A third shift in agricultural policy under Salinas was embodied in NAFTA, which facilitated tariff-free import of agricultural products. Many products, such as bananas and coffee, which are produced by only one NAFTA signatory—Mexico—were allowed into the U.S. tariff-free beginning in 1994. Other crops considered sensitive, such as corn and beans, remained protected by import quotas and tariffs for as long as fourteen years. Beginning in 2008, corn and beans could cross the U.S.–Mexico border without tariffs or quotas, just as manufactured goods did.[140]

Mexican planners felt that NAFTA would result in land, labor, and capital being shifted from corn to other crops, such as fruit and horticultural production, in which Mexico has a comparative advantage. Many displaced agricultural workers, it was assumed, would enter the labor market and be employed in jobs with higher productivity. Philip Martin, an agricultural economist at the University of California, Davis, commented: "We understood that the transition from corn to strawberries would not be smooth. But we did not think there would be almost no transition." Instead of switching to export crops, the farmers exported themselves.[141]

A few thousand large growers, roughly 5 percent of all producers exporting fruits, vegetables, and livestock, have found considerable success under NAFTA. Most of these farms are relatively large and are associated with foreign firms. Between 1994 and 2005, Mexican agricultural exports tripled to $8.3 billion.[142]

NAFTA has produced some not-so-welcome trends. Between 1982 and 2007, agricultural imports soared from $1.8 billion to $19.3 billion. Between 1993 and 2007, Mexican agricultural output increased by 1.5 percent annually. However, this growth was spotty. Grain and oilseed production plateaued at 30 million tons, the level reached at the beginning of the 1980s. The anticipated investment in agriculture never arrived. FDI in agriculture declined from 1.6 percent of all investment in 1990 to 0.02 percent in 2001. As investment has been directed to manufacturing exports and oil development, agriculture declined from 12 percent of GDP in 1970 to 6 percent in 2007.[143]

A major reason for this lack of investment and growth is that, as a result of NAFTA, Mexican agriculture must compete with U.S. agriculture, which enjoys fertile, well-watered soil, a temperate climate, and massive government subsidies. While commodity prices have fallen to international levels, Mexican farmers are saddled with expensive credit, machinery, and electricity, as well as high transportation costs as a result of poor highways. U.S. farmers have higher yields than their Mexican counterparts. U.S. corn farmers, for example, produce nine tons per hectare, while Mexicans produce only 2.9.[144]

The results of competing with U.S. agriculture are both social and economic. A study by the Carnegie Endowment found that in the decade after NAFTA took effect some 1.3 million small farms had been displaced by the flood of farm imports. Mexico became increasingly dependent on food imports from the United States. In 2008, 53 percent of the wheat Mexico consumed, 80 percent of the rice, and 27 percent of the corn were imported.[145]

Small corn growers, who produce a dietary mainstay that is regarded as a symbol of life itself, have been especially hard hit by the imports permitted under NAFTA. Three million corn producers suffered when the price of corn in Mexico plunged from $5 a bushel in 1995 to $1.80 in 2000 due to the opening of the market to international competition. Many corn producers had few other alternatives and thus were reluctant to give quit producing, even if the economics of growing corn were poor.[146]

The risk that comes with dependence on imported grain became apparent as the use of biofuels in the United States surged. Between 1993 and 2008, Mexican corn production increased from 18 million tons to a record 24 million tons. However, as there were increases in both population and meat consumption, the dependency on imports to feed both people and livestock increased. In addition, as almost 20 percent of the U.S. corn crop was devoted to producing ethanol, U.S. corn prices doubled within a year. Since Mexico imports so much U.S. corn, the increase in U.S. corn prices resulted in Mexican tortilla prices rising by more than 60 percent in some places. Speculators added to the price increase. Rather than the free market neoliberal planners had envisioned, at each stage of the food supply chain there is a very high degree of concentration that makes food prices ripe for speculation. Grupo Maseca, for example, controls 85 percent of the market for corn flour.[147]

This spike in tortilla prices threatened social stability since it is the dietary staple of Mexico's poor. To keep tortillas affordable, the government allowed the import of an additional 650,000 tons of corn above the 8 million tons imported in 2006. As ecologist Lester Brown commented, "In this world of high oil prices, supermarkets and service stations will compete in commodity markets for basic food commodities such as wheat, corn, soybeans, and sugarcane."[148]

UNSUSTAINABILITY

As regards the environment, the inadequacies of Mexican policies on water, forestry, land use, fisheries, alternative energy sources, public transportation, urban growth, regional

> development, and—not least important—population growth are becoming acute as these problems overwhelm the government's ability to address them . . . Air and water pollution, encroaching urbanization, and inadequate disposal of industrial and household waste continue unabated.
>
> Víctor Urquidi, 2003[149]

During the last forty years of the twentieth century, Mexico lost 30 percent of its forest and jungle and continues to lose between 600,000 and 800,000 hectares a year. Roughly 95 percent of this loss is due to the clearing of land for cattle raising or for poor peasants to farm.[150]

Erosion resulting from deforestation causes the loss of millions of tons of soil annually. In the Sierra Petatlán y Coyuca de Catatlán region in Guerrero, the erosion rate more than quadrupled as a result of deforestation. Denuded hillsides shed water much more quickly, and flood waters rise higher as river channels silt up. In 1999, after a week of storms in southeastern Mexico, at least 373 were confirmed dead from flooding. In 2007, massive flooding in Tabasco cost an estimated $3.1 billion. In addition to exacerbating flooding, deforestation results in lost biodiversity and huge releases of carbon dioxide. An estimated quarter of the world's carbon dioxide emissions result from forest clearing.[151]

In 2000, the value of Mexico's standing forests was 6.5 times the value of timber harvested. The value of standing timber results from trees mitigating flooding and evening out water flow. Despite forests playing this vital role, Mexico spends only a minuscule 0.11 percent of GDP to maintain forests. Given this minimal commitment to preservation, as the economy expanded under NAFTA there was, not surprisingly, a significant increase in deforestation.[152]

Roughly 66 percent of Mexico's land area shows some signs of degradation and 36 percent is classified as desertified—the most degraded. In addition, 35 percent of irrigated land has been abandoned a due to erosion or its being hopelessly contaminated. The amount of arable land in the Mixtec region of Oaxaca has been reduced by 70 percent due to erosion. The result is massive job loss and out-migration of the area's indigenous population.[153]

Mexican rivers are often contaminated by silt, raw sewage, and residue from the 15,000 tons of pesticide applied annually. Rivers are further abused by the extraction of water for irrigation and municipal use. One of the most abused rivers is the Lerma, which rises west of Mexico City. It is born in a weakened state since its headwaters are diverted to supply Mexico City. The Lerma later accumulates raw sewage, industrial waste, and silt from land that has been eroded due to overgrazing and illegal logging. It is further weakened by the extraction of irrigation water before eventually flowing into Lake Chapala, south of Guadalajara. The volume of the lake, which once covered 428 square miles, has been substantially reduced. This loss of volume results from the multiple demands on water in the Lake Chapala basin, including supplying the 5 million residents of Guadalajara.[154]

Mexicans rely on aquifers to supply water for irrigation and domestic use. Some 41 percent of this water is pumped from aquifers that are being depleted faster than they are being recharged. Each year the stock of water available in Mexican aquifers declines by eight cubic kilometers. Irrigation consumes 80 percent of this water, which is often supplied by the government at highly subsidized prices, so there is little incentive to conserve.[155]

As aquifers are exhausted, the need to import food is likely to rise. Global warming may also lead to the need for increased grain imports. According to one model, the percentage of Mexico's area suitable for unirrigated corn production will decline from 40.0 percent to 18.5 percent as a result of global warming. This would not be so worrisome if world per capita grain production were still increasing. However, production peaked in 1985 at 343 kilograms per capita and has been declining since.[156]

Mexico is not blameless in global warming, since hydrocarbons meet 80 percent of its energy needs. Even though it lags far behind the U.S. rate of 19.0 tons of annual carbon-dioxide emissions per capita, its rate of 3.97 tons per capita is increasing rapidly. Between 2000 and 2006 hydrocarbon emissions increased rapidly, as the demand for gasoline increased by 35 percent and for diesel by 21 percent. This demand increase was driven by heavy fuel subsidies and by massive road construction projects. In addition, by international standards Mexico uses energy inefficiently.[157]

Studies predict that global warming will have a particularly detrimental effect on Mexico. The severest impacts will be increased temperature in the north and northwest and reduced rainfall in this already arid area. Rising sea levels and more severe hurricanes are other negative effects. By one calculation, global warming could cost Mexico 30 percent of its GDP by 2100.[158]

NGOs have attempted to steer Mexico on a less environmentally destructive path. They have had some defeats and some victories. Their outstanding defeat was the failure to prevent the construction of the Laguna Verde nuclear power plant in Veracruz. One of their outstanding victories was blocking the construction by Mitsubishi of the world's largest salt factory on the Laguna de San Ignacio in Baja California. This protected natural area is the last untouched calving grounds for the California gray whale. A well-coordinated campaign against the salt works resulted in 750,000 letters arriving at Mitsubishi headquarters in Tokyo, a growing consumer boycott, and a coordinated alliance of fifty Mexican environmental groups that had solid foreign support. One letter in opposition to the project, signed by thirty-three scientists, including seven Nobel-prize winners, questioned trading the survival of the whale for the production of salt. The 1,000 residents of nearby of Punta Abreojos, which would have been overwhelmed by the project, joined the opposition to the salt works. After visiting the site and viewing the whales, President Zedillo declared, "Taking into account its national and world importance and its singularity, I have made the decision to instruct representatives of the Mexican government . . . to propose a permanent halt to the project."[159]

The government has set aside large areas for preservation. However, given the lack of strong government protection, these natural areas fall victim to squatters, illegal loggers, traffickers in plants and animals, and drug dealers who plant marijuana and opium poppies. Just to cite one example, the preserve set aside in Michoacán to protect the monarch butterfly lost 20 percent of its forest cover in twenty-five years due to illegal logging.[160]

An alternative to simply decreeing land to be protected has been to allow communities to manage their forests. By the middle of the twentieth century, the notion arose that communities could manage their forests as well as their farmland. Beginning in the 1970s and 1980s, many communities assumed responsibility for forest management. Residents established agro-forestry enterprises that supported the community. Over the years, forests managed by communities have fared as well as, if not better than, those simply decreed to be protected. This led environmental studies professor David Barton Bray to comment, "The forest communities in Mexico are demonstrating that they are excellent custodians of the forests and that they deserve the support of the government and of the populace in their efforts to manage forests in a sustainable manner."[161]

In the early 1990s, as the possibility of Mexico joining NAFTA was being discussed, the environmental impact of such an agreement was sharply debated. NAFTA promoters claimed that the treaty would lead to increased per capita income in Mexico. They claimed the resulting affluence would make Mexicans willing to sacrifice to fight environmental degradation. In contrast, NAFTA opponents warned that the agreement would allow dirty industries to move to Mexico to escape more stringent environmental regulations in the United States and Canada.

As it turned out, neither NAFTA critics nor its proponents were correct. Those who felt that polluting industries would migrate to Mexico were mistaken. Such industries did not move south since the costs of relocating large facilities was too high and many dirty producers wished to remain close to their markets. As Mexican exports almost doubled during the first seven years of NAFTA, exports by less polluting industries such as apparel increased more rapidly than did those of highly polluting industries such as chemicals. However, as exports soared, total production increased, leading to increased pollution. In 2000, Mexico produced nearly 9 million tons of hazardous waste, but had only one safe waste disposal facility, with a capacity of 550,000 tons.[162]

Even though Mexico has many sound environmental laws on the books, they are not vigorously enforced due to corruption, poor administration, or high short-term economic cost. In the decade after NAFTA went into effect, the number of plant-level inspections dropped precipitously, suggesting that Mexico had become less assiduous about enforcement. The average OECD country spends six times more per capita on environmental enforcement than Mexico does. In 2005, economist Kevin Gallagher described the result of poor environmental infrastructure and lax law enforcement:

> Here in Mexico, just about every environmental measure has worsened since about 1985. If you look at levels of soil erosion, municipal solid waste, urban air pollution, urban water pollution, they've all grown faster than the economy itself and population growth in Mexico. According to the Mexican government's own estimates, that environmental degradation has cost the Mexican government about 10 percent of its GDP each year or about $45 billion each year in a country where half its hundred million people live in poverty, less than two dollars a day.[163]

NAFTA: THE SECOND DECADE

> Mexico's experience with NAFTA provides a cautionary tale. The goal of economic integration should be to raise living standards, but it is clear that trade liberalization by itself is not sufficient to achieve this. There is no doubt that trade and development are vitally important for economic growth but the real challenge is to pursue liberalization in a manner which promotes sustainable development, in which those at the bottom and middle see incomes rising.
>
> Joseph Stiglitz and Andrew Charlton, 2005[164]

Wal-Mart, which opened its first Mexican store in 1991, is emblematic of economic change in Mexico. In 2002, the company became the largest private employer in Mexico, and in 2004 it became the largest private corporation in Mexico as measured by sales. As with many other new investments, Wal-Mart displaces existing businesses. Since retailing until recently has been in the hands of small shops and street vendors, its impact has been even greater than the impact Wal-Mart had in small U.S. towns. For example, prior to its 2005 arrival in Juchitán, Oaxaca, population 86,000, there were 4,100 merchants, 98 percent of whom were considered small. At the same time that it devastates small retailers, Wal-Mart raises the standard of living of millions who take advantage of its everyday low prices to stretch their incomes further.[165]

As the 2006 presidential election indicated, there is no consensus concerning the course of Mexican economic development. Those favoring the current course share the views laid out in Thomas L. Friedman's book *The Earth is Flat*. They see Mexico successfully plunging into a global marketplace and benefiting from the opportunity to develop specialized niches and to achieve economies of scale in manufacturing. Advocates of NAFTA and globalization cite a wealth of data to support their position:

- During the eight-year period before NAFTA went into effect, FDI averaged only $3.47 billion a year, while during the following eight-year period it exceeded $13 billion a year. During the Fox administration, FDI averaged $17 billion annually.[166]
- Between 1995 and 2005, Mexican GDP increased from $310 billion to $700 billion and average per capita income rose from $3,100 to $7,000. Mexico moved from seventh place in Latin American per capita income in 1995 to first by 2005, ahead of Brazil and Argentina.[167]

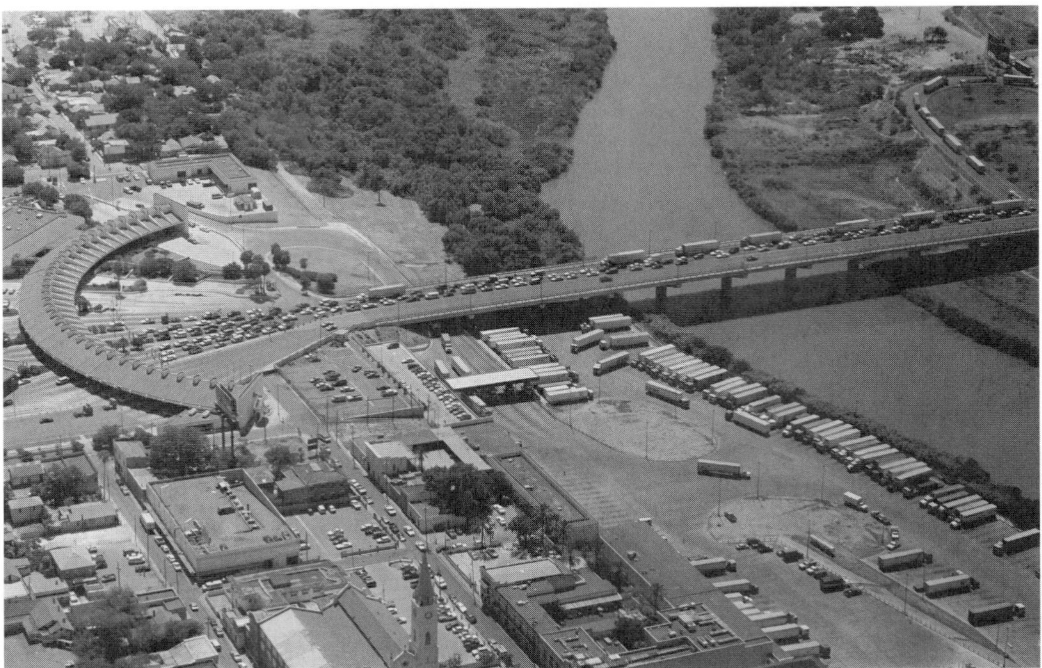

Figure 25.1 *NAFTA traffic on International Bridge at Laredo*
Source: J. Michael Short

- Between 1993 and 2004, U.S. exports to Mexico increased by 166 percent, while Mexican exports to the United States rose by 290 percent.[168]

In 1994, Mexicans put aside their reservations about U.S. domination and accepted NAFTA as a stepping-stone to developed-world standards in wages, health, and education.[169] While NAFTA delivered the anticipated benefits to a minority of Mexicans, such benefits failed to reach broad swaths of the population. Critics of NAFTA seized on this to condemn the treaty and call for its repeal or modification. These are some of the NAFTA shortcomings they cited:

- Between 1994 and 2003, the buying power of manufacturing wages declined by 5.2 percent, while those in maquiladora plants declined by 3.5 percent.[170]
- NAFTA has exacerbated existing regional disparities since most foreign investment goes to the wealthier states. Mexico's five poorest states received only 0.34 percent of direct foreign investment during NAFTA's first nine years and much of that went to already developed tourist spots such as Acapulco.
- Rather than creating new jobs, foreign investment has simply bought out existing enterprises, such as banks and supermarket chains.
- NAFTA supporters claim that those who benefit from NAFTA-induced growth can provide compensation to those who fail to benefit or are harmed by it. Critics note that such compensation has seldom occurred.[171]
- Even though NAFTA was billed as a promoter of exports, between 1994 and 2002 Mexico accumulated a $43.7 billion trade deficit. Negative trade balances continued after 2002.[172]

- Between 1983 and 2009, Mexican gross domestic increased at an annual rate of 2.1 percent a year. Per capita GDP rose by only 0.4 per cent a year.[173]
- NAFTA supporters promised that exports would become the engine of growth, but this has not happened, since exporting firms, by and large, are not connected to national production. They remain as enclaves with few linkages to the rest of the economy. Companies that export bring in components, assemble them in Mexico, and then export them. As the import of components and worker productivity have increased, relatively few manufacturing jobs have been created even though the volume of exports has risen. Between 1993 and 2003, Mexico gained roughly 450,000 new manufacturing jobs.[174]
- Job creation in the economy as a whole has also lagged behind. Between 1994 and 2004, almost 13 million entered the workforce, but only 2.7 million jobs were created. Furthermore, the rate of job creation has been declining. New, permanent jobs covered by social security increased by 1.75 million during Salinas's term (1988–1994), by 390,000 during Zedillo's (1994–2000), and by only 62,000 during Fox's (2000–2006).[175]
- Since wages declined from 37.5 percent of GDP in 1980 to 18.7 percent in 2000, there have not been enough buyers to sustain the domestic economy.[176]
- Productivity per worker between 1981 and 2005 declined by 0.7 percent a year, while between 1940 and 1981 it increased by 3.1 percent.[177]
- Among the world's nations, in 1982 Mexico ranked forty-third in terms of per capita GDP. By 2007, it had fallen to sixty-first place.[178]

While NAFTA opponents want to tinker with (if not abolish) the treaty itself, NAFTA's backers seek to tinker with Mexican society so that NAFTA can deliver its full potential. Between 1980 and 2001, even though it grew faster than the Brazilian and Argentine economies, the Mexican economy lagged behind that of regional star performer, Chile. During these years, Mexico's economy increased by 67.2 percent, while that of Chile grew by 140.8 percent. In 1980, South Korea's per capita income was less than a third of Mexico's, while by 2001 its per capita income was more than double Mexico's. NAFTA backers cite both of these nations as examples of Mexico's potential, were change to be instituted.[179]

Trade policy is important for developing countries, but is not a substitute for reform and investment within the country. There is a general consensus that needed reforms include increasing competition within Mexico, combating corruption, and improving schools, roads, sanitation, and housing. Lowering Mexico's high energy and telecommunications costs would also stimulate investment. There is much less agreement on how to raise the money to carry out these reforms and on how to confront vested interests supporting the status quo.[180]

Doing business in Mexico as compared to Singapore is the equivalent of having a 20 percent tax increase due to higher levels of corruption. Mexican officials estimate that as much as 9 percent of Mexico's GDP is siphoned off due to corruption. In 2005, that amounted to $69 billion—more than the nation spent on defense and education combined. Transparency International, a non-profit organization measuring levels of corruption, found that in 2001, Mexico ranked fifty-first in level of corruption. By 2007–2008, Mexico had slid to seventy-second (out of 180 nations) in its level of corruption. In other words, when it comes to attracting foreign investment, there are seventy-one countries where less of the investment will be consumed by corruption. Ironically, the PAN came to power in 2000 promising to fight corruption.[181]

Another area to be improved is business competitiveness, which measures the ease of conducting business. Factors lowering competitiveness include the failure to enforce contracts, a high crime rate, a poor judicial system, and a mind-numbing bureaucracy. One indicator of competitiveness is the time required to establish a business. In 2001, establishing a new business in Mexico required 112 days, while in Canada it required only one. Between 2004 and 2008–2009, the World

Economic Forum's Global Competitiveness Report lowered Mexico's competitiveness rating from fifty-second to sixtieth (among 134 nations) due to corruption, inefficient government bureaucracy, and the lack of credit. The report found only seven nations in the world that had worse problems with organized crime than Mexico.[182]

Mexico needs a fiscal reform since the current rate of tax collection is so low that the government is unable to adequately carry out such basic tasks as providing good education and infrastructure. In Mexico, tax collection is only 12 percent of GDP, compared to 34 percent in the United States and 37 percent in Brazil.[183]

During the twenty-first century, China has exercised a strong influence on Mexico. The world's most populous nation attracts investment that might otherwise have gone to Mexico by guaranteeing manufacturers the absence of militant unions and providing workers who will work for wages that are only a quarter of Mexican wages. A large, fast-growing market and well-developed infrastructure (roads, ports, etc.) also attract investment. China's prodigious growth in recent decades has been based on gradually implementing and carefully sequencing its development strategy. China began to grow rapidly in the late 1970s, but trade liberalization did not start until the late 1980s.[184]

China impacts the Mexican economy since it competes with Mexico for FDI. Between 2001 and 2003, Mexico lost an estimated 400,000 jobs to China. China also competes with Mexico in the U.S. market. In 1990, China exported only $3.08 billion to United States, while Mexico exported $6.09 billion. In 2008, U.S. imports from China totaled $356 billion, while Mexican imports totaled only $218 billion. Finally, China's highly efficient, low-wage industries are successfully competing for Mexico's domestic market. Between 2000 and 2008, Mexico's trade deficit with China rose from $2.6 billion to $32.7 billion, as China exported to Mexico a wide range of clothing, toys, and housewares, not to mention Mexican flags and porcelain figurines of the Virgin of Guadalupe.[185]

Nobel-prize winning economist Joseph Stiglitz commented that even though globalization has led to economic crisis and hurt the environment and the poor, the answer is not to abandon it, noting that is "neither feasible nor desirable." Felipe Calderón indicated during his 2006 presidential campaign that he would follow Stiglitz's advice and continue to globalize. However, those advocating a shift away from globalization to an emphasis on the domestic economy may yet prevail due to some of the inherent contradictions in neoliberalism. The current model has too many nations attempting to export, while ignoring the impossibility of the whole world running a trade surplus. These exporters currently are trying to sell in a global economy where too few workers can afford to buy what they make. Neoliberalism is based on cheap energy to move goods long distances for assembly and final sales. Finally, Mexico's neoliberal model has even more closely linked Mexico to the market provided by the United States—a nation that even before the 2008–2009 economic crisis was experiencing unsustainable trade and budget deficits.[186]

Neoliberal economic policies led to exports increasing by 11.1 percent a year between 1993 and 2005. Nevertheless, between 1981 and 2005, the Mexican economy grew at a lower rate than that of Latin America and the Caribbean, that of the developed world, or that of the world as a whole.[187]

As a result of neoliberal economic policies, Mexico finds itself trapped between nations offering low-cost labor—a market in which it can no longer compete—and those offering high-tech manufacturing, which it has yet to develop. The economy has been unable to absorb the large number of workers entering the labor force—those born in the 1980s and 1990s—in high-productivity sectors. Rather, the majority of new entrants find employment in low-productivity, informal jobs. Had there been more investment, sufficient jobs might have been created in the relatively high-productivity export sector. Factors limiting investment since 1980 include: 1) an overvalued peso, 2) the low level of bank lending, 3) the lack of a government industrial policy to stimulate investment in specific sectors, and, 4) in keeping with neoliberal ideology, a low level of government investment.[188]

The foreign investment that occurred did not have the transformative effect that investment in East Asia had. In China and the nations often referred to as the Asian Tigers, governments deliberately nurtured the capacities of domestic firms to learn and innovate. They did so through a variety of policy and institutional interventions, including targeted-industry policies and investment in education, research and development, and science and technical training. In the absence of such explicit policies, technical, financial, and human-capital transfers are largely kept within foreign companies, and local firms do not move up the value chain. In such cases, as economists Kevin Gallagher and Lyuba Zarsky observed, "The benefits of FDI [foreign direct investment] are captured primarily within the foreign enclave rather than diffused through the economy." After studying how neoliberal policies decimated Guadalajara's once promising computer industry, they concluded, "The Guadalajara experience confirms the finding of other studies, supportive public policies are needed to nurture domestic industries and capture the benefits from FDI."[189]

Chapter 26

The End of Nationalism, 1971–2000

> No country in the Western Hemisphere, and very few anywhere, affects the United States more than Mexico. No other country (not even Canada) is more pervasively influenced by the United States than our neighbor to the south. Probably no bilateral relationship in the world is more complex.
>
> Abraham Lowenthal, 1990[1]

FROM DISTANT NEIGHBOR TO NAFTA PARTNER

For six Mexican presidential terms after the Second World War, the United States did not publicly meddle in Mexican affairs. Officials in Washington showed unusual flexibility concerning the notion of democracy. Stability was preferred over the more unpredictable consequences of political reform. U.S. policy makers viewed Mexican stability as essential for national security and protecting U.S. investment in Mexico. In 1972, a secret U.S. government document stated, "It is important to our security that there be in Mexico a friendly, cooperative, and politically stable government and that no hostile power have access to the territory of Mexico."[2]

The ambassadors each country sent to the other highlighted an inescapable reality—the asymmetry of power. Mexican ambassadors in Washington were unimportant political figures with rare access to the White House, while the U.S. ambassador to Mexico dominated the local diplomatic scene and frequently met with the Mexican president. While few Americans ever learned the name of the Mexican ambassador to the United States, Washington's choice of ambassador to Mexico was viewed as a barometer of U.S.–Mexico relations and he, for better or worse, was constantly in the news. When President Reagan appointed as his ambassador, John Gavin, a former actor who was best know in Mexico for his TV spots advertising Bacardi rum, Mexicans felt slighted by the presence of such a lightweight. Some Mexicans quipped that the appropriate response to Gavin's appointment would be to send movie comic Cantinflas to Washington as Mexico's ambassador.[3]

President Echeverría (1970–1976) sought to diversify Mexico's international political and economic relations. His administration played a leading role in formulating the proposal for a new international economic order that was endorsed by the United Nations (UN) General Assembly. The Mexican president stridently proclaimed Mexico's "victimization" at the hands of the "colossus of the north." He also irritated U.S. policy makers by warmly embracing and exchanging visits with Chilean president Salvador Allende. Echeverría's taking up the cause, on a rhetorical level, of a more egalitarian distribution of the world's wealth served more to aggravate Washington than to actually redistribute wealth. His policies did cause U.S. Ambassador Robert H. McBride to move from the usual acceptance of incumbent Mexican regimes to open criticism when he declared:

> Let me say candidly that I have noted an attitude, not with alarm but with a certain degree of preoccupation. Many are no longer certain if Mexico wants foreign investment or if it has changed the rules, not only concerning new investment but already established firms.[4]

During Echeverría's term, his rhetoric about sovereignty and independence notwithstanding, Mexican reliance on the United States, as measured by foreign investment, external debt, foreign trade, and the role of American banks, increased. Ironically, the United States, rather than Echeverría's Third World allies, bailed him out of his end-of-term financial crisis by providing a $600-million loan to support the peso.[5]

During both Echeverría's term and that of his successor, Central America emerged as a thorn in the side of U.S.–Mexican relations. For U.S. policy makers, conflicts in Nicaragua and El Salvador were part of the Cold War fomented by Cuba and the Soviet Union. This led them to view each Central American nation as a potential domino that could spread revolution and endanger the United States.

Mexican policy makers viewed the violence in Central America not as falling dominos but as an attempt to right social injustice and end political oppression. They felt conflicts there were a prelude to political modernization that the United States and local oligarchies sought to thwart. Mexicans felt that U.S. policy was not only destabilizing Central America by buttressing the status quo and preventing needed change but also threatening to plunge Mexico into a refugee crisis.

Despite López Portillo's attempt to set a more independent foreign policy, U.S. economic domination of Mexico increased during the years of the oil boom. Between 1977 and 1980, U.S.–Mexico trade increased by 42 percent a year. U.S. investment likewise increased. In 1981, as two-way trade between the two nations exceeded $26 billion, Mexico became the third largest U.S. trading partner.[6]

U.S. influence over Mexico increased still further after the 1982 debt crisis, since the U.S. and the IMF (in which the United States exercised strong influence) conditioned their loans on certain financial behavior. At the time, the United States became seriously concerned about the collapse of the Mexican economic and political system. International investors, the U.S. media, the U.S. Congress, and U.S. officials began to express concern about the lack of democracy in Mexico, due not so much to deeply felt democratic convictions but to a sudden awareness of the danger a chaotic situation in Mexico augured for the United States.[7]

In 1986, doubts that many Americans held concerning Mexico were most conspicuously aired in congressional subcommittee hearings chaired by Senator Jesse Helms, a Republican senator from North Carolina. The hearings highlighted corruption, poor administration, election fraud, and Mexico's lack of will to combat drug trafficking. These hearings broke with the long-held U.S. government policy of not publicly criticizing Mexico.[8]

Most Mexicans, who automatically assumed the United States government was as centralized as Mexico's, concluded that the hearings, as well as sharply increased negative media reports on Mexico, represented U.S. government policy. The hearings produced an upswelling of Mexican nationalism and made it very difficult for anyone, especially those from opposition political parties, to challenge the government without leaving themselves open to charges of being a tool of the United States. A few Mexicans, however, publicly welcomed open discussion of Mexico's problems. Pro-democracy activist Sergio Aguayo, for example, commented on the United States failing to criticize undemocratic practices for so long:

> I believe that the PRI's capacity to survive has been greatly enhanced by the support of the international community, and in particular the United States. Neither the amount and timeliness of the financial aid provided, nor the massive indifference toward Mexico's pro-democracy movements have any precedent or comparison in the world's recent history.[9]

As the Reagan administration's dissatisfaction with the Mexican incumbents increased, it abandoned the long-held U.S. policy of ignoring opposition to the PRI. It also had to decide if the PAN should be considered as politically significant. Answering this question took time. In the early

1980s, no consensus existed concerning the PAN's future. In 1981, the U.S. consul in Monterrey sent a secret cable describing the PAN as "a fly biting the rump of the state."[10]

Once the PAN showed its mettle, the Reagan administration established contact with it in various highly visible ways since the PAN shared Reagan's views on Central America and on the desirability of privatizing government-owned corporations and reducing the size of the state. In 1984, U.S. Ambassador Gavin met with Hermosillo Archbishop Carlos Quintero Arce and PAN regional director Carlos Amaya Rivera. This unprecedented meeting with the political opposition was widely denounced as U.S. intervention into Mexican politics. The opening to the PAN was again highlighted when that party, but not the PRI, was invited to send representatives to the 1984 Republican Party convention in Dallas.[11]

In 1986, the Reagan administration began to back away from its flirtation with the PAN. It returned to supporting the PRI since that party was more strongly committed to paying Mexico's foreign debt than the PAN. In 1988, as leftist candidate Cuauhtémoc Cárdenas emerged as the main political challenger to the PRI, the United States strengthened its embrace of the incumbent De la Madrid administration. Political scientist Denise Dresser noted: "Mexico's successes in economic stabilization and restructuring (along with the fears awakened by the near-triumph of a perceived leftist [Cárdenas] in 1988) dramatically reduced interest in political change in Mexico."[12]

The U.S. embrace of the Mexican incumbents tightened with the meeting of Carlos Salinas de Gortari and George H. W. Bush in Houston, when both were presidents-elect. They established a rapport, and during their terms the cordiality of U.S.–Mexico relations was described as reflecting "the spirit of Houston." The spirit of Houston indicated U.S. awareness that, as the 1988 Mexican election showed, Salinas had a weak political base, which could easily result in instability. Other factors contributing to improved U.S.–Mexican relations were the 1980s crisis forcing Mexico into adopting economic policies that won U.S. approval and the demise of the Soviet block, which ended confrontation over Central America. As Lorenzo Meyer noted in 1989:

> From the rabid right to the moderate left—not to mention the big banks and corporations—almost everyone agrees, for now, that the U.S. national interest requires real, open support for the Salinas government because there are few options, and all the others are worse.[13]

The marked improvement in U.S.–Mexican relations provided tangible results for both nations. The Clinton administration invested considerable political capital to secure the passage of NAFTA and then went out on a limb to arrange a massive economic bailout early in 1995. The U.S.-sponsored Brady Plan reduced the amount of debt and the amount of payments due to the nearly 500 participating banks. Finally, the United States did not allow specific issues, such as drug trafficking or immigration, to cast a pall over U.S.–Mexican relations in general.[14]

The United States gained as Mexico ceased its traditional gringo-baiting. As analyst (and later foreign minister) Jorge G. Castañeda noted:

> It made no sense, on the one hand to put all of Mexico's eggs in one basket (namely the one that held foreign financing, business confidence, and U.S. support) and then proceed to kick and quarrel with the owner of the basket.

Mexico also refrained from promoting a Latin American debtors' cartel when many saw that as an attractive option and muted its protests when the United States invaded Panama to oust Manuel Noriega. Mexico increased oil shipments to the United States by 100,000 barrels a day after the Iraqi invasion of Kuwait. Mexico also dropped its long-standing ban on extraditing Mexican citizens to the United States for trial.[15]

Presidents Zedillo (1994–2000) and Clinton met at least once a year and continued their predecessors' efforts to develop a cooperative bilateral relationship. Several indicators show the depth of the relations that had developed by the end of their terms. The U.S. embassy in Mexico City employed roughly 1,000 people, making it the largest U.S. embassy in the world. Some fifty different bilateral commissions addressed problems concerning agriculture, transportation, NAFTA rules of origin, health standards, customs cooperation, labor matters, and the environment. The number of NGOs, media outlets, and corporations linking the two nations soared. By the end of the 1990s, roughly 600,000 U.S. citizens lived in Mexico.[16]

In February 2001, President George W. Bush emphasized both the cordiality and importance of U.S.–Mexican relations by making his first foreign presidential trip to President Vicente Fox's ranch. Fox later commented, "You cannot imagine what a sensation it caused in Mexico when the president of the United States chose our family ranch in Guanajuato for his foreign state visit."[17]

On the occasion of President Vicente Fox's September 5, 2001 state visit to Washington, Bush declared, "The United States has no more important relationship in the world than our relationship with Mexico." Even the most critical press in Mexico was forced to acknowledge that never before had a Mexican president been received as well in the U.S. capital.[18]

The terrorist attacks of September 11, 2001 interrupted the rapprochement between the United States and Mexico. In the wake of the attacks, some officials in the Bush administration felt the Mexican government failed to sufficiently manifest public support for the United States. U.S. concerns shifted from relations with Mexico to securing its borders against terrorists. Relations were further chilled as the Bush administration invoked the doctrine of preemptive war—a concept that provided an unwelcome reminder of prior unilateral U.S. interventions in the western hemisphere. The refusal by Mexico, which at the time occupied a non-permanent seat on the UN Security Council, to endorse the U.S. invasion of Iraq was seen as a betrayal by the Bush administration. During the rest of the Fox administration, U.S.–Mexican relations never again resumed their pre-9/11 cordiality, as the U.S. stand on the International Criminal Court, drug trafficking, and immigration concerns constantly irritated relations.[19]

At the beginning of the twenty-first century, Mexico and the United States were becoming increasingly important to each other. In 1990, 60 percent of Mexico's trade was with the U.S., while by 2002 that figure had reached 78 percent. The links were also demographic, environmental, musical, and gastronomic, to name just a few areas. Hollywood movies and pop music inundated Mexico, while at the same time hundreds of Spanish-language newspapers, magazines, and radio and TV stations flourished in the United States. Prosperity on one side of the border increased prosperity on the other, just as economic decline on one side inexorably led to lost jobs in the export sector of the other partner.[20]

Increased ties between the two nations produced a major social cleavage in Mexico that transcended region and wealth. It divided those who were linked to the U.S. economy and those who were not. Castañeda referred to this as "the most significant rift in Mexico's society." Mexicans linked to the United States worked in export industries and the tourist industry, and included business people, their employees, accountants, and lawyers working for firms in these sectors. Other groups with economic links to the U.S. economy included Mexicans working in the United States, those receiving remittances from family members working in the United States, and those who smuggled drugs and unauthorized immigrants into the U.S. Even though these links undoubtedly benefited millions, as Castañeda noted, Mexico

> is simply too populous for all those excluded from this cross-cutting cohort to be embraced by it within any reasonable time frame. Many in the United States and Mexico do not yet grasp a fundamental demographic constraint: there are simply not enough tourists from Chicago, export firms in Monterrey, or low-skill jobs in California to go around.[21]

THE BORDER

> The huge US-Mexican border connects two vastly unequal regions. It is both—the paradoxes are endless—the most porous border in the world and the most heavily guarded. It is a line that at once separates and unites two cultures, two languages, two economies.
>
> Marcelo Suárez-Orozco, 1999[22]

Of the nine Mexican states with the highest level of well-being, six are border states, and all have high levels of foreign investment. (By comparison, the three states with the lowest well-being are Chiapas, Guerrero, and Oaxaca, with very low levels of foreign investment.) Since the adoption of the neoliberal economic model, the economic gap between the border states and the rest of Mexico has widened, as foreign investment became concentrated along the border. Between 1975 and 2000, Mexican GDP increased at an annual rate of 0.8 percent, while in the border states it increased by 1.2 percent.[23]

Just as the greater wealth of the United States attracted job seekers from Mexico, the greater wealth of the border states attracted job seekers from further south. Job availability, plus the presence of many who came to use the border as a jumping-off place for entry into the United States, resulted in the border population increasing more rapidly than that of the rest of Mexico. Between 1975 and 2000, the border population increased by 2.5 percent annually, while that of Mexico increased by 2.3 percent. However, by the start of the twenty-first century, job creation away from the border exceeded that on the border. Between 2000 and 2005, of the six Mexican states with the most rapid population growth, only one—Baja California—was a border state.[24]

The U.S.–Mexican border, with 350 million crossings a year, is the most crossed border in the world. A substantial share of these crossings results from traffic generated by the maquiladora industry. The first maquiladoras were usually small operations located in old buildings and generating little cross-border traffic. However, more recently, the trend has been to locate maquiladoras—which are now much larger—in gleaming industrial parks built on city peripheries in locations well supplied with utility service and transport linkages. Ironically, by linking the border area even closer to the United States, the growth of the maquiladora reversed the gains of the National Border Program (PRONAF) of the 1960s.[25]

In 1998, Francisco Gaytán, of the economic development agency of the State of Chihuahua, estimated that 95 percent of the economy of Ciudad Juárez was based on the maquiladora. Gaytán commented, "Everything revolves around the maquiladora, and we have given absolute priority to its development."[26]

***Table 26.1** Border state populations, 1970–2000*

State	1970	2000	Percentage change
Baja California	870,421	2,487,700	186
Sonora	1,098,720	2,213,370	101
Chihuahua	1,612,525	3,047,667	89
Coahuila	1,114,956	2,295,808	106
Nuevo León	1,694,689	3,826,240	126
Tamaulipas	1,456,858	2,747,114	88
Total	7,848,169	16,617,899	112
Percentage of total Mexican population	16.3	17.1	

Source: INEGI (1994: 15-24; 2007: 36–41)

This "absolute priority" accorded the maquiladora has come at the expense of the environment. Legislation protecting the environment is on the books, but enforcement is at best spotty, leading to worsening environmental problems. In addition to lax enforcement, there is a lack of infrastructure for treating hazardous substances, which results in endangerment of both workers and communities adjacent to maquiladora plants. The result of lax enforcement and non-existent hazardous-waste infrastructure was described in a 2001 *New York Times* article, "All along the border, the land, the water and the air are thick with industrial and human waste."[27]

The border towns evolved into substantial cities whose population totaled 5.5 million in 2005. Their growth has been fueled not only by the maquiladora but by soaring cross-border traffic generated by NAFTA. The six largest border cities (in descending order by population) were Tijuana, Ciudad Juárez, Mexicali, Reynosa, Matamoros, and Nuevo Laredo. Their populations ranged from 1.4 million to 356,000. As Héctor Aguilar Camín and Lorenzo Meyer observed in 1993, "A new Northern Mexico is appearing at an astonishing rate, subject increasingly to a process of reindustrialization and integration with the U.S. economy."[28]

DRUG TRAFFICKING

> Most Mexican specialists who track drug-related security challenges are far from sanguine about conditions improving, at least in the short term. They point to the growing strength, proliferation, and fragmentation of the country's myriad drug traffickers, making them much harder to contain, along with the insufficient resources and instruments at the disposal of the Mexican government to deal effectively with the problem.
>
> Michael Shifter, 2007[29]

In the 1950s and 1960s, opium poppies were cultivated in the north-central states of Sinaloa, Durango, and Chihuahua. During this period, Mexico supplied 10–15 percent of the heroin consumed in the United States and as much as 75 percent of the imported marijuana. Drugs were usually grown on small farms and then spirited into the United States by members of well-established smuggling families, some of which got their start running alcohol across the border during Prohibition. Such trafficking involved the bribing of local and regional officials, but did not lead to significant violence.[30]

The modern era of drug trafficking between Mexico and the United States began on September 21, 1969, as the U.S. government launched Operation Intercept to pressure the Mexican government into taking a more active role in halting drug trafficking. Some 2,000 U.S. customs officials began to thoroughly search all cars crossing into the United States from Mexico. Quite predictably enormous traffic jams ensued, and local economies on both sides of the border suffered. The chief architect of this operation was G. Gordon Liddy, later of Watergate fame. Operation Intercept responded to the huge increase in marijuana imports from Mexico and indicated Nixon's desire to project a "tough-on-crime" image. Customs chief Myles Ambrose called the operation "shock treatment" for the Mexican government, stating that afterward "the Mexican ministers promised everything." The bi-national negotiations were secret and it will never be known what "everything" was.[31]

Through the 1960s, Turkey was the principal source of heroin consumed in the United States. However, after the Turkish government, under intense U.S. pressure, banned opium production and implemented a strict control program in 1972, production shifted to a logical and much closer alternative—Mexico. By 1975, an estimated 80 percent of the heroin consumed in the United States came from Mexico.[32]

Mexico responded to U.S. pressure to combat drug trafficking with Operation Condor, one of the most ambitious drug eradication efforts ever undertaken by any country. During 1975 and 1976, Mexico spent $35 million to deploy 5,000 soldiers and 350 police to eradicate drugs in the states of Sinaloa, Durango, and Chihuahua. Troops in the field manually eradicated drug plants, and aircraft sprayed herbicides on fields. The results were dramatic—Mexico's share of marijuana exports to the United States fell from 75 percent in 1976 to as low as 4 percent in 1981. Similarly, Mexico's share of heroin exports to the U.S. fell to 25 percent. Strikingly, even though hundreds of peasants were detained, tortured, and jailed, not a single major trafficker was arrested.[33]

In the late 1970s and early 1980s, cocaine was flown from Colombia to the Bahamas or to any of various Caribbean islands and then on to the United States. To close this smuggling route, U.S. surveillance planes blanketed the Caribbean. However, rather than abandoning the U.S. market, Colombian traffickers diverted their cocaine flights to Mexico and from there across the U.S. border. Increased scrutiny of cross-border flights soon led traffickers to fly cocaine to clandestine airstrips south of the border. Then the drugs would be spirited across some isolated border region or hidden in one of the hundreds of thousands of vehicles that cross the border daily. Mexico's emergence as a transshipment point for northbound cocaine can easily be quantified. In 1982–1983, only 300 kilograms of cocaine were seized in Mexico. By 1991, this figure had risen to more than fifty tons.[34]

U.S. actions to combat drug trafficking increased during the 1980s. During Reagan's tenure (1981–1989), Washington consistently demonstrated its preference for preventing drugs from reaching the U.S. consumer over, as historian Oscar Martínez expressed it, "seriously facing up to the voracious consumption of drugs in U.S. society and coming up with effective means to reduce demand." In the late 1980s, to interdict drug smuggling, National Guardsmen and U.S. army troops were stationed along the border. At least thirty U.S. DEA agents were stationed in Mexico to support the campaign.[35]

In response to increased enforcement efforts, marijuana growers retreated into inaccessible regions of the Sierra Madre Occidental and moved many of their operations to the city of Guadalajara. Increased interdictions forced traffickers into entrepreneurial organizations that were fewer in number, financially stronger, and more dangerous to society and government. Traffickers increasingly bribed and employed violence to protect themselves. At a 1987 U.S. Senate subcommittee hearing, U.S. Customs Commissioner William Von Raab stated: "The good news is that we are catching more drugs because we are getting better at doing our jobs. We have more resources. The bad news is that we are catching more because more is coming across."[36]

During the early 1990s, drug culture permeated border society. Narrative ballads known as *corridos* glorified the drug traffickers, who became celebrities not unlike rock stars. One of the best known celebrity traffickers was Amado Carrillo Fuentes, who flew cocaine into Mexico in privately owned Boeing 727s, a tactic that earned him the nickname "the Lord of the Skies." Country club doors opened to traffickers so long as they paid their dues and hosted lavish weddings for their sons and daughters. These trafficking celebrities never missed an opportunity to exhibit their flashy jewelry, customized pickups, flamboyant clothes, and bodacious babes.[37]

During Salinas's term (1988–1994) more than 102,000 were jailed for trafficking, and drug seizure and plant eradication reached record levels. Prisons were filled with small-time traffickers and those subject to dubious arrests, thus earning praise from U.S. officials as a sign of getting tough on drugs. Despite the arrests, at the end of the Salinas administration, 20 percent of heroin, 60 percent of marijuana, and 60 percent of cocaine that the United States imported crossed the border from Mexico. At that time, traffickers were estimated to bring in more dollars than oil or tourism.[38]

Increased enforcement did little to stem the flow of drugs from Mexico. In 2000, an estimated 20–30 percent of heroin, 50–60 percent of cocaine, and up to 80 percent of marijuana imported by the United States came from Mexico. NAFTA greatly facilitated drug trafficking as smugglers simply inserted drugs into legal cargo loaded onto commercial trucks. They relied on the inability of customs to thoroughly inspect each shipment. Traffickers also used shipping containers and individuals known as "mules" who would walk across the border carrying drugs.[39]

Despite the training and receipt of equipment, illegal drugs continued to flow across the border. At the end of the Fox administration in 2006, an estimated 70 to 90 percent of the drugs illegally imported into the United States came from Mexico. That year the level of trafficking was indicated by a single DC-9 that was busted in Campeche with 5.6 tons of cocaine aboard. Its cargo was to have been part of the estimated 300 tons of cocaine that annually arrives in the United States from Mexico. A 2007 raid in the upscale Lomas de Chapultepec neighborhood in Mexico City indicated the financial power of the traffickers. Police searched a drug safe-house there and found 205 million U.S. dollars in cash, thought to be the product of smuggling amphetamines into the United States.[40]

In order to keep the drugs flowing north, traffickers altered their modus operandi. The most significant change was a relentless increase in violence as enforcement fragmented long-established distribution systems and more young bucks attempted to enter the business. The end of PRI rule shattered the cozy relationship that had existed between politicians and traffickers. The rapid increase in domestic drug consumption also led to increased violence as traffickers fought to control neighborhoods where they sold drugs. Drug-related murders increased to more than 5,000 in 2008. Violence was directed at members of rival cartels, government officials whose efforts at drug enforcement were seen as an obstacle to trafficking, and journalists who brought unwelcome attention. Traffickers turned to increasingly lethal arms including machine guns, bazookas, and hand grenades.[41]

At the same time that they were unleashing lethal force against fellow traffickers, dealers ceased flaunting their lifestyle and began to behave more like low-profile businessmen, since they realized that their behavior attracted unwelcome attention. Flamboyance was replaced by cell phones, faxes, pagers, and the internet, using the latest encryption technology to keep their messages secret.[42]

There are few issues on which there is greater consensus than that the drug war has been a failure. As Mexican analyst Jorge Chabat noted in 2005:

> The good news is that there are more capos in jail; the bad news is that it doesn't change anything. There's no change in the amount of drugs available on the street, and you have more violence. The logical question is, "What are we doing this for?"[43]

The financial cost of this failure is enormous. The United States spends $50 billion annually in its attempt to control narcotics, not including the cost of arresting half a million drug offenders and incarcerating them. In Mexico, supporting soldiers and narcotics agents deprives other projects of funding. The courts are full of drug cases, limiting what can be accomplished in other areas of domestic law. Increased funding to combat drug trafficking strengthens the one state institution that least needs strengthening—the military.[44]

Another cost of the failed drug war is corruption linked to drug trafficking. In 2009, by one estimate drug traffickers provided employment to 450,000 Mexicans. Estimates of Mexican traffickers' receipts ranged between $10 and $24 billion. A notebook recovered from Juan García Abrego at the time of his arrest included a list of payoffs, ranging from $1 million to the commander of the Federal Judicial Police down to $100,000 paid to the federal police commander in the border city of Matamoros. Such payments purchase an essential service monopolized by government officials—the non-enforcement of the law. Those in charge of enforcement must be bribed because they cannot be entirely bullied or bypassed.[45]

The efforts to combat drug trafficking have had a pernicious effect throughout Mexican society. Special anti-drug military units have track records of abuse of power and human rights violations.[46] False accusations of drug trafficking are used to taint rivals, just as false charges to the colonial Inquisition were used.

One of the few points of agreement is that rural development offers a long-term solution to drug trafficking by providing producers with legal income sources. However, as it is, neither the state nor the private sector can offer poor rural residents alternatives that match opportunities offered by traffickers. Whole regions depend on the production of illegal drugs. A 1993 study found that the state of Sinaloa's economy was growing at twice the national rate as a result of drug production. An economist at the University of Sinaloa commented, "You'll notice that despite the economic downturn, there is still a great deal of new construction going in Culiacán [the state capital]." At the individual level, a farmer earns as much money growing one kilogram of marijuana as he earns producing a ton of corn.[47]

EXODUS

> People used to think of Mexico City as the mecca, as "the" city. Now it's Los Angeles. California offers jobs. Not glamorous jobs, but the young people believe that there are jobs there. And California, to a young Indian from Oaxaca, or to people with no real possibilities of jobs in Mexico, offers also and especially a new way of life, a freer and smarter way of life they don't have in the countryside or in the slums.
>
> Carlos Monsiváis, 1999[48]

The end of the *bracero* program in 1965 essentially moved the same people, or their fellow villagers, from the category of *bracero* to unauthorized entrant. In 1964, 86,597 deportable aliens (the term used by the U.S. government) were located, while by 1970 that number had increased to 345,353. These increased numbers reflect the low number of jobs created in Mexico, as well as the enormous gap between U.S. and Mexican per capita income. In 1970, U.S. per capita income was more than $5,000, compared to about $700 in Mexico. The 1982 economic crisis led to increased immigration to the United States as wages and job creation declined in Mexico.[49]

Before 1986, border enforcement to deter illegal crossings was largely a ritualized performance. All parties understood that after being repatriated would-be migrants would attempt to cross the border again and that on the next or subsequent attempt they would probably enter the United States successfully. In 1974, Commissioner of Immigration Leonard F. Chapman virtually decreed the border to be open when he declared that unauthorized workers apprehended outside the border area would no longer be detained or returned to their homelands.[50]

Between 1965 and 1986, an estimated 28.0 million Mexicans entered the United States as unauthorized immigrants, compared to just 1.3 million legal immigrants and a mere 46,000 contract workers. Of the 28.0 million, 23.4 million worked for a short period and then voluntarily returned to Mexico.[51]

As a result of the U.S. recession that began in 1973, the presence of so many unauthorized workers became a source of preoccupation, just as had occurred during earlier recessions. *Washington Post* reporter Lou Cannon commented that the presence of so many Hispanic immigrants posed "a threat to the American melting pot ideal greater than ever faced from the Irish, the Czechs, the Italians and the Poles." While concern was expressed about the issue, there was no immediate legislative response due to the political and economic influence of those who profited from employing unauthorized workers.[52]

Interest groups favoring high levels of immigration included Hispanic organizations, growers, service providers, and border state industrialists who had come to rely on immigrant labor. The AFL-CIO, the main U.S. labor federation, sought to end temporary worker programs and illegal entry, as well as to increase tariff protection against Mexican imports. Joining labor in opposing immigration was the National Association for the Advancement of Colored People (NAACP).[53]

This Hispanic support for high levels of immigration reflected a shift in the immigration dynamic within the United States. During the middle of the century self-identified Mexican–Americans dominated the discourse. By the 1980s, the media began to use the term "Hispanic." Mexican–American interest groups coalesced with the large number of arrivals from other Latin American nations, especially Cuba and Central America, who arrived after their homelands were wracked by social upheaval. As Mexican immigrants increasingly worked in urban settings, they were frequently co-workers, employees, or customers of long-established Mexican–Americans. New arrivals were viewed as economic assets who conferred added political clout to the Hispanic population.[54]

As early as 1981, the Reagan administration raised the prospect of immigration reform in response to perceived problems that included: 1) the number of immigrants exceeding the economic and demographic limits U.S. society could absorb, 2) the non-European origin of the bulk of immigrants, and 3) the exercise of national sovereignty and upholding of the law. This last notion was often summarized by the phase, "take control of our borders."[55]

Finally, Congress passed the Immigration Reform and Control Act of 1986 (IRCA). The main provisions of the bill were: 1) economic sanctions against U.S. employers who "knowingly employed" unauthorized workers, 2) permanent amnesty for unauthorized workers who could prove continuous unlawful residence in the United States since January 1, 1982, 3) an additional amnesty for agricultural workers who had worked at least ninety consecutive days between May 1, 1985 and May 1, 1986, 4) and sharply increased border enforcement.[56]

IRCA reflected the diverse pressures on Congress as it considered the bill. Proof necessary for amnesty as an agricultural worker, a provision that favored agribusiness, was so lax that a U.S. government commission declared its implementation to have been "one of the most extensive immigration frauds ever perpetuated against the U.S. government." The ease with which the provision was used fraudulently reflects its being drafted in haste and appended to IRCA as a political necessity to garner needed votes from members of Congress representing agribusiness constituencies.[57]

IRCA granted amnesty to more than 3 million previously unauthorized workers, 75 percent of whom were estimated to be from Mexico. Once legalized, beneficiaries of IRCA legally brought in close relatives and offered a base to millions of friends and fellow villagers who immigrated illegally. Those who had arrived after 1982 remained as unauthorized workers.[58]

For several years, IRCA did convince the U.S. public that it had regained control of its borders. It also decreased apprehensions for illegal entry from 1.77 million in 1986 to 0.95 million in 1989 as those who had been apprehended crossing illegally now crossed the border legally.[59]

After 1989, this trend reversed, and illegal immigration, as reflected in the number of apprehensions, began a steady increase. This resulted from job creation in Mexico languishing and immigrant networks providing jobs, housing, and economic support for the newly arrived. In addition, the 1994 economic crash resulted in Mexican wages plummeting, which more than offset wage gains attributable to NAFTA. This surge in illegal immigration also reflected the almost total absence of the enforcement measures mandated by IRCA. In 1990, only fifteen firms were fined more than $5,000 for hiring unauthorized immigrants. The number of sanctioned firms subsequently declined, reaching zero in 2004, even as illegal immigration surged.[60]

One reason for IRCA's failure to limit the flow of unauthorized workers during the 1990s was Congress's unwillingness to include in the law a reliable method for employers to verify the legal status of those whom they were hiring. As a result, more than two dozen different kinds of documents could be used to prove legal residence. Most of these documents were easy to counterfeit, and not surprisingly, a cottage industry producing fake IDs soon sprang up. IRCA's failure to mandate a readily verifiable national ID system reflected pressure exerted by growers, other employers, Latin American rights groups, and church organizations. This failure also reflected Americans' generalized fear that a national ID card would create a Big Brother state.[61]

During the 1990s and into the next decade, Mexican immigrants departed from more varied locations, including Mexico City and the southern Mexican states of Oaxaca, Chiapas, and Guerrero. At the same time, Mexican immigrants spread out from the traditional receiving states. For the first time the big five destination states—New York, California, Illinois, Texas, and Florida—received fewer than 60 percent of Mexicans. Increasingly immigrants settled in "new destination" areas, often small towns that offered an increasing supply of poorly paid, difficult, dirty, and sometimes dangerous jobs.[62]

President Clinton (1993–2001) was confronted with both push and pull forces in immigration. The U.S. economy was generating many low-wage (by U.S. standards) low-status jobs that the native-born were generally unwilling to fill. At the same time, Mexicans born in the 1970s and 1980s were coming of age and finding Mexico offered either no jobs or low-wage (even by Mexican standards) jobs. Millions of Mexicans responded by crossing the border to work. The U.S. government in turn responded with an escalation of law enforcement activity.[63]

This escalation began with Operation Blockade, which was launched in El Paso, Texas in 1993. To implement this new strategy, later known as Operation Hold the Line, the Border Patrol stationed 400 officers along the border on an around-the-clock basis. As a result of this increased Border Patrol presence, between October 1, 1993 and February 7, 1994, apprehensions in the El Paso sector declined to 22,156, compared to 84,119 the previous year. On closer inspection it became apparent that migrants simply detoured around the end of the Border Patrol line to cross the border

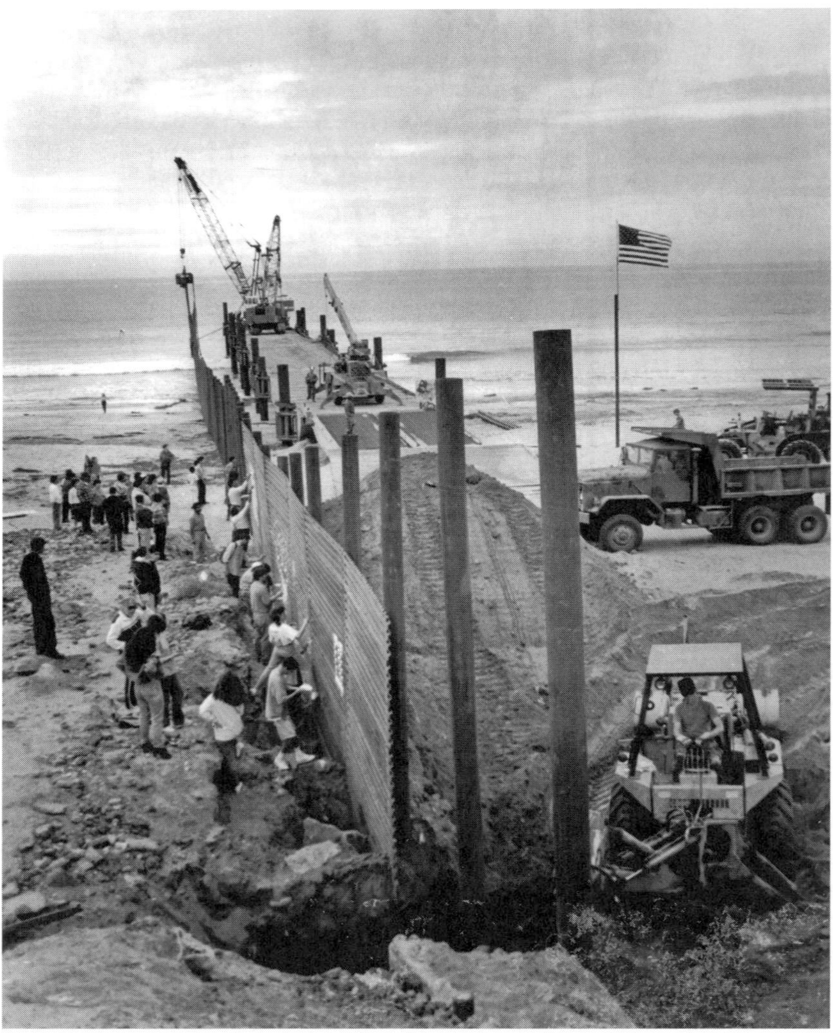

Figure 26.1 *Protest rally where border fence reaches Pacific*
Source: John Nelson/*San Diego Union-Tribune*

and those who had commuted to El Paso from Ciudad Juárez on a daily basis took up residence north of the river. Despite these flaws in the plan, which came to light later, the measure proved highly popular. Silvestre Reyes, the El Paso Border Patrol sector chief who devised the plan, was subsequently elected to the U.S. Congress by the largely Hispanic City of El Paso.[64]

Even before a serious evaluation of Operation Blockade was made, the model was extended to the fourteen westernmost miles of the border just south of San Diego. This was the area where the most illegal crossings—as many as 10,000 a night—occurred. Some $300 million was spent to station 2,000 Border Patrol agents along this sector of the border and to install fences, motion detectors, infrared scopes, trip wires, and high-intensity lights. Thanks to this measure, known as Operation Gatekeeper, or informally as the "tortilla curtain," illegal entry in this area plummeted.[65]

The theory behind Operations Blockade and Gatekeeper was that heightened enforcement would force unauthorized entrants into more dangerous areas, which in turn would lead to an increase in fees charged by smugglers. This, so the reasoning went, would cause unauthorized entry to decline as the cost increased. As it turned out, the most significant result of heightened enforcement in urban areas such as El Paso and San Diego was that unauthorized immigrants began crossing the border in isolated desert regions.[66]

Even though it did not deter illegal entry, heightened enforcement in urban areas did have several significant effects. Rather than simply walking across the border on their own, those seeking unauthorized entry into the United States increasingly hired smugglers at a cost ranging from $1,200 to $1,500 a person. As would-be entrants were scattered over a broader area, the cost to the Border Patrol for each unauthorized entrant it apprehended increased from $300 in 1992 to $1,700 ten years later. Given isolation, rugged terrain, and temperature extremes in the areas where unauthorized entry was attempted, the number dying increased and has remained high ever since, averaging 413 a year between 2004 and 2006. Finally, given the increased cost and danger of illegal entry, unauthorized Mexican workers, once they arrived in the United States, remained. Before IRCA, 25 to 30 percent of unauthorized workers returned annually on a voluntary basis. However, after 1998 only 10 percent did. As sociologist Douglas Massey noted, "Paradoxically, the principal effect of border militarization has been to reduce the odds of going home, not of coming in the first place."[67]

By FY 2001, the Immigration and Naturalization Service (INS) budget had reached $4.3 billion, triple the amount appropriated at the beginning of the Clinton administration. The INS had more officers authorized to carry guns and make arrests than any other federal agency. The U.S. military was brought in to assist border enforcement. Even though the military was prevented from making arrests, they assisted the INS by operating communications and surveillance equipment and by building and maintaining roads and fences.[68]

Despite the deployment of increased manpower and equipment, the number of those apprehended crossing the border illegally rose inexorably, reaching 1.81 million in 2000. The chief accomplishment during the Clinton years, as political scientist Peter Andreas noted, was "symbolically reaffirming the state's territorial authority" and drawing attention "away from the more politically awkward and divisive task of formally recognizing and regularizing a well-entrenched clandestine cross-border labor market." Enforcement along the border proved to be more politically palatable than workplace enforcement, which not only damaged vested economic interests but led to separation of families, many of which included U.S.-born children.[69]

Soon after his 2000 election, Vicente Fox began to vigorously promote the one foreign policy initiative sure to play well at home—calling for European-style open borders within the NAFTA region. Early in 2001, Presidents Bush and Fox both seemed to be moving toward an agreement on the management of Mexican labor migration to the United States. The Mexicans' proposals, which became known as the "whole enchilada," included: 1) an amnesty for Mexicans already in the United States, 2) a temporary work program to address U.S. labor market demands and the needs of potential Mexican migrants, 3) more visas for family reunification, 4) heightened border security, and 5) regional development plans for areas in Mexico that traditionally sent migrants. The likelihood of progress toward at least some of these goals appeared so high that, as then-Mexican Foreign Minister Jorge G. Castañeda later observed, "Fox's resounding state visit to Washington on the eve of the September 11 terrorist attacks further lifted the new initiatives and underscored both leaders' commitment to them."[70]

The year 2001 was not propitious for immigration reform. Had the 9/11 terrorist attacks not occurred, it is far from clear that a substantial portion of the whole "enchilada" would have been enacted by the Republican-dominated Congress, which was inclined much less favorably toward substantial reform than was President Bush. After the September 11 attacks occurred, the U.S. government shifted its attention to security matters. As Fox later commented, "Immigration reform was dead for now, as the United States turned inward and isolationists in Washington began talking about building a fortress America." Furthermore, recession in the United States reduced the demand for immigrant labor.[71]

Even though none of the "enchilada" was enacted into law, there were significant changes affecting unauthorized Mexican residents in the United States. Fox embraced the expat Mexican population as no other president before him had. He created a cabinet-level position to attend to the needs of Mexicans living abroad and instructed Mexican consulates to intensify their support of hometown associations within the United States. Increased competition and pressure from the Fox administration drastically lowered the cost of sending remittances across the border. Mexican consulates began issuing IDs called *matrículas consulares* which could be used in transactions such as opening a bank account. Finally, for the first time Mexicans living abroad were allowed to vote absentee in Mexico's 2006 presidential election.[72]

Offsetting these gains was the inability of the Mexican economy to create jobs that would retain labor in Mexico. As political scientist Wayne Cornelius noted, Mexico's neoliberal capital-intensive development model "has much less capacity to create employment than the old import-substituting industrial model that it replaced. Indeed, the new model's goals of efficiency and global competitiveness are inversely related to job creation." Nor could the Fox administration address other causes of migration such as degradation of cropland and low-cost grain imports.[73]

As former U.S. ambassador to Mexico Jeffrey Davidow observed, "At base the emigration phenomenon is largely the product of a massive increase in national population during the second half of the twentieth century." Even though millions of jobs were created in Mexico between 1950 and 2000, the job market was overwhelmed by a population increase of 72 million during this period. Many chose to move north across the border. In 2006, the U.S. government estimated the number of unauthorized residents, the majority of whom were from Mexico, at 11 million, up from 8.5 million in 2000.[74]

In a 2007 publication, Cornelius concluded that "tightened border enforcement since 1993 has not stopped, nor even discouraged unauthorized migrants from entering the United States. . . . even with an unprecedented level of border enforcement, the vast majority of unauthorized migrants are able to enter without being detected."[75]

Cornelius's observation was based on data collected in previous years. However, after years of steady increase there was a distinct decline in Mexican immigration to the United States beginning in roughly 2007. The number detained by the Border Patrol for illegal entry was 705,000 in the twelve-month period ending in September 30, 2008, down from 858,638 during the previous twelve months. Similarly, after rising for years, the remittances sent to Mexico peaked at $24.0 billion in 2007, and then began to decline—the first such decline since remittance data began to be compiled in 1995. There was a similar decline in the number of illegal entries in 2001 as the U.S. economy slowed down. It remains to be seen if the number of illegal entries will increase again with U.S. economic recovery, or if increased enforcement and lower job growth in the United States has produced a long-term decline in illegal entry.[76]

Immigration policy involves many complex decisions, including how many to admit, whether to criminalize unauthorized entry, whether to give preference by skills or by relationship with current U.S. residents or by refugee status, whether to admit permanent immigrants or guest workers or both, and whether Mexico is to be given special consideration. Finally, the most complex question is how to deal with the millions of unauthorized residents currently living in the United States. Legalization of their presence, while it infuriates conservatives who view it as an amnesty, is vital for allowing them to upgrade their skills and thus make an increased contribution to the economy, just as occurred with those legalized under IRCA.[77]

Progress on immigration legislation is glacially slow since not only must Congress decide each of these questions, but each of these questions attracts vociferous interest groups that cut across party lines. Actors changing sides on the issue further slows progress. In 2000, the AFL-CIO shifted from opposing immigration to favoring legalization of undocumented workers so that management could not use the threat of deportation to prevent low-wage workers from organizing. The U.S. population remains firmly divided on the immigration issue, with 52 percent responding to a 2007 poll by saying that immigration hurts the United States, while 39 percent declared it helped. As *Texas Monthly* writer Michael Ennis noted: "There's a reason why immigration policy never works: It's hard to find solutions when we aren't, as a nation, sure about the problem."[78]

The immigration issue is complicated by competing interest groups within the political parties and outside them and by the difficulty of allocating scarcity (the opportunity to work in United States). By definition, scarcity means some win and some lose. Even free marketers such as Nobel-prize winning economist Gary Becker feel the United States cannot admit unlimited numbers of immigrants as it did in the nineteenth century since government spending per resident is now far higher than it was in the nineteenth century. The implications of no limits are indicated by a 2009 Pew Research Center poll that indicated that a third of Mexicans wanted to move to the United States.[79]

Studies published during the Fox administration emphasized that it was not joblessness or extreme poverty that caused individuals to emigrate from Mexico to the United States. Rather it was the widening gap between Mexican wages and U.S. wages. The ironic implication of this finding is that alleviating poverty in Mexico may actually increase emigration, since as individuals leave poverty, they become able to afford travel and the costs of hiring someone to smuggle them across the border.[80]

Part Nine

The New Millennium

Chapter 27

The 2000 Election

The Mexican electorate didn't vote against Zedillo. It voted against the PRI.

Carlos Fuentes, 2002[1]

CANDIDATE SELECTION

As the year 2000 approached, the Revolutionary Institutional Party (PRI) faced a task that it had never before confronted—deciding how it would choose its presidential candidate. Between the party's founding in 1929 and 1934, Calles had personally selected the party's presidential candidates. After 1934, incumbent presidents had made the selection. However, in his inaugural speech Zedillo pledged, "I will not interfere, in any way at all, in my party's decision-making process." In 1997, using the traditional political slang term *dedazo*, Zedillo reiterated his unwillingness to select his successor when he declared: "This kind of determinism is past. For the year 2000, we want to put forward a candidate who will appeal to the voters. Every vote counts. We have driven away the ghost of the dedazo."[2]

Leaders of the PRI decided that the party would hold a primary election to select the party's presidential candidate. This appeared to be the best alternative to the *dedazo* since the party had organized ten primary elections to select gubernatorial candidates during the Zedillo administration and eight of the primary victors had subsequently won the general election. PRI leaders had also identified "democracy" as a key demand of voters and felt that a primary would cause the electorate to associate the PRI with democracy. Since the PRI had never had a membership list, any registered voter would be allowed to vote in the primary.[3]

Although there were four names on the primary ballot, for all practical purposes the PRI primary race was between Francisco Labastida and Roberto Madrazo. Labastida began his government career in 1962 and had served as governor of Sinaloa, as secretary of energy in the 1980s, and in Zedillo's cabinet as secretary of agriculture and as secretary of the interior. Having held both elected office and cabinet positions, he straddled the two camps within the PRI. One camp contained foreign-trained neoliberal economists while the other was made up of old guard politicians who blamed economic policies of the neoliberals for a drop in the standard of living and thus support for the PRI.[4]

During the campaign, Labastida faced charges that he had stolen his gubernatorial election, a feeling shared by the 20,000 who had marched in protest the day before he took office as governor. The other charge that confronted him was that he was the "official candidate" supported by Zedillo and that the primary election was merely a smokescreen for an old fashioned *dedazo*. Labastida never could shake this perception, even though Zedillo repeatedly declared his neutrality.[5]

Labastida's main primary opponent was Tabasco Governor Roberto Madrazo. Madrazo first reached national prominence when the Party of the Democratic Revolution (PRD) contested his 1994 victory in Tabasco's gubernatorial election. Zedillo had tried to ease him out of office, but he had clung to the position, thus helping create what was to become his trademark—a maverick image. Madrazo even remained in office after the federal attorney general determined that Madrazo had far exceeded the state-imposed campaign finance limit. However, since the spending limit was a state law and Madrazo kept Tabasco under tight control, the state courts never took action on this flagrant violation of spending limits.

During the primary campaign, Madrazo spent some $25 million on TV commercials funded by the State of Tabasco. The commercials, broadcast nationwide, supposedly served to boost the state's image, but mainly boosted Madrazo's.[6]

Madrazo's campaign blended slightly risqué humor with the appealing image of the little man against the system. In a televised debate for primary candidates, Madrazo charged that Labastida "just wants to continue the same failed policies we have now." Madrazo charged that these "failed policies" included economic reforms that left so many in poverty. He declared, correctly as it turned out, that Labastida would be no match for Vicente Fox, the leading contender for the PAN presidential nomination. To cap off what for Mexico was unprecedented negative campaigning, Madrazo accused Labastida of being favored by the then-reviled former president Salinas.[7]

When the primary was held on November 7, 1999, Labastida sailed to an easy victory, drawing 5.3 million votes compared to the 3.8 million votes for the other three candidates. The primary indicated that the PRI still retained enormous organizational and mobilizational strength as it set up 64,200 polling places and involved more than 450,000 individuals who served as voting officials and poll watchers. Despite charges from Madrazo and others that Zedillo had tipped the scales in favor of Labastida by using his influence over local party organizations, most evaluations of the primary were positive. The losers accepted defeat, remained in the party, and campaigned for Labastida.[8]

The 2000 presidential election saw several changes from previous practice. One was that governors, in addition to the incumbent president's cabinet members, had become serious contenders for the presidency. In addition to Madrazo, Vicente Fox, the governor of Guanajuato, cast his hat into the ring. Even though Fox supposedly lost his hotly disputed gubernatorial race in 1991, he won the governorship in 1995 with almost twice as many votes as his PRI opponent. In July 1997, Fox announced that he was seeking the PAN nomination for president. Fox broke with past PAN practices by declaring his candidacy three years prior to the presidential election. He sensed that the traditional wing of the party, which viewed him as newcomer and a populist leader with little attachment to the PAN's ideological principles, would never allow him to be a candidate unless he built up sufficient political momentum to make himself unstoppable. He commented: "I know that I do not stand a chance of winning the party's nomination if I leave it to the party apparatus. My strength lies in my capacity to appeal to the public at large."[9]

In order to build support for his nomination, Fox organized an independent group known as the Friends of Fox, which raised funds to finance his run for the PAN presidential nomination. He recruited as members a wide variety of people, many of whom had no ties to the PAN. Eventually the Friends of Fox became a bigger organization than the PAN, claiming a membership of 3 million throughout Mexico. Fox spent so much time outside Guanajuato building support for his candidacy that critics charged him with governing the state by fax.[10]

Fox—a towering figure, over six foot six in his trademark cowboy boots—took the PAN by storm. While touring around the country, he emphasized that he wanted to bring the success he had as governor of Guanajuato to the entire nation. In fact, in 1998, he enjoyed an 86 percent approval rating as governor, a rating above that of Zedillo. The central theme of his campaign was the need for change after seventy-one years of PRI misrule. He courted business by declaring, "The private sector will be completely integrated into the task of governing." At the same time, he cast himself as a plain talking, no-nonsense populist who had been raised on a ranch.[11]

His down-home image belied his upper-middle-class background and his having reached the peak of the multinational corporate world before plunging into politics. He was born into a ranching family and grew up on a ranch purchased by his American paternal grandfather, thus his decidedly non-Spanish surname. He left the ranch to study business administration at the Universidad Iberoamericana and then in 1964 signed on as a route manager for Coca-Cola. He was transferred to Mexico City in 1972 and in 1975 became president of Coca-Cola of Mexico. In 1979, rather than accepting an offer to direct Coke's Latin American operations from Miami, he left the company to manage the family's two footwear factories and its 1,100-acre vegetable farm.

For almost a decade, he struggled to turn a profit freezing broccoli and making cowboy boots at his family businesses. He blamed his lack of business success on an inept state that had created an unfavorable business climate. Given his frustration with government, he was easily recruited to run for Congress in 1988 by the PAN's presidential candidate, Manuel Clouthier. He won the election and received national attention at Salinas's inauguration for having fashioned ballots into giant ears which parodied Salinas's prominent natural ears.[12]

After his stint in the Chamber of Deputies, he "lost" his first election for governor and then was elected as governor of Guanajuato in 1995. During his term as governor, he improved schools, attracted foreign investment, and started a bank that granted credits of as little as $50 to 45,000 entrepreneurs.[13]

While he was president of Coca-Cola of Mexico and while he was serving as governor, Fox formed close ties to the business community. He drew on these ties when he formed the Friends of Fox, which financed his efforts to secure the PAN nomination. Industrialists seeking a personal meeting with him were expected to drum up $300,000 for the campaign.[14]

When he started his quixotic quest for the presidential nomination, funds were so limited that he relied on free media, constantly endeavoring to make his campaign newsworthy and thus attract coverage. Fox's self-promotion paid off. In July 1997, fewer than 18 percent of voting-age Mexicans could identify him, while a year-and-a-half later that figure was almost 70 percent. By the fall of 1999, he had built up so much political momentum that no other candidate registered for the PAN presidential primary, leaving Fox as the PAN candidate by default.[15]

In contrast to Labastida and Fox, who both emerged from relative obscurity to capture their party's nomination, the PRD's candidate for the 2000 presidential election, Cuauhtémoc Cárdenas, had enjoyed extremely high name recognition since his 1988 candidacy. In April 1999, while still serving as Mexico City mayor, Cárdenas announced he would seek the presidency for a third time. In fact, he had been campaigning for the presidency virtually non-stop since 1988 and faced no serious competition for the PRD nomination.

THE CAMPAIGN

At the end of November 1999, 43 percent of voters polled declared they would vote for Labastida, while Fox's support was 27 percent and Cárdenas's 8 percent, with 22 percent undecided. This poll indicated that each of the three major candidates had a different task. Labastida's task was to maintain his lead. Fox's was to build broad support beyond the PAN's traditional base so he could oust the PRI from Los Pinos—the presidential residence. Cárdenas, who never moved beyond a distant third place, was faced with the choice of soldiering on alone to election day or forming an alliance with Fox to oust the PRI and thus share in the credit for democratizing Mexico.[16]

The three main presidential candidates agreed there was a pressing need for foreign investment and fiscal discipline. None of the three advocated turning away from the policies set in place by former president Carlos Salinas and his successor Ernesto Zedillo. One of the reasons for this consensus on leaving economic policy largely unchanged was that during the first nine months of 2000, Mexico's economy was growing at a brisk 7.5 percent.[17]

More than ever before, the 2000 Mexican presidential campaign was media-driven, taking on the trappings of U.S. presidential campaigns. The resemblance to U.S. campaigns was hardly surprising since the Labastida campaign hired James Carville, the political consultant who managed Bill Clinton's 1992 campaign. Dick Morris, another political consultant who had advised Clinton,

Figure 27.1 *Fox campaigning*

Source: Benjamín Flores/*Proceso*

joined the Fox campaign. Fox summed up the crucial role of TV during the campaign, "Have charisma, and look good on TV, and you can become president." PRD leader Andrés Manuel López Obrador was less upbeat on the role of media, declaring, "Combine money, television, and the large number of Mexican voters who are nearly illiterate, and you could elect a cow as president."[18]

At the beginning of the official campaign in January 2000, Labastida looked practically invincible, since he had the legendary PRI political machine at his service, the incumbent PRI president Ernesto Zedillo was popular, the economy was growing, and his opposition was divided between the PRD and the PAN.[19]

Although his campaign adopted the slogan of "the new PRI," Labastida stood for anything but change. In three decades in government, he had never rocked the PRI boat even slightly. The changes he promised were so innocuous as to be almost imperceptible. In addition, as political scientist Denise Dresser commented, "He's a gray figure, not a stellar personality, he hasn't accomplished much, he doesn't speak very well, he's been lackluster in every job."[20]

Fox, using salty language and attired in denim and cowboy boots, was anything but gray. Rather he exuded freshness, manliness, renewal, and an end of the PRI's stiff style. To reinforce this image, he headhunted a public relations coordinator. Eventually he selected Francisco Ortiz, who had worked for thirteen years at Procter & Gamble and for seven at Televisa. Ortiz had never met Fox before he was hired. Since there was general consensus on the economic model Mexico had adopted, Fox focused on the notion of *change.* His campaign motto was "the change which is right for you." Rather than focusing on what change would lead to, Fox unremittingly portrayed change as leading away from the PRI's innumerable disasters and disliked presidents. Rather than suggesting changes in the economic model, he simply promised more economic growth—7 percent—than any other candidate.[21]

Fox focused on winning over constituencies outside the PAN's traditionally restricted base. He wooed Cárdenas's supporters by speaking of the "useful vote" ("*voto útil*") that if cast for Fox would get the PRI out of office. Casting a vote for Cárdenas, who continued to trail badly at the polls, was described simply as a vote wasted. To build bridges to the left, Fox paid tribute to Cárdenas's role in building democracy in 1988. His deliberate use of crude language, combined with his ranch attire, targeted what he defined as the 40 percent of the population without money or education, few of whom would normally vote for the PAN.[22]

The Fox campaign highlighted the candidate's character and personal life while downplaying issues and party platforms. It relied heavily on denouncing existing problems, which candidate Fox promised to resolve. He declared, "The narcos took over the PRI long ago." Rather than accusing Labastida of any failing that the PRI candidate could respond to, Fox simply belittled his opponent, whose name he would deliberately mispronounce so that it came out "*la vestida*" ("the cross-dresser"). On one occasion, Fox referred to Labastida as "a faggot tied to his wife's apron strings."[23]

Cárdenas's campaign never recaptured the political magic of 1988. By his third presidential campaign, he was no longer a novelty. Also, after having served as mayor of Mexico City, he was considered more as an administrator than as a challenger to the system—a mantle that Fox had inherited. Rather than relying on a catchy notion such as "change," Cárdenas's most dramatic proposal was a revision of the North American Free Trade Agreement (NAFTA)—a proposal that had failed to attract much support when he proposed it in 1994. He dismissed pleas for a political alliance with the PAN to topple the PRI by declaring Fox's party too pro-business. He similarly dismissed Fox when he declared, "I don't think he represents the real and deep change that Mexico needs."[24]

With the first of two nationally televised debates on April 25, the political momentum shifted definitively to Fox. No lofty intellectual discussion occurred, but instead, each time Labastida launched a verbal attack on Fox, the PAN candidate deftly responded. When Labastida chided Fox for using vulgar language, Fox shot back that he could clean up his language, but the PRI could never clean up corruption. When Labastida said he was the candidate for change, Fox responded, "Labastida talks about change, but he's been in the PRI for 37 years." Sometimes Fox did not even need to respond. In the debate, Labastida, speaking of Fox, stated, "In the last few weeks, he has called me shorty, he has called me a little sissy, he called me a stuffed suit, has called me henpecked, has made obscene gestures on television referring to me . . .." Labastida's repeating Fox's insults not only reinforced the image of weakness Fox sought to portray but provided the Fox campaign with video footage that was incorporated into future campaign ads.[25]

By May, a poll in the newspaper *Reforma* indicated that Labastida was favored by 42 percent of likely voters, while Fox was at 40 percent. Cárdenas had virtually faded from the race, with only 16 percent support. These figures were particularly ominous for Labastida since his poll numbers were falling and Fox's were rising. To salvage an electoral victory, Labastida shed his notion of the "new PRI" and publicly embraced members of the party's old guard, such as Manuel Bartlett. Members of the old guard were best known for their ability to fix elections, not for their commitment to democracy. It had been Bartlett, in his role of secretary of the interior, who had been overseeing the vote count in 1988 when the computer "crashed."

As the date of the July election approached, most polls showed Labastida remained ahead of Fox, but the difference between the two candidates was less than the margin of error. What was clear was that in the five months before the election, there had been a 12 percent shift in voter preferences away from Labastida and toward Fox. It was the campaign itself that had caused this shift, not voters' political beliefs at the start of the 2000 campaign.[26]

ELECTION DAY

At 8 a.m., July 2, 2000, almost all of the 113,000 polling places around Mexico opened on time. Returns coming into the presidential residence during the day indicated that Fox was building up a commanding lead. To head off conflicting claims as to who won, Liébano Sáenz, Zedillo's personal secretary, repeatedly informed Labastida that he was behind and that the results of the

Table 27.1 *2000 presidential election results*

Candidate	Percentage of vote
Fox	43.43
Labastida	36.89
Cárdenas	17.00
Others	2.68
Total	100.00

Source: Lawson (2004: 10, Table 1.1)

election would be respected. After the polls closed, both TV networks broadcast results of exit polls indicating that Fox enjoyed a substantial lead. At 11 p.m., José Woldenberg, president of the Federal Electoral Institute (IFE), announced on television that Fox had won. He declared, "We are a country in which a change of government can be accomplished peacefully by means of a regulated competition, without recourse to force by the loser, without risk of retrogression." Immediately after Woldenberg spoke, Zedillo preempted any attempt by the PRI to challenge the results. He confirmed Fox's victory and declared, "For the good of our beloved Mexico, I sincerely hope for the success of the next government which will be led by Vicente Fox."[27]

Rather than resorting to the standard litany of election losers, "We wuz robbed," all the losing candidates accepted Fox's victory. The PRI had little choice but to accept the results of the election since it had few of the levers of power that it had held in 1988. Given the strength of the opposition, any challenge would likely have left it even worse off.[28]

Polls before the election failed to project the margin of Fox's victory since most poll takers assumed "undecided" voters would split along the same lines as those who declared a preference. However, as it turned out, most of the "undecideds" opted for Fox. Even though Fox won the presidential election, in the congressional balloting on the same day the PRI retained the largest delegations in both houses of Congress. In addition, the PRI held nineteen governorships and a majority in twenty-one state legislatures.[29]

Many voters split their tickets, casting a ballot for Fox and for the congressional candidate of some other party. In forty-two of Mexico's 300 congressional districts, the representative elected to the Chamber of Deputies was from a different party than the winner of the presidential balloting. As a result of this split vote, Fox would face a divided Congress, making it much harder to deliver on his campaign promise of "change."[30]

Political scientist Lorenzo Meyer reflected the consensus on the elections when he stated, "In July 2000, Mexico underwent its first orderly and relatively peaceful change of political regime in its history as an independent country." Immediately after the elections, a majority of Mexicans, regardless of their party affiliation, considered that Mexico was a democracy. Writing later, the then-president of the IFE, José Woldenberg, declared the 2000 presidential election was a success in terms of: 1) massive voting, 2) alternatives presented to voters, 3) good administration, and 4) its not being marred by major incidents.[31]

Despite having successfully brought about regime change via elections, Mexico remained under the heavy influence of very non-democratic entities such as multinational corporations (MNCs) and drug traffickers. Notions such as "freedom" had a very different meaning to Mexicans living in poverty, as Nobel-price winning economist Amartya Sen noted, "People are only free where they can provide for their basic needs and realize their innate abilities."[32]

Historian Héctor Aguilar Camín observed even before the 2000 election that democratic elections alone would not solve Mexico's pressing social problems. He stated, "Mexico could become democratic tomorrow and have clean elections, but in no way would that create the million jobs the country needs each year for its young people."[33]

WHY FOX WON

Fox won the 2000 elections by drawing in many voters from beyond the traditional PAN base and by causing many traditional PRI supporters to remain at home as a result of his attacks on Labastida. Sixty-six percent of those voting for Fox cited "change" as the reason they voted for him. Fox could successfully wear the mantle of "change" since the PAN was associated with social transformation in Mexico going back to the PAN challenges to the PRI in the 1980s. The change most Fox voters envisioned was bringing in leaders who could competently manage the economy, fight crime, and reduce corruption.[34]

Fox's macho bravura, reminiscent of a traditional Mexican strongman, or caudillo, appealed to the Mexican public. His charisma and the independence of the media enabled this image to fly. Fox realized that it was only possible to communicate with 60 million voters through the mass media and organized his campaign accordingly.[35]

Fox successfully attracted voters by referring to the *voto útil* (strategic vote). After framing the election around the issue of change, he then drove home the notion that he was the most likely one to bring about this change. He directly appealed to Cárdenas supporters, declaring that the PRD candidate was destined to lose, and thus anyone desiring change and voting for Cárdenas was wasting a vote.

Fox portrayed his record as governor of Guanajuato as a success in terms of honesty, education, job creation, economic growth, and foreign investment. These same results, he promised, would occur at the national level during his presidency.[36]

Given Mexico's rate of economic growth at the time, neoliberalism appealed to voters. It also suited the political proclivities of the 57 percent of the Mexicans who defined themselves as being on the political right.[37]

Fox's 2000 victory was a resounding win for the PAN and especially for Fox. The PAN candidate received 106 percent more votes than the party had received in the 1997 mid-term elections. In 2000, Fox outpolled the PAN candidates for the Chamber of Deputies by 1.8 million votes. Key constituencies voting for Fox included: 1) people who had traditionally identified with the PAN, 2) independent voters, and 3) PRI partisans who were dissatisfied with the party and who probably voted for Madrazo in the party's primary. In addition, some 10 percent of Fox voters identified themselves with the center-left PRD. Young people favoring economic growth and accepting U.S.–Mexican economic integration turned out heavily for Fox. A final constituency turning out for Fox was the anti-PRI vote. In the disputed 1988 election this vote went for Cárdenas, in 1994 it went to the PAN, in 1997 to the PRD, and then in 2000, back to the PAN.[38]

One-round elections in which the candidate with the plurality wins are essentiality zero-sum games, and thus the negatives of losing candidates are as just as important as the positives of the winner. Given its recent track record, the PRI never was able to convince voters it stood for either "change" or "democracy" even though it clearly understood that voters were demanding both. Voters remembered, and blamed the PRI for, an assortment of outrages and debacles ranging from the 1968 massacre of students to the 1994–1995 economic collapse.[39]

Demographics ran against the PRI. Those who had parents alive during Porfiriato, those who could remember Lázaro Cárdenas's reforms of the 1930s, and those remembering the rapid economic growth from the 1930s through the 1970s were rapidly being overwhelmed by new generations. Labastida outpolled Fox among voters over sixty and those who had less than a high school education, but that was decidedly not the new Mexico. Among eighteen-to-twenty-five-year olds, Labastida ran twenty percentage points behind Fox. Among those with a college education, Labastida ran twenty-nine percentage points behind Fox. Key elements of the old PRI coalition, such as organized labor and rural voters, had become come less important in percentage terms and harder to mobilize.[40]

The PRI was burdened not only by unfavorable demographics and long-held grudges against it for sins past but by its failure to offer a new vision. Before the 1997 mid-term elections *New York Times* correspondent Julia Preston wrote of the PRI, "Since it rarely has to defend its position in elections, it no longer has a definite platform of ideas to offer." Labastida failed to emphasize that as president he would continue Zedillo's popular policies. Rather he unsuccessfully attempted to wear the mantle of change. Labastida was unable to shake the image of his representing the old PRI, in large part due to Madrazo having so portrayed him in the PRI primary.[41]

In 2000, Cárdenas repeated many of the mistakes that dogged his unsuccessful 1994 presidential campaign. He had trouble articulating an economic alternative, perhaps reflecting the party's lack of clarity on the subject. Cárdenas's traditional nationalist, anti-American themes appealed to an ever-shrinking sector of the population. To compound his problems, he continued to emphasize the campaign rally over the use of mass media.[42]

The PRD itself became more of a liability than an asset. Since, by its own admission, the March 1999 internal election for party president that the PRD organized was so crooked that it had to be annulled, many felt they did not want the PRD running the nation. The expelling from the party of co-founder Porfirio Muñoz Ledo in January 2000 for having accepted the presidential nomination of the PARM, a small, ill-defined party, raised the question of just what the PRD leadership stood for (other than power).[43]

With these liabilities, not surprisingly Cárdenas obtained 17 percent fewer votes than the PRD had obtained in the mid-term elections of 1997. Presidential candidate Cárdenas even received 689,186 fewer votes than the PRD candidates for the Chamber of Deputies received in 2000.[44]

WHY DEMOCRACY TRIUMPHED

In the 1934 presidential elections, the official party received 98.2 percent of the vote, a figure that steadily declined after that. By 1994, it received only 50.2 percent. Thus in a sense the question was not if, but when, the PRI would lose the presidency. This decline reflects a variety of changes in Mexico, such as a better-educated, more urban population. In addition, with privatization the government had less ability to intervene in the election process. As Mexico changed, more opposition political victories were recognized at the state level. Just before the July 2, 2000 election, the PAN governed 29.6 percent of the population at the state level and the PRD 20.7 percent. As these victories were recognized and people became accustomed to not being under a PRI state administration, they increasingly decided that a vote for the opposition would be respected and voted against the PRI in increasing numbers. Also, once they saw opposition administrations functioning at the state level, the notion of an opposition administration at the national level appeared less intimidating.[45]

The creation of a truly independent IFE was crucial for the emergence of electoral democracy. Granting independence to the IFE in 1994 was a risk the Salinas administration took because it was seen as necessary to keep the PRD from abandoning electoral politics and joining the rebel movement in Chiapas. Then-president Salinas, believing his own rhetoric, felt that his economic reforms were so successful that the PRI would be able to retain power on its own merits. Once election administration was removed from the executive branch to the IFE, the PRI could not reverse this reform since it lacked sufficient seats in the Chamber of Deputies to change the law on its own.[46]

After 1994, the IFE made decisions affecting the entire electoral process, down to and including the location of polling places. In a process analogous to jury selection in the United States, the IFE chose citizens by lot to staff the polling stations. In addition, between 1994 and 2000 the IFE spent $1.2 billion to produce a tamper-proof electoral infrastructure, including photo ID cards for each voter. In 2000, under IFE auspices, the political parties mobilized 346,958 poll watchers who were joined by 38,433 independent election observers. It also provided public financing for political parties, so among other things, Fox could blanket Mexico with his call for change.[47]

Much of the movement towards democracy in the 1990s occurred thanks to non-governmental organizations (NGOs) that brought together youthful reformers, environmentalists, old leftists, feminists, and other reform-minded people. These NGOs formed the non-partisan Civic Alliance (Alianza Cívica) which observed the 1994 elections. It continued to observe elections and press for further reform to correct the faults in the electoral process that it had observed. Rather than mobilizing to support any one candidate, the Civic Alliance remained strictly non-partisan and dedicated itself to ensuring electoral fairness.[48]

Independent media was also crucial to the emergence of democracy. In the 2000 elections, the all-important TV coverage was generally balanced. In addition, repeated press reports on scandals had undermined the establishment. Finally, the publication of polling data proved crucial to efforts by civic groups to monitor elections and prevent fraud.[49]

The PRI lost power because it implemented too many political reforms. Each reform was designed to placate the opposition while maintaining hegemony. After economic crises, it offered political reform, since it had nothing else to offer. Eventually these reforms created a relatively even playing field, forcing the PRI candidate to run on his own merits, which the voters found lacking.[50]

THE 2000 U.S. AND MEXICAN ELECTIONS COMPARED

The progress Mexico made toward democratization during the last quarter of the twentieth century can be put into perspective by comparing Mexico's 2000 presidential election with the presidential election held in the United States the same year:

- In Mexico, each vote has equal weight. In the United States, as a result of the Electoral College, the votes from states with low population count more. Thus it is possible, as occurred in the 2000 U.S. presidential elections, for the winner to receive fewer votes than his principal opponent.
- In Mexico, the non-partisan IFE organizes elections so that the administration of elections does not favor any one party. In the United States, elections are in the hands of partisan local officials, who may, wittingly or unwittingly, make decisions favoring their own party.
- In Mexico, there are uniform paper ballots that are marked with a pen and then hand counted at the polling station. The standardized design of the ballot, across the nation and from one election to another, avoids the introduction of new designs—such as Palm Beach County's famed butterfly ballot—which voters might fail to interpret correctly. The paper ballot also avoids machine malfunction rendering large numbers of votes questionable, such as the Florida votes left in question by hanging chads. Since they leave a verifiable paper trail, paper ballots, as opposed to computerized voting, give the voter greater confidence that the count will be honest. In Mexico, any citizen could monitor vote tabulation from polling station to the national level. Vote totals were posted in written form in front of each polling station. As vote totals came in, they were posted on the internet in real time. Poll watchers ensured that polling-place counts were accurate and that the numbers posted in front of the polling places matched those on the internet.[51]
- The candidates of all parties in the Mexican presidential elections were allowed into the first round of the televised debates. After the public had had a chance to hear their views, the three most popular candidates were selected, based on their polling numbers, to participate in the second round. Opening the debate to all parties allows the airing of ideas not widely voiced in the mainstream. For example, minor party candidate Gilberto Rincón Gallardo denounced intolerance against minority groups. He specifically mentioned the murder of homosexuals in Chiapas. In the U.S. election, only the Democratic and Republican candidates were allowed to debate.[52]

- In Mexico, political parties and elections were publicly funded, and presidential campaigns had a $52-million spending limit. Individual private donations were limited to $80,000 and corporate donations were prohibited. In 2000, the IFE distributed $300 million to the parties to maintain their organizations and to carry out campaigns. This sharply reduces the influence of moneyed interests in the electoral process. The IFE takes these funding limitations seriously. The PAN and its coalition partner in the 2000 election were fined $48.8 million for failure to disclose donations of $8.1 million, for exceeding spending limits by $1.6 million, and for receiving $4 million from corporations. The PRI was fined $98 million for receiving $45 million that Pemex channeled through the oil workers union to support the Labastida campaign.[53]
- As a condition for receiving radio and TV licenses, Mexican broadcasters were required to allow candidates free access to the media. In Mexico, each party received 200 free TV hours and 250 hours of radio time and could use public funding to buy more airtime. This made candidates less beholden to moneyed groups than they were in the United States.[54]
- A larger proportion of the electorate was involved in selecting Mexico's president in 2000. In Mexico, voter turnout was 64 percent. Only 51 percent voted in the U.S. elections. The difference in the percentage of adults voting is even wider than these figures would indicate since Mexico has a proactive voter registration program. Registrars go from house to house to register voters. In 2000, 93 percent of those over eighteen had been issued a voter ID. Only 63.9 percent of the U.S. population over eighteen was registered.[55]

Chapter 28

The Fox Administration, 2000–2006

> The year 2000 didn't lead to a new legal framework, but to a continuation of the old order . . .The economy remains lifeless, the social structure is just as, if not more, skewed, than before, and the institutional structure is just as inefficient . . . The same can be said for corrupt politicians and administrators.
>
> Lorenzo Meyer, 2007[1]

When Vicente Fox took the oath of office in December 2000, he enjoyed an 80 percent approval rating. Even though many had predicted that replacing the experienced PRI administration with the novice PAN would plunge Mexico into chaos, the transition was impeccably smooth. The future seemed to bode socioeconomic change every bit as radical and far-reaching as the political change Fox's election victory represented.[2]

Since Fox had structured his presidential campaign around the group known as the Friends of Fox, whose members were largely from the private sector, not surprisingly he selected eight experienced private-sector managers for his cabinet. His choice of Francisco Gil Díaz as treasury secretary underscored his commitment to continue the free market policies of previous administrations. Gil Díaz, a University of Chicago-trained economist, had served previously with the Salinas administration and the Banco de México. Fox's non-economic cabinet appointments were more innovative and included as foreign relations minister Jorge G. Castañeda, a former member of the Mexican Communist Party and one of Mexico's best known intellectuals. Other cabinet members came from Fox's own inner circle from Guanajuato, academia, and in two cases, the PRI. While his cabinet was talented, its members were largely ignorant of federal public service rules and demands. Its members preferred self-expression to teamwork, which led to its being nicknamed the Montessori cabinet—its members could do whatever they wanted.[3]

In 2000, tax revenues were roughly 12 percent of gross domestic product (GDP)—below the level of other Latin American countries with similar per capita income and well below that of the OECD countries. To expand this meager tax base, Fox proposed that the 15 percent value-added tax (VAT) be extended to food, medicine, books, and school fees. He felt that he could go over the heads of politicians and appeal directly to the people, who in turn would pressure legislators into passing the measures he sought. In one of the many interviews designed to drum up support for the tax reform, he declared, "We will raise the fiscal income needed precisely to combat poverty in Mexico, to build up the universities, the schools, the hospitals that we need, also to build up roads and infrastructure."[4]

Congress failed to pass Fox's proposed tax reform for several reasons. While the World Bank might argue the increase in tax revenues he proposed would finance poverty alleviation, most of the electorate felt a tax increase would simply take money out of their pockets and finance profligate spending. As Fox soon learned, the constitutional instruments available to the president to promote legislative change are rather limited. This proved decisive, since Fox's PAN held only 41 percent of the seats in the Chamber of Deputies and 36 percent in the Senate.[5]

Fox's attempt to appeal directly to the public via the media was rendered ineffective by Congress jealously guarding the political power that it had only recently begun to wield independently of the president. Many PRI members opposed Fox's tax reform proposal because they were reluctant to allow a PAN administration to increase its political stature. Another factor underlying Fox's legislative defeat was his scant interest in involving the PRI and the PRD in the legislative process and thus acknowledging the surging pluralism of the Mexican political system. Fox's failure to form coalitions also doomed his efforts to change labor and energy policy.[6]

In mid-2002, political scientist Lorenzo Meyer noted: "Fox is not the captain of the ship. We are just floating. I worry that the rest of his term is going to be characterized by just surviving." After his initial legislative defeats, rather than being able to regroup and seize the initiative, Fox found the media focused on his romance with his spokesperson Marta Sahagún, his marriage to her, her presidential aspirations, and the subsequent controversies involving the bride and groom having their previous marriages annulled by the Catholic Church.[7]

The mid-term elections in 2003 only compounded Fox's legislative problems. As a result of the elections, the PAN's delegation in the Chamber of Deputies shrank from 207 to 151, while that of the PRI increased from 211 to 224 and that of the PRD from 50 to 97.[8]

In 2003 voters punished the PAN for failing to deliver the 7 percent annual economic growth Fox had promised during his campaign, thus indicating that while campaign promises are cheap, they are not without cost. They slammed the PAN for Fox's failure to enact major fiscal reform. Also, as has happened throughout Latin America, the coming of democracy created high expectations that governments were not able to address immediately in terms of poverty elimination and reduced economic inequality. The low turnout in 2003, as compared to 2000, also reflected the large number of voters who voted to oust the PRI in 2000 but who saw no reason to vote again in 2003. As a result, turnout for the mid-term elections was only 41.7 percent compared to 63.97 percent in 2000. In states with no local elections, only 37.44 percent of voters cast a ballot.[9]

The removal of the PRI from power and Fox taking office forced all three major parties—the PAN, the PRI and the PRD—to realign their images. These parties all moved toward the political center and increasingly focused on who would secure nominations and on maneuvering within the party, as opposed to contesting elections outside the party. Party switching—especially by PRI members denied a desired nomination—was rampant. Former PRI-deputy Demetrio Sodi, who moved from the PRI to the PRD, was an extreme case. After losing the PRD's 2000 Mexico City mayoral nomination to Andrés Manuel López Obrador, he switched to the PAN, which nominated him to be its mayoral candidate in 2006. With no compelling messages and fewer public-sector jobs with which to reward supporters, the public lost interest in the parties. Given the massive federal subsidies the parties received, party leaders could ignore their members between elections.[10]

The PAN under Fox faced three challenges: 1) forging a working relationship between the PAN congressional delegation and the president; 2) forging a working relationship between the PAN congressional delegation (which remained a minority) and the delegations of other parties so that legislation could be passed; and 3) projecting a clear message of what the party stood for once the PRI had been removed from the presidency. The first task was made more difficult by Fox having bypassed the party to win the PAN nomination and the presidential election, by his failure to appoint sufficient PAN members to his cabinet, and by PAN old-timers considering him an outsider who came late to the party after having had a career in business. The party's poor showing in the 2003 elections made the second task even more difficult. The party never rose to the third task facing it—clearly stating that it had something to offer beyond economic orthodoxy and a continuation of PRI social policies.[11]

The PRI, long accustomed to receiving orders from the incumbent president, faced two major challenges under Fox—determining who would be its leader and determining what the party stood for now that it was an opposition party. The party did in fact drift rudderless and clueless for a period after Fox's inauguration. Finally, Roberto Madrazo, the former governor of Tabasco, was selected PRI president, giving the party direction. Madrazo's leadership, the party's still formidable grass-roots machine, and its loyal base that almost instinctively voted for the PRI enabled the party to rebound and win numerous gubernatorial and municipal elections as well as a plurality in the 2003 mid-term congressional elections. The party failed to convey a coherent message as it remained torn between following the neoliberal course charted by its last three presidents or joining the growing throngs throughout Latin America who believed that the reduction of the role of the state by the neoliberals had only increased poverty and inequality.[12]

Elba Esther Gordillo, head of the powerful teachers union, led the neoliberal faction within the PRI. Eventually she lost out in a power struggle with Madrazo, left the PRI, and created a new political party. Given her influence over the teachers union—the most important get-out-the-vote machine in Mexico—this was a major blow to the PRI.[13]

Showing its ambivalence about neoliberalism, the party simply dodged the issue of economic policy, as is illustrated by a 2006 PRI candidate for the Federal District Legislative Assembly who stated: "We are not the intolerant right-wing and radical like the PAN, and we are also not populist and violent like the leftists in the PRD. We are in the center. We represent prudence, maturity and responsibility."[14]

The PRD also faced an identity crisis, since it, like the PAN, had been founded to challenge the PRI for power. As with the left throughout Latin America, it had to determine what it meant to be on the left in an increasingly globalized world. The party's message was further blurred by its becoming a haven for former members of the PRI, many of whom left the PRI when they failed to receive a desired nomination. As of early 2007, two-thirds of the party presidents had come from the PRI, as well as four of the seven governors who had been elected on the PRD ticket. The party's lack of a clear message is reflected in it receiving fewer votes than the PRI or the PAN in the 2003 congressional elections.[15]

From the time of its formation up until 2000, the PRD was under the influence of Cuauhtémoc Cárdenas. After Cárdenas's third defeat as presidential candidate, Andrés Manuel López Obrador, mayor of Mexico City, became the dominant personality within the party. In opposition to these two strong leaders a caucus arose within the party. This group, known as the New Left (Nueva Izquierda), was much more willing to negotiate with whoever was in power than Cárdenas or López Obrador were. Even though this group did not capture the party presidency during the Fox administration, it did enjoy strong grass-roots support.[16]

It was inevitable that Fox's presidency would lead to disappointment simply because problems resulting from seventy-one years of PRI rule were so systemic and because Fox had raised such high expectations. In addition, Fox was saddled with problems over which he had no control, including the economic downturn in the United States, the impact of the 9/11 attacks, and an unscrupulous PRI opposition determined to make his administration fail.[17]

By promising 7 percent annual economic growth, Fox had promised more than he could deliver. The 2001–2003 recession in the United States and the lack of a counter-cyclical policy response by his administration resulted in annual economic growth only averaging 0.7 percent during the first half of his administration. From 2004 to 2007, as the U.S. economy recovered and the price of oil rose, economic growth averaged 4 percent. Such levels of growth, the worst since the De la Madrid administration (1982–1988), led to a worsening of the employment situation. In Japan, with its near constant population, stagnation simply means lack of change. In Mexico, where huge numbers enter the job market annually, anything approaching stagnation leads to sharply increased social problems.[18]

The two main accomplishments for which Fox will be remembered are defeating the PRI and maintaining macroeconomic stability. Looking at the positive side of Fox's record, at the end of 2005, his former foreign minister Jorge G. Castañeda declared: "This has been better by far than any other government in the last 30 years. None of the catastrophes have occurred—devaluations, inflation, assassinations and uprisings . . . This is not a minor achievement."[19]

There are several other accomplishments of the Fox administration. Extreme poverty declined from 24.1 to 13.8 percent of the population between 2000 and 2006, likely the result of wage increases, his anti-poverty program Oportunidades, and remittances sent from the United States. He instituted a very popular, voluntary health insurance program (Seguro Popular), which by 2006 served 3.7 million families, 95 percent of whom were in the bottom fifth of income earners. He also introduced a popular microcredit program that distributed $660 million. Finally, legislation established a transparency-in-government program analogous to that created by the U.S. Freedom of Information Act.[20]

Marketed on television, Fox made a far better candidate than he did president. He failed to take charge and provide cabinet leadership, failed to set priorities, and turned a blind eye to alliance building. Fox's style reflected his belief that the state had a limited role in any matter related to the individual. By 2006, as political scientist Soledad Loaeza noted, "The eager candidate became a reluctant president who avoided tough choices and appeared hesitant and unable to hide the weariness caused by the responsibilities and constraints of the office."[21]

These shortcomings prevented substantial progress and in some cases even led to backsliding on a number of the priorities Fox had set. He had little success at fighting crime. Even though he maintained the macroeconomic stability inherited from his predecessor, economic growth barely exceeded the rate of population increase. Similarly, the lack of fiscal reform left tax collection at a rate similar to that of Haiti, which is not known for the quality of its public services. Finally, during Fox's administration, only 1.4 million formal-sector jobs were created, leading to massive emigration to the United States and an explosive increase in informal employment.[22]

Even though the sums involved were less than those involved in the Salinas administration scandals, corruption tainted the Fox administration. First Lady Marta Sahagún de Fox's young sons became millionaires almost overnight. An auditor estimated that a housing transaction involving her sons and the government cost the government $30 million since they purchased government land at only a small fraction of its appraised value. *Proceso* writer Daniel Lizárraga characterized the entire Fox administration as "marked by extravagance, public funds flowing into the president's personal accounts, and his illegally failing to declare property he owned". After Fox left office, Congress formed a commission to investigate how his family members had accumulated wealth so rapidly. However, in the venerable Mexican tradition of impunity, no action was taken before the commission's mandate expired. [23]

History will undoubtedly regard Fox as a transitional figure, much like Boris Yeltsin and Lech Walesa. As *Los Angeles Times* reporter Sam Enríquez noted just before the 2006 elections: "His accomplishments since booting out Mexico's long-ruling party six years ago have fallen short of his promises. He needs a Calderón and PAN victory to cement his legacy." Despite his failing to fulfill many of his promises, since people liked him as a person Fox left office with an approval rating of 61 percent.[24]

Chapter 29

The 2006 Elections

For the first time in a century, the right and the left are clearly defined as dominant political forces.

Sergio Aguayo, 2006[1]

CANDIDATE SELECTION

Andrés Manuel López Obrador

The 2006 election cycle started out with a clear front runner—Andrés Manuel López Obrador, widely referred to simply as AMLO. The frontrunner, the son of a shopkeeper of modest means, attended the National University in the early 1970s, at a time when the university was a hotbed of radicalism. He then returned to his native state of Tabasco, on the Gulf Coast, and for six years worked as state director of the National Indigenous Institute (INI). During this time, he carried out community development projects among the Chontal, an impoverished indigenous group.[2]

López Obrador became Tabasco state chair for the PRD and began to attract national attention. To protest the rigging of municipal elections in 1991, he organized a march to Mexico City, almost 500 miles away. AMLO ran for governor in 1994 and was defeated by Roberto Madrazo, who far exceeded campaign-spending limits to win the governorship. This resulted in López Obrador organizing a second protest march to Mexico City. In 1996, AMLO led a four-week occupation of Tabasco oil fields to protest environmental damage. After federal troops forcibly dislodged the protestors, he appeared on national TV with his head drenched in his own blood.[3]

In 1996, AMLO was elected national president of his party, the PRD. Under his leadership, the PRD gained votes and increased its number of office holders. In addition to bolstering the party at election time, he repeatedly hammered on the theme of the FOBAPROA (Bank Savings Protection Fund) bank bailout, which he described as "the corrupt being rewarded for irresponsibility."[4]

In 2000, López Obrador was elected mayor of Mexico City. He benefited from Cárdenas having resigned as mayor to run for president, since his replacement, the more popular Rosario Robles, boosted the standing of the PRD in the city. PRD popularity, plus López Obrador's natural gifts as a campaigner, enabled him to edge out two formable opponents—well-known lawyer and former PAN deputy Santiago Creel and former Mexican ambassador to the United States Jesús Silva-Herzog.[5]

As mayor, AMLO provided monthly stipends of $60 to the elderly, the handicapped, and single mothers—a program that proved to be extremely popular. At the same time, he double-decked an expressway and undertook other road projects, currying the favor of more affluent auto owners. He demonstrated his concern for education by providing school supplies to public school children without charge, opening nine high schools catering to low-income students, and founding the Autonomous University of Mexico City, whose students are selected by lottery, not entrance exams.[6]

If nature abhors vacuums, political establishments abhor highly popular challengers. López Obrador was indeed such a challenger. A 2004 opinion poll found that 39 percent of those polled favored him for the 2006–2012 presidential term, compared to only 23 percent for his closest rival, who at the time was First Lady Marta Sahagún. In an attempt to decrease AMLO's popularity, in 2004 several videos were leaked to the media. One showed his finance chief Gustavo Ponce smoking a cigar and playing high stakes baccarat in Las Vegas. This was followed by another video depicting his chief political operator René Bejarano stuffing thousands of dollars in cash, provided by a city contractor, into his pockets. Since none of the videos directly implicated López Obrador, their airing left him largely unscathed. Indeed, since a prominent PAN senator admitted having seen the videos before they went on the air, they convinced many that the videos were establishment dirty tricks aimed at undercutting AMLO.[7]

Two months after the video scandals, as they became known in Mexico, the Fox administration called for the removal of López Obrador's immunity from criminal prosecution. The Mexico City mayor, along with other top government officials, can only be indicted if Congress votes to strip of him of his immunity. According to Mexican law, those who are under indictment cannot run for office.

The indictment the Fox administration sought resulted from López Obrador supposedly having ignored a judge's order to halt construction on a road that crossed private property to provide access to a hospital. AMLO not only denied any wrongdoing but declared that removing his immunity was a desperate attempt to keep him off the 2006 ballot. On April 7, 2005, Congress voted 360 to 127 to strip AMLO of his criminal immunity, a process known as *desafuero*. In response, on April 24 more than 1 million staged a peaceful demonstration to protest the *desafuero*. Foreign media almost universally viewed the *desafuero* as being a politically motivated maneuver keep a formidable rival off the ballot. Fox, afraid that the whole effort might lead to instability and spook investors, dismissed his attorney general, who was handing the matter, and did not raise the question of AMLO's supposed offence again. Rather than keeping AMLO off the ballot, the *desafuero* enhanced his popularity by casting him as an underdog standing up to the powerful.[8]

In July 2005, López Obrador resigned as mayor to campaign full-time for the PRD presidential nomination. His accomplishments as mayor, his Spartan life style, and his apparent lack of interest in self-enrichment resulted in his leaving office with an unprecedented 76 percent approval rating. AMLO enjoyed such overwhelming popularity that the PRD did not even bother with a primary election. López Obrador simply became its presidential candidate, thus effecting a generational change from Cuauhtémoc Cárdenas, who was nineteen years his senior.[9]

Felipe Calderón

While López Obrador gained national prominence as an outsider challenging the system, the PAN's 2006 presidential candidate began life as a political insider. His father was Luis Calderón Vega, an early PAN leader. The younger Calderón spent his childhood in a highly politicized environment, handing out leaflets and painting political signs on walls—the main form of political discourse before television—to promote PAN candidates. With years of activism under his belt, he formally joined the PAN in 1980—at age eighteen.

In 1987, Calderón graduated from Mexico City's Escuela Libre de Derecho with a law degree. He later received a Master's in economics from the Autonomous Technological Institute of Mexico (ITAM) and another Master's in public administration from the JFK School of Government at Harvard.

At age nineteen, Calderón faced his first political crisis when his father resigned from the PAN to protest its having fallen under the influence of businessmen and its accepting campaign financing from the federal government—funds that Calderón père felt would compromise the party's independence. At the time, the younger Calderón decided not to follow his father, but rather to remain in the party and "take it back" from the outsiders.[10]

After his father's resignation from the PAN, Calderón came under the influence of Carlos Castillo Peraza, whom he described as his mentor. This mentor, who is considered the last intellectual to head the PAN, sought to inculcate traditional PAN values in the many new party members who had shifted from business to politics. Castillo Peraza, who was serving as PAN president, appointed Calderón as PAN secretary general in 1993. Two years later, Calderón ran for governor in his native Michoacán, a PRD stronghold. The 25 percent of the vote he received was 14 percent above the vote the previous PAN gubernatorial candidate had received.[11]

At thirty-three, Calderón became the PAN's youngest president ever after winning the party's internal election with the slogan, "Take power without losing the party." This slogan challenged the willingness of many to shed the party's original principles in an attempt to win elections. Calderón benefited from his having Castillo Peraza's support and from his having served previously as PAN youth director.[12]

As party president, 1996–1999, Calderón began to attract national attention. In 1996, he played a major role in drafting the political reform legislation that would allow Fox to take the presidency in 2000. In contrast to López Obrador, he supported the bank bailout known as FOBAPROA because he felt it vital to Mexico's economic health. Calderón also oversaw the continued expansion of the party, as the PAN won gubernatorial races in Aguascalientes, Nuevo León, and Querétaro.[13]

From 2000 to 2003, Calderón served as the PAN coordinator in the Chamber of Deputies. He failed to make much of an impression there, simply because the Fox administration had few legislative victories. In 2003, President Fox appointed him as head of the government–owned Public Works Bank. This was correctly viewed as a lightweight position for someone obviously wanting to move up the political ladder. Calderón did not have to wait long for such an opportunity, since in September of that year Fox appointed him secretary of energy.

In May 2004, the governor of Jalisco organized a rally—which Calderón and some 3,000 others attended—to show the governor's support for a Calderón presidential candidacy in 2006. Fox publicly reprimanded Calderón's "imprudence" for plunging into presidential politics while still a cabinet member, especially since the election was two years in the future. Calderón immediately resigned his cabinet post, declaring he had been unjustly criticized. This resignation proved to be an astute political move, since it turned the spotlight on the still poorly known Calderón. The resignation also gave him something of a maverick image, which the quite bland politician needed. Leaving the cabinet also allowed him to distance himself from the underachieving Fox administration.[14]

His resignation allowed Calderón to tour Mexico full-time to seek the PAN presidential nomination. However, his absence from the cabinet kept him out of the limelight while his chief rival for the nomination, Santiago Creel, remained as secretary of the interior—a position that ensured constant media exposure.

For the 2006 presidential race, the PAN decided that it would hold a primary election to select its presidential candidate, rather than making the selection in a party convention, as it had in the past. However, unlike the PRD and PRI primaries, in which any registered voter could participate, the PAN restricted voting to its 200,000 members and 800,000 activists. This proved to be decisive for Calderón, since although he was not well known to the public at large, he enjoyed very high name recognition among his party's faithful. The small size of the primary electorate enabled Calderón to effectively travel around the country promoting himself to PAN loyalists, without having to spend huge sums—which he lacked—to buy media. His message was simple—elect me to restore the party's conservative, Catholic values.[15]

Calderón won the PAN presidential candidacy in a three-round primary (one round in each of three geographical areas) with 51.79 percent of the vote. Several factors enabled Calderón to overtake Creel, who had started his campaign with 62 percent support, compared to Calderón's

8 percent. Calderón proved to be an effective campaigner, his deep roots in the party appealed to party stalwarts who were less than enthusiastic about Creel, who only joined the party in 1999, and he did well in a debate among those aspiring to the PAN nomination. Creel was hurt by one of his last acts as interior secretary, which was to grant 130 twenty-five-year gaming licenses to Apuestas Internacionales, a firm linked to Televisa. The deal smelled of favors in exchange for support from the dominant TV network. A final factor behind Calderón's victory was that 70 percent of those eligible failed to vote, skewing the voting population to those sharing Calderón's traditional party values. The burst of media attention surrounding his surprise victory over Creel gave Calderón a major boost in the polls and, for the first time, indicated that López Obrador had a serious rival.[16]

Roberto Madrazo

As was the case with Calderón, Roberto Madrazo, the PRI's 2006 presidential candidate, was born into a political family. His father was Carlos Madrazo, a would-be reformer of the party in the 1960s. The younger Madrazo first reached national prominence in 1994 when he was elected governor of Tabasco. However, the publicity he received was not what politicians normally seek. First came López Obrador's charges that he had stolen the elections. At his swearing-in ceremony on January 1, 1995, Madrazo was surrounded by 3,000 soldiers and police who kept protesters at bay. That image had hardly faded before documents were leaked showing that he had spent $70 million dollars—far in excess of the legal limit—during his gubernatorial campaign. Given these images, it is not surprising that Madrazo failed to win his party's 2000 presidential nomination.[17]

In 2002, Madrazo won the presidency of the PRI in an internal party election plagued with irregularities. After having used his stint as party president to position himself for a presidential race, Madrazo emerged as a strong contender to be the PRI presidential candidate in 2006. Many PRI leaders decided that, given his tawdry reputation, a Madrazo candidacy would be the kiss of death for the party, so they formed an informal caucus within the party known as "Everyone United Against Madrazo." This caucus decided to promote the PRI member with the best chance of defeating Madrazo in a primary and then winning the presidency. The person selected for this role was Arturo Montiel, former governor of the vote-rich State of Mexico. Shortly before the primary, information was leaked to the press on Montiel's financial dealings while he was serving as governor. He had deposited $2.8 million in a Merrill-Lynch account, had funneled a long list of other transactions through foreign and domestic bank accounts, and had diverted state funds to a PRI campaign in Michoacán. Overwhelmed by these revelations, Montiel withdrew from the PRI primary, leaving Madrazo unchallenged. These revelations provided Madrazo with a Pyrrhic victory since, instead of causing the public to view Montiel as corrupt, it reinforced the belief that PRI politicians in general were corrupt.[18]

THE CAMPAIGNS

Six major polls in January 2006 showed PRD candidate López Obrador with a 5 to 10 percent lead over his closest rival, Felipe Calderón. These same polls showed the PRI in a distant third place, where it would remain.[19]

On January 19, 2006, to emphasize his commitment to the poor, López Obrador formally inaugurated his campaign in Metlatónoc, Guerrero, the poorest municipality in Mexico. His campaign style was reminiscent of Cárdenas's in that there was a heavy emphasis on face-to-face contact at rallies held around the country. These rallies played to AMLO's great strength—his campaign charisma. As his biographer George Grayson noted:

> If AMLO hadn't gone into politics, he would have made a great evangelist. He is incredibly astute in relating to the public, identifying the concerns of the average person, creating his own pulpit to push ideas and present himself as the paladin of neoliberalism's victims.

To avoid becoming a creature of the mass media, the López Obrador campaign initially avoided TV spots and exclusive interviews. This campaign style seemingly served ALMO well, as is indicated by an early March poll, which placed his support at 42 percent, a full ten points above Calderón.[20]

AMLO made the focus of his campaign clear with the slogan, "For the good of everyone, the poor first." He shared with all the candidates a commitment to address Mexico's chronic poverty. The differences lay in what they considered to be the cause of poverty and the remedies for it. López Obrador was not hesitant to attribute the cause to the neoliberal development model:

> The principal problem of the neoliberal model has been precisely the lack of economic growth. Between 1982 and 2003, the GDP has grown at an average annual rate of 2.2 percent. But if we consider the population increase, *per capita* growth is barely 0.3 percent, that is, the economic policies of the last two decades measured merely quantitatively—without considering other factors such as income distribution—have been a failure and have not led to progress for Mexico.[21]

AMLO preached a return to the values of the 1917 Constitution—justice for workers, indigenous rights, nationalism, and anti-imperialism. His stand on the oil industry indicated these last two values, "We consider that petroleum is an extraordinary business and that, as General Cárdenas said, petroleum has to be a business for Mexican, not for private, interests."[22]

López Obrador proposed shifting the focus of the economy away from exports to the domestic market and promised increased government support for education and housing. He also pledged more federal spending for agriculture, transportation, and infrastructure. AMLO claimed to be able to do this not by raising taxes but with government austerity, cutting high government salaries, fighting corruption, and controlling tax evasion.[23]

While AMLO attributed Mexico's problems to the neoliberal development model, Calderón embraced neoliberalism, promising to refine it by passing a flat tax, making it easier for employers to hire and fire workers, and opening the energy sector to private investment. While both AMLO and Calderón promised massive job creation, the PAN candidate differed from his main rival in declaring that during his administration job creation would be based on attracting foreign investment. Were he to be elected, Calderón promised:

> I am going to invest the people's money in four things: 1) quality education, so the poorest boys and girls can advance in life and triumph, 2) healthcare beginning with a children's insurance program that will cover all medical service beginning at birth, 3) basic services such as drinking water and sewage treatment, which a fourth of Mexican families lack, and 4) public safety, so that our children can walk the streets in peace. And I want the door to employment to be wide open so that people can overcome poverty. For that, we need our economy to be competitive because, to put it bluntly, the world is competing with us and winning.[24]

March was the turning point for the Calderón campaign. The PAN candidate began campaigning with the slogan, "A firm hand, a passion for Mexico." Since that slogan was not gaining traction, he abandoned it and reinvented himself as the "jobs president". To emphasize his personal integrity, Calderón adopted the slogan "clean hands." Josefina Vázquez Mota, who had resigned as Fox's secretary of social development to work with the campaign, was selected to coordinate his hitherto somewhat disorganized campaign staff.[25]

For the public, the most visible shift in PAN strategy was a blitz of negative TV spots, which began in March. These ads emphasized that AMLO was a "danger to Mexico" and were influenced by U.S. political consultant Dick Morris who advised the Calderón campaign. Some ads juxtaposed AMLO and Venezuelan President Hugo Chávez, whose policies have dismayed conservatives throughout Latin America. Another ad declared (with considerable exaggeration) that as mayor AMLO had bankrupted Mexico City with expensive public works projects. Other ads attempted to portray AMLO as an authoritarian, messianic, irresponsible populist who had ties to the revolutionary left and who was surrounded by corruption. As political scientist Denise Dresser noted in April, the PAN "feels that AMLO should be stopped and is using all the instruments at its disposal, including covering him with mud."[26]

The López Obrador campaign filed complaints concerning the attack ads with the IFE, which initially refused to take action, citing freedom of expression. Eventually, however, the explicit use of AMLO's image and attacks on him that could be considered defamatory tipped the scales, and the attack ads were ordered off the air. The order suppressing the attack ads was controversial, with AMLO backers declaring the ads were illegal and that authorities should have taken action sooner, while Calderón supporters argued that attacks on AMLO were an exercise in freedom of speech.[27]

Two other ad campaigns targeted López Obrador. President Fox used roughly $154 million in public funds to air almost half a million radio and TV spots extolling the success of his government. Their clear massage was, "If you elect AMLO, progress achieved during my administration will be endangered." Ironically, in 2000, the Fox campaign had criticized President Zedillo for airing the same type of self-promotional spots. Eventually the Supreme Court prohibited Fox's use of public funds for broadcasting such messages. After Fox's ads were ordered off the air, the Businessmen Coordinating Council (CCE) spent roughly $12 million to broadcast its own spots declaring that AMLO, if elected, would wreck the economy.[28]

The same six polling organizations that had placed López Obrador in the lead at the start of the campaign indicated that Calderón, after having resorted to attack ads, had overtaken AMLO. One poll indicated that Calderón took the lead in March, three reported the lead change in April, and two in May. As columnist Jorge Volpi wrote, "The terrible truth of the PAN TV spots is that, despite their evident lack of truth, they have proved to be effective."[29]

Finally, AMLO's campaign reorganized and launched its own attacks directed at Calderón, undermining his credibility with charges that his relatives were profiting from government contracts and that despite the PAN having promised jobs, it had failed to deliver during the Fox administration. The ads mocked Calderón's claim to honesty and linked him to the PAN-supported FOBAPROA bank bailout, which he declared to be "the biggest scam in history." The ads linked Calderón to an ultra-conservative wing of the PAN known as El Yunque and declared him to be a friend of the rich and a threat to the achievements of the Mexican Revolution.[30]

In mid-May, polls showed Calderón leading AMLO by about five percentage points. Then as the PRD also went negative with its ads and AMLO did well in the second presidential debate on June 6, this gap closed, with late June polls showing a dead heat. The burning question was whether AMLO was just shy of closing the gap or whether had closed it.[31]

AFTER THE ELECTION

On election day July 2, 2006, roughly 913,000 citizen functionaries reported for duty at more than 130,000 polling places across Mexico. To ensure that no one resorted to old election tricks, the election was scrutinized by some 1.24 million party representatives as well as 25,000 domestic and 693 accredited foreign election observers. On election day 2006, the IFE did not receive a single report of anyone attempting to rig the vote. The election proceeded so smoothly that the next day the *New York Times* ran the following headline, "On a peaceful election day across Mexico, growing signs of a maturing democracy."[32]

The IFE devised three vote tabulation systems to provide certainty and quick cloture to the election. The first to come into play, called the "rapid count," compiled the returns from 7,636 polling places that were preselected to represent the nation as a whole. It was designed to allow authorities to call the election by 11 p.m. on election day. The second, called the Preliminary Election Results Program (PREP), was a tabulation of all the tally sheets as they were delivered to 300 district headquarters around Mexico. The formal count—known as the district count—began on Wednesday, July 5, after all the ballots and tally sheets had been received in the district headquarters. It involved a careful examination of tally sheets and ballots, the resolution of arithmetic errors by recounting the ballots, and the transmission of data to the national IFE office. To prevent the alteration of vote totals during this process, party representatives were allowed to observe data collection. In addition, the vote count from each polling place was posted on the internet, so party representatives could ensure they were not altered once the ballots were removed from the polling place.[33]

At 11 p.m. on election day, IFE President Luis Carlos Ugalde appeared on national television and announced that the election was too close to call based on the rapid count. On Monday, July 3, the IFE reported that the PREP count gave Calderón a 1.04 percent advantage. What the public was not told was that 8 percent of the tally sheets, representing 3.5 million votes, were not included in the total since they showed arithmetic errors. This was in keeping with the IFE protocol for the PREP, but created a public relations disaster as AMLO supporters cried fraud. At 8 a.m. on Wednesday July 5 the definitive district count began at each of the 300 district headquarters where the ballots were stored. Finally, on Thursday, the count ended with Calderón being credited with 0.58 percent more votes than López Obrador.[34]

López Obrador, rather than conceding what appeared to be an extremely close election, charged election fraud and mobilized his supporters to defend the victory he claimed. On July 8, 500,000 AMLO supporters rallied in Mexico City's main plaza to protest "election fraud." On July 16, more than a million gathered in the plaza in one of the largest political demonstrations in Mexican history. On July 30, AMLO called for a massive sit-in in the plaza, known as the Zócalo, and along a major commercial avenue, the Paseo de la Reforma. The five-mile-long sit-in was the equivalent in length and impact to a prolonged sit-in blocking New York's Broadway from Houston Street to 92nd Street. This occupation lasted until September 15—a month and a half—creating a strong visual presence to remind Mexicans that AMLO did not accept the official results. Demonstrators prevented President Fox from entering the Zócalo to give his usual Independence Day "grito." PRD legislators in the Chamber of Deputies seized the podium and prevented Fox from delivering his annual state of the nation address to Congress on September 1. PRD legislators also attempted, but failed, to prevent Calderón from taking the oath of office before Congress on December 1.

In addition to mobilizing his supporters, López Obrador called for the Federal Electoral Tribunal to order a recount of all ballots in hopes of erasing his vote deficit. He also called on the Tribunal to consider irregularities that had occurred before election day. In response, on August 5, the Tribunal ordered a recount of ballots from 9 percent of the polling places, selected from areas where the PAN was strong and the PRD weak. Presumably this would be where the PAN had rigged the vote count, if in fact it had been rigged.[35]

On September 5, the Federal Electoral Tribunal ruled that, after taking into consideration the slight modification found by the recount, Calderón had won by 233,831 of the 41.6 million votes cast. According to Mexican law, decisions by the Federal Election Tribunal are final and cannot be appealed.

The Tribunal acknowledged that both the Fox administration and the Businessmen Coordinating Council had orchestrated media campaigns against López Obrador. However, it concluded this was not sufficient cause to nullify the election:

> The negative effects of a campaign of this nature cannot be measured precisely, since there are no objective criteria which will allow one to establish a cause-effect relationship between negative campaigning and the votes cast in an election.[36]

Table 29.1 *2006 presidential election results*

Candidate	Total votes	Percentage of vote
Calderón	14,916,927	35.71
López Obrador	14,683,096	35.15
Robert Madrazo	9,237,000	22.11

Source: *El Financiero*, September 6, 2006, p. 4

Total does not equal 100 percent due to the presence of two small parties on the ballot, some votes being cast for unregistered candidates, and some ballots being nullified

The Tribunal did not clarify just what type of behavior would be sufficient to cause the election to be annulled. Clearly it did not feel that either Fox spending 60 percent more on his anti-AMLO campaign between January 19 and May 22 than Calderón was spending on his own campaign ads or the Businessmen Coordinating Council (CCE) spending $12 million illegally were sufficient.[37]

For the PAN, the July 2 elections, while not the resounding endorsement its members had hoped for, did provide six more years during which to administer the country and promote reform. This task was facilitated by the party receiving 206 seats in the Chamber of Deputies, a fifty-five-seat increase from 2003–2006, and fifty-two senate seats, a five-seat increase.[38]

The PRD, depending on one's point of view, was either defrauded of the presidency or more than doubled the presidential vote it had won in 1994 and 2000. The party emerged as the second power in the Chamber of Deputies with 127 seats, a thirty-seat increase from 2003–2006, and twenty-six senate seats, an eleven-seat increase.

The PRI's showing, the worst in its history, resulted from: 1) Madrazo going into the race with the highest negative rating—more than 40 percent—of any candidate, 2) his being unpopular in the State of Mexico for having driven favorite son Arturo Montiel out of the primary election, 3) his reminding people, as historian Enrique Krauze put it, of "the PRI's dark past of manipulation, corruption, and disinformation", and 4) the inability of the PRI and Madrazo to enunciate a clear ideology with which to appeal to voters. Even though the party's vote fell far below its past levels, the returns did show that, despite many predictions, it was still far from dead. It retained 106 seats in the Chamber of Deputies and with thirty-three senate seats it had the second largest delegation in that chamber. Although the PRI remained a minority party, its strength was enhanced by the PAN desperately needing allies to pass legislation.[39]

The 2006 election only appears to be close when viewed in the aggregate. When viewed on a state-by-state basis, the results are strikingly different. In the sixteen states where Calderón was declared to be the winner, his average margin of victory was 21 percent. Voters in these predominantly northern states strongly backed the increased integration to the world market that he promised. In the Federal District and the fifteen states that López Obrador won, voters provided him with a 17 percent margin of victory. These are the states further south where few of the benefits of NAFTA have arrived and where the government, rather than being viewed as the problem, is still considered to be the solution to pressing social problems.

The attack ads—referred to by former PRD President Porfirio Muñoz Ledo as "the repeated propagation of lies"—undermined López Obrador. The Election Tribunal commented that Fox's many publicly funded TV spots "put at risk the validity" of the election. Finally, the Business Coordinating Council's massive media buys, despite the prohibition on anyone other than political parties buying political ads, constituted an unfair advantage. As historian Enrique Semo noted, "Never before has the Mexican business elite intervened as flagrantly and directly in a political campaign."[40]

Calderón's team, after its reorganization in March, ran a well organized, media-driven campaign. To a large extent, Calderón successfully transformed the election into a referendum on the Fox administration. By mid-2006, Fox had chalked up enough success in lowering inflation and interest

Figure 29.1 *Map of 2006 election results* Source: Reproduced courtesy *New Left Review*

rates, increasing foreign reserves and consumer credit, and maintaining anti-poverty programs that voters opted to continue with the PAN.[41]

In contrast, AMLO and his election team made repeated mistakes, including the following:

- AMLO repeated the errors of Cuauhtémoc Cárdenas's earlier campaigns since he was more at home in town squares with a loudspeaker than on TV and radio. One of AMLO's collaborators lamented, "Unfortunately, at the beginning of the campaign, we didn't realize that a TV spot is worth more than three plazas full of people."[42]
- AMLO was slow to respond to the PAN attack ads that proved so effective. Mexican presidential campaigns have become Americanized and a failure to respond promptly in the media is fatal.[43]
- In February, when polls showed him to be well ahead, AMLO referred to President Fox as a chattering bird (the *chachalaca*) and told him to "shut up" and stay out of the campaign. For a period, López Obrador treated this as a joke and supporters even brought caged *chachalacas* to his rallies as campaign mascots. Eventually the PRD candidate realized this lack of respect for the office of the president was costing him support among swing voters and ceased using the term.
- AMLO skipped the first of two debates on April 25 to prevent all the other candidates from ganging up on him. For the same reason, in Brazil's 2006 presidential election, front-runner Luiz Inácio Lula da Silva skipped the debate and went on to win. However, in AMLO's case, his debate absence was widely seen as a sign of arrogance and contemptuousness of others' viewpoints.[44]
- By early 2006, most voters had made up their minds. The election was lost by AMLO's failure to hold the middle ground—those making roughly $1,000 a month. Calderón addressed them, declaring that their level of well-being resulted from the macroeconomic stability Mexico had enjoyed since 1995 and that electing AMLO would produce an economic crisis that would drag them back into poverty. AMLO never addressed their concerns, since he focused on the poor, who were in his camp already. Between February and July, AMLO lost 13 percent of his support among this group—more than enough to swing the election.[45]

Rather than letting the public forget AMLO's missteps, PAN propaganda kept them alive in voters' minds. One PAN attack ad juxtaposed AMLO's *chachalaca* remark with images of Venezuelan President Chávez dissing Fox, while another commented that AMLO skipped the first debate "because he can't explain unemployment in Mexico City."[46]

The AMLO campaign blamed (and continues to blame) his loss on election fraud. Some of these claims area easily refuted. Just after the election, López Obrador went on national TV to provide an example of what he considered fraud. A video clip of polling place 2227 in Salamanca, Guanajuato, showed the president of the polling place dropping several ballots in the ballot box. It turned out that voters had simply placed the ballots in the wrong ballot box. With the consent of the poll watchers, including the PRD representative, the ballots were simply being deposited in the correct box. AMLO, rather than admitting a mistake, suggested the woman serving as the PRD poll watcher had been suborned. Similarly, as results from the first full count, the PREP, came in, López Obrador's computer experts claimed an algorithm was altering the order in which data was tabulated, thus putting Calderón at an advantage. Those imagining such an algorithm failed to consider the mathematical principle of commutativity, which holds that regardless of the order numbers are added, adding the same numbers will yield the same sum. The apparent statistical anomaly favoring Calderón resulted from urban votes, which favored the PAN candidate, being reported earlier than rural votes. Furthermore, as former IFE president José Woldenberg commented, rigging the PREP would be fruitless since it is the district count, not the preliminary PREP, that determines the winner.[47]

Other charges, given the failure of the Federal Electoral Tribunal to order a full recount, simply hang in limbo. The interests of Mexican democracy would have been better served if the Federal Electoral Tribunal had followed the Costa Rican example and ordered a full recount. In the 2006 presidential elections in Costa Rica, Oscar Arias was declared winner by a 3,648-vote margin. A full recount confirmed his victory.

This leaves the question of whether a well-organized fraud—as opposed to Fox using the bully pulpit of the presidency, the private sector's massive ad buys, and the PAN using social welfare rolls to drum up support—actually occurred. Negative propositions are notoriously hard to prove, but placing the vote handling in the hands of almost a million citizens makes such a conspiracy unlikely. As Woldenberg commented:

> I share the idea that an orchestrated fraud, understood as a conspiracy to change the result of the elections, is impossible. This I strongly affirm, not as an act of faith, but due to the way the electoral process is structured . . . One must distinguish between errors, irregularity, and fraud. It is part of human nature to make mistakes, especially when the elections are administered by so many non-professionals who generously donate their time.[48]

López Obrador's post-election protests did not overturn the election, but they did undermine the broad base of support that he had built up during the campaign. On August 3, 140 intellectuals signed a statement denouncing the occupation of Mexico City streets. The next day another 500 artists and intellectuals, including Elena Poniatowski and Carlos Monsiváis signed a similar statement. While López Obrador's core supporters occupied protest encampments, business owners and auto drivers grew increasingly resentful of the protestors' presence. Finally, and most importantly, the public in general remained unconvinced that fraud had actually occurred. A poll published August 27 by the newspaper *Reforma* found only 33 percent of those queried believed the election had been fraudulent.[49]

Chapter 30

The Calderón Administration, 2006–2009

THE EARLY YEARS, 2006–2009

When Calderón assumed office, many questioned whether he would be able to govern, given the disputed election and vehement protests. Four months later, political analyst Rossana Fuentes-Berain commented, "He has left behind the doubts over whether he will be able to govern." This shift in perception largely resulted from Calderón's aggressive response to drug traffickers—a move that could be implemented without having to wait for legislative assent.[1]

During the first two years of his administration, Calderón sent more than 40,000 soldiers and federal police on anti-drug operations in several states. In the short term, this increased pressure on drug traffickers resulted in an upward surge in violence. Pressure on drug kingpins, many of whom were killed or arrested, fragmented large organizations into ever smaller units that increasingly resembled terrorist cells or guerrilla units. These smaller groups then turned their guns on each other in an attempt to control markets.[2]

In 2007 and 2008, in marked contrast to the previous presidential term, Congress passed several of Calderón's reforms. The president put his experience as a legislator to use and consulted with Congress members to draft legislation that would enjoy majority support. Key to his legislative success was his striking a working relationship with the PRI congressional delegation.

One of Calderón's reforms addressed Mexico's very low rate of tax collection, which in turn limited the effectiveness of government. His fiscal reform included a minimum tax on business enterprise, marking the first time corporate income has been taxed directly. A special fee for large bank deposits in cash was instituted in an attempt to tax the informal sector. Gasoline and diesel prices were increased. Though far from the major restructuring some thought was needed, the reforms increased government revenue by an estimated 1.1 percent of GDP.[3]

Another major reform addressed issues raised by the 2006 presidential election. A new law governing elections lowered levels of campaign financing, cut the length of campaigns, and explicitly prohibited individuals, trade unions, or business groups from buying air time to influence elections. Political parties were granted free air time on radio and TV. The power of the IFE was greatly increased as it was placed in the position of middleman between political parties and broadcast media. Parties would deliver their spots to the IFE, which would then place them with broadcasters. This provision was designed to eliminate ads for which no one claimed responsibility—a frequent occurrence in 2006. In what some considered to be an undue restriction on freedom of expression, Article 41 of the political reform law stated, "Political and electoral propaganda which political parties distribute should abstain from denigrating institutions and the political parties and from personal calumny." Ironically, this article prohibited exactly the kind of attack ads that won Calderón the presidency.[4]

By far the most controversial of the reforms passed during the early Calderón administration was the energy reform. The president proposed overhauling the legal framework of Pemex and expanding areas where private service contracts were allowed–a move that would permit the utilization of foreign capital and expertise. In response, PRD legislators seized the tribunals of both houses of Congress to force debate on the issue before the passage of the bill. The final bill coming out of Congress gave Pemex more administrative autonomy and allowed it to provide cash incentives in the contracts it wrote with other companies. However, it fell short of the sweeping changes many felt were needed to draw in major foreign oil companies. By keeping oil firmly in government hands, the law reflected the feelings of a substantial majority of Mexicans that oil production should remain nationalized.[5]

One of the biggest political surprises of the early Calderón administration was the political recovery of the PRI, under the leadership of savvy president Beatriz Paredes, former governor of Tlaxcala. Of the 297 state legislative seats up for election in 2007, the PRI won 43 percent, as well as 59 percent of the mayoral elections. The party, rather than trying to embarrass the president as it did during the Fox administration, sought to emphasize that he was a capable administrator.[6]

The PRD's fortunes under Calderón were the direct opposite of the PRI's. López Obrador's prolonged demonstrations protesting the presidential election and his refusal to recognize Calderón as president played well to the PRD's radical wing, but cost substantial support among other voters. To compound its problems, the party was sharply divided between more radical followers of López Obrador and the more moderate faction known as the New Left (Nueva Izquierda), which sought to reposition the PRD as a moderate social democratic force. This dispute spilled over into an internal party election to choose the PRD president. Protests flooded into the IFE, claiming that PRD members were trying to steal their own election. The messy election and the failure to recognize Calderón seriously undermined the party's attempts to build its image as a party capable of managing Mexico.

As the mid-term of the Calderón administration approached, Mexico found itself gripped in the world recession. The government's rather tepid response was criticized by many, including former Mexico City Mayor Manuel Camacho Solís, who stated, "The government did not anticipate the severity of the crisis and still lacks a response which reassures the markets and society." Even before the full impact of the 2009 recession was felt, the progress the Fox administration had made on poverty reduction was reversed. In 2006, 42.6 percent of the population lived in poverty. Two years later, 47.6 percent of the population—50.6 million Mexicans—lived in poverty. Much of this increase in poverty was produced by an increase in food costs.[7]

THE 2009 MID-TERM ELECTIONS

In July 2009 Mexico held its mid-term congressional elections in which all 500 members of the Chamber of Deputies were elected, as well as the governors of six states. Since candidates for the Chamber of Deputies are generally not well known, even before the first ballot was cast this election was widely viewed as a referendum on the Calderón presidency.[8]

As in past elections, polling places were managed by citizens who had been randomly selected and trained by the IFE. Detracting from the sound organization was a voter turnout of only 44.72 percent, just slightly above the percentage that voted in the 2003 mid-term elections. The chief complaints were that President Calderón, with a $160 million media budget, unfairly promoted the PAN using government funds. Similar complaints were voiced concerning Enrique Peña Nieto, the PRI governor of the State of Mexico and a 2012 presidential hopeful.[9]

The PAN courted voters based on the presumed success of Calderón's war on drugs. At the same time, the party portrayed the PRI as corrupt and unwilling to tackle drug gangs. This message failed to resonate with voters, who castigated the PAN for multiple shortcomings. These included a failure to combat corruption, an inadequate response to the global economic crisis, and the PAN's inability to develop a model of governing that clearly distinguished it from the PRI. The PAN vote,

Table 30.1 *2009 congressional elections results*

Party	Number of votes (in millions)	Percentage votes	Number of Chamber of Deputies seats won	Change in number of seats, 2006 to 2009
PRI	12.5	36.7	237	+135
PAN	9.5	28.0	143	−63
PRD	4.2	12.2	71	−55
Other parties	5.8	16.9	48	
Null votes	1.8	5.4		
Total votes	34.1			

Source: *El Financiero* (August 24, 2009, p. 37) and Political Data Base of the Americas

which reached 33 percent in 2006, sunk to 28 percent. The number of PAN deputies in the Chamber of Deputies fell from 206 to 143 for the 2009–2012 session.[10]

The election resulted in a significant weakening of Calderón's presidency. Columnist Lorenzo Meyer wrote that the president ran the "risk of becoming a political zombie." In the wake of the election, PAN president Germán Martínez assumed blame for the PAN' poor showing and resigned.[11]

The PRI received 36.7 percent of the vote, a remarkable rebound from its 2006 showing of 22 percent. In addition to increasing its number of seats in the Chamber of Deputies to 237, it won five of the six contested governorships. The successful PRI campaign adopted the slogan, "Today's PRI. Proven Experience. New attitude." In addition to its catchy slogan the PRI victory combined: 1) attractive candidates, 2) television, 3) money, 4) a nationwide political machine, and 5) party unity.[12]

The PRI did well since it occupied a vaguely defined political center, while the leadership of both the PRD and the PAN had become more polarized than the electorate. Lorenzo Meyer described the PRI as "searching for power for power's sake." Luis Rubio, the head of a Mexico City think tank, paraphrased the position of the PRI as, "We might be corrupt, but we're more efficient than the other guys."[13]

The biggest loser in the 2009 election was the PRD, which in 2006 had received 29 percent of the vote—a record for the party. The party receiving only 12 percent in 2009 reflected the PRD's on-going, very public internal struggles. In 2009, it failed to articulate a clear position. The PRD failed to take advantage of the elections to publicize a response to the economic crisis. Its internal splits were highlighted by the election itself. Rather than disseminating PRD policies, the media fixated on the fact that its 2006 presidential candidate ALMO had supported the candidacy of a small left party in Ixtapalapa (a borough of Mexico City) because one of his supporters did not receive the PRD nomination. His successful promotion of another party's candidate left the party leadership with a dilemma after the election as to whether it should expel López Obrador, its record vote getter, for his clear violation of party rules.[14]

The election set the political field for the upcoming 2012 presidential elections. The strong PRI showing favored State of Mexico Governor Enrique Peña Nieto, the front-runner for the 2012 PRI nomination. Pundits began labeling Calderón a "lame duck" and felt he would merely tread water until the end of his term. Finally, the election plunged the political left into disarray. This left the political spectrum devoid of a group that could effectively respond to the high degree of social inequality.[15]

BEYOND THE 2009 ELECTIONS

National moods undergo wide swings. In 2000, Mexico's national mood bordered on euphoria. That year the economy grew at 6.6 percent, and oil production was rising. That was also the year that, after seventy-one years in power, the PRI was ousted from the presidency.

Less than a decade later the optimism of 2000 had been replaced by something much closer to despair. Economic growth between 2001 and 2008 averaged only 2.2 percent. Then with the world economic crisis, during the first half of 2009 the economy declined at an annual rate of 9 percent. To make matters worse, the volume of oil production was plummeting, and the swine flu epidemic had just cost the tourist economy $2 billion. At the same time, the recession in the United States produced a sharp decline in the amount of remittances sent by Mexicans working in the United States.[16]

This economic contraction came at a particularly inopportune time because of the record number of births that had occurred in the mid-1990s. Those born then created an unprecedented demand for employment just as Mexico sank into severe recession.

Further adding to the Mexican malaise was the record number of deaths—more than 12,000 during the first half of the Calderón administration—resulting from the offensive targeting drug cartels. This struggle became the leitmotiv of the first half of his administration. Rather than showing signs of success, the soaring number of deaths raised the question as to whether the cartels or the government was winning and whether the notion of "failed state" applied to Mexico.[17]

Mexico's political system did nothing to improve the national mood. The novel aspect of the 2009 mid-term congressional elections was not an original idea to address Mexico's problems. Rather, it was a well-publicized campaign urging voters to cast a blank ballot to protest the political parties becoming closed clubs staffed by individuals looking out for their own interests. These interests included not only nomination to public office but the extremely generous cash subsides provided to political parties by the government.

Essayist Sergio Aguayo, who spearheaded the drive for democracy during the last decades of PRI rule, endorsed the blank-ballot movement, noting it should be seen in the context of seeking such reforms as independent candidates, reelection of deputies, and reduced financial support for political parties. Another advocate of the blank-ballot movement was political scientist Denise Dresser, who commented, "Voting for the least bad party is like buying the least rotten fruit, rather than pressuring the fruit vendor to supply fresher fruit."[18]

Nationwide, the blank-ballot movement attracted 5.39 percent of the vote in 2009, compared to 3.36 percent in 2003. In the better informed Federal District blank votes totaled 10.3 percent. Among the strongest supporters of the blank-ballot movement were young, internet-savvy voters.[19]

It remains unclear how Mexico's political system will move beyond the current disenchantment. Options include:

- one of the major parties producing a candidate and a platform that capture public imagination;
- a political reform that will correct problems, such as excessive funding for political parties and the lack of reelection, that leave officeholders at the mercy of party functionaries, not the citizens;
- the emergence of one of the several small political parties. One of the significant trends during the first decade of the century has been the steady increase in the vote for the several registered parties besides the PRI, the PAN, and the PRD.

Disenchantment with the political process became so great that many felt change would come from social movements outside the formal political process. Often these social movements reflected the age-old demand for land, since even though the rural population as a percentage of Mexico's total population was declining, the number of people living in rural Mexico steadily increased. Closely related to the demand for land were movements protesting construction projects, such as dams and airports, which deprived people of lands they already owned. Innumerable other groups demanded lower electric rates, housing, gay rights, rights for sex workers, and restrictions on the importation of grain.

Those placing their hopes in such movements emphasize that leadership in these movements is much closer to the social status of the average Mexican than that of the elite-dominated political parties. They recall how the 1968 student movement and the Zapatista Army of National Liberation (EZLN) reshaped Mexico's political and social reality without formally taking part in the political process.

However, these social movements suffer from a number of limitations. None of the social movements—not the 1968 student movement or the EZLN—remotely contested state power, leaving final decision-making in the hands of the political establishment. Most of the movements were highly localized. Thus, for example, the APPO (Popular Assembly of the Peoples of Oaxaca) movement, despite its intensity, was basically a movement affecting the city of Oaxaca. Also, most social movements were limited by their specificity of their demands. Thus whatever the merits of ousting Oaxaca governor Ruiz or blocking the construction of an airport were, it was hard to build broad-based movements on these demands. Finally, even social movements that built a national organization generally faded once their demands were addressed or they were co-opted. A debtors' movement known as Barzón nearly vanished once financial issues resulting from the 1994–1995 economic crisis were resolved. Similarly, the broad-based urban popular movement of the 1970s and 1980s largely disappeared as Salinas's Solidarity Program bought off communities.

Appendix

Mexican Presidents

Juan Álvarez	1855
Ignacio Comonfort	1855–1858
Benito Juárez	1858–1872
Sebastián Lerdo de Tejada	1872–1876
Porfirio Díaz	1876–1880
Manuel González	1880–1884
Porfirio Díaz	1884–1911
Francisco León de la Barra	1911
Francisco I. Madero	1911–1913
Victoriano Huerta	1913–1914
(Revolutionary factions struggle for power)	1914–1916
Venustiano Carranza	1917–1920
Adolfo de la Huerta	1920
Álvaro Obregón	1920–1924
Plutarco Elías Calles	1924–1928
Emilio Portes Gil	1928–1930
Pascual Ortiz Rubio	1930–1932
Abelardo L. Rodríguez	1932–1934
Lázaro Cárdenas	1934–1940
Manuel Ávila Camacho	1940–1946
Miguel Alemán Valdés	1946–1952
Adolfo Ruiz Cortines	1952–1958
Adolfo López Mateos	1958–1964
Gustavo Díaz Ordaz	1964–1970
Luis Echeverría Álvarez	1970–1976
José López Portillo	1976–1982
Miguel De la Madrid	1982–1988
Carlos Salinas de Gortari	1988–1994
Ernesto Zedillo	1994–2000
Vicente Fox	2000–2006
Felipe Calderón	2006–

Glossary

adobe sun-dried bricks made of earth and some organic material such as straw or dung.

agave a genus of succulent plants that includes lechuguilla (the source of ixtle), henequen, and the century plant (Spanish: *maguey*), different varieties of which produce pulque, mescal, and tequila.

alcabala a colonial tax paid on the sale of goods, and, after 1694, on moving goods from one tax zone (*suelo alcabalatorio*) into another. After independence these tax zones were replaced by state boundaries, with each state being free to set its own rates, in effect creating internal tariffs. The tax was abolished in 1896.

Alta California the term used before 1848 to refer to the area now comprising the state of California.

amaranth a grain-producing plant cultivated in pre-Conquest Mexico.

Anglo non-Hispanic of European descent (in the U.S. southwest).

atole a hot beverage formed by mixing finely ground corn with water or milk.

Aztecs the people whose empire dominated central Mexico when the Spanish arrived in 1519.

Bajío a fertile plain that lies in Guanajuato and Michoacán.

cacique 1) in colonial times, the leader of an Indian village; 2) in modern times, a local political boss, typically rural, who exercises a wide range of extralegal political and economic powers.

Caddo one of at least twenty-five distinct but closely affiliated indigenous groups that inhabited northeast Texas and adjacent areas before the mid-nineteenth century.

calzones pants made of coarse white cotton cloth.

camote sweet potato.

campesino peasant. Daniel Nugent (1993: 30) observed, "In the Mexican literature, the term *campesino* has been weighted with such a variety of meanings that its exact meaning is unclear; all it seems in the end to connote is politically dominated rural peoples."

Carlos V King of Spain (1515–1556) and Holy Roman Emperor (1519–1556). He was Carlos I, King of Spain, but Carlos V, Emperor of the Holy Roman Empire. Thus Carlos V precedes Spanish King Carlos III.

Castile one of several kingdoms that united to form modern Spain. This unification process was under way at the time of the Spanish conquest of Mexico.

caudillo a nineteenth-century individual who commanded private armies and competed for national power. In the twentieth century, caudillos were military officers who built regional power bases with mass followings.

chachalaca one of several species of large noisy birds of the genus *Ortalis*.

Chamber of Deputies the lower house of the Mexican Congress.

chia a plant of the genius *Salvia*. Its seeds are ground for use in drinks and food.

chinampa an intensively cultivated artificial island.

comal a metal or earthenware disk used to heat tortillas.

consulado the colonial merchant guild.

corn (*Zea mays*) an annual cereal widely cultivated in pre-Conquest America. This plant is also referred to as "maize," a word derived from its Spanish name, *maíz*, a word that is derived from the Taino name for the plant.

corporate refers to legally defined groups of individuals, such as workers or peasants, that a government deals with *en masse* rather than individually. Within the PRI, the three corporate groups, known as "sectors," were the peasants, the workers, and the popular sector.

corte "parliament" or "royal court" in the singular. When capitalized in the plural, it refers specifically to the Spanish parliament convened after the French invasion of 1808. The plural construction emphasizes that the parliament represented the many ancient kingdoms of Spain.

curandero a traditional healer.

dedazo the incumbent president's practice of selecting candidates for nominally elective office; literally, "the finger pointing."

disappeared those detained by authorities who subsequently deny any knowledge of those persons' detention or whereabouts, despite eyewitnesses and other credible evidence of their detention.

ejidatario one who has received ejido land.

ejido a farm established by the land reform program. The term also refers to the community formed by those who received land and the administrative apparatus making decisions concerning those farming the *ejido*. Proponents of the *ejido* claimed it harkened back to both a pre-Columbian communal land tenure regime and a Spanish tradition of public lands. However, it was less a resurrection of a past system than a compromise between warring post-revolutionary factions Johnson (2001: 293). Existing communities could petition the government for land on the grounds that land had been illegally taken from them (restitution) or because they lacked land and someone nearby owned land in excess of the legal limit.

empresario an entrepreneur. In Mexican Texas, the term specifically referred to those licensed to bring in colonists.

encomendero the holder of an *encomienda* grant.

encomienda a grant made to Spaniards that allowed them to collect tribute from Indians living in a certain area. In theory, the grantee reciprocated by assuming responsibility for Christianizing those paying tribute.

FOBAPROA acronym for Fondo Bancario de Protección al Ahorro (Banking Fund for the Protection of Savings), a Mexican government agency analogous to the U.S. FDIC. The acronym is also shorthand for the highly controversial move by which the government converted the agency's liabilities into public debt after the 1994–1995 peso collapse.

float to determine the value of a currency, not by government-fiat but by supply and demand.

fray a member of certain religious orders.

fuero special legal privileges enjoyed by members of groups such as priests, soldiers, and more recently, holders of public office.

Good Neighbor Policy Franklin D. Roosevelt's Latin American policy, which repudiated military intervention.

gringo a person from the United States.

grito Hidalgo's September 16, 1810 call to arms. The term also refers to reenactments of the original grito to commemorate anniversaries of Hidalgo's call.

guava the fruit of a tropical shrub.

hacendado the owner of a hacienda.

hacienda a large estate, typically producing a variety of crops and livestock.

henequen the fiber—formerly used to make binders twine—that is extracted from the leaves of an agave of the same name (*Agave fourcroydes*).

huarache a crude sandal. In modern times the sole is typically cut from a used auto tire.

Interior Secretary the cabinet position in charge of internal security, and up until the 1990s, the organization of elections.

ixtle the fiber, formerly used for making cordage and basketry, which is extracted from an agave known as lechuguilla.

Jefe Máximo Plutarco Elías Calles, during the period 1928–1934, when he served as the power behind the presidency.

jícama the tuber of a Mexican vine.

kiva an underground room used by the Pueblo for religious rituals.

land reform a government-mandated transfer of land from large landholders to those with little or no land, also called "agrarian reform."

mamey the fruit of a tropical vine.

Manifest Destiny the nineteenth-century belief that the United States was destined, even divinely ordained, to spread across North America.

Maximato the period 1928–1934, during which Calles served as Jefe Máximo. The term also refers to the political machine controlled by Calles during this period.

mercantilism the set of principles that guided Spanish economic policy from the sixteenth to the eighteenth centuries, associated with the notion that the wealth of a nation depended on the accumulation of precious metals. Unlike free traders, who view trade as leading to increased wealth and benefits for both trading parties, mercantilists view trade as a zero-sum game, with benefits accruing to one trading partner at the expense of the other.

mescal the distilled beverage produced from fermented agave juice, but which does not meet the standards imposed on tequila.

Mesoamerica a pre-Conquest cultural area based on extensive corn and bean cultivation and vegetable gardening, using irrigation, terracing, crop rotation, and chinampas. Its northern limit stretched from present-day Sinaloa in the northwest to the mouth of Pánuco River (the present boundary between Veracruz and Tamaulipas) in the northeast. The region extended south to embrace Nicaragua's Pacific Coast and part of Costa Rica (García de León 1988: 19, n. 4).

mestizo 1) a person of mixed race; 2) today a term often used to identify someone who is not an Indian, as in "the interaction between Indians and mestizos."

metate a rectangular stone upon which corn is ground.

metlapil (also known as *mano*) a handstone slid across the *metate* to grind corn.

milpa cornfield.

Moors the Moslem people of mixed Arab and Berber descent who invaded Spain in the eighth century.

mordida a bribe paid to a government official to expedite a legal procedure or to avoid persecution for an illegal act.

Nahuatl the language spoken by the Aztecs and other related groups in Central Mexico.

nixtamal corn kernels that have been boiled in water with slaked lime. *Nixtamal* is milled into dough (Spanish: *masa*), which is then fashioned into tortillas or tamales.

Nueva Galicia the colonial administrative unit covering the present state of Jalisco and parts of adjacent states.

Nueva Vizcaya the colonial administrative unit covering the present states of Chihuahua and Durango and parts of adjacent states.

Pápago an indigenous people inhabiting the Sonoran desert of the southwestern U.S. and northwestern Mexico. They now refer to themselves as the Tahono O'odham.

paseo promenade.

Pico de Orizaba also known as Citlatépetl; the highest mountain in Mexico, on the border between Puebla and Veracruz. Its elevation is 18,405 feet (5,610 meters).

Pima an indigenous people inhabiting Arizona and Sonora, closely related to the Pápago. They now call themselves the Akimel O'odham.

plan a call for revolt that usually incorporated a justification for toppling the established order.

presidio a military post on the northern frontier, usually built to protect a mission.

Pueblo any of several ethnically distinct indigenous peoples living in flat-roofed communal dwellings at the time of the Spanish arrival in New Mexico and Arizona. When not capitalized, the term refers to any town, regardless of the ethnicity of its inhabitants.

pulque the beverage produced by fermenting agave juice.

Quetzalcoatl 1) a pre-Conquest deity depicted as a plumed serpent; 2) A Toltec ruler who took the name of the deity. He left Tula during his reign, never to return. According to some accounts, the initial Spanish arrival was mistaken for a return of the ruler Quetzalcoatl. The plumed serpent has become a symbol of the Mexican spirit second only to the Virgin of Guadalupe. The continued strength of the image is indicated by artist Rufino Tamayo's painting of a plumed serpent on the wall of the National Museum of Anthropology and History and by the fossil of a giant flying reptile discovered in West Texas being named *Quetzalcoatlus*.

ranchería a diffuse cluster of homes.

real one eighth of a peso; also, a royal mining claim, as in real de Catorce.

Reconquest the prolonged process by which Christian forces expelled Moors from the Iberian Peninsula, concluding in 1492 with the fall of Granada.

sarape a shawl, with vivid colors and a hole for the head, worn over the shoulders.

sector one of the three major divisions (labor, peasant, and popular) of the PRI.

secular priest a priest who lives in civil society, as opposed to those living in a cloister or who are members of religious orders.

Seven Years' War The 1756–1763 war pitting Great Britain and its allies against France and its allies, including Spain. In the U.S., it is referred to as the French and Indian War.

Sierra Madre Oriental the mountain range running north from Mexico City parallel to the Gulf Coast.

Sinarquista a member of a mass, quasi-military movement of the late 1930s and early 1940s. Its members opposed government land reform and anticlericalism. It was strongest in areas that had been dominated by the Cristero movement. As an adjective, the term is used to refer to the movement itself, which was known as "sinarquismo."

slash-and-burn agriculture the practice of clearing and farming a plot for a few years and then letting it lie fallow for a longer period to restore its fertility. Also known as "swidden agriculture."

soldadera a woman accompanying military forces, often supplying support services such as food preparation and care for wounded.

tamale Spanish: *tamal*; corn dough stuffed with meat or other filling, which is wrapped in a banana leaf or cornhusk and then steamed or baked.

Tarascan the name the Spanish used to refer to the people they encountered in Michoacán. These indigenous people now refer to themselves as the Purépecha.

Tejas any of the Caddoan people who lived in northeast Texas.

Tenochtitlan The Aztec capital, captured by Cortés in 1521.

tequila the beverage produced by distilling the fermented juice of a specific variety of agave grown in Jalisco.

tortilla a round flatbread made of corn.

tribute a payment imposed on indigenous people to sustain the monarchy.

Valley of Mexico the oval depression, undrained before Spanish times, where the Aztec capital and, later, Mexico City were founded. It measures roughly seventy miles from north to south and forty-five miles from east to west.

viceroy an administrative official ruling a large area (a viceroyalty) as a representative of the king.

Virgin of Guadalupe according to Church teachings, the Virgin who appeared in 1531 to an Indian named Juan Diego and instructed him in Nahuatl to inform Bishop Zumárraga that she wanted a chapel built in her honor at the point of her appearance. In fulfillment of this request, the Basilica of the Virgin of Guadalupe was constructed on Tepeyac Hill just north of Mexico City. Anthropologist Eric Wolf (1979: 115) observed: "The Guadalupe symbol links together family, politics and religion; colonial past and independent present; Indian and Mexican. . . . It is, ultimately, a way of talking about Mexico: a 'collective representation' of Mexican society."

wattle and daub a wall lattice formed by interlacing thin branches daubed with a sticky material, such as wet soil.

wetback an undocumented Mexican entrant into the U.S. The "wet" refers to the entrant having swum the Rio Grande. The term was widely used in the 1950s by the U.S. government, journalists, Hispanic and Anglo academics, and by illegal entrants themselves.

Zapatista 1) a follower of Emiliano Zapata's 1909–1919 revolutionary movement in Morelos; 2) the eponymous rebel movement in Chiapas which went public January 1, 1994 as the Zapatista Army of National Liberation (EZLN).

zapote a soft, edible fruit.

Zócalo Mexico City's main plaza, and by extension, the main plaza in any Mexican municipality.

Notes

1 MESOAMERICA

1 Coe & Koontz (2002: 20–27) and González et al. (2003).
2 Coe & Koontz (2002: 24–27).
3 Coe & Koontz (2002: 22–23) and Knight (2002a: 17–18).
4 Knight (2002a: 18), Coe (1999: 59), and Coe & Koontz (2002: 40).
5 Knight (2002a: 11–19) and Coe & Koontz (2002: 40).
6 Stuart & Stuart (2008: 14), Knight (2002a: 31, 153), Smith (2008: 8), and Sharer (2006: 158).
7 Tedlock (1985: 163–64).
8 Ortiz Monasterio (1987: 76), Bonfil Batalla (1996: 4–5), Warman (1988: 41–49), Coe & Koontz (2002: 30–33), and Pope et al. (2001).
9 Knight (2002a; 22–26).
10 Coe (1999: 61), Coe & Koontz (2002: 68), and Diehl (2004: 11–12).
11 Coe & Koontz (2002: 68) and Tate (2008: 37).
12 Tate (2008: 34), Diehl (2004: 63), Coe & Koontz (2002: 68–70), and Knight (2002a: 32).
13 Vanderwarker (2006: 31, 108) and Florescano (2007: 6).
14 Sharer (2006: 629).
15 Diehl (2004: 82) and Knight (2002a: 47).
16 Coe & Koontz (2002: 42) and Sharer (2006: 155).
17 Coe (2005: 22), Knight (2002a: 54–56), and Stuart & Stuart (2008: 120).
18 Knight (2002a: 52) and Florescano (2006: 18).
19 Ezcurra et al. (1999: 33), Coe & Koontz (2002: 119–120), Thomas (2003: 463), and Verástique (2000: 6).
20 Knight (2002a: 87), Coe (2005: 59), and Sharer (2006: 223).
21 Coe (2005: 87–95) and Sharer (2006: 705).
22 Coe (2005: 148, 206), Stuart & Stuart (2008: 15), and Sharer (2006: 71, 120).
23 Sharer (2006: 89, 715).
24 Knight (2002a: 91, 100) and Sharer (2006: 94).
25 Knight (2002a: 94), Sharer (2006: 645), Coe (1999: 58), and Peña (2005: 51).
26 Sharer (2006: xxvii) and Knight (2002a: 100).
27 Coe (1999: 193; 2005: 24) and Stuart & Stuart (2008: 19, 165).
28 Stuart & Stuart (2008: 11).
29 Sharer (2006: 559–60, 585–86).
30 Coe (2005: 162) and Sharer (2006: 525).
31 Sharer (2006: 508–12), Diamond (2005: 164–76, 431), Sabloff (1995), Gill (2000), Kerr (2001), and Andrews, Andrews & Robles Castellanos (2003: 151).
32 Coe & Koontz (2002: 128–29) and Knight (2002a: 107).
33 Sharer (2006: 156).
34 Florescano (2006: 32).
35 Coe & Koontz (2002: 152–58) and Smith (2008: 23–24).
36 Knight (2002a: 123–24) and Coe & Koontz (2002: 158).
37 Knight (2002a: 131) and Coe & Koontz (2002: 154, 171).
38 Coe & Koontz (2002: 186).
39 Pérez de Salazar V. (1995: 62), Thomas (1993: 3, 18, 58, 277), and Kinsbruner (2005: 15).
40 Smith (2008: 178).

41 Smith (2008: 2–23).
42 Smith (2008: 37–39, 183), Diel (2008: 2–4), and Lockhart (1992: 15).
43 Thomas (1993: 5; 2003: 466). Bakewell (1997: 24) and Florescano (1997: 162–63) speculated on the reasons the Aztecs sought to create an empire.
44 Knight (2002a: 175–76, 188).
45 Cortés (1971: 103) and Díaz del Castillo (1996: 215).
46 Smith (2008: 155, 191).
47 Coe & Koontz (2002: 206–07).
48 Sharer (2006: 6).
49 Coe (1964: 90–93), Armillas (1971), Knight (2002a: 163), Miller (2007: 21) and Melville (2000: 220). Ferriss (2004) described surviving twenty-first-century chinampas and threats to their continued production.
50 Knight (2002a: 166), Tortolero Villaseñor (2000: 23, 27, 128), and Musset (1992: 144).
51 Knight (2002a: 9), Sharer (2006: 44) and Coe & Koontz (2002: 34).
52 Coe & Koontz (2002: 17).

2 THE CONQUEST OF MEXICO 1519–1521

1 Bonfil Batalla (1996: xv).
2 Coe (1999: 71) and Crespo (2009: 30–31).
3 Coe (1999: 71) and Thomas (2003: 463).
4 Grunberg (1994: 261–62), Thomas (1993: 85–115; 2003: 474–78), and Weddle (1985: 55–79).
5 León-Portilla (1992b: 13) quoted the Indian.
6 Thomas (1993: 117) cited this date. He noted (1993: 665, n. 9) that there is no certainty as to Cortés's birth date. In an interview subsequent to the publication of his book (*Excélsior,* September 7, 1994, p. 29A), Thomas mentioned 1481 or 1482 as likely birth dates for Cortés.
7 Phillips (1993), Keen (1996: 38–53), and Verástique (2000: 36–65) described sixteenth-century Spain. Elliott (1984) described the institutions developed to administer conquered Moorish territory.
8 Elliott (2006: 20) and Restall (2003: 65).
9 Elliott (2006: 4). The text of the instructions can be found in Martínez (1993: 45–57).
10 Ruiz (1992: 41).
11 Thomas (1993: 150–53) and Farriss (1984: 29).
12 Guerrero was killed in 1536 as he fought with his adopted people against the Spanish. For a summary of what little is known of Guerrero, see Johnson (1988), Sharer (2006: 758–59), and Rodríguez (2007: 4).
13 Thomas (1993: 680, n. 85) and Karttunen (1994: 5–6) discussed the origin of Malinche's name.
14 Díaz del Castillo (1996: 86) and Pastor Bodmer (1992: 61–62).
15 Díaz del Castillo (1996: 71), León-Portilla (1992b: 33), and Thomas (2003: 482).
16 Semo (1981: 199), Thomas (1993: 199), Nader (2000: 37–40), Elliott (2006: 4), and Restall (2003: 20–21).
17 Restall (2003: 19) and Elliott (2006: 4).
18 Cortés (1971: 66).
19 Cortés (1971: 69–70).
20 Benítez (1957: 157), Castro (2007: 61), and Restall (2003: 87).
21 For comments on the *requerimiento,* see Cortés (1971: 453–55, n. 27), Muldoon (1994: 26–27, 136–38), and Seed (1992). Hanke (1973: 93–95) provided an English translation of the *requerimiento.*
22 Flórez Miguel (1992: 66–68), Muldoon (1994: 15–22), and Restall (2003: 68).
23 Thomas (1993: 243).
24 Smith (2008: 185). For comments on the possible reasons for the massacre, see Cortés (1971: 465–66, n. 27).
25 Casas (1992: 45).
26 Thomas (1993: 263) evaluated evidence for a plan to attack the Spanish. Pastor Bodmer (1992: 88–89) and Restall (2003: 112) commented on the massacre.
27 Díaz del Castillo (1996: 190–91).
28 León-Portilla (1992b: 66).
29 Prescott (1964: 398).
30 Thomas (1993: 383–87; 2003: 486) reviewed the evidence, inconclusive at best, of a planned Aztec attack.
31 Padden (1967: 197).
32 Chávez Balderas (2008: 180), Cortés (1971: 477–78, n. 89), Gibson (1964: 509, n. 9), Gillespie (2008: 51), Hassig (1994: 94), and Wright (1992: 41–42) considered possible causes of Montezuma's death.
33 Prescott (1964: 450) and Thomas (1993: 412). As Kamen (2004: 526, n. 9) noted, there is disagreement concerning the exact date of the Noche Triste.

34 Hassig (1994: 97) and Thomas (1993: 397, 422).
35 Freidel, Schele & Parker (1993: 294–95).
36 Prescott (1964: 470–71) and Thomas (1993: 427–28).
37 Kandell (1988: 120), McNeill (1976: 207), Oldstone (1998: 30–33) and Watts (1997: 91) commented on the epidemic.
38 Hassig (1994: 102).
39 Thomas (1993: 490) and Restall (2003: 47).
40 Cortés (1971: 208–65) and Thomas (1993: 489–525) described the siege.
41 Padden (1967: 224) reported Indian death estimates. Grunberg (1994: 261) reported Spanish deaths.
42 Díaz del Castillo (1996: 131).
43 Thomas (2003: 489), Coe & Koontz (2002: 149), and Storey & Widmer (2006: 74).
44 Coe & Koontz (2002: 204, 228), Kamen (2004: 28), and Knight (2002a: 231).
45 Coe & Koontz (2002: 227) and Thomas (1993: 153).
46 Thomas (1993: 533).
47 Restall (2003: 20, 26, 91, 142) and Elliott (2006: 20).
48 Thomas (2003: 488–90) and Richards (2003: 2).
49 Townsend (2003: 680). Diamond (1997) described the Spanish technology (especially ships and weapons) that contributed to repeated Spanish victories over the peoples of the New World and discussed why the Europeans, but not the Indians, had developed such technology.
50 Coe & Koontz (2002: 225–27), Kamen (2004: 100), and Townsend (2003: 683).
51 Prescott (1964: 524) and Thomas (1993: 470; 2003: 536).
52 Casas (1992: 13).
53 For a black-and-white reproduction of Rivera's mural, see *The Wilson Quarterly* (Summer 1979, p. 116). Krauze (1997a: 40–50) discussed Cortés's negative image. The reputation of historical figures can be quantified by counting the street names included in the *2000 Guía Roja*, a street map of Mexico City.

Historical figure	Number of street names
Cortés	6
Montezuma	139
Cuauhtémoc	351
Hidalgo	735
Morelos	667
Iturbide	110
Guerrero	357
Santa Anna	28
Zaragoza	334
Juárez	758
Díaz	100
Madero	360
Villa	298
Zapata	310
Carranza	209
Cárdenas	346

54 *Mexico Journal* (February 27, 1989, p. 27; October 16, 1989, p. 5). Stern (1992) discussed how various observers have viewed the Conquest since it occurred. Not surprisingly, Mexicans never agreed on how to observe the five-hundredth anniversary of Columbus's arrival. *La Jornada* (October 13, 1992, pp. 3–6) reported that there was a gala event at the Spanish embassy to commemorate the anniversary, as well as thousands in Mexico City's main plaza to protest at such a commemoration. Yet another group honored Cuauhtémoc at the last Aztec emperor's statue and insulted Columbus at the Genoese mariner's statue. Chorba (2007: 30–34) discussed the controversy surrounding the anniversary.

3 THREE CENTURIES OF COLONIAL RULE, 1521–1810

1 Florescano (1994: 65).
2 Restall (2003: 70).
3 Cortés (1971: 518, n. 52) and Restall (2003: 148–57).
4 Warren (1963: 3).
5 Bakewell (1997: 104, 107–08) and Richards (2003: 349).
6 Sharer (2006: 767–72), Coe (2005: 202), Bricker (1981: 13–19), Elliott (1984: 186), Farriss (1984: 12), and Stuart & Stuart (2008: 10).
7 Florescano (1980: 56), Knight (2002b: 7), and Reff (1991: 26–27).
8 Florescano (1976: 21–22).
9 MacLachlan (1988: x).
10 Carmelo (1985: 149–50), MacLachlan (1988: 8, 13), Verástique (2000: 45), and Pagden (1990: 5–6).
11 MacLachlan (1988: 3, 21, 45).
12 Fuentes (1992: 153–54), Kamen (2004: 50), Elliott (2006: 121), and Thomas (2003: 446–50).
13 Bakewell (1997: 120–21) and Jiménez (2005: 4).
14 MacLachlan & Rodríguez O. (1980: 141–42).
15 Lockhart (1976: 6) and Burkholder & Johnson (1998: 83–84).
16 Gibson (1952: 175) and Lynch (1992b: 73).
17 Hamnett (1999: 71) and Burkholder (2000: 120).
18 Cline (1972: 23). Anna (1998a: 38) noted that the terms province and kingdom were often used interchangeably. In addition, some kingdoms, such as Nuevo León, were provinces, and some, such as Guatemala, contained several provinces.
19 Diel (2008: 4), Jiménez (2005: 4), Bakewell (1997: 217), Borah (1985a: 30–31), Carmelo (1985: 157), and Rubio Mañe (1971: 164–65).
20 Bakewell (1997: 123), Diel (2008: 4), Cline (1972: 23–24), Knight (2002b: 55), MacLachlan & Rodríguez O. (1980: 108–09), and Cunniff (1966: 62–63).
21 Chance (1978: 2), Bakewell (1997: 77), Restall (2003: 19), and Dobado González et al. (2008: 762).
22 Ricard (1950: 325).
23 Booker (1993: 29). Borah (1974), and Early (1994: 39–49) discussed the establishment of urban centers.
24 Parry (1953: 18, 27).
25 Borah (1985a: 44), Martin (1996: 88), and Burkholder & Johnson (1998: 172–73).
26 Knight (1993b: 44; 2002b: 56, 61) and Jiménez (2005: 19).
27 Himmerich y Valencia (1991: 99).
28 MacLachlan (1988: 36), Bakewell (1997: 117–19), Kessell (2002: 54), and Elliott (2006: 125).
29 Kandell (1988: 156), Ruiz Medrano (1991: 89) and Bakewell (1997: 79–81).
30 Bakewell (1997: 83–85) and Thomas (2003: 180).
31 John (1975: 9), Nutini (1995: 213), Moreno Toscano (1976: 51–52, 58), Calderón (1988: 197), Lockhart (1992: 430), and Bakewell (1997: 122).
32 Gibson (1964: 78), Knight (2002b: 14), Lockhart (1992: 430), Florescano (1984: 164), Liss (1975: 97), and Elliott (2006: 89).
33 Elliott (2006: 40), Gibson (1984: 387), Knight (2002b: 17), Calderón (1988: 167), Burkholder (2000: 127), and MacLachlan & Rodríguez O. (1980: 115). As Farriss (1984: 39) observed, until 1786, the *encomienda* continued in Yucatán, where Indians continued to organize production.
34 McAlister (1963: 360), Gibson (1966: 60–61), Bakewell (1997: 154) and Himmerich y Valencia (1991: 17).
35 Gómez de Cervantes (1944: 94).
36 Castro (2007: 114–15, 124), Hall (1989: 61), MacLachlan (1988: 59), Ruiz Medrano (1991: 118), and Chance (1978: 48).
37 Borah (1991: 6–7, 13), Thomas (1993: 593), Prem (1991: 33), Mörner (1967: 32), and Newson (2006: 146).
38 Verástique (2000: 84) and Florescano (1997: 184). Melville (2000: 223–25), and Livi-Bacci (2006: 201–02, 224) discussed the factors leading to high death rates. A variety of methods have been used to estimate Mexico's population at the time of the Spanish arrival. Livi-Bacci (2006: 200) cites estimates ranging from 3.2 million to 33.8 million.

Bethell (1984: 145), Denevan (1992: 77–84), and Thomas (1993: 609–14) discussed the widely varying estimates of pre-Conquest population and subsequent population decline. Whitmore (1992: 1–30) reviewed mortality estimates, the methodology used to estimate population loss, and the causes of mortality. As Rabell Romero (1993: 19) noted, scholars have waged a politically charged numerical war concerning post-Conquest population decline. For a critique of these estimates, especially the higher ones, see Henige (1998). For a critique of Henige, see Newson (2000).

The area now included in the United States underwent the same catastrophic population decline as Mexico did. As Chanda (2007: 232) noted, in 1500, the area now included in the United States had an estimated population of 2 million. The indigenous population there declined to 750,000 in 1700 and to 325,000 by 1820.

39 Florescano (1984: 165), Knight (2002b: 83), Monteiro (2006: 194), Newson (2006: 175), and Cope (1994: 12).

40 Knight (2002b: 22, 82–83).

41 Florescano (1984: 165–66) and MacLeod (1984b: 228). As Weber (1992: 410, n. 19) noted, the terms *encomienda* and *repartimiento* were sometimes used interchangeably during the colonial period, and even more often the institutions were used extrajudicially.

42 Knight (2002b: 56) and Kessell (2002: 11).

43 Florescano (1980: 32–33). For a discussion of seventeenth-century Mexico, see Boyer (1977).

44 Moreno Toscano (1976: 63).

45 Brading (1971: 4) and Randall (1977: I, 78–79).

46 Borah & Cook (1962: 11), Miller (2007: 62), and Simon (1997: 23).

47 Monteiro (2006: 201), Tandeter (2006: 326), Burkholder & Johnson (1998: 120–21), Calderón (1988: 247–48), Knight (2002b: 83, 93), Florescano (1984: 167), and Weber (1992: 411, n. 24).

48 Florescano (1984: 169).

49 Arnold (1988: 3–5).

50 Poole (1992: 110–11), Bakewell (1997: 292), and Rodríguez (1978: 2).

51 Guardino (1996: 66–67), Florescano & Rojas (1996: 30), MacLachlan (1988: 90), Burkholder (2000: 145), Hall (1989: 135), and Hobsbawm (1996: 22). There are strong parallels between the Bourbon reforms and the stamp and tea taxes the British imposed on their North American colonies. As Tenenbaum (1994a: 283) remarked, had these taxes not led to the American Revolution, they might have been known as the Hanoverian Reforms.

52 Miller (1985: 167), Bakewell (1997: 274), and Weber (2005: 110).

53 Brading (1971: 27; 1991: 468; 1994a: 3–4; 2007a: 362), MacLachlan & Rodríguez O. (1980: 265–67), J. Meyer (1976: 3), and Elliott (2006: 309, 319).

54 Elliott (2006: 304), Burkholder & Johnson (1998: 274–5), Brading (1994b: 36), Florescano (1997: 271), Hernández Chávez (2006: 95), Gerhard (1986: 17), and Buve (1992: 7–8).

55 Anna (1998a: 41–42) and Elliott (2006: 320).

56 Hernández Chávez (2006: 94), Gonzalbo Aizpuru (1987a: 142), Florescano (1994: 196), Ramírez (1986: 37), Bernstein (1964: 12), and Miller (1985: 176).

57 Brading (1971: 33; 2007a: 366), Miller (1985: 167), Lockhart (1976: 14), Guardino (1996: 32–32), Farriss (1984: 359–60), and Castro Gutiérrez (1994: 26).

58 Santoni (1988: 269), González Pedrero (1993: I/xxxiii), Marichal (2007: 27), Rodríguez O. (2007: 228), and Elliott (2006: 292–301).

59 Hart (1987: 22), Knight (2002b: 224, 230), Tutino (1986: 61–64), and Garner (1993: 1).

60 Moreno-Brid & Ros (2009: 20), Brading (1971: 14), INEGI (1994: 13), Garner (1993: 17), and Turner & Butzer (1992: 42).

61 Knight (2002b: 205, 243–44), Marichal (2007: 54), and Lynch (1989: 21). Van Young (1988b) reviewed literature on Bourbon administration.

62 Humboldt (1966: I, 184).

63 Bakewell (1997: 166), Coatsworth (2006: 262), and Arrom (1994: 92).

64 Farriss (1984: 212) and Weber (2005: 102).

65 Farriss (1984: 176).

66 Chance & Taylor (1977: 474).

67 McAlister (1963: 364).

68 Weckmann-Múñoz (1993: 22), Couturier (2003: 24), and Brading (1973b: 399).

69 Ladd (1976: 6, 58, 163), Couturier (2003: 159), and Kicza (1982: 449).

70 Kandell (1988: 216).

71 Florescano (1994: 187, 191) and Hamnett (1994b: 78).

72 Hoberman (1991: 222).

73 Lockhart (1976: 6), Camp (2003: 30), and Seed (1982: 579–80).

74 Brading (1971: 111) and Lockhart (1976: 13).

75 Halperín-Donghi (1993: 7), Couturier (2003: 77), and Anna (1978: 16).

76 Hoberman (1991: 72–73, 77).

77 Ladd (1976: 50), Coatsworth (1982: 35), and Taylor (1972: 122).

78 Kicza (1983: 24–25) and Harris (1975: 27, 94–96, 99).

79 Booker (1993: 4–5), Couturier (2003: 33), Hoberman (1991: 20, 221), and Brading (1971: 105).

80 Florescano (1984: 179) and Hobsbawm (1996: 20).

81 Hoberman (1991: 18–19), Brading (1974: 635), and Kicza (1983: 229).

82 Offutt (2001: 65) and Knight (2002b: 227).
83 Hoberman (1991: 70, 72, 89–90, 136) and Brading (1971: 105).
84 Kicza (1983: 60, 230–31).
85 Brading (1974: 619), Hoberman (1977: 500; 1991: 257), and Cope (1994: 122).
86 Burkholder & Johnson (1998: 212) and Hoberman (1991: 64, 232, 240, 261).
87 Lindley (1983: 43–44), Tenenbaum (1986: 6), and Kicza (1982: 447).
88 Kinsbruner (2005: 37) and Elliott (2006: 175).
89 Lockhart (1992: 14).
90 Grafe & Irigoin (2006: 249), Reina (2007: 92), Florescano (1997: 249), Chassen-López (2004: 286), Knight (2002b 108), Buve (1992: 5), and Marichal (2007: 95).
91 Jackson (1998: 3), Borah (1983: 53), Ruiz Medrano (1991: 164), Brading (1994a: 6), Rodríguez O. (2000: 133, n. 5), and Florescano & Rojas (1996: 13).
92 Van Young (1989a: 114), Elliott (2006: 386), and Hernández Chávez (2006: 80–82).
93 Florescano (1997: 281–85).
94 Semo (1993: 42–43), Restall (2003: 73), and Guardino (1996: 26).
95 Richards (2003: 340–43).
96 Fisher (1934: 164), Richards (2003: 340–43), Chassen-López (2004: 298), Taylor (1974: 400, 406–09), and *La Jornada* (July 16, 2009, p. 18).
97 Bauer (2001: 149), Knight (2002b: 188–92), and Salvucci (1987: 19–20).
98 Kellogg (1995: xix), Gibson (1952: viii), Taylor (1979: 23), and Assadourian (2006: 294, 301, 313–14).
99 Farriss (1984: 283).
100 Gibson (1952: 150), Farriss (1984: 185), Kamen (2004: 123), Patch (2000: 184), and Nutini (1995: 181).
101 Gibson (1952: 143) and Brading (2007a: 362).
102 Chance (1978: 124) and Couturier (1981: 364).
103 Coatsworth (2006: 250).
104 Kessell (1989: 33), Florescano (1997: 192), Guardino (1996: 42), and Olivera & Crété (1991: 182).
105 Semo (1981: 225), Guardino (1996: 25), Carmagnani (1988: 63), Gerhard (1986: 28), Morse (1984: 84), Prem (1991: 47), and Whitmore (1992: 79).
106 Florescano (1994: 112) and Warman (2003: 121).
107 Tutino (1988: 99).
108 Brading (1971: 5), Chance (1976: 614; 1978: 91), and Tutino (1988: 100).
109 Chance (1976: 622, 625), Kellogg (1995: 34, n. 29), and Cope (1994: 91).
110 *Boletín del Archivo General de la Nación* (January–March 1938, p. 13).
111 Van Young (2007: 34) and Simon (1997: 25).
112 Gibson (1964: 196), Borah (1983: 53), Patch (2000: 204–05), Knight (2002b: 75, 125; 1990c: 75), Van Young (2001: 385–86), Coatsworth (1988: 58; 2006: 252), Katz (1988: 77), and Taylor (1979: 115, 120, 124, 131, 145).
113 Taylor (1979: 121, 145).
114 Florescano (1994: 169).
115 Florescano (1994: 107–08) and Miller (1985: 114–15).
116 Patch (2000: 187, 192).
117 Patch (2000: 211).
118 Gosner (1992) described the rebellion in detail. Florescano (1994: 155–56) reported its goals.
119 Florescano (1994: 160–61), Patch (2000: 210), Reed (2001: 51–52), and Katz (1988: 90).
120 Castro (2007: 161).
121 Richards (2003: 355) and Ahern (1998: 70).
122 Powell (1952: 114).
123 Chipman (1992: 50) and Bakewell (1997: 93).
124 Powell (1952) described the Spanish-Chichimeca conflict. Frye (1996: 45) and Martínez Baracs (1993: 208) discussed the incentives given to Tlaxcalans.
125 Sheridan (2005: 132) and Weber (2005: 96).
126 Marks (1993: 55), Palmer (1976: 6) and Aguirre Beltrán (1944: 412).
127 Aguirre Beltrán (1989a: 20–21), Naveda Chávez-Hita (1987: 14), Kamen (2004: 136), Stein & Stein (2000: 36), and Rout (1976: 37–39).
128 Carroll (1991: 45, 145), Cope (1994: 13), Palmer (1976: 2), Thomas (1997: 211), Blackburn (1997: 150), and Bennett (2003: 23).
129 Rout (1976: 11, 33), Carroll (1991: 94), and Naveda Chávez-Hita (1987: 34).
130 Thomas (1997: 216).
131 Rout (1976: 34), Palmer (1976: 170), and Blackburn (1997: 154).

132 Rout (1976: 23–24, 140) and Ruiz (1992: 108). As Brading (1991: 75) noted, Las Casas later condemned African slavery.
133 Davidson (1966: 237), Palmer (1976: 187), and Blackburn (1997: 143–44).
134 Blackburn (1997: 144).
135 Naveda Chávez-Hita (1987: 105), Bakewell (1997: 197), Pi-Sunyer (1957: 240), and Thomas (1997: 144).
136 Kiple (1987: 8), Palmer (1976: 47), Aguirre Beltrán (1989a: 236), and Pi-Sunyer (1957: 240).
137 Carroll (1995: 411).
138 Naveda Chávez-Hita (1987: 123), Palmer (1976: 189), and Davidson (1966: 241).
139 Rout (1976: 146).
140 MacLachlan & Rodríguez O. (1980: 218).
141 Carroll (1991: 77, 93), Cope (1994: 14), King (1944: 392), Humboldt (1966: I, 236), and Palmer (1976: 187).
142 Davidson (1966: 242–43, 244).
143 Davidson (1966: 242, 243) and Palmer (1976: 139–40).
144 Cope (1994: 18).
145 Carroll (1991: 97; 1995: 405) and Naveda Chávez-Hita (1987: 136).
146 Palmer (1976: 124, 143), Davidson (1966: 243–46), and Naveda Chávez-Hita (1987: 125).
147 Davidson (1966: 246) and Carroll (1991: 91).
148 Davidson (1966: 247), Palmer (1976: 128), and Trens (1947: II, 313).
149 Palmer (1976: 129).
150 Palmer (1976: 130), Naveda Chávez-Hita (1987: 130–31), and Carroll (1991: 92).
151 Brading (1971: 23) and Hernández Chávez (2006: 76).
152 Cope (1994: 83), Bakewell (1997: 166), and Chance & Taylor (1977: 457–60).
153 Chance & Taylor (1977: 482), Knight (2002b: 112), and De la Teja (2005: xvii).
154 Love (1971: 81), Parkes (1960: 120), Sierra (1969: 130–31), and MacLachlan & Rodríguez O. (1980: 209).
155 Stein & Stein (1970: 57).
156 Elliott (2006: 171) and Kinsbruner (2005: 89).
157 Kandell (1988: 215), Lockhart (1976: 15), Mörner (1967: 57, 61, 101), and Cope (1994: 16, 19).
158 Brading (1994a: 120), Chance (1978: 101–02), and Mörner (1967: 61).
159 Humboldt (1966: I, 246).
160 King (1953: 56) and Lavrin (2000: 263).
161 Lavrin (2000: 263), Lavrin & Couturier (1981: 279, 303), and Kinsbruner (2005: 111).
162 Benítez (1965: 35).
163 Gonzalbo Aizpuru (1987b: 38) and Tostado Gutiérrez (1991: 18, 21).
164 Arrom (1985a: 55–58, 61) and Lavrin & Couturier (1981: 279).
165 Arrom (1985a: 67) and Lavrin (1978: 30).
166 Lavrin & Couturier (1981: 286–87) and Dore (2000: 12).
167 Arrom (1985a: 61, 129–32), Giraud (1987: 74), and Lavrin (1976: 253).
168 Gonzalbo Aizpuru (1987a: 53), Giraud (1987: 70), and Lavrin (1989: 11).
169 Arrom (1985a: 158–60), Gonzalbo Aizpuru (1987a: 123, 125, n. 43; 1998: 401), and Lavrin (1978: 40–47; 2000: 266).
170 Lavrin (2000: 266–68).
171 Arrom (1985a: 26, 161–63, 205) and Gonzalbo Aizpuru (1987a: 123).
172 Gonzalbo Aizpuru (1987a: 115), Lavrin (1978: 31), and Tuñón (1999: 25–26).
173 Tutino (1983: 380).
174 Arrom (1985a: 62), Couturier (1985: 296, 301), and Lavrin (1978: 33; 2000: 253).
175 Arrom (1985a: 208–11).
176 Arrom (1985a: 208, 335, n. 1).
177 Gonzalbo Aizpuru (1987a: 9, 129) and Lavrin (2000: 258).
178 Lavrin (2000: 267).
179 Gonzalbo Aizpuru (1987a: 30) and Lavrin (1983: 77).
180 Arrom (1985a: 143), Gonzalbo Aizpuru (1987a: 152) and Tostado Gutiérrez (1991: 21).
181 Lavrin (1972: 367; 2000: 269) and Benítez (1985: 45–49).
182 Lavrin (1976: 256–57, 263, 268; 2000: 269–70) and O. Paz (1988: 119).
183 O. Paz (1988: 65).
184 Schons (1991: 39).
185 Vázquez (1981: 12).
186 Trueblood (1988: 212). O. Paz (1988: 100–13) discussed her decision to become a nun. The quotation is from p. 110.
187 Trueblood (1988: 210).

188 O. Paz (1988: 480).
189 De la Cruz (1995: 86). Translation by the author.
190 Trueblood (1988: 226).
191 Trueblood (1988: 200).
192 The translated text of the *Reply to Sor Filotea* can be found in Trueblood (1988: 205–43). The quotation is from p. 237.
193 Chinchilla-Aguilar (1983: 54–55), Franco (1989: 54), O. Paz (1988: 449), and Schons (1991: 56–57) discussed Sor Juana's decision to end scholarly pursuits.
194 O. Paz (1988: 470).
195 Schwaller (1985: 1; 2000: xiii) and Kamen (2004: 42). A subsequent treaty between Spain and Portugal moved the imaginary line 270 leagues to the west.
196 Elliott (1984: 304), Greenleaf (1961: 6), Muldoon (1978), Poole (1992: 18), Vander Linden (1916), and Weckmann-Múñoz (1976) discussed Alexander VI's grant. The Latin texts and English translations of the Alexandrine bulls can be found in Davenport (1917–37), vol. 1, pp. 56–78.
197 Bakewell (1997: 130), Poole (1992: 8–9), Gutiérrez (1991: 95), Seed (1988a: 166–67), Padden (2000: 29), and Graham (1994: 24). Schmitt (1984: 352) listed the powers transferred to the Spanish Crown by the patronato.
198 Poole (1992: 8, 32, 125), Ricard (1966: 23), Curcio-Nagy (2000: 155), and Knight (2002b: 32).
199 Knight (2002b: 36) and Cline (2000: 75).
200 Florescano (2006: 70), Brading (1991: 102), Taylor (1990: 286), Bonfil Batalla (1996: 87), Knight (2002b: 41), and MacLachlan & Rodríguez O. (1980: 130).
201 Ricard (1966: 54–55), Brading (1994a: 21–22), Florescano (2002: 101–02), Schwaller (2000: xx), Poole (1992: 121), and Lafaye (1984: 667).
202 Greenleaf (1961: 46), Knight (2002b: 33–34), Castro (2007: 167), and Ricard (1966: 91). Benavente is often referred to by the name Motolinía, a Nahuatl word for "poor," which he adopted after he heard the Aztecs using that word to describe him.
203 Greenleaf (1961: 47) and Reff (1991: 269).
204 Reff (1991: 278), Knight (2002b: 48), and Greenleaf (1961: 49–50).
205 Gibson (1952: 32), Schwaller (2000: xxi) and Gruzinski (1993: 178; emphasis in the original).
206 Sharer (2006: 723), Van Young (1989b: 85; 2001: 482), and Farriss (1984: 297).
207 Florescano (2006: 83).
208 Hanke (1937: 69, 71).
209 Hanke (1937: 72) and Castro (2007: 99).
210 Ricard (1966: 81).
211 Buve (1992: 5), Blackburn (1997: 151–2), Greenleaf (1961: 74), and Gruzinski (1993: 67).
212 Ricard (1966: 244).
213 Taylor (1979: 142–43), Wu (1984: 290), Verástique (2000: 104), Knight (2002b: 129), and MacLachlan (1994: 512–13).
214 Van Young (2001: 204).
215 Farriss (1968: 91–92, 101–02), Brading (1994a: 127–28), and Taylor (1996: 163–69).
216 Sharer (2006: 126) and Florescano (2006: 81).
217 Florescano (2006: 137), Ruiz (1992: 19), and Lafaye (1984: 666).
218 Coe & Koontz (2002: 203). Krauze (1997a: 35), Lafaye (1976: 142), Florescano (2002: 160, 163, 189–92; 2006: 163), and León-Portilla (1999: 29; 2002: 4, 9).
219 Lafaye (1984: 666), Kamen (2004: 148), Bakewell (1997: 144–46), and León-Portilla (2002: 8). Systematic study of Nahuatl flourished again in the twentieth century. León-Portilla (2004) described modern scholarship in the field.
220 Greenleaf (1961: 36), Moreno Toscano (1976: 50), C. Castañeda (2000: 87), León-Portilla (2002: 113), and Gruzinski (1993: 48–59).
221 Gruzinski (1993: 67).
222 Ricard (1966: 99, 210–11).
223 Elliott (2006: 333) and Kinsbruner (2005: 82).
224 Marichal (2007: 123–24), Schwaller (1985: 184), Brading (1994a: 220), Knight (2002b: 76), Ladd (1976: 56–57), and Taylor (1972: 168).
225 Taylor (1994: 165).
226 Poole (1992: 129), Taylor (1972: 182), Booker (1993: 75–78), Brading (1994a: 27), Kennedy (1993: 41), and Manchester (1992: 11).
227 Graham (1994: 25) and Elliott (2006: 204).
228 Poole (1992: 129), Semo (1993: 96), Bauer (2001: 122), Kicza (1983: 58–59), Humboldt (1966: III, 102), Ladd (1976: 98), and Costeloe (1967: 107).
229 Semo (1993: 57).

230 Ricard (1966: 243).
231 Paz (1976: xiv), Early (1994: 15), Krauze (1997a: 68), and Bayón (1984: 716).
232 Bayón (1984: 710–11) and Early (1994: 18, 117).
233 Early (1994: 17, 63).
234 Greenleaf (1961: 32–33), Krauze (1997a: 36), and Miller (1985: 150).
235 Warren (1963: 86).
236 Krauze (1997a: 36) and Curcio-Nagy (2000: 154).
237 Castro (2007: 10).
238 Zavala (1974: 143) and Assadourian (1989: 425).
239 Brading (1990: 185), Gutiérrez (1993: 88), and Poole (1992: 86).
240 Zavala (1974: 150).
241 Poole (1992: 86–87), Hanke (1959: 30, 69), and Wallerstein (2000: 13).
242 Brading (1991: 94–95) and Castro (2007: 129–30).
243 Bakewell (1997: 147–48), Hanke (1959: 76), and Mires (1987: 131).
244 Elliott (2006: 77).
245 Poole (1992: 85, 126) and Castro (2007: 145).
246 Castro (2007: 5, 9, 14, 113).
247 Deeds (2005: 99) and Camp (2003: 27).
248 Greenleaf (1969: 162), Knight (2002b: 51), Bennett (2003: 53), and Alberro (1988: 172–73).
249 Greenleaf (1969: 104, 117, 202).
250 Tambs (1965: 168), Greenleaf (1961: 5; 1969: 173, 184), and Curcio-Nagy (2000: 170).
251 Greenleaf (1961: 22) and Tambs (1965: 168).
252 Franco (1989: 58) and Tambs (1965: 181).
253 Greenleaf (1961: 24), Miller (1985: 148), Parkes (1960: 106), Tambs (1965: 169, 175–76), Curcio-Nagy (2000: 172), and Burkholder & Johnson (1998: 102–03).
254 Alberro (1988: 168) and Tambs (1965: 179).
255 Greenleaf (1961: 14, 103).
256 Lopes Don (2008: 604–06), Borah (1992: 189), Brading (1991: 103), and Ricard (1966: 272–73).
257 Alberro (1988: 10) and Kandell (1988: 210).
258 Tambs (1965: 177, 178) and Florescano (1987: 275; 1994: 201).
259 Greenleaf (1961: 130) and Manchester (1992: xiv).
260 Lopes Don (2008: 605), Alberro (1988: 43), Klor de Alva (1981: 139), and Greenleaf (1961: 22, 109; 1969: 13–14, 39, 111).
261 Early (1994: 7–8).
262 Gómara (1964: 297).
263 Burkholder (2000: 129).
264 Cervantes de Salazar (1953: 49, 40).
265 Cervantes de Salazar (1953: 58, 62, 63, n. 100) and Pomeranz & Topik (1999: 83).
266 Cervantes de Salazar (1953: 75–76).
267 Simon (1997: 64), Calderón (1988: 476), Gibson (1964: 305), Kandell (1988: 197–98), Musset (1992: 64–65), and Miller (2007: 73).
268 Díaz del Castillo (1996: 191).
269 Simonian (1995: 39).
270 Musset (1992: 64–65).
271 Kandell (1988: 199) and Humboldt (1966: II, 126–27). Hoberman (1981) discussed the political, economic, and technical questions raised by the drainage system, known as the *desagüe*. Simon (1997: 66–67) noted an unanticipated effect of the *desagüe* was the emergence of salt flats as Lake Texcoco dried. The wind whipped the salty soil into blinding dust storms. These salt flats remain a source of air pollution to this day. Calderón (1988: 475–97) described the project and subsequent flooding and drainage efforts. The *desagüe* tunnel proved to be too small to handle the volume of flood waters, so it was converted into an open cut. This conversion, completed in 1788, is called the Tajo de Nochistongo and still functions today.
272 Calderón (1988: 488–89), Kandell (1988: 199–200), and Musset (1992: 194).
273 Kicza (1983: 133, 187) and Arrom (1985a: 7–10).
274 Kicza (1983: xiii, 1–3, 227), Wasserman (2000: 37–38), Burkholder & Johnson (1998: 277), and Hernández Jaimes (2007: 61).
275 Lafaye (1976: 131) and Early (1994: 144).
276 Lafaye (1976: 81) and Reimers (2006: 432).
277 Domínguez (1980: 42) and C. Castañeda (2000: 84).
278 Manrique (2000: 452), C. Castañeda (2000: 95), and Lafaye (1984: 676).
279 Manrique (2000: 451–52) and Lafaye (1984: 675).

280 Earle (2001: 17), Rodríguez-Buckingham (1985: 42), Verástique (2000: 106), Tarragó (1996: 24–26), Meyer, Sherman, & Deeds (2007: 200), Lafaye (1976: 82), and Neal (1966: 93).
281 Benjamin (1997b: 646). Thomas (1996) commented on Bernal Díaz del Castillo and his history.
282 Manrique (2000: 446–48) and Paz (1976: xv).
283 Krauze (1997a: 81).
284 Florescano (2006: 227), Ronan (1977: 344–51), and Lafaye (1976: 109).
285 Florescano (2002: 276–78).
286 Humboldt (1966: I, 211–12), Brading (1985: 50; 2007a:364), Olivera & Crété (1991: 227–28), and Florescano (1994: 196–98).

4 FROM CORN TO CAPITALISM, 1521–1810

1 Semo (1993: xv) [retranslated by author].
2 Anonymous Conqueror (1972: 15).
3 Bassols Batalla (1984: 86–126), Chevalier (1963: 8–12), and Tortolero Villaseñor (2007: 156, n. 2).
4 Bakewell (1997: 3).
5 Ouweneel & Bijleveld (1989: 487).
6 Calderón (1988: 454–45).
7 Gage (1958: 43, 50–51, 111–12).
8 MacLachlan (1988: 48).
9 Calderón (1988: 143) and Semo (1993: 49).
10 Calderón (1988: 7, 98), Thomas (1993: 591), and Turner & Butzer (1992: 18).
11 Calderón (1988: 344–45). Erosion was not the only environmental disaster to befall the Jesús del Monte lands. In colonial times, the property was situated three leagues from Mexico City. By the 1990s, the estate lands, in Cuajimalpa, had been engulfed by urban sprawl extending out from Mexico City and had been extensively quarried to facilitate the building of the Cuajimalpa–Naucalpan Expressway.
12 Crosby (1986: 151–52). For a discussion of ecological change resulting from the Conquest, see Turner & Butzer (1992), Melville (1994), and Wright (1986).
13 Melville (1994: 1), Kandell (1988: 152), and Simon (1997: 21).
14 Turner & Butzer (1992: 41).
15 Mörner (1967: 22–23), Randall (1977: I, 66), and Chance (1978: 71).
16 Bonfil Batalla (1996: 89), Aguirre Beltrán (1989a: 203), and Van Bath (1979: 57).
17 Semo (1993: 38).
18 García Icazbalceta (1858–66), vol. I, p. 489.
19 Semo (1993: 25).
20 Marichal (2007: 62) and Farriss (1984: 83).
21 Calderón (1988: 167), Semo (1993: 40), MacLeod (1984a: 362–64; 1984b: 237), Florescano (1984: 165–66), and Bonfil Batalla (1996: 90).
22 Semo (1993: 107).
23 Semo (1993: 109).
24 Farriss (1984: 51).
25 Semo (1993: 21–22).
26 Calderón (1988: 8).
27 Bakewell (1971: 225).
28 Knight (2002b: 178, 182).
29 Garner (1988: 904), TePaske & Klein (1981: 132), Hamnett (1999: 115), and Calderón (1988: 369).
30 McNeill (2000: 5), *Harper's* (January 2000, p. 11), and *Economist* (December 31, 1999, p. 10).
31 TePaske & Klein (1981: 120).
32 Arcila Farías (1974: I, 29; II, 183–84, 197) and Coatsworth (1998a: 29).
33 Poole (1992: 110), Arcila Farías (1974: II, 184, 186), Anna (1983: 8), Semo (1978a: 52), Tenenbaum (1986: 3–5; 1989a: 201), Brading (1971: 29, 53), Bakewell (1984: 146), Coatsworth (1986: 27), Velasco A. (1980: 243, 256), and Marichal (2007: 20–22).
34 Moreno-Brid & Ros (2009: 20), Stein & Stein (2003: 225), and Marichal (2006a: 427).
35 Arcila Farías (1974: II, 187–88).
36 Brading (1971: 14) and Marichal (2007: 185).
37 Lynch (1985: 15, 20).
38 Garner (1993: 108).
39 Burkholder & Johnson (1998: 136), Bernstein (1964: 10), Semo (1993: 11), Calderón (1988: 353–55), and Richards (2003: 367).

40 Kandell (1988: 185, 190), Burkholder (2000: 116), Knight (2002b: 175), INEGI (1994: I, 527), Dobado González et al. (2008: 761), and Moreno-Brid & Ros (2009: 21).
41 Calderón (1988: 371), Tandeter (2006: 318, Table 9.1), Burkholder & Johnson (1998: 137), Couturier (2003: 64), and Romero Sotelo (1997: 41).
42 Coatsworth (2008: 548) and Semo (1993: 12, 15).
43 Humboldt (1966: III, 238).
44 Humboldt (1966: III, 197) and Brading (1991: 525–26).
45 Motten (1950: 12), Tandeter (2006: 319), Knight (2002b: 173), Stein & Stein (2003: 227), and Calderón (1988: 601–02).
46 Alamán (1942: I, 102), Romero Sotelo (1997: 32), Humboldt (1966: II, 444; III, 201), and Semo (1993: 12).
47 Calderón (1988: 201), Knight (2002b: 8, 63), Kandell (1988: 185), and Offutt (2001: 176–77).
48 Gilmore (1956: 33–36).
49 Brading (2007b: 85–86), Tandeter (2006: 338), Romero Sotelo (1997: 19, 24–26, 197–98), and Butzer (2001: 80).
50 Moreno-Brid & Ros (2009: 21), Jacobsen & Puhle (1986: 21), Van Young (2001: 70), Knight (2002b: 195), Coatsworth (1986: 41), and Salvucci & Salvucci (1987: 71).
51 Ortiz Monasterio (1987: 119), Mendoza Vargas et al. (2007: 140), and Richards (2003: 368–70).
52 Calderón (1988: 352).
53 Coatsworth (1986: 37) and Knight (2002b: 213).
54 Melville (2006: 121).
55 Chevalier (1963: 2), Semo (1977b: 12; 1993: 155), Florescano (1984: 182), and Van Young (1986a: 70).
56 Chevalier (1963: 277), Melville (2000: 240), and Knight (2002b: 96–97).
57 Semo (1993: 21) and Calderón (1988: 310–11).
58 Taylor (1972: 132) and Van Young (1986a: 75).
59 Moreno-Brid & Ros (2009: 21, Table 2.1) and Knight (2002b: 162).
60 Florescano (1984: 175–79), Kicza (1982: 436), Hernández Chávez (2006: 85), and MacLachlan & Rodríguez O. (1980: 159).
61 Coatsworth (1978: 87–88).
62 Ladd (1976: 69).
63 Lynch (1992a: 19) and Chevalier (1963: 294–95).
64 Florescano (1984: 134).
65 Lockhart (1969: 426) and Mörner (1967: 91).
66 Halperín-Donghi (1993: 7) and MacLachlan & Rodriguez O. (1980: 151).
67 Katz (1986b: 146).
68 Brading (1973b: 392), Humboldt (1966: III, 101), Knight (2002b: 79, 187), and Wu (1984: 277).
69 Knight (2002b: 121), Bauer (2001: 88), and Offutt (2001: 84, 88).
70 Bakewell (1997: 184), Humboldt (1966: III, 2), Warman (1980: 33), and Chevalier (1963: 74).
71 Carroll (1991: 65), Chevalier (1963: 78), MacLachlan & Rodríguez O. (1980: 159–60), Warman (1980: 37), and Semo (1993: 83).
72 Chevalier (1963: 93–94, 106).
73 Chevalier (1963: 93–94).
74 Mendoza Vargas et al. (2007: 138).
75 Chevalier (1963: 84) and Richards (2003: 344, 362–64).
76 Chevalier (1963: 106).
77 Calderón (1988: 341–42) and Burkholder & Johnson (1998: 283).
78 Melville (1994: 14).
79 Simon (1997: 23) and Melville (2000: 236).
80 Van Young (1986a: 82).
81 INEGI (1994: I, 425–26), Salvucci (1987: 175), Stein & Stein (2003: 249), and Van Young (1986a: 71).
82 Florescano (1986: 114), Brading (1971: 18), Moreno-Brid & Ros (2009: 21, Table 2.1), and Bushnell & Macaulay (1994: 56).
83 Coatsworth (2006: 260–61).
84 Salvucci (1987: 12, 19) and Proctor (2003: 37).
85 Fisher (1926: 118), González Angulo & Sandoval Zarauz (1980: 208), Semo (1993: 86–87), Deans-Smith (2007: 76–90), and Calderón (1988: 402–04).
86 Kicza (1983: 209–12).
87 Illades (1996: 251, 254) and Pérez Toledo (1996: 229).
88 Salvucci (1987: 4), Thomson (1986: 173), and Wolf (1982: 275).
89 Proctor (2003: 35).

90 Humboldt (1966: III, 463–64).
91 Greenleaf (1968: 370), Hoberman (1991: 128), and Salvucci (1987: 98).
92 Salvucci (1987: 14, 38, 139), Calderón (1988: 415), and Palmer (1976: 74).
93 Thomson (1986: 195), Viqueira & Urquiola (1990: 95), and Wu (1984: 277).
94 Proctor (2003: 36).
95 Salvucci (1987: 13, 39), Lockhart (1976: 18), Cárdenas (2003: 34), and Stein & Stein (2003: 126).
96 Jacobsen & Puhle (1986: 15) and Deans-Smith (1992: 14).
97 Deans-Smith (1992: xii, xx, 24).
98 Deans-Smith (1992: 54, 63).
99 Deans-Smith (1994: 78).
100 Deans-Smith (1992: 13, 30, 197).
101 Deans-Smith (1992: 100, 104).
102 Deans-Smith (1992: 217–18, 239).
103 Deans-Smith (1992: 31–32).
104 Hoberman (1991: 1).
105 Melville (1994: 10) and Márquez (2006: 395).
106 Burkholder & Johnson (1998: 146–47).
107 Booker (1993: 2–4), Calderón (1988: 552), and Garner (1993: 169–70).
108 Garner (1993: 171–72), Marichal (2006b: 76–77), and INEGI (1994: I, 424).
109 Garner (1993: 169), Elliott (2006: 21), Miño Grijalva (2005: 170), and Kandell (1988: 185).
110 Burkholder & Johnson (1998: 147).
111 Adelman (2006: 29), Hernández Chávez (2006: 90), Poole (1992: 110), Arcila Farías (1974: II, 186), Anna (1983: 8), Semo (1978a: 52), Tenenbaum (1989a: 201), Brading (1971: 115), and Stein & Stein (2003: 258).
112 Stein & Stein (2003: 15, 313, 333) and Hoberman (1991: 41).
113 Humboldt (1966: III, 91–92).
114 Stein & Stein (2003: 279–80), Melville (2006: 139), and Adelman (2006: 157).
115 Ringrose (1996: 318), Hernández Chávez (2006: 89), and MacLachlan (1988: 93).
116 Arcila Farías (1974: I, 152; II, 185–86), Stein & Stein (2003: 158), and Romero Sotelo (1997: 39).
117 Arcila Farías (1974: II, 125–26) and Márquez (2006: 421).
118 Carroll (1991: 59, 154).
119 Calderón (1988: 447–48).
120 Calderón (1988: 451), Fisher (1934: 120), and Ouweneel (1996: 117).
121 Semo (1993: 17) and Calderón (1988: 451).
122 Calderón (1988: 450).
123 Ouweneel & Bijleveld (1989: 487–89), Salvucci, Salvucci & Cohen (1994: 106–07), Salvucci (1987: 41), Calderón (1988: 454), Garner (1993: 181), and Brading (1971: 17).
124 Márquez (2006: 404).
125 Bakewell (1997: 67, 201), Miller (1985: 116), Burkholder & Johnson (1998: 146), Hoberman (1991: 27), and Olivera & Crété (1991: 95).
126 O'Brien (2006: 29), Manning (2006: 56), Márquez (2006: 398), Marichal (2006a: 423; 2006b: 25–26, 46), Elliott (2006: 355), and Chanda (2007: 230).
127 Wolf (1982: 113).
128 Semo (1969: 12) and Salvucci (1987: 174).
129 Thomson (1985: 128) and Coatsworth (1990: 143).
130 Brading (1971: 14) and Garner (1993: 5).
131 Burkholder & Johnson (1998: 150), Stein & Stein (2003: 353), Knight (2002b: 157), Borah (1993: 952), and Garner (1993: 10, 215). Spanish intervention in economic affairs is not surprising, since as Wallerstein (1989: 80) noted, the British industrial revolution, which served as a model for Spain, involved extensive government regulation. In addition to destroying textile production in India, Britain offered a subsidy to exporters, forbade the export of machinery, and prohibited imports, thus providing producers with a domestic monopoly as well as an export market.
132 Garner (1993: 124, 139).
133 Semo (1993: 137).
134 Garner (1993: 141), Camp (2003: 30), and Carroll (1991: 95).
135 Harrer (1979: 28).
136 Calderón (1988: 405).
137 Ladd (1976: 96–97), Grafe & Irigoin (2006: 251), and Marichal (2006b: 44–46).
138 Cope (1994: 112), Garner (1993: 243), and Semo (1993: 89).
139 Durand (1956: 60), Semo (1993: 100), and Calderón (1988: 295).

140 Coatsworth (2006: 248. 260–71).
141 Chua (2007: 134–35).
142 Ruiz (1992: 34), Rout (1976: 34), Krooth (1995: 28), Kandell (1988: 189), Elliott (1984: 204), Semo (1993: 56), and Wallerstein (1980: 37).
143 Kennedy (1987: 33–38, 45), Stein & Stein (2003: 351), and Calderón (1988: 15).
144 Randall (1977: I, 99) and Ringrose (1996: 106).
145 Stein & Stein (2003: 225).
146 Knight (2002b: 158, 195, 233).
147 Galbraith (1975: 12), MacLeod (1984a: 387–88), and Simonian (1995: 37).

5 THE FAR NORTH, 1598–1810

1 M. Meyer (1984: 22).
2 M. Meyer (1984: 3). Ganster & Lorey (2008: 8–13) noted that various modern definitions of the term "borderlands" define the area as transboundary watersheds, as the Mexican *municipios* and U.S. counties abutting the U.S.–Mexico boundary, or as land within 100 kilometers of the boundary (the definition used in the 1982 La Paz Agreement on the environment).
3 Chapman (1921: 307) and Hernández Chávez (2006: 75).
4 Weber (1992: 310).
5 M. Meyer (1984: 48, 50).
6 Salvucci (1987: 95) and Kessell (1989: ix).
7 Calderón (1988: 11), Peña (2005: 70), and Jones (1979: 3, 4).
8 Weber (1992: 327, 328), De la Teja (1995: 25), and Alonso (1995: 52–55).
9 Weber (1992: 327).
10 Bannon (1970: 188), Cutter (1995: 22), Weber (1992: 146), and Patch (2000: 195).
11 Beck (1962: 52), Bannon (1970: 33), and Hall (1989: 76).
12 Rodríguez-Sala, Gómezgil & Cué (1995: 216), Cutter (1995: 17), and Hall (1989: 81–82).
13 Bannon (1970: 35), Beck (1962: 53), and Simmons (1977: 37). As Cutter (1990: 4) observed, the Spanish continued to search for the Straight of Anián, as this imagined passage from the Atlantic to the Pacific was known, until the 1790s.
14 Fontana (1994: 58).
15 Knaut (1995: 49–51) and Bannon (1970: 38–39).
16 De la Teja (1995: 15).
17 Weber (1992: 148) and Bannon (1970: 94).
18 Bannon (1970: 96–97) and Chipman (1992: 83–84). The *Austin American-Statesman* (June 22, 2000, p. E1) described the 2000 excavation of Ft. St. Louis.
19 Foster (1995: 17–18) and Campbell (2003: 45).
20 Bannon (1970: 97) and Faulk (1964: 14).
21 Fontana (1994: 122), Jones (1979: 39–40), Chipman (1992: 99), and Poole (1992: 116).
22 Foster (1995: 46) and Chipman (1992: 18).
23 Lugan (1994: 54) and Weber (1992: 157–58).
24 Jones (1979: 44).
25 Weber (1992: 40) and Gómez (2000: 41).
26 Weber (1992: 238; 2005: 143) and Williams & Williams (1984: 29).
27 Chapman (1921: 223).
28 Weber (1992: 245).
29 Weber (1992: 246).
30 Jackson (1992b: 389) and Ortega Soto (2001: 34).
31 Poole (1992: 117), Jackson & Castillo (1995: 8), Ortega Soto (2001: 28, 61), and Bannon (1970: 164).
32 Bannon (1970: 158), Chapman (1921: 283), and Fontana (1994: 173).
33 Fontana (1994: 203).
34 Bannon (1970: 61). Stern and Jackson (1988) described colonial Sonora, and especially, the Pimería Alta.
35 M. Meyer (1984: 11).
36 Logan (2006: 28–30).
37 Humboldt (1966: II, 336, 299–300).
38 Boyle (1997: 9–10) and Weber (1982: 123).
39 De la Teja (1995: 128, 137).
40 Weber (1992: 176) and Poyo (1996: 11).
41 Cutter (1995: 24) and Raat (1992: 59).

42 Poyo (1996: 12) and Faulk (1964: 97–98).
43 Castañeda (1942: 429).
44 Bannon (1970: 80), Knaut (1995: 130–31), Reff (1991: 121), Beck (1962: 63), Cutter (1995: 23), Hall (1989: 75, 146), and Boyle (1997: 2).
45 Beck (1962: 100).
46 Cutter (1995: 23).
47 Chapman (1921: 3), Bannon (1970: 200), Ortega Soto (2001: 168), and Weber (1992: 247; 2005: 122).
48 Ortega Soto (2001: 149, 168, 177, 180, 184), Bannon (1970: 226–27), and Weber (1982: 125).
49 Weber (1982: 159–60; 1992: 176, 280) and Jackson (1998: 4).
50 Weber (1992: 194), Cutter (1995: 22), and Jones (1979: 47).
51 Knaut (1995: 131).
52 Bannon (1970: 231).
53 Weber (1992: 265), Ortega Soto (2001: 124, 134), and Chapman (1921: 418).
54 Officer (1987: 31), Fontana (1994: 149), Weber (1992: 209), and Bannon (1970: 231).
55 Jackson (1998: 4).
56 Bannon (1970: 73, 235), Lafaye (1984: 673), Jackson (1992b: 391), and Spicer (1962: 5).
57 Weber (1992: 108, 123) and Alonso (1995: 57).
58 Jackson & Castillo (1995: 6) and Wade (2003: 181).
59 Ahlborn (1985: 36–38) and Torres (1993: 21).
60 Lavender (1980: 54) and Jackson & Castillo (1995: 35, 58, 71).
61 Weber (2004: 31) and Jackson & Castillo (1995: 17–19, 29). Serra was not alone in coming under criticism. As Leyva (2007) noted, in the late twentieth century, many Spanish figures such as Juan de Oñate, long considered as benefactors, were sometimes portrayed as perpetrators of genocide. Often Mexican–Americans were divided on the issue, with some considering their Spanish forebears as illustrious civilizers, while others, identifying with their indigenous heritage, condemned them.
62 Sandos (2005: 270–71).
63 Jackson & Castillo (1995: 7, 78–80, 108) and Ortega Soto (2001: 57).
64 Ricard (1966: 97), Reff (1991: 271–72), and Poole (1992: 123–24).
65 Weber (1992: 186–87; 2005: 102) and F. Smith (2005: 4–5).
66 Weber (2005: 92), F. Smith (2005: 15), and De la Teja et al. (2004: 108).
67 Weber (2004: 49, 50, 56; 2005: 99).
68 Weber (2004: 39, 45–46, 50) and Ortega Soto (2001: 14, 55).
69 Eggan (1979) described Pueblo culture.
70 Knaut (1995: xi), Weber (1992: 110), and Adams (1953: 112).
71 Fontana (1994: 86–87), Spicer (1962: 160–61), and Weber (1992: 92).
72 Gutiérrez (1991: 105), Hall (1989: 84), and Knight (2002b: 139).
73 Hall (1989: 88) and Weber (1992: 134).
74 Spicer (1962: 162), Weber (1992: 134), and Gutiérrez (1991: 131–32).
75 Hall (1989: 88).
76 Bannon (1970: 83) and Gutiérrez (1991: 135).
77 Poole (1992: 78), Simmons (1977: 69), Knaut (1995: 10, 174), and Gutiérrez (1991: 136).
78 Roberts (2004: 169).
79 Weber (1992: 136–37) and Knaut (1995: 175).
80 Kessell (1989: 55) and Beck (1962: 85–87).
81 Hall (1989: 92) and Knaut (1995: 177).
82 Beck (1962: 88) and Kessell (1989: 62).
83 Weber (1992: 141), Beck (1962: 92), Bannon (1970: 90), Lavender (1980: 61), Frank (2005: 83), and Simmons (1977: 83–84).
84 Knight (2002b: 129).
85 Chipman (1992: 16–17).
86 Chipman (1992: 135), Hall (1989: 94, 104), Beck (1962: 37–38), F. Smith (2005: 8–9), and Weber (2005: 12, 72).
87 Hall (1989: 78, 107) and Beck (1962: 28).
88 Hall (1989: 94, 100), Faulk (1964: 57), Lavender (1980: 77), De la Teja (1995: 9), and Weber (2005: 75).
89 Worcester (1979: xviii).
90 Weber (1992: 191).
91 Weber (1992: 214) and Gutiérrez (1991: 185).
92 Bannon (1970: 183).
93 Katz (1998a: 12, 17).
94 Simmons (1977: 85) and Wade (2003: 215).

95 Nugent (1993: 44), Simmons (1990: 26), and Alonso (1995: 31).
96 Bobb (1954: 34) and Faulk (1964: 68).
97 Dobyns (1976: 82, 93) and Beck (1962: 96).
98 Weber (2004: 10), F. Smith (2005: 35), and Hall (1989: 120, 131).
99 Simmons (1977: 91–92) and Weber (2005: 193).
100 Weber (2005: 259).
101 Hall (1989: 122), F. Smith (2005: 46), and Weber (2005: 193–94).
102 Fontana (1994: 134) and Spicer (1962: 332).
103 Coatsworth (1982: 34–35).
104 Dobyns (1976: 140).
105 Stannard (1992: 138–39).
106 Foster (1995: 65), John (1975: 523), Knaut (1995: 154–55), and Reff (1991: 229–30).
107 Jackson (1992a: 142) and Weber (1992: 263).
108 Jackson (1992a: 144), Cook (1976: 30–31), Stannard (1992: 136), and Archibald (1978: 184).

6 THE END OF SPANISH RULE, 1810–1821

1 Bakewell (1997: 356).
2 Lynch (1986a: 10) and Florescano & Rojas (1996: 35).
3 Archer (1994a: 263), Pastor (1985: 231), and Lynch (1992b: 78).
4 Florescano & Rojas (1996: 38), Cárdenas (2003: 36), Lynch (1986a: 11), Rodríguez O. (2008: 247), Garner (1993: 220), and Coatsworth (1978: 94).
5 Humboldt (1966: IV, 246).
6 Lynch (1986a: 14–15).
7 Hann (1966: 156), Langley (1996: 330, n. 34), Lynch (1986a: 14), and MacLachlan (1988: 130).
8 Brading (1974: 643; 1991: 526), Castro Gutiérrez (1994: 27), and Archer (1977: 141–56) & (1986: 199, 204).
9 MacLachlan & Rodríguez O. (1980: 283), Archer (1977: 242; 1986: 209, 219–20), and Brading (1991: 467).
10 Florescano (1986: 111), García de León (1988: 26), Ibarra (1988: 29), Garner (1993: 3), and Van Young (1989b: 88).
11 Van Young (2007: 25–26), Burkholder & Johnson (1998: 277), Cárdenas (2003: 50), and Florescano (1986: 82).
12 Marichal (2007: 20, Table 1.1). Graham (1994: 69–78) outlined events leading to these conflicts.
13 Archer (2007: 26) and Tandron (1976: 28–49).
14 Burkholder & Johnson (1998: 304–05), Brading (1984: 435), Lynch (1985: 24), and Ringrose (1996: 122).
15 Abad y Queipo (1994: 111) and Ibarra (1988: 33).
16 Lynch (1986a: 303), Von Wobeser (2007: 22), and Rodríguez O. (2008: 250).
17 Abad y Queipo (1994: 115), Costeloe (1967: 111), Marichal (2007: 148), Von Wobeser (2007: 19–21, 26), Lynch (1986a: 303, 304), and Flores Caballero (1974: 31).
18 Rodríguez O. (2008: 257).
19 Ávila (2007: 261) and Rodríguez O. (2008: 274).
20 Rodríguez O. (2008: 272–75).
21 Rodríguez O. (2008: 259–60).
22 Domínguez (1980: 149), Guedea (1991a: 22), and González Pedrero (1993: I/xxv-xxvi).
23 Rodríguez O. (2008: 277).
24 MacLachlan & Rodríguez O. (1980: 306–07), Rodríguez O. (2007: 229–30; 2008: 283), Archer (2007: 34), Anna (1998a: 50), DePalo (1997: 13), and Domínguez (1980: 149).
25 Miller (1986: 12).
26 Rodríguez O. (1991a: 10), Gracida & Fujigaki (1989: 125), and Anna (1978: 56).
27 Abad y Queipo (1994: 156, 161–62).
28 Descriptions of the Bajío at the time of independence can be found in Anna (1985a: 62), García de León (1988: 55), Pérez Herrero (1991: 216–20), Rodríguez O. (2007: 232), Tutino (1986: 41–98), and Wolf (1972: 84–85).
29 Humboldt (1966: II, 407).
30 Torre Villar (1982: I, 112), Von Wobeser (2007: 23), Domínguez (1980: 155), and J. Meyer (1996: 33).
31 Krauze (1997a: 93–94), Galeana (2007: 247), Von Wobeser (2007: 25–26), Van Young (2001: 1–2), Brading (1970: 19), Taibo (2007: 15), J. Meyer (1996: 27), and Herrejón Peredo (1997: 35–36).
32 Fernández Tejedo & Nava Nava (2001: 5–6) and Taibo (2007: 31).
33 Graham (1994: 96), J. Meyer (1996: 35), and Rodríguez O. (1989: 31). Fernández Tejedo & Nava Nava (2001: 7–11) discussed the content of the Grito.

34 J. Meyer (1996: 36), Rodríguez O. (2007: 232), and Fernández Tejedo & Nava Nava (2001: 11).
35 Tutino (1986: 31, 119, 131).
36 Alamán (1942: I, 352).
37 Ibarra (1988: 47–48).
38 Lynch (1986a: 309).
39 Chavarri (1973: 71) and J. Meyer (1996: 38).
40 Cumberland (1968: 116) and Alamán (1942: I, 354).
41 Kandell (1988: 275) and J. Meyer (1996: 45).
42 Anna (1978: 72), *Siempre!* (March 29, 1972, p. 53), Van Young (2001: 358), and J. Meyer (1996: 45).
43 Tutino (1986: 147, 243).
44 Hart (1987: 54).
45 Archer (1981b: 62).
46 Hamill (1989: 174) and Tutino (1986: 152).
47 Archer (1989b: 26–27).
48 Krauze (1997a: 100), Tutino (1986: 170–71, 182), and Van Young (1988a: 186–92).
49 MacLachlan & Rodríguez O. (1980: 319) and Anna (1978: 85).
50 Archer (1989a: 94–95; 1992a: 37).
51 J. Meyer (1996: 52–53) and Archer (1989a: 90).
52 Villalpando César (1996: 19).
53 Ibarra (1988: 57) and Archer (1992c: 80–81).
54 Miller (1986: 57). For an account of how Spanish sympathizers in the area organized the capture of Hidalgo, see Harris (1975: 129–35).
55 Harris (1975: 136).
56 J. Meyer (1996: 57).
57 J. Meyer (1996: 57).
58 Carrera Stampa (1995: 81).
59 Ávila (2007: 256) and Ibarra (2007: 267, 272).
60 Archer (1991: 150) and J. Meyer (1996: 37).
61 Tutino (1986: 46).
62 Archer (1992c: 79; 1991: 155) and Lynch (1986a: 311; 1992a: 77).
63 Anna (1978: 138).
64 Brading (2007a: 74). Archer (1992c: 77) commented on how various historians have interpreted Hidalgo.
65 Carroll (1991: 131) stated that Morelos was of black, white, and Indian ancestry. Of the twenty-nine leaders of the independence movement before Iturbide, Vincent (1994: 266) found eight to be Africans or mulattos.
66 Florescano (1994: 220) and Lynch (1992a: 78).
67 Gracida & Fujigaki (1989: 156).
68 Guardino (1996: 70).
69 Cumberland (1968: 134), Alamán (1942: IV, 123), and Archer (1989a: 93; 1992d: 126–27; 1994a: 261).
70 Lynch (1992a: 78), Timmons (1963: 50), Herrejón Peredo (1996: 28), Krauze (1997a: 108–09), and Archer (1989b: 25).
71 Timmons (1950: 473) and Krauze (1997a: 106).
72 Gracida & Fujigaki (1989: 160–61).
73 Florescano (1994: 220; 2006: 240) and Herrejón Peredo (1996: 41).
74 Suchlicki (1996: 57).
75 Lynch (1992a: 79), Rodríguez O. (2007: 236), and Van Young (2001: 33).
76 Guedea & Rodríguez O. (1997: 24).
77 Teja Zabre (1959: 277–79) and Herrejón Peredo (1996: 57–59).
78 Timmons (1963: 83) and Herrejón Peredo (1996: 37).
79 Anna (1978: 208) and Lynch (1986a: 317–18, 315).
80 Morris (2007: 440–41) and Archer (2007: 39).
81 Antuñano Maurer (1987: 21).
82 Antuñano Maurer (1987: 22) and Bethell (1985: 230).
83 Antuñano Maurer (1987: 23).
84 Abad y Queipo (1813). Note that in modern usage the author's name is written, "Manuel Abad y Queipo," and is so cited in the bibliography. However the title page of the 1813 book omits the "y." In modern usage the title would also require several more acute accent marks. However, the title as it appears in the book has only one such accent. Perhaps the typesetter had only one accented vowel.
85 Hamill (1991: 60–61).
86 Anna (1978: 69) and Hamill (1966: 151, 175).
87 Anna (1978: 81–82), Archer (1997: 6), and Van Young (2001: 327).

88 Brading (2007a: 373) and MacLachlan & Rodríguez O. (1980: 318).
89 Florescano (2006: 245).
90 Van Young (2001: 332, 479).
91 Domínguez (1980: 199), Timmons (1950: 453–54), and Villalpando César (1996: 41).
92 Kentner (1975: 33, 175).
93 Kinsbruner (1994: 104).
94 Gracida & Fujigaki (1989: 168), Rodríguez O. (1994: 5), Burkholder & Johnson (1998: 335), Tutino (1998: 404), Archer (1991: 165), and Van Young (2001: 30).
95 Langley (1996: 205–06), Van Young (2001: 142), and Archer (1991: 158).
96 Archer (1989b: 30; 1991: 159; 1993: 26). Rodríguez O. (1990: 172) quoted Guedea.
97 Archer (1989b: 28; 1991: 149).
98 Van Young (1989b: 89).
99 Brading (1996: 50) and Anna (1998a: 42–43).
100 Lynch (1986a: 36) and Anna (1998a: 46).
101 Gracida & Fujigaki (1989: 118), Guedea (1993: 47), and Rodríguez O. (2007: 231).
102 Berry (1966: 14) and Gracida & Fujigaki (1989: 135).
103 Ibarra (1988: 69–72).
104 Graham (1994: 77), Brading (1996: 53), and Kinsbruner (1994: 3, 117).
105 Garza (1966: 47), Weber (2005: 264), and Anna (1998a: 52). Neither the Spanish constitution of 1812, the rebels' 1814 constitution, nor any of the Mexican constitutions promulgated between 1824 and 1917 explicitly denied women the vote. Their drafters simply assumed that women could not vote.
106 Rodríguez O. (2000: 144) and Graham (1994: 77).
107 Rodríguez O. (2007: 233–34) and Guedea (1993: 51–55).
108 Rodríguez O. (2007: 233–34) and Domínguez (1980: 184).
109 Guedea (1994: 50).
110 Brading (1985: 45).
111 Benson (1992: 5), Rodríguez O. (1994: 102; 2007: 233), Anna (1998a: 55–58), and González Pedrero (1993: I/251).
112 Anna (1998a: 63), Vázquez (1996a: 15), and Nutini (1995: 232).
113 Brading (1996: 48–49) and Graham (1994: 108).
114 Cunniff (1966: 80), Blaufarb (2007: 755), Weber (2005: 264–54), and Berry (1966: 28).
115 Vázquez (1996a: 15) and Anna (1998a: 66).
116 Benson (1992: 38–39).
117 Graham (1994: 109) and Hann (1966: 175).
118 Berry (1966: 41), Rodríguez O. (2007: 235), Vázquez (1996a: 12), and Neal (1966: 94–95).
119 Ducey (1995: 15).
120 Crespo (2009: 105–07).
121 Iturbide (1971: 6).
122 Villalpando César (1996: 44), Anna (1990: 2; 1998a: 83), and Krauze (1997a: 121–22).
123 Archer (2008: 35) and Anna (1990: 2–3).
124 Archer (2008: 357), Rodríguez O. (1994: 117–18), DePalo (1997: 20), and Ferrer Muñoz (1995: 81).
125 Vázquez (1996a: 37), Graham (1994: 124), and Anna (1998a: 78).
126 Rodríguez O. (1994: 123). An English translation of the Plan can be found in Joseph & Henderson (2002: 192–95).
127 The Plan of Iguala did not spring full-blown from Iturbide's brain. Benson (1953: 440–43) and Rodríguez O. (1994: 118–21) commented on the intellectual history of the Plan.
128 Archer (1994b: 94) and Vázquez (1992: 167).
129 Rodríguez O. (1994: 125) and Guardino (1996: 77).
130 Vázquez (1996a: 39) and Archer (1989b: 41).
131 Rodríguez O. (1994: 126), Archer (2008: 359), and Macaulay (1966: 151).
132 Anna (1978: 211).
133 Rodríguez O. (1994: 125), Graham (1994: 125), and Archer (1989b: 43).
134 Vázquez (1996a: 43) and Anna (1998a: 70). As Ferrer Muñoz (1995: 98) noted, due to a final colonial reorganization, the official title of O'Donojú and his immediate predecessors was not viceroy, but Captain General y Jefe Superior de Nueva España.
135 Benson (1953: 442), Anna (1990: 1, 11), Ferrer Muñoz (1995: 104), Vázquez (1996a: 43), and Crespo (2009: 109).
136 The text of the Treaty of Córdoba can be found in Tena Ramírez (1992: 116–19).
137 Benson (1992: 44) and Ferrer Muñoz (1995: 106).
138 Fernández Tejedo & Nava Nava (2001: 19).

139 Vázquez (1996a: 52–53).
140 The full text of the Declaration of Independence can be found in Tena Ramírez (1992: 122–23).
141 Anna (1990: 8).
142 Van Young (2001: 504).
143 Brading (1985: 48), Lynch (1986a: 25), Van Young (2001: 523), Tortolero Villaseñor (2007: 156), Taylor (2007: 237), and Hernández Jaimes (2007: 68–70).
144 Rodríguez O. (1989: 21) and Anna (1998a: 74).
145 Hamill (1966: 170).
146 Van Young (1989b: 94; 1984: 21; 1988a: 183), Hernández Jaimes (2007: 68), Anna (1994: 19), and Archer (1994a: 268–69).
147 Morris (2007: 438) and Van Young (2007: 42).
148 Lynch (1986a: 322), Van Young (1989b: 76–80), Knight (2004: 489–91), and Taylor (1985: 160).
149 Taylor (1987: 23; 2007: 224) and Archer (1992c: 85).
150 Ducey (1995: 2, 24, 30) and Ouweneel (1996: 328).
151 Domínguez (1980: 189), Bethell (1985: 230), and Brading (1991: 571).
152 Domínguez (1980: 201).
153 Brading (1985: 56) and Graham (1994: 125).
154 Arrom (1985a: 32–34), Villalpando César (1996: 34), Guedea (1992: 81–88), and Kentner (1975: 1).
155 Kentner (1975: 71–73, 77, 81).
156 Kentner (1975: 201), Kinsbruner (1994: 104), and Arrom (1985a: 38).
157 Taylor (2007: 232–33) and Kentner (1975: 71–73, 77, 81).
158 Van Young (2001: 436; 2004: 570).
159 Katz (2007: 184–85) and Guerra (2007: 133).
160 Kentner (1975: 201), Elliott (2006: 394), Rodríguez O. (1991a: 9–11), and Nugent (2008: 40).
161 Anna (1998a: 74), Elliott (2006: 391), Crespo (2009: 106–111), Brading (2007a: 375), and Archer (1989a: 108).
162 Coatsworth (2006: 248).
163 Anna (1983: 55), Humboldt (1966: IV, 95), and Rydjord (1935: 16).
164 Dawson (1990: 10), Halperín-Donghi (1985: 302), and Kaufmann (1951: 7).
165 Salvucci (1987: 153–69) and Booker (1993: 114).
166 Gortari Rabiela (1989: 135–37), Booker (1993: 126), Archer (1989a: 106), and Gracida & Fujigaki (1989: 171).
167 Lynch (1986a: 328), Van Young (2001: 80–81), Romero Sotelo (1997: 14–16, 92), and Coatsworth (1986: 42).
168 Salvucci, Salvucci & Cohen (1994: 104), and Gortari Rabiela (1989: 132, 139, 145).
169 Salvucci (1987: 160, 161), Dobado González et al. (2008: 767–68), and Potash (1983: 10).
170 Archer (1981b: 77; 1992b: 300), Deans-Smith (1992: 99), Rodríguez O. (1983: 26), and Lynch (1986a: 326).
171 Carroll (1991: 57), Hamill (1976: 48), and Romero Sotelo (1997: 57).
172 Booker (1993: 128) and Archer (1992b: 287; 1989c: 6).
173 TePaske (1989: 68, 73), Cárdenas (2003: 55), and Gortari Rabiela (1989: 138).
174 Cárdenas (1997a: 67), Archer (1985: 131), and Hamill (1976: 49).
175 Cortada (1978: 38), Whitaker (1941: 98), and Blaufarb (2007: 761.
176 McDougall (1997: 64, 68), Liss (1984: 15), and Schmitt (1974: 21).
177 Blaufarb (2007: 753) and Griffin (1937: 97–98).
178 Langley (1996: 203), Gracida & Fujigaki (1989: 172–76), and *El Universal* [on line] (December 14, 2008), "México y el mundo."
179 Vázquez & Meyer (1985: 21), Gleijeses (1992: 483), and Green (1971: 3).
180 Jiménez Codinach (1991: 93, 96, 295), Gleijeses (1992: 486), and Johnson (1990: 115).

7 NATIONHOOD, 1821–1855

1 Anna (1990: x).
2 Rodríguez O. (1992a: 2).
3 Anna (1990: 53) and Halperín-Donghi (1973: 116).
4 Anna (1990: 64).
5 Iturbide (1971: 42).
6 Anna (1990: 76–78; 1998a: 94).
7 Anna (1990: 75).
8 Anna (1990: 24–25, 1989: 195; 1998a: 94–95).

9 Lynch (1986a: 323), Rodríguez O. (1992a: 3), Bushnell & Macaulay (1994: 63), and Neal (1966: 109).
10 Anna (1990: 112–13, 118).
11 Iturbide (1971: 67).
12 Anna (1990: 152) and Lynch (1986a: 324).
13 Benson (1945: 46) and Anna (1998a: 104).
14 Anna (1990: 161, 175; 1998a: 105–06) and Rodríguez O. (1992a: 4).
15 Anna (1998a: 106), Rodríguez O. (1992a: 5), and González Pedrero (1993: I/254).
16 Anna (1990: 171–72).
17 Krauze (1997a: 128).
18 Anna (1994: 33; 1998a: 91, 107) and Rodríguez O. (1992b: 316).
19 Benson (1945: 55) and Anna (1994: 33; 1998a: 111; 1989: 199).
20 Krauze (1997a: 128) and Anna (1990: 231; 1998a: 97).
21 Anna (1990: 230–33).
22 Anna (1990: 236).
23 Anna (1990: 84–85, 94, 119), Tenenbaum (1988: 201), and Rodríguez O. (1992a: 2). Anna (1990: 239–40) commented on Iturbide's negative historical legacy. See Chapter 2, n. 53 for the number of streets named after him.
24 Anna (1990: 137), Tenenbaum (1988: 208), and Di Tella (1996: 131, 135).
25 Camp (2003: 31).
26 Anna (1998a: 135–39) and Rodríguez O. (1992a: 15).
27 Anna (1998a: 138), DePalo (1997: 29), and Rodríguez O. (1992a: 20).
28 Russell (1984: 13–19).
29 Rodríguez O. (2007: 242).
30 Anna (1998a: 125) and Florescano (2002: 319).
31 Alamán (1942: V, 751).
32 Anna (1998a: 179, 180) and Wasserman (2000: 216).
33 Tenenbaum (1996: 8) and Guardino (1996: 120).
34 Carroll (1991: 133), Fowler (2007: 109), and González Pedrero (1993: I/389). Guerrero's racial background is far from certain. Historian David Brading (1985: 93) stated that Guerrero was "probably by colonial classification a mulatto."
35 Guardino (1996: 125), DePalo (1997: 35), and Arrom (1996b: 82–83).
36 Carroll (1991: 132).
37 Anna (1998a: 211–12).
38 Carroll (1991: 109) and Lynch (1986a: 332).
39 Carroll (1991: 93), Aguirre Beltrán (1970: 12), and Rodríguez O. (1991a: 13). For a description of surviving black communities, see Aguirre Beltrán (1989b) and *Mexico Journal* (May 1, 1989, pp. 23–25).
40 Guardino (1996: 64), Arrom (1996b: 83), Sims (1990: 6, 18), and Brading (1985: 93).
41 Sims (1990: 6, 207), Burkholder & Johnson (1998: 341–42), and Booker (1993: 147).
42 Crespo (2009: 116).
43 Anna (1998a: 225), DePalo (1997: 37–38), Fowler (2007: 120–22), González Pedrero (1993 I/497, 503–04), and Sims (1990: 151).
44 DePalo (1997: 38) and Santa Anna (1988: 24).
45 Guardino (1996: 130), Anna (1998a: 227), and Florescano (2006: 266).
46 Tenenbaum (1986: 35), Guardino (1996: 131), Anna (1998a: 212, 217), and DePalo (1997: 38).
47 Florescano (2002: 323) and Vázquez (1976: 25).
48 Anna (1998a: 239).
49 Guardino (1996: 134–35).
50 Anna (1998a: 240–41).
51 Anna (1998a: 243), DePalo (1997: 39), Bazant (1985a: 434), and Sierra (1969: 200).
52 Krauze (1994: 124). See Chapter 2, n. 53 for the number of streets named after Guerrero.
53 Anna (1998a: 228–231, 237).
54 Rodríguez O. (1992c: 149), Harris (1975: 276–77), Tenenbaum (1992b: 193), and Anna (1998a: 233, 236).
55 Anna (1998a: 233, 246), Fowler (2007: 133–38), and Rodríguez O. (1992c: 157).
56 Rodríguez O. (1992c: 161) and Anna (1998a: 255).
57 Anna (1998a: 256).
58 Fowler (2007: 347).
59 Archer (1989c: 11) and González Pedrero (1993: I/55).
60 Fowler (2007: x), Poinsett (1969: 14), and Bakewell (1997: 391).
61 Fowler (2007: 142).
62 Bakewell (1997: 397).

63 Bushnell & Macaulay (1994: 72–73), Bakewell (1997: 397–98), Tenenbaum (1992b: 195–97; 1993: 100), Graham (1994: 145), Anna (1998a: 258), and Rodríguez O. (1994: 11).
64 Anna (1997: 234; 1998a: 259) and Vázquez (1987: 559). For the arguments used to justify Santa Anna's takeover, see Costeloe (1988a).
65 Sims (1990: 202–03).
66 Anna (1998a: 259–261), Wasserman (2000: 50), Hernández Chávez (2006: 132), Hart (1987: 80), and Guardino (1996: 152).
67 Guardino (1996: 140).
68 Bushnell & Macaulay (1994: 74) and Rugeley (1996: 62).
69 González Pedrero (1993: II, 505–11).
70 González Navarro (1993: 10), Bushnell & Macaulay (1994: 76), and Fowler (2007: 188–89).
71 Fromson (1996: 119–20).
72 Ruiz Massieu (1996: 155–75). The number of Santa Anna presidencies is in question due to his frequently leaving office to avoid difficult decisions or to command armies. It is unclear if his absences mark the end of one presidency and the beginning of another or are merely hiatuses occurring during one presidency.
73 Arrom (1996a: 9–10) and Beezley (1987: 128).
74 Vázquez (1987: 563) and Costeloe (1989b: 417).
75 Florescano (2006: 278), Fowler (2007: 291), and Guardino (1996: 180).
76 Harris (1975: 291–92), Bazant (1985a: 451–52), Hamnett (1994c: 15), Guardino (1996: 181), Fowler (2007: 298), Tenenbaum (1986: 183), and Fromson (1996: 120).
77 Krauze (1997a: 149) and Garber (1923: 152).
78 Fowler (2007: 303, 310).
79 Bazant (1985a: 452), Galeana (2006: 26–27), and Vázquez (1997c: 34). The text of the Plan of Ayutla can be found in Tena Ramírez (1992: 492–98).
80 Guardino (1996: 188), DePalo (1997: 86), Tenenbaum (1986: 137), and Thomson (1991: 274).
81 Thomson (1991: 274), Fowler (2004: 36), and Bazant (1985a: 453).
82 Thomson (1990: 36), Galeana (2006: 27), and Hamnett (1996a: 87).
83 Fowler (2007: 192–93, 354–56). Fowler (2007: 349–52) discusses the basis of Santa Anna's Veracruz support.
84 Olivera & Crété (1991: 241) and Fowler (2007: xix). See Chapter 2, n. 53 for the number of streets named after Santa Anna.
85 Fowler (2007: 347–48) and Crespo (2009: 119).
86 Weber (1982: xvii).
87 L. Meyer (1996: 18) and Costeloe (1993: 239).
88 Katz (1986a: 42), Hernández Chávez (1992: 207–08; 1993: 35), Garner (2001: 33), and Anna (1998b: 627).
89 Anna (1998a: 16).
90 Anna (1998a: 89).
91 Anna (1998a: 14) and *El Universal* [on line] (November 9, 2008), "México y el mundo."
92 Taylor (1985: 118) and Anna (1998a: 87).
93 Graham (1994: 154–55), Walker (1986: 25), and Anna (1998a: 35).
94 Anna (1998a: 21).
95 Rodríguez O. (1992a: 9).
96 Anna (1998a: 108).
97 Anna (1998a: 139–41).
98 Vázquez (1987: 563–64) and Tenenbaum (1989b: 73).
99 Anna (1998a: 182, 187–88) and Benson (1966: 209).
100 Anna (1998a: 217, 222–23) and González Pedrero (1993: I/298, 303).
101 Olivera & Crété (1991: 17).
102 Safford (1985: 419), Walker (1986: 5), Anna (1998a: 75), Vázquez (1976: 34), Marichal (2007: 119), and Tenenbaum (1992b: 189). Chile, almost alone among the Spanish American nations, enjoyed a high degree of stability during the early independence period. Between 1831 and 1871, it had only four presidents, each serving ten years. As Moreno-Brid & Ros (2009: 41) noted, taxes on the export of copper and temperate agricultural products, especially wheat, were key to this stability.
103 Wasserman (2000: 67) and Marichal (2006a: 446–47).
104 Cárdenas (1997a: 73), Pi Suñer (1992: 139), Di Tella (1996: 212–13), Tenenbaum (1979: 335; 1986: 10–11, 21), Stevens (1991: 18), Vázquez (1976: 40), and Moreno-Brid & Ros (2009: 31).
105 Santoni (1996a: 43), Hernández Chávez (1993: 53), and Costeloe (1993: 4–5).
106 Di Tella (1996: 213) and Costeloe (1993: 243).
107 Bosch García (1983–85: II, 180).
108 Buve (1992: 12) and Vázquez (1976: 56).

109 Costeloe (1993: 5), González Pedrero (1993: I/xxxix), Wasserman (2000: 46), Vázquez (1976: 57), and Sierra (1969: 191).
110 Costeloe (1993: 9, 26, 303), Hamnett (1987: 586), and Brading (1985: 68).
111 Santoni (1996b: 172–73).
112 Stevens (1986: 648) and Costeloe (1993: 7–8).
113 Vázquez (1976: 55), Hamnett (1994b: 92–93), and Santoni (1996a: 140).
114 Lynch (1994: 380).
115 Bakewell (1997: 389) and Lynch (1992a: 405).
116 Lynch (1992a: 184) and Anna (1998a: 22, 257).
117 Anna (1993: 134).
118 Bazant (1985a: 430).
119 Tenenbaum (1986: 89) and C. Cardoso (1980: 150).
120 Stevens (1991: 43), Brading (1973a: 181–83), and Tenenbaum (1986: 88).
121 *New York Times* (November 1, 1988, p. 11).
122 Santoni (1996a: 2), Bakewell (1997: 400), Paz (1985: 124), Hale (1989: 3–4), Brading (1985: 70), and Urías Hermosillo (1979: 33). This last study described the competing ideas on economic development in early nineteenth-century Mexico.
123 Brading (1985: 95).
124 Carbó (1988: 88), Chevalier (1985: 136), and L. Meyer (1983: 137).
125 Stevens (1991: 32, 36) and Weber (1982: 34).
126 Guardino (1996: 144–45).
127 Murray (1997: 189).
128 Hale (1968: 298), Stevens (1991: 38, 42, 105), Brading (1973a: 147), and Costeloe (1993: 22–23).
129 Brading (1973a: 146–49) and Lynch (1992a: 118).
130 Krauze (2006b: 80).
131 Costeloe (1993: 14) and Hamnett (1996b: 660).
132 Guerra (2007: 135) and Tutino (2007: 231).
133 Hansen (1971: 134).
134 Humphreys & Lynch (1966: 265–66).
135 Brading (1985: 54), Vázquez (1994a: 261), and L. Meyer (1996: 18).
136 Bethell (1985: 231–32).
137 Chevalier (1964: 460).
138 Lynch (1986b: 529) and Bethell (1985: 232).
139 Stevens (1991: 32), Staples (1994: 235), and Bushnell & Macaulay (1994: 34).
140 Safford (1985: 352) and Lynch (1986b: 529–30).
141 Lynch (1986b: 531) and Bakewell (1997: 394–95).
142 Mörner (1967: 83).
143 Thompson (1846: 166).
144 Olivera & Crété (1991: 242) and Safford (1985: 379).
145 Olivera & Crété (1991: 242), Carroll (1991: 153), and Lynch (1986a: 333).
146 Lynch (1994: 380), Di Tella (1994: 122), and Tutino (1998: 375–78, 414).
147 Guerra (1988, I: 368), Hernández Jaimes (2007: 66), and Langley (1996: 259).
148 Graham (1994: 147).
149 Hamnett (1994a: 56) and Katz (1988: 9–10).
150 Olivera & Crété (1991: 242–43), Arrom (1985a: 20), Domínguez (1980: 19), and Vaughan (1982: 14–16).
151 García de León (1988: 64), Argüello (1989: 205), McCaa (1993: 100), and INEGI (1994: 13).
152 Sartorius (1961: 103).
153 Wasserman (2000: 30, 54).
154 Sartorius (1961: 69) and Beezley (1987: 85). Mining engineer Allen H. Rogers described a similar dwelling in *Engineering and Mining Journal* (April 4, 1908, p. 701).
155 Sartorius (1961: 55, 102–03, 105, 126).
156 Sartorius (1961: 102).
157 Adams (1967: 474), Borah (1983: 412), Ibarra (1988: 78), and León-Portilla (1997: 17).
158 Santiago (2006: 37, 38).
159 Tutino (1988: 119) and Anna (1996: 11).
160 Brading (1985: 73).
161 Bonfil Batalla (1996: 106) and Lynch (1986a: 333).
162 Brading (1985: 91), González Navarro (1954: 117), Adams (1967: 474), and Borah (1983: 412).
163 Ibarra (1988: 78).
164 Bonfil Batalla (1972: 118) and Calderón de la Barca (1966: 445).

165 Spicer (1962: 334), Langley (1996: 244), and León-Portilla (1997: 18).
166 Santiago (2006: 43) and Weber (2005: 265).
167 Hart (1987: 33–34, 74), Hernández Chávez (1993: 40), and Weber (2005: 276).
168 Levinson (2005: 48–49) and Hart 2005: 43).
169 Tutino (2007: 233), Joseph (1982: 21), Reed (2001: 5, 10–11), and Rugeley (1997: 205; 1996: 185).
170 Rugeley (1996: 124) and Reed (2001: 55).
171 González Navarro (1970a: 309).
172 Joseph (1982: 22) and Rugeley (1996: 157).
173 Reed (2001: 95).
174 Wright (1992: 258–59), Careaga Viliesid (1997: 135), and Bricker (1981: 102).
175 Levinson (2005: 90) and Careaga Viliesid (1997: 161, 182–83).
176 Thomas (1997: 760).
177 Sharer (2006: 723–25) and Bricker (1981: 110–13).
178 Rugeley (1996: 181), Wright (1992: 261–62), and Bazant (1985a: 448, n. 18).
179 Arrom (1985a: 255).
180 Wasserman (2000: 32) and Tutino (1998: 377).
181 Wasserman (2000: 41–43) and Arrom (1985a: 164–65).
182 Arrom (1985a: 4, 20–21).
183 Arrom (1985a: 21–22, 171).
184 Calderón de la Barca (1966: 533).
185 Arrom (1985a: 42, 267–68) and Costeloe (1997: 23).
186 Arrom (1985a: 40, 76–77).
187 Sims (1990: 10), Arrom (1985a: 7, 9–10, 285), Thompson (1846: 147), and Lynch (1994: 380).
188 Wasserman (2000: 35).
189 O. Paz (1988: 478) and Fuentes (1996: 18). Martin (1998: 4–6) discussed European artistic influence in Latin America.
190 Berlandier (1980: 92).
191 Poinsett (1969: 73).
192 Olivera & Crété (1991: 243), Rodríguez O. (1992a: 8), and Fromson (1996: 119).
193 Heller (2007: 191).
194 Fromson (1996: 120) and Rodríguez O. (1992c: 158).
195 Vázquez (2000b: 45).
196 Henderson (2007: 4).
197 Paz (1982: 6, 16), Sokoloff & Zolt (2007: 93), Machinea & Kacef (2007: 2), and Detweiler & Ruiz (1978: 3).
198 Bourguignon & Walton (2007: 105) and Sokoloff & Zolt (2007: 88–90).
199 *L.A. Weekly* (March 9, 1984, p. 8). For more recent musings on Mexican national character, see Knight (2007b).

8 THE DAWN OF INDUSTRIALIZATION, 1821–1855

1 Levy & Bruhn (2001: 40).
2 Walker (1986: 1), Bulmer-Thomas (1994a: 28–29), Cárdenas (2003: 23), Prados de la Escosura (2006: 466), and Heath (1993: 263).
3 Romero Sotelo (1997: 145), Gilmore (1956: 51), and Poinsett (1969: 159).
4 Gilmore (1963: 38) and Vázquez (1976: 43).
5 Randall (1972: 33), Lynch (1986a: 328), and Rippy (1947a: 129).
6 Randall (1972: xi), Grillo (2003: 56), and Dawson (1990: 89).
7 Gilmore (1956: 65).
8 Randall (1972: 52–53, 55–60).
9 Gilmore (1956: 68).
10 Randall (1972: 109) and Marichal (1989: 52, n. 28).
11 Randall (1972: xi, 73), Grillo (2003: 57), and Walker (1986: 194). After U.S. independence, the Mexican silver peso was used as a model for the dollar. Up until 1873, the U.S. dollar and the Mexican peso were equal in value. After that date, the silver-based peso declined in value relative to the dollar, which was linked to gold. This occurred because the price of silver relative to gold declined. The symbol $ when used in this work to refer to sums after 1873, refers only to the U.S. dollar.
12 Gilmore (1956: 169–70) and Walker (1986: 194).
13 Vázquez (1976: 45) and Gilmore (1956: 237–39).
14 Cárdenas (1997a: 75), Bakewell (1997: 402), and Halperín-Donghi (1985: 309).

15 Guardino (1996: 114) and Staples (1992: 106).
16 Halperín-Donghi (1973: 71) and Lynch (1986a: 329).
17 Staples (1992: 116), Gilmore (1956: 220), and Randall (1972: 127, 144).
18 Dobado González (2002: 693–94), Thomson (1985: 131), Gilmore (1956: 135–37), and Berlandier (1980: 220).
19 Prados de la Escosura (2006: 498) and Hernández Chávez (2006: 120–22).
20 Dobado González et al. (2008: 797).
21 Salvucci (1987: 135) and Dobado González et al. (2008: 771).
22 Anderson (1976: 10–12).
23 Pérez Toledo (1996: 240–41) and Novelo (1997: 105).
24 Pérez Toledo (1996: 237) and Bulmer-Thomas (1994a: 132).
25 Potash (1983: 45).
26 Calderón de la Barca (1966: 409).
27 Porter (2003: 52–54).
28 Walker (1986: 138), Calderón de la Barca (1966: 408–09), and Olivera & Crété (1991: 155–56).
29 Walker (1986: 138), Potash (1983: 122–23), and Ortiz Monasterio (1987: 178).
30 Bakewell (1997: 405) and Potash (1983: 52, 73, 77, 92, 102).
31 Dobado González et al. (2008: 772), Heath (1993: 288), Cárdenas (2003: 89), Kinsbruner (1994: 130), Ramos Escandón (1988: 24, 29), and Halperín-Donghi (1985: 328).
32 INEGI (1994: 616) and Potash (1983: 162).
33 Walker (1986: 162–63) and Thomson (1985: 136).
34 Potash (1983: 160).
35 Vázquez (1976: 45), Salvucci & Salvucci (1987: 74), and Haber (1992: 9).
36 Bulmer-Thomas (1994a: 39), Thomson (1986: 198), Gómez-Galvarriato (2006: 394), Heath (1993: 270), and Walker (1986: 151–53).
37 Argüello (1989: 226), Cárdenas (1997a: 84), and Bakewell (1997: 405, 416).
38 Argüello (1989: 200) and Wasserman (2000: 71).
39 Tutino (1975: 510), Keen (1996: 188), and Bushnell & Macaulay (1994: 59).
40 Olivera & Crété (1991: 146–50).
41 Hernández Jaimes (2007: 65) and Harris (1975: 162, 166, 169, 169, 205).
42 Harris (1975: 205, 218, 222, 312), Wasserman (2000: 25), and Olivera & Crété (1991: 146).
43 Bushnell & Macaulay (1994: 58), Miller (1990: 242), and Vázquez (1976: 48).
44 Beato (1993: 71) and Calderón de la Barca (1966: 592).
45 Tutino (1997: 1303) and Brading (1978: 149).
46 Poinsett (1969: 106), Walker (1986: 9), and Guardino (1996: 80).
47 Halperín-Donghi (1985: 301).
48 Heath (1993: 269, 272), Halperín-Donghi (1973: 82–83), and J. Mayo (1996: 174).
49 Graham (1994: 138), Heath (1993: 262–64), Calderón de la Barca (1966: 72), and Walker (1986: 61).
50 Johnson (1990: 107).
51 Kaufmann (1951: 178), Halperín-Donghi (1973: 50; 1985: 300), Tenenbaum (1979: 333), and Knight (2008: 30).
52 Flores (1998: 35).
53 Olivera & Crété (1991: 95), Guardino (1996: 114), and J. Mayo (1996: 178).
54 Hernández Chávez (1993: 52) and Heath (1993: 267).
55 Costeloe (1993: 86) and INEGI (1994: 783).
56 Marichal (1989: 17) and Halperín-Donghi (1985: 306, 327).
57 Brading (1985: 92), Halperín-Donghi (1985: 327), Guardino (2003: 254), and Marichal (1989: 22).
58 Hernández Chávez (2006: 126), Cárdenas (1997a: 69), and Bulmer-Thomas (1994a: 38, Table 2.4).
59 Olivera & Crété (1991: 70), Cárdenas (2003: 73), and Summerhill (1997: 95).
60 Weber (1982: 149, 150).
61 Tenenbaum (1979: 320), Heath (1993: 266, 270), Reynolds (1970: 6), and Thomson (1985: 131).
62 Marichal (1989: 14, 27) and Rodríguez O. (1989: 217–19).
63 Dawson (1990: 1), Marichal (1989: 39), and Gilmore (1956: 7).
64 Dawson (1990: 11), Fishlow (1995: 34), Aggarwal (1996: 1–2), and Rodríguez O. (1989: 216).
65 Vázquez (1976: 37), Marichal (1989: 39), and Rodríguez O. (1989: 218).
66 Rodríguez O. (1989: 234) and Vázquez (1976: 37).
67 Rodríguez O. (1989: 227, 234) and Bazant (1985a: 429).
68 Marichal (1989: 34).
69 Dawson (1990: xi) and Gilmore (1956: 16).
70 Aggarwal (1996: 22).

71 Tenenbaum (1993: 100) and Marichal (1989: 49).
72 Dawson (1990: 2).
73 Walker (1986: 5–6), Marichal (1989: 64), and Vázquez (1976: 39). Costeloe (1999) described the complex negotiations leading to the $2.5 million transfer.
74 Knight (2008: 41).
75 Dobado González et al. (2008: 762) and Moreno-Brid & Ros (2009: 19).
76 Haber (1992: 1, 6) and Prados de la Escosura (2006: 482).
77 Marichal (2006a: 454–56).
78 Lewis (2007: 16–17) and Fernández Arena & May (1971: 10–11).
79 Hobsbawn (1996: 106) and Tenenbaum (1979: 338).
80 Randall (1972: 163).
81 Prados de la Escosura (2006: 470).
82 Marichal (2006a: 446).
83 Rodríguez O. & Vincent (1997: 8) and McDougall (1997: 50).
84 Johnson (1990: 13–15), Vázquez (2000a: 340), Rodríguez O. (1989: 3), and Bairoch (1982: 291).
85 Rodríguez O. (1989: 5).
86 Coatsworth (1998a: 26; 2008: 547) and L. Meyer (1991c: 33).

9 THE DIPLOMATS ARRIVE, 1822–1855

1 Robertson (1918: 251) and *Annals of Congress*, House of Representatives, 17th Congress, 1st Session, col. 825.
2 Richardson (1917: II, 686).
3 U.S. (1822: 8).
4 Robertson (1918: 260–61).
5 In this book, the contemporary term "ambassador" has been used instead of "minister." Poinsett's official title was "envoy extraordinary and minister plenipotentiary." The first U.S. diplomatic representative to Mexico who officially bore the title "ambassador" was Powell Clayton, who served from 1899 to 1905.
6 Guedea & Rodríguez O. (1997: 36) and Schmitt (1974: 31).
7 Johnson (1990: 184) and Vázquez (1986: 148).
8 Johnson (1990: 74) and Rippy (1929: 247).
9 Guedea & Rodríguez O. (1997: 37) and Rippy (1929: 285).
10 Fuentes Mares (1982: 128) and Benson (1989: 293).
11 Manning (1916: 246).
12 The texts of the border and commercial treaties Poinsett negotiated can be found in Bevans (1972, pp. 760–80).
13 Lamar (1981: 100).
14 Letter dated Oct. 28, 1827, *Poinsett Papers,* vol. IV, p. 151, Historical Society of Pennsylvania, Philadelphia. The original is in Spanish.
15 Green (1987: 92) and Rippy (1935: 129).
16 Price (1967: 20–21) and Bassett (1929: IV, 80).
17 Brack (1975: 66) and Bosch García (1957: 147).
18 Herrera (2007: 86–87) and Barker (1907: 797).
19 *Congressional Globe,* vol. XII, pt. 2, col. 1531.
20 Baker (1934: 17–18).
21 Price (1967: 25).
22 Kearney & Knopp (1991: 30–31).
23 Hart (1987: 110).
24 U.S. (1976: 904, 907) and Heath (1993: 266).

10 THE NORTH ADRIFT, 1821–1845

1 Weber (1982: 242).
2 Alonso (1995: 39) and Weber (1982: 112, 115).
3 Weber (1982: 36, 121, 241).
4 Weber (1982: 41–42, 241) and Ortega Soto (2001: 326).
5 McCarty (1997: 112).
6 Weber (1982: 46, 62; 2005: 108), De la Teja et al. (2004: 111), Spicer (1962: 335), and McCarty (1997: 18).
7 Kennedy (1993: 19) and Weber (1982: 54–56).

8 Weber (1982: 63).
9 Haas (1995: 45, 48–49).
10 Haas (1995: 40), Jackson & Castillo (1995: 91–95), and Ortega Soto (2001: 331, 341–42).
11 Weber (1982: 208; 1994: 67) and Ortega Soto (2001: 339, 349, 377).
12 Ulibarri (1974: 141).
13 W. Brown (1988: 6).
14 Hall (1989: 148). Simmons (1986: 9) suggested that Santa Fe was Becknell's intended destination when he left Missouri. In any case, he initiated trade along the trail.
15 Beck (1962: 110–11), McCullough (1992: 20), and Moyano Pahissa (1976: 36).
16 Boyle (1997: 28) and Poinsett (1846b: 29).
17 Ulibarri (1974: 85), W. Brown (1988: 24), and Boyle (1997: 33).
18 Moyano Pahissa (1976: 36), W. Brown (1988: 36), and Boyle (1997: 27).
19 W. Brown (1988: 33), Ulibarri (1974: 87), Wasserman (1984: 74), and Beck (1962: 102).
20 Boyle (1997: 45–46).
21 Simmons (1986: 46, 72) and Boyle (1997: xv, 42, 57, 63–64).
22 Simmons (1986: 31), W. Brown (1988: 35), and Boyle (1997: xiv-xv).
23 Ulibarri (1974: 106, 304).
24 Beck (1962: 110) and W. Brown (1988: 12).
25 Ulibarri (1974: 117) and Beck (1962: 117).
26 Fontana (1994: 218) and Weber (1982: 138–41, 146).
27 Weber (1982: 136).
28 Ortega Soto (2001: 395–96, 412).
29 Weber (2005: 269).
30 Weber (1982: 100; 2005: 267) and Katz (1998a: 13).
31 DeLay (2007: 44–45).
32 Katz (2006: 31), R. Smith (1963: 35–36, 48), Weber (1982: 86), Rodríguez (1995: 71, 92), and Hatfield (1998: 12).
33 DeLay (2007: 42, 44).
34 Officer (1987: 4) and Weber (1988: 126; 1982: 105; 2005: 267).
35 Weber (1982: 95; 1988: 122).
36 Weber (1988: 122) and R. Smith (1963: 34).
37 Weber (1982: 212) and Gutiérrez (1991: 152).
38 Weber (1982: 109; 1988: 119–20).
39 R. Smith (1963: 52), McCarty (1997: 101), and Rodríguez (1995: 71).
40 R. Smith (1963: 44–45), Katz (1998a: 14), Márquez Terrazas (1998: 38), Hatfield (1998: 13), and DePalo (1997: 240, n. 67).
41 Weber (1982: 87).

11 SHIFTING BOUNDARIES, 1845–1855

1 McDougall (1997: 92–93).
2 See Chapter 9, n. 5.
3 Richardson (1917: V, 2195).
4 Manning (1932–39: VIII, 177).
5 Alcaraz et al. (1970: 26), Martínez (1988: 14), and *Congressional Globe,* 29th Congress, 2nd Session, Appendix, p. 242.
6 Montejano (1987: 19).
7 Brack (1975: 181).
8 Schmitt (1974: 69).
9 Pletcher (1973: 255) and Winders (1997: 29).
10 Grant (1996: 43), Foos (2002: 15), and L. Mayo (1996: 163).
11 Sellers (1966: II, 265).
12 Robertson (1955: 209), Santoni (1996a: 106), Costeloe (1993: 290), and Pletcher (1973: 372).
13 U.S. (1848, p. 90).
14 Bauer (1974: 33).
15 Grant (1996: 45) and Richardson (1917: V, 2290).
16 *Congressional Globe,* 29th Congress, 2nd Session, Appendix, p. 241 and Beck & Haase (1989: 22).
17 Bauer (1974: 47).
18 Brack (1975: 117) and Zorrilla (1977: I, 182).

19 Bauer (1974: 42).
20 DePalo (1997: 99) and Henderson (2007: 155).
21 Pletcher (1973: 377), R. Miller (1991: xv), Vázquez (2000b: 48–49), Ulibarri (1974: 245), and Quaife (1910: I, 384).
22 Richardson (1917: V, 2332).
23 Pletcher (1973: 439).
24 Schoultz (1998: 28).
25 This account of the Battle of Palo Alto is based on Bauer (1974: 52–57), DePalo (1997: 100), Dillon (1973: 110–15), McFeely (1981: 31), Eisenhower (1989: 76–80), Haecker & Mauck (1997: 29–48), L. Mayo (1996: 164–65), and Singletary (1960: 29–30).
26 This account of the Battle of Resaca de la Palma is based on Bauer (1974: 59–62), Eisenhower (1989: 81–84), Wheelan (2007: 140), Johannsen (1985: 127), and L. Mayo (1996: 165).
27 González Ramos (2005: 54).
28 Vázquez (1976: 80).
29 Weems (1974: 211) and L. Mayo (1996: 168–69).
30 This account of the Battle of Monterrey is based on Bauer (1974: 90–100), Dillon (1973: 116–18), Eisenhower (1989: 127–51), L. Mayo (1996: 169), Montemayor Hernández (1971: 123–42), Pletcher (1973: 464), and Singletary (1960: 33–43).
31 Henderson (2007: 159).
32 Lynch (1992a: 346–47).
33 Crespo (2009: 140).
34 Bauer (1974: 206–09), DePalo (1997: 110), Haecker & Mauck (1997: 95), Wheelan (2007: 276), and Krauze (1997a: 143).
35 This account of the Battle of Buena Vista is based on Alcaraz et al. (1970: 92), Bauer (1974: 209–17), DePalo (1997: 113–14), Dillon (1973: 118–24), Eisenhower (1989: 182–91), Johannsen (1985: 96), L. Mayo (1996: 171), Pletcher (1973: 48–49), and Singletary (1960: 49–54).
36 Benton (1856: II, 680).
37 Richardson (1917: VI, 2393) and Singletary (1960: 71).
38 Pacheco & Reséndez (1997: 21).
39 Singletary (1960: 111), Bauer (1974: 358–59), and Pletcher (1973: 459).
40 Eisenhower (1989: xvii) and Price (1967: 92).
41 Thoreau (1970: 459).
42 Richardson (1917: VI, 2323) and Wheelan (2007: 258).
43 Winders (1997: 49), Caruso (1991: 147), Grant (1996: 75), and Vázquez (1976: 81).
44 L. Mayo (1996: 174) and Florescano (2002: 332).
45 Zeh (1995: 10). Frederick Zeh emigrated from Bavaria to the United States, joined the army in 1846, and wrote a first-person account of his experiences in the Mexican–American War.
46 DePalo (1997: 119) and Bauer (1974: 252).
47 Bauer (1974: 259) and L. Mayo (1996: 174).
48 Alcaraz et al. (1970: 192).
49 Pletcher (1973: 497) and C. Castañeda (1949: 463–64).
50 Ohrt (1997: 123).
51 L. Mayo (1996: 177).
52 Vázquez (1997d: 13), Foos (2002: 107), and Pacheco & Reséndez (1997: 26).
53 The account of fighting on August 20 is drawn from Alcaraz et al. (1970: 251–58), Bauer (1974: 295–301), DePalo (1997: 127–32), Dillon (1973: 156–63), Eisenhower (1989: 316–27), Pletcher (1973: 512–13), Santa Anna (1988: 109), and Singletary (1960: 89–92).
54 Pletcher (1973: 515) and Richardson (1917: V, 2388).
55 Pletcher (1973: 519).
56 Pacheco & Reséndez (1997: 28) and Olavarría y Ferrari (1974: 693).
57 Ohrt (1997: 132).
58 Bauer (1974: 322).
59 Alcaraz et al. (1970: 327), Bauer (1974: 322), Levinson (2005: 60), and Vázquez (1985: 92).
60 R. Miller (1989: 176).
61 Meltzer (1974: 203).
62 Meltzer (1974: 196–206) and Foos (2002: 105–08).
63 Fowler (2007: 278–79).
64 Bauer (1974: 397), Wasserman (2000: 87), Foos (2002: 25), and Eisenhower (1986: 35).
65 Ohrt (1997: 104).
66 Tenenbaum (1989b: 81) and Quaife (1910: III, 358).

67 Vázquez (1985: 93–94).
68 Griswold del Castillo (1990: 38, 53).
69 Price (1967: 91) and Vázquez (1997d: 129).
70 Tenenbaum (1989b: 79–83) and Marichal (2002: 96).
71 Graebner (1978: 331) and Bauer (1974: 382).
72 Rippy (1935: 229), Johannsen (1985: 299), Moyano Pahissa (1985: 115), Johnson (1990: 196), and Schoultz (1998: 36).
73 McCormac (1922: 552).
74 This brief statement by no means exhausts the discussion of the causes of the war. Interpretations of its causes have varied according to the observers' political persuasion, nationality, and the historical period in which the observations were made. For more on the question, see Benjamin (1979), Benjamin & Velasco Márquez (1997: 100–04), Brack (1975: 1–13), DePalo (1997: 92–93), Harstad & Resh (1964), Pletcher (1973: 1–5), Price (1967: 33), Singletary (1960: 20–21), and Vázquez (2000b).
75 Cazadero (1973: 113–14) and Johannsen (1985: 308).
76 Medina Castro (1971: 74) and Foos (2002: 96–97).
77 Dillon (1973: 233–35), Houston (1972: 273, 281), Haecker & Mauck (1997: 77), and DePalo (1997: 139). For a description of the flying artillery, see Winders (1997: 89).
78 Haecker & Mauck (1997: 59–60) and Wheelan (2007: 135). As Haecker & Mauck (1997: 59, 71–72) noted, even though the era of smooth-bore weaponry was coming to an end, the musket was still the standard weapon of both armies of the Mexican–American War. At that time, rifles were so slow to load that they were of limited utility on the battlefield. The Mississippi volunteers did fight with rifles, which they used effectively at Buena Vista. Regular troops, however, were not issued with rifles.
79 Winders (1997: 54) and Weigley (1984: 185).
80 Johannsen (1985: 21, 27, 53).
81 Harstad & Resh (1964: 297) and Johannsen (1985: 196).
82 Johannsen (1985: 14).
83 Moyano Pahissa (1985: 171).
84 Mexico (1827: 14) and Humboldt (1966: IV, 270).
85 Brack (1975: 119).
86 Wasserman (2000: 77) and Tenenbaum (1986: 76; 1989b: 79).
87 Alcaraz et al. (1970: 137), Henderson (2007: 161–63), and Santoni (1996a: 182–95). Some claim the term "polko" derives from President Polk, since the revolt was seen as favoring the United States. Others claim that the name derives from the polka, then in vogue among the wealthy.
88 Zorrilla (1977: I, 195–96), Moyano Pahissa (1985: 112), Santoni (1996b: 171–72), and Brack (1975: 171).
89 *El Siglo XIX,* June 1, 1848, p. 3.
90 Santa Anna (1988: 98) and González Navarro (1977: 17).
91 Eisenhower (1989: 267), García Cantú (1971: 80–81), and Moyano Pahissa (1985: 113).
92 Suárez Argüello (1987: 178), Levinson (2005: 15), Chassen-López (2004: 320), Hale (1957: 157), and Santiago (2006: 41).
93 DeLay (2007: 58–62).
94 Harris (1975: 242–43) and Foos (2002: 120, 137).
95 Wasserman (2000: 79).
96 García Cantú (1971: 112), Vázquez (1997d: 77), Haecker & Mauck (1997: 96), and Zeh (1995: 47).
97 Brack (1975: 174) and Henderson (2007: 148).
98 Vázquez & Meyer (1985: 41).
99 Brack (1975: 172).
100 Haecker & Mauck (1997: 87, 137), Eisenhower (1989: xxii–xxiii), Moyano Pahissa (1985: 114), and Zeh (1995: 35).
101 See Tuchman (1988: 20) for comments on envelopment and frontal attack.
102 DePalo (1997: 125) and Florescano (2002: 333).
103 Cazadero (1973: 124), Guardino (1996: 169–70), Wasserman (2000: 86), L. Meyer (2008: 13), and Bauer (1974: 218, 221).
104 Cazadero (1973: 124), Levinson (2005: 24, 68–69), and Bauer (1974: 269).
105 Elliott (1937: 448).
106 Santoni (1996a: 232) and Vázquez (2000b: 59).
107 Raat (1992: 72) and Griswold del Castillo (1990: 59).
108 Benjamin & Velasco Márquez (1997: 105) and Griswold del Castillo (1990: 130).
109 *Review of the Economic Situation of Mexico* (January 2002, p. 35) reported that in 2000 Mexico's GDP was $575 billion. That year the product of the four border states was $2.224 trillion (www.bea.gov/regional/gsp/).
110 Olliff (1981: 28).

111 Hart (1987: 110).
112 Rippy (1926: 88).
113 Moyano Pahissa (1985: 214).
114 Rippy (1926: 98–99).
115 Stout (1972: 354–55) and Zorrilla (1977: I, 308).
116 Moyano Pahissa (1985: 241).
117 Benítez (1998: 76).
118 Rippy (1926: 102. 178–79).
119 Hatfield (1998: 1, 15).
120 Katz (1998a: 13).
121 Rippy (1926: 129, 135).
122 Rippy (1926: 75).
123 Park (1961: 138).
124 Park (1961: 141, 142) and Weber (1988: 132).
125 Alonso (1995: 26).
126 Quijada Hernández (1997: 67), Katz (1998a: 13), and Rippy (1919: 386).
127 Schoultz (1998: 46), Martínez (1988: 19), and Tenenbaum (1986: 127).
128 Santa Anna (1988: 143) and Fowler (2007: 307).
129 Perkins (1933: 320–22) and Terrazas Basante (1997: 309).
130 Schmidt (1961: 245).
131 DeLay (2007: 67).
132 Tena Ramírez (1992: 493).
133 Tinker Salas (1997: 102).

12 JUÁREZ AND DÍAZ, 1856–1909

1 Paz (1985: 88).
2 Schettino (2007: 65).
3 Negretto & Aguilar-Rivera (2000: 375) and Camp (2003: 32).
4 Bushnell & Macaulay (1994: 182, 194), Wasserman (2000: 103), Cosío Villegas (1997a: 99), Hamnett (1994c: 35, 49; 1996a: 97), Katz (1986a: 4), Leal (1975c: 13), Mallon (1988: 43), Schmitt (1984: 365), and Velasco Á. et al. (1988: 120) discussed 1850s Mexican liberalism.
5 Bazant (1985a: 457).
6 Ocampo (1900–01: III, 592–93).
7 Krauze (1997a: 155).
8 Ocampo (1900–01: I, 41–42).
9 Krauze (1997a: 168).
10 Hamnett (1996a: 88).
11 Guardino (1996: 188–89).
12 Mallon (1988: 20), Bazant (1985a: 453), and Hamnett (1996a: 88).
13 Tenenbaum (1986: 145), Bazant (1985a: 454), and Hamnett (1999: 160).
14 Lira (1994: 340) and García Ugarte (2007: 151).
15 García Ugarte (2007: 155–56).
16 Sinkin (1979: 117–18), Tutino (1988: 120), and Bazant (1985a: 456). Debate concerning the amount of Church wealth became politically charged. Matson (1979: 602) compared various estimates of Church wealth and observed, "No one knew the value of all these holdings, which were divided among various orders, individuals, and societies, and were disguised, even if inadvertently, by poor record-keeping."
17 Carbó (1988: 93), Katz (1986a: 5), and Tutino (1998: 119).
18 Bazant (1976: 163).
19 Hamnett (1999: 162).
20 Brading (1985: 73).
21 Carbó (1988: 104).
22 Hamnett (1996a: 90).
23 Tutino (1986: 259) and Tenenbaum (1986: 143).
24 González Navarro (2006–7: I, 335), Hamnett (1996a: 89), Ruiz Guerra (2007: 422), and Galeana (2006: 47).
25 Cosío Villegas (1997a), Galeana (2006: 48), Garrido (1986: 29), Hart (1987: 81), and Katz (1986a: 3) discussed the 1857 constitution.
26 Hale (1989: 52), Weldon (1997: 228) and Hamnett (1996a: 92; 1996b: 668).

27 Hamnett (1996a: 90), Santoni (1996a: 234), Bushnell & Macaulay (1994: 197), Hale (1989: 8), Hernández Chávez (1993: 58), and Thomson (1995: 33).
28 Cockcroft (1968: 28) and Staples (1989: 38).
29 Arriaga (1959: 10).
30 Vanderwood (2000: 371) and Camp (2003: 32–33).
31 Cosío Villegas (1997a: 124, 128).
32 Hamnett (1996a: 95), González Navarro (2006–7: I, 148), and Benítez (1998: 109).
33 Hamnett (1996a: 87; 1994c: 59) and Vanderwood (1970: 325).
34 Hamnett (1994c: 102).
35 Benítez (1998: 15–21), González Navarro (2006–7: I, 15), Galeana (2006: 177–80), Gugliotta (1992: 20), Hamnett (1994c: 22), and Krauze (1997a: 160).
36 Benítez (1998: 23–24), Hamnett (1994c: 22), and González Navarro (2006–7: III, 9).
37 Krauze (1997a: 162), Benítez (1998: 44), McNamara (2007: 31), and Hamnett (1994c: 35, 45).
38 Wasserman (2000: 95), Galeana (2006: 199), McNamara (2007: 34), and Krauze (1997a: 163, 166).
39 Krauze (1997a: 167), Galeana (2006: 196), Crespo (2009: 218), and Ruiz (1992: 235).
40 Benítez (1998: 77–78), Krauze (1997a: 167), Galeana (2006: 201), and Hamnett (1994c: 58).
41 Roeder (1947: I, 161).
42 Bazant (1977: 75), Langley (1996: 279), Bushnell & Macaulay (1994: 198–99), Cardoso & Hermosillo (1980: 19), and Kandell (1988: 330–31).
43 Hamnett (1996b: 661), Katz (1986a: 7), Bertola et al. (1993: 119), Bushnell & Macaulay (1994: 199), Langley (1996: 279), Chevalier (1964: 472), and Knight (1985a: 69).
44 Ruiz (1992: 238).
45 Bazant (1977: 80).
46 Díaz (1976: 110), Hamnett (1994c: 117, 120), and Marichal (1989: 65).
47 Thomson (1991: 273) and Krauze (1997a: 170).
48 Sierra (1974: 178).
49 Kandell (1988: 331).
50 Bazant (1985a: 464) and Hamnett (1994c: 126).
51 U.S. (1862: 12).
52 Hamnett (1994c: 168) and Terrazas Basante (1990: 53).
53 Bazant (1985a: 465). The text of the Tripartite Convention of London, which is in French, can be found in *British and Foreign State Papers*, vol. 51, pp. 63–65.
54 Hart (2002: 9) and Perkins (1933: 366).
55 Tenenbaum (1991: 81).
56 O'Connor (1971: 69–71).
57 Vázquez & Meyer (1985: 68–69).
58 Vanderwood (2000: 381).
59 Rivera Cambas: (1987: I, 706–15).
60 See Chapter 2, n. 53 for the number of streets named after Zaragoza.
61 Hamnett (1994c: 171).
62 Díaz (1976: 133) and O'Connor (1971: 79).
63 Hamnett (1994c: 176).
64 Díaz (1976: 135) and Pani (2002: 19).
65 Krauze (1997a: 173) and Galeana (2006: 101).
66 Duncan (1996: 32).
67 O'Connor (1971: 99).
68 Hamnett (1996c: 550) and Galeana (2006: 121–22).
69 Kandell (1988: 341–42), Pitner (1993: 3), and O'Connor (1971: 93, 112).
70 Duncan (1996: 35, 61), González Navarro (2006–7: I, 236), Díaz (1976: 106), Crespo (2009: 186), Bazant (1977: 89), Hart (1987: 38), and Mallon (1995: 78–79).
71 Bakewell (1997: 394) and Díaz (1976: 142).
72 Vanderwood (2000: 382) and *New York Times* (October 9, 1864, p. 4).
73 Díaz (1976: 137), Miller (1985: 246; 1973: 7), and Benítez (1998: 249).
74 Bazant (1985a: 468), Krauze (1997a: 196), and Hamnett (1994c: 119, 138).
75 Miller (1973: 6–7).
76 Díaz (1976: 142) and O'Connor (1971: 155, 158).
77 O'Connor (1971: 127) and Duncan (1996: 38, 42).
78 Miller (1985: 246).
79 Benítez (1998: 262), Perkins (1933: 518–21), Tenenbaum (1991: 88), Krauze (1997a: 185), and Coerver (1999: 25).

80 Pitner (1993: 144) and Hamnett (1994c: 186).
81 Galeana (2006: 146) and Hamnett (1994c: 186).
82 Kandell (1988: 351), Safford (1985: 360), and Hamnett (1994c: 194).
83 Cockcroft (1998: 76) and Gugliotta (1992: 23–25).
84 Knight (1994a: 146), Guerra (1988: I, 47), Wasserman (2000: 10), and Katz (1986a: 8).
85 Hamnett (1999: 168) and Wasserman (2000: 125–26).
86 Fuentes (1996: 65), Mörner (1967: 89), Krauze (1997a: 202), Florescano (1997: 434), and Anna (1998a: 15).
87 Wasserman (2000: 123).
88 Hamnett (1997: 720).
89 E. Meyer (1996: 26), Katz (1986a: 7), Knight (1985a: 66; 1992a: 125), Hamnett (1994c: 200), Hale (1986: 369; 1989: 22), and Krauze (1997a: 199).
90 Cosío Villegas (1997a: 103) and McNamara (2007: 72).
91 Díaz y de Ovando (1972: 52), Hamnett (1996b: 674, 680; 1999: 181), Katz (1986a: 11–14), and Krauze (1997a: 199).
92 Hamnett (1996b: 663, 666).
93 Katz (1986a: 11) and Bulmer-Thomas (1994a: 94).
94 Katz (1986a: 11).
95 Ruiz (1992: 242), Miller (1985: 237), and Stevens (1991: 117).
96 Thomson (1995: 34) and L. Meyer (1974: 722).
97 Hamnett (1996b: 683).
98 Hamnett (1994c: 207, 228).
99 Krauze (1997a: 201), Cosío Villegas (1997a: 103), and Meyer, Sherman & Deeds (2007: 355).
100 Crespo (2009: 232–33), Hamnett (1996b: 684), and Benítez (1998: 322).
101 Hale (1989: 100).
102 *Historia documental de México*, vol. 2, p. 350. This last sentence is still frequently quoted in Mexico. In Spanish it reads, "Entre los individuos, como entre las naciones, el respeto al derecho ajeno es la paz."
103 Calderón (1972: 19) and Katz (1986a: 8–9).
104 Garrido (1986: 30), Wasserman (2000: 113), Sinkin (1979: 105), Vernon (1963: 37), Fuentes (1996: 65), and L. Meyer (1996: 20).
105 Paz (1985: 128), Crespo (2009: 235), and Brading (1985: 75). See Chapter 2, note 53 for the number of streets named after Juárez. He was a polarizing figure. González Navarro (2006–7, vol. 3) reviews the voluminous commentary concerning him.
106 Fromson (1996: 120–21) and Krauze (1997a: 203).
107 Krauze (1997a: 203), Hernández Chávez (1993: 59) and *New York Herald Tribune* (December 16, 1866, p. 3).
108 Hamnett (1994c: 37), Reimers (2006: 435, Table 11.1), and Benítez (1998: 311–12).
109 Guerra (1988, I, 404).
110 Reina (1980: 48–49).
111 Guerra (1988: I, 32).
112 Krauze (1997a: 207), González y González (1986: 163–64), and Kandell (1988: 355–56).
113 González y González (1986: 165), Hart (2002: 60), and Krauze & Zerón-Medina (1993: III, 20).
114 McNamara (2007: 89).
115 Guerra (1988: I, 78, 94) and Garner (2001: 50).
116 Hart (1987: 106, 122–23; 2002: 62, 66).
117 Hart (1987: 125; 2002: 67) and Garner (2001: 62).
118 Cosío Villegas (1955: I, 773–74) and Foster (1909: I, 79).
119 Cosío Villegas (1997a: 105), Mallon (1994: 102), Chassen-López (2004: 358), and Haber, Razo & Maurer (2003: 42).
120 Hamnett (1999: 197) and Kuntz Ficker (1995: 42).
121 Collado (1987a: 38) and Bushnell & Macaulay (1994: 207).
122 Hamnett (1999: 201).
123 Guerra (1988: I, 218).
124 DePalo (1997: 161) and Lieuwen (1968: 3).
125 Johns (1997: 68), Vanderwood (1997: 1323), Chassen-López (2004: 360), and Katz (1986a: 39).
126 Hansen (1971: 151), Krauze (1997a: 10), and Ruiz (1980: 19).
127 Cardoso & Hermosillo (1980: 24), Katz (1986a: 40), and Madero (1986: 116).
128 Guerra (1988: I, 436) and Fromson (1996: 121).
129 Ruiz (1980: 30; 1992: 299), Kandell (1988: 347), Katz (1986a: 35), and Knight (1986a: I, 17). At the federal level, the Senate was reestablished in 1874.
130 Johns (1997: 6), Guerra (2007: 140; 1988: I, 41), and Cosío Villegas (1997a: 100–01).

131 Cosío Villegas (1997a: 100–01).
132 Bertola *et al.* (1993: 125) and Katz (1986a: 36).
133 Guerra (2007: 141), Britton (1997: 740), and Hale (1989: 253).
134 Wasserman (1984: 84), Foster (1997: 145) and Anderson (1976: 243).
135 Raat (1967: 15) and Bakewell (1997: 420).
136 Bakewell (1997: 421–22), Buchenau (1997: 261), Guerra (1988, I, 382), and Hale (1989: 4).
137 Sierra (1969: 359).
138 Guerra (1988: I, 211) and Brown (1987: 392).
139 Ruiz (1980: 40).
140 Cott (1978: 146, 171), Ramos-Escandón (1990a: 12), and Krauze & Zerón-Medina (1993: IV, 64).
141 Gilly (1983: 60) and Katz (1986a: 63–67).
142 Ruiz (1980: 27; 1992: 300), McNamara (2007: 96), and Mallon (1994: 103).
143 Hart (1987: 176), Katz (1986a: 71), Guerra (2007: 142), Vanderwood (1989b: 159), and Hansen (1971: 154).
144 Guerra (1988: I, 439; II, 14, 16) and Haber et al. (2008: 22).
145 Guerra (1988: I, 441; II, 17).
146 Albro (1992: 19) and Guerra (1988: II, 23).
147 Albro (1992: 10).
148 Albro (1992: 12, 16), Bakewell (1997: 431), and Guerra (1988: I, 437).
149 Katz (1998a: 44), Raat (1981: 31), and Albro (1992: 7–16).
150 Albro (1992: 22) and Katz (1986a: 67; 1998a: 45).
151 Cockcroft (1968: 133).
152 Guerra (1988: I, 53) and Raat (1981: 121–22).
153 Albro (1992: 30–32, 60) and Katz (1998a: 44–45). Ricardo Flores Magón remained in the United States where he embraced anarchism and called for total revolution against both capital and the state. In 1922, he died in Fort Leavenworth, to which he had been sentenced for urging Americans not to fight in the First World War on the grounds that they would only serve as cannon fodder for capitalist ruling classes. Such statements were declared to be a violation of the U.S. Espionage Act of 1917.
154 Katz (1986a: 69) and Wasserman (2000: 221).
155 Ruiz (1980: 14), Tinker Salas (1997: 176–77), Raat (1981: 69–73), and Gonzales (2002: 24).
156 Raat (1981: 74–75) and Tinker Salas (1992: 442).
157 Anderson (1976: 110), Bernstein (1964: 58), and O'Brien (1999: 78).
158 Albro (1992: 39), Hart (1987: 67), and Ruiz (1980: 69–70).
159 Gonzales (2002: 68), Anderson (1976: 112, 117), and Raat (1981: 88).
160 Anderson (1976: 157–160, 163, 169; 1997: 684), Cárdenas (2003: 229–30), and Hart (1987: 69–71).
161 Garner (2001: 195).
162 Anderson (1976: 286–87), Cockcroft (1968: 36), Katz (1986a: 64; 1998a: 48), McNamara (2007: 175–76), Randall (1977: I, 178), Knight (2007a: 159), Ganster & Lorey (2008: 59), and Wasserman (1984: 80).
163 Tutino (1986: 335–36), Guerra (1988: II, 106), and Moreno-Brid & Ros (2009: 64).
164 *Pearson's Magazine* (March 1908, p. 237, 242).
165 *Pearson's Magazine* (March 1908, p. 244).
166 Chassen-López (2004: 496), Knight (1986a: I, 48), L. Meyer (2008: 13), and Henderson (2000: 25–26).
167 Anderson (1976: 243), and Guerra (1988: II, 105).
168 Katz (1986a: 70), Hart (1987: 96–97), and Wasserman (1984: 142, 150).
169 Madero (1986: 50) and Guerra (1988: II, 184).
170 Krauze (1997a: 235), Katz (2006: 185), Guerra (2007: 145), and Ulloa (1985: 17).
171 Guerra (1988: II, 193), Garciadiego Dantan (2007: 46), and Anderson (1976: 254, 261).
172 Anderson (1976: 265, 271), Henderson (2000: 27), and Guerra (1988: II, 186).
173 Guerra (1988: II, 209), Kandell (1988: 394), Wasserman (2000: 277), and Knight (1986a: I, 75).
174 Raat (1973: 32–33) and Beato (1993: 83–84).
175 Guerra (1988: I, 347).
176 Katz (1986a: 55), Moreno-Brid & Ros (2009: 65), and Guerra (1988: I, 245).
177 Torres Gaytán (1980: 99), Anderson (1976: 31, 63), and Thorp (1998: 332).
178 Guerra (1988: I, 338), Carr (1973: 322), Katz (1986a: 28, 43), and French (1999: xxvii).
179 Florescano (1997: 462–63), Jaques (1989: 276), and Tinker Salas (1997: 102–03, 203).
180 Anderson (1976: 18), Connolly (1999a: 141), Hart (2002: 258), González y González (1974: 100), and Jaques (1989: 345). As early as 1873, a display advertisement appeared in a Mexico City newspaper for Singer sewing machines, noting different models for home, shop, and shoemaking (*Siglo Diez y Nueve*, September 22, 1873, p. 4).
181 Guerra (1988: I, 357–58) and Beatty (2001: 40).
182 Hernández Chávez (1993: 47) and Knight (1986a: I, 2).

183 González y González (1974: 56, 72–73).
184 Anderson (1976: xv) and González y González (1974: 82, 98).
185 Wasserman (2000: 12). Bauer (2001: 152), Knight (1986a: 5–6), and Van Young (2001: 520).
186 Beatty (2001: 193).
187 Tello Díaz (1993: 107) and Lomnitz & Pérez-Lizaur (1987: 19).
188 Meyers (1977: 425), Brown (1993a: 90), Haber et al. (2008: 22), Cárdenas (2003: 104), Haber (1991: 567), and Molina Enríquez (1978: 138).
189 Walker (1981: 268), Gonzales (2002: 34), and Anderson (1976: 102).
190 Bulmer-Thomas (1994a: 94), Brown (1987: 393), Alonso (1995: 133), Hart (1998a: 75–76), and Moreno-Brid & Ros (2009: 8).
191 Hamnett (1999: 172), Katz (1998a: 14–16), Wasserman (1985: 648–51), Alonso (1995: 142), Haber, Razo, & Maurer (2003: 296–97), Lloyd (1998), and Guerra (1988: I, 95).
192 Vaughan (2006b: 158).
193 Tenenbaum (1996: 13), Hansen (1971: 151), and Camp (2003: 38–39).
194 Ruiz (1992: 312–13).
195 Ruiz (1980: 44; 1992: 300), Katz (1981: 10–11; 2006: 181), and Anderson (1976: 66).
196 Anderson (1976: xix).
197 Rosenweig (1965b: 421), Lear (1998b: 65) and *El Monitor Republicano* (August 12, 1877, p. 3).
198 Anderson (1976: 66, 44).
199 Anderson (1976: 51–53, 59–60) and Ramos-Escandón (1988: 45).
200 Porter (2003: 76–77), Anderson (1976: 93), and Lear (1998b: 60).
201 Lear (1996: 282; 1998b: 59) and Katz (1986a: 60).
202 Anderson (1976: 91; 1997: 684), Niemeyer (1994: 34), and Walker (1981: 267).
203 Anderson (1976: 37).
204 *Engineering and Mining Journal* (October 5, 1907, p. 624).
205 Ruiz (1992: 304), Ramos-Escandón (1988: 75), Anderson (1997: 685), and Brown (1993b: 789, 801–02, 816).
206 Bauer (1986: 185).
207 Ruiz (1980: 86–88).
208 Chassen-López (2004: 181) and Porter (2003: xiii, 103–04, 154–55).
209 Tutino (2007: 234–35).
210 Guerra (1988: I, 359) and Bauer (1986: 160).
211 Tortolero Villaseñor (1995: 30–31), Bauer (1986: 166, 181), Anderson (1976: 185–86), and Glade (1986c: 38).
212 Alonso (1995: 125) and Knight (1992b: 108–09; 1985a: 77).
213 Guerra (1988: I, 269), Anderson (1976: 303), and Vanderwood (1989b: 152).
214 Hernández Chávez (1993: 73–74), Hart (2002: 122), and Hamnett (1994c: 208, 215).
215 Lorey (1999: 59) and Nugent & Alonso (1994: 217).
216 Sokoloff & Zolt (2007: 98). The U.S. figure is for 1900.
217 Ruiz (1980: 75), Alonso (1995: 131), Katz (1986a: 48), Colegio de México (1964: 148), and Suárez Gaona (1987: 14).
218 Florescano (1997: 487), Chevalier (1985: 140), León-Portilla (1997: 20), and Mallon (1995: 78–79).
219 Tinker Salas (1997: 64).
220 González y González (1956: 28) and Márquez Terrazas (1998: 47).
221 Alonso (1995: 28), Márquez Terrazas (1998: 48), and Worcester (1979: 313).
222 Rodríguez (1995: 53, 92).
223 Spicer (1962: 305) and Hu-DeHart (1984: 81).
224 Tinker Salas (1997: 61).
225 Troncoso (1905: 22).
226 Troncoso (1905: 342).
227 Troncoso (1905: 302).
228 Troncoso (1905: 239).
229 Hu-DeHart (1984: 147).
230 Katz (1986a: 46) and Hamnett (1999: 191). Evans (2007: 67–90) described Yaqui removal to Yucatán.
231 Bonfil Batalla (1996: 103).
232 Trens (1950: VI, 91–92).
233 Chassen-López (2004: 80–81).
234 Stevens (1982: 166) and Gibson (1964: 235).
235 Tenorio Trillo (1996: 100), Raat (1967: 200–03), and Stabb (1994: 316).
236 Powell (1968: 21), Florescano (1997: 369), and Chassen-López (2004: 352).

237 Hatfield (1998: 3) and Powell (1968: 23).
238 León-Portilla (1997: 20) and González Navarro (1970b: 152).
239 González y González (1996: 164–68).
240 Chassen-López (2004: 11, 24, 345).
241 Arrom (1985a: 85).
242 Arrom (1994: 88).
243 Ramos-Escandón (1990a: 5).
244 Arrom (1994: 94). The text of the law, including the Epistle of Melchor Ocampo, can be found in Tena Ramírez (1992: 642–47).
245 Arrom (1985a: 43) and Vallens (1978: 25, 55).
246 Ramos-Escandón (1987a: 146).
247 Ramos-Escandón (1987a: 152), Macías-González (2000: 1, 2–3, 15), and Porter (2003: 163).
248 Niemeyer (1994: 27–28), Vázquez (1981: 16), García Quintanilla (1997: 1625), Vallens (1978: 15), and Lau (2009: 6–7).
249 Vallens (1978: 14–15), Ruiz (1992: 284), and Ramos-Escandón (1987a: 159).
250 Towner (1977: 99), Vázquez (1981: 16), and Ramos-Escandón (1990b: 35).
251 Porter (2003: 79–81, 94–96), González Navarro (1957: 310–11), and Vallens (1978: 68–69).
252 García Quintanilla (1997: 1624), Ramos-Escandón (1990b: 36), Towner (1977: 99), Gutmann & Porter (1997: 576), and Chassen-López (2004: 246).
253 INEGI (1994: 353), Deutsch (1991: 262), Lear (2001: 73), and Macías (2002: 50–51).
254 Alvarado (1991: 14), Hernández Carballido (1998: 49–54), and Alvarado (2005: 14, 25, 37).
255 Macías (2002: 35–39).
256 Vallens (1978: 15).
257 Ramos-Escandón (1998a: 89).
258 Bulnes (1916: 142).
259 Brachet-Márquez (1997: 1161–62) and Garner (2001: 174).
260 Bulmer-Thomas (1994a: 85).
261 Case (1917: 61).
262 Bulmer-Thomas (1994a: 89), Cumberland (1968: 191), and Cott (1978: 316).
263 González Navarro (1993: 19), Bauer (1986: 184), and Tinker Salas (1997: 224–25).
264 Staples (1989: 16).
265 Thomson (1995: 32), Katz (2006: 424), Krauze (1997a: 169), and Lynch (1986b: 530).
266 Miller (1985: 235).
267 Cosío Villegas (1997a: 76).
268 Lynch (1986b: 581) and Galeana (2006: 107–08).
269 Bauer (1986: 178) and Staples (1989: 27; 1994: 240).
270 Hamnett (1994c: 206) and Guerra (1988: I, 220).
271 Lynch (1986b: 533, 582–85), Krauze (1997a: 227), Guerra (1988, I, 400), Katz (1986a: 40), and Miller (1985: 263).
272 González y González (1974: 87).
273 Guerra (1988: I, 227) and Gonzales (2002: 11).
274 Anderson (1976: 184) and J. Meyer (2006: 282).
275 Hart (2002: 44), Garner (2001: 121–22), Ruiz Guerra (2007: 423), and Warman (2003: 183).
276 Benítez (1998: 234), Hale (1989: 37), Martínez Assad (2005: 33), and Duncan (1996: 48–49).
277 Buchenau (2004: 53).
278 Johns (1997: 11–17).
279 Scobie (1986: 234, 258).
280 Johns (1997: 16, 30).
281 Miller (1985: 263–65), Johns (1997: 22), Tenenbaum (1994b: 143), and Ross (1955: 21).
282 Wasserman (2000: 111), Kandell (1988: 332), Johns (1997: 22), Benítez (1998: 310–11), and *El Imparcial* (December 18, 1907, p. 1).
283 Johns (1997: 12, 33, 42).
284 Anderson (1976: 44), Johns (1997: 32–33, 35, 43), and Tortolero Villaseñor (2007: 170).
285 Brown (1993b: 802) and Lear (1993: 59; 1998b: 57).
286 Johns (1997: 45) and La Botz (1991: 24).
287 Miller (2007: 147) and Simonian (1995: 70).
288 Davies (1974: 133, 151), Guerra (1988: I, 338), Scobie (1986: 237–38), Johns (1997: 15–16, 41), and Miller (2007: 172).
289 Wilkie (1989: 104–05).
290 Garciadiego Dantan (2007: 42), Martínez Assad (2005: 79–98), Johns (1997: 89), and Krauze (1997a: 1).

291 Molina Enríquez (1978: 147).
292 Katz (1986a: 77).
293 Galeana (2006: 172).
294 Hale (1989: 139), Krauze (1999a: 21), Mabry (1982: 3), and Vaughan (1982: 73).
295 Hale (1989: 64).
296 Katz (1986a: 62) and Cosío Villegas (1972a: 545).
297 Raat (1967: 111–12), Aguilar Plata (1998), and López-Portillo y Rojas (1975: 342). The paper, *El Universal,* subsidized by Díaz, closed in 1901. An entirely new paper with the same name began publication in 1916 and is still published.
298 Navarrete Maya (1998: 108, 116).
299 Griswold del Castillo (1990: 119), A. Schmidt (1997), and Stabb (1994: 315).
300 Brading (1988a: 47–48) and Sierra (1969: 368).
301 Córdova (1978: 23), Brading (1995: 104), Ruiz (1980: 11–12), and Molina Enríquez (1978: 306). Córdova (1978) provides an excellent discussion of Molina Enríquez and his book.
302 Johns (1997: 2), Monsiváis (1986c: 12), Martin (1998: 37), and García Quintanilla (1997).
303 Foster (1997: 146) and Martin (1998: 80).
304 Frank (1998: 5) and Johns (1997: 64–65).
305 Vaughan (1982: 35, 39–40, 65) and Guerra (1988: I, 440).
306 Henderson (1998: 30).
307 Vaughan (1982: 39, 48, 51, 67), Guerra (1988: I, 399), and Brown (1993a: 2–3).
308 Vaughan (1982: 65–66), Hart (1998a: 82), and Ruiz (1980: 15).

13 PLUNGING INTO THE INTERNATIONAL MARKET, 1856–1909

1 Knight (1998a: 42).
2 Cardoso & Hermosillo (1980: 18–19) and Katz (1986a: 5–6).
3 Cott (1978: 9, 42) and Pitner (1993: 91).
4 Deger (1979: 18) and Pletcher (1953: 570).
5 Passananti (2007: 106) and *Siglo Diez y Nueve* (September 22, 1873, p. 1).
6 Bulmer-Thomas (1994a: 46), Aguilar Monteverde (1974: 196), and Katz (1986a: 6).
7 Haber (2002: 327).
8 Bortz & Haber (2002: 16), Haber (2006: 549), and Haber, Razo & Maurer (2003: 345).
9 Cott (1978: 69) and Garner (2001: 170).
10 Coatsworth (1985: 50).
11 Pletcher (1998: 101), Colegio de México (1964: 144), and Tischendorf (1961: 116).
12 Coatsworth (1978: 99), Coerver (1979: 230), and Marichal (1997b: 134–35).
13 Garner (2001: 169), Maurer & Haber (2007: 220), Moreno-Brid & Ros (2009: 52), and Maurer & Gomberg (2004: 1088, 1100, 1103, Table 6).
14 Cott (1978: 189), Raat (1981: 16–17), Batou (1992: 9), and Pletcher (1958a: 216).
15 Krauze & Zerón Medina (1993: III, 60), Zabludowsky (1984: 65), Topik (2000: 720), and Marichal (2002: 95, 106).
16 Marichal (1997b: 136) and Newell G. & Rubio F. (1984: 13).
17 Marichal (1986: 263–64; 1997b: 127), Bátiz. V. (1986: 280), and Sánchez Martínez (1983: 41).
18 Moreno-Brid & Ros (2009: 52–53, 66).
19 Hart (1987: 143, 168), Hansen (1971: 21), and Ruiz (1980: 122).
20 Weiner (1999: 46), Topik (1992: 228) and A. Schmidt (1997: 747).
21 Moreno-Brid & Ros (2009: 57, Table 3.2) and Lains (2007: 69).
22 Wells (2000a: 183).
23 Coerver (1979: 202).
24 Marichal (1989: 79) and Wells (1992: 173).
25 Pletcher (1950: 26), Tischendorf (1961: 50), and Garner (1995: 350).
26 Pletcher (1959: 6). As Pletcher (1953: 568) noted, once built, the railroad was irresistible. Chavero later traveled to the United States on the very rail lines he had warned against.
27 Randall (1985b: 18).
28 Cott (1978: 37), Randall (1985b: 7), and Kuntz Ficker (1995: 53).
29 Cott (1978: 81).
30 Cott (1978: 82).
31 Riguzzi (1996: 56).
32 Bushnell & Macaulay (1994: 207), Passananti (2007: 107), Torres Gaytán (1980: 74), and Hart (2002: 123).

33 Summerhill (1997: 98), Wells (1992: 161), Marichal (1995: 18), Kuntz Ficker (1995: 115), and Hart (1987: 131–33).
34 Riguzzi (1995: 165), Grunstein Dicter (1996: 173), and Cott (1978: 223).
35 Pletcher (1998: 92–94), Summerhill (2006: 302), and Riguzzi (1996: 34).
36 Moreno-Brid & Ros (2009: 50), Coatsworth (1981: 95, 103), and Anderson (1976: 20).
37 Bushnell & Macaulay (1994: 205) and Tischendorf (1961: 42–43).
38 Powell (1921: 175), Grunstein Dicter (1999: 72), Weiner (1999: 51), and Coatsworth (1979: 941; 1985: 52). For a discussion of late Porfirian economic nationalism, see Topik (1990: 107–120), and Garner (1995: 341–44).
39 A. Schmidt (1997: 748), Anderson (1976: 235), and Raat (1967: 187).
40 Hernández Chávez (1993: 115) and Tischendorf (1961: 48).
41 Thomson (1985: 131), Randall (1985b: 25), Summerhill (2006: 318), Solbrig (2006: 351), and Riguzzi (1996: 83).
42 Moreno-Brid & Ros (2009: 50).
43 Ruiz (1980: 14) and Kuntz Ficker (1995: 338).
44 Wells (1992: 159).
45 Riguzzi (1996: 48), Kuntz Ficker (1995: 121; 1999: 22), U.S. (1906: 20–21), Moreno-Brid & Ros (2009: 49–51), Jaques (1989: 296), and Coatsworth (1979: 956).
46 Coatsworth (1978: 100; 1981: 123) and Tinker Salas (1997: 118).
47 Coatsworth (1981: 123), Tinker Salas (1997: 140), and Flores (1998: 36).
48 Simonian (1995: 61), Wells (1992: 171), and Simon (1997: 139–40).
49 Beatty (2000: 430).
50 Keegan (1999: 10–11) and Beatty (2001: 32).
51 Pomeranz & Topik (1999: 48–49), Haber (2002: 881), Bértola & Williamson (2006: 16), and Tischendorf (1961: 58).
52 Summerhill (2006: 318), INEGI (1994: 785), and Bulmer-Thomas (1994a: 74).
53 Salvucci (2006: 288).
54 Marichal (1989: 68; 1999: 768, 771–72) and Katz (1981: 51; 1986a: 21).
55 Reina (2007: 100) and Bulmer-Thomas (1994a: 49–50).
56 Bulmer-Thomas (1994a: 109, 146–47) and Thorp (1998: 346).
57 Colegio de México (1960: 172), Garner (2001: 170), and Bulmer-Thomas (1994a: 65). As Bulmer-Thomas (1994a: 153–54) noted, the mathematical correlation between per capita exports and per capita incomes in pre-First World War Latin America is r squared = 0.82.
58 Coatsworth (1985: 41).
59 Pletcher (1998: 101).
60 Glade (1986c: 16), Haber, Maurer & Razo (2003: 21), and Hart (1987: 142).
61 L. Meyer (1977b: 244, n. 24).
62 Mexico (1884: 4–5; 1892: 13), Bernstein (1964: 28), Brown (1993a: 93), Coerver (1979: 219), and Pletcher (1958b: 35).
63 Tischendorf (1961: 71), Tinker Salas (1992: 434), and Cott (1978: 281).
64 Bernstein (1964: 44, 42) and French (1999: xxvi).
65 Bernstein (1964: 44), Nava Otero (1980: 354), Rankine (1992: 45), and *Engineering and Mining Journal* (July 27, 1907, p. 160).
66 Tinker Salas (1997: 198, 245).
67 Cárdenas (2003: 196) and INEGI (1994: 542–54).
68 Coatsworth (1985: 42) and Guerra (1988: I, 355).
69 Beatty (2001: 9), Hart (2002: 145–46), Hamnett (1999: 186), Jaques (1989: 335), Catão (1992: 38, 45–46), Pomeranz & Topik (1999: 185), and Beatty (2000: 409).
70 Simonian (1995: 54–55) and Tinker Salas (1997: 257).
71 Bulmer-Thomas (1994a: 134).
72 Cardoso (1980: 154–55), Bakewell (1997: 428), and Bulmer-Thomas (1994a: 132).
73 Bulmer-Thomas (1994a: 100–01), Haber (1989: 79–80; 2002: 881), and Moreno-Brid & Ros (2009: 66).
74 Gonzales (2002: 56), Haber (2006: 550), and Beatty (2001: 4–5; 2002: 207).
75 Esquivel & Márquez (2007: 335), Anderson (1976: 19), Guerra (1988: I, 329), Haber (2006: 540), and Ramos-Escandón (1988: 54).
76 Cárdenas (1997a: 84), Hall & Spalding (1986: 327), Márquez (1998: 407), Katz (1986a: 29), Lewis (1986: 278), Haber (1989: 4; 2006: 553) and Beatty (2000: 419).
77 Ramos-Escandón (1988: 84), INEGI (1994: 616), Sánchez Martínez (1983: 21), Haber (2006: 542, Table 13.1), and Hall & Spalding (1986: 326–27).
78 Ramos-Escandón (1988: 67–68) and INEGI (1994: 616).

79 Hibino (1992: 26), Ortiz Monasterio (1987: 183), Montemayor Hernández (1971: 254), Saragoza (1988: 59, 71), and Lorey (1990: 1188–89).
80 Saragoza (1988: 42, 64) and Hibino (1992: 34).
81 Hibino (1992: 29–30).
82 Meyers (1977: 425), Haber (1989: 68) and *New York Times* (December 13, 1902, p. 1).
83 Rosenweig (1965a: 425).
84 Beatty (2001: 4, 78), Haber, Razo & Maurer (2003: 188), and Bulmer-Thomas (1994a: 137, Table 5.3).
85 Beatty (2000: 401).
86 Suárez Gaona (1987: 14) and Knight (1985b: 21).
87 Hart (1998a: 73) and J. Meyer (1986a: 482–83).
88 Hatfield (1998: 5), Katz (1998a: 27), Henderson (2000: 149), Alonso (1995: 142), Santiago (1998: 173), and Womack (1999: 61–62).
89 Holden (1994: 133) and Molina Enríquez (1978: 175).
90 Brown (1993a: 74).
91 Holden (1990: 581), Haber, Razo & Maurer (2003: 292), and Tortolero Villaseñor (1995: 18).
92 Holden (1994: 17).
93 Holden (1990: 607) and Simonian (1995: 60).
94 Holden (1994: 39, 90, 130; 1990: 596), and Haber, Razo & Maurer (2003: 294).
95 Tutino (1997: 1304), Krauze (1997a: 219), and J. Meyer (1986a: 484).
96 Ruiz (1980: 81), Bulmer-Thomas (1994a: 96), Tortolero Villaseñor (1995: 19, 205), and Kay (1997: 171).
97 Bulmer-Thomas (1994a: 129–30).
98 INEGI (1994: 581) and Summerhill (1997: 99).
99 Hamnett (1994a: 52), Torres Gaytán (1980: 62), and Evans (2007: 85).
100 Hamnett (1994a: 52), Bauer (1986: 179), Evans (2007: 16), and Joseph (1986: 57).
101 Fry (1996: 28) and Wells (1985: 61–62).
102 Evans (2007: 41, 61) and Wells (2006: 304, 312–14).
103 Evans (2007: 50–51).
104 Ruiz (1980: 104) and Hart (1998a: 72).
105 Wasserman (1979: 10) and Hart (1998a: 76–77).
106 Bulmer-Thomas (1994a: 122).
107 Tortolero Villaseñor (1995: 27), U.S. (1906: 8) and *New York Times* (October 31, 1901, p. 1).
108 Cárdenas (2003: 221) and Tena Ramírez (1992: 713).
109 Haber, Maurer & Razo (2003: 3).
110 Brown & Linder (1998: 126–28) and Brown (1992: 3).
111 Brown & Linder (1998: 156–57) and Brown (1993a: 40).
112 Brown & Linder (1998: 132–33), Brown (1987: 390), and Hoffmann (1942: 94–96).
113 Ansell (1998: 55), Haber, Maurer & Razo (2003: 4), and L. Meyer (1977b: 23).
114 Santiago (2006: 18, 23, 29, Table 1.2).
115 Santiago (2006: 73, 79, 85, 91–92).
116 Brown (1993a: 42–43).
117 Hoffmann (1942: 104–06), Rippy (1926: 317), Brown (1993a: 36, 45), and Ansell (1998: 85).
118 Brown (1993a: 28) and L. Meyer (1977b: 22–23).
119 Santiago (2006: 65), La Botz (1991: 32), and Brown (1993a: 39).
120 Bethell (1989: 9).
121 Haber, Razo & Maurer (2003: 196), Brown (1987: 403; 1993a: 63), and Santiago (1998: 174).
122 Brown (1993a: 60–61).
123 Brown (1987: 406–07), Young (1966: 126), and Santiago (1998: 178; 2006: 138). The ecological damage from the Dos Bocas fire remained apparent in the twenty-first century. In 2004, Myrna Santiago, author of a book on the environmental impact of oil development, visited the site and noted that one could still smell hydrogen sulfide and see oil slicks on the water-filled crater. Santiago (2006: 1, 141).
124 Brown (1993a: 61) and Hamilton (1966: 76).
125 Brown (1987: 412; 1993a: 68), Cronon (1960: 34), and Young (1966: 134).
126 Krauze & Zerón-Medina (1993: V, 43), Connolly (1999b: 34), Garner (1995: 348), and Haber, Razo & Maurer (2003: 196).
127 Garner (1995: 349) and Brown (1987: 399; 1993a: 99).
128 Brown (1987: 414), Katz (1981: 27), and Haber, Maurer & Razo (2003: 4).
129 Brown (1987: 401).
130 Ansell (1998: 83), D'Olwer (1965: 1129), and Brown (1993a: 65).
131 Santiago (2006: 67), Haber, Razo & Maurer (2003: 193), and Brown (1993a: 8, 83).

132 Brown & Linder (1998: 175), Brown (1993a: 71, 82), and Santiago (1998: 6, 171).
133 Haber, Razo, & Maurer (2003: 198) and Topik & Wells (1998: 220).
134 Catão (1992: 44).
135 Coatsworth (1978: 82; 1998a: 26), Cárdenas (2003: 318, Table VII. 1), Moreno-Brid & Ros (2009: 254–55), and Guerra (1988: I, 305).
136 Bulmer-Thomas (1994a: 69, 84, 119).
137 Katz (1986a: 30) and Bulmer-Thomas (1994a: 102). In an essay entitled "Why Isn't the Whole World Developed?" Easterlin (1981) argued that a nation's educational level largely determines whether sustained development incorporating imported technology will occur.
138 Randall (1977: I, 161).
139 Brandenburg (1964: 221) and INEGI (1994: 347).
140 Cockcroft (1972: 47), Wasserman (1979: 21), and Beatty (2000: 416).
141 Anderson (1976: 32).
142 Kandell (1988: 371), Ruiz (1980: 111), and Reina (2007: 100).
143 Beatty (2001: 79) and Torres Gaytán (1980: 56).
144 Haber (2002 329).
145 Wasserman (2000: 8).

14 A SUPERPOWER EMERGES NEXT DOOR, 1856–1909

1 Fry (1996: 279).
2 Congressional Globe, 35th Congress, 1st session, p. 1682.
3 Berbusse (1958: 227).
4 Schoultz (1998: 46–48).
5 Krauze (2006b: 83).
6 Manning (1932–39: IX, 235).
7 Coerver (1999: 17–18) and Hamnett (1994c: 148).
8 Terrazas Basante (1990: 16) and Zorrilla (1977: I, 379–80).
9 Richardson (1917: VII, 3044).
10 Callahan (1909: 7–8) and Coerver (1999: 18–19).
11 Coerver (1999: 19).
12 Hamnett (1994c: 238) and Benítez (1998: 131–32).
13 Terrazas Basante (1990: 27), Coerver (1999: 19–20), and Randall (1985b: 15).
14 Perkins (1933: 342), Zorrilla (1977: I, 390), and Coerver (1999: 19–20).
15 Rippy (1926: 226).
16 Terrazas Basante (1990: 33) and Zorrilla (1977: I, 397).
17 Callahan (1909: 17).
18 Schoonover (1978: 33), Hamnett (1994c: 154), and Coerver (1999: 23).
19 Zorrilla (1977: I, 430).
20 Miller (1973: 10), Hamnett (1994c: 161), and Terrazas Basante (1990: 120).
21 Sandoval Hernández (2008: 76).
22 Ellis (1973: 224), Rolle (1965: 30), González Ramos (2005: 77–118), Scott (1880–1901: 937), and Martínez (1978: 15).
23 Ellis (1973: 208), Cerutti (1999: 65), González Ramos (2005: 118), Kearney & Knopp (1991: 124), and Hart (1987: 112–14).
24 González Ramos (2005: 78–79), Cerutti (1999: 26–28, 57), and Montemayor Hernández (1971: 167).
25 Rolle (1965: 9, 24, 176–82) and Casellas (1993: 61).
26 Coerver (1999: 25).
27 Miller (1973: 8) and Coerver (1999: 24).
28 Díaz (1976: 155) and O'Connor (1971: 183).
29 Miller (1973: 16) and Rippy (1926: 279).
30 Romero (1986: 168) and Schoonover (1978: xx).
31 Ampudia (1993: 53).
32 A detailed report of this incident can be found in the Historical Archives of the Naval Historical Museum at the Washington Naval Yard.
33 Kearney & Knopp (1991: 153–54), Foster (1909: I, 89), and U.S. (1878: 117, 190–91).
34 Coerver (1999: 28).
35 Foster (1909: I, 19) and U.S. (1976: 904–06).

36 Johnson (1990: 189) and Schoonover (1978: 254).
37 Coerver & Hall (1999: 35) and Schoultz (1998: 83).
38 Schoultz (1998: 236) and Katz (1986a: 22).
39 Coerver (1999: 30) and Hatfield (1998: 26–27).
40 Pletcher (1998: 87) and Katz (2007: 187).
41 Coerver (1999: 30), Cosío Villegas (1997b: 150), Herrera (2007: 206), Buchenau (1997: 502), and Devine (1981: 19).
42 Hamnett (1994c: 148).
43 Holden (1994: 6).
44 Bernstein (1964: 75), U.S. (1976: 903–07), and Moreno-Brid & Ros (2009: 54).
45 Deger (1979: 76), Herrera (2007: 168, 197), Clendenen (1969: 82), Hatfield (1998: 2, 53), and Cosío Villegas (1997b: 229). The text of the treaty permitting reciprocal crossings can be found in Mallory (1910–38, vol. 1, pp. 1144–45).
46 Tischendorf (1961: 21, 129).
47 Pletcher (1998: 106–07) and Beatty (2000: 412, 432).
48 Tischendorf (1961: 130) and Hamilton (1982: 45).
49 Wilkins (1970: 113, 127), Beatty (2000: 417), Krauze (1997a: 6), Schell (2001: 115), and Schoultz (1998: 237).
50 Raat (1992: 105), Knight (1998a: 50), U.S. (1920b: II, 2342), and Tinker Salas (1992: 445).
51 Hale (1989: 254), O'Brien (1999: 77), and Cott (1978: 297).
52 Vázquez (1991: 35).
53 Knight (1998a: 31–32).
54 Cott (1978: 305), Katz (1986a: 75; 2007: 189), and Brown (1993a: 99).
55 Raat (1981: 16) and Leonard (1999: 9).
56 Schoultz (1998: 238).
57 Katz (1986a: 75) and Krauze (1994: 28).
58 González Quiroga (1999: 127), Olmsted (1978: 160), González Quiroga (1999: 115, 118, Table 1).
59 Castañeda (2007: 27) and Rodríguez (2007: 129–30).
60 Ganster & Lorey (2008: 56).
61 Gamio (1969: 20), Anderson (1976: 48), Jaques (1989: 68), Deger (1979: 74, 126), Cárdenas (1975: 67), and Rodríguez (2007: 133–35).
62 Deger (1979: 127–28), U.S. (1920b: II, 2328), and Gonzales (1994: 661).

15 THE REVOLUTION, 1910–1916

1 Knight (1986a: I, 2).
2 Gonzales (2002: 263).
3 The text of the Plan of San Luis Potosí can be found in Mexico (1945: 37–47).
4 Knight (1986a: I, 177), Garciadiego Dantan (2007: 48), and Womack (1986: 84).
5 Knight (1986a: I, 181).
6 Krauze (1997a: 257), Hart (1987: 252), and Katz (2006: 188).
7 Katz (1998a: 87–88), Gonzales (2002: 16–17), Wasserman (2000: 218–19), and Hamnett (1999: 181).
8 Guerra (1988: II, 302), Wasserman (2000: 131), and Henderson (2000: 29).
9 Tortolero Villaseñor (2007: 164).
10 Womack (1968a: 42–43), Hart (2005: viii), Haber, Razo & Maurer (2003: 295), Garciadiego Dantan (1986: 32), and Tutino (1986: 322).
11 Hart (1997: 848), Hart (2005: 7), and Warman (1980: 51–52, 63, 65).
12 Katz (2006: 158).
13 Brunk (1995: 6) and Sotelo Inclán (1970: 534).
14 LaFrance (1990a: 30), Anderson (1976: 295–96), Henderson (2000: 38–39), and Katz (1998a: 94).
15 Katz (1994: 399–400; 1998a: 105), Tortolero Villaseñor (2007: 164), and Vanderwood (1976: 579).
16 An English translation of the Treaty of Ciudad Juárez can be found in Henderson (2000: 241–42).
17 Katz (1998a: 107) and Henderson (2000: 43–44).
18 Collado (1987a: 115), Henderson (2000: 24), Anderson (1976: 299), and Katz (2006: 194).
19 Guilpain Peuliard (1991: 10). See Chapter 2, n. 53 for the number of streets named after Díaz.
20 Knight (1986a: I, 247).
21 Cárdenas (2003: 248), Henderson (2000: 111, 175, 238), and Katz (2006: 195).
22 Brunk (1995: 51–59), Krauze (1997a: 262), and Henderson (2000: 250).
23 Hart (2000: 439).

24 Knight (1986a: I, 398–99) and Silva Herzog (1972: I, 232).
25 Katz (1994: 406), Hart (1986: 8), and Ruiz (1980: 147).
26 Hart (1987: 259) and L. Meyer (1977b: 28).
27 Krauze & Zerón-Medina (1993: VII: 46), Mandujano Jacobo (1998: 186, 191), and Krauze (1993: 12).
28 Joseph & Henderson (2002: 339–43) and Womack (1968a: 400–04) provided a translations of the Plan. The quoted passage is from page 402.
29 Knight (1986a: I, 309).
30 Womack (1968a: 138–39).
31 French (1999: xxxiii).
32 Henderson (2000: 45, 177) and Katz (1998a: 121).
33 Hart (1987: 252, 260), Katz (2006: 207), Schettino (2007: 66), and Kandell (1988: 410).
34 Henderson (2000: 199), Cumberland (1952: 234), Hart (1987: 261), and Krauze (1997a: 269).
35 Hart (2000: 445).
36 Ermolaev (1976: 90), Richmond (1983: 42), Katz (2006: 199), and Hernández Chávez (2006: 216).
37 Beezley & Maclachlan (2009: 17).
38 Katz (2006: 198–99).
39 Córdova (1973: 33), LaFrance (2003: xviii), and Millon (1969: 19).
40 Del Villar (2005: 52–53) and Ross (1955: 340). See Chapter 2, n. 53 for the number of streets named after Madero.
41 Henderson (1998: 47).
42 Henderson (2000: 201), Wilkie (1970a: 160), LaFrance (2003: xxii), Hart (1987: 263; 2000: 446), Katz (1998a: 195), and French (1999: xxxiv).
43 Schettino (2007: 68) and Hernández Chávez (2006: 218–19). An English translation of the Plan of Guadalupe can be found in Eisenhower (1993: 343–45).
44 Katz (1998a: 202).
45 Córdova (1973: 23). Clearly no single term suffices to describe the variety of revolutionaries below the elite and above the peasant. See Knight (1986a: II, 225–37) for a discussion of middle-class leaders.
46 Womack (1968a: 165).
47 Hart (2000: 446), Katz (1989: 112), and Ulloa (1979a: 8).
48 Katz (1998a: 2, 65, 806), Taibo (2006: 1–46), and Krauze (1997a: 306–07).
49 Knight (1986a: I, 412) and Krauze (2009: 3).
50 Gilly (1983: 102) and Knight (1986a: II, 26).
51 Katz (1998a: 203–04) and M. Meyer (1972: 90).
52 Knight (1986a: II, 77).
53 Katz (1981: 119).
54 Brown (1993a: 181), Mandujano Jacobo (1998: 193), Knight (1986a: II, 62–63), and M. Meyer (1972: 99).
55 Katz (1998a: 224).
56 Taibo (2006: 40) and Katz (1998a: 237, 808; 2006: 258).
57 Katz (1976a: 269; 1998a: 431, 511).
58 Katz (1998a: 406).
59 Katz (1976a: 261; 1981: 141).
60 Katz (1976a: 269–70; 1998a: 429).
61 Knight (1986a: II, 143).
62 Knight (1986a: II, 142) and Katz (1998a: 216).
63 Katz (1998a: 208) and Knight (1986a: II, 55).
64 Knight (1986a: II, 46).
65 Joseph (1982: 4).
66 Katz (1998a: 344–48, 353), Taibo (2006: 373–75), and Eisenhower (1993: 143).
67 Krauze (1997a: 322), Katz (1998a: 354), and Taibo (2006: 393). Alternate reasons have been suggested for Villa's failure to continue his drive toward Mexico City. Hart (2000: 451) stated that U.S. customs authorities denied Villa coal. Knight (1986a: II, 169) attributed Villa's failure to advance further south to his desire to protect his home base in Chihuahua.
68 Kandell (1988: 426), Welsome (2006: 57), Eisenhower (1993: 184–85), and Hernández Chávez (2006: 219).
69 Hamnett (1999: 214–15) and Córdova (1973: 192).
70 Womack (1986: 107).
71 Gilly (1983: 128).
72 Eisenhower (1993: 328).
73 Hart (1987: 279).
74 Córdova (1973: 165) and Ávila Espinosa (2007: 96).

75 Knight (1986a: II, 262) and Taibo (2006: 427, 435).
76 Hall (1981: 91–93), Beezley & Maclachlan (2009: 32), and Katz (1981: 268; 1998a: 385).
77 Katz (1998a: 385).
78 Katz (1998a: 379).
79 Katz (1981: 124; 1998a: 435–36).
80 Ulloa (1979a: 58).
81 Gilly (1983: 165), Knight (1986a: II, 307), and Katz (1998a: 456).
82 Womack (1986: 107–08) and Katz (1998a: 388).
83 Katz (1998a: 469).
84 Newell G. & Rubio. F. (1984: 25–26), LaFrance (2003: 59, 89, 115), and Ulloa (1979b: 37).
85 Richmond (1983: 84) and Lear (1993: 314).
86 Córdova (1989: 69).
87 Knight (1986a: II, 285).
88 Knight (1986a: I, 323–25).
89 Katz (1998a: 497).
90 Womack (1968a: 210).
91 Gilly (1983: 240) [retranslated by author].
92 Gilly (1983: 240), Womack (1968a: 241), and Tutino (2007: 240).
93 Womack (1968a: 253) and Brunk (1995: 189).
94 Gilly (1983: 257).
95 Krauze (1997a: 299).
96 Córdova (1973: 195).
97 Katz (1981: 292).
98 Herr (1999: 96).
99 LaFrance (2003: 60, 75, 86–87, 116).
100 González y González (1974: 125).
101 Knight (1992a: 128–29).
102 Tutino (1990: 66), Rugeley (2002: 253), LaFrance (2003: 69), and Guerra (1988: I, 219).
103 Womack (1969b: xi).
104 Millon (1969: 103).
105 Pozas (1962: 38–39).
106 Katz (1998a: 434).
107 *Proceso* (November 18, 1985, p. 13).
108 Knight (1986a: II, 500, 513–17, 521).
109 Womack (1968a: 41) and Knight (1985b: 16).
110 Katz (1998a: 291), Macías (1980: 73), and Reséndez Fuentes (1995: 544).
111 Reséndez Fuentes (1995: 540), Salas (1994: 103), and Reed (1969: 70).
112 Lear (1993: 357–58), Soto (1979: 21), and Rocha (2007: 25). Macías (2002: 41–75) has vivid descriptions of various women's actions, ranging from fighting with Zapata to opposing the Constitutionalists' anti-clericalism.
113 Macías (1974: 592) and Molyneaux (2000: 77, n. 43).
114 Henderson (2000: 172).
115 Macías (1974: 595); 1992: 614; 2002: 91–92), S. Smith (2007: 40), Soto (1979: 49–50), and LaFrance (2003: 133).
116 Soto (1979: 53–55) and Macías (1974: 597–98; 1992: 617).
117 Knight (1985b: 25), Lomnitz & Pérez-Lizaur (1987: 24), and Camp (1995a: 65–66, 73).
118 Sánchez-Albornoz (1986: 124–25), Knight (1986a: II, 420), Womack (1986: 86), Cárdenas (2003: 291), and U.S. (1913: 188; 1922: 299).
119 Katz (2000: 1).
120 Tutino (1986: 363) and Knight (2007a: 159–60).
121 Córdova (2007: 326).
122 Ávila Espinosa (2007: 93).
123 Benjamin (2000b: 147) and Knight (1992b: 161–65).
124 Bailey (1978: 69) and Knight (1992b: 163).
125 Bailey (1978: 73) and Benjamin (2000b: 160).
126 Benjamin (2000b: 158–59) and Ávila Espinosa (2007: 102).
127 Knight (1992b: 165), Lear (1993: 7–9), Wasserman (1990: 1–3), L. Meyer (2000: 838) and *Proceso* (April 4, 1999, p. 55). For twenty-first-century views of the Revolution, see a review essay by Wasserman (2008).
128 Lear (1993: 10).

16 DESTRUCTION AND DEVELOPMENT, 1910–1916

1 Womack (1978: 83) and Haber, Razo, & Maurer (2003: 325).
2 Womack (1978: 90), Florescano (1991: 94), and Katz (1998a: 730).
3 Holden (1994: 122) and Vernon (1963: 78–79).
4 Schell (2001: 189–90).
5 Lorey (1999: 41) and Wilkins (1970: 130–34).
6 Martínez (1978: 50).
7 French (1989: 238), Bernstein (1964: 101), Ruiz (1980: 276), LaFrance (2003: 119), and Womack (1978: 84).
8 Wasserman (1993: 18), Bernstein (1964: 99, 102), Lorey (1999: 42), O'Brien (1999: 86), and *Engineering and Mining Journal* (January 10, 1914, p. 137).
9 Katz (1998a: 416) and French (1989: 236).
10 L. Meyer (2000: 837), Bernstein (1964: 100–01, 105), and INEGI (1994: 390).
11 Katz (1998a: 513).
12 Sanderson (1986: 36) and Wasserman (1993: 19).
13 LaFrance (2003: 129) and Womack (1978: 90, 101).
14 Haber (1989: 125), Haber, Razo & Maurer (2003: 155), J. Meyer (1986b: 174), LaFrance (2003: 121), Villarreal (1988: 280), Hernández Chávez (2006: 229), and INEGI (1994: 609).
15 Gómez-Galvarriato (1998: 355), Aggarwal (1996: 189), and Torres Gaytán (1980: 123).
16 Aggarwal (1996: 193–94) and Cárdenas & Manns (1987: 378).
17 Herr (1999: 38), Knight (1986a II, 408–09), and Suárez Dávila (1988: 353).
18 Cárdenas & Manns (1987: 376, 381, 384), Cortés Conde (2006: 221), and Whitehead (1989: 195).
19 Katz (1998a: 514), Torres Gaytán (1980: 129, 140), and Gómez-Galvarriato (1998: 365).
20 INEGI (1994: 981–82), Cárdenas & Manns (1987: 386), and Moreno-Brid & Ros (2009: 74–75).
21 Lerman Alperstein (1989: 7) and U.S. (1976: 903–06).
22 INEGI (1994: I, 559) and L. Meyer (1979: 10).
23 Brown (1993a: 146), Ansell (1998: 124), L. Meyer (1976a: 30), and Santiago (2006: 154).
24 Brown (1993a: 128) and Ansell (1998: 141).
25 Brown (1993a: 172, 204), Santiago (2006: 93–95), Katz (1998a: 452), and Gonzales (2002: 173).
26 Wilkins (1998: 204), Brown (1993a: 131), and Womack (1978: 95).
27 Brown (1993a: 105, 151).
28 Evans (2007: 102, 109–110) and Joseph (1982: 6).
29 Wasserman (1993: 22, 28) and Tutino (1990: 64).
30 Solís (1973: 90–91).

17 TRYING TO PICK A WINNER, 1910–1916

1 Eisenhower (1993: 328).
2 Wilson (1927: 176–78).
3 Winkler (1929: 275).
4 Pérez (1982: 170).
5 Hart (1987: 248), Katz (1986a: 76), Garciadiego Dantan (2007: 45, n. 30), and L. Meyer (1977b: 26).
6 Wilson (1927: 210).
7 Holcombe (1968: 18–19).
8 Pringle (1939: 700) and Cosío Villegas (1963: v, pt. 2, p. 403).
9 Turner (1969: 186). Katz (2007: 209, n. 14) cites some sources that implicate oil companies in toppling Díaz and some that exonerate them.
10 Pringle (1939: 704).
11 Cline (1971: 129), Hart (1987: 283), Katz (1998a: 157), and U.S. (1919: 745–46).
12 Wilson (1927: 333) and Coerver & Hall (1999: 61).
13 L. Meyer (1977b: 31), Womack (1986: 90) and Haber, Maurer & Razo (2003: 5).
14 Katz (1981: 47).
15 Holcombe (1968: 41).
16 Cline (1971: 130) and Katz (1981: 97–106).
17 Wilson (1927: 263).
18 Vázquez & Meyer (1985: 108).
19 Kandell (1988: 416–17) and Eisenhower (1993: 25).
20 Wilson (1927: 284) and Pringle (1939: 710–11).

21 Kandell (1988: 420).
22 Wilson (1927: 282).
23 Fuentes (1988, p. 20).
24 Pringle (1939: 710) and Eisenhower (1993: 33).
25 L. Meyer (1991b: 223), Ulloa (1997: 168), and *Mexican Herald* (February 19, 1913, p. 1).
26 Vázquez & Meyer (1985: 109–110).
27 Gilderhus (2000: 49) and R. Smith (1986: 107).
28 Richardson (1917: XVII, 7907).
29 Cline (1971: 142–43), Katz (1989: 103), Knight (1986a: II, 138), and Richardson (1917: XVII, 7888).
30 Holcombe (1968: 69–70).
31 Daniels (1924: 180), Yankelevich (2007: 128), Katz (1998a: 355), Cárdenas (2003: 265), and U.S. (1922b: 447–48).
32 Pringle (1939: 711), Yankelevich (2007: 128), and Dunkerley (1999: 25).
33 Katz (1981: 135, 161).
34 Taibo (2006: 347).
35 Tuchman (1963: 47).
36 Daniels (1924: 184).
37 Daniels (1924: 183).
38 Eisenhower (1993: 121) and Perret (1996: 71).
39 French (1989: 235), Brown (1993a: 207), and Knight (1987: 32).
40 Holcombe (1968: 77–79) and Katz (1998a: 356, 500).
41 Schoultz (1998: 247).
42 Eisenhower (1993: 133), Yankelevich (2007: 130), Katz (1981: 201), Womack (1986: 104), and Ulloa (1997: 173).
43 Hall (1981: 63), L. Meyer (1977b: 44), Holcombe (1968: 91), and Katz (1998a: 372).
44 Katz (2006: 234–37).
45 Katz (1981 152; 1989: 102–03) and Richmond (1983: 75).
46 Katz (1989: 102; 1998b: 239).
47 Katz (1989: 102) and Holcombe (1968: 106–07).
48 Hart (1987: 280, 301, 312; 2000: 453) and Katz (1998a: 502).
49 Ulloa (1979b: 240), R. Smith (1972: 39), Katz (1998a: 508–09, 514), and Raat (1992: 111).
50 Hart (1987: 295).
51 Hart (1987: 296), M. Smith (1995: 160–61, 169), and Katz (1981: 564; 1998a: 466, 503; 2007: 191).
52 Tuchman (1963: 89), Katz (1977: xi), and U.S. (1924: 780–81).
53 Katz (1989: 105; 1998a: 528–29; 1998b: 248).
54 Knight (1986a: II, 346–47), Taibo (2006: 573–74), and Eisenhower (1993: 191).
55 *El Universal* (June 22, 1922, Sec. 2, p. 7).
56 Katz (1989: 106).
57 Eisenhower (1993: 234) and Welsome (2006: 170).
58 R. Smith (1972: 50–53) and Holcombe (1968: 134).
59 Clendenen (1969: 290).
60 Taibo (2006: 690) and Welsome (2006: 308).
61 Katz (1989: 106; 1998a: 817) and Hart (2000: 460). For a blow-by-blow, or, more accurately, a hoof-by-hoof account of the Columbus raid and the Pershing expedition, see Eisenhower (1993: 217–307).
62 Katz (1998a: 666), R. Smith (1972: 64), and L. Meyer (1977b: 52).
63 Rippy (1926: 350).
64 Vázquez & Meyer (1985: 103).
65 Huizer (1970a: 31) and Katz (1996: 28).
66 Katz (1998a: 413), Knight (1998a: 52), and Roman (1976: 55).
67 Bilateral Commission (1989: 82), Massey, Durand & Malone (2002: 28), and Lorey (1999: 70).
68 Martínez (1978: 41) and Rodríguez (2007: 137).

18 INSTITUTIONALIZING THE NEW REGIME, 1917–1940

1 Knight (1990d: 3).
2 Cumberland (1968: 259–60), Niemeyer (1974: 33), Sherman (1998: 359), LaFrance (2003: 106), and Gonzales (2002: 162).
3 Niemeyer (1974: 42) and P. Smith (1973: 365).
4 Niemeyer (1974: 32), Brachet-Márquez (1997: 1119), and Brown (1993a: 224).

5 Niemeyer (1974: 59), P. Smith (1973: 382), Vaughan (1982: 83), Brown (1993a: 225), and Krauze (1997a: 387).
6 Wilkie (1970a: 160) and Ruiz (1992: 337).
7 Brading (1995: 105) and Moreno-Brid & Ros (2009: 69).
8 Hart (1987: 332) and Hellman (1983: 22).
9 Knight (1984: 78), Roman (1976: 126), and Brachet-Márquez (1996: 239).
10 Weldon (1997: 227, 235).
11 Carpizo (1985) discussed nineteenth- and twentieth-century attitudes and restrictions on reelection.
12 Knight (1986a: II, 471), L. Meyer (2007a: 288), and Hartlyn & Valenzuela (1998: 11).
13 Knight (1986a: II, 478) and L. Meyer (1992a: 50).
14 Wasserman (1993: 31), Knight (1996b: 573), Haber, Razo, & Maurer (2003: 309), and Bruhn (1997a: 33).
15 Knight (1980: 50–51), Benjamin (2000b: 66), and Katz (1998a: 617).
16 Katz (1998a: 620) and Haber, Razo, & Maurer (2003: 287).
17 Ruiz (1980: 161) and Haber, Razo, & Maurer (2003: 306).
18 Gilly (1979: 43), Beals (1923: 57), Medin (1972: 13), Medina Peña (1994: 33), and Vernon (1963: 67).
19 Córdova (1973: 218) and Womack (1986: 133).
20 Gilly (1983: 317).
21 Hall (1981: 229) and Benjamin (2000c: 472–73).
22 Krauze (1997a: 390).
23 Hamilton (1982: 74), Hart (1987: 334), and Buchenau (2007: 84).
24 Krauze (1997a: 371), L. Meyer (1985: 80), and LaFrance (2003: 203). As Buchenau (2007: 89) noted, the details of Carranza's death have never been conclusively elucidated.
25 Hall (1981: 251–52).
26 Aguilar Camín & Meyer (1993: 62) and Katz (1998a: 617).
27 Richmond (1997: 200), R. Smith (1972: 76), and Knight (1996a: 574).
28 Ankerson (1984: 192).
29 Katz (1998a: 732) and E. Meyer et al. (1986: 171).
30 E. Meyer et al. (1986: 179).
31 Pozas Horcasitas (1988: 43).
32 Garrido (1986: 56) and L. Meyer (1992a: 51).
33 Benjamin (1990: 71–73).
34 L. Meyer (2000: 827).
35 Hernández Chávez (2006: 239–40).
36 L. Meyer (1977b: 75).
37 Kandell (1988: 448), Knight (1986a: II, 464), Medin (1972: 8), and Dulles (1961: 96).
38 Wasserman (1993: 71), L. Meyer (2000: 839), Aguilar Camín & Meyer (1993: 114), and Katz (1996: 33).
39 Benjamin (1990: 71).
40 Beals (1923: 105), Huizer (1970a: 42–50), and Ruiz (1980: 257).
41 Gilly (1983: 322).
42 *El Universal*, June 14, 1922, sec. 2, p. 7.
43 *El Universal*, June 16, 1922, sec. 2, p. 1.
44 *El Universal*, June 18, 1922, sec. 2, p. 3.
45 Katz (1998a: 780, 781). Raat (1987: 626) noted that at the time U.S. military intelligence also concluded that Obregón and Calles arranged for Villa's assassination to prevent his aiding De la Huerta. As with all high-profile assassinations, conspiracy theories abounded. Taibo (2006: 807–22) described some of them.
46 López Villafañe (1986: 28), Ruiz (1980: 376), and L. Meyer (2000: 828).
47 Aguilar Zínser (1990: 294).
48 Cockcroft (1998: 115), Beezley & Maclachlan (2009: 64), Dulles (1961: 442), Hamilton (1982: 75), L. Meyer (1974: 728), Needler (1961: 310), Benjamin (1990: 80), and Brachet-Márquez (1994: 63).
49 J. Meyer (1986b: 161).
50 Garrido (1986: 62).
51 Cumberland (1968: 242, 257), Hansen (1971: 30), and INEGI (1994: 609).
52 Córdova (1973: 33) and Ruiz (1980: 179).
53 L. Meyer (1991b: 224).
54 Macías (1988: 64; 1997: 181) and Krauze (1997a: 409–11).
55 Córdova (1995: 24).
56 Knight (1987: 7), Buchenau (2007: 103), and L. Meyer (2000: 827).
57 INEGI (1994: 381), Fowler-Salamini (1997: 15), Benjamin (2000c: 488, 491), and Collado (2005: 135–36).
58 Cornelius (1973: 419), Markiewicz (1993: 48), Hamnett (1999: 226), Knight (1990d: 6), and Ankerson (1984: 115).

59 Campa (1985: 23) and Garrido (1986: 79).
60 Raat (1992: 187), Brachet-Márquez (1994: 58–59), Weldon (1997: 250), and Aguilar Camín & Meyer (1993: 123, Table 1).
61 Wasserman (1990: 9; 1993: 51, 134, 163).
62 Cline (1971: 193), Garrido (1986: 76), J. Meyer (1986b: 155), Aguilar Camín (1980: 117), and Babb (2001: 28).
63 L. Meyer (2000: 831) and Buchenau (2007: 135).
64 Ruiz (1992: 346), Garrido (1986: 72), and L. Meyer (1992a: 52).
65 *Proceso*, September 28, 1997, pp. 58–64.
66 Krauze (1997a; 401), Garrido (1986: 71–73), and L. Meyer (1992a: 52).
67 For a description of conspiracy theories relating to Obregón's death, see *Proceso*, July 19, 1998, p. 56.
68 Aguilar Camín & Meyer (1993: 93), L. Meyer (1977c: 456), and Buchenau (2007: 146).
69 *Excélsior*, September 2, 1928, p. 1.
70 Benjamin (2000b: 93) and Markiewicz (1993: 60).
71 Garrido (1997: 1058) and Medina Peña (1994: 50).
72 Garrido (1986: 102).
73 Medina Peña (1994: 77), Hernández Chávez (2006: 247), Garrido (1986: 121), and Lajous (1981: 56–59).
74 Garrido (1986: 92, 142), Fuentes (2003: 7A), Wasserman (1993: 41), and Aguilar Camín & Meyer (1993: 111, 131–32).
75 Hellman (1983: 33).
76 Loyola Díaz (1980: 145), López Villafañe (1986: 31), and L. Meyer (1977c: 460–61; 2000: 832).
77 Lajous (1981: 65–67), J. Meyer (1976: 66), and L. Meyer (1985: 88).
78 L. Meyer (1985: 88; 2000a: 830).
79 L. Meyer (1974: 731), J. Meyer (1986b: 170), and Ruiz (1992: 349).
80 Garrido (1986: 140).
81 Dulles (1961: 537).
82 L. Meyer (1977b: 297, n. 4), Gonzales (2002: 218–19), Benjamin (1990: 81), and Dulles (1961: 555).
83 Hernández Chávez (1979: 4) and *El Universal*, December 29, 1929, p. 5.
84 Cumberland (1968: 275).
85 Fuentes Díaz (1969: 250).
86 Krauze (1987: III, 48) and Córdova (1995: 426).
87 Aguilar Camín & Meyer (1993: 99, 107), Moreno-Brid & Ros (2009: 85), and Córdova (1995: 352, 447).
88 Weyl & Weyl (1939: 53), Katz (2006: 270), Fowler Salamini (1978: 116–17), and Fallaw (2001: 11).
89 Cornelius (1973: 434), Knight (1990d: 11), and Córdova (1995: 462).
90 Cornelius (1973: 420) and *El Nacional*, May 18, 1934, p. 1.
91 Garrido (1986: 216).
92 Benjamin (1990: 84), L. Meyer (2000: 833–34), Middlebrook (1995: 27), Córdova (1995: 282), and Hamnett (1999: 227–28).
93 Buchenau (2007: 174).
94 Cornelius (1973: 450), Gilly (1994: 208), and L. Meyer (2000: 865).
95 Hernández Chávez (1979: 60) and Krauze (1987: III, 102).
96 Krauze (1997a: 457) and Bantjes (1998: 65).
97 Ankerson (1984: 148–49).
98 Snodgrass (2000: 7; 2006: 323).
99 Snodgrass (1998: 115; 2006: 325), Basurto (1983: 61), and Hernández Chávez (1979: 67).
100 Snodgrass (2000: 9).
101 Snodgrass (2006: 326–27) and Mexico (1966: vol. 5, 760). Ashby (1963: 34–35) listed the fourteen points Cárdenas proclaimed in Monterrey.
102 Garrido (1986: 256) and Kandell (1988: 478).
103 Camp (1992: 20).
104 Coatsworth (1999: 145), Babb (2001: 6), and Rivera Marín (1955: 192).
105 Cornelius (1973: 403).
106 Gordillo (1985: 299).
107 Olcott (2005: 185).
108 Middlebrook (1995: 92) and Weyl & Weyl (1939: 350).
109 Middlebrook (1995: 93), Brown (1986: 155), and Ashby (1963: 80).
110 Fallaw (2001: 130), Garrido (1986: 304, 385), Calderón & Cazés (1994: 30), and Garciadiego Dantan (1999: 17).
111 Bennet & Sharpe (1985: 26), Hamilton (1982: 190), and L. Meyer (1977b: 227).
112 Villarreal (1988: 302) and González Marín & Moreno (1992: 422).

113 Wilkie (1970a: 81), Ruiz (1992: 407), Sherman (1998: 365), and Knight (1994c: 100; 1985c: 304).
114 Ankerson (1984: 165).
115 Krauze (1997a: 479).
116 Ochoa (2000: 46–47) and Aguilar Camín & Meyer (1993: 142).
117 *Excélsior*, June 27, 1975, p. 30a.
118 Santiago (2006: 240, n. 110), Boyer (1998: 422–23), De la Peña (1998: 302), Hamilton (1980: 356), and Michaels (1971: 90).
119 Michaels (1971: 92), Hamnett (1999: 248), and L. Meyer (2000: 859).
120 Hamilton (1982: 280–86), Cothran (1994: 43), and Krauze (1997a: 489).
121 María y Campos (1939: 358).
122 Sherman (1998: 371), Campa (1985: 56), and Hamilton (1982: 262).
123 L. Meyer (1985: 95), Gilbert (2007: 58), Michaels (1971: 122–23), and Sherman (1998: 373).
124 Reich (1995: 68), Bantjes (1998: 224), Cockcroft (1998: 134), and Aguilar Camín & Meyer (1993: 142).
125 Sherman (1998: 371), Hamilton (1980: 357), and González del Rivero (1994: 18).
126 Knight (1994c: 105), Hamilton (1982: 264), and Cockcroft (1998: 135).
127 *Excélsior*, February 23, 1940, p. 1.
128 Kirk (1942: 237).
129 Contreras (1977: 189) discussed abuses before election day. Election-day events are described in Garrido (1986: 379), Santos (1986: 707–15), L. Meyer (2000: 860), and *Excélsior*, July 8, 1940, p. 1.
130 Garrido (1986: 390) and L. Meyer (1985: 98).
131 Contreras (1977: 196), Garrido (1986: 379), and *New York Times* (September 3, 1940, p. 7).
132 Fuentes (1996: 72) and Castañeda (1993c: 48).
133 Basurto (1999: 78), Murillo (2001: 41), Moreno-Brid & Ros (2009: 88), and L. Meyer (1992a: 54).
134 Loaeza (1999: 59), Wilkie (1970a: 36), Córdova (2007: 331), Benjamin (2000c: 488), Knight (1990d: 7), Hamilton (1982: 120), and Hartlyn & Valenzuela (1998: 16–17).
135 Sherman (1998: 369), Katz (2000: 4–6), Weyl & Weyl (1939: 246), and Krauze (1997a: 476).
136 Simonian (1995: 85, 90, 94) and Galicia (1941: 107–10).
137 Simonian (1995: 3, 91–92, 140) and Boyer (2007: 118–30).
138 Krauze (1997a: 489).
139 Fuentes (1996: 156). Bantjes (1997) discussed various interpretations of Cárdenas's legacy. See also Chapter 2, n. 53 for the number of streets named after him.
140 Medina Peña (1994: 20), Camp (1992: 67), and Katz (1981: 572; 1998a: 618).
141 Richmond (1983: 238) and Ruiz (1980: 260).
142 Benjamin (2000c: 472), Camp (1992: 18–19; 2005: 19, 40–41), Raat (1992: 134), Hodges & Gandy (1983: 29), Lieuwen (1968: 153), and Gonzales (2002: 185).
143 Krauze (1977: 80), Basáñez (1981: 58), Tannenbaum (1950: 91), and Brachet-Márquez (1994: 209, n. 26).
144 Hernández Chávez (2006: 246).
145 Hernández Chávez (1979: 79), Cockcroft (1998: 122), Prewett (1941: 616), and Camp (1992: 21, 67).
146 Townsend (1952: 216).
147 Córdova (1995: 50), Cothran (1994: 30), and Matute (1980: 186).
148 Middlebrook (1995: 87) and Aguilar Camín & Meyer (1993: 147).
149 L. Meyer (1985: 97–98).
150 Loaeza (1999: 108, 152) and Reynoso (2005: 32).
151 Maxfield (1990: 42), Mabry (1973: 23, 32–33), and Arriola (2008: 20–24).
152 Loaeza (1999: 106, 124).
153 *Uno más Uno* (September 17, 1989, p. 9).
154 Mabry (1973: 16, 34), Mizrahi (2003: 20–21), Nuncio (1986: 32), and Loaeza (1999: 149, 152).
155 Loaeza (1999: 116).
156 Loaeza (1999: 177).
157 Mabry (1973: 37–38) and Jarquín Gálvez & Romero Vadillo (1985: 36–37).
158 Brunk (1995: 232).
159 Knight (1986a: II, 518–19) and Wasserman (1993: 149).
160 Krauze (1997a: 366) and Ruiz (1992: 387).
161 Ruiz (1992: 382), Gilly (1994: 189), and Redfield (1930: 46, 52–53).
162 Krauze (1997a: 482–83), Medina (1998: 138), Benjamin (2000b: 95), Ochoa (2000: 62), and Fuentes (1996: 71).
163 Huxley (1934: 237–38).
164 Warman (1980: 165) and Raat (1992: 119).
165 INEGI (1994: 42).
166 Tannenbaum (1950: 70).

167 Gruening (1928: 468) and Warman (1980: 153).
168 Saragoza (1988: 116), Ruiz (1992: 384), and Krauze (1997a: 391).
169 Cárdenas García (1986: 27–40), Valdés Ugalde (1996: 133), and Córdova (1995: 260).
170 Katz (1996: 33) and Wasserman (1993: 76, 146).
171 Knight (1990d: 5), Wasserman (1993: 72–73, 88), Brewster (1998: 268), and Krauze (1997a: 451).
172 Hamilton (1980: 350).
173 Saragoza (1988: 208), Katz (2006: 273), and Brachet-Márquez (1994: 77).
174 Middlebrook (1995: 72).
175 Bortz (2000: 682) and Middlebrook (1995: 45).
176 Middlebrook (1995: 75) and L. Meyer (2000: 842).
177 Aguilar García (1997: 294).
178 Aguilar García (1997: 295) and Beals (1923: 137).
179 Beals (1923: 134–35), Aguilar Camín & Meyer (1993: 124), Gómez-Galvarriato (1998: 362), and Ruiz (1992: 360).
180 Brachet-Márquez (1994: 80) and Middlebrook (1995: 77).
181 Brachet-Márquez (1994: 58–61), Aguilar Camín & Meyer (1993: 123), Hale (1986: 437), and Aguilar García (1997: 296).
182 L. Meyer (2000: 844), Middlebrook (1995: 77), and Haber (2006: 563, 568).
183 Brachet-Márquez (1994: 65, 81), Middlebrook (1995: 80), Aguilar Camín & Meyer (1993: 121), and Haber, Razo & Maurer (2003: 153).
184 L. Meyer (2000: 843), Cornelius (1973: 405), and Garrido (1986: 67).
185 Benjamin (2000c: 494) and Saragoza (1988: 157).
186 Benjamin (2000c: 494), Aguilar García (1997: 297), Huizer (1970b: 458), and Middlebrook (1995: 81).
187 Porter (2003: 184), Hernández Chávez (2006: 251), and Middlebrook (1995: 51).
188 Aguilar Camín & Meyer (1993: 126).
189 Aguilar Camín & Meyer (1993: 126) and Córdova (1995: 234–35).
190 Aguilar García (1997: 283–84).
191 Knight (1990d: 36–37) and Ashby (1963: 73).
192 Benjamin (2000c: 496), Ashby (1963: 76), Basurto (1983: 102), and Medina Peña (1994: 149).
193 Ashby (1963: 276, 284), O'Brien (1996: 295), Knight (1990d: 35), Carr (1997: 690), L. Meyer (1974: 740), Murillo (2001: 41), and Collado (1996: 53).
194 Purnell (1999: 191).
195 Herrera Serna (1986: 55).
196 Purnell (1999: 215, n. 54) and Craig (1990: 65). Early land reform legislation failed to state the size of estates subject to expropriation. The 1922 land-reform law allowed the expropriation of irrigated parcels of land in excess of 370 acres, of rain-fed parcels in excess 617 acres, and of lesser quality parcels in excess of 988 acres. Later laws revised these figures and allowed exemptions if certain high-value crops were grown. Sanderson (1984: 46–48) described how successive land-reform laws changed the size and type of landholding subject to expropriation.
197 Bartra (1985: 25) and Sanderson (1984: 72).
198 Becker (1995: 17) and Warman (1980: 134).
199 Knight (1991b: 94), Fowler Salamini (1978: 156), Friedrich (1977: 64), and Becker (1995: 38).
200 Weyl & Weyl (1939: 79–80).
201 Hernández Chávez (1979: 167) and Markiewicz (1993: 88–89).
202 Krauze (1997a: 461), Bartra (1985: 17–18), and Ashby (1963: 148).
203 Huizer (1970a: 71).
204 Hodges & Gandy (1983: 61–62) and Warman (2003: 261).
205 INEGI (1994: 381), L. Meyer (2000: 861), Markiewicz (1993: 189, Table 17), Warman (1980: 179), and Mexico (1963a: 50). The discrepancy between the area distributed and the area cultivated resulted from much of the land serving as pasture and woodlot.
206 Knight (1990d: 26), Hernández Chávez (2006: 259), Jacobs (1982: 166), and Henderson (1998: 71).
207 Markiewicz (1993: 87).
208 Markiewicz (1993: 55, 97).
209 Henderson (1998: 223), Ashby (1963: 174), and Weyl & Weyl (1939: 171).
210 Weyl & Weyl (1939: 171).
211 Huxley (1934: 216).
212 Knight (1990c: 78), Roman (1976: 44–45), Edmonds-Poli & Shirk (2009: 225), and Weyl & Weyl (1939: 134).
213 Knight (1990c: 82) and Stavenhagen (1986: 406).

214 Knight (1990c: 77, 80).
215 Limón (1998: 43–44).
216 Brading (1988b: 80; 1995: 103).
217 Benjamin (2000c: 481) and Lewis (1997: 840).
218 Rus (1994: 270).
219 Gilly (1994: 423–24).
220 Becker (1995: 70) and L. Cárdenas (1940: 8).
221 Knight (1990d: 30) and Rus (1994: 278–79).
222 Lombardo Toledano (1973: 107).
223 Matute (1995: 84–85), Krauze (1997a: 401), and Knight (1986a: II, 374–75).
224 Vázquez León (1981: 9), Bantjes (1998: 215), and Dwyer (2008: 132–35).
225 Ruiz (1992: 403), Weyl & Weyl (1939: 326), and Raby (1974: 52–53).
226 Knight (1990d: 30) and Benjamin (1996: 191).
227 Valdés & Menéndez (1987: Cuadro Ib & Cuadro II) and Mörner (1967: 2).
228 Morton (1962: 6, 7) and Ramos-Escandón (1994: 200–01).
229 Macías (1974: 599), Ramos-Escandón (1994: 2000), and Tuñón (2009: 34).
230 Olcott (2005: 16, 18, 72–76, 114).
231 Benjamin (2000c: 486) and Macías (1992: 619; 2002: 138).
232 Soto (1979: 37).
233 Ramos-Escandón (1998a: 94) and Olcott (2005: 162).
234 Morton (1962: 17).
235 Morton (1962: 22) and *Excélsior,* September 2, 1935, p. 3.
236 Ramos-Escandón (1994: 203–04; 1998a: 95), Macías (2002: 155), and Olcott (2005: 111, 114, 117 223–27).
237 *Excélsior*, September 2, 1937, p. 10.
238 Becker (1994: 258), Morton (1962: 23), Contreras (1977: 150), Olcott (2005: 180), and Macías (2002: 186).
239 *Excélsior*, September 2, 1939, p. 15.
240 Morton (1962: 44), Ramos-Escandón (1994: 204), and Farías Mackey (1988: 707).
241 Vaughan (1990: 152), Olcott (2005: 13), and Bonifaz de Novelo (1975: 53).
242 Beezley & Machlachlan (2009: 90).
243 Ramos-Escandón (1994: 201; 2007: 56) and INEGI (1994: 353–54). Vaughan (1982: 212–13) commented on changes in post-Revolutionary female employment.
244 Warman (1980: 165), Olcott (2005: 148), and Bauer (2001: 190–91).
245 Tortolero Villaseñor (2000: 111) and Weyl & Weyl (1939: 334).
246 PNR (1937: 57) and Haiman (1997: 1166).
247 Ordorica & Lezama (1993: 43, Table 1 & 47, Table 6).
248 Ordorica & Lezama (1993: 51, Table 8) and INEGI (1994: 65). As with many of the older statistics in this book, these population statistics should not be accepted as exact. The 1921 census, especially, has been viewed as flawed. Population totals were also affected by the many Mexicans who returned to Mexico from the United States to Mexico during the 1920s due to the end of Revolution in Mexico and the Depression in the United States as well as by the departure of others who sought employment in the United States.
249 Vaughan (1997a: 46).
250 Raby (1974: 12), Vaughan (1982: 126), and Wilkie (1970a: 160).
251 Vaughan (1982: 44, 123).
252 Florescano (2002: 399) and Vaughan (2006b: 158).
253 Knight (1990c: 86), Wilkie (1970a: 160), Haddox (1967: 6) and Meyer, Sherman & Deeds (2007: 501–02).
254 Vaughan (1982: 149; 1992: 894; 1975: 27).
255 Knight (1990a: 243) and Vaughan (1982: 174–80; 1994: 112).
256 Vaughan (1982: 147–48).
257 Vaughan (1982: 100, 134, 153, 157, 164).
258 Vaughan (1982: 158, 164).
259 Knight (1990d: 27), Arriola (2008: 24), Muro (2007: 404), and Reich (1995: 47).
260 Lerner (1979: 88), Raby (1974: 55), and Benjamin (2000c: 485).
261 Córdova (1974: 79, 87), Raby (1974: 42, 138), and Weyl & Weyl (1939: 317).
262 Bantjes (1998: 29) and Gonzales (2002: 243).
263 Krauze (1997b: 26), Benjamin (2000c: 481), and Vaughan (1997a: 134).
264 Vaughan (1997a: 86, 122, 153).
265 Raby (1974: 42) and Vaughan (1997a: 6–7).
266 Lerner (1979: 127), Knight (1990d: 31), and Vaughan (1997b: 445).
267 Bush & Mumme (1994: 364, n. 40).

268 Benjamin (2000c: 482) and Roman (1976: 96). Bantjes (2009: 472) discusses the complex roots of Mexican anti-clericalism.
269 Niemeyer (1974: 74).
270 Tangeman (1995: 36) and Reich (1995: 12).
271 Martínez Assad (1979: 22) and Fowler Salamini (1978: 92).
272 Ridgeway (2001: 147), Benjamin (1990: 76), and Martínez Assad (1979: 71; 1997: 556). It is unfortunate that Garrido Canabal is remembered only for his anti-clericalism since his administration successfully converted Tabasco into an efficient banana-producing enterprise—a badly needed income source as the supply of mahogany that the state had relied on became depleted. As Ridgeway (2001: 161) noted, rather than creating a typical enclave export operation, Garrido Canabal regulated the banana industry and used revenue from it to increase wages, extend infrastructure, and improve medical care and education.
273 Purnell (1999: 74), Macías (1988: 71), and Calles (1926: 1–2).
274 J. Meyer (1976: 23, 41–42) and *El Universal*, January 19, 1926, p. 5.
275 Bailey (1974: 63–65) and Wilkie (1966: 222).
276 The text of the Calles Law can be found in *Diario Oficial*, July 2, 1926, pp. 1–4.
277 J. Meyer (1997c: I, 27).
278 Purnell (1999: 72), Lynch (1986b: 592), and Aguilar Camín & Meyer (1993: 86–88).
279 J. Meyer (2006: 287) and Purnell (1999: 79, 81).
280 Purnell (1999: 91–102).
281 Olivera de Bonfil (1976: 303) and Purnell (1999: 79).
282 J. Meyer (1997c: IV, 82–85).
283 Reich (1995: 14) and Purnell (1999: 86–87).
284 Miller (1981: 57–58) and J. Meyer (1997c: III, 12–22, 85).
285 Olivera de Bonfil (1994: 306).
286 *Proceso*, April 8, 2001, p. 14.
287 Córdova (1995: 270).
288 J. Meyer (1997c: I, 90 & II, 77), Buchenau (2007: 130) and *El Universal* [on line] (June 21, 2009), "Hace 80 años, los arreglos."
289 Cornelius (1973: 459) and Reich (1995: 55, 73).
290 Gilly (1994: 255) and Reich (1995: 55, 65).
291 Huxley (1934: 280).
292 Unikel (1974a: 193), Izazola (2001: 294, Table 2), Schell (2006: 113), and Krauze (1977: 279).
293 Davis (1994: 21–22).
294 Collado (2003: 9).
295 Lear (2001: 355–58), Beals (1923: 126), and Huxley (1934: 280).
296 Connolly (1999a: 192).
297 Davis (1994: 84–85, 92).
298 Davis (1994: 93–95).
299 Davis (1994: 96–97).
300 Davis (1994: 77–78).
301 Hennessy (1991: 681).
302 Brading (1995: 100–01) and Hennessy (1991: 687).
303 Vaughan (1997a: 443), Paz (1990: 33), Ades (1989: 165), Vaughan (2006b: 158), and Wolfe (1963: 145).
304 Delpar (2000: 553), Vaughan (1982: 262), Marnham (1998: 178–79), Ruiz (1992: 373), and Hennessy (1991: 687).
305 Delpar (2000: 554).
306 Wolfe (1963: 144).
307 Hennessy (1991: 685).
308 Cockcroft (1991: 106–10) and Delpar (2000: 571).
309 Florescano (2002: 392) and Azuela (1992: 51).
310 Monsiváis (2000b: 1006–10) and Delpar (2000: 565).
311 Hennessy (1991: 687).
312 Vaughan (1982: 136), Meyer, Sherman & Deeds (2007: 502), and Fuentes (1996: 194).
313 Matute (1995: 265).
314 Weyl & Weyl (1939: 319) and González Marín & Moreno (1992: 427).
315 Schuler (1998: 149).
316 Esteva (1982b: 75).
317 Granados Chapa (1982: 347), Rubenstein (2000: 645), Fox (1995: 523), and Niblo (1999: 342).
318 Hayes (2000: 33), Rubenstein (2000: 644–45), and Miller (1998: 71–72).

19 PICKING UP THE PIECES, 1917–1940

1 Hansen (1971: 8).
2 Knight (1984: 77; 1986a: II, 413), and Katz (1981: 320).
3 Hernández Chávez (2006: 228), Thorp (1986: 60), and Krauze (1977: 15).
4 L. Meyer (2000: 826), Newell G. & Rubio F. (1984: 35), Medina Peña (1994: 86), Newell G. & Rubio F. (1984: 35), Cárdenas García (1986: 36), and O'Brien (1996: 41).
5 Krauze (1997a: 415), Knight (1990d: 9), Aguilar Camín & Meyer (1993: 101), and Haber et al. (2008: 49).
6 FitzGerald (1984: 246) and Krauze (1977: 22–23; 1997a: 416).
7 Knight (1998a: 62) and Córdova (1973: 30).
8 Hamilton (1982: 104–05), Wilkins (1974: 55, Table III.1), L. Meyer (1977b: 300, n. 13), and J. Meyer (1986b: 173).
9 E. Cárdenas (1987: 17, Table 2.1) and Keesing (1969: 724).
10 Krauze (1977: 213) and Villarreal (1988: 281, 289).
11 Hamilton (1982: 115), E. Cárdenas (1984: 227), and Moreno-Brid & Ros (2009: 77).
12 Katz (2006: 269), Suárez Dávila (2008: 10), E. Cárdenas (1984: 226), and Villarreal (1988: 301).
13 E. Cárdenas (1984: 225), L. Meyer (2000: 863), and Haber (1989: 154–55, 174–75).
14 E. Cárdenas (1984: 230), Cornelius (1973: 414), Villarreal (1988: 292), and INEGI (1994: 800).
15 Babb (2001: 7) and Knight (1992c: xii).
16 Wilkie (1970a: 32, Table 2–1).
17 L. Cárdenas (1972: I, 233).
18 Glade (1963: 77), FitzGerald (1985: 211), Lains (2007: 65), Labastida Martín del Campo (1981: 330), Suárez Dávila (1988: 374–77), and Simonian (1995: 87).
19 Pastor & Castañeda (1988: 221), Medin (1972: 129), and *Fortune* (January 1956, p. 105).
20 *Excélsior* (September 28, 1974, p. 7a).
21 Bulmer-Thomas (1994a: 232–33, 219, Table 7.6), Anglade & Fortín (1985: 33), and Michaels & Burnstein (1976: 703).
22 Glade (1963: 87) and Moreno-Brid & Ros (2009: 88).
23 Flores Olea (1972: 465), Glade (1963: 43), and Villarreal (1988: 335–36).
24 Lewis (1959: 20).
25 Haber, Maurer, & Razo (2003: 29) and Knight (2000: 142, n. 17).
26 Bernstein (1964: 118–20, 137–38), Haber, Razo, & Maurer (2003: 236, 273), L. Meyer (2000: 837), and Hart (2002: 414).
27 Bernstein (1964: 171), FitzGerald (2000a: 223), Aguilar Camín & Meyer (1993: 106), and Bantjes (1998: 158).
28 Bernstein (1964: 183, 192).
29 Beals (1923: 112).
30 González Gómez (1990: 51).
31 Topik (1990: 121) and Krauze (1977: 102).
32 Simpson (1937: 315), Hansen (1971: 60, Table 3–12—data is for 1935–1939), González Gómez (1990: 53), and INEGI (1994: 692, 694).
33 Knight (1990a: 259).
34 Niblo & Niblo (2008: 35), Banco de México (1941: 20, Table 4, 42, Table 7), Berger (2006: 4, 21), and E. Cárdenas (1984: 235).
35 Waters (2006: 233, 254–55).
36 Edminster (1961: 342).
37 Hamnett (1999: 221), Ankerson (1984: 93), and Tutino (2007: 243).
38 Krauze (1977: 165) and L. Meyer (2000: 842).
39 Krauze (1977: 164, Table 6) and Haber, Razo, & Maurer (2003: 288–90, 313).
40 L. Meyer (2000: 838) and Haber, Razo, & Maurer (2003: 287, 314).
41 L. Meyer (2000: 836), Tortolero Villaseñor (2000: 101–02), and E. Cárdenas (1987: 20).
42 Evans (2007: 275, 180, 225).
43 Beezley & Machlachlan (2009: 119) and L. Cárdenas (1972: I, 247).
44 Haber et al. (2008: 30), L. Meyer (2000: 861), Markiewicz (1993: 189, Table 17) and Glade (1963: 64).
45 Glade (1963: 57–59) and E. Cárdenas (1987: 43).
46 Aguilar Camín & Meyer (1993: 135), Hernández Chávez (2006: 258), Glade (1963: 69, 96), and Knight (1998a: 38).
47 Davis (1994: 21).
48 Haber, Razo, & Maurer (2003: 175), E. Cárdenas (1984: 238), and Ruiz (1992: 345).
49 Thorp (1986: 80), Medina Peña (1994: 114), and Bennett & Sharpe (1979a: 32).

50 Esquivel & Márquez (2007: 337) and Haber, Razo & Maurer (2003: 149–53).
51 Haber (2006: 560–61), Wilkins (1974: 55, Table III.1), and Hamilton (1982: 73).
52 Haber (1989: 143), Haber, Razo & Maurer (2003: 175), Winkler (1929: 224–25), R. Smith (1972: 231), and Wilkins (1974: 74).
53 Krauze (1977: 198) and O'Brien (1999: 125).
54 Gruening (1928: 381–82) and O'Brien (1996: 41).
55 E. Cárdenas (1987: 25. Table 2.3), Lewis (1986: 280, 286), and Pozas Horcasitas (1987: 113).
56 O'Brien (1999: 124), Mexico (1966: vol. 3, 983), and Wilkie (1970a: 71).
57 PNR (1937: 36), FitzGerald (1984: 256), Schuler (1998: 64, 91–92), Medina Peña (1994: 130), and E. Cárdenas (1987: 38).
58 Brachet-Márquez (1996: 109) and E. Cárdenas (1984: 233).
59 E. Cárdenas (1984: 233), Ruiz (1992: 401), Garza (1985: 142, Table IV-2), and Suárez (2000: 80).
60 L. Meyer (2000: 862) and Knight (1992c: 121, n. 19).
61 L. Meyer (1977b: 61), Wilkins (1998: 203), Haber, Razo, & Maurer (2003: 190), and Raat (1992: 123).
62 Hamilton (1982: 217) and Catão (1992: 45).
63 Santiago (2006: 149, 163). Santiago (2006: 206, n. 2) commented on the difficulty of determining the exact number of oil workers and provided various estimates of their number.
64 Krauze (1977: 251), Haber, Razo, & Maurer (2003: 213), Moreno-Brid & Ros (2009: 74), Gonzales (2002: 246), Suárez (2000: 78), and Brown (1985: 373).
65 Santiago (1998: 181–82; 2006: 112, 126, 147, 256–57).
66 Múgica (1984: 77).
67 L. Meyer (2000: 836–37).

20 UNCLE SAM CONFRONTS REVOLUTIONARY NATIONALISM, 1917–1940

1 Richmond (1983: 194–96).
2 Krenn (1990: 47), Schoultz (1998: 274), and R. Smith (1972: 45).
3 Krenn (1990: 26) and Ruiz (1980: 387).
4 Katz (1981: 493), Schmitt (1974: 155), and R. Smith (1972: 93).
5 Garciadiego Dantan (1986: 100), Gilderhus (1972: 214), and Coatsworth (1999: 146).
6 Cline (1971: 185) and Tuchman (1963: 199–200).
7 Richmond (1983: 194).
8 Knight (1987: 78) and R. Smith (1972: 101).
9 Brown (1993a: 248) and Hall (1990: 192).
10 Richmond (1983: 200).
11 Knight (1987: 144) and Warman (1980: 139).
12 Thorp (1986: 57), Winkler (1929: 3, 222–23), Henderson (1998: 126), and Hamilton (1982: 69).
13 Winkler (1929: 224, 284–85).
14 Cline (1971: 192) and Aguilar Camín & Meyer (1993: 80).
15 Gilderhus (2000: 63) Beals (1923: 275) and Cronon (1960: 45).
16 Schoultz (1998: 274), Kane (1975: 303), L. Meyer (1977b: 78, 92), Schuler (2000: 514), and Rippy (1926: 358).
17 L. Meyer (2000: 847).
18 Hall (1990: 193) and Aggarwal (1996: 241).
19 Kane (1973: 346), Medina Peña (1994: 90), and Marichal (2003: 454–55).
20 Kane (1975: 303) and King (1989: 503–04).
21 Russell (1984: 27).
22 Michaels (1968: 57), Cronon (1960: 46), and Gilderhus (2000: 64).
23 Beelen (1984: 189) and Schuler (2000: 510). The Teapot Dome Scandal involved illegal oil leasing on land set aside as a naval petroleum reserve. Albert Fall, who was elected senator from New Mexico in 1912, was appointed as Secretary of the Interior in 1921. Fall was subsequently convicted of accepting illegal payments in exchange for no-bid oil leasing of the land. One of the lease holders was Edward Doheny.
24 L. Meyer (1991b: 217; 2000: 849) and Schoultz (1998: 277).
25 Weyl & Weyl (1939: 69), Cockcroft (1974: 257), L. Meyer (1977b: 283, n. 194), and the *New York Times* (December 30, 1923, p. 1).
26 Thorp (1998: 104; 1986: 61) and Marichal (1989: 225; 2003: 455).
27 Córdova (2007: 329).
28 Bemis (1943: 217) and Gilderhus (2000: 64).
29 Dulles (1961: 320), Collado (2005: 55), and Santiago (2006: 280–81).

30 L. Meyer (1977b: 108).
31 U.S. (1940: II, 518).
32 L. Meyer (1977b: 110).
33 L. Meyer (1977b: 18–19).
34 L. Meyer (1977b: 124, 128) and Haber, Maurer, & Razo (2003: 8–9).
35 Schoultz (1998: 29).
36 Dulles (1961: 324–25) and Collado (2005: 10).
37 L. Meyer (1977b: 130) and Nicolson (1935: 317).
38 Nicolson (1935: 295–98).
39 Knight (1992c: 91), Schmitt (1974: 167), and L. Meyer (2000: 851).
40 Nicolson (1935: 335, 382).
41 Nicolson (1935: 313).
42 Ross (1958: 514, 527) and Córdova (1995: 166).
43 U.S. (1966: vol. 3, 823).
44 J. Meyer (1976: 18) and Dulles (1961: 448).
45 U.S. (1976: 903–06), Mexico (1931: 444–45), Saragoza (1988: 144), and Ruiz (1992: 383).
46 *New York Times* (March 5, 1933, sec. 1, p. 3).
47 Raymont (2005: 25–64) and L. Meyer (1977b: 145, 297, n. 9).
48 Hamilton (1982: 107) and Gilderhus (2000: 81).
49 L. Meyer (1977b: 185) and Schuler (1998: 41).
50 Cronon (1960: 159).
51 Cronon (1960: 135).
52 L. Meyer (1977b: 154–55), Gonzales (2002: 247), and Brown (1997b: 58).
53 Kirk (1942: 160) and Knight (1992c: 91–92).
54 Hamilton (1982: 221), Mejía Prieto (1976: 127), and L. Meyer (1977b: 158–59).
55 Cronon (1960: 171).
56 L. Meyer (1977b: 160) and Kirk (1942: 162—emphasis in original).
57 Cronon (1960: 182).
58 Santiago (2006: 346–47), Knight (1992c: 97), and Brown (1997b: 67).
59 *Excélsior*, March 19, 1938, p. 4.
60 Hamilton (1982: 229).
61 Hamilton (1982: 216) and L. Meyer (1977b: 152).
62 Gilderhus (2000: 88).
63 Tannenbaum (1955: 39).
64 Dwyer (2008: 177).
65 Huasteca Petroleum Co. (1938: 31) and L. Meyer (1977b: 188, 207).
66 Blum (1959: 496), Bernstein (1964: 185), Dwyer (2008: 224), P. Smith (1996: 79), and Schuler (1998: 121).
67 Marks (1988: 221) and L. Meyer (1977b: 194).
68 Daniels (1947: 227–28) and Cronon (1960: 196).
69 Marks (1988: 222) and Dwyer (2008: 200).
70 Cronon (1960: 202), L. Meyer (1977b: 177), M. Paz (1988: 79), and Pazos (1976: 72).
71 M. Paz (1988: 76).
72 Dwyer (2008: 220, 271).
73 Cornelius (1973: 470).
74 L. Meyer (1992b: 160) and Mexico (1940: 582–83).
75 Basurto (1983: 158).
76 Bemis (1943: 349), Daniels (1947: 265), Gellman (1979: 55), Hamilton (1982: 234), L. Meyer (1977b: 224), and P. Smith (1996: 80).
77 L. Meyer (1977b: 224).
78 Fuentes (1988: 20).
79 Marichal (1989: 227; 2003: 457), Dwyer (2008: 159–61), Cronon (1960: 269), and Niblo (1995: 56–57).
80 Knight (1992c: 119–20), Niblo (1995: 45), Brown (1997b: 66), and O'Brien (1996: 305).
81 Knight (1992c: 116–19) and L. Meyer (1971: 5).
82 Hamilton (1982: 264), L. Meyer (2000: 859–60), and Schuler (2000: 534).
83 Schuler (1998: 195) and Marks (1988: 224).
84 The text of the 1917 Act can be found in U.S. (1917: 874–98).
85 Rodríguez (2007: 145) and Morales (1989: 82–84).
86 Balderrama & Rodríguez (1995: 10) and Morales (1989: 86).
87 U.S. (1976: I, 107) and Balderrama & Rodríguez (1995: 8).

88 Hall (1992: 758), L. Cardoso (1980: 101–02) and Morales (1989: 86).
89 Massey, Durand, & Malone (2002: 33) and U.S. (1976: I, 105). The text of the 1921 Act can be found in U.S. (1928: 5–7).
90 Cárdenas (1975: 69), Balderrama & Rodríguez (1995: 6, 19–20), Heller (1992: 68), and Lorey (1999: 73).
91 Bustamante (1972: 269–70), Cárdenas (1975: 73–74), and Rodríguez (2007: 147).
92 Rodríguez (2007: 147), Morales (1989: 89), Balderrama & Rodríguez (1995: 59), Bustamante (1972: 271), and Mirandé (1987: 106).
93 Castells (1978: 76–79).
94 Rodríguez (2007: 145), U.S. (1976: I, 105–07; 1932: 27, Table 35, 63, Table 59).
95 L. Cardoso (1980: 128) and Bustamante (1972: 264–68).
96 *Congressional Record*, vol. 70, pt. 4, p. 3619.
97 Gamio (1930: 184) and L. Cardoso (1980: 109).
98 Balderrama & Rodríguez (1995: 6–7), L. Cardoso (1980: 91–95), and Valdés (1988: 2).
99 L. Cardoso (1980: 145) and Mirandé (1987: 116).
100 Balderrama & Rodríguez (1995: 101) and Beezley & Machlachlan (2009: 126).
101 Mirandé (1987: 116–17) and Balderrama & Rodríguez (1995: 55).
102 Bustamante (1972: 272), Hoffman (1978: 238), and Balderrama & Rodríguez (1995: 103).
103 Hoffman (1978: 227–29).
104 Córdova (1995: 227).
105 Balderrama & Rodríguez (1995: 117–18), Dinwoodie (1977: 195), and Hoffman (1978: 232).
106 U.S. (1976: I, 107).
107 Corwin (1978: 117) and Balderrama & Rodríguez (1995: 121–22).
108 Lorey (1999: 41) and Martínez (1978: 161, Table 4).
109 Wasserman (1993: 130) and Lorey (1999: 46–47).
110 Wasserman (1993: 57) and Lorey (1999: 47).
111 Lorey (1999: 81) and Martínez (1978: 83, 166, Table 8). Border-crossing data is for fiscal years.
112 Martínez (1978: 75), Ganster & Lorey (2008: 68, 77), and Lorey (1999: 48).

21 AFTER CÁRDENAS, 1941–1970

1 Silva Herzog (1975: 100).
2 *Excélsior* (December 2, 1940, p. 11).
3 Jarquín Gálvez & Romero Vadillo (1985: 38), Garrido (1986: 389, 413, 431), and Krauze (1997a: 495).
4 *Hoy* (September 21, 1940, p. 10).
5 Schuler (1985: 466–67), Davis (1995: 180), Kirk (1942: 264–328), Rankin (2007: 25), and the *New York Times Magazine* (June 7, 1942, p. 13).
6 Suárez Gaona (1987: 85), Buchenau (2007: 193), and *Excélsior* (September 26, 1942, p. 5).
7 Huizer (1970b: 476–77), Gilbert (2007: 61), and Hernández Chávez (2006: 262).
8 Medina Peña (1994: 155–56) and Hellman (1978: 49–50).
9 Medina Peña (1994: 118), Niblo (1999: 109, 115, 116–17, 363), Garciadiego Dantan (1999: 37), Katz (2007: 203), Davis (1995: 181–83), and González Casanova (1979b: 5).
10 Niblo (1999: 139–40, 281).
11 Medina Peña (1994: 162), Molinar Horcasitas (1991: 27), and Medina (1979: 62).
12 Molinar Horcasitas (1991: 25–28), Haber et al. (2008: 29), Edmonds-Poli & Shirk (2009: 168), and Bruhn (1997a: 41). Legislation requiring a party to carry out an activity in two-thirds of the states considers the Federal District as a state.
13 Niblo (1999: 156) and Camp (2005: 25).
14 Krauze (1997a: 525), Contreras (1977: 179), Loaeza (2005: 118), Rankin (2007: 27), and González Casanova (1979b: 4).
15 Sherman (2000: 576).
16 Medin (1990: 44), P. Smith (1990: 99), Medina (1979: 93), Camp (2005: 25, 40), and Needler (1987: 77).
17 *Excélsior* (January 20, 1947, p. 1).
18 González Casanova (1979b: 7) and *Excélsior* (October 13, 1951, p. 10A [emphasis in original]).
19 Medin (1990: 51), Medina (1979: 95–110), and Wilkie (1970a: 103).
20 *New York Times* (April 9, 1953, p. 14) and Hodges & Gandy (1983: 119).
21 Niblo (1999: 258–59).
22 Niblo (1999: 162) and CIA (1951: 9).
23 CIA (1951: 69).
24 Huizer (1970b: 489), Servín (2001: 108), and Riding (1985: 57).

25 Niblo (1999: 258) and Cosío Villegas (1975a: 84).
26 P. Smith (1990: 100), Niblo (1999: 363), Paz (1975a: 253), and Sherman (2000: 576).
27 Reyna (1985: 107), Suchlicki (1996: 137), and P. Smith (1990: 106–07).
28 Pellicer de Brody & Reyna (1978: 44–50), Servín (2001: 189–98), and Reyna (1985: 107).
29 Pellicer de Brody & Reyna (1978: 52–54), Piñeyro (1987: 152), Martínez Assad (1982: 32), and *Excélsior* (July 30, 1951, pp. 1a, 9a).
30 Servín (2001: 341–52), Cosío Villegas (1975b: 134), and *New York Times* (July 10, 1952, p. 6).
31 Semo (1987: 60), Servín (2001: 336–41), and Pellicer de Brody & Reyna (1978: 60).
32 Cline (1971: 332) and Pellicer de Brody & Reyna (1978: 10).
33 P. Smith (1990: 108), Niblo (1999: 169), *Hispanic American Report* (January 1953, p. 8), and *New York Times* (July 13, 1952, sec. 4, p. 6; March 25, 1954, p. 8).
34 Wilkie (1970a: 32), Sherman (2000: 588–90), Pellicer de Brody & Reyna (1978: 19–20), and Ramírez (1989: 63–64).
35 *Excélsior* (November 5, 1957, p. 1a).
36 Krauze (1997a: 614).
37 Taylor (1960: 724, n. 7).
38 Vernon (1963: 131).
39 Servín (2001: 390–92), Molinar Horcasitas (1991: 36), and *Diario Oficial* (January 7, 1954). See n. 12 above.
40 Maldonado (1960: 13).
41 Krauze (1997a: 658), Miller (1985: 337–38), and L. Meyer (1992a: 204).
42 Ramírez (1989: 80), I. Semo (1982: 61), Suárez Gaona (1987: 99), and Wilkie (1970a: 32).
43 Medina Peña (1994: 202), *The Wall Street Journal* (November 18, 1963, p. 14), and *Hispanic American Report* (July 1964, p. 591).
44 CIA (1964: 152).
45 Cline (1963: 167).
46 Guevara Niebla (2004: 15–17) and Basáñez (1981: 171).
47 Aguilar Camín & Meyer (1993: 201) and Krauze (1997a: 700).
48 Scherer García & Monsiváis (1999: 186).
49 Fuentes (1971: 152).
50 Zermeño (1978: 180) and Monsiváis (2008: 141–52, 164–65).
51 Agee (1975: 555), Monsiváis (2008: 33), and Stevens (1974: 204–07). Braun (1997) discussed student political beliefs.
52 Scherer García & Monsiváis (1999: 193) and Paz (1975a: 243).
53 Fuentes (1971: 153), Poniatowska (1971: 207), Stevens (1974: 237), Boils (1975: 119), and *New York Times* (October 6, 1969, p. 16). Loaeza (2005: 506, n. 2) noted that during the Fox administration (2000–2006), the government declared forty-two died at Tlatelolco. Despite this feeble attempt at candor, impunity and cover up extended into the twenty-first century. Security expert Carlos Montemayor (*Proceso*, March 1, 2009, p. 46) compared various fatality estimates. Montemayor also reported (2007: 193, 200) that the massacre was filmed by multiple motion-picture cameras. Of the twenty-two hours of film shot, only eight minutes have been made public.
54 *Proceso* (October 2, 1999, pp. 43–49), Scherer García & Monsiváis (1999), Montemayor (2007: 217) and Preston & Dillon (2004: 381) reported on the marksmen. *Reforma* (October 2, 2003, p. 10A) described the U.S. Defense Department documents.
55 *Proceso* (March 1, 2009, p. 47).
56 Cothran (1994: 93), Zermeño (1978: 60), and Medina Peña (1994: 206).
57 *Excélsior* (September 2, 1969, pp. 29–30a).
58 Paz (1972: 12–13).
59 Semo (2003: 94) and Gellert (1998).
60 Ramírez (1989: 46), Womack (1968b: 30), L. Meyer (2005b: 23–24), and Cothran (1994: 69, Table 3.4).
61 Krauze (1997a: 525).
62 L. Meyer (2000: 857), Boils (1975: 75), DePalo (1997: 162), and Lieuwen (1968: 144).
63 Chacón (2000: 311, 314, 341), Schuler (1998: 161), Boils (1975: 159), Camp (2005: 25), and Servín (2001: 42).
64 Rankin (2007: 28) and Tudor (1997).
65 Boils (1975: 154) and *NACLA's Latin America and Empire Report* (July–August 1973, pp. 26–27).
66 Boils (1975: 103, Table 4).
67 Benítez Manaut (2001: 60, Table 1) and Boils (1975: 105, Table 6).
68 P. Smith (1990: 118), Story (1986: 100), Camp (2005: 76, Table 4.1), and L. Meyer (1983: 145).
69 Arreola Ayala (1988: 169).
70 L. Meyer (1992a: 56).

71 Loaeza (1999: 78–79) and P. Smith (1990: 94).
72 Greene (2007: 7) and González Casanova (1970: 12, 132).
73 Loaeza (1999: 282–84), Ashby (1985: 295), Becerra, Salazar & Woldenberg (2005: 115).
74 Story (1986: 47), Pacheco Méndez (1988: 14), Molinar Horcasitas (1991: 85–86), and Rodríguez & Ward (1994: 46).
75 Schettino (2007: 256).
76 Agee (1975: 499).
77 L. Meyer (2000: 924) and Carr (1997: 280; 1992: 249).
78 CIA (1951: 14; 1964: 154) and Angell (1998: 129).
79 L. Meyer (1989a: 100), Bartra (2008: 186), and Monsiváis (2008: 65).
80 Medin (1990: 80), Loaeza (1999: 182–84, 201–06, 231), Krauze (1997a: 517), Greene (2007: 79), and J. Meyer (2003: 137).
81 Loaeza (1999: 198–99) and L. Meyer (2000: 921).
82 Medina (1978: 201), Loaeza (1999: 216), Mabry (1973: 47), and L. Meyer (2000: 921).
83 Loaeza (1999: 24, 229–30) and Arriola (2008: 30–31).
84 Johnson (1984: 148), Loaeza (1999: 268), and Mabry (1973: 49).
85 Cosío Villegas (1966: 148). "Sex appeal" appeared in English in the original.
86 Mabry (1973: 48, 52) and Loaeza (1999: 224, 234–37).
87 Mabry (1973: 72–73).
88 Loaeza (1999: 273–74), Story (1987: 267), and González Morfín (1973: I, 188).
89 L. Meyer (2000: 922), Marván Laborde (1988: 196), and Molinar Horcasitas (1987a: 29, n. 8).
90 Álvarez (2006: 101).
91 Mizrahi (2003: 24), Preston & Dillon (2004: 120), and Cosío Villegas (1972a: 69).
92 P. Smith (1990: 83).
93 Vargas Llosa (1991).
94 L. Meyer (2000: 910–11) and Cothran (1994: 97).
95 González Casanova (1970: 31), Garrido (1997: 1059), and Hellman (1978: 53). Garrido (1987c) listed the metaconstitutional powers.
96 L. Meyer (2000: 912; 1974: 750) and Hellman (1978: 97).
97 De la Garza (1972: xii) and Rodríguez Araujo (1985a: 56, Table 6 bis).
98 L. Meyer (2000: 913) and Molinar Horcasitas (1991: 37).
99 Cothran (1994: 61, Table 3.2).
100 Edmonds-Poli & Shirk (2009: 78) and Guillermoprieto (1994: 59).
101 Garrido (1997: 1059), Aguilar Camín & Meyer (1993: 256), González Casanova (1970: 12), and CIA (1964: 152).
102 The author, in the process of arranging to travel with all six 1988 presidential campaigns, compared floor space.
103 Azuela de la Cueva & Cruz Rodríquez (1989: 127).
104 Hellman (1986: 249–51) and Basáñez (1981: 11).
105 Johnson (1984: 251, Table 1) and Hellman (1978: 96).
106 Medina (1979: 85), Servín (2001: 254), and *Hispanic American Report* (January 1958, p. 9).
107 ADESE (1988) described these and other colorfully named election scams. Gómez Tagle (1994: 54–56) listed 57 common ways the PRI manipulated elections, ranging from locating polls well away from concentrations of opposition voters to manipulating vote totals after polls had closed.
108 Johnson (1971: 134–40), Needler (1971: 36), and *La Jornada* (July 8, 1989, p. 15).
109 Mexico (1941: 7). Stevens (1974: 253) noted the maximum penalty for social dissolution was later extended to 12 years. The offense was removed from the books in 1970 (*Proceso*, Special Number 23, (2008), p. 32).
110 *Proceso* (June 14, 1998, p. 49).
111 Stevens (1974: 289) and Cline (1971: 328).
112 *Proceso* (September 24, 2000, p. 13).
113 Silva Herzog (1975: 108) and the *Los Angeles Times* (December 13, 1994, p. B7).
114 Stavenhagen (1975: 162).
115 Knight (1990a: 230, 254), Levy & Székely (1983: 126–27), and INEGI (1994: 13, 42).
116 Sherman (2000: 575) and Hellman (1978: 67).
117 Cornelius (1969: 838), Brea (2003: 27), and L. Meyer (2000: 933).
118 Alba (1982: 67, Table 4.5).
119 Cabrera Acevedo (1985: 124), INEGI (1994: 35), and Trejo Reyes (1975: 674).
120 Oliveira & Roberts (1994: 276) and Trejo Reyes (1975: 675).
121 Niblo (1999: 22).
122 Ward (1976: 330).
123 Turner (1968: 360).

124 Turner (1968: 357).
125 Portes (1970: 16–17).
126 Camp (2003: 131).
127 Tello (1971: 637, 640–42).
128 Rock (1994: 267), Bortz (1992: 221–22), and Krauze (1999c: VI, 67).
129 Bortz (1992: 231) and Flores de la Peña (1970: 215).
130 Barkin (1974: 199), Martínez de Navarrete (1970: 21), and P. Smith (1990: 87). Hewitt de Alcántara (1984: 110–11) and Portes (1985: 31) discussed the political overtones of the term "marginal."
131 L. Meyer (2000: 933).
132 González Casanova (1970: 92).
133 Niblo (1975: 122).
134 Scott (1964: 83), Alcazar (1970: 2), S. Schmidt (1997: 1122), and Maxfield (1990: 44).
135 Hellman (1978: 54) and L. Meyer (2000: 910).
136 Martínez de Navarrete (1970: 26), L. Meyer (2000: 907–08), Pellicer de Brody & Reyna (1978: 8), FitzGerald (2000b: 83), Niblo (1999: 365), and *Reforma* (February 25, 2002, p. 17A).
137 L. Meyer (2000: 895), Aguilar Camín & Meyer (1993: 177), Cypher (1990: 73, Table 3.2), Babb (2001: 86), and Urquidi (1970: 10).
138 L. Meyer (1988: 81).
139 Cothran (1994: 77), Loaeza (1984a: 55–56), and Oliveira & Roberts (1994: 268).
140 González Casanova (1962: 27).
141 Ruiz (1992; 410) and Hamnett (1999: 249–50).
142 Gilbert (2007: 64), P. Smith (1990: 113), L. Meyer (1988: 80), and Medin (1990: 59).
143 Medina Peña (1994: 157).
144 López Cámara (1971: 71) and L. Meyer (2000: 942).
145 Trejo Delarbre (1976: 133).
146 Middlebrook (1995: 95, 160) and Roxborough (1998: 258).
147 Middlebrook (1995: 50) and Saragoza (1988: 164).
148 Bortz (1995: 50), Córdova (1995: 345), and *Mexican Labor News & Analysis,* vol. 3, no. 4 (February 16, 1998).
149 Middlebrook (1995: 153).
150 Edmonds-Poli & Shirk (2009: 211).
151 Hellman (1986: 252–53), Cook (2007: 154), and Middlebrook (1995: 180).
152 Rivera Marín (1955: 110), Loyo Brambila & Pozas H. (1977: 85, n. 19), and Stevens (1974: 104).
153 Pozas Horcasitas (1977: 58), Roxborough (1998: 257), *The Wall Street Journal* (January 6, 1984, p. 21), and Niblo (1999: 277).
154 Hellman (1986: 244), Haber et al. (2008: 34) and Burgess (2003: 80).
155 La Botz (1992: 47–49), Burgess (2003: 79), and *Hispanic American Report* (February 1962: 111).
156 Hellman (1986: 251), Middlebrook (1995: 150), Katz (2006: 447), and Roxborough (1998: 256).
157 Spenser (2008: 388) and Monsiváis (2008: 48).
158 Beezley & Machlachlan (2009: 143).
159 Trejo Delarbe (1979: 124, Table 1), Oliveira & Roberts (1994: 292), Burgess (2003: 77), and Loyo Brambila (1979: 27).
160 Bachelor (2008: 258) and Haber et al. (2008: 15, 33–35).
161 Sherman (2000: 578) and Krauze (1997a: 572).
162 Niblo (1995: xiv), Bizberg (2003a: 314), and Seligman (1956: 173).
163 Zapata (1997: 695), Cothran (1994: 66), Roxborough (1998: 264), Newell & Rubio (1984: 160, Table VI-1), and Burgess (2003: 77).
164 Hellman (1978: 66), Krauze (1997a: 640), Middlebrook (1995: 221), and Krauze (1997a: 577).
165 Barry (1995: 2).
166 Ávila (1969: 71–73), González y González (1974: 222), and Niblo (1999: 10).
167 Lewis (1963: xiii).
168 Hernández Laos & Córdova Chávez (1982: 67, Table I. 1), Sanderson (1984: 99), Cabrera Acevedo (1985: 123), Urquidi (1977: 6), and Grindle (1986: 113, Table 6.1).
169 Hewitt de Alcántara (1977: 23), Sanders (1986: 277), Bergsman (1980: 33), Aguilar Camín (1988: 151), and Bartra (1976: 24–25).
170 Warman (2001: 193; 1980: 222) and Bartra (1976: 17).
171 Warman (2001: 119) and Hodges & Gandy (2002: 60).
172 Thiesenhusen (1996: 43), Rus (1994: 285–86), and Hewitt de Alcántara (1976: 179; 1984: 127).
173 Hewitt de Alcántara (1984: 126), Bergsman (1980: 36–37), and De Janvry (1981: 125).
174 Barry (1995: 26–27) and Montes de Oca (1977: 57).
175 CDIA (1974: 417–18) and Stavenhagen (1966: 483).

176 Stavenhagen (1975: 147) and Warman (1980: 188; 2001: 73).
177 Warman (1978: 686; 2001: 192), Tello (1971: 653), and Bartra (1976: 18).
178 Servín (2001: 34) and Warman (1980: 236).
179 Monsiváis (1986b: 264), Esteva (1975: 1312), Martínez Vázquez (1975: 156, 162–63), and Becker (1995: 122–23).
180 Gonzales (2002: 207, 235–38), Kuntz Ficker (2002c: 26–27), and *Nexos* (February 1996, p. 46).
181 Stanford (1997: 286), Hellman (1978: 45; 1986: 245), and Haber et al. (2008: 33).
182 Basurto (1983: 105), Hellman (1986: 251), and Warman (1980: 189).
183 Bizberg (2003a: 317–18), Hellman (1986: 245), and Warman (1979: 117; 2001: 216).
184 Mexico (1972: 259, 265), González Casanova (1970: 83), and *Anuario Estadístico de los Estados Unidos Mexicanos 1970–1971*, Mexico (1973: 47).
185 Bonfil Batalla (1991: 21), Doremus (2001: 382), and Aguirre Beltrán (1967: 565).
186 Villa Rojas (1971b: 1025–26) and Rus (1994: 287).
187 Medina (1974b: 16) and Hewitt de Alcántara (1984: 55).
188 Doremus (2001: 376).
189 Aguirre Beltrán (1975: 418).
190 Ramos-Escandón (1998a: 99), Monsiváis (2006b: 17), and Molyneux (2000: 52).
191 Ramos-Escandón (1994: 205) and Rodríguez (2003: 101).
192 Ramos-Escandón (1998a: 100) and *La cultura en México* (January 3, 1973, p. xii).
193 Gutmann & Porter (1997: 577) and Camp (1995a: 158–60).
194 Cline (1963: 167).
195 Camp (1979a: 421), Martínez de Navarrete (1969: 101, Table 10), Riddell (1976: 266), and Ramos-Escandón (1994: 205; 1997: 50–51).
196 Trejo Reyes (1975: 672), Oliveira & Roberts (1994: 317), Cabrera Acevedo (2000: 25, Table 3), Merrick (1994: 37), and Arizpe (1989: 231).
197 *Punto Crítico* (December 1972, pp. 36–39), and Elu de Leñero (1975: 55–57).
198 Alba (1993: 78).
199 *Economist* (August 24, 2002, p. 21).
200 Alba (1993: 79, Table 3).
201 Tortolero Villaseñor (2000: 126), Vaughan (1994: 117), Engelman (2008: 196), Alba & Potter (1986: 51, Table 1), Brea (2003: 14), and Alba (1993: 77–78).
202 P. Smith (1990: 92) and Aguilar Camín & Meyer (1993: 174).
203 Turner (1974: 11) and Tutino (2007: 246).
204 Cabrera Acevedo (2000: 27) and Urquidi (1970: 12).
205 Loaeza (1988: 169) and Knight (1990a: 258).
206 Vaughan (1994: 117; 1997a: 104–05) and Redfield (1950: 134–35).
207 NAFINSA (1977: 417), Martínez de Navarrete (1970: 31), and Latapí (1974: 335).
208 Alba (1982: 52) and Fuentes Molinar (1979: 231).
209 Barkin (1971: 37).
210 Latapí (1974: 334, 341) and Fuentes Molinar (1979: 235).
211 Bergsman (1980: 25) and Hernández Laos & Córdova Chávez (1979: 509).
212 Miller (1985: 331).
213 López Portillo T. (2001: 71).
214 Niblo (1999: 36) and Basáñez (1981: 217, Appendix 3).
215 Niblo (1999: 36), Hibino (1992: 31), Camp (2002: 136), Fuentes Molinar (1979: 232), INEGI (1994: 107–08), and Laurell (1995: 1352–53).
216 Barkin (1971: 45), Martínez de Navarrete (1969: 29), Zaid (1979: 338), Basáñez (1981: 113), and Loaeza (1984a: 56).
217 L. Meyer (2000: 908).
218 Loaeza (1985a: 46), Mexico (1972: 147) and Wilkie (1970b: 97, Table 4).
219 *Hoy* (September 21, 1940, p. 8).
220 *Excélsior* (May 31, 1942, sec. 1, p. 15 [emphasis in original]).
221 Reich (1995: 3), L. Meyer (2000: 908), Loaeza (1988: 158), and González Casanova (1970: 40).
222 González Casanova (1970: 39) and *Time* (May 9, 1955, p. 57).
223 Blancarte (1992: 127, 132, 167–68) and Monsiváis (1995: 148).
224 Blancarte (1992: 170) and *Tiempo* (August 14, 1961, p. 13).
225 Bailey (1986: 240), Pilcher (2001: 193), Tangeman (1995: 47), and Blancarte (1992: 237).
226 Blancarte (1992: 250, 252–54; 2005: 245).
227 Tangeman (1995: 52) and Reich (1995: 106).
228 Bastian (1981: 1947, 1954), Mexico (1943a: 14; 1972: 147), and Tangeman (1995: 42).

229 Tangeman (1995: 43–44), Bastian (1993: 37, 48), and Mexico (1972: 147–48).
230 Davis (1994: 2).
231 INEGI (1994: 31), Ward (1998: 57), Sobrino & Ibarra (2008: 169–71), Aguilar Camín (1988: 153), and Miller (2007: 174).
232 Ronfeldt (1986: 245), Simon (1997: 77), Garza (1985: 284), Ezcurra et al. (1999: 55), Davis (1994: 108), and Alba (1993: 91).
233 Covarrubias Gaitán (1988: 636) and Rowland & Gordon (1996: 176, Table 8.2).
234 Davis (1994: 125; 2002: 259, n. 4), Ward (1998: 47), and Unikel (1974a: 195).
235 Pensado & Correa (1996: 17).
236 Garza (1985: 267–68), Tortolero Villaseñor (2000: 107), and Ortiz Monasterio (1987: 256–57).
237 Covarrubias Gaitán (1988: 627).
238 Tello (1979: 37) and Davis (1994: 2).
239 Alba (1982: 69, Table 4.6) and Ezcurra et al. (1999: 42).
240 Ward (1998: 72), Garza & Schteingart (1984: 597), and Unikel (1974a: 201–02).
241 Ward (1998: 197).
242 Mexico (1963c: 59); 1971: 15/23; 1983–84: II/49).
243 Ferras (1977: 12–13, 21), Ward (1998: 138), *Excélsior* (November 4, 1975, p. 1a), and Ferras (1977: 21). Joseph & Henderson (2002: 536–44) provide a graphic description of life in 1982 Nezahualcóyotl.
244 Hennessy (1991: 681).
245 Krauze (1997c: 24), Bayón (1998: 401), and Paz (1990: 34).
246 Monsiváis (2000b: 1035) and Cuevas (1959: 120).
247 Manrique (2000: 956).
248 Barnet-Sánchez (1997: 246–47).
249 Delpar (2000: 569) and Barnet-Sánchez (1997: 248).
250 Bayón (1998: 402) and Delpar (2000: 569).
251 Miller (1998: 154) and Herrera (1990: 1).
252 Barnet-Sánchez (1997: 249) and Alemán Velasco (1997: 272).
253 Delpar (2000: 572). Barnet-Sánchez (1997) reviewed the nine works. Herrera (1990) and Tuchman (2002) describe Fridamania.
254 Florescano (2006: 322).
255 King (1995: 468; 2000: 46–47), Miller (1998: 88), and Pineda & Paranaguá (1995: 33).
256 Rubenstein (2000: 651), Fein (2001: 197, n. 73), Krauze (1997a: 521), and King (1995: 471).
257 Niblo (1999: 42), Martínez Assad (1990: 345), Fein (2001: 168), Mora (1989: 59), and Rubenstein (2000: 652).
258 Krauze (1997a: 521), Miller (1998: 88, 98), and Knight (1990a: 260).
259 Fein (1999: 128), Paranaguá (1995: 4), Niblo (1999: 45–46), Doremus (2001: 395–96), and Hershfield (1996: 55).
260 Davis (1994: 103), De la Vega Alfaro (1999: 168), and Mora (1989: 84–85).
261 Martínez Assad (1990: 346), Rubenstein (2000: 652), and Monsiváis (2000b: 1057).
262 Mora (1989: 98), Paranaguá (1995: 9), and Fein (1999: 143, 149–50).
263 Granados Chapa (1982: 353) and Rubenstein (2000: 663–64).
264 Rubenstein (2000: 665).
265 Monsiváis (2000b: 1043).
266 Standish (1997: 133).
267 Egan (2001: xiv) and Martin (1998: 171).
268 Krauze (1999e: 248–49).
269 McDuffie (1996: 327–28).
270 *Le Monde* (November 14, 1968, p. 4) and Paz (1972: 45).
271 Hellman (1986: 250).
272 Levy & Székely (1983: 115).
273 Rubenstein (2000: 640), Jiménez de Ottalengo (1974: 777), and Cole (1972: 105).
274 Krauze (1997a: 577).
275 Camp (1982: 48), Krauze (1997a: 642), and Rodríguez Munguía (2007: 80).
276 Camp (1982: 48) and Rodríguez Munguía (2007: 180–87).
277 Story (1986: 103) and Niblo (1999: 287).
278 Krauze (1997a: 582) and Story (1986: 103).
279 González Casanova (1970: 61–63).
280 González Pedrero (1969: 75).
281 Levy & Székely (1983: 90).
282 FitzGerald (1994: 96), Krauze (1997a: 520), Monsiváis (2000b: 1037), and Camp (1985: 188).

283 Silva Herzog (1975) is an English translation of the 1943 article.
284 Cosío Villegas (1975a) is an English translation of the 1947 article. The quotations are from pp. 76 and 85, respectively, of the English version.
285 Krauze (1997a: 598) and Rajchenberg (1999: 165).
286 Bortz (1987: 155) and Medina Peña (1994: 169, 205).
287 Krauze (1999c: vi, 52; 1999e: 423) and Rubenstein (2000: 667).
288 Miller (1998: 66, 70), Hayes (2000: 33), and Fernández & Paxman (2001: 106).
289 Camp (1982: 40) and Bernal Sahagún (1974: 117).
290 Arreola (2006: 242), Fernández & Paxman (2001: 59) and Alisky (1981: 60). Lawson (2002: 223, n. 16) described the ties between the political elite and early television concessionaires.
291 Alisky (1981: 60), Arreola (2006: 242), and Fernández & Paxman (2001: 66).
292 Fox (1995: 533) and Fernández & Paxman (2001: 67).
293 Fernández & Paxman (2001: 68, 164) and Rubenstein (2000: 663).
294 Fernández & Paxman (2001: 143–44, 165–66, 201).
295 *Latin America,* February 20, 1976, p. 59, Bernal Sahagún (1974: 110–15), and O'Brien (1999: 146).
296 Paz (1975a: 252).

22 THE MEXICAN ECONOMIC MIRACLE, 1941–1970

1 Hewitt de Alcántara (1977: 13).
2 Niblo (1988a: 19–20; 1995: 92–93).
3 Niblo (1988a: 10) and Reynolds (1970: 395).
4 Niblo (1988a: 8).
5 Guillén Romo (1984: 28) and the *New York Times* (September 10, 1941, p. 33).
6 Mizrahi (2003: 69), Peschard, Puga & Tirado (1986: 22), Ramírez (1997: 116), Reynolds (1970: 155), Suárez Dávila (2008: 12), and Newell & Rubio (1984: 84).
7 Thorp (1994b: 47, Table 5), Aguilar Camín & Meyer (1993: 167), and E. Cárdenas (2000b: 183).
8 Esquivel & Márquez (2007: 338), Glade (1963: 20), and Bethell & Roxborough (1988: 174).
9 Niblo (1988a: 14).
10 Rivera Marín (1955: 141) and Niblo (1988a: 4).
11 *The Inter-American,* October 1943, p. 4.
12 Aguilar Camín & Meyer (1993: 167).
13 Medin (1990: 105), Wionczek (1986: 292), Rajchenberg (1999: 158–59), and Simpson (1953: 515).
14 Thorp (1998: 129).
15 Niblo (1995: 13; 1999: 361).
16 Niblo (1995: 191) and Seligman (1956: 104–05).
17 Topik & Wells (1998: 21), Velasco (2002: 45), Bauer (2001: 172), and FitzGerald (1994: 99).
18 E. Cárdenas (2000b: 187), Haber et al. (2008: 52), Simpson (1953: 522), Davis (1994: 117), and Niblo (1995: 208).
19 Vernon (1963: 104), Wilkie (1970a: 36), Chang (2008: 112), Niblo (1995: 193, 195), Petricciolí (1988: 855), and L. Meyer (2000: 893).
20 Pereyra (1974: 57).
21 Seligman (1956: 104, 173) and Ramírez (1989: 46).
22 Brachet-Márquez (1994: 84) and Moreno & Flores Caballero (1995: 72), and Urquidi (2001: 117).
23 Gollás (2003: 271), Brachet-Márquez (2004: 251), and Haber (2006: 538).
24 Knight (2007a: 169).
25 De la Peña (1975: 1353), Izquierdo (1964: 269), and P. Smith (1990: 119).
26 L. Meyer (2000: 886), Reynolds (1970: 191), and Seligman (1956: 105).
27 Seligman (1956: 103).
28 Esquivel & Márquez (2007: 341).
29 Moreno & Flores Caballero (1995: 97), Romero (2003: 178), Maxfield (1990 74), and Gil Díaz (1984: 337–38).
30 Villarreal (1988: 316). Mexico (1963a: 112) provided the average urban minimum wage for 1960–1961.
31 Wilkins (1974: 354), Glade (1963: 83), Ramírez (1989: 60), Hansen (1971: 4), and Centeno (1994: 178).
32 Rubio (1992: 74), Beatty (2001: 198), Marichal (2003: 458–60), and Hodges & Gandy (2002: 164).
33 Marichal (2003: 452–53, 461–62) and Sánchez Aguilar (1973: 36).
34 Sánchez Aguilar (1973: 227, 234).
35 Newell & Rubio (1984: 101).
36 Niblo (1995: 202).
37 Bennett & Sharpe (1979c: 152–53) and Middlebrook (1995: 225).

38 Bachelor (2008: 256).
39 Bennett & Sharpe (1985: 109–11) & (1979d: 87).
40 Bennett & Sharpe (1985: 115; 1979d: 66) and INEGI (1994: 640).
41 INEGI (1994: 559)
42 Powell (1956: 73), L. Meyer (2000: 862), Morales (1992: 210), and Philip (1982: 329).
43 Philip (1982: 333).
44 Philip (1982: 331).
45 Grayson (1980: 24–25) and Roxborough (1992: 202).
46 Morales (1992: 213, 228), Grayson (1980: 31), and *New York Times*, March 5, 1952, p. 49.
47 Torres (1979: 286), Randall (1989: 2), Simon (1997: 158), Morales (1992: 224, Table 3), and Pellicer de Brody (1977: 51).
48 Philip (1982: 340–41), Grayson (1980: 33), Brown (1997b: 67), and Grayson (1980: 38).
49 *The Wall Street Journal* (January 26, 1967, p. 1).
50 Mora (1989: 9, 73) and Nolan & Nolan (1988: 16).
51 Brandenburg: (1964: 306), Hart (2002: 3), Robinson (2008: 128), Kastelein (2005b: 29), and López Rosado (1970: 173).
52 Hamnett (1999: 57).
53 Saragoza (2001: 102), Jud (1974: 25–26), and López Rosado (1970: 185).
54 Bulmer-Thomas (1994a: 284, n. 15) and Jud (1974: 20, 32, 34).
55 Sonnenfeld (1992: 31–32).
56 Medina (1978: 231) and Sanderson (1986: 36, Table 1.1).
57 Simonian (1995: 118), Grindle (1986: 101), and McNeill (2000: 221).
58 Grammont (2003: 350), Niblo (1999: 172), Glade (1963: 66), and Warman (1979: 109).
59 Glade (1963: 66) and Evans (2007: 87), Redclift & Goodman (1991: 68, Table 3.10), and United Nations (1951: 181; 1962: 266; 1973: 261).
60 Hewitt de Alcántara (1976: 101) and Medina Peña (1994: 143).
61 Tortolero Villaseñor (2000: 118), Simon (1997: 47–48), Ortiz Monasterio (1987: 236), Wright (1990: 62), USDA (1976: 6), Hewitt de Alcántara (1976: 162), and Murray (1994: 35).
62 Hellman (1978: 193, n. 65), Hamnett (1999: 263), Barry (1995: 31), CDIA (1974: 875), and Hewitt de Alcántara (1976: 154, 309).
63 Fitzgerald (1986: 469), Barkin (1975: 72), CDIA (1974: 200), ECLA (1970: 207, Table 142), and Tortolero Villaseñor (2000: 117).
64 Grindle (1986: 100), E. Cárdenas (2000b: 189), and Hewitt de Alcántara (1976: 23).
65 CDIA (1974: 1028, 1042).
66 Niblo (1995: 267), Hewitt de Alcántara (1976: 312), Warman (1979: 111), and Simpson (1953: 521).
67 Paré (1990: 82), Appendini (2001: 14), Esteva (1975: 1313), Gollás (2003: 296, 270), and Barkin & DeWalt (1988: 31).
68 Gollás (2003: 233, 237) and Schettino (2007: 238).
69 Wionczek (1974: 136), L. Meyer (2000: 887), and Bernstein (1964: 250, 254, 257).
70 French (1988: 92), L. Meyer (2000: 887), and Lustig (1981: 64).
71 Pereyra (1974: 58) and Roxborough (1994: 260).
72 Moreno-Brid & Ros (2009: 4, 255), Ojeda (1972: 300, Table 1), Palma (2003: 127), and Romero (2003: 206, Table VIII).
73 Hansen (1971: 87), E. Cárdenas (2000b: 194–96), and Babb (2001: 117).
74 FitzGerald (2000b: 75), Jenkins (1987: 146), ECLA (1966: 97, Table 97 & 102), E. Cárdenas (2000b: 195), and Banco Nacional de Comercio Exterior (1974: 199).
75 FitzGerald (2000b: 78) and Bennett & Sharpe (1985: 146).
76 Bulmer-Thomas (1994a: 327–28), Thorp (1998: 169), Newfarmer & Mueller (1975: 19), Gómez-Galvarriato (2002: 311), and Cothran (1994: 84).
77 Jenkins (1987: 103, Table 6.1) and Bennett & Sharpe (1985: 100).
78 Urquidi (1967: 187), Bulmer-Thomas (1994a: 312, Table 9.5), and Sepúlveda & Chumacero (1973: 82, Table 16).
79 O'Brien (1999: 145) and Newfarmer & Mueller (1975: 63).

23 THE NEW PARTNERSHIP, 1941–1970

1 Maddison (1985: 31).
2 Torres (1986: 68).
3 Buchenau (2004: 132).

4 Paz (1997: 48, 64–65, 236), L. Meyer (2000: 927), Chacón (2000: 333–34), and Ampudia (1993: 138).
5 L. Meyer (2000: 926), Rankin (2007: 22–23), Dwyer (2008: 258), Thorp (1994a: 123), R. Smith (1997: 191–92), Marichal (2008: 97), Hediger (1943: 80–82), Hart (2002: 414), Aguilar Camín & Meyer (1993: 192–93), and Niblo (1995: 95).
6 Niblo (1999: 78), Thorp (1994b: 45), and Torres (1986: 73).
7 Roxborough (1992: 194–95), Niblo (1995: 90), and Hart (2002: 414).
8 Pike (1995: 274–75), Raymont (2005: 70), and Niblo (1995: 249).
9 Rock (1994: 29), G. Smith (1994: 43), Rabe (1978: 281), Mosk (1950: 17–19), and Niess (1990: 138).
10 Rankin (2007: 32–32) and Bethell (1991: 58–59).
11 Latham (1998: 229), Niblo (1995: 206), Rabe (1978: 291), and Chang (2008: 55).
12 Niblo (1999: 176), Alemán Valdés (1987: 263–77), and Truman (1956: II, 104).
13 P. Smith (1996: 148).
14 CIA (1951: 2).
15 Bethell (1991: 60), P. Smith (1996: 148), and Knight (1987: 13).
16 Krauze (1997a: 655).
17 Bucheneau (1997: 512), Pellicer de Brody & Mancilla (1978: 111), and Langley (1991: 58).
18 Edmonds-Poli & Shirk (2009: 335).
19 Agee (1975: 531) and Suárez Argüello (1989: 3).
20 Information on the declassified documents came from a March 2, 2003 article in *Proceso* by Kate Doyle. The documents and an English-language version of the article can be found at the National Security Archive website. White (2007: 113–20) described Pámanes's spying in detail.
21 Herrera (2007: 216–18), Griswold del Castillo (1990: 160–63), and Martínez (1978: 116).
22 Niemeyer (1986: 185–86) and CIA (1967: 2).
23 L. Meyer (2000: 928) and CIA (1964: 152).
24 Rubio (1992: 74, Table 2.1), Banco Nacional de Comercio Exterior (1977: 227), and Loaeza (1988a: 153).
25 Agee (1975: 525–26, 535) and *Proceso* (October 14, 2001, p. 15).
26 Bustamante (1983: 266), Arizpe (1981: 627), González & Fernández (2002: 25), García (1980: 4, 12), Heyman (1997: 894), and Massey, Durand & Malone (2002: 36).
27 Bustamante (1983: 267) and Ganster (1996: 403).
28 Galarza (1964: 53), Raat (1992: 152), Spenser (2008: 389), Ruiz (1992: 420), Ganster (1996: 404), and Calavita (1997: 158).
29 Matthiessen (1973: 14–15) and Pellicer de Brody & Mancilla (1978: 63).
30 Corwin (1973: 568).
31 Ngai (2004: 161).
32 Ganster & Lorey (2008: 120) and Ngai (2004: 159–160).
33 Ngai (2004: 165), Corwin (1973: 587), Langley (1991: 61), and the *Christian Science Monitor* (September 20, 1999, p. 5).
34 *Congressional Record*, 88th Congress, December 3, 1964, 1st session, p. 23,172.
35 Ngai (2004: 165).
36 Martin (2002: 1128–29), Calavita (1997: 159), and Wilson (2000: 197).
37 Galarza (1964: 244) and Aguilar Camín & Meyer (1993: 194).
38 Bustamante (1987b: 196, Table 2), Galarza (1964: 61), and Martin (2002: 1129).
39 Alba (1976: 155, Table 1) and Bustamante (1983: 268; 1997a: 241–43).
40 Heyman (1997: 893), Cothran (1994: 64, Table 3.3), and Heer (1990: 26, Table. 2.5).
41 Galarza (1964: 48).
42 Langley (1991: 60–61), García (1980: 140), Bustamante (1988: 941), and Ampudia (1993: 146–47).
43 Langley (1991: 45).
44 Bustamante (1983: 260; 1972: 272), García (1980: 227–228), and Lorey (1999: 121–22).
45 Langley (1991: 45), García y Griego (1996: 57), Bustamante (1988: 939), and Simpson (1953: 531).
46 Glade (1963: 205, n. 35), Arizpe (1981: 641), Marshall (1978: 175), Alba (1982: 5), Simpson (1953: 527), and Martínez (1978: 114).
47 Alba (1982: 4), Marshall (1978: 169), Bustamante (1997a: 227), Samora (1971: 19), and Galarza (1964: 62).
48 García (1997: 204), Samora (1971: 5), Turner (1965: 16), and *El Malcriado* [Special Edition] No. 6, p. 3.
49 Lyons (1977: 41).
50 Lorey (1999: 140) and Bustamante (1982: 14–15).
51 Lorey (1999: 121) and Pick (2003: 8).
52 Ganster & Lorey (2008: 83, Table 4.1), Fernández (1977: 124), and Martínez (1978: 114).
53 Lorey (1999: 95–98) and González & Fernández (2002: 47).

54 Clement (1982: 180, Table 9), Herrera (2007: 338–39), and Urquidi & Méndez Villarreal (1978: 143).
55 Urquidi & Méndez Villarreal (1978: 143) and Proffitt (1994: 155).
56 Martínez (1978: 109).
57 Hamnett (1999: 261).
58 Martínez (1978: 144–45) and Lorey (1999: 130–31).
59 Martínez (1978: 99, 123).
60 Lorey (1999: 103–04), Ganster & Lorey (2008: 100–01), and Martínez (1978: 117–19).

24 POLITICS IN TIMES OF CRISIS, 1971–2000

1 Schmidt (1991: 5), Newell & Rubio (1984: 123), Camp (2000: 618), Krauze (1999c: VI, 24), Cothran (1994: 140), and Cornelius (1987: 23).
2 Saldívar (1988: 92), Scherer García & Monsiváis (1999: 205), and Krauze (1999c: VII, 26, 31).
3 Gómez Tagle (1988b: 274: Table 6) and Woldenberg (2002: 91).
4 Newell & Rubio (1984: 130) and FitzGerald (1978: 270).
5 Basáñez (1981: 141), Newell & Rubio (1984: 125, 133), Brachet-Márquez (1996: 186), and Krauze (1997a: 748).
6 Raat (1992: 157), Krauze (1997a: 747), Grayson (1976: 84), and Domínguez & Fernández de Castro (2001: 56).
7 Cornelius (1985: 89), Del Villar (2005: 57–58), Basáñez (1981: 161), Brachet-Márquez (1996: 187, n. 17), Gollás (2003: 238), and Grindle (1977: 532, Table 5).
8 Pellicer de Brody (1977: 47).
9 Del Villar (2005: 57–58).
10 Schmidt (1991: 76).
11 Schmidt (1981: 28; 1991: 100–01), Saldívar (1988: 191), and Story (1986: 36).
12 Whitehead (1980: 498), Cothran (1994: 101), and P. Smith (1990: 132).
13 Cothran (1991: xxiv), Krauze (1997a: 743), Green (1979: 42), Pellicer de Brody (1977: 45–46), and Labastida Martín del Campo (1977: 206).
14 Cothran (1991: xvii), Maxfield (1990: 122), and Aguilar Rivera (2003: 15).
15 Suárez Dávila (2008: 14), Newell & Rubio (1984: 204), Brachet-Márquez (1996: 189), and *New York Times* (December 3, 1976, p. 14A).
16 Hellman (1983: 218) and Holt (1979: 139).
17 Molinar Horcasitas (1991: 81). The law appeared in the *Diario Oficial* (December 6, 1977).
18 Mirón & Pérez (1988: 48) and Sánchez Ruiz (2005: 417).
19 Cothran (1994: 120), Krauze (1997a: 758), and L. Meyer (2003b: 23).
20 Vega (2001: 37), Basáñez (1990: 61–62) and Bazdresch & Levy (1991: 249).
21 Mirón & Pérez (1988: 118, 137), Kraft (1984: 7), P. Smith (1997a: 94), Aguilar Camín & Meyer (1993: 211), FitzGerald (1985: 227), and Maxfield (1990: 130).
22 Bazdresch & Levy (1991: 251), Mirón & Pérez (1988: 134), and Gollás (2003: 240).
23 Kraft (1984: 9, 17–19, 46).
24 *Tiempo* (September 13, 1982, p. 29).
25 McColm (1984: 14) and Maxfield (1990: 49, 142–43, 145).
26 Aguilar Camín (1988: 61) and Mizrahi (2003: 74).
27 Cornelius (1985: 91–92).
28 Aguilar Camín (1982b: 14) and Loaeza (1999: 53).
29 *Fortune* (October 12, 1987, p. 189).
30 Riding (1985: 71) and P. Smith (1990: 143).
31 Hellman (1983: 233), Cornelius (1987: 26), Granados Chapa, Köppen & González Casanova (1985: 197), and *Proceso* (November 9, 1981, p. 29).
32 Hellman (1986: 247–48).
33 Martínez Assad (1987: 36) and *Le Monde* (July 6, 1982, p. 4).
34 Cothran (1994: 120), FitzGerald (1985: 231), Cline (1982–83: 112–13), and Kraft (1984: 46).
35 Cornelius (1985: 93–94; 1986: 8), and De la Peña (1988: 101).
36 Cornelius (1985: 123), Hellman (1983: 231) and Pérez Fernández del Castillo (1999: 94).
37 Garrido (1989: 418), Haber et al. (2008: 124), and Loaeza (1989a: 279).
38 Rodríguez (2003: 198) and Molinar Horcasitas (1991: 124).
39 Riding (1985: 110) and Loaeza (1989a: 281).
40 Aguilar Camín (1988: 72).
41 Aguilar Camín & Meyer (1993: 226) and Story (1986: 72).

42 Cornelius (1987: 24, 27).
43 Alvarado (1985: 2), Granados Chapa, Köppen & González Casanova (1985: 198), Molinar Horcasitas (1991: 159; 1987d: 220, Table 6), Klesner (2005: 107, Table 1), and Gómez Tagle (1988b: 278, Table 10).
44 Castañeda (1985–86: 288) and *The Wall Street Journal* (July 12, 1985, p. 23).
45 Becerra, Salazar & Woldenberg (2005: 56) and *El Norte* (June 15, 2003, p. 10a).
46 The *Diario Oficial* (December 15, 1986, pp. 2–3) published the constitutional amendments that implemented the reform.
47 Becerra, Salazar & Woldenberg (2005: 186–87, 193).
48 Alcocer (1994: 150–51).
49 De la Peña (1988: 105–06), Brachet-Márquez (1996: 206), and Brooks (1987: 30).
50 Brachet-Márquez (1996: 206), Guillén Romo (1990: 83–86), P. Smith (1990: 149), De la Peña (1988: 87), Guillén Romo (1990: 86), Cornelius (1985: 114), Maxfield (1990: 153), and Suárez Dávila (2008: 15).
51 Aguilar Camín & Meyer (1993: 227), L. Meyer (2000: 929), and Arriola (2008: 72).
52 Cornelius (1986: 8), Cothran (1994: 181), Aguilar Camín (1988: 38), and Aguilar Camín & Meyer (1993: 227).
53 Klesner (1994: 159).
54 Garrido (1993: 147) and Grayson (2006: 72).
55 La Botz (1995: 90) and Garrido (1993: 154).
56 *El Cotidiano* (May-June 1987, p. 138).
57 J. Castañeda (2000: 67–70) and *New York Times* (October 8, 1987, p. A39).
58 Aguilar Zínser (1995: 57, 59), Bruhn (1997a: 128, 190), Semo (2001: 52–53), Dresser (1994: 132), and *New York Times* (April 27, 1988, p. A4).
59 Aguilar Camín & Meyer (1993: 241) and WGBH (1988: 12).
60 *Mexico Journal* (April 4, 1988, p. 9).
61 Cothran (1994: 170). In the interest of full disclosure, the author flew on the 727.
62 Gómez Tagle (1994: 65), *Proceso* (July 11, 1988, p. 6), Domínguez & McCann (1996: 151), and *New York Times* (June 22, 1994, p. D5).
63 J. Castañeda (2000: 231–39).
64 *Los Angeles Times* (August 20, 1989, p. 1), Barberán et al. (1988: 74), Preston & Dillon (2004: 173–75), and Cornelius, Gentleman & Smith (1989: 20).
65 *New York Times* (June 22, 1994, p. D5) and Aziz Nassif & Molinar Horcasitas (1990: 170).
66 Grayson (2006: 75) and Krauze (1997a: 770–72).
67 L. Meyer (1989b: 325) and Aziz Nassif (1996: 38).
68 Camp (2003: 255), Dresser (1994: 129), Brachet-Márquez (1996: 215), Reding (1989: 685, 711), Russell (1994: 13), and Domínguez & McCann (1996: 118).
69 L. Meyer (2001: 40) and Del Villar (2005: 73).
70 L. Meyer (1989a: 122).
71 Cothran (1994: 183), L. Meyer (1991d: 29–30), Morris (1995: 100), and Monsiváis (2001: 19).
72 Alcocer (1994: 151–52), L. Meyer (1994: xv-xvi), Loaeza (2003: 86), and Crespo (1995: 61).
73 Langston (2003: 309), Rodríguez & Ward (1994: 38, 42), Hernández Vicencio (2001: 90–98), and Russell (1994: 18–31).
74 The *Diario Oficial* published the constitutional amendments implementing the reform on April 6, 1990 and the implementing legislation (COFIPE) on August 15, 1990.
75 Cansino (2000: 225), Becerra, Salazar & Woldenberg (2005: 274), Klesner (2005: 105, Table 1), *Este País* (September 1991, p. 11), and Cornelius (1991: iii).
76 Basurto (1999: 91).
77 Crespo (1995: 197), Weintraub (1995: 41), Jaime (2004: 29) and *Economist* (February 13, 1993, "Mexico Survey," p. 4).
78 The *Diario Oficial* published the reform legislation (September 3 and September 24, 1993).
79 Hodges & Gandy (2002: 134), Knight (1994b: 64), and Monsiváis (2001: 22).
80 Medina Peña (1994: 250).
81 *The Washington Post* (May 17, 1991, p. A1).
82 Moncayo (1995: 47) and Larrosa & Valdés (1998: 33–34).
83 *Los Angeles Times* (November 2, 1994, p. A4) and *The Miami Herald* (February 6, 1995, p. 11A).
84 Fuentes (1996: 130).
85 *El Financiero* (January 13, 1994, p. 47) and Russell (1995: 55).
86 *La Jornada* (March 7, 1994, pp. 1, 14).
87 *The New York Times* (November 1, 1994, p. A4).
88 *The Wall Street Journal* (April 5, 1994, p. A14) and L. Meyer (2001: 41–42).
89 *El Financiero* (April 4, 1991, p. 19).

90 *Proceso* (April 4, 1994, pp. 6–11).
91 *El Financiero International* (April 4, 1994, p. 14).
92 Bierma (1995: 71), Levy & Bruhn (1999: 546), La Botz (1995: 197), Aguayo (1995: 165), Aziz Nassif & Alonso Sánchez (2003: 69), and Benítez Manaut (1996: 559).
93 Crespo (1995: 244–46).
94 Domínguez & McCann (1996: 202–03) and Aguilar Zínser (1995: 287, 331).
95 *Excélsior* (September 20, 1994, p. 2I). For other evaluations of the 1994 election, see Benítez Manaut (1996: 563, n. 113).
96 Becerra, Salazar & Woldenberg (2005: 371–72) and La Botz (1995: 222).
97 Presidencia de la República (2001: 212) and ECLAC (1999: 238).
98 Dresser (1997a: 65–66) and Jaime (2004: 44).
99 *Wall Street Journal* (July 6, 1995, p. A4).
100 Franko (2003: 207–08).
101 Stamos & Schmidt (1996: 6), Weintraub (1995: 42), and Preston & Dillon (2004: 251).
102 *Wall Street Journal* (July 6, 1995 p. A4).
103 Stamos & Schmidt (1996: 5).
104 *New York Times* (February 1, 1995, pp. A1, A10), *Economist*, February 8, 1995, p. 17, and Stamos & Schmidt (1996: 8).
105 *New York Times* (March 10, 1995, p. 1A) and Cue Mancera (2001: 76).
106 ECLAC (1998: 244), Lorey (1997: 15), Dresser (1997b: 54), Rodríguez (2003: 54), and Aguilar Zínser (1995: 459).
107 Aguilar Zínser (1995: 456), *Wall Street Journal* (June 30, 2000, p. A1), Camp (2000: 628), Aziz Nassif (2003: 401), and Bierma (1995: 86).
108 Molinar Horcasitas (1996: 39) and Domínguez & Fernández de Castro (2001: 108).
109 Haber et al. (2008: 141) and Córdova & Murayama (2006: 19). The text of the reform appeared in the *Diario Oficial* (November 22, 1996).
110 Becerra, Salazar & Woldenberg (2005: 457) and Reyes del Campillo (1997: 7, 9).
111 *Wall Street Journal* (July 11, 1997, p. A15), Greene (2007: 115) and *Los Angeles Times* (July 10, 1997, p. B9).
112 Dresser (1997a: 71), Becerra, Salazar & Woldenberg (2005: 475), ECLAC (2002: 198), and *New York Times* (March 8, 2000, p. C4).
113 Quintana (2001: 149) and *Miami Herald* (July 9, 2000, p. 1E).
114 *Wall Street Journal* (June 30, 2000, p. A1) and *Reforma* (September 1, 2000, p. 1A).
115 Global Exchange (2000: xi).
116 Basáñez (1981: 58), Granados Roldán (1982: 26), and *Proceso* (September 22, 1980, p. 7).
117 Grayson (1998: 9) and Piñeyro (1997: 178–79).
118 *Reforma* (May 23, 2001, p. 4A), Dresser (2003: 343), *Wall Street Journal* (January 31, 2000, p. A13), and Human Rights Watch (1990: 17).
119 Grayson (1998: 9).
120 Grayson (1998: 9), McSherry (1998: 22), *Los Angeles Times* (February 10, 1997, A14).
121 *Proceso*, November 11, 1991, p. 20.
122 *Austin American-Statesman* (February 20, 1997, p. A15), Domínguez & Fernández de Castro (2001: 44), Isacson & Olson (1998: 82), and *Wall Street Journal* (January 31, 2000, p. A1).
123 Domínguez & Fernández de Castro (2001: 46), Isacson, Olson & Haugard (2004: 5), and Camp (2005: 271). See also www.ciponline.org/facts (last updated June 8, 2007). The "717" figure for personnel trained is for the 2001–2004 period.
124 Military balance, 1970–1971 through 2007.
125 *The Other Side of Mexico* (May–June 1991, p. 3) and Bruhn (1998: 119).
126 *Proceso* (July 20, 1997, pp. 20–21) and Bruhn (1998: 124, 132).
127 Bruhn (1999: 95).
128 Palma (2000: 201), Bruhn (1998: 128) and Ross (2000: 221).
129 Meyenberg & Carrillo (1999: 65–66), Levy & Bruhn (2001: 99), and *Proceso* (August 17, 1997, p. 12; May 14, 2000, p. 60).
130 Nuncio (1986: 71).
131 Mizrahi (2003: 64, 76) and Loaeza (1999: 305).
132 Reveles Vázquez (1994: 115) and Mizrahi (1998: 97).
133 Loaeza (1999: 325).
134 Loaeza (1999: 342), Semo (2001: 50), Jarquín Gálvez & Romero Vadillo (1985: 12), and Mizrahi (2003: 67).

135 Middlebrook (2001: 28) and Loaeza (1989a: 290, 310; 1989b: 360–61).
136 Shirk (2001: 59).
137 Bruhn (1998: 130).
138 Cothran (1994: 166–67) and Loaeza (1989a: 166).
139 Preston & Dillon (2004: 198) and L. Meyer (2005b: 29–30).
140 Loaeza (1997: 30; 1999: 102).
141 Oppenheimer (1996: 167) and *La Nación* (September 9, 1994, pp. 4–7).
142 *Etcétera* (November 23, 1995, p. 10) and S. Schmidt (1997: 1125).
143 Hernández Vicencio (2001: 125), Loaeza (2003: 74), *Proceso* (April 12, 1998, p. 19), Espinoza Valle (1999: 235), and Lujambio (2001: 85).
144 Mizrahi (2003: 75) and Loaeza (1999: 567).
145 *El Financiero International* (February 14, 1994, p. 6).
146 Russell (1995: 17)
147 Harvey (1994: 30–31).
148 Le Bot (1997: 45).
149 Montemayor (2001: 91–92), Le Bot (1997: 47), and *Proceso* (January 18, 1998, p. 14).
150 Ross (2003: 11).
151 Benítez Manaut (2001: 363).
152 *El Financiero* (January 2, 1994, p. 16—emphasis in original).
153 *Proceso* Special Edition No. 13 (January 2004, p. 71) and *Los Angeles Times* (May 10, 1998, p. M3).
154 Le Bot (1997: 243) and *Excélsior* (March 3, 1994, p. 46A).
155 *Proceso* Special Number (January 1, 1999, p. 19).
156 Cleaver (2004).
157 Harvey (1999: 257).
158 *Proceso* (January 4, 1998, p. 6).
159 Harvey (1998: 240) and Nadal (1998: 21–22).
160 Womack (1999: 347), Ross (2000: 241), and Hirales (2003: 18).
161 *Washington Report on the Hemisphere* (July 17, 1999, p. 4). See Higgins (2001: 895, n. 14) for references to these UN reports.
162 *Proceso* Special Number No. 13 (January 2004, p. 20).
163 López Monjardin (2000: 140–41) and Preston & Dillon (2004: 460).
164 Levy & Bruhn (2001: 82) and Physicians for Human Rights & Human Rights Watch (1994: 25).
165 Human Rights Watch (1990: 7).
166 Panizza (1993: 209).
167 Panizza (1993: 209–10).
168 *Proceso,* July 27, 2008, p. 35.
169 Krauze (1997a: 742), Cothran (1991: xv), Amnesty International (2007b: 183–84), and *Proceso* (April 16, 2000, p. 27).
170 Amnesty International (1977: 147) and Amnesty International (1982: 154).
171 Amnesty International (1987: 183).
172 Preston & Dillon (2004: 209), Cleary (1997: 30), and Concha Malo (1988: 170–71).
173 Mazza (2001 70), Human Rights Watch (2008: 10–16) and Human Rights Watch (1991: 278–81).
174 Human Rights Watch (1999: 28–29) and Cleary (1997: 35).
175 Amnesty International (1995: 210).
176 Author's interview with Acosta, September 1999.
177 *Miami Herald* (September 20, 1997).
178 *Proceso* (February 1, 2004, p. 9) and Rozental (2004: 111, n. 1).
179 *Proceso* (November 16, 2003, p. 23), Human Rights Watch (2006: 203; 2007: 215), Amnesty International (2007b: 181), and *Noticias* [Oaxaca] (June 7, 2006, p. 8A).
180 *Los Angeles Times* (February 14, 2007), Nathan (2003: 5–6, 8), and Human Rights Watch (2007: 216).
181 *Los Angeles Times* (September 27, 2006), Esteva (2007: 143), *Proceso* (December 24, 2006, p. 26), Stephen (2007: 97), and *El Gráfico* [on line] (March 16, 2007).
182 *El Universal* [on line] (May 29, 2008), "AI: México fracasó en derechos humanos."
183 Panizza (1993: 210) and Amnesty International (2007a).
184 Amnesty International (1991: 42), *La Jornada* (December 8, 1990, p. 3), Human Rights Watch (1997: 127), and Americas Watch (2009: 2).
185 Hellman (1986: 254–55), Panizza (1993: 206), and *Fresno Undercurrent*, at www.fresnoundercurrent.net/node/151.
186 Edmonds-Poli & Shirk (2009: 270).

187 Davis (1993: 51), Centeno (1994: 183), Lustig (1996: 161), Boltvinik (2003: 388; 1994: 102), De Ferranti et al. (2004: 43), and *La Jornada* (November 23, 1999, p. 22).
188 Laurell (1992: 38) and Lustig (1996: 159).
189 Centeno (1994: 202, 207), Boltvinik & Hernández Laos (1999: 151), De Ferranti et al. (2004: 43), Kelly (1999: 23), and Boltvinik (2003: 418).
190 Boltvinik (2000: 20), Rivera et al. (2004: 2564), Oliveira & García (1997: 212), Lustig (2001: 104), *La Jornada* (May 26, 2000 p. 28) and Laurell (2003: 342–44).
191 *Canada Watch* (July 2001, p. 120).
192 Huesca (2006: 63), Levy (2008: 71) and *El Financiero* (August 18, 2006, p. 38).
193 Boltvinik (2004: 337, 345).
194 Alarcón (2003: 481).
195 LaFrance (1996: 219), Zapata (2002: 22), Camarena & Zepeda Patterson (2007: 207), and Bizberg & Meyer (2003: 581).
196 Oliveira, Ariza & Eternod (2001: 886) and *Review of the Economic Situation of Mexico* (June 2001, p. 261).
197 Castells & Portes (1989: 15).
198 *Economist* (January 1, 2005, p. 58).
199 L. Meyer (2000: 935) and *Comercio Exterior* (October 2007, p. 804).
200 Garza (2003: 502–03), CONAPO (2001: 109), and Oliveira & Roberts (1994b: 258–59).
201 Lustig (1988: 11), Portes & Hoffman (2003: 67), Ungar (2006: 171), and *El Universal* [on line] (September 6, 2007), "Presidencia del empleo."
202 Reina, Servín & Tutino (2007: 5).
203 Alarcón (2003: 452, Table 12.3—both per capita GDP figures are in 1990 dollars) and *El Financiero* (March 24, 2004, p. 10).
204 Bizberg & Meyer (2003: 589), De la Garza Toledo (2004: 107), Lustig (2001: 103), Gereffi & Martínez (2005: 144), Heredia (1996: 35), Alarcón (2003: 458–59), and Hufbauer & Schott (2005: 46).
205 Bizberg & Meyer (2003: 589), De la Garza Toledo (2004: 107), Lustig (2001: 103), Gereffi & Martínez (2005: 144), Heredia (1996: 35), and Alarcón (2003: 458–59).
206 Reygadas (2006: 128).
207 *El Universal* [on line] (January 6, 2007), "Salarios paupérrimos."
208 *La Jornada* (November 23, 1999, p. 22) and *Wall Street Journal* (August 4, 2007, p. A8).
209 Portes & Hoffman (2003: 52, Table 2) and Portes (1985: 9–10).
210 *Forbes* listed the billionaires (July 23, 1990, p. 188; July 18, 1994, pp. 194–95) and commented on them (January 30, 1995, p. 46). ECLAC (1996: 248) provided the growth figure.
211 *La Jornada* (August 26, 2000), *Proceso* (December 11, 2005, p. 57), and *Forbes,* (March 26, 2007, p. 136).
212 Camarena & Zepeda Patterson (2007: 201).
213 *Forbes* (March 24, 2008, p. 128).
214 Woldenberg (1988: 203) and Camp (1995b: 69).
215 L. Meyer (2000: 938) and Loaeza (1985c: 222).
216 Aguilar Camín & Meyer (1993: 260–61) and Loaeza (1985b: 271).
217 Lustig (1996: 160) and Samaniego de Villarreal (1990: 55, 64).
218 Loaeza (1989b: 360; 1985c: 236) and Tarrés B. (1990: 87–88).
219 Gilbert (2007: 38, 87, 92).
220 Reid (2007: 219–20) and Gilbert (2007: 99).
221 Camarena & Zepeda Patterson (2007: 115), *USA Today* (February 11, 2008, p. 2A), and Pazos (2006: 10–11). (Interest rates refer to 91-day Certificados de la Tesorería.)
222 González Rodríguez (2005: 468).
223 *El Universal* [on line] (March 31, 2008), "¿Cuál es la solución?"
224 Aguilar García (2001: 399), Payne (1998: 33), and Bizberg (2003c: 201).
225 Bizberg (1993: 301), Whitehead (1987: 173), Boltvinik (1994: 102), and Portes & Hoffman (2003: 49).
226 Middlebrook (1989: 293) and Zapata (1990: 174).
227 Burgess (2003: 81, 87) and Cook (2007: 162).
228 Burgess (1999: 124).
229 Burgess (1999: 123).
230 Middlebrook (1995: 321).
231 Acosta & Culebro (1992: 21).
232 *Christus,* April 1990, p. 56 and Middlebrook (1995: 261).
233 Gutiérrez Garza (1990: 207).
234 Faux (2006: 137).
235 Bachelor (2008: 267).

236 Bizberg (1993: 308) & (1990: 717).
237 Cook (1995: 81–86), Alarcón & McKinley (1997: 506), and Middlebrook (1995: 298).
238 *Houston Chronicle* (May 2, 1995, p. 10A) and *Mexico Labor News & Analysis*, vol. 2, no. 9 (May 2, 1997).
239 Camarena & Zepeda Patterson (2007: 277), Fairris & Levine (2004: 11), Aguilar García (2004a: 103), Quiroz Trejo (2004: 173), and Bacon (2002: 19).
240 Payne (1998: 33) and Bierma (1998: 8).
241 Middlebrook (1989: 302) and *Los Angeles Times* (January 21, 1989, sec. I, p. 8).
242 Hathaway (2000: 198) and Payne (1998: 32).
243 Burgess (2003: 89) and Cook (2007: 166).
244 *Mexico Labor News & Analysis*, vol. 5, no. 9 (December 2000), vol. 8, no. 1 (January 15, 2003), vol. 8, no. 2 (February 2003), vol. 9, no. 1 (January 2004), vol. 10, no. 1 (January 2005).
245 *Proceso* (February 17, 2002, p. 48), Camarena & Zepeda Patterson (2007: 276–77, 269), La Botz (2001: 17), and *Mexico Labor News & Analysis*, vol. 10, no. 8 (August 2005), vol. 11, no. 2 (February 2006).
246 *Financial Times* (December 13, 2005, Special Report, p. 1).
247 Bartra (2004: 36).
248 Harvey (1990: 188), Kelly (1999: 95), and Ochoa (2000: 10).
249 Gordillo (1985: 305), Warman (2001: 160), Fox (1994: 245–46), and Nuijten (2003: 4).
250 Bizberg (2003b: 322), Gordillo (1985: 301), and Harvey (1990: 184).
251 Warman (2001: 167), Favela et al. (2003: 20), Riding (1985: 196), and Warman (2001: 176).
252 Arroyo Picard et al. (2003: 100) and Tello (1991: 59).
253 Levy & Bruhn (2001: 79) and Harvey (1998: 26).
254 Levy & Bruhn (2001: 80), Bacon (2004: 45), and *New York Times* (April 18, 2000, p. C4).
255 Calva (2004a: 16), Stanford (2004: 186), and Fox (1994: 247–48).
256 Davis (2004: 19), Appendini (2003: 262–68), Gereffi & Martínez (2005: 141), and Buckley (2005: 42).
257 L. Meyer (2000: 933) & (2005a: 685), Bartra (2002: 20), Weintraub (2004: 59–60), Levy (2008: 74), *Comercio Exterior* (December 2008, p. 877), and Gollás (2003: 268).
258 O'Boyle (2004: 10) and Appendini (2003: 255).
259 Beals (1975: 15) and A. Bartra (2005: 8).
260 Kelly (1999: 111).
261 Appendini (2003: 260) and *New York Times* (June 17, 2001, I, p. 1).
262 Appendini (2003: 258), Zendejas (1996: 313–16), and Warman (2001: 26).
263 *Proceso* (December 14, 2003, p. 29).
264 INEGI (2003: 3, 14, 499), *Proceso* (March 11, 2001, p. 30), and *Canada Watch* (July 2001, p. 114).
265 Warman (2003: 56) and McSweeney & Arps (2005: 16, Table 2).
266 ORDPI & INI (2002: 33), López & Munro (1999: 130), Cook (2003: 212), and Calderón (1994: 39–41).
267 Pepin Lehalleur (1997: 70) and Warman (2003: 18).
268 Barajas (2002: 69).
269 Harvey (2005: 16), Trejo (2002: 29), and Sarmiento Silva (1996: 376).
270 Hindley (1996: 228) and Sarmiento Silva (1996: 374).
271 Ross (2000: 146).
272 Harvey (1999: 248) and *El Universal* (March 25, 1991, p. 2).
273 Harvey (1999: 247), Pérez Ruiz & Thacker Moll (1994: 377), and Cook (2003: 203–04). The text of the amendment appeared in the *Diario Oficial*, January 28, 1992, p. 5.
274 Díaz-Polanco (1997b: 171).
275 Díaz-Polanco (1997b: 208) and Díaz-Polanco & Sánchez (2002: 40).
276 *Wall Street Journal*, November 2, 2005, p. A14, Mattiace (2005: 245), Sarmiento Silva (1996: 365), and *Proceso* (December 8, 1996, p. 23).
277 Warman (2001a: 207), *Este País* (December 2003, p. 69), and *La Jornada* (September 25, 2000, p. 8).
278 Álvarez (2006: 353) and Gutiérrez Chong (2004: 33).
279 La Botz (2001: 16).
280 Díaz-Polanco (2004: 338).
281 CDI (2005: 88–91, 138).
282 Hernández, Paz, & Sierra (2004: 11), CDI (2005: 138), and *Proceso* (January 15, 2006, p. 32).
283 Nahmad (2008: 137).
284 Lamas (2003: 127).
285 Taino (1997: 258).
286 CONAPO (2001: 156), INEGI (2003: 230), Haber et al. (2008: 178), and *Nexos* (January 2002, p. 82).
287 Rodríguez (2003: 61), *Este País* (May 2000, p. 16), IDB (1995: 68–71), Chant (1991: 16), Taino (1997: 253), Suárez Aguilar (1996: 138), Appendini (2003: 259), and *El Universal* [on line] (September 21, 2008), "Aumenta 40% número de mujeres profesionistas".
288 IDB (1995: 66–67) and *Excélsior* (September 5, 1970, p. 9a).

289 Ramos-Escandón (1994: 200), Stevenson (1999: 558), *Enfoque,* March 6, 2005, pp. 12–23 and *El Universal* [on line] (October 17, 2006).
290 Rodríguez (2003: 188–91, 196, 228) and *Reforma* (March 9, 1997, p. 10A).
291 Lamas (2003: 137).
292 *New York Times* (April 25, 2007, p. A8) and *Proceso* (April 29, 2007, p. 40).
293 *Latin America Monitor—Mexico,* ISSN 0969-5974 (October 2009, p. 6).
294 Brito Domínguez (2001: 21), Lamas (2003: 128), *Proceso* (July 26, 1998, p. 26), and *La Jornada* (May 29, 1997, p. 54).
295 Paz (1972: 45).
296 Levy & Székely (1983: 40) and *Tiempo* (December 7, 1970, p. 12).
297 Zavala de Cosío (1993: 117), Turner (1974: 13), Alba (1982: 117), and Goodwin (1977: 146).
298 Haiman (1997: 1167) and Zavala de Cosío (1993: 120). The 1973 Population Law was published in the *Diario Oficial,* January 7, 1974 and its implementing legislation on November 17, 1976.
299 Salinas de Gortari (1988: 40).
300 INEGI (2003: 3).
301 INEGI (2003: 69), Engelman (2008: 205), and Eberstadt (2001: 47).
302 *Inter-American Development Bank Newsletter,* April 1997, p. 4.
303 Méndez (2001: 41).
304 González Montes (2003: 370).
305 Alba & Potter (1986: 64).
306 INEGI (2003: 74).
307 Tuirán (2002: 75) and *Reforma* (May 4, 2007, p. 13 Nacional.)
308 *El Universal* [on line] (June 29, 2007), "Explosión demográfica."
309 *El Universal* [on line] (April 2, 2007), "Aniversario del CONAPO."
310 J. Castañeda (2004: 121).
311 Padilla López (1996: 193), Bizberg & Meyer (2003: 581), Aguayo (2008: 58), and Cortez (2001: 1911).
312 INEGI (1994: 108; 2003: 235), Ornelas (2001: 187–88), and Aguayo (2008: 57).
313 INEGI (2003: 228) and *El Universal* [on line] (March 4, 2008), "Los que faltan por atender."
314 World Economic Forum (2006: 23), Soria (2002: 99), and *El Universal* [on line] (May 21, 2007), "Bajo reserva."
315 INEGI (2007: 97), Aguayo (2008: 57) and *El Universal* [on line] (March 4, 2008), "Los que faltan por atender."
316 INEGI (2007: 99), Aguayo (2008: 57) and *El Universal* [on line] (March 4, 2008), "Los que faltan por atender."
317 INEGI (1994: 108; 2003: 240), Aguayo (2008: 57), *Este País* (November 2002, p. 53), World Economic Forum (2006: 292) and *El Universal* [on line] (March 4, 2008), "Los que faltan por atender."
318 J. Castañeda (2004: 124, 128), Escobar Latapí & Roberts (1991: 104), Castaños-Lomnitz (2001: 342), Porter & Schwab (2008), *New York Times* (April 20, 2000, p. A3), and *El Universal* [on line] (January 16, 2008), "Mexico y el mundo."
319 *El Universal* [on line] (July 11, 2007), "Discriminación educativa."
320 De la Fuente (2003: 12–13) and *Business Mexico* (November 2003, p. 23).
321 *Proceso* (February 13, 2000, p. 41).
322 Camp (2003: 168).
323 Davis (2006: 4), Ward (2004: 77), Ezcurra & Mazari-Hiriart (1996: 10), and González Salazar (1990: 19, 43).
324 Ward (2004: 108), Niblo & Niblo (2008: 43), and Rodríguez (1997: 228).
325 Ward (2004: 77, 161) and Davis (1994: 276–79).
326 Brea (2003: 27), Izazola & Marquette (1999: 113–14), Villa & Rodríguez (1996: 32), and Davis (1994: 280).
327 Davis (2005: 255), Cornelius (1986: 35), and Bennett (1998: 122–23).
328 Preston & Dillon (2004: 102), La Botz (1995: 72), and Ward (1998: 248).
329 Davis (1994: 281), Preston & Dillon (2004: 98–110), and La Botz (1995: 69).
330 Vite Pérez (2005: 536), Ward (2004: 11, 83), Iracheta Cenecorta (2004: 534), Cano Escalante (2002: 153), Ward & Durden (2002: 5), and *Business Mexico* (September 2005, pp. 34–35).
331 Preston & Dillon (2004: 408).
332 Monsiváis (1996: 39), Pérez Gay (2003: 40), and Preston & Dillon (2004: 410–11).
333 Monsiváis (2000b: 1046) and Schuessler (2003: 321).
334 Riding (1985: 298), Newell & Rubio (1984: 197), Fuentes (1971: 166), and Preston & Dillon (2004: 412). Quesada quipped about the plane crash to Miguel Ángel Corzo, who conveyed remark to the author, personal communication, December 7, 2000.
335 *Proceso* (June 21, 1998, p. 58).
336 P. Smith (1990: 126) and Preston & Dillon (2004: 411–18).
337 Preston & Dillon (2004: 142).

338 Monsiváis (1996: 41–42) and Preston & Dillon (2004: 420–21, 425–6).
339 Pérez Gay (2003: 36).
340 Preston & Dillon (2004: 426) and Camp (2003: 150).
341 Aguilar Rivera (2003: 14).
342 Riding (1985: 83, 124, 126).
343 Cotheran (1994: 170), Oppenheimer (1996: 135), and Lawson (2002: 32). In the interest of full disclosure, the author received free room, board, and transportation while covering Salinas's 1988 campaign. However, no cash was received.
344 Hughes (2003: 9–10) and Lawson (2002: 126).
345 Loaeza (2006: 17).
346 Krauze (1999c: VII: 63) and Vargas (1976: 45).
347 Vargas (1976: 47–48). In 2006, businessman Olegario Vázquez purchased *Excélsior* and hired a new staff, giving the paper a new lease a new on life (*Proceso*, January 15, 2006, p. 18).
348 Granados Chapa (2001: 79) and *La Cultura en México* (August 10, 1976, pp. II-III).
349 Preston & Dillon (2004: 88), Krauze (1984: 10) and *Proceso* (October 9, 1978, pp. 10–11).
350 *Los Angeles Times* (April 18, 1999, p. A26).
351 Fuentes-Berain (2003: 328), Hughes (2003: 19) and *La Jornada* (September 20, 1999, Special Supplement, p. 4).
352 Hughes (2003: 16), Lawson (2002: 72), and *Washington Post* (June 23, 2000, p. A20).
353 Fromson (1996: 131–32), *Forbes* (April 24, 1995, p. 134), and *San Antonio Examiner* (August 22, 1993, p. 16).
354 Lawson (2002: 78), Oppenheimer (1996: 280), Granados Chapa (2001: 82), *Business Mexico* (November 2000, p. 60), *Expansión* (July 10, 2002, p. 34), and *Forbes* (April 24, 1995, p. 134).
355 *Washington Post* (June 23, 2000, p. A20), Lawson (2002: 71), and Hughes (2003: 25- 26).
356 Lawson (2002: 65, 120, 145).
357 Lawson (2004: 187).
358 Fernández & Paxman (2001: 212).
359 Sánchez Ruiz (2005: 414), Granados Chapa (1982: 351), *Wall Street Journal* (February 21, 2001, p. A18), and Hernández & McAnany (2001: 395–96).
360 Lawson (2002: 30) and *Proceso* (July 4, 1994, pp. 6–7).
361 Lawson (2002: 159) and Sánchez Ruiz (2005: 428, Table IV).
362 Fernández & Paxman (2001: 17), Hernández & McAnany (2001: 396), *Forbes* (July 18, 1994, p. 194), and *Los Angeles Times* (March 10, 2005, p. A21).
363 Aguilar Camín & Meyer (1993: 262), Pineda & Paranaguá (1995: 54), Riding (1985: 83), and Fernández & Paxman (2001: 269).
364 Preston & Dillon (2004: 307).
365 Hernández & McAnany (2001: 397, 404), Sutter (1996: 15), *New York Times* (July 22, 1996, pp. C1–3), and Hughes & Lawson (2005: 13, Table 1).
366 *Houston Chronicle* (April 18, 1997 p. 1A) and Fernández & Paxman (2001: 21, 413–14, 642).
367 Lawson (2002: 109).
368 Lawson (2002: 174).
369 Lawson (2002: 159–60; 2004: 189, Table 8.1).
370 Lawson (2002: 119) and Hughes & Lawson (2004: 83–84).
371 Fernández & Paxman (2001: 625–26).
372 *Wall Street Journal* (February 10, 2006, p. A19) and *Christian Science Monitor* (January 23, 2007, p. 12).
373 Sánchez Ruiz (2005: 447) and *Proceso* (July 20, 2008, p. 54).
374 Hughes & Lawson (2005: 11), *Amnesty International* (Fall 2008, p. 13), *Miami Herald* (October 21, 2005; August 11, 2005), *Washington Post* (May 30, 2007), and *Austin American-Statesman* (February 8, 2006, p. A4).
375 Camp (1997: 111).
376 Blancarte (2005: 252), Camp (1997: 216–17), and Riding (1985: 90).
377 D. Bailey (1986: 241) and Loaeza (1984b: 162).
378 Camp (2000: 621) and Blancarte (2005: 277).
379 Blancarte (2005: 280) and Loaeza (1996: 107).
380 J. Meyer (1997b: 260). The *Diario Oficial* (January 28, 1992, pp. 3–6) published the constitutional changes.
381 Camp (1997: 32–34, 219).
382 Blancarte (2002: 47), *Este País* (August 1991, p. 5), and *El Universal* [on line] May 29, 2007.
383 Patterson (2003: 14), Blancarte (2005: 225), and *Este País* (March 2001, p. 69).
384 Patterson (2003: 7–8).
385 Gill (1999: 20–23), Patterson (2003: 5), and *Economist* (July 27, 2002, p. 35).
386 *El Heraldo* [on line] (April 20, 2007).

25 PLUNGING BACK INTO THE INTERNATIONAL MARKET, 1971–2000

1 Roxborough (1994: 248).

2 Gentleman (1987: 43) and Alba Vega & Valencia Lomelí (2003: 247).

3 L. Meyer (2000: 896), De la Garza Toledo (1994: 196), Dussel Peters (2000: 84) and Gentleman (1987: 53).

4 Gollás (2003: 265) and Arroyo Picard et al. (2003: 18). Many feel that had sound economic policies been adopted, the "Mexican miracle" need not have ended in an economic bust. For example, Alejandro Gertz Manero speculated on what might have occurred if fiscally conservative treasury secretary (1958–1970) Antonio Ortiz Mena, widely viewed as the man behind the miracle, had been selected as president for the 1970–1976 term rather than the fiscally reckless Echeverría (*El Universal* [on line] (March 21, 2007), "Políticos excepcionales").

5 Bizberg (2003a: 106).

6 Lustig (1992: 29). As Stiglitz & Charlton (2005: 21) note, some observers consider that the Latin American debt crisis resulted, not from a fatally flawed import-substitution model, but from poor debt management compounded by devastating increases in interest rates.

7 Jaime (2004: 39), P. Smith (1990: 150), and Cypher (1990: 189).

8 Briggs (1995: 40), Calva (2004b: 102), and Ros (1992: 56, Table 1).

9 Gutiérrez R. (1989: 5–7).

10 Portes (1997: 238), Chang (2008: 12), and Ibarra (2005: 56).

11 Calva (2004b: 122–23).

12 Luna, Tirado & Valdés (1987: 25), Cypher (1990: 181), Abruch Linder (1983: 28), and Davis (1992: 656, 665).

13 De la Madrid (2004: 379). Lowenthal (1992–93: 78) noted the lack of credible alternatives facilitated similar policy shifts throughout Latin America.

14 Félix (1992: 32).

15 Camp (2000: 613), Babb (2001: 171–84), and Massey, Durand, & Malone (2002: 78).

16 Ibarra (2005: 74), Stiglitz & Charlton (2005: 16), Greider (1997: 279), Ibarra (2005: 74), and Stiglitz (2002: 92).

17 Torres (2005: 209) and Russell (1994: 183).

18 *Tiempo* (May 3, 1990, p. 59).

19 Lustig & Ros (1999: 30).

20 *Le Figaro* (August 1, 1991, p. 4) and *Business Week* (August 12, 1991, p. 34).

21 RMALC (1991: 7).

22 *Business America* (August 24, 1992, p. 25) and Hufbauer & Schott (2005: 5).

23 *Business Week* (July 27, 1992, p. 45).

24 *New York Times* (February 18, 2007, Sec. 4, p. 4).

25 Hufbauer & Schott (1993: 47–60), Lustig (2001: 97), and *The Other Side of Mexico* (March–April 1991, p. 6).

26 *Wall Street Journal* (March 30, 1990, p. A14).

27 Romero (2003: 205).

28 Pastor & Wise (2005: 101) and *Los Angeles Times* (March 7, 2000, p. B7).

29 Rockefeller (1969: 87).

30 Russell (1994: 161), Marichal (2005: 681), and Babb (2001: 9). Before 1970, Mexico had largely financed industrial expansion with agricultural exports, domestic investment, and FDI. During the 1960s, factors such as uncertainty generated by the Cuban Revolution, the radical rhetoric of Mexican leaders, and Mexico's requiring 51 percent domestic ownership in firms in which foreigners invested caused FDI to decline. To compensate for declining foreign investment, Mexico began to borrow abroad, causing the foreign debt to increase from $813 million in 1960 to $3.2 billion in 1970.

31 Crandall (2005: 65).

32 Aguilar Camín & Meyer (1993: 170) and Moreno & Flores Caballero (1995: 169, 180, 213).

33 Marichal (1997d: 26) and L. Meyer (2003b: 23).

34 Dussel Peters (2000: 60) and Blanco (1985: 425).

35 Marichal (1997d: 27) and Moreno & Flores Caballero (1995: 207).

36 Vásquez (1997: 267) and Marichal (2003: 472).

37 Moreno & Flores Caballero (1995: 209) and Marichal (2003: 484).

38 Davis (2006: 148).

39 Centeno (1994: 198).

40 P. Smith (1997a: 95), Payer (1991: ix), and M. Miller (1991: 64).

41 IDB (1990: 307), Moreno & Flores Caballero (1995: 214), Salinas de Gortari (2002: 531), and *The Other Side of Mexico* (November–December 1989, p. 8).

42 Sachs (1989: 87).

43 *Proceso* (February 12, 1990, p. 30) and *Forbes* (March 6, 1989, p. 39).
44 Ros (2003: 224), IDB (1996: 398, Table E-7), Salinas de Gortari (2002: 531), and Haber et al. (2008: 174).
45 *Este País* (April 2006, p. 19), Alarcón (2003: 452, Table 12.3), and *La Jornada* (March 12, 2000, p. 17).
46 *El Economista* (August 11, 2006, p. 9) and *Wall Street Journal* (August 11, 2006, p. A5). As with many statistics, politicians choose figures which favor them. By 2008, according to conventional accounting, Mexico's foreign debt had declined to $25.7 billion (*El Universal* [on line] April 27, 2008). Calva (2004b: 111) totaling not only government borrowing, but private corporate borrowing, bank debt, and securities, as well debts of Pemex, which are usually calculated separately from the government's debt, found Mexico to owe foreigners $372 billion.
47 Marichal (2003: 473) and Russell (1994: 164, 168–69).
48 *Expansión* (August 22, 2001, p. 73), *La Jornada* (August 19, 2006, p. 26; August 16, 2006, p. 31).
49 *New York Times* (August 23, 1997, p. 3).
50 Székely (1999: 28) and Prager (1992: 304–05).
51 Prager (1992: 301).
52 Hernández Chávez (2006: 302), La Botz (1992: 95), and Teichman (1996: 155).
53 Chaffin (1997: 39).
54 Bacon (2002: 17), *Business Mexico,* Special Edition, 2004, p. 10, and *Expansión* (March 22, 2006, p. 108; March 3, 2008, p. 30).
55 Marichal (1997c: 30) and Heredia (1996: 35).
56 *Business Latin America* (October 16, 2006, p. 4), *Financial Times* (December 13, 2005, Special Report p. 3), and *Wall Street Journal* (August 4, 2007, p. A8).
57 *Wall Street Journal* (June 9, 2000, p. A19; February 10, 2006, p. A19).
58 *Financial Times,* July 5, 1995, p. 5 and *Business Mexico* (February 2001, p. 29).
59 *Reforma* (August 15, 2006, p. 2 "Nacional") and *Los Angeles Times* (April 20, 2007, p. A3).
60 Székely (1999: 14) and Ebrard (1999: 38).
61 Doman (1998: 156) and *Wall Street Journal* (November 3, 1995, p. A15).
62 *Business Mexico* (September 2004, p. 38), *New York Times* (December 31, 1994, p. 53), and Rosen (1998: 13).
63 Grayson (2006: 142).
64 *Vértigo* (August 13, 2006, p. 59), *La Jornada* (July 4, 2006, p. 26), and *Este País* (February 2003, p. 14).
65 Rubio (1999: 100) and Chang (2008: 120).
66 Voljc & Draasima (1993: 126).
67 Cahill (2001: 23).
68 Teichman (1988: 56).
69 Kraft (1984: 34) and Rousseau (2006: 28).
70 Williams (1979: 42) and Urquidi (2005: 308–09).
71 Grayson (1980: 47) and *Wall Street Journal* (June 15, 2005, p. A9).
72 Urquidi (2001: 120), L. Meyer (1979: 6), and Philip (1982: 355).
73 Teichman (1988: 58) and *Comercio Exterior de México* (October 1976, p. 372).
74 Philip (1988: 32) and Székely (1983: 69).
75 Riding (1985: 169) and Williams (1982: 31).
76 Lomnitz & Pérez-Lizaur (1987: 50), Riding (1985: 168), *Forbes* (August 15, 1977, p. 28), and *Petroleum Economist* (September 1977, p. 374).
77 Székely (1983: 77), Urquidi (2005: 319), Teichman (1983: 9), *Petroleum Economist* (December 1982, p. 484), and Moreno & Flores Caballero (1995: 190).
78 Grayson (1981: 379; 1988: 54) and NAFINSA (1984: 262). Brower (2007: 22) discusses the interplay between oil, population, and development.
79 *Proceso* (March 27, 1978, p. 31) and Teichman (1983: 15; 1988: 80).
80 Matías Alonso (1996: 26–27) and Simon (1997: 159). Maxfield (1990: 123) summarized the arguments of those advocating a go-slow approach to oil development.
81 Burger (1997: 30, Table 2.1) and Williams (1982: 39–40).
82 Loyola Díaz & Martínez Pérez (1994: 306), *Expansión* (March 17, 1999, p. 46), Teichman (1996: 165, n. 1), and *El Universal* [on line] (August 29, 2008), "Regreso de la leyenda negra."
83 *Business Week* (August 12, 1991, p. 35), Grayson (1992: 12), and *Zeta* (June 21, 1991, pp. 2B-3B).
84 Riding (1985: 171) and Grayson (1991: 7).
85 Riding (1985: 171), Loyola Díaz & Martínez Pérez (1994: 297–98), and Rousseau (2006: 48).
86 *Los Angeles Times* (April 24, 1996, p. 1A), *Petroleum Economist* (September 2006, p. 47), and *Wall Street Journal* (June 2, 2000, p. A15).
87 *World Oil* (February 2006, p. 61) and *Petroleum Economist* (October 2004, p. 48).
88 *Petroleum Economist* (April 2007, p. 47; July 2009, p. 39).
89 *Petroleum Economist* (November 2006, p. 36), Shields (2006: 28), and *El Universal* [on line] (July 22, 2008), "Tiene México petróleo para 6 años más."

90 *Offshore* (January 2005, p. 42) and Shields (2005: 60). If these deep-water finds reverse the production decline, Mexico's production curve, rather than having a classic bell shape, will have three humps, one from 1921, one from the Fox administration, and one from deep water production. For an example of a two-humped production curve, see *Oil & Gas Journal* (April 3, 2006, p. 40).
91 *Wall Street Journal* (June 15, 2005, p. A9), *Latin American Mexico & NAFTA Report,* ISSN 0968-2724 (September 2008, p. 12), and Olson (2005: 4).
92 *El Universal* [on line] (February 8, 2007; June 1, 2007), "Una reforma para Pemex," Muñoz Leos (2006: 122), Shields (2005: 11, 23), *Proceso* (March 2, 2008, p. 25), *El Universal* [on line] (November 13, 2007), "El dilema de Pemex," and Greenpeace Mexico (2006: 12). By accounting convention, Pemex's foreign debt obligations are not included as part of Mexico's foreign debt.
93 *Latin American Mexico & NAFTA Report* (June 2008, p. 1).
94 *New York Times* (October 10, 2003, p. 1) and *Wall Street Journal* (June 15, 2005, p. A9).
95 Bennett & Sharpe (1985: 3).
96 Shaiken (1994: 43), Ramírez de la O (1983: 171), *Automotive News* (January 11, 1982, p. 26), and *Review of the Economic Situation of Mexico* (September 1994, p. 325).
97 Shaiken (1994: 43), Carrillo (1995: 88), and Carr (1996: 224).
98 Ramírez de la O (1998: 63, Table 3.3) and Carrillo (1995: 89–91).
99 *Ward's Auto World* (January 1987, p. 40), Carrillo (1995: 90–91), and Bayón (1997: 66).
100 Ramírez de la O (1998: 63, Table 3.3).
101 *Comercio Exterior* (April 2004, p. 358), Middlebrook & Zepeda (2003: 20), *Expansión* (June 25, 2007, p. 219), and *Business Mexico* (October 2001, p. 40).
102 Máttar, Moreno-Brid & Peres (2003: 147), *Expansión* (September 17, 2003, p. 59), *Ward's Auto World* (February 2006, p. 23), and *Automotive News* (January 28, 2008, p. 17).
103 Vega & de la Mora (2003: 176, n. 18) and *Expansión* (September 28, 2005, p. 89).
104 *Automotive News* (January 10, 2005, p. 54), (January 15, 2007, p. 53; January 28, 2008, p. 17), *Review of the Economic Situation of Mexico* (December 2006–January 2007, p. 447), *Expansión* (June 25, 2007, p. 219), *Latin American Mexico & NAFTA Report* (November 2006, p. 11), and *Latin America Monitor* (December 2006, p. 6).
105 *Latin America Monitor: Mexico* (September 2008, p. 6; October 2009, p. 6).
106 Gereffi & Martinez (2005: 130) and Faux (2006: 208).
107 *Latin American Mexico & NAFTA Report* (May 2007, p. 11) and *El Financiero* (July 14, 2009, p. 12).
108 David Ibarra, *El Universal* [on line] (February 21, 2007), "Un ensayo importante."
109 *El Financiero* (November 14, 1990, p. 42).
110 Russell (1994: 203).
111 Russell (1994: 203).
112 Ros (2008: 543).
113 *Forbes* (September 2, 1991, p. 78) and Robinson (2008: 108).
114 *Twin Plant News* (January–February 1994, p. 41; May 2001, pp. 54–55; January 2004, pp. 54–55; March 2007, pp. 54–55), Robinson (2008: 111), Faux (2006: 137), *El Universal* [on line] (February 21, 2007), "Un ensayo importante," and INEGI (2007: 390, Table 13.30). Exact figures for the increase in maquiladora employment after 2002 are unavailable since INEGI, the government statistical agency, ceased compiling this data (Mike Patten, editor, *Twin Plant News,* personal communication, October 13, 2008).
115 Sinkin (1989: 45–56).
116 Spalding (2000: 78–79) listed forty-seven types of environmental problems. Pombo (2000: 275) commented on Tijuana. Greenpeace Mexico (2006: 10) reported on Otay Mesa.
117 Reygadas (1991: 19), Roman & Velasco Arregui (2001: 60), and *Maclean's* (December 3, 1990, p. 51).
118 *Twin Plant News* (May 2006, p. 5) and Russell (1994: 209).
119 *MB* [*Mexico Business*] (April 2000, p. 3).
120 Budd (1986: 14–15), Kastelein (2005a: 33), and *Latin America Monitor: Mexico* (June 2006, p. 6).
121 *Latin America Monitor: Mexico* (August 2009, pp. 6–8).
122 Budd (1986: 16).
123 Martí (1985: 7), *New York Times* (July 31, 1994, Sec. 5, p. 3), and Clancy (1995: 7–8, 10).
124 Martí (1985: 49) and Clancy (1995: 10- 11).
125 *Wall Street Journal* (November 29, 2005, p. D3), *Financial Times* (December 19, 2005, p. 4), and INEGI (2006: 11).
126 Budd (1986: 14), *MB* [*Mexico Business*] (April 2000, p. 36), Clancy (1995: 10), and *New York Times* (January 19, 2007, Sec. F, p. 1).
127 *Proceso* (October 8, 2000, pp. 43–44).
128 *Business Mexico* (May 2003, p. 21) and *Reforma* (February 3, 2003, pp. 1A, 12A).
129 Cooper (2003: 17–18).

130 ECLA (1976: 282), De Janvry (1981: 130), Gollás (2003: 232), Maxfield (1990: 68, Table 1), and Warman (1978: 686; 1983: 206–07).
131 Kelly (1999: 94), Grindle (1986: 103-chart), Warman (1983: 218), and Ortiz Monasterio (1987: 234).
132 Barkin & De Walt (1988: 33–34, 40).
133 Mares (1982: 81–82, 87).
134 Esteva (1982a: 60–61) and Zermeño (1993: 289).
135 Davis (1994: 19) and Stiglitz & Charlton (2005: 24).
136 Appendini & Liverman (1994: 155, 161), A. Bartra (2004: 23), Suárez & Pérez (1993: 95), Gates (1996: 44, 47), Pollan (2008: 68), Grammont (2003: 352), Medina Peña (1994: 271–71), and *El Universal* [on line] (May 22, 2008), "Cuándo se hundió el campo?"
137 Zermeño (1995: 61), Grammont (2003: 364), Appendini & Liverman (1994: 161), and Jaime (2004: 54).
138 Grindle (1995: 48), L. Meyer (2000: 942), Gates (1996: 55), Nuijten (2003: 161), Thiesenhusen (1995: 46–47), and *Nexos* (April 1999, p. 15). The text of the amendment to Article 27 can be found in *Diario Oficial* (January 6, 1992) and the implementing legislation in *Diario Oficial* (February 26, 1992).
139 Jaime (2004: 53), Thiesenhusen (1996: 41–44), and Toledo (1996: 248–49, 257). The ejido has long been a source of controversy, with conservatives railing against it and the left defending it. Jaime (2004: 64, n. 22) takes the middle ground and, while seeing the ejido as positive, suggests that it would have been better to have ended the land reform in 1940.
140 Jaime (2004: 64, n. 24).
141 Nadal (2003: 152–53) and *New York Times* (February 18, 2007, sec. 4, p. 4).
142 Grammont (2003: 376–77), Alarcón (2003: 455), and *Los Angeles Times* (April 1, 2006, p. C3; March 3, 2008, p. 5A).
143 *Los Angeles Times* (April 1, 2006, p. C3), Mella & Mercado (2006: 168), *La Jornada* (June 7, 2006, p. 27), Cortés et al. (2005: 229, n. 8), Veeman, Veeman & Hoskins (2002: 10), *Comercio Exterior* (October 2007, p. 801), and *El Universal* [on line] (May 22, 2008), "Cuándo se hundió el campo?"
144 A. Bartra (2005: 10), Faux (2003b: 36; 2006: 133), Jaime (2004: 56), *Euromoney* (September 2001, p. 148), and *Proceso* (December 30, 2007, p. 11).
145 *Los Angeles Times* (April 23, 2004, p. B13), *Reforma* (July 21, 2009, p. 1), and *El Universal* [on line] February 7, 2007, "Agricultura y políticas públicas."
146 *Los Angeles Times* (January 17, 2000, p. A1).
147 *Proceso* (December 30, 2007, p. 11), *Economist* (January 26, 2008, p. 38), *El Financiero* (December 29, 2008, p. 10), and *El Universal* [on line] (May 24, 2008), "Carestía de alimentos".
148 *Chemical & Engineering News* (May 7, 2007, p. 50), *Wall Street Journal* (January 18, 2007, p. A10), *Los Angeles Times* (January 12, 2007, p. C3), L. Brown (2006: 7), and *El Universal* [on line] (January 20, 2007).
149 Urquidi (2003: 575).
150 Knochenhauer (2003: 20).
151 *Business Mexico* (April 2001, p. 48), *Austin American-Statesman* (October 14, 1999, p. A2), Aguayo (2008: 17), Brown, Gardner & Halweil (1999: 68), and Warman (2003: 140).
152 Greenpeace México (2006: 4, 14) and Arroyo Picard et al. (2003: 28).
153 Knochenhauer (2003: 20) and Mumme (1992: 123).
154 *Expansión* (July 7, 2008, pp. 84–88) and L. Brown (2006: 9, 52).
155 L. Brown (2006: 48), Quadri de la Torre (2006: 88), and Greenpeace México (2006: 6).
156 *Excélsior* (February 5, 2007, p. 17) and Worldwatch Institute (2008: 23).
157 Sheinbaum (2008: 8), Quadri de la Torre (2007: 128), *Wall Street Journal* (October 6, 2008, p. R4), and *El Universal* [on line] (May 20, 2008), "Datos soberanos."
158 Luis Miguel Galindo, *La economía del cambio climático en México* (available on-line), summarized in *El Universal* [on line] (June 3, 2009).
159 Russell (2000: 16–18) and *Proceso* (March 5, 2000, p. 81).
160 *Proceso* (January 21, 2001, p. 32; October 20, 2002, p. 46).
161 Bray (2007: 54–56).
162 Gallagher (2004: 27), Schatan (2003: 139), and Malkin (2000: 23).
163 Levy & Bruhn (2001: 18), Gallagher (2003: 123), and "Living on Earth," *National Public Radio*, July 8, 2005.
164 Stiglitz & Charlton (2005: 24).
165 *Proceso* (November 4, 2001, p. 53), *Wall Street Journal* (March 5, 2007, p. A24), and *Expansión* (September 18, 2002, p. 33; September 1, 2004, p. 66). By 2009, Wal-Mart had slipped behind América Móvil in sales (*Expansión*, June 22, 2009, p. 156).
166 *Foreign Policy* (September–October 2002, p. 60) and *Twin Plant News* (December 2006, p. 9).
167 *Latin Trade* (May 2006, p. 34).
168 Hufbauer & Schott (2005: 18).
169 *Los Angeles Times* (January 2, 2004, p. A36).
170 Hufbauer & Schott (2005: 45, Table 1.9).

171 Arroyo Picard et al. (2003: 18, 32) and Stiglitz & Charlton (2005: 28).
172 Arroyo Picard et al. (2003: 25) and *Business Latin America* (May 14, 2007, p. 6).
173 José Luis Calva, "Modelo de desarrollo," *El Universal* [on line] (August 20, 2009).
174 Arroyo Picard et al. (2003: 27, 41) and Faux (2006: 135).
175 A. Bartra (2005: 11) and *La Jornada* (June 9, 2006, p. 33).
176 Cypher (2001: 21).
177 Ros (2008: 538, Table 1).
178 *El Universal* [on line] (July 27, 2008), "México en 2008."
179 *El Economista* (July 6, 2006, p. 8). Ranking is based on purchasing power parity.
180 Stiglitz & Charlton (2005: 40), Levy (2008: 2), and *Economist* (January 1, 2005, p. 58).
181 *Economist* (January 16, 1999, p. 23), *Los Angeles Times* (August 6, 2006, p. C1) and Hufbauer & Schott (2005: 51–52). Transparency International reports can be found at www.transparency.org.
182 *Business Week* (August 6, 2001, p. 43) and cnnexpansion.com accessed 5/17/07, *El Universal* [on line] (September 9, 2007), "México y el mundo." Global Competiveness Reports can be found at www.weforum.com.
183 Weintraub (2004: 58).
184 *Business Week* (December 8, 2003, p. 30), Chang (2008: 99), and Stiglitz & Charlton (2005: 38).
185 Gallagher & Porzecanski (2008: 197), *Wall Street Journal* (December 31, 2007 p. A3), *Expansión*, (January 21, 2008, p. 73), *Business Week* (September 23, 2002, p. 60), *Wall Street Journal* (March 5, 2004, p. A8), *Business Mexico* (November 2005, p. 6), IMF (2009: 402–03), *Comercio Exterior* (August 2009, p. 626), *Los Angeles Times* (December 14, 2003, p. A3), and *Business Latin America* (May 15, 2006, p. 4). Chinese-made Virgin of Guadalupe figures are indeed sold at the Basilica of the Virgin. One of them graces the author's desk.
186 Stiglitz (2002: 214), Greider (2001: 23), and Faux (2006: 200).
187 Ros (2008: 539, Table 2, 540).
188 Moreno-Brid & Jaime Ros (2009: 240–43).
189 Gallagher & Zarsky (2007: 4, 5, 10). In drafting regulations for investment during both the import-substitution and neoliberal eras, the Mexican government ignored its previous success in requiring technology transfer. In the 1920s, as Waters (2006: 223) noted, the Mexican government required U.S. construction firms to employ Mexicans in technical positions. These technicians soon became so proficient at roadbuilding that Mexico no longer need the expertise of foreign firms.

26 THE END OF NATIONALISM, 1971–2000

1 Lowenthal (1990: 70).
2 *Este País* (November 1996, p. 38), Harvey (1998: 239), and *Proceso* (July 6, 2003, p. 28).
3 Riding (1985: 324–25).
4 Domínguez & Fernández de Castro (2001: 19), Purcell (1998: 103), P. Smith (1990: 128), and *Comercio Exterior* (October 1972, p. 939).
5 Grayson (1980: 161) and Moreno & Flores Caballero (1995: 180–81).
6 Pellicer de Brody (1982: 22) and Riding (1985: 333).
7 Mazza (2001: 16), Purcell (1997: 139), and Loaeza (1995: 22).
8 *Los Angeles Times* (July 2, 1986, Pt. II, p. 5), Ojeda (1987: 27), and *Proceso* (July 6, 2003, p. 28).
9 Ronfeldt (1988: 54) and Mazza (2001: 152).
10 Mazza (2001: 16).
11 L. Meyer (1991b: 217), Nuncio (1986: 72–73), and Mazza (2001: 26).
12 Mazza (2001: 45), L. Meyer (1991b: 217), and Dresser (1993: 90).
13 L. Meyer (2003b: 142), Domínguez & Fernández de Castro (2001: 34), and *World Press Review* (January 1989, p. 64).
14 Mazza (2001: 68).
15 J. Castañeda (1990: 410–12).
16 Domínguez & Fernández de Castro (2001: 14, 27, 31, 131, 133).
17 Fox (2007: 195).
18 *Economist* (September 22, 2001, p. 35).
19 Davidow (2004: 8), Ross (2006: 110), Valenzuela (2005: 60), and *Christian Science Monitor* (March 15, 2006, p. 9).
20 Gómez Muñoz (2004: 30), Domínguez & Fernández de Castro (2001: 6), and Weintraub (1990: 4).
21 J. Castañeda (1996: 95–100).
22 Suárez-Orozco (1999: 239).
23 Bizberg & Meyer (2003: 580) and Ocegueda Hernández & Plascencia López (2004: 878, Table 2).
24 INEGI (2006: 11) and Herrera (2007: 338).

25 *Proceso* (February 20, 2005, p. 68), Arreola & Curtis (1993: 204), and Herrera (2007: 334).
26 *Expansión* (October 7, 1998, p. 119) and *New York Times* (March 28, 2007, p. C8).
27 Alfie (2002: 29), Greenpeace México (2006: 10), and *New York Times* (February 11, 2001, sec. 1, p. 6).
28 Herrera (2007: 338, 342), Aguayo (2007: 183–209), Ganster & Lorey (2008: 126–27), and Aguilar Camín & Meyer (1993: 267).
29 Shifter (2007: 61).
30 Hernández (2006: 21) and P. Smith (1999: 194).
31 Andreas (2000: 41), Toro (1995: 62), Del Villar (1988: 200), *Rolling Stone* (July 19, 1973, p. 26), Doyle (1993: 85) and Carlsen (2007).
32 Andreas (2000: 40) and Doyle (1993: 85).
33 Toro (1995: 18), Andreas (2000: 41), and Freeman & Sierra (2005: 288).
34 Massing (2000: 29) and Toro (1995: 44).
35 Bagley & Tokatlian (1999: 221, 229), Martínez (2006: 146), Andreas (2000: 56), and Doyle (1993: 85).
36 Raat (1992: 168–69), P. Smith (1997b: 127), and Andreas (2000: 46).
37 Benítez Manaut (2001: 404–05), Massing (2000: 28), Ruiz (1998: 180), and *El Universal* [on line] (January 2, 2007), "Consumo y narcocultura."
38 *Tiempo* (December 13, 1988, p. 39), Salinas de Gortari (2002: 350), Freeman & Sierra (2005: 285), Andreas (1996: 56; 2000: 60), and *El Financiero International* (August 2, 1993, p. 14).
39 P. Smith (1999: 193) and Payan (2006: 103).
40 Shifter (2007: 61), Rocha (2005: 214), *Proceso* (April 16, 2006, p. 32), and *El Universal* [on line] (March 19, 2007), "Pulso político."
41 P. Smith (1999: 199), Camarena & Zepeda Patterson (2007: 330), *Los Angeles Times* (November 14, 2006, p. A4), and *El Universal* [on line] (December 3, 2008), "Ejecuciones ropen récord: van cinco mil."
42 Massing (2000: 28) and *Economist* (March 6, 2004, p. 34).
43 *Washington Post* (June 16, 2005, p. 1A) quoted Chabat. Others declaring that the drug war has been a failure include AFSC (1999: 7, 18), Aguiar (2006: 120), Andreas (2000: 21), Bagley & Tokatlian (1999: 231), Benítez Manaut (2001: 410), Bertram & Sharpe (1997: 22), Carpenter (2003: 121), Doyle (1993: 88), Freeman & Sierra (2005: 263, 294), Isacson (2005: 56), Massing (2000: 29), L. Meyer (2000: 931), Neild (2005: 61–62), Payan (2006: 95, 109), Preston & Dillon (2004: 347), Sierra Guzmán (2003: 1), Toro (1995: 36), Youngers & Rosin (2005: 4–5), and *Wall Street Journal* (February 21, 2006, p. A19).
44 *Wall Street Journal* (February 21, 2006, p. A19) and Toro (1995: 68).
45 P. Smith (1999: 204), Andreas (1998: 161–63), *Wall Street Journal* (March 20, 2009, p. A9), and *Latin American Weekly Report* (March 19, 2009, p. 14).
46 Neild (2005: 74), Freeman & Sierra (2005: 264), and Davidow (2004: 58).
47 *El Financiero International* (August 2, 1993, p. 14) and Toro (1995: 39).
48 Thelen (1999: 618).
49 U.S. (2006: 91) and Marshall (1978: 167).
50 Andreas (2000: 36), Massey, Durand & Malone (2002: 47), and Briggs (1978: 212).
51 Massey, Durand & Malone (2002: 45).
52 Alba (1978: 502), *Washington Post* (March 26, 1978, p. A1), and Marshall (1978: 178).
53 Weintraub (1990: 193), L. Meyer (1989c: 19), Grayson (1980: 173), and Echaveste (2005: A10).
54 Rodríguez (2007: 228) and Hirshman & Massey (2008: 2).
55 García y Griego (1982: 108).
56 Martin (2002: 1132), Meissner (1988: 95), and Davidow (2004: 113).
57 Martin (2002: 1133) and Meissner (1988: 99).
58 Cothran (1994: 63), Rodríguez (2007: 238–39), and Massey, Durand & Malone (2002: 140).
59 Bustamante (1987a: 17).
60 Cornelius (2002: 301, n. 15) and Jencks (2007: 49–50).
61 Meissner (2005: A8), Castañeda (2007: 29), and Davidow (2004: 113).
62 Rodríguez (2007: 217), *NACLA Report on the Americas* (September–October 2008, p. 23), Hirschman & Massey (2008: 6–8), and Castañeda (2007: 61)
63 Payan (2006: 74).
64 Massey (2003b: 17) and Fried (1994: 33).
65 Cornelius (1998: 129; 2001: 663), Andreas (2000: 93), and Massey, Durand & Malone (2002: 94).
66 Cornelius (1998: 129).
67 Cornelius (2001: 668), Massey (2005: 7; 2003a: 27; 2003b: 19), and *Latin American Mexico & NAFTA Report* (February 2007, p. 15).
68 Cornelius (2001: 661–62) and Andreas (2000: 90–91).
69 U.S. (2006: 91) and Andreas (2000: 85). While the total number of apprehensions includes non-Mexicans and some individuals were are apprehended more than once in the same year, it does give a good indication of the

change in the flow of Mexicans into the United States. In 2005, 86 percent of those arrested for being in the U.S. illegally were Mexicans (*Wall Street Journal*, April 9, 2007, p. A3).

70 York (2001: 14), Massey (2003a: 28), Corona (2003: 19), and J. Castañeda (2003: 71).

71 *Economist* (March 1, 2003, p. 35; November 29, 2003, p. 33) and Fox (2007: 239–40). Castañeda (2007), who was Mexico's foreign minister at the time of the 9/11 attacks, described in detail how the "whole enchilada" could be implemented.

72 Davidow (2004: 209–10), *New York Times* (June 17, 2001, sec. 1, p. 1), Rodríguez (2007: 249), Imaz (2007: 66), and Rozental (2004: 102).

73 Andreas (2000: 104) and L. Brown (2006: 91).

74 Davidow (2004: 124) and *Reforma* (August 19, 2006, p. 2, "Internacional").

75 Cornelius (2007: 11).

76 *The Wall Street Journal* (February 13, 2009, p. A14), *Expansión* (November 10, 2008, p. 70) and *Review of the Economic Situation of Mexico* (December–January 2008–2009, p 456).

77 Tienda (2007: A10–11) and *Wall Street Journal* (May 7, 2007, p. A2).

78 Rozental (2004: 97), Faux (2006: 210), *The Wall Street Journal* (December 20, 2007, p. A13) and Ennis (2006: 80).

79 *Expansión* (April 6, 2005, p. 82), J. Castañeda (2007: 48) and *Latin America Monitor: Mexico* (October 2009, p. 13).

80 Bortz & Águila (2006: 7) and Morales Castañeda (2006: 99, Table 9).

27 THE 2000 ELECTION

1 *Este País* (April 2002, p. 19).

2 *Comercio Exterior* (December 1994, p. 1138) and *Der Spiegel* (October, 6, 1997, p. 172). ["Dedazo" was in the German original.]

3 Klesner (2000: 9), Bruhn (2004: 125), and Langston (2000: 6–7).

4 McCann (2004: 160) and *New York Times* (November 1, 1999, p. A10).

5 *Proceso* (April 25, 1999, p. 13) and *New York Times* (November 3, 1999, p. A6).

6 Preston & Dillon (2004: 485).

7 McCann (2004: 162), *Economist* (August 21, 1999, p. 28), and Shirk (2005: 139).

8 *Proceso* (November 14, 1999, p. 17), *New York Times* (November 8, 1999, p. A24), Schedler (2000: 10), and Bruhn (2004: 125).

9 *Proceso* (June 5, 1995, p. 7) and Mizrahi (2003: 100–01).

10 Mizrahi (2003: 101) and Wallis (2001: 310).

11 Preston & Dillon (2004: 6), Ruiz-Healy (2000: 21), *New York Times* (May 9, 1999, Sec. 3, p. 11), and Loaeza (2006: 9–10).

12 Preston & Dillon (2004: 7).

13 *New York Times* (May 11, 1998, p. A4) and *The Wall Street Journal* (July 5, 2000, p. A8).

14 Klesner (2000: 6) and Preston & Dillon (2004: 483).

15 *Proceso,* Special No. 7 (December 2000, p. 64) and *Proceso* (July 4, 2000, p. 20; November 21, 1999, p. 16).

16 Becerra, Salazar & Woldenberg (2005: 530).

17 *Business Mexico* (April 2000, p. 26) and *The Wall Street Journal* (November 20, 2000, p. 40).

18 *Los Angeles Times* (August 27, 1999, p. A1), *Washington Post* (November 5, 1999), and *New York Times* (September 9, 1993, p. 3).

19 Preston & Dillon (2004: 487) and Domínguez (2004: 323).

20 Preston & Dillon (2004: 8) and *Washington Post* (July 22, 1999, p. A18).

21 Loaeza (2003: 100), Wallis (2001: 312), *Proceso* (February 13, 2000, p. 30), Rottinghaus & Alberro (2005: 148), and Bruhn (2004: 142).

22 Bruhn (2004: 133), Ruiz-Healy (2000: 276), and *Proceso,* Special No. 7 (December 2000, p. 7).

23 Loaeza (2006: 5), *New York Times* (March 12, 2000, Sec. 1, p. 1), Shirk (2005: 155), and *Nation* (July 3, 2000, p. 6).

24 Chambers & Smith (2002: 17) and *New York Times Magazine* (July 2, 2000, p. 37).

25 Preston & Dillon (2004: 493) and Bruhn (2004: 148, 153, n. 2).

26 Bruhn (2004: 149), Greene (2007: 233), and Lawson (2004: 11).

27 Preston & Dillon (2004: 12, 499), *Proceso* (July 4, 2000, p. 18; November 26, 2000, p. 18), and Becerra, Salazar & Woldenberg (2005: 542).

28 Magaloni (2005: 146).

29 Becerra, Salazar & Woldenberg (2005: 540).

30 *Proceso* (August 6, 2000, p. 16).

31 L. Meyer (2005b: 33), *Este País* (November 2003, p. 49), and Woldenberg (2002: 53).

32 *Cultural Survival Quarterly* (Fall 2003, p. 74).
33 Zermeño (1992: 198).
34 Camp (2004: 33), *La Jornada* (July 6, 2000, p. 18), and Magaloni & Poiré (2004: 315).
35 Preston & Dillon (2004: 7), Loaeza (2003: 71), and Lawson (2004: 17).
36 Preston & Dillon (2004: 6).
37 Magaloni & Romero (2008: 122) and Camp (2004: 28–29).
38 Becerra, Salazar & Woldenberg (2005: 532–34), Pacheco Méndez (1988: 30), Magaloni & Poiré (2004: 270), Middlebrook (2001: 30, n. 56), Riding (2000: 12–13), and Lawson (1999: 149).
39 Bruhn (2004: 123–24).
40 *New York Times* (July 4, 2000, p. A1).
41 *New York Times* (July 2, 1997, p. A1), Greene (2007: 234–35), and Camarena & Zepeda Patterson (2007: 114).
42 Bruhn (2004: 143 & 147) and *Los Angeles Times* (July 24, 2000, p. A1).
43 Bruhn (2004: 135) and Prud'homme (2003: 128).
44 Becerra, Salazar & Woldenberg (2005: 532–34).
45 Wallis (2001: 307, Table 1), Cook, Middlebrook & Molinar Horcasitas (2007: 55), Woldenberg (2002: 42), and Domínguez (2004: 336).
46 Magaloni (2005: 135–36, 145–46).
47 Bizberg (2003b: 152), Preston & Dillon (2004: 12), Becerra, Salazar & Woldenberg (2005: 515), and *New York Times* (July 4, 2000, p. A1).
48 La Botz (2005: 70) and Bizberg (2001: 97).
49 Lawson (2002: 110, 132, 151).
50 Edmonds-Poli & Shirk (2009: 93–96).
51 Schedler (2000; 15) and Becerra, Salazar & Woldenberg (2005: 514).
52 *Proceso* (April 30, 2000, p. 29).
53 IFE (2000b, sec. 5, p. 12), Becerra, Salazar & Woldenberg (2005: 510), and *Los Angeles Times* (October 11, 2003, p. A 7). What the Mexican system has yet to overcome is impunity. No individuals were ever put on trial, despite massive violations of campaign funding regulations.
54 Schedler (2000: 12).
55 *Proceso* (August 6, 2000, p. 18), *Economist* (March 18, 2006, p. 13), IFE (2000b: 23), and U.S. Census Bureau (2002).

28 THE FOX ADMINISTRATION, 2000–2006

1 *El Universal* [on line] (July 27, 2007), "El espejismo democrático."
2 *Proceso* (December 1, 2002, p. 37) and *Financial Times* (December 13, 2005, p. 1 "Special Report").
3 Camp (2002: 269), González Velázquez (2002: 138), Loaeza (2006: 14), and Grayson (2005: 24).
4 Ros (2003: 235), Starr (2002: 62–63), and *Business Mexico* (April 2001, p. 11).
5 Cue Mancera (2004: 53) and Aguilar & Castañeda (2007: 116).
6 Grayson (2005: 23), Loaeza (2006: 5), Aguilar & Castañeda (2007: 128, 224), and Jaime (2004: 58).
7 *Washington Post* (June 23, 2002, p. A22) and Loaeza (2006: 12).
8 Camarena & Zepeda Patterson (2007: 312).
9 Loaeza (2006: 24–25), Carrillo Luvianos & Toscana Aparcio (2005: 46), Peschard (2006: 33), IFE (2006a: 2), Tejeda (2007: 433) and Reyes del Campillo (2003: 7).
10 Aguayo (2007: 120), Naím (2004: 103) and Semo (2007: 239).
11 Davidow (2004: 133), Starr (2002: 60), Treviño de Hoyos (2007: 42). Carlos Monsiváis provocatively examined the values represented by the PAN as the ruling party: *El Universal* [on line] (April 15, 2007).
12 Starr (2002: 62), Córdova & Murayama (2006: 22–23), and *Los Angeles Times* (August 3, 2006, p. A4).
13 *Mexico Labor News & Analysis* (December 2005).
14 *Christian Science Monitor* (June 19, 2006, p. 7).
15 *El Universal* [on line] (April 3, 2007).
16 Reynoso (2005: 33), *Latin America Weekly Report* (February 15, 2007, p. 11), and *El Universal* [on line] (February 12, 2007).
17 *Financial Times* (December 13, 2005, p. 5 "Special Report").
18 Suárez Dávila (2008: 17) and *El Universal* [on line] (October 18, 2006).
19 *Financial Times* (December 13, 2005, p. 1, "Special Report").
20 *Reforma* (July 19, 2008, p. 2, "Nacional"), Edmonds-Poli & Shirk (2009: 286), and Haber et al. (2008: 169). Economist Julio Boltvinik suggested that part of the reported reduction in poverty stemmed from redefining the way poverty was measured. *Comercio Exterior* (December 2008, p. 877).

21 Grayson (2005: 24) and Loaeza (2006: 14–16, 29).
22 Camarena & Zepeda Patterson (2007: 325), *Business Latin America* (December 4, 2006, p. 1), L. Meyer (2007b: 34), and Grayson (2006: 20–21).
23 Hernández (2006: 16, 199, 200–01, 216) and *Proceso* (February 18, 2007, p. 7; May 4, 2008, pp. 28–30).
24 *Los Angeles Times* (June 16, 2006, p. A35) and *Reforma* (November 30, 2006, p. 1, "Nacional").

29 THE 2006 ELECTIONS

1 *Miami Herald* (June 8, 2006, p. 10A).
2 Grayson (2006: 20).
3 Grayson (2006: 99–100) and Giordano (2006: 13).
4 Grayson (2006: 123, 141).
5 Grayson (2006: 179).
6 Giordano (2006: 16) and Grayson (2006: 203–04).
7 *Reforma* (February 23, 2004, p. 1A), *Wall Street Journal* (June 12, 2006, p. A6), Arreola (2006: 45–47), Grayson (2006: 9), and Belejack (2004: 6).
8 Grayson (2006: 256), Tello Díaz (2007: 71), Arreola (2006: 54–55), and López Obrador (2005; 2007: 162–80).
9 Grayson (2006: 225–26) and *Reforma* (July 29, 2005, p. 1A).
10 Aristegui (2006: 126).
11 Calderón (2006: 16), Cuéllar (2003: 50–51), and Camarena (2006: 69).
12 Cuéllar (2003: 41).
13 Alcocer & Musacchio (2006: 92–93).
14 *Reforma* (May 30, 2004, p. 2A; May 31, p. 1; June 1, p. 1) and Alcocer & Musacchio (2006: 90–91).
15 Camarena (2006: 88–91).
16 *Nación* (October 31, 2005, p. 4), Aristegui (2006: 202), *Proceso* (September 18, 2005, pp. 8, 11), and *Reforma* (May 9, 2007).
17 Grayson (2006: 99–100), Ugalde (2008: 70–71), and Estrada & Poiré (2007: 76).
18 *Proceso* (February 17, 2002, pp. 33–35; February 24, 2002, pp. 28–31; March 3, 2002, pp. 9–14, October 16, 2005, p. 7; October 23, 2005, pp. 14–15; January 29, 2006, p. 22), Estrada & Poiré (2007: 76), and Ugalde (2008: 72).
19 *Voz y voto* (June 2006, pp. 9–14). López Obrador was candidate of not only of the PRD, but of two small parties, the Labor Party (PT) and Convergencia, which formed the Coalition for the Good of All (CPBT). For simplicity, his candidacy will simply be referred to as that of the PRD. Similarly, Madrazo was the candidate of a PRI-led coalition with the Green Party known as the Alliance for Mexico.
20 Grayson (2006: 10, 183), Berumen (2007: 33), and *Proceso* (March 19, 2006, p. 21).
21 López Obrador (2004: 43).
22 Grayson (2006: 11) and *Financial Times* (March 29, 2005). López Obrador (2004) presented his platform in detail.
23 Grayson (2006: 270) and *New York Times* (June 28, 2006, p. A21).
24 *Financial Times* (May 10, 2006, p. 8), *Wall Street Journal* (July 7, 2006, p. A2), and Calderón (2006: 91).
25 Valverde Loya (2007: 29).
26 *Proceso* (March 18, 2007, pp. 22–23), Tello Díaz (2007: 77), and *Proceso* (April 23, 2006, p. 69).
27 Valverde Loya (2007: 31) and Tello Díaz (2007: 77). The Federal Election Code (COFIPE), art. 38, sec. p) prohibits parties from engaging in "diatribes, calumny, opprobrium, insult, defamation, or from denigrating citizens, public institutions, other political parties, and their candidates, particularly during electoral campaigns . . ."
28 Camacho Guzmán & Almazán (2006: 90–91), *Proceso* (January 15, 2006, p. 8), and Tello Díaz (2007: 176, 183, n. 10).
29 *Voz y voto* (June 2006, pp. 9–14) and *Proceso* (April 23, 2006, p. 66).
30 Berumen (2007: 34), Ugalde (2008: 111–12), and Tello Díaz (2007: 77).
31 Tello Díaz (2007: 231).
32 Tello Díaz (2007: 13, 41), Schedler (2007: 92), and *New York Times* (July 3, 2006, p. A8). In the interest of full disclosure, the author was one of the 693 foreign observers.
33 Schedler (2007: 95).
34 Giordano (2006: 5).
35 Córdova Vianello (2006: 25).
36 Tello Díaz (2007: 193).
37 *Proceso* (May 27, 2007, p. 14). COFIPE art. 49, sec. 2, Subsection (g) outlaws corporate donations to political campaigns.
38 Camarena & Zepeda Patterson (2007: 312–14).

39 *Financial Times* (December 13, 2005, p. 4), Grayson (2006: 276), *Proceso* (January 15, 2006, p. 14), and Tello Díaz (2007: 67).
40 Tello Díaz (2007: 183, n. 10) and *Proceso* (August 20, 2006, p. 14).
41 *Los Angeles Times* (May 10, 2006).
42 Camacho Guzmán & Almazán (2006: 19).
43 *Proceso* (April 30, 2006, p. 8).
44 *New York Times* (May 23, 2006, A6).
45 Miranda (2006: 19).
46 Berumen (2007: 33).
47 Tello Díaz (2007: 93) and *Vértigo* (July 23, 2006, p. 17). Thanks to Catherine Carroll for her discussion of commutativity.
48 *Vértigo* (July 23, 2006, pp. 16, 18).
49 Lajous (2007: 466, 482).

30 THE CALDERÓN ADMINISTRATION, 2006–2009

1 *Austin American-Statesman* (March 26, 2007, p. A6) and Selee (2008: 68).
2 *Wall Street Journal* (February 28, 2009, p. A6), *El Universal* [on line] (July 6, 2009), "De los 'zetas' a los 'matazetas.'"
3 Haber et al. (2008: 162) and *El Universal* [on line] (September 26, 2007), "Reforma fiscal."
4 Heredia & Rodríguez Guillén (2008: 65–68), Ugalde (2008: 136), *Milenio* (February 16, 2009, p. 6), González-Martínez (2008: 11), and Ugalde (2008: 103–04, 114).
5 *Business Latin America* (May 12, 2008, p. 1), *Oil & Gas Journal* (May 5, 2008, p. 38), *El mundo de petróleo* (February–March 2009, pp. 54–56), Shields (2008: 44), and Castañeda (2007: 100).
6 *Indigomedia* (April 25, 2008, p. 3) and Selee (2008: 68).
7 *El Universal* [on line] (July 6, 2009), "Del ilusionsismo a la dura realidad," and *Reforma* (July 21, 2009, p. 6, "Negocios.").
8 *Proceso* (July 12, 2009, p. 56).
9 *El Financiero* (July 14, 2009, p. 31) and *Proceso* (July 7, 2009, p. 28).
10 *Wall Street Journal* (July 7, 2009, p. A8), *Enfoque* (July 19, 2009, p. 7), *Reforma* (July 12, 2009, p. 13 "Opinión"), *El Universal* (July 16, 2009, p. A22), and *El Financiero* (July 14, 2009, p. 22).
11 *Reforma* (July 9, 2009, p. 9) and *Poder y Negocios* (July 17, 2009, p. 30).
12 *Wall Street Journal* (July 7, 2009, A8) and *Reforma* (July 13, 2009, p. 19, "Opinión").
13 Bruhn & Greene (2007: 143), *Reforma* (July 9, 2009, p. 9), and *Wall Street Journal* (July 7, 2009, p. A8).
14 *La Jornada* (July 16, 2009, p. 17).
15 *Proceso* (July 12, 2009, p. 53) and *Reforma* (July 13, 2009, p. 12, "Opinión").
16 *El Financiero* (July 10, 2009, p. 21; July 21, 2009, p. 1).
17 *El Universal* (July 17, 2009, p. 2).
18 *Voz y Voto* (July 2009, p. 9).
19 *Reforma* (July 12, 2009, p. 12 Opinión) and *La Jornada* (July 10, 2009, p. 28).

Bibliography

Abad y Queipo, Manuel (1813) *Coleccion de los escritos mas importantes que en diferentes epocas dirigió al gobierno d. Manuel Abad Queipo, obispo electo de Michoacan.* Mexico City: En la oficina de d. Mariano Ontiveros.

Abad y Queipo, Manuel (1994) *Colección de escritos.* Mexico City: Consejo Nacional para la Cultura y las Artes.

Abruch Linder, Miguel (1983) "La cruzada empresarial," *Nexos* 64 (April): 25–28.

Acosta, Mariclaire & Rocío Culebro (1993) "El poder frente a los derechos humanos," *Cemos Memoria* 51 (February): 5–16.

Adams, Eleanor B. (1953) "Bishop Tamarón's Visitation of New Mexico, 1760," *New Mexico Historical Review* 28 (April): 81–114.

Adams, Richard N. (1967) "Nationalization," pp. 469–89, *Handbook of Middle American Indians,* vol. 6, Manning Nash, ed. Austin TX: University of Texas Press.

Adelman, Jeremy (2006) *Sovereignty and Revolution in the Iberian Atlantic.* Princeton NJ: Princeton University Press.

Ades, Dawn (1989) *Art in Latin America.* New Haven CT: Yale University Press.

ADESE (1988) *Manual de vigilancia y defensa del voto.* Mexico City: Asamblea Democrática por el Sufragio Efectivo.

AFSC (1999) *Still Pulling Strings.* Philadelphia PA: American Friends Service Committee.

Agee, Philip (1975) *Inside the Company.* New York: Stonehill.

Aggarwal, Vinod K. (1996) *Debt Games.* Cambridge: Cambridge University Press.

Aguayo, Sergio (1995) "A Mexican Milestone," *Journal of Democracy* 6 (April): 157–67.

—— (2007) *Almanaque mexicano.* Mexico City: Aguilar.

—— (2008) *México: todo en cifras.* Mexico City: Aguilar.

Aguiar, José Carlos (2006) "Las políticas de seguridad pública en América Latina," *Revista Europea de Estudios Latinoamericanos y del Caribe* 81 (October): 115–21.

Aguilar, Rubén & Jorge G. Castañeda (2007) *La diferencia: radiografía de un sexenio.* Mexico City: Grijalbo.

Aguilar Camín, Héctor (1980) "The Relevant Tradition: Sonoran Leaders in the Revolution," pp. 92–123, *Caudillo and Peasant in the Mexican Revolution,* D. A. Brading, ed. Cambridge: Cambridge University Press.

—— (1982a) "La transición política," *Nexos* 51 (March): 9–14.

—— (1982b) "A través del túnel," *Nexos* 60 (December): 13–25.

—— (1988) *Después del milagro.* Mexico City: Cal y Arena.

Aguilar Camín, Héctor & Lorenzo Meyer (1993) *In the Shadow of the Revolution.* Austin TX: University of Texas Press.

Aguilar García, Javier (1997) "Confederación de Trabajadores de México (CTM)," pp. 283–86, and "Confederación Regional Obrera Mexicana (CROM)," pp. 294–97, *Encyclopedia of Mexico,* Michael S. Werner, ed. Chicago IL: Fitzroy Dearborn.

—— (2001) *La población trabajadora y sindicalizada en México en el período de la globalización.* Mexico City: Fondo de Cultura Económica (FCE) and Universidad Nacional Autónoma de México (UNAM).

—— (2004a) "La CTM y la tasa de sindicalización," *Estudios Políticos* 2 (May–August): 101–17.

—— (2004b) "Notes on Unemployment in Mexico," *Voices of Mexico* 67 (April–June): 63–67.

Aguilar Monteverde, Alonso (1974) *Dialéctica de la economía mexicana* (5th ed.). Mexico City: Nuestro Tiempo.

Aguilar Plata, Blanca (1998) "La imagen de Porfirio Díaz en la prensa capitalina de su tiempo," pp. 141–60, *La prensa en México,* Laura Navarrete Maya & Blanca Aguilar Plata, eds. Mexico City: Addison, Wesley, Longman de México.

Aguilar Rivera, José Antonio (2003) "Crónicas de la sociedad abierta," *Nexos* 302 (February): 14–18.

Aguilar Zínser, Adolfo (1990) "Las relaciones cívico-militares en México," pp. 291–312, *Los militares y la democracia,* Louis W. Goodman, Johanna S. R. Mendelson, & Juan Rial, eds. Montevideo: PEITHO.

—— (1995) *¡Vamos a ganar!* Mexico City: Océano.

Aguirre Beltrán, Gonzalo (1944) "The Slave Trade in Mexico," *Hispanic American Historical Review* 24 (August): 412–31.

—— (1967) "Un postulado de política indigenista," *América Indígena* 27 (July): 559–65.

—— (1970) "The Integration of the Negro into the National Society of Mexico," pp. 11–27, *Race and Class in Latin America,* Magnus Mörner, ed. New York: Columbia University Press.

—— (1975) "Etnocidio en México," *América Indígena* 35 (April–June): 405–18.

—— (1989a) *La población negra de México.* Mexico City: Fondo de Cultura Económica.

—— (1989b) *Cuijla* (2nd ed.) Mexico City: Fondo de Cultura Económica.

Ahern, Maureen (1998) "Fronteras mudables: un informe náhuatl de la Guerra Chichimeca, 1563," pp. 61–76, *Indigenismo hacia el fin del milenio,* Mabel Moraña, ed. Pittsburgh PA: Instituto Internacional de Literatura Iberoamericana.

Ahlborn, Richard Eighme (1985) *The San Antonio Missions.* Fort Worth TX: Amon Carter Museum.

Alamán, Lucas (1942) *Historia de Méjico* (5 vols.). Mexico City: Jus.

Alarcón, Diana (2003) "Income Distribution and Poverty Alleviation in Mexico," pp. 447–86, *Confronting Development,* Kevin J. Middlebrook & Eduardo Zepeda, eds. Palo Alto CA: Stanford University Press & San Diego CA: UCSD Center for U.S.–Mexican Studies.

Alarcón, Diana & Terry McKinley (1997) "The Paradox of Narrowing Wage Differentials and Widening Wage Inequality in Mexico," *Development & Change* 28 (July): 505–30.

Alba, Francisco (1976) "Éxodo silencioso: la emigración de trabajadores a Estados Unidos," *Foro Internacional* 27 (October–December): 152–79.

—— (1978) "Mexico's International Migration as a Manifestation of its Development Pattern," *International Migration Review* 12 (no. 4): 502–13.

—— (1982) *The Population of Mexico.* New Brunswick NJ: Transaction.

—— (1993) "Crecimiento demográfico y transformación económica, 1930–1970," pp. 74–95, *El poblamiento de México,* vol. 4. Mexico City: Consejo Nacional de Población (CONAPO).

Alba, Francisco & Joseph E. Potter (1986) "Population and Development in Mexico since 1940," *Population & Development Review* 12 (March): 47–76.

Alba Vega, Carlos & Enrique Valencia Lomelí (2003) "Agotamiento de un modelo de desarrollo," pp. 233–57, *México al inicio de siglo XXI,* Alberto Aziz Nassif, ed. Mexico City: Centro de Investigaciones y Estudios Superiores en Antropología Social (CIESAS).

Alberro, Solange (1988) *Inquisición y sociedad en México: 1571–1700.* Mexico City: Fondo de Cultura Económica.

Albro, Ward S. (1992) *Always a Rebel: Ricardo Flores Magón and the Mexican Revolution.* Ft. Worth: TCU Press.

Alcaraz, Ramón, Alejo Barreiro, José María Castillo, Félix María Escalante, José María Iglesias, Manuel Muñoz, Ramón Ortiz, Manuel Payno, Guillermo Prieto, Ignacio Ramírez, Napoleón Soborio, Francisco Schiafino, Francisco Segura, Pablo María Torrescano, & Francisco Urquidi (1970) *Apuntes para la historia de la guerra entre México y los Estados Unidos.* Mexico City: Siglo XXI.

Alcazar, Marco Antonio (1970) *Las agrupaciones patronales en México.* Mexico City: Colegio de México.

Alcocer, Jorge (1994) "Party System and Political Transition in Mexico," pp. 149–57, *The Politics of Economic Development,* Maria Lorena Cook, Kevin J. Middlebrook, & Juan Molinar Horcasitas, eds. San Diego CA: UCSD Center for U.S.–Mexican Studies.

Alcocer, Jorge & Humberto Musacchio (2006) *México 2006.* Mexico City: Fondo de Cultura Económica.

Alemán Valdés, Miguel (1987) *Remembranzas y testimonios.* Mexico City: Grijalbo.

Alemán Velasco, Miguel (1997) *No siembro para mí.* Mexico City: Diana.

Alfie, Miriam (2002) "Alianzas y desafíos," *Revista Europea de Estudios Latinoamericanos y del Caribe* 73 (October): 23–42.

Alisky, Marvin (1981) *Latin American Media.* Ames IA: Iowa State University Press.

Alonso, Ana María (1995) *Thread of Blood.* Tucson AZ: University of Arizona Press.

Alvarado, Arturo (1985) "Introduction," pp. 1–16, *Electoral Patterns and Perspectives in Mexico,* Arturo Alvarado, ed. UCSD Center for U.S.–Mexican Studies Monograph Series, 22. San Diego CA: UCSD Center for U.S.–Mexican Studies.

Alvarado, Lourdes (1991) *El siglo XIX ante el feminismo.* Mexico City: Coordinación de Humanidades, Universidad Nacional Autónoma de México.

——, ed. (2005) *Educación y superación femenina en el siglo XIX: dos ensayos de Laureana Wright. Cuadernos del Archivo Histórico de la UNAM* 19.

Álvarez, Luis H. (2006) *Medio siglo.* Mexico City: Plaza y Janés.

Americas Watch (2009) *Uniform Impunity.* New York: Americas Watch.

Amnesty International (1977) *Amnesty International Report 1977.* London: Amnesty International.

—— (1982) *Amnesty International Report 1982.* London: Amnesty International.

—— (1987) *Amnesty International Report 1987.* London: Amnesty International.

—— (1991) *Torture with Impunity.* New York: Amnesty International.

—— (1995) *Human Rights Violations in Mexico.* New York: Amnesty International.

—— (2007a) *Mexico: Laws without Justice.* New York: Amnesty International.

—— (2007b) *Amnesty International Report 2007.* London: Amnesty International.

Ampudia, Ricardo, ed. (1993) *Estados Unidos de América en los informes presidenciales de México.* Mexico City: Instituto Matías Romero de Estudios Diplomáticos.

Anderson, Rodney (1976) *Outcasts in their Own Land.* DeKalb IL: University of Northern Illinois Press.

—— (1997) "Industrial Labor: 1876–1910," pp. 681–86, *Encyclopedia of Mexico,* Michael S. Werner, ed. Chicago IL: Fitzroy Dearborn.

Andreas, Peter (1996) "U.S.–Mexico: Open Markets, Closed Border," *Foreign Policy* 103 (Summer): 51–69.

—— (1998) "The Political Economy of Narco-Corruption in Mexico," *Current History* 97 (April): 160–65.

—— (2000) *Border Games.* Ithaca NY: Cornell University Press.

Andrews, Anthony P., E. Wyllys Andrews & Fernando Robles Castellanos (2003) "The Northern Maya Collapse and its Aftermath," *Ancient Mesoamerica* 14 (Spring): 151–56.

Angell, Alan (1998) "The Left in Latin America since *c.* 1920," pp. 75–144, *Latin America: Politics and Society since 1930,* Leslie Bethell, ed. Cambridge: Cambridge University Press.

Anglade, Christian & Carlos Fortín (1985) "The State and Capital Accumulation in Latin America," pp. 1–51, *The State and Capital Accumulation in Latin America,* vol. 1, Christian Anglade & Carlos Fortín, eds. Pittsburgh PA: University of Pittsburgh Press.

Ankerson, Dudley (1984) *Agrarian Warlord.* DeKalb IL: Northern Illinois University Press.

Anna, Timothy E. (1978) *The Fall of the Royal Government in Mexico City.* Lincoln NE: University of Nebraska Press.

—— (1983) *Spain and the Loss of America.* Lincoln NE: University of Nebraska Press.

—— (1985a) "The Independence of Mexico and Central America," pp. 51–94, *Cambridge History of Latin America* (vol. 3), Leslie Bethell, ed. Cambridge: Cambridge University Press.

—— (1985b) "The Rule of Agustín de Iturbide," *Journal of Latin American Studies* 17 (May): 79–110.

—— (1989) "The Iturbide Interregnum," pp. 185–99, *The Independence of Mexico and the Creation of a New Nation,* Jaime E. Rodríguez O., ed. Los Angeles CA: UCLA Latin American Center and Mexico/Chicano Program of the University of California, Irvine.

—— (1990) *The Mexican Empire of Iturbide.* Lincoln NE: University of Nebraska Press.

—— (1993) "Demystifying Early Nineteenth Century Mexico," *Mexican Studies/Estudios Mexicanos* 9 (Winter): 119–37.

—— (1994) "Iturbide, Congress, and Constitutional Monarchy in Mexico," pp. 17–38, *The Political Economy of Spanish America in the Age of Revolution, 1750–1850,* Kenneth J. Andrien & Lyman L. Johnson, eds. Albuquerque NM: University of New Mexico Press.

—— (1996) "Inventing Mexico: Provincehood and Nationhood after Independence," *Bulletin of Latin American Research* 15 (January): 7–18.

—— (1997) "Review of *National Popular Politics in Early Independent Mexico, 1820–1847* by Torcuato S. Di Tella," *American Historical Review,* (February): 233–34.

—— (1998a) *Forging Mexico, 1821–1835.* Lincoln NE: University of Nebraska Press.

—— (1998b) "Review of *Mexicans at Arms* by Pedro Santoni," *American Historical Review* 103 (April): 627–28.

Anonymous Conqueror (1972) *Narrative of Some Things of New Spain.* Boston MA: Milford House.

Ansell, Martin R. (1998) *Oil Baron of the Southwest.* Columbus OH: Ohio State University Press.

Antuñano Maurer, Alejandro de (1987) "Miguel Hidalgo frente al dogma y la política de 1810," *Revista de la UNAM* 440 (September): 20–24.

Appendini, Kristen (2001) *De la milpa a los tortibonos* (2nd ed.) Mexico City: Colegio de México.

—— (2003) "The Challenges to Rural Mexico in an Open Economy," pp. 255–75, *Mexico's Politics and Society in Transition,* Joseph S. Tulchin & Andrew D. Selee, eds. Boulder CO: Lynne Rienner.

Appendini, Kristen & Diana Liverman (1994) "Agricultural Policy, Climate Change and Food Security in Mexico," *Food Policy* 19 (April): 149–64.

Archer, Christon (1977) *The Army in Bourbon Mexico, 1760–1810.* Albuquerque NM: University of New Mexico Press.

—— (1981a) "Bourbon Finances and Military Policy in New Spain, 1759–1812," *The Americas* 37 (January): 315–50.

—— (1981b) "The Royalist Army in New Spain: Civil-Military Relationships," *Journal of Latin American Studies* 13 (May): 57–82.

—— (1985) "Recent Work on Mexico," *Mexican Studies/Estudios Mexicanos* 1 (Winter): 125–33.

—— (1986) "Military," pp. 197–226, *Cities and Society in Colonial Latin America,* Louisa Schell Hoberman & Susan Migden Socolow, eds. Albuquerque NM: University of New Mexico Press.

—— (1989a) "'*La causa buena*': The Counterinsurgency Army of New Spain and the Ten Years' War," pp. 85–108, *The Independence of Mexico and the Creation of a New Nation,* Jaime E. Rodríguez O., ed. Los Angeles CA: UCLA Latin American Center & Mexico/Chicano Program of the University of California, Irvine.

—— (1989b) "Where Did all the Royalists Go? New Light on the Military Collapse of New Spain, 1810–1822," pp. 24–43, *The Mexican and Mexican American Experience in the 19th Century,* Jaime E. Rodríguez O., ed. Tempe AZ: Bilingual Press.

—— (1989c) "The Young Antonio López de Santa Anna," pp. 1–16, *The Human Tradition in Latin America,* Judith Ewell & William H. Beezley, eds. Wilmington DE: Scholarly Resources.

—— (1991) "'¡*Viva Nuestra Señora de Guadalupe*!' Recent Interpretations of Mexico's Independence Period," *Mexican Studies/Estudios Mexicanos* 7 (Winter): 143–65.

—— (1992a) "The Cutting Edge: The Historical Relationship between Insurgency, Counterinsurgency, and Terrorism during Mexican Independence, 1810–1821," pp. 29–45, *Terrorism: Roots, Impact, Responses,* Lawrence Howard, ed. New York: Praeger.

—— (1992b) "The Militarization of Mexican Politics: The Role of the Army, 1815–1821," pp. 285–302, vol. 1, *Five Centuries of Mexican History/Cinco siglos de historia de México,* Virginia Guedea & Jaime E. Rodríguez O., eds. Mexico City: Instituto Mora & Irvine CA: University of California.

—— (1992c) "Bite of the Hydra: The Rebellion of Cura Hidalgo, 1810–1811," pp. 69–93, *Patterns of Contention in Mexican History,* Jaime E. Rodríguez O., ed. Wilmington DE: Scholarly Resources.

—— (1992d) "La revolución desastrosa," pp. 113–32, *Tres Levantamientos Populares,* J. Meyer, ed. Mexico City: Centre d'Etudes Mexicaines et Centramericaines.

—— (1993) "Politicization of the Army of New Spain during the War of Independence, 1810–1821," pp. 17–43, *The Evolution of the Mexican Political System,* Jaime E. Rodríguez O., ed. Wilmington DE: Scholarly Resources.

—— (1994a) "What Goes Around Comes Around: Political Change and Continuity in Mexico, 1750–1850," pp. 261–80, *Mexico in the Age of Democratic Revolutions, 1750–1850,* Jaime E. Rodríguez O., ed. Boulder CO: Lynne Rienner.

—— (1994b) "Insurrection—Reaction—Revolution—Pigmentation: Reconstructing the Choreography of Meltdown in New Spain during the Independence Era," *Mexican Studies/Estudios Mexicanos* 10 (Winter): 63–98.

—— (1997) *Fighting for Small Worlds: Wars of the People during the Independence Era in New Spain, 1810–1821.* Paper Presented at the XX International Congress of the Latin American Studies Association (LASA), Guadalajara, Jalisco.

—— (2007) "México en 1810: el fin del principio, el principio del fin," pp. 21–39, *México en tres momentos: 1810–1910–2010* (vol. 1), Alicia Mayer, ed. Mexico City: Instituto de Investigaciones Históricas, Universidad Nacional Autónoma de México.

—— (2008) "Royalist Scourge or Liberator of the Patria?" *Mexican Studies/Estudios Mexicanos* 24 (Summer): 325–61.

Archibald, Robert (1978) *The Economic Aspects of the California Missions.* Washington DC: Academy of American Franciscan History.

Arcila Farías, Eduardo (1974) *Reformas económicas del siglo XVIII en Nueva España* (2 vols.). Mexico City: SepSetentas.

Argüello, Gilberto (1989) "El primer medio siglo de vida independiente, 1821–1867," pp. 197–307, *México: un pueblo en la historia,* vol. 2, Enrique Semo, ed. Mexico City: Alianza Editorial Mexicana.

Aristegui, Carmen (2006) *Uno de Dos.* Mexico City: Grijalbo.

Arizpe, Lourdes (1981) "The Rural Exodus in Mexico and the Mexican Migration to the United States," *International Migration Review* 15 (Winter): 626–49.

—— (1989) *La mujer en el desarrollo de México y de América Latina.* Mexico City: Universidad Nacional Autónoma de México.

Armillas, Pedro (1971) "Gardens on Swamps," *Science* 174 (November 12): 653–61.

Arnold, Linda (1988) *Bureaucracy and Bureaucrats in Mexico City: 1742–1835.* Tucson AZ: University of Arizona Press.

Arreola, Daniel & James R. Curtis (1993) *The Mexican Border Cities.* Tucson AZ: University of Arizona Press.

Arreola, Federico (2006) *La lucha de la gente contra el poder del dinero.* Mexico City: Nuevo Siglo/Aguilar.

Arreola Ayala, Álvaro (1988) "La ley electoral de 1946," *Revista Mexicana de Sociología* 50 (July–September): 169–87.

Arriaga, Ponciano (1959) *Voto particular.* San Luis Potosí: Centro Regional del Instituto de Estudios Políticos, Económicos y Sociales del PRI.

Arriola, Carlos (2008) *El miedo a gobernar.* Mexico City: Océano.

Arrom, Silvia M. (1985a) *The Women of Mexico City, 1790–1857.* Palo Alto CA: Stanford University Press.

—— (1985b) "Changes in Mexican Family Law in the Nineteenth Century: The Civil Codes of 1870 and 1884," *Journal of Family History* 10 (Fall): 305–17.

—— (1994) "Changes in Mexican Family Law in the Nineteenth Century," pp. 87–102, *Confronting Change, Challenging Tradition,* Gertrude M. Yeager, ed. Wilmington DE: Scholarly Resources.

—— (1996a) "Introduction," pp. 1–16, *Riots in the Cities,* Silvia M. Arrom & Servando Ortoll, eds. Wilmington DE: Scholarly Resources.

—— (1996b) "Popular Politics in Mexico City: The Parián Riot, 1828," pp. 71–96, *Riots in the Cities,* Silvia M. Arrom & Servando Ortoll, eds. Wilmington DE: Scholarly Resources.

Arroyo Picard, Alberto, Sarah Anderson, John Dilion, John Foster, Manuel Ángel Gómez Cruz, Karen Hansen-Kuhn, David Ranney, & Rita Schwentesius (2003) *Impacts of the North American Free Trade Agreement in Mexico.* Mexico City: Red Mexicana de Acción Frente al Libre Comercio (RMALC).

Ashby, Joe C. (1963) *Organized Labor and the Mexican Revolution under Lázaro Cárdenas.* Chapel Hill NC: University of North Carolina Press.

—— (1985) "The Dilemma of the Mexican Trade Union Movement," *Mexican Studies/Estudios Mexicanos* 1 (Summer): 277–302.

Assadourian, Carlos Sempat (1989) "La despoblación indígena en Perú y Nueva España durante el siglo XVI y la formación de la economía colonial," *Historia Mexicana* 38 (January–March): 419–54.

—— (2006) "Agriculture and Land Tenure," pp. 275–314, *Cambridge Economic History of Latin America* (vol. 1) Victor Bulmer-Thomas, John H. Coatsworth, & Roberto Cortés Conde, eds. New York: Cambridge University Press.

Ávila, Alfredo (2007) "Para una historia del pensamiento político del proceso de Independencia," pp. 255–65, *México en tres momentos: 1810–1910–2010* (vol 1), Alicia Mayer, ed. Mexico City: Instituto de Investigaciones Históricas, Universidad Nacional Autónoma de México.

Ávila, Manuel (1969) *Tradition and Growth.* Chicago IL: University of Chicago Press.

Ávila Espinosa, Felipe Arturo (2007) "Las transformaciones sociales de la Revolución Mexicana," pp. 91–105, *México en tres momentos: 1810–1910–2010* (vol. 1), Alicia Mayer, ed. Mexico City: Instituto de Investigaciones Históricas, Universidad Nacional Autónoma de México.

Aziz Nassif, Alberto (1996) *Territorios de alternancia.* Mexico City: Centro de Investigaciones y Estudios Superiores en Antropología Social.

—— (2003) "La construcción de la democracia electoral," pp. 367–428, *Historia contemporánea de México* (vol. 1), Ilán Bizberg & Lorenzo Meyer, eds. Mexico City: Océano.

Aziz Nassif, Alberto & Jorge Alonso Sánchez (2003) "Votos, reglas y partidos," pp. 65–96, *México al inicio del siglo XXI,* Alberto Aziz Nassif, ed. Mexico City: Centro de Investigaciones y Estudios Superiores en Antropología Social.

Aziz Nassif, Alberto & Juan Molinar Horcasitas (1990) "Los resultados electorales," pp. 138–71, *Segundo informe sobre la democracia,* Pablo González Casanova, ed. Mexico City: Siglo XXI.

Azuela, Mariano (1992) *The Underdogs.* Pittsburgh PA: University of Pittsburgh Press.

Azuela de la Cueva, Antonio & Ma. Soledad Cruz Rodríguez (1989) "La institucionalización de las colonias populares y la política urbana en la Ciudad de México (1940–1946)," *Sociológica* 4 (January–April): 111–34.

Babb, Sarah (2001) *Managing Mexico.* Princeton NJ: Princeton University Press.

Bachelor, Steven J. (2008) "Industrial Workers and the Promise of Americanization in the Cold War Mexico," pp. 253–72, *In from the Cold,* Gilbert M. Joseph & Daniela Spenser, eds. Durham NC: Duke University Press.

Bacon, David (2002) "Off the Grid," *Multinational Monitor* 23 (January–February): 17–19.

—— (2004) *Children of NAFTA.* Berkeley CA: University of California Press.

Bagley, Bruce M. & Juan Tokatlian (1999) Dope and Dogma," pp. 219–35, *Neighborly Adversaries,* Michael LaRosa & Frank O. Mora, eds. Lanham MD: Rowman & Littlefield.

Bailey, David C. (1969) "Álvaro Obregón and Anticlericalism in the 1910 Revolution," *The Americas* 26 (October): 183–98.

—— (1974) *¡Viva Cristo Rey!* Austin TX: University of Texas Press.

—— (1978) "Revisionism and Recent Historiography of the Mexican Revolution," *Hispanic American Historical Review* 58 (February): 62–79.

—— (1986) "The Church since 1940," pp. 236–42, *Twentieth-Century Mexico,* W. Dirk Raat & William H. Beezley, eds. Lincoln NE: University of Nebraska Press.

Bairoch, P. (1982) "International Industrialization Levels from 1750 to 1980," *Journal of European Economic History* 11 (Fall): 269–333.

Baker, Miriam (1934) *The Diplomatic Career of Colonel Powhatan Ellis.* Masters Thesis, University of Texas.

Bakewell, P. J. (1971) *Silver Mining and Society in Colonial Mexico: Zacatecas, 1546–1700.* Cambridge: Cambridge University Press.

—— (1984) "Mining in Colonial Spanish America," pp. 105–152, *Cambridge History of Latin America* (vol. 2), Leslie Bethell, ed. Cambridge: Cambridge University Press.

—— (1997) *A History of Latin America.* Oxford: Blackwell.
Balderrama, Francisco E. & Raymond Rodríguez (1995) *Decade of Betrayal.* Albuquerque NM: University of New Mexico Press.
Banco de México (1941) *El turismo norteamericano en México, 1934–1940.* Mexico City: Gráfica Panamericana.
Banco Nacional de Comercio Exterior (1974) *México 1973.* Mexico City: Banco Nacional de Comercio Exterior.
—— (1977) *México 1976.* Mexico City: Banco Nacional de Comercio Exterior.
Bannon, John Francis (1970) *The Spanish Borderlands Frontier, 1513–1821.* New York: Holt, Rinehart and Winston.
Bantjes, Adrian A. (1997) "Cardenismo: Interpretaciones," pp. 195–99, *Encyclopedia of Mexico,* Michael S. Werner, ed. Chicago IL: Fitzroy Dearborn.
—— (1998) *As if Jesus Walked on Earth.* Wilmington DE: Scholarly Resources.
—— (2009) "Mexican Revolutionary Anticlericalism," *The Americas* 65 (April): 467–80.
Barajas, Gabriela (2002) "Las políticas de administración de la pobreza en México," *Foro Internacional* 42 (January–March): 63–98.
Barberán, José, Cuauhtémoc Cárdenas, Adriana López Monjardin, & Jorge Zavala (1988) *Radiografía del fraude.* Mexico City: Nuestro Tiempo.
Barker, Eugene C. (1907) "President Jackson and the Texas Revolution," *American Historical Review* 12 (July): 778–810.
Barkin, David (1971) "Acceso a la educación en México," *Revista Mexicana de Sociología* 33 (January–March): 33–50.
—— (1974) "La persistencia de la pobreza en México," pp. 186–207, *La sociedad mexicana,* Miguel S. Wionczek, ed. Mexico City: Fondo de Cultura Económica.
—— (1975) "Mexico's Albatross: The U.S. Economy," *Latin American Perspectives* 2 (Summer): 64–80
Barkin, David & Billie R. DeWalt, (1988) "Sorghum and the Mexican Food Crisis," *Latin American Research Review* 23 (no. 3): 30–59.
Barnet-Sánchez, Holly (1997) "Frida Kahlo," *Latin American Research Review* 32 (no. 3): 243–47.
Barry, Tom (1995) *Zapata's Revenge.* Boston MA: South End.
Bartra, Armando (1976) "Sobre las clases sociales en el campo mexicano," *Cuadernos Agrarios* 1 (January–March): 7–29.
—— (1985) *Los herederos de Zapata.* Mexico City: Era.
—— (2002) "Los campesinos del milenio." *Revista de la UNAM* 612 (June): 13–23.
—— (2004) "Rebellious Cornfields," pp. 18–36, *Mexico In Transition,* Gerardo Otero, ed. London: Zed.
—— (2005) "Crónica de un desastre anunciado: México y el TLC," *Cemos Memoria* 199 (September): 5–13.
—— (2008) "Yearnings and Utopias," pp. 186–214, *The New Latin American Left,* Patrick Barrett, Daniel Chávez & César Rodríguz-Garavito, eds. London: Pluto.
Basáñez, Miguel (1981) *La lucha por la hegemonía en México, 1968–1980.* Mexico City: Siglo XXI.
—— (1990) *El pulso de los sexenios.* Mexico City: Siglo XXI.
Bassett, John Spenser, ed. (1929) *Correspondence of Andrew Jackson* (7 vols.). Washington DC: Carnegie Institution.
Bassols Batalla, Ángel (1984) *Geografía económica de México* (5th ed.). Mexico City: Trillas.
Bastian, Jean-Pierre (1981) "Protestantismo y política en México," *Revista Mexicana de Sociología* 43 (Special Number): 1947–66.
—— (1993) "The Metamorphosis of Latin American Protestant Groups," *Latin American Research Review* 28 (no. 2): 33–61.
Basurto, Jorge (1983) *Cárdenas y el poder sindical.* Mexico City: Era.
—— (1999) "Populism in Mexico: From Cárdenas to Cuauhtémoc," pp. 75–96, *Populism in Latin America,* Michael L. Conniff, ed. Tuscaloosa AL: University of Alabama Press.
Bátiz V., José (1986) "Trayectoria de la banca en México hasta 1910," pp. 267–97, *Banca y poder en México, 1800–1925,* Leonor Ludlow & Carlos Marichal, eds. Mexico City: Grijalbo.
Batou, Jean (1992) "Le Tiers Monde avant le Tiers Monde, 1770–1870," *Revue Tiers-Monde* (January–March): 7–29.
Bauer, Arnold (1986) "Rural Spanish America, 1870–1910," pp. 151–86, *Cambridge History of Latin America* (vol. 4), Leslie Bethell, ed. Cambridge: Cambridge University Press.
—— (2001) *Goods, Power, History.* New York: Cambridge University Press.
Bauer, Karl Jack (1974) *The Mexican War, 1846–1848.* New York: Macmillan.
Bayón, Damián (1984) "The Architecture and Art of Colonial Spanish America," pp. 709–46, *Cambridge History of Latin America* (vol. 2), Leslie Bethell, ed. Cambridge: Cambridge University Press.
—— (1998) "Art, c. 1920-c. 1980," pp. 393–454, *A Cultural History of Latin America,* Leslie Bethell, ed. Cambridge: Cambridge University Press.
Bayón, María Cristina (1997) *El sindicalismo automotriz mexicano frente a un nuevo escenario.* Mexico City: Juan Pablos.

Bazant, Jan (1976) "Desamortización y nacionalización de los bienes de la Iglesia," pp. 155–90, *La economía mexicana en la época de Juárez.* Mexico City: SepSetentas.

—— (1977) *A Concise History of Mexico.* Cambridge: Cambridge University Press.

—— (1985a) "Mexico from Independence to 1867," pp. 423–70, *Cambridge History of Latin America* (vol. 3), Leslie Bethell, ed. Cambridge: Cambridge University Press.

—— (1985b) "La iglesia, el Estado y la sublevación conservadora de Puebla en 1856," *Historia Mexicana* 35 (July–September): 93–109.

Bazdresch, Carlos & Santiago Levy (1991) "Populism and Economic Policy in Mexico, 1970–1982," pp. 223–62, *The Macroeconomics of Populism in Latin America,* Rudiger Dornbusch & Sebastian Edwards, eds. Chicago IL: University of Chicago Press.

Beals, Carleton (1923) *Mexico: An Interpretation.* New York: B. W. Huebsch.

Beals, Ralph L. (1975) *The Peasant Marketing System of Oaxaca, Mexico.* Berkeley CA: University of California Press.

Beato, Guillermo (1993) "Principales aspectos de la economía, la sociedad y la política en México, 1821–1920," pp. 60–89, *El poblamiento de México,* vol. 3. Mexico City: Consejo Nacional de Población.

Beatty, Edward (2000) "The Impact of Foreign Trade in the Mexican Economy," *Journal of Latin American Studies* 32 (May): 399–433.

—— (2001) *Institutions and Investment.* Palo Alto CA: Stanford University Press.

—— (2002) "Commercial Policy in Porfirian Mexico," pp. 205–52, *The Mexican Economy, 1870–1930,* Jeffrey Bortz & Stephen Haber, eds. Palo Alto CA: Stanford University Press.

Becerra, Ricardo, Pedro Salazar & José Woldenberg (2005) *La mecánica del cambio político en México* (3rd ed.) Mexico City: Cal y Arena.

Beck, Warren A. (1962) *New Mexico: A History of Four Centuries.* Norman OK: University of Oklahoma Press.

Beck, Warren A. & Ynez D. Haase (1989) *Historical Atlas of the American West.* Norman OK: University of Oklahoma Press.

Becker, Majorie (1994) "Torching La Purísima, Dancing at the Altar," pp. 247–64, *Everyday Forms of State Formation,* Gilbert M. Joseph & Daniel Nugent, eds. Durham NC: Duke University Press.

—— (1995) *Setting the Virgin on Fire.* Berkeley CA: University of California Press.

Beelen, George D. (1984) "The Harding Administration and Mexico," *The Americas* 41 (October): 177–89.

Beezley, William H. (1987) *Judas at the Jockey Club.* Lincoln NE: University of Nebraska Press.

Beezley, William H. & Colin M. Maclachlan (2009) *Mexicans in Revolution 1910–1946.* Lincoln NE: University of Nebraska Press.

Belejack, Barbara (2004) "La lotería más grande," *Texas Observer* 96 (July 16): 4–7.

Bemis, Samuel Flagg (1943) *The Latin American Policy of the United States.* New York: Harcourt, Brace & Co.

Benítez, Fernando (1957) *In the Footsteps of Cortés.* London: Peter Owen.

—— (1965) *The Century after Cortés.* Chicago IL: University of Chicago Press.

—— (1985) *Los demonios en el convento.* Mexico City: Era.

—— (1998) *Un indio zapoteco llamado Benito Juárez.* Mexico City: Taurus.

Benítez Manaut, Raúl (1996) "La ONU en México. Elecciones presidenciales de 1994," *Foro Internacional* 36 (July–September): 533–65.

—— (2001) "Las fuerzas armadas mexicanas y los retos del siglo XXI," pp. 55–77, *¿Estamos unidos mexicanos?* Mexico City: Planeta.

Benjamin, Thomas (1979) "Recent Historiography of the Origins of the Mexican War," *New Mexico Historical Review* 54 (July): 169–81.

—— (1990) "Laboratories of the New State, 1920–1929," pp. 71–90, *Provinces of the Revolution,* Thomas Benjamin & Mark Wasserman, eds. Albuquerque NM: University of New Mexico Press.

—— (1996) *A Rich Land, A Poor People,* revised ed. (1996). Albuquerque NM: University of New Mexico Press.

—— (1997a) "The War between the United States and Mexico, 1846–1848, pp. 97–124, *Myths, Misdeeds, and Misunderstandings,* Jaime E. Rodríguez O. & Kathryn Vincent, eds. Wilmington DE: Scholarly Resources.

—— (1997b) "Historiography," pp. 646–50, *Encyclopedia of Mexico,* Michael S. Werner, ed. Chicago IL: Fitzroy Dearborn.

—— (2000a) "A Time of Reconquest," *American Historical Review* 105 (April): 417–50.

—— (2000b) *La Revolución.* Austin TX: University of Texas Press.

—— (2000c) "Rebuilding the Nation," pp. 467–502, *Oxford History of Mexico,* Michael C. Meyer & William H. Beezley, eds. New York: Oxford University Press.

Benjaman, Thomas & Jesús Velasco Márquez (1997) "The War between the United States and Mexico, 1846–1848," pp. 97–124, *Myths, Misdeeds, and Misunderstandings,* Jaime E. Rodríguez & Kathryn Vincent, eds. Wilmington DE: Scholarly Resources.

Bennett, Douglas & Kenneth Sharpe (1979a) "El Estado como banquero y empresario," *Foro Internacional* 20 (July-September): 29–72.

—— (1979b) "Transnational Corporations and the Political Economy of Export Promotion," *International Organization* 33 (Spring): 177–201.

—— (1979c) "Formación de la industria automotriz, 1958–1964," pp. 151–85, *Dinámica de la empresa mexicana.* Mexico City: Colegio de México.

—— (1979d) "Agenda Setting and Bargaining Power," *World Politics* 32 (October): 57–89.

—— (1985) *Transnational Corporation Versus the State.* Princeton NJ: Princeton University Press.

Bennett, Herman L. (2003) *Africans in Colonial Mexico.* Bloomington IN: University of Indiana Press.

Bennett, Vivienne (1998) "Everyday Struggles: Women in Urban Popular Movements and Territorially Based Protests in México," pp. 116–30, *Women's Participation In Mexican Political Life,* Victoria Rodríguez, ed. Boulder CO: Westview.

Benson, Nettie Lee (1945) "The Plan of Casa Mata," *Hispanic American Historical Review* 25 (February): 45–56.

—— (1953) "Iturbide y los planes de Independencia," *Historia Mexicana* 2 (January–March): 439–46.

—— (1966) *Mexico and the Spanish Cortes, 1810–1822.* Austin TX: University of Texas Press.

—— (1989) "Territorial Integrity and Mexican Politics, 1821–1833," pp. 275–307, *The Independence of Mexico and the Creation of a New Nation,* Jaime E. Rodríguez O., ed. Los Angeles CA: UCLA Latin American Center & Mexico/Chicano Program of the University of California, Irvine.

—— (1992) *The Provincial Deputation in Mexico.* Austin TX: University of Texas Press.

Benton, Thomas Hart (1856) *Thirty Years' View.* New York: Appleton.

Berbusse, Edward J. (1958) "The Origins of the McLane–Ocampo Treaty of 1859," *The Americas* 14 (January): 223–45.

Berger, Dina (2006) *The Development of Mexico's Tourism Industry.* New York: Palgrave Macmillan.

Bergsman, Joel (1980) *Income Distribution and Poverty in Mexico.* World Bank Staff Working Paper no. 395. Washington DC: World Bank.

Berlandier, Jean Louis (1980) *Journey to Mexico During the Years 1826 to 1834.* Austin TX: Texas State Historical Association.

Bernal Sahagún, Víctor (1974) *Anatomía de la publicidad en México.* Mexico City: Nuestro Tiempo.

Bernstein, Marvin D. (1964) *The Mexican Mining Industry, 1890–1950.* Albany NY: State University of New York.

Berry, Charles R. (1966) "The Election of the Mexican Deputies to the Spanish Cortes, 1810–1822," pp. 10–42, *Mexico and the Spanish Cortes, 1810–1822,* Nettie Lee Benson, ed. Austin TX: University of Texas Press.

Bertola, Elisabetta, Marcello Carmagnani & Paolo Riguzzi (1993) "Federación y estados: Espacios políticos y relaciones de poder en México (siglo XIX)," pp. 117–36, *The Evolution of the Mexican Political System,* Jaime E. Rodríguez O., ed. Wilmington DE: Scholarly Resources.

Bértola, Luis & Jeffrey G. Williamson (2006) "Globalization in Latin America before 1940," pp. 11–56, *Cambridge Economic History of Latin America* (vol. 2) Victor Bulmer-Thomas, John H. Coatsworth, & Roberto Cortés Conde, eds. New York: Cambridge University Press.

Bertram, Eva & Kenneth Sharpe (1997) "The Drug War's Phony Fix," *Nation* (April 26): 18–22.

Berumen, Edmundo (2007) "A la distancia," *Este País* 191 (February): 32–35.

Bethell, Leslie (1984) "A Note on the Native American Population on the Eve of the European Invasions," pp. 145–46, *Cambridge History of Latin America* (vol. 1), Leslie Bethell, ed. Cambridge: Cambridge University Press.

—— (1985) "A Note on the Church and the Independence of Latin America," pp. 229–34, *Cambridge History of Latin America* (vol. 3), Leslie Bethell, ed. Cambridge: Cambridge University Press.

—— (1989) "Britain and Latin America in Historical Perspective," pp. 1–24, *Britain and Latin America: a Changing Relationship,* Victor Bulmer-Thomas, ed. Cambridge: Press Syndicate of the University of Cambridge.

—— (1991) "From the Second World War to the Cold War: 1994–1954," 41–70, *Exporting Democracy,* Abraham Lowenthal, ed. Baltimore MD: Johns Hopkins University Press.

Bethell, Leslie & Ian Roxborough (1988) "Latin America between the Second World War and the Cold War," *Journal of Latin American Studies* 20 (May): 167–89.

Bevans, Charles, ed. (1972) *Treaties and Other International Agreements of the United States of America, 1776–1949,* vol. 9. Washington DC: Government Printing Office.

Bierma, Paige (1995) *Mexican Elections 1994.* Palo Alto CA: Master's thesis, Stanford University.

—— (1998) "Work in Progress," *Business Mexico* (February): 8–12.

Bilateral Commission (1989) *The Challenge of Interdependence.* Lanham MD: University Press of America.

Bizberg, Ilán (1993) "Modernization and Corporativism in Government-Labour Relations," pp. 298–317, *Mexico: Dilemmas of Transition,* Neil Harvey, ed. London: Institute of Latin American Studies, University of London (ILAS).

—— (2001) "Clientele and Citizens in the Mexican Political Transition," *Iberoamericana* 1 (June): 87–105.

—— (2003a) "Introducción," pp. 103–10 & "Auge y decadencia del corporativismo," pp. 313–66, *Historia contemporánea de México* (vol. 1), Ilán Bizberg & Lorenzo Meyer, eds. Mexico City: Océano.

—— (2003b) "Transition or Restructuring of Society?" pp. 143–75, *Mexico's Politics and Society in Transition,* Joseph S. Tulchin & Andrew D. Selee, eds. Boulder CO: Lynne Rienner.

—— (2003c) "Estado, organizaciones corporativas y democracia," pp. 183–229, *México al inicio del siglo XXI*, Alberto Aziz Nassif, ed. Mexico City: Centro de Investigaciones y Estudios Superiores en Antropología Social.

Bizberg, Ilán & Lorenzo Meyer, eds. (2003) *Una historia contemporánea de México*, vol. 1. Mexico City: Océano.

Blackburn, Robin (1997) *The Making of New World Slavery*. London: Verso.

Blancarte, Roberto J. (1992) *Historia de la Iglesia Católica en México*. Mexico City: Fondo de Cultura Económica.

—— (2002) "Religiones y creencias en México," *Este País* 133 (April): 44–49.

—— (2005) "Religiosidad, creencias e Iglesias en la época de la transición democrática," pp. 225–298, *Historia contemporánea de México* (vol. 2), Ilán Bizberg & Lorenzo Meyer, eds. Mexico City: Océano.

Blanco, José (1985) "Política económica y lucha política," pp. 399–435, *México ante la crisis*, vol. 1, Pablo González Casanova & Héctor Aguilar Camín, eds. Mexico City: Siglo XXI.

Blaufarb, Rafe (2007) "The Western Question: The Geopolitics of Latin American Independence," *American Historical Review* 112 (June): 742–63.

Blum, John Morton (1959) *The Morgenthau Diaries*. Boston MA: Houghton Mifflin.

Bobb, Bernard (1954) "Bucareli and the Interior Provinces," *Hispanic American Historical Review* 34 (February): 20–36.

Boils, Guillermo (1975) *Los militares y la política en México, 1915–1974*. Mexico City: El Caballito.

Boltvinik, Julio (1994) "La satisfacción de la necesidades esenciales en México en los setenta y ochenta," pp. 99–175, *Desarrollo, desigualdad y medio ambiente*, Pablo Pascual Moncayo & José Woldenberg, eds. Mexico City: Cal y Arena.

—— (2000) "El diseño de Progresa," *La Jornada* (June 2): 20.

—— (2003) "Welfare, Inequality, and Poverty in Mexico, 1970–2000," pp. 385–446, *Confronting Development*, Kevin J. Middlebrook & Eduardo Zepeda, eds. Palo Alto CA: Stanford University Press and San Diego CA: UCSD Center for U.S.–Mexican Studies.

—— (2004) "Políticas focalizadas de combate a la pobreza en México, El Progresa/Oportunidades," pp. 315–47, *La pobreza en México y el mundo*," Julio Boltvinik & Arceli Damián, eds. Mexico City: Siglo XXI.

Boltvinik, Julio & Enrique Hernández Laos (1999) *Pobreza y distribución del ingreso en México*. Mexico City: Siglo XXI.

Bonfil Batalla, Guillermo (1972) "El concepto de indio en América," *Anales de Antropología*, vol. 9: 105–24.

—— (1991) "La identidad, en su hora cero," *Ojarasca* 1 (October): 19–24.

—— (1996) *México Profundo*. Austin TX: University of Texas Press.

Bonifaz de Novelo, María (1975) *Análisis histórico de la mujer mexicana*. Mexico City: SPI.

Booker, Jackie R. (1993) *Veracruz Merchants, 1770–1829*. Boulder CO: Westview.

Borah, Woodrow (1974) "La influencia cultural europea en la creación de los centros urbanos hispanoamericanos," pp. 66–94, *Ensayos sobre el desarrollo urbano de México*. Mexico City: SepStentas.

—— (1983) *Justice by Insurance*. Berkeley CA: University of California Press.

—— (1985a) *El gobierno provincial en la Nueva España, 1570–1787*. Mexico City: Instituto de Investigaciones Históricas, Universidad Nacional Autónoma de México.

—— (1985b) "El status jurídico de los indios en Nueva España," *América Indígena* 45 (April–June): 257–76.

—— (1991) "Introduction," pp. 3–19, "*Secret Judgments of God," Old World Disease in Colonial Spanish America*, Noble David Cook & W. George Lovell, eds. Norman OK: University of Oklahoma Press.

—— (1992) "Reflections on Conversion," pp. 187–98, *Five Centuries of Mexican History/Cinco siglos de historia de México*, vol. 1. Mexico City: Instituto Mora & the Irvine CA: University of California.

—— (1993) "Review of *Economic Growth and Change in Bourbon Mexico*, by Richard L. Garner," *Journal of Economic History* 53 (December): 951–52.

Borah, Woodrow & Sherburne F. Cook (1962) "La despoblación en el México central en el siglo XVI," *Historia Mexicana* 12 (July–September): 1–12.

Bortz, Jeffrey L. (1987) "The Post-War Mexican Economy," *Mexican Studies/Estudios Mexicanos* 3 (Winter): 151–62.

—— (1992) "The Effect of Mexico's Postwar Industrialization on the U.S.–Mexico Price and Wage Comparison," pp. 214–34, *U.S.–Mexico Relations*, Jorge A. Bustamante, Clark W. Reynolds, & Raúl A. Hinojosa Ojeda, eds. Palo Alto CA: Stanford University Press.

—— (1995) "The Genesis of the Mexican Labor Relations System," *The Americas* 52 (July): 43–69.

—— (2000) "The Revolution, the Labour Regime and Conditions of Work in the Cotton Textile Industry in Mexico, 1910–1927," *Journal of Latin American Studies* 32 (October): 671–703.

Bortz, Jeffrey & Marcos T. Águila (2006) "Emigración y bajos salarios," *Cemos Memoria* 213 (November): 5–8.

Bortz, Jeffrey L. & Stephen Haber (2002) "The New Institutional Economics and Latin American Economic History," pp. 1–20, *The Mexican Economy, 1870–1930*, Jeffrey Bortz & Stephen Haber, eds. Palo Alto CA: Stanford University Press.

Bosch García, Carlos (1957) *Material para la historia diplomática de México*. Mexico City: Universidad Nacional Autónoma de México.

—— (1983–85) *Documentos de la relación de México con los Estados Unidos,* 4 vols. Mexico City: Universidad Nacional Autónoma de México.

Bourguignon, François & Michael Walton (2007) "Is Greater Equity Necessary for Higher Long-Term Growth in Latin America?" pp. 95–125, *Economic Growth with Equity,* Ricardo Ffrench-Davis & José Luis Machinea, eds. Basingstoke: Palgrave Macmillan.

Boyer, Christopher (1998) "Old Loves, New Loyalties: Agrarismo in Michoacán, 1920–1928," *Hispanic American Historical Review* 78 (August): 419–55.

—— (2007) "Revolución y paternalismo ecológico," *Historia Mexicana* 225 (July–September): 91–138.

Boyer, Richard (1977) "Mexico in the Seventeenth Century: Transition of a Colonial Society," *Hispanic American Historical Review* 57 (August): 455–78.

Boyle, Susan Calafate (1997) *Los Capitalistas.* Albuquerque NM: University of New Mexico Press.

Brachet-Márquez, Viviane (1994) *The Dynamics of Domination.* Pittsburgh PA: University of Pittsburgh Press.

—— (1996) *El pacto de dominación.* Mexico City: Colegio de México.

—— (1997) "Politics and Government, 1910–46," pp. 1118–21, & "Population: 1821–1910," pp. 1159–64, *Encyclopedia of Mexico,* Michael S. Werner, ed. Chicago IL: Fitzroy Dearborn.

—— (2004) "El estado benefactor mexicano," pp. 240–72, *La pobreza en México y el mundo,* Julio Boltvinik & Arceli Damián, eds. Mexico City: Siglo XXI.

Brack, Gene M. (1975) *Mexico Views Manifest Destiny, 1821–1846.* Albuquerque NM: University of New Mexico Press.

Brading, D. A. (1970) "La situación económica de los hermanos don Manuel y don Miguel Hidalgo y Costilla, 1797," *Boletín del Archivo General de la Nación* 11 (January–June): 15–81.

—— (1971) *Miners and Merchants in Bourbon Mexico, 1793–1810.* Cambridge: Cambridge University Press.

—— (1973a) "Creole Nationalism and Mexican Liberalism," *Journal of Interamerican Studies and World Affairs* 15 (May): 139–90.

—— (1973b) "Government and Elite in Late Colonial Mexico," *Hispanic American Historical Review* 53 (August): 389–414.

—— (1974) "Gobierno y élite en el México colonial durante el siglo XVIII," *Historia Mexicana* 23 (April–June): 611–45.

—— (1978) *Haciendas and Ranchos in the Mexican Bajío: León, 1700–1860.* Cambridge: Cambridge University Press.

—— (1984) "Bourbon Spain and its American Empire," pp. 389–439, *Cambridge History of Latin America* (vol. 1), Leslie Bethell, ed. Cambridge: Cambridge University Press.

—— (1985) *The Origins of Mexican Nationalism.* Cambridge: Centre of Latin American Studies, Cambridge University.

—— (1988a) "Liberal Patriotism and the Mexican Reforma," *Journal of Latin American Studies* 20 (May): 27–48.

—— (1988b) "Manuel Gamio and Official Indigenismo in Mexico," *Bulletin of Latin American Research* 7 (no. 1): 75–89.

—— (1990) "Images and Prophets: Indian Religion and Spanish Conquest," pp. 184–204, *The Indian Community of Colonial Mexico,* Arij Ouweneel & Simon Miller, eds. Amsterdam: Centre for Latin American Research and Documentation.

—— (1991) *The First America.* Cambridge: Cambridge University Press.

—— (1994a) *Church and State in Bourbon Mexico.* Cambridge: Cambridge University Press.

—— (1994b) "La Monarquía Católica," pp. 19–43, *De los imperios a las naciones: Iberoamérica,* Antonio Annino L. Castro Leiva & F.-X. Guerra, eds. Zaragoza: IberCaja.

—— (1995) "Nationalism and State-Building in Latin American History," pp. 89–107, *Wars, Parties and Nationalism,* Eduardo Posada-Carbó, ed. London: Institute of Latin American Studies, University of London.

—— (1996) *Apogeo y derrumbe del imperio español.* Mexico City: Clío.

—— (2007a) "La ideología de la Independencia mexicana y la crisis de la Iglesia católica," pp. 357–75, *México en tres momentos: 1810–1910–2010* (vol. 1), Alicia Mayer, ed. Mexico City: Instituto de Investigaciones Históricas, Universidad Nacional Autónoma de México.

—— (2007b) "Silver: Zacatecas in the Eighteenth Century," *Artes de México* 86 (October): 84–87.

Brandenburg, Frank (1964) *The Making of Modern Mexico.* Englewood Cliffs NJ: Prentice-Hall.

Braun, Herbert (1997) "Protests of Engagement: Dignity, False Love, and Self-Love in Mexico during 1968," *Comparative Studies in Society and History* 39 (July): 511–49.

Bray, David Burton (2007) "Buenas noticias acerca de los bosques mexicanos," *Este País* 192 (March): 54–56.

Brea, Jorge (2003) "Population Dynamics in Latin America," *Population Bulletin* 58 (March): 3–36.

Brewster, Keith (1998) "Gabriel Barrios Cabrera: The Anti-Agrarian Friend of the Campesino," *Bulletin of Latin American Research* 17 (September): 263–83.

Bricker, Victoria Reifler (1981) *Indian Christ, the Indian King.* Austin TX: University of Texas Press.

Briggs, Vernon M., Jr. (1978) "Labor Market Aspects of Mexican Migration to the United States in the 1970s," pp. 204–35, *Views across the Border,* Stanley Ross, ed. Albuquerque NM: University of New Mexico Press.

—— (1995) "Mass Immigration, Free Trade, and the Forgotten American Worker," *Challenge* 38 (May–June): 37–44.

Brito Domínguez, Myriam (2001) "Abortion in Mexico, Year 2000," *Voices of Mexico* 55 (April–June): 19–26.

Britton, John A. (1997) "Liberalism," pp. 738–42, *Encyclopedia of Mexico,* Michael S. Werner, ed. Chicago IL: Fitzroy Dearborn.

Brooks, David (1987) "Mexico: Whose Crisis, Whose Future?" *NACLA Report on the Americas* 21 (September–December): 13–39.

Brower, Derek (2007) "The Cost of Oil," *Petroleum Economist* (May): 22.

Brown, Jonathan C. (1985) "Why Foreign Oil Companies Shifted Their Production from Mexico to Venezuela During the 1920s," *American Historical Review* 90 (April): 362–85.

—— (1987) "Domestic Politics and Foreign Investment: British Development of Mexican Petroleum, 1889–1911," *Business History Review* 61 (Autumn): 387–416.

—— (1992) "The Structure of the Foreign-Owned Petroleum Industry in Mexico, 1880–1938," pp. 1–35, *The Mexican Petroleum Industry in the Twentieth Century,* Jonathan C. Brown & Alan Knight, eds. Austin TX: University of Texas Press.

—— (1993a) *Oil and Revolution in Mexico.* Berkeley CA: University of California Press.

—— (1993b) "Foreign and Native-Born Workers in Porfirian Mexico," *American Historical Review* 98 (June): 786–818.

—— (1997a) "Petroleum, pre-1938" pp. 1076–82, *Encyclopedia of Mexico,* Michael S. Werner, ed. Chicago IL: Fitzroy Dearborn.

—— (1997b) "Acting for Themselves," pp. 45–71, *Workers' Control in Latin America, 1930–1979,* Jonathan C. Brown, ed. Chapel Hill NC: University of North Carolina Press.

Brown, Jonathan C. & Peter S. Linder (1998) "Oil," pp. 125–87, *The Second Conquest of Latin America,* Steven C. Topik & Allen Wells, eds. Austin TX: University of Texas Press.

Brown, Lester (2006) *Plan B 2.0.* New York: Norton.

Brown, Lester, Gary Gardner & Brian Halweil (1999) *Beyond Malthus.* New York: Norton.

Brown, Lyle C. (1986) "The Calles-Cárdenas Connection," pp. 146–58, *Twentieth-Century Mexico,* W. Dirk Raat & William H. Beezley, eds. Lincoln NE: University of Nebraska Press.

Brown, William E. (1988) *The Santa Fe Trail.* St. Louis MO: Patrice.

Bruhn, Kathleen (1997a) *Taking on Goliath.* University Park PA: Pennsylvania State University Press.

—— (1997b) "Cuauhtémoc Cárdenas," pp. 189–92, *Encyclopedia of Mexico,* Michael S. Werner, ed. Chicago IL: Fitzroy Dearborn.

—— (1998) "The Partido de la Revolución Democrática," pp. 114–36, *Governing Mexico,* Mónica Serrano, ed. London: Institute of Latin American Studies, University of London.

—— (1999) "The Resurrection of the Mexican Left in the 1997 Elections," pp. 88–113, *Toward Mexico's Democratization,* Jorge Domínguez & Alejandro Poiré, eds. New York: Routledge.

—— (2004) "The Making of the Mexican President, 2000," pp. 123–56, *Mexico's Pivotal Democratic Election,* Jorge Domínguez & Chappell H. Lawson, eds. Palo Alto CA: Stanford University Press and San Diego CA: UCSD Center for U.S.–Mexican Studies.

Bruhn, Kathleen & Kenneth Greene (2007) "Optimismo moderado," *Foreign Affairs en español* (January–March): 132–43.

Brunk, Samuel (1995) *Emiliano Zapata.* Albuquerque NM: University of New Mexico Press.

Buchenau, Jürgen (1997) "Científicos," pp. 260–65, & "Foreign Policy: 1876–1910," pp. 501–06, *Encyclopedia of Mexico,* Michael S. Werner, ed. Chicago IL: Fitzroy Dearborn.

—— (2004) *Tools of Progress.* Albuquerque NM: University of New Mexico Press.

—— (2007) *Plutarco Elías Calles and the Mexican Revolution.* Lanham MD: Rowman & Littlefield.

Buckley, Tom (2005) "Supermarket Sweep" *Business Mexico* 15: 40–42.

Budd, Jim (1986) "Mexico Builds more Acapulcos," *Américas* 38 (May–June): 14–19.

Bulmer-Thomas, Victor (1994a) *The Economic History of Latin America since Independence.* Cambridge: Cambridge University Press.

—— (1994b) "The Latin American Economies, 1929–1939," pp. 65–115, *Cambridge History of Latin America* (vol. 6, pt. 1), Leslie Bethell, ed. Cambridge: Cambridge University Press.

Bulnes, Francisco (1916) *Whole Truth About Mexico.* New York: Bulnes.

Burger, Joanna (1997) *Oil Spills.* New Brunswick NJ: Rutgers University Press.

Burgess, Katrina (1999) "Loyalty Dilemmas and Market Reform," *World Politics* 52 (October): 105–34.

—— (2003) "Mexican Labor at a Crossroads," pp. 73–107, *Mexico's Politics and Society,* Joseph Tulchin & Andrew D. Selee, eds. Boulder CO: Lynne Rienner.

Burkholder, Mark (1976) "The Council of the Indies in the Late Eighteenth Century: A New Perspective," *Hispanic American Historical Review* 56 (August): 404–23.

—— (2000) "An Empire Beyond Compare," pp. 115–49, *Oxford History of Mexico,* Michael C. Meyer & William H. Beezley, eds. New York: Oxford University Press.

Burkholder, Mark & Lyman L. Johnson (1998) *Colonial Latin America* (3rd ed.). New York: Oxford University Press.

Bush, Diane Mitsch & Stephen P. Mumme (1994) "Gender and the Mexican Revolution," pp. 343–65, *Women and Revolution in Africa, Asia, and the New World,* Mary Ann Tétreault, ed. Columbia NC: University of South Carolina Press.

Bushnell, David & Neill Macaulay (1994) *The Emergence of Latin America in the Nineteenth Century* (2nd. ed.). New York: Oxford University Press.

Bustamante, Jorge A. (1972) "The Historical Context of Undocumented Mexican Immigration to the United States," *Aztlan* 3 (Fall): 257–81.

—— (1978) "Commodity Migrants," pp. 183–203, *Views across the Border,* Stanley Ross, ed. Albuquerque NM: University of New Mexico Press.

—— (1982) "La conceptualización y programación del desarrollo de la zona fronteriza norte de México," pp. 1–30, *Administración del desarrollo de la frontera norte,* Mario Ojeda, ed. Mexico City: Colegio de México.

—— (1983) "Mexican Migration," pp. 259–76, *U.S.–Mexican Relations,* Clark Reynolds & Raúl A. Hinojosa Ojeda, eds. Palo Alto CA: Stanford University Press.

—— (1987a) "La migración de los indocumentados," *El Cotidiano* Special no. 1: 13–29.

—— (1987b) "Commodity Migrants," pp. 183–203, *Views Across the Border,* Stanley R. Ross, ed. Albuquerque NM: University of New Mexico Press.

—— (1988) "Migración indocumentada México-Estados Unidos," pp. 917–44, *México: 75 años de Revolución—desarrollo social,* vol. 2. Mexico City: Fondo de Cultura Económica.

—— (1997a) "Undocumented Migration from Mexico to the United States," pp. 215–50, *Myths, Misdeeds, and Misunderstandings,* Jaime E. Rodríguez O. & Kathryn Vincent, eds. Wilmington DL: Scholarly Resources.

—— (1997b) "Mexico-United States Labor Migration Flows," *International Migration Review* 31 (Winter): 1112–21.

Butzer, Elisabeth (2001) *Historia social de una comunidad tlaxcalteca.* Saltillo: Archivo Municipal de Saltillo.

Buve, Raymond (1992) "Political Patronage and Politics at the Village Level in Central Mexico," *Bulletin of Latin American Research* 11 (January): 1–28.

Cabrera Acevedo, Gustavo (1985) "El desarrollo demográfico en el período posrevolucionario," pp. 107–25, *El desarrollo en México después de la revolución de 1910,* Mario M. Carrillo & Gabriel Reyes, eds. Mexico City: Colegio de México.

—— (1993) "Introducción," pp. 8–31, *El poblamiento de México,* vol. 4. Mexico City: Consejo Nacional de Población.

—— (2000) "Del México rural al México urbano," *El Mercado de Valores* 60 (March): 22–33.

Cahill, Simon (2001) "No Quick Fix," *MB* 7 (March): 22–28.

Calavita, Kitty (1997) "The Bracero Program," pp. 157–60, *Encyclopedia of Mexico,* Michael S. Werner, ed. Chicago IL: Fitzroy Dearborn.

Calderón, Enrique & Daniel Cazés (1994) *Tecnología ciudadana para la democracia.* Mexico City: La Jornada Ediciones.

Calderón, Felipe (2006) *El hijo desobediente.* Mexico City: Nuevo Silgo/Aguilar.

Calderón, Francisco R. (1988) *Historia económica de la Nueva España.* Mexico City: Fondo de Cultura Económica.

Calderón, José María (1972) *Génesis del presidencialismo en México.* Mexico City: El Caballito.

Calderón, Leticia (1994) "Migración indígena a Estados Unidos y a la frontera norte," *El Cotidiano* 62 (May–June): 38–42.

Calderón de la Barca, Fanny (1966) *Life in Mexico.* Garden City NY: Anchor/Doubleday.

Callahan, James Morton (1909) *Evolution of Seward's Mexican Policy.* Morgantown WV: West Virginia University.

Calles, Plutarco Elías (1926) "The Policies of Mexico Today," *Foreign Affairs* 5 (October): 1–5.

Calva, José Luis (2004a) "Ajuste estructural y TLCAN," *El Cotidiano* 124 (March–April): 14–22.

—— (2004b) "La economía mexicana en perspectiva," pp. 100–32, *La pobreza en México y el mundo,"* Julio Boltvinik & Arceli Damián, eds. Mexico City: Siglo XXI.

Camacho Guzmán, Óscar & Alejandro Almazán (2006) *La victoria que no fue.* Mexico City: Grijalbo.

Camarena, Salvador (2006) "Felipe Calderón: el precoz," pp. 53–94, *El Presidente,* Jorge Zepeda Patterson, ed. Mexico City: Planeta.

Camarena, Salvador & Jorge Zepeda Patterson (2007) *El presidente electo.* Mexico City: Planeta.

Camp, Roderic A. (1979a) "Women and Political Leadership in Mexico," *Journal of Politics* 41 (May): 417–41.

—— (1979b) "Mexico in Crisis," *Latin American Digest* 13 (Summer): 1–4, 28.

—— (1982) "Censure: Media et via intellectuelle," *Etudes Mexicaines* 5: 29–58.

—— (1985) *Intellectuals and the State in Twentieth-Century Mexico.* Austin TX: University of Texas Press.

—— (1992) *Generals in the Palacio.* New York: Oxford University Press.

—— (1995a) *Political Recruitment Across Two Centuries.* Austin TX: University of Texas Press.

—— (1995b) "The PAN's Social Bases," pp. 65–80, *Opposition Government in Mexico,* Victoria E. Rodríguez & Peter M. Ward, eds. Albuquerque NM: University of New Mexico Press.

—— (1997) *Crossing Swords.* New York: Oxford University Press.

—— (2000) "The Time of the Technocrats and Deconstruction of the Revolution," pp. 609–36, *Oxford History of Mexico,* Michael C. Meyer & William H. Beezley, eds. New York: Oxford University Press.

—— (2002) *Mexico's Mandarins.* Berkeley CA: University of California Press.

—— (2003) *Politics in Mexico* (4th ed.). New York: Oxford University Press.

—— (2004) "Citizen Attitudes Toward Democracy and Vicente Fox's Victory in 2000," pp. 25–46, *Mexico's Pivotal Democratic Election,* Jorge I. Dominguez & Chappell H. Lawson, eds. Palo Alto CA: Stanford University Press & San Diego CA: UCSD Center for U.S.–Mexican Studies.

—— (2005) *Mexico's Military on the Democratic Stage.* Westport CT: Praeger Security International.

Campa, Valentín (1985) *Mi testimonio* (revised ed.). Mexico City: Ediciones de Cultura Popular.

Campbell, Randolph B. (2003) *Gone to Texas.* New York: Oxford University Press.

Cano Escalante, Francisco (2002) "El desarrollo económico de la Ciudad de México," pp. 153–61, *¿Una ciudad para todos?* Lucía Álvarez Enríquez, María Concepción Huarte Trujillo, Cristina Sánchez-Mejorada Fernández, & Carlos San Juan Victoria, eds. Azcapotzalco: Universidad Autónoma Metropolitana (UAM).

Cansino, César (2000) *La transición mexicana 1977–2000* (2nd ed.). Mexico City: Centro de Estudios de Política Comparada.

Carbó, Margarita (1988) "La oligarquía," pp. 13–131, *Oligarquía y Revolución (1876–1920)*, México: un pueblo en la historia, vol. 3. Mexico City: Alianza Editorial Mexicana.

Cárdenas, Enrique (1984) "The Great Depression and Industrialisation: The Case of Mexico," pp. 222–41, *Latin America in the 1930s,* Rosemary Thorp, ed. New York: St. Martin's Press.

—— (1987) *La industrialización mexicana durante la Gran Depresión.* Mexico City: Colegio de México.

—— (1997a) "A Macroeconomic Interpretation of Nineteenth-Century Mexico," pp. 65–92, *How Latin America Fell Behind,* Stephen Haber, ed. Palo Alto CA: Stanford University Press.

—— (1997b) "Great Depression," pp. 612–13, *Encyclopedia of Mexico,* Michael S. Werner, ed. Chicago IL: Fitzroy Dearborn.

—— (2002a) "The Great Depression and Industrialisation," pp. 195–211, *An Economic History of Twentieth-Century Latin America,* (vol. 2), Enrique Cárdenas, José Antonio Ocampo & Rosemary Thorp, eds. Houndsmills, Basingstoke: Palgrave.

—— (2000b) "The Process of Accelerated Industrialization in Mexico, 1919–82," pp. 176–204, *An Economic History of Twentieth-Century Latin America,* (vol. 3), Enrique Cárdenas, José Antonio Ocampo & Rosemary Thorp, eds. Houndsmills, Basingstoke: Palgrave.

—— (2003) *Cuando se originó el atraso económico de México.* Madrid: Biblioteca Nueva.

Cárdenas, Enrique & Carlos Manns (1987) "Inflation and Monetary Stabilization in Mexico during the Revolution," *Journal of Development Economics* 27 (October): 375–94.

Cárdenas, Gilberto (1975) "United States Immigration Policy toward Mexico," *Chicano Law Review* 2 (Summer): 66–91.

Cárdenas, Lázaro (1940) *El problema indígena de México.* Mexico City: Departamento de Asuntos Indígenas.

—— (1972) *Apuntes* (4 vols.). Mexico City: Dirección General de Publicaciones, Universidad Nacional Autónoma de México.

Cárdenas García, Nicolás (1986) "La Revolución mexicana y los inicios de la organización empresarial, 1917–1918," *Secuencia* 4 (January–April): 24–41.

Cardoso, Ciro F. S. (1980) "Las industrias de transformación (1821–1880)," pp. 147–65, *México en el siglo XIX (1821–1910),* Ciro Cardoso, ed. Mexico City: Nueva Imagen.

Cardoso, Ciro F. S. & Francisco G. Hermosillo (1980) "Las clases sociales durante el estado liberal de transición y la dictadura porfirista (1867–1910)," pp. 7–100, *De la dictadura porfirista a los tiempos libertarios,* Ciro F. S. Cardoso, Francisco G. Hermosillo, & Salvador Hernández, eds. *La clase obrera en la historia de México,* vol. 3. Mexico City: Siglo XXI.

Cardoso, Lawrence (1980) *Mexican Emigration to the United States, 1897–1931.* Tucson AZ: University of Arizona Press.

Careaga Viliesid, Lorena (1997) "Filibusteros, mercenarios y voluntarios: los soldados norteamericanos en la Guerra de Castas de Yucatán, 1848–1850," pp. 123–200, *Política y negocios,* Ana Rosa Suárez Argüello & Marcela Terrazas Basante, eds. Mexico City: Universidad Nacional Autónoma de México & Instituto Mora.

Carlsen, Laura (2007) "Militarizing Mexico: The New War on Drugs," *Foreign Policy in Focus* (July 12).

Carmagnani, Marcello (1988) *El regreso de los dioses.* Mexico City: Fondo de Cultura Económica.

Carmelo, Rosa (1985) "El cura y el alcalde mayor," pp. 149–65, *El gobierno provincial en la Nueva España: 1570–1787,* Woodrow Borah, ed. Mexico City: Instituto de Investigaciones Históricas, Universidad Nacional Autónoma de México.

Carpenter, Ted (2003) *Bad Neighbor Policy.* New York: Palgrave Macmillan.

Carpizo, Jorge (1985) "El principio de no reelección," pp. 119–28, *Las elecciones en México,* Pablo González Casanova, ed. Mexico City: Siglo XXI.

Carr, Barry (1973) "Las peculiaridades del norte mexicano, 1880–1927," *Historia Mexicana* 22 (January–March): 320–46.

—— (1992) *Marxism & Communism in Twentieth-Century Mexico.* Lincoln NE: University of Nebraska Press.

—— (1996) "Labor Internationalism in the Era of NAFTA," pp. 209–32, *Neoliberalism Revisited,* Gerardo Otero, ed. Boulder CO: Westview.

—— (1997) "Communism and Communist Parties," pp. 279–282, & "Industrial Labor: 1910–40," pp. 687–691, *Encyclopedia of Mexico,* Michael S. Werner, ed. Chicago IL: Fitzroy Dearborn.

Carrera Stampa, Manuel (1995) "Hidalgo y su plan de operaciones," pp. 73–87, *La revolución de independencia,* Viriginia Guedea, ed. Mexico City: Colegio de México.

Carrillo, Jorge (1995) "Flexible Production in the Auto Sector," *World Development* 23 (no. 1): 87–101.

Carrillo Luvianos, Mario & Alejandra Toscana Aparcio (2005) "El Partido Acción Nacional y sus saldos electorales (1997-2003)" *El Cotidiano* 133 (September–October): 45–55.

Carroll, Patrick J. (1991) *Blacks in Colonial Veracruz.* Austin TX: University of Texas Press.

—— (1995) "Los mexicanos negros, el mestizaje y los fundamentos olvidados de la 'Raza Cósmica': una perspectiva regional," *Historia Mexicana* 175 (January–March): 403–38.

Caruso, A. Brooke (1991) *The Mexican Spy Company.* Jefferson NC: McFarland.

Casas, Bartolomé de las (1992) *A Short Account of the Destruction of the Indies.* London: Penguin.

Case, Alden Buell (1917) *Thirty Years with the Mexicans.* New York: Revell.

Casellas, Roberto (1993) "Confederate Colonization of Mexico," *Voices of Mexico* 22 (January–March): 56–62.

Casino, César (2000) *La transición mexicana, 1977–2000* (2nd ed.). Mexico City: Centro de Estudios de Política Comparada.

Castañeda, Carlos E. (1942) *Our Catholic Heritage in Texas, 1519–1936,* vol. 5. Austin TX: Von Boeckmann-Jones.

—— (1949) "Relations of General Scott with Santa Anna," *Hispanic American Historical Review* 29 (November): 455–73.

—— (2000) "The Beginnings of University Life in America," pp. 81–100, *New Foundations: Preliminary Studies of the Texas Catholic Historical Society,* vol. 3, Jesús F. de la Teja, ed. Austin TX: Texas Catholic Historical Society.

Castañeda, Jorge G. (1985–86) "Mexico at the Brink," *Foreign Affairs* 64 (Winter): 287–303.

—— (1990) "Salinas' International Gamble," *Journal of International Affairs* 43 (Winter): 407–22.

—— (1993a) "Can NAFTA Change Mexico?" *Foreign Affairs* 72 (September-October): 66–80.

—— (1993b) "The Intellectuals and the State in Latin America," *World Policy Journal* 10 (Fall): 89–96.

—— (1993c) *Utopia Unarmed.* New York: Knopf.

—— (1996) "Mexico's Circle of Misery," *Foreign Affairs* 75 (July–August): 92–105.

—— (2000) *Perpetuating Power.* New York: New Press.

—— (2003) "The Forgotten Relationship," *Foreign Affairs* 82 (May-June): 67–81.

—— (2004) *Somos muchos.* Mexico City: Planeta.

—— (2007) *Ex Mex.* New York: New Press.

Castaños-Lomnitz, Heriberta (2001) "La educación como lugar de mediación individuo-sociedad," pp. 339–54, *¿Estamos unidos mexicanos?* Mauricio de María Campos & Georgina Sánchez, eds. Mexico City: Planeta.

Castells, Manuel (1978) "Trabajadores inmigrantes y lucha de clases," *Cuadernos Políticos* 18 (October–December): 71–93.

Castells, Manuel & Alejandro Portes (1989) "World Underneath," pp. 11–37, *The Informal Economy,* Alejandro Portes & Lauren A. Benton, eds. Baltimore MD: Johns Hopkins University Press.

Castro, Daniel (2007) *Another Face of Empire.* Durham NC: Duke University Press.

Castro Gutiérrez, Felipe (1994) "Del paternalismo autoritario al autoritarismo burocrático: los éxitos y fracasos de José de Gálvez (1764–1767)," pp. 21–33, *Mexico in the Age of Democratic Revoutions,* Jaime E. Rodríguez O., ed. Boulder CO: Lynne Rienner.

Catão, Luis (1992) *The Failure of Export-Led Growth in Brazil and Mexico, c. 1870–1930.* London: Institute of Latin American Studies, University of London.

Cazadero, Manuel (1973) "¿Pudo México ganar la guerra contra los Estados Unidos?" *Anglia* 5: 113–25.

CDI (Comisión Nacional para el Desarrollo de los Pueblos Indígenas) (2005) *Acciones de gobierno para el desarrollo integral de los pueblos indígenas: Informe 2003–2004.* Mexico City: Comisión Nacional para el Desarrollo de los Pueblos Indígenas.

CDIA (Centro de Investigaciones Agrarias) (1974) *Estructura Agraria y Desarrollo Agrícola en México.* Mexico City: Fondo de Cultura Económica.

Centeno, Miguel Ángel (1994) *Democracy Within Reason.* University Park PA: Pennsylvania State University Press.

Cerutti, Mario (1999) "Comercio, guerras y capitales en torno al Río Bravo," pp. 13–111, *El Norte de México y Texas (1848–1880).* Mexico City: Instituto Mora.

Cervantes de Salazar, Francisco (1953) *Life in the Imperial and Loyal City of Mexico in New Spain.* Austin TX: University of Texas Press.

Chacón, Susana (2000) "La negociación del acuerdo militar entre México y los Estados Unidos, 1940–1942," *Foro Internacional* 40 (April–June): 307–44.

Chaffin, Joshua (1997) "The Great Railway Sale," *US/Mexico Business* 4 (November): 32–43.

Chambers, Edward & Peter Smith (2002) "NAFTA in the New Millennium" pp. 1–24, *NAFTA in the New Millennium,* Edward J. Chambers & Peter H. Smith, eds. San Diego CA: Center for U.S.–Mexican Studies and Edmonton: University of Alberta Press.

Chance, John K. (1976) "The Urban Indian in Colonial Oaxaca," *American Ethnologist* 3 (November): 603–32.

—— (1978) *Race and Class in Colonial Oaxaca.* Palo Alto CA: Stanford University Press.

Chance, John K. & William B. Taylor (1977) "Estate and Class in a Colonial City: Oaxaca in 1792," *Comparative Studies in Society and History* 19 (October): 454–87.

Chang, Ha-Joon (2008) *Bad Samaritans.* New York: Bloomsbury.

Chanda, Nayan (2007) *Bound Together.* New Haven CT: Yale University Press.

Chant, Sylvia (1991) *Women and Survival in Mexican Cities.* Manchester: Manchester University Press.

Chapman, Charles E. (1921) *A History of California: The Spanish Period.* New York: Macmillan.

Chassen-López, Francie R. (2004) *From Liberal to Revolutionary Oaxaca.* University Park PA: Pennsylvania State University Press.

Chavarri, Juan N. (1973) *Historia de la guerra de independencia de 1810 a 1821.* Mexico City: Diana.

Chávez Balderas, Ximena (2008) "Death during the Conquest Era," pp. 167–84, *Invasion and Transformation,* Rebecca Brienen & Margaret A. Jackson, eds. Boulder CO: University Press of Colorado.

Chevalier, François (1963) *Land and Society in Colonial Mexico.* Berkeley CA: University of California Press.

—— (1964) "Conservateurs el libéraux au Mexique," *Cahiers d'Historie Mondiale* 8 (no. 3): 457–74.

—— (1985) "Conservadores y liberales en México," *Secuencia* 1 (March): 136–49.

Chinchilla-Aguilar, Ernesto (1983) "El Siglo XVII novohispano y la figura de Sor Juana Inés," *University of Dayton Review* 16 (Spring): 53–62.

Chipman, Donald E. (1992) *Spanish Texas, 1519–1821.* Austin TX: University of Texas Press.

Chorba, Carrie C. (2007) *Mexico, from Mestizo to Multicultural.* Nashville TN: Vanderbilt University Press.

Chua, Amy (2007) *Day of Empire.* New York: Random House.

CIA (Central Intelligence Agency) (1951) *Mexico.* Washington DC: CIA.

—— (1964) *Survey of Latin America.* Washington DC: CIA.

—— (1967) "Security Conditions in Mexico," Special National Intelligence Estimate, 81–67, October Washington DC: CIA.

Clancy, Michael (1995) *Exporting Paradise.* Paper presented at Latin American Studies Association Meetings. Washington, DC.

Cleary, Edward (1997) *The Struggle for Human Rights in Latin America.* Westport CT: Praeger.

Cleaver, Harry (2004) "*The Zapatistas* and the Electronic *Fabric* of Struggle," Symposium on Indigenous Rights and the Law in Mexico, August 28, 2004, the University of Texas at Austin TX.

Clement, Norris (1982) "Perspectivas sobre el desarrollo económico de la región fronteriza del sudoeste de Estados Unidos," pp. 141–84, *Administración del desarrollo de la frontera norte,* Mario Ojeda, ed. Mexico City: Colegio de México.

Clendenen, Clarence C. (1969) *Blood on the Border.* New York: Macmillan.

Cline, Howard F. (1963) *Mexico: Revolution to Evolution, 1940–1960.* New York: Oxford University Press.

—— (1971) *The United States and Mexico* (revised ed.). New York: Atheneum.

—— (1972) "Introductory Notes on Territorial Divisions of Middle America," pp. 17–62, *Handbook of Middle American Indians,* vol. 12. Austin TX: University of Texas Press.

Cline, Sarah (2000) "The Spiritual Conquest Reexamined," pp. 73–101, *The Church in Colonial Latin America,* John F. Schwaller, ed. Wilmington DE: Scholarly Resources.

Cline, William R. (1982–83) "Mexico's Crisis," *Foreign Policy* 49 (Winter): 107–18.

Coatsworth, John H. (1978) "Obstacles to Growth in Nineteenth-Century Mexico," *American Historical Review* 83 (February): 80–100.

—— (1979) "Indispensable Railroads in the Mexican Economy," *Journal of Economic History* 39 (December): 939–60.

—— (1981) *Growth Against Development.* DeKalb IL: Northern Illinois University Press.

—— (1982) "The Limits of Colonial Absolutism: The State in Eighteenth Century Mexico," pp. 25–52, *Essays in the Political, Economic, and Social History of Colonial Latin America,* Karen Spalding, ed. Newark NJ: Latin American Studies Program, University of Delaware.

—— (1985) "El Estado y el sector externo en México, 1800–1910," *Secuencia* 2 (August): 40–54.

—— (1986) "The Mexican Mining Industry in the Eighteenth Century," pp. 26–45, *The Economies of Mexico and Peru During the Late Colonial Period, 1760–1810,* Nils Jacobsen & Hans-Jürgen Puhle, eds. Berlin: Colloquium Verlag.

—— (1988) "Patterns of Rural Rebellion in Latin America: Mexico in Comparative Perspective," pp. 21–62, *Riot, Rebellion, and Revolution,* Friedrich Katz, ed. Princeton NJ: Princeton University Press.

—— (1990) *Los orígenes del atraso.* Mexico City: Alianza Editorial Mexicana.

—— (1998a) "Economic and Institutional Trajectories in Nineteenth-Century Latin America," pp. 23–54, *Latin America and the World Economy since 1800,* John H. Coatsworth & Alan M. Taylor, eds. Cambridge MA: David Rockefeller Center for Latin American Studies.

—— (1998b) "Measuring Influence: The United States and the Mexican Peasantry," pp. 64–71, *Rural Revolt in Mexico,* 2nd ed., Daniel Nugent, ed. Durham NC: Duke University Press.

—— (1999) "The United States and Democracy in Mexico," pp. 141–55. *The United States and Latin America: The New Agenda,* Victor Bulmer-Thomas & James Dunkerly, eds. London: Institute of Latin American Studies, University of London.

—— (2006) "Political Economy and Economic Organization," pp. 237–73, *Cambridge Economic History of Latin America* (vol. 1) Victor Bulmer-Thomas, John H. Coatsworth, & Roberto Cortés Conde, eds. New York: Cambridge University Press.

—— (2008) "Inequality, Institutions and Economic Growth in Latin America," *Journal of Latin American Studies* 40 (August): 545–69.

Cockcroft, James D. (1968) *Intellectual Precursors of the Mexican Revolution, 1900–1913.* Austin TX: University of Texas Press.

—— (1972) "Social and Economic Structure of the Porfiriato: Mexico, 1877–1911," pp. 47–70, *Dependence and Underdevelopment,* James D. Cockcroft, André Gunder Frank, & Dale L. Johnson, eds. Garden City NY: Anchor/Doubleday.

—— (1974) "Mexico," pp. 222–303, *Latin America: The Struggle with Dependency and Beyond,* Ronald H. Chilcote & Joel C. Edelstein, eds. New York: Wiley.

—— (1991) *Diego Rivera.* New York: Chelsea House.

—— (1998) *Mexico's Hope.* New York: Monthly Review.

Coe, Michael D. (1964) "The Chinampas of Mexico," *Scientific American* 211 (July): 90–98.

—— (1999) *Breaking the Code* (revised ed.). New York: Thames & Hudson.

—— (2005) *The Maya* (7th ed.). London: Thames & Hudson.

Coe, Michael D. & Rex Koontz (2002) *Mexico from the Olmecs to the Aztecs* (5th ed.). New York: Thames & Hudson.

Coerver, Don M. (1979) *The Porfirian Interregnum.* Fort Worth TX: Texas Christian University Press.

—— (1999) "Mexico: Conflicting Self-Interests," p. 11–34, *United States-Latin American Relations, 1850–1903,* Thomas M. Leonard, ed. Tuscaloosa AL: University of Alabama Press.

Coerver, Don M. & Linda B. Hall. (1999) *Tangled Destinies.* Albuquerque NM: University of New Mexico Press.

Cole, Richard Ray (1972) *The Mass Media of Mexico.* PhD. Dissertation. Minneapolis MN: University of Minnesota.

Colegio de México (1960) *Estadísticas económicas del Porfiriato: comercio exterior de México 1877–1911.* Mexico City: Colegio de México.

—— (1964) *Estadísticas económicas del Porfiriato: fuerza de trabajo y actividad económica por sectores.* Mexico City: Colegio de México.

Collado, María del Carmen (1987a) *La burguesía mexicana, el emporio Braniff y su participación política, 1865–1920.* Mexico City: Siglo XXI.

—— (1987b) "El régimen porfirista y la privatización del subsuelo petrolero," *Secuencia* 8 (August): 53–69.

—— (1996) "De los empresarios y la Revolución," *Universidad de México* 545 (June): 50–53.

—— (2003) *Private and Public Interests in Mexico's Growth.* Dallas TX: Latin American Studies Association.

—— (2005) *Dwight W. Morrow.* Mexico City: Secretaría de Relaciones Exteriores & Instituto Mora.

CONAPO (Consejo Nacional de Población) (2001) *La población de México en el nuevo siglo* (2nd ed.). Mexico City.

Concha Malo, Miguel (1988) "Las violaciones a los derechos humanos individuales en México (período: 1971–1986)" pp. 115–87, *Primer Informe sobre la democracia: México 1988,* Pablo González Casanova & Jorge Cadena Roa, eds. Mexico City: Siglo XXI.

Connolly, Pricilla (1999a) "Introducción," pp. 141–64, & "El desagüe del Valle de México," pp. 191–219, *Ferrocarriles y obras públicas.* Mexico City: Instituto Mora.

—— (1999b) "Pearson y la deuda pública porfirista," *Casa del Tiempo* 8 (September): 26–37.

Contreras, Ariel José (1977) *México 1940.* Mexico City: Siglo XXI.

Cook, Maria Lorena (1995) "Mexican State-Labor Relations and the Political Implications of Free trade," *Latin American Perspectives* 22 (Winter): 77–94.

—— (2007) *The Politics of Labor Reform in Latin America*. University Park PA: Pennsylvania State University Press.

Cook, Maria Lorena, Kevin Middlebrook & Juan Molinar Horcasitas (2007) "Las dimenciones políticas del ajuste structural," pp. 37–76, *Sistema Político Mexciano*. Mexico City: Facultad de Ciencias Sociales y Políticas, Universidad Nacional Autónoma de México.

Cook, Scott (2003) "Struggling to Understand Complexity," *Mexican Studies/Estudios Mexicanos* 19 (Winter): 203–41.

Cook, Sherburne F. (1976) *The Conflict Between the California Indian and White Civilization*. Berkeley CA: University of California Press.

Cooper, Marc (2003) "Behind Globalization's Glitz," *Nation* 277 (September 22): 17–20.

Cope, R. Douglas (1994) *The Limits of Racial Domination*. Madison WI: University of Wisconsin Press.

Córdova, Arnaldo (1973) *La ideología de la Revolución Mexicana*. Mexico City: Era.

—— (1974) "Los maestros rurales en el cardenismo" *Cuadernos Políticos* 2 (October–December): 77–92.

—— (1978) "El pensamiento social y político de Andrés Molina Enríquez," pp. 9–68, *Los grandes problemas nacionales*, Andrés Molina Enríquez. Mexico City: Era.

—— (1989) *La Revolución y el estado en México*. Mexico City: Era.

—— (1995) *La Revolución en crisis; la aventura del maximato*. Mexico City: Cal y Arena.

—— (2007) "La ideología de la Revolución Mexicana en la perspectiva de un silgo," pp. 325–32, *México en tres momentos: 1810–1910–2010* (vol. 2), Alicia Mayer, ed. Mexico City: Instituto de Investigaciones Históricas, Universidad Nacional Autónoma de México.

Córdova, Lorenzo & Ciro Murayama (2006) *Elecciones, dinero y corrupción: Pemexgate y Amigos de Fox*. Mexico City: Cal y Arena.

Córdova Vianello, Lorenzo (2006) "El 'recurso líder' de la Coalición por el Bien de Todos," *Nexos* 344 (August): 25–27.

Cornelius, Wayne A. (1969) "Urbanization as an Agent in Latin American Political Institutions," *American Political Science Review* 63 (September): 883–57.

—— (1973) "Nation Building, Participation, and Distribution: The Politics of Social Reform Under Cárdenas," pp. 392–498, *Crisis, Choice, and Change*, Gabriel A. Almond, Scott C. Flanagan & Robert J. Mundt, eds. Boston MA: Little, Brown.

—— (1985) "The Political Economy of Mexico Under De la Madrid," *Mexican Studies/Estudios Mexicanos* 1 (Winter): 83–124.

—— (1986) "The Political Economy of Mexico Under De la Madrid," UCSD Research Report Series, 43. San Diego CA: UCSD Center for U.S.–Mexican Studies.

—— (1987) "Political Liberalization in an Authoritarian Regime" pp. 15–39, *Mexican Politics in Transition*, Judith Gentleman, ed. Boulder CO: Westview.

—— (1991) "Las elecciones de 1991," *Cuadernos de Nexos* 40 (October): pp. iii–iv.

—— (1998) "The Structural Embeddedness of Demand for Mexican Immigrant Labor," pp. 113–55, *Crossings*, Marcelo M. Suárez-Orozco, ed. Cambridge: David Rockefeller Center for Latin American Studies.

—— (2001) "Death at the Border," *Population & Development Review* 27 (December): 661–85.

—— (2002) "Impacts of NAFTA on Mexico-to-U.S. Migration," pp. 287–304, *NAFTA in the New Millennium*, Edward J. Chambers & Peter H. Smith, eds. San Diego CA: UCSD Center for U.S. Mexican Studies and Edmonton: University of Alberta Press.

—— (2007) "Introduction" pp. 1–15, *Impacts of Border Enforcement on Mexican Immigration*, Wayne A. Cornelius, ed. San Diego CA: Center for Comparative Immigration Studies, University of California, San Diego.

Cornelius, Wayne, Judith Gentleman & Peter Smith (1989) "Overview," pp. 1–51, *Mexico's Alternative Political Futures*, Wayne Cornelius, Judith Gentleman, & Peter H. Smith, eds. UCSD Center for U.S.–Mexican Studies Monograph Series, 30. San Diego CA: UCSD Center for U.S. Mexican Studies.

Corona, Carlos (2003) "El debate de la migración entre México y Estados Unidos después del 11 de septiembre de 2001," *El Cotidiano* 120 (July–August): 17–25.

Cortada, James W. (1978) *Two Nations Over Time: Spain and the United States, 1776–1977*. Westport CT: Greenwood.

Cortés, Fernando, Daniel Hernández, Enrique Hernández Laos, Miguel Székely, & Hadid Vera Llamas (2005) "Evolución y características de la pobreza en México en la última década del siglo XX," pp. 223–51, *Números que mueven al mundo: la medición de la pobreza en México*, Miguel Székely, ed. Mexico City: Miguel Ángel Porrúa.

Cortés, Hernán (1971) *Letters from Mexico*. New York: Grossman.

Cortés Conde, Roberto (2006) "Fiscal and Monetary Regimes," pp. 209–47, *Cambridge Economic History of Latin America* (vol. 2) Victor Bulmer-Thomas, John H. Coatsworth, & Roberto Cortés Conde, eds. New York: Cambridge University Press.

Cortez, Willy (2001) "What is Behind Increasing Wage Inequality in Mexico?" *World Development* 29 (no. 11): 1905–22.

Corwin, Arthur F. (1973) "Causes of Mexican Emigration to the United States," pp. 557–635, *Perspectives in American History*, vol. 7. Cambridge MA: The Charles Warren Center for Studies in American History, Harvard University.

—— (1978) "¿Quién Sabe?" pp. 108–35, *Immigrants—and Immigrants,* Arthur F. Corwin, ed. Westport CT: Greenwood.

Cosío Villegas, Daniel (1955) *La República Restaurada, La vida política.* Historia moderna de México, vol. 1. Mexico City: Hermes.

—— (1963) *El Porfiriato.* Historia moderna de México, vol. 5, pt. 2. Mexico City: Hermes.

—— (1966) *Ensayos y Notas,* vol. 1. Mexico City: Hermes.

—— (1972a) *Historia moderna de México: el Porfiriato: La vida política interior,* pt. 2. Mexico City: Hermes.

—— (1972b) *El sistema político mexicano.* Mexico City: Joaquín Mortiz.

—— (1975a) "Mexico's Crisis," pp. 73–86, *Is the Mexican Revolution Dead?* (2nd ed.), Stanley R. Ross ed. Philadelphia PA: Temple University Press.

—— (1975b) *La sucesión presidencial.* Mexico City: Joaquín Mortiz.

—— (1997a) *La constitución de 1857 y sus críticos.* Mexico City: Clío.

—— (1997b) *Estados Unidos contra Porfirio Díaz.* Mexico City: Clío.

Costeloe, Michael P. (1967) *Church Wealth in Mexico.* London: Cambridge University Press.

—— (1988a) "Federalism to Centralism in Mexico: The Conservative Case for Change, 1834–1835," *The Americas* 45 (October): 173–85.

—— (1988b) "The Mexican Press of 1836 and the Battle of the Alamo," *Southwestern Historical Quarterly* 91 (April): 533–43.

—— (1989a) "Generals versus Politicians: Santa Anna and the 1842 Congressional Elections in Mexico," *Bulletin of Latin American Research* 8 (no. 2): 257–74.

—— (1989b) "Los generales Santa Anna y Paredes y Arrillaga en México, 1841–1843," *Historia Mexicana* 39 (October–December): 417–40.

—— (1993) *The Central Republic in Mexico, 1835–1846.* Cambridge: Cambridge University Press.

—— (1997) "The Junta Patriótica and the Celebration of Independence in Mexico City, 1825–1855," *Mexican Studies/Estudios Mexicanos* 13 (Winter): 21–53.

—— (1999) "The Extraordinary Case of Mr. Falconnet and 2,500,000 Silver Dollars: London and Mexico, 1850–1853," *Mexican Studies/Estudios Mexicanos* 15 (Summer): 261–89.

Cothran, Dan A. (1991) "The Echeverría Years," pp. xi–xxvi, *The Deterioration of the Mexican Presidency* by Samuel Schmidt. Tucson AZ: University of Arizona Press.

—— (1994) *Political Stability and Democracy in Mexico.* Westport CT: Praeger.

Cott, Kennett S. (1978) *Porfirian Investment Policies, 1876–1910.* Ph.D. Dissertation. Albuquerque NM: University of New Mexico.

Couturier, Edith (1981) "Marcela Angela Carrillo: Widow and Pulque Dealer," pp. 362–75, *Struggle and Survival in Colonial America,* David G. Sweet & Gary B. Nash, eds. Berkeley CA: University of California Press.

—— (1985) "Women and the Family in Eighteenth-Century Mexico: Law and Practice," *Journal of Family History* 10 (Fall): 294–304.

—— (2003) *The Silver King.* Albuquerque NM: University of New Mexico Press.

Covarrubias Gaitán, Francisco (1988) "El desarrollo urbano en México," pp. 611–92, *Mexico: 75 años de Revolución: Desarrollo Social II,* Mexico City; Fondo de Cultura Económica.

Craig, Ann L. (1990) "Legal Constraints and Mobilizing Strategies in the Countryside," pp. 59–77, *Popular Movements and Political Change in Mexico,* Joe Foweraker & Ann L. Craig, eds. Boulder CO: Lynne Rienner.

Crandall, Russell (2005) "Mexico's Domestic Economy," pp. 61–87, *Mexico's Democracy at Work,* Russell Crandall, Guadalupe Paz, & Riordan Roett, eds. Boulder CO: Lynne Rienner.

Crespo, José Antonio (1995) *Urnas de Pandora.* Mexico City: Espasa Calpe.

—— (2009) *Contra la historia official.* Mexico City: Debate.

Cronon, E. David (1960) *Josephus Daniels in Mexico.* Madison WI: University of Wisconsin Press.

Crosby, Alfred W. (1986) *Ecological Imperialism.* Cambridge: Cambridge University Press.

Cue Mancera, Agustín (2001) "El error de diciembre y *el libro verde,*" *El Cotidiano* 105 (January–February): 70–79.

—— (2004) "Panorama de la política económica en México (1984-2004)," *El Cotidiano* 126 (July–August): 39–54.

Cuéllar, Mireya (2003) *Los panistas.* Mexico City: La Jornada Ediciones.

Cuevas, José Luis (1959) "The Cactus Curtain," *Evergreen Review* 2 (Winter): 111–20.

Cumberland, Charles C. (1952) *Mexican Revolution: Genesis under Madero.* Austin TX: University of Texas Press.

—— (1968) *Mexico: The Struggle for Modernity.* New York: Oxford University Press.

Cunniff, Roger L. (1966) "Mexican Municipal Electoral Reform 1810–1822," pp. 56–86, *Mexico and the Spanish Cortes, 1810–1822,* Nettie Lee Benson, ed. Austin TX: University of Texas Press.

Curcio-Nagy, Linda A. (2000) "Faith and Morals in Colonial Mexico," pp. 151–81, *Oxford History of Mexico,* Michael C. Meyer & William H. Beezley, eds. New York: Oxford University Press.

Cutter, Charles R. (1995) *The Legal Culture of Northern New Spain, 1700–1810.* Albuquerque NM: University of New Mexico Press.

Cutter, Donald C. (1990) *California in 1792.* Norman OK: University of Oklahoma Press.

Cypher, James (1990) *State and Capital in Mexico.* Boulder CO: Westview.

—— (2001) "Developing Disarticulation Within the Mexican Economy," *Latin American Perspectives* 118 (May): 11–37.

D'Olwer, Luis Nicolau (1965) "Las inversiones extranjeras," pp. 973–1185, *Historia Moderna de México,* vol. 7, Pt. 2, Daniel Cosío Villegas, ed. Mexico City: Hermes.

Daniels, Josephus (1924) *The Life of Woodrow Wilson.* Philadelphia: John C. Winston Co.

—— (1947) *Shirt-Sleeve Diplomat.* Chapel Hill NC: University of North Carolina Press.

Davenport, Frances Gardiner (ed.) (1917–37) *European Treaties Bearing on the History of the United States and its Dependencies to 1648* (4 vols.). Washington DC: Carnegie Institution of Washington.

Davidow, Jeffrey (2004) *The U.S. and Mexico: The Bear and the Porcupine.* Princeton NJ: Markus Wiener.

Davidson, David M. (1966) "Negro Slave Trade and Resistance in Colonial Mexico, 1519–1650," *Hispanic American Historical Review* 46 (August): 235–53.

Davies, Keith A. (1974) "Tendencias demográficas urbanas durante el siglo XIX en México," pp. 131–74, *Ensayos sobre el desarrollo urbano de México.* Mexico City: SepSetentas.

Davis, Diane E. (1992) "Mexico's New Politics," *World Policy Journal* 9 (Fall–Winter): 655–71.

—— (1993) "The Dialectic of Autonomy," *Latin American Perspectives* 29 (Summer): 46–75.

—— (1994) *Urban Leviathan.* Philadelphia PA: Temple University Press.

—— (1995) "Uncommon Democracy in Mexico," pp. 161–89, *The Social Construction of Democracy, 1870–1990,* George Reid Andres & Herrick Chapman, eds. New York: New York University Press.

—— (2002) "Mexico City," pp. 227–63, *Capital City Politics in Latin America,* David J. Myers & Henry A. Dietz, eds. Boulder CO: Lynne Rienner.

—— (2005) "Reverberations: Mexico City's 1985 Earthquake and the Transformation of the Capital," pp. 255–80, *The Resilient City,* Lawrence J. Vale & Thomas J. Campanella, eds. New York: Oxford University Press.

Davis, Mike (2004) "Planet of Slums," *New Left Review* 26 (March–April): 5–34.

—— (2006) *Planet of Slums.* New York: Verso.

Dawson, Frank Griffith (1990) *The First Latin American Debt Crisis.* New Haven CT: Yale University Press.

De Ferranti, David Guillermo E. Perry, Francisco H. G. Ferreira & Michael Walton (2004) *Inequality in Latin America.* Washington DC: World Bank.

De Janvry, Alain (1981) *The Agrarian Question and Reformism in Latin America.* Baltimore MD: Johns Hopkins University Press.

De la Cruz, Sor Juana (1995) *Inundación Castálida.* Toluca: Instituto Mexiquense de Cultura.

De la Fuente, Juan Ramón (2003) "La universidad pública en América Latina," *Cuadernos Americanos* 101 (September–October): 11–25.

De la Garza, Rodolfo (1972) *The Mexican Chamber of Deputies and the Mexican Political System.* Ph.D. Dissertation. Tucson AZ: University of Arizona.

De la Garza Toledo, Enrique (1994) "The Restructuring of State-Labor Relations in Mexico," pp. 195–217, *The Politics of Economic Restructuring,* Maria Lorena Cook, Kevin J. Middlebrook & Juan Molinar Horcasitas, eds. UCSD Center for U.S.–Mexican Studies Contemporary Perspectives Series, 7. San Diego CA: UCSD Center for U.S.–Mexican Studies.

—— (2004) "Manufacturing Neoliberalism," pp. 104–120, *Mexico in Transition,* Gerardo Otero, ed. London: Zed.

De la Madrid, Miguel (2004) *Cambio de rumbo.* Mexico City: Fondo de Cultura Económica.

De la Peña, Guillermo (1998) "Rural Mobilizations in Latin America since *c.* 1920," pp. 291–394, *Latin America: Politics and Society since 1930,* Leslie Bethell, ed. Cambridge: Cambridge University Press.

De la Peña, Sergio (1975) "Estado, desarrollo económico y proletariado," *Comercio Exterior* 25 (December): 1352–60.

—— (1988) "La política económica de la crisis," pp. 73–114, *Primer Informe sobre la democracia: México 1988,* Pablo González Casanova & Jorge Cadena Roa, eds. Mexico City: Siglo XXI.

De la Teja, Jesús F. (1995) *San Antonio de Béxar.* Albuquerque NM: University of New Mexico Press.

—— (2005) "Introduction," pp. xi-xxi, *Choice, Persuasion and Coercion,* Jesús F. de la Teja & Ross Frank, eds. Albuquerque NM: University of New Mexico Press.

De la Teja, Jesús F., Paula Marks & Ron Tyler (2004) *Texas: Cross Roads of North America.* Boston MA: Houghton Mifflin.

De la Vega Alfaro, Eduardo (1999) "The Decline of the Golden Age and the Making of the Crisis," pp. 165–96, *Mexico's Cinema,* Joanne Hershfield & David R. Maciel, eds. Wilmington DE: Scholarly Resources.

Deans-Smith, Susan (1992) *Bureaucrats, Planters, and Workers.* Austin TX: University of Texas Press.

—— (1994) "State Enterprise, Work, and Workers in Mexico: The Case of the Tobacco Monopoly, 1765–1850," pp. 63–93, *The Political Economy of Spanish America in the Age of Revolution, 1750–1850,* Kenneth J. Andrien & Lyman L. Johnson, eds. Albuquerque NM: University of New Mexico Press.

—— (2007) "'This Noble and Illustrious Art': Painters and the Politics of Guild Reform in Early Modern Mexico City, 1674–1768," pp. 67–98, *Mexican Soundings,* Susan Deans-Smith & Eric Van Young, eds. London: Institute for the Study of the Americas.

Deeds, Susan (2003) *Defiance and Deference in Mexico's Colonial North.* Austin TX: University of Texas Press.

—— (2005) "Subverting the Social Order," pp. 95–119, *Choice, Persuasion and Coercion,* Jesús F. de la Teja & Ross Frank, eds. Albuquerque NM: University of New Mexico Press.

Deger, Robert John, Jr. (1979) *Porfirian Foreign Policy and Mexican Nationalism.* Ph.D. Dissertation. Bloomington IN: Indiana University.

Del Villar, Samuel I. (1988) "The Illicit U.S. Drug Market," pp. 191–208, *Mexico and the United States,* Riordan Roett, ed. Boulder CO: Westview.

—— (2005) "El voto que cuajó tarde," pp. 49–88, *Historia contemporánea de México* (vol. 2), Ilán Bizberg & Lorenzo Meyer, eds. Mexico City: Océano.

DeLay, Brian (2007) "Independent Indians and the U.S.–Mexican War," *American Historical Review* 112 (February): 35–68.

Delpar, Helen (2000) "Mexican Culture, 1920–1945," pp. 543–72, *Oxford History of Mexico,* Michael C. Meyer & William H. Beezley, eds. New York: Oxford University Press.

Denevan, William M. (1992) *The Native Population of the Americas in 1492* (2nd ed.). Madison WI: University of Wisconsin Press.

DePalo, William A., Jr. (1997) *The Mexican National Army, 1822–1852.* College Station TX: Texas A&M University Press.

Detweiler, Robert & Ramón Ruiz (1978) "Introduction," pp. 1–17, *Liberation in the Americas,* Robert Detweiler & Ramón Ruiz, eds. San Diego CA: Campanile Press.

Deutsch, Sandra McGee (1991) "Gender and Sociopolitical Change in Twentieth-Century Latin America," *Hispanic American Historical Review* 71 (May): 259–306.

Devine, Michael J. (1981) *John W. Foster.* Athens OH: Ohio University Press.

Di Tella, Torcuato (1994) "Ciclos políticos en la primera mitad del siglo XIX," pp. 111–33, *La fundación del Estado mexicano,* Josefina Vázquez, ed. Mexico City: Nueva Imagen.

—— (1996) *National Popular Politics in Early Independent Mexico, 1820–1847.* Albuquerque NM: University of New Mexico Press.

Diamond, Jared (1997) *Guns, Germs, and Steel.* New York: Norton.

—— (2005) *Collapse.* New York: Viking.

Díaz, Lilia (1976) "El liberalismo militante," pp. 85–162, *Historia general de México,* vol. 3. Mexico City: Colegio de México.

Díaz del Castillo, Bernal (1996) *The Discovery and Conquest of Mexico.* New York: Da Capo.

Díaz-Polanco, Héctor (1997a) *Indigenous Peoples in Latin America.* Boulder CO: Westview.

—— (1997b) *La rebelión zapatista y la autonomía.* Mexico City: Siglo XXI.

—— (2004) "Reconocimiento y redistribución," pp. 333–56, *El Estado y los indígenas en tiempos del PAN,* Rosalva Aída Hernández, Sarela Paz, & María Teresa Sierra, eds. Mexico City: Miguel Ángel Porrúa.

Díaz-Polanco, Héctor & Consuelo Sánchez (2002) *México Diverso.* Mexico City: Siglo XXI.

Díaz y de Ovando, Clementina (1972) "Julio de 1872," *Revista de la UNAM* 26 (July): 51–61.

Diehl, Richard A. (2004) *The Olmecs.* London: Thames & Hudson.

Diel, Lori Boornazian (2008) *The Tira de Tepechpan.* Austin TX: University of Texas Press.

Dillon, Lester R., Jr. (1973) "American Artillery in the Mexican War, 1846–1847," pp. 7–29, 109–27, 149–170, and 233–50, *Military History of Texas and the Southwest,* vol. 11. Austin TX: Military History Press.

Dinwoodie, D. H. (1977) "Deportation," *New Mexico Historical Review* 52 (July): 193–206.

Dobado González, Rafael (2002) "El monopolio estatal del mercurio en Nueva España durante el siglo XVIII," *Hispanic American Historical Review* 82 (November): 685–718.

Dobado González, Rafael, Aurora Gómez Galvarriato & Jeffrey G. Williamson (2008) "Mexican Exceptionalism: Globalization and De-Industrialization, 1750–1877," *Journal of Economic History* 68 (September): 758–811.

Dobyns, Henry F. (1976) *Spanish Colonial Tucson.* Tucson AZ: University of Arizona Press.

Doman, Matthew (1998) "Crying Out for Corporate Funding," *Euromoney* 353 (September): 156–62.

Domínguez, Jorge I. (1980) *Insurrection or Loyalty.* Cambridge MA: Harvard University Press.

—— (2004) "Why and How did Mexico's 2000 Presidential Elections Matter?" pp. 321–44, *Mexico's Pivotal Democratic Election,* Jorge Domínguez & Chappell H. Lawson, eds. Palo Alto CA: Stanford University Press and San Diego CA: UCSD Center for U.S.–Mexican Studies.

Domínguez, Jorge I. & James A. McCann (1995) "Shaping Mexico's Electoral Arena," *American Political Science Review* 89 (March): 34–48.

Domínguez, Jorge I. & Rafael Fernández de Castro (2001) *The United States and Mexico.* New York: Routledge.

Dore, Elizabeth (2000) "One Step Forward, Two Steps Back: Gender and State in the Long Nineteenth Century," pp. 3–32, *Hidden Histories of Gender and the State in Latin America,* Elizabeth Dore & Maxine Molyneux, eds. Durham NC: Duke University Press.

Doremus, Anne (2001) "Indigenism, Mestizaje, and National Identity in Mexico during the 1940s and the 1950s," *Mexican Studies/Estudios Mexicanos* 17 (Summer): 375–402.

Doyle, Kate (1993) "The Militarization of the Drug War in Mexico," *Current History* 92 (February): 83–88.

Dresser, Denise (1993) "Exporting Conflict," pp. 82–112, *The California–Mexico Connection,* Abraham F. Lowenthal & Katrina Burgess, eds. Palo Alto CA: Stanford University Press.

—— (1994) "Embellishment, Empowerment, or Euthanasia of the PRI?" pp. 125–47, *The Politics of Economic Restructuring,* Maria Lorena Cook, Kevin J. Middlebrook, & Juan Molinar Horcasitas, eds. UCSD Center for U.S.–Mexican Studies Contemporary Perspectives Series, 7. San Diego CA: UCSD Center for U.S.–Mexican Studies.

—— (1997a) "Falling from the Tightrope: the Political Economy of the Mexican Crisis," pp. 55–80, *Mexico 1994,* Sebastian Edwards & Moisés Naím, eds. Washington DC: Carnegie Endowment for Int. Peace.

—— (1997b) "Mexico: Uneasy, Uncertain, Unpredictable," *Current History* 96 (February): 49–54.

—— (2003) "Mexico: from PRI Predominance to Divided Democracy," pp. 321–47, *Constructing Democratic Governance in Latin America* (2nd ed.), Jorge I. Domínguez & Michael Shifter, eds. Baltimore: Johns Hopkins University Press.

Ducey, Michael T. (1995) *Indigenous Insurgents and Constitutionalism in Northern Veracruz, 1810–1821.* Paper presented at the XIX Congress of the Latin American Studies Association. Washington, DC.

Dulles, John W. F. (1961) *Yesterday in Mexico.* Austin TX: University of Texas Press.

Duncan, Robert H (1996) "Political Legitimization and Maximilian's Second Empire in Mexico, 1864–1867," *Mexican Studies/Estudios Mexicanos* (Winter) 27–66.

Dunkerley, James (1999) "The United States and Latin America in the Long Run (1800–1945)," pp. 3–31, *The United States and Latin America,* Victor Bulmer-Thomas & James Dunkerley, eds. London: Institute of Latin American Studies, University of London and Cambridge MA: David Rockefeller Center for Latin American Studies, Harvard University.

Durand, José (1956) "El lujo indiano," *Historia Mexicana* 6 (July–September): 59–74.

Dussel Peters, Enrique (2000) *Polarizing Mexico.* Boulder CO: Lynne Rienner.

Dwyer, John (2008) *The Agrarian Dispute.* Durham NC: Duke University Press.

ECLA (Economic Commission for Latin America) (1966) *Economic Survey of Latin America 1964.* New York: United Nations.

—— (1970) *Economic Survey of Latin America 1969.* New York: United Nations.

—— (1976) *Economic Survey of Latin America 1974.* New York: United Nations.

ECLAC (Economic Commission for Latin America and the Caribbean) (1996) *Economic Survey of Latin America and the Caribbean 1995–1996.* Santiago: United Nations.

—— (1998) *Economic Survey of Latin America and the Caribbean 1997–1998.* Santiago: Unlited Nations.

—— (1999) *Economic Survey of Latin America and the Caribbean 1998–1999.* Santiago: United Nations.

—— (2002) *Economic Survey of Latin America and the Caribbean 2001–2002.* Santiago: United Nations.

Earle, Rebecca (2001) "The Role of Print in the Spanish American Wars of Independence," pp. 9–33, *The Political Power of the Word,* Iván Jasic, ed. London: Institute of Latin American Studies, University of London.

Early, James (1994) *The Colonial Architecture of Mexico.* Albuquerque NM: University of New Mexico Press.

Easterlin, Richard A. (1981) "Why Isn't the Whole World Developed?" *Journal of Economic History* 41 (March): 1–19.

Eberstadt, Nicholas (2001) "The Population Implosion," *Foreign Policy* (March-April): 42–53.

Ebrard, Marcelo (1999) "FOBAPROA: la oportunidad perdida," pp. 33–73, *FOBAPROA e IPAB.* Mexico City: Océano.

Echaveste, Maria (2005) "Target Employers," *American Prospect* 16 (November): A10–11.

Edminster, Robert (1961) "Mexico," pp. 326–65, *Economic Development,* Adamantios Pepelasis, Leon Mears, & Irma Adelman, eds. New York: Harper.

Edmonds-Poli, Emily & David A. Shirk (2009) *Contemporary Mexican Politics.* Lanham MD: Rowman & Littlefield.

Egan, Linda (2001) *Carlos Monsiváis.* Tucson AZ: University of Arizona Press.

Eggan, Fred (1979) "Pueblos: Introduction," pp. 224–35, *Handbook of North American Indians,* vol. 9. Washington DC: Smithsonian Institution.

Eisenhower, John S. D. (1986) "Polk and his Generals," pp. 34–65, *Essays on the Mexican War,* Douglas W. Richmond, ed. College Station TX: Texas A&M University Press.

—— (1989) *So Far From God.* New York: Random House.

—— (1993) *Intervention!* New York: Norton.

Elliott, Charles Winslow (1937) *Winfield Scott.* New York: Macmillan.

Elliott, J. H. (1984) "The Spanish Conquest and Settlement of America," pp. 149–206 & "Spain and America in the Sixteenth and Seventeenth Centuries," pp. 287–340, *Cambridge History of Latin America* (vol. 1), Leslie Bethell, ed. Cambridge: Cambridge University Press.

—— (2006) *Empires of the Atlantic World.* New Haven CT: Yale University Press.

Ellis, L. Tuffly (1973) "Maritime Commerce on the Far Western Gulf, 1861–1865," *Southwestern Historical Quarterly* 77 (October): 167–226.

Elu de Leñero, María del Carmen (1975) *El trabajo de la mujer en México.* Mexico City: Instituto Mexicano de Estudios Sociales.

Engelman, Robert (2008) *More Population, Nature, and What Women Want.* Washington DC: Island Press.

Ennis, Michael (2006) "North toward Home," *Texas Monthly* (April): 78–84.

Ermolaev, V. (1976) "México de 1870 a 1917," pp. 83–94, *Ensayos de historia de México.* Mexico City: Ediciones de Cultura Popular.

Escobar Latapí, Augstín & Bryan R. Roberts (1991) "Urban Stratification, the Middle Classes, and Economic Change in Mexico," pp. 91–113, *Social Responses to Mexico's Economic Crisis of the 1980s,* Mercedes González de la Rocha & Agustín Escobar Latapí, eds. UCSD Center for U.S.–Mexican Relations Contemporary Perspectivas Series, 1. San Diego CA: UCSD Center for U.S.–Mexican Studies.

Espinoza Valle, Víctor Alejandro (1999) "Review of *El Partido Acción Nacional* by Soledad Loaeza," *Revista Mexicana de Sociología* 6 (July–September): 235–40.

Esquivel, Gerardo & Graciela Márquez (2007) "Some Economic Effects of Closing the Economy: The Mexican Experience in Mid-Twentieth Century," pp. 333–61, *The Decline of Latin American Economies,* Sebastian Edwards, Gerardo Esquivel, & Graciela Márquez, eds. Chicago IL: University of Chicago Press.

Esteva, Gustavo (1975) "La agricultura en México de 1950 a 1975," *Comercio Exterior* 25 (December): 1311–22.

—— (1982a) "Las transnacionales y el taco," pp. 33–67, *Transnacionales, agricultura y alimentación,* Rodolfo Echeverría Zuno, ed. Mexico City: Nueva Imagen & Colegio Nacional de Economistas.

—— (1982b) "Prensa, derecho a la información y democratización de la sociedad mexicana," pp. 74–96, *Foro internacional de comunicación social.* Mexico City: El Día en Libros.

—— (2007) "The Asamblea Popular de los Pueblos de Oaxaca," *Latin American Perspectives* 34 (January): 129–44.

Estrada, Luis & Alejandro Poiré (2007) "Taught to Protest, Learning to Lose," *Journal of Democracy* 18 (January): 73–87.

Evans, Sterling (2007) *Bound in Twine.* College Station TX: Texas A&M University Press.

Ezcurra, Exequiel & Marisa Mazart-Hiriat (1996) "Are Megacities Viable? A Cautionary Tale from Mexico City," *Environment* 38 (January–February): 6–15, 26–29.

Ezcurra, Exequiel, Marisa Mazari-Hiriart, Irene Pisanty, & Adrián Guillermo Aguilar (1999) *The Basin of Mexico: Critical Environmental Issues and Sustainability.* Tokyo: United Nations University Press.

Fairris, David & Edward Levine (2004) "Declining Union Density in Mexico, 1984–2000," *Monthly Labor Review* 127 (September): 10–17.

Fallaw, Ben (2001) *Cárdenas Compromised.* Durham NC: Duke University Press.

Farías Mackey, María Emilia (1988) "La participación de la mujer en la política," pp. 693–816, *México: 75 años de revolución—desarrollo social,* vol. 2. Mexico City: Fondo de Cultura Económica.

Farriss, Nancy M. (1968). *Crown and Clergy in Colonial Mexico, 1759-1821.* London: Athlone.

—— (1984) *Maya Society under Colonial Rule.* Princeton NJ: Princeton University Press.

Faulk, Odie B. (1964) *The Last Years of Spanish Texas.* The Hague: Mouton.

Faux, Jeff (2003a) "Corporate Control of North America," *American Prospect* 13 (January 13): 24–27.

—— (2003b) "How NAFTA Failed Mexico." *American Prospect* 14 (July–August): 35–37.

—— (2006) *The Global Class War.* Hoboken: John Wiley & Sons.

Favela, Alejandro, Miriam Calvillo, Alfonso León, Israel Palma, & Pablo Martínez, (2003) *El combate a la pobreza en el sexenio de Zedillo.* Mexico City: Plaza y Valdés.

Fein, Seth (1999) "From Collaboration to Containment," pp. 123–63, *Mexico's Cinema,* Joanne Hirschfield & David R. Maciel, eds. Wilmington DE: Scholarly Resources.

—— (2001) "Myths of Cultural Imperialism and Nationalism in Golden Age Mexican Cinema," pp. 159–98, *Fragments of a Golden Age,* Gilbert Joseph, Anne Rubenstein & Eric Zolov, eds. Durham NC: Duke University Press.

Félix, David (1992) "Privatizing and Rolling Back the Latin American State," *CEPAL Review* 46 (April): 31–46.
Fernández, Claudia & Andrew Paxman (2001) *El Tigre* (2nd ed.). Mexico City: Grijalbo.
Fernández, Raúl (1977) *The United States-Mexico Border.* Notre Dame IN: University of Notre Dame Press.
Fernández Arena, José Antonio & Hebert K. May (1971) *El impacto económico de la inversión extranjera en México.* Mexico City: Tabasco.
Fernández Tejedo, Isabel & Carmen Nava Nava (2001) "Images of Independence in the Nineteenth Century: the Grito de Dolores," pp. 1–41, *¡Viva México! ¡Viva la independencia!,* William H. Beezley & David E. Lorey, eds. Wilmington DE: Scholarly Resources.
Ferras, Robert (1977) *Ciudad Nezahualcoyotol.* Mexico City: Colegio de México.
Ferrer Muñoz, Manuel (1995) *La formación de un estado nacional en México.* Mexico City: Universidad Nacional Autónoma de México.
Ferriss, Susan (2004) "Paradise Lost?" *Austin American-Statesman* (October 22): A1, A7.
Fisher, Lillian Estelle (1926) *Viceregal Administration in the Spanish–American Colonies.* Berkeley CA: University of California Press.
—— (1934) *The Background of the Revolution for Mexican Independence.* Boston MA: Christopher.
Fishlow, Albert (1995) "Latin American Nineteenth Century Public Debt: Theory and Practice," pp. 23-45, *La deuda pública en América Latina en perspectiva histórica,* Reinhard Liehr, ed. Frankfurt am Main: Vervuer & Madrid: Iberoamericana.
Fitzgerald, Deborah (1986) "Exporting American Agriculture," *Social Studies of Science* 16 (August): 457–83.
FitzGerald, E. V. K. (1978) "The State and Capital Accumulation in Latin America," *Journal of Latin American Studies* 10 (November): 263–82.
—— (1984) "Restructuring Through the Depression: The State and Capital Accumulation in Mexico, 1925–40," pp. 242–72, *Latin America in the 1930s,* Rosemary Thorp, ed. New York. St. Martin's Press.
—— (1985) "The Financial Constraint on Relative Autonomy: The State and Capital Accumulation in Mexico, 1940–82, pp. 210–40, *The State and Capital Accumulation in Latin America,* vol. 1, Christian Anglade & Carlos Fortín, eds. London: Macmillan.
—— (1994) "ECLA and the Formation of Latin American Economic Doctrine," pp. 89–108, *Latin America in the 1940s,* David Rock, ed. Berkeley CA: University of California Press.
—— (2000a) "Restructuring Through the Depression: The State and Capital Accumulation in Mexico, 1925–40," pp. 212–32, *An Economic History of Twentieth-Century Latin America* (vol. 2), Enrique Cárdenas, José Antonio Ocampo & Rosemary Thorp, eds. Houndsmills, Basingstoke: Palgrave.
—— (2000b) "ECLA and the Theory of Import Substitution Industrialization in Latin America," pp. 58–97, *An Economic History of Twentieth-Century Latin America* (vol. 3), Enrique Cárdenas, José Antonio Ocampo & Rosemary Thorp, eds. Houndsmills, Basingstoke: Palgrave.
Flores, Mario (1998) "Tiempos de Auge," *Vuelo* (February): 34–37.
Flores Caballero, Romero (1974) *Counterrevolution.* Lincoln NE: University of Nebraska Press.
Flores de la Peña, Horacio (1970) "La educación superior y la investigación científica," pp. 205–220, *El Perfil de México en 1980,* vol. 2. Mexico City: Siglo XXI.
Flores Olea, Víctor (1972) "Poder, legitimidad y política en México," pp. 461–502, *El Perfil de México en 1980,* vol. 3. Mexico City: Siglo XXI.
Florescano, Enrique (1976) *Origen y desarrollo de los problemas agrarios de México, 1500–1821.* Mexico City: Era.
—— (1980) "La formación de los trabajadores en la época colonial, 1521–1750," pp. 9–124, *De la Colonia al imperio,* La clase obrera en la historia de México, vol. 1. Mexico City: Siglo XXI.
—— (1984) "The Formation and Economic Structure of the Hacienda in New Spain," pp. 153–88, *Cambridge History of Latin America* (vol. 2), Leslie Bethell, ed. Cambridge: Cambridge University Press.
—— (1986) *Precios del maíz y crisis agrícola en México, 1708–1810.* Mexico City: Era.
—— (1987) *Memoria mexicana.* Mexico City: Joaquín Mortiz.
—— (1991) *El nuevo pasado mexicano.* Mexico City: Cal y Arena.
—— (1994) *Memory, Myth, and Time in Mexico.* Austin TX: University of Texas Press.
—— (1997) *Etnia, estado y nación.* Mexico City: Aguilar.
—— (2002) *Historia de las historias de la nación mexicana.* Mexico City: Taurus.
—— (2006) *National Narratives in Mexico: A History.* Norman OK: University of Oklahoma Press.
—— (2007) "Los olmecas: el primer reino de Mesoamérica," *Revista de la UNAM* 38 (April): 5–18.
Florescano, Enrique & Rafael Rojas (1996) *El ocaso de la Nueva España.* Mexico City: Clío.
Flórez Miguel, Marcelino (1992) *Ambición y muerte en la conquista de América.* Valladolid: Ámbito.
Fontana, Bernard L. (1994) *Entrada.* Albuquerque NM: University of New Mexico Press.
Foos, Paul (2002) *A Short, Offhand, Killing Affair.* Chapel Hill NC: University of North Carolina Press.
Foster, John W. (1909) *Diplomatic Memoirs* (2 vols.). Boston MA: Houghton Mifflin.
Foster, Lynn V. (1997) *A Brief History of Mexico.* New York: Facts on File.

Foster, William C. (1995) *Spanish Expeditions into Texas, 1689–1786*. Austin TX: University of Texas Press.

Fowler, Will (2004) "Joseph Welsh: A British *Santanista* (Mexico, 1832)," *Journal of Latin American Studies* 36 (February): 29–56.

—— (2007) *Santa Anna of Mexico*. Lincoln NE: University of Nebraska Press.

Fowler Salamini, Heather (1978) *Agrarian Radicalism in Veracruz, 1920–38*. Lincoln NE: University of Nebraska Press.

—— (1997) "Agrarian Policy: 1910–1940," pp. 13–17, *Encyclopedia of Mexico*, Michael S. Werner, ed. Chicago IL: Fitzroy Dearborn.

Fox, Elizabeth (1995) "Latin American Broadcasting," pp. 519–68, *Cambridge History of Latin America* (vol. 10), Leslie Bethell, ed. Cambridge: Cambridge University Press.

Fox, Jonathan (1994) "Political Change in Mexico's New Peasant Economy," pp. 243–76, *The Politics of Economic Restructuring*, Maria Lorena Cook, Kevin J. Middlebrook, & Juan Molinar Horcasitas, eds. UCSD Center for U.S.–Mexican Studies Contemporary Perspectives Series, 7. San Diego CA: UCSD Center for U.S.–Mexican Studies.

Fox, Vicente (2007) *Revolution of Hope*. New York: Viking.

Franco, Jean (1989) *Plotting Women*. London: Verso.

Frank, Patrick (1998) *Posada's Broadsheets*. Albuquerque NM: University of New Mexico Press.

Frank, Ross (2005) "Controlling Social and Ethnic Mobility in Late Colonial New Mexico," pp. 77–94, *Choice, Persuasion and Coercion*, Jesús F. de la Teja & Ross Frank, eds. Albuquerque NM: University of New Mexico Press.

Franko, Patrice (2003) *The Puzzle of Latin American Economic Development*, 2nd ed. Lanham MD: Rowman & Littlefield.

Freidel, David, Linda Schele & Joy Parker (1993) *Maya Cosmos*. New York: Morrow.

Freeman, Laurie & Jorge Luis Sierra (2005) "Mexico: The Militarization Trap," pp. 231–302, *Drugs and Democracy in Latin America*, Coletta Youngers & Eileen Rosin, eds. Boulder CO: Lynne Rienner.

French, William E. (1988) "Mining and the State in Twentieth-Century Mexico," *Journal of the West* 27 (October): 85–93.

—— (1989) "Business as Usual: Mexico North Western Railway Managers Confront the Mexican Revolution," *Mexican Studies/Estudios Mexicanos* 5 (Summer): 221–38.

—— (1999) "Introduction," pp. xix–xlii, in *An American Family in the Mexican Revolution*, Robert Woodmansee Herr. Wilmington DE: Scholarly Resources.

Fried, Jonathan (1994) *Operation Blockade: A City Divided*. Philadelphia PA: American Friends Service Committee.

Friedrich, Paul (1977) *Agrarian Revolt in a Mexican Village*. Chicago IL: University of Chicago Press.

Fromson, Murray (1996) "Mexico's Struggle for a Free Press," pp. 115–37, *Communication in Latin America*, Richard R. Cole, ed. Wilmington DE: Scholarly Resources.

Fry, Joseph A. (1996) "From Open Door to World Systems," *Pacific Historical Review* 44 (May): 277–303.

Frye, David (1996) *Indians into Mexicans*. Austin TX: University of Texas Press.

Fuentes, Carlos (1971) *Tiempo mexicano*. Mexico City: Joaquín Mortiz.

—— (1988) "The Experience of Mexico," *CALC Report* (Summer): 20.

—— (1992) *The Buried Mirror*. Boston MA: Houghton Mifflin.

—— (1996) *A New Time for Mexico*. New York: Farrar, Straus and Giroux.

—— (2003) "Colores electorales," *El Norte* (July 3): 7A.

Fuentes-Berain, Rossana (2003) "Los medios como factor de cohesión social," pp. 321–36, *¿Estamos unidos mexicanos*? Mauricio de María Campos & Georgina Sánchez, eds. Mexico City: Planeta.

Fuentes Díaz, Vicente (1969) *Los partidos políticos en México*. Mexico City: Altiplano.

Fuentes Mares, José (1982) *Poinsett: historia de una gran intriga*. Mexico City: Océano.

Fuentes Molinar, Olac (1979) "Educación pública y sociedad," pp. 230–65, *Mexico Hoy*, Pablo González Casanova & Enrique Florescano, eds. Mexico City: Siglo XXI.

Gage, Thomas (1958) *Thomas Gage's Travels in the New World*. Norman OK: University of Oklahoma Press.

Galarza, Ernesto (1964) *Merchants of Labor*. Charlotte NC: McNally & Loftin.

Galbraith, John Kenneth (1975) *Money*. Boston MA: Houghton Mifflin.

Galeana, Patricia (2006) *Juárez en la historia de México*. Mexico City: Miguel Ángel Porrúa.

—— (2007) "La idea de República en Hidalgo y Morelos," pp. 245–53, *México en tres momentos: 1810–1910–2010* (vol. 1), Alicia Mayer, ed. Mexico City: Instituto de Investigaciones Históricas, Universidad Nacional Autónoma de México.

Galicia, Daniel F. (1941) "Mexico's National Parks," *Ecology* 22 (January): 107–110.

Gallagher, Kevin (2003) "The CEC and Environmental Quality," pp. 117–32, *Greening NAFTA*, David Markell & John H. Knox, eds. Palo Alto CA: Stanford University Press.

—— (2004) *Free Trade and the Environment: Mexico, NAFTA & Beyond*. Palo Alto CA: Stanford University Press.

Gallagher, Kevin & Roberto Porzencanski (2008) "China Matters," *Latin American Research Review* 43 (no. 1): 185–200.

Gallagher, Kevin & Lyuba Zarsky (2007) *The Enclave Economy.* Cambridge MA: MIT Press.

Gamio, Manuel (1930) *Mexican Immigration to the United States.* Chicago IL: University of Chicago Press.

—— (1969) *El inmigrante mexicano.* Mexico City: Universidad Nacional Autónoma de México.

Ganster, Paul (1996) "Bracero," pp. 403–04, *Encyclopedia of Latin American History and Culture* (vol. 1), Barbara Tenenbaum, ed. New York: C. Scribner's Sons.

Ganster, Paul & David E. Lorey (2008) *The U.S.–Mexican Border into the Twenty-First Century* (2nd ed.). Lanham MD: Rowman & Littlefield.

Garber, Paul Neff (1923) *The Gadsden Treaty.* Philadelphia PA: Press of the University of Pennsylvania.

García, Juan Ramón (1980) *Operation Wetback.* Westport CT: Greenwood.

García, Mario T. (1997) "Mexican Immigration in U.S.–Mexican History," pp. 199–213, *Myths, Misdeeds, and Misunderstandings,* Jaime E. Rodríguez O. & Kathryn Vincent, eds. Wilmington DE: Scholarly Resources.

García Cantú, Gastón (1971) *Las invasiones norteamericanas en México.* Mexico City: Era.

García de León, Antonio (1988) "Las grandes tendencias de la producción agraria," pp. 13–85, *Historia de la cuestión agraria mexicana,* vol. 1. Mexico City: Siglo XXI.

García Icazbalceta, Joaquín (ed.) (1858–66) *Colección de documentos para la historia de México* (2 vols.). Mexico City: J. M. Andrade.

García Quintanilla, Alejandra (1997) "Women's Status and Occupation: 1821–1910," pp. 1622–26, *Encyclopedia of Mexico,* Michael S. Werner, ed. Chicago IL: Fitzroy Dearborn.

García Ugarte, Marta Eugenia (2007) "Church and State in Conflict," pp. 140–68, *Mexican Soundings,* Susan Deans-Smith & Eric Van Young, eds. London: Institute of Latin American Studies, University of London.

García y Griego, Manuel (1982) "La comisión selecta, la administración Reagan y la política norteamericana sobre indocumentados," pp. 97–130, *México-Estados Unidos 1982,* Lorenzo Meyer, ed. Mexico City: Colegio de México.

—— (1996) "The Importation of Mexican Contract Laborers to the United States, 1942–1945," pp. 45–85, *Between Two Worlds,* David G. Gutiérrez, ed. Wilmington DE: Scholarly Resources.

Garciadiego Dantan, Javier (1986) "El Estado moderno y la Revolución Mexicana," pp. 19–108*, Evolución del Estado mexicano,* vol. 2. Mexico City: Caballito.

—— (1999) "Del antiguo al nuevo régimen," pp. 11–40, *México en el Siglo XX,* vol. 1. Mexico City: Archivo General de la Nación (AGN).

—— (2007) "1910: del viejo al nuevo Estado mexicano," pp. 11–49, *México en tres momentos: 1810–1910–2010* (vol. 1), Alicia Mayer, ed. Mexico City: Instituto de Investigaciones Históricas, Universidad Nacional Autónoma de México.

Garner, Paul (1995) "The Politics of National Development in Late Porfirian Mexico," *Bulletin of Latin American Research* 14 (September): 339–56.

Garner, Richard L. (1988) "Long-Term Silver Mining Trends in Spanish America," *American Historical Review* 93 (October): 898–935.

—— (1993) *Economic Growth and Change in Bourbon Mexico.* Gainesville FL: University of Florida Press.

—— (2001) *Porfirio Díaz.* Harlow: Longman.

Garrido, Luis Javier (1986) *El partido de la revolución institucionalizada.* Mexico City: Secretaría de Educación Pública.

—— (1987a) "El Partido del Estado ante la sucesión presidencial en México (1929–1987)," *Revista Mexicana de Sociología* 49 (July–September): 59–82.

—— (1987b) "Un partido sin militantes," pp. 61–76*, La vida política mexicana en la crisis.* Mexico City: Colegio de México.

—— (1987c) "Las quince reglas de la sucesión presidencial," pp. 85–106*, La sucesión presidencial en 1988,* Abraham Nuncio, ed. Mexico City: Grijalbo.

—— (1989) "The Crisis of *Presidencialismo,*" pp. 417–34, *Mexico's Alternative Poliltical Futures,* Wayne Cornelius, Judith Gentleman, & Peter H. Smith, eds. UCSD Center for U.S.–Mexican Studies Monograph Series, 30. San Diego CA: UCSD Center for U.S.–Mexican Studies.

—— (1993) *La ruptura.* Mexico City: Grijalbo.

—— (1997) "Partido Revolucionario Institucional," pp. 1058–62, *Encyclopedia of Mexico,* Michael S. Werner, ed. Chicago IL: Fitzroy Dearborn.

Garza, David T. (1966) "Mexican Constitutional Expression in the Cortes of Cádiz," pp. 43–58, *Mexico and the Spanish Cortes, 1810–1822,* Nettie Lee Benson, ed. Austin TX: University of Texas Press.

Garza, Gustavo (1985) *El proceso de industrialización en la Ciudad de México, 1821–1970.* Mexico City: Colegio de México.

—— (2003) "The Dialectics of Urban and Regional Disparities in Mexico," pp. 487–521, *Confronting Development,* Kevin J. Middlebrook & Eduardo Zepeda, eds. Palo Alto CA: Stanford University Press and San Diego CA: UCSD Center for U.S.–Mexican Studies.

Garza, Gustavo & Martha Schteingart (1984) "Ciudad de México," *Demografía y Economía* 18 (no. 4): 581–604.

Gates, Marilyn (1996) "The Debt Crisis and Economic Restructuring," pp. 43–62, *Neoliberalism Revisited,* Gerardo Otero, ed. Boulder CO: Westview.

Gellert, Peter (1998) "Mexico Marks 1968 Massacre," *Mexico Labor News & Analysis,* vol. 3, no. 17.

Gellman, Irwin F. (1979) *Good Neighbor Diplomacy.* Baltimore MD: Johns Hopkins University Press.

Gentleman, Judith (1987) "Mexico after the Oil Boom," pp. 41–62, *Mexican Politics in Transition,* Judith Gentleman, ed. Boulder CO: Westview.

Gereffi, Gary & Martha Martínez (2005) "Mexico's Economic Transformation under NAFTA," pp. 119–50, *Mexico's Democracy at Work,* Russell Crandall, Guadalupe Paz, & Riordan Roett, eds. Boulder CO: Lynne Rienner.

Gerhard, Peter (1986) *Geografía histórica de la Nueva España, 1519–1821.* Mexico City: Universidad Nacional Autónoma de México.

—— (1993) *Guide to the Historical Geography of New Spain,* revised edition. Norman OK: University of Oklahoma Press.

Gibson, Charles (1952) *Tlaxcala in the Sixteenth Century.* New Haven CT: Yale University Press.

—— (1964) *The Aztecs under Spanish Rule.* Palo Alto CA: Stanford University Press.

—— (1966) *Spain in America.* New York: Harper & Row.

—— (1984) "Indian Societies under Spanish Rule," pp. 381–419, *Cambridge History of Latin America* (vol. 2), Leslie Bethell, ed. Cambridge: Cambridge University Press.

Gilbert, Dennis (2007) *Mexico's Middle Class in the Neoliberal Era.* Tucson AZ: University of Arizona Press.

Gilderhus, Mark T. (1972) "The United States and Carranza, 1917," *The Americas* 39 (October): 214–31.

—— (2000) *The Second Century.* Wilmington DE: Scholarly Resources.

Gil Díaz, Francisco (1984) "Mexico's Path from Stability to Inflation," pp. 333–76, *World Economic Growth,* Arnold C. Harberger, ed. San Francisco CA: Institute for Contemporary Studies.

Gill, Anthony (1999) "The Struggle to be Soul Provider: Catholic Responses to Protestant Growth in Latin America," pp. 17–42, *Latin American Religion in Motion,* Christian Smith & Joshua Prokopy, eds. New York: Routledge.

Gill, R. B. (2000) *The Great Maya Droughts.* Albuquerque NM: University of New Mexico Press.

Gillespie, Susan D. (2008) "Blaming Moteuczoma," pp. 25–55, *Invasion and Transformation,* Rebecca Brienen & Margaret A. Jackson, eds. Boulder CO: University Press of Colorado.

Gilly, Adolfo (1979) "La guerra de clases en la revolución mexicana," pp. 21–53, *Interpretaciones de la revolución mexicana.* Mexico City: Nueva Imagen.

—— (1983) *The Mexican Revolution.* London: Verso.

—— (1994) *El cardenismo, una utopía mexicana.* Mexico City: Cal y Arena.

Gilmore, Newton R. (1956) *British Mining Ventures in Early National Mexico.* Ph.D. Dissertation, Berkeley CA: University of California.

—— (1963) "Henry George Ward, British Publicist for Mexican Mines," *Pacific Historical Review* 32 (February): 35–47.

Giordano, Al (2006) "Mexico's Presidential Swindle," *New Left Review* 41 (September–Oct): 5–27.

Giraud, François (1987) "Mujeres y familia en Nueva España," pp. 61–78, *Presencia y Transparencia: la mujer en la historia de México.* Mexico City: Colegio de México.

Glade, William (1963) "Revolution and Economic Development: A Mexican Reprise," pp. 1–101, *The Political Economy of Mexico.* Madison WI: University of Wisconsin Press.

—— (1986a) "How Will Economic Recovery Be Managed?" pp. 47–72, *Mexico's Political Stability: The Next Five Years,* Roderick A. Camp, ed. Boulder CO: Westview.

—— (1986b) "Distributional and Sectoral Problems in the New Economic Policy," pp. 73–99, *Mexico's Political Stability, the Next Five Years,* Roderick A. Camp, ed. Boulder CO: Westview.

—— (1986c) "Latin America and the International Economy, 1870–1914," pp. 1–56, *Cambridge History of Latin America* (vol. 4), Leslie Bethell, ed. Cambridge: Cambridge University Press.

Gleijeses, Piero (1992) "The Limits of Sympathy: The United States and the Independence of Spanish America," *Journal of Latin American Studies* 24 (October): 481–505.

Global Exchange (2000) *Always Near, Always Far: The Armed Forces in Mexico.* San Francisco: Global Exchange.

Goldman, Robert K. & Daniel Jacoby (1978) *Report of the Commission of Enquiry to Mexico.* New York: International League for Human Rights.

Gollás, Manuel (2003) "Breve relato de cincuenta años de política económica," pp. 223–312, *Historia contemporánea de México* (vol. 1), Ilán Bizberg & Lorenzo Meyer, eds. Mexico City: Océano.

Gómara, Francisco López de (1964) *Cortés.* Berkeley CA: University of Califormia Press.

Gómez, Adriana (2000) "Baja California Sur," *Nexos* (January-March): 49–46.

Gómez de Cervantes, Gonzalo (1944) *La vida económica y social de Nueva España al finalizar el siglo XVI.* Mexico City. Antigua Librería Robredo, de José Porrúa e Hijos.

Gómez-Galvarriato, Aurora (1998) "The Evolution of Prices and Real Wages in Mexico from the Porfiriato to the Revolution," pp. 347–78, *Latin America and the World Economy since 1800,* John H. Coatsworth & Alan M. Taylor, eds. Cambridge MA: David Rockefeller Center for Latin American Studies.

—— (2002) "Measuring the Impact of Institutional Change in Capital–Labor Relations in the Mexican Textile Industry, 1900–1930," pp. 289–323, *The Mexican Economy, 1870–1930,* Jeffrey Bortz & Stephen Haber, eds. Palo Alto CA: Stanford University Press.

—— (2006) "Premodern Manufacturing," pp. 357–64, *Cambridge Economic History of Latin America* (vol. 1) Victor Bulmer-Thomas, John H. Coatsworth, & Roberto Cortés Conde, eds. New York: Cambridge University Press.

Gómez Muñoz, Bibiana (2004) "Ten Years of NAFTA," *Voices of Mexico* 66 (January–March): 29–32.

Gómez Tagle, Silvia (1988a) "Conflictos y contradicciones en el sistema electoral mexicano," *Estudios Sociológicos* 6 (January–April): 3–38.

—— (1988b) "Los partidos, las elecciones y la crisis," pp. 209–84, *Primer Informe sobre la democracia: México 1988,* Pablo González Casanova & Jorge Cadena Roa, eds. Mexico City: Siglo XXI.

—— (1994) *De la alquimia al fraude.* Mexico City: García y Valadés.

Gonzalbo Aizpuru, Pilar (1987a) *Las mujeres en la Nueva España.* Mexico City: Colegio de México.

—— (1987b) "Tradición y ruptura en la educación femenina del siglo XVI," pp. 33–59, *Presencia y transparencia: la mujer en la historia de México,* Carmen Ramos-Escandón, ed. Mexico City: Colegio de Mexico.

—— (1998) "La familia en México colonial: Una historia de conflictos cotidianos," *Mexican Studies/Estudios Mexicanos* 14 (Summer): 389–406.

Gonzales, Michael J. (1994) "United States Copper Companies, the State and Labour Conflict in Mexico, 1900–1910," *Journal of Latin American Studies* 26 (October): 651–82.

—— (2002) *The Mexican Revolution, 1910–1940.* Albuquerque NM: University of New Mexico Press.

González, Gilbert G. & Raúl Fernández (2002) "Empire and the Origins of Twentieth-Century Migration from Mexico to the United States," *Pacific Historical Review* 71 (February): 19–57.

González, Silvia, José Concepción Jiménez-López, Robert Hedges, David Huddart, James C. Ohman, Alan Turner, & José Antonio Pompa y Padilla (2003) "Earliest Humans in the Americas: New Evidence from Mexico," *Journal of Human Evolution* 44 (March): 379–87.

González Angulo, Jorge & Roberto Sandoval Zarauz (1980) "Los trabajadores industriales de Nueva España, 1750–1810," pp. 173–238, *De la colonia al imperio,* La *clase obrera en la historia de México,* vol. 1. Mexico City: Siglo XXI.

González Casanova, Pablo (1962) "México: el ciclo de una revolución agraria," *Cuadernos Americanos* 120 (January–February): 7–29.

—— (1970) *Democracy in Mexico.* New York: Oxford University Press.

—— (1979a) "El partido del estado, I," *Nexos* 16 (April): 3–32.

—— (1979b) "El partido del estado, II," *Nexos* 17 (May): 3–19.

González del Rivero, Leticia (1994) "La oposición almazanista y las elecciones de 1940," *Historia y Grafía* (no. 3): 11–33.

González Gómez, Ovidio (1990) "Construcción de carreteras y ordenamiento del territorio," *Revista Mexicana de Sociología* 52 (July–September): 49–67.

González Marín, Silvia & Raúl Moreno (1992) "Análisis paralelo de las elecciones presidenciales," pp. 420–37, *Five Centuries of Mexican History/Cinco siglos de historia de México,* Virginia Guedea & Jaime E. Rodríguez O., eds. Mexico City: Instituto Mora & Irvine CA: University of California.

González-Martínez, Carlos (2008) "Decalogue of Challenges for the New Mexican Electoral Reform," *Voices of Mexico* 81 (January–April): 11–14.

González Montes, Soledad (2003) "La 'desindianización' de una población en el siglo XX en el contexto de la transición económica y demográfica," pp. 355–76, *Las dinámicas de la población indígena,* François Lartigue & André Quesnel, eds. Mexico City: Centro de Investigaciones y Estudios Superiores en Antropología Social.

González Morfín, Efraín (1973) *Discursos de su campaña presidencial: 1970,* vol. 1. Mexico City: Jus.

González Navarro, Moisés (1954) "Instituciones indígenas en México independiente," pp. 113–69, *Métodos y resultados de la política indigenista en México,* Memorias del INI, vol. 6. Mexico City: Instituto Nacional Indigenista.

—— (1957) "La vida social," pp. 1–979, *Historia moderna de México,* vol. 4, Daniel Cosío Villegas, ed. Mexico City: Hermes.

—— (1970a) *Raza y tierra.* Mexico City: Colegio de México.

—— (1970b) "*Mestizaje* in Mexico During the National Period," pp. 145–69, *Race and Class in Latin America,* Magnus Mörner, ed. New York: Columbia University Press.

—— (1977) *Anatomía del poder en México, 1848–1853.* Mexico City: Colegio de México.
—— (1993) "Introducción," pp. 9–21, *El poblamiento de México,* vol. 3. Mexico City: Consejo Nacional de Población.
—— (2006–07) *Benito Juárez.* (3 vols.) Mexico City: Colegio de México.
González Pedrero, Enrique (1993) *País de un solo hombre: el México de Santa Anna* (2 vols.). Mexico City: Fondo de Cultura Económica.
González Pedrero, José (1969) "La responsabilidad social de los medios de comunicación de masas," pp. 56–82, *Los medios de comunicación de masas en México.* Mexico City: Facultad de Ciencias Políticas y Sociales, Universidad Nacional Autónoma de México.
González Quiroga, Miguel (1999) "Los trabajadores mexicanos en Texas," pp. 115–81, *El Norte de Mexico y Texas (1948–1880).* Mexico City: Instituto Mora.
González Ramos, Manuel Humberto (2005) *Historia del Puerto de Bagdad.* Matamoros: Imprenta Impresa.
González Rodríguez, Sergio (2005) "Del libro a la pantalla," pp. 455–85, *Historia contemporánea de México* (vol. 2), Ilán Bizberg & Lorenzo Meyer, eds. Mexico City: Océano.
González Salazar, Gloria (1990) *El Distrito Federal* (2nd ed.). Mexico City: Instituto de Investigaciones Económicas, Universidad Nacional Autónoma de México.
González Velázquez, Carlos Enrique (2002) "Crisis y rearticulación del PRI," pp. 129–44, *El primero año del gobierno foxista,* Ana Alicia Solís de Alba, ed. Mexico City: Itaca.
González y González, Luis (1956) "El hombre y la tierra," pp. 1–146, *Historia moderna de México,* vol. 3, Daniel Cosío Villegas, ed. Mexico City: Hermes.
—— (1974) *San José de Gracia.* Austin TX: University of Texas Press.
—— (1986) "La dictadura de Díaz," pp. 161–78, *Dictaduras y dictadores,* Julio Labastida Martín del Campo, ed. Mexico City: Siglo XXI.
—— (1996) *El indio en la era liberal.* Mexico City: Clío.
Goodwin, R. Kenneth (1977) "Mexican Population Policy," pp. 145–68, *The Future of Mexico,* Lawrence Koslow, ed. Tempe AZ: Center for Latin American Studies, Arizona State University.
Gordillo, Gustavo (1985) "Estado y movimiento campesino en la coyuntura actual," pp. 295–311, *México ante la crisis,* vol. 2, Pablo González Casanova & Héctor Aguilar Camín, eds. Mexico City: Siglo XXI.
Gortari Rabiela, Hira de (1989) "La minería durante la guerra de independencia y los primeros años del México independiente, 1810–1824," pp. 129–61, *The Independence of Mexico and the Creation of a New Nation,* Jaime E. Rodríguez O., ed. Los Angeles CA: UCLA Latin American Center and Mexico/Chicano Program of the University of California, Irvine.
Gosner, Kevin (1992) *Soldiers of the Virgin: The Moral Economy of a Colonial Maya Rebellion.* Tucson AZ: University of Arizona Press.
Gracida, Elsa & Esperanza Fujigaki (1989) "La revolución de independencia," pp. 109–96, *México: un pueblo en la historia,* vol. 2, Enrique Semo, ed. Mexico City: Alianza Editorial Mexicana.
Graebner, Norman A. (1978) "Lessons of the Mexican War," *Pacific Historical Review* 47 (August): 325–42.
Grafe, Regina & Maria Alejandra Irigoin (2006) "The Spanish Empire and its Legacy," *Journal of Global History* 1 (July): 241–67.
Graham, Richard (1994) *Independence in Latin America* (2nd ed.). New York: McGraw-Hill.
Grammont, Hubert C. de (2003) "The Agricultural Sector and Rural Development in Mexico," pp. 350–81, *Confronting Development,* Kevin J. Middlebrook & Eduardo Zepeda, eds. Palo Alto CA: Stanford University Press & San Diego CA: UCSD Center for U.S.–Mexican Studies.
Granados Chapa, Miguel Ángel (1982) "El estado y los medios de comunicación" pp. 341–56, *El estado mexicano,* Jorge Alonso, ed. Mexico City: Nueva Imagen.
—— (2001) "Males y (re)medios," *Proceso* Special no. 9 (November): 78–85.
Granados Chapa, Miguel Ángel, Elkie Köppen & Pablo González Casanova (1985) "Las elecciones de 1982," pp. 195–209, *Las elecciones en México,* Pablo González Casanova, ed. Mexico City: Siglo XXI.
Granados Roldán, Otto (1982) "Ejército: ¿Regreso a las armas?" *Nexos* 50 (February): 25–29.
Grant, U. S. (1996) *Personal Memoirs of U.S. Grant.* Lincoln NE: University of Nebraska Press.
Grayson, George W. (1976) "The Making of a Mexican President, 1976," *Current History* 70 (February) 49–52, 83–84.
—— (1980) *The Politics of Mexican Oil.* Pittsburgh PA: University of Pittsburgh Press.
—— (1981) "Oil and Politics in Mexico," *Current History* 80 (November): 379–83.
—— (1988) *Oil and Mexican Foreign Policy.* Pittsburgh PA: University of Pittsburgh Press.
—— (1991) "Incremental Change in Pemex," *Petroleum Economist* 58 (October): 7–9.
—— (1992) "Pemex Given Modern Image," *Petroleum Economist* 59 (October): 10–12.
—— (1998) "Civilians Order Army out of the Barracks," *Hemisfile* 9 (May–June): 8–11.
—— (2005) "Running After a Fallen Fox," *Harvard International Review* 27 (Spring): 22–27.
—— (2006) *Mesías mexicano.* Mexico City: Grijalbo.
Green, David (1971) *The Containment of Latin America.* Chicago IL: Quadrangle.

Green, Rosario (1979) "Todos los caminos llevan a Washington," *Nexos* 13 (January): 41–44.

Green, Stanley C. (1987) *The Mexican Republic: The First Decade, 1823–1832.* Pittsburgh PA: University of Pittsburgh Press.

Greene, Kenneth (2007) *Why Dominant Parties Lose.* New York: Cambridge University Press.

Greenleaf, Richard E. (1961) *Zumárraga and the Mexican Inquisition: 1536–1543.* Washington DC: Academy of American Franciscan History.

—— (1968) "Viceregal Power and the Obrajes of the Cortés Estate, 1595–1708," *Hispanic American Historical Review* 48 (August): 365–79.

—— (1969) *The Mexican Inquisition of the Sixteenth Century.* Albuquerque NM: University of New Mexico Press.

Greenpeace México (2006) *La destrucción de México.* Mexico City.

Greider, William (1997) *One World, Ready or Not.* New York: Simon & Schuster.

—— (2001) "A New Giant Sucking Sound," *Nation* 273 (December 31): 22–24.

Griffin, Charles (1937) *The United States and the Disruption of the Spanish Empire, 1810–1822.* New York: Columbia University Press.

Grillo, Ioan (2003) "English a la Mexicana," *Business Mexico* 13 (May): 56–60.

Grindle, Merilee S. (1977) "Policy Change in an Authoritarian Regime," *Journal of Interamerican Studies and World Affairs* 19 (November): 523–55.

—— (1986) *State and Countryside.* Baltimore MD: Johns Hopkins University Press.

—— (1995) "Reforming Land Tenure in Mexico," pp. 39–56, *The Challenge of Institutional Reform in Mexico,"* Riordan Roett, ed. Boulder CO: Lynne Rienner.

Griswold del Castillo, Richard (1990) *The Treaty of Guadalupe Hidalgo.* Norman OK: University of Oklahoma Press.

Gruening, Ernest (1928) *Mexico and its Heritage.* New York: Century.

Grunberg, Bernard (1994) "The Origins of the Conquistadores of Mexico City," *Hispanic American Historical Review* 74 (May): 259–84.

Grunstein Dicter, Arturo (1996) "¿Competencia o monopolio? Regulación y desarrollo ferrocarrilero en México, 1885–1911," pp. 167–221, *Ferrocarriles y vida económica en México, 1850–1950,* Sandra Kuntz Ficker & Paolo Riguzzi, eds. Zinacantepec: Colegio Mexiquense & Xochimilco: Universidad Autónoma Metropolitana.

—— (1999) "De la competencia al monopolio: la formación de los Ferrocarriles Nacionales de México," pp. 71–104, *Ferrocarriles y obras públicas,* Sandra Kuntz Ficker & Priscilla Connolly, eds. Mexico City: Instituto Mora.

Gruzinski, Serge (1993) *The Conquest of Mexico.* Cambridge: Polity.

Guardino, Peter F. (1996) *Peasants, Politics and the Formation of Mexico's National State: Guerrero, 1800–1857.* Palo Alto CA: Stanford University Press.

—— (2003) "Postcolonialism as Self-Fulfilled Prophecy? Electoral Politics in Oaxaca, 1814–1828," pp. 248–71, *After Spanish Rule,* Mark Thurner & Andrés Guerrero, eds. Durham NC: Duke University Press.

Guedea, Virginia (1991a) "El golpe de Estado de 1808," *Revista de la UNAM* 488 (September): 21–24.

—— (1991b) "Las primeras elecciones populares en la Ciudad de México: 1812–1813," *Mexican Studies/Estudios Mexicanos* 7 (Winter): 1–28.

—— (1992) *En busca de un gobierno alterno: los guadalupes de México.* Mexico City: Instituto de Investigaciones Históricas, Universidad Nacional Autónoma de México.

—— (1993) "The First Popular Elections in Mexico City, 1812–1813," pp. 45–69, *The Evolution of the Mexican Political System,* Jaime E. Rodríguez O., ed. Wilmington DE: Scholarly Resources.

—— (1994) "El pueblo de México y la política capitalina, 1808 y 1812," *Mexican Studies/Estudios Mexicanos* 10 (Winter): 27–61.

Guedea, Virginia & Jaime E. Rodríguez O. (1997) "How Relations between Mexico and the United States Began," pp. 17–46, *Myths, Misdeeds, and Misunderstandings,* Jaime E. Rodríguez O. & Kathryn Vincent, eds. Wilmington DE: Scholarly Resources.

Guerra, François-Xavier (1988) *México del antiguo régimen a la Revolución.* Mexico City: Fondo de Cultura Económica.

—— (2007) "Mexico from Independence to Revolution," pp. 129–52, *Cycles of Conflict, Centuries of Change,* Elisa Servín, Leticia Reina, & John Tutino, eds. Durham NC: Duke University Press.

Guevara Niebla, Gilberto (2004) *La libertad nunca se olvida.* Mexico City: Cal y Arena.

Gugliotta, Bobette (1992) "A First Lady's Courageous Voyage," *Américas* 44 (March–April): 20–25.

Guillén Romo, Héctor (1984) *Orígenes de la crisis en México: 1940–1982.* Mexico City: Era.

—— (1990) *El sexenio de crecimiento cero.* Mexico City: Era.

Guillermoprieto, Alma (1994) *The Heart that Bleeds.* New York: Knopf.

Guilpain Peuliard, Odile (1991) *Felipe Ángeles y los destinos de la Revolución mexicana.* Mexico City: Fondo de Cultura Económica.

Gutiérrez, Gustavo (1993) *Las Casas.* Maryknoll NY: Orbis.

Gutiérrez, Ramón A. (1991) *When Jesus Came, the Corn Mothers Went Away.* Palo Alto CA: Stanford University Press.

Gutiérrez Chong, Natividad (2004) "Mercadotenica en el 'indigenismno' de Vicente Fox," pp. 27–51, *El Estado y los indígenas en tiempos del PAN,* Rosalva Aída Hernández, Sarela Paz, & María Teresa Sierra, eds. Mexico City: Miguel Ángel Porrúa.

Gutiérrez Garza, Esthela (1990) "La crisis laboral y la flexibilidad del trabajo," pp. 178–220, *Testimonios de la crisis,* vol. 4, Esthela Gutiérrez Garza, ed. Mexico City: Siglo XXI.

Gutiérrez R., Roberto (1989) "La década perdida de los 80s," *El Cotidiano* 32 (November-December): 3–10.

Gutmann, Mathew C. & Susie S. Porter (1997) "Gender: 1910–1996," pp. 575–80, *Encyclopedia of Mexico,* Michael S. Werner, ed. Chicago IL: Fitzroy Dearborn.

Haas, Lisbeth (1995) *Conquests and Historical Identities in California, 1769–1936.* Berkeley CA: University of California Press.

Haber, Stephen H. (1989) *Industry and Underdevelopment: The Industrialization of Mexico, 1890–1940.* Palo Alto CA: Stanford University Press.

—— (1991) "Industrial Concentration and the Capital Markets: A Comparative Study of Brazil, Mexico, and the United States, 1830–1930," *Journal of Economic History* 51 (September): 559–80.

—— (1992) "Assessing the Obstacles to Industrialisation: The Mexican Economy, 1830–1940," *Journal of Latin American Studies* 24 (February): 1–32.

—— (2002) "The Commitment Problem and Mexican Economic History," pp. 324–36, *The Mexican Economy, 1870–1930,* Jeffrey L. Bortz & Stephen Haber, eds. Palo Alto CA: Stanford University Press.

—— (2006) "The Political Economy of Industrialization," pp. 537–84, *Cambridge Economic History of Latin America* (vol. 2) Victor Bulmer-Thomas, John H. Coatsworth, & Roberto Cortés Conde, eds. New York: Cambridge University Press.

Haber, Stephen, Noel Maurer, & Armando Razo (2003) "When the Law Does not Matter: The Rise and Fall of the Mexican Oil Industry," *Journal of Economic History* 63 (March): 1–32.

Haber, Stephen, Armando Razo, & Noel Maurer (2003) *The Politics of Property Rights.* New York: Cambridge University Press.

Haber, Stephen, Herbert S. Klein, Noel Maurer, & Kevin J. Middlebrook (2008) *Mexico since 1980.* New York: Cambridge University Press.

Haddox, John H. (1967) *Vasconcelos of Mexico.* Austin TX: University of Texas Press.

Haecker, Charles M. & Jeffrey G. Mauck (1997) *On the Prairie at Palo Alto.* College Station TX: Texas A&M University Press.

Haiman, Richard L. (1997) "Population: 1910–1996," pp. 1165–69, *Encyclopedia of Mexico,* Michael S. Werner, ed. Chicago IL: Fitzroy Dearborn.

Hale, Charles A. (1957) "The War with the United States and the Crisis in Mexican Thought," *The Americas* 14 (October): 153–73.

—— (1968) *Mexican Liberalism in the Age of Mora, 1821–1853.* New Haven CT: Yale University Press.

—— (1986) "Political and Social Ideas in Latin America, 1870–1930," pp. 367–441, *Cambridge History of Latin America* (vol. 4), Leslie Bethell, ed. Cambridge: Cambridge University Press.

—— (1989) *The Transformation of Liberalism in Late Nineteenth-Century Mexico.* Princeton NJ: Princeton University Press.

Hall, Linda B. (1981) *Álvaro Obregón.* College Station TX: Texas A&M University Press.

—— (1990) "Banks, Oil, and the Reinstitutionalization of the Mexican State, 1920–1924," pp. 189–211, *The Revolutionary Process in Mexico,* Jaime E. Rodríguez O., ed. Los Angeles CA: UCLA Latin American Center & Irvine CA: Mexico/Chicano Program, University of California.

—— (1992) "Álvaro Obregón and Mexican Migrant Labor to the United States, 1920–1924," pp. 757–69, *La ciudad y el campo en la historia de México,* vol. 2. Mexico City: Universidad Nacional Autónoma de México.

Hall, Michael M. & Hobart A. Spalding, Jr. (1986) "The Urban Working Class and Early Latin American Labour Movements, 1880–1920," pp. 325–46, *Cambridge History of Latin America* (vol. 4), Leslie Bethell, ed. Cambridge: Cambridge University Press.

Hall, Thomas D. (1989) *Social Change in the Southwest, 1350–1880.* Lawrence KS: University Press of Kansas.

Halperín-Donghi, Tulio (1973) *The Aftermath of Revolution in Latin America.* New York: Harper & Row.

—— (1985) "Economy and Society in Post-Independence Spanish America," pp. 299–345, *Cambridge History of Latin America* (vol. 3), Leslie Bethell, ed. Cambridge: Cambridge University Press.

—— (1993) *The Contemporary History of Latin America.* Durham NC: Duke University Press.

Hamill, Hugh M., Jr. (1966) *The Hidalgo Revolt.* Gainesville FL: University of Florida Press.

—— (1973) "Royalist Counterinsurgency in the Mexican War for Independence: The Lessons of 1811," *Hispanic American Historical Review* 53 (August): 470–89.

—— (1976) "Was the Mexican Independence a Revolution?" pp. 43–61, *Dos revoluciones: México y los Estados Unidos.* Mexico City: Fomento Cultural Banamex.

—— (1989) "Caudillismo and Independence: A Symbiosis?" pp. 163–174, *The Independence of Mexico and the Creation of a New Nation,* Jaime E. Rodríguez O., ed. Los Angeles CA: UCLA Latin American Center and Mexico/Chicano Program of the University of California, Irvine.

—— (1991) "The Rector to the Rescue: Royalist Pamphleteers in the Defense of Mexico, 1808–1821," pp. 49–61, *Los intelectuales y el poder en México,* Roderic A. Camp, Charles A. Hale, & Josefina Zoraida Vázquez, eds. Mexico City: Colegio de México.

Hamilton, Charles W. (1966) *Oil Tales of Mexico.* Houston TX: Gulf Publishing.

Hamilton, Nora (1980) "The State and Class Conflict: Mexico During the Cárdenas Era," pp. 346–63, *Classes, Class Conflict, and the State,* Maurice Zeitlin, ed. Cambridge MA: Winthrop.

—— (1982) *The Limits of State Autonomy.* Princeton NJ: Princeton University Press.

Hamnett, Brian R. (1987) "Partidos políticos mexicanos e intervención militar, 1823–1855," pp. 573–91, *America Latina dallo Stato Coloniale allo Stato Nazione.* Milano: Franco Angeli.

—— (1994a) "Between Bourbon Reforms and Liberal Refoma: The Political Economy of a Mexican Province—Oaxaca, 1750–1850," pp. 39–62, *The Political Economy of Spanish America in the Age of Revolution,* Kenneth J. Andrien & Lyman L. Johnson, eds. Albuquerque NM: University of New Mexico Press.

—— (1994b) "Faccionalismo, constitución y poder personal en la política mexicana, 1821–1854," pp. 75–109, *La fundación del estado mexicano, 1821–1855,* Josefina Zoraida Vázquez, ed. Mexico City: Nueva Imagen.

—— (1994c) *Juárez.* London: Longman.

—— (1996a) "The Comonfort Presidency, 1855–1857," *Bulletin of Latin American Research* 15 (January): 81–100.

—— (1996b) "Liberalism Divided: Regional Politics and the National Project during the Mexican Restored Republic," 76 *Hispanic American Historical Review* (November): 659–689.

—— (1996c) "Maximilian," pp. 550–51, *Encyclopedia of Latin American History and Culture* (vol. 3), Barbara Tenenbaum, ed. New York: C. Scribner's Sons.

—— (1997) "Benito Juárez," pp. 718–22, *Encyclopedia of Mexico,* Michael S. Werner, ed. Chicago IL: Fitzroy Dearborn.

—— (1999) *A Concise History of Mexico.* Cambridge: Cambridge University Press.

Hanke, Lewis (1937) "Pope Paul III and the American Indians," *Harvard Theological Review* 30 (April): 65–102.

—— (1959) *Aristotle and the American Indians.* Chicago IL: Henry Regnery.

Hanke, Lewis, ed. (1973) *History of Latin American Civilization* (2nd ed.), vol. 1. London: Hollis & Carter.

Hann, John H. (1966) "The Role of the Mexican Deputies in the Proposal and Enactment of Measures of Economic Reform Applicable to Mexico," pp. 153–84, *Mexico and the Spanish Cortes, 1810–1822.* Nettie Lee Benson, ed. Austin TX: University of Texas Press.

Hansen, Roger D. (1971) *The Politics of Mexican Development.* Baltimore MD: Johns Hopkins University Press.

Harrer, Hans-Jürgen (1979) *Raíces económicas de la revolución mexicana.* Mexico City: Taller Abierto.

Harris, Charles H., III. (1975) *A Mexican Family Empire.* Austin TX: University of Texas Press.

Harstad, Peter T. & Richard W. Resh (1964) "The Causes of the Mexican War," *Arizona and the West* 6 (Winter): 289–302.

Hart, John Mason (1986) "Agrarian Reform," pp. 6–16, *Twentieth-Century Mexico,* W. Dirk Raat & William H. Beezley, eds. Lincoln NE: University of Nebraska Press.

—— (1987) *Revolutionary Mexico.* Berkeley CA: University of California Press.

—— (1997) "Mexican Revolution: Causes," pp. 847–50, *Encyclopedia of Mexico,* Michael S. Werner, ed. Chicago IL: Fitzroy Dearborn.

—— (1998a) "Social Unrest, Nationalism, and American Capital in the Mexican Countryside, 1876–1920," pp. 72–88, *Rural Revolt in Mexico,* Daniel Nugent, ed. Durham NC: Duke University Press.

—— (1998b) "The Evolution of the Mexican and Mexican-American Working Classes, pp. 1–26, *Border Crossings,* John Mason, ed. Wilmington DE: Scholarly Resources.

—— (2000) "The Mexican Revolution, 1910–1920," pp. 435–65, *Oxford History of Mexico,* Michael C. Meyer & William H. Beezley, eds. New York: Oxford University Press.

—— (2002) *Empire and Revolution.* Berkeley CA: University of California Press.

Hart, Paul (2005) *Bitter Harvest.* Albuquerque NM: University of New Mexico Press.

Hartlyn, Jonathan & Arturo Valenzuela (1998) "Democracy in Latin American since 1930," pp. 3–66, *Latin America; Politics and Society since 1930,* Leslie Bethell, ed. Cambridge: Cambridge University Press.

Harvey, Neil (1990) "Peasant Struggles and Corporatism in Chiapas," pp. 183–98, *Popular Movements and Political Change in Mexico,* Joe Foweraker & Ann L. Craig, eds. Boulder CO: Lynne Rienner.

—— (1994) *Rebellion in Chiapas.* UCSD Center for U.S.–Mexico Studies Transformation of Rural Mexico Series, 5. San Diego CA: UCSD Center for U.S.–Mexican Studies.

—— (1998) *The Chiapas Rebellion.* Durham NC: Duke University Press.

—— (1999) "Resisting Neoliberalism," pp. 239–65, *Subnational Politics and Democratization in Mexico,* Wayne A. Cornelius, Todd Eisenstadt & Jane Hindley, eds. San Diego CA: UCSD Center for U.S.–Mexican Studies.

—— (2005) "Inclusion through Autonomy: Zapatistas and Dissent," *NACLA Report on the Americas* 39 (September–October): 12–17

Hassig, Ross (1994) *Mexico and the Spanish Conquest.* London: Longman.

Hatfield, Shelley Bowen (1998) *Chasing Shadows.* Albuquerque NM: University of New Mexico Press.

Hathaway, Dale (2000) *Allies Across the Border.* Cambridge MA: South End.

—— (2002) "El problema de la organización de los sindicatos de las maquiladoras en una economía global antidemocrática," *El Cotidiano* 116 (November–December): 45–54.

Hayes, Joy Elizabeth (2000) *Radio Nation.* Tucson AZ: University of Arizona Press.

Heath, Hilarie J. (1993) "British Merchant Houses in Mexico, 1821–1860," *Hispanic American Historical Review* 73 (May): 261–90.

Hediger, Ernest (1943) "Impact of War on Mexico's Economy," *Foreign Policy Reports* (June 15): 78–87.

Heer, David M. (1990) *Undocumented Mexicans in the United States.* Cambridge: Cambridge University Press.

Heller, Karl Bartolomeus (2007) *Alone in Mexico.* Tuscaloosa: University of Alabama Press.

Heller, Thomas (1992) "Immigration and Regulation," pp. 42–74, *U.S.–Mexico Relations,* Jorge A. Bustamante, Clark W. Reynolds, & Raúl A. Hinojosa Ojeda, eds. Palo Alto CA: Stanford University Press.

Hellman, Judith Adler (1978) *Mexico in Crisis.* New York: Holmes & Meier.

—— (1983) *Mexico in Crisis* (2nd ed.). New York: Holmes & Meier.

—— (1986) "Social Control and the Mexican Political System," pp. 243–56, *Twentieth-Century Mexico,* W. Dirk Raat, Clark W. Reynolds & Raúl A. Hinojosa, eds. Lincoln NE: University of Nebraska Press.

Henderson, Peter V. N. (2000) *In the Absence of Don Porfirio.* Wilmington DE: Scholarly Resources.

Henderson, Timothy J. (1998) *The Worm in the Wheat.* Durham NC: Duke University Press.

—— (2007) *A Glorius Defeat.* New York: Hill & Wang.

Henige, David (1998) *Numbers from Nowhere.* Norman OK: University of Oklahoma Press.

Hennessy, Alistair (1991) "The Muralists and the Revolution," pp. 681–93, IYPN.

Heredia, Carlos A. (1996) "Downward Mobility," *NACLA Report on the Americas* 30 (November-December): 34–40.

Heredia, Juan & Raúl Rodríguez Guillén (2008) "Nueva reforma electoral," *El Cotidiano* 151 (September-October): 59–74.

Hernández, Anabel (2006) *Fin de fiesta en los Pinos.* Mexico City: Grijalbo.

Hernández, Omar & Emile McAnany (2001) "Cultural Industries in the Free Trade Age: A Look at Mexican Television," pp. 389–414, *Fragments of a Golden Age,* Gilbert Joseph, Anne Rubenstein & Eric Zolov, eds. Durham NC: Duke University Press.

Hernández, Rosalva, Sarela Paz & María Teresa Sierra (2004) "Introducción," pp. 7–24, *El estado y los indígenas en tiempos del PAN,* Rosalva Aída Hernández, Sarela Paz, & María Teresa Sierra, eds. Mexico City: Miguel Ángel Porrúa.

Hernández Carballido, Elvira Laura (1998) "La prensa femenina en México durante el siglo XIX," pp. 45–63, *La prensa en México.* Mexico City: Addison, Wesley, Longman de México.

Hernández Chávez, Alicia (1979) *La mecánica cardenista,* Historia de la Revolución Mexicana, vol. 16. Mexico City: Colegio de México.

—— (1992) "La Guardia Nacional y movilización política de los pueblos," pp. 207–25, *Patterns of Contention in Mexican History,* Jaime E. Rodríguez O., ed. Wilmington DE: Scholarly Resources.

—— (1993) *La tradición republicana del buen gobierno.* Mexico City: Colegio de México & Fondo de Cultura Económica.

—— (2006) *Mexico: A Brief History.* Berkeley CA: University of California Press.

Hernández Jaimes, Jesús (2007) "Crisis de subsistencia e insurgencia popular en la Nueva España: entre la infidencia y la lealtad," pp. 61–74, *México en tres momentos: 1810–1910–2010* (vol. 1), Alicia Mayer, ed. Mexico City: Instituto de Investigaciones Históricas, Universidad Nacional Autónoma de México.

Hernández Laos, Enrique & Jorge Córdova Chávez (1979) "Estructura de la distribución del ingreso en México," *Comercio Exterior* 29 (May): 505–20.

—— (1982) *La distribución del ingreso en México.* Mexico City: Centro de Investigación para la Integración Social.

Hernández Rodríguez, Rogelio (2000) "La historia moderna del PRI," *Foro Internacional* 40 (April–June): 278–306.

Hernández Vicencio, Tania (2001) *De la oposición al poder.* Tijuana: Colegio de la Frontera Norte.

Herr, Robert Woodmansee (1999) *An American Family in the Mexican Revolution.* Wilmington DE: Scholarly Resources.

Herrejón Peredo, Carlos (1996) *Morelos.* Mexico City: Clío.

—— (1997) "Hidalgo: les raisons de la révolte," *Cahiers des Amériques Latines,* no. 26: 25–40.

Herrera, Hayden (1990) "Why Frida Kahlo Speaks to the 90s," *New York Times,* October 28, sec. 2, pp. 1, 41.

Herrera, Octavio (2007) *El lindero que definió a la nación.* Mexico City: Secretaría de Relaciones Exteriores.

Herrera Serna, Laura (1986) "Plutarco Elías Calles y su política agraria," *Secuencia* 4 (January–April): 42–65.

Hershfield, Joanne (1996) *Mexican Cinema/Mexican Woman, 1940–1950.* Tucson AZ: University of Arizona Press.
Hewitt de Alcántara, Cynthia (1976) *Modernizing Mexican Agriculture.* Geneva: United Nations Research Institute for Social Development.
—— (1977) *Ensayo sobre la satisfacción de necesidades básicos del pueblo mexicano entre 1940 y 1970.* Cuadernos del CES no. 21. Mexico City: Colegio de México.
—— (1984) *Anthropological Perspectives on Rural Mexico.* London: Routledge & Kegan Paul.
Heyman, Josiah (1997) "Migration to the United States, 1940–96," *Encyclopedia of Mexico,* Michael S. Werner, ed. Chicago IL: Fitzroy Dearborn, pp. 892–98.
Hibino, Barbara (1992) "Cervecería Cuauhtémoc," *Mexican Studies/Estudios Mexicanos* 8 (Winter): 23–43.
Higgins, Nicholas (2001) "Mexico's Stalled Peace Process," *International Affairs* 77 (October): 855–903.
Himmerich y Valencia, Robert (1991) *The Ecomenderos of New Spain: 1521–1555.* Austin TX: University of Texas Press.
Hindley, Jane (1996) "Towards a Pluricultural Nation," pp. 225–43, *Dismantling the Mexican State?* Robert Aitken, Nikki Craske, Gareth A. Jones & David E. Stansfield, eds. New York: St. Martin's.
Hirales, Gustavo (2003) "La matanza de Acteal," *Nexos* 312 (December): 17–21.
Hirschman, Charles & Douglas Massey (2008) "Places and Peoples: The New American Moasic," pp. 1–21, *New Faces in New Places,* Douglas Massey, ed. New York: Russell Sage Foundation.
Hoberman, Louisa Schell (1977) "Merchants in Seventeenth-Century Mexico City," *Hispanic American Historical Review* 57 (August): 479–503.
—— (1981) "Enrico Martínez: Printer and Engineer," pp. 331–46, *Struggle and Survival in Colonial America,* David G. Sweet & Gary B. Nash, eds. Berkeley CA: University of California Press.
—— (1991) *Mexico's Merchant Elite, 1590–1660.* Durham NC: Duke University Press.
Hobsbawm, Eric (1996) *The Age of Revolution, Europe: 1789–1848.* New York: Barnes & Noble.
Hodges, Donald & Ross Gandy (1983) *Mexico 1910–1982: Reform or Revolution?* London: Zed.
—— (2002) *Mexico, the End of the Rebellion.* Westport CT: Praeger.
Hoffman, Abraham (1978) "Mexican Repatriation during the Great Depression," pp. 225–47, *Immigrants—and Immigrants,* Arthur F. Corwin, ed. Westport CT: Greenwood.
Hoffmann, Fritz L. (1942) "Edward L. Doheny and the Beginnings of Petroleum Development in Mexico," *Mid-America* 24 (April): 94–109.
Holcombe, Harold Eugene (1968) *United States Arms Control and the Mexican Revolution, 1910–1924.* Ph.D Dissertation. Birmingham AL: University of Alabama.
Holden, Robert H. (1990) "Priorities of the State in the Survey of Public Lands in Mexico, 1876–1911," *Hispanic American Historical Review* 70 (November): 579–608.
—— (1994) *Mexico and the Survey of Public Lands.* DeKalb IL: Northern Illinois University Press.
Holt, Donald (1979) "Why Bankers Suddenly Love Mexico," *Fortune* (July 16): 138–45.
Houston, Donald E. (1972) "The Role of Artillery in the Mexican War," *Journal of the West* 11 (April): 273–84.
Hu-DeHart, Evelyn (1984) *Yaqui Resistance and Survival.* Madison WI: University of Wisconsin Press.
Huasteca Petroleum Co. (1938) *Expropriation.* New York.
Huesca, Robert (2006) "A Workers' Agenda for Social Change in Mexico's Maquiladoras," *Canadian Journal of Latin American and Caribbean Studies* 31 (no. 62): 131–65.
Hufbauer, Gary Clyde & Jeffrey J. Schott (1993) *NAFTA: An Assessment.* Washington DC: Institute for International Economics.
—— (2005) *NAFTA Revisited.* Washington DC: Institute for International Economics.
Hughes, Sallie (2003) *How 'Institutional Entrepreneurs' Transformed the Mexican Press.* Paper presented at the XXIV Conference of the Latin American Studies Association, Dallas TX.
Hughes, Sallie & Chappell Lawson (2004) "Propaganda and Crony Capitalism," *Latin American Research Review* 39 (October): 81–105.
—— (2005) "The Barriers to Media Opening in Latin America," *Political Communication* 22 (January–March): 9–25.
Huizer, Gerrit (1970a) *La lucha campesina en México.* Mexico City: Centro de Investigaciones Agrarias.
—— (1970b) "Peasant Organization in Agrarian Reform in Mexico," pp. 445–502, *Masses in Latin America,* Irving Louis Horowitz, ed. New York: Oxford University Press.
Human Rights Watch (1990) *Human Rights in Mexico: A Policy of Impunity.* New York: Human Rights Watch.
—— (1991) *World Report 1992.* New York: Human Rights Watch.
—— (1996) *Mexico: Labor Rights and NAFTA.* New York: Human Rights Watch.
—— (1997) *World Report 1997.* New York: Human Rights Watch.
—— (1999) *Systemic Injustice.* New York; Human Rights Watch.
—— (2006) *World Report 2006.* New York: Human Rights Watch.
—— (2007) *World Report 2007.* New York: Human Rights Watch.
—— (2008) *Mexico's National Human Rights Commission: A Critical Assessment.* New York: Human Rights Watch.

Humboldt, Alexander (1966) *Political Essay on the Kingdom of New Spain* (4 vols.). New York: AMS Press.

Humphreys, R. A. & John Lynch, eds. (1966) *The Origins of the Latin American Revolutions.* New York: Knopf.

Huxley, Aldous (1934) *Beyond the Mexique Bay.* New York: Harper.

Ibarra, Ana Carolina (2007) "El concepto *Independencia* en la crisis del orden virreinal," pp. 276–79, *México en tres momentos: 1810–1910–2010* (vol. 1), Alicia Mayer, ed. Mexico City: Instituto de Investigaciones Históricas, Universidad Nacional Autónoma de México.

Ibarra, Antonio (1988) "Tierra, sociedad y revolución de independencia, 1800–1824," pp. 1–81, *Historia de la cuestión agraria mexicana,* vol. 2. Mexico City: Siglo XXI.

Ibarra, David (2005) *Ensayaos sobre economía mexicana.* Mexico City: Fondo de Cultura Económica.

IDB (Inter-American Development Bank) (1990) *Economic and Social Progress in Latin America 1990.* Washington DC: IDB.

—— (1996) *Economic and Social Progress in Latin America 1996.* Washington DC: IDB.

—— (1995) *Women in the Americas: Bridging the Gender Gap.* Washington DC: Inter-American Development Bank.

IFE (Instituto Federal Electoral) (2000a) *The Mexican Electoral Regime and the Federal Elections of the Year 2000.* Mexico City: Federal Electoral Institute.

—— (2000b) *Federal Electoral Process.* Mexico City: Federal Electoral Institute.

—— (2006) *Elecciones federales en México: evolución histórica de registros básicos 1994-2006.* Mexico City: IFE.

Illades, Carlos (1996) "Organizaciones laborales y discurso asociativo en el siglo XIX," pp. 245–74, *Ciudad de México,* Carlos Illades & Ariel Rodríguez Kuri, eds. Zamora: Colegio de Michoacán.

Imaz, Cecilia (2007) "Percepciones de la migración en México y Estados Unidos," *Metapolítica* 11 (January–February): 62–67.

IMF (International Monetary Fund) (2009) *Direction of Trade Statistics.* Washington DC: IMF.

INEGI (Instituto Nacional de Estadística, Geografía e Informática) (1994) *Estadísticas históricas de México* (2 vols.). Aguascalientes: INEGI.

—— (2003) *Mujeres y hombres en México, 2003* (7th ed.): Aguascalientes: INEGI.

—— (2006) *Mujeres y hombres en México, 2006* (10th ed.): Aguascalientes: INEGI.

—— (2007) *Anuario estadística de los Estados Unidos Mexicanos, edición 2006.* Aguascalientes: INEGI.

Iracheta Cenecorta, Alfonso (2004) "Estado de México: la otra cara del la megaciudad," pp. 491–607, *México megaciudad.* Mexico City: Migel Ángel Porrúa.

Isacson, Adam (2005) "The U.S. Military in the War on Drugs," pp. 15–56, *Drugs and Democracy in Latin America,* Coletta Youngers & Eileen Rosin, eds. Boulder CO: Lynne Rienner.

Isacson, Adam & Joy Olson (1998) *Just the Facts.* Washington DC: Latin America Working Group.

Isacson, Adam, Joy Olson, and Lisa Haugard (2004) *Blurring the Lines.* Washington DC: Latin American Working Group & Washington Office on Latin America (WOLA).

Iturbide, Agustín de (1971) *Memoirs of Agustín de Iturbide.* Washington DC: Documentary Publications.

Izazola, Haydea (2001) "Agua y sustentabilidad en la Ciudad de México," *Estudios Demográficos y Urbanos* (May-August): 285–320.

Izazola, Haydea & Catherine Marquette (1999) "Emigración de la Ciudad de México," pp. 113–35, *Hacia la demografía del siglo XXI,* vol. 3. Mexico City: Universidad Nacional Autónoma de México.

Izquierdo, Rafael (1964) "Protectionism in Mexico," pp. 241–89, *Public Policy and Private Enterprise in Mexico,* Raymond Vernon, ed. Cambridge MA: Harvard University Press.

Jackson, Robert H. (1992a) "The Dynamic of Indian Demographic Collapse in the Mission Communities of Northwestern New Spain," pp. 139–56, *Five Centuries of Mexican History/Cinco siglos de historia de México,* Virginia Guedea & Jaime E. Rodríguez O., eds. Mexico City: Instituto Mora & Irvine CA: University of California.

—— (1992b) "The Changing Economic Structure of the Alta California Missions—A Reinterpretation," *Pacific Historical Review* 61 (August): 387–415.

—— (1998) "Introduction," pp. 1–8, "Northwestern New Spain," pp. 73–106, *New Views of Borderlands History,* Robert H. Jackson, ed. Albuquerque NM: University of New Mexico Press.

Jackson, Robert H. & Edward Castillo (1995) *Indians, Franciscans, and Spanish Colonization.* Albuquerque NM: University of New Mexico Press.

Jacobs, Ian (1982) *Ranchero Revolt.* Austin TX: University of Texas Press.

Jacobsen, Nils & Hans-Jürgen Puhle (1986) "Introduction," pp. 1–25, *The Economies of Mexico and Peru During the Late Colonial Period, 1760–1810,* Nils Jacobsen & Hans-Jürgen Puhle, eds. Berlin: Colloquium Verlag.

Jaime, Edna (2004) "Fox's Economic Agenda," pp. 35–64, *Mexico under Fox,* Luis Rubio & Susan Kaufman Purcell, eds. Boulder CO: Lynne Rienner.

Jaques, Mary J. (1989) *Texan Ranch Life; with Three Months* through *Mexico in a "Prairie Schooner."* College Station TX: Texas A&M University Press.

Jarquín Gálvez, Uriel & Jorge Javier Romero Vadillo (1985) *Un PAN que no se come.* Mexico City: Ediciones de Cultura Popular.

Jencks, Christopher (2007) "The Immigration Charade," *New York Review of Books* (September 27): 49–52.
Jenkins, Rhys (1987) *Transnational Corporations and the Latin American Automobile Industry.* Pittsburgh PA: University of Pittsburgh Press.
Jiménez, Alfredo (2005) "Who Controls the King?" pp. 1–25, *Choice, Persuasion and Coercion*, Jesús F. de la Teja & Ross Frank, eds. Albuquerque NM: University of New Mexico Press.
Jiménez Codinach, Guadalupe (1991) *La Gran Bretaña y la independencia de México, 1808–1821.* Mexico City: Fondo de Cultura Económica.
Jiménez de Ottalengo, Regina (1974) "Un periódico mexicano, su situación social y sus fuentes de información," *Revista Mexicana de Sociología* 36 (October–December): 767–806.
Johannsen, Robert (1985) *To the Halls of the Montezumas.* New York: Oxford University Press.
John, Elizabeth A. H. (1975) *Storms Brewed in Other Men's Worlds.* College Station TX: Texas A&M University Press.
Johns, Michael (1997) *The City of Mexico in the Age of Porfirio Díaz.* Austin TX: University of Texas Press.
Johnson, J. Holbrook (1988) "Father of the Mexican Mestizos," *Américas* 40 (March-April): 26–29.
Johnson, John J. (1990) *A Hemisphere Apart.* Baltimore MD: Johns Hopkins University Press.
Johnson, Kenneth F (1971) *Mexican Democracy: A Critical View.* Boston MA: Allyn & Bacon.
—— (1984) *Mexican Democracy: A Critical View* (3rd ed.). New York: Praeger.
Johnson, Nancy (2001) "*Tierra y libertad*: Will Tenure Reform Improve Productivity in Mexico's Ejido Agriculture?" *Economic Development and Cultural Change* 49 (January): 291–309.
Jones, Oakah L. (1979) *Los Paisanos.* Norman OK: University of Oklahoma Press.
Joseph, Gilbert M. (1982) *Revolution from Without.* Cambridge: Cambridge University Press.
—— (1986) *Rediscovering the Past at Mexico's Periphery.* University AL: University of Alabama Press.
Joseph, Gilbert M. & Timothy J. Henderson (2002) *The Mexico Reader.* Durham NC: Duke University Press.
Jud, G. Donald (1974) "Tourism and Economic Growth in Mexico since 1950," *Inter-American Economic Affairs* 28 (Summer): 19–44.
Kamen, Henry (2004) *Empire.* New York: HarperCollins.
Kandell, Jonathan (1988) *La Capital.* New York: Random House.
Kane, N. Stephen (1973) "Bankers and Diplomats: The Diplomacy of the Dollar in Mexico, 1921–1924," *Business History Review* 47 (Autumn): 335–52.
—— (1975) "American Businessmen and Foreign Policy," *Political Science Quarterly* 90 (Summer): 293–313.
Karttunen, Frances (1994) *Between Worlds.* New Brunswick NJ: Rutgers University Press.
Kastelein, Barbara (2005a) "Traveling in Style", *Business Mexico* 17 (February): 32–35.
—— (2005b) "Acapulco Revival," *Business Mexico* 27 (September): 28–31.
Katz, Friedrich (1976a) "Agrarian Changes in Northern Mexico in the Period of Villista Rule, 1913–1915," pp. 259–73, *Contemporary Mexico,* James W. Wilkie, Michael C. Meyer & Edna Monzón de Wilkie, eds. Berkeley CA: University of California Press.
—— (1976b) "Peasants in the Mexican Revolution of 1910," pp. 61–85, *Forging Nations,* Joseph Spielberg & Scott Whiteford, eds. East Lansing MI: Michigan State University Press.
—— (1977) "¿A dónde íbamos con Pancho Villa?," *Siempre!* 780 (January 26): ix–xii.
—— (1981) *The Secret War in Mexico.* Chicago IL: University of Chicago Press.
—— (1986a) "Mexico: Restored Republic and Porfiriato, 1867–1910," pp. 3–78, *Cambridge History of Latin America* (vol. 5), Leslie Bethell, ed. Cambridge: Cambridge University Press.
—— (1986b) "Commentary," pp. 143–49, *The Economies of Mexico and Peru during the Late Colonial Period, 1760–1810,* Nils Jacobsen & Hans-Jürgen Puhle, eds. Berlin: Colloquium Verlag.
—— (1988) "Introduction: Rural Revolts in Mexico," pp. 3–17, "Rural Uprisings in Preconquest and Colonial Mexico," pp. 65–94, *Riot, Rebellion, and Revolution,* Friedrich Katz, ed. Princeton NJ: Princeton University Press.
—— (1989) "Pancho Villa y la revolución mexicana," *Revista Mexicana de Sociología* 51 (June): 87–113.
—— (1994) "The Demise of the Old Order on Mexico's Haciendas: 1911–1913," *Ibero-Amerikanisches Archiv* 20 (no. 3–4): 399–435.
—— (1996) "The Agrarian Policies and Ideas of the Revolutionary Mexican Factions Led by Emiliano Zapata, Pancho Villa, and Venustiano Carranza," pp. 21–34, *Reforming Mexico's Agrarian Reform,* Laura Randall, ed. Armonk NY: M. E. Sharpe.
—— (1998a) *The Life and Times of Pancho Villa.* Palo Alto CA: Stanford University Press.
—— (1998b) "From Alliance to Dependency: The Formation and Deformation of an Alliance between Francisco Villa and the United States," pp. 239–57, *Rural Revolt in Mexico* (2nd ed.), Daniel Nugent, ed. Durham NC: Duke University Press.
—— (2000) "Mexico, Gilberto Bosques and the Refugees," *The Americas* 57 (July): 1–12.
—— (2006) *Nuevos ensayos mexicanos.* Mexico City: Era.

—— (2007) "International Wars, Mexico, and U.S. Hegemony," pp. 184–210, *Cycles of Conflict, Centuries of Change,* Elisa Servín, Leticia Reina, & John Tutino, eds. Durham NC: Duke University Press.

Kaufmann, William W. (1951) *British Policy and the Independence of Latin America, 1804–1828,* New Haven CT: Yale University Press.

Kay, Cristóbal (1997) Review of *Landlords and Haciendas in Modernizing Mexico* by Simon Miller. *Journal of Peasant Studies* 25 (October): 170–72.

Kearney, Milo & Anthony Knopp (1991) *Boom and Bust: The Historical Cycles of Matamoros and Brownsville.* Austin TX: Eakin.

Kellogg, Susan (1995) *Law and the Transformation of Aztec Culture, 1500–1700.* Norman OK: University of Oklahoma Press.

Keegan, John. (1999) *The First World War.* New York: Knopf.

Keen, Benjamin (1996) *A History of Latin America* (5th ed.). Boston MA: Houghton Mifflin.

Keesing, Donald B. (1969) "Structural Change Early in Development: Mexico's Changing Industrial and Occupational Structure from 1895 to 1950," *Journal of Economic History* 29 (December): 716–38.

Kelly, Thomas (1999) *The Effects of Economic Adjustment on Poverty in Mexico.* Aldershot: Ashgate.

Kennedy, Paul (1987) *The Rise and Fall of the Great Powers.* New York: Random House.

Kennedy, Roger G. (1993) *Mission.* Boston MA: Houghton Mifflin.

Kentner, Janet R. (1975) *Socio-Political Role of Women in the Mexican Wars of Independence, 1810–1821.* Ph.D. Dissertation. Chacago IL: Loyola University of Chicago.

Kerr, Richard A. (2001) "A Variable Sun and the Maya Collapse," *Science* 292 (May 18): 1293.

Kessell, John, ed. (1989) *Remote Beyond Compare.* Albuquerque NM: University of New Mexico Press.

Kessell, John (2002) *Spain in the Southwest.* Norman OK: University of Oklahoma Press.

Kicza, John E. (1982) "The Great Families of Mexico: Elite Maintenance and Business Practices in Late Colonial Mexico City," *Hispanic American Historical Review* 62 (August): 429–57.

—— (1983) *Colonial Entrepreneurs.* Albuquerque NM: University of New Mexico Press.

King, James F. (1944) "The Latin-American Republics and the Suppression of the Slave Trade," *Hispanic American Historical Review* 24 (August): 387–411.

—— (1953) "The Colored Castes and American Representation in the Cortes of Cádiz," *Hispanic American Historical Review* 33 (February): 33–64.

King, John (1995) "Latin American Cinema," pp. 455–518, *Cambridge History of Latin America* (vol. 10), Leslie Bethell, ed. Cambridge: Cambridge University Press.

—— (2000) *Magic Reels* (new ed.). London: Verso.

King, Robin (1989) "Propuesta mexicana de una moratoria de la deuda a nivel continental (1933)," *Historia Mexicana* 38 (January–March): 497–522.

Kinsbruner, Jay (1994) *Independence in Spanish America.* Albuquerque NM: University of New Mexico Press.

—— (2005) *The Colonial Spanish–American City.* Austin TX: University of Texas Press.

Kiple, Kenneth F. (1987) "A Survey of Recent Literature on the Biological Past of the Black," pp. 7–34, *The African Exchange,* Kenneth F. Kiple, ed. Durham NC: Duke University Press.

Kirk, Betty (1942) *Covering the Mexican Front.* Norman OK: University of Oklahoma Press.

Klesner, Joseph (1994) "Realignment or Dealignment?" pp. 159–91, *The Politics of Economic Restructuring,* Maria Lorena Cook, Kevin J. Middlebrook & Juan Molinar Horcasitas, eds. UCSD Center for U.S.–Mexican Studies Contemporary Perspective Series, 7. San Diego CA: UCSD Center for U.S.–Mexican Studies.

—— (2000) *The 2000 Mexican Presidential and Congressional Elections.* Washington DC: Center for Strategic and International Studies.

—— (2005) "Electoral Competition and the New Party System in Mexico," *Latin American Politics and Society* 47 (Summer): 103–42.

Klor de Alva, J. Jorge (1981) "Martin Ocelotl: Clandestine Cult Leader," pp. 128–41, *Struggle and Survival in Colonial America,* David G. Sweet & Gary B. Nash, eds. Berkeley CA: University of California Press.

Knaut, Andrew L. (1995) *The Pueblo Revolt of 1680.* Norman OK: University of Oklahoma Press.

Knight, Alan (1980) "Peasant and Caudillo in Revolutionary Mexico, 1910–1917," pp. 17–58, *Caudillo and Peasant in the Mexican Revolution,* D. A. Brading, ed. Cambridge: Cambridge University Press.

—— (1984) "The Working Class and the Mexican Revolution, *c.* 1900–1920," *Journal of Latin American Studies* 16 (May): 51–79.

—— (1985a) "El liberalismo mexicano desde la Reforma hasta la Revolución (una interpretación)," *Historia Mexicana* 35 (July–September): 59–91.

—— (1985b) "The Mexican Revolution: Bourgeois? Nationalist? Or just a 'Great Rebellion?'" *Bulletin of Latin American Research* 4 (no. 2): 1–37.

—— (1985c) "The Political Economy of Revolutionary Mexico, 1900–1940," pp. 288–317, *Latin America, Economic Imperialism and the State,* Christopher Abel & Colin M. Lewis, eds. London: Athlone.

—— (1986a) *The Mexican Revolution* (2 vols.). Cambridge: Cambridge University Press.

—— (1986b) "Mexican Peonage: What Was It and Why Was It?" *Journal of Latin American Studies* 18 (May): 41–74.

—— (1987) *U.S.–Mexican Relations, 1910–1940.* UCSD Center for U.S.–Mexican Studies Monograph Series, 28. San Diego CA: UCSD Center for U.S.–Mexican Studies.

—— (1990a) "Revolutionary Project, Recalcitrant People: Mexico, 1910–1940," pp. 227–64, *The Revolutionary Process in Mexico,* Jaime E. Rodríguez O., ed. UCLA Latin American Center and Mexico/Chicano Program, University of California, Irvine.

—— (1990b) "Interpretaciones recientes de la Revolución Mexicana," pp. 193–210, *Memorias del Simposio de Historiografía Mexicanista.* Mexico City: Comité Mexicano de Ciencias Históricas, Gobierno de Estado de Morelos & Comité Mexicano de Ciencias Históricas, UNAM.

—— (1990c) "Racism, Revolution and *Indigenismo*: Mexico, 1910–1940," pp. 71–113, *The Idea of Race in Latin America, 1870–1940,* Richard Graham, ed. Austin TX: University of Texas Press.

—— (1990d) "Mexico, *c.* 1930–1946," pp. 3–82, *Cambridge History of Latin America* (vol. 7), Leslie Bethell, ed. Cambridge: Cambridge University Press.

—— (1991a) "Intellectuals in the Mexican Revolution," pp. 141–71, *Los intelectuales y el poder en México,* Roderic A. Camp, Charles A. Hale, & Josefina Zoraida Vázquez, eds. Mexico City: Colegio de México.

—— (1991b) "Land and Society in Revolutionary Mexico: The Destruction of the Great Haciendas," *Mexican Studies/Estudios Mexicanos* 7 (Winter): 73–104.

—— (1992a) "The Peculiarities of Mexican History: Mexico Compared to Latin America, 1821–1992," *Journal of Latin American Studies* 24 (Quincentenary Supplement): 99–144.

—— (1992b) "Revisionism and Revolution," *Past & Present* 134 (February): 159–99.

—— (1992c) "The Politics of Expropriation" pp. 90–128*, The Mexican Petroleum Industry in the Twentieth Century,* Jonathan C. Brown & Alan Knight, eds. Austin TX: University of Texas Press.

—— (1992d) "Mexico's Elite Settlement: Conjuncture and Consequences," pp. 113–45, *Elites and Democratic Consolidation in Latin America and Southern Europe,* John Higley & Richard Gunther, eds. Cambridge: Cambridge University Press.

—— (1993a) "Revolución social: una perspectiva latinoamericana," *Secuencia* 27 (September–December): 141–83.

—— (1993b) "State Power and Political Stability in Mexico," pp. 29–63, *Dilemmas of Transition,* Neil Harvey, ed. London: Institute of Latin American Studies, University of London & British Academic Press.

—— (1994a) "Peasants into Patriots: Thoughts on the Making of the Mexican Nation," *Mexican Studies/Estudios Mexicanos* 10 (Winter): 135–61.

—— (1994b) "Weapons and Arches in the Mexican Revolutionary Landscape," pp. 24–66, *Everyday Forms of State Formation,* Gilbert M. Joseph & Daniel Nugent, eds. Durham NC: Duke University Press.

—— (1994c) "Cardenismo: Juggernaut or Jalopy?" *Journal of Latin American Studies* 26 (February): 73–108.

—— (1996a) "Lázaro Cárdenas del Río," pp. 553–55, *Encyclopedia of Latin American History and Culture* (vol. 1), Barbara Tenenbaum, ed. New York: C. Scribner's Sons.

—— (1996b) "Venustiano Carranza," pp. 572–74, *Encyclopedia of Latin American History and Culture* (vol. 1), Barbara Tenenbaum, ed. New York: C. Scribner's Sons.

—— (1998a) "The United States and the Mexican Peasantry, circa 1880–1940," pp. 25–63, *Rural Revolt in Mexico* (2nd ed.), Daniel Nugent, ed. Durham NC: Duke University Press.

—— (1998b) "Mexico and Latin America in Comparative Perspective," pp. 71–91, *Elites, Crisis, and the Origins of Regimes,* Mattei Dogan & John Higley, eds. Lanham MD: Rowman & Littlefield.

—— (2000) "Export-Led Growth in Mexico, *c.* 1900–30," pp. 119–52, *An Economic History of Twentieth-Century Latin America,* vol. 1, Enrique Cárdenas, José Antonio Ocampo, & Rosemary Thorp, eds. New York: Palgrave.

—— (2002a) *Mexico from the Beginning to the Spanish Conquest.* Cambridge: Cambridge University Press.

—— (2002b) *Mexico: The Colonial Era.* Cambridge: Cambridge University Press.

—— (2004) "Eric Van Young, *The Other Rebellion* y la historiografía mexicana," *Historia Mexicana* 214 (October–December): 445–515.

—— (2007a) "Mexico's Three Fin de Sièle Crises," pp. 153–83, *Cycles of Conflict, Centuries of Change,* Elisa Servín, Leticia Reina, & John Tutino, eds. Durham NC: Duke University Press.

—— (2007b) "Mexican National Identity," pp. 192–214, *Mexican Soundings,* Susan Deans-Smith & Eric Van Young, eds. London: Institute of Latin American Studies, University of London.

—— (2008) "Rethinking British Informal Empire in Latin America, (Especially Argentina)," pp. 23–48, *Informal Empire in Latin America,* Matthew Brown, ed. Oxford: Blackwell.

Knochenhauer, Guillermo (2003) "Apertura commercial agropecuario," *Este País* 143 (February): 18–23.

Kraft, Joseph (1984) *The Mexican Rescue.* New York: Group of Thirty.

Krauze, Enrique (1977) *La reconstrucción económica,* Historia de la Revolución mexicana, vol. 10. Mexico City: Colegio de México.

—— (1984) "Por una democracia sin adjetivos," *Vuelta* 86 (January): 4–13.

—— (1987) *Biografía del poder* (8 vols.) Mexico City: Fondo de Cultura Económica.

—— (1993) "Madero vivo," *Vuelta* 17 (March): 11–14.

—— (1994) *Siglo de caudillos*. Mexico City: Tusquets.

—— (1997a) *Mexico: Biography of Power*. New York: HarperCollins.

—— (1997b) "El estado mexicano: las fuentes de su legitimidad," *Vuelta* 247 (June): 8–14.

—— (1997c) *La presidencia imperial*. Mexico City: Tusquets.

—— (1999a) "Los últimos nihilistas," *Letras Libres* 8 (August): 20–26.

—— (1999b) "El parto que viene," *Letras Libres* 12 (December): 82.

—— (1999c) *México siglo XX. Los sexenios* (7 vols.). Mexico City: Clío.

—— (1999d) "Ser viejos y nuevos, y administrar los desacuerdos," pp. 41–62. *México en el Siglo XX*, vol. 1. Mexico City: Archivo General de la Nación.

—— (1999e) *Mexicanos eminentes*. Mexico City: Tusquets.

—— (2006a) "Furthering Democracy in Mexico," *Foreign Affairs* 85 (January–February): 54–65.

—— (2006b) "Mirándolos a *ellos*," pp. 79–100, *La brecha entre América Latina y Estados Unidos*, Francis Fukuyama, ed. Buenos Aires: Fondo de Cultura Económica de Argentina.

—— (2009) "El vértigo de la victoria," *Reforma*, February 22, p. 3 (cultural supplement).

Krauze, Enrique & Fausto Zerón-Medina (1993) *Porfirio* (6 vols.) Mexico City: Clío.

Krenn, Michael L. (1990) *U.S. Policy toward Economic Nationalism in Latin America, 1917–1929*. Wilmington DE: Scholarly Resources.

Krooth, Richard (1995) *Mexico, NAFTA, and the Hardships of Progress*. Jefferson NC: McFarland.

Kuntz Ficker, Sandra (1995) *Empresa extranjera y mercado interno: el Ferrocarril Central Mexicano, 1880–1997*. Mexico City: Colegio de México.

—— (1999) "Introducción" pp. 9–38, *Ferrocarriles y obras públicas* (2nd ed.). Mexico City: Instituto Mora.

—— (2002a) "Institutional Change and Foreign Trade in Mexico, 1870–1911," pp. 161–204, *The Mexican Economy, 1870–1930*, Jeffrey Bortz & Stephen Haber, eds. Palo Alto CA: Stanford University Press.

—— (2002b) "Tracing U.S. Predominance in Mexico's Foreign Trade (1870–1948)," *Voices of Mexico* 60 (July–September): 28–32.

—— (2002c) "¿Qué nos dejó la Revolución mexicana?" *Revista de la UNAM* 617 (November): 23–30.

La Botz, Dan (1991) *Edward L. Dohney*. New York: Praeger.

—— (1992) *Mask of Democracy*. Boston MA: South End Press.

—— (1995) *Democracy in Mexico*. Boston: South End.

—— (2001) "Mexico: The Fox Era Begins," *Against the Current* 16 (May–June): 16–18.

—— (2005) "Mexico's Labor Movement in Transition," *Monthly Review* 57 (June): 62–72.

Labastida Martín del Campo, Julio (1977) "Proceso político y dependencia en México (1970–1976)," *Revista Mexicana de Sociología* 39 (January-March): 193–227.

—— (1981) "De la unidad nacional al desarrollo estabilizador, 1940–1970," pp. 328–76, *América Latina: Historia de medio siglo*, vol. 2, Pablo González Casanova, ed. Mexico City: Siglo XXI.

Ladd, Doris M. (1976) *The Mexican Nobility at Independence, 1780–1826*. Austin TX: Institute of Latin American Studies.

Lafaye, Jacques (1976) *Quetzalcóatl and Guadalupe*. Chicago IL: University of Chicago Press.

—— (1984) "Literature and Intellectual Life in Colonial Spanish America," pp. 663–704, *Cambridge History of Latin America* (vol. 2), Leslie Bethell, ed. Cambridge: Cambridge University Press.

LaFrance, David (1990a) "Many Causes, Movements, Failures, 1910–1913," pp. 17–40, *Provinces of Revolution*, Thomas Benjamin & Mark Wasserman, eds. Albuquerque NM: University of New Mexico Press.

—— (1990b) "The Myth and the Reality of 'El Negro' Durazo: Mexico City's 'Most-Wanted' Police Chief," *Studies in Latin American Popular Culture* 9: 237–48.

—— (1996) "Francisco Madero," pp. 487–79, *Encyclopedia of Latin American History and Culture* (vol. 3), Barbara Tenenbaum, ed. New York: C. Scribner's Sons.

—— (2003) *Revolution in Mexico's Heartland*. Wilmington DE: Scholarly Resources.

Lains, Pedro (2007) "Before the Golden Age," pp. 59–81, *The Decline of Latin American Economies*, Sebastian Edwards, Gerardo Esquivel, & Graciela Márquez, eds. Chicago IL: University of Chicago Press.

Lajous, Alejandra (1981) "El Partido Nacional Revolucionario y la campaña vasconcelista," pp. 53–78, *La sucesión presidencial en México*, Carlos Martínez Assad, ed. Mexico City: Nueva Imagen.

—— (2007) *Vicente Fox: el presidente que no supo gobernar*. Mexico City: Océano.

Lamar, Curt (1981) "Genesis of Mexican-United States Diplomacy: A Critical Analysis of the Alamán-Poinsett Confrontation, 1825," *The Americas* 38 (July): 87–110.

Lamas, Marta (2003) "The Role of Women in the New Mexico," pp. 127–41, *Mexico's Politics and Society in Transition*, Joseph S. Tulchin & Andrew D. Selee, eds. Boulder CO: Lynne Rienner.

Langley, Lester D. (1991) *Mexico and the United States.* Boston MA: Twayne.
—— (1996) *The Americas in the Age of Revolution, 1750–1850.* New Haven CT: Yale University Press.
Langston, Joy (2000) *The Death of the Dedazo.* Paper presented at the XXII Latin American Studies Association Conference, Mexico City.
—— (2003) "Reorganizing and Unifying the PRI's State Party Organizations after Electoral Defeat," *Comparative Political Studies* 36 (April): 293–318.
Larrosa, Manuel & Leonardo Valdés (1998) *Elecciones y partidos politicos en México,* 1994. Ixtapalapa: Universidad Autónoma Metropolitana.
Latapí, Pablo (1974) "Las necesidades del sistema educativo nacional," pp. 330–58, *La sociedad mexicana,* Miguel S. Wionczek, ed. Mexico City: Fondo de Cultura Económica.
Latham, Michael (1998) "Modernization and the Kennedy-Era Alliance for Progress," *Diplomatic History* 22 (Spring): 199–229.
Lau, Ana (2009) "Todas contra la dictadura: las precursoras," pp. 4–11, *Proceso Bi-Centenario* 3.
Laurell, Asa Cristina (1992) "Democracy in Mexico: Will the First be the Last?" *New Left Review* 194 (July–August): 33–53.
—— (1995) "La cuestión social mexicana y el viraje en la política social," pp. 117–33, *México: ¿Fin de un régimen?* José C. Valenzuela, ed. Ixtapalapa: Universidad Autónoma Metropolitana.
—— (2003) "The Transformation of Social Policy in Mexico," pp. 320–49, *Confronting Development,* Kevin J. Middlebrook & Eduardo Zepeda, eds. Palo Alto CA: Stanford University Press & San Diego CA: UCSD Center for U.S. Mexican Studies.
Lavender, David (1980) *The Southwest.* Albuquerque NM: University of New Mexico Press.
Lavrin, Asunción (1972) "Values and Meaning of Monastic Life for Nuns in Colonial Mexico," *The Catholic Historical Review* 58 (October): 367–87.
—— (1976) "Women in Convents: Their Economic and Social Role in Colonial Mexico," pp. 250–77, *Liberating Women's History,* Berenice A. Carroll, ed. Urbana IL: University of Illinois Press.
—— (1978) "In Search of the Colonial Woman in Mexico: The Seventeenth and Eighteenth Centuries," pp. 23–59, *Latin American Women,* Asunción Lavrin, ed. Westport CT: Greenwood.
—— (1983) "'Unlike Sor Juana?' The Model Nun in the Religious Literature of Colonial Mexico," *University of Dayton Review* 16 (Spring): 75–92.
—— (1989) "The Scenario, the Actors, and the Issues," pp. 1–43 & "Sexuality in Colonial Mexico: A Church Dilemma," pp. 47–95, *Sexuality and Marriage in Colonial Latin America,* Asunción Lavrin, ed. Lincoln NE: University of Nebraska Press.
—— (2000) "Women in Colonial Mexico," pp. 245–73, *Oxford History of Mexico,* Michael C. Meyer & William H. Beezley, eds. New York: Oxford University Press.
Lavrin, Asunción & Edith Couturier (1979) "Dowries and Wills: A View of Women's Socioeconomic Role in Colonial Guadalajara and Puebla," *Hispanic American Historical Review* 59 (May): 280–304.
—— (1981) "Las mujeres tienen la palabra: Otras voces en la historia colonial de México," *Historia Mexicana* 31 (October–December): 278–313.
Lawson, Chappell (1999) "Why Cárdenas Won—The 1997 Elections in Mexico City," p. 147–73, *Toward Mexico's Democratization,* Jorge Domínguez & Alejandro Poiré, eds. New York: Routledge.
—— (2002) *Building the Fourth Estate.* Berkeley CA: University of California Press.
—— (2004) "Introduction," pp. 1–21, *Mexico's Pivotal Democratic Election,* Jorge I. Domínguez & Chappell H. Lawson, eds. Palo Alto CA: Stanford University Press & San Diego CA: UCSD Center for U.S.–Mexican Studies.
Le Bot, Yvon (1977) *La Rêve Zapatiste.* Paris: Du Seuil.
—— (1997) El sueño zapatista. Barcelona: Plaza & Janés.
Leal, Juan Felipe (1975a) "El estado y el bloque en el poder en México: 1867–1914," *Latin American Perspectives* 5 (Summer): 34–47.
—— (1975b) "The Mexican States: 1915–1973: An Historical Interpretation," *Latin American Perspectives* 5 (Summer): 48–63.
—— (1975c) *México: estado, burocracia y sindicatos.* Mexico City: Caballito.
Lear, John (1993) *Workers,* Vecinos *and Citizens: The Revolution in Mexico City, 1909–1917.* Ph.D. dissertation. Berkeley CA: University of California.
—— (1996) "Del mutualismo a la resistencia," pp. 275–309, *Ciudad de México,* Carlos Illades & Ariel Rodríguez Kuri, eds. Zamora: Colegio de Michoacán.
—— (1998a) "La XXVI Legislatura y los trabajadores de la ciudad de México (1912–1913)," *Secuencia* 40 (January–April): 5–41.
—— (1998b) "Mexico City: Popular Classes and Revolutionary Politics," pp. 53–87, *Cities of Hope,* Ron Pineo & James A. Baer, eds. Boulder CO: Westview.

—— (2001) *Workers, Neighbors, and Citizens: The Revolution in Mexico* City. Lincoln NE: University of Nebraska Press.

León-Portilla, Miguel (1992a) *The Aztec Image of Self and Society.* Salt Lake City UT: University of Utah Press.

—— (1992b) *The Broken Spears.* Boston MA: Beacon.

—— (1992c) "Men of Maize," pp. 147–75, *America in 1492,* Alvin M. Josephy, Jr., ed. New York: Knopf.

—— (1997) "Pueblos originarios y globalización," *Cuadernos Americanos* 4 (July–August): 11–31.

—— (1999) "Sahagún antropólogo," *Letras Libres* 12 (December): 26–30.

—— (2002) *Bernardino de Sahagún.* Norman OK: University of Oklahoma Press.

—— (2004) "Lengua y cultura Nahuas," *Mexican Studies/Estudios Mexicanos* 20 (Summer): 221–30.

Leonard, Thomas M. (1999) "Introduction," pp. 1–10, *United States-Latin American Relations, 1850–1903,* Thomas M. Leonard, ed. Tuscaloosa AL: University of Alabama Press.

Lerman Alperstein, Aída (1989) *Comercio exterior e industria de transformación en México: 1910–1920.* Mexico City: Plaza y Valdés.

Lerner, Victoria (1979) *La educación socialista.* Historia de la Revolución Mexicana, vol. 17. Mexico City: Colegio de México.

Levinson, Irving W. (2005) *Wars Within War.* Fort WorthTX: Texas Christian University Press.

Levy, Daniel C. & Kathleen Bruhn (1999) "Mexico: Sustained Civilian Rule and the Question of Democracy," pp. 519–73, *Democracy in Developing Countries: Latin America* (2nd ed.) Larry Diamond, Jonathan Hartlyn, Juan J. Linz, & Seymour Martin Lipset, eds. Boulder CO: Lynn Rienner.

—— (2001) *Mexico: The Struggle for Democratic Development.* Berkeley CA: University of California Press.

Levy, Daniel & Gabriel Székely (1983) *Mexico: Paradoxes of Stability and Change.* Boulder CO: Westview.

Levy, Santiago (2008) *Good Intentions, Bad Outcomes.* Washington DC: Brookings Institution Press.

Lewis, Colin M. (1986) "Industry in Latin America before 1930," pp. 267–323, *Cambridge History of Latin America* (vol. 4), Leslie Bethell, ed. Cambridge: Cambridge University Press.

Lewis, Daniel (2007) *Iron Horse Imperialism.* Tucson AZ: University of Arizona Press.

Lewis, Oscar (1959) "Mexico Since Cárdenas," *Social Research* 26 (Spring): 18–30.

—— (1963) *Life in a Mexican Village: Tepoztlán Restudied.* Urbana IL: University of Illinois Press.

Lewis, Stephen E. (1997) "Mestizaje," pp. 838–42, *Encyclopedia of Mexico,* Michael S. Werner, ed. Chicago IL: Fitzroy Dearborn.

Leyva, Yolanda (2007) "Commemorating and Protesting Oñate on the Border," *New Mexico Historical Review* 82 (Summer): 343–67.

Lieuwen, Edwin (1968) *Mexican Militarism.* Albuquerque NM: University of New Mexico Press.

Limón, José E. (1998) *American Encounters.* Boston MA: Beacon.

Lindley, Richard B. (1983) *Haciendas and Economic Development.* Austin TX: University of Texas Press.

Lira, Andrés (1994) "La Nación contra los agentes colectivos en México," pp. 329–46, *De los imperios a las naciones: Iberoamérica,* A. Annino, L. Castro Leiva, & F.-X. Guerra, eds. Zaragoza: IberCaja.

Liss, Peggy K. (1975) *Mexico under Spain: 1521–1556.* Chicago IL: University of Chicago Press.

—— (1984) "Creoles, the North American Example and the Spanish American Economy, 1760–1819," pp. 13–25, *The North American Role in the Spanish Imperial Economy, 1760–1819,* Jacques A. Barbier & Allan J. Kuethe, eds. Manchester: Manchester University Press.

Livi-Bacci, Massimo (2006) "The Depopulation of Hispanic America after the Conquest," *Population and Development Review* 32 (June): 199–232.

Lloyd, Jane-Dale (1998) "*Rancheros* and Rebellion: The Case of Northwestern Chihuahua, 1905–1909," pp. 107–33, *Rural Revolt in Mexico* (2nd ed.), Daniel Nugent, ed. Durham NC: Duke University Press.

Loaeza, Soledad (1984a) "El estudio de las clases medias mexicanas después de 1940," *Estudios Políticos* 3 (April–Jun.): 52–62.

—— (1984b) "La Iglesia católica mexicana y el reformismo autoritario," *Foro Internacional* 25 (October–December): 138–65.

—— (1985a) "Notas para el estudio de la Iglesia en el México contemporáneo," pp. 42–58, *Religión y política en México,* Martín de la Rosa & Charles A. Reilly, eds. Mexico City: Siglo XXI.

—— (1985b) "Clases medias," pp. 263–72, *El desafío mexicano.* Mexico City: Océano.

—— (1985c) "Las clases medias mexicanas y la coyuntura económica actual," pp. 221–37, *México ante la crisis,* vol. 2, Pablo González Casanova & Héctor Aguilar Camín, eds. Mexico City: Siglo XXI.

—— (1988) *Clases medias y política en México.* Mexico City: Colegio de México.

—— (1989a) *El llamado de las urnas.* Mexico City: Cal y Arena.

—— (1989b) "The Emergence and Legitimization of the Modern Right, 1970–1988," pp. 351–65, *Mexico's Alternative Political Futures,* Wayne Cornelius, Judith Gentleman, & Peter H. Smith, eds. UCSD Center for U.S.–Mexican Studies Monograph Series, 30. San Diego CA: UCSD Center for U.S.–Mexican Studies.

—— (1995) "Contexts of Mexican Policy," *Challenge* 38 (March–April): 20–25.

—— (1996) "Las relaciones Estado-Iglesia católica en México 1988–1994, *Foro Internacional* 36 (January–June): 107–32.
—— (1997) "Partido Acción Nacional," pp. 23–35, *Mexico: Assessing Neo-Liberal Reform,* Mónica Serrano, ed. London: Institute of Latin American Studies, University of London.
—— (1999) *El Partido Acción Nacional.* Mexico City: Fondo de Cultura Económica.
—— (2003) "Acción Nacional en la antesala del poder: 1994–2000," *Foro Internacional* 43 (January–March): 71–102.
—— (2005) "Gustavo Díaz Ordaz" pp. 117–55, *Historia contemporánea de México* (vol. 2), Ilán Bizberg & Lorenzo Meyer, eds. Mexico City: Océano.
—— (2006) "Vicente Fox's Presidential Style and the New Mexican Democracy," *Mexican Studies/Estudios Mexicanos* 22 (Winter): 1–32.
Lockhart, James (1969) "Encomienda and Hacienda," *Hispanic American Historical Review* 49 (August): 411–29.
—— (1976) "Introduction," pp. 3–28, *Provinces of Early Mexico,* Ida Altman & James Lockhart, eds. Los Angeles CA: UCLA Latin American Center.
—— (1992) *The Nahuas after the Conquest.* Palo Alto CA: Stanford University Press.
Logan, Michael F. (2006) *Desert Cities.* Pittsburgh PA: University of Pittsburgh Press.
Lombardo Toledano, Vicente (1973) *El problema del indio.* Mexico City: SepSetentas.
Lomnitz, Larissa Adler & Marisol Pérez-Lizaur (1987) *A Mexican Elite Family.* Princeton NJ: Princeton University Press.
Lopes Don, Patricia (2008) "The 1539 Inquisition and Trial of Don Carlos of Texcoco in Early Mexico," *Hispanic American Historical Review* 88 (November): 573–606.
López, Felipe H. & Pamela Munro (1999) "Zapotec Immigration," *Aztlan* 24 (Spring): 129–49.
López Cámara, Francisco (1971) "La clase media mexicana," *Revista Mexicana de Ciencia Política* 65 (July–September): 69–79.
López Monjardin, Adriana (2000) "Los nuevos zapatistas y la lucha por la tierra," *Chiapas* (no. 9): 139–57.
López Obrador, Andrés Manuel (2004) *Un proyecto alternativo de nación.* Mexico City: Grijalbo.
—— (2005) *Contra el desafüero.* Mexico City: Grijalbo:
—— (2007) *La mafia nos robó la presidencia.* Mexico City: Grijalbo.
López Portillo T., Felícitas (2001) "El gobierno de Miguel Alemán (1946–1952) y la Universidad Nacional de México," *Cuadernos Americanos* 89 (September–October): 57–72.
López-Portillo y Rojas, José (1975) *Elevación y caída de Porfirio Díaz* (2nd ed.). Mexico City: Porrúa.
López Rosado, Diego G. (1970) "El turismo," pp. 169–85, *El perfil de México en 1980,* vol. 2. Mexico City: Siglo XXI.
López Villafañe, Víctor (1986) *La formación del sistema política mexicano.* Mexico City: Siglo XXI.
Lorey, David E. (1990) "Monterrey, Mexico, during the Porfiriato and the Revolution," *Statistical Abstract of Latin America* 28 (1990): 1183–1203.
—— (1997) "The Status of Development under Zedillo," pp. 14–19, *Zedillo's First Year,* M. Delal Baer & Roderic Ai Camp, eds. Washington DC: Center for Strategic and International Studies.
—— (1999) *The U.S.–Mexican Border in the Twentieth Century.* Wilmington DE: Scholarly Resources.
Love, Edgar F. (1971) "Marriage Patterns of Persons of African Descent in a Colonial Mexico City Parish," *Hispanic American Historical Review* 51 (February): 79–91.
Lowenthal, Abraham (1990) *Partners in Conflict* (revised ed.). Baltimore MD: Johns Hopkins University Press.
—— (1992–93) "Latin America: Ready for Partnership?" *Foreign Affairs* 72 (no. 1): 74–92.
Loyo Brambila, Aurora (1979) *El movimiento magisterial de 1958 en México.* Mexico City: Era.
Loyo Brambila, Aurora & Ricardo Pozas H. (1977) "La crisis política de 1958" *Revista Mexicana de Ciencias Políticas y Sociales* 89 (July–September): 77–118.
Loyola Díaz, Rafael (1980) *La crisis Obregón-Calles y el estado mexicano.* Mexico City: Siglo XXI.
Loyola Díaz, Rafael & Liliana Martínez Pérez (1994) "Petróleos Mexicanos," *Estudios Sociológicos* 35 (May–August): 287–317.
Lugan, Bernard (1994) *La Louisiane Française, 1682-l804.* Paris: Perrin.
Lujambio, Alonso (2001) "Democratization through Federalism?" pp. 47–94, *Party Politics and the Struggle for Democracy in Mexico,* Kevin Middlebrook, ed. UCSD Center for U.S.–Mexican Studies Contemporary Perspective Series, 17. San Diego CA: UCSD Center for U.S.–Mexican Studies.
Luna, Matilde, Ricardo Tirado & Francisco Valdés (1987) "Businessmen and Politics in Mexico, 1982–1986," pp. 13–43, *Government and Private Sector in Contemporary Mexico,* Sylvia Maxfield & Ricardo Anzaldúa M, eds. UCSD Center for U.S.–Mexican Studies Monograph Series, 20. San Diego CA: UCSD Center for U.S.–Mexican Studies.
Lustig, Nora (1981) *Distribución del ingreso y crecimiento en México.* Mexico City: Colegio de México.
—— (1986) "Balance de sombras," *Nexos* 106 (October): 27–31.

—— (1988) "La desigualdad económica," *Nexos* 128 (August): 8–11.
—— (1992) *Mexico: The Remaking of an Economy.* Washington DC: Brookings Institution.
—— (1996) "The 1982 Debt Crisis, Chiapas, and Mexico's Poor," pp. 157–65, *Changing Structure of Mexico,* Laura Randall ed. Armonk NY: M.E. Sharpe.
—— (2001) "Mexico's Quest for Stability and Growth," *Journal of Economic Perspectives* 15 (Winter): 85–106.
Lustig, Nora & Jaime Ros (1999) "Economic Reforms, Stabilization Policies, and the 'Mexican Disease'" pp. 17–52, *After Neoliberalism,* Lance Taylor, ed. Ann Arbor MI: University of Michigan Press.
Lynch, John (1985) "The Origins of Spanish American Independence," pp. 3–50, *Cambridge History of Latin America* (vol. 3), Leslie Bethell, ed. Cambridge: Cambridge University Press.
—— (1986a) *The Spanish American Revolutions* (2nd ed.). New York: Norton.
—— (1986b) "The Catholic Church in Latin America, 1830–1930," pp. 527–95, *Cambridge History of Latin America* (vol. 4), Leslie Bethell, ed. Cambridge: Cambridge University Press.
—— (1989) *Bourbon Spain, 1700–1808.* Oxford: Basil Blackwell.
—— (1992a) *Caudillos in Spanish America, 1800–1850.* Oxford: Clarendon Press.
—— (1992b) "The Institutional Framework of Colonial Spanish America," *Journal of Latin American Studies* 24 (Quincentenary Supplement): 69–81.
—— (1994) "Conclusion," pp. 373–84, *Latin American Revolutions, 1808–1826,* John Lynch, ed. Norman OK: University of Oklahoma Press.
Lyons, Gene (1977) "Inside the Volcano," *Harper's* 254 (June): 41–55.
Mabry, Donald J. (1973) *Mexico's Acción Nacional.* Syracuse NY: Syracuse University Press.
—— (1982) *The Mexican University and the State.* College Station TX: Texas A&M University Press.
McAlister, Lyle. N. (1963) "Social Structure and Social Change in New Spain," *Hispanic American Historical Review* 43 (August): 349–70.
Macaulay, Neill (1966) "The Army of New Spain and the Mexican Delegation to the Spanish Cortes," pp. 134–52, *Mexico and the Spanish Cortes, 1810–1822,* Nettie Lee Benson, ed. Austin TX: University of Texas Press.
McCaa, Robert (1993) "El poblamiento del México decimonónico," pp. 90–113, *El poblamiento de México,* vol. 3. Mexico City: Consejo Nacional de Población.
McCann, James A. (2004) "Primary Priming," pp. 157–83, *Mexico's Pivotal Democratic Election,* Jorge I. Domínguez & Chappell H. Lawson, eds. Palo Alto CA: Stanford University Press and San Diego CA: UCSD Center for U.S.–Mexican Studies.
McCarty, Kieran, ed. (1997) *A Frontier Documentary.* Tucson AZ: University of Arizona Press.
McColm, R. Bruce (1984) "Mexico: The Coming Crisis," *Journal of Contemporary Studies* 7 (Summer): 3–26.
McCormac, Eugene (1922) *James K. Polk: A Political Biography.* Berkeley CA: University of California Press.
McCullough, David (1992) *Truman.* New York: Simon & Schuster.
McDougall, Walter A. (1997) *Promised Land, Crusader State.* Boston MA: Houghton Mifflin.
McDuffie, Keith (1996) "Octavio Paz," pp. 327–28, *Encyclopedia of Latin American History and Culture* (vol. 4), Barbara Tenenbaum, ed. New York: C. Scribner's Sons.
McFeely, William S. (1981) *Grant.* New York: Norton.
Machinea, José Luis & Osvaldo I. Kacef (2007) "Growth and Equity: In Search of the 'Empty Box'" pp. 1–23, *Economic Growth with Equity,* Ricardo Ffrench-Davis & José Luis Machinea, eds. Basingstoke: Palgrave Macmillan.
Macías, Anna (1974) "The Mexican Revolution Was No Revolution for Women," *Latin America: A Historical Reader,* Lewis Hanke, ed. Boston MA: Little, Brown.
—— (1980) "Women and the Mexican Revolution, 1910–1920," *The Americas* 37 (July: 53–82.
—— (1992) "Rural and Urban Women in Revolutionary Yucatán, 1915–1923," pp. 613–20, *La ciudad y el campo en la historia de México.* Mexico City: Instituto de Investigaciones Históricas, Universidad Nacional Autónoma de México.
—— (2002) *Contra viento y marea.* Mexico City: Centro de Investigaciones y Estudios Superiores en Antropología Social.
Macías, Carlos (1988) "Las ideas sociales de Plutarco Elías Calles," pp. 63–72, *Estadistas, caciques y caudillos,* Carlos Martínez Assad, ed. Mexico City: Instituto de Investigaciones Sociales, Universidad Nacional Autónoma de México.
—— (1997) "Plutarco Elías Calles," pp. 181–83, *Encyclopedia of Mexico,* Michael S. Werner, ed. Chicago IL: Fitzroy Dearborn.
Macías-González, Víctor M. (2000) *The Philanthropy of Elite Porfirians: Affirmation and Contestation.* Paper presented at the 20th Latin American Studies Association Conference, Miami FL.
MacLachlan, Colin M. (1988) *Spain's Empire in the New World.* Berkeley CA: University of California Press.
—— (1994) "Review of *The Conquest of Mexico* by Serge Gruzinski," *American Historical Review* 99 (April): 512–13.

MacLachlan, Colin M. & Jaime E. Rodríguez O. (1980) *The Forging of the Cosmic Race.* Berkeley CA: University of California Press.

MacLeod, Murdo J. (1984a) "Spain and America: The Atlantic Trade: 1492–1720," pp. 341–88, *Cambridge History of Latin America* (vol. 1), Leslie Bethell, ed. Cambridge: Cambridge University Press.

—— (1984b) "Aspects of the Internal Economy of Colonial Spanish America: Labour, Taxation, Distribution, and Exchange," pp. 219–64, *Cambridge History of Latin America* (vol. 2), Leslie Bethell, ed. Cambridge: Cambridge University Press.

McNamara, Patrick J. (2007) *Sons of the Sierra.* Chapel Hill NC: University of North Carolina Press.

McNeill, William H. (1976) *Plagues and Peoples.* Garden City NY: Anchor/Doubleday.

—— (2000) *Something New Under the Sun.* New York: Norton.

McSherry, J. Patrice (1998) "The Emergence of 'Guardian Democracy,'" *NACLA Report on the Americas* 32 (November–December): 16–24.

McSweeney, Kendra & Shahna Arps (2005) "A 'Demographic Turnaround,'" *Latin American Research Review* 40 (no. 1): 3–29.

Maddison, Angus (1985) *Two Crises: Latin America and Asia 1929–38 and 1973–1983.* Paris: Organization for Economic Cooperation and Development.

Madero, Francisco (1986) *La sucesión presidencial.* Mexico City: EPESSA.

Magaloni, Beatriz (2005) "The Demise of Mexico's One Party Regime," pp. 121–467, *The Third Wave of Democratization in Latin American,* Frances Hagopian & Scott P. Mainwaring, eds. New York: Cambridge University Press.

Magaloni, Beatriz & Alejandro Poiré (2004) "Strategic Coordination in the 2000 Mexican Presidential Race," pp. 269–92, & "The Issues, the Vote, and the Mandate for Change," pp. 293–319, *Mexico's Pivotal Democratic Election,* Jorge Domínguez & Chappell H. Lawson, eds. Palo Alto CA: Stanford University Press and San Diego CA: UCSD Center for U.S.–Mexican Studies.

Magaloni, Beatriz & Vidal Romero (2008) "Partisan Cleavages, State Retrenchment, and Free Trade," *Latin American Research Review* 43 (no. 2): 107–35.

Maldonado, Braulio (1960) *Baja California.* Mexico City: Costa-Amic.

Malkin, Elizabeth (2000) "Uphill Battle," *Amicus* (Summer): 21–23.

Mallon, Florencia (1988) "Peasants and State Formation in Nineteenth Century Mexico: Morelos, 1848–1858," *Political Power and Social Theory* 7: 1–54.

—— (1994) "Reflections on the Ruins: Everyday Forms of State Formation in Nineteenth-Century Mexico," pp. 69–106, *Everyday Forms of State Formation,* Gilbert M. Joseph & Daniel Nugent, eds. Durham NC: Duke University Press.

—— (1995) "Authoritarianism, Political Culture, and the Formation of the State," pp. 67–109*, Agrarian Structure and Political Power,* Evelyne Huber & Frank Saffordeds, eds. Pittsburgh PA: University of Pittsburgh Press.

Mallory, William, ed. (1910–38) *Treaties, Conventions, International Acts, Protocols, and Agreements Between the United States of America and Other Powers* (4 vols.), publication information. Washington DC: Government Printing Office.

Manchester, William (1992) *A World Lit Only by Fire.* Boston MA: Little, Brown.

Mandujano Jacobo, Pilar (1998) "El periodismo humorístico y satírico en la primera etapa de la Revolución Mexicana, pp. 179–94, *La prensa en México (1810–1915),* Laura Navarrete Maya & Blanca Aguilar Plata, eds. Mexico City: Addison Wesley Longman de México.

Manning, Patrick (2006) "African Connections with American Colonization," pp. 43–71, *Cambridge Economic History of Latin America* (vol. 1) Victor Bulmer-Thomas, John H. Coatsworth, & Roberto Cortés Conde, eds. New York: Cambridge University Press.

Manning, William R. (1913) "Poinsett's Mission to Mexico," *American Journal of International Law* 7 (October): 781–822.

—— (1916) *Early Diplomatic Relations between the United States and Mexico.* Baltimore MD: Johns Hopkins Press.

Manning, William R., ed. (1932–39) *Diplomatic Correspondence of the United States: Inter-American Affairs, 1831–1860* (12 vols.). Washington DC: Carnegie Endowment for International Peace.

Manrique, Jorge Alberto (2000) "Del barroco a la Ilustración," pp. 431–88 & "El proceso de las artes (1910–1970)," pp. 945–56, *Historia general de México: Versión 2000.* Mexico City: Colegio de México.

Mares, David (1982) "Agricultural Trade," pp. 79–132, *Mexico's Political Economy,* Jorge Domínguez, ed. Beverly Hills CA: Sage.

María y Campos, Armando de (1939) *Múgica: crónica biográfica.* Mexico City: Compañía de Ediciones Populares.

Marichal, Carlos (1986) "El nacimiento de la banca mexicana en el contexto latinoamericano," pp. 231–65*, Banca y poder en México (1800–1925),* Leonor Ludlow & Carlos Marichal, eds. Mexico City: Grijalbo.

—— (1989) *A Century of Debt Crises in Latin America.* Princeton NJ: Princeton University Press.

—— (1995) "Introducción," pp. 11–25, *Las inversiones extranjeras en América Latina, 1850–1930,* Carlos Marichal, ed. Mexico City: Colegio de México & Fondo de Cultura Económica.

—— (1997a) "Avances recientes en la historia de las grandes empresas y su importancia para la historia económica de México," pp. 9–38, *Historia de las grandes empresas en México, 1850–1930*, Carlos Marichal & Mario Cerutti, eds. Mexico City: Fondo de Cultura Económica.

—— (1997b) "Obstacles to the Development of Capital Markets in Nineteenth-Century Mexico," pp. 118–45, *How Latin America Fell Behind,* Stephen Haber, ed. Palo Alto CA: Stanford University Press.

—— (1997c) "The Rabid Rise of the *Neobanqueros," NACLA Report on the Americas* 30 (May–June): 27–31.

—— (1997d) "The Vicious Cycles of Mexican Debt," *NACLA Report on the Americas* 31 (November–December): 25–31.

—— (1999) "De la banca privada a la gran banca. Antonio Basagoiti en México y España, 1880–1911," *Historia Mexicana* 48 (April–Jun.): 767–93.

—— (2002) "The Construction of Credibility," pp. 93–119, *The Mexican Economy, 1870–1930,* Jeffrey Bortz & Stephen Haber, eds. Palo Alto CA: Stanford University Press.

—— (2003) "La deuda externa," pp. 451–92, *Historia contemporánea de México* (vol. 1), Ilán Bizberg & Lorenzo Meyer, eds. Mexico City: Océano.

—— (2005) "¿Existen ciclos de la deuda externa en América Latina?" *Comercio Exterior* 55 (August): 676–82.

—— (2006a) "Money, Taxes, and Finance," pp. 423–60, *Cambridge Economic History of Latin America* (vol. 1) Victor Bulmer-Thomas, John H. Coatsworth, & Roberto Cortés Conde, eds. New York: Cambridge University Press.

—— (2006b) "The Spanish-American Silver Peso," pp. 25–52, and "Mexican Cochineal and the European Demand for American Dyes, 1550–1850," pp. 76–92, *From Silver to Cocaine,* Steve Topik, Carlos Marichal, & Zephyr Frank, eds. Durham NC: Duke University Press.

—— (2007) *Bankruptcy of Empire.* New York: Cambridge University Press.

—— (2008) "The Finances of Hegemony in Latin America," pp. 90–113, *Empire and Dissent,* Fred Rosen, ed. Durham NC: Duke University Press.

Markiewicz, Dana (1993) *The Mexican Revolution and the Limits of Agrarian Reform, 1915–1946.* Boulder CO: Lynne Rienner.

Marks, Frederick W., III (1988) *Wind over Sand: The Diplomacy of Franklin Roosevelt.* Athens GA: University of Georgia Press.

Marks, Richard Lee (1993) *Cortés.* New York: Knopf.

Marnham, Patrick (1998) *Dreaming with his Eyes Open.* Berkeley CA: University of California Press.

Márquez, Gaciela (1998) "Tariff Protection in Mexico, 1892–1909," pp. 407–42, *Latin America and the World Economy since 1800,* John H. Coatsworth & Alan M. Taylor, eds. Cambridge MA: David Rockefellar Center for Latin American Studies.

—— (2006) "Commercial Monopolies and External Trade," pp. 395–422, *Cambridge Economic History of Latin America* (vol. 1) Victor Bulmer-Thomas, John H. Coatsworth, & Roberto Cortés Conde, eds. New York: Cambridge University Press.

Márquez Terrazas, Zacarías (1998) *Terrazas y su siglo.* Chihuahua: Centro Librero la Prensa.

Marshall, F. Ray (1978) "Economic Factors Influencing the International Migration of Workers," pp. 163–80, *Views Across the Border,* Stanley R. Ross, ed. Albuquerque NM: University of New Mexico Press.

Martí, Fernando (1985) *Cancún, fantasía de banqueros.* Mexico City: F. Martí.

Martin, Cheryl (1996) *Governance and Society in Colonial Mexico.* Palo Alto CA: Stanford University Press.

Martin, Gerald (1998) "Literature, Music and the Visual Arts, *c.* 1820–1870," pp. 3–45, "Literature, Music and the Visual Arts, 1870–1930," pp. 47–130 & "Narrative since *c.* 1920," pp. 133–225, *A Cultural History of Latin America,* Leslie Bethell, ed. Cambridge: Cambridge University Press.

Martin, Philip (2002) "Mexican Workers and U.S. Agriculture," *International Migration Review* 36 (Winter): 1124–42.

Martínez, José Luis, ed. (1993) *Documentos cortesianos,* vol. I. Mexico City: Fondo de Cultura Economica.

Martínez, Oscar J. (1978) *Border Boom Town.* Austin TX: University of Texas Press.

—— (1988) *Troublesome Border.* Tucson AZ: University of Arizona Press.

—— (2006) *Troublesome Border* (revised ed.) Tucson AZ: University of Arizona Press.

Martínez Assad, Carlos (1979) *El laboratorio de la Revolución.* Mexico City: Siglo XXI.

—— (1982) *El henriquismo.* Mexico City: Martín Casillas.

—— (1987) "State Elections in Mexico," pp. 33–42, *Electoral Patterns and Perspectives in Mexico,"* Arturo Alvarado Mendzoa, ed. UCSD Center for U.S.–Mexican Studies Monograph Series, 22. San Diego CA: UCSD Center for U.S.–Mexican Studies.

—— (1990) "El cine como lo vi y como me lo contaron," pp. 339–60, *Entre la guerra y la estabilidad política,* Rafael Loyola, ed. Mexico City: Grijalbo.

—— (1997) "Anticlericalism," pp. 60–62, & "Tomás Garrido Canabal," pp. 556–57, *Encyclopedia of Mexico,* Michael S. Werner, ed. Chicago IL: Fitzroy Dearborn.

—— (2005) *La Patria en el Paseo de la Reforma*. Mexico City: Universidad Nacional Autónoma de México & Fondo de Cultura Económica.

Martínez Baracs, Andrea (1993) "Colonizaciones tlaxcaltecas," *Historia Mexicana* 43 (October–December): 195–250.

Martínez de Navarrete, Ifigenia (1969) *La mujer y los derechos sociales*. Mexico City: Oasis.

—— (1970) "La distribución del ingreso en México" pp. 15–71, *El perfil de México en 1980*, vol. 1. Mexico City: Siglo XXI.

Martínez Vázquez, Víctor Raúl (1975) "Despojo y manipulación campesina," pp. 148–94, *Caciquismo y poder político en el México rural*. Mexico City: Siglo XXI.

Marván Laborde, María (1988) "El Partido Acción Nacional (1949–1962)," *Revista Mexicana de Sociología* 50 (July–September): 189–99.

Massey, Douglas S. (2003a) "Closed-Door Policy," *American Prospect* 14 (July–August): 26–28.

—— (2003b) "Una política de inmigración disfuncional," *Letras Libres* 53 (May): 16–20.

—— (2005) "Beyond the Border Buildup," *Immigration Policy in Focus* 4 (September): 1–11.

Massey, Douglas S., Jorge Durand & Nolan J. Malone (2002) *Beyond Smoke and Mirrors*. New York: Russell Sage Foundation.

Massing, Michael (2000) "The Narco-State?" *New York Review of Books* 47 (June 15): 24–29.

Matías Alonso, Marcos (1996) "El oro, el petróleo y otros recursos estratégicos en las regiones indígenas de México," *Anuario Indigenista*, pp. 21–42.

Matson, Robert W. (1979) "Church Wealth in Nineteenth-Century Mexico: A Review of Literature," *Catholic Historical Review* 65 (October): 600–09.

Máttar, Jorge, Juan Carlos Moreno-Brid & Wilson Peres (2003) "Foreign Investment in Mexico after Economic Reform," pp. 123–60, *Confronting Development*, Kevin Middlebrook & Eduardo Zepeda, eds. Palo Alto CA: Stanford University Press and San Diego CA: UCSD Center for U.S.–Mexican Studies.

Matthiessen, Peter (1973) *Sal Si Puedes* (revised ed.) New York: Random House.

Mattiace, Shannan (2005) "Representation and Rights," *Latin American Research Review* 40 (no. 1): 237–50.

Matute, Álvaro (1980) *La carrera del caudillo*, Historia de la Revolución Mexicana, vol. 8. Mexico City: Colegio de México.

—— (1995) *Las dificultades del nuevo Estado*," Historia de la Revolución Mexicana, vol. 7. Mexico City: Colegio de México.

Maurer, Noel & Andrei Gomberg (2004) "When the State is Untrustworthy," *Journal of Economic History* 64 (December): 1087–1107.

Maurer, Noel & Stephen Haber (2007) "Related Lending: Manifest Looting or Good Governance?" pp. 213–42, *The Decline of Latin American Economies*, Sebastian Edwards, Gerardo Esquivel, & Graciela Márquez, eds. Chicago IL: University of Chicago Press.

Maxfield, Sylvia (1990) *Governing Capital*. Ithaca NY: Cornell University Press.

Mayo, John (1996) "English Commercial Houses on Mexico's West Coast, 1821–1867," *Ibero-Amerikanisches Archiv* 22 (no. 1–2): 173–90.

Mayo, Lida (1996) "The Mexican War and After," pp. 163–83, *American Military History*, vol. 1, Maurice Matloff, ed. Conshohocken PA: Combined Books.

Mazza, Jacqueline (2001) *Don't Disturb The Neighbors*. New York: Routledge.

Medin, Tzvi (1972) *Ideología y praxis política de Lázaro Cárdenas*. Mexico City: Siglo XXI.

—— (1990) *El sexenio alemanista*. Mexico City: Era.

Medina, Andrés (1974a) "Etnología o literatura? El caso de Benítez y sus indios," pp. 109–40, *Anales de Antropología*, vol. 11.

—— (1974b) "Antropología e indigenismo." *Revista de la UNAM* 29 (October): 13–29.

—— (1998) "Los pueblos indios en la trama de la nación: notas etnográficas," *Revista Mexicana de Sociología* 40 (January–March): 131–68.

Medina, Luis (1978) *Del cardenismo al avilacamachismo*, Historia de la Revolución Mexicana, vol. 18. Mexico City: Colegio de México.

—— (1979) *Civilismo y modernización del autoritarismo*, Historia de la Revolución Mexicana, vol. 20. Mexico City: Colegio de México.

Medina Castro, Manuel (1971) *El gran despojo*. Mexico City: Diógenes.

Medina Peña, Luis (1994) *Hacía el nuevo estado*. Mexico City: Fondo de Cultura Económica.

Meissner, Doris (1988) "The New Immigration Law and Mexico," pp. 94–103, *Mexico in Transition*, Susan Kaufman Purcell, ed. New York: Council on Foreign Relations.

—— (2005) "Learning from History," *American Prospect* 16 (November): A6–9.

Mejía Prieto, Jorge (1976) *Llámeme Pepe*. Mexico City: Editores Asociados.

Mella, José María & Alfonso Mercado (2006) "La economía agropecuaria mexicana y el TLCAN," *Comercio Exterior* 56 (March): 181–93.

Meltzer, Milton (1974) *Bound for the Rio Grande.* New York: Knopf.
Melville, Elinor G. K. (1994) *A Plague of Sheep.* Cambridge: Cambridge University Press.
—— (2000) "Disease, Ecology, and the Environment," pp. 213–43, *Oxford History of Mexico,* Michael C. Meyer & William H. Beezley, eds. New York: Oxford University Press.
—— (2006) "Land Use and the Transformation of the Environment," pp. 109–42, *Cambridge Economic History of Latin America* (vol. 1) Victor Bulmer-Thomas, John H. Coatsworth, & Roberto Cortés Conde, eds. New York: Cambridge University Press.
Méndez, Kristopher (2001) "Mexico's New Hope," *Harvard International Review* 22 (Winter): 38–41.
Mendoza Vargas, Héctor, Pedro S. Urquijo, Narisco Barrera-Bassols, & Gerardo Bocco (2007) "México y el cambio geográfico: dos siglos de Historia (1810–2010)" pp. 135–52, *México en tres momentos: 1810–1910–2010* (vol. 2), Alicia Mayer, ed. Mexico City: Instituto de Investigaciones Históricas, Universidad Nacional Autónoma de México.
Merrick, Thomas W. (1994) "The Population of Latin America, 1930–1990," pp. 3–64, *Cambridge History of Latin America* (vol. 6, pt. 1), Leslie Bethell, ed. Cambridge: Cambridge University Press.
Mexico (1827) *Dictamen que dió la Junta de Fomento de Californias al Exmo. Señor Presidente de la República.* Mexico City: Junta de Fomento de Californias.
—— (1884) *Código de minería de la República Mexicana.* Mexico City: Secretaría de Fomento.
—— (1892) *Ley minera de los Estados Unidos Mexicanos.* Monterrey: Tip. del Gobierno en Palacio.
—— (1931) *Anuario estadístico de los Estados Unidos Mexicanos 1930.* Mexico City: Dirección General de Estadística.
—— (1940) *Anuario estadístico de los Estados Unidos Mexicanos 1939.* Mexico City: Dirección General de Estadística.
—— (1941) *Diario de los debates de la Cámara de Senadores,* October 24. Mexico City: Cámara de Senadores.
—— (1943a) *Censo de población 1940: resumen general.* Mexico City: Dirección General de Estadística.
—— (1943b) *Censo de población 1940.* Mexico City: Dirección General de Estadística.
—— (1945) *Documentos de la revolución mexicana,* vol. 79. Mexico City: Secretaría de Educación Pública.
—— (1963a) *50 años de Revolución mexicana en cifras.* Mexico City: Presidencia de la República & Nacional Financiera.
—— (1963b) *VII censo general de población-1960. Distrito Federal.* Mexico City: Dirección General de Estadística.
—— (1963c) *VII censo general de población-1960. Estado de México.* Mexico City: Dirección General de Estadística.
—— (1966) *Los presidentes de México ante al Nación.* Mexico City: XLVI Legislatura de la Cámara de Diputados.
—— (1971) *IX censo general de población.* Mexico City: Dirección General de Estadística.
—— (1972) *IX Censo general de población. 1970. Resumen general.* Dirección General de Estadística.
—— (1973) *Anuario estadístico de los Estados Unidos Mexicanos 1970–1971.* Mexico City: Dirección General de Estadística.
—— (1983–84) *X Censo general de población. 1980.* Dirección General de Estadística.
Meyenberg, Yolanda & Ulises Carrillo (1999) "El Partido de la Revolución Democrática," *Revista Mexicana de Sociología* 61 (July–September): 53–68.
Meyer, Eugenia (1996) "Liberalismo, federalismo y modernidad," *Eslabones* 12 (July-December): 22–37.
Meyer, Eugenia, María Alba Pastor, Ximena Sepúlveda, & María Isabel Souza, (1986) "La vida con Villa en la Hacienda del Canutillo," pp. 170–83, *Secuencia* (May–August): 170–83.
Meyer, Jean A. (1976) *The Cristero Rebellion.* Cambridge: Cambridge University Press.
—— (1986a) "Haciendas y ranchos, peones y campesinos en el Porfiriato. Algunas falacias estadísticas," *Historia Mexicana* 35 (January–March): 477–509.
—— (1986b) "Mexico: Revolution and Reconstruction in the 1920s," pp. 155–94, *Cambridge History of Latin America* (vol. 5), Leslie Bethell, ed. Cambridge: Cambridge University Press.
—— (1996) *Hidalgo.* Mexico City: Clío.
—— (1997a) "El zapatismo va a la Cristiada," *Nexos* 231 (March): 37–38.
—— (1997b) "Church and State: 1910–1996," pp. 257–60, *Encyclopedia of Mexico,* Michael S. Werner, ed. Chicago IL: Fitzroy Dearborn.
—— (1997c) *La Cristiada* (4 vols.) Mexico City: Clío.
—— (2003) *El sinarquismo, el cardenismo y la Iglesia: 1937–1947.* Mexico City: Tusquets.
—— (2006) "An Idea of Mexico: Catholics in the Revolution," pp. 282–96, *The Eagle & the Virgin,* Mary Kay Vaughan & Stephen E Lewis, eds. Durham NC: Duke University Press.
Meyer, Lorenzo (1971) "Los límites de la política cardenista," *Revista de la UNAM* 25 (May): 1–8.
—— (1974) "El Estado mexicano contemporáneo," *Historia Mexicana* 92 (April–June): 722–52.
—— (1976a) *El primer tramo del camino (1920–1940),* Historia de México, etapa nacional, vol. 5. Mexico City: Edutex.
—— (1976b) "La campaña presidencial de 1976," *Comercio Exterior* 26 (June): 644–46.
—— (1977a) "Historic Roots of the Authoritarian State in Mexico," pp. 3–22, *Authoritarianism in Mexico,* José Luis Reyna & Richard S. Weinert, eds. Philadelphia PA: Institute for the Study of Human Issues.

—— (1977b) *Mexico and the United States in the Oil Controversy, 1917–1942.* Austin TX: University of Texas Press.

—— (1977c) "La etapa formativa del Estado mexicano contemporáneo (1928–1940)," *Foro Internacional* 17 (April–June): 453–76.

—— (1979) "Petróleo mexicano," *Nexos* 20 (August): 3–13.

—— (1983) "México en el siglo XX: la concentración del poder político, pp. 131–47, *La unidad nacional en América Latina,* Marco Palacios, ed. Mexico City: Colegio de México.

—— (1985) "La Revolución mexicana y sus elecciones presidenciales, 1911–1940," pp. 69–99, *Las elecciones en México,* Pablo González Casanova, ed. Mexico City: Siglo XXI.

—— (1988) "La debilidad histórica de la democracia mexicana," pp. 73–83, *Mexico: El reclamo democrático,* Rolando Cordera Campos, Raúl Trejo Delarbre & Juan Enrique Vega, eds. Mexico City: Siglo XXI.

—— (1989a) *La segunda muerte de la Revolución Mexicana.* Mexico City: Cal y Arena.

—— (1989b) "Democratization of the PRI: Mission Impossible?" pp. 325–48, *Mexico's Alternative Political Futures,* Wayne A. Cornelius, Judith Gentleman, & Peter H. Smith, eds. UCSD Center for U.S.–Mexican Studies Monograph Series, 30. San Diego CA: UCSD Center for U.S.–Mexican Studies.

—— (1989c) "El año político," pp. 11–25, *México-Estados Unidos, 1987,* Gerardo Bueno & Lorenzo Meyer, eds. Mexico City: Colegio de México.

—— (1991a) *Su majestad británica contra la revolución mexicana, 1900–1950.* Mexico City: Colegio de México.

—— (1991b) "Mexico: The Exception and the Rule," pp. 215–32, *Exporting Democracy,* Abraham F. Lowenthal, ed. Baltimore MD: Johns Hopkins University Press.

—— (1991c) "De vecinos distantes al amor sin barreras," *Este País* 2 (May): 32–34.

—— (1991d) "El límite neoliberal," *Nexos* 163 (July): 25–34.

—— (1992a) *La segunda muerte de la Revolución Mexicana.* Mexico City: Cal y Arena.

—— (1992b) "The Expropriation and Great Britain," pp. 154–72, *The Mexican Petroleum Industry in the Twentieth Century,* Jonathan C. Brown & Alan Knight, eds. Austin TX: University of Texas Press.

—— (1994) "México o la cultura de la desconfianza," *Cuadernos de Nexos* 67 (January): xiv–xvii.

—— (1996) "La crisis del presidencialismo mexicano. Recuperación espectacular y recaída estructural, 1982–1996," *Foro Internacional* 36 (January–June): 11–30.

—— (2000) "La institucionalización del nuevo régimen," pp. 823–79 & "De la estabilidad al cambio," pp. 881–943, *Historia general de México: Versión 2000.* Mexico City: Colegio de México.

—— (2001) "La brega por el poder," *Proceso* Special no. 9: 34–45.

—— (2003a) "La sorpresa: una rebelión indígena al final del antiguo régimen," *Foro Internacional* 43 (January–March): 249–67.

—— (2003b) "La visión general," pp. 13–31 & "Estados Unidos; de vecindad distante a la proximidad difícil," pp. 111–53, *Historia contemporánea de México* (vol. 1), Ilán Bizberg & Lorenzo Meyer, eds. Mexico City: Océano.

—— (2005a) "La pobreza en México," *Comercio Exterior* 55 (August): 684–91.

—— (2005b) "La visión general," pp. 15–33, *Historia contemporánea de México* (vol. 2), Ilán Bizberg & Lorenzo Meyer, eds. Mexico City: Océano.

—— (2007a) "The Second Coming of Mexican Liberalism," pp. 271–304, *Cycles of Conflict, Centuries of Change,* Elisa Servín, Leticia Reina, & John Tutino, eds. Durham NC: Duke University Press.

—— (2007b) *El espejismo democrático.* Mexico City: Océano.

—— (2008) "El Ocho," *Reforma* (January 24): 13, "Opinión."

Meyer, Michael C. (1972) *Huerta: A Political Portrait.* Lincoln NE: University of Nebraska Press.

—— (1984) *Water in the Hispanic Southwest.* Tucson AZ: University of Arizona Press.

Meyer, Michael, William L. Sherman, & Susan Deeds (2007) *The Course of Mexican History* (8th ed.). New York: Oxford University Press.

Meyers, William K. (1977) "Politics, Vested Rights, and Economic Growth in Porfirian Mexico," *Hispanic American Historical Review* 57 (August): 425–54.

Michaels, Albert L. (1968) "Lázaro Cárdenas y la lucha por la independencia económica de México," *Historia Mexicana* 18 (July–September): 56–78.

—— (1971) "Las elecciones de 1940," *Historia Mexicana* 21 (July–September): 80–134.

Michaels, Albert L. & Marvin Bernstein (1976) "The Modernization of the Old Order," pp. 687–710, *Contemporary Mexico,* James W. Wilkie, Michael C. Meyer, & Edna Monzón de Wilkie, eds. Berkeley CA: University of California Press.

Middlebrook, Kevin J. (1989) "The CTM and the Future of Government-Labor Relations," pp. 291–305, *Mexico's Alternative Political Futures,* Wayne Cornelius, Judith Gentleman, & Peter H. Smith, eds. UCSD Center for U.S.–Mexican Studies Monograph Series, 30. San Diego CA: UCSD Center for U.S.–Mexican Studies.

—— (1995) *The Paradox of Revolution.* Baltimore MD: Johns Hopkins University Press.

—— (2001) "Party Policies and Democratization in Mexico," pp. 3–44, *Party Politics and the Struggle for Democracy in Mexico,* Kevin Middlebrook, ed. UCSD Center for U.S.–Mexican Studies Contemporary Perspective Series, 17. San Diego CA: UCSD Center for U.S.–Mexican Studies.

Middlebrook, Kevin & Eduardo Zepeda (2003) "On the Political Economy of Mexican Development Policy," pp. 3–52, *Confronting Development,* Kevin J. Middlebrook & Eduardo Zepeda, eds. Palo Alto CA: Stanford University Press & San Diego CA: UCSD Center for U.S.–Mexican Studies.

Miller, Barbara (1981) "Women and Revolution: The Brigadas Femeninas and the Mexican Cristero Rebellion, 1926–29," pp. 57–66, *Women and Politics in Twentieth Century Latin America,* Sandra F. McGee, ed. Williamsburg VA: Dept. of Anthropology, College of William & Mary.

Miller, Hubert J. (1986) *Padre Miguel Hidalgo.* Edinburg TX: Pan American University Press.

Miller, Michael (1998) *Red, White, and Green.* El Paso TX: Texas Western Press.

Miller, Morris (1991) *Debt and the Environment.* New York: United Nations.

Miller, Robert Ryal (1973) "Arms across the Border," *Transactions of the American Philosophical Society* 63 (December): 1–68.

—— (1985) *Mexico: A History.* Norman OK: University of Oklahoma Press.

—— (1989) *Shamrock and Sword.* Norman OK: University of Oklahoma Press.

Miller, Robert Ryal, ed. (1991) *The Mexican War Journal and Letters of Ralph W. Kirkham.* College Station TX: Texas A&M University Press.

Miller, Shawn William (2007) *An Environmental History of Latin America.* New York: Cambridge University Press.

Miller, Simon (1990) "Mexican Junkers and Capitalist Haciendas, 1810–1910: The Arable Estate and the Transition to Capitalism between the Insurgency and the Revolution," *Journal of Latin American Studies* 22 (May): 229–63.

Millon, Robert P. (1969) *Zapata: The Ideology of a Peasant Revolutionary.* New York: International.

Miño Grijalva, Manuel (2005) "La Ciudad del México," pp. 161–91, *Revolución, independencia y las nuevas naciones de América,* Jaime E. Rodríguez O., ed. Madrid: Fundación Mapfre Tavera.

Miranda, René (2006) "El PREP a detalle," *Nexos* 344 (August): 12–16.

Mirandé, Alfredo (1987) *Gringo Justice.* Notre Dame IN: University of Notre Dame Press.

Mires, Fernando (1987) *La colonización de las almas.* San José Costa Rica: Editorial DEI.

Mirón, Rosa María & Germán Pérez (1988) *López Portillo: auge y crisis de un sexenio.* Mexico City: Plaza y Valdés.

Mizrahi, Yemile (1998) "The Costs of Electoral Success: The Partido Acción Nacional in Mexico," pp. 95–113, *Governing Mexico,* Mónica Serrano, ed. London: Institute of Latin American Studies, University of London.

—— (2003) *From Martrydom to Power.* Notre Dame IN: University of Notre Dame Press.

Molina Enríquez, Andrés (1978) *Los grandes problemas nacionales.* Mexico City: Era.

Molinar Horcasitas, Juan (1987a) "Vicisitudes de una reforma electoral," pp. 25–40, *La vida política mexicana en la crisis,* Soledad Loaeza & Rafael Segovia, eds. Mexico City: Colegio de México.

—— (1987b) "Regreso a Chihuahua," *Nexos* 111 (March): 21–32.

—— (1987c) "The 1985 Federal Elections in Mexico," pp. 17–32, *Electoral Patterns and Perspectives in Mexico,* Arturo Alvarado, ed. UCSD Center for U.S.–Mexican Studies Monograph Series, 22. San Diego CA: UCSD Center for U.S.–Mexican Studies.

—— (1987d) "Las elecciones de 1985 y sus consecuencias," pp. 189–223, *17 ángulos de un sexenio,* Germán Pérez & Samuel León, eds. Mexico City: Plaza y Valdés.

—— (1991) *El tiempo de la legitimidad.* Mexico City: Cal y Arena.

—— (1996) "Renegotiating the Rules of the Game," pp. 25–39, *Rebuilding the State,* Mónica Serrano & Victor Bulmer-Thomas, eds. London: Institute of Latin American Studies, University of London.

Molyneux, Maxine (2000) "Twentieth-Century State Formations in Latin America," pp. 33–81, *Hidden Histories of Gender and State in Latin America,* Elizabeth Dore & Maxine Molyneux, eds. Durham NC: Duke University Press.

Moncayo, Pablo Pascual, ed. (1995) *Las elecciones de 1994.* Mexico City: Cal y Arena.

Monsiváis, Carlos (1986a) "Civilización y Coca-Cola," *Nexos* 104 (August): 19–30.

—— (1986b) "Sociedad y cultura," pp. 259–80, *Entre la guerra y la estabilidad política,"* Rafael Loyola, ed. Mexico City: Grijalbo.

—— (1986c) "Prologue," *El Zarco,* Ignacio Manuel Altamirano. Mexico City: Océano.

—— (1995) "All the People Came and Did Not Fit Onto the Screen: Notes on the Cinema Audience in Mexico," pp. 145–52, *Mexican Cinema,* Paulo Antonio Paranaguá, ed. London: British Film Institute.

—— (1996) "Los intelectuales mexicanos a fin de siglo," *Viento del Sur* 8 (Winter): 37–44.

—— (2000a) "La era del PRI y sus deudos" *Letras Libres* 20 (August): 16–22.

—— (2000b) "Notas sobre la cultura mexicana en el Siglo XX," pp. 957–1075, *Historia general de México—Versión 2000.* Mexico City: Colegio de México.

—— (2001) "La muerte del semidiós," *Proceso* Special no. 9: 12–25.

—— (2006a) "Imágenes del editor Julio Scherer," *Revista de la UNAM* 23 (January): 5–9.

—— (2006b) "When Gender Can't Be Seen Amid the Symbols," pp. 1–20, *Sex in Revolution*, Jocelyn Olcott, Mary Kay Vaughan, & Gabriela Cano, eds. Durham NC: Duke University Press.

—— (2008) *El 68*. Mexico City: Era.

Monteiro, John M. (2006) "Labor Systems," pp. 185–233, *Cambridge Economic History of Latin America* (vol. 1) Victor Bulmer-Thomas, John H. Coatsworth, & Roberto Cortés Conde, eds. New York: Cambridge University Press.

Montejano, David (1987) *Anglos and Mexicans in the Making of Texas, 1836–1986*. Austin TX: University of Texas Press.

Montemayor, Carlos (2001) "La guerrilla recurrente," pp. 69–104, *Chiapas en perspectiva histórica*. Barcelona: El Viejo Topo.

—— (2007) *La guerrilla recurrente*. Mexico City: Debate.

Montemayor Hernández, Andrés (1971) *Historia de Monterrey*. Monterrey: Asociación de Editores y Libreros de Monterrey.

Montes de Oca, Rosa Elena (1977) "The State and the Peasants," pp. 47–63, *Authoritarianism in Mexico*, José Luis Reyna, & Richard S. Weinert, eds. Philadelphia PA: Institute for the Study of Human Issues.

Mora, Carl J. (1989) *Mexican Cinema*. Berkeley CA: University of California Press.

Morales, Isidro (1992) "The Consolidation and Expansion of Pemex, 1947–1958," pp. 208–32, *The Mexican Petroleum Industry in the Twentieth Century*, Jonathan C. Brown & Alan Knight, eds. Austin TX: University of Texas Press.

Morales, Patricia (1989) *Indocumentados Mexicanos*. Mexico City: Grijalbo.

Morales Castañeda, Raúl (2006) "El crecimiento de la economía mexicana en los últimos veinticinco años," *El Cotidiano* 139 (September–October): 86–100.

Moreno, María de los Ángeles & Romero Flores Caballero (1995) *Evolución de la deuda pública externa de México: 1950–1993*. Monterrey: Ediciones Castillo.

Moreno-Brid, Juan Carlos & Jaime Ros (2009) *Development and Growth in the Mexican Economy*. New York: Oxford University Press.

Moreno Toscano, Alejandra (1976) "El siglo de la conquista," pp. 1–81, *Historia general de México*, vol. 2. Mexico City: Colegio de México.

Mörner, Magnus (1967) *Race Mixture in the History of Latin America*. Boston MA: Little, Brown.

Morris, Mark (2007) "The Nahuatl Counterinsurgency Propaganda of 1810," *Hispanic American Historical Review* 87 (August): 433–70.

Morris, Stephen D. (1995) *Political Reformism in Mexico*. Boulder CO: Lynne Rienner.

Morse, Sanford A. (1984) "The Urban Development of Colonial Spanish America," pp. 67–104, *Cambridge History of Latin America* (vol. 2), Leslie Bethell, ed. Cambridge: Cambridge University Press.

Morton, Ward M. (1962) *Woman Suffrage in Mexico*. Gainesville FL: University of Florida Press.

Mosk, Sanford A. (1950) *Industrial Revolution in Mexico*. Berkeley CA: University of California Press.

Motten, Clement G. (1950) *Mexican Silver and the Enlightenment*. Philadelphia PA: University of Pennsylvania Press.

Moyano Pahissa, Ángela (1976) *El comercio de Santa Fe y la guerra de 47*. Mexico City: SepSetentas.

—— (1985) *México y Estados Unidos: Orígenes de una relación, 1819–1861*. Mexico City: Secretaría de Educación Pública.

Múgica, Francisco (1984) "De San Luis a Tampico," *Desdeldiez* (September): 76–86.

Muldoon, James (1978) "Papal Responsibility for the Infidel: Another Look at Alexander's VI's *Inter Caetera*," *The Catholic Historic Review* 44 (April): 168–84.

—— (1994) *The Americas in the Spanish World Order*. Philadelphia PA: University of Pennsylvania Press.

Mumme, Stephen (1992) "System Maintenance and Environmental Reform in Mexico," *Latin American Perspectives* 72 (Winter): 123–43.

Muñoz Leos, Raúl (2006) *Pemex en la encrucijada*. Mexico City: Nuevo Siglo Aguilar.

Murillo, María Victoria (2001) *Labor Unions, Partisan Coalitions, and Market Reforms in Latin America*. Cambridge. Cambridge University Press.

Muro, Víctor Gabriel (2007) "La Iglesia católica ante los procesos sociopolíticos del siglo XX en México," pp. 319–415, *México en tres momentos: 1810–1910–2010* (vol. 1), Alicia Mayer, ed. Mexico City: Instituto de Investigaciones Históricas, Universidad Nacional Autónoma de México.

Murray, Douglas L. (1994) *Cultivating Crisis: The Human Cost of Pesticides in Latin America*. Austin TX: University of Texas Press.

Murray, Pamela (1997) "Diverse approaches to Nineteenth-Century Mexican History," *Latin American Research Review* 32 (no. 3): 187–92.

Musset, Alain (1992) *El agua en el Valle de México: Siglos XVI-XVIII*. Mexico City: Pórtico de la Ciudad de México & Centro de Estudios Mexicanos y Centroamericanos.

Nadal, Alejandro (1998) "Terror in Chiapas," *Bulletin of the Atomic Scientists* 54 (March–April): 18–25.

—— (2003) "Corn in NAFTA Eight Years After," pp. 152–72, *Greening NAFTA*, David Markell & John H. Knox, eds. Palo Alto CA: Stanford University Press.

Nader, Helen (2000) "The Spain that Encountered Mexico," pp. 11–45, *Oxford History of Mexico*, Michael C. Meyer & William H. Beezley, eds. New York: Oxford University Press.

NAFINSA (National Financiera) (1977) *Statistics on the Mexican Economy.* Mexico City: Nacional Financiera.

—— (1984) *La economía mexicana en cifras 1984.* Mexico City: Nacional Financiera.

Nahmad, Salomón (2008) "Mexico: Anthropology and the Nation-State," pp. 128–49, *A Companion to Latin American Anthropology,* Debora Poole, ed. Oxford: Blackwell.

Naím, Moisés (2004) "From Normalcy to Lunacy," *Foreign Policy* 141 (March–April): 103–04.

Nathan, Debbie (2003) "The Juárez Murders," *Amnesty Now* 29 (Spring): 4–9.

Nava Otero, Guadalupe (1980) "La minería bajo el porfiriato," pp. 339–79, *Mexico en el siglo XIX (1821–1910),* Ciro Cardoso, ed. Mexico City: Nueva Imagen.

Navarrete Maya, Laura (1998) "La prensa satírica durante él régimen de Lerdo de Tejada," pp. 103–21, *La prensa en México,* Laura Navarrete Maya & Blanca Aguilar Plata, eds. Mexico City: Addison, Wesley, Longman de México.

Naveda Chávez-Hita, Adriana (1987) *Esclavos negros en las haciendas azucareras de Córdoba, Veracruz, 1690–1830.* Jalapa: Universidad Veracruzana.

Neal, Clarice (1966) "Freedom of the Press in New Spain, 1810–1820," pp. 87–112, *Mexico and the Spanish Cortes, 1810–1822,* Nettie Lee Benson, ed. Austin TX: University of Texas Press.

Needler, Martin C. (1961) "The Political Development of Mexico," *American Political Science Review* 55 (June): 308–12.

—— (1971) *Politics and Society in Mexico.* Albuquerque NM: University of New Mexico Press.

—— (1987) *The Problem of Democracy in Latin America.* Lexington MA: Heath.

Negretto, Gabriel L. & José Antonio Aguilar-Rivera (2000) "Rethinking the Legacy of the Liberal State in Latin America," *Journal of Latin American Studies* 32 (May): 361–97.

Neild, Rachel (2005) "U.S. Police Assistance and Drug Control Politics," pp. 61–98, *Drugs and Democracy in Latin America,* Coletta Youngers & Eileen Rosin, eds. Boulder CO: Lynne Rienner.

Newell G., Roberto & Luis Rubio F. (1984) *Mexico's Dilemma: The Political Origins of Economic Crisis.* Boulder CO: Westview.

Newfarmer, Richard S. & Willard F. Mueller (1975) *Multinational Corporations in Brazil and Mexico.* 94th Congress, 1st Session. U.S. Government Printing Office.

Newson, Linda A. (2000) Review of *Numbers from Nowhere* by David Henige. *Journal of Latin American Studies* 32 (February): 265–66.

—— (2006) "The Demographic Impact of Colonization," pp. 143–84, *Cambridge Economic History of Latin America* (vol. 1) Victor Bulmer-Thomas, John H. Coatsworth, & Roberto Cortés Conde, eds. New York: Cambridge University Press.

Ngai, Mae (2004) *Impossible Subjects.* Princeton NJ: Princeton University Press.

Niblo, Stephen R. (1975) "Progress and the Standard of Living in Contemporary Mexico," *Latin American Perspectives* 2 (Summer): 109–24.

—— (1988a) *The Impact of War: Mexico and World War II.* La Trobe University Institute of Latin American Studies Occasional Paper no. 10. Melbourne: La Trobe University.

—— (1988b) "Mexico: Development Without the People," *Journal of the West* 37 (October): 50–63.

—— (1995) *War, Diplomacy, and Development.* Wilmington DE: Scholarly Resources.

—— (1999) *Mexico in the 1940s.* Wilmington DE: Scholarly Resources.

Niblo, Stephen R. & Diane M. Niblo (2008) "Acapulco in Dreams and Reality," *Mexican Studies/Estudios Mexicanos* 24 (Winter): 31–51.

Nicolson, Harold (1935) *Dwight Morrow.* New York: Harcourt, Brace & Co.

Niemeyer, E. Victor, Jr. (1974) *Revolution at Querétaro.* Austin TX: University of Texas Press.

—— (1986) "Personal Diplomacy: Lyndon B. Johnson and Mexico, 1963–1968," *Southwestern Historical Quarterly* 90 (October): 159–86.

—— (1994) *Bernardo Reyes.* Monterrey: Gobierno del Estado de Nuevo León.

Niess, Frank (1990) *A Hemisphere to Itself.* London: Zed.

Nolan, Mary Lee & Sidney Nolan (1988) "The Evolution of Tourism in Twentieth-Century Mexico," *Journal of the West* 27 (October): 14–25.

Novelo, Victoria (1997) "Artisans and Artisanal Production," pp. 105–07, *Encyclopedia of Mexico,* Michael S. Werner, ed. Chicago IL: Fitzroy Dearborn.

Nugent, Daniel (1993) *Spent Cartridges of Revolution.* Chicago IL: University of Chicago Press.

Nugent, Daniel & Ana María Alonso (1994) "Multiple Selective Traditions in Agrarian Reform and Agrarian Struggle," pp. 209–46 *Everyday Forms of State Formation*, Gilbert M. Joseph & Daniel Nugent, eds. Durham NC: Duke University Press.

Nugent, Walter (2008) *Habits of Empire*. New York: Knopf.

Nuijten, Monique (2003) *Power, Community, and the State*. London: Pluto.

Nuncio, Abraham (1986) *El PAN*. Mexico City: Nueva Imagen.

Nutini, Hugo G. (1995) *The Wages of Conquest*. Ann Arbor MI: The University of Michigan Press.

O'Boyle, Michael (2004) "Nafta's Birthday Party," *Business Mexico* 14 (February): 28–33.

O'Brien, Patrick Karl (2006) "The Global Economic History of European Expansion Overseas," pp. 7–42, *Cambridge Economic History of Latin America* (vol. 1) Victor Bulmer-Thomas, John H. Coatsworth, & Roberto Cortés Conde, eds. New York: Cambridge University Press.

O'Brien, Thomas (1996) *The Revolutionary Mission*. Cambridge: Cambridge University Press.

—— (1999) *The Century of U.S. Capitalism in Latin America*. Albuquerque NM: University of New Mexico Press.

Ocampo, Melchor (1900–01) *Obras completas de Melchor Ocampo* (3 vols.) Mexico City: F. Vázquez.

Ocegueda Hernández, Juan Manuel & Gladys Plascencia López (2004) "¿Convergencia o divergencia regional en la frontera de México con Estados Unidos?" *Comercio Exterior* 54 (October): 874–83.

Ochoa, Enrique (2000) *Feeding Mexico*. Wilmington DE: Scholarly Resources.

O'Connor, Richard (1971) *The Cactus Throne*. New York: Putnam.

Officer, James E. (1987) *Hispanic Arizona, 1536–1856*. Tucson AZ: University of Arizona Press.

Offutt, Leslie S. (2001) *Saltillo, 1770–1810*. Tucson AZ: University of Arizona Press.

Ohrt, Wallace (1997) *Defiant Peacemaker: Nicholas Trist in the Mexican War*. College Station TX: Texas A&M University Press.

Ojeda, Mario (1972) "El perfil internacional de México en 1980," pp. 289–324, *El Perfil de México en 1980*, vol. 3. Mexico City: Siglo XXI.

—— (1987) "La doble agenda en las relaciones entre México y Estados Unidos," pp. 21–40, *México-Estados Unidos, 1986*, Gerardo M. Bueno, ed. Mexico City: El Colegio de México.

Olavarría y Ferrari, Enrique (1974) "México independiente, 1821-1855," vol. 4, *México a través de los siglos* (11th ed.), Vicente Riva Palacio, ed. Mexico City. Editorial Cambre.

Olcott, Jocelyn (2005) *Revolutionary Women in Postrevolutionary Mexico*. Durham NC: Duke University Press.

Oldstone, Michael B.A. (1998) *Viruses, Plagues, and History*. New York: Oxford University Press.

Oliveira, Orlandina de, Marina Ariza & Marcela Eternod (2001) "La fuerza de trabajo de México," pp. 873–923, *La población de México*, José Gómez de León Cruces & Cecilia Rabell Romero, eds. Mexico City: Fondo de Cultura Económica & Consejo Nacional de Población.

Oliveira, Orlandina de & Brígida García (1997) "Socioeconomic Transformation and Labor Markets in Urban Mexico," pp. 211–32, *Global Restructuring, Employment, and Social Inequality in Urban Latin America*. Coral Gables FL: North-South Center Press.

Oliveira, Orlandina de & Bryan Roberts (1994) "Urban Growth and Urban Social Structure in Latin America, 1930–1990," pp. 253–324, *Cambridge History of Latin America* (vol. 6, pt. 1), Leslie Bethell, ed. Cambridge: Cambridge University Press.

Olivera, Ruth R. & Liliane Crété (1991) *Life In Mexico under Santa Anna, 1822–1855*. Norman OK: University of Oklahoma Press.

Olivera de Bonfil, Alicia (1976) "La Iglesia en México, 1926–1970," pp. 295–316, *Contemporary Mexico*, James W. Wilkie, Michael C. Meyer, & Edna Monzón de Wilkie, eds. Berkeley CA: University of California Press.

—— (1994) "Cómo se forjó un mártir: vida y milagros del padre Pro," pp. 303–30, *A Dios lo que es de Dios*, Carlos Martínez Assad, ed. Mexico City: Aguilar.

Olivera Rivera, Alberto J. (1997) "Transformaciones económicas, cambios politicos y movimientos sociales en el campo," pp. 65–89, *La democracia de los de abajo en México*, Jorge Alonso & Juan Manuel Ramírez Sáiz, eds. Mexico City: La Jornada Ediciones.

Olliff, Donathon C. (1981) *Reforma Mexico and the United States*. University AL: University of Alabama Press.

Olmsted, Frederick Law (1978) *A Journey through Texas*. Austin TX: University of Texas Press.

Olson, Robert (2005) "A Shrinking Giant," *Petroleum Economist* 72 (March): 4–8.

Oppenheimer, Andrés (1996) *Bordering on Chaos*. Boston MA: Little, Brown.

Ordorica, Manuel & José Luis Lezama (1993) "Consecuencias demográficas de la Revolución Mexicana," pp. 32–54, *El poblamiento de México*, vol. 4. Mexico City: Consejo Nacional de Población.

Ornelas, Carlos (2001) "La educación mexicana y la cohesión social," pp. 175–92, *¿Estamos unidos mexicanos?* Mauricio de María Campos & Georgina Sánchez, eds. Mexico City: Planeta.

ORDPI & INI (Oficina de Representación para el Desarrollo de los Pueblos Indígenas & Insitituto Nacional Indigenista) (2002) *Programa Nacional para el Desarrollo de los Pueblos Indígenas 2001–2006*. Mexico City: ORDPI & INI.

Ortega Soto, Martha (2001) *Alta California: una frontera olvidada del noroeste de México 1769–1846.* Mexico City: Plaza y Valdés.

Ortiz Monasterio, Fernando (1987) *Tierra profanada: historia ambiental de México.* Mexico City: Instituto Nacional de Antropología e Historia (INAH).

Ouweneel, Arij (1996) *Shadows over Anáhuac.* Albuquerque NM: University of New Mexico Press.

Ouweneel, Arij & Catrien, C. J. H. Bijleveld (1989) "The Economic Cycle in Bourbon Central Mexico," *Hispanic American Historical Review* 69 (August): 479–530.

Pacheco, José Emilio & Andrés Reséndez (1997) *Crónica del 47.* Mexico City: Clío.

Pacheco Méndez, Guadalupe (1988) *El PRI en los procesos electorales de 1961 a 1985.* Xochimilco: Universidad Autónoma Metropolitana.

Padden, Robert C. (1967) *The Hummingbird and the Hawk.* Columbus OH: Ohio State University Press.

—— (2000) "The Ordenanza del Patronazgo of 1574," pp. 27–47, *The Church in Colonial Latin America,* John F. Schwaller, ed. Wilmington DE: Scholarly Resources.

Padilla López, Raúl (1996) "Educación y cultura en México," pp. 187–213, *Los compromisos con la Nación.* Mexico City: Plaza y Janés.

Pagden, Anthony (1990) *Spanish Imperialism and the Political Imagination.* New Haven CT: Yale University Press.

Palma, Esperanza (2000) "El PRD," *El Cotidiano* 100 (March-April): 198–205.

Palma, Gabriel (2003) "The Latin American Economies during the Second Half of the Twentieth Century," pp. 125–51, *Rethinking Development Economics,* Ha-Joon Chang, ed. London: Anthem.

Palmer, Collin A. (1976) *Slaves of the White God: Blacks in Mexico, 1570–1650.* Cambridge MA: Harvard University Press.

Pani, Erika (2002) "Dreaming of a Mexican Empire," *Hispanic American Historical Review* 82 (February): 1–31.

Panizza, Francisco (1993) "Human Rights: Global Culture and Social Fragmentation," *Bulletin of Latin American Research* 12 (no. 2): 205–14.

Paranaguá, Paulo Antonio (1995) "Ten Reasons to Love or Hate Mexican Cinema," pp. 1–14, *Mexican Cinema,* Paulo Antonio Paranaguá, ed. London: British Film Institute.

Paré, Luisa (1990) "The Challenge of Rural Democratization in Mexico," *Journal of Development Studies* 26 (July): 79–96.

Park, Joseph F. (1961) "The Apaches in Mexican–American Relations, 1848–1861," *Arizona and the West* 3 (Summer): 129–46.

Parkes, Henry Bamford (1960) *A History of Mexico.* Boston MA: Houghton Mifflin.

Parry, J. H. (1953) *The Sale of Public Office in the Spanish Indies under the Hapsburgs.* Ibero-Americana: 37. Berkeley CA: University of California Press.

Passananti, Thomas F. (2007) "Managing Globalization in Early Porfirian Mexico," *Latin American Research Review* 42 (November): 101–28.

Pastor, Manuel & Carol Wise (2005) "The Fox Administration and the Politics of Economic Transition," pp. 89–118, *Mexico's Democracy at Work,* Russell Crandall, Guadalupe Paz, & Riordan Roett, eds. Boulder CO: Lynne Rienner.

Pastor, Robert A. & Jorge G. Castañeda (1988) *Limits to Friendship.* New York: Knopf.

Pastor, Rodolfo (1985) "El repartimiento de mercancías y los alcaldes mayores novohispanos," pp. 201–36, *El gobierno provincial de Nueva España, 1570–1787,* Woodrow Borah, ed. Mexico City: Instituto de Investigaciones Históricas, Universidad Nacional Autónoma de México.

Pastor Bodmer, Beatriz (1992) *The Armature of Conquest.* Palo Alto CA: Stanford University Press.

Patch, Robert W. (2000) "Indian Resistance to Colonialism," pp. 183–211, *Oxford History of Mexico,* Michael C. Meyer & William H. Beezley, eds. New York: Oxford University Press.

Patterson, Eric (2003) *Faith in a Changing Mexico.* Paper presented at the XXIV Latin American Studies Association Meetings, Dallas TX (March).

Payan, Tony (2006) *The Three U.S.–Mexico Border Wars.* Westport: Praeger Security International.

Payer, Cheryl (1991) *Lent and Lost.* London: Zed.

Payne, Douglas (1998) "Los trabajadores mexicanos," *Este País* 86 (May): 32–37.

Paz, María Emilia (1988) "La expropiación petrolera y el contexto internacional," *Revista Mexicana de Sociología* 1 (July-September): 75–96.

—— (1997) *Strategy, Security, and Spies.* University Park PA: Pennsylvania State University Press.

Paz, Octavio (1972) *The Other Mexico.* New York: Grove.

—— (1975a) "Mexico: The Last Decade," pp. 241–62, *Is the Mexican Revolution Dead?* (2nd ed.), Stanley R. Ross, ed. Philadelphia PA: Temple University Press.

—— (1975b) "Thinking Back to the Student Revolt" *Dissent* 22 (Spring): 148–53.

—— (1976) "Foreword," *Quetzalcóatl and Guadalupe,* Jacques Lafaye. Chicago IL: University of Chicago Press.

—— (1982) "Mexico and the United States: Positions and Counterpositions," pp. 1–21, *Mexico Today,* Tommie Sue Montgomery, ed. Philadelphia PA: Institute for the Study of Human Issues.

—— (1985) *The Labyrinth of Solitude.* New York: Grove.

—— (1988) *Sor Juana or, the Traps of Faith.* Cambridge MA: Harvard University Press.

—— (1990) "Will for Form" pp. 3–38, *Mexico: Splendors of Thirty Centuries.* New York: Metropolitan Museum of Art.

Pazos, Luis (1976) *Devaluación y estatismo en México.* Mexico City: Diana.

—— (2006) *6 años de PAN con Fox.* Mexico City: Centro de Investigaciones sobre la Libre Empesa.

Pellicer de Brody, Olga (1977) "La crisis mexicana: hacia una nueva dependencia," *Cuadernos Políticos* 14 (October–December): 44–55.

—— (1982) "Política exterior," *Nexos* 50 (February): 21–24.

Pellicer de Brody, Olga & Esteban L. Mancilla (1978) *El entendimiento con los Estados Unidos y la gestión del desarrollo estabilizador,* Historia de la Revolución mexicana, vol. 23. Mexico City: Colegio de México.

Pellicer de Brody, Olga & José Luis Reyna (1978) *El afianzamiento de la estabilidad política,* Historia de la Revolución mexicana, vol. 22. Mexico City: Colegio de México.

Peña, Devon G. (2005) *Mexican Americans and the Environment. Tierra y Libertad.* Tucson AZ: University of Arizona Press.

Pensado, Patricia & Leonor Correa (1996) *Mixcoac.* Mexico City: Instituto Mora.

Pepin Lehalleur, Marielle (1997) "Évolutions Culturelles au Mexique. Approches Anthropologiques," *Cahiers des Amériques Latines,* no. 25: 67–77.

Pereyra, Carlos (1974) "México: los límites del reformismo," *Cuadernos Políticos* 1 (July–Sept): 52–65.

Pérez, Louis A., Jr. (1982) "Intervention, Hegemony, and Dependency: The United States in the Circum-Caribbean, 1898–1980," *Pacific Historical Review* 51 (May): 165–194.

Pérez de Salazar V., Francisco (1995) "Mexico City: Growth and Development" *Voices of Mexico* 33 (October-December): 61–66.

Pérez Fernández del Castillo, Germán (1999) "Del presidencialismo absoluto al presidencialismo acotado," pp. 63–110, *México en el siglo XX,* vol. 1. Mexico City: Archivo General de la Nación.

Pérez Gay, Rafael (2003) "Entre las ruinas y el jardín" *Nexos* 302 (February): 30–47.

Pérez Herrero, Pedro (1991) "Los factores de la conformación regional en México, 1700–1850," pp. 207–36, *Región e Historia en México, 1700–1850.* Mexico City: Instituto Mora & Universidad Autónoma Metropolitana.

Pérez Ruiz, Maya Lorena & Majorie Thacker Moll (1994) "Los indígenas en México," pp. 347–88, *Desarrollo, desigualdad y medio ambiente,* Pablo Pascual Moncayo & José Woldenberg, eds. Mexico City: Cal y Arena.

Pérez Toledo, Sonia (1996) "Artesanos y gremios en la ciudad de México," pp. 223–44, *Ciudad de México,* Carlos Illades & Ariel Rodríguez Kuri, eds. Zamora: Colegio de Michoacán.

Perkins, Dexter (1933) *The Monroe Doctrine:* 1826–1867. Baltimore MD: Johns Hopkins Press.

Perret, Geoffrey (1996) *Old Soldiers Never Die.* New York: Random House.

Peschard, Jacqueline (2006) "Quince años de cambios en la política mexicana," *Este País* 181 (April): 31–34.

Peschard, Jacqueline, Cristina Puga, and Ricardo Tirado (1986) "De Ávila Camacho a Miguel Alemán," pp. 19–58, *Evolución del estado mexicano,* vol. 3. Mexico City: El Caballito.

Petriccioli, Gustavo (1988) "Economía mixta," pp. 840–65, *México: setenta y cinco años de revolución I—desarrollo económico 2.* Mexico City: Fondo de Cultura Económica.

Philip, George (1982) *Oil and Politics in Latin America.* Cambridge: Cambridge University Press.

—— (1988) "Petroleum in Mexico," *Journal of the West* 27 (October): 26–32.

Phillips, Carla Rahn (1993) "Spain," pp. 63–77, *Encyclopedia of the North American Colonies,* vol. 1. New York: Charles Scribner's Sons.

Physicians for Human Rights & Human Rights Watch (1994) *Waiting for Justice in Chiapas.* Boston MA & New York: Physicians for Human Rights & Human Rights Watch.

Pi Suñer, Antonia (1992) "La relaciones hispano-mexicanas en manos de los prestamistas," pp. 136–53, *Five Centuries of Mexican History/Cinco siglos de historia de México,* Virginia Guedea & Jaime E. Rodríguez O., eds. Mexico City: Instituto Mora & Irvine CA: University of California.

Pi-Sunyer, Oriol (1957) "Historical Background to the Negro in Mexico," *Journal of Negro History* 42 (October): 237–46.

Pick, James B. (2003) *Population and Urban Change in the U.S.–Mexican Border Cities, 1900–2020.* Paper Presented at XXIV Conference of the Latin American Studies Association, Dallas TX.

Pike, Fredrick B. (1992) *The United States and Latin America.* Austin TX: University of Texas Press.

—— (1995) *FDR's Good Neighbor Policy.* Austin TX: University of Texas Press.

Pilcher, Jeffrey M. (2001) *Cantinflas and the Chaos of Mexican Modernity.* Wilmington DE: Scholarly Resources.

Pineda, Alexandra & Paulo Antonio Paranaguá (1995) "Mexico and Its Cinema" pp. 15–61, *Mexican Cinema,* Paulo Antonio Paranaguá, ed. London: British Film Institute.

Piñeyro, José Luis (1987) "El Henriquismo y las elecciones presidenciales en 1952," *El Cotidiano* 17 (May–Jun.): 152–54.

—— (1997) "Las fuerzas armadas en la transición política de México," *Revista Mexicana de Sociología* 59 (January–March): 163–89.

Pitner, Ernst (1993) *Maximilian's Lieutenant.* Albuquerque NM: University of New Mexico Press.

Pletcher, David M. (1950) "The Building of the Mexican Railway," *Hispanic American Historical Review* 30 (February): 26–62.

—— (1953) "México, campo de inversiones norteamericanas: 1867–1880," *Historia Mexicana* 2 (April–Jun.): 564–74.

—— (1958a) *Rails, Mines, and Progress.* Ithaca NY: Cornell University Press.

—— (1958b) "The Fall of Silver in Mexico, 1870–1910, and its Effect on American Investments," pp. 33–55, *Journal of Economic History* 18 (March): 33–55.

—— (1959) "Mexico Opens the Door to American Capital, 1877–1880," *The Americas* 16 (July): 1–14.

—— (1973) *The Diplomacy of Annexation.* Colombia MO: University of Missouri Press.

—— (1998) *The Diplomacy of Trade and Investment.* Columbia MO: University of Missouri Press.

PNR (Partido Nacional Revolucionario) (1937) *Plan Sexenal.* Mexico City: Partido Nacional Revolucionario.

Poinsett, Joel Roberts (1846a) "The Mexican War," *Debow's Review* (July): 21–24.

—— (1846b) "The Republic of Mexico," *Debow's Review* (July): 27–42.

—— (1969) *Notes on Mexico, Made in the Autumn of 1822.* New York: Praeger.

Pollan, Michael (2008) *In Defense of Food.* New York: Penguin.

Pombo, Alberto (2000) "Water Use and Sanitation Practices in Peri-Urban Areas of Tijuana," pp. 276–92, *Shared Space,* Lawrence A. Herzog, ed. UCSD Center for U.S.–Mexican Studies Contemporary Perspectives Series, 16. San Diego CA: UCSD Center for U.S.–Mexican Studies.

Pomeranz, Kenneth & Steven Topik (1999*) The World That Trade Created.* Armonk NY: M.E. Sharpe.

Poniatowska, Elena (1971) *Massacre in Mexico.* New York: Viking.

Poole, Stafford (1992) "Iberian Catholicism Comes to the Americas," pp. 1–129, *Christianity Comes to the Americas, 1492–1776,* Charles H. Lippy, Robert Choquette, & Stafford Poole, eds. New York: Paragon House.

Pope, Kevin O., Mary E. D. Pohl, John G. Jones, David L. Lentz, Christopher von Nagy, Franciso J. Vega, & Irvy R. Quitmyer (2001) "Origin and Environmental Setting of Ancient Agriculture in the Lowlands of Mesoamerica," *Science* 292 (May 18): 1370–73.

Porter, Michael E. & Klaus Schwab (2008) *Competitiveness Report 2008–2009.* Geneva: World Economic Forum.

Porter, Susie S. (2003) *Working Women in Mexico City.* Tucson AZ: University of Arizona Press.

Portes, Ajejandro (1970) "El proceso de urbanización y su impacto en la modernización de las instituciones políticas locales," *Revista de la Sociedad Interamericana de Planificación* 4 (March–June): 5–21.

—— (1985) "Latin American Class Structure," *Latin American Research Review* 20 (no. 3): 7–39.

—— (1997) "Neoliberalism and the Sociology of Development," *Population and Development Review* 23 (June): 229–59.

Portes, Alejandro & Kelly Hoffman (2003) "Latin American Class Structures," *Latin American Research Review* 38 (no. 1): 41–82.

Potash, Robert A. (1983) *Mexican Government and Industrial Development in the Early Republic: The Banco de Avío.* Amherst MA: University of Massachusetts Press.

Powell, Fred (1921) *The Railways of Mexico.* Boston MA: Stratford.

Powell, J. Richard (1956) *The Mexican Petroleum Industry: 1938–1950.* Berkeley CA: University of California Press.

Powell, Philip Wayne (1952) *Soldiers, Indians & Silver.* Berkeley CA: University of California Press.

Powell, T. G. (1968) "Mexican Intellectuals and the Indian Question, 1876–1911," *Hispanic American Historical Review* 48 (February): 19–36.

Poyo, Gerald E. (1996) "Community and Autonomy," pp. 1–14, *Tejano Journey, 1770–1850,* Gerald Poyo, ed. Austin TX: University of Texas Press.

Pozas, Ricardo (1962) *Juan the Chamula.* Berkeley CA: University of California Press.

Pozas Horcasitas, Ricardo (1977) "El movimiento médico en México, 1964–1965," *Cuadernos Políticos* 11 (January–March): 57–70.

—— (1987) "Del desorden a la crisis (120-1929)," *Revista Mexicana de Sociología* (July–September): 105–21.

—— (1988) "De Hermosillo a la silla. La presidencia de Adolfo de la Huerta," pp. 39–52, *Estadistas, caciques y caudillos,* Carlos Martínez Assad, ed. Mexico City: Instituto de Investigaciones Sociales, Universidad Nacional Autónoma de México.

Prados de la Escosura, Leandro (2006) "The Economic Consequences of Independence In Latin America," pp. 463–504, *Cambridge Economic History of Latin America* (vol. 1) Victor Bulmer-Thomas, John H. Coatsworth, & Roberto Cortés Conde, eds. New York: Cambridge University Press.

Prager, Jonas (1992) "Is Privatization a Panacea for LDC?" *Journal of Developing Areas* 26 (April): 301–22.

Prem, Hanns J. (1991) "Disease Outbreaks in Central Mexico during the Sixteenth Century," pp. 20–48, *"Secret Judgments of God": Old World Disease in Colonial Spanish America,* Noble David Cook & W. George Lovell, eds. Norman OK: University of Oklahoma Press.

Prescott, William H. (1964) *History of the Conquest of Mexico.* New York: Bantam.

Presidencia de la República (2001) *Informe del Gobierno 1 de septiembre 2001: anexo.* Mexico City.

Preston, Julia & Samuel Dillon (2004) *Opening Mexico.* New York: Farrar, Straus and Giroux.

Prewett, Virginia (1941) "The Mexican Army," *Foreign Affairs* 19 (April): 609–20.

Price, Glenn W. (1967) *Origins of the War with Mexico.* Austin TX: University of Texas Press.

Pringle, Henry F. (1939) *The Life and Times of William Howard Taft* (2 vols.) New York: Farrar & Rinehart.

Proctor, Frank T., III (2003) "Afro-American Slave Labor in the Obrajes de Paños of New Spain, Seventheenth and Eighteenth Centuries," *The Americas* 60 (July): 33–58.

Proffitt, T. D., III (1994) *Tijuana.* San Diego CA: San Diego State University Press.

Prud'homme, Jean François (2003) "El Partido de la Revolución Democrática," *Foro Internacional* 43 (January–March): 103–40.

Purcell, Susan Kaufman (1997) "The Changing Nature of U.S.–Mexican Relations," *Journal of Interamerican Studies and World Affairs* 39 (Spring): 137–52.

—— (1998) "The New U.S.–Mexico Relationship," pp. 101–25, *Mexico under Zedillo,* Susan Kaufman Purcell & Luis Rubio. eds. Boulder CO: Lynne Rienner.

Purnell, Jennie (1999) *Popular Movements and State Formation in Revolutionary Mexico.* Durham NC: Duke University Press.

Quadri de la Torre, Gabriel (2006) "Más allá de 2006: políticas públicas, sustentibilidad y medio ambiente," *Este País* 181 (April): 82–90.

—— (2007) "Calentamiento global, bienes públicos y mercado de carbono," *Foreign Affairs en español* 7 (July–Sept): 109–31.

Quaife, Milo Milton (1910) *The Diary of James K. Polk* (4 vols). Chicago IL: McClurg.

Quijada Hernández, Armando (1997) "Periódo México Independiente, 1831–1883," pp. 15–109, *Historia general de Sonora,* vol. 3. Hermosillo: Gobierno del Estado de Sonora.

Quintana, Enrique (2001) "La economía durante la transición electoral en México," pp. 137–55, *México 2000,* Luis Salazar, ed. Mexico City: Cal y Arena.

Quiroz Trejo, José Othón (2004) "Veinte años de desarticulación obrera," *El Cotidiano* 1265 (July–August): 166–75.

Raat, William Dirk (1967) *Positivism in Díaz Mexico: 1876–1910.* Ph.D. Dissertation. Salt Lake City UT: University of Utah.

—— (1973) "Ideas and Society in Don Porfirio's Mexico," *The Americas* 30 (July): 32–53.

—— (1981) *Revoltosos.* College Station TX: Texas A&M University Press.

—— (1987) "U.S. Intelligence Operations and Covert Action in Mexico, 1900–47," *Journal of Contemporary History* 22 (October): 615–38.

—— (1992) *Mexico and the United States: Ambivalent Vistas.* Athens: University of Georgia Press.

Rabe, Stephen G. (1978) "The Elusive Conference: United States Economic Relations with Latin America, 1945–1952," *Diplomatic History* 2 (Summer): 279–94.

Rabell Romero, Cecilia (1993) "El descenso de la población indígena durante el siglo XVI y las cuentas del gran capitán," pp. 18–35, *El poblamiento de México,* vol. 2. Mexico City: Consejo Nacional de Población.

Raby, David L. (1974) *Educación y revolución social en México (1921–1940).* Mexico City: SepSetentas.

Rajchenberg (1999) "¿Milpas o chimeneas?" pp. 153–74, *México en el Siglo XX.* Mexico City: Archivo General de la Nación.

Ramírez, Miguel D. (1989) *Mexico's Economic Crisis.* New York: Praeger.

—— (1997) "Mexico," pp. 111–48, *The Political Economy of Latin America in the Postwar Period,* Laura Randall, ed. Austin TX: University of Texas Press.

Ramírez, Susan E. (1986) "Large Landowners," pp. 19–45, *Cities and Society in Colonial Latin America,* Louisa Schell Hoberman & Susan Migden Socolow, eds. Albuquerque NM: University of New Mexico Press.

Ramírez de la O, Rogelio (1983) *De la improvisación al fracaso.* Mexico City: Océano.

—— (1998) "The Impact of NAFTA on the Auto Industry in Mexico," pp. 48–91, *The North American Auto Industry under NAFTA,* Sidney Weintraub & Christopher Sands, eds. Washington DC: CSIS Press.

Ramos-Escandón, Carmen (1987a) "Señoritas porfirianas: mujer e ideología en el México progresista, 1880–1910," pp. 143–61, *Presencia y transparencia: la mujer en la historia de México,* Carmen Ramos Escandón, ed. Mexico City: Colegio de México.

—— (1987b) "La política obrera del Estado Mexicano," *Mexican Studies/Estudios Mexicanos* 3 (Winter): 19–48.

—— (1988) *La industria textil y el movimiento obrero en México.* Iztapalapa: Universidad Autónoma Metropolitana.

—— (1990a) *Gender Construction in a Progressive Society: Mexico, 1870–1917.* Institute of Latin American Studies Working Paper 90–07, University of Texas at Austin.

—— (1990b) "Mujeres trabajadoras en el México porfiriano," *Revista Europea de Estudios Latinoamericanos y del Caribe* 48 (June): 27–44.

—— (1994) "Women's Movements, Feminism, and Mexican Politics," pp. 199–221, *The Women's Movement in Latin America* (2nd ed.), Jane S. Jaquette, ed. Boulder CO: Westview.

—— (1997) "Mujeres de ayer: participación femenina en México: 1190–1960," *Estudios Políticos* 15 (May–August): 27–52.

—— (1998a) "Women and Power in Mexico: The Forgotten Heritage, 1880–1954," pp. 87–102, *Women's Participation in Mexican Political Life,* Victoria E. Rodriguez, ed. Boulder CO: Westview.

—— (1998b) "Gender, Labor, and Class Consciousness in the Mexican Textile Industry, 1880–1910," pp. 71–92, *Border Crossings,* John Mason Hart, ed. Wilmington DE: Scholarly Resources.

—— (2007) "Challenging Legal and Gender Constraints in Mexico," pp. 53–71, *The Women's Revolution in Mexico, 1910–1953,* Stephanie Mitchell & Patience A. Schell, eds. Lanham MD: Rowman & Littlefield.

Randall, Laura (1977) *A Comparative Economic History of Latin America, 1500–1914* (4 vols.). Ann Arbor MI: University Microfilms International.

—— (1989) *The Political Economy of Mexican Oil.* New York: Praeger.

Randall, Robert W. (1972) *Real del Monte.* Austin TX: University of Texas Press.

—— (1985a) "British Company and Mexican Community: The English at Real del Monte, 1824–1849," *Business History Review* 59 (Winter): 622–44.

—— (1985b) "Mexico's Pre-Revolutionary Reckoning with Railroads," *The Americas* 42 (July): 1–28.

Rankin, Monica (2007) "Mexico: Industrialization through Unity," pp. 17–35, *Latin America during World War II,* Thomas Leonard & John F. Bratzel, eds. Lanham MD: Rowman & Littlefield.

Rankine, Margaret E. (1992) "The Mexican Mining Industry in the Nineteenth Century with Special Reference to Guanajuato," *Bulletin of Latin American Research* 11 (January): 29–48.

Raymont, Henry (2005) *Troubled Neighbors.* Boulder CO: Westview.

Redclift, Michael & David Goodman (1991) "The Machinery of Hunger," pp. 48–78, *Environment and Development in Latin America,* David Goodman & Michael Redclift, eds. Manchester: Manchester University Press.

Redfield, Robert (1930) *Tepoztlan.* Chicago IL: University of Chicago Press.

—— (1950) *A Village that Chose Progress.* Chicago IL: University of Chicago Press.

Reding, Andrew (1989) "Mexico Under Salinas," *World Policy Journal* 6 (Fall): 685–729.

Reed, John (1969) *Insurgent Mexico.* New York: Simon & Schuster

Reed, Nelson A. (2001) *The Caste War of Yucatán* (revised ed.). Palo Alto CA: Stanford University Press.

Reff, Daniel T. (1991) *Disease, Depopulation, and Culture Change in Northwestern New Spain, 1518–1764.* Salt Lake City UT: University of Utah Press.

Reich, Peter Lester (1995) *Mexico's Hidden Revolution.* Notre Dame IN: University of Notre Dame Press.

Reid, Michael (2007) *Forgotten Continent.* New Haven CT: Yale University Press.

Reimers, Fernando (2006) "Education and Social Progress," pp. 427–80, *Cambridge Economic History of Latin America* (vol. 2) Victor Bulmer-Thomas, John H. Coatsworth, & Roberto Cortés Conde, eds. New York: Cambridge University Press.

Reina, Leticia (1980) *Las rebeliones campesinas en México, 1819–1906.* Mexico City: Siglo XXI.

—— (2007) "Local Elections and Regime Crisis," pp. 91–125, *Cycles of Conflict, Centuries of Change,* Elisa Servín, Leticia Reina, & John Tutino, eds. Durham NC: Duke University Press.

Reina, Leticia, Elisa Servín & John Tutino (2007) "Introduction," pp. 1–20, *Cycles of Conflict, Centuries of Change,* Elisa Servín, Leticia Reina, & John Tutino, eds. Durham NC: Duke University Press.

Reséndez Fuentes, Andrés (1995) "Battleground Women: Soldaderas and Female Soldiers in the Mexican Revolution," *The Americas* 51 (April): 525–53.

Restall, Matthew (2003) *Seven Myths of the Spanish Conquest.* New York: Oxford University Press.

Reveles Vázquez, Francisco (1994) "El desarrollo organizativo del Partido Acción Nacional," *Revista Mexicana de Ciencias Políticas y Sociales* 156 (April–June): 101–26.

Reyes del Campillo, Juan (1997) "La transición se consolida," *El Cotidiano* 85 (September-October): 4–12.

—— (2003) "2003: Elecciones después de la transición," *El Cotidiano* 122 (November–December): 6–15.

Reygadas, Luis (1991) "Libertad laboral y tratado de Libre comercio," *El Cotidiano* 43 (Sept–October): 16–21.

—— (2006) "Latin America: Persistent Inequality and Recent Transformations," pp. 120–43, *Latin America after Neoliberalism,* Eric Hershberg & Fred Rosen, eds. New York: NACLA & New Press.

Reyna, José Luis (1985) "Las elecciones en el México Institucionalizado, 1946–1976," pp. 101–18, *Las elecciones en México,* Pablo González Casanova, ed. Mexico City: Siglo XXI.

Reynolds, Clark W. (1970) *The Mexican Economy.* New Haven CT: Yale University Press.

Reynoso, Víctor Manuel (2005) "Tres institucionalidades partidarias," *El Cotidiano* 133 (Sept–October): 28–34.

Ricard, Robert (1950) "La Plaza Mayor en España y en América española," *Estudios Geográficos* 11 (May): 321–27.

—— (1966) *The Spiritual Conquest of Mexico.* Berkeley CA: University of California Press.

Richards, John F. (2003) *The Unending Frontier.* Berkeley CA: University of California Press.

Richardson, James D. (1917) *A Compilation of the Messages and Papers of the Presidents* (20 vols.) New York: Bureau of National Literature.

Richmond, Douglas W. (1983) *Venustiano Carranza's Nationalist Struggle, 1893–1920.* Lincoln NE: University of Nebraska Press.

—— (1997) "Venustiano Carranza," pp. 199–202, *Encyclopedia of Mexico,* Michael S. Werner, ed. Chicago IL: Fitzroy Dearborn.

Riddell, Adaljiza (1976) "Female Political Elites in Mexico: 1974," pp. 257–67, *Women in the World,* Lynne B. Iglitzin & Ruth Ross, eds. Santa Barbara CA: Clio.

Ridgeway, Stan (2001) "Monoculture, Monopoly, and the Mexican Revolution: Tomás Garrido Canabal and the Standard Fruit Company in Tabasco (1920–35)," *Mexican Studies/Estudios Mexicanos* 17 (Winter): 143–69.

Riding, Alan (1985) *Distant Neighbors.* New York: Knopf.

—— (2000) *¿Cambiará México ahora?* Mexico City: Joaquín Mortiz.

Riguzzi, Paolo (1995) "Inversión extranjera e interés nacional en los ferrocarriles mexicanos, 1880–1914," pp. 159–77, *Las inversiones extranjeras en América Latina, 1850–1930.* Carlos Marichal, ed. Mexico City: Fondo de Cultura Económica & Colegio de México.

—— (1996) "Los caminos del atraso: tecnología, instituciones e inversión en los ferrocarriles mexicanos, 1850–1900," *Ferrocarriles y vida económica en México, 1850–1905,* Sandra Kuntz Ficker & Paolo Riguzzi, eds. Zinacantepec: Colegio Mexiquense and Xochimilco: Universidad Autónoma Metropolitana.

Ringrose, David R. (1996) *Spain, Europe, and the "Spanish Miracle," 1700–1900.* Cambridge: Cambridge University Press.

Rippy, J. Fred (1919) "The Indians of the Southwest in the Diplomacy of the United States and Mexico, 1848–1853," *Hispanic American Historical Review* 2 (August): 363–96.

—— (1926) *The United States and Mexico.* New York: Knopf.

—— (1929) *Rivalry of the United States and Great Britain over Latin America: 1808–1830.* Baltimore MD: Johns Hopkins Press.

—— (1935) *Joel R. Poinsett, Versatile American.* Durham NC: Duke University Press.

—— (1947a) "Latin America and the British Investment 'Boom' of the 1820s," *Journal of Modern History* 19 (June): 122–29.

—— (1947b) "British Investments in Latin America, End of 1913," *Journal of Modern History* 19 (September): 226–34.

Rivera, J. A., D. Sotres-Álvarez, J.-P. Habicht, T. Shamah, & S. Villalpando (2004) "Impact of the Mexican Program for Education, Health and Nutrition (*Progresa*) on Rates of Growth and Anemia in Infants and Young Children," *Journal of the American Medical Association* 291 (June 2): 2563–70.

Rivera Cambas, Manuel (1987) *Historia de la intervención* (3 vols.). Mexico City: Instituto Nacional de Estudios Históricos de la Revolución Mexicana.

Rivera Marín, Guadalupe (1955) *El mercado de trabajo.* Mexico City: Fondo de Cultura Económica.

RMALC (Red Mexicana de Acción Frente al Libre Comercio) (1991) *¿Libre comercio o explotación libre?* Mexico City: Red Mexicana de Acción Frente al Libre Comercio.

Roberts, David (2004) *The Pueblo Revolt.* New York: Simon & Schuster.

Robertson, Frank D. (1955) *The Military and Political Career of Mariano Paredes y Arrillaga, 1797–1849.* Ph.D dissertation, University of Texas.

Robertson, William Spence (1918) "The Recognition of the Hispanic American Nations by the United States," *Hispanic American Historical Review* 1 (August): 239–69.

Robinson, William I. (2008) *Latin America and Global Capitalism.* Baltimore: Johns Hopkins University Press.

Rocha, Martha Eva (2007) "The Faces of Rebellion," pp. 15–35, *The Women's Revolution in Mexico, 1910–1953,* Stephanie Mitchell & Patience A. Schell, eds. Lanham MD: Rowman & Littlefield.

Rocha, Oscar (2005) "Civil-Military Relations and Security Policy in Mexico," pp. 185–229, *Mexican Governance,* Armand B. Peschard-Sverdrup & Sara R. Rioff, eds. Washington DC: CSIS Press.

Rock, David (1994) "War and Postwar Intersections: Latin America and the United States," pp. 15–40, & "Conclusion," pp. 265–73, *Latin America in the 1940s,* David Rock, ed. Berkeley CA: University of California Press.

Rockefeller, Nelson A. (1969) *The Rockefeller Report on the Americas.* Chicago IL. Quadrangle.

Rodríguez, Gregory (2007) *Mongrels, Bastards, Orphans, and Vagabonds.* New York: Pantheon.

Rodríguez, Mario (1978) *The Cádiz Experiment in Central America, 1808 to 1826.* Berkeley CA: University of California Press.

Rodríguez, Martha (1995) *Historias de resistencia y exterminio: los indios de Coahuila durante el siglo XIX.* Mexico City: Centro de Investigaciones e Estudios Superiores en Antropología Social & Instituto Nacional Indigenista.

Rodríguez, Victoria E. (1997) "La centralización de la política contra las políticas descentralizadoras en México, 1970–1995," pp. 223–53, *El cambio del papel del estado en América Latina,* Menno Vellinga, ed. Mexico City: Siglo XXI.

—— (2003) *Women in Contemporary Mexican Politics.* Austin TX: University of Texas Press.

Rodríguez, Victoria & Peter M. Ward (1994) *Political Change in Baja California.* UCSD Center for U.S.–Mexican Studies Monograph Series, 40. San Diego CA: UCSD Center for U.S.–Mexican Studies.

Rodríguez Araujo, Octavio (1985a) "Partidos políticos y elecciones en México, 1964 a 1985," *Revista Mexicana de Sociología* 47 (January–March): 41–104.

—— (1985b) "Iglesia, partidos y lucha de clases en México," pp. 26–67, *Religión y Política en México,* Martín de la Rosa & Charles A. Reilly, eds. Mexico City: Siglo XXI.

Rodríguez-Buckingham, Antonio (1985) "The First Forty Years of the Book Industry in Sixteenth-Century Mexico," *Iberian Colonies, New World Societies: Essays in Memory of Charles Gibson,* Richard L. Garner & William B. Taylor, eds. Private printing.

Rodríguez Munguía, Jacinto (2007) *La otra guerra secreta.* Mexico City: Debate.

Rodríguez O., Jaime E. (1983) *Down from Colonialism.* Los Angeles CA: Chicano Studies Research Center, UCLA.

—— (1989) "Introduction," pp. 1–14, "From Royal Subject to Republican Citizen," pp. 19–43, & "Mexico's First Foreign Loans," pp. 215–35, *The Independence of Mexico and the Creation of a New Nation,* Jaime E. Rodríguez O., ed. Los Angeles CA: UCLA Latin American Center & Mexico/Chicano Program of the University of California, Irvine.

—— (1990) "Two Revolutions: France 1789 and Mexico 1810," *The Americas* 47 (October): 161–76.

—— (1991a) "La paradoja de la independencia de México," *Secuencia* 21 (Sept–December): 7–17.

—— (1991b) "La Constitución de 1824 y la formación del Estado mexicano," *Historia Mexicana* 40 (January–March): 507–36.

—— (1992a) "The Struggle for the Nation: The First Centralist–Federalist Conflict in Mexico," *The Americas* 49 (July): 1–22.

—— (1992b) "The Formation of the Federal Republic," pp. 316–28, *Five Centuries of Mexican History/Cinco siglos de historia de México,* vol. 1, Virginia Guedea & Jaime E. Rodríguez O., eds. Mexico City: Instituto Mora & Irvine CA: University of California.

—— (1992c) "The Origins of the 1832 Rebellion," pp. 145–62, *Patterns of Contention in Mexican History,* Jaime E. Rodríguez O., ed. Wilmington DE: Scholarly Resources.

—— (1994) "Mexico in the Age of Democratic Revolutions," pp. 1–17, & "The Transition from Colony to Nation: New Spain, 1820–1821," pp. 97–132, *Mexico in the Age of Democratic Revolutions,* Jaime E. Rodríguez O., ed. Boulder CO: Lynne Rienner.

—— (2000) "The Emancipation of America," *American Historical Review* 105 (February): 131–52.

—— (2007) "¿Dos revoluciones: la política y la insurgencia?" pp. 227–42, *México en tres momentos: 1810–1910–2010* (vol. 1), Alicia Mayer, ed. Mexico City: Instituto de Investigaciones Históricas, Universidad Nacional Autónoma de México.

—— (2008) "New Spain and the 1808 Crisis of the Spanish Monarchy," *Mexican Studies/Estudios Mexicanos* 24 (Summer): 247–87.

Rodríguez O., Jaime & Kathryn Vincent (1997) "'It Takes Two to Tango,'" pp. 1–16, *Myths, Misdeeds, and Misunderstandings,* Jaime E. Rodríguez O. & Kathryn Vincent, eds. Wilmington DE: Scholarly Resources.

Rodríguez-Sala, María Luisa, Ignacio Gómezgil & María Eugenia Cué (1995) *Exploradores en el Septentrión Novohispano.* Mexico City: Miguel Ángel Porrúa.

Roeder, Ralph (1947) *Juárez and his Mexico* (2 vols.). New York: Viking.

Rolle, Andrew F. (1965) *The Lost Cause.* Norman OK: University of Oklahoma Press.

Roman, Richard (1976) *Ideología y clase en la Revolución Mexicana.* Mexico City: SepSetentas.

Roman, Richard & Edur Velasco Arregui (2001) "Neoliberalism, Labor Market Transformation, and Working-Class Responses," *Latin American Perspectives* 28 (July): 52–71.

Romero, José (2003) "Crecimiento y comercio," pp. 155–221, *Historia contemporánea de México* (vol. 1), Ilán Bizberg & Lorenzo Meyer, eds. Mexico City: Océano.

Romero, Matías (1986) *Mexican Lobby.* Lexington KY: University of Kentucky Press.

Romero Sotelo, María Eugenia (1997) *Minería y Guerra: la economía de Nueva España, 1810–1821.* Mexico City: Colegio de México & Universidad Nacional Autónoma de México.

Ronan, Charles E. (1977) *Francisco Javier Clavijero, S. J. (1731–1787), Figure of the Mexican Enlightenment, his Life and Works.* Chicago IL: Loyola University Press.

Ronfeldt, David F. (1986) "The Modern Mexican Military," pp. 224–61, *Armies and Politics in Latin America* (revised ed.), Abraham F. Lowenthal & Samuel Fitch, eds. New York: Holmes & Meier.

—— (1988) "Questions and Cautions about Mexico's Future," pp. 53–66, *Mexico in Transition,* Susan Kaufman Purcell, ed. New York: Council on Foreign Relations.

Ros, Jaime (1992) "Free Trade Area or Common Capital Market?" *Journal of Interamerican Studies and World Affairs* 34 (Summer): 53–92.

—— (2003) "The Mexican Economy," *Latin American Research Review* 38 (no. 3): 223–36.

—— (2008) "La desaceleración del crecimiento económico en México desde 1982," *Trimestre Económico* 29 (July–Sept): 537–60.

Rosen, Fred (1998) "The $55 Billion Bank-Bailout Scandal," NACLA *Report on the Americas* 32 (November–December): 11–14.

Rosenzweig, Fernando (1965a) "El desarrollo económico de México de 1877 a 1911," *El Trimestre Económico* 32 (July–Sept): 405–54.

—— (1965b) "La industria," pp. 311–481, *Historia Moderna de México*, vol. 7, pt. 1, Daniel Cosío Villegas, ed. Mexico City: Hermes.

Ross, John (2000) *The War Against Oblivion.* Monroe ME: Common Courage.

—— (2003) "The Zapatistas at Ten," *NACLA Report on the Americas* 37 (November–December): 11–15.

—— (2006) *¡Zapatistas! Making Another World Possible.* New York: Nation Books.

Ross, Stanley R. (1955) *Francisco I. Madero: Apostle of Mexican Democracy.* New York: Columbia University Press.

—— (1958) "Dwight Morrow and the Mexican Revolution," *Hispanic American Historical Review* 38 (November): 506–28.

Rottinghaus, Brandon & Irina Alberro (2005) "Rivaling the PRI," *Latin American Politics and Society* 47 (Summer): 143–58.

Rousseau, Isabelle (2006) "Las transformaciones de la política de hidrocarburos en México en el contexto de la transición democrática," *Foro Internacional* 46 (January–March): 21–50.

Rout, Leslie B., Jr. (1976) *The African Experience in Spanish America.* Cambridge: Cambridge University Press.

Rowland, Allison & Peter Gordon (1996) "Mexico City: No Longer a Leviathan?" pp. 173–202, *The Mega-City in Latin America,* Alan Gilbert, ed. Tokyo: United Nations University Press.

Roxborough, Ian (1992) "Mexico," pp. 190–216, *Latin America between the Second World War and the Cold War, 1944–1948,* Leslie Bethell & Ian Roxborough, eds. Cambridge: Cambridge University Press.

—— (1994) "Labor Control and the Postwar Growth Model in Latin America," pp. 248–64, *Latin America in the 1940s,* David Rock, ed. Berkeley CA: University of California Press.

—— (1998) "Urban Labour Movements in Latin America since 1930," pp. 219–90, *Latin America: Politics and Society since 1930,* Leslie Bethell, ed. Cambridge: Cambridge University Press.

Rozental, Andrés (2004) "Fox's Foreign Policy Agenda," pp. 87–114, *Mexico Under Fox,* Luis Rubio & Susan Kaufman Purcell, eds. Boulder CO: Lynne Rienner.

Rubenstein, Anne (2000) "Mass Media and Popular Culture in the Postrevolutionary Era," pp. 637–70, *Oxford History of Mexico,* Michael C. Meyer & William H. Beezley, eds. New York: Oxford University Press.

Rubio, Luis (1992) "Japan in Mexico," pp. 69–100, *Japan and Latin America in the New Global Order,* Susan Kaufman Purcell & Robert M. Immerman, eds. Boulder CO: Lynne Rienner.

—— (1999) *Tres ensayos: FOBAPROA, privatización y TLC.* Mexico City: Cal y Arena.

Rubio Mañe, J. Ignacio (1971) "Organización de las instituciones del virreinato de la Nueva España," *Boletín del Archivo General de la Nación* 12 (January–June): 129–74.

Rugeley, Terry (1996) *Yucatán's Maya Peasantry and the Origins of the Caste War.* Austin TX: University of Texas Press.

—— (1997) "Rural Political Violence and the Origins of the Caste War," *The Americas* 53 (April): 469–96.

—— (2002) "Indians Meet the State, Regions Meet the Center: Nineteenth-Century Mexico Revisited," *Latin American Research Review* 37 (no. 1): 245–58.

Ruiz, Ramón Eduardo (1980) *The Great Rebellion.* New York: Norton.

—— (1992) *Triumphs and Tragedy.* New York: Norton.

Ruiz, Samuel (1998) "The Politics of Marginalization: Poverty and the Rights of the Indigenous People of Mexico," *Journal of International Affairs* 52 (Fall): 85–100.

Ruiz Guerra, Rubén (2007) "La aceptación de la diversidad religiosa. Una ruta ardua," pp. 417–28, *México en tres momentos: 1810–1910–2010* (vol. 1), Alicia Mayer, ed. Mexico City: Instituto de Investigaciones Históricas, Universidad Nacional Autónoma de México.

Ruiz-Healy, Eduardo (2000) *En voz de Vicente Fox: Entrevistas a Fox.* Mexico City: Oxford University Press Mexico.

Ruiz Massieu, Armando (1996) *El gabinete en México.* Mexico City: Océano.

Ruiz Medrano, Ethelia (1991) *Gobierno y sociedad en Nueva España: segunda audiencia y Antonio de Mendoza.* Zamora: Gobierno del Estado de Michoacán & Colegio de Michoacán.

Rus, Jan (1994) "The 'Comunidad Revolucionaria Institucional,' 1936–1968," pp. 265–300, *Everyday Forms of State Formation,* Gilbert M. Joseph & & Daniel Nugent, eds. Durham NC: Duke University Press.

Russell, Dick (2000) "David: 1; Goliath: 0," *Amicus* (Summer): 16–18.

Russell, Philip (1977) *Mexico in Transition.* Austin TX: Colorado River Press.

—— (1984) *El Salvador in Crisis.* Austin TX: Colorado River Press.

—— (1994) *Mexico under Salinas.* Austin TX: Mexico Resource Center.

—— (1995) *The Chiapas Rebellion.* Austin TX: Mexico Resource Center.

Rydjord, John (1935) *Foreign Interest in the Independence of New Spain.* Durham NC: Duke University Press.

Sabloff, Jeremy A. (1995) "Drought and Decline," *Nature* 375 (June 1): 357.

Sachs, Jeffrey (1989) "Making the Brady Plan Work" *Foreign Affairs* 68 (Summer): 87–104.

Safford, Frank (1985) "Politics, Ideology and Society in Post-Independence Spanish America," pp. 347–421, *Cambridge History of Latin America* (vol. 3), Leslie Bethell, ed. Cambridge: Cambridge University Press.

Salas, Elizabeth (1994) "The Soldaderas in the Mexican Revolution," pp. 93–105, *Women of the Mexican Countryside, 1850–1990,* Heather Fowler-Salamini & Mary Kay Vaughan, eds. Tucson AZ: University of Arizona Press.

Saldívar, Américo (1988) *Ideología y política del Estado mexicano: 1970–1976* (6th ed.). Mexico City: Siglo XXI.

Salinas de Gortari, Carlos (1988) *Challenges.* Mexico City: Office of the President-Elect of Mexico.

—— (2002) *México: un paso difícil de la modernidad* (4th ed.). Mexico City: Plaza y Janés.

Salvucci, Richard J. (1987) *Textiles and Capitalism in Mexico.* Princeton NJ: Princeton University Press.

—— (2006) "Export-led Industrialization," pp. 249–92, *Cambridge Economic History of Latin America* (vol. 2) Victor Bulmer-Thomas, John H. Coatsworth, & Roberto Cortés Conde, eds. New York: Cambridge University Press.

Salvucci, Richard J. & Linda K. Salvucci (1987) "Crecimiento económico y cambio en la productividad de México, 1750–1895," *HISLA* 10 (July–December): 67–89.

Salvucci, Richard J., Linda K. Salvucci & Aslán Cohen (1994) "The Politics of Protection," pp. 95–114, The *Political Economy of Spanish America in the Age of Revolution, 1750–1850,* Kenneth J. Andrien & Lyman L. Johnson, eds. Albuquerque NM: University of New Mexico Press.

Samaniego de Villarreal, Norma (1990) "Algunas reflexiones sobre el impacto económico de la crisis," pp. 51–67, *Las clases medias en la coyuntura actual,* Soledad Loaeza & Claudio Stern, eds. Mexico City: Colegio de México.

Samora, Julian (1971) *Los mojados.* Notre Dame IN: University of Notre Dame Press.

Sánchez Aguilar, Edmundo (1973) *International Activities of U.S. Commercial Banks: A Case Study, Mexico.* Ph.D. Dissertation. Cambridge MA: Harvard University.

Sánchez-Albornoz, Nicolás (1986) "The Population of Latin America, 1850–1930," pp. 121–51, *Cambridge History of Latin America* (vol. 4), Leslie Bethell, ed. Cambridge: Cambridge University Press.

Sánchez Martínez, Hilda (1983) "El sistema monetario y financiero mexicano bajo una perspectiva histórica: el porfiriato," pp. 15–94, *La banca: pasado y presente,* José Manuel Quijano, ed. Mexico City: Centro de Investigación y Docencia Económicas (CIDE).

Sánchez Ruiz, Enrique E. (2005) "Los medios de comunicación masiva en México, 1968–2000," pp. 403–47, *Historia contemporánea de México* (vol. 1), Ilán Bizberg & Lorenzo Meyer, eds. Mexico City: Océano.

Sanders, Thomas G. (1986) "Mexico's Food Problem," pp. 267–85, *Twentieth-Century Mexico,* W. Dirk Raat & William H. Beezley, eds. Lincoln NE: University of Nebraska Press.

Sanderson, Steven E. (1986) *The Transformation of Mexican Agriculture.* Princeton NJ: Princeton University Press.

Sanderson, Susan R. Walsh (1984) *Land Reform in Mexico: 1910–1980.* Orlando FL: Academic.

Sandos, James A. (2005) "Social Control within Missionary Frontier Society; Alta California, 1769–1821," pp. 253–75, *Choice, Persuasion and Coercion,* Jesús F. de la Teja & Ross Frank, eds. Albuquerque NM: University of New Mexico Press.

Sandoval Hernández, Efrén (2008) "El espacio económico Monterrey-San Antonio," *Frontera Norte* 39 (January–Jun.): 69–100.

Santa Anna, Antonio López de (1988) *The Eagle.* Austin TX: State House Press.

Santiago, Myrna I. (1998) "Rejecting Progress in Paradise," *Environmental History* 3 (April): 169–188.

—— (2006) *The Ecology of Oil.* New York: Cambridge University Press.

Santoni, Pedro (1988) "A Fear of the People: The Civic Militia of Mexico in 1845," *Hispanic American Historical Review* 68 (May): 269–88.

—— (1996a) *Mexicans at Arms.* Fort Worth TX: Texas Christian University Press.

—— (1996b) "The Failure of Mobilization: The Civic Militia of Mexico in 1846," *Mexican Studies/Estudios Mexicanos* 12 (Summer): 169–94.

Santos, Gonzalo (1986) *Memorias.* Mexico City: Grijalbo.

Saragoza, Alex M. (1988) *The Monterrey Elite and the Mexican State, 1800–1940.* Austin TX: University of Texas Press.

—— (2001) "The Selling of Mexico: Tourism and the State, 1929–1952," pp. 91–115, *Fragments of a Golden Age,* Gilbert M. Joseph, Anne Rubenstein & Eric Zolov, eds. Durham NC: Duke University Press.

Sarmiento Silva, Sergio (1996) "Movimiento indio, autonomía y agenda nacional," pp. 355–95, *Neoliberalismo y organización social en el campo mexicano,* Hubert Carton de Grammont, ed. Mexico City: Plaza y Valdés.

Sartorius, Carl (1961) *Mexico about 1850.* Stuttgart: Brockhaus.

Schatan, Claudia (2003) "The Environmental Impact of Mexican Manufacturing Exports under NAFTA," pp. 133–51, *Greening NAFTA,* David L. Markell & John H. Knox, eds. Palo Alto CA: Stanford University Press.
Schedler, Andrea (2000) "The Democratic Revolution," *Journal of Democracy* 11 (October): 5–19.
—— (2007) "The Mobilization of Distrust," *Journal of Democracy* 18 (January): 88–102.
Schell, Patience A. (2006) "Gender, Class, and Anxiety at the Gabriela Mistral Vocational School, Revolutionary Mexico City," pp. 112–26, *Sex in Revolution,* Jocelyn Olcott, Mary Kay Vaughan, & Gabriela Cano, eds. Durham NC: Duke University Press.
Schell, William, J. (2001) *Integral Outsiders.* Wilmington DE: Scholarly Resources.
Scherer García, Julio & Carlos Monsiváis (1999) *Parte de guerra.* Mexico City: Aguilar.
Schettino, Macario (2007) *Cien años de confusión.* Mexico City: Taurus.
Schmidt, Arthur (1997) "José Yves Limantour," pp. 746–49, & "Justo Sierra," pp. 1343–44, *Encyclopedia of Mexico,* Michael S. Werner, ed. Chicago IL: Fitzroy Dearborn.
Schmidt, Louis Bernard (1961) "Manifest Destiny and the Gadsden Purchase," *Arizona and the West* 3 (Autumn): 245–64.
Schmidt, Samuel (1981) *Democracia mexicana.* Centro de Estudios Latinoamericanos, Universidad Nacional Autónoma de México.
—— (1991) *The Deterioration of the Mexican Presidency.* Tucson AZ: University of Arizona Press.
—— (1997) "Politics and Government: 1946–1996," pp. 1121–27, *Encyclopedia of Mexico,* Michael S. Werner, ed. Chicago IL: Fitzroy Dearborn.
Schmitt, Karl M. (1974) *Mexico and the United States, 1821–1973.* New York: Wiley.
—— (1984) "Church and State in Mexico: A Corporatist Relationship," *The Americas* 40 (January): 349–76.
Schons, Dorothy (1991) "Some Obscure Points in the Life of Sor Juana Inés de la Cruz," pp. 38–60, *Feminist Perspectives on Sor Juana Inés de la Cruz,* Stephanie Merrim, ed. Detroit MI: Wayne State University Press.
Schoonover, Thomas David (1978) *Dollars over Dominion.* Baton Rouge LA: Louisiana State University Press.
Schoultz, Lars (1998) *Beneath the United States.* Cambridge MA: Harvard University Press.
Schuessler, Michael (2003) *Elenísima.* Mexico City: Diana.
Schuler, Friedrich E. (1985) "Germany, Mexico and the United States During the Second World War," pp. 457–76, *Jahrbuch für Geschichte van Staat, Wirtschaft und Gesellschaft Lateinamerikas.*
—— (1998) *Mexico Between Hitler and Roosevelt.* Albuquerque NM: University of New Mexico Press.
—— (2000) "Mexico and the Outside World," pp. 503–41, *Oxford History of Mexico,* Michael C. Meyer & William H. Beezley, eds. New York: Oxford University Press.
Schwaller, John Frederick (1985) *Origins of Church Wealth in Mexico.* Albuquerque NM: University of New Mexico Press.
—— (2000) "Introduction," pp. xi–xxiii, *The Church in Colonial Latin America,* John F. Schwaller, ed. Wilmington DE: Scholarly Resources.
Scobie, James R. (1986) "The Growth of Latin American Cities, 1870–1930," pp. 233–65, *Cambridge History of Latin America* (vol. 4), Leslie Bethell, ed. Cambridge: Cambridge University Press.
Scott, Robert E. (1964) *Mexican Government in Transition* (revised ed.). Urbana IL: University of Illinois Press.
Scott, Robert N. (1880–1901) *The War of Rebellion: A Compilation of the Official Records of the Union and Confederate Armies,* series I, vol. xlviii. Washington DC: Government Printing Office.
Seed, Patricia (1982) "Social Dimensions of Race: Mexico City, 1753," *Hispanic American Historical Review* 62 (November): 569–606.
—— (1988a) *To Love, Honor, and Obey in Colonial Mexico.* Palo Alto CA: Stanford University Press.
—— (1988b) "Marriage Promises and the Value of a Woman's Testimony in Colonial Mexico," *Signs* 13 (Winter): 253–76.
—— (1992) "Taking Possession and Reading Texts: Establishing the Authority of Overseas Empires," *William and Mary Quarterly* 49 (April): 183–209.
Selee, Andrew (2008) "Back from the Brink in Mexico," *Current History* 107 (February): 65–70.
Seligman, Daniel (1956) "The Maddening, Promising Mexican Market," *Fortune* 53 (January): 102–112.
Sellers, Charles (1966) *James K. Polk: Continentalist, 1843–1846.* Princeton NJ: Princeton University Press.
Semo, Enrique (1969) "El desarrollo de capitalismo en la minería y la agricultura de Nueva España, 1760–1810," *Historia y Sociedad* 15 (January–March): 3–17.
—— (1977a) "Clases sociales y partidos en la revolución de independencia," *Plural* 6 (October): 34–44.
—— (1977b) "Introducción," pp. 9–18, *Siete ensayos sobre la hacienda mexicana, 1780–1880,* Enrique Semo, ed. Mexico City: Instituto Nacional de Antropología e Historia.
—— (1978a) *Historia mexicana: economía y lucha de clases.* Mexico City: Era.
—— (1978b) "El origen del capitalismo en México," *Coyuntura* 1 (April–June): 36–54.
—— (1981) "Conquista y colonia," pp. 178–332, *México: un pueblo en la historia,* vol. 1. Enrique Semo, ed. Mexico City: Nueva Imagen.

—— (1987) "La sucesión en la historia: 1910, 1940, 1952," pp. 47–61, *La sucesión presidencial en 1988*, Abraham Nuncio, ed. Mexico City: Grijalbo.
—— (1993) *The History of Capitalism in Mexico*. Austin TX: University of Texas Press.
—— (2001) "La utopía extraviada," *Proceso* Special no. 9: 46–55.
—— (2003) *La búsqueda*. Mexico City: Océano.
—— (2007) "Un centauro llamado PRD," pp. 227–45, *Sistema político mexicano*. Mexico City: Facultad de Ciencias Sociales y Políticas, UNAM.
Semo, Ilán (1982) "El ocaso de los mitos, 1958–1968," pp. 9–154, *México: un pueblo en la historia*, vol. 4, Enrique Semo, ed. Mexico City: Nueva Imagen.
Sepúlveda, Bernardo & Antonio Chumacero (1973) *La inversión extranjera en México*. Mexico City: Fondo de Cultura Económica.
Servín, Elisa (2001) *Ruptura y oposición*. Mexico City: Cal y Arena.
Shaiken, Harley (1994) "Advanced Manufacturing and Mexico," *Latin American Research Review* (no. 2): 39–71.
Sharer, Robert (2006) *The Ancient Maya* (6th ed.). Palo Alto CA: Stanford University Press.
Sheinbaum, Claudia (2008) "El petróleo es de los mexicanos," *Enfoque* (March 2): 8–9.
Sheridan, Cecilia (2005) "Social Control and Native Territoriality in Northeastern New Spain," pp. 121–48, *Choice, Persuasion and Coercion*, Jesús F. de la Teja & Ross Frank, eds. Albuquerque NM: University of New Mexico Press.
Sherman, John W. (1998) "Reassessing Cardenismo," *The Americas* 54 (January): 357–78.
—— (2000) "The Mexican 'Miracle' and its Collapse," pp. 575–607, *Oxford History of Mexico*, Michael C. Meyer & William H. Beezley, eds. New York: Oxford University Press.
Shields, David (2005) *Pemex: la reforma petrolera*. Mexico City: Planeta.
—— (2006) "Despite Falling Output, Mexican Politics Keep Foreign Operators Out," *Offshore* 66 (September): 28–30.
—— (2008) "Faced with Sharp Decline, Mexico Eyes Deepwater," *Offshore* 68 (June): 44–46.
Shifter, Michael (2007) "Latin America's Drug Problem," *Current History* 106 (February): 58–63.
Shirk, David A. (2001) "El PAN, un partido en construcción," pp. 58–80, *La experiencia del PAN*. Tania Hernández Vicencio & José Negrete Mata, eds. Mexico City: Plaza y Valdés.
—— (2005) *Mexico's New Politics*. Boulder CO: Lynne Rienner.
Sierra, Justo (1969) *The Political Evolution of the Mexican People*. Austin TX: University of Texas Press.
—— (1974) *Juárez: su obra y su tiempo* (3rd ed.). Mexico City: Porrúa.
Sierra Guzmán, Jorge Luis (2003) "Mexico's Military in the War on Drugs," *WOLA Drug War Monitor* (April): 1–18.
Silva Herzog, Jesús (1972) *Breve historia de la Revolución Mexicana* (2 vols., 2nd ed.) Mexico City: Fondo de Cultura Económica.
—— (1975) "The Mexican Revolution is Now a Historical Fact," pp. 99–109, *Is the Mexican Revolution Dead?* (2nd ed.), Stanley R. Ross, ed. Philadelphia PA: Temple University Press.
Simmons, Marc (1977) *New Mexico: A Bicentennial History*. New York: Norton.
—— (1986) *Along the Santa Fe Trail*. Albuquerque NM: University of New Mexico Press.
—— (1990) *Spanish Government in New Mexico* (2nd ed.). Albuquerque NM: University of New Mexico Press.
Simon, Joel (1997) *Endangered Mexico*. San Francisco CA: Sierra Club Books.
Simonian, Lane (1995) *Defending the Land of the Jaguar: A History of Conservation in Mexico*. Austin TX: University of Texas Press.
Simpson, Eyler N. (1937) *The Ejido: Mexico's Way Out*. Chapel Hill NC: University of North Carolina Press.
Simpson, Lesley Byrd (1953) "Unplanned Effects of Mexico's Planned Economy," *Virginia Quarterly Review* 29 (Autumn): 514–32.
Sims, Harold Dana (1990) *The Expulsion of Mexico's Spaniards: 1821–1836*. Pittsburgh PA: Pittsburgh University Press.
Singletary, Otis A. (1960) *The Mexican War*. Chicago IL: University of Chicago Press.
Sinkin, Richard (1979) *The Mexican Reform, 1855–1876*. Austin TX: Institute of Latin American Studies, University of London, and University of Texas.
—— (1989) "Mexico's Maquiladoras," *Twin Plant News* 4 (Jul.): 43–58.
Smith, F. Todd (2005) *From Dominance to Disappearance: The Indians of Texas and the Near Southwest, 1786–1859*. Lincoln NE: University of Nebraska Press.
Smith, Gaddis (1994) *The Last Years of the Monroe Doctrine: 1945–1993*. New York: Hill and Wang.
Smith, Michael (1995) "*Carrancista* Propaganda and the Print Media in the United States," *The Americas* 52 (October): 155–74.
Smith, Michael E. (2008) *Aztec City-State Capitals*. Gainesville FL: University Press of Florida.
Smith, Peter H. (1973) "La política dentro de la Revolución: El Congreso Constituyente de 1916–1917," *Historia Mexicana* 22 (January–March): 363–95.

—— (1990) "Mexico since 1946," pp. 83–157, *Cambridge History of Latin America* (vol. 7), Leslie Bethell, ed. Cambridge: Cambridge University Press.

—— (1996) *Talons of the Eagle*. New York: Oxford University Press.

—— (1997a) "Acenso y caída del Estado desarrollista en América Latina," pp. 74–102, *El cambio del papel del Estado en América Latina*, Menno Vellinga, ed. Mexico City: Siglo XXI.

—— (1997b) "Drug Trafficking in Mexico," pp. 125–54, *Coming Together*? Barry Bosworth, Susan Collins, & Nora Lustig, eds. Washington DC: Brookings Institution.

—— (1999) "Semiorganized International Crime: Drug Trafficking in Mexico," pp. 193–216, *Transnational Crime in the Americas*, Tom Farer, ed. New York: Routledge.

Smith, Ralph A. (1963) "Indians in American-Mexican Relations Before the War of 1846," *Hispanic American Historical Review* 43 (February): 34–64.

Smith, Robert Freeman (1972) *The United States and Revolutionary Nationalism in Mexico, 1916–1932*. Chicago IL: University of Chicago Press.

—— (1986) "Latin America, the United States and the European Powers, 1830–1930," pp. 83–119, *Cambridge History of Latin America* (vol. 4), Leslie Bethell, ed. Cambridge: Cambridge University Press.

—— (1997) "The United States and the Mexican Revolution, 1921–1950," pp. 181–97, *Myths, Misdeeds, and Misunderstandings*, Jaime E. Rodríguez O. & Kathryn Vincent, eds. Wilmington DE: Scholarly Resources.

Smith, Stephanie J. (2007) "Educating the Mothers of the Nation," p. 37–51, *The Women's Revolution in Mexico, 1910–1953*, Stephanie Mitchell & Patience A. Schell, eds. Lanham MD: Rowman & Littlefield.

Snodgrass, Michael (1998) "The Birth and Consequences of Industrial Paternalism in Monterrey, 1890–1940," *International Labor and Working-Class History* 53 (Spring): 115–36.

—— (2000) *Patriots and Proletarians: Industrial Workers and National Identity in Revolutionary Mexico (1920–1940)*. Paper presented at the 2000 Latin American Studies Association Conference, Miami FL.

—— (2006) "Workers, Patriotism and Union Struggles in Monterrey," pp. 314–34, *The Eagle and the Virgin*, Mary Kay Vaughan & Stephen E Lewis, eds. Duke NC: Duke University Press.

Sobrino, Jaime & Valentín Ibarra (2008) "Movilidad intrametropolitana en la Ciudad de México," pp. 161–205, *El dato en cuestión*, Beatriz Figueroa Campos, ed. Mexico City: Colegio de México.

Sokoloff, Kenneth L. & Eric M. Zolt (2007) "Inequality and the Evolution of Taxation," *The Decline of Latin American Economies*, Sebastian Edwards, Gerardo Esquivel, & Graciela Márquez, eds. Chicago IL: University of Chicago Press.

Solbrig, Otto T. (2006) "Economic Growth and Environmental Change," pp. 329–76 & "Structure, Performance, and Policy in Agriculture," pp. 483–536, *Cambridge Economic History of Latin America* (vol. 2) Victor Bulmer-Thomas, John H. Coatsworth, & Roberto Cortés Conde, eds. New York: Cambridge University Press.

Solís, Leopoldo (1973) *La realidad económica mexicana* (4th ed.). Mexico City: Siglo XXI.

Sonnenfeld, David A. (1992) "Mexico's 'Green Revolution,' 1940–1980," pp. 29–52, *Environmental History Review* 16 (Winter): 29–52.

Soria, Víctor (2002) "La política de desarrollo social y lucha contra la pobreza de Vicente Fox," pp. 87–117, *El primero año del gobierno foxista*, Ana Alicia Solís de Alba, ed. Mexico City: Itaca.

Sotelo Inclán, Jesús (1970) *Raíz y razón de Zapata*. Mexico City: Editorial CFE.

Soto, Shirlene Ann (1979) *The Mexican Woman: A Study of Her Participation in the Revolution, 1910–1940*. Palo Alto CA: R&E Research Associates.

Spalding, Mark J. (2000) "The NAFTA Environmental Institution and Sustainable Development on the U.S.–Mexican Border," pp. 75–98, *Shared Space*, Lawrence Herzog, ed. San Diego CA: UCSD Center for U.S.–Mexican Studies.

Spenser, Daniela (2008) "Standing Conventional Cold War History on its Head," pp. 381–95, *In From the Cold*, Gilbert M. Joseph & Daniela Spenser, eds. Durham NC: Duke University Press.

Spicer, Edward H. (1962) *Cycles of Conquest*. Tucson AZ: University of Arizona Press.

Stabb, Martin S. (1994) "The Essay," pp. 305–39, *Mexican Literature: A History*, David William Foster, ed. Austin TX: University of Texas Press.

Stamos, Stephen C., Jr. & Samuel Schmidt (1996) "La crisis del peso mexicano," *Este País* 63 (June): 3–17.

Standish, Peter (1997) "The Boom," pp. 133–34, *Encyclopedia of Latin American Literature*. London and Chicago IL: Fitzroy Dearborn.

Stanford, Lois (1997) "Confederación Nacional Campesina (CNC)," pp. 286–89, *Encyclopedia of Mexico*, Michael S. Werner, ed. Chicago IL: Fitzroy Dearborn.

—— (2004) "The Binational Integration of the U.S.–Mexican Avocado Industries," pp. 186–203, *Mexico in Transition*, Gerardo Otero, ed. London: Zed.

Stannard, David E. (1992) *American Holocaust*. New York: Oxford University Press.

Staples, Anne (1989) "El Estado y la Iglesia en la república restaurada," pp. 15–53, *El dominio de la minorías*. Mexico City: Colegio de México.

—— (1992) "Las vicisitudes de un empresario minero decimonónico," pp. 106–18, *Five Centuries of Mexican History/Cinco silgos de historia de México,* vol. 2. Mexico City: Instituto Mora and Irvine CA: University of California.

—— (1994) "Clerics as Politicians: Church, State, and Political Power in Independent Mexico," pp. 233–42, *Mexico in the Age of Democratic Revolutions, 1750–1850,* Jaime E. Rodríguez O., ed. Boulder CO: Lynne Rienner.

Starr, Pamela K. (2002) "Fox's Mexico," *Current History* 201 (February): 58–65.

Stavenhagen, Rodolfo (1966) "Social Aspects of Agrarian Structure in Mexico," *Social Research* 33 (Autumn): 463–85.

—— (1975) "Collective Agriculture and Capitalism in Mexico," *Latin American Perspectives* 2 (Summer): 146–63.

—— (1986) "Congreso de pueblos, el indigenismo cuestionado," pp. 405–07, *La quiebra política de la antropología social en México,* vol. 2, Carlos García Mora & Andrés Medina, eds. Mexico City: Instituto de Investigaciones Antropológicas, Universidad Nacional Autónoma de México.

Stein, Stanley J. & Barbara H. Stein (1970) *The Colonial Heritage of Latin America.* New York: Oxford University Press.

—— (2000) *Silver, Trade, and War.* Baltimore MD: Johns Hopkins University Press.

—— (2003) *Apogee of Empire.* Baltimore MD: Johns Hopkins University Press.

Stephen, Lynn (2007) "Women Leaders in the Oaxaca Rebellion," *Socialism and Democracy* 21 (July): 97–112.

Stern, Peter & Robert Jackson (1988) "Vagabundaje and Settlement Patterns in Colonial Northern Sonora," *The Americas* 44 (April): 461–81.

Stern, Steve J. (1992) "Paradigms of Conquest: History, Historiography, and Politics," *Journal of Latin American Studies* 24 (Quincentenary Supplement): 1–33.

Stevens, Donald Fithian (1982) "Agrarian Policy and Instability in Porfirian Mexico," *The Americas* 39 (October): 153–66.

—— (1986) "Economic Fluctuations and Political Instability in Early Republican Mexico," *Journal of Interdisciplinary History* 16 (Spring): 645–65.

—— (1991) *Origins of Instability in Early Republican Mexico.* Durham NC: Duke University Press.

Stevens, Evelyn P. (1974) *Protest and Response in Mexico.* Cambridge MA: MIT Press.

Stevenson, Lynda (1999) "La política de género en el proceso de democratización en México," *Estudios Sociológicos* 17 (May–August): 519–58.

Stiglitz, Joseph E. (2002) *Globalization and Its Discontents.* New York: Norton.

Stiglitz, Joseph & Andrew Charlton (2005) *Fair Trade for All.* New York: Oxford University Press.

Storey, Rebecca & Randolph J. Widmer (2006) "The Pre-Columbian Economy" pp. 73–106, *Cambridge Economic History of Latin America* (vol. 1) Victor Bulmer-Thomas, John H. Coatsworth, & Roberto Cortés Conde, eds. New York: Cambridge University Press.

Story, Dale (1986) *The Mexican Ruling Party.* New York: Praeger.

—— (1987) "The PAN, the Private Sector, and the Future of the Mexican Opposition," pp. 261–79, *Mexican Politics in Transition,* Judith Gentleman, ed. Boulder CO: Westview.

Stout, Joe A., Jr. (1972) "Filibustering in Northern Mexico, 1850–1855," *Journal of the West* 11 (April): 348–60.

Stuart, David & George Stuart (2008) *Palenque.* New York: Thames & Hudson.

Suárez, Alfonso & Eduardo Pérez (1993) "Caída y recuperación: los salaries en México 1987–1993, *El Cotidiano* 59 (December): 94–101.

Suárez, Eduardo L. (2000) "Capital extranjero y desarrollo económico en Mexico" *Comercio Exterior* 50 (Special Anniversary Issue no. 1): 75–82.

Suárez Aguilar, Estela (1996) "The Impact of Regional Integration on Women," pp. 134–45, *Look at the World through Women's Eyes,* Eva Friedlander, ed. New York: Women Ink.

Suárez Argüello, Ana Rosa (1987) "Los temores de Texas a la reconquista mexicana, 1836–1845," *Secuencia* 8 (May–June): 177–85.

—— (1989) "México, los Estados Unidos y la política interamericana durante el gobierno de Lyndon B. Johnson (1963–1968)," *Iztapalapa* 17 (January–June): 51–66.

Suárez Dávila, Francisco (1988) "Política hacendaria y economía política en el México posrevolucionario," pp. 341–444, *México: Setenta y cinco años de Revolución I— desarrollo económico,* vol. 1. Mexico City: Fondo de Cultura Económica.

—— (2008) "La dialéctica del desarrollo mexicano en su bicentenario (1810–2010)," *Este País* 205 (April): 8–18.

Suárez Gaona, Enrique (1987) *¿Legitimación revolucionaria del poder en México?* Mexico City: Siglo XIX.

Suárez-Orozco, Marcelo (1999) "Latin American Immigration to the United States," pp. 227–44, *The United States and Latin America,* Victor Bulmer-Thomas & James Dunkerley, eds. London: Institute of Latin American Studies, University of London and David Rockefeller Center for Latin American Studies, Harvard University.

Suchlicki, Jaime (1996) *Mexico: From Montezuma to NAFTA, Chiapas and Beyond.* Washington DC: Brassey's.

Summerhill, William (1997) "Transport Improvements and Economic Growth in Brazil and Mexico," pp. 93–117, *How Latin America Fell Behind,* Stephen Haber, ed. Palo Alto CA: Stanford University Press.

—— (2006) "The Development of Infrastructure," pp. 293–326, *Cambridge Economic History of Latin America* (vol. 2) Victor Bulmer-Thomas, John H. Coatsworth, & Roberto Cortés Conde, eds. New York: Cambridge University Press.

Sutter, Mary (1996) "Home-Grown Programming Takes Off," *Business Mexico* 6 (August): 12–15.

Székely, Gabriel (1983) *La economía política del petróleo en México.* Mexico City: Colegio de México.

—— (1999) "Presentación," pp. 13–31, *FOBAPROA e IPAB,* Gabriel Székely, ed. Mexico City: Océano.

Taibo, Paco Ignacio, II (2006) *Pancho Villa.* Mexico City: Planeta.

—— (2007) *El cura Hidalgo.* Mexico City: Ediciones B.

Taino, Susan (1997) "The Role of Women," pp. 237–69, *Understanding Contemporary Latin America,* Richard Hillman, ed. Boulder CO: Lynne Rienner.

Tambs, Lewis A. (1965) "The Inquisition in Eighteenth-Century Mexico," *The Americas* 22 (October): 167–81.

Tandeter, Enrique (2006) "The Mining Industry," pp. 315–56, *Cambridge Economic History of Latin America* (vol. 1) Victor Bulmer-Thomas, John H. Coatsworth, & Roberto Cortés Conde, eds. New York: Cambridge University Press.

Tandron, Humberto (1976) *El comercio de Nueva España y la controversia sobre la libertad de comercio, 1796–1821.* Mexico City: Instituto Mexicano de Comercio Exterior.

Tangeman, Michael (1995) *Mexico at the Crossroads.* Maryknoll NY: Orbis.

Tannenbaum, Frank (1950) *Mexico: The Struggle for Peace and Bread.* New York: Knopf.

—— (1955) "Reflections on the Mexican Revolution," *Journal of International Affairs* 9 (no. 1): 37–46.

Tarragó, Rafael E. (1996) "The Presses Roll in Colonial Times," *Américas* 48 (no. 6): 22–27.

Tarrés B., María Luisa (1990) "Participación social y política de las clases medias," pp. 83–119, *México en el umbral del milenio.* Mexico City: Colegio de México.

Tate, Carolyn E. (2008) "Landscape and a Visual Narrative of Creation and Origin at the Olmec Ceremonial Center of La Venta," pp. 31–65, *Pre-Columbian Landscapes of Creation and Origin,* John Edward Staller, ed. New York: Springer.

Taylor, Philip B., Jr. (1960) "The Mexican Elections of 1958," *Western Political Quarterly* 13 (September): 722–44.

Taylor, William B. (1972) *Landlord and Peasant in Colonial Oaxaca.* Palo Alto CA: Stanford University Press.

—— (1974) "Landed Society in New Spain: A View from the South," *Hispanic American Historical Review* 54 (August): 387–413.

—— (1979) *Drinking, Homicide, and Rebellion in Colonial Mexican Villages.* Palo Alto CA: Stanford University Press.

—— (1985) "Between Global Process and Local Knowledge," pp. 115–90, *Reliving the Past,* Olivier Zunz, ed. Chapel Hill NC: University of North Carolina Press.

—— (1987) "The Virgin of Guadalupe in New Spain: An Inquiry into the Social History of Marian Devotion," *American Ethnologist* 14 (February): 9–33.

—— (1990) "Conflict and Balance in District Politics," pp. 270–94, *The Indian Community of Colonial Mexico,* Arij Ouweneel & Simon Miller, eds. Amsterdam: Centre for Latin American Research and Documentation.

—— (1994) "Santiago's Horse: Christianity and Colonial Indian Resistance in the Heartland of New Spain," pp. 153–89, *Violence, Resistance, and Survival in the Americas,* William B. Taylor & Franklin Pease G. Y., eds. Washington DC: Smithsonian Institution Press.

—— (1996) *Magistrates of the Sacred.* Palo Alto CA: Stanford University Press.

—— (1997) *The Slave Trade.* New York: Simon & Schuster.

—— (2007) "La Virgen de Guadalupe, Nuestra Señora de Remedios y la cultura política del período de Independencia," pp. 213–38, *México en tres momentos: 1810–1910–2010* (vol. 2), Alicia Mayer, ed. Mexico City: Instituto de Investigaciones Históricas, Universidad Nacional Autónoma de México.

Tedlock, Dennis (tr.) (1985) *Popol Vuh.* New York: Simon & Schuster.

Teichman, Judith (1983) *Petroleum and Political Crisis in Mexico, 1976–1981.* Centre for Research on Latin America and the Caribbean Working Paper no. 4. York: York University.

—— (1988) *Policymaking in Mexico.* Boston MA: Allen & Unwin.

—— (1996) "Economic Restructuring, State-Labor Relations, and the Transformation of the Mexican Corporation," pp. 149–66, *Neo-Liberalism Revisited,* Gerardo Otero, ed. Boulder CO: Westview.

Teja Zabre, Alfonso (1959) *Vida de Morelos.* Mexico City: Instituto de Historia, Universidad Nacional Autónoma de México.

Tejeda, José Luis (2007) "A mital del recorrido," pp. 413–34, *Sistema politico mexicano.* Mexico City: Facultad de Ciencias Sociales y Politicas, UNAM.

Tello, Carlos (1971) "Notas para el análisis de la distribución personal del ingreso en México," *Trimestre Económico* 150 (April–June): 629–57.

—— (1979) *La política económica en México: 1970–1976*. Mexico City: Siglo XXI.

—— (1991) "Combating Poverty in Mexico," pp. 57–65, *Social Responses to Mexico's Economic Crisis of the 1980s,* Mercedes González de la Rocha & Agustín Escobar Latapí, eds. UCSD U.S.–Mexican Studies Contemporary Perspective Series, 1. San Diego CA: UCSD Center for U.S.–Mexican Studies.

Tello Díaz, Carlos (1993) *El exilio: un relato de familia*. Mexico City: Cal y Arena.

—— (2007) *2 de Julio*. Mexico City: Planeta.

Tena Ramírez, Felipe (1992) *Leyes fundamentales de México, 1808–1992* (17th ed.) Mexico City: Porrúa.

Tenenbaum, Barbara A. (1979) "Merchants, Money, and Mischief: The British in Mexico, 1821–1862," *The Americas* 35 (January): 317–39.

—— (1986) *The Politics of Penury*. Albuquerque NM: University of New Mexico Press.

—— (1988) "El poder de las finanzas y las finanzas del poder en México durante el siglo XIX," *Siglo XIX* 3 (January–June): 197–221.

—— (1989a) "Taxation and Tyranny: Public Finance During the Iturbide Regime, 1821–1823," pp. 201–13, *The Independence of Mexico and the Creation of a New Nation,* Jaime E. Rodríguez O., ed. Los Angeles CA: UCLA Latin American Center & Mexico/Chicano Program of the University of California, Irvine.

—— (1989b) "'Neither a Borrower Nor a Lender Be': Financial Constraints and the Treaty of Guadalupe Hidalgo," pp. 68–84, *The Mexican and Mexican American Experience in the 19th Century,* Jaime E. Rodríguez, ed. Tempe AZ: Bilingual Press.

—— (1991) "Development and Sovereignty: Intellectuals and the Second Empire," pp. 77–88, *Los intelectuales y el poder en México,* Roderic A. Camp, Charles A. Hale, & Josefina Zoraida Vázquez, eds. Mexico City: Colegio de México.

—— (1992a) "The Chicken and the Egg: Reflections on the Mexican Military, 1821–1846," pp. 355–70, *Five Centuries of Mexican History/Cinco siglos de historia de México,* Virginia Guedea, ed. Mexico City: Instituto Mora and Irvie CA: University of California.

—— (1992b) "'They Went Thataway:' The Evolution of the *Pronunciamento,* 1821–1856," pp. 187–205, *Patterns of Contention in Mexico History,* Jaime E. Rodríguez O., ed. Wilmington DE: Scholarly Resources.

—— (1993) "The Making of a Fait Accompli: Mexico and the Provincias Internas, 1776–1846," pp. 91–115, *The Evolution of the Mexican Political System,* Jaime E. Rodríguez O., ed. Wilmington DE: Scholarly Resources.

—— (1994a) "The Emperor Goes to the Tailor," pp. 281–302, *Mexico in the Age of Democratic Revolutions, 1750–1850,* Jaime E. Rodríguz O., ed. Boulder CO: Lynne Rienner.

—— (1994b) "Streetwise History: The *Paseo de la Reforma* and the Porfirian State, 1876–1910," pp. 127–50, *Rituals of Rule, Rituals of Resistance,* William H. Beezley, Cheryl English Martin & William E. French, eds. Wilmington DE: Scholarly Resources.

—— (1996) "Mexico, 1810–1919," pp. 6–14, *Encyclopedia of Latin American History and Culture* (vol. 4), Barbara Tenenbaum, ed. New York: C. Scribner's Sons.

Tenorio Trillo, Mauricio (1996) "1910 Mexico City: Space and Nation in the City of the *Centenario,*" *Journal of Latin American Studies* 21 (February): 75–104.

TePaske, John J. (1989) "The Financial Disintegration of the Royal Government During the Epoch of Independence," pp. 63–83, *The Independence of Mexico and the Creation of a New Nation,* Jaime E. Rodríguez O., ed. Los Angeles CA: UCLA Latin American Center & Mexico/Chicano Program of the University of California, Irvine.

TePaske, John J. & Herbert S. Klein (1981) "The Seventeenth-Century Crisis in New Spain," *Past & Present* 90 (February): 116–35.

Terrazas Basante, Marcela (1990) *Los intereses norteamericanos en el noroeste de México.* Mexico City: Universidad Nacional Autónoma de México.

—— (1997) "Los especuladores y el debate parlamentario norteamericano en torno al Tratado de la Mesilla," pp. 293–373, *Política y negocios,* Ana Rosa Suárez Argüello & Marcela Terrazas Basante, eds. Mexico City: Universidad Nacional Autónoma de México & Instituto Mora.

Thelen, David (1999) "Mexico's Cultural Landscapes," *Journal of American History* 86 (September): 613–22.

Thiesenhusen, William C. (1995) *Broken Promises.* Boulder CO: Westview.

—— (1996) "Mexican Land Reform, 1934–91," pp. 35–47, *Reforming Mexico's Agrarian Reform,* Laura Randall, ed. Armonk NY: M.E. Sharpe.

Thomas, Hugh (1993) *Conquest: Montezuma, Cortés, and the Fall of Old Mexico.* New York: Simon & Schuster.

—— (1996) "Introduction," pp. xi-xviii, *The Discovery and Conquest of Mexico,* Bernal Díaz del Castillo. New York: Da Capo.

—— (1997) *The Slave Trade.* New York: Simon & Schuster.

—— (2003) *Rivers of Gold.* New York: Random House.

Thompson, Waddy (1846) *Recollections of Mexico.* New York: Wiley & Putnam.

Thomson, Guy P. C. (1985) "Protectionism and Industrialization in Mexico, 1821–1854: The Case of Puebla," pp. 125–46, *Latin America, Economic Imperialism and the State,* Christopher Abel & Colin M. Lewis, eds. London: Athlone.

—— (1986) "The Cotton Textile Industry in Puebla during the Eighteenth and Early Nineteenth Centuries," pp. 169–202, *The Economies of Mexico and Peru During the Late Colonial Period, 1760–1810,* Nils Jacobsen & Hans-Jürgen Puhle, eds. Berlin: Colloquium Verlag.

—— (1990) "Bulwarks of Patriotic Liberalism: The National Guard, Philharmonic Corps, and Patriotic Juntas in Mexico, 1847–88," *Journal of Latin American Studies* 22: (February): 31–68.

—— (1991) "Popular Aspects of Liberalism in Mexico, 1848–1888," *Bulletin of Latin American Research* 10 (no. 3): 265–92.

—— (1995) "Federalism and Cantonalism in Mexico, 1824–1892: Sovereignty and Territoriality," pp. 27–54, *Wars, Parties and Nationalism,* Eduardo Posada-Carbó, ed. London: Institute of Latin American Studies, University of London.

Thoreau, Henry D. (1970) *The Annotated Walden.* New York: Potter.

Thorp, Rosemary (1986) "Latin America and the International Economy from the First World War to the World Depression," pp. 57–81, *Cambridge History of Latin America* (vol. 4), Leslie Bethell, ed. Cambridge: Cambridge University Press.

—— (1994a) "The Latin American Economies, 1939–*c.* 1950," pp. 117–58, *Cambridge History of Latin America* (vol. 6), Leslie Bethell, ed. Cambridge: Cambridge University Press.

—— (1994b) "The Latin American Economies in the 1940s," pp. 41–58, *Latin America in the 1940s,* David Rock, ed. Berkeley CA: University of California Press.

—— (1998) *Progress, Poverty and Exclusion.* Washington DC: Inter-American Development Bank.

Tienda, Marta (2007) "Don't Blame Immigrants for Poverty Wages," *American Prospect* 18 (May): A10–11.

Timmons, Wilbert H. (1950) "Los Guadalupes: A Secret Society in the Mexico Revolution for Independence," *Hispanic American Historical Review* 30 (November): 453–79.

—— (1963) *Morelos: Priest, Soldier, Statesman of Mexico.* El Paso TX: Texas Western College Press.

Tinker Salas, Miguel (1992) "Sonora: The Making of a Border Society, 1880–1910," *Journal of the Southwest* 34 (Winter): 429–56.

—— (1997) *In the Shadow of the Eagles.* Berkeley CA: University of California Press.

Tischendorf, Alfred (1961) *Great Britain and Mexico in the Era of Porfirio Díaz.* Durham NC: Duke University Press.

Toledo, Víctor (1996) 'The Ecological Consequences of the 1992 Agrarian Law of Mexico," pp. 247–60, *Reforming Mexico's Agrarian Reform,* Laura Randall, ed. Armonk NY: M.E. Sharpe.

Topik, Steven (1990) "La revolución, el Estado y el desarrollo económico en México," *Historia Mexicana* 40 (July–Sept): 79–144.

—— (1992) "The Emergence of Finance Capital in Mexico," pp. 227–42, *Five Centuries of Mexican History/Cincos siglos de historia de México,* vol. 2, Virginia Guedea & Jaime E. Rodríguez O., eds. Mexico City: Instituto Mora & Irvine: University of California.

—— (2000) "When Mexico Had the Blues," *American Historical Review* 105 (June): 714–38.

Topik, Steven C. & Allen Wells (1998) "Introduction: Latin America's Response to International Markets during the Export Boom," pp. 1–36, & "Retrospect and Prospect: The Dance of the Commodities," pp. 215–26, *The Second Conquest of Latin America,* Steven C. Topik & Allen Wells, eds. Austin TX: University of Texas Press.

Toro, María Celia (1995) *Mexico's "War" on Drugs.* Boulder CO: Lynne Rienner.

Torre Villar, Ernesto de la (1982) *La independencia mexicana* (3 vols.). Mexico City: Fondo de Cultura Económica.

Torres, Blanca (1979) *México en la Segunda Guerra Mundial,* Historia de la Revolución mexicana, vol. 19. Mexico City: Colegio de México.

—— (1986) "La guerra y la posguerra en las relaciones de México y Estados Unidos, pp. 65–82, *Entre la guerra y la estabilidad política en el México de los 40,* Rafael Loyola, ed. Mexico City: Grijalbo.

—— (2005) "Actores no estatales y la apertura comercial," pp. 201–24, *Historia contemporánea de México* (vol. 2), Ilán Bizberg & Lorenzo Meyer, eds. Mexico City: Océano.

Torres, Luis (1993) *San Antonio Missions National Historic Park.* Tucson AZ: Southwest Parks and Monuments Association.

Torres Gaytán, Ricardo (1980) *Un siglo de devaluaciones del peso mexicano.* Mexico City: Siglo XXI.

Tortolero Villaseñor, Alejandro (1995) *De la coa a la máquina de vapor.* Mexico City: Siglo XXI.

—— (2000) *El agua y su historia.* Mexico City: Siglo XXI.

—— (2007) "Entre las revoluciones y el desarrollo: el agua en México, siglos XIX y XX," pp. 155–74, *México en tres momentos: 1810–1910–2010* (vol. 2), Alicia Mayer, ed. Mexico City: Instituto de Investigaciones Históricas, Universidad Nacional Autónoma de México.

Tostado Gutiérrez, Marcela (1991) *El álbum de la mujer,* vol. 2: *Época colonial.* Mexico City: Instituto Nacional de Antropología e Historia.

Towner, Margaret (1977) "Monopoly Capitalism and Women's Work during the Porfiriato," *Latin American Perspectives* 4 (Winter-Spring): 90–105.

Townsend, Camilla (2003) "Burying the White Gods: New Perspectives on the Conquest of Mexico," *American Historical Review* 108 (June): 659–87.
—— (2006) *Malintzin's Choices.* Albuquerque NM: University of New Mexico Press.
Townsend, William Cameron (1952) *Lázaro Cárdenas.* Ann Arbor MI: George Wahr.
Trejo, Guillermo (2002) "Indígenas," *Nexos* 289 (January): 28–30.
Trejo Delarbre, Raúl (1976) "The Mexican Labor Movement: 1917–1975," *Latin American Perspectives* 3 (Winter): 133–53.
—— (1979) "El movimiento obrero: situación y perspectivas," pp. 121–51, *Mexico Hoy,* Pablo González Casanova & Enrique Florescano, eds. Mexico City: Siglo XXI.
Trejo Reyes, Saúl (1975) "El desempleo en México," *Trimestre Económico* 42 (July–Sept): 671–94.
Trens, Manuel B. (1947) *Historia de Veracruz* (vol. 2). Jalapa: Enríquez.
—— (1950) *Historia de Veracruz* (vol. 6). Mexico City: La Impresora.
Treviño de Hoyos, Miguel B. (2007) "El PAN—¿ahora sí?—al poder," *Letras Libres* 97 (January): 42–45.
Troncoso, Francisco (1905) *Las guerras con las tribus Yaqui y Mayo del Estado de Sonora.* Mexico City: Tipografía del Departamento de Estado Mayor.
Trueblood, Alan S. (1988) "Introduction," pp. 1–23, *A Sor Juana Anthology.* Cambridge MA: Harvard University Press.
Truman, Harry (1956) *Memoirs* (2 vols.) Garden City NY: Doubleday.
Tuchman, Barbara W. (1963) *The Zimmermann Telegram.* New York: Dell.
—— (1988) *Guns of August.* New York: Macmillan.
Tuchman, Phyllis (2002) "Frida Kahlo," *Smithsonian* 33 (November): 50–60.
Tudor, W. G. (1997) *Flight of Eagles.* Ph.D. Dissertation. Fort Worth TX: Texas Christian University.
Tuirán, Rodolfo (2002) "Los desafíos demográficos de México en el siglo XXI," *Este País* 138 (Sept): 69–78.
Tuñón, Enriqueta (2009) "Las feministas y la Constitución del 17," *Proceso Bi-Centenario* 3, pp. 24–34.
Tuñón, Julia (1999) *Women in México.* Austin TX: University of Texas Press.
Turner II, B. L. & Karl W. Butzer (1992) "The Colombian Encounter and Land-Use Change," *Environment* 34 (October): 16–20.
Turner, Frederick (1974) *Responsible Parenthood.* Washington DC: American Enterprise Institute for Public Policy Research.
Turner, J. (1968) "Squatter Settlement: An Architecture that Works," *Architectural Design* 38 (August): 355–60.
Turner, John Kenneth (1969) *Barbarous Mexico.* Austin TX: University of Texas Press.
Turner, William (1965) "No Dice for Braceros," *Ramparts* 4 (Sept): 14–24.
Tutino, John (1975) "Hacienda Social Relations in Mexico: The Chalco Region in the Era of Independence," *Hispanic American Historical Review* 55 (August): 496–528.
—— (1983) "Power, Class, and Family: Men and Women in the Mexican Elite, 1750–1810," *The Americas* 39 (January): 359–81.
—— (1986) *From Insurrection to Revolution in Mexico: Social Bases of Agrarian Violence, 1750–1940.* Princeton NJ: Princeton University Press.
—— (1988) "Agrarian Change and Peasant Rebellion in Nineteenth-Century Mexico: The Example of Chalco," pp. 95–140, *Riot, Rebellion, and Revolution,* Friedrich Katz, ed. Princeton NJ: Princeton University Press.
—— (1990) "Revolutionary Confrontation, 1913–1917," pp. 41–70, *Provinces of the Revolution,* Thomas Benjamin & Mark Wasserman, eds. Albuquerque NM: University of New Mexico Press.
—— (1997) "Rural Economy and Society: 1821–1910," pp. 1302–09, *Encyclopedia of Mexico,* Michael S. Werner, ed. Chicago IL: Fitzroy Dearborn.
—— (1998) "The Revolution in Mexican Independence," *Hispanic American Historical Review* 78 (August): 367–418.
—— (2007) "The Revolutionary Capacity of Rural Communities," pp. 211–68, *Cycles of Conflict, Centuries of Change,* Elisa Servín, Leticia Reina, & John Tutino, eds. Durham NC: Duke University Press.
Ugalde, Luis Carlos (2008) *Así lo viví.* Mexico City: Grijalbo.
Ulibarri, Richard Onofre (1974) *American Interest in the Spanish-American Southwest, 1803–1848.* San Francisco CA: R & E Research Associates.
Ulloa, Berta (1979a) *La revolución escindida,* La historia de la Revolución mexicana, vol. 4. Mexico City: Colegio de México.
—— (1979b) *La encrucijada de 1915,* La historia de la Revolución mexicana, vol. 5. Mexico City: Colegio de México.
—— (1985) "La revolución maderista," pp. 13–26, *El desarrollo de México después de la Revolución de 1910.* Puebla: Colegio de Puebla & Mexico City: Colegio de México.
—— (1997) "The U.S.-Government versus the Mexican Revolution, 1910–1917," pp. 159–79, *Myths, Misdeeds, and Misunderstandings,* Jaime E. Rodríguez O. & Kathryn Vincent, eds. Wilmington DE: Scholarly Resources.
Ungar, Mark (2006) "Crime and Citizen Security in Latin America," pp. 171–92, *Latin America after Neoliberalism,"* Eric Hershberg & Fred Rosen, eds. New York: NACLA & New Press.

Unikel, Luis (1974a) "La dinámica del crecimiento de la Ciudad de México," pp. 175–206, *Ensayos sobre el desarrollo urbano en México*. Mexico City: SepSetentas.

—— (1974b) "Urbanización y urbanismo," pp. 254–88, *La sociedad mexicana*, Miguel S. Wionczek, ed. Mexico City: Fondo de Cultura Económica.

United Nations (1951) *FAO Production Yearbook*. New York: Food and Agriculture Organization of the United Nations.

—— (1962) *FAO Production Yearbook*. New York: Food and Agriculture Organization of the United Nations.

—— (1973) *FAO Production Yearbook*. New York: Food and Agriculture Organization of the United Nations.

—— (2008) *World Urbanization Prospects: The 2007 Revision—Highlights*. New York: United Nations Department of Economics and Social Affairs. Online at www.un.org/esa/population/publications/wup2007/2007WUP_Highlights_web.pdf (accessed February 5, 2010).

Urías Hermosillo, Margarita (1979) "México y los proyectos nacionales, 1821–1857," *Nexos* 2 (August): 32–41.

Urquidi, Víctor (1967) "Fundamental Problems of the Mexican Economy," pp. 173–202, *Mexico's Recent Economic Growth*. Austin TX: University of Texas Press.

—— (1970) "Perfil general: economía y población," pp. 1–13, *El perfil de México en 1980*, vol. 1. Mexico City: Siglo XXI.

—— (1977) "México en la encrucijada," *Vuelta* 1 (July): 4–7.

—— (2001) "Los efectos de la política económica y cohesión social," pp. 115–30, *¿Estamos unidos mexicanos?* Mauricio de María y Campos & Georgina Sánchez, eds. Mexico City: Planeta.

—— (2003) "Mexico's Development Challenges," pp. 561–76, *Confronting Development*, Kevin J. Middlebrook & Eduardo Zepeda, eds. Palo Alta CA: Stanford University Press & San Diego CA: UCSD Center for U.S.–Mexican Studies.

—— (2005) *Otro siglo perdidio*. Mexico City: Colegio de México & Fondo de Cultura Económica.

Urquidi, Víctor & Sofía Méndez Villarreal (1978) "Economic Importance of Mexico's Border Region," pp. 141–62, *Views Across the Border*, Stanley R. Ross, ed. Albuquerque NM: University of New Mexico Press.

U.S. (1822) *Report of the Committee on Foreign Relations*, to which was referred the President's message concerning the recognition of the late Spanish Provinces in America. 17th Congress, 1st Session. Washington DC: Journal of the House of Representatives.

—— (1848) *Hostilities by Mexico*. House Executive Document no. 60, 30th Congress, 1st Session. Washington DC: Journal of the House of Representatives.

—— (1862) *The Present Condition of Mexico*. House Executive Document no. 100, 37th Congress, 2nd Session. Washington DC: Government Printing Office.

—— (1878) *Relations of the United States with Mexico*. House Report no. 701, 44th Congress, 2nd Session. Washington DC: Government Printing Office.

—— (1906) *Report on Trade Conditions in Mexico*, Senate Document no. 246, 59th Congress, 1st Session. Washington DC: Government Printing Office.

—— (1913) *Thirteenth Census of the United States Taken in the Year 1910: Abstract of the Census*. Washington DC: Government Printing Office.

—— (1917) *United States Statutes at Large*, vol. 39. Washington, DC: Government Printing Office.

—— (1919) *Papers Relating to the Foreign Relations of the United States, 1912*. Washington DC: Government Printing Office.

—— (1920a) *Affairs in Mexico*. Senate Report no. 645, 66th Congress, 2nd Session. Washington DC: Government Printing Office.

—— (1920b) *Investigation of Mexican Affairs*. Senate Document 285, 66th Congress, 2nd Session. Washington DC: Government Printing Office.

—— (1922a) *Fourteenth Census of the United States Taken in the Year 1920*. Washington DC: Government Printing Office.

—— (1922b) *Papers Relating to the Foreign Relations of the United States, 1914*. Washington DC: Government Printing Office.

—— (1924) *Papers Relating to the Foreign Relations of the United States, 1915*. Washington DC: Government Printing Office.

—— (1928) *United States Statutes at Large*, vol. 42. Washington, DC: Government Printing Office.

—— (1932) *Fifteenth Census of the United States: 1930*, vol. 3, pt. 1. Washington DC: U.S. Government Printing Office.

—— (1940) *Papers Relating to the Foreign Relations of the United States*, 1925. Washington DC: Government Printing Office.

—— (1976) *Historical Statistics of the United States, Colonial Times to 1970* (2 vols.). Washington DC: Bureau of the Census.

U.S. (2006) *2005 Yearbook of Immigration Statistics*. Springfield VA: National Technical Information Service. Online at www.dhs.gov/xlibrary/assets/statistics/yearbook/2005/OIS_2005_Yearbook.pdf (accessed February 7, 2010).

U.S. Census Bureau (2002) Internet Release, February 27.

USDA (1976) *The Mexican Cotton Industry.* Foreign Agricultural Service, U.S. Dept. of Agriculture.

Valdés, Dennis (1988) "Mexican Revolutionary Nationalism and Repatriation during the Great Depression," *Mexican Studies/Estudios Mexicanos* 4 (Winter): 1–23.

Valdés, Luz Ma. & Ma. Teresa Menéndez (1987) *Dinámica de la población de habla indígena (1900–1980).* Mexico City: Instituto Nacional de Antropología e Historia.

Valdés Ugalde, Francisco (1996) "The Private Sector and Political Regime Change in Mexico," pp. 127–47, *Neoliberalism Revisited,* Gerardo Otero, ed. Boulder CO: Westview.

Valenzuela, Arturo (2005) "Beyond Benign Neglect," *Current History* 104 (February): 58–63.

Valenzuela, Liliana (1988) *Mexico's La Malinche.* Masters Report, Austin TX: University of Texas.

Vallens, Vivian M (1978) *Working Women in Mexico during the Porfiriato, 1880–1910.* San Francisco CA: R & E Research Associates.

Valverde Loya, Miguel Ángel (2007) "La estrategia del ataque," *Este País* 191 (February): 28–31.

Van Bath, Bernard Slicher (1979) "Economic Diversification in Spanish America around 1600," pp. 53–96, *Jahrbuch für Geschichte von Staat, Wirtschaft und Gesellschaft Lateinamerikas 1979.* Cologne: Böhlau Verlag.

Van Young, Eric (1984) "'Who Was that Masked Man, Anyway?': Symbols and Popular Ideology in the Mexican Wars of Independence," *Proceedings of the Rocky Mountain Council on Latin American Studies,* vol. 1. Tucson AZ: Rocky Mountain Council of Latin American Studies.

—— (1986a) "The Age of Paradox: Mexican Agriculture at the End of the Colonial Period, 1750–1810," pp. 64–90, *The Economies of Mexico and Peru During the Late Colonial Period, 1760–1810,* Nils Jacobsen & Hans-Jürgen Puhle, eds. Berlin: Colloquium Verlag.

—— (1986b) "Millennium on the Northern Marches: The Mad Messiah of Durango and Popular Rebellion in Mexico, 1800–1815," *Comparative Studies in Society and History* 28 (July): 385–413.

—— (1988a) "Moving toward Revolt: Agrarian Origins of the Hidalgo Revolt in the Guadalajara Region," pp. 176–204, *Riot, Rebellion, and Revolution,* Friedrich Katz, ed. Princeton NJ: Princeton University Press.

—— (1988b) "A modo de conclusión: El siglo paradójico," pp. 206–231, *Empresarios, indios y estado,* Arij Ouweneel & Cristina Torales Pacheco, eds. Amsterdam: Centrum voor Studie en Documentatie van Latijns Amerika.

—— (1989a) "Quetzalcóatl, King Ferdinand, and Ignacio Allende Go to the Seashore; or Messianism and Mystical Kingship in Mexico, 1820–1821," pp. 109–27, *The Independence of Mexico and the Creation of a New Nation,* Jaime E. Rodríguez O., ed. Los Angeles CA: UCLA Latin American Center & Mexico/Chicano Program of the University of California, Irvine.

—— (1989b) "The Raw and the Cooked: Elite and Popular Ideology in Mexico, 1800–1821," pp. 75–102, *The Middle Period in Latin America.* Boulder CO: Lynne Rienner.

—— (2001) *The Other Rebellion.* Palo Alto CA: Stanford University Press.

—— (2004) "De aves estatuas: Respuesta a Alan Knight," *Historia Mexicana* 214 (October–December): 417–73.

—— (2007) "Of Tempests and Teapots," pp. 23–59, *Cycles of Conflict, Centuries of Change,* Elisa Servín, Leticia Reina, & John Tutino, eds. Durham NC: Duke University Press.

Vander Linden, H. (1916) "Alexander VI and the Demarcation of the Maritime and Colonial Domains of Spain and Portugal, 1493–1494," *American Historical Review* 22 (October): 1–20.

Vanderwarker, Amber (2006) *Farming, Hunting and Fishing in the Olmec World.* Austin TX: University of Texas Press.

Vanderwood, Paul J. (1970) "Genesis of the Rurales," 50 *Hispanic American Historical Review* (May): 323–44.

—— (1976) "Response to Revolt," *Hispanic American Historical Review* 56 (November): 551–79.

—— (1989a) "Comparing Mexican Independence with the Revolution: Causes, Concepts, and Pitfalls," pp. 311–22, *The Independence of Mexico and the Creation of a New Nation,* Jaime E. Rodríguez O., ed. Los Angeles CA: UCLA Latin American Center & Mexico/Chicano Program of the University of California, Irvine.

—— (1989b) "Resurveying the Mexican Revolution: Three Provocative New Syntheses and Their Shortfalls," *Mexican Studies/Estudios Mexicanos* 5 (Winter): 145–63.

—— (1997) "Rurales," pp. 1323–24, *Encyclopedia of Mexico,* Michael S. Werner, ed. Chicago IL: Fitzroy Dearborn.

—— (2000) "Betterment for Whom? The Reform Period: 1855–1875," pp. 371–96, *Oxford History of Mexico,* Michael C. Meyer & William H. Beezley, eds. New York: Oxford University Press.

Vargas, Armando (1976) "The Coup at Excelsior," *Columbia Journalism Review* (Sept–October): 45–48.

Vargas Llosa, Mario (1991) "Mexico: The Perfect Dictatorship," NPQ 8 (Winter): 23–24.

Vásquez, Ian (1997) 'The IMF through a Mexican Lens," *Orbis* 41 (Spring): 259–76.

Vaughan, Mary Kay (1975) "Education and Class Struggle in the Mexican Revolution" *Latin American Perspectives* 5 (Summer): 17–33.

—— (1982) *The State, Education, and Social Class in Mexico, 1880–1928.* DeKalb IL: Northern Illinois University Press.

—— (1990) "Women School Teachers in the Mexican Revolution," *Journal of Women's History* 2 (Spring): 143–68.

—— (1992) "The Implementation of National Policy in the Countryside: Socialist Education in Puebla in the Cárdenas Period," pp. 893–904, *La ciudad y el campo en la historia de México,* vol. 2. Mexico City: Insituto de Investigaciones Históricas, Universidad Nacional Autónoma de México.

—— (1994) "Rural Women's Literacy and Education during the Mexican Revolution," pp. 106–34, *Women of the Mexican Countryside, 1850–1990,* Heather Fowler-Salamini & Mary Kay Vaughan, eds. Tucson AZ: University of Arizona Press.

—— (1997a) *Cultural Politics in Revolution.* Tucson AZ: University of Arizona Press.

—— (1997b) "Education: 1889–1940," pp. 441–445, *Encyclopedia of Mexico,* Michael S. Werner, ed. Chicago IL: Fitzroy Dearborn.

—— (2006a) "Pancho Villa, the Daughters of Mary, and the Modern Woman," pp. 21–32, *Sex in Revolution,* Jocelyn Olcott, Mary Kay Vaughan, & Gabriela Cano, eds. Durham NC: Duke University Press.

—— (2006b) "Nationalizing the Countryside: Schools and Rural Communities in the 1930s," pp. 157–75, *The Eagle and the Virgin,* Mary Kay Vaughan & Stephen E Lewis, eds. Durham NC: Duke University Press.

Vázquez, Josefina Zoraida (1976) "Los primeros tropiezos," pp. 1–84, *Historia general de México,* vol. 3. Mexico City: Colegio de México.

—— (1981) "La educación de la mujer en México en los siglos XVII y XVIII," *Diálogos* 17 (March–April): 10–16.

—— (1985) "Lo positivo de la guerra de 1847 entre México y EU," *Contenido* (January): 85–94.

—— (1986) "México y Estados Unidos desde el Foreign Office, 1833–1846," *Secuencia* 5 (May–August): 148–54.

—— (1987) "La crisis y los partidos políticos, 1833–46," pp. 557–72, *America Latina dallo Stato Coloniale allo Stato Nazione.* Milano: Franco Angeli.

—— (1991) "La influencia de Estados Unidos en México," *Secuencia* 19 (January–April): 33–42.

—— (1992) "Los pronunciamientos de 1832: Aspirantismo político e ideología," pp. 163–86, *Patterns of Contention in Mexican History,* Jaime E. Rodríguez O., ed. Wilmington DE: Scholarly Resources.

—— (1993) "Colonización y pérdida de territorio, 1819–1857," pp. 114–33, *El poblamiento de México,* vol. 3. Consejo Nacional de Población.

—— (1994a) "Una difícil inserción," pp. 259–81, *De los imperios a las naciones: Iberoamérica,* Antonio Annino et al., eds. Zaragoza: IberCaja.

—— (1994b) "Women's Liberation in Latin America: Toward a History of the Present," pp. 18–25, *Confronting Change, Challenging Tradition: Women in Latin American History.* Wilmington DE: Scholarly Resources.

—— (1996a) *La patria independiente.* Mexico City: Clío.

—— (1996b) "Political Plans and Collaboration between Civilians and the Military, 1821–1846," *Bulletin of Latin American Research* 15 (January): 19–38.

—— (1997a) "The Colonization and Loss of Texas: A Mexican Perspective," pp. 47–77, *Myths, Misdeeds, and Misunderstandings,* Jaime E. Rodríguez O. & Kathryn Vincent, eds. Wilmington DE: Scholarly Resources.

—— (1997b) "El origen de la guerra con Estados Unidos," *Historia Mexicana* 186 (October–December): 285–309.

—— (1997c) "Liberales y conservadores en México: diferencias y similitudes," *Estudios Interdisciplinarios de América Latina y el Caribe* 8 (no. 1): 19–39.

—— (1997d) *La intervención norteamericana,* 1846–1848. Mexico City: Secretaría de Relaciones Exteriores.

—— (2000a) "War and Peace with the United States," pp. 339–69, *Oxford History of Mexico,* Michael C. Meyer & William H. Beezley, eds. New York: Oxford University Press.

—— (2000b) "Causes of the War with the United States," pp. 41–65, *Dueling Eagles,* Richard V. Francaviglia & Douglas W. Richmond, eds. Fort Worth TX: Texas Christian University Press.

Vázquez, Josefina Zoraida & Lorenzo Meyer (1985) *The United States and Mexico.* Chicago IL: University of Chicago Press.

Vázquez León, Luis (1981) "La práctica de la antropología social durante el cardenismo," *Cuicuilco* 4 (July): 8–17.

Veeman, Michele M., Terrence Veeman, & Ryan Hoskins (2002) "NAFTA and Agriculture," pp. 305–29, *NAFTA in the New Millennium,* Edward Chambers & Peter H. Smith, eds. San Diego CA: UCSD Center for U.S.–Mexican Studies and Edmonton: University of Alberta Press.

Vega, Eduardo (2001) "La sustentabilidad en México," *Gaceta Ecológica* no. 61: 30–45.

Vega, Gustavo & Luz María de la Mora (2003) "Mexico's Trade Policy," pp. 163–94, *Confronting Development,* Kevin Middlebrook & Eduardo Zepeda, eds. Palo Alto CA: Stanford University Press & San Diego CA: UCSD Center for U.S.–Mexican Studies.

Velasco, Andrés (2002) "Dependency Theory," *Foreign Policy* 133 (November–December): 44–45.

Velasco, Cuauhtémoc, Eduardo Flores Clair, Alma Laura Parra Campos, & Edgar Omar Gutiérrez López (1988) *Estado y minería en México (1767–1910).* Mexico City: Fondo de Cultura Económica.

Velasco A., Cuauhtémoc (1980) "Los trabajadores mineros en la Nueva España, 1750–1810," pp. 239–301, *De la Colonia al imperio, La clase obrera en la historia de México,* vol. 1. Mexico City: Siglo XXI.

Verástique, Bernardino (2000) *Michoacán and Eden.* Austin TX: University of Texas Press.
Vernon, Raymond (1963) *The Dilemma of Mexico's Development.* Cambridge MA: Harvard University Press.
Villa, Miguel & Jorge Rodríguez (1996) "Demographic Trends in Latin America's Metropolises, 1950–1990," pp. 25–52, *The Mega-City in Latin America,* Alan Gilbert, ed. Tokyo: United Nations University Press.
Villa Rojas, Alfonso (1971a) "Antropología e indigenismo en América Latina," *América Indígena* 31 (January): 5–44.
—— (1971b) "El resurgimiento del indigenismo mexicano," *América Indígena* 31 (October): 1021–31.
Villalpando César, José Manuel (1996) *En pie de guerra.* Mexico City: Clío.
Villarreal, René (1988) "El desarrollo industrial de México: una perspectiva histórica, pp. 257–339, *México: Setenta y cinco años de Revolución I— desarrollo económico,* vol. 1. Mexico City: Fondo de Cultura Económica.
Vincent, Ted (1994) "The Blacks Who Freed Mexico," *Journal of Negro History* 79 (Summer): 257–76.
Viqueira, Carmen & José I. Urquiola (1990) *Los obrajes en la Nueva España, 1530–1630.* Mexico City: Consejo Nacional para la Cultura y las Artes.
Vite Pérez, Miguel Ángel (2005) "Reflexiones sobre la política social en la Ciudad de México," *Comercio Exterior* 55 (June): 533–40.
Voljc, Marko & Joost Draaisma (1993) "Privatization and Economic Stabilization in Mexico," *Columbia Journal of World Business* 28 (Spring): 122–34.
Von Wobeser, Gisela (2007) "La Consolidación de los Vales Reales como antecedente de la lucha de Independencia (1804–1808)," pp. 15–28, *México en tres momentos: 1810–1910–2010* (vol. 2), Alicia Mayer, ed. Mexico City: Instituto de Investigaciones Históricas, Universidad Nacional Autónoma de México.
Wade, Maria F. (2003) *The Native Americans of the Texas Edwards Plateau, 1582–1799.* Austin TX: University of Texas Press.
Walker, David W. (1981) "Porfirian Labor Politics," *The Americas* 37 (January): 257–89.
—— (1986) *Kinship, Business, and Politics.* Austin TX: University of Texas Press.
Wallerstein, Immanuel (1980) *The Modern World-System II.* New York: Academic.
—— (1989) *The Modern World-System III.* New York: Academic.
—— (2000) "The Albatross of Racism," *London Review of Books* 22 (May 18): 11–14.
Wallis, Darren (2001) "The Mexican Presidential and Congressional Elections of 2000 and Democratic Transition," *Bulletin of Latin American Research* 20 (July): 304–22.
Ward, Peter (1976) "The Squatter Settlement as Slum or Housing Solution: Evidence from Mexico City," *Land Economics* 52 (August): 330–46.
—— (1998) *Mexico City* (2nd ed.) Chichester, West Sussex: John Wiley & Sons.
—— (2004) *México Megaciudad.* Mexico City: Miguel Ángel Porrúa.
Ward, Peter & Elizabeth Durden (2002) "Government and Democracy in Mexico's Federal District, 1997–2001," *Bulletin of Latin American Research* 21 (no. 1): 1–39.
Warman, Arturo (1978) "Frente a la crisis: ¿Política agraria o política agrícola?" *Comercio Exterior* 28 (June): 681–87.
—— (1979) "El problema del campo," pp. 108–20, *Mexico, Hoy,* Pablo González Casanova & Enrique Florescano, eds. Mexico City: XXI.
—— (1980) *We Come to Object.* Baltimore MD: Johns Hopkins University Press.
—— (1983) "The Future of a Crisis: Food and Agrarian Reform," pp. 205–24, *U.S.–Mexican Relations,* Clark Reynolds & Carlos Tello, eds. Palo Alto CA: Stanford University Press.
—— (1988) *La historia de un bastardo: maíz y capitalismo.* Mexico City: Fondo de Cultura Económica & Instituto de Investigaciones Sociales, Universidad Nacional Autónoma de México.
—— (2001) *El campo mexicano en el Siglo XX.* Mexico City: Fondo de Cultura Económica.
—— (2003) *Los indios mexicanos en el umbral del milenio.* Mexico City: Fondo de Cultura Económica.
Warren, Fintan B. (1963) *Vasco de Quiroga and his Pueblo-Hospitals of Santa Fe.* Washington DC: Academy of American Franciscan History.
Wasserman, Mark (1979) "Foreign Investment in Mexico, 1876–1910: A Case Study of the Role of Regional Elites," *The Americas* 36 (July): 3–21.
—— (1984) *Capitalists, Caciques, and Revolution.* Chapel Hill NC: University of North Carolina Press.
—— (1985) "Enrique C. Creel: Business and Politics in Mexico, 1880–1930," *Business History Review* 59 (Winter): 645–62.
—— (1990) "Introduction," pp. 1–14, *Provinces of the Revolution,* Thomas Benjamin & Mark Wasserman, eds. Albuquerque NM: University of New Mexico Press.
—— (1993) *Persistent Oligarchs.* Durham NC: Duke University Press.
—— (2000) *Everyday Life and Politics in Nineteenth Century Mexico.* Albuquerque NM: University of New Mexico Press.
—— (2008) "You Can Teach an Old Revolutionary Historiography New Tricks," *Latin American Research Review* 43 (no. 2): 260–71.

Waters, Wendy (2006) "Remapping Identities: Road Construction and Nation Building in Postrevolutionary Mexico," pp. 221–42, *The Eagle & the Virgin*, Mary Kay Vaughan & Stephen E Lewis, eds. Durham NC: Duke University Press.

Watts, Sheldon (1997) *Epidemics and History.* New Haven CT: Yale University Press.

Weber, David J. (1982) *The Mexican Frontier, 1821–1846.* Albuquerque NM: University of New Mexico Press.

—— (1988) *Myth and the History of the Hispanic Southwest.* Albuquerque NM: University of New Mexico Press.

—— (1992) *The Spanish Frontier in North America.* New Haven CT: Yale University Press.

—— (1994) "The Spanish-Mexican Rim," pp. 45–77, *The Oxford History of the American West,* Clyde A. Milner II, Carol A. O'Connor, and Martha A. Sandweiss, eds. New York: Oxford University Press.

—— (2004) *Spanish Bourbons and Wild Indians.* Waco TX: Baylor University Press.

—— (2005) *Bárbaros.* New Haven CT: Yale University Press.

Weckmann-Múñoz, Luis (1976) "The Alexandrine Bulls of 1493: Pseudo-Asiatic Documents," pp. 201–09, *First Images of América,* vol. 1, Fredi Chiappelli, ed. Berkeley CA: University of California Press.

—— (1993) "Spain Transmitted to America Many of Her Medieval Accomplishments," pp. 19–26, *People and Issues in Latin American History,* Lewis Hanke & Jane M. Rausch, eds. New York: Markus Wiener.

Weddle, Robert S. (1985) *Spanish Sea.* College Station TX: Texas A&M University Press.

Weems, John Edward (1974) *To Conquer a Peace.* Garden City NY: Doubleday.

Weigley, Russell F. (1984) *History of the United States Army* (2nd ed.). Bloomington IN: Indiana University Press.

Weiner, Richard (1999) "Competing Market Discourses in Porfirian Mexico," *Latin American Perspectives* 26 (January): 44–64.

Weintraub, Sidney (1990*) A Marriage of Convenience.* New York: Oxford University Press.

—— (1995) "Mexico's Foreign Economic Policy," *Challenge* 38 (March–April): 39–44.

—— (2004) "Scoring Free Trade," *Current History* 103 (February): 56–60.

Weldon, Jeffrey (1997) "Political Sources of *Presidencialismo* in Mexico," pp. 225–58, *Presidentialism and Democracy in Latin America,* Scott Mainwaring & Matthew Soberg Shugart, eds. Cambridge: Cambridge University Press.

Wells, Allen (1985) *Yucatán's Gilded Age.* Albuquerque NM: University of New Mexico Press.

—— (1992) "All in the Family: Railroads and Henequen Monoculture in Porfirian Yucatán," *Hispanic American Historical Review* 72 (May): 159–210.

—— (2000a) "Out from the Shadows," *Latin American Research Review* 35 (no. 1): 172–86.

—— (2000b) Review of *The Life and Times of Pancho Villa* by Friedrich Katz, *Hispanic American Historical Review* 80 (February): 141–46.

—— (2006) "The Life and Times of Yucatecan Henequen," pp. 300–20*, From Silver to Cocaine,* Steven Topic, Carlos Marichal, and Zephyr Frank, eds. Durham NC: Duke University Press.

Welsome, Eileen (2006) *The General and the Jaguar.* New York: Little, Brown & Co.

Weyl, Nathaniel & Sylvia Weyl (1939) *The Reconquest of Mexico.* New York: Oxford University Press.

WGBH (1988) *Mexico.* Transcript of program produced by WGBH-TV, broadcast November 30.

Wheelan, Joseph (2007) *Invading Mexico.* New York: Carroll & Graf.

Whitaker, Arthur Preston (1941) *The United States and the Independence of Latin America, 1800–1830.* Baltimore MD: Johns Hopkins Press.

White, Christopher M. (2007) *Creating a Third World.* Albuquerque NM: University of New Mexico Press.

Whitehead, Laurence (1980) "La política económica del sexenio de Echeverría" *Foro Internacional* 20 (January–March): 484–513.

—— (1987) "The Mexican Economy," *Third World Quarterly* (July): 970–76.

—— (1989) "Political Change and Economic Stabilization," pp. 181–213, *Mexico's Alternative Political Futures,* Wayne A. Cornelius, Judith Gentleman and Peter H. Smith, eds. UCSD Center for U.S.–Mexican Studies Monograph Series, 30. San Diego CA: UCSD Center for U.S.–Mexican Studies.

Whitmore, Thomas M. (1992) *Disease and Death in Early Colonial Mexico.* Boulder CO: Westview.

Wilkie, James (1966) "The Meaning of the Cristero Religious War against the Mexican Revolution," *Journal of Church and State* 8 (Spring): 213–33.

—— (1970a) *The Mexican Revolution: Federal Expenditure and Social Change since 1910* (2nd ed.). Berkeley CA: University of California Press.

—— (1970b) "Statistical Indicators of the Impact of National Revolution on the Catholic Church in Mexico, 1910–1967," *Journal of Church and State* 12 (Winter): 89–106.

—— (1989) *Statistical Abstract of Latin America,* vol. 27. Los Angeles CA: UCLA Latin American Center.

Wilkins, Mira (1970) *The Emergence of the Multinational Enterprise.* Cambridge MA: Harvard University Press.

—— (1974) *The Maturing of Multinational Enterprise.* Cambridge MA: Harvard University Press.

—— (1998) "An Alternative Approach," pp. 188–214*, The Second Conquest of Latin America,* Steven C. Topik & Allen Wells, eds. Austin TX: University of Texas Press.

Williams, Edward J. (1979) *The Rebirth of the Mexican Petroleum Industry.* Lexington MA: D.C. Heath.
—— (1982) "Petroleum and Political Change," pp. 23–77, *Mexico's Political Economy,* Jorge Domínguez, ed. Beverly Hills CA: Sage.
Williams, Martha N. & John Hoyt Williams (1984) "The Route to Riches," *Américas* 36 (November–Dec): 24–29.
Wilson, Henry Lane (1927) *Diplomatic Episodes in Mexico, Belgium and Chile.* Garden City NY: Doubleday, Page & Co.
Wilson, Tamar (2000) "Anti-Immigrant Sentiment and the Problem of Reproduction/Maintenance in Mexican Immigration to the United States," *Critique of Anthropology* 20 (no.2): 191–213.
Winders, Richard Bruce (1997) *Mr. Polk's Army.* College Station TX: Texas A&M University Press.
Winkler, Max (1929) *Investments of United States Capital in Latin America.* Boston MA: World Peace Foundation.
Wionczek, Miguel S. (1974) "La inversión extranjera privada," pp. 135–57, *La sociedad mexicana: presente y futuro.* Mexico City: Fondo de Cultura Económica.
—— (1986) "Industrialization, Foreign Capital and Technology Transfer: The Mexican Experience 1930–85," *Development and Change* 17 (April): 283–302.
Woldenberg, José (1988) "La negociación político-social en México," pp. 188–208, *Primer informe sobre la democracia: México 1988,* Pablo González Casanova & Jorge Cadena Roa, eds. Mexico City: Siglo XXI.
—— (2002) *La construcción de la democracia.* Mexico City: Plaza y Janés.
Wolf, Eric (1972) "El Bajío en el siglo XVIII," pp. 63–95, *Los beneficiarios del desarrollo regional,* David Barkin, ed. Mexico City: SepSetentas.
—— (1979) "The Virgin of Guadalupe: A Mexican National Symbol," pp. 112–15, *Reader in Comparative Religion* (4th ed.), William A. Lessa & Evon Z. Vogt, eds. New York: Harper & Row.
—— (1982) *Europe and the People without History.* Berkeley CA: University of California Press.
Wolfe, Bertram (1963) *The Fabulous Life of Diego Rivera.* New York: Stein & Day.
Womack, John (1968a) *Zapata and the Mexican Revolution.* York: Vintage.
—— (1968b) "Unfreedom in Mexico," *New Republic* (October 12): 27–31.
—— (1969a) "The Mexican Revolution, 1920–1940: Genesis of a Modern State," pp. 298–339, *Latin American History: Select Problems.* New York: Harcourt, Brace & World.
—— (1969b) *Zapata y la Revolución mexicana.* Mexico City: Siglo XXI.
—— (1978) "The Mexican Economy During the Revolution, 1910–1920: Historiography & Analysis," *Marxist Perspectives* 1 (Winter): 80–123.
—— (1986) "The Mexican Revolution, 1910–1920," pp. 79–153, *Cambridge History of Latin America* (vol. 5), Leslie Bethell, ed. Cambridge: Cambridge University Press.
—— (1999) "Acteal," *Nexos* 258 (June): 63–69.
Worcester, Donald E. (1979) *The Apaches.* Norman OK: University of Oklahoma Press.
World Economic Forum (2006) *The Global Competiveness Report 2006–2007.* Houndsmills: Palgrave Macmillan.
Worldwatch Institute (2008) *Vital Signs, 2006–2007.* Washington DC: Worldwatch Institute.
Wright, Angus (1986) *The Social History of Mexican Pesticide Use.* Paper presented at the XIII Congress of the Latin American Studies Association, Boston MA.
—— (1990) *The Death of Ramón González.* Austin TX: University of Texas Press.
Wright, Ronald (1992) *Stolen Continents.* Boston MA: Houghton Mifflin.
Wu, Celia (1984) "The Population of the City of Querétaro in 1791," *Journal of Latin American Studies* 16 (November): 277–307.
Yankelevich, Pablo (2007) "Quemar la selva para cazar el tigre. Coordenadas internacionales de la Revolución Mexicana, pp. 121–31, *México en tres momentos: 1810–1910–2010* (vol. 2), Alicia Mayer, ed. Mexico City: Instituto de Investigaciones Históricas, Universidad Nacional Autónoma de México.
York, Anthony (2001) "Howdy, Partner," *MB* 8 (July): 14–16.
Young, Desmond (1966) *Member for Mexico.* London: Cassell.
Youngers, Coletta & Eileen Rosin (2005) "The U.S. 'War on Drugs,'" pp. 1–13, *Drugs and Democracy in Latin America,* Coletta Youngers & Eileen Rosin, eds. Boulder CO: Lynne Rienner.
Zabludowsky, Jaime Enrique (1984) *Money, Foreign Indebtedness and Export Performance in Porfirist Mexico.* Ph.D. Dissertation. New Haven CT: Yale University.
Zaid, Gabriel (1979) *El progreso improductivo.* Mexico City: Siglo XXI.
Zapata, Francisco (1990) "Participación social y política en México," pp. 157–88, *México en el umbral del milenio.* Mexico City: Colegio de México.
—— (1997) "Automobile Industry," pp. 111–15, & "Industrial Labor, 1940–1996," pp. 691–98, *Encyclopedia of Mexico,* Michael S. Werner, ed. Chicago IL: Fitzroy Dearborn.
—— (2002) "NAFTA: Few Gains for Mexico's Workers," *Perspectives on Work* 6 (no. 1): 22–24.
Zavala, Silvio (1974) "Las Casas ante la encomienda," *Cuadernos Americanos* 194 (May–June): 143–55.

Zavala de Cosío, María Eugenia (1993) "El contexto social y el cambio de la política de población, 1960–1973," pp. 106–25, *El poblamiento de México*, vol. 4. Mexico City: Consejo Nacional de Población.

Zeh, Frederick (1995) *An Immigrant Soldier in the Mexican War.* College Station TX: Texas A&M University Press.

Zendejas, Sergio (1996) "U.S.-Bound Migration and the Future of the Ejido," pp. 305–21, *Reforming Mexico's Agrarian Reform*, Laura Randall, ed. Armonk NY: M.E. Sharpe.

Zermeño, Felipe (1995) "La crisis agrícola," pp. 55–64, *México: ¿Fin de un régimen?* José Valenzuela, ed. Iztapalapa: Universidad Autónoma Metropolitana.

Zermeño, Sergio (1978) *México: una democracia utópica.* Mexico City: Siglo XXI.

—— (1992) "Los intelectuales y el Estado en la década perdida," pp. 195–233, *El nuevo Estado mexicano*, vol. 3. Mexico City: Nueva Imagen.

—— (1993) "Intellectuals and the State in the 'Lost Decade'," pp. 279–98, *Mexico: Dilemmas of Transition*, Neil Harvey, ed. London: Institute of Latin American Studies, University of London & British Academic Press.

Zorrilla, Luis G. (1977) *Historia de las relaciones entre México y los Estados Unidos de América, 1800–1958* (2nd ed., 2 vols.). Mexico City: Porrúa.

Index

There are multiple spellings for many of the words in the text and multiple words one can use in discussing Mexico. In the text and index: 1) word forms more familiar to English-language readers have been used, thus "Montezuma" (rather than "Moctezuma") and "Aztec" (rather than "Mexica"), 2) following Sharer (2006), accents have not been placed on indigenous words, thus "Tenochtitlan" and 3) following (Weber 1992) accents have not been placed on words of Spanish origin which have become U.S. place names, such as "San Jose, California" (but San José, Costa Rica).